E-Learn 2002

World Conference on E-Learning in Corporate, Government, Healthcare, & Higher Education

Edited by
Margaret Driscoll
Thomas C. Reeves

Proceedings of E-Learn 2002

World Conference on E-Learning in Corporate, Government, Healthcare, & Higher Education

October 15-19, 2002; Montréal, Canada

Association for the Advancement of Computing in Education

A CONFERENCE OF AACE
www.aace.org

Volume 3

From AACE, the Conference organizer: This is to confirm that all Conference paper submissions are peer-reviewed by at least 2 referees prior to acceptance in the Final Program and prior to publication in the Proceedings book and CD.

See AACE Review Policy: www.aace.org/reviewpolicy.htm

Published by

Association for the Advancement of Computing in Education (AACE)
P.O. Box 3728
Norfolk, VA 23514-3728 USA
www.aace.org

Printed in the USA

ISBN: 1-880094-46-0

Special thanks to – AACE Technical Coordinator: Jerry Price, University of Houston.

PROGRAM COMMITTEE

EXECUTIVE ADVISORY BOARD

8ᵀᴴ ANNUAL

CALL FOR PARTICIPATION

E-Learn 2003

World Conference on E-Learning in Corporate, Government, Healthcare, & Higher Education

November 7-11, 2003
Phoenix, Arizona, USA

Proposals Due: April 30, 2003

www.aace.org/conf/elearn

- Keynote & Invited Speakers
- Full & Brief Papers
- Panels
- Roundtables
- Video Festival **NEW**
- Interactive Sessions **NEW**
- Tutorials & Workshops
- Posters/Demonstrations
- Corporate Posters/Showcases
- SIG (SPECIAL INTEREST GROUP) Discussions

Authors notified:
May 28, 2003
Proceedings file deadline:
September 15, 2003
Early registration deadline:
September 15, 2003
Advance registration deadline:
October 24, 2003

AACE
Estab. 1981

Association for the Advancement of Computing in Education

*Advancing Knowledge & Learning
with Information Technology Worldwide*

A CONFERENCE OF AACE • www.aace.org

CO-SPONSORED BY

International Journal on E-Learning
Corporate, Government, Healthcare, & Higher Education

E-Learn 2003 — World Conference on E-Learning in Corporate, Healthcare, Government, and Higher Education is an international conference organized by the Association for the Advancement of Computing in Education (AACE). This annual conference series serves as a multidisciplinary forum for the exchange of information on the research, development, and applications on all topics related to E-Learning.

Information for Presenters

Details of presentation formats are given on the following pages. The general principles applying to all are:

- All communication will be with the principal presenter who is responsible for communicating with co-presenters of that session.
- The conference will attempt to secure all equipment for presenters, with the exception of poster/demonstration presenters. However, where special equipment is needed, presenters may need to bring or rent equipment. The name of a rental firm can be provided.
- All presenters must register and pay the registration fee. Early registration fee will be approximately $395 (US) with a discount for AACE members.

Proceedings

Accepted papers will be published in the Proceedings (book and CD-ROM formats) as well as in the AACE Digital Library. These proceedings serve as major sources of information and reflect the current state of the art for the E-Learning community. In addition, selected papers may be invited for publication in AACE's respected journals especially in the *International Journal on E-Learning*. See: www.aace.org/pubs

Paper Awards

All presented papers will be considered by the Program Committee for Outstanding Paper Awards. There will also be an award for Outstanding Student Paper (therefore, please indicate if primary author is a full-time student).

Hotel & Travel Arrangements

Special hotel room rates will be available to conference attendees. Discount airfares will be available from a designated airline carrier.

Background

The E-Learn Conference series originated as the WebNet World Conference on the WWW and Internet which was held as a major international conference in San Francisco, CA (1996); Toronto, Canada (1997); Orlando, Florida (1998); Honolulu, HI (1999); San Antonio, TX (2000); Orlando, FL (2001); and Montréal, Canada (2002). E-Learn 2003 is the eighth in this series of internationally respected events.

Corporate Participation

A variety of opportunities are available to present research-oriented papers or to showcase and market your products and services.

E-Learn is Unique

The E-Learn Conference series is an international forum designed to facilitate the exchange of information and ideas on the research, issues, developments, and applications of a broad range of E-Learning topics.

E-Learn is an innovative collaboration between E-Learning researchers and practitioners from the corporate, government, healthcare, and higher education sectors. All presentation proposals are reviewed and selected by a respected international Program Committee, based on merit and the perceived value for attendees.

Broad Range of Important Topics: Coverage of a wide range of interrelated topics is just one of the features that distinguishes the E-Learn conference series. Attendees are able to mix and match sessions to focus on the combination of topics that are of the most interest, concern and benefit to them.

Participatory Event: While there are Keynote and Invited talks delivered by internationally recognized technology experts, E-Learn is more of a participatory event. This means that all attendees play an important, interactive role, offering valuable feedback and insight gained from their own experiences. The atmosphere at E-Learn is exciting and energizing. A wealth of knowledge is gathered and exchanged, as professionals from disparate but related fields come from all over the world to meet one-on-one or in small groups and learn about new developments that impact their respective activities.

Not a Trade Show: While E-Learn does encourage commercial participation, it is not a trade show, and there is not an exhibition. Instead, the conference uniquely relates and displays commercial activities throughout the E-Learn program in the form of Corporate Showcases and Demonstrations and other presentations by companies.

900+ Participants from 50 Countries

TOPICS

The scope of the conference includes, but is not limited to, the following topics as they relate to E-Learning in Corporate, Government, Healthcare, and Higher Education.

Application Domains
- General & Cross-Domain
- Corporate
- Government
- Health Care
- Higher Education
- Informal Learning (Museums, Communities, Homes)
- K-12
- Military Training
- Professional Associations & Non-Profits

Major Topics relating to or technologically supporting E-Learning
- Content Development
- Evaluation
- Implementation Examples and Issues
- Instructional Design
- Policy Issues
- Research
- Social and Cultural Issues
- Standards and Interoperability
- Tools and Systems
- Other

FULL PAPERS

Presentation time: 25 minutes
Submission length: 4-6 pages (2,500-3,750 words)
Proceedings length: 6 pages maximum
AV equipment provided: PC, Projector, Internet, VCR

Papers present reports of significant work or integrative reviews in research, development, applications, and societal issues related to all aspects of the conference topics.

Systems & Resources
Papers related to projects, technical developments, systems, and resources.
The paper should include:

- Whether this work is just beginning, on-going, or completed;
- The partners involved;
- The major goals and the basic approach - this includes the educational problem addressed or the new educational opportunity created;
- A brief review of previous work as a background;
- A clear description of what has been developed, including schematic overviews and screen dumps (if applicable);
- Any validation (usability testing, pilot testing, expert evaluation, etc.) that has taken place; and
- Future work and implications for others.

The reference list for this kind of paper should include URLs for the work, and at least a few literature references.

Conceptual & Empirical Studies
Reviews, conceptual overviews, evaluations, and empirical studies.
The paper should include:

- The topic;
- The motivation for the work;
- The major questions addressed;
- The general process and conceptual framework, with references to literature;
- The concrete method, with sufficient detail on instruments and procedures;
- Major points or results; and
- Implications.

This paper category requires a strong and up-to-date well synthesized literature review, with work from a variety of sources (not just the research team of the author), and also an appropriate writing and presentation style for a scholarly review or overview.

Case Studies
Papers related to local experiences (e.g., a course or a prototype tested in a local situation).
The paper should include:

- The most important features of the context;
- A description of the problem in both local and conceptual terms;
- A description of who, what, why, and how, including screen dumps if relevant;
- Implications for the local setting or the local prototype; and
- Implications for others outside the local setting.

This paper category should include a reference list with relevant URLs, and a few citations to papers related to the local problem, but from outside the local setting. The latter is to indicate that the author can see the local situation in a broader and more general context.

Other
For authors who do not feel they fit in any of the above. The Program Committee may request that the author revise the paper to relate to one of the above categories, or may accept it as submitted.

BRIEF PAPERS

Presentation time: 15 minutes
Submission length: 2-3 pages, 1,250-1,875 words
Proceedings length: 2 pages maximum
AV equipment provided: PC, Projector, Internet, VCR

These papers are brief, more condensed presentations or work-in-progress projects.

New Developments
Descriptions of new extensions to existing projects or newly initiated projects.

Project Opportunities
Descriptions of projects underway that include opportunities for additional project partners.

Demonstrations

Other
For authors who do not feel they fit in any of the above. The Program Committee may request that the author revise the paper to relate to one of the above categories, or may accept it as submitted.

The submission should include:

- What is going to be shown or demonstrated or offered;
- The major aspects;
- The context or motivation; and
- Relevant URLs or literature references.

PANELS

Presentation time: 1 hour
Submission length: 2-3 pages, 1,250-1,875 words
Proceedings length: 4 pages maximum
AV equipment provided: PC, Projector, Internet, VCR

A panel offers an opportunity for 3-5 people (including the chair) to present their views or results on a common theme, issue, or question and discuss them with the audience. Panels should cover timely topics related to the conference areas of interest. Panel selection will be based on the importance, originality, focus, and timeliness of the topic; expertise of proposed panelists; as well as the potential for informative (and even controversial) discussion.

Panels must allot at least 50% of the time for interaction and discussion with the audience.
The panel proposals should include:

- Description of the panel topic, including why this topic is important to Conference attendees; and
- Brief position statement and qualifications of each panelist.

ROUNDTABLES

Presentation time: 1 hour
Submission length: 2-3 pages, 1,250-1,875 words
Proceedings length: 150 words (to be published only in Abstract Book)
AV equipment provided: electricity

These sessions allow maximum interaction in informal, small-group discussions on a single topic. The format is appropriate for papers, projects, or works-in-progress that encourage discussion. Roundtables share a room with 2-3 other concurrently held Roundtables.

VIDEO FESTIVAL

Presentation time: 1 hour
Submission length: 2-3 pages, 1,250-1,875 words
Proceedings length: 2 pages
AV equipment provided: VCR, PC, Projector, Internet

The field has matured to the point that we have a growing number of video resources – cases, classroom/training video clips, and many other forms. Presenters should have a short handout on the video and use most of the time showing the video.

INTERACTIVE SESSIONS

Presentation time: 1 hour
Submission length: 2-3 pages, 1,250-1,875 words
Proceedings length: 3 pages
AV equipment provided: PC, Monitor, Internet

If you have mastered a new piece of software (or a new version) that others would be interested in learning about, submit a proposal for an Interactive Session. In this informal session, you will demonstrate the software, illustrate the process of using it, show participants some of the complexities and tricks about it, and give them an opportunity to try it themselves.

These sessions are also appropriate for instructional strategies, procedures, and evaluation procedures. The idea is not to give a definitive workshop on the topic, but to provide participants with enough information to help them decide whether their needs can be met with the program or procedure.

Include a description of the software to be used by participants, the objectives of the session, and the intended audience (experience level and prerequisites).

These presentations share a room with 2-3 other concurrently held Interactive Sessions.

TUTORIALS / WORKSHOPS

Presentation time: 3.5 or 7 hours
Submission length: see information below
Proceedings length: no pages
AV equipment provided: PC, Projector, Internet (Tutorial);
PC, Projector, PC Lab, Internet (Workshop)

Tutorials and Workshops are intended to enhance the skills and broaden the perspective of their attendees. They should be designed to introduce a rigorous framework for learning a new area or to provide advanced technical training in an area. Submissions will be selected on the basis of the instructors' qualifications for teaching the proposed Tutorial or Workshop and their contribution to the overall conference program. Workshops differ from Tutorials by involving hands-on experience with hardware/software provided.

Note: Few Workshops are selected because a lab of equipment is required for each. If you submit a Workshop proposal, please indicate if your proposal is also appropriate for presentation as a non-hands on Tutorial.

Tutorial/Workshop proposals should include:

- Clear description of the objectives;
- Intended audience (experience level and prerequisites);
- Proposed length (3.5 hours or 7 hours);
- 200-word abstract;
- 1-page topical outline of the content; and
- Summary of the instructor's qualifications.

POSTER / DEMONSTRATIONS

Presentation time: 2 hours
Submission length: 2-3 pages, 1,250-1,875 words
Proceedings length: 2 pages
AV equipment provided: 4'x8' poster board, 6' table, 2 chairs, electricity, Internet if wireless card & PC brought

Poster/Demonstration sessions enable researchers and non-commercial developers to demonstrate and discuss their latest results and developments in progress in order to gain feedback and to establish contact with similar projects.

Poster/Demonstration proposals should include:

- Description of the planned Poster/Demonstration; should emphasize the problem, what was done, and why the work is important.

Poster/Demonstration presenters will be required to arrange for their own systems software and hardware.

CORPORATE DEMONSTRATIONS/ LITERATURE

Presentation time: 2 hours
Submission length: 1-2 paragraphs
Proceedings length: no pages
AV equipment provided: 4'x8' poster board, 6' table, 2 chairs, electricity, Internet if wireless card & PC brought

Demonstrate and discuss your company's products, services, developments, applications and research, inform the audience of your future directions, gain feedback, and establish contacts.

Scheduled with Poster/Demonstrations grouped together in open exhibition-style, usually all in one hall. This is an informal event with a circulating conference-wide audience. Sales are permitted. You may stock and sell your product at your table.

CORPORATE SHOWCASES

Presentation time: 30 minutes
Submission length: 1-2 paragraphs
Proceedings length: 150 words (to be published only in Abstract Book)
AV equipment provided: PC, Projector, Internet, VCR

Demonstrate and discuss your company's products, services, developments, applications and research, inform the audience of your future directions, gain feedback, and establish contacts.

Scheduled concurrently only with other Showcases. Presentation rooms generally accommodate 50-150 people, theatre-style. This is more of a formal presentation than the Corporate Demonstration.

SIG (SPECIAL INTEREST GROUP) DISCUSSIONS

Presentation time: 1 hour
Submission length: 1-3 pages (625-1,875 words)
Proceedings length: no pages
AV equipment provided: PC, Projector, Internet, VCR

To encourage informal interaction among individuals with common interests, SIG discussion groups will be formed based upon proposals accepted under the Call for Participation. Also, new SIG discussion groups may be formed either formally or on an impromptu basis when at the conference.

SIG Discussion proposals should include:

- Description of the discussion topic emphasizing the problem or issue and why the work is important; and
- Indication of whether you are willing to chair the discussion.

SUBMISSION REQUIREMENTS

Submit all proposals by completing the Web form at: http://www.aace.org/conf/elearn

All proposals must be submitted by uploading PDF, Word, RTF, or Postscript file using the Web form. No hard copy paper, faxed, or e-mail submissions will be accepted.

Please send your proposal only ONE time.

Questions? Contact AACE at:

E-mail: conf@aace.org

Phone: 757-623-7588
Fax: 703-997-8760
www.aace.org/conf/edmedia

Phoenix Arizona

Offering unique Southwest culture and a desirable climate, Phoenix is located along the banks of the Salt River, where early Hohokam Indians first settled. Phoenix, the state's capital, is saddled between dramatic mountain ranges.

Year-round sunshine and mild autumn temperatures make Phoenix an ideal location for E-Learn 2003. This premier desert city is located 1,117 feet above sea level and the weather is warm, sunny and usually dry.

ATTRACTIONS/NIGHTLIFE/PERFORMING ARTS: A variety of museums offer indigenous history and art, as well as imported works. The Heard Museum in downtown Phoenix is well known for its Native American art exhibits. The Phoenix Art Museum, host of the Cowboy Artists Show, has a permanent collection of 16,000 paintings, sculptures, costumes and other works of art from the 15th through 20th centuries. Other interesting and informative museums are the Arizona Science Center, the Phoenix Museum of History, the Hall of Flame Fire Fighting Museum, Scottsdale Center for the Arts and the Champlin Fighter Aircraft Museum.

With 20 theater groups in the area, there is no shortage of entertainment. Phoenix offers everything from Broadway plays to lyric opera. The Herberger Theater Center plays host to many fine performances, including Ballet Arizona, the Arizona Opera Company and the Arizona Theatre Company.

The Phoenix Symphony Orchestra has been performing for more than 35 years with a season that runs from fall through spring. There are many opportunities to enjoy other music as well, including rock, jazz, country and more.

SIGHTSEEING: Arizona is known for its contrasts. Visitors will see everything from northern Arizona's tall, cool pines to the cactus-filled scenery of the Sonoran Desert. And if there's a "must-see," it's Arizona's majestic Grand Canyon, one of the world's seven natural wonders. This breathtaking sight is open year-round and may be experienced through nature walks or mule rides into the Canyon, or by taking a leisurely drive along its outer edges. Before reaching the Grand Canyon, be sure to stop at Sedona, a cultural community providing a wide array of boutiques and art galleries selling everything from Native American and Southwestern arts and crafts to fine jewelry.

Arizona also is home to Lake Powell on the northern border. Lake Powell is 186 miles long and has more miles of shoreline than the entire Pacific coast of the United States. The lake, which extends into southern Utah. Located in east-

ern Arizona, the White Mountains stand at an elevation of some 9,000 feet. The White Mountains are rich in trout-stocked lakes. With temperatures about 30 degrees cooler than Phoenix.

Other scenic trips worth taking include venturing to: Prescott - site of the historic 1857 John C. Fremont House, the first territorial governor's mansion, and Whiskey Row; Apache Trail - a world-famous trail that twists through the Superstition Mountains and was once traveled by the Apache Indians; and Montezuma's Castle - a 12th-century Aztec-designed dwelling carved into a steep cliff, once inhabited by the Pueblo Indians.

These destinations can be reached in as a few hours by car from Phoenix.

ACTIVITIES: With so many sunshine-filled days, Phoenix is the perfect place to experience a range of outdoor activities. Horseback riding is a great way to see the spectacular Sonoran Desert, as is a rugged jeep ride. Spending an afternoon tubing or rafting the Verde or Salt rivers is another way to enjoy the outdoors. For the thrill seeker, a glider or hot-air balloon flight will take you high above the desert plateau and offer splendid views for miles.

Dependable sunshine and great weather make outdoor sports a way of life. Golf, tennis, hiking, mountain biking and in-line skating are popular activities. Visitors can also choose from water skiing, sailing and fishing in the region's lakes and rivers.

DINING: Endless dining possibilities exist in Phoenix. With some of the world's best chefs, taste buds will be tantalized by indulging in a variety of foods including Fusion, Italian, Chinese, Mexican, Continental, Thai and Moroccan, just to name a few. It also is possible to taste a bit of the Old West by sampling a genuine cowboy mesquite-grilled steak at one of the many restaurants specializing in authentic Southwestern cuisine.

SHOPPING: When shopping you'll find a wonderful selection of upscale souvenirs such as beautifully handcrafted Native American turquoise jewelry and elegant leather goods. Everything from the latest in fashionable apparel to collectible artwork can be found at one of the many large shopping malls or tiny boutiques.

Sound like a great place for a conference? You bet! Plan to join us for E-Learn 2003, in Phoenix, Arizona, USA, November 7-11, 2003.

Explore Phoenix online at: www.phoenixcvb.com

P.O. Box 3728, Norfolk, VA 23514-3728 USA

Educational Technology Review – Electronic Journal

Educational Technology Review

International Forum on Educational Technology Issues & Applications

AACE's member journal is the focal point to exchange information between disciplines, educational levels, and information technologies. Its purpose is to stimulate the growth of ideas and practical solutions which can contribute toward the improvement of education through information technology.

CITE – Electronic Journal

CITE

CONTEMPORARY ISSUES IN TECHNOLOGY & TEACHER EDUCATION

An electronic publication of the Society for Information Technology and Teacher Education (SITE), established as a multimedia, interactive electronic counterpart of the *Journal of Technology and Teacher Education.*

International Journal on E-Learning

(formerly WebNet Journal & International Journal of Educational Telecommunications)

(IJEL)   ISSN# 1537-2456   Quarterly

IJEL serves as a forum to facilitate the international exchange of information on the current theory, research, development, and practice of E-Learning in education and training. This journal is designed for researchers, developers and practitioners in schools, colleges, and universities, administrators, policy decision-makers, professional trainers, adult educators, and other specialists in education, industry, and government.

Journal of Computers in Mathematics & Science Teaching

(JCMST)   ISSN# 0731-9258   Quarterly

JCMST is the only periodical devoted specifically to using information technology in the teaching of mathematics and science. The *Journal* offers an in-depth forum for the exchange of information in the fields of science, mathematics, and computer science.

Journal of Educational Multimedia & Hypermedia

(JEMH)   ISSN# 1055-8896   Quarterly

Designed to provide a multidisciplinary forum to present and discuss research, development and applications of multimedia and hypermedia in education. The main goal of the *Journal* is to contribute to the advancement of the theory and practice of learning and teaching using these powerful and promising technological tools that allow the integration of images, sound, text, and data.

Journal of Interactive Learning Research

(JILR)   ISSN# 1093-023X   Quarterly

Journal Of INTERACTIVE LEARNING RESEARCH
Formerly Journal of Artificial Intelligence in Education

The *Journal's* published papers relate to the underlying theory, design, implementation, effectiveness, and impact on education and training of the following interactive learning environments: authoring systems, CALL, assessment systems, CBT, computer-mediated communications, collaborative learning, distributed learning environments, performance support systems, multimedia systems, simulations and games, intelligent agents on the Internet, intelligent tutoring systems, micro-worlds, and virtual reality-based learning systems.

Journal of Technology and Teacher Education

(JTATE)   ISSN# 1059-7069   Quarterly

A forum for the exchange of knowledge about the use of information technology in teacher education. *Journal* content covers preservice and inservice teacher education, graduate programs in areas such as curriculum and instruction, educational administration, staff development, instructional technology, and educational computing.

Information Technology in Childhood Education Annual

(ITCE)   ISSN# 1522-8185

Information Technology in Childhood Education Annual
(formerly Journal of Computing in Childhood Education)

A primary information source and forum to report the research and applications for using information technology in the education of children – early childhood, preschool, and elementary. The annual is a valuable resource for all educators who use computers with children.

The exchange of ideas and experiences is essential to the advancement of the field and the professional growth of AACE members. AACE sponsors conferences each year where members learn about research, developments, and applications in their fields, have an opportunity to participate in papers, panels, poster/demonstrations and workshops, and meet invited speakers.

ED-MEDIA 2003

World Conference on Educational Multimedia, Hypermedia & Telecommunications

JUNE 23-28, 2003 HONOLULU, HAWAII, USA

ED-MEDIA - World Conference on Educational Multimedia, Hypermedia & Telecommunications

This annual conference serves as a multidisciplinary forum for the discussion of the latest research, developments, and applications of multimedia, hypermedia, and telecommunications for all levels of education.

E-Learn 2003

World Conference on E-Learning in Corporate, Government, Healthcare, & Higher Education

NOVEMBER 7-11, 2003 PHOENIX, ARIZONA, USA

E-Learn 2003 - World Conference on E-Learning in Corporate, Government, Healthcare, & Higher Education

E-Learn is a respected, international conference enabling E-Learning researchers and practitioners in corporate, government, healthcare, and higher education to exchange information on research, development, and applications. This interdisciplinary dialogue is further supported by satellite events such as by the WebNet Symposium on the WWW and Internet.

SOCIETY FOR INFORMATION TECHNOLOGY & TEACHER EDUCATION

2003
14TH INTERNATIONAL CONFERENCE

MARCH 24-29, 2003 ALBUQUERQUE, NEW MEXICO, USA

SITE - Society for Information Technology and Teacher Education International Conference

This conference, held annually, offers opportunities to share ideas and expertise on all topics related to the use of information technology in teacher education and instruction about information technology for all disciplines in preservice, inservice, and graduate teacher education.

Co-Sponsored Conferences

ICCE—International Conference on Computers in Education

ICCE is an annual event focusing on a broad spectrum of interdisciplinary research topics concerned with theories, technologies and practices of applying computers in education. It provides a forum for interchange among educators, cognitive and computer scientists, and practitioners throughout the world, especially from the Asia-Pacific region.

DECEMBER 3-6, 2002 AUCKLAND, NEW ZEALAND

Membership Application

Join today and keep up-to-date on the latest research and applications!

Name: _____

Address: _____

City: _____ State: _____ Code: _____ Country: _____

E-mail: _____ ❏ New Member ❏ Renewal Membership ID # _____

AACE Journals

Please check below the journal(s) you wish to receive:

❏ *International Journal on E-Learning (IJEL)*
   (formerly WebNet Journal & International Journal of Educational Telecommunications (IJET)

❏ *Jrl. of Educational Multimedia and Hypermedia (JEMH)*

❏ *Jrl. of Computers in Math and Science Teaching (JCMST)*

❏ *Jrl. of Interactive Learning Research (JILR)*

❏ *Jrl. of Technology and Teacher Education (JTATE)*
   Includes membership in Society for Information Technology and Teacher Education (SITE)

❏ *Information Technology in Childhood Education Annual (ITCE)*

Professional & Student Memberships

Annual membership includes a choice of AACE sponsored journals, subscriptions to *Educational Technology Review* and *CITE* (electronic journals), discounts for conferences, proceedings books & CD-Roms, and more.

Please check below the Journal(s)/membership(s) you wish to receive:

	Professional Membership	Student Membership*	
1 Journal	$ 85	$ 45	$ _____
2 Journals	$140	$ 80	$ _____
3 Journals	$195	$ 115	$ _____
4 Journals	$250	$150	$ _____
5 Journals	$305	$185	$ _____
All 6 Journals	$360	$220	$ _____

*If you selected a Student Membership rate above, you must be registered full-time in an accredited educational institution and you must provide the following information:

Expected graduation date: _____

Educational Institution: _____

Non-U.S. postage: add $15 for shipping EACH Journal outside the U.S. $ _____

TOTAL $ _____

Library/Institutional Subscriptions

❏ *Int'l Jrl. on E-Learning (IJEL)* $130

❏ *Jrl. of Educational Multimedia and Hypermedia (JEMH)* $130

❏ *Jrl. of Computers in Math and Science Teaching (JCMST)* $130

❏ *Jrl. of Interactive Learning Research (JILR)* $130

❏ *Jrl. of Technology and Teacher Education (JTATE)* $130

❏ *Information Technology in Childhood Education Annual (ITCE)* $85

Non-U.S. postage: add $15 for shipping EACH Journal outside the U.S. $ _____

TOTAL$ _____

Method of Payment (US Dollars)

Membership extends for 1 year from the approximate date of application. Please allow 6-8 weeks for delivery.

Enclosed: ❏ **Check** (U.S. funds & bank, payable to AACE)
         ❏ **Purchase Order** (PO must be included)

Credit Card: ❏ **MasterCard** ❏ **VISA** ❏ **AMEX** ❏ **Discover**

Card # |_|_|_|_|_|_|_|_|_|_|_|_|_|_|_|_|_|_|_|

Card Exp. Date |_|_| / |_|_|

Signature: _____

Total: $ _____

Return to: AACE, PO Box 3728, Norfolk, VA 23514-3728 USA
757-623-7588   Fax: 703-997-8760
E-mail: info@aace.org   www.aace.org

AACE
Association for the Advancement of Computing in Education

PO Box 3728, Norfolk, VA 23514-3728 USA

Not-for-Profit Organization
U.S. Postage PAID
Charlottesville, VA
Permit #564

Current members:
Please give to a colleague

Preface

Welcome to E-Learn 2002 in exciting Montreal, Quebec, CANADA. The first E-Learn conference organized by the Association for the Advancement of Computing in Education (AACE) comes at an auspicious time. The past two years have been quite sobering for anyone interested in the topics encompassed in this inaugural E-Learn conference.

First, the downturn in the economy that began to affect North America two years ago (and even earlier in Asia and other parts of the world) has prompted many enterprises to take a hard look at their education and training initiatives, including those that might be described as e-learning, m-learning, virtual learning, Web-based learning, and so forth. As a result, these enterprises are, more than ever, looking to education and training programs as investments that must show a return.

Second, the shocking events of September 11, 2001, awoke many of us in North America and Europe to a vulnerability that others in less fortunate countries have lived with for decades. In the wake of these tragic events, managers and workers alike are considering e-learning in its many variants as an increasingly attractive alternative to traditional face-to-face education and training events that require people to travel great distances and/or be away from loved ones for long periods of time.

So what do the recent economic downturn and global terrorism have to do with E-Learn 2002? The answer is the importance of diverse professionals sharing research and development papers, tutorials, workshops, posters, demonstrations, panels, showcases and other events. E-Learn, like the other AACE conferences, is all about high quality research and development efforts. Unlike most commercial conferences, E-Learn presentations have been rigorously refereed by people who are the leaders in their respective fields. Thus, the quality of the sharing that goes on at this conference, and continues through the dissemination of these proceedings, becomes crucial to the realization of the return-on-investment we all seek, and the extension of learning and professional development opportunities beyond specific times and places.

In 2002, and in the wake of the aforementioned calamities, some might question the value of holding face-to-face conferences for which the submissions are due months in advance. After all, changes in technologies occur at an ever faster pace, and last month's cutting-edge development is sometimes this month's e-flop. Nevertheless, most of us recognize that as conference participants, we are not so much interested in technologies as ideas: ideas that are best shared, critiqued, and reshaped through personal dialogue and group discussion. While this could occur online, we recognize that many of the most important exchanges at conferences take place informally away from the formal sessions. Indeed, the face-to-face interactions are often the most valued and long-remembered aspects of any conference we attend, and we look forward to sharing these with you in Montreal.

E-Learn 2002 would not exist without the efforts of scores of volunteers, and so we would like to express our gratitude to the members of the Conference Steering and Program Committees as well as the local volunteers in Montreal who have made this event possible. Further appreciation is due to the highly professional staff at AACE who have worked tirelessly to ensure that this professional event is among the best of its kind. Finally, and most importantly, we wish to thank all of the researchers, developers, and others whose outstanding work is reported in these proceedings. Without you, there would be no quality to celebrate.

The more than 600 papers in this volume and on the accompanying CD-ROM come from contributors representing more than 50 countries. This is truly an international event. A year of preparation will soon be over, and E-Learn will be a pleasant memory. It is our hope that this memory will be refreshed each time you open this volume or access the conference CD-ROM, providing the wisdom and inspiration you seek. Further evidence of that living memory will be your continued participation in E-Learn conferences, and toward that end, we look forward to seeing you again next year at E-Learn 2003 in Phoenix, Arizona, USA; Nov. 7-11th (http://www.aace.org/conf/elearn).

E-Learn 2002 Program Chairs:
- Margaret Driscoll
IBM Mindspan Solutions, USA
- Thomas C. Reeves,
The University of Georgia, USA

TABLE OF CONTENTS

PANELS

BRIEF PAPERS

INTERACTIVE SESSIONS

VIDEO FESTIVAL

POSTER/DEMONSTRATION PAPERS

OTHER PAPERS

ABSTRACT

The George Washington University has developed an enterprise portal solution to fulfill the varied needs of students, faculty, alumni, staff and friends. The ability to integrate email, online student registration, courseware software, enterprise data and other existing resources into a comprehensive single-sign-on portal allowed for greater application interoperability, extended usage, and enhanced University wide communication.

PAPER

In late 1998, The George Washington University (GW) started conceptualizing innovative ways to use web technologies to replicate its sense of community in the online world and to enable more agile communication within its constituencies. GW needed an all-in-one comprehensive and integrated enterprise portal; a solution that would allow all types of constituents – students, alumni, faculty, staff or some combination of these roles - the ability to use services and receive information tailored to their specific needs. Moreover, the system was to provide the ability to integrate applications such as email, online student registration, courseware development and management, and other existing resources into a comprehensive single-sign-on portal.

GW decided to build its own portal and named it GWeb. The Interactive Multimedia Applications Groups (IMAG), a team within the Administrative Applications department of GW's Information Systems and Services, spearheaded the development of GWeb. Initial features were based on student, staff, faculty, and alumni interests, focus groups, GW administrative guidance, including the Web Advisory Committee of GW's Information Technology Advisory Council and the Technology Committee of GW's Board of Trustees. GWeb went officially live in September 2001 after a "test drive" period that lasted eight months, as we collected and responded to user feedback to improve services and features.

Developing the University portal independently allowed GW to focus on its specific needs and opportunities distinctive to GW. While the challenge of building a portal may have been greater than using a generic product, the autonomy and independence generated allowed GW to provide solutions responsive to the community's needs and values. Furthermore, the ability to integrate existing resources into a comprehensive single-sign-on portal allowed for greater application interoperability, extended usage, and enhanced University-wide communication.

The GWeb portal is based upon a mix of academic, collaborative, informative and personal services to encourage use and promote community interaction. Services of personal nature, such as weather from around the globe, movie show time listings, comics, and classified ads provide resources that would otherwise require users to search elsewhere for these features. The aggregation of the GWeb services increased usage and the effectiveness of communication between the University and its constituencies.

Today, thanks to its proven infrastructure, more and more applications are being built on top of the GWeb architecture to facilitate the University's operations and academic learning.

Currently, GWeb includes the following features:

- Role-based configuration. Users are presented with applications and communication that are relevant to their affiliation within the University (i.e. student, staff, faculty, alumni, or guest).

-

- Role-based polling and surveys. Users are presented with polls and surveys that are relevant to their affiliation within the University.
- Content management and distribution. Organizations and departments within the University can post news and events on the portal and have the same content syndicated out to their own website on the University's main web server.
- Online directory: Users can search email and campus addresses for faculty and staff. Student and alumni email addresses may also be searched.
- Access to external applications. The portal provides single sign-on to Email, library catalogues, and the University's online courseware application.
- Secure distribution: Staff and faculty can obtain instant, secure access to their personal identification numbers (PINs) for accessing BANNER, the University's enterprise system, over the web.
- Employment listings and employment applications: This application allows users to browse and apply online for GW employment opportunities. The data feeds directly from the BANNER database.
- Training registration: Allows training providers to manage GW employee training.. The system feeds data back to the BANNER system to record, track and report on fulfilled employee-training requirements.
- Bookmarks and Web Notes. Users can bookmark web sites or save the contents of various web pages through GWeb. These bookmarks and notes can then be shared with other GWeb users and accessed from any computer.
- Instant Messaging: Users can send instant messages within the GW network and to other popular networks, including AOL, MSN, Yahoo and ICQ.
- Alumni Mentoring Program: Students may browse through alumni profiles to select a mentor.
- Student Elections: Students may vote online for their school board representatives.
- Entertainment: GWeb modules include news from washingtopost.com, weather from around the world, comics, horoscopes, movie show time listings, live broadcasts of GW's radio station, real-time robotic cameras from around campus, news feeds from and classified ads.

Developing the portal required three predominant types of activities occurring almost concurrently: business development, technical development, and design and usability. Each is outlined below:

Business Development

It was necessary to build relationships throughout the University and beyond to make GWeb happen. Two types of relationships were required. First, relationships needed to be established within the University to secure commitment to GWeb. Second, relationships with content providers were required to enable GW to provide services such as news and movie listings. GW established a partnership with the Washington Post that became a win-win solution. While integrating washingtonpost.com with the portal, the Post developed the standards for content distributions, which will later be used with other washingtonpost.com customers.

Technical Development

GW's in-house knowledge of the systems that were to be integrated was one of the reasons for the successful design of the portal solution. IMAG's ability to easily reach for knowledge and expertise within the Administrative Application division made the links between the portal, the administrative data and the systems relatively simple.

Scalability issues were addressed carefully to ensure GWeb's ability to handle a growing user base and an expanded service offering. Furthermore, the University's high standard of and commitment to security demanded particular attention to preserving the integrity of University data.

Design and Usability

Crucial to the success and adoption of GWeb was making it easy to use and understandable for the user. Early on, mock-ups were created and their practicability examined. Special efforts went into creating an environment that would be friendly, inviting, and intuitive. Focus groups were used to assess ease of use, intended audience and future development needs. The personalization aspect of GWeb allowed for each user to see a specific page made especially for them. Whether the feature being used is a particular discussion group, a favorite news section, or weather reports from a hometown region, each user can easily personalize GWeb to their needs and preferences. Additionally, applications like email, instant messaging, and the courseware application are made accessible without additional logins.

The evidence of the success of the GWeb portal comes from the usage that we are registering. Whether because of the email integration, the instant messaging, or the comics column, users are valuing the application and are using it every day. Because of its successful adoption, the University has used the portal as one of the major means of communication. Surveys are proposed to users over the portal. The ability to then correlate the survey data with enterprise data provides the University with a powerful tool for strategic planning initiatives.

The self-service aspect of the portal has reduced the cost associated with providing direct assistance. The portal has eliminated the need for publishing a hardcopy version of the GW phone directory and reduced the costs associated with maintaining directory entries.

The portal has assisted with identification of data quality issues in our enterprise database. A few staff and faculty members who tried accessing one of the portal applications, which required the submission of personal data, learned that their birthdate or social security number was recorded incorrectly in the enterprise database and then were able to take steps to correct their information. Staff and faculty members can easily view their online directory entry and update it with a few clicks.

The employment vacancies listing program allows for the display of job descriptions, which were previously not available through the web. Job applicants can submit their resume online, thereby improving the quality of staff by increasing the pool of resumes from which University managers can choose.

There are several elements which give GWeb sustainability throughout the University. Its capabilities have changed the way we develop and deploy applications. For example, by being able to access our enterprise database, users are now able to provide correct and updated information ranging from birth dates to office phone numbers with only a few clicks. With our online directory, finding a department contact number or email address is simple. With the new calendar, users are able to add events into one consolidated calendar, which can be sorted by various user groups such as student organizations, classes, departments.

GWeb Portal has been well received throughout the GW community and has received support from Vice Presidents and the Board of Trustees, as well as becoming a permanently bookmarked site for thousands of students, faculty, administrators, and staff that populate the GW community. All these elements further sustain the University by providing information in a single consolidated portal, accessible to anyone, customizable by any user, and further projects The George Washington University's online presence in the world wide web.

Although GWeb has been live since September 2001, it is a work in progress. We have already added new features such as a robotic camera that allows the user to control viewing of various parts of the GW community. With such innovative modules being developed every day, GWeb has become a powerful tool and resource that will further sustain access to services and communication among the many constituencies that make up the GW community.

The fact that thousands of University constituents have incorporated use of the portal into their daily use of on-line services speaks for itself. An integrated tool such as this is the direction of the future for access to services and information. The business process, technical and usability challenges already identified and solved during this project should prove beneficial to any other higher education institution wishing to take the next step into the future of web-based services, integrated information and targeted communications.

Issues in Rural Uptake of Online Learning: an Australian Perspective

Dr. Ann Deden
a.deden@ecu.edu.au
Learning and Development Services
Edith Cowan University
Perth, Western Australia

Abstract: Worldwide, many hopes for improved access to tertiary education have been pinned on Internet-based telecommunications. This presentation reports the extent and success of attempts to encourage rural and remote Australian secondary school students to use the Internet to participate in tertiary education, and identifies key features of successful programs.

The Discrepancy Between Metropolitan And Rural Rates Of Tertiary Participation

Based on 1996 census data, the Australian Department of Education, Training and Youth Affairs (DETYA)[1] calculated that 28.4 percent of metropolitan Australians between the ages of 19 and 21 were enrolled in higher education, as compared with 18.3 per cent of their peers from rural and isolated locations. Yet rural Australians constitute 46 percent of the total population. In rural and especially in remote areas, populations tend to be very sparse, spread over vast distances. Transportation and communication are often minimal and seasonally unreliable. And a significant proportion of rural and remote Australians are disadvantaged not only by location but by socioeconomic status as well. Taken together, these factors make the issue of rural and remote education equity a challenge of daunting proportions. Many state and national government leaders expect that online learning offers a panacea that will happily resolve this dilemma.

The presentation reports the results of an investigation into whether this expectation is likely to be realised with current approaches, and derives a criterion list of potential success factors that should be piloted.

Project description

The investigation took the form of a structured survey of existing programs, and an analysis of those programs in terms of factors identified in the research literature as affecting secondary students' tertiary education decisions. We assessed the extent and methods used to address both factors that encourage tertiary participation and those that discourage it.

Most programs that met the criteria for inclusion is this study are limited to vocationally oriented in-School offerings, known as VET in School programs. Typically, these programs focus primarily on encouraging students to complete school through Year 12 by providing local access to an expanded range of attractive vocational subjects. Many such programs offer TAFE Certificate I or II qualifications, along with high school completion awards.

Programs such as the Nhulunbuy High School, New South Wales Access Clusters, and the New England Institute of TAFE programs integrate significant participation by the local secondary school, relevant local industries, community telecentres[2] and TAFE institutions. By engaging active local business and community support, the programs help create a climate in which further education, as well as the use of distance learning technologies, can become normative, and reinforced by social interaction. Furthermore, they demonstrate the relevance of advanced learning to careers in local

---

[1] Name changed in 2002 to: Department of Education, Science, and Training (DEST)

[2] Telecentres are community-managed facilities that offer Internet access and skills training. Many also support video-based lectures and student assessment for tertiary vocational programs.

industries. This shows students that they will not necessarily have to abandon their communities if they pursue tertiary goals. Experiences with supportive distance learning facilities and staff can also help secondary students feel more comfortable with the idea of engaging in tertiary study via distributed learning approaches.

It was extremely rare to find university-initiated rural tertiary participation programs using technology. A number of universities, particularly those with regional campuses, conduct at least some rural student recruitment programs. However, there is at present no university program that uses online learning as part of a program guiding rural and remote Australian students through either an enriched conventional or an alternative pathway to university.

Edith Cowan University's Harvey Aspirations program is in the early days of a three-year pilot trial, seeking to adapt the Upward Bound model from the U.S. to Western Australian requirements, and to incorporate online learning as part of the process. While Aspirations provides more of the elements that the research suggests are essential for the success of tertiary encouragement programs, it continues to rely on a substantial amount of face-to-face contact, and as yet makes little use of the Internet. ECU is able to provide that at Harvey due to the proximity of its Bunbury campus. Thus, we were unable to identify any working model of a rural/remote tertiary encouragement program in which a metropolitan university campus provides the university component and uses distributed learning technologies to support any significant portion of its interaction and contact with distant school students.

However, from the analysed programs and related research, it was possible to generate at least a starting set of recommended features that would contribute to the effectiveness of any tertiary encouragement programs that used distributed learning technologies to reach rural and remote secondary students.

Toward a Best Practice Model

To be successful, model programs will need to effectively address as many of the factors that currently discourage country students from pursuing further tertiary learning, as well as incorporate a number of strongly encouraging elements (James et al. *op. cit.* 1999). Based on analysis of the data gathered, the following features can contribute strongly to the potential success of tertiary encouragement programs for rural and remote Australian students:

- Early intervention, perhaps as early as Year 7 and certainly by year 9 or 10, to help ensure secondary completion to a level appropriate for each students' tertiary study goals, to broaden students' exposure to career and related study options, and to begin to address any academic deficits or enrichment needs

- Inclusion of self-management and independent learning and living skills, including the use of distributed learning technologies

- Effectively addressing students' and families' financial concerns regarding the costs of leaving home for tertiary study

- Engagement of family, school and community members, and of local telecommunications resources, so that students experience more social support and continuity between home and away tertiary locales

- Focus on tertiary study pathways to careers that require university as well as TAFE preparation

- Active, well-integrated partnerships across participating educational sectors

- Community and family involvement in selection of subjects and provision of relevant work experience and work-based learning

- Residential camp experiences conducted on university campuses

- Incorporation of regional clusters of schools interested in the same program, with shared contribution to program teaching

- Use of distance learning and telecommunications technologies to foster ongoing high levels of interaction among cluster schools and with linked universities

- Technical and curricular support from state education agencies

- Active involvement with a specific university and/or faculty that offers courses seen as relevant and beneficial to the economic life of the community—whether it is geographically close or not

- Exploration of careers requiring tertiary preparation

- Tertiary level learning skills and academic remediation, bridging, and enhancement as appropriate to each student's goals and skill levels

- Provision of additional social, counselling, and academic skills support once students embark upon tertiary study

It is likely that such programs will also need to encompass some professional development for both secondary and tertiary teaching, counselling and advising staff. Significant professional and organisational learning will be involved as staff from different institutions and sectors work together to develop well-articulated pathways for rural and remote students, to track student progress, and to provide appropriate and effective programs and advice, both face-to-face and via distributed learning modes.

Next Steps

The findings of this study can help to guide strategic planning for tertiary access in any country facing the challenges of distance, culture, and socioeconomic status in its attempts to upgrade the educational attainment of its rural and remote citizens. The full government-sponsored report (to be published this year) includes a number of recommendations that will be considered at the national level, including the funding of pilot project designed to develop varied working best practice models.

References and relevant links:

Australian Bureau of Statistics:
http://www.abs.gov.au/

Australian Department of Education, Science and Technology Home Page:
http://www.detya.gov.au/highered/index1.htm

Deden, A. (2002, in press) *Distributed Learning in Non-metropolitan Australia.* Department of Education, Science and Technology, Canberra, ACT, Australia.

James, R., Wyn, J., Baldwin, G., Hepworth, G., McInnis, C. and Stephanou, A. (1999). *Rural and Isolated School Students and their Higher Education Choices.* Commissioned Report No. 63, National Board of Employment, Education and Training Higher Education Council, Canberra.

University Strategies in the Online Learning Marketplace

Ann Deden
Learning and Development Services
Edith Cowan University
Perth, Australia
a.deden@ecu.edu.au

Jan Herrington
School of Communications and Multimedia
Edith Cowan University
Perth, Australia
j.herrington@ecu.edu.au

Abstract: Universities worldwide are faced with enormous challenges as they decide on how the rapid changes in technology and the widespread availability of the Internet will impact upon their modes of operation. This paper examines the strategic planning implications of cost, risk, quality, and potential outcomes driving universities' investments in online learning. It explores a continuum of valid strategic positions universities can adopt, based on their analysis of these factors.

Universities attracted to Web-based delivery need well-defined policies and strategies in place that will give the them the best chance of promoting effective learning, gaining market share, generating profits, and demonstrating leadership in the quality of the online learning experiences they offer. In order to achieve such ends, a university must partner strategically, build its capacity wisely, and manage its online business commercially.

What Options Does A University Have In Defining Its Online Profile?

Every university needs to make a choice among 'big picture' strategy alternatives. For example, five possible options are suggested below, ranging from simple Web-assisted learning (effectively opting out of the competition) to one requiring a significant university commitment to Web-based delivery. In Australia, the national government's Department of Education, Science and Training (DEST) definitions of mode levels A, B, and C indicate the degree of Web-dependence a course displays. They do not and should not be taken to indicate that, for instance, Mode C is necessarily best in all circumstances. Rather, the choice of mode should be seen as reflective of the university's strategic market focus and pedagogical philosophy.

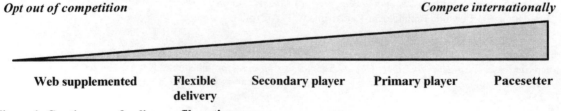

Figure 1: Continuum of online profile options

Option 1: Web-supplemented (DEST Mode A)

This option uses Web components to enrich the learning of a student cohort that is primarily campus and classroom based. Web use is recommended by the teacher, but is not strictly required in order for students to achieve unit outcomes. Universities may opt to offer this level of Web enhancement for some or all of its courses as a result of any of the following considerations:

- The course content is primarily hands-on laboratory or technical work.
- Students are unlikely to have good online access.
- The institution has decided to very gradually use the Web as one way to enrich the high-quality face to face learning experience that is already a distinguishing, marketable feature of the university.
- The particular course caters for only a small, local student population, and that population finds it relatively easy to attend regularly scheduled classes.

Online resources provided at this level can range from basic unit information to inclusion of other resources such as access to databases, and other topically relevant Websites, links to the university library and other student services. Given the traditional emphasis on on-campus teaching, it is likely that a university will find the largest number of its online learning resources and units will be at this level. Some institutions also start their online endeavours at this level. Though this is changing as student expectations rise, many courses marketed as 'online' have been primarily delivered via traditional print distance education.

Funding implications: Costs depend on features that are included and the condition of pre-existing course and unit resources. Average costs would range from a minimum of $500 to $5000 for the development of the materials.[1]

Option 2: Flexible Delivery using Web-dependent Units (DEST Mode B)

At this level, Web use is required, but other learning resources and/or experiences are also essential unit components. The Flexible Delivery option packages a mix of learning resources to support substantially online unit delivery. At this level, units and courses usually need at least moderate redesign to take advantage of Web affordances to create a more learner-centred environment. Hence, instructional designers, multimedia and Web-production personnel are typically involved. If this is the teacher's first foray at this level, then supportive professional development is also essential.

Universities may opt to offer this level of online engagement for some or all of its courses as a result of any of the following considerations:

- It can enhance quality assurance for offshore programs.
- It aligns with the needs of an older local student population with work and home commitments that make traditional university attendance problematic.
- Students can be expected to have good online access.
- The university's IT infrastructure can provide reliable, reasonably high-speed access to remote learners, and to at least the library.
- The university has made a strategic commitment to using the Web to create more learner-centred teaching, and has aligned the necessary financial resources and support services.

Funding implications: Bates (2000) estimates costs for the development of a Web-based new unit to be around $28,300 Canadian dollars. Any such figure is simply an estimate. Bates gives four ways to estimate: 'wild guesses', 'marginal costs', 'careful estimates' and 'actual costs.' Multiplying such a figure by the number of units to estimate the cost of whole courses denies the possibility of economies of scale with template developments and other savings. The figure is also rubbery because the total cost will depend on the nature of the unit itself, and the tasks and resources that need to be produced.

Option 3: Secondary Player

---

[1] Unless otherwise stated, all dollar values are given in Australian dollars. With the exchange rate typical in mid-2002, the Australian dollar is worth a little more than half a US dollar.

A Secondary Player profile would involve offering Mode B or Mode C (fully online) units and courses. The critical feature here is the use of external providers (e.g., Open Learning Australia or OLA) for course management and marketing, in return for a percentage of enrolment income.

Universities may choose this approach for some or all of their online courses. For example, Curtin University of Technology offers most of its online courses through OLA, but also administers some directly. The decision to go to the market through a large broker or distributor can be influenced by factors such as:

- A determination that at least some programs can reach larger markets.
- The costs of reaching that wider audience are shared through a consortium approach.
- An opportunity to join with a larger provider that offers the IT infrastructure and support, and perhaps administrative support as well, that would be too costly for the individual university.
- A desire to enhance the university's name recognition through association with more widely known consortium members.

Funding implications: Funding implications will depend on the nature of the relationship, for example, whether the outside provider pays the university for unit development, or whether the university underwrites and contributes units. Administration, infrastructure and maintenance costs would need to be covered. However, the cost of joining a consortium can be significant.

Option 4: Primary Player

A primary player provides a fully e-commerce-enabled, e-learning Web Portal for all student-university interactions; may host secondary players' courses in non-competing areas; and markets through direct channels (e.g., Website, direct mail, advertising) as well as indirect channels (e.g., brokers, links to consortia and other accrediting universities).

Universities can reasonably consider this option when, for example:
- Their IT infrastructure and administrative systems are all integrated, online, robust on a 24x7 basis, and secure, allowing for all student transactions and services, as well as units, to be delivered entirely via the Web.
- They have identified programs with strong actual or potential online learning markets. These markets offer enough income to cover not only course development, delivery, and upgrading but also marketing and at least a portion of significant ongoing IT infrastructure and administrative system improvements.
- They have developed and debugged the online courses for these markets.
- They have strong name recognition in their selected market segments, and have experienced success in marketing their online courses.
- They have developed and implemented policies and practices that assure quality staffing, quick response times from teaching and support staff, and reasonable workload formulas for delivering online courses that will meet the quality standards of their face-to-face programs.
- They have made the financial commitment to continued updating and enhancement of all of the above.

Funding implications: Infrastructure and development costs for the portal would be needed, together with management and maintenance costs. It is important to remember that the rapid pace of IT evolution, coupled with increasingly intense competition for online learners means any primary players will need to commit very significant funding on a long-term basis.

Option 5: Pacesetter

Pacesetters may be traditional universities or commercial entities. *Pacesetters* contribute to the advancement of online learning, pushing the boundaries and defining the rules of the game. In addition to being a primary player, *Pacesetters* make major contributions such as:

- development of software for student-centred online teaching and learning

- development of new benchmark virtual university environments
- models for online interactive support of online students
- evaluation of virtual university outcomes
- business models for an online virtual university
- models and templates for effective online course development
- adaptation or development of effective administrative systems
- integration of on-campus and online flexible delivery
- models for the management of staffing and workload issues
- partnerships with other providers
- commercialisation of intellectual property

Funding implications: *Pacesetter* status results from a strategic commitment to deliberately pursue this position on the playing field. It requires significant prompt and ongoing realignment of resources, as well as resource enhancement through major grants, partnerships, and commercial arrangements.

Conclusion: Strategic Planning Recommendations

A university may target different levels of Web involvement for different markets or different curricular areas. A key criterion for targeting resources should be identification of the university's strong and strategic course offerings, as well as those of emerging strengths and strategic significance. However, the university as a whole must also choose appropriate targets to provide the underlying marketing, and technology and staffing arrangements required by the academic programs.

Online teaching and learning does not offer universities a 'sure bet' opportunity for increasing enrolments, reducing costs, or enhancing their reputations. The online learning market is highly competitive, yet the parameters of success in that market are not yet clearly defined. A prudent business-like approach to the possibilities, challenges, and risks e-learning presents would encompass market research including identification and analysis of potential partners and competition, analysis of expertise and resources within the university, strategic direction and priority-setting, an evaluation of the university's technical and staff readiness, plus careful cost-benefit and risk analysis.

Reference

Bates, A.W. (2000). *Managing technological change: Strategies for college and university leaders*. San Francisco: Jossey-Bass.

Designing E-Learning Success:
Curriculum Design that Encourages Student Success

Stephanie Delaney
Instructional Design
Highline Community College
United States
sdelaney@highline.edu

Abstract: It can be challenging for some students to succeed in an e-learning environment. One way that instructors can insure online success is to design success elements into the curriculum of the course. Success elements are, quite simply, components of a course that facilitate student success. This brief paper explores the idea of success elements as a tool for reviewing whether new or existing e-learning courses facilitate student success. The paper goes on to explore several types of success elements that instructors can integrate into their curricula that will improve student success without significantly adding to the instructor's workload. Success elements will also help the instructor to have a better idea of how the class as a whole is absorbing the course material.

Introduction

Faculty in higher education complain regularly about how the work of their students disappoints them. Students are unable to write well, unable to cite properly, unable evaluate the quality of research sources . . .the list goes on. Rather than complain about poor student work, this paper proposes identifying the elements which are most troublesome and giving the students the tools they need to do what is required and to do it right. These tools are identified here as success elements. Many will view this as handholding that should not be necessary with today's college students. However, for those who are willing to accept that students are not as prepared as they wish and are willing to do something about it, they will be rewarded with higher quality work, less time spent grading and much less teaching related frustration.

Evaluating Curriculum

The first step in creating success elements is to identify the problem areas in a course. This is most easily done while grading student work or after calculating final grades. Determine the areas where students tend to falter or fail to live up to your expectations.

Case Study – Inadequate Papers

One instructor notes frustration with students who fail to ask questions about an assignment before turning them in. Rather than ask for clarification on an assignment, students would e-mail the assignment with a note saying that they hoped the work was ok since they had run into some hurdle that they could not get over.

To address this problem, the instructor began providing web links to the type of information that students claimed they could not find. She gave them as starting points and discouraged the students from using the provided resources in the papers. However, once the students saw what type of site they were looking for, they were able to find additional resources and consequently turn in better work.

Most instructors can quickly and easily list the top five or ten problem areas for students. Go through your own class and start a list of the problems that crop up. You may want to keep a running list while you are grading student work. Note any comment that you make more than twice – that is probably a place where a student success element would be useful.

Keep in mind that student inadequacy often goes beyond academic concerns. Students may be unable to manage time well enough to turn in a paper in time, may not have a computer at home, or may have domestic issues which interfere with the ability to study and complete assignments. While few faculty wish to get involved in the personal lives of students, simple success elements can assist the student in managing personal shortcomings more effectively. Interestingly, the elements designed to help the struggling student often assist the high achieving students as well.

Determining Success Elements and Incorporating them into the curriculum

After you have determined where students are having problems, you can begin to identify solutions. Sometimes a solution is as easy as giving the students more information. Other times, an assignment may need to be restructured to assist students in surmounting common hurdles. Here are a few practical suggestions that you might find useful in your own class. Keep on mind that finding the appropriate success elements is often an ongoing experiment. Soliciting student feedback throughout the class can result in some great ideas.

Pre Class Assignment

Online classes often require certain basic technical skills – the ability to download a document, to send an attachment, to do basic web searching, and so on. Students may say they know how to do these things, but they sometimes overestimate their abilities until it is too late. To address this problem, a pre-class assignment may be a good tool.

In one case, the pre class assignment is given to students about 2 weeks before the class begins. Students are asked to complete a series of simple tasks before the first day of class or on the first day of class. Tasks include finding a basic piece of information on the Internet, downloading needed software, buying the textbook and creating a schedule with the proposed hours of study. Students are asked to e-mail the assignment to the instructor as an attachment, testing that skill as well. This assignment gives students the opportunity to test their abilities in a non-stressful situation, outside of class. The two-week time period gives students the time to acquire some of the more basic skills before the class begins. If the student realizes that they do not posses needed skills, they still have time to select a different class.

Week One Monitoring

The first week of class can be challenging to e-learning students. They may be confused about how to start the class or how to proceed once class begins. Students may not realize the importance of reading and following *all* of the directions and as a result miss important information. Also, students new to e-learning are often challenged by technical problems in the early days of a class. Detailed monitoring of students can make the process much easier for the student and, in the long run, for the teacher as well. The monitoring generally consists of tracking each student on a daily basis and following up immediately when the student fails to meet a deadline.

A simple first step in week one monitoring is to ask each student to contact the instructor by email on the first day to insure the instructor that the student has been able to access the course materials and is doing ok. Students who fail to contact the instructor get a follow-up e-mail the following day and a telephone call the day after that. This helps identify those students who did not think to check their e-mail for information about their online class or those who got stuck and figured the problem would somehow resolve itself. The personal contact from the instructor makes students feel less isolated in the online environment.

Another week one monitoring activity is to have something simple due early on. Examples include biographies, student home pages, textbook exercises and the like. Those who fail to submit work in a timely manner are contacted by e-mail and telephone.

Another, more time consuming, monitoring project is to reply to all email within an hour of getting the message, when possible. The downside for the instructor is that they are practically glued to their computer for the first week. The upside is that students get a sense that the instructor is there, cares for them and is attentive to their needs. This impression lasts throughout the term, even after response times return to normal. This connection with the instructor also results in higher retention rates.

It is generally advisable to notify the students when the intense monitoring period is over (though they may not have been aware it was going on) and to set out contact expectations in that message.

Syllabus Quiz

Students frequently disregard information in the syllabus, even when that information is read to them in class. In the early days of an online class, students suffer from information overload and are likely quickly scan the syllabus or to skip it altogether. A short syllabus quiz is an ideal way to insure that students are attentive (at least at the beginning of the course) to the important elements of the syllabus.

Most courseware enables faculty to set up objective, automatically graded quizzes so that, once the quiz is created, it is little work for the instructor to administer. For those without a course management tool, a quick short answer or objective quiz can achieve a similar result. Encourage retention of the important elements of the syllabus by including syllabus questions in every quiz or exam as a bonus point or easy question.

Hyperlinked Rubric or Criteria list

Many faculty members have lists of criteria or rubrics that they use to evaluate student work. One way to improve student work is to give students access to that criteria and hyperlink each of the elements to an example and additional information.

For example, proper formal essay structure may be required in an assignment. List that in a criteria list or rubric and hyperlink it to an example of a properly formed essay. Identify the portions of the essay that make it particularly noteworthy and explain why. Ideally, this example would be a student answer, letting students know that the level of expected work really is possible. In addition to the example, the instructor could link to campus and online resources where the student who has trouble with essays can go for help. This might include links to the campus writing center and reference librarians as well as online writing labs and tutorials on essay writing.

The instructor can benefit in two ways. First, the general quality of work improves. Second, when students do turn in problem work, rather than writing lengthy explanations about what was wrong with the essay, the instructor can refer the students to the existing helpful resources. Some instructors even ask the student to write a comparison of their own work to the model and to rewrite the problem area(s) based on that critique.

Peer Grading

There are many ways to incorporate peer grading into a curriculum. From the perspective of student success, peers can review the first draft work of classmates using a set of criteria set by the instructor. This enables the peers to catch common problems overlooked in the haste of assignment preparation – poor grammar and spelling, improper formatting, and other basic problems. Depending on the class and the students, more sophisticated problems can be corrected. Either way, the result is improved work from the student and less grading time by the professor.

Incorporating peer grading into the curriculum is generally as simple as adding an additional due date a few days before the final assignment is due. Sometimes additional days will be required so that the reviewer has time to read it and to make meaningful comments and that the reviewed student has time to rewrite the assignment.

Summary

The ideas presented here are, for the most part, not new ones. What may be new is the holistic and systematic approach to improving student performance by taking greater responsibility student success. The concept of incorporating success elements into the curriculum is a series of actions that a faculty member can take to improve the quality of student work while reducing time spent grading and banging ones head against the wall in frustration. The initial investments of time are often modest and the products can frequently be used in more than one class, term after term. The next time you identify a frustrating yet typical student behavior, take action and address it.

A DISTRIBUTED LEARNING MODEL FOR PROBLEM SOLVING AND PROGRAM DEVELOPMENT

Fadi P. Deek and Idania Espinosa

ABSTRACT

Technological advances are paving the way for improvements in many sectors of society. Traditional education has primarily been teacher driven, lectured-based in one location. Distributed learning is an emerging paradigm that can contribute significantly to the learning process. This paper explores the difficulties novice programmers' face when learning to program and proposes how distributed learning can be used in learning problem solving and program development.

INTRODUCTION

Novice programmers have difficulties in breaking down a given problem, designing a working solution, and debugging a program. Many programming environments, software applications, and learning tools have been developed to address these difficulties [2][3][4][5]. Several factors play a role in developing problem solving skills and program development in students. Achieving these skills is based on the internal cognition of the individual, the instructor abilities, environmental factors and the programming language. Why do novices have such difficult time learning to program? This question is answered from different angles: student, teacher, and programming language. Novice programmers normally find programming frustrating and difficult. They may not have the sufficient preparation to grasp concepts that are abstract and complex. Novices are not familiar with designing and testing logical structures for solving problems by computer. They lack an adequate mental model about the internals of a computer and how it operates. Some programming teaching methods are also a factor that hinders students' ability to learn, such as the over-emphasis in introductory computing courses on language construct and programming syntax [2][6] and not on problem solving skills.

LEARNING STYLES

Educational research shows that students have different styles of learning. These learning styles can be identified based on the type of information students prefer to receive: sensory or intuitive, visual or verbal, inductive or deductive, actively or reflectively, and sequentially or globally [1]. Instructors should mold their teaching styles to that of students' learning styles in order to effectively maximize learning in classroom.

Sensing learners tend to retain information like facts and observations. They process information more effectively through sights, sounds, and physical sensations. They are detailed oriented and prefer solving problems using well-defined steps. They are practical and complain when information is not related to the real world. Intuitive individuals, on the other hands, are more imaginative and thus prefer abstract concepts and information that is open to interpretation. They rely on memory, ideas, and their own insights. Sensing learners tend to get lower grades than intuitive learners do on lectured courses.

Visual learners retain information through images more so than verbally. They perceive information more effectively via diagrams. If a lecture does not incorporate some visual representation of a concept, visual learners have the tendency to forget the material. Research shows that most students in science classes are visual learners [1]. Lectures are mostly verbal with abstract concepts, formulas, and few diagrams. Verbal learners learn based on written and spoken words.

Inductive learners learn based on first specific scenarios and then more general principles. Students tend to use given facts and observations to infer principles. Deductive learners, on the other hand, prefer general principles first and then deduce consequences. Research shows that inductive learning promotes a deeper understanding and retention of information. Classrooms tend to use deductive approach [9].

Active learners prefer group discussions and exchanging ideas with others. Reflective learners tend to think things through and then experiment. They prefer individual work or in pairs. In a lectured course, both groups are actually neglected and enforce a passive approach to learning. Studies show that students in an active environment excel in comprehension, memory retention, and problem solving. [7]

Sequential learners gain an understanding of information in small, connected pieces. They solve problems efficiently, but may lack an understanding of the larger problem domain. Global learners' approach is all-or-nothing. Initially, they may appear to be slow students, but once they grasp the larger picture, they can make connections that sequential learners do not identify.

DISTRIBUTED LEARNING: AN ALTERNATIVE TO LEARNING PROBLEM SOLVING AN PROGRAMMING

A new model of learning has emerged which collectively brings together these models. This is distributed learning. This section describes this model of learning and also describes the solutions to existing problems in programming. According to Syllabus Magazine in 1995, distributed learning is not just a new term to replace distance learning. Rather, it comes from the concept of distributed resources. Distributed learning is an instructional model that allows instructors, students, and content to be located in different, non-centralized locations so that instruction and learning occur independent of time and place.

Programming using distributed learning model serves as microcosm of the future of learning whereby learning can take place both inside and outside of classrooms. The boundaries have been removed and interactions with people from different locations and different times are possible. The use of distributed learning in computer classrooms provides a new direction for teaching. It resolves the many difficulties that have been observed by novice programmers in learning software development. Below is a summary of difficulties encountered by students and the provisions needed along with a distributed learning environment to resolve these issues.

1. Lack a mental model to visualize abstract relationships
2. Instructors in traditional learning hold an important role in transferring knowledge. If instructor is lacking social skills necessary for interacting with students, technical ability, or effective speaking, an impediment for learning results
3. Students fall behind in classrooms and miss fundamental concepts.
4. Lack of motivation

5. Limited knowledge in a scientific area which may result in difficulty in interacting and following complex discussions
6. Students passivity in class
7. Small programming assignments which tend to lead to individualistic work habits
8. Deficiencies with traditional teaching methods, esp. lectured-based teaching
9. Emphasis on competition for grades rather than learning
10. Programming language paradigms do not associate with natural tendencies of problem solving.

The difficulty of mentally representing abstract concepts is overcome by the use of visual modeling tools. Sensory immersion devices assist in visualizing abstract concepts. These devices have been successful in areas of science and medicine. Once this is extended to the computer world, novices will be better able to model abstractions.

Distributed learning provides alternate means of learning than traditional teaching methods. By allowing students to engage in collaborative learning exercises and to use visual modeling tools, they can spread their depth of learning. The goal is to provide a more enriched curriculum that can guide students to achieve maximum learning potential. Interacting with students could enhance cognitive skills and complement individual cognition.

Distributed learning offers a solution to the third difficulty described whereby students fall behind in class. Virtual classrooms can provide additive means of learning, such as discussion forums, so in the event that a student falls behind, other sources of information are readily available to bring students up to speed on misunderstood materials. For students who prefer learning at their own pace, distance learning course can facilitate this.

CONCLUSIONS

Distributed learning has great potential to be the wave of the future in academic development in support of learning without boundaries to time and distance. It offers a wider spectrum of instructors, advisors, and collaborators than in any single educational institution. It provides a means of attaining skills from remote sources and collaborating with dispersed team members. Technology provides the essential tools for establishing interactions, but these tools, if misused, could lead to adverse effects. A balance is necessary between virtual and direct communication within group members in order to develop and sustain a sense of community. Interactions based on phone conversations alone lack the vibrancy of face-to-face. Also, while technology-mediated communication (i.e. teleconferencing, digital and video) will open the doors of virtual interactions over various information mediums, it will not completely replace personal contact. In order to optimize the use of the distributed learning model, provisions must be made and new inventions devised which provide the best of both worlds for learning. The future of distributed learning is via collaborative virtual workspaces and sensory immersion devices [8]. Further studies are necessary to measure the performance of dispersed team members using CVW. More research is also needed in the area of sensory immersion to study the impacts of these devices in the (virtual) classroom. High performance computing will gradually enable virtual communities to make possible face-to-face interactions and sensory immersion to be an integrated part of everyday life.

REFERENCES

1. W. B. Barbe and M. N. Milone, "What We Know About Modality Strengths," *Educational Leadership*, vol. 38, pp. 378-380, February 1981.

2. F. P. Deek, H. Kimmel, and J. McHugh, "Pedagogical Changes in the Delivery of the First Course in Computer Science: Problem Solving Then Programming," *Journal of Engineering Education*, vol. 87, no. 3, pp. 313-320, July 1998.

3. F. P. Deek and J. McHugh, "Problem Solving and the Development of Critical Thinking Skills," *Journal of Computer Science Education – ISTE SIGCS*, vol. 14, no. 1/2, pp. 6-12, April 2000.

4. F. P. Deek and J. McHugh, "Prototype Software Development Tools for Beginning Programming," *Journal of Computer Science Education – ISTE SIGCS*, vol. 14, no 3/4, pp. 14-20, April 2001.

5. F. P. Deek and J. McHugh, "A Survey and Critical Analysis of Tools for Learning Programming," *Journal of Computer Science Education*, vol. 8, no. 2, pp. 130-178, August 1998.

6. F. P. Deek, M. Turoff, and J. McHugh, "A Common Model for Problem Solving and Program Development," *Journal of the IEEE Transactions on Education*, vol. 42, no. 4, pp. 331-336, November 1999.

7. W. J. McKeachie, *Teaching Tips: A Guidebook for the Beginning College Teacher*, 8th Edition, Lexington, Massachusetts, 1996.

8. M. C. Salzman, C. Dede, and B. Loftin, "ScienceSpace: Virtual realitics for learning complex and abstract scientific concepts," *Proceedings of IEEE Virtual Reality Annual International Symposium*, New York, pp. 246-253, 1996.

9. L. K. Silverman and R. M. Felder, "Learning and Teaching Styles in Engineering Education," *Engineering Education*, vol. 78, no. 7, pp. 674-681, April 1988.

Building and Accessing E-Learning Resources

Bich-Liên Doan and Yolaine Bourda
Supélec, Plateau de Moulon, 3 rue Joliot Curie, 92192 Gif/Yvette.
France
E-mail : (Bich-Lien.Doan , Yolaine.Bourda)@emse.fr

Abstract: This paper shows the importance of taking account of the structure in order to describe and retrieve educational resources. Each educational resource is associated to metadata and structure. We propose combining the structural and the textual analysis of the resources to improve the performance of the system. The user is able to manipulate information at several levels of abstraction, for example a set of resources, images, chapters dealing with one particular area.

Building Educational Resources

Nowadays, more and more educational resources are published and accessed through the World Wide Web (WWW). But educational resources on the WWW lack explicit semantics and structure. This can be improved by the use of metadata to describe the semantic content and by the use of typed links to represent the structure of the resources. Standardized metadata such as Dublin Core Education [1], LOM [2] bring better understanding of the educational resources content and aim, but there is a little description of the structure of these resources.

In order to underline the importance of taking into account of the structure, we classify various types of links that we can find to relate educational resources. Links of structure: they represent the logical structure of a resource, either the inclusion, the sequencing of parts of a resource (for example, the list of prerequisites).
Links of semantic association: these links reflect a semantic association between two pages, or two concepts and are very diverse because they concern the cognitive aspects of the author. Indeed according to the context, the term "winter" can suggest cold, season, country etc. Links of navigation: purely functional, they are used to physically cut out a text in a set of pages limited in volume (number of bytes). They are used for navigation between the pages, for example back link, return to the home page. Links of references: they are used to reference to pages in connection with the subject, for example the bibliographical references, or the references to similar sites and personal pages.

All of these links are often chosen by the author during the building of pages, but the types of links are not explicit with the Hypertextual Markup Language (HTML). To mitigate these problems, we consider that a educational resource is either an atomic unit of information such as an image, a passage, a title…, or a composition of other resources. A resource can be defined as a semantic unit of information, autonomous in the sense that it can be given as a response to a user request. From there, we can consider different levels of resources. A global resource can be structured in a hierarchy of several resources, it is composed of structured elements representing either section, paragraph, image, sound, graph called resources too. Each level in the hierarchy corresponds to a different level of granularity. We choose a tree structure of nodes for our example to be understandable, but in fact, we can have a Directed Acyclic Graph (DAG) structure. For example we can have a first organization level, composed of several domains, sub-domains and so on. Each hierarchical level represents a level of granularity, the lowest level of granularity is that of the components of the atomic resources (not decomposable). This concept of granularity is significant because it intervenes in all the stages of our new information retrieval system. Indeed, during the description of the resources, our formalism makes it possible to describe resources, to express the structural or semantic relations between the resources, to adapt this description to structured pages with the HTML format (META tags) or XML (the tags are defined by the author of the pages according to a particular DTD). Thus, it is possible to explicit the various types of relations between resources, between components of various natures (multi-media like its, image, video) or of various types like paragraphs, references, summaries...

The semantics and the structure of resources as we specified previously may be done by the author of the pages, manually, thanks to metadata. A classical hierarchical clustering algorithm can determine the hierarchy of resources and provide the summary of each cluster. The first solution enables a precise control and the labeling of each represent of clusters by the author, but it requires human help. The second solution is completely automatic but the drawback is that the labels are a list of keywords extracted from the resources and maybe some concepts are omitted. For a quality reason and to enable the author to control the indexing phase, we build the structured resources with the help of the author of resources.

In the building phase of the educational resources, we propose to describe the resources using the IEEE LOM[2] semantics and to apply the RDF serialization[3] with the XML syntax[4].

In the following sections, we take the same example of an E-learning Web course delivered at Supelec's school. In this example, there is one "computer science course" resource which is composed of other resources. The educational resource material has been created by Yolaine Bourda. The domain of the resource is the database management systems (DBMS), including the SQL language. The courses are currently used by students both in Paris and in different geographical places of the Supelec's school: Metz and Rennes. Firstable, the audience is the Supelec's students but it can also be extended to any e-learner who can access the http://wwwlsi.supelec.fr/www/yb/poly_bd/ site. This is an example of the LOM metadata describing three resources:

```
<?xml version="1.0" encoding="iso-8859-1" ?>
<educational_resources>
<General>
<title><langstring xml:lang="en">"Learning databases"</langstring></title>
<identifier><entry>"http://wwwlsi.supelec.fr/www/yb/poly_bd/"</entry></identifier>
<keyword>"course, computer science"</Keyword>
</General>
<LifeCycle>
        <contribute><entity> Yolaine Bourda </entity><date>"1997 september"</date>
        </contribute>
</LifeCycle>
<Educational>
<intenteduserrole>"2nd year Supelec's students"</intenteduserrole>
</Educational>
</educational_resources>


<educational_resources>
<General>
<title><langstring xml:lang="en">What is a DBMS?</langstring></titel>
<identifier><entry>"http://wwwlsi.supelec.fr/www/yb/poly_bd/tdm"</entry></identifier>
<keyword>"DBMS"</Keyword>
</General>
<Relation>
        <kind>"isPartOf"</kind>
        <resource><identifier>"http://wwwlsi.supelec.fr/www/yb/poly_bd/"</identifier></resource>
</Relation>
</General>
</educational_resources>

<educational resources>
<General>
<title><langstring xml:lang="en">"Learning SQL"</langstring></titel>
<identifier><entry>"http://wwwlsi.supelec.fr/www/yb/poly_bd/tdm_sql"</entry></identifier>
<keyword>"SQL"</Keyword>
</General>
<Relation>
        <kind>"isPartOf"</kind>
        <resource><identifier>"http://wwwlsi.supelec.fr/www/yb/poly_bd/"</identifier></resource>
</Relation>
</General>
</educational_resources>
```

The e-learning resources and their organization are partially illustrated in figure 1. Through this example, the same author is responsible for the publication of the three documents (described beyond and illustrated in figure 1 by *d, d1 and d2*), and the date of the creation is the same for the whole documents too; nevertheless, this piece of information has been omitted when the resources composing the root document have been described. This omitted information may be deduced thanks to the dynamic propagation of the metadata along the structural links. The first resource *d* represents the Web site as a collection of E-learning resources. Each resource is described thanks to the LOM metadata. *d* is composed of the two resources *d1* and *d2*. The classification of links categorizes the "isPartOf" and "requires" attributes as structural ones. Each attribute can be static or dynamic. Static means that the attributes are local to the resource and that they can't be propagated along the hierarchy of the metadata. For example, the "kind" and "identifier" attributes are static. "Dynamic ascending" and "dynamic descending" respectively mean that the attributes can be propagated along the hierarchy towards the root or towards the leaves. For example, in figure 1, "author" is a dynamic descending attribute, therefore every resources composing *d* inherit from the value of author. "Keyword" is both an ascending and a escending attribute, so *d21* is indexed by keyword = syntaxe + query whereas *d211* and *d212* are indexed by keyword = course + computer science + SQL + query.

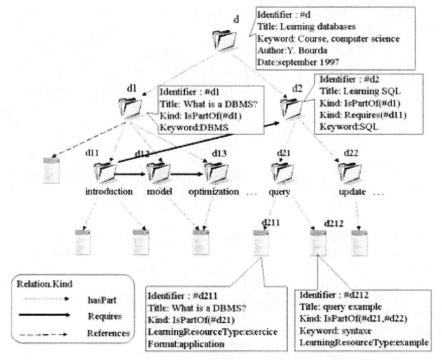

Figure 1: A partial organization of a hierarchy of educational resources

Accessing Educational Resources

Let's assume that DB is the corpus of the resources. In order to support the new functionalities we introduced in our paper, we defined a new query language that supports:
- dynamic granularity of the response, i.e. the granularity of the resource (a chapter, a section, an image) is not expressed in the query but determined by the information retrieval system with the evaluation function at the request time,
- querying on metadata attributes of each resource,
- combination of multi-typed requests allowing the system to manage requests against resources of various types.

The relevant documents in response to a query can be computed with the following evaluation function: where R is the relevance rate of the document and p_i is the weight of each attribute of metadata. d_i is a distance associated to the level of propagation of the attribute.

$$R = \sum_{i=1}^{n} p_i \times \frac{1}{1+|d_i|}$$

$$p_i = \frac{1}{n}$$

We opt for an OQL-like syntax defined by the ODMG[5].
We give two examples showing the power of expressiveness of the query using both metadata and

structure.

Query 1: find documents dealing with both "query" and "update" whose author is "Yolaine Bourda"

```
Select   d   from   DB   where   d.lifeCycle.contribute.entity="Yolaine   Bourda"   and
d.general.keyword="query"+ "update"
```

Thanks to the ascending propagation of the "keyword" attribute (figure 2), the evaluation function returns *d2* as the most relevant answer with the score: 1/2.

Query 1: find SQL courses in computer science published after 1995

```
Select d from DB where d.lifeCycle.contribute.date > "1995" and d.general.keyword="SQL"+
"course" + "computer science"
```

Thanks to the descending propagation of the "keyword" attribute (figure 3), the evaluation function returns *d2* as the most relevant answer with the score: 1. *d21* and *d22* where candidates too, but their scores : 1/3 are less than *d,* (note that the level of granularity of *d* is bigger than the *d21* or *d22* one) .

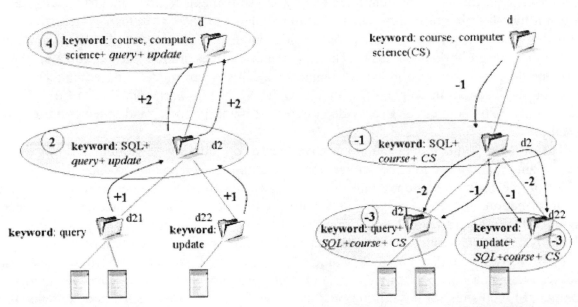

Figure 2 : ascending attribute   **Figure 3** : descending attribute

Conclusion

Classical information retrieval systems provide static responses (fixed by the pre-defined granularity of resources), without taking into account neither the structure of a resource nor its semantics. Here we explain how to explicit the structure of educational resources, and we suggest a new information retrieval system that can index and search educational resources organized into multi-typed resources. This will enable end-users to request in a powerful semantic query language and to provide more suitable responses at several levels of granularity.

References

[1]http://www.dublincore.org/documents/education-namespace/

[2] http://ltsc.ieee.org/wg12/index.html

[3] http://www.w3c.org/XML

[4] Walid Kekhia and Yolaine Bourda. Implementing Learning Object Metadata using RDF. Ed-Media, Tampere, 2001

[5] http://www.odmg.org/

Connecting the Dots: Uniting Education Around the World

Laura Diggs, Ph.D. & John Wedman, Ph.D.
University of Missouri-Columbia

This paper describes a current and ongoing effort to increase global awareness by providing a unique use of Internet2 and video for English instruction with international teachers and students, exchanging cultural information, addressing needs of learners from diverse cultures, and understanding the importance of providing enabling technology experiences that learners cannot have otherwise. The University of Missouri-Columbia College of Education (MU CoE) has implemented a globalization initiative and there are currently 4 schools in Taipei, Taiwan that are connected with K-12 schools in Missouri as well as MU faculty and pre-service teachers. This year, the MU CoE sent three faculty and staff members to Taipei to develop and implement a literature-based English curriculum for students to share with their American counterparts. The goals of this globalization initiative are a critical 3-part model that is a unique experience that currently does not exist. This experience evolves around information and learning, enabling technology, and global connections. This 3-part model is based on: 1) connecting a K-12 school in Taipei, 2) with a K-12 school in Missouri, and 3) MU CoE Literacy faculty. The connection is provided through utilizing Internet2 and video conferencing equipment.

The process of this globalization initiative focuses on individual school needs, but all involve utilizing technology to allow students to have email as well as face-to-face conversations to practice online communication, establish friendships with students of other cultures, exchange cultural information, and develop and understanding and tolerance for other cultures. Students from both cultures benefit from the opportunity to improve their English language (written and verbal) skills as well as identifying the benefits and limitations of online communications.

Current projects where partners include schools in Taipei working with Missouri schools include two elementary schools, one K-9 school, and one senior high school. Projects include development of web sites for descriptions and pictures of participating teacher and students, the school and surrounding community, special events and holidays, as well as information on foods and day-to-day life for students their age. Schools have participated in paired reading of English children's literature books and had face-to-face video conversations around the books. Several schools are participating in science projects together where they collect samples of vegetation, water, and wild life to compare and contrast on the web site with their partner school With the time difference between Taipei and Missouri being a complicating factor, partners are sharing information through threaded discussions and emails as well.

The impact of this globalization initiative has proven to be beneficial to the Taiwanese students having authentic conversations with native speaking English speaking students their own age and improving their English writing and oral skills. The Missouri students have discovered a new cultural appreciation as well as developing friendships. The MU CoE faculty and pre-service teachers have acted as cyber-tutors to help in the writing process as well as professional development for the Taiwanese teachers.

This summer, three of the Taiwan schools are planning trips to Missouri to visit their partners and learn more about living in the United States. One school will have the opportunity to participate in the ThinkQuest Internet2 conference in Seattle, Washington after spending time in St. Louis, Missouri, taking field trips to Boeing corporation, St. Louis Science Center, and other points of interest. Students will collect digital photographs, movies, and other media objects to share as part of the conference and globalization initiative.

E-Learning : The Design of Cognitive Crutches in the 21st Century

Koen DePryck, Ph.D.
Center for Adult Education, Antwerp (Belgium)
Institute of Knowledge Management, Brussels (Belgium)

Abstract

This paper deals with the implications of evolutionary epistemology for the design of Learning and Knowledge Tools. Evolutionary epistemology brings to the table a set of concepts that allow us to construct new cognitive tools that, embedded in or connected to our evolutionary past, may contribute to our cognitive future.

Human cognition is neither static nor deterministic but has evolved, under evolutionary pressure, into a set of tools capable of interacting with those aspects of reality bound to enhance our potential for survival as individual beings or as a group.

Any meaningful design of IT-based Knowledge Tools will need to take that double evolutionary context into consideration. It must address

1. the issue of providing input to a wide range of cognitive modules, many of which serve multiple cognitive function.
2. the issue of compatibility with a wide range of cognitive styles.

We try to point at the relevant characteristics of our mental system and explore the systemic conditions the evolutionary context imposes on knowledge tools and knowledge management systems.

Paper

The history of human tool-making is also a history of crutch-design. A hammer is a fist. Power (most often electric power) has added a new dimension to tools but did not really change their nature—it just made them even more powerful. We have not only developed tools to decrease our physical limitation, we also developed tool to decrease our cognitive restrictions: magnifying glasses and telescopes, clocks, books, …[1]

Every tool is somehow connected to our cognitive wiring if not but for the simple reason that we use them. If that connection goes wrong because it is too complex or because it is poorly designed, the tool quickly looses its attraction and usefulness. The study of cognitive tools is therefore also a study in ergonomics and a study of interfaces.[2]

The study of our tools is a study of ourselves. In a sense, tools are a magnifying glass trough which we can look at our own design. Looking at the cognitive tools that we use can help us to peek inside our minds and to take a look behind the curtains of evolutionary pressure. But an understanding of how our mind functions should allow us to come up with new and exciting cognitive tools without having to rely too much on trial and error.

---

[1] Slide: list of physical and cognitive tools
[2] Slides: examples of how tools connect to our neural circuitry

When we look at educational software, for example, we find an incredible amount of utterly useless products. They simply don't resonate with our cognitive processes. They are like a beautifully sculptured hammer made out of glass: nice to look at, perhaps, but utterly impractical.

A VCR is a wonderful tool. Let us take a look at the buttons. Record (memory storage), play (retrieval), ff, fb, pauze, index (use of markers to facilitate retrieval), … It is not clear if each successful and often used function of the machine corresponds to a primitive 'human' cognitive function, although it is safe to assume that unsuccessful gadgets probably fail to connect to such a human function, except perhaps for a small and marginal group of people.[3]

Human cognition is neither static nor deterministic but has evolved, under evolutionary pressure, into a set of tools capable of interacting with those aspects of reality bound to enhance our potential for survival as individual beings or as a group (and thus indirectly as individuals). New technologies and e-learning will only be successful if they connect to our evolutionary history. At the same time, successful new tools are likely to profoundly change our thinking, our behaviour, our values, …

At the level of the species (or, if one prefers, at the level of individual selection) evolution has constructed, over millions of years, a set of cognitive modules and clusters of such modules. Individual modules define operations over inputs. The input can be either external, as in the case of sensory inputs, or internal, generated by the module itself or generated by some other mental subsystem. Furthermore, it is reasonable to assume that several modules originated as either backup or add-on to older modules, resulting in a by all means complex system.

Cognitive modules and clusters of such modules interact with proper as well as actual input domains. In the case of a module (perhaps constituted by more fundamental modules) for syntactic pattern recognition, actual sentence patterns make up the proper input domain, whereas a rather large set of auditory constructs (from babies' 'talking' to songs of birds and sometimes even mechanical noise produced by machinery) would belong to the actual domain without belonging to the proper domain.

As human beings, we generate huge amounts of actual but improper inputs. The use of IT in general and in education more specifically allows us to explore the boundaries of our mental modules and their interaction. Furthermore, it is not unreasonable to assume that the increasingly large amounts of improper input have an effect on the microcircuits of our cognition. Since a reduction of visual experience causes a reduction of the number and size of synapses in the visual areas of the cortex, a culturally increased amount of specific visual experience (such as we would find in specific types of interaction with computers) could lead to an increase in the amount and size of synapses required to handle that input to cognitive modules. The cortex of wild animals may be up to one-third thicker in wild animals than in domesticated ones, something Darwin already noted.

---

[3] Slide: picture of VCR as a cognitive tool, relating buttons to cognitive functions.

For obvious reasons, the production of improper input to our mental system is greatly restricted by the characteristics of that system and its larger environment, although some degree of randomness, noise, and perhaps coincidence may not be avoided.

In this paper, we try to point at the relevant characteristics of our mental system and explore the systemic conditions or the constraints that the evolutionary context imposes on knowledge tools and knowledge management systems.

Our cognitive system can be described by number of aspects:[4]

- Input
    - Visual, auditory, tactile, kinaesthetic, olfactory
    - Verbal, non-verbal
    - Proper, improper
    - Focus
- Content
    - Paradigms
    - Need-based, interest-based, …
- Processes and operations
    - Differentiation, categorization, seriation, logical deduction or induction, analogy, counting, mapping, …
- Learning
    - Implicit, explicit
    - Speed, …
- Level of abstraction
    - Distance from information present in sensory input
- Level of complexity
    - Number of units of information, degree of novelty, ..
- Storage
    - Memory
    - Retrieval
- Output
    - Cfr. Input
    - Communication

The specifics of each of these aspects have been shaped under evolutionary pressure in a relatively stable context. IT and E-Learning dramatically change that context. In order to maximize the usefulness of cognitive tools, we must identify their strengths as well as their weaknesses and compare those with our 'innate' tools. It is only on the basis of such an inventory (perhaps also including characteristics of successful 'older tools, such as books) that we will be able to integrate existing E-learning tools successfully and to design new tools that are even more powerful than the ones we have available today.

Mathematics is bound to play an essential role in the development of meaningful new tools. Pattern recognition, typically something humans are fairly good at, can be enhanced by teaching computers how to deal with pattern. Understanding how we

---

[4] Slides: overview of the aspects of a human cognitive system

handle patterns will allow us build tools that are even better at doing that than we ourselves are.

Nevertheless, the relationship between innate and the set of new tools is typically ambiguous. Computers make it easier to count. Databases enhance our memory. On the one hand, new tools obviously outshine a number of our innate functions, perhaps contributing to their decline. On the other hand, they make it possible to train our innate functions or to compensate for deficiencies. Children playing games on their computers develop superior eye-hand coordination. Foreign languages are more easily learned using speech technology and sound analysis, vocabulary is more easily memorized with the help of appropriate software. Even common word processors can help people with language problems (dyslexics, …) by incorporating tools such as speech recognition, spelling correction and functions to find homonyms.

E-Learning exists at the somewhat paradoxical crossroad of making us less dependent on the restrictions of some of our innate functions and the enhancement of others. E-Learning must therefore be approached as part of a larger epistemic system that includes our innate as well as the totality of the cognitive tools that we have developed throughout our history.

That is especially important if we take the distribution of cognitive functions in a population into consideration. At the level human social interacting, (or, if one prefers, at the level of group selection) evolution has come up with a range of cognitive styles, ranging from the predominantly verbal to the predominantly non-verbal, from the predominantly inductive to the predominantly deductive, from the predominantly synthetic to the predominantly analytic, and so on.

Any meaningful design of IT-based Knowledge Tools will need to take that double evolutionary context into consideration.

1. At the level of the individual, it must address the issue of providing input to a wide range of cognitive modules, many of which serve multiple cognitive functions.
2. It must also address the issue of compatibility with a wide range of cognitive styles, avoiding a simplistic reduction of human cognition to a single evolutionary thread or, worse, a single static set of cognitive functions.

In conclusion, I argue that E-Learning tools must be sufficiently 'traditional' in order to change our traditional ways. In the design of educational software, all too often too much energy is spent trying to make something 'unique', something 'different'. While that may appeal at first, in the long run it tends to decrease the chances to make a truly lasting contribution to a genuine learning society.

Providing Higher Education Degrees Through Telecommunications and Collaborations

Rita L. Dobbs, Ph.D., Department of Technology, The University of Texas at Tyler, USA, rdobbs@mail.uttyl.edu

W. Clayton Allen, Ed.D., Department of Technology, The University of Texas at Tyler, USA, callen@mail.uttyl.edu

Abstract: **This paper will provide critical information to interested higher education personnel for designing/implementing undergraduate/graduate degree programs utilizing telecommunications, collaborations, and technical support services. Collaborations among the Mexia State School, a MHMR facility, The University of Texas at Tyler (UTT), and the UT TeleCampus, a virtual university designed as a central support system for the 15 component campuses and research facilities that comprise the U T System, allow students to obtain degrees that would have previously remained unattainable. The Department of Technology at UTT provides custom designed degree plans through a combination of interactive television courses, web-based courses, and academic credit for work experience to grant degrees in appropriate fields. Technological support, tutorial programs, and digital libraries are among the essential support services provided to participating students.**

As The University of Texas at Tyler (UTT) steps into the new millennium, a new era will be much more complex and demanding than the last one. It will be characterized by rapid changes in demographics, growth of an information-age economy, and revolutionary technological advances. The 21st Century will also place new pressures and demands on universities to be more accountable and more affordable, to serve an increasingly diverse society, and to deliver education using alternative models. The University must be positioned to meet these realities in order to prepare students to meet the challenges of a fast-paced and shrinking world. The University of Texas at Tyler welcomes the challenge, and in doing so will become the distinctive choice for those seeking academic excellence, opportunity for personal and professional growth, and a dynamic environment for learning in the new millennium.

UTT was established by the Texas Legislature in 1971 as Tyler State College and was renamed Texas Eastern University four years later; it became a component of The University of Texas System in 1979. UTT became a four-year university by action of the legislature in 1997; it had been created as an upper-level university.

Challenges for Students

University students will need to *take more responsibility for their learning*, for exploring and understanding complex concepts, and for accurate analysis and creative synthesis. They must become fully engaged, active partners in the educational process, learning to navigate through the rich information environment that exists outside of the classroom and challenging themselves to become intellectually vigorous in order to acquire, evaluate and use the information available to them. In short, students must not only learn, they must also acquire the skills to learn effectively on their own.

Challenges for The University of Texas at Tyler

The University of Texas at Tyler is transforming itself into a four-year, comprehensive, regional university with a full range of undergraduate and graduate degree programs. Only a comprehensive university that emphasizes the integration of liberal arts and professional education can provide the depth and breadth of knowledge, skills, and attitudes that students will need for success in the new millennium.

The University will respond by creating the "U. T. Tyler Tradition"-a solid foundation for successful learning that is based in the humanities, arts, and sciences and that fosters rigorous intellectual growth and academic development in all disciplines. The "U. T. Tyler Tradition" will provide the "cornerstone" for preparing students to accept and even anticipate the multiple transitions they will make during their lives. This distinctive curriculum will provide the necessary base of knowledge and engage students in self-discovery where they develop the art of reflection and embrace intellectual challenges.

The Department

The Department of Technology is a student-centered department committed to conducting multi-option programs targeted at preparing technical professionals, instructors, and educators who exceed standards. In accordance with this statement, the Department of Technology continually strives to improve the array of managerial and technical knowledge and skills of individuals by offering programs and courses based on industry's need for applications oriented, technically competent, flexible and internationally competitive employees. In order to ensure that the program offerings are technically up-to-date, the Department employs laboratory instruction based on tabletop technology and computer-based simulation.

The Department of Technology has adopted the NAIT definition of Industrial Technology. It is viewed as a field of study designed to prepare technical and/or technical management oriented professionals for employment in business and industry. The programs in the Department include:

1. The application of theories, concepts, and principles found in the humanities and the social and behavioral sciences, including a thorough grounding in communication skills.

2. The understanding of the theories and the ability to apply the principles and concepts of mathematics and science and the application of computer fundamentals.

3. The application of concepts derived from, and current skills developed in, a variety of technical and related disciplines which may include, but is not limited to, materials and production processes, industrial management and human relations, marketing, communications, electronics, and graphics.

These concepts have served as the basis of an ongoing program and curriculum improvement process throughout the history of the Department. As a result of this commitment, the Department of Technology entered into an agreement with the personnel of the Mexia State School to offer undergraduate and graduate programs via interactive television classes (ITV) and through web-based courses offered through the UT TeleCampus component.

Mexia State School

Mexia is located approximately 100 miles southwest of Tyler. Personnel at the Mexia State School previously had to travel to Waco to take courses from Baylor University, a private institution where tuition rates were proving to be prohibitive for the personnel wishing to continue their education.

Today the school employs almost 1,500 individuals. The school operated exclusively from wooden barracks until June 1951, when the first permanent brick buildings were completed with beds for 312 boys. In September 1953, a second group of buildings was completed with 425 beds. Money for this early construction came from a one cent a pack cigarette tax levied by the Texas Legislature. Construction of new buildings continued through the 1950's with the completion of additional dormitories. A 50-bed infirmary was opened in 1958. In 1963 the peak period of construction ended with the dedication of 14 new buildings on the state school campus.

During the past years, the school's population has changed as other services became available in the community. From its origin has a home for young men and women with various levels of mental retardation, the school has become a place where individuals with profound and severe retardation in addition to behavior and medical problems live. The average age of the school's residents is now 45 years old. Mexia State School is a regional operation of the Texas Department of Mental Health and Mental Retardation. (Mexia State School)

Providing Degrees for Mexia Students

In order to meet the needs of the Mexia students, a special undergraduate degree was made available to the students, the Bachelor of Applied Arts and Sciences (BAAS). This degree program has been identified with the "inverted curriculum." It gives primary consideration to areas of emphasis meeting the educational and career goals of community and junior colleges. Only students who have specialized at the junior college or community college level in technical or vocational studies and desire to continue in their pursuit of a degree may follow a program leading to the Bachelor of Applied Arts and Sciences degree.

The courses, which lead to the degree, may differ from student to student, making it possible to customize the degree program to fit a student's needs. The purpose of this program is to provide opportunities for those individuals planning to enter the technical or vocational occupations, or for those who have already entered the technical or vocational occupations but have decided that additional educational preparation will strengthen their previous training and improve career advancement opportunities. A student may also prepare a professional dossier of past work experience for consideration of academic credit up to 18 semester hours. This allows the personnel at the Mexia State School to complete their undergraduate degree. The courses for the BAAS are offered to the Mexia State School through ITV courses that originate at UTT and are transmitted to Mexia through a T1 line via compressed video. Mexia students are able to conduct counseling sessions and student conferences through the ITV system. Professors from the Department of Technology travel to Mexia at least one time during the semester to make a personnel contact with students and to help assimilate them into campus life.

UTT library provides digital resources for the remote students. Complete instructions for accessing the electronic databases as well as instructions for requesting interlibrary materials are in place on the library homepage found at http://library.uttyler.edu/distance.htm

Students in Mexia who are pursuing the Masters of Science in Technology/Human Resource Development (HRD) option have two options available to them. They may take courses through the ITV system or they may take courses through the UT TeleCampus. The HRD degree option can be customized to meet the particular student's area of interest and can accommodate the interests and special skills of each student. Professors in the department meet with each degree-seeking student individually to construct a degree plan that is perfect for that student's career goals. The success of the program has been tremendous with the growth of the program exceeding double digit increases each year.

Human Resource Development is a professional field of practice that focuses on education and training of adults in diverse settings. It is organized learning activities arranged within an organization in order to prepare young people to manage the dual roles of family member and wage earner, to enable them to gain entry-level employment in a high-skill, high-wage job and/or to continue their education.

The online Master of Science degree/HRD option utilizes the resources of UTT, The University of Texas at Galveston (UTG), The University of Texas at Permian Basin (UTPB), The University of Texas at Arlington (UTA), and the UT TeleCampus. The Department of Technology assumed responsibility for developing nine (9) courses in the

MS degree option and utilizes 6 courses from the component institutions. This truly makes the MS degree in Technology/HRD option a unique opportunity, not only for the personnel of the Mexia State School, but also for the citizens of Texas and beyond.

The UT TeleCampus (UTTC) is the support center for online learning within the University of Texas System's fifteen component campuses. Online courses and degree programs can be completed entirely at a distance and meet the same high-quality academic standards as their onsite equivalents. The UT TeleCampus provides everything a student needs to participate, including admission applications, registration and financial aid information, classrooms and academic resources. The goal of the TeleCampus in placing programs online was the creation of collaborative degrees, utilizing the best resources in faculty expertise from all campuses. This was the model followed in developing the Master of Science Degree in Technology/HRD option.

"An excellent example of the expanding e-learning programs offered by state university systems, the UT TeleCampus was launched in 1998 by the University of Texas System. Students may earn an MBA, Masters in Computer Science, and various other online degrees from a school within the UT system. Students who wish to earn a degree must first apply and be admitted to one of the universities in the UT system. That campus will then serve as the student's "home" campus, and ultimately award the degree," Dr. Darcy Hardy, Asst. Vice Chancellor for Academic Affairs and UT TeleCampus Director.

Conclusions

In order to participate in a UT TeleCampus online course, certain computer requirements and browser configurations and plug-ins are needed to enable a successful experience. Online students must also have a confident level of computer literacy.

An important part of an online course will involve Web conferencing and other interactivity such as synchronous chat. These tools provide a means for communicating with the instructor and classmates much like a student would in a face-to-face environment.

By using the "Getting Started" CD-ROM, published by the UT TeleCampus, a student can start the semester with the advantage of being able to receive all multimedia aspects of any given course. Necessary software requirements are consolidated on one easy-to-use CD provided by the UT TeleCampus and mailed to each student enrolled in the online program. (UT TeleCampus)

Extensive support services are provided by TeleCampus staff in the way of instructional design and course development, as well as faculty training in bringing courses from the lecture-based classroom to the Web-based classroom. Technological support, policy, marketing research and external communications are among the other essential support services provided to the campus from the UT TeleCampus (UT TeleCampus).

The Department of Technology at The University of Texas at Tyler is striving to provide quality educational programs to students who wish to pursue their educational career goals. By collaborating with specific institutions, UT components, and the UT TeleCampus, the Department of Technology is bringing higher education degrees to the citizens of Texas and the world.

Resources

Mexia State School, (2000-2002) [Online], Available: http://www.mhmr.state.tx.us/Schools/MexiaSS/MexiaSS.html

The University of Texas at Tyler, (2000-2001) Undergraduate /Graduate Catalog [Online]. Available: http:// www.uttyler.edu

UT Telecampus, The University of Texas System [Online], Available: http://www.telecampus.uttsystem.edu

Technology, Education and Knowledge:
Digital Divide or Knowledge Leverage ?
-Some Thought Following a Pilot Project of the European Commission-

Patrick-Yves Badillo and Dominique Bourgeois
Research Center on Media, Information and Knowledge
University of Aix-Marseille II (Université de la Méditerranée)
France
badillo@ejcm.univ-mrs.fr

Abstract: Knowledge is a key factor in the new information society and technology induces a considerable demand to the education systems. The virtues of a "socratic school", resting on four pillars: to learn how to know, to learn how to make, to learn how to live together, to learn how to be, must be accessible thanks to the use of the information and communication technologies. Form-Ami is a pilot project of the European Commission with a view to promoting new university training courses in the specialized skills required by the information industries. Form-Ami can be considered as a reference for the diffusion of a new pedagogical paradigm. We will show how the new pedagogical and knowledge mediation is a key for the future. But, to break the digital divide will be more and more costly at the beginning. Only later the fruits of these efforts will be available...

> *"The illiterate of the future will not be the person who cannot read.*
> *It will be the person who does not know how to learn."*
> *A. TOFFLER quoted by I. PRIGOGINE, letter, 1999*

Need for Radical Teaching Innovations... to Surmount the Knowledge Gap

The harmonious development of the information society depends *on the coherence of the "triptyque": technology - education - social diffusion. The technological push* made possible to develop networks which store, treat and convey an increasingly significant quantity of information. A new training paradigm appears with the rise of the Information and Communication Technologies (ICT); the usual teaching actors have to make a difficult and long adjustment: training and knowledge are accessible with new methods thanks to new technologies. Remote teaching becomes a distributed teaching in which the learner plays an increasingly active role in interaction with the teacher. *Beyond the technological development much more significant breaks become visible concerning "Knowledge" and its diffusion.* In the context of the information society the Universe of Knowledge is recombining. In a rather traditional way one can distinguish "data", which are simply data recorded in a system (discrete, objective data, which record facts on the world and are easily structured, organized and transferred) and information which makes possible to transmit a message; thus Picasso passes a message through Guernica, and influences minds. According to T. H. Davenport and L. Prusak (1997), knowledge constitutes "a fluid mix of framed experience, values, contextual information, and expert insight that provides a framework for evaluating and incorporating new experiences and information. It originates and is applied in the minds of knowers. In organizations, it often becomes embedded not only in documents or repositories, but also in organizational routines, processes, practices, and norms" (p. xii).
In short, knowledge is a key factor of the firm competitiveness in the new economy based on information. Consequently, work and knowledge which were two relatively distinct values in the taylorist universe are mixing. Then training and the control of knowledge become a new stake. Acquired knowledge is becoming obsolete almost instantaneously and any individual must learn throughout his life. Taking into account the economic importance of the stakes, it is not astonishing to observe that, beyond the traditional places of knowledge, the Schools and the Universities, new training places are set up: companies develop training structures, such as for example Motorola University, Hewlett Packard or Sun University; one also sees, for example, Microsoft diffuse its own certification labels, equivalent to professional diplomas.

Form-Ami: a Pilot Project of the European Commission to Apply the "Socratic" Teaching Method

Technological progress thus modifies radically the relation between man and information and induces a considerable demand with respect to the education systems (See J. Richarson, 1996). *Virtues of a "socratic school"* resting on four pillars (on this topic see the publication of the European Commission, 1998): to learn how to know, to learn how to make, to learn how to live together, to learn how to be, must be accessible thanks to the use of ICT. Indeed, ICT must help the teachers to set up a teaching approach supporting not only training but also an hypothetico-deductive reasoning mode which will permit the learners to acquire an autonomy vis-a-vis the life events (see the document of the European Commission, 1998, p. 11). It is on this condition that the Knowledge Gap will be surmounted.

The Socratic Approach: a Process or "The Art to Be Confined"

"[...] research and knowledge are on the whole only reminiscence"
PLATO, Menon, translation from Les Belles Lettres, tome III, 2, 1923

Form Ami [1] is a pilot project of the European Commission with a view to promoting new university training courses in the specialized skills required by the information industries, through the socratic method and on the basis of an important consortium which includes academic institutions and information firms. *The socratic approach refers to the philosophy of education and to the teaching method presented by Plato. One will retain in particular the idea of the socratic "maïeutique", which is an art of obstetrician, and the conditions of the knowledge learning: the role of the teacher is that of a guide and the learner is responsible for his learning, which cannot be an accumulation of knowledge, but rather a search of knowledge by reminiscence.*
Within the framework of the Form-Ami project the socratic approach is implemented gradually, so that the students adapt to work as a group, by using more and more the multimedia tools and while trying more and more to solve by themselves the problems which they encounter. Thus two stages can be distinguished each one corresponding to a part of the teaching and to the realization of multimedia products: in the first stage all the students attend the same courses which give them the bases in art and mechanics of information; in the second stage the students follow specialized courses in the option which they have chosen: Security, Geographical Information Systems or multimedia Pedagogy. So they are very few in each option (between 5 and 12) and the follow-up work by the teachers is very effective. Obviously it is during the second stage that the socratic approach is the most applied, but the first stage is essential for a transition between a traditional teaching and a teaching based on the socratic approach with the intensive use of ICT.

Implementation of the Socratic Method for the Realization of Multimedia Products

For the academic year 2000-2001 among 500 European candidates finally 28 students obtained their diploma. The students were of 11 different nationalities; they represented largely the European Union and there were also non European students. Five multimedia products linked to the courses were realized on the following subjects: Theory of Information, Information market, Security, Geographical Information Systems, Pedagogy. The socratic method is in the heart of the teaching and of the realization of the multimedia products. From a pedagogical point of view the thread rests on a flexible process during which the students learn how to learn by working in group and with the multimedia tools. Of course, the students benefit from the help of the teachers, in particular from the content of research and work carried out for many years by the teachers-researchers-experts. The principles of the implementation of the socratic method are best described by the process of realization of the multimedia product "pedagogy". For this multimedia product, realized during the second stage of the Form-Ami project, the socratic approach is reinforced, because the students are accustomed to work together, have better ability to use multimedia tools and also because of the number of students (only 12 students). So the teachers ask the students 12 questions to define progressively the outline of the multimedia product with the students. Questions are the guideline for the construction of the multimedia on line product and socratic exercises. The students define themselves 4 groups of 3 students and then work together; each group works on 4 questions, of course with the permanent help of different teachers (from the University of Aix-Marseille II -

---

[1] The Form-Ami backgrounds were defined by D. Deberghes, Administrateur Principal, European Commission, Information Society DG.

Université de la Méditerranée/EJCM-, the University of Tampere, the University of Koblenz-Landau and the CJD Maximiliansau). There is a high level of interactivity between the students and the teachers.

The Pedagogical and Knowledge Paradigm[2]

The Old Pedagogical Paradigm Confronted with the New Knowledge Diffusion Model

The old pedagogical paradigm can be defined as a knowledge push. In this framework, which is dominant since the beginning of the Gutenberg's Galaxy, teachers are the holders and have the monopoly of knowledge; they produce and diffuse knowledge with a specific place in the society.

Old pedagogical paradigm:
Knowledge push: teachers produce and diffuse knowledge

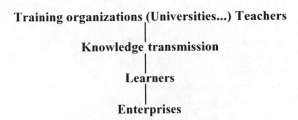

But today this old paradigm is questioned by changes which affect the universities. The whole university world will switch over tomorrow; according to P. Lévy (2000), "the universities will depend more and more exclusively on their customers (...) the students can now learn elsewhere (...) by shopping around in cyberspace where the on-line training offers are daily becoming more varied, more precise, better organized" (p. 95).

A Key for the Future: the New Pedagogical and Knowledge Mediation Paradigm

The Socratic approach is a new pedagogical model with the realization of multimedia on-line products: Form-Ami can be considered as a reference because it is perfectly adapted to the new information and knowledge society. *We define Form-Ami as a new interactive knowledge mediation paradigm: in the context of the new pedagogical paradigm teachers share knowledge and produce knowledge in collaboration with students and enterprises or training organizations.*

Interactive Knowledge
Teachers, learners and enterprises share, produce and diffuse knowledge

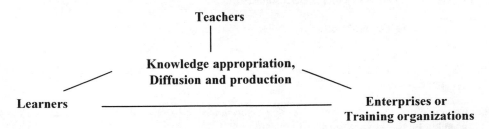

In this new interactive knowledge mediation paradigm the learning process becomes more and more a common construction and collaboration: "*Young people will be guiding their teachers to new kind of learning models*", predicts Mr. Juha Lipianen from Nokia (ED-MEDIA 2001, Hypermedia Laboratory, University of Tampere, June 2001). "*Knowledge is not delivered; it grows in unpredictable ways because learners move through this space according to their own needs, intentionally connected to others. Participation in this space makes it grow for you, over time and through your use and interaction.*"(P. Clifford and S. Friesen,2001).

---

[2] source: P.-Y. Badillo, communications to different conferences and Final Form-Ami Report, July 2001.

Form-Ami is a useful reference because its pedagogical principle, defined about five years ago, anticipated the more up-to-date present research. According to D. Jonassen (2001) learning process is efficient if it is organized as a "solving problem" system; students are confronted to a problem and they have to solve it; the only professional legitimated goal of everybody is "problem solving" (decision making, modeling...). Form-Ami has been a rich pedagogical experiment because the students, of course with the help of the teachers, have had to solve problems: how to apply in practice the courses, how to produce a multimedia product, how to organize their practical training. Teachers have also to adapt their pedagogical approach and the educational organization to help the students to solve the problems. This new pedagogical paradigm is also described, for example, by B. Collis (2001): "What is our first aim? Learning from experiences, from one's own and from those in one organization, and building upon these experiences....".

Conclusion: From Digital Divide to Knowledge Leverage ?

The Socratic approach based on ICT permits the following results:
- *The Internet is a vast set of knowledge resources for the students: students often learn more effectively by discovery (constructivism) and by interaction (collaboration) than by lecture (direct traditional training).*
- *The students learn to work together, to be together and to collaborate in the context of different nationalities, different scientific backgrounds, but with a common objective and a common work: they learn to realize multimedia on-line products.*

But the new pedagogical model needs high investment in software, material and an intensive involvement of all the actors: very high intensive work of the learners (in Form-Ami: evening until 9.00 p.m. and some Saturdays, intense exchanges par e-mail), high investment of the teachers anywhere, anytime..., a lot of help by tutors. We have also to highlight the fact there is a danger: students can be hypnotized by new technologies; it is imperative to ask them to work on the content and to produce content through exercises.

In conclusion, with its Socratic organization Form-Ami has introduced a new pedagogical model. Form-Ami must be considered as a reference; this project was several years in advance and is fully adapted to the new pedagogical paradigm based on problem solving pedagogy and learners experience. However it is obvious, for cost reasons, that the generalization of the socratic method to standard courses is impossible. We will recommend to adopt this method for specializations for which today the needs are essential. *New technologies multiply the knowledge, learning and diffusion possibilities but also the cost; new technologies in pedagogy are submitted to the well known network effect: to launch a network is very expensive, then it is cheaper and cheaper. So, to break the digital divide thanks to new technology and new pedagogical method like the socratic approach will cost more and more at the beginning. Only later the fruits of these efforts will be available...*

References

Clifford P. and Friesen S. (2001). Bringing learning to learners: the Galileo Educational Network. *ED-MEDIA 2001*, Hypermedia Laboratory, University of Tampere, June 2001.

Collis B. (2001). Linking Organizational Knowledge and Learning *ED-MEDIA 2001*, Hypermedia Laboratory, University of Tampere, June 2001.

Davenport, T. H. and Prusak, L. (1997). *Working Knowledge: How Organizations Manage What They Know*. Cambridge, MA: Harvard University Press.

European Commission (1998). *Teaching, Learning, Information: towards an open Socratic school.* Luxembourg: Official Office of the publications of the European Community.

Jonassen D. (2001). E-Learning to solve problems. *ED-MEDIA 2001*, Hypermedia Laboratory, University of Tampere, June 2001.

Lévy P. (2000). *World Philosophie, Le marché,le cyberespace, la conscience.* Paris: Editions Odile Jacob.

Richarson J. (1996). *Information technology: a new path to creativity in education.* Paris: Editions Eska.

CARA
A Constructivist Approach to E/C Resource Management and Administration

Michael Draper and Yves Perrin, – CERN, Geneva
(11 July 2002)

Abstract

Very often extremely valuable Education & Communication (E/C) material gets forgotten about and is buried in a drawer or computer file system once the event for which it was originally developed is over. CARA aims at making these resources, developed in various corners of CERN, wider known and available to as many people as possible. Our target audiences are the community of High Energy Particle (HEP) physicists but also high school teachers and the media. Such an approach saves both developer time by providing a source of inspiration and of documents and will help in gradually improving resource quality by building on what has been done before. CARA will be based on the CERN Document Server (CDS) which already hosts a large database relating to HEP containing more than 500,000 records. CDS also offers many related utilities including a document format converter and an automated information submission system. It uses the MARC based CDS metadata set extended for E/C material.

Why?

- re-usability of E/C material such as presentation slides, articles, brochures, leaflets, pieces of text, diagrams, photos, screen shots, web pages, video clips, animations, simulations, games, etc
- availability to other user communities (high school teachers, media, etc)
- automatic review of resource validity and characteristics.
- Reduce effort spent on duplication

Related benefits

- enlarge source of information and inspiration
- complement and/or improve quality of E/C material on a given topic by building on top of what already exists rather then re-inventing the wheel.

How?

Step #1

- identify potential sources of E/C material and types of available resources
- make inventory of existing resources

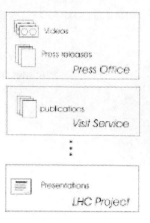

Step #2

Resource's metadata ⟷ Resources

- specify appropriate set of metadata to describe resources as fully as possible (identify the characteristics that potential users of the resource are likely to use when searching for resources and the characteristics that are useful to control the relevance of the resources over time)
- test relevance of this metadata with representatives of the targeted user communities on a few typical resources
- review specification of the metadata set accordingly

title: CERN in 2 minutes, Du Big au Bang, Technology at CERN

location: Press Office, Photo service, CMS

media type: poster, film, leaflet, picture, presentation, etc

topic: General information about CERN, Assembly of CMS detector

size (as seen by user): 23 pages, 800x600, 2m x 1.5m, 23mn

archive size: 47 KB, 3 video tapes

available formats: Word, Illustrator, Power Point, JPEG

original event/context: Open Day, Dalai-Lama visit, webcast

author(s) identification: John Smith / CERN-EP

ownership: CERN, Scientific American

creation date: July 1975

last modification date: May 1999

language: English, Italian

interactivity level: none, medium, high

correctness confidence :	unknown, Press Office validated, DG validated
sub-topics / keywords :	WWW, Tim Berners Lee
identified components :	not analyzed, resource_id1, resource_id2
intended audience (level, age, etc):	general public, physics students, pupils
estimated interest in year:	edu/2001, info/1999, history/2000, etc
resource id :	unique identifier of the resource within the system
next review year:	2003, 2005

```
General public    history  info  edu
Pupils            history  info  edu
Students          history  info  edu
Teachers          history  info  edu
Physicists        history  info  edu
```

Example of how the interest of an E/C resource might drift and survive over time for the community it was developed for and for other communities

Step #3

review all existing resources and for each of them:
- decide on the validity, redundancy, and usefulness
- if useful, record the metadata values corresponding to the resource

Hosting platform

- The CERN Document Server (CDS) is one of the major information sources for High Energy Physics. It containing links to more than 500,000 resources (mostly scientific papers within the field of HEP, but also photos, videos and posters).
- The E/C resources will be catalogued in a separate "sub-base" inside CDS. Authors and/or system managers will use on-line submission procedures to add new material or modify existing resources.
- A customized, and easy-to-use (c.f. Google), user interface to ease E/C resource search, retrieval, submission as well as document format conversion.

CERN Document Server

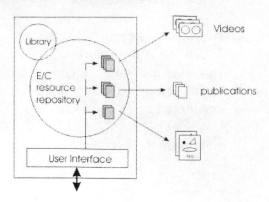

Criteria to measure system operation and maintenance quality

- how populated does the system get ?
- how accurate/up-to-date are hosted documents' metadata?
- how frequently is the system used?
- how much its use crosses CERN organization and targeted user communities boundaries?

Related issues

- responsibility of content (individual, group, project, lab) on expressed opinion, information sensitivity, data correctness, etc)
- čopyright issues
- automatic signaling that metadata needs reviewing

Effects of Social Interaction on Learning in a Hybrid Model of an Online Course, Child Abuse Detection and Reporting

Brenda Dressler, Ph.D
Instructional Technology & Teacher Education
New York Institute of Technology
United States
brendres@aol.com

Abstract: The paper is a report on the findings of the effect of social interaction on learning in this online course, Child Abuse Detection and Reporting. The course is delivered in the hybrid format, a mixture of asynchronous and synchronous models. A one-way analysis of variance was used to examine the scores on the questionnaires of 101participants for evidence of the effect of the chat on learning outcomes. Findings indicate no significant between the scores of Group I, the participants who completed the questionnaire before attending the chat and the scores of Group II, the participants who completed the questionnaire after attending the chat. Participants' evaluations of the course's interactivity reveal that the chat is viewed positively both by Groups I and II. Educators need to develop distance-learning models that encourage social interactivity.

Introduction

Given the tremendous growth of online courses educators and psychologists are investigating whether learning takes place in this format. Learning is defined as a "change in human disposition or capability that persists over a period of time and is not simply ascribable to processes of growth." (Gagne, 1985, p.2). A permanent change in knowledge, skill, attitude or interest or value develops from the learning experience. A fundamental aspect of learning is social interaction. Learning is accomplished when students are actively engaged (Leider & Jarvenpaa, 1993). Furthermore, educators who teach distance-learning courses concur that for these courses to be successful the student learner must be actively involved (Catchpole, 1993; Webster & Hackley, Dec. 1997). When a learner is actively involved learning is facilitated.

Adults learn through life experiences and then reflect on the knowledge gained and skills acquired. These are important factors in adult learning (Webster & Hackley, Dec.1997). Some educators of adult learners view successful learning as including "collaboration, interactivity, application, democracy, constructivist, and a sense of community" (Eastmond &Summer, 1998, p.34). In the Child Abuse online course, participants collaborate when they analyze their experience with witnessing or reporting suspected abuse/neglect and with the case studies imbedded in the course readings.

New York State Department of Education mandates a two-hour workshop on Child Abuse Detection and Reporting Course for teachers and other school personnel. The United Federation of Teachers (UFT), a state approved provider offers this class in two formats. One format is the traditional face-to-face classroom setting. The second format is an online course and is the focus of this research proposal. Two models of this online course, hybrid and asynchronous, has been ongoing for over five years. The hybrid course is the subject of this research paper.

The hybrid online course was offered each month from October 1996 through June 1998, excluding July and August to pre-service and in-service teachers, assistant principals, school secretaries and paraprofessionals. Participants are given two weeks to complete the assignments and access to AOL is required. The course consists of six parts: an introduction, four reading assignments that include six (6) questions, a myth and fact questionnaire consisting of 19 questions and a series of open-ended evaluation question and a synchronous one-hour chat. For purposes of this study, asynchronous learning is defined as learning that can take place in any location and at any time using a computer with Internet access. Synchronous learning is defined as learning that takes place at a distance but at the same time.

America Online's message boards are the electronic analog of the old familiar corkboard and pushpins. Participants post their answers and read messages at any time. Folders are posted on boards (the messages are inside the folder). The folders are organizational tools placed on the board to help you locate topics. The instructor asks additional questions, encourages class members to read and react to each other's responses. The instructor also posts questions based on participants' responses that appear on the electronic message board. Participants are required to write one or two sentences explaining their answers to the myth and fact questionnaire and e-mail their answers to the instructor. After the answers are received, the instructor then e-mails the correct answers to the individual participant. All required reading and responses are in the asynchronous format. Participants can complete their work when it is convenient for them. At the end of the two-week period participants are required to meet in a chat room for one-hour to discuss case studies in the reading assignments and in the newspapers and to respond to additional questions raised by the instructor. During the chat, participants collaborate and determine whether reasonable cause to suspect child abuse/neglect is present in these cases studies.

The Study

This research examines the following hypotheses regarding the distance learning hybrid model:
Hypothesis 1: Participants (Group II) who complete the myth and fact questionnaire after their participation in the interactive chat has significantly higher scores that those participants (Group I) who completed the myth and fact questionnaire before they participated in the interactive chat.
Hypothesis 2: Participants (Group II) who complete the myth and fact questionnaire after their participation in the interactive chat express greater levels of satisfaction than those participants (Group I) who complete the myth and fact questionnaire before they participated in the interactive chat.

Participants consist of new teachers who need to meet New York State Department of Education's requirement for certification and experienced teachers who need to take the course to be certified as an assistant principal and /or principal. These participants teach in the New York City public schools. Other school personnel such as paraprofessionals and school secretaries also take this course.

This study uses quantitative and qualitative data obtained during a one and one half-year period from 101 participants who have completed this hybrid online course. The quantitative information derives from the scores on the myth and fact questionnaire used to measure learning outcomes. Learning outcomes are operationalized by performance on the myth and fact questionnaire. The scores of the participants in Group I (n=71) who complete the myth and fact questionnaire before participating in the chat and the scores of the participants in Group II (n= 30) who complete the myth and fact questionnaire after participating in the chat are compared. A one-way analysis of variance was conducted to determine whether the mean scores of Group I and Group II were significantly different from each other.

In the Learning Hall (chat) The instructor asks questions such as, " how can the barriers to reporting suspected child abuse/neglect be removed?" and " do you know the name of the designated reporter and the members of the School Child Abuse Team?" and " do you agree or disagree that this case should be reported and explain why or why not?"

The qualitative data presented is taken from three courses, consists of open-ended evaluation questions. Participants are asked to evaluate the course. They are also asked whether the course was interactive and if they have any suggestions to improve the course. In addition, qualitative information from participants' interactive discussions with online classmates and with the instructor during the chat and at the electronic message board has been collected.

Findings

A one-way analysis of variance conducted to determine whether the mean scores of Group I and Group II were significantly different from each other indicated there was no significant difference between the two groups. Participants' responses to assigned questions posted on to the message board were brief, no more that a sentence or two. Answers were not well developed nor were they reflective. There was little response to the instructor's additional questions posted on the message board. Similarly, very few participants responded to each other's comments that were posted on the message board.

The following are comments made by Group I and Group II participants in three (3) classes in the evaluation section.

Group I: "Miss personal reactions and look forward to the chat; very efficient; reading others responses made it interactive; more convenient if my computer skills were better; looking forward to the interactive conference; look forward to chat room segment in which we will be able to "talk" at a more conversation-like atmosphere; driving me crazy is the message board people are responding to me and then some one responding to them or me; suggest that it would be more interactive-maybe meet twice to discuss the topics at hand other than at the end of the class; incorporate the video into the course; turned out to be a course on learning to do more on the computer as well as the child abuse course; I couldn't have asked for more convenience; sometimes online learning is a much more social experience than traditional forms of distance learning, such as correspondence study; Info and materials were every bit as effective as taking the course in a classroom; In their hearts, I believe most teachers would report child abuse. With this information, they now have it in their heads as well; I am looking forward to "chatting" with other participants. Even though I cannot see or hear other participants, I still feel I have classmates. At this point I don't find this course to be interactive. However the day of the conference will be interactive."

Group II: "I enjoyed the online chat the most. It was interesting to see how we each interpret the information we had regarding child abuse. I believe there should be required refresher courses available. The course was great. I would love to take another course on the Internet; I did not find it to be very interactive for me since none of my questions were ever addressed on the conference chat. It was interactive enough because each person could post responses to other students' posts and because of the meeting in the Learning Hall. It was informative and fun using on-line technology to talk with colleagues."

Conclusions

There was no significant difference in the scores measuring learning outcomes of Group I and Group II. It may be that studies on distance learning should consider other aspects of student learning such as what did they learn, did they learn to analyze and did they learn to be critical about the subject matter, is there student participation and collaboration and was interactivity encourage by the instructor. A model that encourages social interactivity needs to be developed for the online course. Also, the extent to which students' technological abilities impact learning and social interactivity in an online class needs to be investigated.

Generally, participants did not click on to the message board to communicate with other classmates. Their answers to the six questions were brief. This was probably due to limited experience with technology as indicated in their evaluations.

In the evaluations, the chat is viewed positively both by Groups I and II. Evaluations indicate that Group II felt connected to each other. Group I looked forward to the chat. Success in the chat room however, depended on good typing skills to keep up with the discussion. Furthermore, if the class had too many students then discussions in the chat room were difficult. The ideal size consisted of 10 students. The chat did give the students the opportunity to collaborate on various cases and situations in the schools.

References

Catchpole, M.J. (1993). Interactive media: The bridge between distance and classroom education. In T. Nunan (Ed.), _Distance Education Futures_ 37-56. Adelaide: University of South Australia Press.

Eastmond, D. (Summer 1998). Adult learners and internet-based distance education. _New Directions for Adult and Continuing Education._ 33-41.

Gagne, R. (1985). _The Conditions of Learning and Theory of Instruction_. FLA: Holt, Rinehart and Winston.

Leider, D.E. & Jarvenpaa, S.I. (1993). The information age confronts education: Case studies on electronic classrooms. _Information Systems Research:_ 4, 24-54.

Webster, J. & Hackley, P, (Dec 1997). Teaching effectiveness in technology-mediated distance learning. _Academy of Management Journal_ 40:6 1282-1309.

Estimating Development Time for E-Learning Programs

Mark Eaton
Cerner Virtual University
Cerner Corporation
E-mail: meaton@cerner.com

Abstract: Project managers and instructional designers face two challenges with every new e-learning project engagement - accurately scoping the project and then controlling it. The former often involves undisciplined practices. The latter is made more difficult because of it. Accurately estimating projects requires detailed analysis that is rarely available prior to signing agreements and contracts. The success or failure of a project is often determined by the quality of estimations since they tend to set client expectations. This paper recommends using estimators that are designed for specific types of e-learning solutions to improve quality and accuracy of scoping. Estimators provide a foundation for terms of reference, project scope, and help set client expectations. There are four steps in developing an estimator – define a learning event, define levels of interaction, identify development activities, and create the estimating matrix.

Methods for Scoping Projects

Project managers face two challenges - accurately scoping the project and then staying within scope. Since scoping sets client expectations, the success or failure of a project is often determined right from the beginning by the quality of these estimations.

There are three basics approaches in estimating projects for fixed fee services. The first is a simple gross estimate with a percentage of time added on for risks. It is quick, but not accurate and doesn't help when there are misunderstandings about the requirements.

The second method is to use a ratio of development time to learning time. Example: it takes 600 hours to develop 1 hour of learning; therefore, a two-hour e-learning program will take 1200 hours to develop.

I use ratios to analyze internal changes to development tools and processes for a specific type of e-learning program. With the exception of the changes, all factors remain the same and it is helpful to measure what effect, if any, these internal changes have on the development timeline. Ratios work when assessing these changes if they are internal to one program or activity.

It is very risky, however, to use ratios in a proposal that involves new technology or for comparing different solutions. Consider two proposed solutions where one is a simple slide presentation and the other has interactive practice exercises. The ratio for one will be significantly less than the other and the reason for the differences is not always as obvious as it is in this example. Ravet & Layte (1997) recognize this and suggest splitting ratios into components like knowledge acquisition, practice, and testing.

The third method is to use a tailored estimator for the specific type of e-learning solution that is proposed. More and more e-Learning content developers are using various types of estimators.

In this paper, we look at the steps to develop an estimator – define a learning event, define levels of interaction, identify development activities, and create the estimating matrix. The estimator is the best method to scope projects because it becomes the terms of reference and clearly communicates types of learning events and levels of interaction.

Process in Developing an Estimator

Step One: Define a Learning Event

It is usually necessary to begin by evaluating the type of analyses the designer will use in the instructional design approach. For example, Task Analysis is a process to identify target and enabling objectives (Gagne, Briggs, & Wager 1992). The analysis can be used to identify an event profile and course map. From this, designers can identify the lowest level of granularity.

This lowest level in the course hierarchy is a recognizable learning event that can be added, removed, or modified somewhat independently within the course. It is consider portable if it meets this criteria and it needs to be defined to help set client expectations. For example,

> A learning event is considered the lowest portable learning object and is an independent set of
> tasks that collectively form a complete piece of instruction. It is a short piece of instruction
> that takes only a few minutes to complete and no more than 10 minutes.

The next step is to classify learning events into various levels of interaction. Ten minutes of instruction that is almost entirely text-based is much different than ten minutes of instruction that includes games, even though both may take the same amount of time to complete.

Step Two: Define Levels of Interaction

There are many classification systems that are available to classify levels of interaction. Schwier (1992) proposes taxonomy of interactions in terms of the user's cognitive engagement. He evaluates interaction on three levels – reactive, proactive, and mutual interaction.

More recent classifications include defining the interaction between the actors – students, instructors, and the system or program (Wagner, E. D. 1998, Sook K. S. & Bonk, Curt J. 1998). Others describe interaction from the developer's perspective and the media components – graphics, text, animations, simulations, user inter-face controls, etc. (Bixler, B. & Spotts, J. 1998, Sims, R. 1997).

I use the classification scale in Table 1. It has six levels to describe types of learning events and how users react to them.

Level	Type	Description
1	Single Document	Characterized as a single document like on-line reference manuals. Controls are limited to scrolling or clicking objects for sequential or non-sequential hypertext navigation within the document.
2	Web Document	Multiple documents. Involves additional branching for specific instructional support (Schaefermeyer, 1990).
3	Multimedia	Includes text, graphics, animation, and audio. User can play, pause, rewind, and advance through the animations.
4	One-True-Path (OTP) Simulations	Simulates basic features of the system or environment. OTPs are usually linear. The prominent feature is that triggers are embedded within the simulation so that navigation occurs by interacting with the simulation.
5	Multiple-True-Path (MTP) Simulations	Limited exploration. MTPs have more effective hands-on realistic experiences than level-4 OTP programs. Multiple parallel pathways exist, but are limited or controlled.
6	Scenario Simulations	The best example of this is an aircraft flight simulator. The learning program not only has the look and feel of the actual system, but also uses underlying algorithms that fully describe the real world system. Great for what-if scenarios.

Table 1: Classification by Levels of Interaction

Step Three: Identify the Design and Development Activities in the Construction of a Learning Event

Designers identify activities that are involved in designing, developing, and producing learning events. These activities are fairly common across e-learning solutions. Table 2 gives a sample of activities.

Activity	Description
Design	Creating the training scenario - writing assignment text or directions, writing any learning support messages that may be required, identifying and describing the scenes or pages, and identifying the conditions that will let the student progress between tasks and events. Output is a detail design document or storyboard.
Database Development	Entering data into the data structure. May include data entry into an actual database or creating other data sources that the event will utilize.
Authoring	Developing learning events using tools or authoring systems that do not require programming.
Programming	Actual programming using high-level languages or scripting languages.
Integration	Integrating tasks together into learning events and integrating events into lessons. Setting triggers for navigation and integrating all the learning support tools the end-user will need.
Testing	Testing - following the development of each learning event or after all learning events have been integrated. Estimations take into account the number of iterations that will be required between development and testing.

Table 2: Development Activities

Step Four: Create the Estimation Matrix

It is here that you document approximate times required for the various activities in developing a learning event. Table 3 shows a sample matrix. Notice that it takes approximately 7 hours to build a level-1 learning event and 110 hours to build a level-6 learning event. Thus the matrix accounts for variations in each activity among the various types (interaction levels) of learning events.

Levels Activities	1: Document	2: Web Document	3: Multimedia	4: OTP Simulation	5: MTP Simulation	6: Scenario Simulation
Design	2	3.5	5	6	12	20
Database	.2	.2	1	4	8	20
Authoring	3	5	7	7	8	15
Programming	0	0	2	4	6	30
Integration	1	1	3	3	6	10
Testing	1	1	3	3	6	15
Total Time	**7.2**	**10.7**	**21**	**27**	**46**	**110**

Table 3: Estimation Matrix

Using the Estimator

Table 4 shows the output of the estimator to scope a proposal. In this example, a learning program will be designed to develop skills on using a word processor. The first column documents the proposed learning events. The second column identifies the level of interaction that is required for each event. The last column is the estimated time to manage the activity based on the estimating matrix in Table 3.

Proposed Learning Events	Level	Development Time
Home Page	1	7.2

Course Overview & Getting Started	2	10.7
Opening the Word Processor	3	21
Creating a New Document	4	27
Enter Text in the Document	5	46
Running Spell Check	5	46
Saving Changes to the Document	5	46
Open and Modify an Existing Document	5	46
Copy and Paste	5	46
Adding Tables and Graphics	5	46
Closing a Document and Exit	5	46
Summary/Review	2	10.7
Total Development		**398.6**

Table 4: Sample Course Plan with Learning Events, Levels, and Estimates

There are several advantages to using this approach. First, it provides scope of the project. At a consulting rate of $120 per hour and approximately 400 hours to develop, the fee is over $47,000. If the client needs the project closer to $40,000, the number of learning events or the interactions can be adjusted to bring the project into range.

Secondly, it sets client expectations right from the start. Any changes (interactions or number of learning events) can be managed as out-of-scope as opposed to absorbing the changes within the fee and timeline of the arrangement.

Finally, estimations are *distributed* across the learning events. It is much simpler to add, remove, or classify learning events instead of re-scoping the entire project each time there is a change.

References

Bixler, B., & Spotts, J. (1998). *Screen design and levels of interactivity in web-based training.* Paper presented at the International Visual Literacy Association 1998 Conference, Athens, GA. Retrieved April 2, 2002, from Pennsylvania State University, Royer Center for Learning and Academic Technologies Web site: http://www.clat.psu.edu/homes/jds100/john/research/ivla1998/ivla98.htm#toc3

Gagne, R. M., Briggs, L. J., & Wager, W. W. (1992). *Principles of instructional design (4th ed.).* New York: Harcourt Brace Jovanovich College Publishers.

Ravet, S., & Layte, M. (1997). *Technology-Based Training: A comprehensive guide to choosing, implementing, managing, and developing new technologies in training.* Houston : Gulf Publishing Company.

Schaefermeyer, S. (1990). Standards for instructional computing software design and development. *Educational technology*, June, 9-15.

Schwier, R. A. (1992). *A taxonomy of interaction for instructional multimedia.* (Eric Document Reproduction Service No. ED352044)

Sims, R. (1997). *Interactivity: A forgotten art?* Retrieved April 2, 2002, from Georgia State University, Instructional Technology Online Web site: http://www.gsu.edu/~wwwitr/docs/interact/

Sook K. S., & Bonk, Curt J. (1998). *Interaction: What does it mean in online distance education?* (Eric Document Reproduction Service No. ED428724)

Wagner, E. D. (1998). *Interaction strategies for online training designs.* (Eric Document Reproduction Service No. ED422881)

SPIDER TUTORING SYSTEM For TEACHING COMPUTER PROGRAMMING LANGUAGES

Mahmoud M. El-Khouly

Mathematics Department, Faculty of Science, Helwan University, Egypt.

melkhouly@yahoo.com

Abstract: This paper presents a spider tutoring system (STS) for teaching computer programming languages through WWW. In this version, spider technique have been used to update the databases used by the blackboard hosted at the tutoring agent (TA) server, with blackboard module a student can exchange his expertise with other students. Due to overwhelming size and growth rate of Internet, spider's discovery had been restricted to direct discovery technique only.

Introduction

Learning one of the computer languages today, is essential for students in both undergraduate and graduate levels. However, when I asked around 300 faculty students about their knowledge about the computer, I found that they almost use it as a tool for typewriting or games. There are many reasons for not learning computer programming languages (e.g. economical reasons, the lack of good instructors, geographical distance, etc...). Egyptian government offered a free internet from beginning of the year 2002, therefore accessing the internet costs only 0.2 \$/hour (previous cost was 2\$/hour) which gives us a good support to provide some web-based tutoring system for teaching computer programming languages.

The movement toward client-server applications began in the late 1980s and so in many organizations there are already many server applications with well-structured APIs for RPC or IPC access by a client. However, in many cases the backend server is a relatively standard database monitor, which provides no logic or protocol specific to the current application. The emergence of network computing, where the client side of the application logic is provided by JAVA applets that are downloaded at runtime to a Web browser, offers a new opportunity for constructing the agent-equivalent of a Web browser (Alper, 1997). With the WWW as an educational platform, it will be feasible for the students to access the multimedia courseware with general-purpose browsers. No special tools are required to start learning. For the courseware provider, it is not necessary to worry about the distribution and maintenance of the copies of the courseware but they just take care of the original on their server (Kiyoshi et al., 1997).

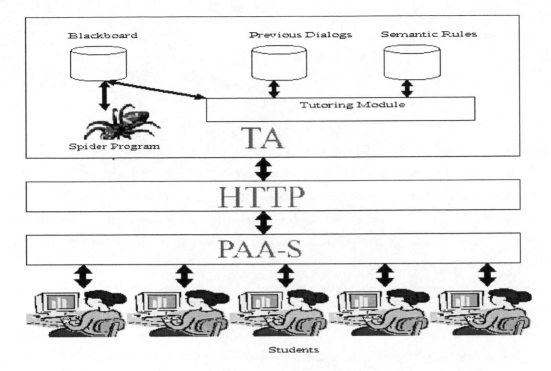

Figure (1): STS system

Lewis Johnson (Lewis Johnson, et al., 1997) support interaction with teachers and students through their project ADE, using off-the-shelf whiteboard and teleconferencing tools. But this required both teachers and students to be on-line.

M.M. El-Khouly, et.al. (2000), presented an expert tutoring system (E-TCL) for teaching computer programming languages through WWW. In this paper, I extend the features of that system to include spider technique. The most common application for spiders is creating and updating the databases used by search engines.

The proposed system consists of two agents representing a server-clients relationship, tutoring agent (TA) as a "server", and personal assistant agent for students (PAA-S) as a "clients". The PAA-S can communicate with TA through WWW to retrieve the tutoring dialog of the command(s) that a student wants to practice, and to access the experiences of other students in blackboard module (as shown in (fig. 1)).

Pedagogical Design

When the structural computer language course content was analyzed, it was clear that the subject matter was topical in nature, and could be organized into a small number of reasonably self-contained modules.

The following form the central core of any procedural computer language curriculum.

- Input/Output statement
- Conditional statement
- Loop
- Array
- Function
- Structure
- Input/Output files

The following was adopted as a model for each module:

1. Introduction: here the basic ideas and concepts were presented. The major goal was the motivation of the central idea of each module.

2. Syntax section: basic understanding of the syntax of the command, and any examples about different forms. After all, a series of multiple choice questions are presented. The student must answer these before progressing to the next activity.

3. Procedural section: algorithmic understanding to reinforce connecting statements together to build more lines of programs pieces.

4. Strategic section: problem solving: after the student is familiar with the basic concepts in the module, more complicated multi-step questions are presented. This reinforces problem solving strategy.

5. practice exercises: at the end of the activities in each module, a series of exercises is presented to the student. Each problem is graded and the student is told whether he/she is correct or not.

6. Graded quiz: after the practice exercises, a series of questions is given to the student. They focus on the procedural and strategic components of the module.

Tutoring Agent

TA contains tutoring module, previous dialogs database, semantic rules base, spider program, and blackboard database.

Spider Program

A spider program creates a database by scanning the Internet and updates by continually scanning the WWW. To index a site, a spider must crawl it, meaning it must find all the pages the site's home page links to. Spiders add the pages they crawl to the search engine's database – a task that can be performed in several ways. Some spiders add every word of a web page to the database index. While others include only words listed in special <Meta> tags embedded in a page. Some spiders are being developed to execute multimedia-oriented searches or the automatic assignment of categories based on content.

Two basic techniques of discovering exist: blind discovery and directed discovery.

- blind discovery entails simply trying to access every IP address is existence
- direct discovery -which is significantly faster than blind discovery -entails scanning a list of known domains to see which ones are still on line and responsive. A list can be constructed or acquired in a number of different ways, but the most extensive approach is to start with the list of top-level domains (TLDs). Directed discovery isn't necessarily limited to the original list of sites: as the spiders crawls each page, it's bound to discover new links. By adding new links to the database of site, more and more pages get introduced to the system (David Pallmann 1999).

Personal Assistant Agent for Students

The personal assistant agent for students (PAA-S) consists of three components, student model, tutoring module and user interface module.

Conclusion

In this paper, STS system had been presented for teaching computer languages. STS consists of two agents, tutoring agent, and personal assistant agent for students. They communicate with each other as client-server through WWW. This allows the system to communicate with other agents to exchange semantic rules and tutoring text for different languages. The spider technique had been used in PAA-S. Such that the blackboard modules hosted at TA, can be updated continually to see whether the student is on-line or off-line and therefore checking whether he/she will contribute to the current inquiry or not? This will safe time for waiting students who are off-line.

References

ALPER C and Colin H (1997) *Agent Source book: A Complete Guide to Desktop, Internet, and Intranet Agents*. John Wiley & Sons, USA.

David Pallmann (1999). Programming Bots, Spiders, and Intelligent Agents in Microsoft Visual C++, Microsoft press.

Kiyoshi Nakabayashi, Mina Maruyama, Yoshimasa Koike, Yasuhisa Kato, Hirofumi Touhei, & Yoshimi Fukuhara. (1997). Architecture of an Intelligent Tutoring System on the WWW. In Proc. 8th World Conference of the AIED Society, Kobe, Japan.

Lewis Johnson & Erin Shaw (1997). Using Agents to Overcome Deficiencies in Web-Based Courseware. AI-ED'97 workshop on intelligent educational systems on the world wide web.

M.M. El-Khouly, B H. Far, & Z. Koono. (2000).Expert Tutoring System for teaching computer languages . Expert Systems with Applications, 18, 27-32.

Semi-online Workshop for Planning and Developing Online Courseware.

Authors: Larisa Enríquez   Interactive Products Department   larisa@piaget.dgsca.unam.mx
Dámaris García   Interactive Products Department   damaris@piaget.dgsca.unam.mx
Erika Nuevo   Interactive Products Department   erika@piaget.dgsca.unam.mx
Elga de la Cruz   Interactive Products Department   elga@piaget.dgsca.unam.mx
Sonia López   Interactive Products Department   sonia@piaget.dgsca.unam.mx
Mariana Vázquez   Interactive Products Department
Gabriela Aranda   Interactive Products Department   gaby@piaget.dgsca.unam.mx

Institution: National Autonomous University of México

Abstract

During this presentation, it will be demonstrated how the Academic Computer Center (at the National University of México) is helping their face-to-face teachers to develop online content for online courses.

Introduction

The Academic Computer Center is nationally recognized as a leader in computers and telecommunications technology. Among other things, it is responsible for bringing computers and telecommunications training to the Mexican population. The Academic Computer Center has over 200 different courses and 300 face-to-face teachers but by the end of the year 2001, only three online courses formed part of the course catalogue. How can we expand our online courses offering? How can we help teachers modify and make their notes more accesible for an online course? How can they experience an online lesson?

In order to answer these questions is that a semi-online workshop for planning and developing online courseware has been designed.

The workshop consists of two modules, the first of them (over three weeks) is to be given through the Internet and the second one (over six weeks) is to be given in a classroom in two-hour sessions per week.

Content

The Semi-online workshop for planning and developing online courseware was designed for those teachers interested in developing online courses. Because we think teachers are the content experts and that they do not necessarily need to know about programming, designing or administering a server, the only pre-requisites that we required the teachers to have prior to the workshop were:
1. Managing the Windows interface
2. Internet connection
3. Being able to use a word processor
4. Have email access
5. Have already selected the coursware's content

The workshop consists of two modules. The first one is theoretical and when finished, the student will be able to understand the significance of the instructional design. The student will be introduced to the distance education concept and the technologies for delivering it.

The first module is based totally on the Internet; forum discussions, handing-in assignments, evaluating online products and suggested readings are some of the activities proposed for this module. The student (in this case, the teacher) faces the situation that his or her own students will also be facing; loneliness, motivation, feedback and evaluation are four basic concepts that are easily explained with words but are difficult to achieve with this media. In order to help them face this issues we worked on each of them, as follows:

Loneliness We regularly send emails to the students; either to tell them we received their homeworks, o to ask them about their feelings being in the course.
Motivation. During the discussions on the forum, we tried to collect some of the students' comments or works, telling the rest of the group about an interesting view or work.

Feedback. Because students are expecting to know if they are doing well in the course, it is important to tell them about their performance as well asto make them feel that the tutor is following the discussions, by asking questions and directing the discussion.

Evaluation. Evaluating a person that is at a distance is difficult, first of all, because we are never sure who is behind the computer. The way we have dealt with this question is by assigning several activities along the course in which students have to work constantly. This system has helped us to, not enhance a proactive interaction among students, but also brings the opportunity to construct related and more complex activitites as the course advances.

During the case of the second module, students are basically developing their courseware content. Face-to-face sessions are used for supervising, consulting and sharing ideas and experiences within the group. A special content delivery system was developed for students in order to help them construct and see their course; they are also able to view the other on going projects.

In México, most teachers do not have any distance education experience; neither as students nor asfacilitators. It is difficult for them to adapt and interact freely at their first online course, and because we know they have good ideas, questions and proposals for teaching we decided that, for the second module, face-to-face sessions would be better than online assistance.

Development

An interdisciplinary group developed the workshop. A graphic designer, two instructional designers, a media integrator, a system developer and an interface designer were integrated into the team.

Planning: We consider that there are two basic problems to solve when someone decides to transfer a face-to-face course to an online one: the content's development and the role the teacher must assume because of the technology. We decided to concentrate on the first problem and help teachers identifying differences, advantages and disadvantages of the Internet for the delivery of information. The workshop's coordinator and the two instructional designers worked on this stage.

Content Selection: Because an online facilitator teaches at a distance, it is important to be aware of this significance. That is why the first two subjects to be overviewed in the workshop are Distance Education and Distance Education Delivery Technologies. The next subject is Internet and online education, concentrating on online courses. The following subjects deal with independent study, instructional design, and web content design usability concepts. All these subjects are taught through the Internet and students have plenty of activities to do. At the end, students are asked to develop their course content and face-to-face sessions are used to show each person's progress and to discuss ideas and doubts. Teachers are asked to put their materials on a server, using a system and an interface designed specially for them. People participating in this stage are the workshop's coordinator, the instructional designers and the interface designer.

Development: Once the program was decided and the content selected, it was time to develop the workshop's site (web pages for the online module and the course delivery system to be used during the second module). The whole team participates at this stage.

Evaluation: When both web sites were finished (the online course and the course delivering system for the teachers), functionality, usability and learning evaluations were applied. We invited teachers to participate on the 6-week workshop. Twelve teachers attended the workshop but only nine finished it. We handed out a questionnaire to those persons who abandoned the course for feedback, as well as those who did finished it.

The main comments we received about the online module were:
- the agenda wasn't very clear to people; they didn't understand how the course content and activities were distributed along the six weeks
- people needed a printable version of the documents
- people thought it would be important to have an a students' space so they could post personal information and thus to get better acquainted with each other
- some notes should be improved by adding specific references

For the course delivery system, they told us:
- they had the possibility of sending 'pdf' documents
- they could see other people's courses
- they wanted to use our delivery course system in the future for their courses

For the didactic aspects, they all agreed:
- time was top limited in order to reach the course's objective
- there were too many activities
- face-to-face assessments could be improved by discussing and analyzing more fully everyone's progress
- they wanted assessments after the workshop was completed

Results

- Four online computer courses were developed as a result of the workshop and three of them are now part of the online course catalogue.
- The workshop site was redesigned and the teacher's notes were improved.
- The workshop now lasts 9 weeks (three to be attended by Internet and 6 face-to-face sessions).
- The workshop was included on the online course catalogue and promoted through the university's web page and newspaper.
- 24 students enrolled in the following workshop.

Bibliography

Ángelez Gutiérrez, Ofelia. (1998).Selección y recopilación del material de apoyo del Seminario-Taller: Evaluación y diseño curricular. ANUIES. México,

Tony Bates (1995) Technology, open learning and distance education, Routledge studies in Distance Education. ISBN 0-415-12799-8

David W. Brooks (1997) <u>Web-teaching, a guide to designing interactive teaching for the worldwide web</u>. New York, plenum publishing. ISBN 0-306-45552-8

Desmond Keegan (1999) <u>Foundations of Distance Education</u>. Great Britain, Routledge publishing. ISBN 0-415-13909-0.

Desmond Keegan, (1994).<u>Otto Peters on Distance Education. The Industrialization of Teaching and Learning</u>. Routledge. London and New York.

Hannafin, Michael J. (1988).<u>The Design, Development, and Evaluation of Instructional Software</u>. Macmillan Publishing Company. New York.

Jakob Nielsen (1999) <u>Designing web usability: The practice of simplicity</u>. New Riders Publishing

Colin McCormack, David Jones (1997). <u>Building a Web-based Education System</u>, John Wiley & Sons. ISBN 0471191620

Gloria Pérez Serrano,. (1994).<u>El profesor-tutor. Perspectiva humana de la educación a distancia</u>. Revista Iberoamericana de la educación superior a distancia. Madrid. UNED, AIESAD, vol. VI, núm 2.

William K. Horton (2000) <u>Designing web-based training: How to teach anyone anything anywhere anytime</u>, John Wiley & Sons

iQUIZ: A Tool Making Internet Quizzes easy to Develop and Use

Hanna Farah, and Abdulmotaleb El Saddik
School of Information Technology and Engineering (*SITE*)
University of Ottawa
161 Louis Pasteur, P.O. Box 450, Stn A, Ottawa, Ontario, Canada, K1N 6N5
Tel: (613) 562-5800 x 6277, Fax: (613) 562-5175
hfarah@farahtech.net, elsaddik@site.uottawa.ca

Abstract

This paper presents a tool called iQUIZ that tries to facilitate composing, distributing and correcting online quizzes for different groups of students in a given course. iQUIZ is a client-server TCP/IP-based application; the server can be used by educators and/or organizations to compose and host online quizzes. The client application will be used by students or any other party (e.g., customers) solving the quiz. iQUIZ is characterized by its ease to use graphical user interface and its high degree security features.

1. Introduction

University teachers spend a lot of time differentiating and correcting exercises and quizzes and posting student marks on the web. They may do it using a web-based learning system like WebCT or just by typing the information using a standard word /and or HTML editor. On the other hand, and based on our own observations, students don't express much interest in assisting to labs or discussion groups. This work tries to facilitate composing, distributing and correcting online quizzes for different groups of students in a given course. We want to give the students a good reason to assist to labs or discussion groups.

2. Architecture

iQUIZ is a client-server application developed in Visual C++ using MFC. The client sends its ClientID and Password to the server for validation, if it is the first time the server will create an account for that verified client (there is an authorization from the server administrator to create an account for that new user by having registered the student number for example so that not all students can create accounts).

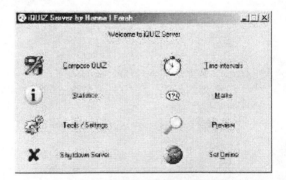

Figure 1. User interface of the iQuiz server

The server hosts the quizzes and sends the quiz version corresponding to the client ID. The communications take place in real time, each time the client answers a question, the answer is automatically sent to the server and stored locally. The communication socket is destroyed when the quiz is over.

2.1 Security issues

- Digital signature:
  - Both the server and the client are digitally signed to prevent malicious users from modifying the code or resources of our application. Unlike Java applets that can be decompiled and modified.
- Encryption:
  - All communications between the server and its clients are encrypted.
  - Local quizzes are stored on disk but using a very strong encryption algorithm(Blowfish 128 bit encryption for example)
  - Data stored on the client's side for high availability purposes are also encrypted using the same algorithm (Blowfish 128 bit).
- Semaphores:

o   To allow only 1 client application to be ran on a single computer by a single user, we create semaphore objects in memory.

2.2 Upload

iQUIZ can communicate with an FTP server using the File Transfer Protocol to upload files to that server. A feature of iQUIZ is automatic marks upload at a given time interval, which will be discussed in the next Section.

3. Implementation / Easy to use UI

Figure 1 represents the user interface of the server. It consists of 8 items which can be described as follow:

3.1 A friendly, easy to use interface to compose the quiz

As can be seen in Figure 2, the educator can compose a question with a maximum of 5 multiple answers. She/He can also specify the difficulty level of this question, and has the option to give a maximum amount of time the student is allowed to have in order to answer the question. In the Scenario field the educator can specify several consecutive questions on a subject which the student can read in a popup window. The total questions field shows the number of already composed questions with their difficulty level respectively.

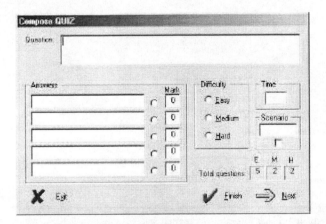

Figure 2. User interface for composing a quiz

3.2 Option to have the quiz available at defined times only

This feature allows only students from a specified group or groups to do the quiz in a specific time interval. It has also a no time restriction option (see Figure 3).

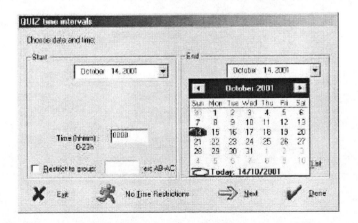

Figure 3. User interface of the quiz time interval

3.3 The statistics tool

This tool allows the educator to view the statistics of using the iQuiz tool. She/he can find the number of submitted quizzes, the average mark, the lowest mark, etc...

3.4 Lookup a mark instantly

This option allows the educator to search for a mark for a specific student in her/his database.

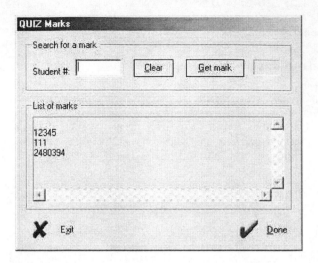

Figure 4. Searching for a specific student marks

3.5 Tools/ settings

Figure 5 displays the various features of the iQUIZ tool: the ability to load with Windows on startup. The quiz can differ from one student to another when Randomize is checked so even in the same group; the order of the questions in the quiz will be based on the student's number. The educator does not need any more to worry about posting marks; iQUIZ will automatically do it for her/him and on regular basis if she/he wishes. Marks are posted via FTP with a single click. The educator can also arrange students in groups and manage them with ease. The iQUIZ server auto-corrects the quiz, put the marks on the educator's desktop and uploads them to the desired FTP site.

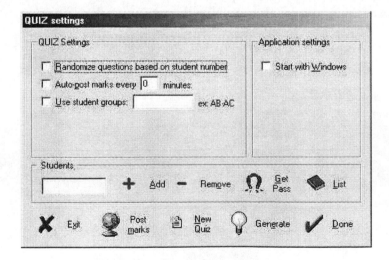

Figure 5. Quiz settings

The educator can also specify how many question of each type (easy, medium, hard or difficult) the quiz should contain and how many different versions of the quiz should be generated (therefore we will have different quizzes for different students in the same group). She/he can also have 1 different version generated for each group.

3.6 Preview

The educator can preview what each generated quiz contains before hosting the quiz and setting the server online. This is to ensure that everything will be done as planned by the educator and give her/him the comfort and more control over the quiz. This feature is based on the well known concept of what you see is what you get (WYSIWYG).

3.7 Set online

This button sets the server online and makes it ready to accept client connections. Note that the educator can set predefined time intervals and iQUIZ will go online and offline automatically. With the ability to startup with Windows, the educator doesn't have to remember to execute the iQUIZ tool each time she/he turns on her/his computer. After the server is set online, this buttons turns into a Set offline button to tell the server to break all connections and stop accepting new connections.

3.8 Shut down server

This button shuts down all communications and terminates the application.

4. Evaluation

The system has been tested by two educators, who generated a number of quizzes for their students. They were very satisfied with the easy to use user interface and the lack of complexity. At the same time we did a network communication in order to study the number of users (students) the system can simultaneously support. Our simulation showed that we could support about 300 users without decreasing the response time from the server. This is due to the fact that we are using TCP/IP communication protocol and therefore we could support virtually thousands of users (every user will be given a special port). Practically and based on our prior experience [elsaddik2001] the server last will increase linearly with the increasing number of users.

5. Conclusion and future work

After the success of our test simulation we are planning to use it in fall 2002 (Course ELG5121 Multimedia communications) at University of Ottawa. We are also planning to add some other features, among others:

- Load several quizzes at once and have a specialized tool to compose the quizzes separating the communication part from the composition part.
- Remote control the server from another computer.
- Email support: we want to be able to send congratulation emails to the students with the highest achievements!

We also plan to use XML-based specification and develop a Java version of this project to ease deployment and allow usage on different operating systems.

6. References

[Belnap(976)] Belnap, N. D., The Logic of Questions and Answers. New Haven: Yale University Press.

[elsaddik2001] El Saddik A., Interactive Multimedia Learning", ISBN: 3-540-41930-6, Springer-Verlag (2001), 200 pp.

[Lee et al. 1995] Lee, W. W., Mamone, R. A., & Roadman, K. H The Computer Based Training Handbook: Assessment, Design, Development, Evaluation. Englewood Cliffs. N.J: Englewood

[Tinoco2002] Tinoco, L. C. QUIZIT Tutorial. Blacksburg, VA: Virginia Tech Computer Science Dept. http://pixel.cs.vt.edu/~ltinoco/quizitdocs/

A DISTRIBUTED WEB-BASED K-12 MANAGEMENT SYSTEM

João Ferreira, Alberto Silva, Rui Azevedo, Gonçalo Borrêga

ISEL / DEI-IST-UTL / INESC-ID Lisboa

(jferreira@deec.isel.ipl.pt, alberto.silva@acm.org)

Abstract: The project "Rent@School - Bringing the Future to the Education" is a research effort to study and prototype information system architectures to support, standardize, and facilitate the management of K12 schools at a national scale. It looks for the sharing and dissemination of relevant information among different stakeholders, based on the ASP model and also on a novel architecture, which we called "distributed and multi-instance web architecture". This architecture means that beyond the existence of a unique central/national Rent@School instance, multiple Rent@School instances can be installed at local/regional scale, in a way that autonomy, performance and flexibility of all the system can be improved. This issue is introduced and discussed in this paper from two complementary perspectives: from the organizational and management information systems perspective; and from the integration and large-scale interoperability.

1 Introduction

Education is considered by modern societies to be one of the most import ant and strategic factors that contributes for the development, wealth creation and solidarity of any Nation [1,5]. In this context, Rent@School (RS) is a research project where we will propose and discuss organizational and information system architectures to support, standardize, and facilitate the management of K-12 (from kinder garden till 12th year) schools at a national scale, as well as, the sharing and dissemination of relevant information among the different stakeholders, such as students, teachers, schools' administrators, parents, and Ministry of Education' support and technical employees. This project is particularly oriented by the Portuguese educational public system (the educational private subsystem has some facets and requirements that we deliberately did not consider).

The RS project is being developed in the context of the ISG (Information System Group of INESC -ID) where we are interested on two main research topics. First, to study organizational systems, architectures and patterns, in particular those with complex, dynamic and distributed features which can be found in different areas of the economy and society, such as public administration, education, transports, logistics, or tourism. Second, to study the best information systems architectures and patterns to support the referred systems, following a technological perspective.

RS is based on the ASP (application service provider) model, however, adopting a novel architecture, which we called "distributed and multi-instance web architecture". This architecture means that beyond the existence of a unique central/national RS instance, multiple RS instances can be installed at local/regional scale, in a way that autonomy, performance and flexibility of all the system can be improved. This issue is particularly interesting and novel and it is introduced and discussed in this paper from two complementary perspectives. First, following the organizational and management information systems perspective. Second, following a more technical perspective, in particular regarding issues of application integration and large-scale interoperability based on the web services concepts.

The main novel contributes of this paper can be summarize in three points. First, we propose and discuss the interest of an information system that can support, standardize, and facilitate the management of K-12 schools at a national scale. Second, the proposed architecture is not restricted by itself to the classic and central ASP model because it allows the installation and configuration of multiple instances promoting, in that way, the autonomy, flexibility and performance of the overall system. Third, we propose and discuss the importance to develop this kind of system with public and open interfaces, promoting integration and large-scale interoperability among different systems.

This paper is organized in 6 sections; including this one (Section 1) that describes the context, the motivation and its main contributes. Section 2 describes briefly the Portuguese educational system, and in particular the subsystem of public K-12 schools. Section 3 identifies the most relevant (functional and non-functional) requirements that the RS design and prototype should take into account. Section 4 presents and discusses issues related to the information system architectures that support the RS, as well as, related to the application integration and large-scale interoperability. Finally, Section 6 refers some considerations related the future work and the research aims.

2   Portuguese Educational System

The educational system in Portugal, like in most of the developed countries, is organized in classical training and/or professional levels. The following educational levels exist in Portugal: pre-primary; primary - 1st cycle (1st to 4th years); 2nd cycle (5th to 9th years); secondary-high school (different areas, like classical, artistic and professional are available); and higher education (divided in University and Polytechnic). The Portuguese educational system is available, at all different levels, either Public or Private. Quoting the official source INE regarding year 2000/2001, the education K-12 has a total population of 1.261.603 students (approximately 12% of the Portuguese population) distributed by 16.984 educational facilities or schools.

The RS formulates his proposal for all K-12 schools and other performers acting in the Public educational sub-system. In Portugal this sub-system in organized as shown in figure 1.

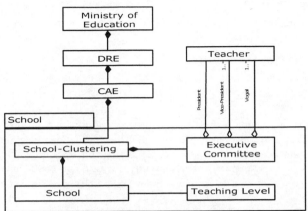

Figure 1: Organization of Portuguese educational system for the first degrees levels.

Schools are the elementary unit of educational activities. For financial reasons, regarding the level of performance on administrative tasks, the schools are organized in groups, called "school-clustering" or just "clusters". Each school can provide and manage more than one educational level. The main objective of the cluster structure is the possibility of different schools sharing a package of resources (e.g., human, technical and others) obtaining a better global costs system performance. The Ministry of Education is responsible for the planning, promotion, follow up and evaluate the available resources for the public education sub-system. This sub-system is divided in various responsibility levels namely the Educational Regional Delegations (DRE) as 1st hierarchical level. As the 2nd level there is Educational Supporting Centers (CAE). Each school is associated to a certain CAE (and therefore to a certain DRE), besides the cluster they belong to.

3   General Requirements of Rent@School

In this section we summarize the main requirements that should be supported by the RS system. Namely, we identify two major groups of requirements: functional requirements, that match the use cases; and non-functional requirements, that match the common needs that the system should satisfy independently of specific functionalities.

3.1   Functional Requirements

RS provides a personalized service for different types of stakeholders. It can be seen as a "multifaceted portal for the Portuguese K-12 teaching system", becoming the personalized portal for schools, students, parents, teachers and administratives. We identify the main functionalities of the RS based on these stakeholders: **Administrator, MinistryOfEducation-User, School-SuperUser, School-Executive, School-Administrative, School-ClassDirector, Student, Teacher and Parent.**

Like other ASP applications, the responsibilities of each user are based on the chained delegation approach and profile management. The "Administrator" actor is the user with more power on the RS, in particular she can manage schools, and for each school she can manage the School-SuperUser accounts. The "School-SuperUser" actor is responsible for the configuration of school data and for the management of other school users, such as "School-Executive" or "School-Administrative" that performs very important roles in school administration and management.

"Student", "Teacher" and "Parent" are not school-level users; they are global-level users. This means that students and teachers should have a global identification, independently of the current school association. The same should be verified for parents: independently of the number of students associated, and the different school registrations, the parent should not have to manage various system user-accounts to access the data of their dependent students.

This issue of global identification of students, teachers and parents (independently of the school and the academic year) is novel and we expect that it can bring a real impact in the quality level regarding the management of the education system. Namely, it can bring the following contributes (1) a better and simple way to record history and curriculum of the different actors; (2) a more integrated and personalized service can make possible a simpler, direct and easier interaction; and (3) a significant simplification in the administrative processes such as school registrations, student transfers and evaluation.

3.2 Non-Functional Requirements

Non-functional requirements have to do with general aspects of the system like performance, robustness, liability, distribution, security, integration with the Internet and opening to standards. We identify in this project the following non-functional requirements: **Usability, Performance and scalability, Local and access type independency, Privacy and confidentiality, Openness and integration with other systems, Messages and alerts delivered through multiple channels.**.

4 Rent@School Architecture

In this section we discuss important topics related the RS architecture, as well as its mechanisms to support open-interface and interoperate with other systems.

4.1 Distributed Single Instance Architecture

In order to satisfy the general requirements identified in Section 3, in particular the non-functional requirement of "local and access type independency", RS should have necessarily to be developed based on a web information systems architecture.

RS follows the typical ASP model, in a way that it provides several functionalities to a selected range of actors that have previously subscribed to the system. Additionally, those functionalities are supported by a complex information system, kept and managed by a credentialed entity and responsible by supporting a number of quality of service parameters, such as performance, security, privacy and confidentiality of data, and liability. This entity – the RS manager – can be a telecommunications operator and/or an institute related to the Ministry of Education.

The main advantages present in this model resides in the fact that the participant actors never have to be worry about technological issues, such as: installation, licensing and configuration of applications; data quality; backups; availability of computing systems; or even issues concerning the updating of new versions. On the other hand, this model requires that the support computing architecture provides extremely large performance and scalability levels (thinking on the huge number of potential users), and doesn't allow for an eventual decentralization and autonomy of the information systems at the regions level (e.g, at DRE and CAE level) or even at the school level.

4.2 Distributed Multiple Instance Architecture

In order to solve the problems referred on the previous paragraph, we propose (to be developed in the second phase of the p roject) a novel architecture based on multiple instances of RS.

This architecture consists in multiple instances of RS, which can be installed at different management levels of the public education system hierarchy. For example (without considered the cent ral/national level): at regional level (e.g., at all DRE); at school-clustering level; or even in a mixed way, such as at the central level and at the school-clustering level for the ones that may have technical conditions to operate one RS instance.

Altho ugh there are some variants in the way the deployment and configuration of the several instances are performed, we assume in this article for the sake of simplicity, that the various instances would be installed at the school-clustering and therefore, every school belonging to its school-clustering share the same RS infrastructure.

The main aspects that this architecture intends to improve, relatively to the single-instance architecture, are:

- *Performance and scalability of the global system* : The fact that there would exist multiple instances has as direct consequence in the multiplication of access points, as well as in the distribution of the total charge of the system along those different points, and so the overall system would provide a better performance and a better scalability.
- *Decentralization and autonomy.* This is one of the main advantages of this architecture, which would allow that RS's instance configuration and management would be as close as possible to the communities that most use it: the sch ools. Among other factors, we may work in a more productive way and answer more quickly and in a more agile way to the identified requirements. In case the central/national instance would be temporarily deactivated, the regional/local instances could be working adequately in the schools. It is important to notice that although a very significant number of functional requirements (e.g., most use-cases that are performed by teachers, students, class directors and school administrative) the accesses are perfomed directly on the regional/local RS's instances; other functional requirements (e.g., the parents authentication, the teacher record and historic search) will still require access to the central/national RS's instance.

On the other hand, in spite the several advantages, this architecture requires significant issues that should be adequately analysed and supported in a concrete implementation of the system. Namely (1) every instance should be installed on machines that have a permanent connection to the internet; (2) the existence of adequate technical support, preferably provided by an entity that is external to the schools; and (3) the existence of adequate management support (typically developed by the school's executive committee).

4.3 Interoperation Mechanisms

One important and complex aspect for the success of the distributed architecture is the existence of interoperation mechanisms between the central/national and the regional/local instances, in the support of the adequate distribution and information management and of some general use-cases.

On the other hand, in order to support normal complementarities between RS and other information systems in the education domain, and in order to satisfy the non-functional requirement "openness and integration with other systems" (§3.2), it is relevant the public specification and exposal of a basic set of interfaces and services according to the common Internet technologies, actually designated as "web services" [6, 7].

There are some ways to describe the concept of "web service". Maybe the simplest one is the following: "a set of operations that are available at the global scale through an electronic address of the type URL". One other one, more generic, defines a web service as "an interface that describes a collection of operations that are accessible from the network through a mechanism of XML standard messages". The web services underlying technology is strongly based on the Internet, its technology and standards, such as TCP/IP, URL, XML, HTTP or SMTP. The TCP/IP, HTTP and SMTP protocols take the general role of guaranteeing the transport of messages between the web services; other protocols may also be used, such as FTP, MQ or IIOP. However, due to its ubiquity, HTTP takes the role of the *de facto* standard as a transport protocol of the exchanged messages between web services. On the other hand, to some levels, XML plays a basic role in web services, such as a mechanism of description of the data independently of the programming languages, operating systems, and computer architectures.

5 Rent@School Current state

As previously referred, RS is a project in development, being on its first iteration, in which a first prototype is being developed based on the distributed single instance architecture, but already with support for the generality of the actors and representative use-cases. For the second iteration we aim to explore the multi-instance architecture and mechanisms related to openness and interoperation.

According our plan, the first iteration takes place until September of 2002 (started in September of 2001), and the second iteration would be developed between May of 2002 and December of 2003. It is still left open the possibility of transferring the RS technology to an institutional or enterprise context that would promote and adequately support it. For more details regarding the utilization or evaluation of the RS's state the reader can consult [2, 3, 4].

6 Conclusion and Future Work

In this paper we propose and discuss the main ideas of an ambitious project that can contribute to a better future for the management of the Portuguese education system.

The RS presentation in this paper was deliberately positioned at a high level, particularly by drafting its main requirements, possible information system architectures, and integration technologies. Other documents describe the current state of the project at a detailed level, namely: the "requirements and business analysis" document [3] or the "end-users point of view" document [4].

We plan the development of this project, in research and prototype terms, along the next sixteen months and based on two iterations. The first iteration has already started and is expected to finish on September of 2002. Its main objective will be the development of a prototype application, based on the distributed and single-instance architecture, to demonstrate the original concept.

The second iteration should start next months and it is expected to finish on December of 2003. Its main interest would be the design and implementation of the RS's open and public API, as well as, the research and discussion related to organizational and information system architectures.

References

[1]   Roberto Carneiro (2001). *O Futuro da Educação em Portugal: Tendências e Oportunidades, Um estudo de reflexão prospectiva*, Departamento de Avaliação Prospectiva e Planeamento do Ministério da Educação.

[2]   Rent@School Web Site. http://berlin.inese-id.pt/rentaschool/

[3]   Alberto Silva, Rui Azevedo, Gonçalo Borrêga. *Rent@School: Relatório Técnico - Descrição dos Requisitos*, February 2002.

[4]   Alberto Silva, Rui Azevedo, Gonçalo Borrêga (March 2002). *Rent@School: Guião de Utilização.*

[5]   E. Hobsbawn (2000). *On the Edge of the New Century,* The New Press.

[6]   W3C, *Web Services Activity*, 2002, http://www.w3.org/2002/ws/

[7]   WebServices.Org, *The Web Services Community Portal*, 2002, http://www.webservices.org

The Challenges of Implementing a University Copyright Policy in the Digital World
by
Donna L. Ferullo

Copyright laws are complex and can be confusing especially when trying to ascertain their applicability to digital works. Many universities have developed copyright policies to define the rights and responsibilities of their faculty, staff and students but there is a great challenge in implementing such policies. Many questions arise such as how does one reach all of the stakeholders in a university; what are the important issues for particular stakeholders such as libraries and distance learning programs; how does one educate the students about their copyright responsibilities; and how does a university navigate the legal potholes of the copyright law?

This brief paper highlights my experiences in establishing a copyright office at a major university. The University Copyright Office (UCO) at Purdue University has been in existence for two years. It was established as a result of a new copyright policy that took effect in July 2000. The policy provides some guidance about the copyright law and the expectations for faculty and staff. Students are included by referencing their honor code. The major focus of the policy is to inform the university community that they have both a legal and moral obligation to comply with the copyright law. The UCO is charged with advising faculty and staff on the use of copyrighted works for research and teaching but does not address questions of ownership of works created at the university. Educating the university community about the copyright law is also a primary responsibility of the Office.

One of the first hurdles was to develop a game plan on the best way to inform the university community that the Office existed. I met with faculty and staff from all levels and all disciplines to determine what were the questions and issues on campus and what did they think would be the best way to convey my message. It became quite apparent during the early stages that many were confused as to how copyright worked in the digital world. There was also a misconception that all educational use is fair use under the copyright law. I also discovered that many people did not even have a basic understanding of the copyright law. Even though the majority of the copyright concerns revolved around digital issues, the university community needed to have a clear, concise understanding of what the copyright law was about before they could move forward and apply the concepts to digital materials.

As I heard the concerns, I began to formulate a strategy for communicating with a diverse group of people who had very different levels of understanding. I embarked on an awareness campaign that was comprised of a combination of print, web, and targeted outreach programs.

A brochure entitled "A Guide to Copyright" was developed that condensed the fundamentals of the copyright law as it pertained to higher education. The brochure was distributed to all faculty, administrative/professional staff, and clerical staff at all of the campuses. The information in the brochure put the university community on notice that they were obligated to comply with the copyright law. As part of the educational component of the UCO, the brochure will be sent to all faculty and staff on an annual basis.

It was important for the UCO to establish a web presence on campus. The information that was included in the brochure was expanded on for the web site. Differences in the copyright law between classroom teaching and distance learning were highlighted with examples. Other components such as a Q & A section as well as a copyright news section were added. This is the second iteration of the web site and the structure and content will be changed according to the needs of the university.

The third approach was to promote the services of the Office through meetings with faculty and presentations to different groups on campus. I've worked with many of the distance learning faculty in assisting them in trying to achieve a win-win situation by using the materials they need to teach the course while still abiding by the spirit and letter of the copyright law.

Libraries also face many challenges in providing e-services and maintaining copyright compliance. There are library exemptions in the copyright law but the digital aspect for a service such as e-reserves is a bit hazy. Many times the only exemption that is applicable is fair use. Licensing access to materials is becoming more the norm for libraries than owning materials. It is therefore more important than ever for librarians to negotiate with all their vendors for the broadest possible use of materials.

The copyright issues around distance learning are certainly many and varied. The majority of concerns about copyright and distant learning revolve around what is allowed and what is not allowed for various formats of materials. Unfortunately, there is no easy answer. Many times it comes down to applying the fair use doctrine when no other copyright exemptions are appropriate.

One of the first myths that needed to be debunked is that distance learning does not necessarily mean that the professors or the students have to be in a far away place. The distance could be from one building to another on campus. Distance learning for the most part means that the professor and students are not in the same place and more often than not the learning is asynchronous.

The second myth is that everything on the Internet is free and clear to use. Many believe that no one owns the material that is posted. It is sometime difficult for many to understand that a work on the Internet enjoys the same copyright protection as a book or a journal article.

The third myth, as mentioned above, is that all educational use is fair use. Granted, fair use is probably the most utilized exemption in higher education for anything that occurs outside face-to-face teaching or classroom teaching but that does not automatically mean that every use falls within that exemption. It is critical that the university community understands the four-factor fair use test and can articulate the applicability of it to their situation. If they have made a good faith determination that their use is fair, a court can reduce the money damages if the university and/or employee are found guilty of copyright infringement.

The student honor code encompasses the rights and responsibilities for students during their tenure at the university. This certainly includes the expectation that they will comply with the copyright law. It has been my observation that students are unaware of exactly what the copyright law is and how it applies to them. Current and future students learn differently than many of their older professors. Their learning style is much more e-based than print based. To many students everything they need is on the Internet and many lack the ability to differentiate and critically evaluate the information and the source of the information such as what is provided for them through the library like full text journal databases and a web page posted by a group or an individual. If they can freely access it then it must be free. In their minds free access is equal to free use. So it is even more critical than ever for students to understand the copyright law. But how does a university make that happen? I maintain that the professors play a crucial role in educating the students not only in their discipline but also in the more fundamental requirements of the academy such as compliance with the copyright law. Educate the professor to educate the student.

In this litigious society universities must take precautions to protect themselves from both frivolous and valid law suits for copyright infringement. One of the best defenses to any such suit is to have developed and implemented a copyright policy. It is also very important that the university community be constantly aware of their responsibilities under the copyright law. A comprehensive and systematic program of copyright education and awareness will go a long way in minimizing the number of lawsuits and protecting the university.

The University Copyright Office at Purdue is still in its infancy stage but certainly great strides have been made. The number of questions that were generated by the brochure, web page and speaking engagements has risen over 500% from the first year to the second year and I fully expect that increase to continue as the Office becomes firmly entrenched in the infrastructure. I have concluded that one of the measures of success is that many people are now able to identify a potential copyright issue. They might not have the answer but they have recognized that there is an issue. The combination of that recognition and the resources of the UCO result in a win-win position for the university.

Interactive Video Content Supporting CSCL Environments

Matthias Finke
Department of Mobile Information Visualization
Computer Graphics Center
Germany
E-mail Matthias.Finke@gris.informatik.tu-darmstadt.de

Abstract: Creating knowledge within a community on the Internet is performed with great success. Thereby, *computer supported collaborative learning* (CSCL) environments use different media formats to convey information content and to establish communication channels between participants. With this paper, we announce a design approach integrating *interactive video* content as the basic media format into a CSCL environment in order to meet the requirements for group discussion concerning knowledge creation. A system prototype has been designed with an emphasis on a navigation model for supporting the community members.

Introduction

The Internet is a global network that relies on user interactivity. The world largest hypermedia system, the World Wide Web (WWW), which is based on the Internet, was introduced in the early 90's. Due to bandwidth limitation text based information was mainly transmitted within the WWW at that time. The development of the Internet enables today's user to transmit and retrieve multimedia content like sound, images, graphics, etc. The use of the medium *video* has become quite popular on the Internet and the amount of available content is growing rapidly. Higher bit rates, which means a faster transmission of data, new compression techniques and new transfer technologies, like the streaming technology, make it possible to transmit video content on the Internet today. A rather new video format that can be found on the Internet is called h*yper video*, also denoted as *interactive video* (IAV). The general target of interactive video is to integrate the user within the presentation and to provide him with an active role that encourages him to exert influence on the way the content is presented.

We denoted interactive video as a composition of video and additional information. Additional information supports the video and can consist of different media formats, like audio, images, graphics, animation, etc. Interactive video content enables us to combine additional information with objects within a video sequence. A number of projects have focused on this subject since the beginning of the 90's as described in (Sawhney 1996 and Stotts 2002). So far, interactive video content over the WWW is determined for presentation purposes, allowing a user to view the video content and to interact with video objects in order to request additional information. This interactive presentation form has been used in e-learning environments to support the process of knowledge creation as described in (Guimarães 1999).

Creating knowledge is a process often performed by a single person, for instance, by utilizing the WWW. A different approach to creating knowledge is *collaborative learning* (CL) within communities. Within these communities, users may discuss topics or problems. Communities can have a number of different objective targets, for instance, to share experiences or to work together on complex problems, which might be very difficult to solve by a single individual. A discussion on the WWW can be of synchronous character, like *chat-rooms* or asynchronous character, like *new groups*. CSCL can be understood as a form of knowledge creation based on group discussion that relies on both the information exchange and retrieval between distributed community members in a network.

The WWW is a basis for many communities exchanging and retrieving information content consisting of different multimedia formats to perform group discussion. So far, little has been done to provide communities with multimedia tool sets allowing them to use video content as a basis for their distributed discussion. With this paper, we announce a concept that provides a system architecture for *video based discussion forums*. The problem which will be dealt with in this paper is: *How do we support video based collaborative learning within distributed environments?*

General System Approach

The popularity and advantages of digital video content on the WWW can be associated with the *dual coding theory* as described in (Paivio 1986), which is especially true for virtual learning environments. This theory attempts to give equal weight to verbal and non-verbal processing. Furthermore, it is assumed that there are two cognitive independent subsystems: one is specialized for non-verbal information and one is for verbal information. Recall or recognition is enhanced by presenting information in both non-verbal and verbal form. This is an important aspect for our design approach, since video content is a carrier for both verbal and non-verbal information content. Learning, on the other hand, is an active process and a high degree of interactivity is important for the success of knowledge creation. Based on the consideration of video as an audiovisual information carrier and the importance of interactivity in relation to learning processes, we chose interactive video content as a hypermedia information structure for our CSCL environment.

A video based discussion forum is based on two main components: the *presentation* and the *authoring* component. The authoring component is responsible for enabling a user to contribute to the community forum. The presentation component is responsible for presenting the information content. Information content in our design approach contains the subsets *video content*, *additional information* and *navigation data*.

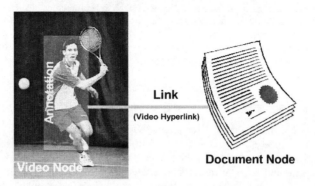

Figure 1: Video Object Linked to Document

The interactive video structure used in this system approach is based on the *Dexter Hypertext Reference Model* (Halasz & Schwartz 1994), including the notation of *links* and *nodes* that is the essence of hypertext. A *video node* can be associated with a video object like a *tennis player* in a tennis match. In contrast to a node in a hypertext document, a video node in an IAV has a spatial and temporal characteristic, since it can move within a video sequence. A video hyperlink consists of two endpoints: a video node that is associated with an object in a video sequence and a document node providing additional information about the video object. The result of the combination of video and additional information with nodes and links spans an information space, which we denote as a *video based hypermedia information structure* (VHIS). The activation of a video node leads via the video hyperlink to the presentation of the associated document node. In addition, the visualization or annotation of the video node within the video sequence supports the user with the navigation. Figure 1 shows the relation between video node, video hyperlink and document node.

An authoring component is needed when a user provides his contribution by extending the interactive video content. The authoring component can be divided into *video node authoring* and *video hyperlink authoring*. Since a video node is associated with a video object, *location data* is needed to determine the position of the video node. The generation of location data is a demanding task, see (Finke 2000). The authoring process concerning the generation of video hyperlinks is rather straightforward. The user selects a video node and defines a new video hyperlink and the document node, which is presented after activating the video node.

The video based hypermedia information structure described here can become very complex and unmanageable for the community participants. This could reduce the effect of knowledge creation within the group. Therefore, we introduce a concept to support the navigation capability of a user in such a CSCL environment. This concept visualizes the hypermedia structure, showing the user the availability of hyperlinks in a video sequence. In addition, when a member provides information for the community discussion, he has to provide additional *meta data* that specifies his contribution. The meta data set includes *user name*, *time*, *media format*, *user comment* and a *contribution category* and will also be visualized in order to support user navigation. Furthermore, this concept will support the communication within the community discussion.

System Design

A first prototype presents the *video content*, the *additional information* and provides an *authoring tool set* to extend the interactive video content with user contribution by combining video nodes with document nodes via video hyperlinks. In addition, a discussion board is implemented in the system design, visualizing in a first approach the video hyperlink structure combined with the meta data, which describes every contribution. The discussion board helps the community members to get an overview of the ongoing discussion. Furthermore, it helps them to navigate within the interactive video structure. These functionalities are important aspects for our CSCL system design.

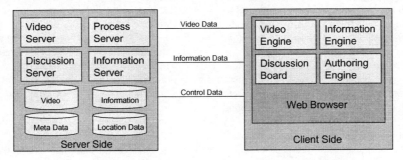

Figure 2: Reference Model

The system is designed as a server-client architecture enabling asynchronous group discussion for community members. Using the Internet, the system is implemented in a WWW environment using a Web browser on the client side to visualize the interactive video content and the discussion board, including a tool for providing user contribution. Figure 2 shows the main system components. On the server side, a video server streams the video content towards the client side. The information server receives the request regarding an activated video hyperlink. In addition, this server receives the meta data and the contribution of the users. The discussion server generates information for client navigation purpose based on the meta data and the dynamic interactive video structure. On the client side, there are four main components. The video engine presents the video content and is the user interface for every interaction regarding the video hyperlinks and the video controlling. The information engine represents the discussion contribution of the community members. The discussion board presents the video based hypermedia information structure in combination with the meta data. Based on the authoring engine, contributions can be provided by the community. Figure 3 shows a screen shot of the Web application. The client application front end is divided into four areas. If a user clicks with the mouse pointer on a video object, which is combined with a video hyperlink, the associated document is presented in the information window. In addition, the content of the discussion board is synchronized with the video *play-time* and will always be updated when an interaction with a video object occurs.

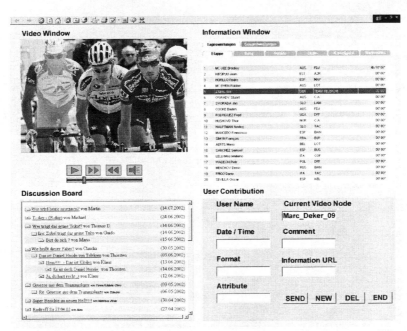

Figure 3: Web User Interface

User Scenario

Figure 3 shows the Web application on the client side. Upon user request, the video nodes are annotated within the video stream, visualizing the video hyperlinks and thus the existence of additional information. When a user wants to activate a video hyperlink, he clicks on a video object in the *video window*. The *information window* then presents the additional information (user contribution) and the *discussion board* is updated. In the *discussion board window*, the meta data *user name*, *user comment* and *time* associated with the contribution is shown and graphically highlighted. If the user clicks on this highlighted data set entry, then the complete meta data set is presented within the *user contribution window*. This is one way to navigate through a video based discussion forum.

Another way to navigate in the video based discussion forum is by scrolling the *discussion board* entries. If a user finds an interesting entry, he clicks on it in the *discussion board window*. The *video window* then jumps to the video sequence in which the video object can be found that is associated with the entry in the *discussion board*. Furthermore, the *information window* presents the user contribution associated with that entry and the full meta data set is presented in the *user contribution window*.

As mentioned above, these two navigation options lead to the presentation of the meta data set in the *user contribution window*. In addition, the *current video node* name is also presented there. If a user wants to provide a contribution to the current video node, she chooses the NEW option and fills out the form in the *user contribution window*. The contribution along with the meta data is then sent to the server with the SEND option. A user can always delete his contribution with the DEL option. At this stage of the development, the additional information denoted as the user contribution is given in form of URL addresses.

Conclusion

We have described a video based discussion forum that takes advantage of interactive video content. Community members can exert influence over the way the interactive video based information is presented. In addition, users can insert additional information in to the interactive video structure by defining new video nodes and links into the interactive video structure. With this approach, users can exchange and share their experiences and views by inserting additional information into the presentation platform and thus into a dynamic *video based hypermedia information structure*. The integration of an advanced discussion board supports the navigation within the information structure for the community members. Since the complexity of such a hypermedia information structure can easily become quite large, a mechanism for navigation purposes is mandatory. This concept along with the integration of meta data sets is the basis for an enhanced navigation model, which provides a better understanding of the information content within a community discussion and supports the success of knowledge creation.

References

Guimarães, N. (1999). Towards Hypervideo on the Web", Proceedings of IMSA 99, Third IASTED International Conference on Internet and Multimedia Systems and Applications, Grand Bahamas.

Finke M. (2000). An Architecture of a Personalized Dynamic Interactive Video System, Digital Content Creation Conference, Bradford, UK.

Halasz, F., & Schwartz, M. (1994). The Dexter Hypertext Reference Model: Hypermedia, Communications of the ACM, Vol. 37, No. 2, pp. 30-39.

Paivio, A. (1986). Mental Representation, A Dual Coding Approach, Oxford, u.a.: Oxford University Press, Inc., , pp. 53-83.

Sawhney, N. (1996). HyperCafe: Narrative and Aesthetic Properties of Hypervideo, Proceedings of the Seventh ACM Conference on Hypertext. New York: Association for Computing Machinery.

Stotts, D.(2002). Hypervideo Support for Distributed Extreme Programming, Technical Report, Department of Computer Science, University of North Carolina, March.

DISTANCE LEARNING AT SECONDARY LEVELS: CONTEXTS AND NORMS FOR THE LEARNING O F MATHEMATICS

Josep M Fortuny ,Universitat Autònoma de Barcelon, Joaquin Giménez, Universitat de Barcelona, Spain. Philippe Richard, University of Montreal , Canada

Distance Learning for Secondary Education

Since 1998 the Departaments de Didàctica de la Matemàtica i les Ciències Experimentals of both Universitat Autònoma de Barcelona & Universitat de Barcelona, develop a research project concerning the use of the Internet to attend those students who are not able to go to school regularly, specially those at the hospital or at home (Gimenez & Fortuny, 2000), and high performance athletes (Figueiras, 2000). In other papers we have discussed some aspects relating the communication model used by tutor and students under the influence of technology - web pages, e-mail, clectronic forums, - and the impact that a virtual tutor has on the students participating in the experience (Figueiras, 2000; Fortuny et al. 1999). Specially in mathematics, the syntax of its language shape some of the learners' actions to make the others know about their progress.

We also detect a great influence of tutor's and students' context arising from the case studies carried out on statistics, algebra and geometry. It is an influence on both the way they manage the experience of learning at a distance, and the way they access to the contents,. This and its contribution to the norms they agree for developing the experience are the discussion points of this paper.

A great amount of the work carried out on distance training and self-learning attend university or professional levels, for it aims to be used by those adults who engage a working society highly influenced by the actual self-learning paradigm. Within this frame, it is supposed that many of the knowledge that people have when access to a job has been acquired using self-learning programs and, moreover, that it is an up to date learning (Duart, 2000; Guigou, 1999). However, this paradigm is quite different wh en adapting and justifying the use of new technologies for communication in secondary levels of education, for aspects such as affect, curricular constraints, and the influence of technology on the motivation and willingness to learn, become more valued (Brieba, 2000): Personal contact among peers and teachers has a high relevance at this level of education and responses to questions concerning why should we introduce distance learning experiences has not an immediate answer. Standards for secondary education emphasise objectives to be carried out in a classroom setting, such as peer- discussion in a community; handling of objects in the space; learning how to speak and moderate a debate; and we are far away from consolidated proposals joining the use of distance learning to the objectives of the actual curricula. Rejecting simplistic approximations concluding if the conversion from a non-technology -oriented course structure to a technology-oriented one led to a quantifiable difference of any sort, our commitm ent in this specific project is a social and politic one: distance education at a secondary level to attend those people for whom it seems to be the best opportunity, specially the use of the Internet.

Dynamic contract, sociomathematical norms and context influences

Different situations led us to adapt learning units for learning at a distance to the different contexts in which the learners develop their activity. Evidence in the cases studied suggests focus in the way it modifies the design of the learning environments and curricula adaptation for each setting.

The influence of the family is an important factor to take into account with hospitalised students (Muria et al. 2000). When students work at home, and even when they communicate with their tutors, usually do it in the company of their relatives, who work with them. If the correspondent activities do not take into account this factor, there is no possibility for the tutor to follow the student by observing only their communication via e-mail, and there is a need to engage the family in the experience and make explicit their role together with the ones of tutors and students. This is the main point to create a new setting for learning and not to force the students to reproduce at a distance the norms and constraints which they have learnt that prevail in the classroom.

This must be also applied to the case of high performance athletes, who due to sport training must be absent from school for long periods of time. However, the role of the family has almost no influence when planning or designing the environment to be used during the tutorial, but the hard training sessions and press of the competition arise as the main factors that mould the learning experience of the student:

> *I am a bit lost with these of determinants. I did not know how to do anything for you and I hope that you will help me tomorrow. The videoconference doesn't work, it may be the change of the modem, I don't know. Let's meet tomorrow at 12h o'clock to communicate by telephone or chat. Maybe that the championships are coming closer and I cannot concentrate.* (Figueiras, 1999)

This kind of assertions are a key to adapt the contents to the special situation of the student, and shows not only the influence of the natural context in the student's activity, but the implicit agreements arising during the experience. It is important for the tutor to recognise it as a new agreement in the relationship that he/she construct with the student. In the example above, the student assumes that the high grade of flexible learning permits him to look for spaces of collaboration in order to cover the program. This occurs not at the beginning of the tutorial but later, while he maintains a personal relationship with his tutor.

Therefore, we face different norms or rules, what we here roughly label as *contract*, some of them implicitly assumed by the learners as a result of their interaction, and some of them stated from the very beginning of the experience (fig. 1). Moreover, these rules are continuously re-negotiated, and new ones appear leading us to a dynamic view of this contract. It is not possible to conduct the experience under the rules of a planned contract unless it deal with this dynamic process. Keys for the construction of these rules need to be recognised by the learners and, in the contexts of distance education we are dealing with, they must look for them in their written conversations via e-mail. For this reason is important to describe and familiarise with the kind of actions that permit us to communicate and collaborate at a distance. If the participants learn how to participate (by writing) on a electronic conversation and how to express ideas related to the specific contents, they mould their actions to make the other know about their own interests, implicitly or explicitly. Distance learning and people who engage on-line courses require a new interpretation of *context* and its dimensions (Badia et al. 2000).

Two main aspects are directly related with the context of the experiences we are discussing: the design of the activities concerning didactical and pedagogical issues of the course proposed, and an important and not yet sufficiently investigated question: the student's rejoining the school setting after the conducted tutorial.

Adapted Design for a dynamic process

For each one of the cases proposed to be attended, a web based environment is prepared for the student to cover the same curriculum which is considered at the corespondent school. Thus, there is a decision to give priority to the program followed by the current teacher. To this extent, the main point in the exploratory studies has been to investigate the way in which this new learning settings permit the student to follow his or her learning activities, more than to innovate or to experiment a new *mosaic* knowledge, as a hypertext system like the Internet suggest.

Interactive points have been used, discussed and analysed to know and let the learners know about socialisation roles of tutor and students, and its influence in the relationship among them and the materials. Internet is the most significant contact with the mathematical activity for these students, and giving references, using reactions, or emotional activation resources, are considered beyond a classical *talk-with-the-tutor* way of interaction. Figure 2 enlighten this points attending a personal experience of a sick student studying at home.

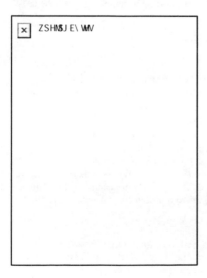

Design of the tutorial units and adapted curriculum

We have analysed some crucial aspects of a unified model of conducted-at a distance tutorial concerning several experiences with secondary students. It is important to emphasise the differences between this kind of precise support for some students, and general courses designed totally to be carried out at a distance, specially what concerns to design, evaluation and implement (Muria et al 2000). In the sections above, starting from some researches on the cases conducted in the project we offered the main points to be taken into account in the planning phase: contact with the family when appropriate; sharing from the beginning the initial rules and objectives to take into account; and flexible -collaborative, personal- design of the virtual learning environment.

But attending the end of the experience, it is more important to ensure the students' rejoining the school setting and the adaptation to the way of assessment of his or her current teacher at the school than evaluate the goals or benefits of the distance environment alone. We have detected that new habits of reading and writing, offering of open responses due to the asynchronicity of the distance conversations; and creativity arising from the contact with a virtual environment contribute to shape the learners' experience after the tutorials. Concerning the cases we are discussing here, this led us in the future to evaluate which of the interactive issues arising in the experience of learning at a distance are used by the students once they came back to their classroom setting.

This project is supported by the DGIGYT, reference PB96-1201 and a grant from the Comissionat per a Universitats i Recerca de la Generalitat de Catalunya.

References

Badia, T, Barberá; E, Giménez, J & Rosich, N. (2000) *Les dimensions del context en l'educació virtual.* (Projecte IN3). Barcelona, Universitat Oberta de Catalunya.

Brieba, C. (2000) *Papel de los aspectos emotivos y afectivos en la tutorización personalizada on-line.* Unpublished manuscript, Universitat Autònoma de Barcelona.

Duart, M. (2000) *Aprendizaje sin distancias*[electronic paper. http://campus.uoc.es/web/cat/articles/josep_maria_duart.html] Universitat Oberta de Catalunya.

Figueiras, L. (1999) [E-mail correspondence from an on-line teaching experience on linear algebra] Unpublished corpus of data.

Figueiras, L. (2000) *Written discourse in virtual environments.* Universitat Autònoma de Barcelona. Manuscript submitted for publication.

Fortuny, J. M., Murillo, J., Martín, J.F., Trevijano, D. (1999). Aprendizaje sin límites. Un modelo de diseño interactivo como soporte y ampliación instruccional en la enseñanza de la geometría en la ESO. *Contextos Educativos: Revista de Educación, 2,* 27-52.

Giménez, J & Fortuny, JM (2000) Télétutorisation en mathématiques et traitement de l'heterogéneité. In: A. Ahmed et al. (eds) *Proceedings of the CIEAEM 1999,* Chichester, Elis Horword eds.

Guigou, J. (1999, December) *L'autonomisation des apprentissages dans la société capitalisée.* Plenary conference presented at the 5è. Col.loqui Europeu sobre l'Autoformació, Barcelona.

Muria, S; Latorre, R; Rosich, N & Giménez, J. (2000) *An exploratory study about the use of a statistics tutorial unit in a rich on line environment: The case Ivan.* Unpublished manuscript, Universitat de Barcelona. [Catalan version available by the authors]

DISTANCE EDUCATION AT SECONDARY LEVELS: CONTEXTS AND NORMS FOR THE LEARNING OF MATHEMATICS

Josep M. Fortuny, Departament de Didàctica de la Matemàtica i de les Ciències Experimentals, Universitat Autònoma de Barcelona, Spain, JosepMaria.Fortuny@uab.es

Joaquin Giménez, Departament de Didàctica de les Ciències Experimentals i la Matemàtica, Universitat de Barcelona, Spain, jgimenez@uoc.edu

Philippe R. Richard, Département de didactique, Université de Montréal , Canada, philippe.r.richard@umontreal.ca

Abstract:

We analysed some crucial aspects of a unified model for conducting distance tutorial concerning several experiences with secondary students. It is important to emphasize the differences between this kind of precise support for some students, and general courses designed totally to be carried out at distance, specially in relation to design, evaluation and implementation. At attending the end of the experience, it is more important to ensure the students' insertion in the school setting and the adaptation to the way of assessment of his or her current teacher at the school than evaluate the goals or benefits of the distance environment alone. We have detected habits for reading and writing, offered open responses due to the asynchronicity of distance conversations; and creativity arising from the contact with a virtual environment contribute to shape learners' experience after the tutorials.

DISTANCE LEARNING FOR SECONDARY EDUCATION

Since 1998 the *Departaments de Didàctica de la Matemàtica i les Ciències Experimentals* of both *Universitat Autònoma de Barcelona* and *Universitat de Barcelona*, develop a research project concerning use of the Internet for students who are not able to go to school regularly, specially those at hospital or at home (Gimenez & Fortuny, 2000), and high performance athletes (Figueiras, 2000). In other papers we have discussed some aspects relating the communication model used by tutor and students under the influence of technology -- web pages, e-mail, electronic forums, -- and the impact of a virtual tutor has on students participating in the experience (Figueiras, 2000; Fortuny et al. 1999). Especially in mathematics, the syntax of its language shape some of the learners' actions to make the others know about their progress.

We also detected a great influence of tutor's and students' context arising from the case studies carried out in statistics, algebra and geometry. It influenced both the way they managed the experience of learning at a distance, and the way they accessed the contents. This and its contribution to the norms they agreed for developing the experience were the discussion points of this paper.

A great amount of research on distance training and self-learning has been conducted at university or professional levels, for it aims to be used by those adults who engage a working society highly influenced by the actual self-learning paradigm. Within this frame, it is supposed that most of the knowledge that people have while accessing to a job has been acquired using self-learning programs and, moreover, that it is an up-to-dated learning (Duart, 2000; Guigou, 1999). However, this paradigm is quite different when adapting and justifying the use of new technologies for communication at secondary levels of education, for aspects such as affect, curricular constraints, and influence of technology on the motivation and willingness to learn, become more valued (Brieba, 2000). Personal contacts among peers and teachers has a high relevance at this level of education and responses to questions concerning why should we introduce distance learning experiences has not an immediate answer.

DYNAMIC CONTRACT, SOCIOMATHEMATICAL NORMS AND CONTEXT INFLUENCES

Different situations led us to adapt learning units for teaching at a distance to the different contexts in which the learners develop their activity. Evidence in the cases studied suggested focus in the way it modifies the design of the learning environments and curricula adaptation for each setting.

The influence of the family is an important factor to take into account with hospitalized students (Muria et al. 2000). When students work at home, and even when they communicate with their tutors, usually they do so in the company of their relatives, who work with them. If the correspondent activities do not take into account this factor, there is no possibility for the tutor to follow the student by observing only their communication via e-mail, and there is a need to engage the family in the experience and make explicit their role together with the ones of tutors and students. This is the main point to create a new setting for learning and not to force the students to reproduce at distance the norms and constraints which they learnt that prevail in the classroom.

This must be also applied to the case of high performance athletes, who due to sport training must be absent from school for long periods of time. However, the role of the family has almost no influence when planning or designing the environment to be used during the tutorial, but the hard training sessions and pressure of the competition arise as the main factors that mould the learning experience of the student:

> I am a bit lost with these of determinants. I did not know how to do anything for you and I hope that you will help me tomorrow. The videoconference doesn't work, it may be the change of the modem, I don't know. Let's meet tomorrow at 12h o'clock to communicate by telephone or chat. Maybe that the championships are coming closer and I cannot concentrate. (Figueiras, 1999)

This kind of assertions is a key to adapt the contents to the special situation of the student, and shows not only the influence of the natural context in the student's activity, but the implicit agreements arising during the experience. It is important for the tutor to recognise it as a new agreement in the relationship that he-she is constructing with the student. In the example above, the student assumes that the high grade of flexible learning permits him to look for spaces of collaboration in order to go through the whole program. This occurs not at the beginning of the tutorial but later, while he maintains a personal relationship with his tutor.

Figure 1: Initial window of Interm@tes web-site [1]

----
[1] English translations of the figures are available: http://www.mapageweb.umontreal.ca/richarp/intermates/aace/index.html

Therefore, we face different norms or rules, what we here roughly label as *contract*, some of them implicitly assumed by the learners as a result of their interaction, and some of them stated from the very beginning of the experience (fig. 1). Moreover, these rules are continuously re-negotiated, and new ones appear leading us to a dynamic view of this contract. It is not possible to conduct the experience under the rules of a planned contract unless it deals with this dynamic process. Keys for the construction of these rules need to be recognized by the learners and, in the contexts of distance education we are dealing with, they must look for them in their written conversations via e-mail. For this reason it is important to describe and familiarize with the kind of actions that permit us to communicate and collaborate at a distance. If the participants learn how to participate (by writing) on an electronic conversation and how to express ideas related to a specific contents, they mould their actions to make the other know about their own interests, implicitly or explicitly. Distance learning and people who engage on-line courses require new interpretation of *context* and its dimensions (Badia et al. 2000).

Two main aspects are directly related with the context of the experiences we are discussing: the design of the activities concerning didactical and pedagogical issues of the course proposed, and an important and not yet sufficiently investigated question: the student's return to the school setting after the conducted tutorial.

ADAPTED DESIGN FOR A DYNAMIC PROCESS

For each one of the cases proposed to be attended, a web-based environment was prepared for the student to cover the same curriculum, which is considered at the correspondent school. Thus, there is a decision to give priority to the program followed by the current teacher. To this extent, the main point in the exploratory studies was to investigate the way in which this new learning setting permits the student to follow his or her learning activities, more than to innovate or to experiment a new *mosaic* knowledge, as a hypertext system like the Internet suggests.

Interactive points have been used, discussed and analysed to know and let the learners know about socialisation roles of tutor and students, and its influence in the relationship among them and the materials. Internet is the most significant contact with the mathematical activity for these students, and giving references, using reactions, or emotional activation resources, are considered beyond a classical *talk-with-the-tutor* way of interaction. Figure 2 enlightens this point attending a personal experience of a sick student studying at home.

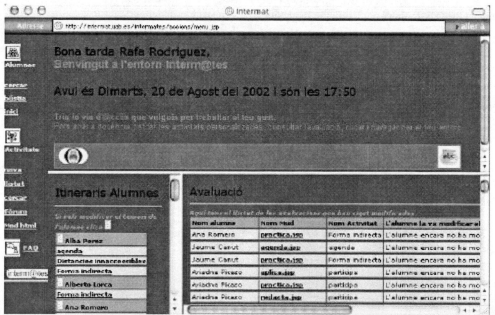

Figure 2: Personalized gate to recognize the actions of the pupils

DESIGN OF THE TUTORIAL UNITS AND ADAPTED CURRICULUM

Mainly, the web-based environment was built in a hypertextual form starting from the disciplinary contents and technological aspects. The disciplinary contents were structured according to a catalogue of key questions which cover of compulsory secondary education, age 12 to 16, adapting at the beginning the modular base and the pedagogical principles of *Bon dia Mates* project -- curricular material which was financed, diffused and published in paper version by the *Departament d'Ensenyament* of *Generalitat de Catalunya*, of which a static web version by the *Programa d'Informàtica Educativa*. However, the access to the contents, which vary with the needs of the users, is possible not only starting from a glossary, blocks of matters, a set of questions-answers game and an internal search engine, but also starting from mini didactic units (fig. 3). The latter were organized to launch a progressive study of the key questions with various points of interactivity, including elements of orientation, regulation and synthesis for the pupil and the teacher, in addition to the possibility of communication with the peers or the tutor. In the case of complex key questions, as on figure 3, we developed the organization of the tutorial units thanks to behavioural research (Richard, 2002).

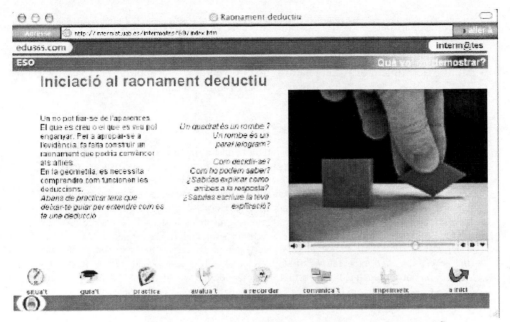

Figure 3: Main window for the study of key question *what means to proof?*

REFERENCES

Badia, T., Barberá, E., Giménez, J. & Rosich, N. (2000). *Les dimensions del context en l'educació virtual* (Projecte IN3). Barcelona: Universitat Oberta de Catalunya.

Brieba, C. (2000). *Papel de los aspectos emotivos y afectivos en la tutorización personalizada on-line.* Unpublished manuscript, Universitat Autònoma de Barcelona.

Duart, M. (2000). *Aprendizaje sin distancias.* Retrieved August 18, 2002, from Universitat Oberta de Catalunya Web site: http://campus.uoc.es/web/cat/articles/josep_maria_duart.html.

Figueiras, L. (1999). [E-mail correspondence from an on-line teaching experience on linear algebra]. Unpublished raw data.

Figueiras, L. (2000). *Written discourse in virtual environments.* Universitat Autònoma de Barcelona. Manuscript submitted for publication.

Fortuny, J. M., Murillo, J., Martín, J.F. & Trevijano, D. (1999). Aprendizaje sin límites. Un modelo de diseño interactivo como soporte y ampliación instruccional en la enseñanza de la geometría en la ESO. *Contextos Educativos: Revista de Educación, 2,* 27-52.

Giménez, J. & Fortuny, J.M. (2000). Télétutorisation en mathématiques et traitement de l'hétérogénéité. In A. Ahmed et al. (Eds.), *Proceedings of the CIEAEM 51.* Chichester: Elis Horword.

Guigou, J. (1999, December). *L'autonomisation des apprentissages dans la société capitalisée.* Plenary conference presented at the 5è Col.loqui Europeu sobre l'Autoformació, Barcelona.

Muria, S., Latorre, R., Rosich, N. & Giménez, J. (2000). *An exploratory study about the use of a statistics tutorial unit in a rich on line environment: The case Ivan.* Unpublished manuscript, Universitat de Barcelona. [Catalan version available by the authors].

Richard, P. R. (in press). *Modélisation du comportement en situation de validation.* Bern: Peter Lang.

ACKNOWLEDGEMENTS

The authors wish to express their gratitude to *Comissionat per a Universitats i Recerca de la Generalitat de Catalunya* and *Proyecto Sur de Ediciones S.L.* for their support. This research has been supported by DGIGYT (Spain) under Grant PB96-1201.

Privacy and Anonymity in an Online Course: Perceptions and Expectations of Distance Education Students

Dannie B. Francis, Department of Adult Learning and Instructional Technology, University of Wyoming, United States, DannieFrancis@email.msn.com

Guy M. Westhoff, Department of Adult Learning and Instructional Technology, University of Wyoming, United States, westhoff@uwyo.edu

Abstract With the emergence of the Internet and the increased use of online courses, email, and chat rooms, the issues of privacy, anonymity and the security of personal information have evolved to a new level of importance. These issues have been discussed extensively as related to open access of online services, but have only lightly been addressed with regard to students in online courses. Online distance education courses bring into play a new set of classroom variables and factors, particularly the attitudes and expectations of distance education students who are making use of the Internet to further their education. This study sought to answer the question: What are the perceptions and expectations of students in an online course with regard to privacy and anonymity? Results indicated that the respondents shared a noncommittal attitude toward privacy and anonymity issues expressed a lack of concern for the issues.

Introduction

"The fundamental concept of distance education is simple enough: teachers and students are separated by distance and sometimes by time" (Moore & Kearsley, 1996, p. 1). Correspondence and independent study courses were the first generation of distance education classes. "The earliest documented home study course offered in the United States was shorthand" (Moore & Kearsley, 1996, p. 20). The State University of Iowa began radio broadcast courses for credit in February of 1925 and followed up in 1934 with courses in oral hygiene and identifying constellations through television broadcasts (Moore & Kearsley, 1996, p. 27). This ushered in the broadcasting and teleconferencing era of distance education. The Open University was introduced as a key player in distance education in the 1960's and 1970's. In 1991 the World Wide Web introduced us to the third generation of distance education classes. "By June 15, 1995 seventy three percent of the countries of the world were Internet connected to some degree" (Khan, 1997, p. 20) and online classes were ready to be launched into homes all across America.

The relatively recent phenomenon of online education has opened the door to many research opportunities. Among the research options have been several studies conducted concerning privacy and anonymity of persons who use the Internet (Bodi, 1998; Descy, 1997; Metivier-Carreiro & LaFollette, 1997; Singleton, 1998). While privacy issues are not unique to the Internet, Holt (1998) reminds us that "risks may be magnified by the power and reach of electronic systems," and to date studies have not addressed students of online classes. This study will specifically address such students and ask the question, "What are the perceptions and expectations of online students with regard to privacy and anonymity?"

Privacy is defined as all information available in an online class, which can be used to identify the student taking the class. Examples of privacy information for students include name, address, phone number, age, gender and social security number. Anonymity is defined as the ability to take a class without other individuals being aware of your identity or personality. An example of this would be allowing students to use an alias for class instead of their real name.

The face-to-face interaction of the traditional classroom usually results in students revealing some components of their personality. Race, gender and age are examples of traits that are immediately open to the scrutiny of other students while grooming habits, shyness or a tendency to be outspoken are traits that might reveal themselves over a period of time. Distance education, and more specifically, online courses bring into play a new set of classroom variables and factors (Holt, Kleiber, Swenson, Reess & Milton, 1998). Students who are typically reserved in a traditional classroom might "blossom" in an online class and with greater participation by a larger number of students, the usually dominant personality might become just another voice in the class.

Because there are environmental differences between traditional classrooms and online courses this study will explore what expectations and perceptions exist with regard to privacy and anonymity in online courses. Other studies have shown that individuals who utilize Web-based commerce such as email and chat rooms do expect some level of security with regard to their privacy, and educators should be aware of this concern for their online students (Holt, 1998).

In a study conducted at the University of Wyoming (Novick & Francis, 2001) a class of twenty-nine students were surveyed for their opinions on privacy and anonymity within their online courses. Of the twenty-nine students surveyed slightly over forty-one percent responded. Of the students who responded, those who had taken two or more online courses showed less concern over privacy and anonymity issues than those who were new to online education. The strongest reactions were to the question, "Should a student be able to use a pseudonym for chats and threaded discussions?" A little over eighty-three percent of the respondents disagreed or disagreed strongly with this concept. Mild concern was expressed over the sharing of home phone numbers and addresses while video streaming for chats and biographies were basically neutral showing no concern against or enthusiasm for the concepts. A copy of this study is available in the 2001 National Meeting proceedings from AECT.

Methods

Students in outreach programs offered by the University of Wyoming were offered the opportunity to complete an online survey regarding attitudes towards issues of privacy, anonymity and personal information sharing in an online educational environment. The survey was offered in April and May of 2002. The survey instrument was built in Macromedia's Dreamweaver 4 software using radio buttons and text boxes as the response method. The URL for accessing the survey was sent to students by email with the assistance of the University of Wyoming Outreach School. Students who chose to participate were asked to select the provided URL and complete a questionnaire consisting of a demographics section and twenty attitude questions. The attitudes questions were rated on a Likert scale with five categories ranging from strongly agree to strongly disagree.

The responses were submitted via the Internet directly to the researcher when the respondent chose a submit button at the end of the survey. Likert responses were weighted one through five. The responses were tallied with a strong concern for privacy or anonymity resulting in a high score (5) while a strong preference for openness or minimal privacy and anonymity resulted in a low score (1). Of the twenty questions ten were related to issues of privacy and ten were related to anonymity. Statistics were performed using SPSS.

Findings and Conclusions

This study showed that online distance education students had similar attitudes towards issues of privacy and anonymity within the online course. These attitudes were noncommittal and expressed a lack of concern or previous thought about the issues of privacy and anonymity. Moss (2000) identified that users of chat rooms and e-commerce expect a certain level of security. However, from the results of this study it appears that students in an online distance education course do not. This result could be attributed to the fact that these online students are interacting within an environment where access is controlled via password protection.

The increase in web-based distance education courses and entire degree programs offered online, it is important to determine student attitudes toward the issues of privacy, anonymity, and sharing personal information and the degree these attitudes impact the success of the course and students in online courses. Future studies need to be conducted to ascertain specific attitudes related to the issues of privacy, anonymity, and the sharing of personal information by the students in an online distance education course.

References

Bodi, S., (1998). Ethics and information technology: Some principles to guide students. *Journal of Academic Librarianship*, 24 (6), 459-63.

Descy, D, (1997). The Internet and Education: Some lessons on privacy and pitfalls. *Educational Technology*, 37 (2), 48-52.

Holt, M. E., (1998). Ethical Considerations in Internet-based adult education. In B. Cahoon (Ed.), *New Directions for Adult and Continuing Education.* Jossey-Bass, San Francisco, CA.

Holt, M. E., Kleiber, P. B., Swenson, J. D., Rees, E. F., and Milton, J., (1998). Facilitating group learning on the Internet. In B. Cahoon (Ed.), *New Directions for Adult and Continuing Education*. Jossey-Bass, San Francisco, CA.

Kahn, B. H., (1997). *Web-Based Instruction*. Englewood Cliffs, New Jersey: Educational Technology Publications.

Metivier-Carreiro, K. and LaFollette, M. C., (1997). Balancing cyberspace promise, privacy and protection: Tracking the debate. *Science Communication*, 19 (1), 3-20.

Moore, M. G. and Kearsley, G., (1996). *Distance Education: A Systems View*. Belmont, California: Wadsworth Publishing Company.

Moss, M., (2000, March 28). SEC's plan to snoop for crime on Web sparks a debate over privacy. *The Wall Street Journal*, p. B1, B4.

Novick, S. L. and Francis, D. B., (2001). Privacy and anonymity: Issues for online students or not? Unpublished manuscript, University of Wyoming.

Singleton, S., (1998). Privacy or freedom on the Internet: What are the conflicts between proposed new privacy laws and freedom on information. *Update on Law Related Education*, 22 (2), 16-19.

Blended Learning: What is it? How does it impact student retention and performance?

Patricia C. Franks

Many institutions have developed educational programs that provide a continuum of totally on-campus courses, supplementary Web-enhanced courses, and completely online courses (Pittinsky, 2001).

Since the early days of universities, a traditional oral lecture has been a keystone of higher education (Brusilovsky, 2000). Even distance learning is not new. Major universities including The University of Michigan and Ball State University in Indiana literally created distance learning 15 years ago as a revenue producer. Rio Salado College, one of ten colleges in the Maricopa County Community College District of Phoenix, Arizona, has provided distance learning for more than twenty years (Walczak, 1999).

Educators who have tried both approaches realize that neither the traditional lecture format nor the distance education approach is appropriate for every student, every teacher, and every course. This leads us to a third option, blended learning.

Blended Learning

A blended approach to learning is accomplished by leveraging technology to make education more accessible. "Simply put, blended learning is learning that employs multiple strategies, methods, and delivery systems ("The Node Learning", 2001)." Blended learning is sometimes referred to as "integrated learning," "hybrid learning," or "multi-method learning." The primary focus of this article is on the integration of classroom- and Internet-based resources in ways that improve conditions for teaching and learning.

To create a successful blended learning approach to teaching and learning, two tools are essential: 1) learning technology and 2) blended learning strategy (McArthur, 2001).

Learning technology enables the instructor to create course materials in different formats including printed textbooks, online textbooks, online lecture notes, QuickTime movies, CDRoms, PowerPoint Presentations, streaming media, and videotapes of lectures and demonstrations. Dr. David Rose, co-director of the Center for Applied Special Technology (CAST), believes in providing students with "multiple representations of information" and a menu of different ways to get the information they need (O'Neill, 2001).

A blended learning strategy must be developed to identify the best "blend" of strategies, methods, and medias to help students meet the course objectives.

Blended Learning as a Process

It's important to understand that instructors don't create successful blended courses in one fell swoop ("The Node Learning", 2001). The best approach is to use your course goals plus identified teaching and learning objectives as a basis for your blended course. Remember, teaching and learning come first, technology follows. Stephen Ehrmann ("The Node Learning", 2001) puts it another way: "If you're headed in the wrong direction, technology won't help you get to the right place."

Once you clarify your goals and objectives, you're ready to determine the best method to achieve them. Technology can help in one of two ways: 1) by providing administrative or logistical support for the instructor and students and 2) by enhancing teaching and learning.

If you want to develop your blended course in stages, it may progress something like this:

1. First, provide administrative and logistical support for your students and yourself by posting your current syllabus, office hours, and a list of course references on line.

2. Then add a discussion forum or chat room for students to ask questions or discuss assignments outside of class.
3. Next, post course materials such as lectures, course notes, and presentation slides online.
4. Finally, revise the entire course to take advantage of some ways in which the web can help create a more active learning environment. For example, for a class that meets for 1 hour and 15 minutes twice a week, deliver live lectures and demonstrations in a large lecture hall one day. Instead of meeting in person the second day, facilitate online group work.

Embrace blended learning if you believe it will enhance teaching and learning in your courses. But don't be disappointed if things don't work out the way you planned the first time you try this approach. Remember, blended learning is a process, and evaluation is an important part of the process. You may need to rethink the ways in which you evaluate student performance. For example, if you assign online discussion questions, you will need to determine criterion on which to base a grade for discussion responses.

Blended Learning at BCC

Until the Fall of 2001, instructors at BCC had only two options: 1) to teach in a traditional fashion without an online component for their students or 2) to teach an entire course online. There was no middle ground. Only students enrolled in distance learning courses through the SUNY Learning Network had the opportunity to interact with others in a flexible but challenging asynchronous environment. All of that changed when WebCT, an online course development and management system, was implemented. It was used to provide an online component for six courses in the Fall of 2001. By the Spring of 2002, the number of WebCT supplemented courses grew to 23.

As stated earlier, the primary focus of this article is to discuss the integration of classroom- and Internet-based resources in ways that improve conditions for teaching and learning. Instructors interested in using WebCT first considered the goals and objectives identified for their own courses and their students. Then they decided how an online supplement using WebCT could help them achieve those goals and objectives. Some decided to post course materials and engage in discussions with students. Others posted lectures and PowerPoint Presentations. Still others created online tests and quizzes.

Traditional classroom instructors weren't the only ones to recognize the benefits of using WebCT to enhance their courses. Three instructors teaching either in our synchronous distance learning room (Luminet) or teaching video-based courses decided to use a WebCT supplement to engage students in discussions, and the instructors of four SLN courses opted to supplement those courses with WebCT in order to utilize the testing component.

Comparison of Student Success Rates Determined By Completion of an Introductory HTML Course and Average Class Grades Earned

The introduction of WebCT at BCC provided many instructors with the option to incorporate web-based technology into their on campus courses. In some cases, sections of those courses had already been taught completely online through the SUNY Learning Network. For the first time, statistics could be compiled to compare the retention rate of students in blended courses with sections of the same course taught in the traditional mode and completely online. One such course is BIT 173 – Basics of Web Page Creation.

Data was gathered from two online sections of BIT 173 taught completely over the SUNY Learning System, two sections of BIT 173 taught completely on campus without the benefit of an online supplement created in WebCT, and two sections taught on campus with an online supplement. Since students taking online courses are not required to take placement tests, it is not possible to compare entry-level skills or knowledge of the students enrolled in any of the sections. Therefore, only retention rates and final grades were used in this comparison. Consistency was provided across all sections and semesters by providing students with the same syllabus; assigning the same readings, activities, and discussions; and requiring students to take the same examinations and complete the same midterm and final projects. The same instructor taught each of the sections included in the study. The main difference was in the delivery method used. The figures are summarized in the table below.

Comparison of Success Rates of Students Enrolled in Different Sections of Basics of Web Page Creation Based on Delivery Method

Retention Rates and Average Grades

Delivery Method	Semester	Number of Students Completing Course	Retention Rate	Average Grade
Traditional – on campus with no web-based material	Spring 2001	49	83% (96% after students who earned a GPA of 0 were excluded)	2.67
Blended - on campus supplemented with WebCT	Fall 2001	50	79% (90.9% after students who earned a GPA of 0 were excluded)	2.896
Completely online through the SUNY Learning Network	Spring 2001 and Fall 2001	30	75% (85.6% after students who earned a GPA of 0 were excluded)	3.346

Limitations

The figures above do take into account some variables, such as the removal of one student who audited the course since no numeric grade was available. Students who earned a GPA of "0" were excluded from the computations since they completely dropped out of school. Their failure to complete may have had more to do with personal problems or second thoughts about school in general than completion of this one course. Of course, a separate study looking at retention within the college system would want to include those students.

Entrance exam scores were not available for online students and students not enrolled in a degree program, and no pre-test was given to students. Therefore, it is not possible to know if the students entered with comparable skills and knowledge.

More detailed information related to the statistics reported above will be available at the conference.

Findings

The table above highlights two outcomes in which this research was interested, retention rate within the course and average class GPA based on the method of course delivery. The traditional courses included in the study were 3 sections of BIT 173 – Basics of Web Page Creation – 2 day sections and 1 evening section. The blended courses were taught in the Fall of 2001 and included 4 sections of the same course – 3 day sections and 1 evening section. Although the retention rate and success rate as evidenced by average GPA was better for the blended course than the traditional, it is not possible to know if the fact that class sizes were slightly smaller had any impact. The completely online courses experienced the lowest retention rate but the highest GPA. One section taught in the Spring of 2001 and one taught in the Fall of 2001 were used in this study. No other sections of these courses were taught on campus in the Fall or Spring 2001 semesters.

In the case of the Internet-only courses, the instructor had been familiar with the software and hardware, having taught at least one online course each semester for the previous four years. In the case of the courses supplemented by WebCT, the technology was new and the semester used in this study being used on campus for the first time. It was as new to the instructor as to the students. It would be useful to compare the retention rates and average GPA by method of delivery in a second semester to this first semester to see if the instructor's familiarity with the technology has any bearing on student retention and achievement. The same instructor is again teaching 3 blended courses and 1 completely online course this semester, which ends the middle of May. The report will be updated to reflect these figures and presented at the conference.

Closing Thoughts

In the very near future, greater bandwidth, faster processing speeds, and better software will enable students to download larger files more quickly. Instructors will be able to create even more interactive and entertaining web courses. Multimedia may actually be viewed as just another teaching tool. And wireless devices will facilitate access to courses anytime and from anywhere.

In the past few years, much emphasis has been placed on the technology. Professors employing the new technology to post course materials are becoming more efficient. Now it's time to concentrate on pedagogical issues related to the use of technology to see if we can help instructors become more effective.

Those individuals who thought distance education would replace traditional classes were wrong. But so were the individuals who predicted that distance education was a passing fad. Both are here to stay – and blended learning is an exciting alternative to both.

References

Brusilovsky, P. (January 2000). Web Lectures: Electronic Presentations in web-based instruction. Syllabus, 13(5), pp. 18-23.

McArthur, J. (September 19, 2001). Blended learning: a multiple training strategy. Video Web-cast. [On-line]. Available: http://www.connectlive.com/events/opm/.

O'Neill, L. (April 2001). Universal design for learning: making education accessible to all learners. Syllabus, 14(9), pp. 31-32.

Pittinsky, M. (July 2001). A convergence opportunity. Converge, 4(7), 54-56.

The Node's Guide to Blended Learning. (2001). [On-line]. Available: http://node.on.ca/guides/blended/.

Walczak, R. (April 1999). Nature abhors a vacuum. Converge, 2(4), pp. 56-61.

The Effect of Interactive Applets in Mathematics Teaching

George Gadanidis
Faculty of Education
University of Western Ontario
Canada
ggadanid@uwo.ca

Abstract: Interactive applets, which are typically web-based, are the most recent manifestation of technological tools used in mathematics education. This paper briefly reports on recent case studies of three grades 5-6 and one grade 10 teacher where the use of web-based applets may have acted as pedagogical models for teachers' classroom practice, shifting the teaching focus from the learning of isolated concepts to algebraic relationships among concepts. The paper also describes an upcoming study of the affect of the availability of interactive applets on the pedagogical thinking of teachers.

Interactive applets, which are typically web-based, are the most recent manifestation of technological tools used in mathematics education. They are unique in their focus on small interactive units, due in large part to the current nature of web-access where large programs are unwieldy and quickly exhaust download capabilities and user patience. Well designed interactive applets enable students to engage in investigations of mathematical relationships without having to spend a lot of time learning how to use the tool that creates the various representations of these relationships. For example, the Maximize Area applet (ExploreLearning, 2000a), shown in Figure 1, enables students to investigate multiple representations of area and perimeter relationships. The focused and user-friendly nature of well-designed interactive applets may make them appropriate as models of mathematical concepts and of new pedagogical directions, as is the case at the Illuminations.nctm.org web site of NCTM (2001).

Some research indicates that "our thinking is deeply molded by material devices and socio-technical collectives" (Levy, 1993, p. 10). Perhaps well designed and easily accessible interactive applets that allow students and teachers to use and explore mathematical relationships may affect what Levy refers to as the "cognitive ecology" of learning environments (Levy, 1993). It may be possible that "new forms of representation change the mathematics being taught" (Confrey, 1993, p. 335). New media not only enable us to express our ideas in new ways – they also affect the ideas we have. "We don't always have ideas and then express them in the medium. We have ideas *with* the medium. Making progress is an episode of materially mediated thinking – reasoning or coming up with a new idea – happens jointly in the mind and in the medium at every stage" (DiSessa, 2000, p. 116). And perhaps more importantly, some research indicates that there may be a spillover effect, where learning to think with material devices affects our thinking even when the devices are not present (Borba & Villarreal, 1998). However, some research also indicates that attempts to change teachers' mathematics conceptions and teaching practice "are minimally effective, in part because teachers filter what they learn through their existing beliefs" (Stipek et al 2001, 214) and teachers assimilate new ideas without substantially altering existing beliefs that drive their practice (Cohen & Ball 1990).

This paper briefly reports on recent case studies of three grades 5-6 and one grade 10 teacher using web-based interactive applets in their teaching of mathematics. The paper also describes an upcoming study of the affect of the availability of interactive applets on the pedagogical thinking of teachers. In the cases described below, teachers were first introduced to a variety of web-based interactive applets. The teachers selected which applets to use in their teaching based on the mathematics topics in their next unit of study. The three grades 5-6 teachers chose an applet dealing with measurement (Figure 1) while the grade 10 teacher chose an applet dealing with the vertex form of a quadratic function. (Figure 2) (ExploreLearning 2000a; 2000b).

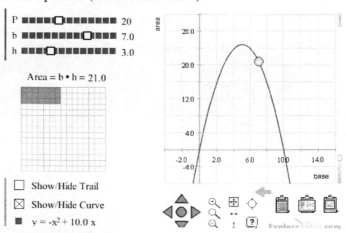

Figure 1. Maximize Area applet.

Brief summary of the use and effect of interactive applets

The Maximize Area applet (Figure 1) may have acted as a pedagogical model for grades 5-6 teachers' classroom practice as the approach to teaching about area and perimeter described above varies from the norm. In previous years, teachers in the study did not focus on the relationships between area and perimeter. Their typical approach to area and perimeter is more reliant on the development and use of formulas, with minimal emphasis on the relationship between area and perimeter. The grade 5 teacher said, "I think I do more the traditional way, separating the two." One of the grade 6 teachers said, "I do perimeter first." The grade 5 teacher reflected on the effect of this difference on students: "When I introduced area and perimeter [in previous years] they didn't see a relationship between the two, but when you fix one at a given constant, and you can manipulate the other, they really found that pretty neat."

The grades 5-6 teachers used the Maximize Area applet in the context of teaching a unit on measurement. They met and decided on the general direction for the classroom and online activities. The grade 5 teacher then used their ideas to develop a detailed lesson that was shared with the grade 6 teachers. The lesson plan started with the following problem: "We're going to build a pen for your dog. Your parents are going to go out and buy 24 metres of fence. You're going to build it with four sides. How are you going to get the biggest area for your dog to play?" In the grade 5 classroom, the teacher drew one possible pen configuration on the board and then asked the students to find and draw all possible configurations on grid paper. Then students developed a table of values, recording the dimensions of the pens they had drawn, and they plotted area versus length on a graph. Students had previous experiences plotting straight line graphs and were surprised that the area graph was curved. "And they said oh that's kind of a neat shape because they're used to [...] getting a straight line [...] and the reason I wanted to do that [in class] was because once they go to the computer that is what they are going to see. [...] I didn't want them to go to the computer right away because [...] I think they would see the graphs and say that's neat but not relate it to any meaning [...] I think that was a big key for their understanding." The next day, the grade 5 students went to the computer lab and were asked to solve the problem where the perimeter is 20 metres. The teacher was impressed with how well students understood and solved the problem of finding the pen with maximum area. "They liked seeing this, they liked seeing the area changing." The teacher was also surprised "because I have some grade fives that are not top grade fives but all of them got it." Some students asked, "is the biggest area always a square? [...] Wouldn't a circle be bigger? [...] They were really thinking."

In contrast, the grade 6 teachers decided to do the computer lab component of the lesson before they did the classroom component. They did this because of minimal access to the computer lab and because of the tight timelines of other classroom activities. In the computer lab, the grade 6 teachers noticed that some students were not focusing on the problem at hand when they were using the Maximize Area activity. "Some of them thought it was a toy [...] changing sliders all over the place." The grade 6 teachers stated that they felt students going to the computer lab were expecting something different, "it seems they were expecting a game or a fun activity." They noted that the activity worked better with the grade 5 students because "your kids knew what to expect when they went to the lab because they had done those kind of activities (in the classroom), and they knew what the problem was all about." The grade 6 teachers said that next time they would reverse the order of the lesson activities, to match the sequence used by the grade 5 teacher.

In the case of the grade 10 teacher, the effect of using the Quadratics: Vertex Form applet (Figure 2) appears to have shifted the pedagogical focus from studying the individual and isolated effects of coefficients of quadratic equations to a holistic and dynamic exploration of relationships between quadratic equations and graphs. The teacher used the applet in a lab setting where each student worked on their own computer. Students however collaborated in some cases to discuss

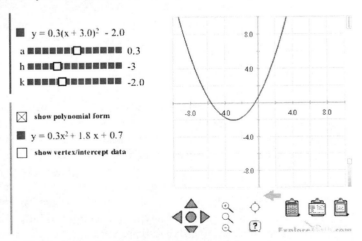

Figure 2. Quadratics: Vertex Form applet.

what they discovered and to check their answers and understanding. Students were provided with a set of worksheets prepared by the teacher. The worksheets included: (1) An explanation of how to log in to the school network and how to access the applet online; (2) a set of guided investigations, questions and instructions; and (3) a self-test section where students manually graphed quadratic functions in vertex form and used the applet to check their answers. As students worked through the worksheets, the teacher was surprised at how focused the students were and how well they seemed to understand. However, he indicated that he would withhold judgement until he saw how well students would do on an upcoming unit test. The teacher used the same unit test that he had used in a previous semester with a different class and compared the results of the two classes. The test scores on the topic of the vertex form of a quadratic of his current students were significantly higher than the test results of students in the previous semester who used graphing calculators (approximately a 30% difference in test scores on average). Although student ability can vary from class to class, the teacher felt that the two classes were generally of similar ability and that the test score difference was significant.

In previous semesters, the teacher taught the vertex form of a parabola using graphing calculators where over a sequence of three different classroom periods, students explored the effect of coefficients a, h and k, respectively, using the graphing calculator and then moving to paper and pencil graphs. A fourth classroom period was used to consider the effect of all coefficients simultaneously. When using the Quadratics: Vertex Form applet, the teacher spent only two classroom periods on the topic: one in the lab (as described above) and one in the classroom to reinforce concepts using paper and pencil activities and graphs. The teacher noted that his approach changed when using the Quadratics: Vertex Form applet in that he started with the big picture first (exploration of relationships between all there coefficients and the graph) rather than considering each coefficient in isolation. He also noted that he spent much less time teaching this topic (about half the time). The teacher felt that in contrast to the Quadratics: Vertex Form applet, his previous use of graphing calculators did not allow students to see the dynamic nature of relationships between coefficients and graphs and that the graphing calculator user interface is relatively primitive.

Both studies involved the use of a single web-based applet on a limited basis. The studies offer some support for existing research that shows that material resources affect the mathematics taught (Levy, 1993; Confrey, 1996; diSessa, 2000) by shifting to some degree the mathematics teaching focus from isolated concepts to relationships among concepts. However, the specific effects in each of the classrooms, including the level of pedagogical success experienced by the teachers, varied. More research is needed to explore the potential use of interactive applets as models of mathematics relationships and teaching practice.

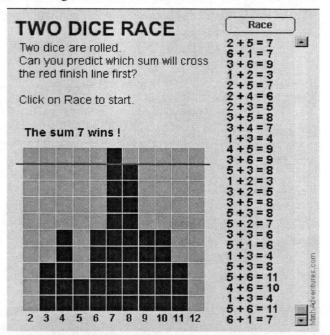

Figure 3. Probability applet.

Upcoming research

In 2002-2003 a follow-up study will be conducted to investigate the nature of the pedagogical thinking, and more specifically the lesson planning, of mathematics teachers when designing lessons on given topics, with and without access to interactive applets similar to those shown in Figure 2 and Figure 3 (MathAdventures.com 2002). Does the availability of interactive applets whose focus is on exploring mathematical relationships affect the lessons designed by teachers? The study will involve 16 teachers and will have four stages. Structured, task-based interviews (Goldin 2000) will be used in the first stage of the study. Each of the teachers will be interviewed for 1 hour each, 30 minutes for each of the two tasks. A laptop will be available to demonstrate the interactive applets. Each of the 30 minute sections of the interviews will be structured as follows:
- The lesson planning task will be presented.
- Teachers may ask clarification questions.

- Teachers will be asked the following sequence of questions:
  - What do you know about the topic?
  - What are your expectations for students?
  - What introductory activity would you use to set the stage for the lesson?
  - What sequence of activities would you plan?
  - How will you know whether students have met your expectations?

In the second stage of the study, lesson plans described by teachers will be analyzed in terms of the level of student mathematical thinking and performance that they facilitate, based on the four-level scheme described in Table 1 (Gadanidis 2002). In the third stage of the study, each teacher will be interviewed for an additional 30 minutes. The analysis of their lesson planning will be shared and questions will be asked to determine: (1) The extent to which the analysis seems appropriate to the teachers; and (2) other insights or explanations they may have that would enrich the analysis. In the last stage of the study, a model will be developed to describe the effect of the availability of interactive applets on the lesson planning of mathematics teachers.

Level	Emphasis
1	Recalling mathematical facts and simple skills.
2	Applying mathematical procedures to solve routine problems.
3	Understanding and explaining mathematical relationships.
4	Extending understanding to new contexts or more general cases.

Table 1. Levels of student thinking

References

Borba, M. & Villarreal, M. (1998). Graphing calculators and the reorganization of thinking: The transition from functions to derivative. In *Proceedings of the 22nd Psychology of Mathematics Education Conference* (Volume 2, pp. 136-143), Stellenbosch, South Africa.

Cohen, D.K., & Ball, D.L. (1990). Relations between policy and practice: A commentary. *Educational Evaluation and Policy Analysis, 12*(3), 331-338.

Confrey, J. (1993). The role of technology in reconceprualizing functions and algebra. In Becker, J.R. & Pence, B.J. (Eds.) *Proceedings of the XV Psychology of Mathematics Education – NA* (Vol. I, pp. 47-74). San Jose, USA: Centre for Mathematics and Computer Science Education at San Jose State University.

Di Sessa, A. (2000). *Changing minds: Computers, learning and literacy.* London, England: The MIT Press.

ExploreLearning.com (2000a). Maximize area. *http://www.ExploreMath.com.* Charlottesville, VA: ExploreLearning.com.

ExploreLearning.com (2000b). Quadratics: Vertex form. *http://www.ExploreMath.com.* Charlottesville, VA: ExploreLearning.com.

Gadanidis, G. (2001), Web-based multimedia activities as pedagogical models. *Asian Technology Conference in Mathematics* (223-232). Melbourne, Australia: RMIT University.

Gadanidis, G. (2002). Tests as performance assessments and marking schemes as rubrics. Available at *http://publish.edu.uwo.ca/george.gadanidis/publications.htm.*

Gadanidis, G., Graham, L., McDougall, D., Roulet, J. (2002 – in press). *Mathematics online: Visions and opportunities, issues and challenges, and recommendations (A White Paper).* The Fields Institute for Research in Mathematical Sciences, Toronto.

Goldin, G.A. (2000). A scientific perspective on structured, task-based interviews in mathematics education research. In A.E. Kelly & R.A. Lesh (eds) *Handbook of research design in mathematics and science education* (pp. 517-545). Mahwah, NJ: Lawrence Erlbaum.

Levy, P. (1993). As technologias da inteligencia. O futuro do pensamento na era da nformatica, trad. C.I. da Costa. Sao Paulo, Editoria 34. (Traducao de Les Technologies de l'Intelligence.) Quoted in M. Villarreal (2000). Mathematical thinking and intellectual technologies: The visual and the algebraic. *For the Learning of Mathematics,* 20(2), 2-7.

MathAdventures.com (2002). Two dice race. *http://www.mathadventures.com.* London, Canada: MathAdventures.com.

National Council of Teachers of Mathematics (2001). Illuminations web site. *http://www.illuminations.nctm.org.* Reston, VA: National Council of Teachers of Mathematics.

Stipek, J.S. et al (2001). Teachers' beliefs and practices related to mathematics instruction. *Teaching and Teacher Education, 17,* 213-226.

Interaction, Distributed Cognition and Web-based Learning

Penny Ann Garcia, Ph.D.
Department of Human Services and Educational Leadership
College of Education and Human Services
University of Wisconsin Oshkosh
Oshkosh, Wisconsin USA
garcia@uwosh.edu

Abstract: The purpose of this paper is to set the stage for future discussions on an expanded definition of the term *interaction* as applied to web-based instruction. The classic definition may be constraining and reductive in that it does not consider the multiplicity of interactions possible within a web course virtual environment. The field of distributed cognition can illuminate the number of interactions that may be considered. A brief overview of distributed cognition is given. Cole and Engestrom's modified mediated triangle is presented prior to suggesting modification of that triangle to reflect the distribution of cognition over the tools and interactions found in web-based courses.

Introduction

Much attention has been focused on the role of *interaction* in virtual classrooms. Interaction has traditionally been defined by examining two categories – individual and social. Individual interaction has been that which occurs between the student and course information in books, computer programs and lab experiments. Social interaction has come to signify that which occurs between a student and teacher or other students. Most discussion concerning interaction in any distance education class has centered on social interaction. However, due to the increased usage of digital tools by faculty to facilitate the students' grasp of understanding and to the very nature of the web interface which houses the web-based course, a dialogue towards a more robust view of interaction in web-based courses should lead to increased awareness of how the interactions between student or students with the tools routinely used within that course impact the learning experience.

Rationale

Just as the sciences have found richness and interdependency in the study of comple x systems, education can expand its view of cognition from the microcosm of the individual to the complexities of distributed cognition. This leads to a renewed interest in the writings of Munsterberg, Luria, Dewey and Vygotsky all of whom recognized the role of interaction in constructing meaning – interaction not only between humans but with tools as well.

Munsterberg (1914) gives one of the first reasoned considerations about distributed cognition. He writes, "A letter, a newspaper…exists outside of the individuals themselves, and yet it intermediates between two or between millions of people in the social group…The book remembers for the social group, and the experiences of the group, objectively recorded in it, shape the social action and the social thought. The letter can connect any distant social neurons; the paper may distribute the excitement from one point of a social group to millions of others. Every objectified expression becomes a social short cut."

Alexandria Luria (1928) asserted that the use of tools and the refinement of these tools was fundamentally unique to humans and stated that these tools "not only radically change his conditions of existence, they even react on him in that they effect a change in him and his psychic condition." These tools included not only basic and advanced technologies but also uniquely human functions such as language. All tools mediate between the person and the task at hand and fundamentally affect human activity.

John Dewey echoed this view of the social nature of human development as well. Dewey's (1938) wrote, "Experience does not go on simply inside a person…we live from birth to death in a world of persons and things which in large measure is what it is because of what has been done and transmitted from previous human activities."

The notion of distributed cognition arises from such consideration of people in action. Certainly activity is enabled by intelligence but the individual does not solely contribute this intelligence. Rather the intellectual resources that shape and enable activity are distributed across people, environments and situations. As Roy Pea (1993) so simply states "…intelligence is accomplished rather than possessed."

In reality, adult students in their daily work interact with a variety of artifacts that significantly enhance their cognitive ability. This cognitive ability, this intelligence, is distributed among other people and tools – cultural artifacts – and, in turn, enables the individual to obtain feedback, gather information, and test hypotheses that extend their mind's potential. As this cognition is distributed, the result obtained is greater than the single whole of the content on which interaction is focused. Instead, each of these distributions across artifacts adds increased dimensions to that content knowledge.

Implications for Web-Based Courses

The traditional classroom and, by extrapolation, the traditional web-based course is founded on the notion of solitary intelligence. Too often, the social, physical, and artifactual surroundings in which cognition takes place have been largely disregarded. Increasingly this view of intelligence has been questioned both by the practitioners of education and the consumers of the education products (or students), business and industry. The observation of what Lave (1988) refers to as Just Plain Folks and experts alike by a wide variety of researchers confirmed that in real-world settings (as opposed to school settings) that the mind rarely works alone. In order to cope with complex activities in an efficient way, human cognition in the real world distributes intelligence among individuals, environments, cultures, symbol systems, tools, and artifacts. In the past much of this distribution was accomplished at a leisurely pace through discussion, shared physical activities, and apprenticeship. Today's society moves at a pace that disables these traditional opportunities for distributed intelligence. Instead, computers and other digital information technologies, while threatening to isolate us even further, also carry the power to create more opportunities for interaction both with the tool and with other humans.

The technologies that deliver web-based courses cannot be viewed as passive neutral delivery systems. These technologies include both the hardware and the software whether it be the web-course building software (e.g. Blackboard or WebCT) or software the students use to construct meaning from the course content. Any technology is a tool that mediates between the subject (learner) and the object (curriculum), creating the classic cultural-historical Vygotsky (1978) mediational triangle. In mediating that transaction, the nature of the object, the subject and the outcome is changed by the technology. In order to truly represent the dynamic nature of this interaction, Cole and Engestrom (1993) added a fourth element, time. In the course of time the two worlds, a student interacting with curriculum delivered through instructor and a student-mediated-by-tool interacting with curriculum, are constantly integrated. This results in the modified mediational triangle shown in figure 1.

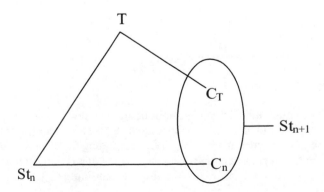

Figure 1: Instructional mediational triangle symbolizing that new states of the student arise from the integration of information obtained both from the mediated (tool) and direct (instructor) connections between the student and the curriculum. [T, mediating tool; St_n, student's state of knowledge at time n; C_T, curriculum as represented via the tool; C_n, curriculum at time n; St_{n+1}, emergent new state of student's knowledge at time $n+1$.]

This triangle deals only with the interactions of a single student with a single tool and the curriculum. Within a web-based course, a myriad of tools can be considered which may impact a student's state of knowledge: the student develops a disposition to learning through the ease (or dis-ease) of interaction with the web courseware, the student interacts with various courseware tools, the student interacts with other students via the courseware tools, the student interacts with content via courseware tools and other tools as required by the instructor for the task at hand.

For instance, consider a web-based course delivered in a traditional web-course environment such as WebCT. First students must interact with the primary tool – their local computer – to access the course. Upon entering the virtual course environment, they are asked to make use of the discussion forum tool, the bulletin-board tool, the e-mail tool, the chat tool and the electronic drop box. They need to download and upload materials, convert documents to various formats, and move to a variety of locations specified on the web. Additionally, they may be required to construct a web-page using web publishing software, storyboard their ideas with a thought-processor software, use presentation software to create a synopsis of research, or create an interactive portfolio using a multimedia software. Each of these tools carries with it a means for interacting with the content from different perspectives. Then consider that students may or may not be acting with these software programs solely as individuals; rather, they may take their Inspiration document, email it to colleagues who create their comments in the notes section, and return it to the individual for consideration. Another consideration would be any of the variety of ways that web-based courses may be structured to include a face-to-face component during the semester. All of these actions, these tools, are neither passive nor neutral. Rather, the experience forms a whole that alters students' perceptions of web-based courses, their own ability, that of their instructor, their relationship with other students, and, most importantly, the sum knowledge of the content interacted with during the course duration.

Recognizing that several interactions occur within a virtual classroom leads to a consideration of how the triangle in figure 1 might be modified to reflect the affect of those interactions as it relates to the student's emergent new state of knowledge. Given that there are now multiple tools mediating the curriculum, will that result in a different emergent knowledge state? If those interactions are successful will that knowledge state be enhanced over that of a traditional classroom? If those interactions are perceived as negative by the student, could the knowledge state be actually be less than what would have been achieved by the classic mediated triangle? Figure 2 is presented as a first step towards modeling this state.

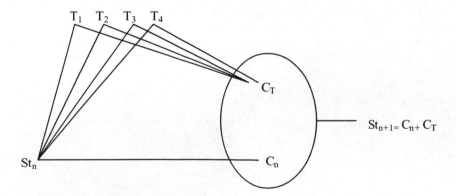

Figure 2: Instructional mediational triangle symbolizing that new states of the student arise from the integration of information obtained from the mediated (tool) and direct (instructor) connections between the student and the curriculum.[T_1,T_2,T_3,T_4 mediating tools; St_n, student's state of knowledge at time n; C_T sum curriculum as represented via the mediating tools; C_n, curriculum at time n; St_{n+1}, emergent new state of student's knowledge at time $n+1$.]

Conclusion

A dialogue towards enlarging the traditional view of interaction in web-based courses should encompass the recognition of the impact of distributed intelligence in the web environment as well as a careful consideration of the means used to deliver a course on the web. This dialogue can serve to inform the creation of better tools for delivery of web-based courses while providing a basis for reflection on student reactions to the both the web course environment and the instructor. It would allow the examination of the role of the instructor in the virtual environment and how that role may differ significantly from that of the face-to-face classroom. Most importantly, it can lead to recognition of learners as inventors of, and users of, distributed-intelligence-as-tool, rather than as passive receivers of intelligence-as-entity.

References

Cole, M. & Y. Engestrom (1993). A cultural-historical approach to distributed cognition. Distributed cognitions: Psychological and educational considerations. G. Salomon. Cambridge, Cambridge University Press.

Dewey, J. (1963 (Originally published 1938)). Experience and Education. New York, Macmillan.

Lave, J. (1988). Cognition in Practice. Boston, MA, Cambridge University Press.

Luria, A. R. (1928). "The problem of the cultural development of the child." Journal of Genetic Psychology 35: 495.

Munsterberg, H. (1914). Psychology: General and applied. New York, Appleton.

Pea, R. D. (1993). Distributed intelligence and designs for education. Distribute cognitions: Psychological and educational considerations. G. Salomon. Cambridge, Cambridge University Press.

Vygotsky, L.S. (1978). Mind in Society: The development of higher psychological processes. Cambridge, Massachusetts: Harvard University Press.

Binding Virtual Molecules Sounds Good! :
Exploring a Novel Way to Convey Molecular Bonding to Students

Miguel Garcia-Ruiz
School of Cognitive and Computing Sciences
University of Sussex
United Kingdom
miguelga@cogs.susx.ac.uk

Abstract: This paper describes a doctoral research that explores a novel way to convey molecular bonding to students by using a multimodal virtual environment system. Twenty-four chemistry students participated in an exploratory experiment to see if non-speech sounds (musical sounds and natural sound effects that represent information) played as feedback and informative aide in a virtual environment, along with 3D visualization of molecular structure, are useful to support molecular bonding understanding. The experiment consisted of four counterbalanced conditions where participants bound virtual molecules in a desktop virtual environment by using a 3D mouse and listening to sounds and visualizing molecular structures in stereo, as well as using a plastic model set. Results indicated positive outcomes from usability and performance analyses, where non-speech sounds were useful to support molecular bonding understanding.

Introduction

This research concerns the application of auditory display, which is the use of sound properties in computer interfaces to convey information (Kramer, 1994), along with visualization techniques, as a way to support understanding of abstract information, such as molecular bonding. Past research (Salzman et al, 1996) shows that a good medium to present both sound properties and visualization techniques is using a virtual environment (a computer-generated 3D graphical environment where the user interacts with it and its contents). Virtual environments offer a unique way to present information in more than one sensory modality with the possibility to complementing or supplementing each, as well as keeping its users from being passive observers, where they interact with the virtual environment, and therefore learn by doing.

Molecular bonding is an abstract topic where students have difficulty to understand how two atoms or molecules bind, as well as the bond characteristics, such as its energy and length, and how both characteristics interact. Literature abounds on showing students' misconceptions and misperceptions about molecular bonding and structure (Hapkiewicz, 1991; Peterson et al, 1989, to name some).

This research suggests that non-speech sounds played in a virtual environment can effectively support students' performance of molecular bonding, and therefore enhance its understanding. To convey bonding information, we used in this research two types of non-speech sounds: *earcons* and *auditory icons*. Earcons are musical tones that convey a message (Blattner et al, 1989), and auditory icons are natural sound effects that have a meaning (Gaver, 1986).

Method

To test the idea of using a multimodal virtual environment to convey bonding, we developed three virtual environments that worked as molecular modelers, and conducted an experiment to test them. It consisted of a within-subjects design, and had four counterbalanced conditions. The conditions can be seen in (Tab. 1).

Condition:	Activity:
A (Traditional tool used for teaching molecular structure)	Participants bound two molecules using a plastic model set, bond energy and length values appeared on a label attached to the bond.
B (Visual condition)	Participants bound two virtual molecules in the virtual environment, color variations from yellow to red represented bond energy, and participants watched bond length and atom charges.
C (Visual + earcons)	Participants bound two virtual molecules in the virtual environment; earcons represented bond energy (pitch variations of a pure sine tone), and trumpet and piano notes represented atom charges. In addition, participants watched the molecular structure.
D (Visual + auditory icons)	Participants bound two virtual molecules in the virtual environment; auditory icons (changes in pitch of an electric discharge sound) represented bond energy, and sounds of hitting metal and crystal represented atom charges. Furthermore, participants watched the molecular structure.

Table 1: Conditions Used in the Experiment

The molecular structures were different in each condition, and they do not exist in nature. We did this to avoid participants' previous knowledge recalls. The charges used for the bindings were arbitrary.

Participants were twenty-four chemistry undergraduates from first and second-years (twelve women and twelve men with ages ranging 23 years) from Sussex University in England (the entire experiment was conducted there), and were paid for their participation. Participants' answers to verbal questions asked prior to the experiment indicated that all of them had enough knowledge about molecular structure to perform the experiment.

We used pre-questionnaires to get participants' characteristics, and questionnaires with Likert scales and open questions to obtain the system usability at the end of each condition and at the end of each experimental session. In addition, we measured participants' performance by timing each condition and getting participants' errors they made during the binding through computer logs and by videotaping the virtual environment for further analysis.

The experiment ran on a desktop virtual environment system consisting of a SGI O2 workstation. We developed the virtual environment using DIVE (Distributed Interactive Virtual Environment), a virtual environments browser and programming interface. Participants watched the virtual environment in stereo by wearing a pair of NuVision shutter (polarizing) glasses, and listened to the non-speech sounds by wearing a pair of high-fidelity headphones Sennheiser model HD 570. Further, participants manipulated the environment's point of view and the virtual molecules using a six-degrees-of freedom mouse (Spaceball 3003). The complete virtual environment system can be seen in (Fig. 1), and a screenshot of one of the virtual environments is shown in (Fig. 2).

   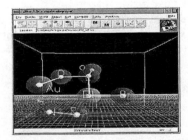

Figure 1: Virtual Environment System   **Figure 2**: Screenshot of the Virtual Molecules

Participants also used a model set (Fig. 3) to see possible differences between the use of a traditional tool for learning mo lecular structure and the developed virtual environments.

Figure 3: Plastic Model Set used in the First Condition

Results

Emergent findings obtained from usability questionnaires shown that manipulation of the molecular structures using the plastic model set was easier than using the virtual environments. However, most participants preferred the virtual environment with musical sounds to perform the bonding, and they stated that the virtual environments with sounds provided better feedback (Fig. 4).

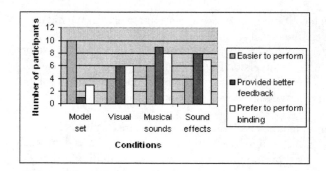

Figure 4: Some Results Obtained From Usability Questionnaires

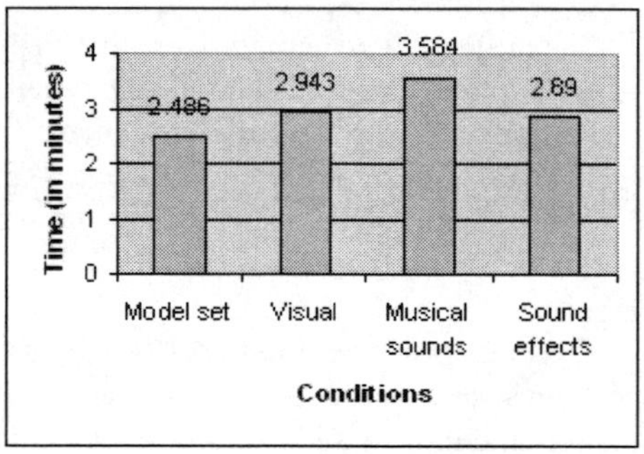

Figure 5: Average of Completion Time in Each Condition

We can see in (Fig. 5) that participants took less time when using the model set. In the conditions with virtual environments, they spent less time when used the virtual environment with sound effects.

Conclusions

The purpose of this paper was to describe preliminary findings of a research on the application of a multimodal virtual environment to support students' performance and understanding of molecular bonding. We carried out an experiment with chemistry students to assess the usability of auditory and visual modalities that represented molecular bonding in a desktop virtual environment. Results showed that although a considerable number of students found the model set easier to manipulate, they preferred the virtual environment with musical sounds to do the bonding. Furthermore, in the conditions that used a virtual environment, participants performed bonding faster in the virtual environment with sound effects.

Acknowledgements

This doctoral research is supported by the Telematics School of the University of Colima and PROMEP grant scheme of the Ministry of Education in Mexico.

References

Blattner, M.M., Sumikawa, D.A., Greenberg, D. (1989). Earcons and Icons: Their Structure and Common Design Principles. *Human Computer Interaction*, 4(1), 11-44.

Gaver, W.W. (1986). Auditory icons -- using sound in computer interfaces. *Human-Computer Interaction*, 2(2), 167-177.

Hapkiewicz, A. (1991). Clarifying chemical bonding. *The Science Teacher*, 58(3), 24-27.

Kramer, G. (1994). An introduction to auditory display. In G. Kramer (Ed.), *Auditory display, sonification, audification and auditory interfaces. Proceedings of the First International Conference on Auditory Display.* Reading, MA: Addison-Wesley, 1-77.

Peterson, R., Treagust, D.F., & Garnett, P. (1989). Development and application of a diagnostic instrument to evaluate grade-11 and 12 students' concepts of covalent bonding and structure following a course of instruction. *Journal of Research in Science Teaching*, 26(4), 301-314.

Salzman, M. C., Dede, C., & Loftin, B. (1996). ScienceSpace: Virtual realities for learning complex and abstract scientific concepts. *In Proceedings of IEEE Virtual Reality Annual International Symposium*, New York: IEEE Press, 246-253.

Accessibility Implications for Multimedia

Multimedia techniques are engaging instructional tools.
> "Everyone benefits from dynamic visual displays and dialog.
> Well, not everyone. Viewers who are deaf miss all audio content
> that is not also presented in a visual form. Those who are blind
> can access only the visual content that is also presented in spoken
> form. It is not difficult to make video and multimedia products
> accessible to viewers with sensory impairments, but special
> considerations should be made at the design phase to assure full
> access to everyone."

(Burgstahler, 2001)

Electronic accommodations can assist those who are deaf by providing text captioning or links to texts. Millions of Americans have enough hearing loss to affect their ability to hear at a typical volume level. Some people are born deaf or are hard-of-hearing, others experience a hearing loss from accident or illness, and some gradually lose their ability to hear. The elderly are the fastest growing group of individuals who are deaf or hard-of-hearing. Text links allow these people to fully access educational materials with fellow students.

Although captions were developed to make home television accessible to viewers who are deaf and hard-of-hearing, they are important to Internet based video. There are several types of captioning. "Off-line captioning" is developed once the video has been created. The captioner types the captions, which are the recorded on the video image. Captions typically appear on the screen as a group and erase as a group since they do not scroll. Captions are either "open" or "closed." Open captioning appears on the screen wherever the video is presented. It is recommended that products be specifically designed for people with disabilities, for training and education. Closed captions appear only when special equipment, called decoders, are purchased by individuals. "Since 1993 all television sets thirteen inches or larger sold for use in the United States must have built-in decoders." (Burgstahler, 2001)

"Real-time captions" are simultaneously created during a video production. They are most frequently used for live programs such as videoconferences. Similar to a courtroom reporter, a trained stenotypist enters spoken content by typing phonetic codes on a special keyboard that facilitates high-speed transcription. Computer software translates the phonetic codes into text that typically scroll across the bottom of the video production in a continuous motion.

Captioning is usually considered when the video production is complete. Special precautions need to be considered to avoid covering critical visual content with captioning. Burgstahler provides several suggestions for making attractive and functional captions, these include:

- Use one or two lines of text.
- Use a sans serif font, such as Helvetica, and proportional spacing.
- Caption the exact wording of speakers, including slang and grammatical errors. Occasionally a few words may be edited to facilitate reading speed.
- Caption sound effects that contribute to the understanding of the content.
- Use italics to indicate the narrator, off-screen voices, sound effects, and other vital information.
- Synchronize captions with the aural content.
- Avoid changing the location of captions on the screen.

(Burgstahler, 2001)

People who are blind cannot access the visual content of a video production unless there is an audio link available. Once a video product is complete, audio content must be added to the production. When pauses occur in the original production, the audio description voice reads the titles and speakers' names, describes the scenery, objects, and other visual information. Because additional audio description is not of value to other audiences it can be distracting. Audio descriptions are usually not included with a standard video but can be provided as an optional format. Providing this option is particularly important for Internet based videos used in educational programs at all levels. The audio link may be used by those who need this service therefore, it is not distracting to other viewers.

The National Center for Accessible Media (NCAM) is a research and development facility that works to make media accessible to disabled persons, minority-language users and people with low literacy skills. This site also maintains separate types of disabilities. NCAM promotes the use of a Web Access symbol and provides model examples of accessible pages. Creators of web and CD-based multimedia projects need an authoring tool to make their materials accessible to persons with disabilities. NCAM meets this need by providing MAGpie, the ideal authoring environment for multimedia providers who want to add captions, subtitles and audio descriptions to their work. The Trace Research and Development Center provide funding for MAGpie. (http://www.wqbh.org/wqbh/pages/ncam)

Instrument Development: Constructing a valid and reliable instrument was essential for this study (found in Appendix C). Validity is expressed by three different approaches: content validity, criterion-related validity and construct validity, however, each is pertinent to the other. The reliability of an instrument expresses the degree an instrument measures whatever it was set out to measure. The more reliable an instrument, the more confidence the instrument scores obtained would be reproduced when administered again to the same participants (test-re-test).

The instrument used a two position forced choice response to the statements. This instrument forces respondents to choose between the two options provided, Agree or Disagree. This format enhances consistency of responses, makes it easier to tabulate and code the data into a database and is easier and quicker for subjects to respond. However the disadvantages of this format may include constraining or limiting the respondents' choice. Some respondents are uncomfortable in completing a scale with no neutral position. The instrument was also jury validated for content. The instrument was then administered to forty-seven (n=47) undergraduate allied health students. The sample distribution was 70% female and 30% male, 40% White Non-Hispanic, 47% Hispanic, 4% Asian-Pacific Islander, 6% Black-Non Hispanic and 2% American Indian or Alaskan Native. The instrument was reviewed and found to be a homogenous instrument with good internal validity and reliability. The Analysis of Variance (ANOVA) was used to test for differences (p<.05) between the group of subjects and the years of computer experience. The subjects grouped based on the following scale: less than 1 year, 1-2 years, 2-5 years and more than 5 years. At this time it was suggested to broaden the years of experience to the following: less than 1 year, 2-5 years, 5-10 years and more than 10 years.

There were no differences in attitudes towards multi media between ethnic backgrounds or gender for the undergraduate allied health students. Ninety-five percent of the respondents reported feeling comfortable using computers, 100% of the females and 86% of the males were comfortable with computers. Sixty-eight percent of the subjects had more than 5 years of experience with computers.

The principle components factor analysis with a varamax rotation identified three factors in addition to measurement of attitudes to assist with the overall assessment of individual reactions to multimedia. The three factors are identified were: 1) Factor one: Learner score for overall Internet delivered multi media as an *effective* learning tool. This factor identified principle components for assessing not only beliefs about multimedia, but also the type of delivery system. 2) Factor two: Learner score of *preference* for courses using Internet delivered multi media. This factor measures learners' preference for learning. The subjects in the study indicated a preference for teacher based delivery over the Internet delivered multi media.　3) Factor three: Learner score for how Internet delivered multi media *enhances* learning. This factor measures attitudes of preference. This is a key underlying assumption that those individuals who perceive that Internet delivered multi media enhances learning are more likely to gain the most advantage from this type of delivery system.

The instrument was rewritten as a final twenty-one-statement instrument with five background and demographic statements A four-point Likert scale was used with a forced choice response: Strongly Agree (SA), Agree (A), Disagree (D), Strongly Disagree (SD). This forced-choice scale omitted the option of neutral or not applicable, which may be troubling to some of the respondents. Four open-ended statements for the respondents to write in their opinion of the strengths, weakness and importance of Internet delivered multi media. This final instrument was used for the remainder of the study.

Subjects: The final target population for this study is undergraduate and graduate students enrolled in Southwest Texas State University statistic courses (n=70). There were three classes of students: Class 1: 22 male and female undergraduate students from various ethnic backgrounds. Class 2: 30 female undergraduate students from various ethnic backgrounds. Class 3: 18 male and female graduate students from various ethnic backgrounds. The total subject demographic information was 74.6% female and 25.4% male, between 19 to 48 years of age although majority of the students were between 19 and 26 years of age, from various ethnic backgrounds. These demographics closely resemble the SWTSU demographic profile.

Study Limitations: This study was affected by the following limitations, sample size, technology, terminology and scoring scale. The sample size (n=70) is a small group. A technological glitch was a factor that may have affected the outcome of the post-test is the technology. The class 1 study may have been tainted by the intervention, an Internet delivered multi media presentation. The technology, Internet access, and RealPlayer plug-ins were not functioning on the day of the pilot study. Class 1 completed the intervention and post-test one day later with out any technological problems. This may have impacted the results of the post-test. The third limitation was the content the Internet delivered multi media segment described, streaming media. This content may have been too abstract for the respondents. The recommendation for future studies would be to use content that is applicable to the audience.

The term "Internet delivered multi media", although defined on the instrument is not a common term and the respondents may not have truly understood the concept when answering the questionnaire. Learners' may be apprehensive about trying new teaching methods especially on-line methods without proper orientation or instruction.

The instrument scoring scale utilized 1 = Strongly Agree to 4=Strongly Disagree. This created some confusion with data interpretation. The scoring scale for the future should be reversed to reflect 4=Strongly Agree to 1=Strongly disagree. This reflects the "normal" thought of a large number being a positive or good result and a low number being a negative or poor result.

Quantitative Results: Numerous surveys have been constructed to measure learners' attitudes towards computers. However, few instruments have been published that measure learners' attitudes towards learning by Internet delivered multi media. This descriptive study constructed an instrument to measure learner's perceptions about Internet delivered multi media.

Of the total sample population for the final instrument administration (n=70), 63 pre and 64 post tests were available for analysis using SPSS software using a factor analysis with a varamax rotation, analysis of variance, chi square and numerous *t*-test. The principle components factor analysis with a varamax rotation identified four factors for the final instrument in addition to measuring attitudes to assist with the overall assessment of individual reactions to multimedia. The four pure constructs are identified :1) Factor one: Learner score for Internet delivered multi media as an *effective* learning tool. The factor measured the overall reaction to this media as an effective tool for learning. This factor identified principal components for assessing not only beliefs about multimedia, but the type of delivery system. Internet delivered multi media places the responsibility of learning on the learner. 2) Factor two: Learners score of Internet delivered multi media as an *interactive* learning tool. This factor identified the importance of activity versus passivity. This factor plays an important roll in the transfer of learning by this medium. The subjects in the study indicated interaction with a person via Internet delivered multi media is important.3) Factor three: Learner score of their *preference* for courses using Internet delivered multi media. This factor measures learners' preference for learning medium. The subjects in the study indicated a preference for teacher based delivery over the Internet delivered multi media. 4) Factor four: Learner score of how *user friendly* the Internet delivered multi media is. This factor identified and measured the learners' attitudes and perceptions towards the convenience and level of difficulty of this media. Many learners are intimidated by media or find it confusing and these can lead to learning barriers.

The analysis of variance (ANOVA) was used to test for differences (p <0.05) in total attitudes toward multimedia between the two groups for comfort using computers. The data is illustrated in Table 3 below.

Table 3. Differences in Attitude Towards Multimedia

		Sum of Squares	df	Mean Square	F	Sig
Pre Total	Between Groups	309.778	1	309.778	5.402	0.024*
	Within Groups	3211.343	56	57.345		
	Total	3521.121	57			
Post Total	Between Groups	170.477	1	170.477	2.446	0.124
	Within Groups	3553.353	51	69.693		
	Total	3724.830	52			

*Significant difference

There is a significant difference in attitudes towards multimedia between the two comfort groups on the pre-test. However a significant difference does not exist on the post-test. It is assumed the intervention is responsible for changing the subjects' attitudes towards Internet delivered multi media. Such that after viewing the short multi media segment, those uncomfortable with computers now have a higher attitude score for multi media. Cross tabulations were calculated for gender verses computer experience groups. There was no significant association found between gender and experience.

The *t* test for independent samples (a =.05) revealed no significant differences between each of the four groups based upon age, race, and gender for the pre and post totals in the attitude instrument.

Qualitative Results: Qualitative results were obtained from the attitudinal survey. Two trends were apparent from the attitudinal survey data. First, overall student response to the effectiveness of Internet delivered media as a learning tool is favorable. Second, attitudes for preference of courses using Internet delivered multi media are not favorable.

Qualitative research results did not support one of the research questions; do learners find Internet delivered multi media learning more effective than traditional classroom learning? Only 31% believe Internet delivered multi media is as effective as traditional lecture instruction. However, 79% believe Internet delivered multi media is an effective tool for learning before the intervention and 87% after the intervention due to the uncomfortable group changing opinions. Seventy-eight percent believe this media enhances the learning process. 53% enjoy learning through streaming media and 61% will tell others about courses using Internet delivered media.

However, majority of the respondents (90%) preferred an instructor to present the course material, 70% valued Internet interaction with the professor or person teaching the material and 98% valued person-to-person contact. Ninety-one percent believe active student participation is important for learning. However, 49% are excited about learning using this medium and only 39% prefer courses that use Internet delivered multi media. The majority (97%)of the respondents like to learn at times convenient to them.

After the intervention, 76% are not fearful of learning through this medium, nor do they find it confusing (70%) or difficult (70%). A large percentage of the respondents believe this medium is not helpful with retaining (75%) or grasping (59%) difficult concepts.

Only 3% of the respondents reported having less than one year of computer experience. Where as, 70% of the respondents have five or more years of experience. Those with more years of computer experience are more comfortable using computers. This may be responsible for the statistical difference in attitudes towards multimedia between the two comfort groups.

Learners Response To Statements: Students were also given an opportunity on the survey to comment on the strengths, weaknesses, and importance of Internet delivered multi media. Three points stand out from their subjective remarks.

First, the greatest weakness of Internet delivered multi media is the lack of teacher-student interaction and direction. Students may waste precious time searching for answers. In the event technological problems arise, precious time may be wasted searching for the contact person. These issues create discouragement and frustration leading to learning barriers.

The strengths and importance of Internet delivered multi media go hand in hand. Internet delivered multi media is important because it allows institutions to reach people in distant places who may not otherwise have access to the information or content. One of the greatest strengths of this media is repetition. Internet delivered multi media allows students to view the information at times convenient to them and as often as needed. This media also meets the needs of the various learning styles.

Overall the qualitative data provides support that learners' attitudes will change after experiencing an Internet delivered multi media segment. Even after the intervention more students believed this media enhances learning and is an effective learning tool, it did not change their preference for traditional instructor lead courses.

REFERENCES

Billig, S., Gibson, D., Sherry, L., and Tavalin, F. (2001). New Insights on Technology Adoption in Communities of Learners. Retrieved May 4, 2002 from http://www.rmcdenver.com/webproject/SITEproc.html.

Boettcher, J.V. (1998, August). How Many Students are "Just Right" in a Web Course? Syllabus Magazine. 12 (1). Retrieved May 4, 2002, from www.syllabus.com/syllabusmagazine/aug98_magcol.html.

Bonk, C.J., and Reynolds, T.H. (1997). Learner-Centered Web Instruction for Higher-Order Thinking, Teamwork, and Apprenticeship. In Khan, B.H. (Ed), Web-Based Instruction (167-178). Englewood Cliffs, NJ: Educational Technology Publications.

Burgstahler, S. (2001). Creating Video and Multimedia Products that are Accessible to People with Sensory Impairments. Retrived from the Internet, May 4, 2002, http://www.washington.edu/doit/Brochures/Technology/vid_sensory.html

Cox, C., and Pratt, S. (2002). The Case of the Missing Students, and How We Reached Them with Streaming Media. Computers in Libraries. 22(3), 40.

Cruver, P. (2001). Broadband and the Future of Learning. Multimedia. 8(4), 28-29, 31.

Dooley, K. (2001). Towards a Holistic Model for the Diffusion of Educational Technologies: An Integrative Review of Educational Innovation Studies. Educational Technology & Society. Vol 2(4), 1999. ISSN 1436-4552. Retrieved May 4, 2002 from http://ifets.ieee.org/periodical/vol_4_99/kim_dooley.html.

Durrington, V., Repman, J., and Valente, T.(2000). Using Social Network Analysis to Examine the Time of Adoption of Computer-Related Services Among University Faculty. Journal of Research on Computing in Education. 33(1), 16-17.

Ellis, T. (2001). Multimedia Enhanced Educational Products as a Tool to Promote Critical Thinking in Adult Students. Journal of Educational Multimedia and Hypermedia, 10((2), 107-123.

Fichter, D. (2000). And..Action! Multimedia on the Intranet. Online. 24(5), 84, 4.

Freeman, M. and Capper, J. (1999). Educational Innovation: Hype, Heresies and Hopes. Asynchronous Learning Network Magazine. 3(2). Retrieved from May 27, 2002 from http://www.aln.org/alnweb/magazine/Vol3_issue2/ALNMag3_2_ma.htm.

Gatlin-Watts, R., Arn, J., Kordsmeier, W. (1999). Multimedia as an Instructional Tool:Perceptions of College Department Chairs. Education, 120(1), 190-196.

Garcia, J.C . (2001). An Instrument to Help Teachers Assess Learners' Attitudes Towards multimedia Instruction. Education. 122(1), 94-102.

Gay, L., and Airasian, P. (2000). Educational Research Competencies for Analysis and Application. Upper Saddle River, New Jersey.

Gloster, A., and Saltzberg, S. (1995). Multimedia and Asynchronous Learning: Changing the Role of Academic Computing. Proceedings of the 1995 CAUSE Annual Conference. Retrieved May 27, 2002 from http://www.educause.edu/asp/doclib/abstract.asp?ID=CNC9540.

Guan, Y., Wang, J., Gable, R., and Young, M. (1998). Student Attitudes Toward Multimedia Classrooms. Paper presented at the Eastern Educational Research Association Conference. Tampa, Fl, February 26, 1998. ED 427774.

Hagner, P. (2000). Faculty Engagement and Support in the New Learning Environment. EDUCAUSE. Sept/Oct, 27-37.

Hayes,B., and Robinson III, E. (2000). Assessing counselor education students' attitudes toward computers and multimedia instruction. Journal of Humanistic Counseling, Education & Development. 38(3), 132-140.

Howles, L.(2002). Streaming Media Tutorial. Wisconsin University, Do It web site. Retrieved May 4, 2002 from http://pocahontus.doit.wisc.edu.

Jaffee, D. (1998). Institutionalized Resistance to Asynchronous Learning. Journal of Asynchronous Learning Network. 2(2), 40-43.

Kolb, D. A. (1985). Learning Style Inventory. Boston, MA: McBer and Company.

Knee, R., Musgrove, A., Musgrove, J. (2000). Learning and Leading with Technology Lights, Camera Action! Streaming Video on Your Web Site. Learning and Leading with Technology. 28(1), 50-53.

Landis, M. (2001). A Comparison of Interaction in AV-based and Internet -based Distance Courses. Eductational Technology and Society. 4 (2), ISSN 1436-4522. Retrieved May 4, 2002 from http://ifets.ieee.org/periodical/vol_2_2001/landis.html

Massy, W and Zemsky, R. (1995) Using Information Technology to Enhance Academic Productivity. Retrieved January 5, 2002, from http://www.educause.edu/nlii/keydocs/massy.html.

McLuhan, M., (2001). The Medium is the Message. Retrieved November 12, 2001, from http://www.nwlink.com/~donclark/hrd/media.html.

Montag, M.. Simson. M.R. & Maurer. M. (1984). Manual for the Standardized Test of Computer Literacy and the Computer Anxiety Index, Iowa State University Research foundation, Inc., Ames.

Nowaczyk, R., Santos, L., and Patron, C. (1998). Student Perception of Multimedia in the Undergraduate Classroom. International Journal of Instructional Media. Vol 25 (4), 367 - 379.

Perry, T., Perry, L. (1998). University Student's Attitudes Towards Multimedia Presentations. British Journal of Educational Technology. 29(4), 375-377.

Rogers, E. (1995). Diffusion of Innovations. New York, New York.

Smith, S., Woody, P. (2000). Computers in Teaching. Teaching of Psychology. Vol 27 (3), 220-223.

Strom, J. (2001). Streaming Video: A Look Behind the Scenes. Cultivate Interactive. Retrieved May 27, 2002 from http://www.cultivate-int.org/issue4/scenes/

Surry, D.W. (1997). Diffusion Theory and Instructional Technology. Retrieved November 12, 2001, from http://intro.base.org/docs/diffusion/.

Takacs, J., Reed, W., Wells, J., Dombrowski, L. (1999). Journal of Research on Computing in Education. 31(4), 341-350.

Tooth, T. (2000). The Use of Multi Media in Distance Education. Retrieved May 4, 2002, from http://www.col.org/Knowledge/ks_multimedia.htm .

U.S. Congress, Office of Technology Assessment, Teachers and Technology: Makin the Connection, OTA-HER-616 (Washington, DC: U.S. Government Printing Office, April 1995).

Van Horn, R. (2001). Streaming Video and Rich Media. Phi Delta Kappan, 82 (7), 561-2.

Vrtacnik, M., Sajovec, M., Dolnicar, D., Pucko-Razdevsek, C., Glazar, Al, Brouwer, N. (2000). An Interactive Multimedia Tutorial Teaching Unit and its Effects on Student Perception and Understanding of Chemical Concepts. Westminister Studies in Education. 23(1), 91-100.

Webopedia. Retrieved May 4, 2002, from www.webopedia.com.

Electronic Portfolios: Effective Assessment Tools in Teacher Education Programs

The School of Education at Northern State University has implemented the electronic portfolio as an assessment tool and as a means of integrating technology throughout teacher education. The electronic portfolio offers a unique opportunity to build preservice teachers' proficiency with technology as well as showcase their expertise in teaching.

The portfolio concept is very popular in education today – and for good reason. First, today's educators have embraced constructivism – the belief that teaching is an active and learner-centered process. This philosophy recognizes that students build their own understanding of the world by using what they already know to interpret new ideas and experiences. Constructivists emphasize not only what students know, but what they do.

Secondly, the growing interest among colleges of education in performance assessment makes a transcript of grades and a score on the National Teachers' Exam (NTE) seem inadequate indicators of competence. A wise person once said: "There is a lot of difference between naming the tools and building the house."

And thirdly, there is still competition for teaching jobs in most areas of the country. It is imperative that prospective teachers be able to demonstrate their teaching competence in concrete ways – to university faculty, to prospective employers, to policy makers at the state and national levels, to parents, the media and the general public.

Why electronic portfolios rather than the paper versions? Electronic portfolios emphasize process as well as product and are multi-sensory in nature, including images, sound, video, text, and multimedia products. It's more fun to see a great bulletin board than to read about it, and it's more effective to hear a university supervisor talking about a preservice teacher's strengths than to read a letter of recommendation. In addition, electronic portfolios facilitate the integration of technology throughout the teacher education program; they provide students with exposure to a wide variety of technology experiences – all in the context of teaching and learning.

The critical phases of portfolio development are collecting, selecting, and reflecting – but the process actually has many phases. Burke, Fogarty, and Belgrad (1994) proposed ten: projecting, collecting, selecting, interjecting, reflecting, inspecting, perfecting, connecting, injecting (and ejecting), and respecting.

As students think about what entries they will collect, how to select those that best convey their abilities, and how to present what they have learned, they are constantly reflecting. Reflective thinking (as defined by Dewey, 1933) is the ability to give serious and persistent consideration to a subject in order to act deliberately and intentionally rather than routinely and impulsively. If teacher educators want preservice teachers to move beyond non-reflective reliance on impulse, tradition, and authority, opportunities for reflection must be provided throughout the teacher education program.

After piloting the use of electronic portfolios with twelve teacher education students during the 1998-1999 academic year, the School of Education at Northern State University began implementing electronic portfolio components into teacher education methods courses. The model used for electronic portfolio implementation solicited proposals from faculty members interested in integrating electronic portfolio components into their methods classes. Faculty received monetary compensation for the creation and integration of electronic portfolio components into their courses.

Each student-created electronic portfolio is original; portfolio components are designed to address one or more of the ISTE National Educational Technology Standards (NETS) and performance indicators for teachers. In addition, students must address each of the five categories of the knowledge base for teacher education at Northern State University: Knowledge of Self as an Individual, Knowledge of Content, Knowledge of the Learner, Knowledge of Pedagogy, and Knowledge of Self as a Teacher and Member of a Learning Community.

Electronic portfolios have been a part of the teacher education programs at Northern State University for four years; current efforts have focused on assessment of the electronic portfolio process and product. Teacher education graduates are asked to complete a self-assessment survey of their technology expertise and their comfort level with technology integration. During their professional semester, preservice teachers showcase their electronic portfolios and receive feedback from university faculty members. Electronic portfolio components are then assessed to determine whether appropriate opportunities have been provided for students to meet the ISTE National Technology Standards (NETS) and performance indicators for teachers as well as the required program outcomes for teacher education graduates of Northern State University.

This presentation will focus on the data collected from the self-assessment surveys as well as the results of the electronic portfolio assessment. Specific components of original student-created electronic portfolios addressing one or more of the ISTE standards and meeting one or more program outcomes will be shared along with accompanying assessment tools, including a newly-developed holistic rubric.

Burke, K., Fogarty, R., & Belgrad, S. (1994). The mindful school: The portfolio connection. Arlington Heights, IL: IRI/Skylight.

Dewey, J. (1904). The relation of theory to practice in education. The Third National Society of Education Yearbook (Part I). Chicago: University of Chicago Press.

Dewey, J. (1933). How we think: A restatement of the relation of reflective thinking to the educative process. Boston: Heath.

Dr. Constance Geier is an Associate Professor of Education at Northern State University in Aberdeen, South Dakota. She has been at NSU since 1991 and has taught courses in Educational Psychology, Educational Assessment, and Educational Research. She currently serves as NSU's LOFTI Coordinator. LOFTI is a $10 million federal technology challenge grant administered by the United States Department of Education. LOFTI stands for Learning Organizations for Technology Integration, and NSU is one of numerous partners in the five-year grant.

The Changing Role for Universities as Life Long Learner Centres

Ralph Genang, Delft University of Technology, the Netherlands, r.r.m.genang@io.tudelft.nl

Sicco Santema, Delft University of Technology, the Netherlands, s.c.santema@io.tudelft.nl

Abstract:
Universities can become Life Long Learner centres if they adapt quickly to the needs of future knowledge workers. Technology enables universities and research institutions to prepare their organizations to serve and develop future life long learners.
By motivating learners with similar interest to collaborate and innovate, universities will develop stronger ties to the corporate world and their knowledge workers, who will need continuous education in order to effectively compete in the ever changing business world.
This working paper will present you some relevant points and questions. Interested persons can contact the authors for more information about this research program.

Introduction

Today 30% of the total work forces are skill-based workers, workers that need a continuous learning environment in order to do their job efficiently. The US Department of Labour in 2000 forecast that by 2015, 85% of our workforce will be a knowledge-or skill-based worker. How can companies feed all the right skills to the right people acknowledging that most of these future skills don't even exist today?

A primary requirement for any company operating in the knowledge-based economy is to structure individual and organizational learning to create a learning environment amongst its employees, partners and clients. Being able to learn at the speed of change and continuously create and share specific knowledge will be a required skill in order to maintain a competitive advantage over both the near and long term.

Businesses are increasingly operating on a global scale, often in a multi-lingual and multi-cultural environment in different time zones. Due to this growing internationalization, learning at the speed of change and providing employees access to the right knowledge at the right time faces an even more challenging task

Access to Knowledge is one of the Keys

A lot of research and knowledge is available in universities and research centres throughout the world. Many companies, especially SME's do not have the resources to create their own knowledge centers and are in no position to maintain their knowledge centers and create new knowledge.
Employees who have access to a knowledge base where they can share their expertise are stimulated to innovate individually and as a team, yielding increased performance of both individuals and teams, resulting in better performance of the company.
Can Universities and their Research Centers Offer the Necessary Life Long Learning Environments and feed individuals with the necessary knowledge?
In order to contribute to a society that learns at the speed of change, universities will have to learn in close contact with the industry what the purpose of learning is in today's world.

What is the purpose of learning?
1. Learn how to solve problems what is a problem?
2. Learn how to communicate and collaborate in a multi-cultural and global society
3. Learn how to address the impacts of external forces and change

4. Learn how to become a transferor of skills
5. Learn how to stimulate a desire to learn

Learners have to develop three sets of skills that will carry them to a life long learning process
1. Has an ability to learn (Intellectual Capital). The ability to learn has to be coupled to the individual learning style of the student.
2. Knows how to define and solve problems (Creative Capital). They have to be able to apply knowledge to innovate and create solutions to problems
3. Knows how to work with people (Emotional Capital). He has to develop the interpersonal skills to work with a diverse group of people

Today's sixth form students are learning problem solving skills beyond the knowledge based A-levels. They live in a different world than their parents. They know how to use the Internet and other information and communication tools to solve problems quicker and differently and are learning to collaborate and exposed to different learning systems, they grow up in a multi-cultural, global environment, they are capable in multi tasking, they are learning teamwork and leadership skills.
What is the relevance of these skills to a university education as it is currently offered? How important are these skills to a university education and beyond?

Qualifications

Our society is obsessed with the term qualification. So what is a qualification?
Is it the ability to memorize and demonstrate any specific knowledge a qualification for anything? Is it a set of skills required for a job? What job are we qualifying these people for? Will today's jobs still exist tomorrow and visa versa? Is it is an arbitrary designation by the Government, school or university? Is it to measure progress of the learner or of the teacher?

What is the value of today's qualification in an ever-changing world? Since today's economy requires continuous learning being able to effectively compete, the university's role must continue beyond issuing degrees. They'll do that by establishing outreach programs where they will offer short courses and seminars on relevant subjects to the community at large. At the same time universities must encourage in-reach programs by utilizing industry experts, establishing research projects with industry and forming cooperative curriculums with other universities on a global basis.

Tools and technology

Tools have to be created that take advantage of technology and contribute to the ongoing learning process. These tools should give learners easy access to knowledge. They must be able to create their own learning material in constant collaboration with their peers and motivate each other to update their knowledge in a manner so others can benefit from it. The offered continuous learning environment should be based on different learning styles. Some learners prefer to learn by hearing, others by watching or by reading and others by doing.
How will we provide learners with these tools?

In order to be effective, learning must be collaborative, particularly between the learners. The best way to accomplish that via electronic media is through simulations using interactive game theories. Rather than a lecturer, the learning is delivered via a facilitator, which can be an independent third person of one or more of the learners.

Before simulations can take place, universities or research institutions will have to focus on accumulating relevant content based on knowledge available within the institution or within its network. Publications are current carriers of knowledge. But the society does need another carrier that will enable users to access data instantly and remotely.

The carrier does need to shift capture and application of knowledge towards the presence and if possible the future.

Knowledge can only exist in the present. In the past knowledge becomes commodity data and in the future, knowledge becomes intelligence. In the future past knowledge can only be useful if it can be communicated by "insiders" to outsiders through a story reflecting the context of the situation in which the knowledge grew. For future users this knowledge will become commodity data. Capturing this data is relevant for future innovation and the process can only be successful if it is captured in the present.

We believe you cannot learn unless you are emotionally involved! So in order for new knowledge and innovation to grow out of commodity data, the learner, must have a special relationship to the situation, he or she must be emotionally involved and peers must approve his or her experience. This will stimulate the learner to take the effort to capture and share the knowledge and allow it to become commodity data for future purposes.

Delivering learning through a technology media such as the Internet requires a completely different approach than that used in the classroom. The vast majority of Internet based canned courses are created by trying to duplicate a lecturer's role by offering either printed text or in some cases audio or video overlays on a screen. Without an intimate classroom environment and synchronous feedback from the lecturer, this method via the Internet is ineffective, at best.

Both the universities and corporations are introducing technology into their learning centres to lower the costs of training, make the material more relevant and to allow employees, partners and clients to access necessary courses at any time from any place. Up to today it is not clear if these learning centres have the right learning effect.

Building effective courses and creating content to be delivered via the electronic media that can be used by people from different backgrounds and with different interests is a very expensive process initially. However, the results that it will yield will give a rapid return on investment

Example: Business to Business marketing at Delft University of Technology

At Delft University of Technology a first prototype of a new carrier was created over the last five years. There are three different levels of knowledge in this knowledge environment: commodity data, commodity knowledge and new knowledge. (Santema, Genang, 1999) Actually all the bodies of knowledge are just bodies filled with interesting data, or as we call it "commodity" data. As Karl Marx (1957) quoted, a commodity is a mysterious thing, a hieroglyphic – a picture thing, a "beautiful" system now taken to be difficult or impossible to decode. Succeeded in motivating the learners to react on this "commodity" data in order to "learn" it, to deepen it and make their own knowledge of it. But this is not enough. The learner should be able to share his or her knowledge with other learners following the course. Can learners be motivated to state what data they found (and where) and what they did to process it in order to make it knowledge for them. And what happens when they discuss it with other learners. Will they motivate their progress, will they change it, will they convince others and therefore deepen the knowledge they derived from the data? Can they add new knowledge? In order to achieve these learners were rewarded on information and knowledge sharing. Groups of learners were deliberately instructed to look at a subject from different angles and using "knowledge" out of our learning environment or any available medium to substantiate their opinions. The focus of education shifts more to the self-expression and judgment of the learner. (Sakamoto, 1999). There are no instructor-based lectures but student-based lectures. The lectures of the instructor are recorded and his commodity knowledge is now accessible through ICT. Learners can access this data (their perspective) and use it to solve problems. They learn how to find, access and apply relevant knowledge to solve a specific knowledge in collaboration with other users. The time saved by not giving lectures anymore is now for learners. They can discuss face-to-face their learning moments, ideas with other learners or experts. (Representatives of the industry are invited to challenge the learners with future problems, which they do have to solve based on available knowledge, creativity, resulting in future intelligence. Learners prepare their own subjects, they have to use their own hunger to learn to motivate their fellow learners, and they become their own instructors. This is one example how learners are motivated to cooperatively use "content" to create "new knowledge" among the participants. The setup is summarized in (figure 1) The process is baptized Learner-Led-Learning. We are currently studying how we can improve knowledge creation by introducing simulations that will connect learners with different or similar backgrounds and interests to increase innovation. There is a huge interest from the industry to access the current knowledge base and use it as a resource for development and innovation. Some students still access the environment after graduating.

	Classic lectures	Workshops
Commodity knowledge (Teachers perspective) = **Commodity data (Students perspective)**	Learning environment, (Bodies of knowledge)	Learner groups
Teacher **New knowledge** Student	Via - Learners - Www - Instructors	Discussion learners Amongst themselves, and With instructor(s) or Guest speaker(s)
	ONLY ICT	**FACE to FACE**

Figure 1: possibilities for ICT based classrooms, Santema Genang, Delft, 2000

Technology has been a tool during this process enabling learners and instructors to speed up the process of solving a problem by having instant access to relevant knowledge and peers.

Summary: Break the Rules

In order for universities to serve a roll as life learning centers they must address intellectual capital, creative capital and emotional capital in the educational process. Universities have to understand that life long learning not a choice but a requirement in today's economy. Their role is to develop life long learners and provide life long learners with the right tools.

Before that will happen, education has to shift from the past towards the future, towards innovation and creativity. Universities and government must question the value of today's qualifications in an ever-changing world and shift the focus towards evaluating problem solving skills, learning skills and people skills. They will have to prepare their content and structure their organization to allow the establishment of outreach programs where they will offer short courses and seminars on relevant subjects to the community at large. Universities must encourage in-reach programs by utilizing industry experts. They must establish research projects with the industry and form cooperative curriculums with other universities on a global basis.

If universities and research centres succeed in creating, attracting and delivering life long learners and succeed in cooperating with other institutions; universities will play an important role in the future as "centres of knowledge and innovation".

Paulo Freire (Freire 1999) had a message to learners: "I'd like to say to us as educators: poor are those among us who lose their capacity to dream, to create their courage to denounce and announce. Poor are those who, instead of occasionally visiting tomorrow, the future, through a profound engagement with today, with the here and now, poor are those who, instead of making this constant trip to tomorrow, attach themselves to a past of exploration and routine."

References:
Freire, P. (1999). Education and Community Involvement. In Donalde Macedo, Critical Education in the new Information Age.
Genang, Santema (1999). Delft University of Technology, Rethinking Education, Ed-Media paper.
Marx, K. (1957). Capital. Translated by Samuel Moore and Edward Aveling, London: Allen and Unwin
Sakamoto, T. (1999). Educational Reform by Information and Communication Technology, National Institute of Multimedia Education, Japan

"Living in the Information Age"
Writing Emphasis Goes Online

David C. Gibbs

Department of Mathematics and Computing

University of Wisconsin-Stevens Point

Stevens Point, WI 54481

dgibbs@uwsp.edu

Abstract

This paper describes a unique course residing at the intersection of two movements: an online offering containing a writing emphasis. The course is entitled "Living in the Information Age" and is offered in a department of Computer Information Systems. The learning activities of the online course are described along with their associated writing activities. Several successful strategies are described in some detail.

1 Introduction

The   University   of   Wisconsin

Stevens Point has been a leader in technology since the earliest days of networked computing. Technology leaders saw the direction of campus computing, and in 1985, having sought out and established corporate partnerships, succeeded in putting a local area network in place. By the early 1990s, all constituents of the university were regularly using the Internet – well ahead of its time for an institution of its size. Online courses followed as early as 1996, when faculty in the school of education recognized an opportunity to take their coursework to practicing teachers.

Almost a decade earlier, in response to a perceived decline in writing skills, the university began to develop "writing emphasis" courses. A writing emphasis course is typically a discipline-specific course in which students are required to research, compose, and revise text to an extent exceeding a normal offering of the course. The university established a writing   emphasis   graduation   requirement   for   all   freshmen   entering   in   the   1981-82 academic year.

This paper describes a unique course residing at the intersection of the two movements: an online offering containing a writing emphasis. The course is offered by the Computer Information Systems department and is entitled "Living in the Information Age[1]". Several successful strategies are described in some detail.

2 The Learning Environment

The semester long course is taught entirely online (via the Internet) using the courseware *Blackboard* [1]. Blackboard provides instructors with a complete set of online course tools, including discussion forums, folders for course information and assignments, an online gradebook, a virtual classroom, and the ability to manage group interactions. The course described here utilizes each of these features.

3 The Course and its Activities

Students are exposed to course material in three separate ways: by reading and writing, by reading and responding to their classmate's writings in the peer editing process, and by reading and replying to their classmates postings in the online (asynchronous) discussion forums.

---

[1] Course Description: Outline of technological developments occurring in information access and storage, and effect s the information revolution is having on everyday life, professions, privacy, security, automation, law, government and employment.

The course is comprised of four principal activities: (1) reading (books and websites) and responding to the readings (by writing or electronic discussions), (2) *e-News* posts (and responses to posts), (3) *"Because-You-Can"* posts (and responses to posts), and (4) *Web-Exercises*. Each activity includes reading and writing.

Readings

The formal readings for the course are intended to prod and provoke the reader. Listed in the order they are examined in the course, they are:

1) *Technopoly,* by Neil Postman;

2) *What Will Be,* by Michael Dertouzos;

3) *Brave New World,* by Aldous Huxley.

Web readings taken from selected URLs are also utilized throughout the course.

A response to a formal reading comes in several forms, varying from a post in a discussion forum to a complete paper. The responses are described in section 4 below.

e-News Posting

An *e-News* post is a current news item of interest that is related to the *Information Age*. The news item may emerge from an online news service, such as Edupage [3], the New York Times Technology page [5], or from another web source. Posting means briefly summarizing the news item, placing the reference (usually a web address) in the appropriate discussion forum along with some provocative questions. Here is an example of an e-news posting (from September 12, 2001) in the discussion forum:

> Use of 911 in cell phones has been talked about for a number of years. Wireless carriers were supposed to have the first phase of the system in place by 1998, and phase 2 was to be established by Oct. 1 of this year.
>
> http://news.cnet.com/news/0-1004-200-7139433.html?tag=mn_hd
>
> But there is an ugly flip side to e-911 - the simple fact that identifying the location of the cell phone usually means identifying your location - any time day or night - when calling or not.
>
> Should wireless phones be required to have 911 built-in? Why or why not? Does it represent yet another loss of individual privacy?

Each student must respond (asynchronously) to the questions. Often they are required to return a day or two later and respond to any previous student post.

"Because-You-Can" Posting

While similar to an *e-News* posting, a *"Because-You-Can"* (BYC) posting is may be somewhat whimsical. Students are asked to find an example of technology for which the only possible answer to the question "Why would they create that?" is *"Because You Can"*.

> Want your hair stimulated and massaged as you brush it? You need the massaging hair brush. It will encourage hair growth by magnetically stimulating your scalp, increasing blood circulation.
>
> I think they should make it with adjustable, programmable settings, though, because my wife and daughter probably have their eye on it and their massaging and detangling needs are way different than mine.
>
> PLEASE tell me what the "blessing" is in this device? And what is the "curse"?

Posting a "BYC" means summarizing the technology and providing the reference (again, usually a URL). Because it is difficult to ask thought-provoking questions in this case, it is sufficient to attempt to establish something *beneficial* (and something *less than beneficial*) about the technology. And then challenge the class to do the same. The point of the exercise, besides having some fun, is to expose the extent to which technology can sometimes presents solutions in search of a problem.

Web-Exercise and Assignment

A web exercise and its assignment will usually involve some exploring of the web leading to a deeper understanding of "Life in the Information Age." Each exercise is organized around a theme [8], such as "Online Education." Sets of questions, accompanied by a series of links, guide the exploration. The written answers to questions are submitted either by e-mail or to a discussion forum established for the exercise.

4   The Writing Assignments

Writing assignments are submitted or exchanged through a variety of techniques, including e-mail (as body text or an attachment), a discussion forum, or the instructor's or the group's drop box.

The types of writing assignments vary from somewhat informal to highly formal. The informal writing assignments include *e-News* and *Because-You-Can* posts and responses. Submitted in a discussion forum created for that purpose, all students are given the opportunity to post, to read, and to respond to the questions raised and their classmates' replies.

Another informal type of writing is found in completing the Web Exercises. Consisting of one or two paragraphs, this writing can be posted in a discussion forum or submitted to the entire class (using a distribution list) or directly to the instructor using e-mail.

Somewhat more formal are responses to readings. These may take the form of answering questions posed by the instructor or posting a "reaction paper." In both cases, students are encouraged to compose text in a word processor making use of spell- and grammar-checking capabilities before copying and pasting into a discussion forum.

The most formal type of writing is the most familiar to college teachers and students, but with some online wrinkles. Given a topic rooted in the readings and discussions, students are asked to address the main points in three or more pages. Peer editing is key. In groups of three, students submit their writing in the digital drop box[2] for their group. Each student will edit two other papers, supplying feedback to their peers using standard word processing strategies. They may insert suggestions directly into the text, add comments using the software's "Insert Comments" ability, or simply use highlighting or font/color changing to draw attention to certain passages or paragraphs. The editor then re-submits the document (using a variation on the filename) to the group's drop box. The author picks up the paper, makes the changes deemed appropriate, and submits it to the instructor's digital drop box. When submitting their final drafts, each student is required to include the peer-edited versions of their papers. The instructor uses the same editing techniques to return marked-up papers to the students.

5   Successful Strategies

The most successful strategies for writing emphasis emerging in this online course are the informal *e-News* and *BYC* posts, the reaction papers, and the longer, more formal papers.

The *e-News* and *Because-You-Can* posts and responses are effective in generating lively electronic discussion, if not quality writing. Students today are well versed in "chatting" and the riposte style that emerges when questioning someone's assumptions. These "discussions" generally remain of high quality due to the implicit moderation provided by the instructor's virtual presence.

Forums for the purpose of discussing reaction papers are restricted to approximately ten students. Each student is required to respond to nine other reactions. Because of the seriousness of issues examined (e.g. personal privacy, ethics of genetic engineering), the dialog taking place here is at an even higher level than the e-News and BYC posts.

According to student evaluations, though they found peer editing of the formal papers a bit of a nuisance, almost all students found it valuable. As writers, they found it valuable in receiving feedback, and as editors, they found it valuable in learning from a classmate's views of the same subject.

6   Summary

Writing emphasis courses were added to the curriculum and graduation requirements in order to improve students' writing skill by increasing the quantity and quality of writing being done. This course presents a variety of writing tasks, from informal to formal, and it does so requiring the interaction of peers. Increasing both time on task and the amount of writing and rewriting with feedback can only assist the goal of improving writing skills.

References

[1] Blackboard Corporation, www.blackboard.com

[2] Dertouzos, Michael. (1998). *What Will Be.* New York: Harper-Collins.

[3] Edupage e-mail list subscription:

---

[2] Blackboard's "digital drop box" is essentially a managed file exchange service for only those members in the group (and the instructor).

www.educause.edu/pub/edupage/edupage.html

[4] Huxley, Aldous. (1932). *Brave New World*. New York: Harper and Row.

[5] New York Times Technology page subscription:
email.nytimes.com/email/email.jsp

[6] Postman, Neil. (1991). *Technopoly: The Surrender of Culture to Technology*. New York: Vintage Books.

[7] University of Wisconsin Stevens Point internal document: "Guidelines for Writing Emphasis Courses." (1981).

[8] Web Exercises in CIS 300 at UW Stevens Point:
www.uwsp.edu/cis/dgibbs/CIS300/WebXINDEX.htm

Building Responsive Dissemination Systems for Education with the Semantic Web: Using the New Open-Source "Liber" Application

Dr. David Gibson
National Institute for Community Innovations
Montpelier, Vermont
dgibson@vismt.org

Dr. Michael B. Knapp
Green River Data Analysis
Guilford, Vermont
mknapp@greenriver.org

Brandt Kurowski
Somerville, MA
E-Learn@BrandtKurowski.com

Abstract. There are numerous web-based survey instruments for educators that determine needs related to professional development, student results, and school performance. However, people receiving survey results also need simultaneous access to proven solutions to the concerns identified in such surveys. This paper explains a portal tool application of the Semantic Web which pre-configures channels of digital library content based on survey analyses and user profiles. The National Institute for Community Innovations (NICI) has developed the open-source code "Liber," that assists in the use of XML/RDF descriptions of digital resources to customize the presentation of digital library content to the needs of individuals and groups involved in K-12 education. The research and development of Liber has been supported with USDOE, and NSF subgrants and contracts from both NICI and the Vermont Institute for Science, Mathematics and Technology.

Introduction. The World Wide Web (WWW) has enjoyed unparalleled success as a tool for the publishing of digital content, but it remains difficult to find appropriate high quality resources online, even though many exist. Two reasons for this are that (1) the staggering quantity of information on the WWW defies any centralized, human cataloging efforts; and, (2) most WWW information is posted with little attention to information structure, making the cataloging of these resources by computers or humans more difficult. Computer scientists, researchers, and librarians have attempted to address this problem in varying ways, and strategies such as the html "meta" tag and the Dublin Core have been most successful. An effort to improve upon these technologies has led to the creation of the Semantic Web, a multidisciplinary initiative with a structure that allows machines to process information for accessibility of web content.

The core of the Semantic Web is the Resource Description Format (RDF), a standard for machine understandable metadata. Because RDF works in such a way as to allow applications to share data, even if they were built independently of one another, the Semantic Web allows catalogs of resources to be built using a decentralized model. Just as anyone can link to any page on the WWW, anyone can describe any resource on the Semantic Web. This allows for the development of intelligent routing of resources to users, based on RDF queries that express a user's interests.

A New Semantic Web Tool: Liber. The Vermont Institute for Science, Mathematics and Technology (VISMT) and the National Institute for Community Innovations (NICI) began piloting the application of the Semantic Web to the field of online education in the fall of 2000. After discussions with leadership from the Dublin Core Metadata Initiative and the W3C Semantic Web activity, we began development of the Liber engine (http://liber.sourceforge.net), now an open-source software application. Liber allows resources to be cataloged using an extensible metadata framework, and presents those resources through an integrated front-end tool.

Liber is a prototype of the application of Semantic Web concepts and technologies to the needs of the educational community. It is a catalog of community-contributed resources that have undergone review by experts and been cataloged by a librarian. At present, Liber uses RDF schemas from Dublin Core and IMS, merging them with custom RDF schemas representing GEM Element Set and NICI's Educational Reform metadata, to form a comprehensive vocabulary for expressing information about resources of interest to educators. Such an approach exhibits some of the principles of metadata as expressed by Duval, Hodgins, Sutton, and Weibel (2002). For example, the *modularity* of the schemas allows different educational groups to use a small set of core elements to tag resources for a wide variety of specialized educational uses. Second, the *namespace* we propose "*edreform:*" adds a new dimension to the existing core data elements available in existing metadata schemas. Third, the *extensibility* of the metadata system produced by Liber allows for an evolution in the vocabularies. Finally, we are proposing a number of *refinements* to concepts that were originally proposed for broader application. For example, we are proposing a scale of "novice to expert" that is commonly used in educational assessment, as a refinement of the dc-ed: audience.

The Liber prototype has powerful ways of searching resources – users can perform simple searches of the metadata, construct complex RDF queries with a simple web interface, or get a list of resources similar to an already discovered resource. With these tools, users can easily traverse the catalog without being confined by disciplinary boundary, intended audience, or other similarly limiting categorizations.

Liber Applications. The first Liber application was developed by NICI under funding from the US Department of Education, and is used to present online resources that are helpful to grantees in addressing the digital divide - disparities in access to online technologies by race, gender, ethnicity, and income. This work resulted in the application currently running at www.digital-equity.org. The PT3 (Preparing Tomorrow's Teachers to Use Technology, www.pt3.org) grant program that funded the work followed our recommendation to establish a metadata working group, and has promulgated an RDF standard at http://www.pt3.org/2002/elements/1.0/elements Following this initial project, in the spring of 2001, under funding from the US Department of Education's technology innovation challenge grant program, NICI began work on a metadata vocabulary to describe educational reform. The prototype educational reform metadata can be viewed at www.edreform.net/metadata.

EdReform Metadata. As we worked to develop the NICI educational reform metadata, we encountered difficulty due to the fact that metadata standards for education are devised from the perspective of practicing education, not researching and improving education. Existing educational metadata standards, such as IEEE LOM and IMS, are useful for cataloging courseware, but criteria of importance to educational improvement, such as urban teacher preparation, equity, and school leadership, are not addressed. Our prototype work demonstrates that existing metadata standards can be integrated, and that additional metadata specific to the needs of educators in the field will have to be added. For example, we have proposed the addition of control vocabulary under a new qualifier we termed systemic values (see http://www.edreform.net/wiki?EducationalReformMetadata/SystemicValues) to describe the beneficiary and mediator of an educational resource. Our intention is to develop an application framework for educational practitioners to propose cataloging terms, and to integrate those terms into both the existing frameworks of cataloging entities and the initiatives of a number of national educational organizations.

Our initial work indicates that this is possible, and we are now preparing to refine and promulgate the educational reform vocabulary, and develop a methodology to allow for the enhancement of the vocabulary based on an analysis of the proposals from the educators using the applications. We believe that this will significantly enhance the ability of field-based educators to use terms and phrases they naturally employ to describe important concepts in order to search for and access information on validated reform strategies and resources. Our goal is to improve the ease and efficiency with which field-based educators locate material on best practices relevant to their priority concerns.

Responsive Dissemination Portals. The second prototype implementation of Liber is under development at www.edreform.net. "Channels" of information are constructed from specific paths in the metadata, which respond to the key phrases and big ideas of expert panels on educational reform. We have thereby extended existing metadata vocabularies (e.g. Dublin Core, LOM) with an EdReform vocabulary, and included a new process of *aggregation* to define topics relevant to K-12 educational reform. These topics, regarded as critical to state and local K12 educators, include ideas such as urban teacher preparation, equity, and technology infusion. We have found that it is at this level of vocabulary that teachers, administrators, educational leaders and other organizational leaders can effectively interact with digital resources. Our proposed mechanism for *aggregation* is a unique addition to the conceptual framework of metadata principles, perhaps as new form of *refinement*. (Duval, et. al., 2002)

The NSF Protocol. Based on the success of these first two prototype implementations of Liber, NICI began collaboration with VISMT to develop a Liber portal for the NSF Funded National Systemic Improvement Initiative Protocol project. VISMT, in collaboration with seven other statewide systemic initiatives (together called the National Systemic Improvement Initiatives consortium), has developed a web-based survey (the "protocol", http://www.nsii.org/survey.cfm). Its purpose is to enable states and local education agencies (LEAs) to self-assess the extent to which systemic reform is established in their organization. Research by Fuhrman, Clune and others (2001) have shown a relationship between the depth and breadth of systemic change and improved student achievement. That portal is currently running at http://catalog.nsii.org, and school systems that complete the assessment instrument are offered a responsively configured channel of resources based on the results of the NSSI survey.

NEA Keys. NICI has also developed an online survey instrument in support of educational reform for the National Education Association (NEA) that can be viewed online at www.keysonline.org/DEMO. Over 5000 users in three states have accessed this survey since it went online in the Fall of 2001. Our intention is to apply the architecture underlying the linkages between the interactive catalog and the NSII application to the NEA's application, as well numerous others. We have recently proposed, for NSF digital library funding, to strengthen the prototype, and to extend it to additional applications.

When a NICI survey is taken, factor analyses are performed on groups of survey questions, which calculate mean scores, priority levels, and standard deviations. Based on these calculations, an index is determined within each metadata category (such as school leadership). An application of the metadata to the factor analysis results matches indices with Liber cataloged resources. Furthermore, because respondents' own personal metadata profiles use the same vocabulary as the other digital resources, it can be used to match people and organizations with one another. Thus, we can expand the definition of cataloged resources to extend to individuals, work groups (such as the classroom), school systems, regional and national educational organizations and other learning organizations.

Conclusion. Liber begins to demonstrate the value and scalability of a responsive dissemination system that (a) queries K-12 educators, students, professional developers, teacher education faculty, and educational leadership via a set of web-based surveys. (b) scores surveys using factor analysis, and generates metadata profiles based on the results. (c) catalogues resources by elements, qualifiers, and controlled vocabularies based on factors assessed in the survey , and (d) presents resources to each user or organization in a channel that is pre-configured according to survey results. When accessed as we are describing, the dissemination of digital resources that are coming online now using XML and RDF standards will be "responsive" to learners, teachers, schools and other kinds of groups and organizations.

References
Fuhrman, S. (2001). From the capitol to the classroom: standards-based reform in the states National Society for the Study of Education. Chicago: University of Chicago Press.

Duval, E., Hodgins, W., Sutton, S., Weibel, S.L., 2002, Metadata Principles and Practicalities. D-Lib Magazine, Vol. 8. No. 4
http://www.dlib.org/dlib/april02/weibel/04weibel.html

Functions of an Online Mentoring and Professional Learning Portal

David Gibson
National Institute for Community Innovations
Montpelier, Vermont
Dgibson@vismt.org

Abstract

How does online collaboration work when a learner is in complete control of the dialog with advisors? How can remote advisors provide high quality feedback on work samples and artifacts? This paper discusses the online Professional Learning Portal project underway at the National Institute for Community Innovations, and presents some of the details of the theory and thinking that is guiding the development. The web-based software is part of work by the National Institute for Community Innovations (NICI at http://nici-mc2.org) to develop tools for enhancing preservice education and supporting increased use of technology, especially in Professional Development Schools.

Introduction

The online Personal Learning Planner is a human and machine web-based assistant site that is based on a theory of dialog recently articulated by myself and Anne Friedrichs (Friedrichs, 2000; Friedrchs and Gibson, 2001). The theory of collaborative interaction for learning is consistent with several writers concerned with authenticity, use of technology to create problem-centered learning teams, representation of complex dynamics in educational settings, and online learning. (Carroll, 2000; Gibson, 1999; Gibson & Clarke, 2000; Newmann & Wehlage, 1995; Stiggins, 1997; Wiggins, 1989, NSDC, 2001).

Friedrichs (2000) discusses four distinct dialogue stages that manifest themselves in the Personal Learning Planning process:

1. Sharing Experience: Listening to own and others' inner speech and natural attitude about a skill or concept.
2. Expressing and Examining Diverse Concepts: Recognizing conflicts; analyzing old and new concepts, models and beliefs; working in one's zone of proximal development.
3. Articulatiing Applications and Understandings: Practicing new skills; combining old and new concepts; using others' ideas, using scaffolds to renegotiate understandings.
4. Communicating New Powers and Creations: Celebrating effects of critical analysis

The online Personal Learning Planner (PLP) provides a structure within an online working space with private and public access controlled by the learner to enable the above framework to work among a learner and any group of people serving as critical friends and advisors to the learner. With funding from the U.S. Department of Education under the "Preparing Tomorrow's Teachers to Use Technology" program (http://www.ed.gov/teachtech/). NICI has developed the first version of the PLP as a "critical friends" online space for future teachers who are assembling portfolios of evidence that they meet the standards required for a teaching license. The PLP is designed to assist learners through the processes of:

- Self-assessment of strengths, interests and aspirations

- Planning preservice education learning goals and projects
- Linking goals and projects to valued outcome standards
- Creating original work and sharing the work with others
- Receiving high quality feedback for the improvement of their work
- Documenting and validating the achievement of learning goals
- Assisting in the selection and preparation of exhibits of learning

Future plans for the PLP include many other learner groups such as K12 students and teachers, trainer-of-trainers programs, leadership programs, and groups as learners, for example, school-based action research teams using the site to develop collaborative products and seeking advice from remote experts to shape and validate the group's work.

Rationale

The rationale for building a web-based tool focused on the improvement of preservice teacher work has two parts. First, there is a need for feedback to come from a diverse audience, yet preservice and induction programs sometimes have limited resources and structures that produce scant feedback to aspiring teachers. As a result, an aspiring teacher's work evolves in isolation, perpetuating the general conditions of teaching present in most schools today. A web-based professional network can help overcome isolation, but even more important, it can provide the future teacher with high quality information that might not otherwise be available. The advantages of "anytime, anyplace" access to experts is an obvious benefit of a web-tool.

The second rationale is that there is a need for effective documentation of learning beyond paper and pencil formats. Ideally, documentation should be a record of the decisions as well as the validation of the work produced. In small personalized programs, preservice teachers benefit from many interviews and observation/feedback sessions related to their work, but in many programs, that experience is limited to the last few months of preparation. An online personal learning planner can help create a longitudinal multimedia record of growth and change in an aspiring teacher's skills and capabilities

The sources of inspiration and rationale led us to ask "What does preservice teacher work look like?" "What would happen if we could build a site for the improvement of a future teacher's work?" "Could the principles of personalization and helpful feedback in a professional network assist teacher education programs?" The online Personal Learning Plan is a way to pose answers to these kinds of questions.

Critical Components in the Online Personal Learning Plan

One of the first questions often raised is whether online learning of any kind can truly be personal. Isn't person-to-person the most *personal* way to learn? In fact, isn't online work one of the most *impersonal* kinds of interaction there is between humans? I don't wish to argue these points here. Online learning is here to stay. It brings remote resources to the desktop anytime, anyplace. Yes, it is in its infancy. Yes, it lacks many important features needed for rich human communication, but so does writing, film, video, and even talking. Using new communication tools in learning is a matter of integration and balance and its effectiveness depends mightily on the attributes of both the learner and teacher. In spite of these challenges, online learning is growing and evolving at a rapid pace.

The Online PLP promotes a uniquely learner-centered approach to the challenge of integration and balance of technology in learning. The following basic assumptions guide the thinking behind the NICI - PLP.

Three bases of planning and action for learning
The purposes of learning can be categorized by three domains:

- Institutional priorities – our shared community goals
- Professional priorities – our scholarly traditions and expectations
- Personal priorities – our source of deep meaning

The Learning Cycle
The Online PLP can be a powerful extension and helpmate in the "action research" process of planning, doing, reflecting and consolidating knowledge.

Focus on the learner's work
The learner's productivity and self-efficacy is the ultimate goal of the Online PLP. Work samples are the critical source for evidence of learning, the documentation of progress, and the verification that high standards have been achieved.

Self-Direction and Making Meaning
Learners produce better and are more highly motivated the more they have decision-making power over their learning. Learners gain from posing questions to advisors, and from knowing about, developing and using a variety of learning assets - their strengths, interests, aspirations, community and personal resources. All learning is a matter of making personal meaning out of the alternatives presented in experience.

Flexible Thinking Tools
Learners gain from scaffolding and assistance in stages and types of thinking, for example, divergent thinking, using multiple frameworks and perspectives, and so forth.

Structure and Roles
The online Personal Learning Planner allows all media formats and a multiplicity of linkages among learning goals, projects, and the evidence of attainment of standards of performance. Distinct from electronic portfolios that concentrate on the presentation and storage of completed work, the PLP concentrates on the improvement of work and the documentation of change of work over time.

Three user levels and a server administrator level are provided. Users levels include the Learner, Advisors, and a Program Administrator. The learner is in charge of their PLP. They create or choose goals, link them to standards or other external sources, create work that stands in relationship to the goals, make decisions on when both goals and work will be shared with advisors, and decide when work and goals are to be archived into permanent storage. Learners can make digital collections from their body of completed work. Each collection is presented as a self-contained website in which each work can independently attach reflections, summative evaluation, and new context-setting narrative and graphics.

Advisors are associated with one or more learners. When a learner's goal or work is being shared for critique and feedback, the Advisor can discuss, offer direct edits or validate the goal or work as adequate for its purpose. For example, a goal might be validated as appropriate to completion of a secondary teaching license in science; a piece of work might be validated as evidence of achieving a standard of performance linked to one or more goals. The validation process can be formalized with rubrics or left as narrative, and any rubric can be associated with any piece of work's link as evidence. When a group of advisors scores a work using a common rubric, a summative rubric can be built upon completion of the work.

The Program Administrator can review all Learners and Advisor records, add and delete Learners and Advisors, set defaults on the number of advisors that need to agree in order for validation to be complete, create rubrics, create and edit standards, and make other selections associated with program management. The Server Administrator controls the hardware and communication decisions needed for site maintenance and archiving.

PLP as a Team Tool

The use of the PLP as a team tool assumes that agency for a group operates much like it does for an individual, once internal communication and trust within the group has been developed. Outside reviewers can be invited to become project advisors. The PLP allows anonymous or "tagged" contributions by group members to facilitate both group and individual accountability. As a collaborative tool, the PLP facilitates building a group's history as well as a collection of validated work products.

References

Bentley, T. (1999, December 8). Students empowered in Montpelier [Our Generation Page]. Times Argus Newspaper.

Carroll, T. (2000). If we didn't have the schools we have today–would we create the schools we have today? Keynote speech at the AACE/SITE conference, San Diego, CA.

Csikszentmihalyi, M. (1996). Creativity: Flow and the psychology of discovery and invention. New York: HarperPerennial, a division of Harper Collins

Fiebelkorn, D. (1997). An ethnography of change: A year in the life of capital city high school. Unpublished draft of doctoral dissertation, University of Vermont, Burlington.

Friedrichs, A. (2000). Continuous learning dialogues: An ethnography of personal learning plans' impact on four river high school learners. Unpublished doctoral dissertation. University of Vermont.

Friedrichs, A. and Gibson, D. (2001) Personalization and secondary school renewal. (Forthcoming from Brown University Regional Laboratory.)

Gibson, D. (1999). Mapping the dynamics of change: A complexity theory analysis of innovation in five Vermont high schools. . Unpublished doctoral dissertation. University of Vermont.

Gibson, D. (2000). Complexity theory as a leadership framework. Montpelier, VT: VISMT. Available: http://www.vismt.org/pub/ComplexityandLeadership.pdf

Gibson, D. & Clarke, J. (1999). Growing towards systemic change. Providence, RI: The Regional Laboratory.

Moffett, J. (1998). The universal schoolhouse: Spiritual awakening through education. Portland, ME: Calendar Island Publishers.

Newmann, F. M. & G.G. Wehlage (1995). Successful school restructuring: A report to the public and educators. Center on Organization and Restructuring: University of Wisconsin.

NSDC (2001). National standards for online learning. Forthcoming. National Staff Development Council.

Stiggins, R. J. (1997). Student-centered classroom assessment. Upper Saddle River, NJ: Merrill, Prentice Hall.

Wiggins, G. (1989). Teaching to the (authentic) test. Educational Leadership, 46: 41-46.

Large-Scale Interaction Strategies for Web-Based Professional Development

Paul J. Giguere, M.S.
Health & Human Development Programs
Education Development Center, Inc. (EDC)
Newton, MA – United States
pgiguere@edc.org

Scott W. Formica, B.A.
Social Science Research & Evaluation, Inc. (SSRE)
Burlington, MA – United States
ssre@gis.net

Wayne M. Harding, Ed.M., Ph.D.
Social Science Research & Evaluation, Inc. (SSRE)
Burlington, MA – United States
wayneh@gis.net

Abstract: The primary purpose of this paper is to briefly discuss five interaction strategies that can be used in large-scale (more than 30 participants) Web-based trainings. Evaluation data are presented from seven Web-based continuing education workshops conducted with United States Department of Education (USED) Middle School Drug Prevention and School Safety Coordinators (MSCs) that utilized two of these large-scale strategies. Results of the evaluation show that, contrary to the current literature, MSCs who participated in large-scale Web-based trainings were highly satisfied with many aspects of the workshops, including the on-line facilitation. The results point to a need to replicate these findings and to further study additional large-scale interaction strategies in Web-based training and professional development.

Introduction

As organizations begin to explore the use of the Web for conducting training and professional development, the issue of workshop or class size inevitably becomes a topic of discussion and debate. Organizations feel pressure to increase the number of participants enrolled in a Web-based training because the costs of creating such trainings (or converting a face-to-face training to the Web) are high and Web-based training can be structured to handle lots of participants (Boettcher, 1999). Increasing the number of participants in Web-based trainings can be an effective way to more quickly recoup development costs by using similar resources for a training of 100 participants that would normally be used for 30 participants. This approach does, however, run contrary to Ko and Rossen's (2001) findings that it is not possible to have a high level of interaction when more than 40 people participate in a Web-based training. Similarly, Palloff and Pratt (1999) indicate that given the large amount of time needed for facilitators and students to engage in substantive interaction, limiting training size seems to be a logical and necessary strategy to maximize the quality of the training. At issue then is the nature of the interaction strategy utilized and how it is impacted when the number of participants exceeds the original design or violates what the literature tells us is good practice. This paper presents five large-scale interaction strategies that, if used properly, should help minimize the potentially detrimental effects of increasing the number of participants in a Web-based training beyond the suggested maximum threshold.

Large-Scale Interaction Strategies

Large-scale interaction strategies allow a large group of learners (in numbers greater than thirty) to engage in some form of asynchronous discussion with a facilitator or instructor in an online environment. The premise behind the use of such strategies is that the objectives of the training have less to do with personal interaction (such as building a community of learners) and more to do with providing a means of reinforcing various elements from the content of the training. For the purposes of this discussion, the five strategies described below are based on the presence of 100 people participating in a Web-based training that utilizes an asynchronous bulletin board-style Web-based discussion area. In each scenario, all participants have unrestricted access to the content of the training (materials, activities, etc.).

1. *Multi-Group Interaction* – This strategy divides the participants into four groups of twenty-five. Each group has its own discussion area and a single facilitator. Groups are not able to view other groups' discussions during the training, however, all groups engage in the same activities and address similar issues in the discussion areas with regard to the content of the training.

2. *Forum Interaction* – Based on topical interests (or through random assignment), participants are divided into four groups of twenty-five. Each group has its own discussion area and a single facilitator but, unlike the Multi-Group strategy, all groups are able to view other group's discussions during the training. This strategy can help achieve a large number of training objectives by having smaller groups of participants exclusively address certain objectives and by making the results available to all groups.

3. *Sub-Group Interaction* – More analogous to an active/auditor model, this strategy selects twenty-five participants who are provided a discussion area with a facilitator (the active group). The remaining 75 participants have "read-only" access to the active group's discussion area, i.e. they can read all of the discussions but cannot make postings. The selection of the active group can be accomplished through a registration process (some participants may prefer to be an auditor since this requires no interaction on their part) or selection can be done randomly.

4. *Large-Group Interaction* – This strategy provides a single discussion area, with one facilitator, for all 100 participants. As the training progresses and amount of participation in the discussion area increases, additional facilitators join in the discussion as needed to accommodate the increasing number of questions or comments.

5. *Meta-Interaction* – This strategy uses a synthesis approach whereby participants are able to submit questions or comments to a facilitator (which may also involve a small team of assistants) through e-mail or a Web-based form. The questions or comments are synthesized and posted by the facilitator (usually with his/her comments or reactions) to a "read-only" discussion area. Participants can then read the synthesis and continue asking questions or making comments.

The five strategies mentioned in this section just barely scratch the surface of what is possible using various interaction strategies in combination with computer-mediated communication tools. Each strategy also has various benefits and problems (the scope of which is beyond this paper).

The Study

Seven continuing education Web-based trainings were held with between 36 and 95 United States Department of Education (USED) Middle School Drug Prevention and School Safety Coordinators (MSCs). These events were meant to supplement a five-day face-to-face training that MSCs were required to attend at the beginning of their grant. The events lasted for five days, and each provided a more in-depth presentation of topics that were just briefly introduced at the face-to-face training. The first three training events utilized the *Sub-Group Interaction Strategy* (#3), and the remaining four events used the *Large Group Interaction Strategy* (#4). Post-event assessment forms were used to assess various aspects of each of the trainings including overall satisfaction, whether or not participants would recommend the event to other MSCs, satisfaction with the role of the facilitator, and usefulness of the information presented. As shown in Table 1, participants gave consistently high ratings to each of these aspects across each of the events.

Table 1. Participant Ratings Web Events 1-7

	Overall Satisfaction (Mean 1-5) [a]	Recommend this event to others (Mean 1-5) [b]	Satisfaction with facilitator (Mean 1-5) [a]	Usefulness of information (Mean 1-4) [c]
1: Using Existing Data to Inform Prevention Program Selection (N=37) [d]	Mean = 4.11	Mean = 4.39	Mean = 4.19	Mean = 3.32
2: Identifying Priorities and Strategies for Your Prevention Initiative (N=82) [d]	Mean = 4.05	Mean = 4.33	Mean = 3.91	Mean = 3.54
3: Promoting Prevention Through School-Community Partnerships (N=56) [d]	Mean = 4.30	Mean = 4.35	Mean = 4.11	Mean = 3.37
4: Selecting Research-Based Programs for Your School (N=93) [e]	Mean = 4.51	Mean = 4.53	Mean = 4.17	Mean = 3.59
5: Implementing Research-Based Prevention Programs in Schools (N=58) [e]	Mean = 4.45	Mean = 4.40	Mean = 4.36	Mean = 3.47
6: Sustaining Your Prevention Initiative (N=72) [e]	Mean = 4.59	Mean = 4.52	Mean = 4.17	Mean = 3.65
7: Linking Violence & Substance Abuse Prevention to Academic Success (N=96) [e]	Mean = 4.58	Mean = 4.57	Mean = 4.46	Mean = 3.65
OVERALL	**Mean = 4.40**	**Mean = 4.46**	**Mean = 4.20**	**Mean = 3.55**

[a] Based on a scale from Very Dissatisfied (1) to Very Satisfied (5)
[b] Based on a scale from Strongly Recommend They NOT Participate (1) to Strongly Recommend They Participate (5)
[c] Based on a scale from Not at All Useful (1) to Very Useful (4)
[d] Utilized the Sub-Group interaction strategy. Results indicated no significant difference between auditors and active participants
[e] Utilized the Large Group interaction strategy.

Conclusions

Results from independent evaluations of seven Web-based continuing education events utilizing the *Sub-Group Interaction Strategy*, and the *Large Group Interaction Strategy* suggest that, contrary to the current literature, the use of large-scale Web-based trainings does not negatively influence participants overall satisfaction with the event, their willingness to recommend the event to other participants, their satisfaction with the role of the facilitator, or their rating of the usefulness of the information provided in the event. Further research is needed determine whether the additional three large-scale interaction strategies would produce similar results and whether similar results would be obtained for Web-based trainings that are designed to be more dependent on close participant-to-facilitator or participant-to-participant interaction. Also, future research should examine the extent to which the positive results here depended on participants' prior participation in an intensive face-to-face training by comparing participants with and without such an experience.

References

Boettcher, J.V. (1999). Cyber course size: Pedagogy and politics. *T.H.E. Journal. 12*(8).

Harding, W.M. & Formica, S.W. (2001a). Evaluation findings for MSC continuing education web event #1: Using existing data in your needs assessment. [Report] Prepared for Education Development Center, Inc., Newton, MA and the United States Department of Education (USED).

Harding, W.M. & Formica, S.W. (2001b) Evaluation findings for MSC continuing education web event #2: Identifying priorities and strategies for your prevention initiative. [Report] Prepared for Education Development Center, Inc., Newton, MA and the United States Department of Education (USED).

Harding, W.M. & Formica, S.W. (2001c) Evaluation findings for MSC continuing education web event #3: Promoting prevention through school-community partnerships. [Report] Prepared for Education Development Center, Inc., Newton, MA and the United States Department of Education (USED).

Harding, W.M. & Formica, S.W. (2002a) Evaluation findings for MSC continuing education web event #4: Selecting research-based programs for your schools. [Report] Prepared for Education Development Center, Inc., Newton, MA and the United States Department of Education (USED).

Harding, W.M. and Formica, S.W. (2002b) Evaluation findings for MSC continuing education web event #5: Implementing research-based prevention programs in schools. [Report] Prepared for Education Development Center, Inc., Newton, MA and the United States Department of Education (USED).

Harding, W.M. and Formica, S.W. (2002c) Evaluation findings for MSC continuing education web event #6: Sustaining your prevention initiatives. [Report] Prepared for Education Development Center, Inc., Newton, MA and the United States Department of Education (USED).

Harding, W.M. and Formica, S.W. (2002d) Evaluation findings for MSC continuing education web event #7: Substance abuse prevention to academic success. [Report] Prepared for Education Development Center, Inc., Newton, MA and the United States Department of Education (USED).

Ko, S. & Rossen, S. (2001). *Teaching online: A practical guide.* New York, NY: Houghton Mifflin Co.

Palloff, R.M. & Pratt, K. (1999). *Building learning communities in cyberspace: Effective strategies for the online classroom.* San Francisco, CA: Jossey-Bass Publishers.

BUILDING A KNOWLEDGE COMMUNITY AMONG HIGHER EDUCATION INSTITUTIONS

Marycarmen Aguilar and Catherine Gihlstorf
Center for Innovation in Learning
Kenan-Flagler Business School
University of North Carolina – Chapel Hill
USA
CIL@bschool.unc.edu

Abstract: A professor's head holds a wealth of knowledge and experience both tacit and explicit; relating both to their chosen field of study and to their classroom teaching. Our Knowledge Community provides a repository and collaborative environment in which to capture, store and share this knowledge with others. It is a complete on-line, searchable archive featuring teaching resources, teaching best practices, faculty publications and working papers, and multimedia showcases of faculty research. The knowledge community also provides a place for collaborating partner schools to share research, exchange best practices and to leverage the intellectual assets of the collaborating schools. This project is in progress and scheduled for completion in September 2002. The current community contains 5 partner schools with plans to expand the number of schools over the next 4 years.

Project background

Kenan-Flagler Business School of the University of North Carolina (UNC) at Chapel Hill is one of the top worldwide research business institutions worldwide that is always looking to innovate and increase international collaboration among top business schools. Kenan-Flagler Business School promotes, enhances and facilitates collaboration and knowledge sharing internally in the business school as well as with its global partners. The Knowledge Community (KC) project emerged looking to enrich the internal and external knowledge sharing and collaborative goals of the Business School, as well as to improve the business school's efficiency by having in one location a website interface and a dynamic data base easy to integrate with other internal systems in the school, the university system, and with the systems of its global partners. Also, the Knowledge Community facilitates access to the faculty by external sources, and creates a global virtual community for the exchange of research publications and teaching best practices.

The Knowledge Community is designed to include Kenan-Flagler Business School and all its international partners such as the members of the OneMBA consortium and Centers for International Business Education and Research, CIBER schools. OneMBA is a global consortium allying 5 top business schools from around the world: South America, North America, Asia, and Europe. The OneMBA consortium is offering a premier global executive MBA program starting in September 2002. This program involves students from these 5 universities working on virtual global projects, as well as the faculty teams collaborating to design and teach courses for all of the students. One of the main funding sources that makes the OneMBA program possible is the CIBER grant that Kenan-Flagler was awarded this year. As part of the faculty development section in the CIBER OneMBA grant, the Knowledge Community project is designed to support the faculty development efforts of the OneMBA program and bolster recognition of faculty research at the associated partner schools.

The Knowledge Community project will assist the teaching and learning efforts within the consortium by documenting and sharing faculty teaching best practices and learning activities. It also strives to increase the visibility, and reputation of the faculty of partnering schools both within the consortium and externally by publicizing their research activities and areas of expertise. The project will be divided into three sections: a teaching and learning community, a listing of faculty publications and research activities, and a multimedia showcase section.

The Kenan-Flagler Knowledge Community will be a dynamic repository and collaborative environment in which to capture, store and share research and teaching materials about business topics. Through this virtual collaborative environment the faculty members will share and update all their actual research, all working papers and publications, in addition to sharing their teaching best practices, experiences, activities and teaching materials. The KC will be an instrument that will provide all the publications, research and information about the faculty experts and their specific areas of expertise.

Project Description

The Kenan-Flagler Knowledge Community (KC) has been a team effort involving different areas of the school, including: the Office of the Dean, Business School Faculty and students, information technology staff, program directors, marketing and communication areas, instructional designers, international areas, knowledge management experts, potential users and more. The project is led by the Business School's Center for Innovation in Learning, and supported by internal funds and a grant obtained from CIBER. The project's design and planning covers all research and teaching knowledge-sharing needs of the Kenan-Flagler Business School. This also includes the OneMBA consortium goals, and general trends in the field toward learning communities, knowledge management and information technologies. The fist stage in the project plan is for the pilot version to include the research publications and teaching materials from Kenan-Flagler. The next version will be offered to the OneMBA consortium, and the following versions will be shared with CIBER schools and other international partners of the Kenan-Flagler Business School.

The features in this first Kenan-Flagler version will have 6 main sections, divided into 3 functional areas: research, teaching, and multimedia information showcases. This version will have a stand-alone interface and will also provide various services to the Business School external website and other Kenan-Flagler program websites.

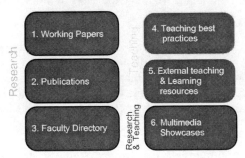

Knowledge Community Sections

Figure 1: Knowledge Community Sections will cover the functional areas of research publications, teaching best practices and materials and the research multimedia showcases.

Research Sections
The first three functions involve capturing existing publication information on faculty research that currently exists in several non-searchable and searchable venues. This information will be collected on the web in a central, searchable location. A dynamic document-based system will allow information entry, retrieval, and reporting from one central interface. External users will access the information via a web browser. No software beyond this will be required.

Working Papers
Centralized repository of pre-published working papers and abstracts. Searchable via the web and linked from the Kenan-Flagler external web site. Faculty members or designates can maintain their individual

entries in this collection. After publication, papers will remain in the archive with the permission of the copyright holder. Currently, these materials reside on individual faculty member web sites, on departmental web sites or on external sites (i.e. SSRN)

Publications
Centralized repository of publications or links to them. Searchable via the web and linked from the Kenan-Flagler external web site. Faculty members or designates can maintain their individual entries in this collection. Currently, these materials reside on individual faculty member web sites, as list entries on the individual faculty member's page, in the faculty directory, in a listing in the annual research report for the Senior Associate Dean, and in a listing in the quarterly Research Newsletter.

Faculty Experts Guide (Faculty Directory)
Central repository for all faculty information with links to resources/papers, personal websites, areas of interest/expertise, contact information, background and recent research.
Searchable via the web and linked from the Kenan-Flagler external web site. Faculty members or designates can maintain their individual entries to this collection. Members of the media, prospective students and other researchers will be the primary users of this section

Teaching Sections
The Teaching sections involve capturing existing best teaching practices from Kenan-Flagler content experts, along with external teaching best practices, and sharing these practices with Kenan Flagler Business School partners and the faculty community. In addition, this section archives existing internal and external teaching resources and tools as a resource to aid faculty in teaching and technology development.

Teaching Best Practices
Centralized repository of Kenan-Flagler Business School faculty and staff teaching best practices. External faculty, specifically from the OneMBA consortium schools and other partner schools may add material to the Kenan-Flagler Business School system once registered in the database. This will allow Kenan-Flagler Business School to expand on an international scale and share the system with its global partners to create a virtual community. This will be searchable via the web and linked from the Kenan-Flagler external web site. Faculty members or Ph.D. students would be the users of this section.

Teaching Resources
The teaching resources section will be a centralized repository of external resources for teaching, including relevant research and best practices. It will include information on Kenan-Flagler Business School's teaching best practices and teaching materials that currently do not exist in any formal or searchable format. At present, some of this information is available at the Program offices or resides with Department Chairs. This information will be available via the web in a central, searchable location.

Multimedia Showcase
This portion of the project highlights the expertise of faculty from various schools. On a rotating basis, select faculty members from each of the schools will be showcased by the Kenan-Flagler Business School and OneMBA consortium. All multimedia showcases will be linked in the marketing website. Faculty will either speak on a current issue or an area of research, or be interviewed. The feature will be delivered via video/audio, audio only, or stills and audio. Each school will have the option of placing this feature on their individual school's pages as well. If feasible, an on-line chat may take place with the speaker during a short designated time or a threaded discussion may be opened to facilitate a dialogue. Faculty members and their schools will receive positive exposure and the program site will gain visitors and attract interest. The first version of the KC will have Kenan-Flagler Business School faculty, Kenan-Flagler guest speakers and faculty of selected global partners.

Data-Base Structure and Technology Tools
The knowledge community project data-base structure is a relation data-base where the two main tables are the Faculty information and the Resources that are written for each faculty member in the community. A best practices table is the third main table in this initial framework. The relationships between tables provide the associations with all the different elements trying to answer all potential questions about the

research and teaching materials from the KC. This first structure will be modified and adapted for the following version to include all the feedback from Kenan-Flagler users and international partners.

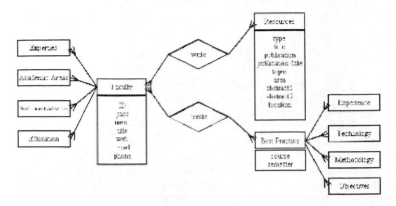

Figure 2: Knowledge Community Relational Data Base Structure

The technology tools that have been used by the team to develop and implement the knowledge community project were selected according to the corporate standards for global information knowledge management systems along with the UNC- Chapel Hill standards. The team will be work with the global partners to assure easy and successful system transfer according to their internal systems. The knowledge community project uses Oracle 8i as a database server and Tomcat 3.2.4/JRun 3.1 as an application server. On the application server, Oracle XDK, Oracle JDBC drivers and JDK would be installed. Additionally, Oracle Client should be installed on the application server to make a connection to the oracle server.

The team is currently working with UNC-Chapel Hill main campus Oracle policies and with the Kenan-Flagler Information Technology administrator to coordinate efficient communication between the different servers, tables and tools used.

Future Challenges

The first version of the KC is on schedule to be up and running at the end of 2002. The challenges confronted during the pilot version have taught us much which can be used for following versions, particularly to include all the lessons learned to increase the success of the future global versions of OneMBA and CIBER. Some of the challenges that the team visualizes for the future versions include: Obtain up to date information from faculty members researchers; Getting and entering the research publications and teaching materials into the system from faculty on a regular basis; Getting faculty to share their teaching best practices, Assuring information quality over quantity .

Knowledge management, global collaboration and knowledge sharing have been some of the university's chief initiatives and challenges in the last decades. For many schools, to open the doors to their latest research initiatives and share their experiences and intellectual production has been a cultural challenge and a difficult goal to achieve. The ones that have accomplished that now enjoy all the benefits and advantages of sharing all their research publications, research initiatives and best practices. This has had a positive impact not only on the organizations' internal cultures, but has also contributed to increasing the visibility of the organizations externally, especially to the various audiences interested in the subjects of business research and business teaching.

The Kenan-Flagler Business School KC project is an example of global collaboration and knowledge sharing. Creating and offering a knowledge community like this will allow all business Faculty from partner institutions to benefit from a virtual community and share their knowledge and experiences through this system in the future.

GEOGRAPHICALLY DISTRIBUTED INTERNATIONAL STUDENT TEAM COLLABORATION

Catherine Gihlstorf and Marycarmen Aguilar
Center for Innovation in Learning
Kenan-Flagler Business School
University of North Carolina – Chapel Hill
United States
CIL@unc.edu

Abstract A partnership of five top-ranked business schools on four continents, this 21-month MBA program develop global leaders and benefits executives through a curriculum that spans business cultures and best practices in Asia, Europe, North and South America. Student teams comprised of one student from each partner school collaborate on projects and coursework in a virtual environment, meeting face-to-face only once every six months. The program's toolbox consists of Blackboard's LMS for asynchronous discussion forums and course material distribution; CentraOne for synchronous collaboration, session recordings and virtual student presentations; and email for asynchronous collaboration and notification. Each student will be geographically distributed. A selection of both web-based synchronous and asynchronous tools was necessary to facilitate the student collaboration. While the program begins in September 2002, the collection of tools has been pilot tested for seven months in another MBA program.

Program Overview

A partnership of 5 top-ranked, international Masters of Business Administration (MBA) programs designed the OneMBA, an Executive MBA degree unlike any existing MBA program. The five partnering schools based in; *North America*; University of North Carolina in Chapel Hill, USA and Monterrey Tech (ITESM) in Monterrey, Mexico; *South America*;, Fundaco Getulio Vargas in Sao Paulo, Brazil; *Asia;* The Chinese University of Hong Kong and *Europe*; Erasmus University-Rotterdam School of Management in Rotterdam, The Netherlands, collaborated to design the program over a year and a half period. The program opened with the inaugural class of approximately 100 students in September 2002.

Each partnering school recruits and contributes students to the program. These students are identified as "local students" or students belonging to a specific partner school. The uniqueness of the program originates with the design of the instruction. Each partnering school designs the basic instruction for their "local" students and a committee of faculty designs a series of globally coordinated courses containing all students from every school. The format for the local instruction remains independent of the other schools. Currently, each school operates on a different schedule and delivery format. The globally coordinated courses however, involve all students and provide identical instruction. Globally coordinated courses begin once every six months with an experiential learning module. All students travel to a designated partner school for the 3 day experiential module. A new business theme organizes each of the 6 month global courses, and the theme, new global student teams and cultural material are introduced during these experiential learning modules. During any 6 month module, a student participates in a series of locally delivered courses as well one team-based, globally coordinated course. This paper focuses on the team-based, globally coordinated courses.

Student Profile/Team Composition

The target student for this program is an accomplished executive with 7-10 years of management experience and responsibility for global activities within his/her respective company. Extensive travel schedules and executive responsibilities functionally eliminate the possibility a traditional two-year full-time MBA program for this audience. The OneMBA program is designed to accommodate part-time executive students with a need for global management and cultural proficiency. Many students possess advanced degrees in areas of study other than business.

All students meet each other "virtually", prior to the debut of the program, by posting short biography pages on a Blackboard course site dedicated to student communication. This site hosts these biographies and all global team discussion forums for the duration of the 21-month program. The first face-to-face meeting between students occurs during a week long "opening week" hosted by the Americans in Washington, D.C. Students participate in cultural exchange activities, group skill-building exercises and engage in learning activities around the first learning module theme: organizational behavior. Global student teams are meticulously selected by a faculty/staff committee to provide representation from each school as well as representation from a variety of professions, industries and quantitative skill levels. Each team contains 5-6 students who participate in a different student team for each module in order to maximize the learning opportunities between colleagues.

Tool Selection

The program's selection of tools resulted from an analysis of our target audience, global coordination challenges and consideration of what each school currently provides. The OneMBA students travel frequently as part of their work responsibilities and accommodate course activities during and after work hours, often in brief time increments such as between meetings or flights. This student group expects superior customer service and support. Partnering schools decided that tool selection would be based primarily on meeting students' needs rather than operating with the lowest common technology denominator among the schools. Each student is required to have a laptop computer with a predefined configuration available for their use.

Team assignments in the globally coordinated courses typically focus on the discussion and analysis of a case study, participation in a simulation or group project preparation and presentation. Geographically dispersed team members represent a time zone span of 12 hours necessitating the availability of an asynchronous communication and collaboration tool. The pilot test of the proposed tools revealed that student of a similar profile to the OneMBA student appreciated the benefits of asynchronous time zone accommodation but realistically had limited time in which to complete assignments and therefore the immediacy of synchronous tools was highly valued. All schools agreed to provide three tools for student collaboration and communication; both asynchronous and synchronous. Student teams were free to use the communication and collaboration method or technology of their choice, but three market leader tools would be provided.

CentraOne

The Centra company located in Massachusetts, USA produces three levels of Internet–based synchronous communication products; E-meeting, Conference and Symposium; increasing in functionality and price with each level. Centra provides ASP services as well as licensing their products as package of a server license and concurrent user licenses. Centra Symposium offers the following features which met the anticipated needs of the program's students: full duplex audio over IP accommodating several hundred participants concurrently, session recording and playback, breakout rooms with the ability to import breakout groups' work back into the main session, application sharing and markup, text chat, whiteboard functionality, web page display and mark-up and one-way video.

As our students travel frequently, the program needed a web-based tool able to perform on a variety of Internet connections, whether from a hotel in Lagos or a corporate network in Las Vegas. The minimum entry requirements for any level of Centra license are a 133 MHz Pentium processor, a microphone and sound card and a 28.8 modem connection to the Internet. This low level of entry satisfied the need of students for flexibility in connecting and participating from a variety work assignments. The recording and playback feature allows students to record their meeting for team members unable to attend or for faculty feedback. Students can also present projects to a team of faculty for evaluation virtually. One way video allows for one group to view the other during the presentation such as the student presenter viewing the faculty member evaluation them.

Virtual office hours become more efficient on-line when faculty can "meet" with more than one student at a time and record the session for those students unable to attend. The application sharing and whiteboard features allow both the instructor and student to share, view and work on a spreadsheet, document or formula at the same time.

The University of North Carolina-Chapel Hill's Kenan-Flagler Business School purchased the Conference product and 10 seats at an educational discount of 50% in December 2001. After a seven month pilot test with a Weekend MBA Human Resources Management class and an online Working Spanish course, the school recommended the product to the OneMBA program with the caveat that the license is upgraded to the Symposium level and 20 additional seats licensed.

The following issues contributed to the recommendation to upgrade. The Conference level license provided excellent duplex voice over IP functionality but limited the number of speaking participants to 5 at any one time. The addition of a sixth student or faculty observer to the meeting necessitated "passing" one of the virtual "microphones" to the extra person and returning it to the originator when the he/she needed to speak again. This "passing the mic" impeded to the smooth flow of conversation. Symposium's inclusion of a whiteboard and integration with Blackboard made it a more appealing choice. The per seat license costs prohibited the purchase of more that 30 total concurrent licenses (seats) but the expectation is that no more than a third of the global student teams will be utilizing Centra Symposium concurrently.

The tool is intended to facilitate student collaboration on their virtual team assignments for the globally coordinated courses. It may also be utilized by any student for their local course collaboration as well. It has also been used as a communication tool for administrative meetings between the partnering schools.

Blackboard

The Blackboard course delivery product incorporates both synchronous and asynchronous tools as well as providing a shell in which to deliver course material. Three of the partnering schools had various levels of Blackboard implementations in use prior to the OneMBA program inception. The remaining partner schools utilized similar delivery products. After considering a number of open market products for course material delivery, the program technology committee selected Blackboard. Since each of the existing Blackboard schools operate a different level of Blackboard license, the OneMBA program itself purchased a level one license from Blackboard, and hosted it in Monterrey, Mexico. As each school maintains their own registration systems, Blackboard's level two or three licenses with registration integration were not needed. The OneMBA program pays the salary of a full-time host master for this server.

A uniform course delivery platform across schools provides students with a consistency and cohesion important when student teams experience the majority of their course interface locally and only 25% of it across the schools. During one module, a student will need to visit only one Blackboard login page for all his/her local and global courses; finding material located consistently within that framework.

Integrated discussion forums with file attachment capabilities provide the base for student team asynchronous collaboration and discussion. Blackboard also allows for the integration and scheduling of Centra Symposium events, therefore students need to enter only one Blackboard site to find all the tools or links to all the tools the program provides. This meets our target audience need for efficiency, consistency and superior support.

Faculty members favor Blackboard for the ability to upload material without knowledge of any scripting or coding language and to do so from any location with an Internet connection.

Email

Email, from either a program provided address or work-related account provides asynchronous communication and collaboration features for virtual teams. Email provides a means for communicating to schedule a virtual meeting or as a backup for other tools or as a means to communicate with faculty members. Each partnering school provides an email account to their "local" students. A roster of all students and clickable email addresses reside in the Student Communication Blackboard course.

Challenges

Support for the globally coordinated courses remains a challenge. Each partner school maintains technology and content support for their local instruction, but the global virtual teams in the coordinated courses fall under no specific school's oversight. The program is experimenting with a global time zone approach to support. The technology support staff at each school troubleshoots technology problems for global course teams during a specific assigned time span. One support email address (support@onemba.org) forwards a help request to the mailboxes of the technology coordinators for each school. The school responsible for that assigned time span (GMT time) answers the request.

Conclusion

Students assigned to global teams for a globally coordinated course meet face to face only once every 6 months. During the interim months, communication and project collaboration relies on a set of synchronous and asynchronous tools provided by the program. Unlike traditional programs, OneMBA students participate both in local courses at their home university as well as in global teams of 5-6 students, with at least one student from each partnering school. Cultural nuances, customs and work and communication styles will need to be negotiated via distance. Part-time executive students accommodate their learning and team collaboration into small time spans and prefer synchronous collaboration.

Areas for further study include the type of tool used for what type of communication/ collaboration, how do the groups dynamics and communication style change if the composition of the team contains more than one student per school, and what alternative technologies and methods, if any, do students use for communication and collaboration beyond what is provided by the program.

European Project:

DELOS (Developing a European eLearning Observation System)

Crsitina Girona

Universitat Oberta de Catalunya

Area of Educational Methodology and Innovation

cgirona@uoc.edu

The Universitat Oberta de Catalunya is participating in the **Delos project** from the beginning of the year 2002 until January 2004.

The project aims at the development, validation and establishment of a sustainable Observation System of experiences and institutions in the **elearning field** to contribute to the decision making process by different stakeholders (European policy makers and market actors). DELOS is a comprehensive and inclusive action that builds convergence and coherence among existing observation & analysis systems and approaches, provided by international organisations, by the various Services and Agencies of the European Union and by other targeted observation projects in European Commission Programmes, such as those in SOCRATES, LEONARDO DA VINCI and IST.

In its first development phase, a specific analysis of the needs and priorities of the two main groups, the one of the "Information Users" and the other of the "Information Collectors", in Education and Training around the world, is being conducted trough a series of interviews, considering the different specialisations and characteristics of the institutions involved and aiming at the definition of the formulation of a comprehensive map of the different competencies and strengths available in Europe.

The mapping activity will consist in the following tasks:

1) Identifying all different E&T observatory systems, bodies (i.e. actors)

2) Recording the aims, structures and practices of the main E&T observatory systems (i.e. Profiling)

3) Identifying the main stakeholders (users) of the observatory systems

4) Recording the information needs and interests of the main stakeholders

This will allow a definition of the state-of-the-art and will contribute to set up proposals for improvement and define the new observatory.

The institution leading the project is MENON (Belgium). The rest of the project partnership is formed by SCIENTER (Italy), FIM (Germany), CEDEFOP (Greece), LRF (Greece), Swedish Agency for Distance Education (Sweden), EENet (Germany) i EDEN (Hungary).

First project results are expected by September 2002.

The European Commission is supporting the project and sees it as one of the best initiatives for decision makers and policy makers in the field of the use of technology in education.

Developing ICT-facilitators Competencies through a Blended Learning Approach

Lisa Gjedde
Research Program for Media and ICT in a Learning Perspective
Department for Curriculum Research
Danish University of Education
lg@dpu.dk

Abstract: A blended learning approach to a diploma course for in-service teachers, studying to become Pedagogical ICT facilitators, may have implications for their learning process in relation to a multimedia production. Drawing on cases from this diploma course in which a blended learning approach is providing experiential resources for teachers, the development of didactic tools will be related to the teacher's experiential problem oriented learning process.

Introduction

The development of Information and Communication Technology (ICT) has been instrumental in setting the arena for a new learning paradigm, calling for new roles for learner and teacher. It has also pointed to the need for a new set of competencies for the teacher, in order to be able not only to deliver instructions in a subject matter, but also to facilitate the learners' independent learning processes in a number of ways. This paper will explore some of the implications for an blended learning approach to a diploma course for in-service teachers, studying to become Pedagogical ICT facilitators and how they through a process of production of an educational multimedia programme have been challenged with making reflections on the didactics of using and integrating multimedia in their teaching, as well as reflections on the design and communication strategies for presenting it.

This study is based on action research methodology involving 3 classes and a follow up study a a year after the finished course which involves 6 students based on qualitative inquiry with research interviews.

Research questions have emerged that are related to the development of new competencies and a didactics for new media.

How may the pedagogical imagination of the teachers be engaged in the construction of learning environments for their students?

How may this process be supported by a blended learning approach ?

Background

Basic to the didactic approach for the introductory course is a learning cycle involving experience as well as analysis and production, leaving space for reflexivity relating to the learners experiences as well as sharing it with teams of fellow students. The experiential learning cycle has been described by Kolb and others (Kolb 1984) as having four stages: Concrete Experience, Reflective Observation, Abstract Conceptualisation and Active Experimentation. This cycle may happen over a period of time, and include second order cycles within it. Basic to it is a view of learning as a transformation of experience into knowledge. (Kolb 1984)

Part of this experiential approach to a didactics for pedagogical ICT -facilitators, is to use new media in a pedagogical context through a process, which draws on experiential learning methodologies and through an initial multimedia production allows for an articulation of experience and reflection on it.

The use of a project-based multimedia production done by teams that collaborate on the internet, combined with seminars that provide cognitive tools for the reflection on this experiential learning process provides the basic experiences on which to anchor the didactics for the teachers further implementation of a learning new paradigm and the potentials it may offer for the integration of ICT in the curriculum.

It can also provide valuable experiences that may serve as a reference point in the development of a didactics for multimedia, both in the planning process through the use of pedagogical scenarios and the production process. In the design process, it has significance that the students having been through an actual production process, in which they have had to develop a structure reflecting their ideas through a process of articulation. This articulation then enters into a learning cycle as the material for further reflection.

Towards new ways of implementing ICT

The teacher's role in this context is seen as a facilitator and coach rather than as transmitter of knowledge to be passively absorbed by students. One of the ways to facilitate this constructivist approach and build skills and competences that may further this is to focus on the role of individual expression and articulation through a process of design, which is enabling a learning-by-doing approach. It also puts a focus on the need for support of different learning strategies and different preferences for learning. One of the strategies for moving beyond the present limitations of most conference based e-learning systems is to integrate approaches that goes beyond the mere text-based approaches and integrates multi-medial approaches while also allowing for the creation of more ambient environments.

The experiences of the primary and secondary school teachers who were studying to become ICT-facilitators brought a wide background of didactic experiences from the classrooms with children with different needs into the production scope as actual target groups. This also brought forth a number of different design strategies, some of which were explicitly targeting special needs groups as well as focusing on the different intelligences and different preferences of children (Gardner 1993). Some of these designs did represent novel and imaginative ways of engaging children though different web-based programmes, as well as cd-rom based programmes. Some productions did for instance provide an interactive learning environment with a rich media use, involving sound, video and text, each supplementing the other – to provide children with different challenges, based on different preferences or skills. Through this support in web-based learning environments it was made possible for the teachers to free up resources to further assist children in the classroom, with special or different needs. In this way a blended-learning environment afforded differentiated teaching and learning in the primary school.

The teacher's experiences with this design process were carried out in a blended learning environment, constituted by a blend of seminars and a first-class conference, with teams of teacher's planning and developing actual productions. This project based learning environment afforded experiences with e-learning as well as actual meetings with fellow students and the sharing of projects and experiences with projects, which helped anchor the learning into a web-based community.

In this learner centred and project-based course, the communication strategies and scope of the production were be defined and argued for by the students based on their communications strategies for the production thus calling for reflection on the choices made in the production.

It further served to provide the prospective ICT-facilitators with an interpretive and hermeneutic perspective that may transfer into their own perceptions and future roles as catalysts for implementing a new learning paradigm involving the use of ICT within a reflexive pedagogical framework.

References:

Bruner, Jerome. (1996). *The culture of education.* Cambridge: Harvard University Press

Gardner, Howard (1993) *Multiple Intelligences. The Theory in Practice.* New York

Kolb (Ed.). (1984). *_Experiential Learning: experience as the source of learning and development.* New Jersey: Prentice-Hall

Tiller, Tom (2000) *Forskende partnerskab. Aktionsforskning og aktionslæring i skolen.* København. Kroghs Forlag.

The Impact of Technology and Distance Learning on Higher Education

Susan J. Goetz, Ed.D.
MAED via distance learning
The College of St. Catherine
United Stated
Sjgoetz@stkate.edu

Abstract: The promise of distance education to provide education programs that can be undertaken anywhere and at any time is not new. With the rapid advances in technology, higher education today can offer educational services where learners choose the services they need for their own educational and training needs. Higher education is presented with the choice of implementing and delivering quality models where each student receives an educational experience customized to his/her individual learning abilities versus a high-volume or quantity model where the information conveyed is directed to a non-specific, abstract student. In such a high-volume model, the variance among the individuals who constitute the class would have to be ignored. This paper discusses how institutions are resolving the quality-quantity trade-off in their distance-learning, technology-based educational programming while supporting a goal of effectively generating net revenues.

Introduction

The promise of distance education to provide education programs that can be undertaken anywhere and at any time is not new. Correspondence study programs were offered early in the 20th century with great enthusiasm, but they quickly faded from favor because they were perceived as designed around quantity rather than quality.

With the recent advances in technology, higher education today can offer educational programs where students choose the services they need and want for their own educational needs. Students can decide when and where they learn. However, higher education again must visit the choice of implementing and delivering quality programs where each student receives an educational experience customized to his or her individual learning abilities versus a high-volume, quantity programs where the information conveyed is directed to a non-specific, abstract student. In the high-volume model, the range of differences among the individuals who constitute the class would have to be ignored.

History of Correspondence Education

Before the Internet, the only ways to learn outside the classroom were enrolling in correspondence courses, watching educational videos, software designed around specific content, or self-study through reading books and journals. None provide frequent opportunities to interact with teachers and other students – the community building so evident in the classroom (Strehle, 2000).

With the introduction of the GI Bill after World War II in the United States, and an increasing emphasis upon the value of a college degree in the marketplace, student enrollments increased in colleges and universities. This had the effect of creating mass lecture courses, particularly in introductory classes. These mass lecture courses dramatically increased the number of students that could be reached, which severely sacrificed quality for the sake of quantity in higher education. This is a model of education that achieves substantial efficiency – if efficiency is measured in terms of cost per student – but it does so at the expense of quality. There are few teachers who would not tell you that it is virtually impossible to establish a relationship with each student in a large class. However, to compensate for increasing class sizes at the introductory level, students expected reduced class sizes in more advanced coursework. It was hoped that as they moved to higher grades, they would begin to experience small classes resembling seminars. Here efficiency would be sacrificed for quality, and relationship building could be recovered.

Today, however, as the cost of higher education increases more rapidly than public support for higher education, colleges and universities are faced with the necessity to both increase revenues from other sources and to become more cost-efficient. "Budget reductions and general resource constraints have become commonplace, while institutions are being asked to serve increasing numbers of students and constituencies" (Alexander, 2002, p. 1). Such pressures make it difficult for colleges and universities to cut down the size of their classes.

To help generate additional revenues, some colleges and universities are looking at distance education as a way to provide subject-matter experts who deliver programs using the latest technologies. However, if the underlying rationale for utilizing distance education is to generate significant financial revenues, distance learning is doomed to the same fate as correspondence education. Students who found it difficult to travel to specific sites at specified times for their education was attracted to correspondence education. Quality would be maintained through frequent written submissions that would be rigorously critiqued by the subject-matter expert. While such a model prevents student and teacher from meeting face-to-face, a relationship can be built upon frequent correspondence between learner and teacher. This model, as it was designed, proved to be too expensive and did not generate significant net revenues. The process required large amounts by the teacher spent critiquing the students' work. The model then evolved to one where the subject-matter expert designed the correspondence courses, but then turned them over to cheaper sources of labor such as graduate students, adjuncts, and instructors to facilitate the instruction. Even this model proved to be unsuccessful, however, as facilitators found the process too labor intensive. The students' work was not carefully and rigorously critiqued, no relationships were build and maintained, and the demand for correspondence education decreased significantly with a resulting decrease in net revenues generated from this source.

One can see that if distance education is designed with the same goal of generating significant revenues, its future may mirror the experience of correspondence education (Herema & Rogers, 2001).

Definition of Distance Education

Distance education as we know it today is a relatively new technology. Its major goal is to provide education to many kinds of populations, especially to some geographically distributed groups.

Distance education is emerging as a viable and vital force in educational delivery systems in recent years, especially in higher education. Much of the growth comes from a rapidly growing demand for educational opportunities directed toward and designed for some specific target groups (Garrison, 1986; 1987; Gaspar & Thompson, 1995). Just as Amundsen and Bernard (1989) pointed out, "…the definitive characteristic of distance education is the separation between 'teacher' and learner and among learners. As a result, interpersonal communication is not a natural characteristic of distance education" (p. 7). According to Gaspar and Thompson (1995), distance education integrates correspondence, instruction, use of periodicals and teaching aids, mass media, audiovisual lessons, social interactions, computer-assisted instruction, and various technologically-advanced formats. In the perspective of Keegan (1986), distance education has six major features: (a) the separation of teacher and learner, (b) the role of the educational organization, (c) the place of the technological medium, (d) two-way communication, (e) the separation of learner and the learning group, and (f) industrialization. In sum, distance education establishes a system that provides learning opportunities to various groups of learners who have no access to the traditional, higher education institutions.

In addition, according to Bates (1986), there are two basically different approaches of distance education. One is based on structured, pre-programmed learning materials and the other is based on the computers' communications functions. These two approaches have completely distinct philosophies of education. The former is called the black box approach. This approach views the computer as a black box to substitute for the traditional face-to-face (FtF) teacher. Therefore, it is the computer or black box that teaches the students. The frequent example is computer-assisted learning (CAL) software. The latter view is called networks approach. This approach views the computer as a channel of communication between learners and teachers. The frequent example is computer-mediated communication (CMC) systems. Therefore, it is the teacher who teaches the students, only with the computer as a channel of facilitating the two-way communication between teachers and students, online but at a distance and asynchronously. These two approaches are not mutually exclusive. They can be combined to become a powerful medium for distance education. Lauzon and Moore (1989) called the integration of these two approaches the fourth generation distance system that has no barriers of time and place.

The Demand for Distance Education

The diversity in America's higher education institutions has led to a wide variety of approaches to using electronic methods both to enhance on-campus learning and to provide distance learning. Although such on-campus uses are frequently a first priority, distance learning is still growing about 30 percent a year if measured by the number of students.

The development of new technologies is creating a revolution in education and training in the United States. Our on-campus students are already receiving information and educational materials for many of their courses through the Internet. They often communicate with teachers and fellow students by e-mail. Based on a recent survey, universities see technology for on-campus uses as a higher priority than distance learning. The two applications are, in fact, closely linked. The best of the on-campus programs provide a growing source of web-based materials for conversion to distance learning.

When one views the future for distance learning, one must make an assumption about the overall size of the higher education market. Glenn Strehle from the Massachusetts Institute of Technology recently posed the question: "do you believe that the total number of students will not be affected by the increased opportunities for receiving an education through distance learning? If you do, then any growth in distance learning must come from a reduction in the number of students learning in the classroom. Distance learning becomes a substitute for classroom learning." Strehle went on to say: "if, instead, you assume there is a global demand for learning that cannot be met by our campus-based universities, then you come to a different conclusion. Distance learning will increase the number of students and, as a result, enhance real economic growth and create a more educated population" (Strehle, 2000, p. 214).

Based on the number of students enrolled in courses, distance learning is growing at a rate of about 30 percent a year in the United States. A survey by the U.S. Department of Education reported there were about 55,000 distance learning courses with over 1.6 million students enrolled in our 1998 academic year. Since many students were taking more than one distance learning course, the number of actual students was about one-half that number. Looking at more recent estimates, the number of courses may be growing faster than the number of students. This is not surprising as many institutions, particularly public universities, are trying to offer a full curriculum of distance learning courses to be combined with their degree programs.

A survey shows that 90% of public four-year institutions were offering, or expected to offer, distance learning courses by next year. By contrast, only 41 percent of private institutions expected to do so, with many of the remainder being colleges with relatively small enrollments. There is a strong correlation between the size of an institution and its offering of distance learning courses. Ninety-five percent of those institutions with more than 10,000 students, both public and private, expected to be offering some distance learning courses by next year.

About 92 percent of the nation's distance learning students at the undergraduate level, including both four-year and two-year colleges, are taking their courses from a public institution. By contrast with only 8 percent at the undergraduate level, private institutions have 42 percent of the distance learning students at the graduate and professional level. Public institutions have the other 58 percent.

Highly selective private universities do not usually offer distance learning programs toward an undergraduate degree. Their faculties see the campus learning experience as particularly important, including the opportunity for learning in the laboratory. These universities, like MIT, have enhanced many on-campus courses with technology while limiting distance learning to selected graduate and non-degree programs.

There can be a difference in the way that technology is used for undergraduate and graduate education. Undergraduate distance learning programs mostly use text-based Internet delivery and are limited by the bandwidth into the homes of their students. By contrast, it is expected that graduate programs will take greater advantage of streaming video, synchronous two-way conferencing and other uses of broadband technology to create some aspects of the live classroom and seminar. Professional and graduate courses delivered at a distance are expected to grow rapidly. For many, the need to earn credit toward a degree will be less important than the need to develop competence in a subject within a minimum time and at the learner's convenience. Many of the students in graduate and professional courses have access to broadband technology at an institutional location or at their workplace (Strehle, 2000).

What Works in Distance Education

Learning at a distance is not easy for many students. The isolation from both the teacher and other students, the unfamiliar format and need to self-pace their learning can be discouraging. While we are aware of outstanding scholars and public leaders who were largely self-taught, we also recognize that this is very difficult for almost all of us. Motion pictures, television and videos were all predicted to have a major impact on education and found only limited success. Is on-line learning just the latest in a series of new technologies that will fail to meet the educational goals of its advocates? This may be true if we fail to develop frequent opportunities for interaction with the teacher and other students.

Most successful examples seem to have one common factor: the opportunity for students to feel they are part of a community of learners. One successful exception is those educational forms that permit the student to be interactive with the learning, although it is all on-line. Even with these tools, students have to be motivated to learn when using self-paced forms of delivery rather than the rigid schedules of on-campus courses (Strehle, 2000).

The academic performance of distance learning students, relative to on-campus students, provides some assurance that the learning is about the same as measured by tests. Learning at a distance may not be the best way to educate either the next generation of teachers and researchers or those that can benefit from the socializing experience of a campus. For a great many people, however, it is either distance learning or no learning. For others, the sacrifices involved in acquiring on-campus learning may be avoided at some benefit to both the learner and the learning. The search is to identify those methods of distance learning that are achieving success and seeing what works well and what doesn't. We need to bring our research rigor to understanding distance learning.

Summary and Conclusion

What is going to drive the development, growth, and change in distance learning? It will take careful planning with a goal first and foremost of providing quality education to the student. Planning by colleges and universities means responsive policy-making, working with faculty to develop positive attitudes toward distance learning and helping them to adopt the technology, listening to the reactions of the learners. If distance students show a marked preference for one form of delivery over another, there will be colleges and universities who will do it their way. If the free market works the way it was designed to work in the United States, then student attitudes, experiences, and innovation that leads to positive learning outcomes will determine the future of distance learning programs. And in order to create and maintain successful distance education, higher education institutions may have to include many of the techniques of successful businesses, including effective marketing, highly reliable distribution, quality assurance and the ability to quickly adopt what works and quickly drops what doesn't - in short, a focus on the customer rather than the supplier.

References

Alexander, F. K. (2002) Financing university performance in the United Kingdom and the United States, *The University: International Expectations,* McGill/Queen's University Press

Amundsen, C. L, & Bernard, R. M. (1989). Institutional support for peer contact in distance education: An empirical investigation. *Distance Education, 10* (1), 7-27.

Bates, T. (1986). Computer assisted learning or communications: Which way for information technology in distance education? *Journal of Distance Education,* 1 (1), 41-57.

Cerny, M. G. & Heines, J. M., Evaluating distance education across twelve time zones, Massachusetts Institute of Technology, Center for Advanced Educational Services, 2000.

Garrison, D. R. (1986). The role of technology. In R. G. Brockett (Ed.), *Continuing education in the year 2000* (pp.41-54). San Francisco: Jossey Bass.

Garrison, D. R. (1987). The role of technology in continuing education. *New Directions for Continuing Education*, 36, 41-53.

Gaspar, R. F., & Thompson, T. D. (1995). Current trends in distance education. *Journal of Interactive Instruction Development, 8* (2), 21-27.

Glass, Gene V (1976). Primary, secondary and meta-analysis. *Educational Researcher 5(10)*, 3-8.

Gottesman, B. & Jennings, J., Peer coaching for educators, Technomic Publishing Co., Lancaster, PA 1994.

Heerema, D. L. & Rogers, R. L., Avoiding the quality/quantity trade-off in distance education," *T.H.E. Journal*, Indiana University, Indianapolis. Dec. 2001.

Keegan, D. (1986). *The foundations of distance education*. Dover, New Hampshire: Croom Helm.

Lauzon, A. C., & Moore, G. A. B. (1989). A fourth generation distance education system: Integrating computer-assisted learning and computer conferencing. *The American Journal of Distance Education, 3* (1), 38-49.

Liv, Y. & Ginther, D., Cognitive styles and distance education, Department of Psychology and Special Education, Texas A & M University, 2002.

Strehle, G. P., Distance learning in America: how institutions and corporations are stimulating growth, MIT Center for Advanced Educational Services, September 26, 2000.

Io, Database Driven Web Art-Work

Nan Goggin and Joseph Squier
Narrative Media Program
School of Art and Design
University of Illinois @ Urbana-Champaign
n-goggin@uiuc.edu, j-squier@uiuc.edu

Abstract: Network-based electronic databases are finding expanded application in the worlds of research and commerce. But artists are increasingly putting this tool to new and unexpected uses. This is not a new phenomenon, but rather the latest iteration of a longstanding tradition of artists appropriating technology in unexpected ways. This paper will explain the database engine that drives a project titled *Io*, and discuss the implications of database technologies for future research into new storytelling forms as well as demonstrate the art piece.

io is based on a Greek myth in which a young maiden, who has attracted the amorous attention of Zeus, is punished by being transformed into a calf. She eventually regains her human form by using her hoof to scratch her name in the sand. The story deals with language and writing as fundamental traits of what is means to be human. The io project explores the boundary between consciousness and machine intelligence.The title refers back to the Greek myth of the same name. The piece is an image/text poem comprised of a database of single words, sentences, short paragraphs, images and sounds and a set of rules for analyzing the statements viewers write.

Intoduction

Network-based electronic databases are finding expanded application in the worlds of research and commerce. But artists are increasingly putting this tool to new and unexpected uses. This is not a new phenomenon, but rather the latest iteration of a longstanding tradition of artists appropriating technology in unexpected ways. This paper will explain the database engine that drives a project titled *Io*, and discuss the implications of database technologies for future research into new storytelling forms.

Database technologies hold much the same promise as earlier technologies from the 19th and 20th Centuries. After all, photography as an art form emerged from the discoveries of entrepreneurs intent on capturing the market for mass-produced realistic pictures. The moving image was born in the research laboratory, and was understood initially as simply an improved tool for scientific observation; that is until artists got their hands on the technology and invented the language that today we call cinema. Database technologies, in the hands of artists, may also yield new communication languages. More than just a container for cataloging inventory, customer information, or research data, networked databases have the potential for exploring new constructions and understandings of narrative and storytelling. This presentation will highlight one such example of artists and programmers working collaboratively to appropriate database technology for its poetic rather than its practical application.

Description

    io is based on a Greek myth in which a young maiden, who has attracted the amorous attention of Zeus, is punished by being transformed into a calf. She eventually regains her human form by using her hoof to scratch her name in the sand. The story deals with language and writing as fundamental traits of what is means to be human. The io project explores the boundary between consciousness and machine intelligence.artwork they were creating titled *Io*. The title refers back to the Greek myth of the same name. The piece is an image/text poem comprised of a database of single words, sentences, short paragraphs, images and sounds and a set of rules for analyzing the statements viewers write

    It's concept is an extension of a simple AI program called ELIZA, which was developed in 1967 by computer scientist Joseph Weisenbaum. In *Io,* unlike ELIZA, the inherent division between audience and author dissolves, and viewers enter into a creative collaboration with the machine." Therefore, *Io* brings us a step closer to realizing the concept of the cyborg; combining human consciousness with machine logic, it becomes part muse and part confidante. Professors Squier and Goggin saw *Io* as a journey into a world of memory and identity, dreams and desires, faith and trust, metaphors and fossil clues.

Project Background

    The original *Io* was written several years ago as a Java Applet, which constrained it's interaction and did not make use of current technical advances, We began by exploring the possibility of using programming as a "toolset" to create a better means for people to interact with a machine. At that time, it was only a text -based interactive system. We realized that we could replace the old Java Applet component of *Io* with a database using flat data files.

    Our shared interest was to re-design *Io* to communicate using several multimedia elements. Together we devised plans to allow *Io* to respond to particular words typed by the viewer, or to allow the viewer to select text from the screen. We also decided that the user should be given a set of options for viewing the information. *Io* became a platform for inventing a rich interactive system utilizing new technologies. Conceived as a web-based image/text/sound hybrid, the *Io* project explores the boundary between machine intelligence and human consciousness. Utilizing simple artificial intelligence and database concepts, *Io* has been constructed to accept keyboard input and can recognize and respond to a vocabulary of keywords. Each user elicits a different 'performance' of *Io*, creating a multimedia collage of poetic text fragments, images, and audio clips. The resulting narrative addresses issues situated at the frontier dividing flesh and machine: history, memory, vision, and desire.

Project Process

Io involves storage of and access to hundreds of data files—word, text, image and sound files. Each of these data formats are quite different, which means that Io must be able to communicate across these file formats so that it can retrieve, display and update the files quickly. Therefore, scalability and flexibility of software became the most important criteria for selecting our system architecture. MySQL + PHP + Flash was our third architecture model, and became the choice we decided to integrate.

Programs used: Mysql, PHP, Flash, Photoshop, Soundedit,
Hardware: Macintosh g4, Dell

But how does this model work? (a sample scenario)

When a user opens Io [image1: front page] and types a keyword into the input box, {image: interface input box] this word is sent back to the server. This triggers a PHP file named 'readIO.php'. This file checks whether the word is in the database system. It executes a query to repeatedly search for this word in a table. If it finds the word, the PHP file will return a true statement, otherwise it will return as false. If a false value is returned, an error message will be sent back to Io to inform the user that Io cannot understand the word, and the user will be asked to try another word. [image of Io not understanding the word] If a true value is returned, the PHP file will find the corresponding text for that word and temporarily store it in a variable. It then searches for any corresponding images and sounds. Because the image and sound data files are located on the web server rather than in the table, the database merely stores a url pointing the PHP file to the correct file on the web server. All this information, as well as the x and y coordinates for where to place the image, is sent back to Io for display in a browser. As long as the Io gets this message package, it will call upon it's many different functions to show text, display image and play sound.

After finalizing our choice of a system architecture by choosing MySQL as the DBMS for the Io project and with the scripting language being MySQL; we were ready to create the database organization.

Xi Zhang created totally 6 tables in which he labeled 'ww', 'wi', 'ws', 'il' and 'userinfo' respectively. Table below shows the function and schema of different database tables.
. ww was used for storing text information for each keyword
        fields: keyWord, outputWord, i

. wi used for storing image url pinter information for each keyword
fields: keyWord, outputImage, imageType, i

. ws used for storing sound url pointer information for each keyword
        fields: keyWord, outputSound, i

. il used for storing xy coordinate values for different image type
        fields: imageType, x1, y1, x2, y2, x3, y3, x4, y4, x5, y5, x6,
y6, x7, y7

. userinfo was used for storing users's profile
fields: userID, userName, userPass, lastAccess, lastText, userEmail, isNew

PHP accesses these tables and how they relate to each other. For each PHP scripting file, there are a total of 8 files that sit on the server waiting to process incoming requests and output them as Flash files. The 8 type files are:serverCheck.PHP, readUser.PHP, checkUser.PHP, registrateUser.PHP, emailUser.PHP, readIO.PHP and logoutUser.PHP.

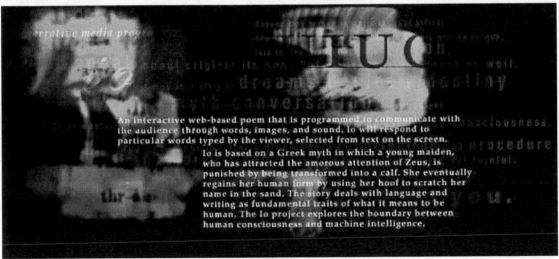

art work: io
artists: joseph squier, nan goggin, xi zhang, eunah kang
url: 128.174.50.18/io/download/html

The Collaborative Study in the Virtual Classroom, Some Practices in Distant Learning Carried Out in a Mexican Public University: Universidad Autónoma Metropolitana-Azcapotzalco (UAM-A), México City.

María Dolores González-Martínez
mdgm@correo.azc.uam.mx
Tatiana Sorókina
t_sorokina@hotmail.com
Miguel Ángel Herrera-Batista
mherrera@correo.azc.uam.mx
Universidad Autónoma Metropolitana
Campus Azcapotzalco, México City

Abstract: We discuss the results of two e-learning experimental courses carried out in Mexico City which are a part of a research project whose goals are: to experience the teaching learning process through the electronic media via Internet. We worked focused on collaborative working and learning with new pedagogical models based on directed group work by means of assignments, goals, questions and problem solving. Some students manifested anguish as a result of the absence of face-to-face professors; there were differences in personalities, participation and collaboration, aspects that will have to be taken into account for future courses. The conclusion is collaborative work among participants must be promoted, not only letting everybody's interventions to be displayed but also encouraging participants to converse about these courses in public working together in solving problems, elaborating team projects, including evaluating each other.

Introduction

After the second half of Twenty century problems in educational systems were perceived. Specialists in the subject started to articulate with more emphasis the low effectiveness related to the teacher-centered classes. At the same time, the educational theories were in search of methods and new practices primordially oriented towards a more personalized process of teaching learning, in which the students take the initiative of their own learning. With these goals in mind, the digitalized technology was considered adequate for the innovative education.

Nowadays the cyberspace offers on one hand, the individualized process of teaching learning; on the other, allows the development of certain skills of study and work in group. In the past, an expert professor used to meet these same goals in a traditional setting (a live class, for example), however, the current *modus vivendi* demands to exchange the chalk and blackboard for a different tool; that is to transform the theoretical-conceptual frame and the pedagogic practice. With these modifications, a number of aspects in the learning process will be possible to change, giving as a result a new educative experience.

The use of technology by faculty members

In our university we find a number of middle age professors who avoid the use of computing and Internet systems. The possible reasons are the insufficient amount of computers on campus and the lack of cyber culture among this age group. Besides, the current system of information on campus is still using printed handouts to give instruction to its members. Trying to promote cultural changes in the way of communication in the academic system, a group of professors from UAM-A in the Design Department in collaboration with Humanities Department, started to develop courses in an experimental manner in order to implement changes in the professors' abilities and attitudes. The first one, cost free, was the training of professors in the area of design education via Internet, form April to August 2001. The objectives of the course were: to test the distant learning model and to experience the teaching learning process through the electronic media, to develop the necessary skills to utilize the Internet' s main tools: navigators, e-mail, FTP, distribution lists, chats and navigation browsers; to let the students know the basic characteristics of the computer systems and the necessary electronic infrastructure to access to the Internet. For this experience a limited private web page Discussion Forum was opened, in which the work plan, the location of the reading material and the modalities of participation where annotated. The most difficult aspect was the monitoring of the participants and activities. After four weeks of the course initiation, a decrease in participation was noted. It was necessary to apply the participants a survey to investigate the cause. Technical problems in the professors' offices' computers discouraged the participants from regularly attend in the class. The desertion rate was high, which probably is an indicator of the lack of interest for the use of computers. Other problems inside the campus facilities were related to the system and connections, lack of adequate browser versions, and some associated with a lack of knowledge of the system itself. The students manifested anguish as a result of the absence of face-to-face professors who usually push them to fulfill their obligations and to turn in papers in a given deadline. It is necessary to continue insisting that professors and mentors direct attention to each student in Mexico; to know why someone is behind, to answer all their e- mail messages, to stimulate those who are dropped the class and to pay attention to the causes of desertion. In spite of that, the results were encouraging in the sense that professors became aware of the need to face changes in the way of working and studying. It is desirable to repeat the experience with participants who come from other distant institutions or places and who will have to pay a fee for the course to see if the results of the experiment change.

Teaching face to face with online support

The second experimental course was about reading and written expression. This course, which lasted from September to December 2001, was addressed to graduate students of design. In an experimental manner the participant professors tried to monitor the students, their attitudes and performance through two forms of deliver courses: the traditional one and the e-learning. Our goal was to explore the possibilities to integrate both; to develop an application of the pedagogical model, which was proposed by our research team in which some part was delivery face to face but count on the support of a virtual classroom. We did it with the *Blackboard* software (www.blackboard.com) in its free version. This software is an e-learning environment with technical infrastructure and various means of academic support that link technology and pedagogy, such as chat, discussion forum, links to web sites, a place to offer the course material and evaluations and statistics of participation. *Blackboard* constitutes one more working option for the e-courses proposed within our group as an element of communication and feedback for students. During the month of December a collaborative practice was made with the purpose of trying to unify the students' opinion about specific and important subjects for the class. The class contribution for team of professors was the experience of an e-class formed by a significant number of students with specific assignments; where differences in personalities, participation and collaboration, creativity, enthusiasm and state of mind were observed.

Trying collaborative working on the virtual environment

Finally, during the period from January through March 2002, we worked in the preparation of the course *Introduction to the e-study in the Improving of Professors,* which took place between June and August. We practice with another e-environment: *Nicenet* software (www.nicenet.org*),* also free, more limited than *Blackboard*, nevertheless more agile and faster. The collaborative effort among professors to create the course has been quite arduous. We have tried first individual work that later will be reviewed by other members of the team who will subsequently contribute with comments and/or changes to the original text. The first sessions ended up in almost total disagreement. After long hours of discussion and the exchange of texts through the e-mail we thought the work was progressing.

Practice showed that we need to develop certain aptitudes and abilities that in each culture are revealed differently. In our case what is important was the presence of the virtual counselor (conceptually different of the traditional trainer) during all the period, therefore emerged the need of share out the content of the course and that each one of the teachers take the responsibility of their part but maintaining the interaction in all the activities; for example: in the interventions of the forum, in the epistolary exchange, with link suggestions, etc. In this step is precisely when the exigency of the collaborative work between the teachers was expressed.

In particular, Faculty should remain in mutual collaboration with students and among themselves. In this way students get involved and participate actively in their learning management. If we understand the management as a set of processes, actions and procedures aimed to fulfill a number of determined objectives, we could talk about formative self-management. In a distant course the collaborative work among participants must be promoted, not only letting everybody's interventions to be displayed but also encourage participants to opine about these courses in public. Other additional collaborative activities may be working together in solving problems, elaborating team projects, debating subjects democratically, including evaluating each other and learning from the process.

From a cognitive point of view, propitiating the unbalance of the individual's mental models will generate the necessary conditions for learning. Such unbalance may be generated by confronting the individual with two options related to the use of computers: databases supported by hypertext and the synchronic or asynchronic interaction assisted by computer. The former is constituted by the databases supported by the hypertext, such as elibraries, interactive educational material, simulators, on line courses, etc. It is also necessary to pay attention to the need to create new writing systems, which allow a more dynamic reading to get to more amount of information.

Our project is focused on the synchronic or asynchronic interaction assisted by computer to exchange knowledge and dialogue with other members of the class through e-mail, discussion groups, video links, etc. These practices allow to enrich the learning experience in a significant manner since they stimulate not only the acquisition of factual knowledge but also emphasize the e- interacting in remote places which facilitates the sharing of common goals.

Conclusions

Our discussion centers on the question: how can we establish a collaborative environment? Some possible answers are making the individual work of students stronger, overcoming isolation, characteristic of crowded live courses, promoting the construction of learning with pedagogical models based on directed group work by means of assignments, goals, questions and problem solving. All these learning activities are based in the principle of learning as a permanent process. Knowledge is acquired in the social process of interaction; the active experience empowers learning. However, it is necessary to evaluate each member of the class to prove that learning has taken place. We have been working on this aspect of distant learning and we hope to organize the last experimental course and from here to draw some conclusions.

References

Delacôte, Goéry (1998). *Enseñar y aprender con nuevos métodos. La revolución cultural de la era electrónica*. Barcelona, Gedisa.

Landow, George P. (1992). *Hypertext. The convergence of contemporary critical theory and technology*. Baltimore & London, The Johns Hopkins University Press.

McLuhan, Marshall (1994). *Understanding Media. The extensions of Man*. Massachusetts Institute of Technology.

Negroponte, Nicholas (1995). Ser digital. México, Océano.

Palloff, Rena M. & Pratt, Keith (1999). *Building Learning Communities in Cyberspace. Effective Strategies for the online classroom*. San Francisco, Jossey-Bass Publishers.

Spiller, Neil (ed.) (2002). Cyber_Reader. Critical writings for the digital era. London, Phaidon Press.

Conquering the Digital Divide in Higher Education Attitudes

Valerie Kesner Greenberg
Communication Arts
University of the Incarnate Word
United States
Greenber@universe.uiwtx.edu

Abstract: Defining the digital divide as an important civil rights issue goes beyond social science to make a political and moral statement about the role communications technology plays in fostering a more inclusive and egalitarian America. Students with a good sense of Internet Literacy and who have Internet access, are able to effectively engage in the global village through access to the global economy, meaningful participation in political discourse, and interaction in a social way within the global village. People who refuse to embrace and use computers with Internet access risk being left behind, disconnected from the global village, the political process, and the global, information-driven, market economy. University faculty are primary change agents for inclusion of the Internet in American society, yet many are hesitant to embrace its use in their own classrooms. This paper is a report of a qualitative study which examines the causes for faculty negative attitudes towards technology inclusion in the classroom.

Introduction

Research has shown that a person's beliefs in their own achievement possibilities determine an individual's success in learning. This key personal variable is *self-efficacy* or belief in oneself to achieve goals. Self-efficacy can influence such achievement behaviors as choice of tasks, effort, persistence, and performance. Compared with learners who doubt their capabilities, efficacious students are more likely to engage in tasks, expend effort, persist to overcome difficulties, and perform at higher levels (Bandura, 1997; Pajares, 1995; Schunk, 1996; Zimmerman, 1994).

Within our fields we are experts and as such have an easy attitude towards learning our subject matter. But when the roles are reversed, and we become novices, then the playing field becomes more difficult.

Although research on general skills (e.g., problem solving and decision making) has a long history in cognitive psychology, the study of expertise within a very specific problem domain (e.g., chess, medical diagnosis) is a relatively new research area. A large portion of this work is descriptive; that is, expert behavior is described and often compared to novice behavior. Glaser (1996) summarize characteristics of expertise that are robust and generalizable across a variety of domains:

Teaching recognition of the role differences between experts and novices can help ease expert professors into the unappetizing role of novice learners of technology incorporation into their classrooms.

Learner's beliefs in their efficacy can be enhanced in several ways. One of the most powerful ways is through mastering challenges. A resilient sense of efficacy requires experience in overcoming obstacles through persevering efforts. Another source is through vicarious experiences. Social modeling serves as a way of building a sense of efficacy. Competent models transmit knowledge, skills, and strategies for managing environmental demands. Seeing people similar to oneself succeed by sustained effort raises the observers' beliefs in their own capability.

The third way is through social persuasion-- that is structuring learning activities for learners in ways that bring success and do not place them prematurely in situations where they are likely to fail. Social persuasion can also increase efficacy through correction of negative perceptions concerning subject matter.

Combining these methods might help to provide a classroom atmosphere conducive to a learning experience filled with grace and ease and most especially the intake of knowledge and skills.

Personal variables and environments also affect one another. According to Bandura (1986), human functioning comprises a series of reciprocal interactions between behavioral, environmental, and personal

variables. When learners with high self-efficacy try to complete an academic task in a distracting environment they may increase their concentration (personal variable) to make the environment less distracting. This type of personal influence has been described as *volitional control*
(Corno & Kanfer, 1993)

Perhaps faculty who have experiences other than excellent with technology have personal influence variables which cause them to think more practically about the integration of technology into their teaching methodologies.

The Study

Six faculty members from liberal arts disciplines at two universities were interviewed concerning attitudes towards incorporation of technology into their classrooms. Instructors ranked from assistant professors to full professors between the ages of 32 and 65 . Some had attended several classes in technology incorporation into the classroom while others had not attended any yet. Some instructors used technology (defined as electronic teaching materials or assignments which included overhead transparencies, online projection systems, Internet research tools, web bas ed postings and chats, and the electronic learning service, Blackboard) heavily-- on a daily basis, while one instructor had never used any of these devices. Most used technology moderately to replace previous versions of non electronic instructional tools, such as paper hand-outs.

Findings

From interviews and observations conclusions were drawn as to the extent and nature of faculty avoidance of technology use. For many, the increased effort necessary to incorporate technology into their class room did not equate to the amount of noticeable improvement in student learning and interaction with presented materials. F says that after spending many hours posting material normally presented as hard copy handouts, his students told him that they preferred the non electronic version of the material. Many faculty declined workshops or tutorials based on anxiety concerns with appearing inexperienced or foolish in their classrooms, a domain in which they normally are the "expert". Experts and novices learn in different fashions, thus feeling inexperienced at mastering new material felt uneasy to the instructors. C states that many faculty in the blackboard (electronic learning environment) workshops she teaches express a fear of failure and avoidance of domains other than their own subject manner of which they are expert, " What is really interesting is that in a sense this is a real role reversal . Here they are the expert in their field, they have a doctorate, they know their fields backwards and forwards. Usually, it has been a long time since they have been in school. And now they are in a class where they know very little. It can totally overwhelm someone."

No wonder then, that a novice in the field of teaching with technology might experience overwhelming feelings of defeat when trying to incorporate the necessary skills to radically change teaching habits.

Novice technology users teaching in the classroom begin to experience a role reversal or what G referred to as "walking in our students' shoes" with feelings of helplessness and sensations of being overwhelmed with incompetence and low skill abilities to complete assigned tasks.

Conclusions

In order to gain the self confidence necessary to believe that one can absorb and effectively complete the "how" of any learning goal, a student must obtain high levels of self-efficacy necessary to succeed in completion of the task.

Our level of self-efficacy influences the choices we make, the effort we put forth, how long we persist when we confront obstacles and how we feel if we fail.

Belief in one's personal efficacy spurs our actions. Unless people believe that they can produce desired effects by their actions, they have little confidence that they will achieve their goal. Self-efficacy buffers the learner's disappointments with failure and provides an unshakable belief in their personal efficacy and a firm belief in the worth of what they are doing. This powerful internal resource enables them to withstand adversity. The slow inclusion of paced innovative additions to classroom technology can help instructors overcome fears of being non-expert. As more technology is placed within their teaching regime, a comfortable level and sense of what is appropriate for their teaching style and what is inconsequential should emerge, raising confidence levels. As confidence is increased, so is usage. When instructors feel competent with the value and competence of their skill level they will begin to model and encourage use among their students of the tools necessary to begin bridging the digital divide.

References

Anderson, Cheryl. Interview. *University of the Incarnate Word, April 1 , 2002*

Bandura, Albert. "Perceived Self-Efficacy in Cognitive Development and Functioning." Educational Psychologist 28.2 (1993): 117-148.

Baxter, Gail P., Anastasia D. Elder, and Robert Glaser. "Knowledge-Based Cognition and Performance Assessment in the Science Classroom." Educational Psychologist 31.2 (1996): 133-140.

Pajares, Frank, and John K. Bengston. "The Psychologizing of Teacher Education: Formalist Thinking and Preservice Teachers' Beliefs." PJE. Peabody Journal of Education 70.3 (1995): 83-98.

Dale H. Schunk, and Barry J. Zimmerman, eds. Self-Regulation of Learning and Performance: Issues and Educational Applications. Hillsdale, NJ: Lawrence Erlbaum Associates, 1994.

Schunk, Dale H., and Barry J. Zimmerman. "Social Origins of Self-Regulatory Competence." Educational Psychologist 32.4 (1997): 195-208.

Sweany, Noelle. Interview. *University of the Incarnate Word,* May 1, 2002.

Wicker, Frank. Interview. *University of Texas at Austin,* May 15, 2002.

Multimedia Instruccional Design *VS* Learning Objects Development
A dynamic process of educational content creation in Open and Distance Learning

Albert Sangrà, Academic director and Director of Edu Lab (UOC)
Lourdes Guàrdia, Director of Multimedia Instructional Design Dp. (UOC)
Francesc Santanach; Multimedia Instructional Designer and computer engineer (UOC)
Xavier Mas; Multimedia Instructional Designer (UOC)
Universitat Oberta de Catalunya, Avda.Tibidabo, 39-43, E-08035 Barcelona
Tel: 34-932532300   http://www.uoc.es

The role of Multimedia Instructional Design (MID) applied to the new information and communication technologies substantially changes in those teaching and learning models based on Open and Distance Learning.

> An intrinsic link exists between instructional design (ID) and open distance learning (ODL). Their inextricability in the real world raises specific problems of interest in the field of ID. In no other teaching/learning situation is ID essential as in ODL. The conditions of ODL make it a necessity to have long-term instructional planning, cost, analysis, curriculum and course development, instructional materials development and maintenance, delivery plans, and detailed evaluation rules. Without all of these components, DL simply could not happen. It took some time for this necessity to be acknowledged, as can be seen in the history of ODL. (Bourdeau, J. and Bates, T.)

The term *Instructional Design* is usually used to describe the process in which:

- the learning needs and the environment where they will manifest are analysed;
- training needs are defined;
- the most appropriate resources regarding the learning processes are chosen:
- contents and activities are developed;
- evaluation is designed.

However, this concept becomes much wider when referring to ODL. We are nowadays facing the challenge of making good use of the possibilities of multimedia technologies in order to offer much more significant learning than those which traditional educational materials would facilitate; so, it is necessary to take into account all the elements intervening in the instructional design of a concrete training action for ODL. In that sense, the coherence of the materials and the teaching strategy, together with the functionalities of the virtual environment and the relations that will be developed will be fundamental.

Gillespie (1995) recently contented that a well-designed piece of courseware should incorporate the most appropriate aspects of each learning theory (Phillips, R.):

> This is what we as instruction and learning environment designers ought to be striving for, using our expertise and knowledge of behaviourist, cognitive, and constructivist learning theory to combine with expertise in other disciplines (multimedia, human factors, systems engineering, telecommunications, etc.) to design and deliver the most appropriate solutions for our performance improvement and learning situations.

The ideal piece of courseware incorporates the most appropriate parts of both theories, and the balance will be different for every application.

Our experience in distance learning has shown us how important it is to have well structured materials which are designed from a pedagogical point of view, and keeping in mind what, how and when we want to teach or encourage learning.

Dr. Michael Moore -the president of American Center for the Study of Distance Education (ACSDE)- said in his last conference, in June 2001, in Barcelona (at UOC) *"It's necessary to invest more in design than in technology...the learning outcomes are related also to design of the course and the tutor's support"*

This implies training the authors (usually specialists in a field of science or other areas of study) in how to elaborate teaching material for distance learning.

Thus, some professors may need to expand their own material or prepare new one. This implies, again a training task, centred not only in the understanding of the distance teaching-learning process, but also in the knowledge of resources and tools to make the elaboration of material easier.

This need will force many distance learning institutions to plan the creation of tools which allow tutoring and continuous training for teachers and authors; so that learning objectives in an ODL model in which technology brings us new opportunities, are fully guaranteed.

In our case, at Universitat Oberta de Catalunya (UOC), the ARM (Methodological Resources Assistant) was created to answer the above mentioned needs.

1. What is the ARM?

The ARM is a system for the design and elaboration of methodological resources adapted to different objectives and training needs, in a virtual learning environment.

Its aim is to provide a wide range of distance learning methodological resources as well as tools to facilitate material creation, for professors and authors.

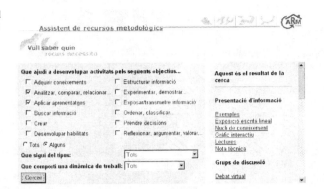

2. What can be found there?

The ARM enables:

- Looking for resources: The user can carry out resource or activity type searches from different criteria using a very simple and intuitive interface.
- Accessing to a concrete resource report by selecting its name.
- Acquiring ideas/Offering ideas. This is a project open to all the new incoming resources and activities that may appear with new needs.
- Consulting methodological aspects.
- Creating instructional activities.
- Giving guidelines or advice of pedagogical use

See in detail each chapter:

- Looking for resources

The user can carry out resource or activity type searches from different criteria using a very simple and intuitive interface. The route that takes the users to the resources that would best fit their needs depends on the desired objectives, the kind of activity and the work dynamics they prefer.

- Accessing to a concrete resource report by selecting its name

Every resource report provides information about the typology or category that the resource belongs to, the goals that can be reached with it or the activity given; the resource description – structure, stages, functioning, etc.; the application – guidelines or directions to improve the possibilities the resource offers; the work dynamics to follow; the view of concrete examples; the elaboration guidelines for the resource; the bibliography reference; and templates and programs to create resources easier.

- Acquiring ideas/Offering ideas

Our idea is to fulfil the potential users' needs in advance. This is a project open to all the new incoming resources and activities that may appear with new needs.

This is why we offer a double use: you can access ARM knowing what you want, and therefore going directly to a concrete resource or you may access to look for new ideas. Every resource has got concrete examples that will help you to decide what you want.

- Consulting methodological aspects.

The functional ARM includes important aspects such as strategy offers to teachers and authors in order to define goals, select contents, make guidelines for material, follow style indications, etc. You can access to ARM methodological contents in various ways: as a course to be followed or as a consulting space for concrete questions.

- Creating activities: the programs and templates

ARM objectives are not only to select resources but to facilitate the creation of new activities. In order to achieve it when choosing a resource, we can access to a template in the shape of a form or other systems, where the necessary steps to create an activity would be given.

Once the form has been filled in, you can print it out and save the written content before being sent to a general database where the technicians in charge of the activity of implementation would give it the corresponding format.

There is a double aim behind these programs and templates. On the one hand, their aim is to help in creating new activities, and on the other hand, to facilitate their later implementation, given that the model's goal is to ensure that every requirement is met for later implementation.

- Giving guidelines or advice of use

We can access the assistant knowing which resource we are looking for and then obtain some guidelines or advice on how to use it in distance learning. Thus, there is a report for every resource with this kind of advice.

3. What is its structure?

The ARM is structured as a system composed of different elements:

- A communication space (forum, FAQs, consulting mailbox...)

In this space the users find a forum and a mailbox for asking questions about or giving their opinion on what ARM provides.

- Help or Guidance about methodological aspects

It helps methodological design explaining, for example, what we are referring to when talking about objectives, how to take decisions about what resources to use, how the learning guide is structured, what is evaluation and how to treat it.

- The searching form

The searching form is the tool that helps the professor or the author to know the best resource features for their material elaboration. The result of the searches is a list of the resources that best suit the user's requirements.

- The resource reports

From the result list you can access to the resource reports, which include the previously mentioned sections. The main aspects are the guidelines for resource elaboration, the examples and the elaboration templates and tool that make the process easier for the author.

> The recent growth of the field of interactive multimedia may be attributed in part to the availability of courseware authoring, which gives the course-ware developer who has no expertise in programming in high–level languages the ability to control the full range of presentation functions.(Inglis, A., Ling, P. and Joosten, V.)

4. What's the future?

After working in this system of design for the last two years, we are just starting and adding a new concept of how to conceptualise learning materials in terms of educational knowledge management (EKM). In this sense, the instructional design is based on learning objects and consists in structuring the educational contents thinking of the interactions between users profile, learning resources and the virtual environment.

Also the EKM tries to consider the artificial intelligence techniques in order to get information about students previous knowledge and to assure the interactions between the learning objects, learners and teaching staff offering learning resources, strategies, and contents that the students may need. An analytical model of teachers' cognitive-interactional activities within an experimental reflective teaching situation would be an interesting research to do.

> In order to carry out educational activities successfully, teachers need to draw on a wide variety of knowledge, such as students' knowledge, the curriculum, teaching methods, classroom organisation, educational goals, and subject matter… we focus on the nature of teacher's knowledge of student's knowledge and on the understanding how teachers acquire it in a form that is appropriate to the specific activity in which they are engaged. (1999, Lund, K. Baker, M.)

The EKM system that our institution is planning to implement has a determinant impact in the creation and edition of learning materials, concerning the optimisation and agility of the process, as much as the increase in the security.

Our interest focuses on assuring the structure of the materials and their pedagogical adequacy, lessening production times and guaranteeing that the original work from authors is being delivered in the best condition.

This is the reason why we need to design certain processes and tools which allow us to reach the stated objectives, by generating contents according to the knowledge management system (standardised –tested- and innovative elements) and that which can be presented on different support systems.

The organising axis of all this is the Methodological Resources Assistant, a pedagogical portal for any educational development of the institution that facilitates all the necessary information, tools and guidance for the creation of learning and teaching resources.

See the graphic below:

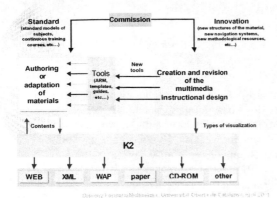

With the creation of this tool, the Knowledge Management system and the constant work as instructional designers in UOC – an institution offering total virtual training – we may firmly contribute to the evolution of the concept of instructional design as a guarantee of pedagogical innovation in learning processes in ODL.

Bibliography

Bates, T.; Bourdeau, J.(1996). "Instructional Design for Distance Learning". *Journal of Science Education and Technology* (Vol. 5, núm. 4).

Edu Lab Documents. The contribution of the Universitat Oberta de Catalunya to the ICDE. Vienna, June 1999. 19th World congress of the International Council for Open and Distance Education (ICDE)

Guàrdia, L *El diseny formatiu: un nou enfocament de diseny pedagògic dels materials didàctics en suport digital.* Duart. J.M., Sangrà. A. (eds) Aprenentatge i virtualitat. Disseny pedagògic de materials didàctics per al WWW. Ediuoc i Pòrtic, Barcelona, 1999

Hall, B. (1997) *Designing courses for the web.* Web-Based Training Cookbook Wiley Computer Publishing,

Hannafin M.. *Designing Resource-Based Learning and Performance Support Systems*

Hill, J. R. (2000). Web-based instruction: Prospects and challenges. In R. M. Branch & M. A. Fitzgerald (Eds.). *Educational Media and Technology Yearbook*

Inglis, A.; Ling, P.; Joosten, V. (1999). "Delivering Digitally. Managing the Transition to the Knowledge Media". London: Kogan Page Limited

Lajoie, S.; Vivet, M. (Eds). (1999). Lund, K. *Teachers' collaborative interpretations of students' computer-mediated collaborative problem solving interactions.* "Artificial intelligence in education. Open Learning Environments: New Computational Technologies to Support Learning, Exploration and Collaboration." The 9th international conference on artificial intelligence education (AA-FD'99), IOS Press, Ohmsha

Merrill, M. D. (1994). *Instructional Design Theory.* Englewood Cliffs: Educational Technology Publications.

Phillips, R. (1997). "The Developer's Handbook to Interactive Multimedia. A practical guide for educational applications". London: Kogan Page Limited

Ritchie, D.; Hoffman, B. *'Web-Based Instruction*. Educational Technology Publications 1997
Rowntree, D. (1994). "Preparing Materials for Open, Distance and Flexible Learning. London: Kogan Page Limited

Wilson, B.; Ryder M. (1998). "Dynamic Learning Communities: an alternative to Designed Instructional Systems". Denver: University of Colorado.

Links

Bren Wilson home page (professor in information and learning technologies (ILT) at the University of Colorado at Denver)

http://carbon.cudenver.edu/%7Ebwilson/index.html

Web-Based Instruction Examples

http://www.wested.org/tie/dlrn/examples.html

The American Center for the Study of Distance Education (ACSDE)

http://www.ed.psu.edu/acsde/aboutacsde.asp

International Council of Distance Education

http://www.icde.org

Course Development for Distance Learning Using PowerPoint

This paper describes the process and procedures for the development of a distance learning course using PowerPoint as the design software.

Multimedia and Distance Learning for Business in Borovichi, Russia funded by the United States Department of State was a grant to provide course materials for Russian business education. These materials were developed by individuals from Broome Community College, in Binghamton, NY and the American - Russian College of Commerce "InterBiz," in Borovichi, Russia. The materials used in the demonstration course were developed by faculty members at Broome Community College (BCC) in Binghamton, N. Y. Anne Blakeslee, Professor of Business at BCC (Blakeslee_a@sunybroome.edu), was responsible for course content; while Alice McNeely, Director of the Teaching Resource Center (mcneely_a@sunybroome.edu), and myself, George Guba, Multimedia Instructional Designer, organized and designed the technical aspects of the project.

The grant required the trainers from Broome Community College and the instructors from Interbiz College in Borovichi, Russia to develop distance learning courses that could be delivered via the Internet, a computer network, or via CD-ROM. An additional requirement was that the materials be convertible to HTML. PowerPoint was chosen because it was available to the grant participants in both locations. It met the requirements for potential tools to: provide the required means of delivery, be available to the Russian instructors, be available in Russian language software, be easy to use, and have a relatively low learning curve.

The sample course, Small Business Marketing, was designed to be instructor paced, with the lectures and most of the supporting materials contained within the course on the CD-ROM. Some of the examples used were selected to fit the Russian culture and included case studies of businesses in Borovichi. The material on the CD- ROM was also designed to coordinate with an available Russian language textbook. The pluses and minuses of the software will be discussed along with course and template design and evaluation.

Contact with the course's instructor was designed to be flexible based on the accessibility, needs and abilities of the students. The course was designed for multiple means of delivery to meet student needs. The content was designed to allow for the possibility of delivery via multiple channels including the Internet, computer networks, CD-ROM, and print.

An Evaluation of an On-line Anatomy Course by Lab Instructors: Building on Instructional Design

Guo, X
Faculty of Kinesiology
University of Calgary
Canada

Katz, L.
Faculty of Kinesiology
University of Calgary
Canada
Email: katz@ucalgary.ca

Maitland, M.
School of Physical Therapy
University of South Florida
United States

Abstract: On-line learning is becoming more popular and realistic with the development of distributed network technology. However, the methods that take advantage of technology and integrate on-line learning into conventional classroom teaching remain controversial. Laboratory instructors evaluated an on-line anatomy lab course at the University of Calgary through questionnaires and direct interviews. Four lab instructors and one professor participated in this study. Results showed that to effectively integrate technology into the curriculum, it was perceived by the instructors as important to set clear teaching objectives, an appropriate amount and depth of information for the level of the students, and teaching strategies related to students' learning style and motivation. Laboratory instructors felt that the dynamic and interactive 3-D animation was motivating for students.

The Study

With the development of distributed internet technology, on-line learning is becoming more prevalent. However, the methods that can take advantage of the internet and integrate it with conventional classroom teaching remain controversial.

There are potential benefits of the Internet for teaching students. The Web:

- is a flexible, dynamic learning environment (Hackbarth, 1997; Ross, 2000)
- allows for multimedia presentations (Palloff & Pratt, 1999; Ross, 2000)
- provides students with access to a potentially rich, collaborative, and powerful learning environment (McGreal, 1997; Ross, 2000).

Kulik's (1994) meta-analysis of the findings of 97 studies on effectiveness of computer-based instructions concluded that students usually learn more in classes that received computer-based instructions, especially in elementary and high school.

However, there are many reports of ineffective distance on-line learning programs (Horton, 1999). Technological possibilities do not automatically transfer into effective teaching and learning (Loveless, 1996; Zhao, 1999). Designing and delivering instruction on the web requires thoughtful analysis and investigation of how to use the Web's potential in concert with instructional design principles (Ritchie & Hoffman, 1997).

There does not appear to be a consensus about the best method to evaluate on-line learning. Traditional evaluation models have concentrated on the empirical and quantitative procedures (Stufflebeam & Shinkfield, 1985; Worthen & Sanders, 1987; Simonsen, 1997). More recently, evaluators of distance

8/27/200211:57 PM

education programs have begun to propose qualitative models incorporated with naturalistic methodologies from more holistic perspectives.

Therefore, a qualitative study of the on-line anatomy lab course in the University of Calgary was conducted from the perspective of instructional design and teaching strategy. The on-line anatomy lab course, which was incorporated into the Kinesiology curriculum, was designed to offer students a wide range of learning media to supplement their study. The website of the program is: www.kin.ucalgary.ca/anatomy.

The on-line computer lab includes four labs (see figure 1). Lab I is an introduction to the computer lab and includes procedures for using this material. Labs II, III, and IV follow the same five-part format (see figure 2): introduction, surface anatomy, dissection, movement and testing. The dissection part is a completely separate program that has been incorporated into the Lab designed specifically for Kinesiology students.

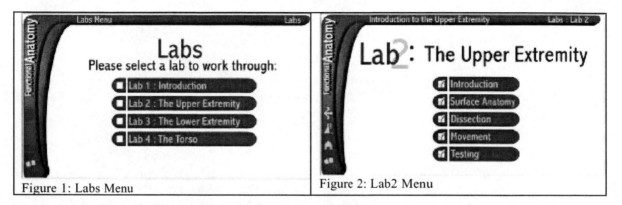

Figure 1: Labs Menu   Figure 2: Lab2 Menu

Methods

Participants

Four lab instructors from the on-line lab course participated in this study.

Instruments and its validity

A five-point Likert scale and ten interview questions were used. The five-point Likert scale is based on Ross' study where he used compared conventional teaching and on-line teaching (Ross, 2000). Some of the interview questions are selected from the reviewed literature and the study of the Integrated Learning system (ILS) in an Alberta middle school conducted by M. Jacobsen (1996). The interview questions were presented under the following four sections:

- demographic information
- comparison with the conventional cadaver laboratory teaching
- students' interaction with other students and lab instructor
- teaching strategies

Procedure

After completing an informed consent form, participants were asked to answer a questionnaire on a five-point Likert scale and then interviewed. All interviews were recorded anonymously on tape.

Analysis of the results

A descriptive statistical analysis was performed on the questionnaires. The interview recordings were transcribed and cross-referenced for both common and unique responses.

Conclusion

Computer technology has provided many new educational possibilities such as distance accessibility, and interactive, dynamic multimedia learning environments. Effective use of educational technology should take into consideration numerous elements. Results of this study highlight the need for instructional design, content, and teaching strategies that take into consideration learner characteristics as well as the classroom environment.

In this study, according to the lab instructors, the 3D animation and interactivity of web-based labs appear to have attracted student attention. Moreover, they suggested that the following factors be taken into consideration in order to develop World Wide Web tools to support classroom activities:

- course content should be current and relevant to learner needs
- expected learning outcomes must be clearly described
- too much text on one page should be avoided
- students should not be overwhelmed with information
- increased access to the Internet, and voluntary lab assignments should be encouraged.

Future study of student work-load and its impact on knowledge mastery, and student comfort with using technology as it relates to performance and attitude, is recommended.

References

Horton, W. (1999). *Designing Web-Based Training.* John Wiley & Sons, Inc. New York, NY.

Jacobsen, M. (1996). *A descriptive study of the implementation of an integrated learning system in an Alberta middle school.* Ottawa: National Library of Canada, repr.1996, c1995.

Kulik, J.A. (1994) Meta-Analytic Studies of Findings on Computer-Based Instruction. *Technology Assessment in Education and Training.* E. L. Barker & H. F. O' Neil. Lawrence Erlbaum Associates, Hillsdale, New Jersey. (pp9-33)

Loveless, T. Why Aren't Computers Used More in Schools? *Educational Policy*, 10(4), 448-467.

McGreal, R. (1997). The internet: A learning environment. In T.E. Cyrs (Ed), *Teaching and Learning at a distance: What it takes to effectively design, deliver and evaluate programs.* (67-74). San Francisco: Jossey-Bass .

Pallof, R.M. & Pratt, K. (1999). *Building Learning communities in cyber space.* San Francisco: Jossey-Bass.

Pennell, R. (1997) Managing online Learning. In *Proceedings of the second Australian World-wide Web Conference.* [Available On-line]. http://elmo.scu.edu.au/sponsored/ausweb/ausweb96/educn/pennel/papers.html

Ritchie, D.C. & Hoffman, B. (1997) Incorporating Instructional Design Principles with the World Wide Web. In Khan, B.H. (Ed.). *Web-based Instruction: What it is and why is it?* Educational Technology Publications, Englwood Cliffs: NJ, USA.

Ross, J.L. (2000). *An exploratory analysis of post-secondary student achievement comparing a web-based and a conventional course learning environment,* PhD thesis, University of Calgary, Canada.

Simonson, M.R. (1997). Evaluating Teaching and Learning at a Distance. In T. E. Cyrs(Editor), *Teaching and Learning at a distance: What it takes to effectively design, deliver and evaluate programs.* (pp 87-94). San Francisco: Jossey-Bass

Zhao, Y. (1998). Design for Adoption: The Development of an Integrated Web-Based Education Environment. *Journal of Research on Computing in Education.* Spring 1998: Volume 30 Number 3. pp307-327.

Using Technology to Aid in the Creation of High-Quality Corporate E-Learning

David A. Guralnick, Ph.D.
Kaleidoscope Learning
386 Park Avenue South
Suite 1900
New York, NY 10016
dguralnick@kaleidolearning.com

Abstract: E-learning has the potential to make a huge impact on the corporate learning field,, but this potential has not yet been realized. In theory, e-learning can provide high-quality, individualized, easily accessible, on-demand, interactive learning and performance support. But in practice, most attempts to migrate to an online learning model have resulted in poor, inefficient training. I suggest that the primary reason for e-learning's failure to this point lies in the focus on technology rather than on learning. In this paper I propose a three-part plan to employ technology differently, with the end result being a focus on high-quality learning.

1. Introduction

E-learning has the potential to make a huge impact on the corporate learning field, but this potential has not yet been realized. In theory, e-learning can provide high-quality, individualized, easily accessible, on-demand, interactive learning and performance support. But in practice, most attempts to migrate to an online learning model have resulted in poor, inefficient training. I suggest that the primary reason for e-learning's failure to this point lies in the focus on technology rather than on learning. This has resulted in the following specific problems:

- People who are skilled in learning theory are often less involved, or not involved, in creating training; rather, the role of computer programmers and graphic artists is increased
- Technical structures often are allowed dictate the design of an e-learning piece, rather than the other way around
- Lack of software tools for trainers—most authoring tools are "pseudo-programming" tools which still require the user to think in terms of programming logic rather than focusing on pedagogy.
- The Web and corporate intranets are typically viewed simply as information repositories, thus failing to take advantage of what technology can offer: personalized, interactive, just-in-time training and performance support
- Technical implementation details take time, preventing trainers from focusing on content and pedagogy.

2. Technology and Pedagogy: Must They Be at Odds with One Another?

There often seems to be a war of sorts between the technology side and the learning side. I suggest here that this conflict is to a large degree unavoidable: there's a huge communication gap between the groups, and there is no easy way around it. These groups have different skills and essentially speak different languages, and their design and development styles often are at odds by their very nature. While an admirable attempt at finding a middle ground, today's authoring tools are "pseudo-programming" tools, designed to let people build Web sites and programs without actually programming—but in practice that means "without writing actual code," rather than "without thinking in terms of programming logic and technical details"; the users of such tools do need to create programming logic even if they do not need to know programming language syntax. Given this difficult situation along with the temptation to garner the benefits of e-learning, many trainers today are trying to "catch up" by following one or more of several plans:

- Outsourcing their e-learning projects
- Hiring a programmer or programming team to help them

- Learning to use authoring tools, which themselves generally fall into two categories: those with a steep learning curve and a programming-like feel; and those which are simple to use but create only very simplistic products with little likelihood of teaching effectively.

The first option, outsourcing, is expensive, and over time also becomes inefficient if the vendor needs to be involved in the updating process as well. The second option, a programmer or programming team, is also quite costly, and it is very difficult to create a good quality product with such a project team; the technical details end up dictating the learning rather than the other way around. The third option, authoring tools, provides trainers with the greatest control over the learning experience; yet the amount of work required is substantial, and much of the work is necessarily focused on technical rather than learning issues. The learning design part is already difficult to do well, and while it is the trainers' core area of expertise, if they spend their time handling technical issues, their skills are going to waste. Imagine if a trainer wanted to produce a print manual and needed to understand how a printing press worked—building training with today's authoring tools can seem just as nonsensical.

What can we do about this problem in order to allow quality e-learning on a large scale? In this paper I propose a three-pronged method to creating effective e-learning on a large scale, and describe some elements of this approach. The three components are:
- "Learning Architectures": technology designed specifically to support good training
- A technical engine, invisible to the users, to support personalization and customization
- An e-learning creation "control center," with authoring methods that are intuitive to trainers, and support tools to help trainers organize and understand their content.

In the following section, I describe this new method in more detail, and draw from real-life examples of works that are either in the prototype stage or have already been deployed.

3. The Approach
3.1 Learning Architectures

Sound learning architectures that make use of the interactive capabilities of the medium are key to creating successful e-learning. In many ways, this is the next logical step in the development of online learning; whenever a new technology is introduced, its first uses closely resemble products designed for old technologies, which fail to make use of the new capabilities. Elearning has remained in that stage for too long. The idea here is to create learning architectures, beyond online manuals or Flash animations. These architectures are built around the learners' goals and, while good training design and good content are also necessary (and the responsibility, as well as the core skill set of the trainer), the architectures provide conceptual building blocks for sound training. Examples of learning architectures include:

Procedural learn-by-doing simulations
- **Goals**: Learn by practicing a real-life task.
- **Description:** The learner is given realistic scenarios and a simulated environment, and must work through them. A teaching component provides guidance and feedback, as a real-life coach would.
- **Uses**: This architecture is best for procedural tasks where there's some notion of a recommended way or ways to do things—examples include operating software or equipment and script-based soft skills such as many customer service jobs.
- **Sample Training Applications:**
  - **Laser Radio Terminal (LRT) Training**: Retail employees use handheld LRT scanners to track store inventory and locate product. The LRT terminals run a set of software applications, and mistakes made by employees can have drastic consequences on the accuracy of the data. The LRT Training simulations present users with real-life tasks in which they must perform actions with LRT software, using a simulated LRT on their computer screen.
  - **Guest Service Video-based Simulation**: Here, retail employees learn about customer service skills and store policies and procedures, by handling customers who appear in video, with realistic consequences played out for each action.

Rate-and-Review training activities
- **Goals**: Learn by observing the performance of a task, reflecting, and discussing it with others.
- **Description**: Users watch a task being performed by someone, generally through video or audio, ad rate the performance along several dimensions, and compare their thoughts with those of peers and experts.
- **Uses**: This is best for tasks which are visual, and/or expensive or difficult to simulate, such as coaching employees, where body language and personal style weigh heavily.
- **Sample Training Applications:**
  - **Coaching Training**: Retail employees watch videos of coaching situations based on real-life problems that they may face in their own jobs. They rate the video coach along several dimensions, then compare their ratings with the way their peers and some experts viewed it. They then can read explanations and see the same situation handled in a better way.
  - **Crisis Training**: Corporate employees watch a crisis situation unfold in video, and see how the company handled the crisis. Again, they rate the quality of the response, and can discuss with peers and experts. The learning goals here are for the users to become more proficient in handling crises.

Solid learning architectures in conjunction with a good trainer can produce excellent e-learning end-products. But the end-product itself is only a piece of the overall puzzle. If we want a way to produce quality e-learning on a large scale, two other areas must be addressed.

3.2 The Technical Engine

The goals of this technology piece are to support customization and personalization—so that content can be reused but in a way that always feels relevant to the user and the situation. For example, suppose a retail chain wants to teach their supervisory employees how to coach their staff. The audience however, is made up of employees with very diverse responsibilities and skills.

Generic coaching tips and instructions will not work - learners are notorious for deciding quickly "that doesn't apply to me." On the other hand, it is ridiculous to expect the trainer to create several entire coaching pieces from the ground up, such as "Coaching Cashiers," "Coaching Unloaders," and "Coaching Food Service Employees."

The basic underlying structure of the technology must allow the trainer to include both general information (in this example, coaching principles such as "coach positively as well as negatively," or "give feedback in private") and position-specific information that makes the training relevant to each different audience. Then, the technology must integrate the two seamlessly when the site is accessed so the end-user, for example, the cashier supervisor, doesn't notice or have to wade through information and examples relevant to the unloading supervisor.

In addition, learners need to be able to quickly and easily find the information, training, or other on-the-job support they need, which requires a good search engine, sound indexing of the content (as opposed to a plain text search which pulls up far too many results to be useful), and a clean interface for the end-user.

Up through this section, with a technical implementation adhering to the above guidelines, we now have the ability to have good training for a large group, including efficient content reuse, when they need it, in a personalized and customized way.

3.3 The Trainer's Control Center

In order for this approach to work, trainers need to be able to actually employ it—on their own, without programmers or outsourcing vendors. This means that they should be able to build e-learning while using minimal technical skills, and also maintain, study, organize, and customize the training and content. A software tool for trainers to do these things requires a focus on content and training rather than a focus on technical structures. The technical structures in section 3.2, along with the learning architectures in section 3.1, combine to form the underlying basis for this approach, but the training development platform itself should support a trainer in the following ways:

- It must have a natural, intuitive interface
- It should use a vocabulary of training and content, not of the technical world—for example, trainers can build "simulated tasks" rather than "branching models".
- It must offer support tools to make the trainer's development process simple and error-free. These tools come in two varieties:
  1. Basic quality assurance, such as spellcheck.
  2. Complex, content-centered tools, such as detailed reports describing the content of a training site.

The Control Center toolkit is currently a work-in-progress and will be completed in December, 2002. For the future, the next generation of these tools can include features that support the learning design process by training the trainers to design better online learning environments.

4. Conclusion

Technology and pedagogy can indeed coexist, and can join forces to create the e-learning that has been long discussed. In order to reach this point, we need to make changes in the way the two fields view each other and work together. Only then can large scale e-learning truly have an impact. Under the plan described here, trainers would still need to become expert at some new skills in order to create training under new, more-complex learning architectures. But these are natural evolutions of the trainer's current skill set. Technology, under this plan, plays a background role and supports and assists in the creation of sound learning, available just-in-time to end-users. With such a learning-focused plan, the true potential of e-learning can be realized on a large scale.

5. References

Guralnick, D. (1996). *An Authoring Tool for Procedural-Task Training*. Ph.D. Dissertation, Northwestern University.
Guralnick, D., & Larson, D. (2000). Using the Web to Improve Manager Performance at Target Stores. *Interactive Multimedia 2000*, American Society for Training and Development, Orlando, FL 65-76.
Guralnick, D. (2000). A Step Beyond Authoring: Process-Support Tools. WebNet 2000, Association for the Advancement of Computing in Education, San Antonio, TX.
Guralnick, D. (2002). The Art of Creating Useful Content and Effective Online Learning. InfoToday 2002, New York.

ESTABLISHING A PEDAGOGICAL PLATFORM FOR DELIVERING POST GRADUATE EDUCATION AS BLENDED E-LEARNING.

Author: Andrew Hall
Institution: University of Manchester, School of Nursing, UK
Email :   andrew.g.hall@man.ac.uk

Abstract: This paper focuses on the implementation of a blended e-learning resource-based learning and tutoring approach for post graduate study and the implications of this for on-campus and off-campus students. In particular the paper address issues of appropriate pedagogy and the use of new media to expand and improve on the traditional lecture based approach.

The project

The conversion of traditional Masters level modules in research methodology for health professionals, which form a key unit of study for postgraduate students, too distributed learning materials for flexible off or on campus delivery. The project has made extensive use of streaming media and use of a VLE. During the project each aspect of teaching and learning has been explored, the pedagogy questioned and the content examined. The process has been of benefit to both staff and students in relation to the nature and content of the learning materials.

Traditionally each unit was delivered through a series of six lectures or teaching sessions over a period of six weeks. After review and development each unit is now a half module and can standalone or be integrated into other study packages and is delivered as blended e-learning over one semester. The core learning material is available on the web; students access this and then undertake individual & group activities, face to face if on-campus, by use of asynchronous web based communication if on-line. After each block of study, students present a review of their work in academic seminars if on-campus or online if not. Assessment is by a summative assignment supported by a portfolio of selected coursework with reflective statements.

The pedagogy

 For Candy (1991) self direction is a process where learners gradually take control of their learning as well as an environment that encourages travel towards an ideal end point of self direction. During the development of materials it be came clear that this is a multi layer model with each layer built on a similar principles; the programme of study was designed to encourage the students to be more independent at the end than at the beginning Caffarella (1993), as was each module and each learning session. The structure of the learning material, the nature and content of the resources, wo rding and nature of the tasks all encourage the development of inquiring and analytical study and the exploration of other related routes of investigation with the assumption that the independence of the learner would grow. Knowles (1980) provides criteria that can be used to judge the value of the learning material in reach this end. In particular do the learning materials promote the ability to formulate questions that are answerable through inquiry and to generalize, apply and communicate the answers to question raised.

Tennant (1997) identifies assumptions within the humanistic concepts of self-development and self-direction, which, he argues, the evidence base does not fully support. The project team had some sympathy for Tennant's argument that there is inherent in the assumption of *self-directed,* a contextualization of the self that is often not addressed in these debates. By placing the self-directed elements of study after more structured elements context could be provided by the expertises that lie within the knowledge and work of the content experts, not in a traditional didactic fashion but through the shaping of tailored learning. As such the self enters a world where initially the context of study is apparent. The student is therefore expected to develop at multiply levels: as a subject expert; as a learner; and as a professional within a given context. The development of open ended linear routes, which draw on the knowledge and experience of the subject expert, guide learners through a pattern of predetermined resources and activities, promote both subject focused learning and the skills of the independent learner, and lead to more open explorative study, provide a framework for such an approach.

 Weil & McGill (1996) argue that the experience of the learner has value and that learning should be active, meaningful and relevant to the agendas of the learners; Laurillard (1998) identifies a conversation framework as key to the development of a critical perspective, necessary for academic understanding. These principles were employed in the structure of the learning materials and assessment. At each key stage students are presented with a number of resources and an activity that is undertaken in two parts. The first allows for consideration and reflection on the requirements & resources and the second requires students to engage with tutor and peer group to consider the contributions made. Within this facilitated dialogue, learning is an active process in the construction of meaning with the experiences and knowledge of the student cohort contributing to knowledge base of the group and its understanding of the issues under investigation. The method rewards collaboration and this is enforced by part of the assessment process being linked to the outcomes of the discussion. The ability to be responsive in this element allows the tutor to develop themes that the students have identified as of particular interest and if so desired to communicate these to the wider group. Additionally at this stage the tutor can facilitate the students learning to learn Wallace (1996), how to learn and direct themselves through information, concepts and tasks. Activities are built around problem solving, knowledge sharing, the construction of an analytical approach and the production of knowledge and as such work focuses on what Salmon (2001) identified as stage 4 skills.

New Media

Much work has been done on the potential of low bandwidth streaming media both video and audio in production of learning resources. A key benefit of which has been the potential for personalisation of the learning programme. Resources can be produced that address the needs and interests of different cohorts of students within the same pedagogical framework. Students of Nursing, Public Health, Socialwork, Medicine and others can view case studies and new media resources particular to their field and then engage with learning materials that draw on areas common to research methodology. This form of personalization would not be possible in a traditional setting and together with the acknowledged advantages of web based delivery in relation to accessibility, provides a strong driver for such development.

Conclusions

Through the development of this project we hope to address the major current pedagogical themes in the delivery of education through new media. In particular we hope to have established an adaptive educational framework which can support and influence the delivery of other post graduate programmes and programmes at other levels of study. We have drawn on elements of different theoretical approaches to develop a methodology that we feel is appropriate to the students in our institution and that may have generalisable outcomes. The course runs live in Sept 2002; we have obtained funding for a two-year research project into the educational experiences of different student cohorts.

References

Caffarella, R. (1993) 'Self-directed learning', in Tennant (2002) 'Psychology & Adult Learning', London: Routledge

Candy, P. (1991) 'Self direction for lifelong learning', San Franciso: Jossey-Bass

Knowles, M (1980) 'The Modern Practice of Adult Education' ', in Tennant (2002) 'Psychology & Adult Learning', London: Routledge

Laurillard, D. (1998) 'Rethinking University Teaching', London: Routledge

Salmon, G. (2001) 'E-Moderating: the key to teaching and learning online', London: KoganPage

Tennant, M. (2002) 'Psychology & Adult Learning', London: Routledge

Wallace, M. (1996) 'When is experiential learning not experiential learning?' in Claxton, G., et al (Ed.) Liberating the Learner' London: Routledge

Weil, S. & McGill, I. (Ed.) (1996) 'A Framework for making sense out of Experiential Learning' Buckingham: SRHE & OUP

Development of a Web-based Learning System for Teaching Web Design and Development: A Problem-Based Progressive-Scaffolding Approach

Richard H. Hall
Information Science and Technology
University of Missouri – Rolla
United States
rhall@umr.edu

Aram Digennaro
Psychology
University of Missouri – Rolla
United States
aram@umr.edu

Jessica Ward
Psychology
University of Missouri – Rolla
United States
Jessica@umr.edu

Nicholas Havens
Biological Science & Psychology
University of Missouri – Rolla
United States
nhavens@umr.edu

Joseph Ricca
Information Science and Technology
University of Missouri – Rolla
United States
jricca@umr.edu

Abstract: This paper describes a model for design of web-based learning system which is guided by two fundamental, and somewhat contrasting, design themes: problem-based interactivity; and progressive scaffolding. It is proposed that effective systems should be built around core problems, which require the active engagement of the learner. It is also proposed that the learner should be provided with scaffolding to support problem solution in a progressive manner going from the most general and minimal guidance to the most specific and detailed. It is then up to the learner to select the tool at the necessary level for problem solution. A prototype system for teaching web design, which was designed to examine the two fundamental components of this approach, and on-going usability testing of the prototype are also discussed.

Introduction

Although the number of web-based learning systems that have been developed in recent years to support distance and face-to-face classes has grown exponentially in recent years, research indicates that much of the promise of these learning systems has not been realized (Reeves, 2002). There are a number of reasons for this. A primary reason is that little thought or effort goes into design and research before the tools are implemented (Hall, Watkins & Ercal, 2000, April). A fundamental characteristic of effective learning environments is that they promote and encourage active learning; and many web-based distance courses, and even elaborate multimedia simulations are simply used to display information, without requiring students to interact with them. At the same time, research in hypermedia learning systems indicates that it is also very important to provide a learner with some level of guidance(Shin, Schallert & Savenye, 1994), and this too, is often lacking in these web-based systems. Finally, the ineffectiveness of these tools is almost surely partly due to the lack of research on these web-based learning technologies (Dillon & Gabbard, 1998). The vast majority of web-based courses and modules have not been pilot tested or evaluated prior to their introduction into the curriculum.

Computer based learning systems and the World Wide Web afford us an opportunity to move education to a new level, both to enrich traditional instruction and to provide instruction at a distance. However, such a transformation can only be realized through the application of systematic principles of instructional media design and through close interaction between content providers and web designers (Hall, Feltrop & Davis, 2001, April).

The purpose of this paper is to: a) Introduce a model for such a Web-Based learning system; b) Describe an example of such a system for teaching Web Design and Development currently under development; and c) Describe an initial usability study currently in progress.

Problem-Based Progressive-Scaffolding

The system currently under development is guided by two fundamental, and somewhat contrasting, design themes: problem-based interactivity; and progressive scaffolding.

At the core of each module is a problem, which requires that the learner actively integrate knowledge from multiple sources and apply basic methods and procedures for its solution. A large body of educational research indicates that learners learn most effectively when they are activity engaged in learning, as opposed to passively reading or listening (Brooks, 1997). Further, problem solving is at the core of meaningful learning.

"Progressive scaffolding" is the term we use to refer to a systematic method of providing learners with and optimal level of guidance(Hall, Watkins & Eller, in press). The system is designed in such a way that supporting materials are offered in a progressive fashion, from the most general and minimal guidance to the most specific and detailed. It is then up to the learner to select the tool at the necessary level for problem solution.

A Prototype System

We are currently developing a series of learning modules based on the system described above for teaching Web Design and Development. The system is intended to support a face-to-face class at the University of Missouri-Rolla on this topic, but it is also intended to be appropriate as a component of a distance learning class.

To begin development of such a system, we first created a prototype module, which is a step-by-step description for how to create a fairly elaborate web page, using the web development tool *Dreamweaver©*. To create the page, the user must apply a number of general procedures including: setting up a site; adding tables & graphics; using tables for page layout; inserting text; creating hyperlinks; creating image rollovers; and creating a disjoint swap image behavior.

This initial system is straightforward and is intended to examine the key components of the model above, so the initial interface is very straightforward in design. The progressive scaffolding is provided in the form of different levels of information for displaying each step in the development process: a) Text; b) Graphics; c) Narrated Video. A screen shot from this prototype system, which is currently under examination is displayed in Figure 1.

Usability Testing

This system is currently undergoing usability testing with students in General Psychology classes at the University of Missouri-Rolla serving as participants. Each student works with the system for forty-five minutes with the specific goal of recreating a model web page that includes all of the components cited above. Each participant's session is recorded including dynamic screen video capture, user facial expressions and audio; using a typical usability testing scenario (Dumas & Redish, 1999).

The principles questions that are being examined in the analysis of these session recordings are:

1. To what degree were students successful in creating the page using this prototype interface?
2. To what degree did students utilize each of the progressively complex types of guidance (text, graphics, and video)?
3. What is the relationship between 1 and 2?

Of course, any other trends or themes that emerge with regard to participants' traversal through the stages of the task and it's relationship to performance are also being noted, and, most importantly, recommendations for the continued development of the Web-Based learning system are being delineated.

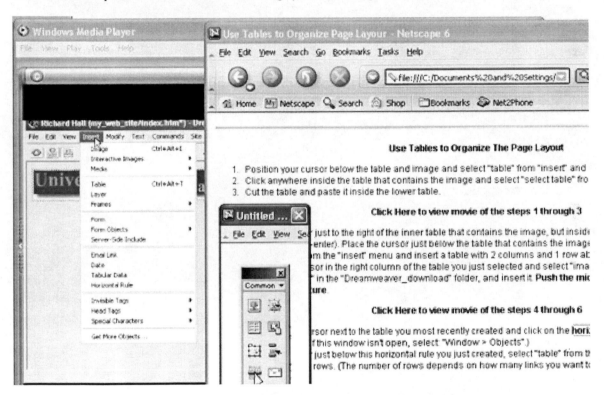

Figure 1: Screen Shot of Prototype Web-Based Learning System Interface

References

Brooks, D. W. (1997). *Web-teaching: A guide to designing interactive teaching for the world wide web*. New York, Plenum Press.

Dillon, A. and Gabbard, R. (1998). Hypermedia as an educational technology: A review of the quantitative research literature on learner comprehension, control, and style. *Review of Educational Research 68*: 322 - 349.

Dumas, J. S. and Redish, J. C. (1999). *A Practical Guide to Usability Testing*. Exeter, England, Intellect.

Hall, R. H., Feltrop, E. J. and Davis, R. L. (2001, April). *The web-based multimedia courseware development process at UMR's instructional software development center*. Paper presented at Higher Education Learning and Information eXchange (HELIX), Osage Beach, MO.

Hall, R. H., Watkins, S. E. and Eller, V. E. (in press). A model of web based design for learning. <u>The Handbook of Distance Education</u>. M. Moore and B. Anderson. Mahwah, NJ, Erlbaum.

Hall, R. H., Watkins, S. E. and Ercal, F. (2000, April). *The horse and the cart in web-based instruction: Prevalence and efficacy.* Paper presented at the Annual meeting of the American Educational Research Association, New Orleans, LA.

Reeves, T. (2002). *Faculty productivity and the World Wide Web.* Paper presented at Annual Meeting of the American Educational Research Association, New Orelans, LA.

Shin, E., Schallert, D. and Savenye, C. (1994). Effects of learner control, advisement, and prior knowledge on young students' learning in a hypertext environment. *Educational Technology Research and Development 42*: 33 - 46.

Acknowledgements

This research was supported by the University of Missouri – Rolla's Instructional Software Development Center.

A return to education as usual: learning complexity in the design and evaluation of a university mathematics course

Tony Hall, Liam Bannon
Interaction Design Centre,
Department of Computer Science and Information Systems,
University of Limerick,
Limerick, Ireland
tony.hall@ul.ie, liam.bannon@ul.ie

Eamonn Murphy
Department of Mathematics and Statistics,
University of Limerick,
Limerick, Ireland
eamonn.murphy@ul.ie

Abstract: In this paper, we describe the design and multidisciplinary evaluation of a new university course for teaching complex topics in probability and statistics. The course combines traditional third-level instructional elements, lectures and tutorials with interactive Internet instruction[1] and quick response e-mail support for students' urgent queries. The design of interaction for the course marks a return to *education as usual*, and a turn from the *Big education* (Stevens, 2002), *business as usual* approach to learning. *Big education* is concerned with using ICT[2] to automate education, premised on the simplistic assumption that learning is simple. This new math course was designed however on the basis that learning is complex and that effective use of ICT in higher education necessitates going beyond simply posting lecture slides to the Web, and furthermore that effective teaching can be supplemented, but not substituted by ICT. In addition, the new course was designed with the intention of preserving and enhancing traditional, but effective aspects of the course pedagogy. However, the new course is at the same time not quite a return to *education as usual* in the sense that its designers wanted with this new course to create a complementary combination of ICT support and offline interaction to try to overcome some limitations traditionally faced in trying to teach the course's complex subject matter to a very large group of students. In evaluating the new course we adopted a multidisciplinary approach, drawing for our critique of the new course on three different perspectives: collaborative learning and work, HCI/usability analysis and instructional design. We document how adopting this particular, 'tripartite' approach helped us to gain some significant perspective on the complex design and delivery of the course. We document also how this approach has enabled us to envision possible improvements to instructional and organisational aspects of the new course.

Introduction – Big education, big possibilities

This has become an era of intense efforts around standards, accountability, and socially consequential tests for the masses. It has become an era of aspiring technology millionaires for whom education is an enormous open market. In short, it has become an era of Big education.

(Stevens, 2002:269-270)

In the age of *Big education*, there are big possibilities. But we need to ensure these possibilities are big for learning. ICT, the Internet and related technologies promise much for education but their real value is to be found, not in determining how they can be used to replace teaching, but how, in combination with more effective teaching and more effective conditions for learning, (within and without the school), these technologies can serve as valuable adjuncts to learning.

The Internet is just one component of a new socio-technical system with great learning potential. Just as it matters which books students read, it matters which Internet software they use. And it matters what activities and social practices surround the process of Internet use in schools and at home.

(Bruckman, 2002:60)

The designers of the new mathematics course aimed to use ICT in concert with more effective teaching to create better conditions for student learning. They also intended "not to use the new media to do the old thing" (Papert, 2001) but to use ICT in combination with face-to-face and other ancillary student support to overcome some of the difficulties of teaching complex mathematics topics to a very large class.

Description of new mathematics course

197 undergraduate students take the MA4704 course in the spring term, each academic year. The course is a required credits course for the students, who all study in cognate disciplines: computer science, engineering and applied mathematics. The course is for many students their first experience of statistics; the presumed knowledge for the course is second-level or K-12 mathematics. Some of the students will previously have studied statistics in other courses or colleges. A multidisciplinary team developed the interactive instructional Web site for the new course. The team-members came from a range of backgrounds, including graphic design, biology, multimedia, computing, science teaching, and computer-based training. The team was composed of an instructional designer; two graphic designers; a software engineer; a Web specialist; a project manager; a content quality assurance lead; one teaching assistant; one tutor; and the lecturer. The Web site for the new course took approximately 9 months to design and implement. Students normally access the site from computer labs in the university; they can also access the site from home. Tutorial sessions are run twice weekly for students and in these they work through problem sheets related both to content in the lectures and to topics on the Web site. If students are experiencing particular difficulties with course topics, they can use the Dr. Dr. e-mail support: they can e-mail a query to the course TA and she will reply within 24 hours. Students can also attend additional help sessions in the Maths Learning Centre, located in the Mathematics and Statistics Department, where they can receive further, one-to-one or small-group tutorial assistance.

Our multidisciplinary approach to evaluation

For our evaluation of the course, we took elements from three disciplinary perspectives, from collaborative learning and work, HCI/usability analysis and instructional design. We had three concerns: (1) to assess the instructional effectiveness and usability of the course tool, the interactive Web site; and (2) to get some sense of the overall pedagogical efficacy of the novel course. And, in addition to our interest in the collaborative work of students, we were also interested in the collaborative work practices of the course designers and teachers, (3) with a view to generating some insights into how these practices might be better supported.

Usability analysis and evaluation of instructional design

We applied the Thinking Aloud protocol in assessing the usability of the Web site. For this part of the evaluation, we asked three students to follow the protocol as they completed a new topic on the Web site. We used an online questionnaire (http://richie.idc.ul.ie/tony/questionnaire ma4704.html) to supplement the feedback we received from the Thinking Aloud evaluation with the small sample of students – we intended to garner some specific results with feedback from the class group in general about instructional and usability aspects of the site. We also held short semi-structured interviews with the three students to get their reflections more generally on the course and its instructional approach. 101 of the 197 students responded to the online questionnaire. In assessing the instructional design of the course Web site, we drew on aspects of Merrill's (2002) First Principles for Effective Instruction, including, for example: is the courseware presented in the context of real world problems? And, are there techniques provided, which encourage learners to integrate new knowledge or skill(s) into their everyday life?

Getting through the 'Net

We found in our evaluation that students can get through the topics online without really having to think critically about them. Asked about the Web site, one of the interviewees said: "more searching questions need to be asked". Examples are the self-tests on the site, which loop continuously until the student gives the right answer. A number of the students we interviewed said that in the self-tests they often just kept trying different answers until they 'got the right one', without reflecting on <u>why</u> it was the right answer. The self-tests also create the fundamental usability problem that the user no longer has control - if a wrong answer is proffered the navigation buttons disappear. And there is also the pedagogical issue that this having to keep doing something until you give the right answer is too traditionally pedantic. One of the interviewees commented: "It's like school, being forced to give the right answer." Of the online animations and the course generally, the students in the interviews and questionnaires reported that they found this a much more interesting and meaningful way to teach statistics. One student remarked: "This is a much better and more interesting way of teaching prob and stats than normal lectures which can be very tedious." However, while students said the new course certainly gave them much more of a sense of how statistics can be applied in the real world, which should help them to integrate their new knowledge of statistics concepts and principles into their future internship or professional work, we found from the interviews, questionnaire and Thinking Aloud evaluations with students that there is perhaps too little *synthetic* interactivity available for students on the Web site. There is not enough, it seems, of a challenge and opportunity for students to actually do (*synthesise*) statistical work and reflect critically on it. To illustrate the use of instructional technology to facilitate creative or *synthetic* interactivity, and to help elicit critical thinking, Merrill (2002) gives the example of courseware that involves the learner in using MS Excel to prepare previous month's sales figures for a friend's shop. The instructional technology facilitates the learner in working through a real world problem. The courseware replicates Excel and the learner creates the workbook; enters the data; and creates the calculations and finally the financial report. In using the instructional technology, the learner is necessarily required to focus and reflect on spreadsheet concepts. The courseware also supports instruction with *non-examples*, which means the learner can make mistakes or take a problematic path through the scenario but she receives feedback on where she is going wrong. Another problem we found from our interviews concerned students' submission of answer sheets over the Web. The response page only informed students their data had been submitted without telling them what they had submitted. Furthermore, when they got back their results, they were just told their mark, and they were not told what they had gotten right or wrong nor why they had gotten certain things right or wrong. We would argue that the instructional design for the course Web site, while generally very good in aesthetic terms and in terms of usability and clarity of explanations, could be changed to better support critical thinking about statistics. In general, instructional artefacts should be designed to facilitate the development of learners' critical aspect and inquiry skills by supporting them in asking the right kinds of questions, and not with giving right answers *per se* (Koschmann, 2002; Hall & Wright, 2002). This change in the site design would need to be complemented with changes in the way feedback is provided on the Web site - students would need to receive feedback as they work through topics, and not just feedback on what they are getting right or wrong, but moreover <u>why</u> they are getting things right or wrong.

Online collaboration - beyond the *electronic soapbox*?

One of the problems we found with the course is the lack of support, ICT or other, for collaboration among students. We argue that online collaboration could be useful pedagogically, particularly for those students who access the course Web site off-campus, to give them some support where peers or tutors are not physically accessible for ideas or to take questions. Some online collaboration, like computer programming developer fora on the Web (for example, see http://forums.internet.com/), where students can post questions and post answers and solutions to problems, and where they can see how other students are approaching problems related to course topics. This online collaboration would be used to complement the critical aspect and real world focus of students' interaction on the Web site. This forum would require moderation but a Netiquette for the forum could be developed so that students use it appropriately. A chat room or unstructured e-mail discussion might not be that useful as we have found these can deteriorate into *electronic soapboxes* – that is students log on and contribute various unrelated comments that lack cohesive or logical threading. Also an online forum could be useful in further grounding statistics for students and in relating it to real world applications by using the Web to link students to practising statisticians in the workplace. It could be used to involve professional mathematicians and statisticians in discussions and in helping students to work through real world statistical scenarios on the Web site. This *community of practice* approach has previously been tried with some promise in teaching Computer Support for Co-operative Work (CSCW) (Eales et al, 2002). Our evaluation also revealed that there is a need to consider again in general how the Web site content sits with the lecture material. One of the students commented: "very useful but all of the information should be on it [Web site] instead of being at 1 level on the web and another in the lectures this was very confusing." In terms of helping students pace their own learning, overall the course has proven very successful. As one student noted: "I found this method very interesting, I could work through it at my own pace and attempt questions before looking at the answers. I could also take detailed notes at my own pace."

Conclusion

The design and delivery of the new MA4704 course marked a turn from *Big education* and the simplistic principle that learning is simple. The new math course was designed on the premise that learning is complex. In this paper, we have attempted to illustrate how a particular multidisciplinary approach to evaluation of this new course helped both to highlight problematic aspects of the course's design and delivery, and to provide insight to possible ways to improve these. Notwithstanding, subsequent research is warranted to investigate how this specific evaluative approach might be enhanced through meaningful combination with other disciplinary perspectives, or elements from. The combined approach we adopted worked well in helping to assess and uncover possibilities for the design of interaction and ICT in the context of a university math course. But different educational settings are likely to require different combinatorial or multidisciplinary approaches to evaluation, appropriate for the respective contexts of learning.

References

Bruckman, A. (2002) The Future of e-learning communities. *Communications of the ACM*, Vol. 45, No.4 (April 2002), pp. 60-63.

Eales, R.T.J., Hall, T., & Bannon, L.J. (2002) The Motivation is the Message: Comparing CSCL in different settings. In the proceedings of CSCL '02. (Ed. Stahl, G.) New Jersey: Lawrence Erlbaum Associates, pp. 310-317.

Hall, T., & Wright, T. (2002) Guess who's coming to lunch? The innovative lunchtime sessions organised for the student volunteers at the CSCL 2002 conference, Boulder, Colorado, US, 7-11 January 2002. *ACM Crossroads Special Edition on Human-Computer Interaction*, Fall 2002, (forthcoming).

Koschmann, T. (2002) Dewey's Contribution to the Foundations of CSCL Research. In *the proceedings of CSCL '02*. (Ed. Stahl, G.) New Jersey: Lawrence Erlbaum Associates, pp. 17-22.

Merrill, D. M. (2002) "A Pebble-in-the-Pond Model of Instructional Development", Guest Lecture, University of Limerick, Ireland, April 12th 2002.

Papert, S. (2001) "The Future of Learning – Let's be serious", MIT MediaLabEurope Guest Lecture, St. Patrick's College of Education, Drumcondra, Dublin, Ireland, June 19th 2001.

Stevens, R. (2002) Keeping it complex in an era of Big education. In *CSCL2 – Carrying forward the conversation*. (Eds. Koschmann, T., Hall, R., and Miyake, N.), Mahwah, New Jersey: Lawrence Erlbaum Associates, pp. 269-273.

[1] Course Web site: http://www.ul.ie/~e-stats;
[2] By ICT (information and communications technology), we mean the panoply of technologies that can be used by people to share information electronically: for example, the Internet and elated technologies like email, instant messaging and the World Wide Web.

An Assessment of Synchronous Online Audio Conferencing for English Language Instruction

Sandy McIntosh
English Language Program, Faculty of Extension
University of Alberta
Canada
sandy.mcintosh@ualberta.ca

Elizabeth Hanlis
TELUS Centre for Professional Development
University of Alberta
Canada
elizabeth.hanlis@ualberta.ca

Abstract: This paper is a report on the findings obtained from a pilot study using a synchronous online audio conferencing tool (CentraOne) for English as a Second Language (ESL) instruction. The study examined the responses of ESL students towards the use of this medium for the purposes of discussion. Students' responses varied, but overall they were positive; they seemed to feel quite comfortable with the tool and enjoyed the discussion, especially when they were broken up into smaller groups. However, many of the students found that inconsistent volume levels and lack of non-verbal cues, hindered communication.

Introduction

The Faculty of Extension's English Language Program (ELP) endeavors to deliver effective distance courses for ESL instruction that include the traditional four language skill areas in online course design: reading, writing, speaking and listening, as well a consideration for academic critical-thinking skills. The existing text -based resources do not meet the requirements for speaking and listening when incorporated into online instruction. While a number of synchronous instructional tools offer multi-point audio conferencing, it is not yet known how well these products work in the instruction of ESL or whether they offer an adequate replacement for existing face-to-face instructional methods. To better understand the strengths and weaknesses of these types of products for online ESL instruction, as well as the appropriate instructional methods for their use, it is necessary to perform careful evaluation of these tools. A pilot study was conducted as an initial step in this evaluation process; it provided a realistic pedagogical context for the evaluation of a mu lti-point synchronous online audio conferencing tool.

Review of relevant literature

Numerous studies deal with the more general issue of computer and Internet mediated communication for education (Gibson & Herrera, 1999; Seagren & Stick, 1999). At the present time, new elements of technology and pedagogical design continue to emerge in language education, resulting in varied program configurations. This inconsistency in design is reflected in Salaberry's (2000) report on a project to determine best practices in computer-mediated communication, specifically for second language learning.

The pilot test in question focused specifically on synchronous, online audio conferencing with both instructor-directed and peer-to-peer activities. Recent studies have examined the effects of synchronous video and audio-based online learning environments (Voice-over-Internet Protocol). In a study of synchronous online instruction with one-way video and two-way audio, Hofmann (2000) observed that the technologies became transparent in the learning process, and content, rather than the medium, became the focus. According to Appelt and Mambrey (1999), synchronous virtual learning environments seemed to increase the quantity and quality of student-to-student and student-to-instructor interaction, subsequently establishing a network of communication and collaboration among participants.

Overview of the Project

The TELUS Center for Professional Development was responsible for the planning and delivery of a pilot project comprising four (4) synchronous online sessions using CentraOne. These sessions were used to supplement the speaking and listening portion of an English as a Second Language course (Business English), at the Faculty of Extension. Participants were international students, mostly in their early 20s, whose ESL proficiency was rated as "advanced." The Business English course was designed as a terminal course, for students who intend to use English in their professional work.

Other participants in the sessions were: a CentraOne facilitator, the project coordinator, and the ESL instructor for Business English. The facilitator was a specialist in Educational technology and offered assistance in both the technological and pedagogical aspects of the project. The project coordinator was a specialist in program development for post-secondary education. The instructor, a specialist in classroom based ESL, provided the students with 20 hours per week of ESL instruction, including one hour per week in the pilot sessions. Apart from the pilot sessions, all ESL instruction for Business English were classroom based.

CentraOne is a web-enabled learning and collaboration environment using Voice-over-Internet Protocol (VoIP) software tool for synchronous conferencing (See Figure 1). Only some of the capabilities of CentraOne were utilized for the project. Specifically the following tools were utilized: audio, chat, whiteboarding and graphical slides, break out rooms, surveys, and evaluation. In the sessions, each participant was assigned a computer with headphones and a microphone, which could be used to speak to the group through the online medium, with permission from the facilitator. Only one participant could speak at a time, but all other participants could hear the speaker. In addition to audio conferencing, participants could communicate freely and synchronously with brief written messages and could also take part in simple communication such as voting or requesting permission to address the group by clicking on various icons.

Each synchronous online session was approximately one hour in duration. An average of 15 students participated in each online session. The first session, which took place near the end of March 2002, consisted of orientation instruction in the use of the tools and a brief discussion session. The remaining sessions occurred once per week during the month of April 2002. The course instructor, students, and facilitator actively participated in these sessions.

Figure 1: Screenshot of a typical CentraOne interface from one of the sessions

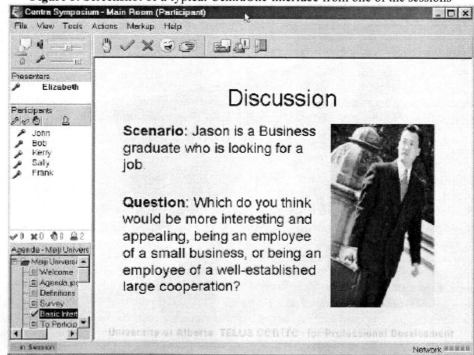

Overview of the Process

The project consisted of two main phases: 1) Planning, 2) Delivery, and 3) Evaluation.

During the planning phase the facilitator set up the synchronous online sessions. For each session, the facilitator created user accounts, created and managed events, and uploaded the agenda and content. The Business English instructor, in collaboration with the students, delivered the content for the sessions verbally or through documents e-mailed to the facilitator. The facilitator spent a maximum of two hours per session preparing the content for synchronous online delivery, uploading the content and preparing the event. For the first session the instructor completed an orientation rehearsal with the facilitator to detect and resolve any potential problems, prior to the actual event, in addition to the instructor, to become comfortable with the technology.

During the delivery phase, the facilitator assisted the instructor and students in the delivery of the synchronous online sessions, giving the microphone to the students and instructor as appropriate. A brief orientation was provided to students at the beginning of the first two sessions. This was intended to familiarize them with the CentraOne tools and to make them feel comfortable with the unfamiliar computer based technology.

Aside from making observational notes of the proceedings, the project coordinator assisted students with start-up, as needed. Both the facilitator and the instructor monitored and participated in the discussions. The facilitator participated in the sessions online and was only accessible to the other participants through the medium of CentraOne. The instructor was physically accessible but participated solely online. The students worked in one computer facility, with the instructor and the project coordinator. The computer facility was designed with limited sight lines that discouraged physical interaction between participants, outside the medium of CentraOne, and interaction was minimal during the sessions.

The assessment process focused on student approval ratings and comments. As simplicity and immediacy were considered to be desirable characteristics of the process, students were given the evaluations as a closing activity for each session. Student responses to rating scales and comments regarding approval or disapproval of the virtual classroom software were recorded within the medium of CentralOne. Ratings and comments were collected throughout the entire project and aggregated over time for analysis. In addition to the collection of data from student surveys, the project coordinator, the facilitator, and the instructor recorded observation notes during each session for the duration of the project. An informal debriefing session for the observers was held at the conclusion of each instructional session. Observational data were compiled and recorded from the three observers, over the duration of the project.

Findings

The pilot study examined the reaction, attitude, and comfort level of ESL students in using a synchronous online audio conferencing tool for discussion purposes. Based on the feedback gathered from the students at the end of each session, the majority of students indicated that they enjoyed using this tool for the purposes of discussion and were comfortable enough with the technology to complete and participate in the sessions.

It was observed that the students' and instructor's levels of enthusiasm and apparent confidence around the technology increased with each session, over the duration of the project. Specifically the students appeared to enjoy the use of break out rooms for smaller group discussions, compared to having larger discussions as a class within the tool. They also found the technology appropriate for communication of ESL students at a distance. Some of the negative comments around the tool focused on the varied microphone levels and the lack of non-verbal cues, which made communication difficult at some points.

An interesting phenomenon was that the From "Session 1" to "Session 2", the "Very Comfortable" rating declined from 27% to 23% and the "Not Very Comfortable" rating increased from 0% to 23%. This may be attributed to variations in lesson formats between the two sessions, as students were asked to participate more actively in the second session than in the first one by being assigned the responsibility of leading parts of the discussion. While they seemed to enjoy being leaders and moderators of the discussions, students found this role quite challenging. By the end of the term satisfaction ratings had almost returned to the original levels, however 10% of the participants emerged to express strong dissatisfaction. By ESL standards, the quality of discourse improved weekly.

Recommendations for Designing and Delivering Synchronous Online Sessions

The following recommendations are based on synthesis and analysis of the data collected from the project:

1. Orientation lessons at the beginning of each may need to be extended across many sessions throughout the course, to ensure that they feel comfortable with the technology. Orientation should include checking microphone and headphone volume levels.
2. The instructor should be given personalized technical assistance throughout the project, as needed.
3. Students should be placed in "break-out rooms" to provide opportunities for discussion in small groups with three to five participants.
4. Students should be given opportunities to lead discussions in a way that empowers them to solicit increased participation from other students. Training for student discussion leaders may be beneficial.
5. Courses using multi-point audio conferencing tools should be scheduled over an extended period of time. This would allow participants to become comfortable and proficient with the delivery technology in the early stages of a course.
6. It is important to engage the instructor in a pilot project early in the planning process. The support and cooperation of the instructor are necessary for the success of a project.

Conclusion and Suggestions for Further Research

As a first step to integrating synchronous online conferencing into ESL instruction, attitudes and the comfort level of students were examined and evaluated. The results from the study were encouraging and useful. However, further research needs to be conducted to determine how well synchronous online audio conferencing tools work in ESL instruction. There are many issues that need to be addressed in further research on this tool; the following are suggestions for further research:

1. Determine if ESL students of a different age group and with different proficiency levels would respond to the tool in the same manner.
2. Examine the responsiveness of ESL students using a synchronous online audio conferencing tool at a distance for a class/course.
3. Examine the achievement of students using a synchronous online audio conferencing tool over an extended period of time.

References

Bump, J. (1990). Radical changes in class discussion using networked computers. Computers & the Humanities, 24(1), 49-65.

Gibson, J. W. & Herrera, J. M. (1999 January). How to go from classroom based to online delivery in eighteen months or less: A case study in online program development. T H E Journal, 26. 6 (57).

Honeycutt, L. (2000). Comparing e-mail and synchronous conferencing in online peer response. Written Communication, 18 (1), 26-60.

Salaberry, M. R. (2000 March). Pedagogical design of computer mediated communication tasks: Learning objectives and technological capabilities. Modern Language Journal, 84. 1(28).

Seagren, A. T. & Stick, S. L. (1999 June). Enhancing quality through distributed education. Phi Delta Kappan, 80. 10 (793).

Sorg, J., & McEihinney, J.H., (2000). A case study describing student experiences of learning in a context of synchronous computer-mediated communication in a distance education environment. (ERIC Document Reproduction Service No. ED 447 794).

Web Access Evaluation and Repair Tools - Automation and Integration
Laurie Harrison
Adaptive Technology Resource Centre, University of Toronto

An increasing number of software utilities to support web accessibility are now appearing on the market, all claiming to automate the process of evaluating and/or repairing Web pages. These tools assist the author in identifying the changes needed in the HTML code in order for the pages in question to conform to standards to ensure access by people with disabilities. Recent developments in this market demand particular attention to two areas: 1) models for integration of evaluation and repair within the html authoring tool and 2) models for integration of authoring tool support within the courseware environment.

There are two sets of standards that are generally used by developers of these evaluation and repair products to set benchmarks for compliance. The first is the Web Content Accessibility Guidelines 1.0 from the Web Accessibility Initiative (WAI) of the World Wide Web Consortium (W3C).[i] and the Section 508 requirements, amended in 1998."[ii] While these two sets of standards provide the context for evaluation and repair, further attention must be paid to the role of authoring tools, such as HTML editors, in development of accessible resources. A grassroots approach including integration of accessible authoring practices and validation processes into the design phase would reduce the need for the evaluation and repair tools. However, as yet, only preliminary steps are evident in the HTML editors currently on the market. An example of this strategy is the 508 Accessibility Suite from UsableNet Inc. for Macromedia Dreamweaver and UltraDev, a downloadable software extension that supports HTML authors in testing Web sites and making them accessible. [iii]

Automation addresses the two key factors that are significant in the current prolific production of inaccessible Web pages. The first is lack of awareness, or more specifically, the possibility of authoring Web pages with little or no understanding of accessibility issues related to HTML programming. A second problem is the lack of motivation to do repetitive, complicated or time consuming activities that may be viewed as unimportant. The key to increasing the accessibility of the Web is to leverage the power of computers to do the repetitive and guideline intensive work instead of asking people to scrutinize and change their own authoring habits. With the proliferation of GUI word processor style HTML editors, a unique opportunity for including accessibility automation presents itself.

In recent years the education sector has witnessed an exponential growth in the area of courseware authoring tools, or learning content management systems (LCMS) to assist in presentation of Web-based curriculum and in performing class management tasks. Significant gains can be made if courseware authoring tool developers take steps to eliminate barriers to access in the web pages generated automatically by their programs, as well as those uploaded from an external source.[iv]

Considerable work in this area has already been completed by WAI in the form of the Authoring Tool Accessibility Guidelines (ATAG) 1.0 .[v] The associated guidelines and checkpoints in the WAI document provide a useful framework for consideration of the current challenges and the opportunities at hand for courseware authoring tool developers. In this paper, the ATAG guidelines have been used as criteria for analysis of several courseware products reviewed in a recent study at the Adaptive Technology Resource Centre, University of Toronto[vi]

Guideline 1. Support accessible authoring practices.
> *1.1 Ensure that the author can produce accessible content in the markup language(s) supported by the tool. [Priority 1]*
> *1.2 Ensure that the tool preserves all accessibility information during authoring, transformations, and conversions. [Priority 1]*

Compliance with checkpoints 1.1, 1.2 and 1.3 relates to two types of HTML authoring. In some cases the products reviewed allow online editing of HTML through a text field in the client browser, allowing the author complete control of the HTML markup. However, a more recent trend toward online WSYWYG editors, based on Java technology is more problematic as the underlying code is not apparent to the author. Courseware products generally allow the course designer to upload documents authored outside of the courseware tool without alteration to the HTML markup or compromising of the accessibility information inherent in the pages. In this latter instance, clearly the author determines how the HTML code will be written or edited.

1.3 Ensure that when the tool automatically generates markup it conforms to the W3C's Web Content Accessibility Guidelines 1.0 [WCAG10]. [Relative Priority]
1.4 Ensure that templates provided by the tool conform to the Web Content Accessibility Guidelines 1.0 [WCAG10]. [Relative Priority]

Checkpoints 1.3 and 1.4 are indeed one of the main areas where developers of courseware authoring tools need to focus their efforts. In most cases, material generated through automatic functions or templates cannot be easily edited by the designer, if at all. Potentially, this may act as a barrier to accessible design. However, with some further effort, it could as easily become an important support in the creation of accessible resources, with no need for specialized knowledge or training on the part of the designer.

Of particular importance is the integration of accessibility features into tools used for synchronous communication. The ATRC has developed a prototype of an accessible chat utility, designed with specific attention to the needs of screen reader users. [vii] E-College has also created an alternative interface for text -based rendering of chat content, which will also be highlighted.

Guideline 2. Generate standard markup.
2.1 Use the latest versions of W3C Recommendations when they are available and appropriate for a task. [Priority 2]

Some of the W3C standards recommended in the context of Checkpoint 2.1 may be seen by courseware authoring tool developers as unfeasible because they are not yet well supported by mainstream browsers. Standards mentioned in this section of the Authoring Tool Guidelines include: MathML, XHTML, CSS and SVG. Even if mainstream browsers are unable to render new standards, they facilitate support accessibility by non-standard browsers and alternative output formats. By ensuring that the authoring tool recognizes and preserves elements that are defined in the relevant specification(s), usability may be enhanced for all users, as legacy documents are used in contexts that support newer standards.

2.2 Ensure that the tool automatically generates valid markup. [Priority 1]
2.3 If markup produced by the tool does not conform to W3C specifications, inform the author. [Priority 3]

Checkpoint 2.2 is another crucial signpost for courseware authoring tool developers. While deprecated elements and nonstandard mark up may produce graphical rendering in a satisfactory manner for mainstream browsers, accessibility issues may arise if content is transformed to an alternative modality based on the users preferences. Examples of common practices include use of a header to change the font size, or BLOCKQUOTE to indent a paragraph. Using markup improperly may create a barrier preventing users with specialized software or preferences from understanding the organization of a page, and navigating through it effectively.

Guideline 3. Support the creation of accessible content.
3.1 Prompt the author to provide equivalent alternative information (e.g., captions, auditory descriptions, and collated text transcripts for video). [Relative Priority]

In addition to supporting authors in creation of materials using standard markup Checkpoint 3.1 recommends support through tools and prompts that further enhance accessibility for students with disabilities. An example can be found in WebCT, a company that has taken steps in recent releases to prompt the author for a description when uploading images to a database.

3.2 Help the author create structured content and separate information from its presentation. [Relative Priority]

Checkpoint 3.2 suggests that courseware developers use new standards such as Cascading Style Sheets, XHTML and XML to separate information from its presentation. While these technologies are relatively recent, it is anticipated that they will become more and more common, as we are faced with management of large web sites and dynamic, database driven resources.

3.3 Ensure that prepackaged content conforms to the Web Content Accessibility Guidelines 1.0 [WCAG10]. [Relative Priority]

Recent developments in the publishing industry may increase the significance of this guideline for courseware developers as they are called upon to partner with companies that have traditionally provided educational resources in print formats. Recognizing the need to move digitize educational materials to meet the demands of today's learner, publishing companies such as McGraw-Hill Ryerson and Pearson have taken steps to offer textbooks as content within a courseware environment.

3.4 Do not automatically generate equivalent alternatives. Do not reuse previously authored alternatives without author confirmation, except when the function is known with certainty. [Priority 1]
3.5 Provide functionality for managing, editing, and reusing alternative equivalents for multimedia objects. [Priority 3]

Issues related to Checkpoints 3.4 and 3.5 may be very simple, or quite complex, depending on the nature of the graphical or multimedia components included in the course. Current products all allow the designer to upload files to be used as course content. Examples where alternative equivalent would be required may range from simple ALT text for an image file to captioning or text transcripts for a video or audio file.

Guideline 4. Provide ways of checking and correcting inaccessible content.
4.1 Check for and inform the author of accessibility problems. [Relative Priority]
4.2 Assist authors in correcting accessibility problems. [Relative Priority]
4.3 Allow the author to preserve markup not recognized by the tool. [Priority 2]
4.4 Provide the author with a summary of the document's accessibility status. [Priority 3]
4.5 Allow the author to transform presentation markup that is misused to convey structure into structural markup, and to transform presentation markup used for style into style sheets. [Priority 3]

The checkpoints found in the *Authoring Tools Accessibility Guidelines* related to automation and provision of a validation and repair process are as yet unresolved by courseware products currently on the market. Online tools such as Bobby[viii], or services such as RetroAccess AccessEnable™ [ix] demonstrate the feasibility of providing such support, potentially within a web-based environment. By including the validation and repair process within the upload utility, content added to the courseware could be monitored for compliance with accessibility benchmarks.

Guideline 5. Integrate accessibility solutions into the overall "look and feel".
5.1 Ensure that functionality related to accessible authoring practices is naturally integrated into the overall look and feel of the tool. [Priority 2]
5.2 Ensure that accessible authoring practices supporting Web Content Accessibility Guidelines 1.0 [WCAG10] Priority 1 checkpoints are among the most obvious and easily initiated by the author. [Priority 2]

At such time as prompts, validation tools and repair tools are integrated into a courseware product, it is hoped that, as recommended by Section 5 of the Guidelines, the interface will be integrated with the overall look and feel of the program. Accessibility should be seen as an essential part of the authoring process, not as an add on to the program or an "extra" external step in the process. In the future, courseware products should use models such as these as they move to include tools to support accessible authoring practices.

Guideline 6. Promote accessibility in help and documentation.
6.1 Document all features that promote the production of accessible content. [Priority 1]
6.2 Ensure that creating accessible content is a naturally integrated part of the documentation, including examples. [Priority 2]
6.3 In a dedicated section, document all features of the tool that promote the production of accessible content. [Priority 3]

Checkpoints 6.1, 6.2 and 6.3 indicate that, in addition to automation of accessible design, validation and repair processes through integration of prompts and utilities to support the page author, help and documentation must include explanations of accessibility problems, and should demonstrate solutions with examples. This will support Web authors who may not be familiar with accessibility issues that arise when creating Web content.

Guideline 7. Ensure that the authoring tool is accessible to authors with disabilities.

7.1 Use all applicable operating system and accessibility standards and conventions (Priority 1 for standards and conventions that are essential to accessibility; Priority 2 for those that are important to accessibility; Priority 3 for those that are beneficial to accessibility).

7.2 Allow the author to change the presentation within editing views without affecting the document markup. [Priority 1]

7.3 Allow the author to edit all properties of each element and object in an accessible fashion. [Priority 1]

7.4 Ensure that the editing view allows navigation via the structure of the document in an accessible fashion. [Priority 1]

7.5 Enable editing of the structure of the document in an accessible fashion. [Priority 2]

7.6 Allow the author to search within editing views. [Priority 2]

This final section of the Authoring Tool Accessibility Guidelines addresses issues related to the designer user interface, emphasizing the importance of providing components and utilities that can be accessed by an author using assistive technology. While it is critical to ensure inclusion of learners with disabilities in development of the student interface, it is equally as important to provide support for the educator, instructor or designer with a disability.

While development of "offline" HTML editing software requires consideration of traditional user interface design standards and conventions, provision of the authoring process through a browser instead requires consideration of Web content accessibility standards. A client browser authoring tool offers many of the access advantages inherent in Web-based delivery, including flexibility in presentation, input and output modalities. Using their browser or adaptive software, the author can enlarge the font, navigate the content and utilize authoring utilities, provided the interface has been designed in compliance with WAI *Web Content Accessibility Guidelines*.

Summary:

In summary, authoring and courseware tool developers face challenges, but also have a great opportunity to improve access for all learners. Given that content developers and instructors rely on these tools to create and delivery content, they play an essential role in ensuring the accessibility of educational resources on the Web. As noted in the *Authoring Tool Accessibility Guidelines* it must be recognized that the Web is "both a means of receiving information and communicating information," and "it is important that both the Web content produced and the authoring tool itself be accessible."

---

[i] Web Content Accessibility Guidelines 1.0 from WAI of W3C (http://www.w3.org/TR/WAI-WEBCONTENT/)

[ii] Guide to the Section 508 Standards for Electronic and Information Technology (http://www.access-board.gov/sec508/guide/index.htm)

[iii] UsableNet - The Macromedia Partnership (http://www.usablenet.com/macromedia/index.htm)

[iv] Harrison. "The Role of the Courseware Authoring Tool Developer". Adaptive Technology Resource Centre, University of Toronto. (http://snow.utoronto.ca/initiatives/access_study/ATrec.html)

[v] Authoring Tool Accessibility Guidelines 1.0 from WAI of W3C (http://www.w3.org/TR/2000/REC-ATAG10-20000203/)

[vi] Inclusion in an Electronic Classroom – 2000 (http://snow.utoronto.ca/initiatives/access_study/inclusion.html)

[vii] Accessibile Chat Utility (http://snow.utoronto.ca/chat)

[viii] Bobby online validation from CAST (Center for Applied Special Technology), (http://www.cast.org/bobby/)

[ix] RetroAcess from AccessEnable™ (http://www.retroaccess.com/)

One World, One Ethics: Lessons Learned Designing an International E-learning Curriculum for Research Ethics

Mary Harvey
PriorityX Internet Services
United States
mary@priorityx.net

Bob Rice
Field, Information and Training Services
Family Health International
United States
rrice@fhi.org

Abstract: Research ethics training is mandated by many funders supporting research that includes human participants. Most programs are developed specifically for a U.S. audience and almost exclusively reference local institutional policies and U.S. regulations. Family Health International (FHI) developed a **Research Ethics Training Curriculum** as an interactive e-Learning aid for international researchers that is easy and fun to use. This curriculum is directed at the "lower end" of computer hardware, common in many international locations. The curriculum is written in non-technical language, was field-tested in four international settings, and is intended and designed for both individual and group educational settings. All materials needed for a group presentation are available "ready-to-go" so that the presenters' preparation work is kept to a minimum. The materials are available as either a stand alone CD-ROM or online through the FHI website at www.fhi.org.

Overview

Family Health International (FHI), an international research and training group that works in the reproductive health field, in collaboration with PriorityX, a web development company, created a *Research Ethics Training Curriculum* (*RETC*). This curriculum is designed to meet the needs of international audiences of biomedical and social science researchers. The curriculum addresses basic elements of research ethics, including the principles of human research ethics, international guidelines, informed consent and ethic review committees. The *Research Ethics Training Curriculum* was developed as an interactive e-Learning aid for international researchers that is easy and fun to use.

This curriculum is directed at the "lower end" of computer hardware, common in many international locations. The curriculum is written in non-technical language, was field-tested in four international settings, and is designed for both individual and group educational settings. The materials are available as either a stand alone CD-ROM or online through the FHI website at www.fhi.org.

To work effectively in low technology settings, no plug-ins, multi-media or single platform programming were used. The program was written entirely in HTML. For the interactive online post-test to store answers and give a final score, JavaScript was utilized. *RETC* was designed for Explorer 3.0 and Netscape 3.0, since those versions are still in use throughout the world. For the web version, large files were divided into smaller files for download purposes keeping in mind 28.8 speed modems. Interactivity was created using pop-up windows for the case study responses to actively involve the learner. Interaction between the learner(s) and the course material is further encouraged via "learner notes" that ask the learner to respond to questions before moving to the next section of the curriculum.

The main messages in the *RETC* are that:

Research is good
Research is a privilege
Social progress requires research
Society must trust its researchers
Researchers earn society's trust

Rational

In October of 2000 the World Medical Association (2000) revised the Declaration of Helsinki. Parts of this controversial reaction were in response to placebo-controlled research in the developing world. In April of 2001 the U.S. President's National Bioethics Advisory Commission (2001) issued a comprehensive report on issues in international research. The report, which included research considerations suggested by FHI, offered sweeping recommendations for those sponsoring and conducting research outside the United States.

Ethics in research involving human participants is important as comments from international research sites indicate:

CIOMS (1993): "the ethical implications for research involving human subjects are identical in principle wherever the work is undertaken"

Sharif, S.K. (1998), Kenya: "one of the major problems in the Third World is the weak ethics and scientific committees that review scientific studies"

Benatar, S.R. (2002), South Africa: "the need to build capacity in research ethics as part of the research endeavor"

The *RETC* employs provocative and culturally interesting reproductive health case studies developed by FHI researchers to highlight and discuss various ethics issues with the training participants. The Council for International Organizations of Medical Science (CIOMS, 1993) Guidelines and World Health Organization "Operational Guidelines for Ethics Committees That Review Biomedical Research" (WHO, 2000) are cited as key sources; complete copies of these documents are included in the reference section of the curriculum. Since publication in June 2001, FHI has received numerous positive comments from international research groups about the curriculum's local relevance and applicability. The *RETC* is now a recommended educational tool for organizations such as United States Agency for International Development (USAID), the Centers for Disease Control and Prevention (CDC) and the National Institutes of Health (NIH), among others.

The goal for this e-Learning program is to verify that research investigators, Internal Review Board (IRB) members and staff maintain continuing knowledge of relevant regulations and institutional policies for the protection of human participants.

Design

For the organizer of the group presentation, the *Research Ethics Training Curriculum* is "ready to go" in that very little preparation time is needed on the part of the facilitator. PowerPoint was selected as the presentation format as it is becoming more available around the world, and is fairly easy to use (and allows the facilitator to tailor slides to the specifics of the audience). All needed programs are supplied on the CD-ROM version of *RETC*, including Internet Explorer, Acrobat Reader and Microsoft PowerPoint Reader.

Case studies, learner notes, and the post-test are structured to encourage interaction between the viewer/learner and the subject matter. Examples include shaded learner notes, pop-up windows for case study answers, and a computer graded self-test. Of course, adults learn best and remember what they have learned longer when they actively participate in the learning experience. After completing the course material, learners are encouraged to contact FHI to receive a "certificate of completion" and to be included on a mailing list that will allow them access to research results and materials appropriate to their field of study. The "certificate of completion" is important to participants as it credentials the attendee of the training course, and is a noteworthy wall decoration in a resource-poor setting.

The *RETC* is attractive and visually appealing. Visual images were selected that appeal to an international audience. For example, the lotus flower graphically highlights the main sections of the RETC as it symbolizes "purity and perfection" in many cultures—the goal of a research design when it is implemented.

The *RETC* is available as either a three-ring binder, a CD-ROM, or on the web, catering to different learning/presenting styles. All three choices "interact" with the audience and demand participation—thereby enhancing retention on the part of the learner(s).

The *RETC* is user-friendly. It uses a tabbing system in both the three-ring binder and the navigational layout of the CD-ROM/web site. The objectives, learner notes and self-evaluations are displayed so that the learner is able to quickly and effortlessly identify the key messages. A post-test helps the learner retain important concepts.

The draft *RETC* was reviewed by a number of international research ethics experts at WHO and other research agencies. After thorough review, the *RETC* was field-tested in India, Kenya, Philippines, Zimbabwe and the U.S. The *RETC* uses simple English, given that many of the users of the curriculum will speak English as a second, or even third, language. For example, during the field-testing it was suggested that the word "oversight" was more authoritarian than a local researcher would expect—hence the word "supervision" was substituted instead. Several words and concepts were modified as a result of the field-testing experiences. The *RETC* is now being widely disseminated, mostly in English-speaking countries, including the WHO collaborating centers. Translations in French, Russian, Chinese, Portuguese, and Spanish will be available soon.

PriorityX collaborated with FHI to develop the Training-of-Trainers program (TOT) to insure that facilitators are well prepared to deliver the *RETC* in their research site. In the TOT package, exercises are presented to encourage training rather than presenting, teaching to different kinds of learning, and utilizing the group's knowledge resources.

E-Learning Conference

At the conference, the presenters intend to present and discuss, in a participative, adult-centered educational format, representative pieces of the *RETC* including the Self-Study guide in action, sample best practices from the Training-of-Trainers guide, sample slides from the PowerPoint presentation for presenters and the post-test. Additionally, attendees will receive copies of the *RETC* CD-ROM.

References

Benatar, S.R. (2002). Reflections and recommendations on research ethics in developing countries. *Social Science and Medicine*, 54 (7) 1131-1141.

Council for International Organizations of Medical Sciences (CIOMS) (1993). International Ethical Guidelines for Biomedical Research Involving Human Subjects. Geneva, Switzerland: World Health Organization.

Sharif, S.K. (1998). Letter to the editor. *The New England Journal of Medicine*, 338 (12) 838.

U.S. President's National Bioethics Advisory Commission (2001). Volume I: Report and Recommendations of the National Bioethics Advisory Commission. Springfield, VA: U.S. Department of Commerce.

World Health Organization. Product Research and Development Team (2000). Operational Guidelines for Ethics Committees That Review Biomedical Research. Geneva, Switzerland: World Health Organization.

World Medical Association (2000). Declaration of Helsinki: Ethical Principles for Medical Research Involving Human Subjects. Edinburgh, Scotland: WMA.

Acknowledgements

This publication was funded by:
U.S. Agency for International Development (USAID)
Andrew W. Mellon Foundation
National Institutes of Health (NIH).
The information contained in the publication does not necessarily reflect FHI, USAID, the Mellon Foundation or NIH policies.

RETC was written by Roberto Rivera, David Borasky, Robert Rice and Florence Carayon.

RETC web site was designed and created by Traci Knight, Mary Harvey, Jeff Martin, Rance McDaniel and the team at PriorityX Internet Services, Houston, Texas.

Special thanks to David Borasky and Roberto Rivera for research assistance.

Introducing the Idea of Sustained Query Exposure in the Context of Language Vocabulary Learning

Daniel C Heesch
Department of Computing, Imperial College
180 Queen's Gate, London SW7 2BZ, England
dh500@doc.ic.ac.uk

Abstract: This paper describes and motivates the novel idea of sustained query exposure as a form of passive knowledge consolidation and illustrates its use in the context of a basic pool-sink vocabulary model. The effectiveness of this technique hinges on a well-designed graphical user interface (GUI) that extends and facilitates the interaction between user and query objects. One such GUI is presented in this paper.

1   Introduction

Most of what we learn is forgotten after a short period of time. Considering the amount of largely redundant data with which our cognitive apparatus is continuously bombarded, this tendency to forget is a blessing and deserves being ranked as a chief adaptation against information overload. It becomes a curse, however, whenever there is a need for selective long-term memorization. As was first described by the German psychologist Ebbinghaus, recall ability decreases at an exponential rate (Ebbinghaus **1913**), a relationship that has been validated ever since (see for example Bahrick **1984** and Bahrick & Phelps **1987**). Methods devised to overcome this degradation tend to belong to one of two learning paradigms, namely associative learning and staggered learning. The latter is based on the observation that each time a periodical review takes place of the information to be learnt, recall ability does not only jump to its initial level but, more importantly, the rate of subsequent decay decreases such that retention is ensured for progressively longer intervals (Bahrick et al. **1993**). The positive effect of staggered learning on recall ability can be enhanced by excluding from reviews items the student has successfully recalled during previous reviews, a learning mode known as selective learning. A few software systems exist that provide support for such selective, staggered learning of foreign language vocabularies (see for example Raedle **2002** which is based on a cardboard predecessor (Leitner **1984**)). Typically, queries that are answered incorrectly are retained in the system for subsequent reviews. For most of its life cycle, a query is hidden away from the user's sight and it is only for brief moments that it is brought back to the attention of the user. In the pre-computer era, practicality may have offered itself as a plausible rationale for this property. However, recognizing the flexibility that can be offered by graphical user interfaces, this seems like an unnecessary constraint and more like a relict of the cardboard era. We instead advocate an approach which we shall refer to as sustained query exposure. The principal idea is to display every query previously answered incorrectly in the periphery of the user interface until that query is posed again and answered correctly. By thus keeping incorrect queries visually accessible following their explicit exposure, further interaction between user and query becomes possible, providing potential for the query to "sink in" further.

This visualization is built around a language learning model which has the desirable property that the number of incorrectly answered queries held back for a subsequent review is kept relatively constant (sink size constancy).

The report is organized in two parts. The first part introduces the underlying model, in particular the method used to achieve sink size constancy, and discusses performance measures that can be derived from it. The second part provides a description of the graphical user interface.

The system presented here is based on a simple pool-sink learning model as depicted in Figure 1. The queries are Spanish verbs which initially reside in a pool that is accessed to obtain a new query with probability p. If the query is answered correctly, it is marked as successfully learnt and excluded from the learning session. If the answer is incorrect, the query enters a sink which is accessed during each round with probability $q = 1-p$. We can thus distinguish between two kinds of queries which we shall refer to as type A (pool) and type B (sink) queries.

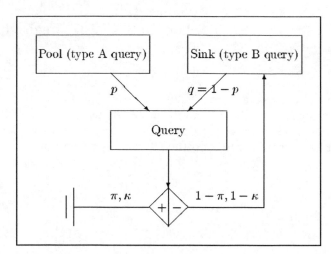

Figure 1: Queries are either drawn from the pool (new queries) or from a sink (incorrectly answered queries). The variables determining the word flow are the probabilities p, q, π and κ (see text for details).

2.1   Fixed sink capacity

The sink is assigned a fixed capacity and the word flow through the system is regulated with the aim of keeping the sink level close to its capacity. This system constraint is desirable not only for the purpose of visualization. For staggered learning to be effective, the user ought not to be exposed to a type B query until some time after the first encounter (time between exposures = TBE). This requirement of a minimum TBE can be met by ensuring that a certain number of queries may enter the sink before they are retrieved. It is not desirable, however, to allow the unlimited accumulation of queries as this would lead to an unacceptable prolongation of the TBE, thus the need for an upper bound. Keeping the sink level constant means that, for a competent user, pressure on the sink is low and TBE will be long. For a less competent user, pressure on the sink is higher and queries need to be retrieved more frequently. Hence, TBE increases with the competency level of the user.

The system variable that regulates the flux through the system is the probability, p, of a query being drawn from the pool. The external variables that affect flow characteristics and on which we have little influence relate to user performance. Specifically, they are the probabilities π and κ of the user correctly answering a query of type A and B, respectively. p, τ and κ provide a complete description of the system. Our aim is to achieve a dynamic equilibrium of the system with the sink level remaining stable and the rate of inflow of new queries being balanced by an equal rate of outflow of correctly answered queries. Let s_t be the sink level at time t, then the state of the sink at time $t + 1$ is given by the stochastic equation

$s_{t+1} = s_t + w$,   where w is a random variable with

$$w = \begin{cases} 1 & \text{with probability} \quad p(1 - \pi) \\ -1 & \text{with probability} \quad (1-p)\kappa \\ 0 & \text{with probability} \quad 1 - p(1 - \pi) - (1-p)\kappa \end{cases}$$

At equilibrium, the expectation of w, $E(w)$, is zero, that is $E(w) = p(1 - \pi) - (1-p)\kappa = 0$ and hence

$$p = \frac{\kappa}{1 - \pi + \kappa}. \tag{1}$$

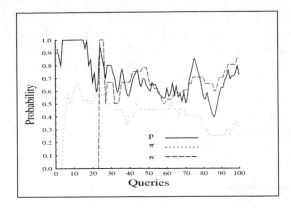 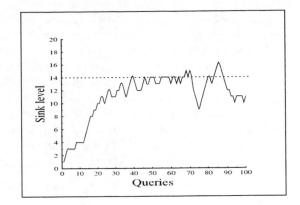

Figure 2: Left: a typical learning session over 100 queries. Initially, a query is likely to come from the pool (p is high) so as to fill the sink. As the sink approaches its capacity, p decreases. Right: sink level constancy is achieved by continuously updating the probability p of a query being obtained from the pool.

As the user performs better on either type of query (increase in κ or π), the probability p of presenting a fresh query in the next round increases. To ensure that the system reaches the equilibrium in the first place and finds back to it when being displaced (as a result of variations in κ and π), we first introduce the random variable w_i, representing the value of w on the $(t+i)$th trial. Then,

$$E(s_{t+n}) = s_t + \sum_{i=1}^{n} E(w_i)$$

and since the random variables w_i are independent and have the same distribution as w, this is just $E(s_{t+n}) = s_t + nE(w)$. To reach the capacity c after d steps, we want to choose p such that

$$E(s_{t+d}) = s_t + dE(w) = s_t + d(p(1 - \pi + \kappa) - d\kappa) = c \qquad \text{and thus}$$

$$p = \frac{c - s_t}{d - d\pi + d\kappa}.$$

The more the current state lies below the capacity, the greater is the influx of new queries. Updating p thus requires knowledge of the values of π and κ. In the present model these performance values are obtained by determining the running average over the last 20 queries of either type.

2.2 Measuring performance

From this model we can derive a simple performance measure, namely the value of the variable p. The higher p the greater the proportion of queries answered correctly. It follows from the sink capacity constraint and directly from equation 1 that $p = 1$ implies that all queries are of type A and are answered correctly ($\pi = 1$), while $p = 0$ implies that all queries are of type B and are answered incorrectly ($\kappa = 0$). p varies during any one particular session owing to user/query specific variations in π and κ. The mean value of p over all queries during one session thus provides an estimate of overall performance while the variance in p is an indicator of the extent of inter-query consistency in performance. The variations in p, π and κ during a typical learning session are depicted in Figure 2. It also illustrates how continuous adjustment of p helps to keep the sink level within narrow bounds around the sink capacity ($c = 14$).

3 Sink visualization

With the sink level thus being kept relatively constant, the stage is now set for a visualization of the sink content. The center of the display accommodates three text fields to display a query, enter a reply and inform the user about correctness and possible alternatives. Incorrectly answered queries are displayed as spheres on a concentric circle around this center as shown in Figure 3. The query string is printed across each sphere and for aesthetic purposes, the radii of the query spheres vary with query length.

To increase interaction between the user and the periphery, each query is assigned an electric charge, with the charge depending on query length and thus the radius of the sphere. Spheres repel each other and whenever a new query is taken up into or leaves the set, the new set of queries are allowed to find a stable arrangement subject to the electrostatic forces acting between them. The movement towards equilibrium is recorded and displayed as a short animation sequence of one to two seconds after which the user is provided with a new query. In addition to thus drawing the user's attention towards the periphery and thereby facilitating interaction between user and incorrectly answered queries, it also gives the user a form of immediate visud feedback. If the current query was obtained from the sink and is again answered incorrectly, the set remains unchanged and no animation sequence will be shown. Instead, the colour of the respective query sphere will turn darker as shown in Figure **3.**

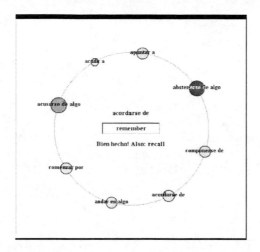

Figure **3: User** interface and sink visualization. **Animation and colour changes are included to facilitate interaction between user and periphery. See text for** details.

4   Outlook

This paper introduces the idea of sustained query exposure and illustrates its potential use in the context of a staggered learning model for Spanish verbs. At this stage comparative performance evaluation becomes a key necessity in order to corroborate our claim about the potential effectiveness of this proposed technique of passive knowledge consolidation. Additional information that may be of interest concerns the predse scope and type of visud interaction between user and interface. This information, which could be gathered using existing eye-tracker technology, is likely to motivate further improvements of the interface.

References

Bahrick H.P. **(1984).** Semantic memory content in permastore: fifty years of memory for Spanish learned in school. *Journal* of *Experimental Psychology: General,* 113(1):1-37.

Bahrick **H.P.**et al. **(1993).** Maintenance of a foreign language vocabulary and the spacing effect. *Psychological Science,* 4(5): **316-321.**

Bahrick H.P. and Phelps E. **(1987).** Retention of Spanish vocabulary over **8** years. *Journal* of *Experimental Psychology: Learning, Memory and Cognition,* **13(2): 344-349.**

Ebbinghaus **H.** (1913). *Memory:* **A** *Contribution to Experimental* Psychology. Teacher's College, Columbia University (New York).

Leitner S. *Asi se aprende.* Herder (Barcelona).

Raedle **P.** (2002). V train. *http://www.pauZ-raedle. de/vtrain/sci.htm*

E-Literacy for the Workforce: Designing Effective Instruction

Heather Hemming
School of Education
Acadia University
Canada
heather.hemming@acadiau.ca

Sonya Symons
Department of Psychology
Acadia University
Canada
sonya.symons@acadiau.ca

Lisa Langille
School of Education
Acadia University
Canada
0146391@acadiau.ca

Abstract: To address the increasing demands placed on adults entering today's workforce, this study involved the development of an instructional approach designed to teach adults strategies for writing effectively in an electronic context through a combination of face-to-face and electronic-based tutorial sessions. The instructional approach was developed based on a reciprocal teaching framework and a goal was to situate the learning within a meaningful, work-related context through electronic discussions. Specifically, the objectives of this study were 1) to understand the experiences of participants enrolled in workforce literacy programs, 2) to assess the impact of an instructional protocol, developed to teach how to express or explain a viewpoint, ask pertinent questions, and write effective responses, on the quality of writing, and 3) to examine if changes occurred in participant attitudes toward writing using computers.

Introduction

Writing in electronic spaces has changed most workplaces. For example, a poll conducted by the Gallup Organization, Inc. estimates that ninety percent of large companies, sixty-four percent of mid-sized companies, and forty-two percent of small firms currently use e-mail systems. The same poll found that more than forty million employees correspond via e-mail, and the number is expected to increase by about twenty percent each year (Kopp, 1998). Further, "e-mail has become the most-used communication tool on the job" in the United States and in Canada (Merrick, 2000, p.17). In addition to the steady increase of e-mail in today's workplaces, there also has been an escalation in the need to write in electronic contexts.

With the continual increase of electronic writing in various workplaces, it becomes evident that workforce literacy programs must begin to reflect the changing demands of today's workplaces to more adequately assist adult learners in finding and maintaining employment. However, given the growing need to communicate effectively within an electronic environment, it must be recognized that computer exposure is not adequate preparation for adults entering the workforce. Research is needed to establish an instructional design that may support individuals in learning how to use literacy skills effectively within a technological context.

The term Digital Divide came to public attention after a 1995 study by the Markle Foundation revealed that the "same divergence found in society along cultural and racial lines is found online and offline" (CNET News.com, 1997). Many participants in workforce preparation programs are involved in these programs because of barriers to maintaining employment. Although these barriers may occur for a variety of reasons, those attending the programs are often dealing with issues of unemployment. Research suggests that patterns of technology access often mirror existing inequalities rather than mitigate them (Schofield & Davidson, 1998) and if corrective steps are not taken, technology may worsen rather than solve equity disparities (Serim, 1999). Thus, it is essential that workforce literacy programs address these issues and provide opportunities for this gap to be lessened. Reddick, Boucher, and Groseilliers (2000), in their report on technology in Canada, stated "the levels of awareness and the use of these new technologies and services are highly polarized along social class and generational lines, creating the digital divide" (p.1).

Technology integration within workforce preparation programs is needed, especially after long-term repercussions are considered in the case that adult learners are not given adequate preparation for electronic environments in the workplace. For many adults attempting to enter or re-enter the workforce, the addition of new technological demands within workplaces only further multiplies the obstacles to overcome. Unfortunately, many workforce literacy programs typically have not adapted their instruction and curricula to reflect the ever-increasing presence of technology within today's workforce, which therefore may impact participant ability to successfully maintain employment. This study involved the development and assessment of an e-learning context designed to provide instructional support for developing strategies for effective e-literacy writing to adults enrolled in workforce preparation programs.

The Study

The goal of this research was to design and assess an e-learning instructional context aimed at facilitating the development of skills for writing in electronic spaces. This study involves the development of an instructional approach designed to teach adults strategies for writing effectively in an electronic context through a combination of face-to-face and electronic tutorial sessions. The instructional approach was developed based on a reciprocal teaching framework and the goal was to situate the learning within a meaningful, work-related context through electronic discussions. The objectives of the study include the following: to understand the experiences of participants enrolled in workforce literacy programs; to assess the impact of an instructional protocol (developed to teach how to express or explain a viewpoint, ask pertinent questions, and write effective responses) on the quality of writing and; to examine if changes occurred in participant attitudes toward writing using computers.

Twenty-two participants (ages 18-48, mean 29.8) from the Annapolis Valley Work Centre took part in this study. All participants had some form of barrier to employment; further, all had been either out of employment for a significant period of time or had never been employed and were receiving social assistance. In all cases, participants felt they would be better prepared for employment if they could improve their ability to communicate electronically.

Basic computer instruction was provided to the participants using IBM Thinkpads, which they used throughout the study. When participants felt comfortable using the laptop computers, they completed an introductory session prior to instruction, which involved making an entry into the electronic discussion group after examining a case study.

Instruction was based on a reciprocal model of instruction and consisted of eleven forty-minute sessions, summarized in Table 1, which focused on three specific writing strategies used when making electronic discussion entries. Instruction was also founded in context pertinent to workforce preparation. Strategy modeling tutorials were primarily grounded in face-to-face interaction. Guided practice sessions involved both face-to-face and electronic instruction and strategy use. Independent practice tutorials consisted of electronic instruction and strategy implementation. Session 10 entailed face-to-face guidance in addition to electronic strategy use while session 11 involved electronic, independent strategy use.

During the instructional phase, participants worked in heterogeneous small groups with a research assistant during their regular class hours at the Annapolis Valley Work Centre. Throughout this time, participants received a protocol for instruction for the three writing strategies. The gradual shifting of responsibility in reciprocal teaching (Palinscar & Brown, 1984) was embedded in the nature of the sessions. Participants used worksheets and study guides prior to making their electronic discussion group entries throughout the tutorial sessions.

Table 1

Description of Instructional Protocol

Session #	Strategy	Description
1	Explaining/Expressing a Viewpoint	Modeling of Strategy
2		Guided Practice
3		Independent Practice
4	Asking Pertinent Questions	Modeling of Strategy
5		Guided Practice
6		Independent Practice
7	Writing Effective Responses	Modeling of Strategy
8		Guided Practice
9		Independent Practice
10	All 3 Strategies	Guided Use of Strategies
11		Independent Use of Strategies

Findings

A computer usage survey completed prior to instruction reflected participant experience with, and attitude toward, computers. Sixty-eight percent of participants had used e-mail while 41% had used chat groups prior to this study. There was also diversity in the frequency of computer use among participants. For example, 14% of the participants categorized themselves as heavy computer users, another 14% felt they were light computer users while another 14% considered themselves to be infrequent users. Additionally, although 59% of the participants had used a computer within seven days prior to participating in the study, 62% of those participants had used a computer for playing games while only 38% used a computer for word-processing and 46% for writing an e-mail message. These findings may suggest that although some participants are using computers, they are not necessarily gaining sufficient experience communicating with computers. Further, at the beginning of the study, 36% of the participants specifically identified writing as a significant barrier for them with regard to finding and maintaining employment.

The instructional protocol was based on reciprocal teaching, in which there was a combination of face-to-face and electronic tutorial sessions, as depicted in Table 1. This blend of instructional delivery proved to be an effective method for teaching adult learners writing strategies necessary for e-literacy. Throughout the sessions, participants consistently requested information regarding computer use. The prompts were aimed primarily at basic computer skills needed to participate in electronic discussions. This suggests that the participants' limited computer experience and comfort level may have prevented independent participation in the instruction, had it been offered without the face-to-face component. One participant's comment reveals the importance of the face-to-face interaction received throughout the instruction: "I liked that you didn't just throw us in there and expect us to know what to do right away."

To assess change in writing quality after instruction, the electronic discussion entries created during an introductory session and entries made during the final independent session were compared. Pre- and post-instruction number of words did not differ (pre-instructional mean 79 and post-instructional mean 68, t (20) = 1.77, p = .092). However, participants used an increased number of sentences after instruction than they did prior to instruction (pre-instructional mean 3.5 and post-instructional mean 4.9 (t (20) = 3.24, p = .004). This suggests that writing processes were changing; it appeared as though participants began to make more intentional, thoughtful decisions about their writing. Further, the comparison of these two groups of entries showed that 95% of participant entries contained an increased amount of explanation to support viewpoints generated. These findings suggest improvements to participants' written communication; relevant viewpoints were explained instead of including irrelevant, isolated opinions. Overall quality of participants' writing was scored using a modification of the TOWL-3. Results suggest significantly higher scores following instruction (pre-instructional mean 19.2 and post-instructional mean of 22.9 with 29 being the maximum score, t (20) = 2.43, p = .024). Explanatory quality of the participants' arguments was also assessed using a 5-point scale. This reliable scale indicated that arguments were stronger after instruction than before (pre-instruction 1.5 and post-instruction 4.7, t (19) = 12.58, p = .001).

Participant attitudes toward writing also appeared to change. Prior to the study, some participants revealed hesitation surrounding the writing process, as they were concerned with the aesthetics of their handwriting (some experienced difficulty with the mechanics of letter formation). After participating in the electronic discussions as a part of the instructional protocol, those same participants described writing using computers as being much more enjoyable than writing via the more traditional methods.

Conclusions

Workforce literacy programs must provide opportunities for learners to gain experience using technologies that are prevalent in the workforce, as it may directly increase participants' chances of successfully finding and maintaining employment. However, it must also be recognized that adequate instruction is needed to assist learners in using these technologies effectively for communication, as a certain level of communication skills is essential to use various components of technology such as e-mail and electronic discussion groups. Due to the overwhelming population of adult learners who do not yet possess the necessary skills to independently participate in electronic instruction, it becomes evident that face-to-face and electronic instruction complement one another through reciprocal teaching and may provide adult learners with an optimum opportunity to gain experience using communication technologies within a meaningful, work-related context while engaging in the process of becoming e-literate for the workforce of the 21st century.

References

CNET News.com. (1997, March 14). *Society's digital divide*. Retrieved June 7, 2002, from http://news.com.com/2100-1023-278007.html

Kopp, K.P. (1998, Summer). Electronic communications in the workplace: E-mail monitoring and the right of privacy. *Seton Hall Constitutional Law Journal*, 1-30.

Merrick, B. (2000). E-mail replaces the water cooler. *Credit Union Magazine*, 66(11), 17.

Palincsar, A. S., & Brown, A. L. (1984). Reciprocal teaching of comprehension-fostering and comprehension-monitoring activities. *Cognition and Instruction*, 1, 117-175.

Reddick, A., Boucher, C., & Grosseilliers, M. (2000). *The dual digital divide: The information highway in Canada*. Ottawa: The Public Interest Advocacy Centre.

Schofield, J. and Davidson, A. (1998). The Internet and equality of educational opportunity. In T. Ottmann and I. Tomek (Eds.). *Proceedings of ED-MEDIA and ED-TELECOM 98-World Conference on Educatioanl Multimedia and Hypermedia and World Conference on Educational Telecommunications* (pp.104-110). Charlottesville, VA: AACE.

Serim, F. (1999). Beyond Y2K: Bridging the digital divide. *Multimedia Schools*, 6(5).

Acknowledgements

This research was funded by a grant provided by Social Sciences Humanities Research Council. The information presented is solely the responsibility of the authors.

Exploring the Effect of Visual Complexity on Music Interval Recognition Tasks Involving User-Generated Images

George J. Henik[1] and Christopher Allen[2]
Educational Communication and Technology Program
New York University
United States
ed.ss.webmaster@nyu.edu[1] and allenchg@shu.edu[2]

Abstract: 36 volunteers were assigned to either a high (19) or low (17) visually complex (VC) treatment group and are given an online drawing environment in which they are to generate images based on musical intervals. They are then tested on their recall of the intervals by using their own images as choices. While the low visually complex group significantly improved, several factors including time may have played a more important role. Results are explained with respect to dual coding theory (Clark & Paivio, 1991; Paivio, 1971, 1990) and the generative theory of reading comprehension (Wittrock, 1990).

When examining multimedia learning environments, the most noticeable omissions occur when applied to music. One of the largest obstacles to designing effective music software has been hardware; that is computers that were being used for instruction were not capable of effectively reproducing authentic sound. Though the hardware has improved, there is little research on how to effectively use computers to teach music. In attempting to design instructional software that seeks to teach any aspect of music (performance, composition, history, or theory), it is imperative to understand how one processes music and how that information relates back to an effective design of musical educational media.

This pilot study will investigate the effect visual complexity may have on music interval recognition tasks to assist in future design decisions. Through the use of user generated images possible connections between aural information, visual information, and verbal information may be explored. By making a connection between these modalities, a more effective method for designing music education software may be possible.

Theoretical Foundation

There are a number of educational theories currently attempting to explain how individuals process new information. Mayer proposes a Cognitive Theory of Multimedia Learning alternately referred to as the Generative Theory of Multimedia Learning (Mayer, 1997, 1999; Mayer & Sims, 1994; Moreno & Mayer, 2000) in which he merges dual coding theory (Clark & Paivio, 1991; Paivio, 1971, 1990) and the generative theory of reading comprehension (Wittrock, 1990). Within the theoretical framework of the Cognitive Theory of Multimedia Learning, an individual perceives the information to be processed in one of two formats: words (verbal) or images (nonverbal) (Mayer, 2001). As the information is received either visually or aurally the learner selects the pieces that are pertinent to their knowledge acquisition. Depending how the individual originally learned or coded the information, either as a word or image, depends on how that information is subsequently recalled.

Cognitive load theory attempts to explain how an individual appropriates a level of mental processing energy to a specific amount of information (Cooper, 1990). In attempting to learn new information, the learner is placed in an environment where they are receiving a variety of information stimuli in potentially different modes. The amount of cognitive load can increase depending on the information itself, the presentation of the information, or the situation in which the learner is engaged. As cognitive load increases the learner becomes frustrated, makes mistakes, and generally performs poorly on the task they are attempting to complete (Keyes & Krul, 1992).

Increasingly, online multimedia systems are integrating greater amounts of visual information and potentially increasing the level of complexity within the information architecture. According to Keyes & Krul (1992), this complexity refers to "the number of information items into the number of relationships among them" (p. 122). Visual complexity is circumscribed as the amount of visual item interactivity contained within an image and limiting that information to the primary representation or more simply how much visual information is "packed" into the primary image. This information is generated through the intersection of lines, colors, tones, and texture gradients (Gibson, 1979). It is therefore believed that by incorporating more information within an image, the greater the level of visual complexity.

Considering cognitive load is increased as the amount of information being processed increases, the conjecture is that visual complexity will affect cognitive load. The greater the visual complexity, the greater the cognitive load. However, there is the possibility that a lack of visual complexity will also affect cognitive load in that the viewer will be required to expend mental energy to fill in the information not being provided.

The research involving educational implications of musical auditory processing with respect to images is scarce. Many studies look at how verbal and visual information are connected (Mayer, 1997, 1999; Mayer & Sims, 1994; Moreno & Mayer, 2000) or verbal and nonverbal information (Clark & Paivio, 1991). Other research indicates a deeper semantic connection between the visual and auditory modalities (Datteri 2000).

Clark, Stamm, Sussman, and Weitz (1974) examined recall of sounds that could be labeled, such as water or a saw, versus those that could not be easily labeled, such as a lathe or a calculator. The designation of "labelable" (p. 177) sounds was determined through a pilot study. When these sounds were mixed in with other sounds and subjects were asked to indicate whether or not they have heard that sound before, the "labelable" sounds were selected significantly more than "nonlabelable" sounds. They concluded that dual coding theory (Clark & Paivio, 1991; Paivio, 1971, 1990) could be expanded to sounds as well.

Lipscomb and Kendall (1994) examined the interaction between music soundtracks and film, suggesting that a model of motion picture perception must focus on the "*source* of meaning within both the auditory and visual modalities" (p. 88). The decisions of the appropriateness of a film score is based on the listener's past experience and is therefore "individual-specific." (p. 91).

In another study that examined verbal labels to music, Hiraoka and Umemoto (1981) used 19th and 20th Century classical excerpts to examine how verbal labels affect the memory recall of musical passages. Creating four groups (three with titles and one without), each group was given a booklet with the six titles. Each passage was played, and the subjects had to read the title of that passage, and then listen to the passage, forming an image of the music based on its title. Participants described their images on paper, and rated the "vividness of the image" on a scale from 1 to 5, with 5 being very vivid, followed by a post-treatment test. The study concluded that since these subjects made their own imagery they seemed to use it as a retrieval cue that resulted in the higher recognition scores.

So it seems that there may be a dual coding process that exists within the auditory modality, and that by having the user generate meaning or images, a stronger connection can be made. Wittrock's generative theory of reading comprehension (1990) discusses the importance in generative meaning through reading. Could this process be similar to verbal information in the sense of language?

There are several known facts about processing music. Whereas the visual modality is distributed spatially the auditory modality is distributed temporally. Also, the assumption that music is processed in the same way as language is far from clear. Sloboda (1985) expounds a clear comparison of music versus language, and finds that the perception in music is not as complete and automatic as it occurs in language, even for trained musicians. In this sense there seems to be two different systems that exist within the auditory modality, one for verbal information and one for auditory information.

Even if there are two different systems that exist, perhaps there are similarities in the way information is processed. Based on these points, it seems that if a user was able to generate an image based on a music interval, then a stronger connection could be made between the visual and aural modalities that would result in the user learning the intervals more effectively. What is the effect of user-generated images on interval recognition? What is the effect of high and low visual complexity on music interval recognition tasks?

Methods

Research Questions:
1. What is the effect of user-generated images on musical interval recognition tasks?
2. What is the effect of high and low visual complexity utilizing user-generated images on musical interval recognition tasks?
3. What is the relationship between user-generated images in high and low visual complexity groups for interval recognition and a) prior music knowledge, b) prior drawing knowledge, c) music interest and d) drawing interest?

Sample: The sample consisted of 36 graduate students who do not have a strong music background though do have a mixed background in graphic design. There were two intact groups from two semesters, each group was assigned to either a high (19) or low (17) visually complex treatment.

Materials: The experiment involved the use of a web-based drawing program developed in Macromedia's Flash 5.0. The user-generated images based on musical intervals were saved in a database and used later to test the participants' interval recognition. One group will have a very simple interface (Low Treatment

Group-LTG) while the other will be more complex (High Treatment Group- HTG) using more elements of interactivity such as a working keyboard (HTG) vs a sound button (LTG), tab-type pallets (HTG) vs all pallets laid out (LTG), and the option to continue (HTG) vs a timed treatment (LTG). Other variables were prior music and drawing experience, the number of times the keyboard or music buttons were pushed, and the time of the second treatment group. Each computer used had access to the Internet, a set of headphones for each user, and the Flash 5 browser plug-in.

Procedures: Learners were given three different musical intervals to memorize (Major 3rd, Perfect 4th, and Tritone). The low visual complex group had 5 minutes for each, while the high VC group could continue at any time. While listening to the intervals they were asked to draw a picture that represents to them what that interval sounds like. After having drawn pictures of all three, a post-test was administered, but this time each user had their own picture that they used as a cue to choose an answer. The entire experiment took between 25 and 35 minutes, with all the data collected through the use of an online database.

Results

For the first question, "What is the effect of user-generated images on interval recognition?" a paired t-test was conducted, using the interval pre- and post- tests as the dependent measure and the drawing program as the independent measure for each group. While the low visually complex group significantly improved (t=2.759, p=.014), the high visually complex group did not (t=.965, p=.349).

For the second question, "What is the effect of high and low visual complexity utilizing user-generated images on musical interval recognition tasks?" an unpaired t-test was conducted between the pre and post-test scores of each group. The pretest was not significant, though the posttest showed the low visually complex group was significantly larger (t=2.156, p=.038).

For the third question, "What is the relationship between user-generated images for interval recognition and a) prior music knowledge, b) prior drawing knowledge, c) music interest and d) drawing interest?" a multiple regression was conducted for the first group using answers from the questionnaire to rate prior music and drawing knowledge as the independent variables, and their answers from the post-test as the dependent measure. A series of multiple regressions for the low visually complex group yielded a significant model (F (4, 12) = 4.284, p = .022) with r^2 = .588. Based on a correlation table that yielded no significant results, multiple regressions were not conducted on the high visually complex group.

Conclusions

For the low treatment group, the treatment was effective in using the generated images as a visual cue for auditory information, and adds to the body of research that addresses the effectiveness of Web-based instruction. In this sense, there seems to be a system that helps connect auditory information and visual information without either one having a designation of "verbal information" as in dual coding theory (Clark & Paivio, 1991; Paivio, 1971, 1990). This connection is made through the user generating an individually meaningful chunk of information (Wittrock, 1990), in this case an image.

An inverse relationship existed between the level of treatment group and performance, indicating that by increasing the level of visual complexity, instruction degraded. The discrepancy between the groups may be explained through two other ways, however. The biggest difference in the two interfaces was time. In the LTG, the participants were forced to wait a full 5 minutes before being able to go on to the next interval. Meanwhile, the participants in the HTG could continue at their discretion. While some participants in the HTG spent approximately 8 minutes on the treatment section, others spent less than 1 minute; far below the 15 minutes the LTG spent on the actual memorization and drawing tasks.

Another possible explanation for between the LTG and HTG results was the class mindset when the treatment was administered. When students in the HTG were administered the treatment, the classroom was very hot and the treatment date fell during a more stressful point in the semester whereas the LTG received the treatment in a relatively comfortable room during a less stressful time in the semester. This might account for some of the more random answers, and helps to explain why some students spent less than a minute on the entire treatment.

Based on the exit surveys in both groups, students were asked to comment on their experience. Qualitative analysis of these comments revealed that many of the students felt the instructions leading up to the treatment were too verbose and could have been accomplished in a more concise manner. However, the ability to understand the goals of the treatment were mixed. Some individuals understood exactly what was expected of them while others felt the requirements were unclear. Clarity appeared to be a continuous theme in many comments, whether it was the clarity of the directions or how to use the interface.

One of the primary differences between the two treatment groups was a change in the interface. In the first treatment individuals indicated problems associated with the fore and background color panels being spaced too close together. This problem seemed to be alleviated in the second treatment by modifying the interface design because no comments focused on a problem differentiating between the two color palettes. In the second treatment, while individuals did comment on difficulties with the interface, these stemmed from problems associated with the aforementioned directions.

While difficult to assess, because of the minor changes associated with an already difficult interface and complex information structure, the addition of a keyboard as a visual cueing mechanism seemed to have no effect on the overall treatment. However, this is supposition considering individuals in the second treatment were not forced to spend a predetermined length of time on each treatment and could skip ahead.

Considering the element of time, a question raised by this study is exactly what effect does time have on the treatment. One final question how would the results differ if this treatment were run with music students as the participants. Considering there is an incentive to learn and not merely gloss through the treatment the potential to understand the basics of the treatment as well as actually incorporate imagery as a learning method would prove interesting. Since the learners generated their own images, the potential for them to undergo a deeper cognitive process may eventually lead to a more effective method for ear training and music education in general.

For an expansion on this article, working demonstrations, and any other research conducted by the authors, please visit http://www.georgehenik.com/

References

Clark, J. M., & Paivio, A. (1991). Dual coding theory and education. *Educational Psychology Review, 3*(3), 149 - 210.

Clark, M., Stamm, S., Sussman, R., & Weitz, S. (1974). Encoding of auditory stimuli in recognition memory tasks. *Bulletin of the Psychonomic Society, 3*(3A), 177-178.

Cooper, G. (1990). Cognitive load theory as an aid for instructional design. *Australian Journal of Educational Technology, 6(2),* 108-113.

Datteri, D. L. (2000). *Music, figures, and words, oh my! The influences of music on stick figures and word perception: An audiovisual gestalt investigation.* Unpublished Dissertation, Texas Christian University, Fort Worth.

Gibson, J.J. (1979). *Ecological approach to visual perception.* London: Houghton Mifflin Co..

Hiraoka, I., & Umemoto, T. (1981). The effect of titles on the memory for music. *Psychologia, 24,* 228-234.

Keyes, E. & Krull R. (1992). User information processing strategies and online visual structure. SIGDOC'92 Proceedings. Tenth Annual International Conference. Toronto 121-128.

Lipscomb, S. D., & Kendall, R. A. (1994). Perceptual judgment of the relationship between musical and visual components in film. *Psychomusicology, 13,* 60-98.

Mayer, R. E. (1997). Multimedia learning: Are we asking the right questions? *Educational Psychology, 32*(1), 1-19.

Mayer, R. E. (1999, April). *When multimedia works: Designing multimedia for meaningful learning.* Paper presented at the American Educational Research Association, Montreal.

Mayer, R. E. (2001). *Multimedia learning.* New York: Cambridge University Press.

Mayer, R. E., & Sims, V. K. (1994). For whom is a picture worth a thousand words? Extensions of a dual-coding theory of multimedia learning. *Journal of Educational Psychology, 86*(3), 389-401.

Moreno, R., & Mayer, E. (2000). A coherence effect in multimedia learning: the case for minimizing irrelevant sounds in the design of multimedia instructional messages. *Journal of Educational Psychology, 92*(1), 117-125.

Paivio, A. (1971). *Imagery and verbal processes.* New York: Holt, Rinehart, & Winston.

Paivio, A. (1990). *Mental representations: A dual-coding approach.* Oxford, England: Oxford University Press.

Paivio, A., & Lambert, W. (1981). Dual coding and bilingual memory. *Journal of Verbal Learning and Verbal Behavior, 20*(532-539), 532-539.

Sloboda, J. (1985). *The musical mind.* New York: Oxford Press.

Wittrock, M. C. (1990). Generative processes of comprehension. *Educational Psychologist, 24*(4), 345-376.

A Systematic Review of Technology to Support Adult Learning in Communities of Practice

Gyeong Mi Heo
Department of Educational and Counselling Psychology
McGill University
Montreal, Canada
gheo@po-box.mcgill.ca

Abstract: This paper presents a systematic review regarding how technology supports adult learning in communities of practice. It presents the systematic review procedure that was developed, based on NHS CRD (2001) protocol, from publication sources relevant to the topic. It includes the identification of research from an initial question that is how technology supports adult learning in communities of practice, a search strategy, a study quality assessment, a data extraction strategy and a synthesis of findings. Because most of the pertinent research is qualitative, a typology of qualitative research and a critical appraisal checklist for quality assessment were designed and are presented. The results presented are synthesizing evidence from studies that meet certain quality criteria and they are discussed in terms of (a) the kinds of technologies applied in communities of practice, and (b) successful features of the technology that seem to contribute to learning.

Introduction

The development of computer-mediated communications has led to rapid changes in learning environments. In the professional development literature, particularly, the concepts of "learning communities" and "communities of practice" with asynchronous and synchronous communications are emphasized. Even though many online learning communities and/or communities of practice are created and maintained (e.g., Brown & Gray, 1995; Burk, 2000), there is a lack of clear and helpful guidelines to increase meaningful learning in these contexts (Wenger, 1998). Most of the relevant literature offers models, programs, and projects in relation to online communities in learning environments. However, there are very few organized accounts of the significant, valuable, and reliable evidence regarding the effectiveness of on-line technology for fostering and supporting learning in communities of practice (Owen, 1998; Simich-Dudgeon, 1999). In this context, a systematic review, such as those currently being conducted in the medical and health care field [1] and considered seriously in education [2], seems to be an appropriate research method to produce general statements about the relationships between technology and learning through the synthesis of individual research results.

The research presented here is a systematic review whose purposes are (a) to present an application of the systematic review protocol in educational research on the question of web-based technology to support learning in communities of practice and, (b) based on the results of the systematic review, to examine the effectiveness of technology in communities of practice. This paper presents a preliminary review of the studies in order to test the systematic review process and its feasibility. The following two objectives are identified

- Objective 1: What kinds of technologies were applied to in communities of practice?
- Objective 2: What features of the technology seem to contribute successfully to learning?

The next section introduces the steps involved in conducting such a review.

---

[1] The Cochrane Collaboration (http://www.cochrane.org/)

[2] The Campbell Collaboration (http://www.campbellcollaboration.org/)

Systematic Review

The systematic review is "a review of the evidence on a clearly formulated question that uses systematic and explicit methods to identify, select, and critically appraise relevant primary research, and to extract and analyze data from the studies that are included in the review" (NHS CRD, 2001). The systematic review is a rigorous methodology that has emerged in the fields of medical and health care. The Campbell Collaboration was initiated recently to study the effects of social and educational policies and practices as a sibling organization to the Cochrane Collaboration that prepares and maintains systematic reviews of the effects of interventions in health care (Boruch, Petrosino, & Chalmers, 1999). According to the CRAG (1996), the characteristics of a systematic review in comparison with a traditional literature review are (1) it is more systematic and objective through whole review procedures, and (2) it makes possible to increase power by synthesizing the results of a number of related smaller studies.

Identification of research

As a first step, to develop a search strategy, the research question should be broken down into facets in terms of population (e.g., *adult learning* that includes university education, professional development and workplace training), interventions (e.g., *communities of practice* and *technology*), outcomes (e.g., unrestricted), and study design (e.g., unrestricted). The search conducted with these keywords in the ERIC database and 253 citations were obtained.

Selection of studies

In this step, the obtained citations were selected through two filters for inclusion and exclusion in order to have more retrieval of relevant documents. For an initial selection, abstracts of citations obtained from the previous ERIC search were scanned and selected using the initial criteria for inclusion and exclusion. The second selection was conducted by reading the full texts. At this stage, more detailed criteria were applied and 60 papers were selected for the next step which consisted in assessing the quality of the studies.

Study quality assessment

Next, the quality of the studies in the corpus thus obtained was assessed. For the quality assessment, at first, the type of evidence is characterized according to research methods in educational research – quantitative research and qualitative research. As for the qualitative research is, typically, needed to be subdivided, because most research papers those are included in the review form as the qualitative research rather than quantitative research and each research method has different report styles and required components. The types of qualitative research were: ethnographic research, action research, evaluation research, case study, and design experiments. Sixty citations were categorized according to the criteria for research methods. Among these citations, thirty-eight citations were classified under descriptive reports and/or opinions of experts, and those were excluded in the review. Among the remaining 22 citations, one was an experimental research with quantitative measures, and 21 citations relate to 20 studies were qualitative researches. Therefore, 21 research papers were included for quality assessment.

Then, a critical appraisal checklist was developed for this review to assess the quality of qualitative research studies in terms of credibility and reliability. Hence, the questions are focused on whether a research paper describes each expected component of a study within the category clearly, appropriately, and reliably. The famework underlying the critical appraisal checklist is largely composed of two parts, one regarding general features of research methods (e.g., Introduction, Methods, and Discussion / Implication), and the other for each specific research method. The remaining 20 research papers, other than the experimental study, were assessed through the critical appraisal checklist. According to the results, 11 qualitative studies and one experimental study were selected for inclusion in the review. Thus, qualified evidence was extracted and synthesized to answer the research questions.

Data extraction and Data synthesis

In this pilot review, initially, the author extracted data into a FileMaker Pro5 database, and then, collated and summarized the results of primary studies included.

Results & Discussion

Objective 1: What kinds of technologies were applied in communities of practice?

The technologies that were applied in 12 studies were e-mail, threaded message board, chat room, web pages, electronic bulletin board, forum, online network, mailing lists, web conferencing, listserv, electronic database. Representative examples of synchronous technology are chat room and video conferencing. However, there none of the studies considered video conferencing. In five studies (Fusco, 2000; Harmon, 2000; Milton, 1999; Ohlund, 1999; Powers, 1997), chat applications were used, and, also, these were combined with one or several asynchronous technologies, such as electronic bulletin board, mailing lists, listserve, and e-mail.

All studies report positive effects of technology in each practice. Technology seems to support learning in the following manners:

- To have multiple conversations (Owen, 1999).
- To expand learning experiences through online networks (Brett, 1997; Rusell, 1999).
- To develop an "out-of-class" classroom community (Burns, 1996; Brett, 1997; Edens, 2000).
- To develop collaborative work (Milton, 1999; Ohlund, 1999)

Objective 2: What features of the technology seem to contribute successfully to learning?

Eight of 12 studies were conducted in formal learning environments. That is, learning communities were built within university-based courses. As for the target learners, six studies involved pre-service and/or in-service teachers. Three studies (Edens, 2000; Milton, 1999; Owen, 1998) explored possible factors contributing to the development of an online learning community.

In conclusion, it is possible from the studies reviewed to synthesize the following features to take into account in order to develop an effective online learning community:

1. The purposes of the group should be determined. (Owen, 1998).
2. An atmosphere of respect is required. Participants should respect others' opinions and ideas (Edens, 2000; Owen, 1999; Harmon, 2000; Simich-Dudgeon, 1999).
3. The role of a moderator or facilitator is one of the critical factors (Edens, 2000; Milton, 1999; Owen, 1998).
4. The participation framework may effect the development of online learning communities (Edens, 2000; Owen, 1999; Harmon, 2000).
5. The strategies for facilitating learners' participation should be considered (Brett, 1997; Fusco, 2000; Hirtle, 2000, Harmon, 2000).
6. On the other hand, Edens (2000) and Milton (1999) indicate two difficulties regarding the use of technology in a community: (a) the problems of the software and network itself, and (b) the lack of non-verbal communication cues, such as eye contact and body expression, in electronic written communication.

According to the results of this systematic review, there are several findings having implications for follow-up reviews and further research. First, the search sources should be expanded, for example by deploying more systematical search strategies in the ERIC database, searching the WWW, and hand searching in proceeding papers or journals not included in ERIC search. Second, in order to increase the validity and reliability for the assessment of study quality, the critical appraisal checklist needs to be continuously developed and validated, and two or more researchers should participate in the review. Third, more research needs to be conducted in non-formal learning contexts emphasizing adult learning and various adult learners.

Conclusions

Computer-mediated communication (CMC) makes it possible to interact asynchronously and synchronously at a distance. It can facilitate sharing, negotiating, developing, sustaining, and building knowledge in communities of practice. During this process, learning can be achieved.

Based on the review of 12 studies, the major factors contributing to facilitate learning in communities of practice are: (a) well-defined purposes for the group, (b) an atmosphere of respect among participants, (c) a moderator or facilitator playing an active role, (d) a structured participation framework, and (e) strategies to trigger and maintain participation.

This systematic review shows the positive potential of the systematic review as an effective research method in educational research, at least in the area of educational technology in practice settings. That is, existing variations in practices and general relationships can be examined by synthesizing related qualified data in smaller studies. It suggests that conducting further systematic reviews in this area will be fruitful.

References

Boruch, R., Petrosino, A., & Chalmers, I. (1999, July). *The Campbell Collaboration: a proposal for systematic, multi-national, and continuous reviews of evidence.* Paper presented at the Planning Meeting on the Campbell Collaboration, School of Public Poliy, University College London, July 1999.

Brett, C. & Woodruff, E. (1997). *Communities of Inquiry among Pre-service Teachers Investigating Mathematics.* Paper presented at the Annual Meeting of the American Educational Research Association (Chicago, IL, March 24-28, 1997).

Brown, J. S. & Gray, E. S. (1995). *The people are the Company: How to build your company around your people.* Retrieved from http://www.fastcompany.com/ online/01/people.html#

Burk, M. (2000). *Communities of Practice.* Retrieved from http://www. tfhrc.gov/pubrds/mayjun00/commprac.htm

Burns, R. C. & Meehan, M. L. (1996). E-Mail Survey of the Interdisciplinary Teamed Instruction (ITI) Listserv Discussion Group: Exploratory Study of an Electronic Community of Learners. Appalachia Educational Lab., Charleston, WV.

Edens, K. M. & Gallini, J. K. (2000). Developing a Discourse Community of Preservice Teachers in a Technology-Mediated Context. *Teacher Educator.* v35 n4 p64-82 Spring 2000.

Fusco, J., Gehlbach, H., & Schlager, M. (2000). *Assessing the Impact of a Large-Scale Online Teacher Professional Development Community.* Proceedings of SITE 2000 (11th, San Diego, California, February 8-12, 2000). Volumes 1-3.

Harmon, S. W. & Jones, M. G. (2000). *A Qualitative Analysis of Situated Web-Based Instruction.* Paper presented at the Annual Meeting of the American Educational Research Association (AERA) (New Orleans, LA, April 24-28, 2000).

Hirtle, J. P., & McGrew-Zoubi, R. (2000) *New Horizons in Distance Education: Re-Mapping the Pedagogical Terrain.* Proceedings of SITE 2000 (11th, San Diego, California, February 8-12, 2000).

Milton, J., Davis, M., & Watkins, K. E. (1999). *Virtual Learning Communities: Creating Meaning Through Dialogue and Inquiry in Cyberspace.* In Qualitative Studies in HRD: Academy of Human Resource Development (AHRD) Conference Proceedings.

NHS Centre for Reviews and Dissemination. (2001). *Undertaking systematic reviews of research of effectiveness.* CRD Report Number 4 (2nd ed.) Retrieved from http://www.york.ac.uk/inst/crd/report4.htm

Ohlund, B., Andrews, S., Yu, C. H., Jannasch-Pennell, A., & DiGangi, S. A. (1999). *Impact of Asynchronous and Synchronous Internet-Based Communication on Collaboration and Performance among K-12 Teachers.* Paper presented at the Annual Meeting of the American Educational Research Association (Montreal, Quebec, Canada, April 19-23, 1999).

Owen, C., Pollard, J., Kilpatrick, S., & Rumley, D. (1998). *Electronic Learning Communities: Lessons from the Ether.* CRLRA Discussion Paper Series.

Powers, S. M. & Mitchell, J. (1997). *Student Perceptions and Performance in a Virtual Classroom Environment.* Paper presented at the Annual Meeting of the American Educational Research Association, (Chicago, IL, March, 1997).

Russell, M. & Ginsburg, L. (1999). *Learning Online: Extending the Meaning of Community.* A Review of Three Programs from the Southeastern United States. IN: National Center for Adult Literacy, Philadelphia, PA.

Simich-Dudgeon, C. (1999). Interpersonal Involvement Strategies in Online Textual Conversations: A Case Study of a Learning Community.

The Critical Reviews Advisory Group [CRAG] (1996). *Introduction To Systematic Reviews by ScHRR.* Retrieved from http://www.shef.ac.uk/~scharr/ triage/docs/systematic/

Wenger, E. (1998a). *Communities of practice: Learning, meaning, and identity.* New York: Cambridge University Press.

The Professional Development of Human Service Professionals in Rural and Remote Areas: Investigating the Affordances of the Internet

Anthony Herrington
School of Education
Edith Cowan University
Australia
a.herrington@ecu.edu.au

Jan Herrington
School of Communications and Multimedia
Edith Cowan University
Australia
j.herrington@ecu.edu.au

Abstract: This paper is a report of work-in-progress on a project that seeks to identify effective ways in which the Internet can be used to overcome the isolation of human service professionals employed in rural and remote areas. Professionals employed in rural locations in Australia will be surveyed and interviewed with regard to their needs, awareness, use and benefits of the Internet for professional development and support. Guidelines will be produced to document strategies for the design and delivery of effective use of the Internet to support and assist professionals in rural and remote areas.

Introduction

Retaining human service professionals—such as teachers and health care workers—is a huge problem in many rural and remote areas of the world. The overall objective of this paper is to report on work-in-progress that seeks to identify effective ways in which the Internet can be used to overcome the isolation of professionals employed in these remote regions. More specifically, the research described will use surveys and interviews to:

- Identify the *level* of professional development and support that is available through the Internet to professionals working in rural Australia;
- Assess the *use* of this professional development and support, and
- Identify the perceived *needs* and *benefits* of the professional development to the professionals in these remote areas.

The findings of this research will provide a basis for informed decision making on the design, development and provision of professional development and support through the Internet for a wide range of professions working in rural Australia as well as the training needs to access such support.

Background

There is a growing concern that reduced outcomes in health, education, employment and technology in rural Australia have the potential to undermine national cohesion (House of Representatives Standing Committee on Primary Industries and Regional Services, 2000; Regional Australia Summit Steering Committee, 2000). As a consequence, strategic support for rural and regional areas has become a national priority (Anderson, 2001). Recommendations from these reports document specific strategies for establishing improved social infrastructures and equity of services to enable improved health and education outcomes, better employment pathways and improved telecommunications. Attracting and retaining professional and paraprofessional staff in regional and rural areas is recognised as a significant factor in improving many of these outcomes.

Compared to their metropolitan counterparts, rural communities face a number of reduced health outcomes. These include higher mortality rates, higher incidence of cardiovascular disease, preventable accidents, cancer and diabetes, higher rates of youth suicide, higher rates of hospitalisation and reduced access to medical practitioners, nurses, midwives, pharmacists, dentists and other allied health professionals (National Rural Health Alliance, 2001). This trend is also observed in American rural communities (National Rural Health Association, 1998).

Similarly, educational outcomes are reduced for rural compared to metropolitan communities. Schools in rural Australia experience a higher turnover rate of staff than metropolitan schools (Tomlinson, 1994). A high turnover of inexperienced staff results in schools lacking stability and program continuity, with clear disadvantages for students (Human Rights and Equal Opportunity Commission, 2000). The commission has documented the reduced quality of educational outcomes achieved by rural students in respect of literacy, numeracy, retention rates and participation in higher education. While there are initiatives in place to attract professionals not enough research attention is being given to determining effective ways to retain them (Collins, 1999; Murphy & Angelski, 1996, National Rural Health Association, 1998).

The innovative use of information communication technologies (ICT) is argued by a number of researchers as a viable option for providing professional development and support for rural professionals in the areas of health (e.g., Striffler, & Fire, 1999; Sykes, & McIntosh, 1999). The National Rural Health Association (1998) in the United States argues that although much effort has been expended in placement of physicians in rural areas, relatively little has been done to enhance their retention. The association argues that professional isolation is often a reason to leave a rural area and, as in Australia, the association suggests that innovations in information technologies such as the Internet and teleinformatics can become resources for diminishing this isolation.

A number of websites have been developed to provide professional development and support to professionals in rural areas. For example, sites have been developed to provide information, resources and channels of communication for medical, nursing and allied health professionals working in the NSW public health system (Wensley, 1999). Shackcloth (1999) describes a CD-ROM and Internet interactive resource that provides professional development for dentists in rural and remote regions.

In response to the need for continuing professional contact for newly appointed teachers, Herrington and Herrington (2001) have developed a website entitled Mathematics Education on the Web (MEOW) to enable new teachers to keep contacts with their peers and lecturers, and to access curriculum resources. The site comprises: a discussion board, where issues of relevance can be discussed; lesson plan resources, where teachers can download lesson plans to use with their classes; exemplary teaching videos, where teachers can view a variety of teaching strategies demonstrated by expert teachers; and links to a variety of websites including mathematics and professional development resources.

There are some insights into the effectiveness of these and similar professional development and support websites. Watson, Bannan, Clark, and Timmerman (1999) report that in early trials of Internet use, web-based discussion forums proved unsustainable mainly because allied health workers appeared not in the habit of accessing them on a regular basis. However, email-based discussion lists (listservs) appeared to be more successful with participants indicating that this form of communication helped reduce their professional isolation.

Methodology

Using a variety of databases and direct contact with a range of individuals and organisations, the researchers are conducting a systematic review of the literature on the use of web-based resources for the professional development and support of professionals working and living in rural communities. This includes Australian and international literature, together with additional sources of information. The review of the literature focuses on such issues as:
- the professional needs and benefits in relation to web-based professional development and support,
- the factors that facilitate/hinder the professional use of web-based professional development and support

- the design and functionality of resources
- approaches to IT training for professionals

Professionals working in rural areas of Western Australia and Queensland will be selected for the study. These states have been chosen as they both have large remote areas with geographically dispersed rural communities, and both have a long history of responding to the special needs of these communities (as evidenced for example, by both states' extensive distance education and health initiatives). As such they provide a diverse sample from which generalisations can be made.

The professionals will be contacted by mail via relevant government agencies which include the Education Departments of Western Australia and Queensland, Health Departments of Western Australia and Queensland and the Aboriginal Medical Services. A postal questionnaire will be developed and sent to each professional identified as working in a rural area. Surveys will be undertaken to elicit information on:

- demographic data (e.g., age, qualifications, period of employment)
- needs, awareness, use and accessibility of professional development and support that uses ICT
- benefits/drawbacks of professional development and support that uses ICT
- their beliefs about the impact of ICT in ameliorating professional isolation
- perceived barriers to using ICT
- their IT competence

The initial data analysis will be conducted by profession, examining in detail the effectiveness of ICT on overcoming professional isolation. The analysis will:

- assess rural professionals' *use* of web-based professional development and support resources. For example, are they aware of relevant sites? Do they access these sites. What level of interactivity do they engage in?
- identify professionals' perceived *benefits* of web-based professional development and support resources. For example, are relevant sites helpful?
- identify professionals' perceived *needs* for web-based professional development and support resources. For example, what other resources and supports are needed? What further training do they need to benefit from these sites?

The findings from this research will be used to develop a broad analysis of the impact of the Internet on professionals working in rural communities, and its effectiveness in ameliorating professional isolation. In this part of the analysis, particular attention will be paid to:

- identifying any generic impacts of ICT on professions
- identifying impacts which are likely to be pertinent to specific professions
- identifying effective generic design and implementation strategies
- identifying effective design and implementation strategies specific to certain professions

The findings of the analysis will be the basis of a concise draft report that will be distributed to various stakeholders (State and Federal Government agencies, tertiary and higher education institutions, and professional associations) seeking further comments and suggestions. Such information may form the basis of a more informed approach to the retention of professional in rural and remote regions of the world.

References

Anderson, J. (2001). *Stronger regions, a stronger Australia.* Canberra: Commonwealth of Australia.

Collins. T, (1999). *Attracting and retaining teachers in rural areas.* Available: www.ael.org/eric/digests/edorc997.htm

Herrington, A., & Herrington, J. (2001). *Web-based strategies for professional induction in rural, regional and remote areas.* Paper presented at the Australian Association for Research in Education Conference, Fremantle, WA, December 2001.

House of Representatives Standing Committee on Primary Industries and Regional Services (2000). T*ime running out: Shaping regional Australia's future. Report of in inquiry into infrastructure and the development* *of Australia's regional areas.* Canberra: The Parliament of the Commonwealth of Australia.

Human Rights and Equal Opportunity Commission (2000). *National Inquiry into Rural and Remote Education (Australia): Emerging Themes.* Sydney: Author.

Murphy, P., & Angelski, K. (1996). Rural teacher mobility. *Rural Educator.* 18(2), 5-11.

National Rural Health Alliance (1998). *Fighting rural decay-Dental heath in rural communities.* Available: http://www.ruralhealth.org.au/

National Rural Health Alliance (2001). *2001 Election Charter.* Available: http://www.ruralhealth.org.au/

National Rural Health Association (1998). *Physician recruitment and retention* Available: www.nrharual.org/dc/issuepapers/paper13/html.html

Shackcloth, S. (1999). Using multimedia technology to overcome the tyranny of distance in delivering education and training in oral health. *5th National Rural Health Conference.* Adelaide Available: http://www.ruralhealth.org.au/

Striffler, N. & Fire, N. (1999). Embedding personnel development into early intervention service delivery: Elements in the process. *Infants and Young Children, 11*(3), 50-61.

Sykes, D. & McIntosh, W.A. (1999). Telemedicine, hospital viability, and community embeddedness: A case study. *Journal of Healthcare Management.* 44(1). 59-71.

Tomlinson (1994). *Schooling in rural Western Australia. The ministerial review of schooling in rural Western Australia.* Perth: Education Department of WA.

Watson, J., Bannan, G., Clark, S. & Timmerman, L. (1999). Strengthening connections in the Bush: On-line communications and collaboration in allied health. *5th National Rural Health Conference.* Adelaide Available: http://www.ruralhealth.org.au/]

Wensley, M. (1999). The NSW health clinical information access project (CIAP) website: Leaping the boundary fence via the Internet. *5th National Rural Health Conference.* Adelaide Available: http://www.ruralhealth.org.au/

Computer Assisted Simulation and Role Playing

Donald R. Hetzner

Department of History/Secondary Social Studies

State University of New York College at Buffalo, USA

Hetznerd@AOL.Com

Social studies education is the least empirical of all the subdisciplines in the social sciences. An influx of computers into classrooms has had little impact on the nature and direction of social studies instruction. E-learning in the social studies usually consists of using materials such as computer based games with simulated environments and the Internet as expository techniques carried out in very traditional classroom settings. This holds true in most classrooms whether there is a computer for every student or every ten students. The average social studies teacher has little experience in integrating e-learning into a complex curriculum that is undergoing mandated change. This is reinforced by college experiences where students model professors housed in traditional academic and professional departments. At most, social studies students are taught to produce Power Point presentations, and the basics of Internet research.

What forms does e-learning take in typical social studies classrooms? Much depends on the school "rules", the use of consumable supplies, and the nature of teacher. At Niagara Falls SHS, where every student has full-time use of a laptop, students are required to keep their computers in backpacks and only take them out at a teacher's request. Why? Because students play computer games, or leave messages for friends. Many schools control access to large numbers of computers by placing them in the library. Unfortunately, in many of those same schools the librarian does not let students sit next to one another. So, there is no such thing as class use of computers in those schools. In other schools there may be several computers or computers for all students but only one printer and that on the teachers desk. Some schools only issue one printer cartridge or one ream of paper to teachers each semester. Last, social studies is so conservative and tradition bound that teachers use computers in ways they recognize.

PowerPoint takes the place of notes and overheads in many classrooms. Teacher after teacher has happily related to me that "I have all my notes and overheads on PowerPoint now." A teacher of Honors Economics in a local high school was given a petition from her students, only half in jest, "no more PowerPoint" one day when I was visiting her student teacher. Teachers in a number of schools have received the same message.

You can tell when teachers are using the Internet rather than manipulative models for instruction. In the not too distant past 5th and 9th grade students built models of the Mesopotamian ziggurat at home and brought them to class. What models are in the rooms are dust covered and usually rather primitive and poorly constructed, the models that were so "dumpy" that students did not take them home. At least one wall is covered with poorly drawn ziggurats. Students search the Web for " ziggurat" and locate and view a rendering of the building and a discussion of ancient Mesopotamia. During this exercise usually at least one student asks, "what do I do now?" Most of the time the teacher's answer is "draw a picture of it!"

Friday is still AV day in the social studies class. Major movies on DVD's such as *Pearl Harbor*, *Enemy at the Gate*, *Band of Brothers*, *Saving Private Ryan*, and *Gladiator* are standard fare despite the on-screen cautions on use. Possibly even more blatant is the use of copyrighted photographs in extensive, 20-30 minute, PowerPoint presentations.

"Experiences in Simulation and Role Playing," a graduate course at the State University College at Buffalo attempts to cope with the above problems by presenting a model of e-learning that is interactive, data-based, and well-integrated with a variety of media. This is a model with the basic purpose of educating secondary social studies students to become active participants in a democracy. Graduate students, all of whom are NYS certified social studies teachers, are instructed in role playing and simulation through participation in activities such as John Gearon's "War or Peace?" and Barbara Olmo's "Pioneers in Arania."

Students are introduced to Statistical Package for the Social Sciences with a data bases from Nan Rothschild's *New York City Neighborhoods: The 18th Century* (Rothschild 1990), and the writer's *Historian: Building a New Nation in 1789* (Hetzner 2000). The Rothschild book focuses on the demographics of NYC Wards in selected years including 1789. *Historian...* is a proprietary database that focuses on the 1st Congress that met in NYC in 1789. It details the socioeconomic, religious, and ethnic backgrounds of the 95 legislators and their fathers, and voting behaviors and political attitudes toward the Constitution and George Washington. Essentially, it is an introduction to quantitative history and the basic evidence used in historical research. To teach students how to ask historical questions they are taught the basics of SPSS and questionnaire design. The process used in class is termed "interviewing the dead." Graduate students work with the database, which contains music clips, cartoons, reproductions of paintings...until they are familiar enough with the processes of historical investigation and materials design to produce their own computer-assisted simulations and role plays. The basic rules are that:

1. Databases must support the simulation/role play, be the basic stand-alone component of the exercise, or gather data from the secondary students on the results of the activity

2. PowerPoint may be used only to present information that would take too long or be awkward/impossible to present in another fashion

3. Audio is the preferred method for having a moderator communicate with participants in an autoinstrucional simulation/role play

4. The E-activity must be designed to fit into or complement the NYS secondary social studies curriculum

What types of computer databases and simulations/role plays do secondary social studies teachers produce under these guidelines? Graduate students have submitted approximately 45 projects since the requirement for computer-assisted databases was added to course requirements. The following 5 descriptions are of typical student produced databases. Each of the databases is associated with a simulation or role play on the same topic.

1. Terrorism (a hypothetical situation). Following a terrorist incident the Draft is reinstated. The database simulates random selection of draftees and compiles demographics and physical attributes of those selected

2. Political involvement. This database explores the connection between students' political involvement, socioeconomic background, interests (including social studies), and knowledge of current events.

3. "Failure is Impossible" draws its name from the 75th anniversary celebration of the 19th Amendment. This database of women goes from Abigail Adams to Nellie Rodgers Schuler, and includes information on age, religion, politics, and marital state.

4. Conjoined twins. The author of this database and role play teaches 4th grade in a Catholic school--data can be displayed by nationality, ethnicity, sex, and family background.

5. Heritage of church members. A class member who is an active member of a largely African-American Baptist church compiled, and is now expanding, a database on the history of the church that focuses on the demographics of parishioners. Family data has been gathered on church founders who moved from the South in the 1860's up to the present day. The database is being used in local elementary schools and in the church to foster community.

A more extensive project, carried out in collaboration with teachers who are former *Experiences in Simulation and Role Play* students, is planned for the 2002-2003 academic year. Arrangements have been made for an architectural firm to complete a reconnaissance study of the architectural/historical significance of 1000 buildings in a Western New York village using "Preserve New York" funding. During or following completion of that component, students in social studies and the leadership program at the high school will work with the writer and an associate to carry out an assets study of the community. Secondary students will design questionnaires and interview schedules, interview village residents, process data, and present the findings at a regularly-scheduled Village Board meeting

References

Rothschild, N.A. (1990). *New York City Neighborhoods: The 18th Century.* New York: Academic Press .

Hetzner, D. Historian: Building a New Nation in 1789. *Creative Interactive Teaching: Case Methods & Other Technique*s, 2000. World Association for Case Method Research & Application, Boston, MA. 487-493.

Computer Assisted Simulation and Role Playing

Donald R. Hetzner

Department of History/Secondary Social Studies

State University of New York College at Buffalo, USA

Hetznerd@AOL.Com

Social studies education is the least empirical of all the subdisciplines in the social sciences. An influx of computers into classrooms has had little impact on the nature and direction of social studies instruction. E-learning in the social studies usually consists of using materials such as computer based games with simulated environments and the Internet as expository techniques carried out in very traditional classroom settings. This holds true in most classrooms whether there is a computer for every student or every ten students. The average social studies teacher has little experience in integrating E-learning into a complex curriculum that is undergoing mandated change. This is reinforced by college experiences where students model professors housed in traditional academic and professional departments. At most, social studies students are taught to produce Power Point presentations, and the basics of Internet research.

What forms does E-learning take in typical social studies classrooms? Much depends on the school "rules", the use of consumable supplies, and the nature of teacher. At Niagara Falls SHS, where every student has full-time use of a laptop, students are required to keep their computers in backpacks and only take them out at a teacher's request. Why? Because students play computer games, or leave messages for friends. Many schools control access to large numbers of computers by placing them in the library. Unfortunately, in many of those same schools the librarian does not let students sit next to one another. So, there is no such thing as class use of computers in those schools. In other schools there may be several computers or computers for all students but only one printer and that on the teachers desk. Some schools only issue one printer cartridge or one ream of paper to teachers each semester. Last, social studies is so conservative and tradition bound that teachers use computers in ways they recognize.

PowerPoint takes the place of notes and overheads in many classrooms. Teacher after teacher has happily related to me that "I have all my notes and overheads on PowerPoint now." Interesting enough, A teacher of Honors Economics in a local high school was given a petition from her students, only half in jest, "no more PowerPoint" one day when I was visiting her student teacher. Teachers in a number of schools have received the same message.

You can tell when teachers are using the Internet rather than manipulative models for instruction. In the not too distant past 5th and 9th grade students built models of the Mesopotamian ziggurat at home and brought them to class. What models are in the rooms are dust covered and usually rather primitive and poorly constructed, the models that were so "dumpy" that students did not take them home. At least one wall is covered with poorly drawn ziggurats. Students search the Web for " ziggurat" and locate and view a rendering of the building and a discussion of ancient Mesopotamia. During this exercise usually at least one student asks, "what do I do now?" Most of the time the teacher's answer is "draw a picture of it!"

Friday is still AV day in the social studies class. Major movies on DVD's such as *Pearl Harbor*, *Enemy at the Gate*, *Band of Brothers*, *Saving Private Ryan*, and *Gladiator* are standard fare despite the on-screen cautions on use. Possibly even more blatant is the use of copyrighted photographs in extensive, 20-30 minute, PowerPoint presentations.

"Experiences in Simulation and Role Playing," a graduate course at the State University College at Buffalo attempts to cope with the above problems by presenting a model of E-learning that is interactive, data-based, and well-integrated with a variety of media. This is a model with the basic purpose of educating secondary social studies students to become active participants in a democracy. Graduate students, all of whom are NYS certified social studies teachers, are instructed in role playing and simulation through participation in activities such as John Gearon's "War or Peace?" and Barbara Olmo's "Pioneers in Arania."

Students are introduced to Statistical Package for the Social Sciences with a data bases from Nan Rothschild's *New York City Neighborhoods: The 18th Century* (Rothschild 1990), and the writer's *Historian: Building a New Nation in 1789* (Hetzner 2000). The Rothschild book focuses on the demographics of NYC Wards in selected years including 1789. *Historian...* is a proprietary database that focuses on the 1st Congress that met in NYC in 1789. It details the socioeconomic, religious, and ethnic backgrounds of the 95 legislators and their fathers, and voting behaviors and political attitudes toward the Constitution and George Washington. Essentially, it is an introduction to quantitative history and the basic evidence used in historical research. To teach students how to ask historical questions they are taught the basics of SPSS and questionnaire design. The process used in class is termed "interviewing the dead." Graduate students work with the database, which contains music clips, cartoons, reproductions of paintings...until they are familiar enough with the processes of historical investigation and materials design to produce their own computer-assisted simulations and role plays. The basic rules are that:

1. Databases must support the simulation/role play, be the basic stand-alone component of the exercise, or gather data from the secondary students on the results of the activity

2. PowerPoint may be used only to present information that would take too long or be awkward/impossible to present in another fashion

3. Audio is the preferred method for having a moderator communicate with participants in an autoinstrucional simulation/role play

4. The E-activity must be designed to fit into or complement the NYS secondary social studies curriculum

What types of computer databases and simulations/role plays do secondary social studies teachers produce under these guidelines? Graduate students have submitted approximately 45 projects since the requirement for computer-assisted databases was added to course requirements. The following 5 descriptions are of typical student produced databases. Each of the databases is associated with a simulation or role play on the same topic.

1. Terrorism (a hypothetical situation). Following a terrorist incident the Draft is reinstated. The database simulates random selection of draftees and compiles demographics and physical attributes of those selected

2. Political involvement. This database explores the connection between students' political involvement, socioeconomic background, interests (including social studies), and knowledge of current events.

3. "Failure is Impossible" draws its name from the 75th anniversary celebration of the 19th Amendment. This database of women goes from Abigail Adams to Nellie Rodgers Schuler, and includes information on age, religion, politics, and marital state.

4. Conjoined twins. The author of this database and role play teaches 4th grade in a Catholic school-- data can be displayed by nationality, ethnicity, sex, and family background.

5. Heritage of church members. A class member who is an active member of a largely African-American Baptist church compiled, and is now expanding, a database on the history of the church that focuses on the demographics of parishioners. Family data has been gathered on church founders who moved from the South in the 1860's up to the present day. The database is being used in local elementary schools and in the church to foster community.

A more extensive project, carried out in collaboration with teachers who are former *Experiences in Simulation and Role Play* students, is planned for the 2002-2003 academic year. Arrangements have been made for an architectural firm to complete a reconnaissance study of the architectural/historical significance of 1000 buildings in a Western New York village using "Preserve New York" funding. During or following completion of that component, students in social studies and the leadership program at the high school will work with the writer and an associate to carry out an assets study of the community. Secondary students will design questionnaires and interview schedules, interview village residents, process data, and present the findings at a regularly-scheduled Village Board meeting

References

Rothschild, N.A. (1990). *New York City Neighborhoods: The 18th Century*. New York: Academic Press.

Hetzner, D. Historian: Building a New Nation in 1789. *Creative Interactive Teaching: Case Methods & Other Techniques*, 2000. World Association for Case Method Research & Application, Boston, MA. 487-493.

Developing a Framework of Electronic Literacy for Post-Compulsory, Remote-Access, Virtual Learning Environments

Anne Hewling,
Institute of Educational Technology, The Open University, UK
a.hewling@open.ac.uk

Abstract

This paper reports on a study to develop a framework of electronic literacy for post-compulsory, remote access, virtual learning environments. The study acknowledges previous work on individual aspects of the online experience but seeks, through a variety of qualitative and quantitative techniques, to formulate an over-arching framework applicable to post-compulsory, remote-access education. This not only enables contextualisation of the many different elements involved but also enables further examination of their nature and relative importance in order that the framework may provide a flexible and robust tool for use in electronic instructional design.

Context

Increased global availability of computing technology, particularly of the Internet, offers the potential for collaborative interaction more or less 'anywhere, anytime'. Along with changes in workplace practices associated with global economic change and the consequent need for lifelong learning, these developments have led to a mushrooming of interest in the potential of virtual (i.e. online) learning environments (VLEs) as education delivery mechanisms.

Virtual Learning Environments

The 1999 Commonwealth of Learning (COL) report on a global evaluation of virtual education notes that *'virtual education is an extremely dynamic phenomenon'* (reported in Farrell 2001). Virtual Learning Environments (VLEs) range from local intranets used to supplement face-to-face and traditional education presentations, to entirely Web-based Internet dependent spaces which may have no terrestrial existence other than through the participation of students using the space. VLEs can be as large or as small as the available access technology, potentially offering a gateway to infinite numbers of learners. Barajas & Owen (2000), define VLEs as *'any combination of distance and face-to-face interaction, where some kind of space and time virtuality is present'*. Postle describes three types: *'supplemental or adjunct'* (online delivery is far from being the primary medium of instruction); *'mixed mode'* (online and face-to-face are both significantly important delivery media) and *'wholly online'* (online delivery is the only medium of instruction), (Postle 2002 p 4).

Electronic Literacy

Traditional and virtual classrooms alike require a certain level of literacy in users. In its most well understood form, literacy can be termed as the ability to read and write in a print-text-based environment. The virtual classroom, in common with the traditional one, is a text based environment but the text is situated within an amorphous electronic environment (Kaplan 2001) where sequence and structure are notably different (Richards 2000; Reinking). The dominance of text in both environments suggests that traditional literacy may form the backbone of electronic literacy. It is clear, however, that traditional literacy practices alone will not guarantee success in the electronic world. There is much debate on and around the nature of electronic literacy, most of it focusing on a single specific aspect. Some authors concentrate on its roots in traditional literacy (Koch 2001). Others, on the skills perceived as essential in a computer based environment (Tapper 1997), or as presented by the learner, in ideas of self-efficacy (Eastin & laRose 1996; Wang & Newlin 2002). Yet others concentrate on adaptation to the specific nature of an environment which lacks social cues (Yates 2001); where presence cannot be assumed (Rourke *et al.* 2000) and where particular opportunities are afforded for constructivist design and practice (Laurillard 1993); collaborative activity (Garrison *et al.* 2000) and vicarious learning (McKendree et al. 1998). Some refer specifically to an academic literacy of the online classroom. Others speak in terms of electronic litera*cies* (Kaplan 1995; Warschauer 1999) implying that there is no one definition applicable to all situations and introducing the idea of literacy as social practice (Lankshear et al. 2002; Snyder 2001), in turn encapsulating the idea that an absolute definition of literacy must be *'preposterous'* since meanings are inherently amorphous (Semali 2001).

Background to the Study

Taking up the challenge, from New Literacy Studies, to broaden the traditionally narrow view of literacy and instead *'capture the complexity of real literacy in contemporary society'* (Snyder 2000 p118) where reading and writing *'are only part of what people have to learn to be literate'*, (Snyder 2001 p119; Barton 2001 p95), the primary aim of this research is to develop a framework of electronic literacy for post-compulsory remote-access virtual learning environments. The secondary aim is to begin the process of understanding the nature of the elements within; to determine whether these are primarily aptitudes or more abstract and conceptual; whether they can be defined purely in terms of skills or whether ideas, such as those of space (Cicognani 1998) and place (Mitra & Schwartz 2001), are implied. This will provide a three-dimensional depth to the study and develop understanding of the inter-relationships of the various elements. Consequent to these aims, the study seeks to map contours rather than to produce definitive answers, quantify elements or prescribe limits and will facilitate discussion of the central question –

> *What does it mean to be an effective, electronically literate, post-compulsory student in a remote-access virtual learning environment?*

The Study

The study has two main stages. First stage data sources have been:
➢ *Case studies of electronic/online literacy* - an investigation of what researchers have deemed appropriate to explore or evaluate rather than the outcomes they have generated.
➢ *Examination of 'grey' literature* - in the form of institutional prospectuses and pre-enrolment materials such as suitability questionnaires and demonstration modules, as indicators of education providers' views of the scope of electronic literacy.

In both cases grounded theorising has been used to identify concepts to assist in mapping the overall scope of electronic literacy. Together with understandings from the researcher's own background and previous experience of online teaching and learning, these concepts have been used to inform:
➢ *Semi-structured interviews* - with online tutors which are being conducted online using synchronous chat facilities. Interviewees have been purposefully sampled from those working in *'wholly online'* and *'mixed-mode'* environments (Postle 2002)
➢ *A self-completion electronic questionnaire* – being sent to 100 online learners *undertaking 'mixed-mode'* or *'wholly online'* courses (Postle 2002). Questions seek to explore concepts emerging from ongoing analysis, in greater depth.

Responses to the above are being used to facilitate the development of the core categories which will become the elements of the desired framework of electronic literacy.

Emerging Themes

Any study of electronic literacy, as Tapper (1997) notes, requires consideration of an almost infinite number of variables. Analysis for this study so far has indicated areas receiving most overall attention to be:
- Previous experience of computers, not just word processing skills but experience which has developed positive learner attitudes towards, and tolerance of, technology
- Time and place management where learners not only have a sense of advance planning but also perceive the need to balance and contain online learning activity within other life priorities
- Self-sufficiency as a learner including self-motivation, self-discipline, determination and acceptance of the need for learner pro-activity
- Writing, including ability to write reflectively and convert conversational thought into coherent text
- Visual and semiotic understanding and interpretation
- Information processing, interpretation and evaluation

with different groups affording a range of priority ratings within any one area.

The key challenge in applying the outcomes of the later stages of analysis will be in creating a framework which is both robust and flexible enough to provide a useful tool for use in electronic instructional design. It will need to be tested against different groups of learners entering post-compulsory learning as the products of the ebb and flow of curriculum and resourcing tides within widely differing compulsory education systems.

References

Barajas, M. and Owen, M. (2000). Implementing Virtual Learning Environments: Looking for Holistic Approach, *Educational Technology & Society*, 3 (3), available online from URL: http://ifets.ieee.org/periodical/vol_3_2000/barajas.html accessed 5/10/2001

Barton, D. (2001). Directions for Literacy Research: Analysing Language and Social Practices in a Textually Mediated World, *Language and Education*, 15 (2&3), 92-104.

Cicognani, A. (1998). On the Linguistic Nature of Cyberspace and Virtual Communities, *Virtual Reality: Research Development and Application*, 3 (1), 16-24.

Eastin, M.S. & LaRose, R. (1996). Internet Self-Efficacy and the Psychology of the Digital Divide, *Journal of Computer-Mediated Communication*, 6 (1). available from URL: http://www.ascusc.org/jcmc/vol6/issue1/eastin.html accessed 28/11/2001

Farrell, G. M. (2001). *The Changing Faces of Virtual Education*, London, Commonwealth of Learning.

Garrison, D. R., Anderson, T. and Archer, W. (1998). Critical Inquiry in a Text-Based Environment: Computer Conferencing in Higher Education *(online)* available online from URL: http://www.atl.ualberta.ca/cmc/CtinTextEnvFinal.pdf
Accessed 22/11/2001

Kaplan, N. (2001). Knowing Practice: A More Complex View of New Media Literacy in *Proceedings of the International Conference on Advances in Infrastructure for Electronic Business, Science and Education on the Internet*. Available online at URL: http://iat.ubalt.edu/kaplan/ssgrr01.pdf accessed 28/11/2001

Kaplan, N. (1995). Eliteracies: Politexts, Hypertexts, and Other Cultural Formations in the Late Age of Print, available on-line from URL: http://iat.ubalt.edu/kaplan/lit/
accessed 7/12/2001

Koch, M. (2001). Information Literacy: where do we go from here, *TECHNOS Quarterly for Education and Technology*, 10 (1) Available online from URL: http://technos.net/journal/volume10/1koch.htm accessed 11/01/2002

Lankshear, C. Peters, M. and Knobel, M. (2002). Information, knowledge and learning: some issues facing epistemology and education in a digital age in Lea, M.R. and Nicholl, K. (eds.) *Distributed Learning: social and cultural approaches to practice*, London, Routledge Falmer.

Laurillard, D. (1993). *Re-thinking University Teaching: A Framework for the Effective Use of Educational Technology*, London, Routledge.

Mitra, A. and Schwartz, R.L. (2001). From Cyber Space to Cybernetic Space: Rethinking the Relationship between Real and Virtual Spaces, *Journal of Computer Mediated Communication*, 7 (1), (online) available from URL: http://www.ascusc.org/jcmc/vol7/issue1/mitra.html accessed 19/11/2001

McKendree, J., Dineen, F., Mayes, T. and Lee, J. (1998). The Vicarious Learner: discussion as learning resource and learning task, *ERCIM news online*, 33 available online from URL: http://www.ercim.org/publication/Ercim_News/enw33/mckendree.html
Accessed 9/11/2001

Postle, G. (2002). Emergence of Fourth Generation Technologies in *e-JIST*, (online) 5 (1) available from URL: http://www.usq.edu.au/electpub/e-jist/docs/html2002/gPos.html accessed 4/4/2002

Reinking, D., (undated). *Electronic Literacy*, available online from URL: http://curry.edschool.virginia.edu/go/clic/nrrc/reinking.html accessed 10/01/2002

Richards, C. (2000). Hypermedia, Internet Communication, and the Challenge of Redefining Literacy in the Electronic Age, *Language, Learning & Technology,* 4 (2), 59-77, available online from URL: http://llt.msu.edu/vol4num2/richards/default.html accessed 12/02/2002

Rourke, L., Anderson, T., Garrison. R., Archer, W. (2001). Assessing Social Presence in Asynchronous Text-based, Computer Conferencing, web-published paper from URL: http://www.atl.ualberta.ca/cmc/social%20presence%20May8.pdf

Semali, L. (2001). Defining New Literacies in Curricular Practice, *Reading Online*, available from URL: http://www.readingonline.org/newliteracies/semali1/index.html
accessed 26/11/2001

Snyder, L. (2001). A New Communication Order: Researching Literacy Practices in the Network Society, *Language and Education,* 15 (2&3), 117-131

Tapper, J. (1997). Integrating Online Literacy into Undergraduate Education: a case study, *Higher Education Research & Development,* 16 (1)

Wang, A. Y. & Newlin, M. H. (2002). Predictors of web-student performance: the role of self-efficacy and reasons for taking an on-line class, *Computers in Human Behavior,* 18 (2), 151-163

Warschauer, M. (1999). *Electronic Literacies: language, culture and power in online education,* Mahwah, New Jersey, Lawrence Erlbaum Associates.

Yates, S. J. (2001). Researching Internet Interaction: Sociolinguistics and Corpus Analysis in Wetherell, M., Taylor, S. and Yates, S.J. (eds.) *Discourse as Data: a guide for analysis,* London, Sage

Differential Indexing: A Problem-Authoring Method for Computer-Based Problem Practice

Tsukasa HIRASHIMA, Akira TAKEUCHI
Kyushu Institute of Technology, JAPAN
e-mail: tsukasa@ai.kyutech.ac.jp

Abstract: In this paper, a problem-authoring method is proposed and an example of the implementation of the method is described. In the problem-authoring method, a new problem is characterized using differences from the basic problem. In the problem-authoring environment, a user can make a new problem by changing the basic problem. The changes represent the differences between the new problem and the basic problem. The new problem is then characterized by the differences from the basic problem. We call the problem authoring method "Differential Indexing".

Introduction

Problem practice is a highly private activity. For example, the next problem in the practice should be decided depending on the student's knowledge, learning context, or mistakes. Computer-based problem practice is, then, a promising approach to deal with the private activity. To realize the elaborate form of the practice, the following three factors are indispensable, (1) student model, (2) practice strategy, and (3) practice material, that is, problems. Such computer-based problem practice is often called Intelligent Problem Practice. There are already many investigations for computer-based problem practice, but most of them are focused on the student modeling or practice strategy. However, we believe that the problems as practice material are the basis of problem practice. The abilities of a student model and practice strategy depend on the quantity and quality of prepared problems. From this viewpoint, how to describe problems and how to get the data are key issues to achieve the advanced practice [Hirashima 93; Ritter 98; Arroyo 00; Hirashima 01]. We call this issue "problem-authoring". There are several types of problem-authoring methods. Our current target is to make various problems that can be solved using the same solution method. We call this type of problem-authoring method "solution based problem-authoring". "Problem-authoring" signifies this "solution based problem-authoring" in this paper.

In this paper, a problem-authoring method is proposed and an example of the implementation of the method is described. In the problem-authoring method, a new problem is characterized using differences from the basic problem. In the problem-authoring environment, a user can make a new problem by changing the basic problem. The changes represent the differences between the new problem and the basic problem. The new problem is then characterized by the differences from the basic problem. We call the problem-authoring method "Differential Indexing".

In section 2, a classification of problem-authoring methods from the viewpoint of problem indexing is described. Then, a method of problem indexing, that is, Differential Indexing is explained. A problem-authoring environment as an implementation of Differential Indexing is also described in section 3.

Problem-Authoring

Level of Indexing

In problem-authoring process, a user usually makes problem sentences that are the body of the problem. However, it is difficult for the computer to interpret the problem sentences directly. Giving indexes to the problem and dealing with the indexes as the content of the problem is a useful as well as a popular way. In this paper, we also adopt this approach and propose an indexing method as a problem-authoring method.

Indexing methods are categorized in the following three levels: (1) flag level indexing, (2) keyword level indexing, and (3) problem structure level indexing. In the case of the flag level indexing, each problem has a flag representing a specific number or symbol. The courseware of the problem practice deals with any problems with the flags. In other words, the flag level index is used to identify a problem but doesn't describe the content of the problem. Therefore, problem-authoring and courseware designing cannot be separated. It is then very difficult

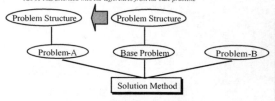

A problem that can be solved by the same solution method with a base problem can be characterized with the differences from the base problem.

Figure 1: Concept of Differential Indexing.

The number of legs of a crane is two.
The number of legs of a turtle is four.
There are cranes and turtles, 20 in total.
The total number of legs of the cranes and turtles is 48.
How many cranes are there?
How many turtles are there?

Figure 2: Problem-1: Base Problem of Crane-Turtle Method.

(Step1) : The supposed total number of legs when it supposed that there were only cranes.

(the total number of cranes and turtles) * (the number of legs of a crane) = A

(Step2): The difference in the above number and actual number of legs.

(the total number of legs of cranes and turtles) -A = B

(Step3): The difference of number of legs when a turtle is substituted to a crane.

(the number of legs of a turtle legs) - (the number of legs of a crane) = C

(Step4): Total difference(Step2) / Individual difference(Step3) is the number of turtles substituted to cranes.

B / C = (the number of turtles)

Figure 3: Crane-Turtle Method.

---

to reuse the problem data with other systems.

In the case of keyword level indexing, indexes of a problem are composed of a set of keywords that describe the content of the problem. In the courseware of the problem practice using the keyword level index, problems that include required keywords are used. Therefore, if the problem author and courseware designer share the meanings of the keywords, the problem authoring and courseware designing can be separated. However, it is often difficult to make the meanings of the keywords clear systematically, because they often depend on the specific system.

If the indexes of a problem include enough information to solve the problem, we call it "problem structure level indexing". To realize such a level of indexing, a problem solving model should be prepared and the indexes should be described based on the model. In order to share the meanings of the indexes, the problem author and courseware designer have to share the model. Although the description ability of the indexes is restricted by the model, the model usually doesn't depend on the specific system and therefore sharing it with the author and the designer is easier. This problem structure level indexing is the target level of this research.

Concept of Differential Indexing

In this research, we give the indexes that describe differences from base problem to a problem. We call the indexing method "Differential Indexing". Figure 1 shows the concept of Differential Indexing. In this method, a combination of a base problem and a solution method is necessary. We call the pair the "Solution Model". This indexing method can then be used to make problems that can be solved using the same solution method with the base problem. For example, if Problem-A can be solved using the same solution method with the base problem, it can be characterized by the difference of problem structure from the base problem. Then, the differences are used as the indexes of the Problem-A. The differences decide the worth of the practical problems, like Problem-A, because all factors a learner has to overcome to master the solution method are included in the differences. Therefore, the index described as the differences is enough from the viewpoint of "solution based problem authoring". This is the concept of Differential Indexing. In the next section, the problem solving model used to describe these differences is explained.

Indexing Method

In Differential Indexing, the following two differences from a base problem can be categorized: (1) an instance difference, and (2) a structure difference. The structure difference is divided as (2a) a structure difference that can be complemented with fact knowledge, and (2b) a structure difference that can be complemented with operational knowledge. In this section, the aforementioned three differences are explained by using the crane-turtle method as an example. The base problem and the calculation procedure of the method are shown in

Figure 2 and 3.

Instance Difference

Figure 4 shows Problem-2 that can be solved using the crane-turtle method. In the problem, an octopus corresponds to a crane, and a squid corresponds to a turtle. This problem is different from the base problem in instances, but the problem structure is the same. This is an example of the instance difference. If this problem is difficult for a learner, it speculates the cause of the difficulty is in the instance differences.

Figure 5 shows Problem-3 that also includes the instance difference. In the problem, a boy corresponds to a crane and the score corresponds to the number of legs. Usually, people judge Problem-3 as more difficult than Problem-2. The cause of this distinction is in the quality of the instance changes. To deal with the quality of the changes, in Differential Indexing, a hierarchical structure of concept classes is prepared. The distance in the hierarchical structure from the class that the base problem belongs to describes the quality of the instance changes. When the distance is longer, a problem becomes more difficult.

Structure Difference

If the following two sentences, that is, "the number of legs of an octopus is eight" and "the number of legs of a squid is ten" are missing in Problem-2, there are structure differences between the base problem and this problem. Here, if a student has the knowledge about "the number of legs of an octopus" and "the number of legs of a squid", the differences can be complemented with them. Therefore, we call this type of the structure difference, "structure difference that can be complemented with fact knowledge". If a learner who can solve Problem-2 cannot solve the problem that includes this structure difference, it is estimated that the difficulty for the learner exists in the structure difference. We call this structure difference "the first-order structure difference", and a problem that includes only this type of structure difference, "the first-order problem".

When "the total score of the pupils" is omitted and then "the average score of the pupils" is given in Problem-3, the problem has another type of structure difference. To apply the crane-turtle method to the problem, "the total score of the pupils" is necessary. In this case, "the total score" can be derived by using both "the average score" and "the total number of the pupils". This is the structure difference that can be complemented by operational knowledge. We call this structure difference, "the second-order structure difference", and a problem that includes this type of difference, "the second-order problem". A problem that only includes the instance difference is called "the zeroth-order problem".

In Differential Indexing, the indexes of a new problem are described with instance differences and structure differences. In the problem-authoring environment described in Section 3, the indexes are represented by XML (eXtensible Markup Language) and the problem data can be made and used through the internet.

Problem-Authoring Environment

We have now implemented a problem-authoring environment. The main component is the problem-making editor where a user can make problems. It can also diagnose problems and acquire knowledge for the diagnosis through the problem-making process.

The main task of the problem-making process is to provide indexes for a new problem. Figure 6 is the interface of the problem-making editor. (Currently, only a Japanese version is implemented. Words in the figures were translated into English). The interface is composed of (a) a problem sentences field, (b) a problem-indexing field, and (c) a problem confirmation field. When a user selects a solution method, the base problem of the solution method is given in the problem-indexing field (in this section, a user means a problem author). In the problem-indexing field, each line is corresponding to a basic relation composed of an object, an attribute, and a numerical value. The left-hand column is the statement of the way to give the value. The "given value" is the value that is given in the problem directly. "Not given (fact)" is the value that is not given in the problem, but can be complemented by fact knowledge. "Not given (operational)" is the value that is not given in the problem, but can be derived by operational knowledge. This is the problem structure of the base problem. By changing the concepts or the statements, the problem structure of the new problem is generated. The indexes of the new problem are described as the changes.

The number of legs of an octopus is eight.
The number of legs of a squid is ten.
There are octopuses and squid, 20 in total.
The total number of legs of the octopuses and squid is 180.
How many octopuses are there?
How many squids are there?

Figure 4: Problem-2: An Example of Instance Difference.

There are 40 pupils in the class.
The total score of the test of the pupils is 2760.
The average score of the test of a boy is 65.
The average score of the test of a girl is 75.
How many boys are there?
How many girls are there?

Figure 5: Problem-3: An Example of Instance Difference.

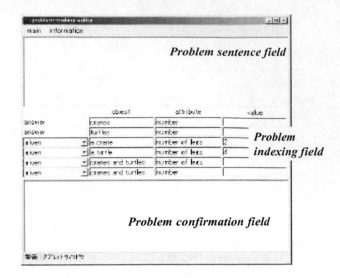

Figure 6: Interface of Problem-Making Editor.

Concluding Remarks

This paper described a problem-authoring method and a problem-authoring environment where the method was implemented. The environment is composed of Problem-Making Editor, Problem Database and Practice Editor. A user can make problem with the Problem-Making Editor. Problems made in the Problem-Making Editor are saved in Problem Database. In Practice Editor, a user can build a simple problem practice CAI by designing a problem sequence. These components can be accessed through the internet. Evaluation of this problem-authoring environment is our future work.

References

[Arroyo 00] Ivon Arroyo. "Animalwatch: an arithmetic ITS for elementary and middle school students", Learning Algebra with the Computer, *Workshop of Fifth International Conference on Intelligent Tutoring Systems.* Montreal, Canada. 2000.
[Hirashima 93] Hirashima, T., T. Niitsu, A. Kashihara and J. Toyoda. "An Indexing Framework for Adaptive Setting of Problems in ITS", *Proc. of AI-ED93*, pp.90-97, 1993.
[Hirashima 01] Tsukasa Hirashima Taichi Umeda, Akira Takeuchi, "An Intelligent Problem Authoring Environment on Web", *Proc. of ICCE2001*, pp.560-562(2001).
[Ritter 98] Ritter, S., Anderson, J., Cytrynowicz, M., and Medvedeva, O., "Authoring Content in the PAT Algebra Tutor", *Journal of Interactive Media in Education*, 98 (9).

Acknowledgements

This research was partially supported by the Telecommunications Advancement Foundation and Atrificial Intelligenced Research Foundation.

Problems and Perils for Digital Libraries in the K-12 Domain

Ellen S. Hoffman
Eastern Michigan University
Ypsilanti, MI USA
ehoffman@online.emich.edu

Marcia Mardis
Merit Network, Inc.
Ann Arbor, MI USA
mmardis@merit.edu

INTRODUCTION

The U. S. National Science, Technology, Engineering, and Mathematics Education Digital Library (NSDL) does not currently exist except as a vision and goal for the STEM community with initial funding from the National Science Foundation (NSF)—a vision that is different from any existing library today. Currently a set of multiple funded grant projects with formal and informal partnerships among universities, K12 schools, professional organizations, government agencies, non-profit organizations, and corporations, the library is moving toward realization. When the NSDL opens its virtual doors in fall 2002, it will be the culmination of over a decade of research and collaboration among librarians, technologists, and educators in the public and private sectors (National Research Council, 1998; Wattenberg, 1998; Zia, 2001).

A community that is a special focus for the program is K-12, one that is in many ways a new challenge for the developers who are predominantly from higher education and the research community (National Research Council, 1999). As part of a project funded by the National Science Foundation, TeacherLIB has provided a review of the issues that arise if the library is to positively impact student achievement in K-12 mathematics and science (Hunter, Mardis & Hoffman, 2002).

A VIRTUAL LIBRARY VISION

Critical barriers for digital libraries today are as much human issues as technological ones. Even when good collections are developed, getting them known and used remains problematic in this age of Internet information overload. Today the Internet offers lots of "stuff," but finding the "right stuff" may be difficult or impossible even when it is available (Zia, 2001). This conclusion is reinforced by the research on search engines by Lawrence and Giles, who noted that popular Internet search engines "could be compared to a phone book which is updated irregularly, is biased toward listing more popular information, and has most of the pages ripped out" (Lawrence & Giles, 1999). Further, when confronted by the overwhelming amount of content, learners may not have the experience or basic knowledge to evaluate and use the resources that are found. Some studies of pre-college students have indicated that they spend increased research time looking for materials and less actually reading and analyzing web-based content.

A prime consideration in building digital libraries is ensuring that users needs are met, which implies that one size will not fit all. The NSDL is viewed as having many kinds of resources and services that go beyond the traditional books and journals of brick-and-mortar libraries, with resources including non-textual sources and educational

This material is based upon work supported by the National Science Foundation under Grant No. 0085866, TeacherLIB. Any opinions, findings, and conclusions or recommendations expressed in this material are those of the author and do not necessarily reflect the views of the National Science Foundation.

materials such as lesson plans, curriculum guidelines, and tutorials. "Beyond providing traditional library functions such as the intelligent retrieval of relevant information, indexing and online annotation of resources, and archiving of materials, the digital library will also enable users to access virtual collaborative work areas, hands-on laboratory experiences, tools for analysis and visualization, remote instruments, large databases of real-time or archived data, simulated or virtual environments, and other new capabilities as they emerge" (National Science Foundation, 2000).

While digital libraries have been widely discussed, the NSDL is different because of its focus on education. At workshops in 2000 organized by the current grant recipients (Manduca, McMartin, & Mogk, 2001), educational goals were defined including:

- Provide quality assurance of resources in the collections;
- Enable contextual learning;
- Empower critical literacy skills;
- Support new pedagogical approaches;
- Advance scientific knowledge and understanding;
- Enable inter- and multi-disciplinary educational opportunities;
- Implement the National Science Education Standards (National Research Council, 1996) and related SMET education reform programs;
- Support independent learning;
- Support learning that is active, and that involves inquiry and discovery;
- Foster a sense of excitement about life-long learning;
- Provide access for all;
- Empower users;
- Support communities of scholars.

CHALLENGES IN K-12 DEPLOYMENT

As the NSDL program moves forward, it moves from issues of creating a technical infrastructure to impacting learning in communities with structures and cultures that emerged long before the digital age and are not always well positioned to take advantage of new technologies. In an examination of those issues, researchers for the TeacherLIB project detailed a range of concerns that must be addressed before the digital library can become a primary tool in K-12 classrooms in the United States (Hunter, Mardis, & Hoffman, 2002). These include social, economic, cultural and technical barriers.

Many challenges are well understood as technology enters K-12 schools, including teacher time, training, skills, and attitudes, issues of access to appropriate hardware and software, technical support, and organizational structures that can make it difficult for teaching reforms to take hold. Further, issues of the digital divide may limit the reach of the new library to those who have the most to gain from new teaching tools.

At the same time there are some new challenges that are particular to envisioned library that are emerging as new structures are being tested. The following are not intended to cover all possible issues but to give a sense of some of the emerging issues that have been discussed as the library is moving towards reality.

Accommodating the diverse curriculum requirements of American schools: Despite a decade of developing national standards, each state (and often local district) has revised the standards to meet local concerns and priorities. Students are assessed through state-mandated tests rather than a national testing system, and increasingly curriculum is driven in K-12 schools to raise test scores. Teachers are pushed to adopt learning materials that are tightly aligned with local standards. As a result, learning materials that are not perceived to meet these needs may face a more difficult struggle in adoption. Can a national library find ways to tie in local standards effectively? Some projects are already examining ways to match state standards to library content so that it is customized for each viewer.

Access to the range of potential high-quality content: U.S. schools that receive federal funds for telecommunications (known as the Universal Service Fund or E-rate) are required by federal law to filter content to protect minors from unacceptable content. Studies of these filtering systems have shown that they may block content that is critical for teaching science or mathematics because it covers subjects such as sexually transmitted diseases or references to male or female anatomy. Library developers will need to work with schools and commercial manufacturers of filtering programs to ensure that the rich resources are available to all students.

Personal portals in a protected world: One of the most powerful concepts being developed for the NSDL is the personalized portal. Through customized portals that "recognize" each user, an individual learner has the potential to gain scaffolded assistance in their educational explorations. Under federal laws and regulations, however, the kinds of personal information that may be needed to make such portals highly effective cannot be released by American schools. As a result, tracking mechanisms that could potentially provide support for each learner may not be possible within this protected environment. Developers will need to find creative ways to advance such technologies while ensuring high levels of security for minors.

Incorporating legacy collections: Many excellent collections that are now in use by K-12 that are developed as the result of intensive local efforts or larger national reform projects were never designed to be used in a more structured library effort. These collections may have a mix of high quality materials and underdeveloped experimental materials that never reached conclusion. As teachers demand that their time be maximized so that they are not required to review hundreds of resources to find the right item for the age group and subject they are teaching, these materials may have insufficient metadata to assist teachers in limiting their search. New ways of labeling may be required that go beyond the traditional library catalog to assist users in finding materials that are reviewed and tested. As yet, the methods and data structures for such reviews remain to be developed and tested in real classrooms. Even further away are the tools that will allow such schema to be readily applied to materials that were not developed with such a labeling process in mind. In many cases, the personnel simply does not exist among these K-12 collections to develop high level metadata that may be needed for ready K-12 access.

FUTURES FOR E-LEARNING

Although technical, informational, and organizational challenges remain, NSDL continues to move forward towards its Fall 2002 launch date. The scope of the overall program is providing new hopes for reforming math and science learning for K-12 students. While the challenges are great, the potential continues to motivate the digital library community to develop new methods for deployment that will work well for children and provide new access to high-quality learning.

REFERENCES

Hunter, B., Mardis, M., & Hoffman, E. S. (2002). *K-12 education considerations for a national SMETE digital library* [PDF document]. Retrieved, from the World Wide Web: http://www.teacherlib.org

Lawrence, S., & Giles, L. (1999). Accessibility of information on the Web. *Nature, 400*, 107-109.

Manduca, C. A., McMartin, F. P., & Mogk, D. W. (2001, March 20, 2001). *Pathways to progress: Vision and plans for developing the NSDL* [PDF document]. Retrieved June, 2001, from the World Wide Web: http://www.smete.org/nsdl/index.html

National Research Council. (1996). *National science education standards*. Washington D.C.: National Academy Press.

National Research Council. (1998). *Developing a digital national library for undergraduate science, mathematics, and technology education: A report*. Washington D.C.: National Academy Press.

National Research Council. (1999). *Serving the needs of pre-college science and mathematics education: Impact of a digital national library on teacher education and practice. Proceedings from a National Research Council workshop*. Washington D.C.: National Academy Press.

National Science Foundation. (2000). *National Science, Mathematics, Engineering, and Technology Education Digital Library (NSDL), Program Solicitation* (NSF00-44). Washington, DC: National Science Foundation.

Wattenberg, F. (1998, October 1998). *A national digital library for science, mathematics, engineering and technology education*. D-Lib Magazine. Retrieved April 7, 2000, from the World Wide Web: http://www.dlib.org/dlib/october98/wattenberg/10wattenberg.html

Zia, L. L. (2001). Growing a national learning environments and resources network for science, mathematics, engineering, and technology education: Current issues and opportunities for the NSDL program. *D-Lib Magazine, 7*(3), (electronic).

An Examination of the Elements and Principles of the Visual Design of Web-Interfaces in the Context of Improving Accessibility for Older Adult Users

Charlotte Holland
School of Education Studies
Dublin City University
Ireland
charlotte.holland@dcu.ie

Abstract: This paper introduces elements and principles of visual design, and examines these in the context of designing web interfaces that are accessible to older adult users. It begins by looking at the background to the projected increases in the aged population and the physiological effects of ageing. The discussion continues by reviewing the elements and principles of visual design, and moves forward to focus on the possible impacts of visual impairments on visual interface interpretation. It concludes by outlining the next stages of this work-in-progress and some of the aspirations of this investigation.

Introduction

Improvements in the life expectancy rate has resulted in projections of a massive increase in the number of older adults in society of the near-future. "Thirty years from now, it is estimated that one in four people in the developed world will be aged 65 and over, an increase from one in seven today" (Preston, 1999).

The 1996 Irish Census (Central Statistics Office, 1996) showed that almost 29% of the population were aged between 25 and 44, with a further 11% aged between 45 and 54. By 2026, these two categories of the population will form the older adult community and, when the improved life expectancy rate is taken into account, this older adult community may represent over thirty-five per cent of the total Irish population.

In Ireland, as in many other countries, government and state agencies, (McCall, 2002), commerce and educational institutions are making significant strides in bringing a wide range of services from life events to career choices and leisure options online. The proliferation of information that is now communicated using web technologies in particular demands that all sectors of society gain access and interact with new technologies.

How accessible is this information transmitted using web technologies to older adults? The ageing process can result in diminished vision, hearing, hand-eye co-ordination and psychomotor impairments, (Vanderheiden, 2000). The most common of these physiological changes associated with longevity is the change in vision. "By age 65, most people have lost at least some of their ability to focus; have a reduced field of vision, ability to resolve images, distinguish colours and adapt to changes in light" (The AgeLight Institute, 2000).

The World Wide Web Consortium, W3C, published the Web Content Accessibility Guidelines 1.0, WCAG 1.0, in May 1999 with the aim of explaining how to make web content accessible to people with disabilities. The specification contained fourteen guidelines, (W3C, 1999), that address barriers in web pages which people with physical, visual, hearing and cognitive/neurological disabilities may encounter.

The White Paper published by the Age Light Institute in 2000 focused on maximising usability and accessibility in web-site design for seniors and older Internet users in particular. It highlighted general design elements to make websites more 'senior-friendly', and as such has "raised awareness of design parameters and usability considerations for the increasingly varied demographics and lifestyles of computer users" (The Agelight Institute, 2000).

Physiological Effects of Ageing on Vision

"As one ages, the likelihood of vision loss increases significantly. For those over age 65, one in nine people experience serious vision loss. This rate increases to one in four for those over 85" (Vision Loss Resources, 1997).

During the aging process, the average person will probably experience some of the following eye conditions and resultant vision changes (National Eye Institute, 2001):

- Yellowing of the Lens occurs when the fibres of the lens take on a yellow hue and results in difficulty in contrasting colours, in particular, blue, green or violet.
- Fixed Lens occurs when the lens becomes more rigid and loses its ability to focus on objects that are close. The lens may also become denser and cloudier, which cuts down on the light that is passed through to the retina, resulting in a loss of visual acuity.
- Loss of Pupil Expansion is where the pupil reduces its ability to expand resulting in less light entering the eye. This combined with a dense lens often means that older people need three times more light to see. It results in a loss of ability to adapt to glare, difficulty seeing in the dark and adapting to light changes, hence causing eye-strain or eye fatigue. "Resistance to glare is 2.5 times greater at 20 than at 65" (Flax & Luchterhand, 1995).
- Floaters are condensations of cells in the gel parts of the eye and take the form of tiny spots, specks or strings that float across the field of vision. "Floaters are very common in the elderly, patients with nearsightedness, diabetes and high-blood pressure" (Ohiolions Eye Research, 2000).

In addition to the age-related vision changes discussed above that occur for most older adults, some older adults will experience eye diseases and resultant effects on vision as outlined below (National Institute on Aging, 2002):

- Age-related Macular Degeneration occurs when the central part of the eye dies off creating a black hole or blind spot in the central field of vision. Whilst peripheral or side vision may be maintained, it leads to difficulty in reading, recognising faces or doing 'close-up' work.
- Cataracts results from the clouding of the lens inside the eye, which reduces light entering the eye, and can cause blurring across the entire field of vision.
- Glaucoma and Retinitis Pigmentosa are different diseases but both result in a gradual loss of peripheral vision, leaving a central field of vision or tunnel vision and eventually blindness.
- Diabetic Retinopathy occurs in long-term diabetics where damage can occur to the retina. The blood vessels leak creating large floaters that move across the field of vision.

Therefore, older adults may experience, in addition to eye-strain and eye fatigue, a reduced field of vision, blurred vision, reduced ability to resolve images, reduced colour discrimination, sensitivity to glare, night blindness, a degree of colour blindness and a loss of visual acuity.

How will these physiological changes in vision, brought about by the ageing process, impact perception of and interaction with the visual elements and principles of the web interface? In order to answer this, we first need to establish the constituents of visual design, namely, the elements and principles of visual design.

Elements of Visual Design

The main elements of visual design as described below are texture, form, line, value, colour, space and shape, (Crystal Production Company, 1996):

Texture refers to the simulated surface quality of artwork. *Form* describes the 3-D aspects of objects that take up place. *Lines* can be expressive and suggestive; they can be used to outline the edges of forms or shapes; they can be used to indicate action and physical movement; they can be used to create value and textures. *Value* refers to dark and light, it can be used to develop suitable contrast between foreground and background and to describe form. *Colour* has three properties; hue, value and chroma. The hue is the name of the colour: red, yellow and blue. Colour value refers to the lightness or darkness of the colour. Chroma is the intensity of the colour or the purity of the hue. *Space* can be empty or filled with objects. *Shape* is an area that is contained within an implied line, or is identified because of colour or value changes. Shapes are 2-D, and can be geometric or free-form.

Principles of Visual Design

The principles of visual design below include rhythm, emphasis, contrast, pattern, visual movement and balance (Crystal Production Company, 1996).

Rhythm is the repetition of the visual movement of each of the elements. It can be regular or irregular, staccato(abrupt and change frequently) or progressive(change size whilst moving). *Emphasis* is where the elements are emphasised to achieve dominance or to create a focal area of interest. *Contrast* is where elements are contrasted to achieve dominance. *Pattern* uses the elements in planned or random repetition. They increase visual excitement by enriching surface interest. *Visual Movement* can be used to direct users to focal areas (Vaughan, 1997), such movement can be along lines, edges, shapes and colours. *Balance* refers to the distribution of visual weight in a work and can be either symmetrical or asymmetrical.

Visual Design Considerations for Web Interfaces

Of elemental concern in the visual perception of the visually impaired older adult, would be the use of colour, value, texture and space. These elements would further be enhanced or detracted by the use of rhythm, pattern, emphasis, contrast, visual movement and balance.

For example, think of an interface that uses a font of appropriate size and colour contrast, but has a shadow added for emphasis. How will a visually impaired adult user perceive the 'shadowed' text? Depth perception difficulties may arise?

How about an interface that displays a font that is marginally lighter in colour than the background, will the adult user who has a loss in colour perception be able to perceive the difference? Are low value/contrast colours a good choice in this case?

What would a user with discoloration in the eye fluids and lens (or yellowing) experience when viewing visual elements on a colour 'co-ordinated' web interface? Would the colour contrast/ value still be significant?

What about the placement of the visual elements on the interface, is the amount of white space surrounding the block/s of text large enough, how will this impact on readability of the text for the visually impaired adult user?

Consider the interface that uses geometric textures/pattern in the background, how do these textures affect the contrast or readability of text/ images? Are organic textures/patterns a better option?

Now consider the web interface that incorporates moving text or images, how does the rhythm and/ or movement of these images affect the visually impaired adult user?

Next Stage

The sample questions above are among many questions that are currently under investigation in a review of the visual design of contemporary web interfaces aimed at the adult population in Ireland, tentative findings will be released over the next few months. It is hoped that this investigation into the impact of visual impairments on perception of visual elements and principles of web interfaces may help establish the current state of accessibility of such sites. Furthermore, it is desired that this investigation will raise an awareness of the need for more detailed research on all aspects of web interface design for an ageing population.

References

Central Statistics Office. (1996). *Census 1996*. Dublin: Stationary Office

Crystal Production Company. (1996). *The Elements and Principles of Design* http://www.snoqualmie.wednet.edu Accessed: 02/02

Flax, M.E. & Luchterhand, C. (1995). *Aging with Developmental Disabilities: Changes in Vision*. http://www.thearc.org Accessed: 07/02

McCall, B. (2002). *Connecting the Citizen*. Dublin: The Sunday Tribune 21/04/02.

National Eye Institute. (2001). *Eye Disease Simulations*. http://www.nei.nih.gov Accessed: 06/02

National Institute on Aging. (2002). *Aging and Your Eyes*. http://www.nih.gov/nia Accessed: 07/02

Ohiolions Eye Research. (2000). *Simulations*. http://www.ohiolionseyeresearch.com/simulati.htm Accessed: 07/02
Preston, P.G. (1999). *Gray Dawn*. New York. Times Books.

The Agelight Institute. (2000). *A Guide for Web Design Usability for users of All Ages*. http://www.agelight.org Accessed: 02/02

Vanderheiden, G. (2000). *Fundamental Principles and Priority Setting for Universal Usability*. http://trace.wisc.edu/docs/ Accessed: O6/02

Vaughan, L. (1997). *Understanding Movement* http://www.acm.org/sigs/sigchi/chi97 Accessed: 04/02

Vision Loss Resources. (1997). *Living with Low Vision Loss* http://www.visionlossresources.com Accessed: 04/02

World Wide Web Consortium W3C. (1999) *Web Content Accessibility Guidelines 1.0*. http://www.w3.org/WAI/GL Accessed: 02/02

Additional Resources

Arditi, A. (2000). *Effective Color Contrast: Designing for People with Partial Sight and Color Deficiencies*. http://www.lighthouse.org/color_contrast.htm Accessed: 05/02

Bearman, M. (1997). *Graphic Design, Interfaces & Usability*. http://www.med.monash.edu.au/informatics/ Accessed : 05/02

Color Matters. (2002). *Color Matters:Computers*. http://www.colormatters.com/ Accessed: 03/02

Department of Education and Science. (2000). *Learning for Life: White Paper on Adult Education*. Government Publications: Ireland

Percoco, G. & Sarti, L. *On the usage of graphics in ICAI systems*. (1996). Istituto Tecnologie Didattiche. C.N.R.

"Bringing Stars into the Classroom"- A unique model for virtual courses

Yona Holtzman-Benshalom, Yoav Yair and Dafna Raviv

TAMID Project, The Open University of Israel, Tel-Aviv, Israel

Astronomy teaching is a challenge even to the veteran science teacher. It is a dynamic and changing field of science, where the constant flow of new discoveries require rapid and continuous updating of the study materials. Alongside the enormous popularity of astronomy and space science amongst children, are found many misconceptions and misinformation about their basic facts. Children may conceive explanations for natural astronomical phenomena from popular resources such as science fiction movies, video games, television series and informal internet resources (mostly on UFOs and aliens). There is an extensive literature on misconceptions in astronomy and their origins, which includes pedagogical ideas and recommendations of how to avoid them, and the most suitable teaching strategies at each age. Since astronomy was introduced into the science curriculum in Israel 6 years ago, there has been an intensive effort to train teachers in this field.

The course we describe here was designed for junior-high school science teachers, who have not received any formal training in astronomy and who have never before taught the subject in their classes. It was a 12-weeks hybrid course consisting of a few face-to-face meetings, independent -learning, and extensive on-line activities, using the Open University's Opus LMS (an internally developed, non-commercial, Hebrew-based set of web tools).

Initially, the course was focused on teaching the subject matter and on forming a active learning community. This involved educating the participants in the use of the course web-site which forms the central axis of their learning, by means of ongoing mentoring and mode rating by the course tutors in the forums. The method of using specific repetitive activities such as "Ask the expert" or "What's up in the sky" have helped teachers overcome their initial shyness and lack of confidence, caused by their feeling of "not knowing anything in astronomy". By giving legitimacy to their questions, a shared resource of answers was rapidly built, shared and later used by the teachers themselves as an extensive data-base. The constant dialog about current celestial events (we were treated to a beautiful comet and a rare planetary conjunction) generated the enthusiasm and motivation to report observations, and teachers soon began to harvest updated astronomy news from the plethora of web resources and the popular media in general. Additionally, teachers were asked to come up with lesson plans, suggestions for overcoming hurdles in teaching and to respond to and discuss the products of their peers.

The teachers became "advocates of astronomy" among their colleagues and soon started teaching the subject in their classes. They presented the feedback and questions of their pupils in the course online forums, and these were discussed and shared amongst the participants. Suggestions, comments and even compliments from their colleagues created a positive learning atmosphere. Consistent accompaniment of the course by subject experts has greatly eased the burden of first-time teaching processes and experiences (of astronomy), and the on-line mentoring was the attribute most noted by the teachers as being central and essential to fulfilling their expectations of the course.

A self-generated model of "learning on-line while teaching in the field" can be successfully implemented in content area courses other than Astronomy, as long as constant concern and care are given in balancing the amounts of basic subject material and didactic activities, with implementation tools and motivating assignments . Essentially, in the Astronomy field, that is what the teachers really need and may use, in order to bring the stars from heaven above down into their classrooms.

.

"Bringing Stars into the Classroom":
(A Unique Model for Virtual Courses for Science Teachers)

Yona Holtzman-Benshalom, Yoav Yair and Dafna Raviv
TAMID Project, The Open University of Israel, Tel-Aviv, Israel

Astronomy teaching is a challenge even to veteran science teachers. It is a dynamic and changing field of science, with a constant flow of new discoveries that require rapid updates to the study materials. The enormous popularity of astronomy and space science among children is too often mixed with conceptual errors and misinformation about the basic facts in these sciences. Children may conceive explanations for the natural astronomical phenomena from popular resources such as science fiction movies, video games, television series and informal internet resources (mostly on UFOs and aliens). There is an extensive literature about misconceptions in astronomy and their origins, with ideas and recommendations of what pedagogy should be used in order to overcome them, and what teaching strategies are best for each age. Since the introduction of astronomy into the science curriculum in Israel 6 years ago, there has been an intensive effort to train teachers in this field.

The course we describe here was designed for junior-high school science teachers, who have not received any formal training in astronomy and who have never before taught the subject in their classes. It was a 12-weeks hybrid course which consisted of a small number of face-to-face meetings, self-learning studies, and extensive on-line activities, using the Open University's Opus LMS (an internally developed, non-commercial, Hebrew-based set of web tools). Initially, the course was focused on teaching the subject matter and on forming a vivid learning community. This involved educating the participants to the use of the course web-site as the center axis for their learning, through constantly mentoring and moderating by the course tutors. Focused and regularly repeated activities such as "Ask the expert" or "What's up in the sky" have helped teachers overcome their shyness and lack of confidence, expressed by the feeling of "not knowing anything in astronomy". By giving legitimacy to their questions, a shared resource of answers was rapidly built, shared and later used by the teachers themselves as an extensive data-base.. The constant dialogue about current celestial events (we were treated to a beautiful comet and a rare planetary conjunction) created enthusiasm and motivation for reporting observations accordingly, and teachers soon began to harvest updated astronomy news from the plethora of web resources and the popular media in general. Additionally, teachers were asked to come up with lesson plans, suggestions to overcome hurdles in teaching and to mutually discuss the products of their peers.

The teachers became "advocates of astronomy" among their schoolmates and soon started teaching the subject in their classes. They brought the feedbacks and questions of their pupils into the online forums, and these were discussed and shared among the participants. Suggestions, comments and even compliments from their colleagues created a positive learning atmosphere. The constant escort by subject experts has greatly eased the burden of first-time teaching processes and experiences (of astronomy), and the on-line mentoring was the attribute most noted by the teachers as central and essential to fulfilling their expectations of the course.

A self-generated model of "learning on-line while teaching in the field" can be a successfully carried out for both Astronomy courses and any other subject matter courses proposed, as long as constant concern and care are given to balancing the amounts of basic subject material and didactic activities, with implementation tools and motivating assignments. Essentially, in astronomy teaching that is what the teachers really need and may use, in order to bring the stars from heaven above down into their classrooms.

.

An Empirical Study of the Learning Motivation, Satisfaction, and Effectiveness among Web-based Learners in Taiwan

Ti Hsu

Department of Business Administration

Tamkang University

Taipei, Taiwan, R. O. C.

E-mail: th4657@yahoo.com

Chihua Wang

Industrial Technology Research Institute, Taiwan R. O. C

Hsiu Fei Wang

Da Yeh University and New York University

ABSTRACT The present study investigated the relationships among e-learners' behaviors in terms of their motivation, satisfaction, and effectiveness. 139 college undergraduates enrolled in a business course offered in an internet learning environment called the VICAS System voluntarily at the National Taiwan University. The system was developed in house and contains six major parts, including course materials, multi-media capability, interactive testing, discussion forum, message, and personal notes. The findings indicated that there displayed strong correlations among the learners' motivation, their learning satisfactio n, and their learning effectiveness. In addition, "richness" of the system was singled out as a critical factor for e-learning.

INTRODUCTION

E-learning may become one of the most popular and cost-effective ways of learning with traditional students as well as lifelong learners. This is because with e-learning, the "same place," the "s ame time" and the "same pace" type of learning is a way of the past. The "learner" is in full control over the time and place of his learning as well as the pace of the learning. She may at a click decide to joint a virtual community for a collaborative learning. Over 70 million people, according to Cisco, were learning on the internet as of 2001. One day, training of all kinds in this world will be available on the Web. In a global society, where knowledge is being viewed as a source of nation's health as well as its economic competitiveness, how to offer the best possible education or training and how to take advantage of lifelong learning opportunities become crucial.

Cooperative (collaborative) learning is one of the strong points in advocating e-learning. In the past, collaborative learning was not widely accepted because academic excellence was defined by individual achievement via competition. However, collaborative le arning is now back on campus (Johnson, Johnson & Smith 1998; Stein & Hurd, 2000). It is believed that e-learning is most effective in collaborative means via learning communities (Alavi, 1994; Azmitia, 1988; Dillenbourg, et al, 1994; Goeller, 1998).

E-learning is one form of the distance learning and can deliver instructional materials to those who would like to learn on the internet. There are lots advantages of using internet for instruction, learning or training. For one, it is not restricted by the time and place of learning. In other words, it is available anywhere and anytime. For another, learners have the full control of the learning process in terms of the speed, contents, subjects, place and time. For yet another, both the learning and the instruction can be interactive. Besides, e -learning may deliver accessibility, opportunity, and accountability.

As Leidner and Jarvenpaa (1998) indicated that learning would be best achieved through an active involvement. Other researchers (Alavi, et al, 1995) also stated that for learning to be successful, course designing must be in such a way to encourage active student involvement beyond passive note taking. Murray (1938) was one of the first to call for the attention to the need of achievement as the desire to perform things well, to accept difficult challenges, to overcome obstacles, to excel in something, or to surpass others. As a result, many researchers (Asbury, 1974; Atkins & Raynor, 1974; Clarke, 1973; Griffore & Lewis, 1978; Matthews & Chan, 1980; Waters & Waters, 1986) attempted to develop achievement motivation instruments. Chiu's (1997) the School Achievement Motivation Rating Scale was also one of these attempts. Pintrich, et al (1991) investigated learning motivation strategies to compare private and public thoughts and behaviors that might contribute to successful learning.

"Motivation theories are built on a set of assumptions about the nature of people and about the factors that give inpetus to action (Deci & Ryan, 1985, p. 3)" Most psychologists like to use the word of "motivation" to describe the process to deal with four things when it comes to learning and education. Those four things are used to 1) arouse and instigate behavior; 2) offer direction and purpose to behavior; 3) allow continually behavior to persist; and 4) lead to choosing or preferring a particular behavior (Wlodkowski, 1985).

There are in essence two types of motivation, namely, the extrinsic motivation, which was established in 1971 and was based on findings of numerous researchers in psychology, according to Skinner (1953), and the intrinsic motivation, which was first advanced by Deci (1971). The former refers to choose an activity for no compelling reason, beyond the satisfaction derived from the activity itself, while the latter deals with motivation to engage in an activity as a means to an end. Individuals who are extrinsically motivated work on tasks because they believe that participation will result in desirable outcomes, such as reward, teacher praise, or avoidance of punishment. It is the intrinsic motivation that this study is intended to focus on.

Deci in 1971 argued for the first time that extrinsic rewards not only could not provide any positive motivation, but also could undermine the intrinsic motivation in some activities because those activities could be intrinsically motivated by their very own nature. His general findings were later replicated by Lepper, Greene, and Nisbett (1973). Nevertheless, this school of thoughts has been continuously considered as the focus of controversy by researchers and practitioners. While the debate continues, this line of thinking has been expanded and can now be classified into three major types of theories. They are motivational theories (Deci, 1971, Deci & Ryan, 1980, 1985, 1991; Ryan, 1982, 1995), behavioral or cognative theories (Scott, 1975; Dickinson, 1989; Flora, 1990; Carton, 1996; Eisenberg & Cameron, 1996), and attributional theories (Kruglanski, 1975; Lepper, 1981; Lepper, Sagoysky, Dafoe, & Greene, 1982; Higgins & Trope, 1990).

Under motivational approaches, rewards are considered to have conflict effects (Deci, Koestner, Ryan ,1999). On the one hand, it is considered as controlling, meaning it may thwart satisfaction of the need for autonomy, and it may also, on the other, be considered as informational, thus offering satisfaction of the need for competence. That is why additional factors have to be added in order to be able to predict the likely effects of such rewards. Those factors may include, but are not lmited to, reward contingencies (Ryan et al, 1983), verbal rewards (Deci, 1971; Ryan, 1982), Symbolic cue value (Harackiewicz, 1979; Harackiewicz, Manaderlink, & Sansone, 1984), and interpersonal contexts (Ryan, 1982 ; Deci, Nezlek, & Sheinman, 1981; Deci, Connell, & Ryan, 1989; Deci &Ryan, 1991; Ryan 1995).

The users' behavior and the effectiveness of e-learning will always be one of the most important considerations in the success of the learning system. However, very few, if any, efforts have been devoted to the understanding of the application portion of the Web-based learning systems and environments despite the fact that substantial efforts have been devoted to the development and design of those teaching/learning systems and their infrastructure. Basically, we know very little about the e-learners and their behavior. This is especially the case in Taiwan. Besides, mobile learning is expected to be the next wave in online education, understanding the types of contents and the behavior of learners will help e-learning instructors, instructional developers, and administrators, if not the system designers, to take the challenges that wireless e-learning technologies will bring in the very near future.

The present research was designed primarily to examine the relationships between the learning effectiveness and the motivation as well the satisfaction among Web-based learners in Taiwan. More specifically, the study was intended:
1. to assess the relationships between the learning motivation and the learning satisfaction among e-learners;
2. to evaluate the relationships between the learning motivation and the learning effectiveness among Web-based learners; and
3. to investigate the relationships between the learning satisfaction and the learning effectiveness among internet-based learners;

RESEARCH METHODOLOGY

The Learning Environment - the VICAS System.

The system was developed by Prof. Ming Chou Hong of the National Taiwan University for learning/training on the internet and has been in use for several years now. It basically contains six major parts, including course materials, multi-media capability, interactive testing, discussion forum, message, and personal notes. The system has the following features: asynchronization, multi-direction, individualization, and self-monitoring.

Subjects.

The sample consisted of 139 undergraduates (51 males) at the National Taiwan University who enrolled voluntarily in an "Introduction to Management" internet course. Of the total, 98 were business majors and the other 41 were none-business majors. 67 subjects were upper-level students and the other 72 were either freshmen or sophomores.

Instruments

The study utilized three instruments. They included the learning motivation scale, the satisfaction questionnaire, and the learning effectiveness scale.

The learning motivation scale was developed by Pan (1997) for his master's thesis and has been used in a number of occasions in Taiwan. They were totally 12 items and scored on a 5-point Likert scale with 1 being not influenced at all and 5 being very influenced. Cronbach's alphas for the 12-item in this sample ranged from 0.8131 to 0.8540.

The learning satisfaction questionnaire was developed after an extensive evaluation of five different scales (Wu, 1992; Cheng, 1995; Lin, 1997; Shiao, 1998; Cooper and Bradshwaw 1999). The instrument had 16 items. The first 12 items were related to specific questions, such as the interconnectivity of the system, the interactions between the instructor and the students, the way the information was shared, the richness of the course materials, the way the final grade was assessed, the instructor's general attitudes toward e-instruction, etc. The other four items were to evaluate the overall satisfaction in the learning performance, the course quality, the learning environment, and the instructional method. They were also scored on a 5-point Likert scale with one being not satisfied at all and 5 being most satisfied. The Fishbein's Satisfaction Model was adopted here to accommodate the use of the learning satisfaction question. More specifically, subjects were asked about their learning satisfaction in terms of their anticipated satisfaction level and the actual satisfaction level. Cronbach's coefficients for the 16-item scale were 0.8613 for the anticipated satisfaction level and 0.8823 for the actual satisfaction level.

The third instrument modified Pan's (1999) Learning Effectiveness Scale to come up with 10 items. The scale was to measure the domain knowledge and concept, the abilities of decision-making, thinking, analytic, and language expression, interpersonal relations, communication skills, negotiation skills, collaborativeness, and the overall learning performance. It was based upon a three-point scale with one being learned a lot and three being learned very little and two being the neutral one.

Procedure.

At the outset of the semester when students were gathered face-to-face in their very first class, they were explained about the study and were asked to provide some general background information, including sex, major, the class year, and prior experience with computers, etc.

When the students gathered again face-to-face for the last class of the semester, they were administered the learning motivation scale, the learning satisfaction questionnaire, and the learning effectiveness instrument. In addition, during the course of the semester, students' participation in the discussion forum of the VICAS were monitored and recorded automatically by the VICAS system via its self-monitoring feature.

RESULTS

The 12-item learning motivation scale and the 9-item learning effectiveness questionnaire (not counting the overall performance item) were factor analyzed, respectively. The former generated three separate factors, whereas the latter came up with two distinguished factors.

The three learning motivation factors were: 1) learning flexibility, which included six items and explained 27.82% of the variance; 2) richness of contents, which consisted of three items and had a 24.75% of variance explained; and 3) lack of pressure in learning, which was composed of three items and was able to explain 17.69% of the variance. Collectively, the three factors explained 70.26% of the total variance.

The two factors derived from the learning effectiveness questionnaire were: 1) socialization, which had five items included and explained 29.52% of the variance; and 2) ability, which consisted of four items and was able to explain 27.99% of the variance. Together, they were able to explain 52.51% of the total variance.

Satisfaction on	Flexibility	Richness	Pressure	Socialization	Ability
Learning outcomes	0.245**	0.311**	-0.064	0.347**	0.387**
Instruction Quality	0.207**	0.366**	-0.161*	0.303**	0.391**
Learning Environment	0.171*	0.235**	-0.074	0.231**	0.256**
Instruction Style	0.033	0.300**	-0.013	0.218**	0.229**

**$p<0.01$ *$p<0.05$

Table 1 Pearson Correlation Analysis

Results of a Pearson correlation analysis between the three-factor learning motivation and the two-factor learning effectiveness indicated that a strongly positive correlation ($r=.43$, $p<.01$) existed between "richness" and "ability" and that "flexibility" was weakly correlated to "socialization" ($r=.196$, $p<0.05$) and moderately correlated to "ability" ($r=.357$, $p<.01$). "Pressure" was not found to be statistically correlated to either "socialization" or "ability."

Table 1 presents the results of a Pearson correlation analysis between the learning satisfaction of the Fishbein model in terms of the last four items, namely the overall satisfaction on the learning effectiveness, the instruction quality, the learning environment, and the instruction style and the three-factor learning motivation and the two-factor learning effectiveness.

SUMMARY

Based upon the findings presented above, it was clear that there were positive correlations between the learning motivation and the learning effectiveness, between the learning motivation and the learning satisfaction, and between the learning satisfaction and the learning effectiveness, respectively.

A number of implications for the findings may be discussed here. First, among the three factors of the learning motivation, the richness was found to be positively and strongly correlated with all four factors of the learning satisfaction, as well as the ability factor of the learning effectiveness. In other words, for learners to be satisfied with the overall learning performance, instruction quality, learning environment, and instruction style, there should be enough information sharing; the contents should be rich enough, and the instructor should have a different teaching style and attitude toward e-learning than the traditional face-to-face learning.

Second, since all four learning satisfaction factors were found to be strongly and positively interrelated to the two learning effectiveness factors, the implications were simple and straightforward. Learners were not satisfied of the learning experience unless the system provided an opportunity for them to improve their abilities in decision-making, thinking, analytic, and/or the domain knowledge and concept, collectively referred to as the "ability," as well as their skills in interpersonal relations, communication, negotiation, language expression, and collaborativeness, classified together as "socialization."

Third, the strong correlations exhibited between the ability factor of the learning effectiveness and the lack of any strong correlations, positively or negatively, between the socialization factor of the learning effectives and the three learning motivation factors could only be interpreted one way. Students signed up for the course primarily to enhance their "ability" factor, not to strengthen their "socialization" factor, which was secondary in their learning objectives in this course. Since the system did help them achieve their primary goal, i.e., to enhance their "abilities," and that is why they were satisfied.

Finally, the fact that the pressure factor of the learning motivation was found to be not correlated to either the four satisfaction factors or the two learning effectiveness factors was not surprising and was understandable. This is because the learning was supposed to be taking place at any time, any place, and any pace. We were not surprised that "pressure" was not found to be a critical factor at all.

REFERENCES (partial list due to limited pages)

Alavi, M., Wheeler, B.C., & Valacich, J.S. (1995) Using IT to reengineer business education: An exploratory investigation of collaborative telelearning .MIS Quarterly ,19: 293-312

Azmitia, M. (1988). Peer interaction and problem solving: When are two heads better than one? Child Development 59:87--96.

Dillenbourg, P.; Baker, M.; Blaye, A.; and O'Malley, C. 1994. The Evolution of Research on Collaborative Learning. http://tecfa.unige.ch/tecfa-research/lhm/ESF-Chap5.text

Goeller, Karen E. Web-based collaborative learning: a perspective on the future. Computer Networks and ISDN systems 30(1998), pp.634-635

Johnson, D. W., Johnson, R., & Smith, K. (1998). Active Learning: Cooperation in the College Classroom (2nd Ed.), Edina, MN: Interaction Book Company.

Pintrich, P.R., and Smith, D.A. F., Garcia, T., & McKeachie, W. J. (1991) A Manual for the use of the Motivated Strategies foe Research to Improve postsecondary Teaching and Learning.

Acknowledgements

This research was supported by a grant from the National Science Council of the Republic of China in Taiwan to the first author. The data presented, the statements made, and the views expressed are solely the responsibility of the author.

Instructional Design, On-Line Classrooms, and Disability

Abstract:

Brief Paper: This brief paper will provide instructional designers with practical suggestions for assisting students with disabilities in college classrooms. Furthermore, it will examine the similarities and differences between the Americans with Disabilities Act (ADA), Section 504 and 508 of the Rehabilitation Act, and these laws affect on instructional design. Included in the brief paper will be suggestions for instructional designers when designing an on-line or web-based class.

Description:

Since the first FTP file was sent circa 1991, the United States and many other countries of the world have been investigating new ways to send information over the realm of the World Wide Web. Many persons can easily send E-mail, perform a Web Search, and design Web pages using a multitude of software products. Universities have begun to explore ways to utilize the World Wide Web to educate and inform their students.

For students at college and universities campuses the use of the World Wide Web by professors is becoming common practice; professors have homepages where students can view syllabi, download readings, and see adjustments to the class schedule. Another example of instructors integrating of technology into classrooms is a class list-server. List serves are mailing lists used by all students in a particular class to post and send information relating to class material. Some instructors require all students participate in discussion on the list-serve for part of their overall course grade. Also, some professors do not collect papers in class anymore; they require the students to submit the papers using email attachments instead. A final example of how technology is being integrated into college and universities course are on-line classes that been developed to allow students to be at a distance and attend classes. Typically these classes utilize software as classroom management tools and include the following areas: discussion posting boards, file exchanges, email applications, course readings posted to the internet, uploaded power point presentation.

These above examples demonstrate how technology is being integrated into higher education. If the information age continues to grow exponentially, the future use of the World Wide Web as an informational and educational tool can be endless for college students. For most students, and professors, this technological integration has made their life simpler; attending classes without leaving the house, getting another copy of a syllabus without visiting the professor, having students view a video tape shown in class, or a web-cast of a lecture they had missed. Yet, for some students the advancement of technologies in the classrooms, either virtual or traditional, has caused distress. Disabled students sometimes have difficulty with the new technologies professors are using in their classrooms to present their course material. Difficulties can stem from not being able to read power point presentations professors project onto a screen, not being able to hear a video playing in a class, and not being able to comprehend information that is presented in large chucks on a computer screen.

Today, there are more students with documented disabilities in higher education than ever before -- 140,142 freshmen reported having a disability in 1996 which represents over 9% of all freshmen (HEATH Resource Center, 1998), as compared with only 2.6% in 1978 (HEATH Resource Center, 1995). The growth in the number of students with learning disabilities has created a new challenge to professors and colleges. Over the years, there has been considerable resistance by professors to alter the way they instruct, particularly if such alteration were to accommodate a student with a mental, as compared to a physical, disability. Many professors prefer that all students meet the same set of requirements, within the same time period, and in the same way, and are ill-prepared either to adapt their instruction to address the individual needs of students or to identify appropriate, fair, and reasonable accommodations (Thomas, 2000). This situation can be improved by the assistance of a university's Student Disability Services (SDS), or similar unit. However, such units often are inadequately funded, given the growth in the number of students requesting accommodation, and seldom have experts on staff who are knowledgeable about the wide range of disabilities that colleges are now attempting to accommodate (Thomas, 2000).

The term disability was modified in 1990, and is broadly defined by congress as "a term that should be used to describe conditions such as perceptual handicaps, brain injury, minimal brain dysfunction, dyslexia and developmental aphasia." Furthermore, Congress has defined a qualified handicapped persons as "an individual with a disability who, with or without reasonable modifications to rules, policies or practices, the removal of architectural, communication or transpiration barriers, or the provision of auxiliary aids, and services meets the essential eligibility requirements for the receipt of services or the participation in programs or activities provided by a public entity." These definitions allow universities to determine if a disabled person is a qualified handicapped person, and if they are, the university must provide accommodations to qualified persons. Thus, these items an instructional designer should become aware of to ensure the materials used in classrooms accommodate disabled students as defined by the law.

The Americans with Disabilities Act (ADA) of 1990, Section 504 of the and Section 508 of the Rehabilitation Act, are laws that exist to protect disabled persons from being discriminated against, and to assure that persons with disabilities are provided with reasonable and proper accommodations. A common theme for each of these laws is they were created, and have been modified, to protect persons with disabilities. Even with this common goal, these laws do have several differences that will be highlighted during the discussion. For example, ADA is designed as an umbrella law, and all United States private and public agencies must comply with the rules and regulation of ADA. The provisions outlined in section 504 only apply to federal agencies and private agencies that accept federal funding (29 U.S.C. § 794(a)). An example of a private institution required to comply with section 504 is a research university that accepts National Science Foundation grants. Finally, section 508 compliance has only been set for federal websites, an example would be the National Aeronautic and Space Administration website.

The main goal of ADA, 504, and 508 are to provide disabled persons with reasonable accommodations and allow them to function at, or near, the same level of non-disabled persons. Currently, the interpretations of these laws intertwine with the moral obligations of society, and form a 'gray area'. In terms of an on-line environment, the moral issue of knowing the University must provide reasonable accommodations for disabled students enrolled in programs the University offers, yet there are no litigations which state technology used outside or during of a face to face is required to be assessable to students. Thus, an interpretation of the gray area can be "it has not been shown that not providing accommodations for disabled students who take classes with technological components is in violation of the law, thus we are doing nothing wrong."

In the context of this brief paper, technology will be defined as materials and devices used by the instructor that goes beyond the traditional lecture. Thus, this brief paper will examine how to modify advanced technology to ensure disabled students are provided the same learning opportunities as non-disabled students. Advanced technology would be considered data posted to websites, projected computer images, on-line classrooms, web-based learning, computer programming software, and list-serves.

The concentration of the brief paper will focus on advanced technology and the considerations instructional designers need to developing course that involves those types of technology. There are solutions, which fit these laws that instructional designers can utilize when technology is incorporated into learning environments to assist student who are visually impaired students, hearing impaired students, and students who have language-processing disorders. For example, when posting a reading to a class website, either in an on-line classroom or a traditional classroom, ensure that the information can be printed in Braille, if not add the proper HTML code to ensure students who are visually disabled can read the information. Another example would be to have all Power Point slides available in printable format for students prior to discussions. This would allow students with disabilities to have a copy of the material in front of them in a format in which they can follow along with the classroom discussion.

Instructional designers need knowledge of disability law so they are able to consider those aspects when designing courses that involve advanced technology. Furthermore, instructional designers need to have knowledge of what should be done to help disabled students in higher education classrooms. These two components will be the start of better instructional design that allows disabled students to excel in college classrooms.

References:

Americans with Disabilities Act of 1990, 42 U.S.C. § 12102 et seq. (1998); title II, § 12131 et seq. (1998); 28 C.F.R. §§ 35.101-35.191 (1998); title III, § 12181 et seq. (1998); 28 C.F.R. §§ 36.101-36.608 (1998); Appendix A to Part 36 (Standards for Accessible Design 1998).

HEATH Resource Center. (1995). College Freshmen with Disabilities. Washington, DC: American Council on Education.

HEATH Resource Center. (1998). Profile of 1996 College Freshmen with Disabilities. Washington, DC: American Council on Education.

Thomas, Steven B. College Students and Disability Law. The Journal of Special Education. Vol.33. NO.4. 2000, pp. 248-257.

The Value of Community Building in an Online Classroom

Debbie Hu

Higher education is changing. The method for education has begun to shift from traditional classroom delivery to at home delivery; better known as online learning. This paper explores changes occurring in the higher education system in relationship to online learning and community building. Many persons involved in traditional classes can have an easier time forming a community of learners among themselves and their professors. Yet, in online classes, variables such as proximity of students can cause difficulty in building community. If an online classroom lacks community it is more prone to students' failing, conflict, problems, frustration for both students and faculty (Lindner 2002). This paper explores some of the problems and solutions for building an online community, and the positive effects community can have on both the students and faculty in online classes.

The reality of online education is that it favors a transition from traditional notions of academic community toward a much narrower, transactions-based model; which is defined as the psychological and communications space between learners and instructors (Moore as sited in Rovai, 2002). Transactional distance is relative and different for each person. Thus, the pedagogy of faculty members in a distance education course needs to change from a teacher-centered approach to being student-centered (Strain, 1987; Beaudoin, 1990; 1998; Berge, 1998). In traditional higher education, a "community of scholars" was a place where the student was mentored as an apprentice and eventually became a co-investigator in research and creative activity. Though, from the student's perspective, the social and physical distance of online education seems to make students need clear, precise, objectives-oriented curricula which may represent a narrowing of education, and may make them unlikely candidates for collegial work on faculty research projects (Online Classrooms 1999). In 1997, T.H. Murphy noted that the instructional effectiveness of distance education is comparable to that delivered on campus. For distance education programs to be successful they must provide "for appropriate and sufficient synchronous and asynchronous interaction between faculty and students and among students" (Murphy, 1997, p. 8).

An obstacle for students in online classes is the physical separation of the students. Separation has a tendency to reduce the sense of community, giving rise to feelings of disconnection (Kerka 1996), isolation, distraction, and lack of personal attention (Edelstein 2002). This could affect student persistence in distance education courses or programs. Tinto (1993) emphasized the importance of community and theorized that students will increase their levels of satisfaction and the likelihood of persisting in a college program if they feel involved and develop relationships with other members of the learning community. The importance of community is supported by empirical research. Wehlage, Rutter and Smith (1989) found that traditional schools with exemplary dropout-prevention programs devoted considerable attention to overcoming the barriers that prevented students from connecting with the school and to developing a sense of belonging, membership, and engagement. The key finding of their report is that effective schools provide students with a supportive community. Finally, Ashar and Skenes (1993) discovered that learning alone appeared strong enough to attract adults to the program, but not to retain them.

Research provides evidence that strong feelings of community may not only increase persistence in courses, but may also increase the flow of information among all learners, availability of support, commitment to group goals, cooperation among members, and satisfaction with group efforts (Rovai 2002). Additionally, learners benefit from community membership by experiencing a greater sense of well being and by having an agreeable set of individuals to call on for support when needed (Rovai 2002).

It is important to clearly state what community means within the context of this paper. We will define community as: a group of people who are socially interdependent, who participate together in discussion and decision making, and who share certain practices that both define the community and are nurtured by the community. Furthermore, community is an environment in which people act in a cohesive manner, continually reflecting on the work of the group while always respecting the differences individual members bring to the group (Rovai 2002). Yet, an online education community can be viewed as what people do together, rather than where or through what means they do them, community becomes separated from geography, physical neighborhoods, and campuses (Wellman, 1999). Advocates of online education argue that an academic community of scholars could be enhanced through technology. Palloff hypothesized that in principle it is possible to maintain and extend values such as mentoring and co-investigation by means of telecommunications.

There are many advantages to creating a sense of community for the online student. This paper will discuss three advantages. First, students who are engaged in collaborative activities are more likely participate within an online community. For example, online discussions within small groups or learning sets offers a powerful environment for adult learning as it enables members to reflect on each other's experience and to engage in a collaborative tasks. In such groups there is likely to be a high sense of presence and a growing sense of community (Hammond 2000). Furthermore, Royal and Rossi (1996) suggest that learners' sense of community is related to their engagement in school activities, with students who have a higher sense of community being less likely to experience class cutting behavior or thoughts of dropping out of school and more likely to report feeling bad when unprepared for classes.

Second, students who have support are more likely to complete their online course and contribute to the online community. Aviv (2000) states that the supportive interaction process occurs when every member helps each other, gives feedback on processing, reflects on the effectiveness of the community, and advocates effort.

Finally, students who participate in online communities will be more receptive to other academic points of view. For example, Hammond's (2000) research on online discussion forums indicated students using community forums keep an open mind on the value of different types of knowledge, take a critical stance to theoretical knowledge, reflect and seek dialogue and debate with others in the community. These discussions can promote and support participation among students in the online class.

We explored online communities to help students become empowered to build online relationships with other participants in the learning environment. This paper examined three community building activities. First, using collaborative activities such as online discussions to increase a sense of community among students. Second, students gaining support from the community to increase interaction among students thus decreasing the student failure rate. Finally, using forums as a mean to support knowledge perspective taking among students.

References:

Aviv, R. (2000). Educational Performance of ALN via Content Anaylsis. *Journal of Asynchronus Learning Networks,* v4, n2.

Beaudoin, M.R. (1998). A new professorate for the new millennium. *DEOSNEWS* 8 (5), Article 98-00004. Retrieved June 30, 2002 from http://www.outreach.psu.edu/ASCDE/DEOS.html

Berge, Z.L. (1998). Changing roles of teachers and learners are transforming the online classroom. *Online-Ed* August 30, 1998, Article 74. Retrieved June 30, 2002 from http://www.edfac.unimelb.edu.au/online-ed

Edelstein, Susan, and Edwards, Jason. *If you Build It, TheyW ill Come: Building Learning Communities Through Threaded Discussions.* Retrieved July 3, 2002. http://www.westga.edu/%7Edistance/ojdla/spring51/edelstein51.html

Hammond, Micheal. *Communication with Online Forums: The Opportunities, The Constraints and the Value of a Communicative Approach.* Computers & Education; v35 n4. p 251-62. December 2000.

Kerka, Sandra, and Micheal E. Wonnacott. *Assessing Learner Online: Practitioner File."* ERIC Clearing house on Adult, Career, and Vocational Education (ERIC/ACVE).

Lindner, James, Dooley, Kim, Kelsey, Kathleen. All for One and One for All: Relationships in a Distance Education Program. *On-Line Learning of Distance Learning Administration.* Retrieved July 3, 2002. http://www.westga.edu/%7Edistance/ojdla/spring51/linder51.html

Miller, W.W., & Webster, J. (1997, December). *A comparison of interaction needs and performances of distance learners in synchronous and a synchronous classes.* Paper presented at the American Vocational Association Convention, Las Vegas, Nevada.

Murphy, T. H. (1997). Five factors to evaluate distance education programs. *NACTA Journal, 42*(3), 6-10.

Creating Online Learning Communities. Online Classroom Apr 2002. p. 7. Feature Article.

Schifter, Catherine. Perception Differences About Participaitng in Distance Education. *On-Line Learning of Distance Learning Administration.* Retrieved July 3, 2002 from *http*://www.westga.edu/%7Edistance/ojdla/spring51/schifter51.html

Strain, J. (1987). The role of the faculty member in distance education. *The American Journal of Distance Education* 1 (2): 61-65.

Tinto, V. (1993). Leaving College: Rethinking the Causes and Cures of Student Attrition. (2nd ed.) Chicago: University of Chicago Press.

Rovai, Alfred (April, 2002). Building Sense of Community at a Distance. *International Review of Research in Open and Distance Learning:* 3, 1

Wehlage, G.G., Rutter, R.A & Smith, G.A. (1998) *Reducing Risk: Schools as Communities of Support.* New York: Falmer Press.

Wellman, B. & Kahne, J. (1993) The Network Basis of Social Support: A network is More than the Sum of its Ties. In B. Wellman (Ed.). *Networks in the Global Village.* P. 1 – 48. Boulder, CO: Westview Press.

On-line Simulations for Health Care Providers

Introduction

This paper will describe the development and implementation of interactive on-line continuing education modules for health care providers. The interactive framework, extensive use of links, pre- and post-testing, and evaluation of outcomes will be featured.

The Internet has become a source for health related continuing education. However, continuing education for health professionals on the Internet must be critically evaluated by the user. Many of these offerings consist of reproduced journal articles or other text-based content. Some of the sites provide few links and offer little or no interactivity.

To address the need for quality continuing education of health care providers, on-line modules were developed as part of a grant-funded nurse practitioner learning project. The feasibility of on-line learning for health professions included the results of a nurse practitioner (n=187) survey of computer availability and skills, topic preference, and their potential for taking on-line continuing education. More than 80% of the respondents had Internet access, and 71% had basic Internet skills. The majority of the respondents indicated their computer met the minimum standards to access an on-line course. Fifty percent of the respondents were very interested in taking an on-line continuing education course. Although the modules were designed from the nurse practitioner data, the modules are appropriate for physicians, physician-assistants, and other allied health professionals.

Designing the Modules

Two modules were designed to be interactive, realistic, self-study simulations that closely resemble clinical practice. "Acute Low Back Pain," and "Common Dermatological Problems in Primary Care" were selected as the topics for development. A preview of the modules is available at http://www.nursing.twsu.edu/clp. This preview was designed to allow learners to explore the modules prior to registration.

The development of the learning materials includes identification of learning objectives, pre-test and post-test construction, extensive search of the Web for related sites, and development of a comprehensive bibliography for further study. In order to establish communication with the learners, the instructors include a brief biographical sketch with photographs. E-mail links for each instructor are provided. An optional area is provided for learners to input information about them and practice as well as questions and comments about the continuing education modules. This is an attempt to establish a learning community for potential communication with one another and the instructors. A "help" section is available for the students who may have technical problems with the program. This link is on-line directly to the educational specialist who assisted with the development of the modules. Following the construction of the modules, each module was submitted to a panel of expert reviewers. Revisions were made based on the expert reviewers' evaluation of the modules.

Learners are guided through the process from registration to completion with on-line submission of the post-test. The course overview presents the learning objectives, the instructors biographies, the module bibliography and related sites, and then explains the structure of the modules. The learner links to the on-line registration process which provides verification of credentials for awarding of continuing education credit. In addition, the registration questionnaire contains additional demographic information and on-line education preferences. The pre-test is automatically graded and the learners immediately receive their scores. The authors elected not to share the answers of the pre-test with the learners until completion of the post-test.

The learner is then directed to begin the case studies. The dermatology module presents 25 brief patient scenarios with presenting history and an image of the condition. The learner is asked to submit the diagnosis and receives immediate feedback. Links are provided for management, additional images, and patient information for each dermatologic condition. "Acute Low Back Pain" contains two extensive, interactive patient case simulations that take the learner through the assessment, diagnosis, and management of the low back pain patient in primary care. Following completion of the case simulations, the learner completes the post-test and electronically submits the answers. The learner must pass with an 80% rate in order to earn their continuing education credit. The modules have been further developed for academic graduate credit ranging from one to three credit hours.

Evaluation

The survey information obtained from the registration submission help to determine a demographic profile of users and motivation for on-line education. To date, 50 learners have completed the modules with others currently enrolled. All learners are Registered Nurses, ranging in age from 25 to 59 years, with learners residing across the United States and internationally. A broad range of nursing specialties are represented including staff nurses, graduate students, directors of nursing, clinical nurse specialists and nurse practitioners. Analysis of data reveals significant differences between the pre-test and post-test knowledge scores.

Learner comments are submitted electronically through an evaluation form and are reviewed for attitudes toward on-line continuing education, satisfaction with the completed module, and the potential for further use. Learners evaluated the modules as innovative, time saving, convenient, available, and economical. Learners particularly liked the case study approach, use of graphics, and the extensive links to other quality web sites. These comments provide feedback for revision of the current modules and future development of additional modules. Outcome data are currently being collected online and will be analyzed for efficacy of this delivery system for continuing education. These data will be analyzed and presented.

Conclusions

Competency-based learning is a preferred method in advanced practice nursing education. Through the use of interactive case studies, we were able to offer time pressed health professionals opportunities for continuing education. The future of on-line continuing health education is dependent on well-structured, interactive, and challenging programs as well as the accessibility and the skill of the user.

Web-Based Instruction—Its Impact on Higher Education

Pei-Wen Nicole Huang
National Huwei Institute of Technology, Taiwan
huang_nicole@hotmail.com

Yung-Hoh Sheu
Kung Shan University of Technology, Taiwan
uu2789@ms52.hinet.net

Abstract: A review of the literature and related research concentrates on the area of Web-based instruction is presented in this paper. An overview of Web-based instruction, including its impact on the higher education learning environment, emerging roles for instructors, synchronous and asynchronous learning environments, and creating learning communities are presented in the section.

Introduction

A review of the literature and related research concentrates on the area of Web-based instruction are presented in this paper. An overview of Web-based instruction, including its impact on the higher education learning environment, emerging roles for instructors, synchronous and asynchronous learning environments, and creating learning communities are presented in this section.

Impact on Higher Education Learning Environments

Web-based instruction (WBI) is defined as an innovative approach for delivering instruction to a remote audience using the World Wide Web as the instructional delivery system (Khan, 1997). It has been used not only in exclusive distance programs but also in supporting face-to-face traditional classroom instruction. Angulo & Bruce (1999), stated in <u>Innovative Higher Education</u> that in 1996 the University of Georgia engaged WBI to supplement their traditional course offerings. Numerous other colleges and universities, such as the University of Colorado at Denver, the University of California system, State University of New York, Arizona State, and other independent "Virtual Universities" where students can apply for admission, register for courses, purchase books, and attend classes without ever visiting a physical place on campus, have launched similar or more extensive programs (Palloff & Pratt, 1999).

Corresponding to the statement by McIsaac & Gunawardena (1996) that distance learning is the fastest growing form of education, there will be a continued expansion of web-based technologies in higher education. As the web will be increasingly used as a teaching and learning medium, it is important to consider the emerging roles of instructors and its learning environment (Shotsberger, 1997).

Emerging Roles for Instructors and Learners in the Web-based Instruction

A number of authors perceived that the instructor's role in a Web-based setting requires a different set of skills than those employed in a traditional face-to-face classroom. According to McIsaac (1995), the role of the teacher of tomorrow will not be an actor of transmission of just consumption, but will become a facilitator of learning and research as a whole process. Duchastel & Turcotte (1996) argued that we may well see a tremendous growth in informal and out-of-class learning, and the impact of this growth will shift the power in the classroom where the instructor is no longer necessarily the expert. The role of the teacher will shift toward a greater emphasis on guidance and mentoring (Thiele, Allen, & Stucky, 1999; Duchastel & Turcotte, 1996). The instructor no longer dispenses knowledge but, rather, guides the student's pursuit of knowledge and provides technical support as educational facilitator (Palloff & Pratt, 1999; Shotsberger, 1997). Rohfeld & Hiemstra (1995) also indicated that the most important role of the online instructor is to model effective teaching and accept "the responsibility of keeping discussions on track, contributing special knowledge and insights, weaving together various discussion threads and course components, and maintaining group harmony" (p. 91).

Those characteristics of instructor roles also corresponding to Berge & Collins' (1996) assertion that categorized the various tasks and roles demanded of the online instructor into four general areas: pedagogical, social, managerial, and technical. They described the pedagogical function as one that revolves around educational facilitation. The social function is the promotion of the friendly social environment, which is essential to Web-based learning. The managerial function involves norms in course setting, pacing, objective setting, and decision making. The technical function depends on the instructor first becoming comfortable and proficient with the technology being used and being able to transfer that level of comfort to the learners.

Shotsberger (1997) mentioned that formalizing and tailoring the interactive environment in the Web-based instruction is considered one of the instructional roles. From a constructivist view, interaction is an important means by which learners construct meaning. Students with higher levels of interaction have more positive attitudes and higher levels of achievement (Thiele, Allen, & Stucky, 1999). By developing Web-based instruction, faculty can create an interactive learning environment that changes the old paradigm of instruction from one of "shoveling knowledge" at the students to one of guiding students through collaborative learning experiences (French, Hale, Johnson, & Farr, 1999; Denning, 1999).

Synchronous and Asynchronous Learning Environments

Eastmond (1995) proclaimed that learners should be given the opportunity to interact, to reflect, and to apply their individual experience in the learning. Also, interactive learning is taking place when the instructor merges both synchronous and asynchronous interactive teaching and learning methods in the Web-based instruction. Berge & Collins (1996) also pointed out that both synchronous and asynchronous interaction teaching and learning methods can be structured as one-to-one (email), one-to-many (listserver managed group), and many-to-many (bulletin boards and dedicated computer conferencing systems).

Relan & Gillani (1997) articulated that WBI offers a new sensibility and means of social interaction employed toward learning. With WBI, cooperative learning extends beyond one classroom to potentially every classroom. Synchronous communication that allows for live interaction (Berge & Collins, 1996) takes the form of interactive messaging systems like computer conferencing tools and chatrooms (Khan, 1997). All participants must be present online at the same time in order to interact. When many people do so, the text on the screen can scroll along at a furious pace with the discussion having much of the flexibility of the spoken word. Harasim, Hiltz, Teles, & Turoff (1995) stressed "The synchronicity of online interactions allows participants time to reflect on a topic before commenting or carrying out online tasks" (p. 27).

Asynchronous communication allows for time-independent interaction that ranges from simple email discussions between individuals that require only the participants have access to an electronic mailbox to feature-rich groupware programs like listserves or bulletin boards (Berge & Collins, 1996). Participants do not have to be online at the same time in order to interact and can do so from any location in which they have access to a networked computer with the appropriate client program.

Theoretically, Web-based learning is available at any hour in which the participant has the ability to access a networked computer. Participants who have access from work, home, or another convenient location may find courses taught by computer conferencing easier to accommodate around work and family responsibilities (Berge & Collins, 1996). Relan & Gillani (1997) also claimed, "the ability of the instructor and students to communicate privately or collectively in a synchronous or asynchronous manner lends a new dimension to the design of instructional strategies" (p. 45). In spite of providing interactive synchronous or asynchronous methods in the Web-based learning environment, Westrom & Pankratz (1997) further stated "the purpose of email, discussion groups, and web pages is to enable communication. These technologies, when combined with procedures designed to facilitate cooperative learning, can lead to the building of learning communities" (p. 2).

Creating a Learning Community

Palloff & Pratt (1999) described the importance of community in the electronic classroom: "In distance education, attention needs to be paid to the developing sense of community within the group of participants in order for the learning process to be successful. The learning community is the vehicle through which learning occurs online" (p. 29). They further concluded that in order to create a successful online learning experience, "the instructor in an online class is responsible for facilitating and making room for the personal and social aspects of an online community" (p. 76). Berge and Collins (1996) referred to this function as "promoting human relationships, affirming and recognizing student's input; providing opportunities for students to develop a sense of group cohesiveness, maintaining the group as a unit, and in other ways helping members to work together in a mutual cause" (p. 7).

Palloff & Pratt (1999) revealed that if a participant logs on to a course site and there has been no activity on it for several days, he or she might become discouraged or feel a sense of abandonment. The situation is related to Berge & Collins' (1996) assertion that

The advantage of computer conferencing includes interaction at a distance with other students and the instructor, rather than studying alone. A virtual community can be built that provides support and encouragement and promote sharing among the participants and can help overcome the isolations of remote areas. (p. 4)

A major finding of Gunawardena's (1995) research pointed out the crucial role of the instructional facilitators of computer conferences in creating a sense of community and collaboration among users. Hiltz (1994) also stated three basic principles concerning the instructor's role in distance instruction for establishing and maintaining a learning community: be responsive, be competent online, and organize the interaction. Hill & Raven (2000) recently conducted empirical research examining the best techniques/strategies to enhance learning and community building in WBI. Their results outlined four main categories: atmosphere, foundation, communication, and technology. The technique of atmosphere is to provide a safe on-line environment that learners perceive to be a space where open communication can occur. The foundation strategy is to create structural dependence and organization to assist learners in overcoming information overload, establish patterns, and set expectations to anticipate certain types of communication. Communication strategy is to encourage learners to keep in touch with others and apply technology techniques to provide flexibility in terms of facilitating multiple learning and interactions and minimize glitches.

Web-based learning is sometimes referred to as asynchronous interactivity or asynchronous learning network (Mayadas, 1997), and is defined as people network, anytime, anywhere learning. Romiszowski (1997) concluded the real meaning and importance of WWW networks consisting of computer networks, conversational networks, information networks, and conceptual networks.

Conclusion

Currently, WBI is growing faster than any other instructional technology. The potential collaborative and interactive benefits of WBI have recently caught the attention of institutions of higher education in a profound way. However, WBI is only a delivery mechanism for designing a learning context to individuals. The various aspects of quality, accountability, productivity, and access of WBI had been discussed constantly. Some authors were concerned that critical issues need to be examined before WBI is adopted into university practices, yet many pedagogical factors and theoretical guidelines involved in WBI require to be investigated fully for the success of WBI (Harasim et al., 1995; Berge, 1999).

Reference

Angulo, A. J., & Bruce, M. (1999). Student perceptive of supplemental Web-based Instruction. Innovative Higher Education, 24 (2), 105-125.

Berge, Z. (1999). Interaction in Post-Secondary Web-based learning. Educational Technology, Jan., 5-11.

Berge, Z., & Collins, M. P. (1996). Facilitating Interaction in Computer Mediated Online Courses. Paper presented at the FSU/AECT Distance Education Conference, Tallahassee, FL. [Online]. Available: http://www. Emoderators.com/moderators/flcc.html

Duchastel, P., & Turcotte, S. (1996). On-line learning and teaching in an information-rich context. Proceedings of the Ineti'96 International Conference, Montreal, Canada.

Eastmond, D. V. (1995). Alone but together: Adult distance study through computer conferencing. Cresskill, NJ: Hampton Press.

French, D., Hale, C., Johnson, C., & Farr, G. (Eds.). (1999). Internet based learning: An introduction and framework for higher education and business. Sterling, VA: Stylus Publishing, Inc.

Gunawardena, C. N. (1995). Social presence theory and implications for interaction and collaborative learning in computer conferences. International Journal of Educational Telecommunications, 1 (2/3), 147-166.

Harasim, L., Hiltz, S. R., Teles, L., & Turoff, M. (1995). Learning networks: A field guide to teaching and learning online. Cambridge, MA: MIT Press.

Hill, J. R., & Raven, A. (2000, October). Online learning communities: If you build them, will they stay? Poster session presented at the ITFORUM. [On-line]. Available: http://it.coe.uga.edu/itforum/paper46/paper46.htm

Hiltz, S. R. (1994). The virtual classroom: Learning without limits via computer networks. Norwood, NJ: Ablex Publishing Corporation.

Khan, B. H. (1997). Web-based instruction (WBI): What is it and why is it? In B. H. Khan (Ed.), *Web based instruction* (pp. 239-244). Englewood Cliffs, NJ: Educational Technology Publications.
Mayadas, F. (1997). Asynchronous learning networks: A Sloan foundation erspective. Journal of Asynchronous Learning Networks, 1 (19), 1-16.

McIsaac, M. S. (1995). Fusion of communications and computing technologies: Impact on Teachers' education. [On-line]. Available: http://seamonkey.ed.asu.edu/~mcisaac/emc523old95/gaby523/finrs.html

McIssaac, M. S., & Gunawardena, C. N. (1996). Distance education. In D. H. Jonassen (Ed.), Handbook of research for educational communications and technology (pp.403-437). New York: Simon and Schuster.

Palloff, R. M., & Pratt, K. (1999). Building learning communities in cyberspace:effective strategies for the online classroom. San Francisco, CA: Jossey-Bass Publishers.

Relan, A., & Gillani, B. B. (1997). Web-based instruction and the traditional classroom: similarities and differences. In B. H. Khan (Ed.), Web based instruction (pp. 41 - 45). Englewood Cliffs, NJ: Educational Technology Publications.

Rohfeld, R. W., & Hiemstra, R. (1995). Moderating discussions in the electronic classroom. In Z. Berge & M. P. Collins (Eds.), Computer Mediated Communication and the Online Classroom: Vol 3, Distance Learning (pp. 91-104). Cresskill, NJ: Hampton Press.

Romiszowski, A. J. (1997). Web-based distance learning and teaching: Revolutionary invention or reaction to necessity? In B. H. Khan (Ed.), Web based instruction (pp. 25- 34). Englewood Cliffs, NJ: Educational Technology Publications.

Shotsberger, P. G. (1997). Emerging roles for instructors and learners in the web-based instruction classroom. In B. H. Khan (Ed.), *Web-based Instruction* (pp. 101-103). Englewood Cliffs, NJ: Educational Technology Publications.

Thiele, J. E., Allen, C., & Stucky, M. (1999). Effects of Web-based instruction on learning behaviors of undergraduate and graduate students. Nursing and Health Care Perspectives, 20(4), 199-209.

Westorm, M., & Pankratz, T. (1997). Creating collaborative communities online. [On-line]. Available: http://star.ucc.nau.edu/~hauweb97/ papers/ westrom.htm

Breaking the unbreakable: addressing the need for cryptanalysis

William J. Hunter

Network security research

Some time ago, the world of Internet security was brought to life by the seminal work of Clifford Stohl, The Cuckoo's Egg. More recently, books have begun to appear that provide good general introductions to cryptography (e.g., The Code Book by Simon Singh) and to network security more generally (e.g., Secrets and Lies: Digital Security in a Networked World by Bruce Schnier. When Stohl told his story of uncovering a major espionage ring that was using university computers as conduits for the invasion of military computers, one of the most remarkable features of the tale was the complete absence of knowledgeable authorities within the police community, including military intelligence and the FBI. Another critical part of the story was the cavalier attitude of many university-based system administrators who might not even know that the computers they installed came with built-in accounts that had standardized usernames and passwords (which was well known in hacker communities).

Much has changed in the dozen years since Stohl's book was published. Singh's account of the history of "the evolution of secrecy from Mary, Queen of Scots to quantum cryptography" draws on resources from the Second World War that are only now becoming public knowledge. Schnier puts cryptography into a broader social context of network security that indicates both that we have come a long way since Stohl's adventures and that we are still a very long way from anything like adequate security in most computing environments. The questions are of sufficient general interest that a major novel, Cryptonimicon by Neil Stephenson, has drawn heavily on both public key cryptography and a fictionalized account centering on the cracking of Enigma in the Second World War. Finally, the fact that international baccalaureate student Aaron Suggs based his theory of knowledge essay (http://www.ktheory.com/write/extendedessay.htm) on this very topic is one concrete example of the potential for student interest in cryptography as an area of inquiry.

Objectives for a new line of inquiry

The current argument that public key cryptography has given us the capacity to develop unbreakable codes rests on estimates of the amount of computing power/time required to decode an encrypted message. The reasoning seems sound, but the assertion that unbreakable codes exist has been made repeatedly throughout history but eventually those codes succumbed to the efforts of analysts. Nevertheless, there is good reason to take the current claims seriously. If we do so and if we believe that a balance between code-breaking and code-making is important to the success of democratic systems of government (e.g., the ability to defeat Nazism or the potential to uncover terrorist plots), then it becomes important to consider what will be necessary to restore that balance. Among other things, we need to begin work that will

- develop network security as a new area of inquiry in educational technology,
- evoke discussion on critical issues regarding education for and about network security not only for education but for social and political policy,
- provide a basis for informed decision making regarding education for and about network security, and
- establish a body of work that would inform course development in this area.

Proposed directions

The lessons of Turing's Bletchley Park project suggest that many diverse talents can be put to use in the development of a cryptanalytic team. Likewise, it seems likely that cryptanalysis and cryptography could serve as useful integrative themes for an interdisciplinary teaching unit that might be used, with different levels of complexity, at several grade levels. There is already an existing body of children's fiction that is based on code-making and code-breaking concepts that dates back to Edgar Allan Poe's short story, The Gold Bug. Working from this literary base, it is clear that social studies questions around the nature of community, conflict, cooperation and crime could be developed. Further, the connections to history (Bletchley Park, e.g.,) are clear and intriguing as Aaron Scuggs work reveals. Similarly, the use of numeric and algebraic tools in the process of making and breaking codes would provide links to concepts in math curricula and the automating of algorithms for code-breaking is a natural introduction to computer science. Connections to DNA research could relate the study to both biology and chemistry. The final version of this paper will include a delineation of a potential curriculum plan.

Part of the rationale for developing such a curriculum is that it might serve to introduce more students to genuinely interesting and socially useful applications of mathematics. If we are to make a dent in the invulnerability of quantum cryptography, we will need to have substantially more bright minds considering the possibilities of new algorithms that would demand significantly fewer calculations, thus rendering it possible for computers to crack codes in a fraction of the times now projected. This is a long term project that, if successful, might see a payoff many decades into the future. It is thus even more important that the curriculum would raise awareness of the social issues involved in having totally secret communications systems.

Raising the level of concern and debate about such questions will be a prerequisite to developing the kind of problem solving culture the code-breaking will require, but it also would focus attention on the need to avoid succumbing to a sense of futility regarding the potential for evil-doers to benefit from unlimited secrecy. That is, a secure code is only a small part of a secure communications system. Governments will need to be aware of other possibilities for preventing or interrupting conspiratorial communications. A brief discussion of some such possibilities and their educational and policy implications will be a part of the final paper.

Much of this presentation has assumed that the readers have the benefit of good and benevolent government, but civil libertarians could be equally concerned about the potential for government secrecy (or government invasions of privacy) to be as problematic as the potential for crime or terrorism. This is an equally compelling reason for importance of restoring equilibrium (or at least tension) between our capabilities for cryptography and our capacities for cryptanalysis. It would seem, then, that objectives and directions proposed here would have near universal appeal; however, it is quite likely that this will not be the case at all. Strong cryptography has developed in recent years largely to meet the demands of commercial interests wishing to conduct business securely on the Internet. People involved in Internet commerce, both producers and consumers, are likely to see any weakening of the security of Internet transactions as a threat to commerce. While this may be true, I will argue that this threat is more perception than reality, that equilibrium serves commercial interests as well, and that, in the final analysis, commercial losses are a fair price to pay for the security of the social order.

ONLINE COURSES, TEACHING AND DEVELOPMENT EXPERIENCES

Larisa Enríquez Vázquez
Productos Interactivos
DGSCA UNAM
Mexico
larisa@piaget.dgsca.unam.mx

Alma Ibarra Obando
Productos Interactivos
DGSCA UNAM
Mexico
alma.io@servidor.unam.mx

Berenice Ramírez Toledo
Productos Interactivos
DGSCA UNAM
Mexico
bere@piaget.dgsca.unam.mx

Abstract

We consider that there are two basic problems to solve when a face-to-face teacher decides to incorporate his course to an online system:

- the content's development and
- the role the teacher must assume because of the delivering technology.

Each of these have issues to be considered. While the content's development stage requires an interdisciplinary team to assist the teacher graphically, didacticly and ergonomically, the facilitator who instructs an online course deals with the student´s new role and his personal circumstances as well as the new learning environment.

During this presentation we will talk about the main problems and solutions we faced to develop, deliver and instruct on-line courses.

Introduction

Distance education systems represent a huge opportunity for those people who, for whatever reason, cannot attend a classroom (geographic, health, work schedule limitations).

In this educational system, the computer and specifically the Internet, are becoming very popular. Secondary educational courses, masters degree programs, certificates, etc., are all offered as web-based courses.

The Academic Computer Center is, among other things, responsible for bringing computers and telecommunications training to the Mexican population. In order to reach more people from different states, as well as those who are unable to attend a classroom, training at a distance has become an important goal for the institution.

The Interactive Products department is focused on developing online learning materials as well as research and helping teachers adapt the curricula and its contents for the web.

Even though web-based courses are constantly increasing, we are just beginning to establish development standards as well as new didactic strategies focused on this media. We are aware that a lot of people are working on this objective and that is why we are considering the sharing of our experiences and ideas.

Content

The Interactive Products department was founded in 1997 with the goal to develop supportive online learning and teaching materials, for the face-to-face courses given at the Computer Centre.

The main reasons for this decision were:

- free teachers from spending too much time developing supportive materials
- facilitating teachers and students supportive materials accessible at all times
- research on educational applications using the new technologies

In two years, on-line tutorials, educational games, quizes and simulators were developed by the department.

The success obtained by the use of these enhanced the research and development of other educational materials. Teachers and researchers came to us for assistance and training to generate on-line materials. As time passed, we saw that training and teaching at a distance was a trend for the university, and becoming stronger each day.

Our first on-line course was a pilot project and was given internally in our department. Conceptual maps was the subject to be taught, in order to know a little bit more about the teaching strategy that teachers were talking about.

The first step was to collect data (from articles, books and on-line materials). Then we decided the curricula to be covered during the three weeks course (aproximately, 30 hours). The next important step was to write the introductory notes for each unit; they were brief notes along with articles, on-line resources and activities to enhanced independent study. At this point, we began to build the interface and to programm the interactive applications that were needed. A graphic designer, an interface designer and a programmer were responsible for these activities.

The website's architecture was simple and easy to use. There were basically two screens. The main screen had general information about the course, and the second screen (after logged in) had several options: instructions, agenda, group information, discussion forum, mail service to the teacher, blibliography, activities and units.

The course started with 20 people, most of them had never taken an on-line course before neither did we had taught at a distance either. The main problems the tutor had to deal with, were:

- Because the course was an obligatory one for all members of the team, some of them were not really interested on the subject.
- Even though all people in the department work with computers and Internet, they were not familiar interacting as a group through the web.
- Most of the persons were not used to studying independently.
- It was difficult to motivate students to interact through the forum and to follow discussions.
- Most people didn't pay attention to the agenda or the deadlines.

Taking into consideration these experiences, we built two more internal courses: UNIX and JavaScript. This time they were not obligatory and only those people interested in the subjects were registered.

We added another option for those students that wanted to review the units already seen and designed more activities to be done through the forum.

In order to offer the first three courses to the public, we had to answer some questions about online instruction.

- How do we administer our time in order to help all students?
- How many e-mails do we respond to daily?
- Which is the optimum way of moderating an online discussion?
- How do we promote students' interaction in the forum?
- How often do we need to participate or ask new questions to be discussed?
- When do we use the e-mail and when do we use the forum?
- How can we make students meet their deadlines?

Even though every online course is different and every teacher and student has their own teaching and learning style, we felt, based on our experiences, that there were some important issues to be considered and that will help answer the questions above:

Independent Study. The online courses we have developed are based on independent study. We encouraged students to read, analyze, investigate, experiment and discuss, in order to construct knowledge. That is why it is important to let the student face the problems, to be a facilitator instead of a tutor; he should provide guidance and not solve problems.

Follow-up. When a student sends an e-mail to the facilitator, it is very useful that he receives a "received message" from the facilitator. Another issue that needs to be tracked is "activity". It is common that at the beginning of the course, students start very enthusiastically, but as the course progresses, they participate less. It is then that the facilitator should encourage them to be active and not passive; by asking them if there are any problems or by proposing a discussion or an activity.

Discussion Forum. This space is designed for students to interact as a group; they will be able to exchange messages, experiences and doubts. It will help student feel part of the group along the course. The tutor follows the discussions and participates when he thinks it is necessary (solving a general doubt, bringing up new questions and maintaining the discussion).

E-mail. Students that need or want to interact exclusively with the tutor are encouraged to use e-mail, either to solve a specific question, to comment on any task or to send assignments. It is very important to specify, at the beginning of the course, the amount of time and specific hours that the tutor will be available, in order to have time to do other activities acide from tutoring.

Evaluation. In order to verify a student's progress and his achievement, several problems to be solved are presented; the level of complexity of each of them increases as the course advances and, at the end, they must develop a project that integrates the most important concepts reviewed and that are related to his daily activities.

Results

The results obtained were satisfactory, so we decided to establish this architecture as a model for the next online courses . At this moment we have seven online courses and four online tutors. It is important to mention that a face-to-face teacher tried to teach at a distance but did not develop the skills needed to interact with students and did not feel comfortable with online teaching. Also we found several teachers that did not finish developing the courses' contents because, either, lacked the time or lacked motivation and commitment.

The following table shows the average results obtained on six courses:

Registered students	111
Students that finished the course	83
Students that obtained the certificate	80
Students that registered on another course, after the first experience	11

Conclusions

> - It is convenient to have an interdisciplinary team to develop online courses.
> - It is important that institutions support teachers developing online content, giving them time and, in some cases, money for their work.
> - An optimal learning environment involves not only instructional materials, but also the interface design, its usability and interactivity.
> - Optimal learning environments enhance students to enroll again to an online course.
> - Online facilitators must be trained.
> - Feedback and interactivity are key elements to success in an online course.
> - Even though students need to change their learning skills, they are ready to make the effort to adapt and incorporate to online courses.

Bibliography

Tony Bates (1997) *Technology, open learning and distance education*, Routledge studies in Distance Eduaction. ISBN 0-415-12799-8

Robert C. Bogdan, Sari Knopp Biklen (1998). *Qualitative research in education*. Allym & Bacon. ISBN 0.205-27564-8

David W. Brooks (1997) *Web-teaching, a guide to designing interactive teaching for the world wide web.* New York, plenum publishing. ISBN 0-306-45552-8

Manuel Gándara, (1995). *Desarrollar o no desarrollar: E ahí el dilema*, en Álvarez-Mailla y Bañuelos , Coords., pp. 17-42. CISE/UNAM.

Jakob Nielsen (1999) *Designing web usability: The practice of simplicity*. New Riders Publishing

Colin McCormack, David Jones *Building a Web-based Education System*, 1997, John Wiley & Sons ISBN 0471191620

The Web Learning Fieldbook: Using the world wide web to build workplace learning environments, Jossey Bass ISBN 0787950238

William K. Horton. *Designing web-based training: How to teach anyone anything anywhere anytime*. 2000, John Wiley & Sons

Preservice Teachers Assess Credibility and Cognitive Load Associated with Websites

Marie Iding
University of Hawaii
Department of Educational Psychology
Honolulu, HI 96822, USA
miding@hawaii.edu

Martha E. Crosby
University of Hawaii
Department of Information and Computer Sciences
Honolulu, HI 96822, USA
crosby@hawaii.edu

E. Barbara Klemm
University of Hawaii
Department of Teacher Education and Curriculum Studies
Honolulu, HI 96822,USA
klemm@hawaii.edu

Abstract In order to discover a potential relationship between instructional interventions and the judgments, confidence, and perceived cognitive load of preservice teachers, we performed a study to examine different instructional methods aimed at facilitating preservice teachers' judgments about the credibility and cognitive load aspects of Web-based resources. Participants were ask to rate whether the web sites were considered objective and accurate, mistaken, or purposely misleading and give reasons for their decision both prior to and after different instructional methods. We found that the confidence ratings varied considerably but the judgments themselves did not. This gives educators hope that evaluation skills may be taught that are general enough that students can apply them to a variety of web sites.

Introduction

As the use of resources from the World Wide Web become more prevalent in today's classrooms at all levels, the need for critical evaluation skills is increasingly important. In our research, we have examined differences between scientists' and preservice teachers' ratings of the credibility of different information sources for learning scientific information and found some interesting differences (Klemm, Iding, & Speitel, 2001). We have also carried out instruction in Web evaluation with high school biology students (Iding, Landsman, & Nguyen, in press) and university-level preservice teachers (Iding & Klemm, 2002), and we have examined differences between preservice teachers and computer science students in their judgments of credibility of Web-based resources (Iding, Auernheimer, Crosby, & Klemm, 2002). In the present paper, we briefly describe findings from this line of research and propose a new study that will examine an instructional intervention aimed at facilitating preservice teachers' judgments about the credibility and cognitive load aspects of Web-based resources.

Research Review

In previous research we compared preservice teachers and scientists' ratings of the credibility of a number of different kinds of information sources for scientific information, including weekly newsmagazines, information from the Internet and resources from museums (Klemm, Iding, & Speitel, 2001). We found interesting differences between scientists' and preservice teachers' ratings. For example, scientists attributed a higher level of credibility to a scientist researching a topic. In contrast, preservice teachers attributed higher credibility ratings to information sources like TV newsmagazines, while scientists rated them less highly. In our conclusion, we argued for the need for instructional interventions.

In subsequent research, we carried out several sessions of instruction with high school biology students about evaluating the credibility of Websites and the science information contained in them (Iding, Landsman, & Nguyen, in press). After instruction students reported that they would spend more time assessing the credibility of websites in the future, provided lists of criteria for assessing websites that were more comprehensive than when they were pretested, and reported increased confidence about their critical evaluation skills with respect to web-based science information.

In other research, we worked with university-level educational psychology and computer science students. We asked them to rate the accuracy and objectivity of information on websites (related to class topics) and their confidence in their abilities to effectively evaluate course-relevant information effectively on the World Wide Web and generally (Iding, Auernheimer, Crosby, & Klemm, 2002). We found that educational psychology students rated their ability to assess the validity of information in their field more highly than computer science students, but educational psychology students rated their ability to assess the validity of information on the Web less highly than computer science students. Notions of website authors' vested interests seemed particularly problematic for some students. We called for the importance of further instruction and research in this area (Iding, Crosby, Auernheimer, & Klemm, 2002).

In another instructional study, we worked with preservice teachers in educational psychology classes to determine what criteria they use when evaluating science websites for credibility and cognitive load (Iding & Klemm, 2002). To provide some background, the concept of cognitive load is particularly relevant to learning effectively with multimedia and media-rich environments, such as those presented on Websites. Chandler and Sweller's (1991) and Sweller and Chandler's (1994) work provides the foundation for much of the current work in this area. Specifically, they argued that cognitive load can be increased and negatively impacted when instructional formats create needless redundancies (i.e., "redundancy effects") or foster integration from multiple, separate information sources (i.e., "split attention effects"). Other factors can contribute to detrimental increases in cognitive load as well, including distracting multimedia effects.

Instructional Intervention

We believe that in addition to making effective judgments about the credibility or validity of information, it is also important for future teachers to be selective and informed about the most effective types of multimedia for students, as it cannot be assumed that because a website or other information sources. Therefore, in this study, in addition to studying we gave preservice teachers a brief introduction to aspects of cognitive load related to instructional formats.

First, we asked students to provide preliminary lists of criteria that they use when determining whether to use information from a website. We provided students with a brief introduction to the concept of cognitive load and to website evaluation criteria that we derived form the work of Farah (1995) and Rader (1998) and adapted in the work of Nguyen (2000) and Iding, Landsman and Nguyen (in press). Then, students worked in pairs to evaluate and rate actual websites for credibility and cognitive load, and in small groups, they engaged in a brainstorming activity around effective credibility criteria. Lastly, we asked them to create rubrics for students assessing the credibility of Website information, and for teachers determining the cognitive loads associated with Websites. Our findings indicated that students had some useful and interesting ideas for rubrics, however our instructional intervention was short and the rubrics created by some students for assessing cognitive load included credibility criteria as well.

In the present research, we describe interventions with preservice teachers. In these intervention methods, we provide specific instruction over several sessions for activities related to helping them develop effective strategies for assessing credibility and cognitive load/multimedia aspects of Websites. In addition to fostering effective credibility judgments (and effective ways to teach this important aspect of technological and scientific literacy to their students), our goal is to also investigate effective ways for them to assess cognitive load associated with websites and multimedia presentations that they might select for their students.

Acknowledgements

This research was supported in part by ONR grant no. N00014970578 awarded to M. E. Crosby and DARPA grant NBCH1020004. We appreciate the participation of graduate students at the University of Hawaii, Manoa.

References

Chandler, P., Sweller, J. (1991). *Cognitive load theory and the format of instruction. Cognition and Instruction, 8,* 293-332.

Farah, B. (1995). Information literacy: retooling evaluation skills in the electronic information environment. *Journal of Educational Technology Systems, 24(2),* 127.

Iding, M. K., Auernheimer, B., Crosby, M. E., & Klemm, E. B. (2002, May). Users' Confidence Levels and Strategies for Determining Web Site Veracity. *Proceedings of The WWW 2002: The Eleventh International World WideWeb Conference.*

Iding, M. K., Crosby, M. E., Auernheimer, B., & Klemm, E. B. (2002). Critical evaluation skills for web-based information: "Lies, damned lies" and web-based information. *Proceedings of the ED-MEDIA 2002: World Conference on Educational Multimedia, Hypermedia & Telecommunications.*

Iding, M., & Klemm, E. B., (2002, July). Teachers critically evaluate scientific information on the World Wide Web. Research presentation at the International Reading Association World Congress on Reading, Edinburgh, Scotland.

Iding, M., Landsman, R., & Nguyen, T. (in press). Critical evaluation of scientific websites by high school students. *WCCE (World Conference on Computers in Education) 2001 Conference Proceedings.* The Netherlands: Kluwer Academic Publishers.

Klemm, E. B., Iding, M., & Speitel, T. (2001). Do scientists and teachers agree on the credibility of media information sources? *International Journal of Instructional Media 28(1),* 83-91.

Nguyen, T. T. (2000). *OASIS: Student Evaluation Methods for World Wide Web Resources.* Unpublished master's thesis, University of Hawai`i, Honolulu, Hawaii, U.S.A.

Rader, H. (1998). Library Instruction and Information Literacy. *Reference Service Review, 26(3/4),* 143.

Sweller, J., & Chandler, P. (1994). Why some material is difficult to learn. *Cognition and Instruction, 12(3),* 185-233.

Trust and the Internet: Findings from the HomeNetToo Project.
Linda A. Jackson, Gretchen Barbatsis, Alexander von Eye, Frank Biocca,
Yong Zhao and Hiram E. Fitzgerald
Michigan State University

HomeNetToo is a longitudinal research project funded by the National Science Foundation to examine the antecedents and consequences of home Internet use in low-income families in the United States.[1] Participants in the project are African American and European American families who agreed to have their Internet use continuously recorded, complete surveys at multiple points during the 18-month project, and participate in home visits during which instruction on how to use the Internet was provided. In exchange, participants received home computers, Internet access, and in-home technical support. Among the antecedents of Internet use considered in the project were trust-related beliefs about the Internet. In this report we focus on relationships between trust-related beliefs, demographic characteristics and Internet use. Structural equations modeling is used to describe these relationships.

Trust has long been recognized as a core personal characteristic that influences a broad range of behaviors (Erikson, 1963). Yet despite recognition that trust is a "quintessentially human trait," much of the research on trust in a networked society has focused more on the technology than on the people who use it. Technological fixes to concerns about trust have filled research agendas. But as May argued (2000), this emphasis on "things" rather than on people will never resolve the central issues surrounding trust in a digital world. Similarly, Rosenbloom (2000) closed the introduction to the Communications of the Association of Computing Machinery special issue on trusting technology with this comment: "answers to questions about technology-mediated trust might ultimately depend on changing human attitudes and behavior - a challenge certainly greater than any of those involving technology alone."

Research and public opinion polls support the view that trust is a critical issue in the future of Internet, and in the use of technology in general. A Gallup poll (February, 2000) reported that half of U.S. Internet users have serious concerns about the trustworthiness of the Internet, particularly about privacy and security of information. A later report by the Pew Internet & American Life Project (August, 2000) found that both users and nonusers of the Internet have serious concerns about privacy. Similarly, the UCLA Internet Reports (2000, 2001) revealed deep concerns about privacy, the ease with which children can access inappropriate content, and the trustworthiness of information on the Internet. In the HomeNetToo project we examined trust-related beliefs about the Internet and how beliefs related to actual Internet use.

Methods

Participants and Procedures

Participants in the HomeNetToo project were 117 adult residents of a low-income, medium-size urban community in the mid-western United States. Participants were primarily African American (67%), female (80%), never married (42%), and earning less than $15,000 annually (49%). The majority reported having some college education (49%) or earning a college degree (13%). Average age of participants was 38.6 years old. Surveys completed at pre-trial, three months, and nine months included measures of trust-related beliefs about the Internet and demographic characteristics. Internet use was automatically server-logged throughout the project period.

Measures

Four measures of Internet use are considered in this report: time online (minutes/day), number of Internet session (log-ins/day), number of unique Web domains visited (per day), and number of e-mails sent (per day). Internet use measures were divided into two time intervals: Time 1: months 1-6; Time 2: months 7-12.

The five trust-related beliefs about the Internet were as follows: There is no privacy on the Internet; Most of the information on the Internet is true; No one can find out what you're doing on the Internet; Children can come to harm if they use the Internet; Using the Internet can cause health problems. Five-point rating scales were used; higher values indicated stronger agreement with the belief statement. Because there was no change in trust-related beliefs between pre-trial and later assessments (i.e., three months and nine months), only pre-trial measures are considered in this report.

Also measured at pre-trial were demographic characteristics (i.e., gender, race, age, income, education) and previous experience using the Internet, assessed by four questions (e.g., How would you rate the extent of your experience with the Internet? 1=no experience, 5=a great deal of experience).

Results and Discussion

Relationships between trust-related beliefs and Internet use are presented in Table 1. During the first six months of home Internet access, believing that most of the information on the Internet is true was *negatively* related to all measures of Internet use. Believing that no one can find out what you're doing on the Internet was *negatively* related to number of Internet sessions and number of e-mails sent. Believing that using the Internet can cause health problems was negatively related to number of domains visited and number of e-mails sent.

Table 1: Relationships between trust-related beliefs and Internet use

	Time online (minutes)	Number of sessions	Number of domains visited	Number of e-mails sent
Time 1 (1-6 months)				
There is no privacy on the Internet.	.11	.15	.17	-.05
Children can come to harm if they use the Internet.	-.01	-.04	-.08	-.19
Most of the information on the Internet is true.	-.19*	-.28*	-.24*	-.30*
Using the Internet can cause health problems.	-.13	-.15	-.22*	-.36*
No one can find out what you're doing on the Internet.	-.09	-.20*	-.11	-.26*
Time 2 (7-12 months)				
There is no privacy on the Internet.	.20*	.20*	.22*	.20*
Children can come to harm if they use the Internet.	-.07	-.15	-.07	-.17
Most of the information on the Internet is true.	-.29*	-.29*	-.31*	-.55*
Using the Internet can cause health problems.	-.14	-.23*	-.20*	-.23*
No one can find out what you're doing on the Internet.	-.21*	-.24*	-.21*	-.22*

Note. Numbers are correlations (Pearson) between belief measures and log transformations of Internet use measures. *$p<.05$.

During the next six months, *negative* correlations between believing that most of the information on the Internet is true and using the Internet were stronger than during the first six months. Similarly, believing that no one can find out what you're doing on the Internet was again *negatively* related to Internet use, not only to number of sessions and number of e-mails sent, as during the first time interval, but also to time online and number of domains visited. Believing that there is no privacy on the Internet was related *positively* to all measures of Internet use during time interval 2, relationships that were not significant during time interval 1. Finally, believing that using the Internet can cause health problems was again negatively related to number of domains visited and number of e-mails sent, as in time interval 1, and also to number of Internet sessions.

Race differences in Internet use were obtained at both time intervals. During the first six months, African Americans participated in fewer Internet sessions ($M=.70$) than did European Americans ($M=1.21$; $F(1,108)=6.83$, $p<.01$). Race differences were more pronounced during the second time interval. African Americans spent less time online ($M=38.08$), participated in fewer Internet sessions ($M=.41$), visited marginally fewer domains ($M=8.43$), and sent fewer e-mails ($M=.14$) than did European Americans ($Ms=45.61, 1.00, 15.61, .99$, respectively; $F(1, 114)=5.83$, $p<.05$, $F(1,114)=8.56$, $p<.01$, $F(1,114)=3.10$, $p<.08$, $F(1,114)=4.96$, $p<.05$, respectively).

Age differences were only marginally significant during the first six months of home Internet access. Older participants (age 38 and above) engaged in somewhat fewer Internet sessions ($M=.68$), and visited fewer domains ($M=7.94$) than did younger participants ($Ms=1.07, 12.27$, respectively; $F(1,108)=3.65$, $p<.06$, $F(1,108)=3.02$, $p<.09$, respectively). Age differences were more pronounced during the second time interval. Older participants spent less time online ($M=30.66$), participated in fewer Internet sessions ($M=.49$), and visited fewer domains ($M=8.80$) than did younger participants ($Ms=52.67, .74, 13.07$, respectively; $Fs(1, 114)=4.65, 4.60, 5.13$, $ps<.05$).

Previous experience using the Internet was only modestly related to Internet use. During the first six months, participants with more experience spent somewhat more time online ($r=.18$, $p<.07$), visited more domains ($r=.21$, $p<.05$), and sent more e-mails ($r=.25$, $p<.05$) than did less experienced participants. During the second six months, more experienced participants spent more time online ($r=.20$, $p<.05$) and visited more domains ($r=.20$, $p<.05$) than did less experienced participants.

Structural equations modeling was used to explore relationships among trust-related beliefs, previous experience, demographic characteristics and Internet use (LISREL, 8.2, Joreskog & Sorbom, 1991). The model presented in Figure 1 is the result of exploratory rather than confirmatory analysis of a theory-based model. Nevertheless it provides a moderately good fit to the data ($P^2(81)=166.81$, $p<.01$, RMSEA=.096, AGFI=.76, NNFI=.85). Moreover, tests of alternative models indicated that none was statistically or conceptually a better fitting model (i.e., changes in PNFI < .06).

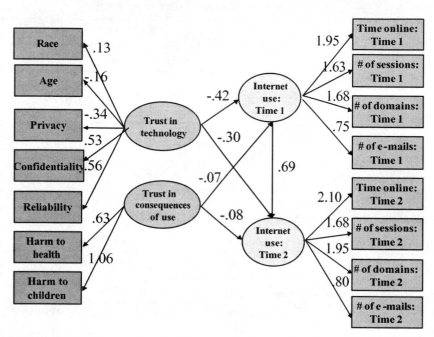

In the model the effects of race and age on Internet use are mediated by their effects on trust-related beliefs about the Internet, specifically, beliefs about privacy, confidentiality, and reliability of information. African American and older participants were more trusting of the technology than were European American and younger participants (respectively), and this trust was related to less Internet use at both time intervals. There was also a tendency for participants who believed that using the Internet may have negative consequences for children and health to use it less, but these effects were not statistically significant. Thus, participants who distrusted the technology but did not believe that using it would harm children or health used it more than did participants who trusted the technology but were concerned about its impact on children and health.

References

Erikson (1963). Childhood and society (2nd Ed.). New York: Norton.

May, T (November 13, 2000). The Digital Economy's Future Banks on Trust.
http://www.computerworld.com/cwi/story/0,1199,NAV47_STO53904,00.html

Pew Internet & American Life Project. (2000a). Trust and Privacy Online: Why Americans want to rewrite the rules. (August, 2000). Pew Foundation, 1100 Connecticut Avenue, Washington, DC.
http://www.pewinternet.org/reports/toc.asp?Report=19

Rosenbloom, R. (2000). Trusting technology. Communications of the ACM, 43, 31-32.

UCLA Internet Report (2000). Surveying the digital future. UCLA Center for Communication Policy. University of California, Los Angeles, CA. www.ccp.ucla.edu

UCLA Internet Report (2001), UCLA Center for Communication Policy, University of California, Los Angeles, CA. http://www.ccp.ucla.edu/pages/NewsTopics.asp?Id=29

Footnotes

[1] This research was supported by a National Science Foundation-Information Technology Research Grant, #085348, September 1, 2000 to September 30, 2003. Linda A. Jackson, Principal Investigator.

[2] Additionally, 140 children of the adult participants described in this report participated in the project.

[3] Other server-logged measures of Internet use were obtained but are not considered in this report (e.g., names of domains and chats visited).

mSupport -- supporting the mobile student

Di James and Nathan Bailey
Flexible Learning and Teaching Program
Monash University

Abstract

Portals provide a valuable mechanism for providing a unified, personalised environment for accessing information -- a one stop shop for students to manage their relationship with the University. Increasingly, however, institutions are looking for ways to disseminate key information to students, while taking care to avoid information overload. This paper explores the way that technologies such as SMS (mobile phone text messaging) and workflow can allow students to direct crucial information, including academic information, in the way that is most convenient for *them* to receive them.

Introduction

Portals are a proven technology and are increasingly used in higher education for learning and teaching, research, staff and student support and administration. They will almost certainly be a part of any Information Technology architecture that is established in the higher education sector, to manage the appropriate, relevant and secure collection, storage, publishing and access and dissemination of information (Information Management). Other technologies that can contribute to the dissemination of information and provide efficient co st and time alternatives to email are emerging as adjuncts to institutional portals. The use of text messages sent to mobile phones (SMS) is an example.

Monash University now uses SMS to distribute examination results at the end of each semester, in conjunction with the online release of results accessed via the university portal. We propose to investigate the use of SMS for additional academic, administrative and social functions. We are however concerned that issues related to Information Management, including privacy and security need to be addressed.

mContact -- taking advantage of a highly 'mobile' demographic

The ownership of mobile phones in Australia is now 69% and there is a higher % ownership among young (15-24) and middle (25-49) age individuals.
(http://www.tnsofres.com/apmcommerce/product.cfm)

The use of text messages by young mobile phone users in Australia prompted an interest several years ago in testing the viability of this medium for communication with students. Consequently, Monash University piloted what was quite possibly a world-first in distributing unit results directly to student's mobile phones. SMS has now been successfully implemented as a cost effective and highly appealing distribution channel for student administrative information. This service continues to be one of the most popular services we offer to students, with continuing positive feedback every semester. Now institutions are starting to look at how to use this valuable avenue for disseminating other kinds of informat ion.

We speculate that the very strong acceptance of text messaging by students could indicate that it has a role to play in other areas, as well as supporting additional administrative functions. General email to class lists requires login to a computer and is often ignored, but SMS is immediate and personal and has the potential to be a more attractive medium for communication with students. Uses might include communication of assignment information, topics, venues and social activities, by teaching staff within individual subjects or courses. It could also be used to comment on topics, readings or current events that come to hand during semester. Pilot programs are now being established to test the potential within higher education of SMS in conjunction with institutional portals to extend functionality and increase effective communication

Some of the issues that arise are related to security and privacy and to the emerging concern with information management systems within higher education generally.

Information dissemination

Much of our support for students is in response to their needs, rather than actually being proactive and taking the information they need to them. Messaging and workflow technologies provide the opportunity for students to profile the information they want, in they way they want it, thereby allowing the University to be much more proactive in information dissemination.

Some courses are beginning to establish announcement forums, either in email or discussion groups. However, such forums can be regarded by students as generic announcement emails, and students ignore them. It would appear that there is no sense of the gravity of the issues or the areas of interest to the recipients.

Technology offers two promising solutions toward this need – choice of content, and choice of forum. Some information is essential for participation in a unit of study (e.g. the time/location of the mid-semester test has changed), other information is merely helpful for those students who choose to pursue it (e.g. "there is another reading on this topic at this URL"). However, it is not always clear what information students regard as urgently important and what information they would prefer to browse at their leisure. Students need to be empowered not only to choose what information they receive, but how they receive it. Instead of them feeling overwhelmed with information that is only of passing interest to them, they should be able to process specific items exactly as they wish to.

This could be achieved using SMS messages (i.e. text messages to mobile phones) and Workflow (i.e. the workflow component on my.monash). In terms of workflow, many of the processes we complete both in our jobs and in learning and teaching can be set up as a series of steps that allow each person involved in the process to pick it up from their in tray, do their bit, and pass it on to the next person's in tray. Sometimes we do this by email, sometimes we do it by phone, but (sadly) often we do it by paper forms that are subsequently entered in to a computer!

Electronically supported workflow ensures that the information is stored electronically, the status of the task is identifiable to everyone involved in the process and the task is automatically distributed to the next person or group of people who need to participate in the process. In increasing transparency to the entire process, students can be sure that their form/request wasn't just "lost in the mail" but has actually been actioned with an identified outcome.

Such workflow could be useful for requesting/granting extensions, proposing/responding to social events (e.g. RSVP for course/department BBQ.

Advantages

Monash has 45,000 students enrolled over 8 campuses – 6 metropolitan or regional Australian campuses and 2 offshore (in Malaysia and South Africa) and frequently studying off campus. Mobile information dissemination is equally as important as mobile academic content delivery. The university portal, online content and use of SMS for administrative services provides for much of the successful management of information services including academic services. An exploration of the use of SMS to provide additional support for academic delivery and student/teacher communication is now seen as potentially beneficial for both enhancing communication and for cost effectiveness.

The cost of publishing to the web and bulk SMS services to nominated phone numbers is highly competitive, compared with the cost of producing and posting hard copy to students, particularly when many are off campus.

Issues

Some of the issues that arise are related to:

- the obvious requirement that technology supports, not drives, learning - core academic activity must be facilitated, not undermined, by technological developments – but innovation must be supported to determine the potential of new technologies.
- security - SMS messages are sent to a mobile phone number nominated by the student. There is some concern that unauthorised persons could have access to the phone and therefore to confidential information (eg exam results). This issue has been managed by ensuring that students read the

security and privacy information when they nominate to receive confidential information via SMS and sign off on a disclaimer.

- privacy – The matter of keeping records of transactions with students, their access to records and the somewhat 'ephemeral' nature of SMS is somewhat more difficult to manage. In this context, it relates to more general issues of information management that are currently of concern to higher education institutions - data storage, collection and dissemination, publishing and access to information etc.
- equity – Use of particular technologies that rely on student ownership of equipment must be considered in the context of any disadvantage caused by students choosing not to use, or being financially or physically unable to use the equipment
- the emerging concern with information management systems within higher education generally.

Conclusion

The use of SMS to mobile phones provides a cost advantage for the delivery of administrative information to students. While this is an obvious benefit to both students and the university and will continue to be used, the use of SMS and other emerging communications technologies for academic purposes needs to be considered carefully and creatively. The place of these technologies in the emerging Information Management systems architecture will also need to be considered along with appropriate policy development.

E-Learning Strategic Planning Utilising a Work Systems Framework

Sam Jebeile
Division of Economic and Financial Studies
Macquarie University
Australia
Sam.Jebeile@mq.edu.au

Associate Professor Robert Reeve
Division of Economic and Financial Studies
Macquarie University
Australia
Robert.Reeve@mq.edu.au

Abstract: This paper examines the various work system elements that should be considered by school administrators when developing e-Learning strategies in traditional teaching and learning contexts. Focus group interviews were conducted with teachers in a secondary school in Sydney, Australia in order to identify the work system elements involved when using the Web for student-centred learning activities. The findings of the analysis are provided and the associated implications for the development of school e-Learning strategies are also discussed.

Introduction

The 'information revolution' has forced most OECD economies into an era which demands 'knowledge workers' for the 'knowledge economy' (OECD 1996). As a result, schools are placed in a situation requiring reassessment of their methods of practice, adapting and improving teaching and learning for the changing needs of a global, digital, and networked economy. While global spending on e-Learning in educational institutions is increasing at unprecedented rates (OECD 1998), the pressing problem for school administrators is that the rate of adoption by teachers across all sectors of education has lagged significantly behind that of industry (Leidner & Jarvenpaa 1995). Latham (1998) suggests that any organisation wishing to make changes to their processes by incorporating information technology (IT) into their activities will require a strategy as an essential part of the management of change. She describes *strategy* in terms of creating a vision of the future and formulating the means and policies that will enable the organisation to reach that vision. Latham points out the potential for schools to effect strategic use of IT in such areas as curriculum delivery and the provision of students and teachers with access to knowledge bases. She argues that in order to achieve these strategic objectives, schools need to identify and develop an information systems strategic plan that should be based on business needs, and derived from an analysis of the business, its environment and business strategies. While most of the literature on information systems (IS) strategy relates to the business goals of making profits and surviving in a competitive environment, schools also have organisational goals and need to manage resources effectively in order to meet those goals. In order to develop IS/IT strategies, school administrators would benefit from adopting a framework for analysing the underlying work systems involved in various aspects of e-Learning.

Work Systems and E-Learning Strategy

Alter (2002) suggests that the use of the *work system framework* will assist organisations in the process of conducting a thorough systems analysis that will assist in the process of strategic integration of information and communication technology. Alter suggests that one common pitfall made in defining e business models, is that the business process is defined so broadly that it involves a wide range of products and customers and is difficult to analyse coherently. He argues that this pitfall can be overcome through a focus on *work systems* defined as "systems in which human participants and/or machines perform a business process using information, technology, and other resources to produce products and/or services for internal or external customers". Alter defines the eight linked elements that can be used to summarise any work system. *Customers* are the people who use and receive direct benefits from the products and services produced by the work system. *Products* are the combination of physical things, information, and services that the work system produces for its customers. The (business) *process* is the set of work steps or activities that are performed within the work system. *Participants* are the people who perform the work steps in the business process. *Information* is the information used by the participants to perform their work. *Technology* is the hardware, software, and other tools and equipment used by the participants to perform their work. *Context* is the organisational, competitive, technical, and regulatory realm within which the work system operates. *Infrastructure* is the shared human and technical resources that the work system relies on even though these resources exist and are managed outside of it. This typically includes human infrastructure such as support and training staff, information infrastructure such as shared databases, and technical infrastructure such as networks and programming technology.

As part of a larger study on eLearning in Australian schools, a small group of four Australian Mathematics, Science, Social Science, and Humanities secondary school teachers were interviewed to conduct an analysis of the work system involved when using the *Web* for student-centred learning activities. In this paper we provide a summary of this analysis and highlight the critical success factors that should be considered when formulating an e-Learning strategic plan in the context of this particular school.

Findings

Prior to conducting the analysis, we first considered the traditional means by which student-centred learning activities are performed and subsequently identified the *rationale* and *strategic goals* associated with the introduction of the *Web for student-centred learning* (Tab. 1).

Rationale: Instead of students going to traditional sources such as for books and/or journal articles in library, encourage them to access the latest information on-line from home, or during class via school computer network.
Strategic Goal: Develop student skills: use of IT and Web, independent learning, information literacy, 'knowledge work', and problem solving.

Table 1: Rationale and strategic goals of the Web for student-learning

The next step in the work system analysis involved the identification of the general work system elements, the associated critical success factors (Alter 2002), and some broad implications for school management when formulating the IS/IT strategic plan (Tab. 2).

Customer: Students use the Web for independent learning activities (research project). *Products:* Completed research project demonstrating student's ability to synthesise information into knowledge applied to the project. Development of students' independent learning skills and other generic skills. Teacher assessment and feedback on student Web research skills. *Success factors:* Product design consistent with customers needs (Alter 2002). *Implications:* In this case, teachers will need to develop projects and student-centred activities commensurate with student information literacy and independent learning skills. The pedagogical implications and objectives of e-Learning will need to be understood by teachers and aligned with student research tasks and appropriate assessment guidelines. Therefore teachers require adequate training, prior research on topic, and alignment with overall curriculum and course objectives.

Process: Teacher sets Web research project. Student uses Web search engines and/or on-line journals from home or via school computer network. Student types in relevant key words and decides which information is relevant. Student analyses and sorts through relevant information and synthesises to produce project (product). Teacher assesses and comments on quality of products (project and student information skills).

Success factors: Fit of process with other elements of the work system; Adequate resources for process; Effective operational management (Alter 2002). *Implications:* Teachers need skills in developing, managing and assessing these projects. They need to ensure students are adequately trained and have developed effective search strategies. For example, Boolean logic (the expressions *and*, *or*, and *not*) requires higher order skills. Teachers also need to ensure that sufficient time, adequate on-line resources are available, and equitable access is available to students conducting the research. Finally, teachers will need to ensure that IT support staff are aware of the process and are attentive to any system disruptions during the project time frame. Teachers therefore need training and support to ensure effective planning and management of student-Web research activities.

Participants: Students using Web. Teachers setting and marking research projects. IT-support staff.

Success factors: Appropriate skills and understanding; Interest in doing this type of work; Motivation to do this work in this setting; Ability to work together to resolve conflicts (Alter 2002). *Implications*: Adequate training for both students and teachers will be integral to the success of the system. Well qualified IT support staff are required, along with accessible, functioning networked terminals. Management needs to foster a collegial working environment. Understanding of the learning implications for students is also crucial. If managed effectively, the above factors will also have implications on the motivation of the participants involved in the work system.

Information: Student gathers: information on research question. Key words for search. Hyperlinks to Web pages. Information on research question. Teacher inputs: Information on research project. Feedback to student on work. Assessment grade into school reporting system.

Success factors: Adequate information quality; Adequate information accessibility; Adequate information presentation; Adequate information security (Alter 2002). *Implications*: Apart from the aspects of training, support and equipment discussed above. Teachers will need to ensure that the browsers, terminals and monitors are adequate for displaying information. Further, that the school network has appropriate security measures in place such as firewalls and up-to-date anti-virus software. Teachers also need to ensure that they have developed adequate methods for presenting students with assigned tasks and feedback.

Technology: Personal computer used by student with modem from home or on school computer network. Computers and networks used by the various search engines.

Success factors: Ease of using the technology; Adequate technology performance (having enough 'horsepower'); Maintainability (how easy it is to keep the technology operating over time); Compatibility with technology in related systems (Alter 2002). *Implications*: The provision of adequate training, maintenance plan, and support staff. Careful consideration of the above factors when planning and acquiring hardware such as PCs and network components. Also important when selecting software, Web browsers, and subscription to ISP.

Table 2: Work system analysis for Web use in student-centred learning

The final step in our analysis involved analysis of teacher comments regarding the current context and infrastructure within which the work system is situated (Tab. 3). The analysis in Table 3 highlights several key *structural* problems related to the *context* and *infrastructure* within which this work system is currently situated. These issues need to be addressed by the highest level of school management as part of the strategic planning process and present major obstacles to the integration of the Web into student learning activities.

Current Context: The timetable (based on 50-minute periods); curriculum requirements; school culture; teacher IT training and skills; and classroom layout; are all consistent with the traditional teaching and learning environment in this secondary school. Student demographics also suggest that a large proportion of students currently do not have access to the Web from home and therefore equity issues affect teacher utilisation of the Web in this work system.

Strategic Implications for Management: Top management support and initiative is required in addressing some of the organisational issues presented above. Management needs to work on changing the school culture to become more compatible with the new work system. They need to facilitate and foster cooperative decision-making regarding the adoption of the new work methods. They need to foster a teaching and learning environment that reduces the level of turmoil and distraction between the various contextual components addressed above and the new work system (Alter 2002). For example, one suggestion is the provision of a single dedicated classroom to each key learning area (e.g. Science) with appropriate layout and a high ratio of networked terminals. Combined with restructuring of the timetable to allow for at least one double period per week for each class in each subject. This set of initiatives would allow for decentralised lesson planning by teachers in each key learning area. Teachers in each faculty could coordinate their use of the room when required and organise integrated student Web activities during the double periods. If the single computers, currently under-utilised in each classroom, were placed in the dedicated classroom, it would potentially lead to more effective utilisation of existing resources.

Infrastructure: Web access exists through school computer network. However, the service is slow and while access is possible through dedicated computer labs and the school library, the facilities are often reserved for dedicated IT classes during normal school periods thus rendering it difficult to integrate with lessons in the other key learning areas such as science. At best, one networked computer may be available in the normal classroom and in many cases these are not functioning properly. Also, it is difficult to access IT support staff when problems arise and further the skills of the support staff do not seem to be sufficient to correct the problem in a timely manner.

Strategic Implications for Management: Need to provide adequate *technical* and *human* infrastructure for the integration of the Web into student learning activities (Alter 2002). For example, at this school, more computers are required in classrooms, more powerful servers and greater bandwidth is required for this school network. A higher ratio of suitably qualified support staff is also necessary. While these issues are costly, the school management has a duty to provide these services in order to achieve the strategic objectives. Leasing arrangements may assist.

Table 3: Current context and infrastructure and strategic implications for management

The analysis in this study highlights the importance of work systems analysis as a framework for strategic planning for the integration of e-Learning in schools. The findings suggest that this framework can be utilised at various phases throughout the systems development process and has several implications including: the design and planning of educational technology courses for teachers; e-Learning resource location and acquisition; and information and communication technology infrastructure planning.

References

Alter, S. (2002). *Information Systems: The Foundation of E-Business* (4th ed.) New Jersey: Pearson Education Inc.

Latham, A. (1998). Strategic Information Systems Planning: a necessary evil for schools? *Journal of Applied Management Studies*, 7 (2), 267-274.

Leidner, D. E., & Jarvenpaa, S. L. (1995). The Use of Information Technology to Enhance Management School Education: A Theoretical View. *MIS Quarterly*, September, 265-291.

Organisation for Economic Cooperation and Development (OECD). (1996). *The Knowledge-based Economy.* http://www.oecd.org/dsti/sti/s_t/inte/prod/kbe.htm

OECD. (1998). *New Developments in Educational Software and Multimedia.*

Strategies for the Diffusion of E-Learning in Traditional Teaching and Learning Contexts: A Study of Web Adoption in an Australian School

Sam Jebeile
Division of Economic and Financial Studies
Macquarie University
Australia
Sam.Jebeile@mq.edu.au

Professor Mohamed Khadra
Pro Vice-Chancellor, Division of Science and Design
University of Canberra
Australia
khadra@scides.canberra.edu.au

Associate Professor Robert Reeve
Division of Economic and Financial Studies
Macquarie University
Australia
Robert.Reeve@mq.edu.au

Abstract: This paper reports the findings of a study which utilised diffusion of innovations theory to examine Web adoption by teachers in a secondary school in Sydney, Australia. Data collected through a survey questionnaire was used to examine teacher perceptions regarding various attributes of the Web as a tool for both teaching preparation and delivery. Our analysis of the data suggests that the innovation attributes of relative advantage, compatibility, visibility, ease of use, result demonstrability, and trialability should be considered by school administrators seeking to increase the rate of Web use by teachers in their schools. The image attribute did not emerge as significant in either of the contexts examined. Implications for the development of strategies for e-Learning diffusion are discussed including practical examples.

Introduction and Background

The adoption and effective utilisation of e-Learning is an important issue to educators around the world. In the context of Australian schools, Gibbons (2001) reports that 98% of teachers from K to 12 are using the Internet but only to perform basic tasks such as e-mail and research via search engines mainly for *teaching preparation*. Gibbons suggests that the majority of Australian teachers are still struggling to incorporate Internet applications such as Web publishing with traditional methods of *teaching delivery*. In this study we use *diffusions of innovations* (DOI) theory to examine factors affecting the *adoption* of the Web by teachers in an Australian secondary school.

Rogers (1983) DOI theory defines five attributes or characteristics of innovations which influence an individual's attitude towards an innovation during the adoption process. These attributes include relative advantage, compatibility, complexity, trialability, and observability. *Relative advantage* is the degree to which an innovation is perceived as better than the idea it supersedes. *Compatibility* is the degree to which an innovation is perceived as being consistent with the existing values, needs, and past experiences of potential adopters. *Complexity* is the degree to which an innovation is perceived as difficult to understand

and use. *Trialability* is the degree to which an innovation may be experimented with on a limited basis. *Observability* is the degree to which the results of an innovation are observable to others.

Based on DOI theory, Moore and Benbasat (1991) developed an instrument to measure an individual's perceptions about using an information and communication technology (ICT) innovation. Moore and Benbasat renamed Rogers' complexity construct as *ease of use*, consistent with Davis (1989). They also developed the *image* construct defined as the degree to which use of an innovation is perceived to enhance one's image or status in one's social system. Also, during the process of developing the instrument, they found that the construct of observability separated into two constructs: result demonstrability and visibility. *Result demonstrability* concentrated on the tangibility of using the innovation, including their observability and communicability. *Visibility*, on the other hand, focused on the physical presence of the innovation in the organisational setting. In the present study we are not concerned with teachers' perceptions of the Web as an IT innovation *per se*, rather we are concerned with teachers' perceptions of *using* the Web in two work-related contexts. We therefore use the instrument to separately examine teacher use of the Web for both *teaching preparation* and *teaching delivery*. The hypotheses tested in this study are:

Hypotheses: The seven adoption variables (relative advantage, compatibility, image, visibility, ease of use, results demonstrability, and trialability) will predict the dependent variables, teachers' future use of the Web for purposes of: (1) *teaching preparation* ; and (2) *teaching delivery*.

Data Analysis and Results

Multiple linear regression models were used to test the hypotheses. The unit of analysis was the individual teacher. The data was collected from one secondary school thus controlling for any between-school differences. All 75 teachers from the participating school were surveyed using a questionnaire that included the items from the short form of the Moore and Benbasat (1991) instrument. All questionnaires were returned and useable thus satisfying our sample size requirements and eliminating concerns of non-response bias. The questionnaire items measured teacher perceptions relating to each of the seven adoption variables forming the *independent variables* in this study. Two single item measures asking teachers about their intended use of the Web for (a) *teaching preparation* and (b) *teaching delivery* were used to measure the *dependent variables* in this study. All items were measured on a seven point Likert scale with polar anchors "strongly agree" and "strongly disagree". The Moore and Benbasat (1991) instrument has been used extensively in the literature demonstrating reliability and validity in a range of contexts. Tests for internal consistency reliability and construct validity provided strong support for the instrument in this study.

A multiple regression analysis (full model) was conducted of all seven ICT adoption variables on the dependent variables: (a) *Web use for teaching preparation* (TPREP); and (b) Web use for *teaching delivery* (TDEL). Tests were conducted to check the regression assumptions of normality, linearity, and homoscedasticity of residuals (Tabachnick & Fidell 2001). The tests revealed that the regression assumptions had not been violated.

Hypothesis 1: A multiple regression analysis (full model) was conducted of all seven adoption variables on the dependent variable *Web use for teaching preparation* (TPREP). The results indicate strong support for Hypothesis 1. The full model regression equation was statistically significant ($p < .0001$) and explained approximately 72% of the variation in TPREP (Adj. $R^2 = .718$). Model reduction techniques (Tabachnick & Fidell 2001) were then used to formulate a reduced model which included only the significant variables of relative advantage, result demonstrability, and trialability. The results indicate that the reduced model regression equation was statistically significant (p < .0001) and there was no significant difference between the full and reduced model in terms of their ability to explain variation in TPREP (Adj. $R^2 = .723$). In the reduced model, *relative advantage (p < .0001), result demonstrability (p = .001)*, and *trialability (p = .012)*, have a positive and significant relationship with TPREP.

Hypothesis 2: A multiple regression analysis (full model) was conducted of all seven adoption variables on the dependent variable *Web use for teaching delivery* (TDEL). The results indicate strong support for Hypothesis 2. The full model regression equation was statistically significant ($p < .0001$) and explained approximately 53% of the variation in TDEL (Adj. $R^2 = .531$). A reduced model was formulated that was statistically significant (p < .0001) and there was no significant difference between the full and reduced model in terms of their ability to explain variation in TDEL (Adj. R^2 = .547). In the reduced model, *compatibility (p = .003)*, *visibility (p = .036)*, and *ease of use (p = .006)*, have a positive and significant relationship with TDEL.

The results also showed that *image* has a negative although not significant relationship with both TREP and TDEL.

Implications for E-Learning Diffusion

As hypothesised our empirical results show that DOI theory as operationalised in this study was successful in predicting the future Web use by secondary teachers for purposes of teaching preparation and teaching delivery. The most interesting aspect of the results was that in each of the two contexts of Web use by teachers three different factors emerged as significant. Of further interest to school principals is the fact that image did not emerge as a significant factor in either of the cases. This finding indicates that strategies that promote the status (or image) of teachers who are currently advanced in their use of the Web may not have any effect on the adoption behaviours of other teachers. Principals seeking to increase the rate of adoption of the Web by teachers should be better served adopting strategies that address the attributes of the Web found to be significant in this study. In the case of Web use for teaching preparation the three most important factors affecting teachers in our sample were relative advantage, result demonstrability, and trialability. This finding suggests that in the context of our sample, strategies to increase the diffusion of teachers' use of the Web for teaching preparation should specifically address these attributes. While in the case of Web use for teaching delivery, strategies should focus on the attributes of compatibility, visibility, and ease of use. The following discussion provides some examples of how this may be achieved in each case.

Strategies for Increasing Web use for Teaching Preparation

Relative advantage was concerned with the degree to which using the innovation is perceived as being *better* than using its precursor. The term *better* related to factors such as quality, efficiency, and effectiveness. Thus, one strategy to increase adoption in this context is to organise professional development programs that require teachers to prepare a lesson on the same topic (eg. The Solar System) using traditional methods followed by use of the Web. Teachers could then be asked to evaluate each lesson in terms of efficiency (ie. time spent), and the quality and effectiveness of the final lesson plan.

Result demonstrability represents the extent to which use of the Web provides teachers with clear, measurable, and observable results. In the case of teaching preparation the results are evident in the final lesson plan and the reaction of students. Therefore in the context of our sample, teachers should be encouraged to formally evaluate lessons that have been prepared with and without the utilisation of the Web. For example, a survey of student satisfaction at the end of each of these lessons may provide the teacher with greater insight and clear evidence regarding the results of using the Web when preparing lessons. In addition, principals could provide teachers with the latest research on student learning in technology rich environments.

Trialability represents the extent to which teachers can trial the use of the Web in teaching preparation prior to adoption. One strategy for increasing the trialability of the Web for teaching preparation is to provide teachers with convenient access to the Web in places where they are most likely to perform this activity. At school these areas would obviously include staffrooms, common rooms, and classrooms. It is also common for teachers to prepare lessons at home and therefore any scheme that subsidises teachers for the costs of Web access from home would increase opportunities for trialing the Web. Good quality peripheral devices, such as colour laser printers and screen projectors, should also be available for teachers to trial when using the Web to prepare lessons. Trial agreements with vendors of e-Learning related products and services could also be utilised to assist in this process. Finally, professional development sessions providing opportunities and advice for teachers to trial the Web for teaching activities would be beneficial.

Compatibility represents whether or not the innovation is perceived to fit teachers' existing values, needs, and past experience. In the context of our study, the move to teaching delivery through the Web represents a dramatic shift from the traditional face to face teaching methods familiar to most teachers. Organisational strategies will need to target this problem in order to increase teacher perceptions regarding the compatibility of this non-traditional teaching mode within their context. Teachers could be supported in this regard through professional development regarding the pedagogical implications of e-Learning. Radical structural changes may also assist increasing the compatibility of Web-based teaching in the traditional school environment. For example, school policy currently requires students and teachers to attend each class in the traditional mode, thus creating an inherent structural limitation for the diffusion of Web-based teaching delivery. That is, any Web-based delivery will be conducted over and above the existing face to face workload of both teachers and students. One organisational strategy to overcome this problem may be the rescheduling of the school timetable in order to facilitate a mixed delivery mode.

Visibility examines how apparent or visible the use of the innovation is in the organisation or school context. In the context of our sample, Web use for teaching delivery is a relatively more recent innovation than Web use for teaching preparation. At this early stage, increasing the rate of adoption of this innovation will require strategies that promote the physical presence of the innovation throughout the school. For example, vendors of Web-based delivery products could be invited by the school Principal to promote their products at staff meetings and most importantly provide sample content for teachers to access on the school network. Teachers in other schools involved in best practice in this area may also be invited to the school to share their experiences.

Ease of use is concerned with the ease of using, learning, and implementing the innovation. In the context of our sample, Web-based teaching delivery is relatively new to teachers and at this stage they may be unfamiliar with the technologies supporting this mode of learning. As such, the school Principal may adopt a number of strategies to assist teacher perceptions during this initial phase including increased time for professional development, the employment of competent e-Learning resource developers, and the provision of adequate user-friendly infrastructure to facilitate the implementation process. Another important strategic consideration is the identification and acquisition of existing e-Learning resources suitable to the teaching and learning context of the school. This process will allow teachers to build on existing modules thereby reducing difficulties of implementation.

References

Davis, F. D. (1989). Perceived Usefulness, Perceived Ease of Use, and User Acceptance of Information Technology. *MIS Quarterly,* 13 (3), 319-333.

Gibbons, P. (2001). Schools get deeper into the Web. *Business Review Weekly* 23(10), 86.

Moore, G.C. & Benbasat, I. (1991). Development of an Instrument to Measure Perceptions of Adopting an Information Technology Innovation. *Information Systems Research,* 2 (3), 192-222.

Rogers, E.M. (1983). *Diffusion of Innovations* (3rd ed.). New York: Free Press.

Tabachnick, B.G., & Fidell, L.S. (2001). *Using Multivariate Statistics* (4th ed.). Needlam Heights, MA: Allyn and Bacon.

The Development of Computer-Based Simulation Laboratory for e-Learning : A Case Study of Non-Electrical Engineering Background at KMUTT in Thailand

Kalayanee Jitgarun
Surachai Suksakulchai
Khanchai Tunlasakun
Department of Electrical Technology Education
School of Industrial Education
King Mongkut's University of Technology Thonburi
Thailand
Kalayanee.jit@kmutt.ac.th
Surachai.suk@kmutt.ac.th
Khanchai.tun@kmutt.ac.th

Abstract: This paper presents the second phase of development of Computer – Based Simulation Laboratory (CBSL) for e-Learning especially for non-electrical engineering background. There were 14 lab sheets used in this study. Each lab sheet was divided into different components in order to help the students get used to the process of thinking properly. The steps of developing CBSL were as follows : 1) taking the students' opinions on CBSL (first phase) into account such as the correctness, and the completeness of the contents for making corrections on CBSL 2) design the computer program, and 3) get validated by 6 experts. The results of the study were that most of the experts were satisfied with CBSL at the good level particularly on the picture/image. However, there was still a need to improve the contents, and others. After all, CBSL was developed on CDR which introduces to the undergraduate students the engineering way of thinking. The computer-based simulation experiments were developed for beginners in science and engineering. Its objective is to facilitate students to experiment, solve problem, gather data, and to engage scientific interpretation in the early studies.

Introduction

What is engineering ? The word itself comes from the Latin word *ingenerare, to create.* It's art and communication, politics and finance, modeling and simulation, invention, approximation, measurement and estimation, and more. It's a way to think about problems. The laboratory is an important component of the lecture where students gain hands-on experience. Thus, to introduce the engineering student the way of thinking is to develop a *Virtual Laboratory*- a set of simulated laboratory experiments that we can perform over the WWW (Karweit, 2001). With the development of new computer technologies, the World Wide Web is now possible to simulate engineering and science laboratory projects on a computer. Computer lab activities such as pre- and post-lab exercises, can help support varied approaches to electrical education (Yaron, 2002). Experiences in laboratory experiments are difficult to provide in typical classroom settings because many interesting physical artifacts are expensive or dangerous to build and practice on. However, Computer-Based Simulation Laboratory (CBSL) will address these problems cheaply and safely. It will also provide coaching for students, in order to help them understand fundamental principles, to help them practice the skills needed to analyze, and to provide the kind of supervision that a good laboratory assistant provides by way of minimizing unenlightening aspects of student explorations (Forbus, 1999).

Findings

The study involved the steps of CBSL development as follows:

1. Design the components of CBSL as follows: 1) Lab Sheets, 2) Instructions on how to conduct physical labs, 3) Step by step guide through experiment 4) Analysis, and 5) Report Writing.

2. Select 14 labs for CBSL development according to the students' opinion particularly on the correctness and completeness of the contents (Jitgarun & Tunlasakun, 19-21 October, 1999) as follows:

2.1 *Compound Motor Laboratory*

A student will be able to adjust Variac, R1 and R2 easier than the real experiment and the output response can be seen promptly and clearly. The color of motor while spinning will stimulate the student's interest in doing the experiments.

2.2 *Series Motor Laboratory*

A student will be able to learn how to connect the circuit for series motor. Then, while adjusting Variac and R1, it is possible to make note of the starting point of the current to be six times while it is running.

2.3 *Shunt Motor Laboratory*

A student will be able to learn how to connect the circuit for shunt motor. Then, while adjusting Variac and R1, the starting point of the current will be six times while it is running.

2.4 *Alternator Laboratory*

A student will be able to adjust the load so that the loss and efficiency of DC Generator can be found.

2.5 *Induction Motor Laboratory*

To connect the control circuit and to test the circuit operation by pushing an *on-off* button, it will help move the motor in a clockwise or anti clockwise direction and/or using on-off lamp.

2.6 *DC Generator Laboratory*

A student will adjust R1, R2 easily and precisely and be able to observe the graphs. A student doesn't have to plot the graphs by him/herself. The colors of the graphs, the motor while working, the primover and the loads will help the student see the steps of operation clearly. This is how it can stimulate the student's interest.

2.7 *3 Phase Rectifier Laboratory*

The circuit will be 3 Phase Half Wave Rectifier. A student can adjust input voltage and graphs will be changed accordingly. Then, all of these graphs can be zoomed in and out. Thus, simulation will be safer for a student as well as the equipment. The different colors will help a student see the signals of different phases clearly.

2.8 *3 Phase Measurement Laboratory*

A student can adjust Variac or push the on-off button to show electrical power output and electrical current value in graphs and/or by the on-off lamps.

2.9 *Single Phase Rectifier Laboratory*

A student can adjust voltage input and observe the changes of voltage output of rectifier circuit which will be shown in graphs.

2.10 *Single Phase Transformer Laboratory*

A student can adjust Variac along with the changes of Volt meter and Amp meter simultaneously. The simulation of virtual lab will be safer for the student as well as the equipment while there are on-off loads and short circuit. It also motivates the student to do more experiments because it will show on-off lamps. However, when over current, there will be a warning with a dialogue box.

2.11 *Single Phase Measurement Laboratory*

A student can push on-off button and observe the changes of Volt meter, Amp meter, Kilo-Watt meter, KiloWatt-hour meter of which the load can be changed accordingly.

2.12 *3 Phase Transformer Connection*

A student can select secondary voltage at 127 V. or 220 V. and observe the changes of Volt meter, Amp meter of each phase.

2.13 *Star-Delta Laboratory*

A student can push on-off switch, setup time delay, and observe on-off lamps when time is over. Then, a student can also see output in the Amp meter as well.

2.14 *SCR Rectifier Laboratory*

A student will be able to adjust Vs (Supply) and Trigger Angle easily, precisely, and be able to see the changes of signal outs that takes place from Vs (Supply) and Trigger adjustment. What's more, the input and output signals are comparable to one another at the same time.

3. Design simulation kits on the computer screen.

4. Construct simulation laboratory instruction with Borland Delphi program, Adobe Photoshop, Visio Technique, and PSpice.

5. Develop the manual for CBSL.

6. Trained experts check for the accuracy which were as follows:

The responses of six trained experts' satisfaction upon CBSL were found to be at the good level with the pictures/images. The synchronous of the contents and their objectives, the simulation capability, the order of the contents, the promotion of thinking process, the convenience, the safety and the fastness were identified at the good level while the accuracy, the completeness, and the promotion of thinking rather than remembrance were still rated at the average level.

Discussion and Conclusions

As the results of the study on Computer-Based Simulation Laboratory (CBSL), the researchers would like to discuss and conclude as follows:

1. Technical educational institutions are crunched between demand for an effective education along with budget constraints. Their ability to deliver effective education can be greatly enhanced by laboratories equipped with modern technologies including computer hardware and software capable to perform data acquisition, statistical data analysis, control experiments, remote instrument control and network communication (Ursutiu, 2002). However, there are some problems in providing experimental instruction as follows: 1) Inadequate equipment and tools matching with the number of students, 2) High number of students in a group, 3) Insufficient teaching time, 4) Out of order equipment and tools used during the experiment, 5) Damage of equipment and tools used during the experiment, 6) Danger of the mistake in experiment for the experimenter, and 7) Too much time used in equipment and tools in the real operation.

Thus, CBSL is an environment in which the students may make *authentic* actions and receive *authentic* responses from the *virtual* equipment (Virtual Laboratory, 2002). There is no additional equipment besides the computer, monitor, and mouse necessary for this type of experience. A teacher creates CBSL where students can conduct experiments that they would otherwise not be able to do because the equipment are too expensive. Experimental results indicate that students who use CBSL prior to conducting the same experiments in a physical laboratory are able to complete the physical laboratory in a much shorter time, require less assistance, and also report that they are very satisfied with their laboratory experience (Mosterman et al., 2002).

2. Engineering sciences and physics education have always been dynamically interrelated with technology change. By solving control problems using software-based instruments and actual hardware, students gain an appreciation of the interaction of process instrumentation and computers. The interaction of instrumentation and networked computers running graphical software reduces manual data collection, analysis, presentation, storage, and transmission tasks, allowing supplemental material to be covered by the professor in the same time span.

3. "…there will be more CBSL in the future. Perhaps five years down the road, one-third of the experiments may be done virtually. However, the CBSL are not established to replace face-to-face teaching, but allow the students to carry out the experiment before or after the real session" (Ko, 2002). Pre-experiment *hands-on* experience for students before they go to the actual laboratory (Zhu, 1997). A teacher has his students use CBSL as a pre-lab so that they can understand the basics of the lab before they actually do it. Thus, CBSL can only augment the lecturers' teaching tools. It can't replace them. While the results of any education are difficult to prove, sufficient evidence exists that CBSL provides a fresh and fun way to supplement traditional education. Though CBSL cannot replace traditional education in many tasks, it may be better than traditional education when used appropriately (VirtualChicago Project, 2002). Computers aid students in laborious data-logging and enable them to perform extensive experiments. Many of the students spent as much time modifying their CBSL as they did on the experiment. It should be emphasized that CBSL is not intended to replace the hands-on laboratory inquiry but to extend it into investigations that are not feasible in the classroom. As CBSL develops and more options become available, student inquiry will become more and more open.

4. Once CBSL has been set up, students or users will be able to conduct actual experiments from remote computers anywhere in the world twenty-four hours a day, as if they were working in actual laboratories. This technology greatly enhances the flexibility of laboratory education, and introduces

students to the new paradigm of remote experimentation (Ko, 2002). The term *CBSL* refers to any learning process that takes place in virtual reality, or a virtual classroom. The location where learning takes place is called *virtual* because it does not exist in reality. Since CBSL is a non-traditional form of education, students and educators should be prepared for different forms of learning.

5. Creating articulate virtual laboratories requires synthesizing advances involving several technologies such as *Qualitative physics* which provides formal representations for the tacit knowledge of scientists and engineers that connects their professional knowledge to their experience-based intuitions, enabling software to use methods and concepts similar to those deemed natural by domain experts;. *Compositional modeling* provides representations and reasoning techniques for computer-assisted modeling (e.g., how to apply professional knowledge of a domain to modeling real-world situations so that they can be formally analyzed); *Truth-maintenance systems* provide reasoning services and the raw material for constructing explanations of the system's results and reasoning in terms that help students understand the domain of study; *Symbolic algebra and constraint propagation* provide mathematical solutions; and *Analogical processing techniques* provide the ability to retrieve and apply results from libraries of worked out designs and examples to novel situations, in order to coach students (Forbus, 1999).

References

Forbus, K.D., Articulate Virtual Laboratories for Science and Engineering Education [Online], Available : http://www.qrg.ils.nwu.edu/projects/NSF/av1.htm [1999, April 22].

Jitgarun, K., & Tunlasakun, K. (19-21 October, 1999). Development of Computer-Based Simulation Laboratory : A Case Study of KMUTT Students in Thailand, A paper presented at Southeast Asian Forum on Technologies for the Classroom, SEAMEO INNOTECH, Quezon City, Philippines.

Ko, CC, Web-based Virtual Laboratories Go Online [Online], Available : http://www.eng.nus.edu.sg/Eresnews/9905/p9.html [2002, July 17].

Karweit, M., What is Engineering? [Online], Available : http://www.jhu.edu/~virtlab/index.htm [2001, August 31].

Mosterman, P.J., Dorlandt, M.A.M., Campbell, J.O., Burow, C., Bouw, R., Broaersen, A.J., & Bourne, J. R., Virtual Engineering Laboratories : Design and Experiments [Online], Available : http://www.op.dir.de/FF-DR-ER/staff/pjm/papers/eed94/p.html [2002, July 17].

Ursutiu, D., Teaching Physics on a Virtual Laboratory [Online], Available : http://rilw.emp.paed.uni-muenchen.de./98/Doru-pap.html [2002, July 17].
VirtualChicago Project, Virtual Education [Online], Available : http://vchicago.org/virtualed/ [2002, July 17].

Virtual Laboratory [Online], Available : http://tiger.coe.missouri.edu/~pgermann/projects2/Scilnq/Virtual_Labor.../virtual_laboratory.htm [2002, July 17].

Yaron, D., The irYdium Project [Online], Available : http://ir.chem.cmu.edu/irproject/lists/Default.asp [2002, August 8].

Zhu, D., Virtual Laboratory – Demo Site [Online], Available : http://www.civil.ubc.ca/home/coursew3/virlab [1997, February 21].

Modelling a Web-based Learning System using Wired and Wireless Technology

Jun H. Jo, Vicki Jones, Greg Cranitch and Kyung-Seob Moon
School of Information Technology
Griffith University, Gold Coast Campus
QLD Australia 4217
{j.jo, v.jones, g.cranitch, k.moon}@gu.edu.au

Abstract: Internet technology has been rapidly developed and had a significant influence on education. However, through implementations, online teaching systems have not shown sufficient flexibility, which is the key element to this new approach. The current use of wireless technology has triggered attempts to inject greater flexibility into e-learning. This paper will propose a new model incorporating wireless technology within an e-learning system. The integration of the new technology in the current hybrid system will be discussed. The system will employ Pull/Push technology to provide efficient communication between educators and students.

Introduction

A number of universities around the world have attempted to use Wireless Local Area Networks (WLANs) in order to provide learning environments with sufficient flexibility. However, the cost of establishing a WLAN system is significant and the flexibility is usually accomplished within the proximity and operational area of a connection point. By including the benefits of wireless technology, this research investigates a new e-learning system with greater flexibility, regardless of time and location. The new Wireless Web-Based Instruction (WWBI) system will integrate a mobile phone and a Personal Digital Assistant (PDA) within an existing online teaching system which has been developed and used at Griffith University in Australia since 1999.

Wireless and Mobile Technology

Wireless Application Protocol (WAP)

WAP was designed to handle the limitations of wireless networks, such as narrow bandwidth, and unstable and unreliable connections. The WAP forum set the specifications for the micro-browser requirements in mobile and wireless devices (Moon, 2001). A micro-browser, as defined by the WAP specification, is the ultimate thin client. In a handheld device, it can operate with a small amount of memory, which suits the limited resources of the device.

The proposed system is designed to deliver teaching materials using:
- Protocols: HTTP and WAP
- Markup languages: HTML for multimedia information and WML for simple text message
- Communication methods: *pull/push*

Wireless Markup Language (WML)

Although HTML is a relatively simple markup language it is still too complex for use with a WAP device. Because of the constraints associated with handheld devices, an alternate model was necessary and WML was developed in 1999. WML and WMLScript (an event-based language, based on JavaScript) provide the functionality needed to reduce the load on the CPU. As a result, WML is a highly simplified markup language, which follows strict XML specifications (Bulbrook, 2001). Like HTML, the use of WML allows designers to specify format and presentation of text, and control navigation through a series of hyperlinks between pages.

Pull/Push Messages

Currently WBI systems are based on pull technology, which means that users request, or pull, information to their handheld device. However, using this method, when information perhaps of an urgent or otherwise important nature needs to be sent to the user, it will not be received until the user logs in and requests information. An example would be: when the university needs to inform students of a change or cancellation of a lecture. The new elearning system will allow students to be contacted by both educators and other students, using pull/push technology. The pull/push technology (see Figure 1.) in the new system can provide an efficient way to transmit information.

The concept of pushing and pulling information is not new. It has been used in the finance industry for some time, in the form of financial paging services. Information is pushed to the user's pager. The user can then pull more information from the website or from call centres. However, in reference to WAP, Push (or WAP Push as it is sometimes called) is slightly different. Using WAP Push a notification message can be sent to the user, who can then pull more information using links embedded in the message. It is made easy to use by allowing the user to just click a button to go to the WAP site (Bellis, 2000).

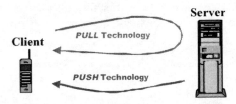

Figure 1: Pull and push technology

Personal Digital Assistant (PDA) Technology

Although some PDAs come with a small keyboard, PDA technology does not require a keyboard, and PDAs also come with a touch sensitive screen operated by a special input/output pen. The built-in graphical interface of a stylus-operated PDA uses both touch-pad technology and handwriting recognition, which allows the user to "write" on the small screen with the stylus pen. Some of the keyboard PDAs also have a pen and touch sensitive screen (Moon, 2001).

The advantages of PDA technology include:
- Convenience – easily accessible when needed
- Portability – easy to carry, small and light-weight
- AT/AP – easy to use the Internet anytime/anyplace
- Ease of use - management of personal information and tasks
- Display screen - generally reasonable and functional in size (capable of displaying thousands, or millions, of colours)
- Extra features - entertainment such as games and music (often includes MP3 and mpeg4 players)

The constraints (disadvantages) include:
- Limited battery life
- Limited CPU power
- Still relatively expensive – although prices will come down
- High running costs

Many PDAs include a wireless communication module, but if not, a mobile phone can be used as a wireless modem for data communication. There are three common methods of data communication: IrDA (Infrared Data Association - inexpensive with high transfer rates; Bluetooth (currently the most common communication method used in wireless communication) and RS232C serial cable (easy to implement, inexpensive, with lower distance limitations than parallel communication). These methods are also used to provide connection between PC and PDA.

Wireless Technology in Education

In the university environment the mobile phone is a common device for both mature-age and younger students. Yet there are significant limitations when using the mobile phone as a WBI device, such as: small screen, limited method of input, and lack of multimedia functionality. The new model aims at employing PDAs to overcome the limitations of mobile phone use.

Some of the promising aspects of wireless technology in e-learning include:

- *The rapid growth of mobile phone use:* There is an estimated 600 million wireless phone users worldwide. This exceeds the current Internet user base of about 420 million, of which 10 percent use wireless Internet (Bulbrook, 2001). The population of mobile phone users provides a significant infrastructure for wireless technology in e-learning.
- *Flexibility:* Many of Australia's tertiary students have part-time jobs, so flexibility is a key issue. However, on-line teaching cannot presently provide all the possible benefits of AT/AP. Wireless technology has the potential to enrich flexibility and offer significant increases in the number of resources available to students.
- *Easy Access:* Wireless e-learning may be an attractive alternative to attending face-to-face learning environments, especially in large metropolitan areas which suffer traffic congestion and lengthy commuting times.

A Hybrid System Model

The hybrid system provides two methods for students to access the main server:

- The use of a networked desktop/laptop PC
- The use of a mobile phone and a PDA

Figure 2 shows the Hybrid System Model. There are three main sections: Students, Mobile Base Station and Service Centre Module.

Students: Students can access the main server using a networked PC either from home or from the university's computer lab. From the computer lab, students generally have access to fast connections, with large memory and large computer screens, compared with access from home. Unless the student has broadband access the connection speed will be considerably lower than using this method. Therefore, to cater for all aspects of the learning environment, the learning materials are not only in text and picture formats but also in multimedia format such as movie, animation or real-time video streaming. The new model uses the online teaching system that Griffith University has developed and used since 1999 (Jones, Jo and Cranitch, 2000). This process is based on the Pull method for HTTP information.

Students can also access the system using a mobile phone and PDA. This feature aims at improving the flexibility of the system. Students can access the main server through the WAP gateway and browse the concise textual information such as: a Table of Contents (TOC), which includes teaching materials and MSN messages; and a Notice board (from educator or the university).

Push technology is used here and information is written in WML using WAP. When the student finds the required information in the TOC and wants to access it, the PDA can be used to display the information in either WML or HTML. This is especially suitable if using multimedia format. The mobile phone can be used as a modem and the PDA as a multimedia device.

Mobile Base Station: The Mobile Base Station is responsible for providing wireless connection to the student module as well as the wired connection to the service centre module. A mobile communication company provides this service.

Service Centre Module: The Service Centre Module shows the gateway, an ISP server and the University Web server. The *WAP gateway* is positioned between the Mobile Base Station and the University Web server. Its job

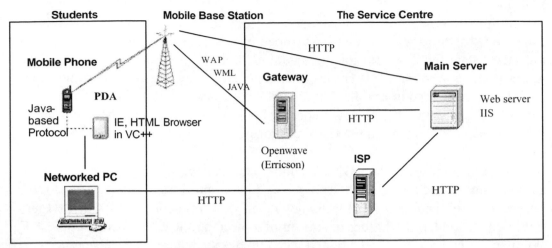

Figure 2: Hybrid System Model

is to transfer information via WAP and HTTP. When students use a PDA with a mobile phone as a modem, the format will be HTTP and does not need to go through the gateway. The use of various expansion cards enable PDAs to access the server or a Wireless LAN. Some expansion cards can also make a PDA act as a mobile phone. However, our system aims at all types of PDA and does not require any special expansion cards. The *ISP* server is the link used by students accessing the university server from home. It consists of a separate, possibly private, company that supplies Internet hours to the students. The *university server* is the main server holding all the data available for the educational learning module.

Conclusion

This paper introduces a Hybrid Delivery System, which includes both wired and wireless technology. The aim is to provide the general online delivery system with more flexibility and to improve the student-learning environment. To overcome the limitations of using a mobile phone, the system has employed the use of PDA technology to provide a larger screen, improved computational functions and increase storage capacity. The new system will adopt *Pull/Push* technology to provide efficient and economical communication between educators and students. Currently, the wired part of the system is complete and is being implemented. The *Pull/Push* technology has been developed and emulated using Openwave and will be applied to the teaching environment in the near future.

References

Bellis, D. (2000) PUSH, *Infinite Technologies in Asia*, Ariel Communications Ltd, [http://www.asia.infinite.com/Solutions/WAP/PUSH.htm] April, 2002.

Bulbrook, D. (2001) *WAP A Beginners's Guide*, Osborne/Macgraw-Hill, CA, U.S.A.

Jones, V., Jo, J.H., and Cranitch, G. (2000) A Study of Students' Response to WBI within a Traditional Learning Environment, *Conference Proceedings AusWeb2K,,* 6th Australian World Wide Web Conference, Cairns, June 2000.

Moon, K. S. (2001) *Innovations in e-Learning with Mobile Phone and Personal Digital Assistant*, unpublished Honours thesis, Griffith University, Gold Coast.

Developing Web-Based Materials for Electronic Learning

Background:
The eMath initiative is one of the first national efforts to create and deliver innovative multimedia instructional mathematics developed by middle school mathematics teachers.. eMath meets state standards for middle school math through its development of state-of-the-art, customized program that changes fundamentally how teachers use multimedia and web-based resources in middle school mathematics classrooms. In particular it has looked to fundamentally change how middle school teachers teach mathematics and how teachers and students engage in the learning process.

Partner schools from seven rural, small school districts in East Texas teamed with the parent company of eSchool Online, ACTV Net, Inc., to produce 30 mathematics modules (10 per grade level) and three staff technology staff development modules that target student learning in identified areas of student high need and teacher professional development. The program uses blended technologies such as video, web-based material, collaborative exercises and imbedded assessment. The math content is being delivered through eSchool Online software optimizing the Internet to deliver not only instructional material but also professional development to approximately 8000 students and 85 educators (teachers, math specialists, administrators, and library media specialists).

Aspects of the Initiative:
The impact of this initiative is felt by teachers and students moving toward an engaged learning and problem based learning model. Each teacher accesses the curriculum through 30 interactive modules delivered on demand via the Internet. This integrative web portal provides for email, program resources, teacher administration, instructional and unit development and a proven project based learning model. Videotapes clips using real life situations are used to demonstrate the mathematics concepts. Module development is targeted toward Texas State performance standards Math objectives 9, 11, 13 as well as the development of algebraic concepts. Students and parents access the modules from their school libraries, classrooms, computer labs, public libraries, ad hojme computers.

Also a select group of 14 teachers have been involved in the development of all the materials through inception to completion. Middle School mathematics teachers were developers of the content of the discovery based materials, its formatting and presentation style. Working with and through math experts from across the state the teachers developed the materials and took enormous ownership in the project. All materials were matched to the instructional learning styles of middle school students and were scrutinized for appeal to all ethnicities and gender.

Presentation information
Initial first year data will be presented. Research questions that will be addressed from data collected from school district administrators and eMath middle school teachers are:

a) what types of changes in thinking about mathematics pedagogy have teachers had since beginning the development of these materials; b) has the interaction between teacher and student changed since beginning this initiative and if so why; c)hat types of skills do classroom teachers need to have to develop online materials; and d) what is it or what was it that significantly changed the way you taught mathematics?

The Technology Mentor Fellowship Initiative: A Study of Cross Generational Learning

The Need

Our fast moving world expects educators to prepare students and teachers for needed future skills, including technology application, which have been underused to date. The current focus of technology in education has moved to curriculum integration and practical uses of the technology to support e-Learning, rather that the former focus of computer skills and isolated application instruction. This change, along with continual change in technology, impacts education directly and requires innovative ways to deliver instruction. Not only do we look to innovative ways to deliver curriculum but we also look for innovative ways to develop preservice teachers who are well versed in technology and its use and who are confident with technology integrations (Elwood-Salinas, 2001; Macers, Browne, & Cooper, 2000; Gillingham & Topper, 2000' Stuhlmann & Taylor, 1999).

The design of this initiative, funded by the US Department of Education, is to address the need for increased faculty proficiency in technology while recognizing the challenge and the potential of the disparity between faculty and students in technology skills. The goals of the project were to facilitate faculty development through both approaches: building capacity and providing tech support. This was done by: 1) developing proficiency of the faculty in the Texas A&M College of Education (COE) in the use of various instructional and communication technologies (building capacity); 2) developing capacity within the Texas A&M COE in digital media that supports the NCATE standards and the International Society for Technology in Education (ISTE) (building capacity); and 3) providing support to faculty transitioning to the new teacher training program by providing support in the area of technology support and infusion into the curriculum and coursework (providing tech support).

Program Description

The Technology Mentor Fellowship Program (TMFP) draws upon successful strategies evolving from programs funded by the Technology Literacy Challenge, specifically the Generation www y program, Gen Y Challenge Grant-Olympia, Washington) and the Profiler and Trackstar tools developed in a partnership with the current High Plains Regional Technology in Education Consortia. Training materials supplied through a partnership with Intel and Microsoft (Gates Foundation) through the Intel Teach to the Future initiative provided additional training and support.

The scope of work for the TMFP is to: 1) Provide teacher education faculty (campus based faculty, cooperating teachers, early experience supervisors) a system for technology training that:
- Provides intensive mentoring and support to faculty, and cooperating teachers in the field from pre-service teachers experienced in the process of integrating technology into instruction at the K-12 level;
- Identifies the growing knowledge base within college and school organizations, among students and faculty, and supports the sharing of both skills and knowledge through collaboration and the development of specific, skill related instructional objects;
- Provides continuous assessment of competence for college and school teacher education faculty, in the area of integration of technology into instruction;
- Provides professional development activities tailored to the particular needs identified by teacher education faculty regarding technology skills/processes for technology integration.

2) Provide teacher education faculty and pre-service teachers access to a repository of instructional objects designed to:
- Develop and use basic technology skills, skills in the instructional application of technology;
- Use technology -congruent pedagogy, such as project based learning and continuous skills assessment;
- Be searchable by their application to specific issues related to the integration of technology into instruction across grade levels, content areas, and national standards.

3) Provide opportunities to organize instructional objects into web-based courses.

Findings

Findings from this study not only address issues related to intergenerational learning and cross-age and cross-gender teamwork but also issues related to organizational change to support technology utilization and faculty change regarding pedagogy used in their classrooms.

- Why use a technical assistance group that ranges in age from about 18 to 24 years of age? First we know that this age group is made up of predominately the Net Generation (sometimes called Generation Y). The Net Generation, having grown up with the new technologies, enters our institutions of higher education with a much better comfort level for technology than the existing university faculty who grew up with television and radio. Consequently an "Intergenerational Digital Divide" exists.

- To compound the problem, a second divide exists in our state: that is, the technology infrastructure gap between public schools and higher education teacher preparation programs in Texas. Texas schools have experienced substantial technology infrastructure changes over the past few years. Colleges of Education, however, are limited in their ability to provide substantial pre-service training in Internet-based technologies so that beginning teachers may take advantage of this increased infrastructure. Rather than presenting exemplary models of technology-enhanced instruction to pre-service teachers, most Texas institutions of higher education are struggling with integrating technology into courses and content areas and in offering of on-line courses.

- Certain structures must be in place organizationally to begin, support, and sustain, technology infusion. These beginning structures consist of such things as support from the Dean and support from each of the Department Heads in the COE. This support cannot only be in the form of verbal support but must also come in the form of monetary support to sustain the technical assistance structure. Included in the organizational structure for technology integration should be a system for rewarding faculty that achieve a certain level of expertise and then model that level of expertise in their teaching. Also in this organizational structure should be a plan to fund the technical support.

- To successfully utilize technology in their teaching situations university faculty must have a certain level of expertise and comfort with the technology. They must have a certain level of "executive control." That is faculty must be able to do particular technical functions without really having to think much about it and must be able to then understand its transferability to their teaching situation.

- Teaching with this new medium has drastically altered the role of the teaching faculty requiring a group, or team effort. When implementing technology we must involve numerous specialists including instructional designers, graphics and multimedia designers, and programmers. Few faculties have the time or enthusiasm to integrate technology without a support team. This support team should provide "just-in-time" assistance to the university faculty.

- In addition to learning to work as a member of a team, instructors may need to change their pedagogical approaches to teaching and learning, moving from being the presenter of information to a facilitator of learning.

- The COE should have a mechanism in place to assess educational technology competency for its preservice students. A number of assessments are on the market to do just this. When deficiencies are found then technical support must be provided to the preservice student either in the form of access to an educational competency course or individual technical assistance.

- Provide in-service teacher mentors to our preservice education programs. These K-12 mentors could provide ideas for collaborative project development with K-12 institutions and institutions of higher education.

References

Elwood-Salinas, S. (2001). Preservice Teachers' Perceptions (Values and Expectations) Regarding Technology-Integrated Experiences in a Secondary Methods Course. Published Dissertation, Texas Tech University.

Gillingham, M. & Topper, A. (1999). "Technology in teacher preparation: Preparing teachers for the future." Journal of Technology and Teacher Education 7 (4): 303-321.

Macers, M., Browne, N., & Cooper, E. (1996). 60 in a 20 zone: Technology and teacher education. In N. Strader, D. Neiderhauser, & N. Hunt (Section Editors). Technology and Teacher Education Annual Proceedings. Allyn and Bacon: Association for the Advancement of Computing in Education.

Stuhlman, J.M. & Taylor, H.G. (1999). "Preparing technically competent student teachers: A three year study of interventions and experiences." Journal of Technology and Teacher Education 7(4): 333-350.

Writing for the Web

David Kim Juniper
Educational Media Development
Athabasca University
Canada
davidj@athabascau.ca

Abstract: The purpose of this brief paper is to explore how the World Wide Web differs from print and to give educators the tools they need to write effectively for this new medium. Topics covered range from paragraph length and sentence structure to fonts and the importance of a minimalist approach. As more educational institutions move their materials online and on CD-ROM, and more students expect digitally-based instruction, instructors are faced with a serious challenge. The first step in putting any written materials online is ensuring that the material is presented in the most usable way possible. As the pioneers of online education, it is up to today's teachers to forge a path that others will follow.

The World Wide Web is rich in pedagogical opportunity. As more educational institutions move their materials online, and more students expect digitally-based instruction, educators are facing an increasingly serious challenge. Unlike print, which has an established history and clear guidelines for its production, online materials are very recent and demand a different approach. Where do we, as educators, go from here?

The first thing to consider when placing educational materials online is the manner in which these materials will be read by the student. Are the materials intended to be read off the monitor or will they be printed by the student? This distinction is of paramount importance, and will inform the manner in which the materials will be presented, the structure of the document, etc. In the next few paragraphs, I will explore these two approaches and highlight the major aspects of each.

The "print" strategy involves using materials to be printed off and read at a later date. This approach will likely be the most familiar to many educators, as most of us have been trained in the print medium and are familiar with its conventions. As with most print-based material, the student will be expected to follow a linear approach to reading the printed document. Online students will navigate the text by scrolling and by using internal links, such as the "back to top" links often seen in longer html documents. Appropriately structured paragraphs and sentences give a sense of coherence to the material and maximize student understanding and retention. The document should be single-spaced, with a double space between paragraphs to enhance online readability.

Sub-headers assume a high degree of importance in longer documents, as they play a major role in its navigation. Using internal links, students can access individual sections of the document through a "Table of Contents" often found at the top of the page. Using the "Print Selection" option offered by most browsers, the student may print out sections of the document instead of the entire document.

Before continuing on the next online strategy, I'd like to take a moment to discuss the use of fonts online. Although a discussion of online typography could easily fill an entire paper in itself, I would like to touch on a few fundamentals with regards to usability. The default font used on the World Wide Web is Times New Roman, a font designed for both legibility and economy of space in the print medium (Bernard et al. 2002). Conversely, according to Ramsden (2000), the most widespread sans-serif font used on the World Wide Web is Arial, which also has a history based in print. The widespread use of these fonts online should not be mistaken for a "best-practice" however, as these fonts have since proven themselves less than efficient when read online.

Among the many alternatives to both Times New Roman and Arial, many designers and usability gurus have chosen either Georgia (serif) or Verdana (sans serif) as the best choice for online text. In an article in *Cre@te Online* magazine, Stuart Dredge describes how the low resolution on the monitor screens (72 dpi as opposed to 2400 in print) can play havoc with the readability of many print-based fonts. Options such as Verdana and Georgia come up winners because they were designed primarily for the monitor screen. In the following example, taken from a web page, you will see the differences between the fonts.

Times New Roman

Arial

Verdana

Georgia

Moving on from the world of print, the other approach to using the Web, and the one which poses the greatest challenge, is material intended to be read from the monitor itself. In addition to choosing the right font, the educator is presented with a host of other design challenges. Unlike traditional readers, the student who is reading online text is always on the verge of going elsewhere. The Back button, the Favorites or Bookmarks menus, all beckon the student to other digital destinations. The challenge then becomes how to capture and hold the student's attention.

There are a few core rules to follow when creating online materials designed to be read online. The foundation upon which these rules and guidelines rest is the fact that students rarely read online materials - they scan them (Nielsen 1997). Rather than reading the entire text in a linear fashion, online users are more likely to jump from paragraph to paragraph, searching for the main ideas or concepts they recognize, or stopping in areas which arouse their interest. Furthermore, because of the abbreviated attention span of many web surfers, large blocks of text are likely to be quickly discarded in favor of shorter more compact fare. To overcome these challenges, effective online text usually adheres to the following guidelines;

1. Keep the lines short. The flickering background of a computer monitor makes reading more difficult, so each line should not be longer than 10-13 words.
2. Short paragraphs of 150 words or less help ensure readers stay on task.
3. Make ample use of headers, sub-headers and bulleted lists.
4. Use the active voice rather than the passive
5. When appropriate, use different media such as images, animation as well as audio and video intermixed with the text.
6. Stay clear of cultural references that might confuse foreign students.

The aim in using the aforementioned guidelines is to create pages that will catch the reader's attention and maintain it. Much like journalistic writing, web writing makes good use of the snappy opening line, short paragraphs and sub-headers. Furthermore, web writing also often make use of the "inverted pyramid" strategy (Nielsen 1996). Starting the text with the conclusion, followed by the most important supporting information, ensures that the reader gets the most important parts of the article right at the beginning. Should the student desire more information, a hypertext link would lead to a more comprehensive treatment of the material which could be printed off and read at a later time. So, in this way we have the two strategies - read online and printed off - working together to provide the student with a quick, efficient online experience.

The Web is in its infancy, and will grow into a powerful force in education. As the pioneers of online education, it is up to today's educators to forge a path that others will follow. Simply transferring print-based materials directly to the Internet is not a viable solution, for different mediums have different requirements. By being aware of the idiosyncrasies and challenges of the online medium, educators can make a smooth transition to online learning and thus make full use of this powerful new pedagogical tool.

References:

Bernard, Lida, Riley, Hackler, & Janzen. (2002). A Comparison of Popular Online Fonts: Which Size and Type is Best? *Usability News* [online]. http://psychology.wichita.edu/surl/usabilitynews/41/onlinetext.htm

Dredge, Stuart. (2002). Getting the text message. *Cre@te Online*. Issue 027.

Nielsen, Jakob. (1997). How Users Read on the Web. *Alertbox* [online]. http://www.useit.com/alertbox/9710a.html

Nielsen, Jakob. (1996). Inverted Pyramids in Cyberspace. *Alertbox* [online]. http://www.useit.com/alertbox/9606.html

Ramsden, A. (2000).Font Surveys. *Annabella's HTML Help*. [Online]. http://www.annabella.net/fontface.html

Teaching or Producing?
Orientation and Motivation of Virtual University Team in the Development of Web Courses

Kirsi Karjalainen & Esko Kähkönen
Educational Technology Centre
University of Joensuu
Finland
kirsi.karjalainen@joensuu.fi
esko.kahkonen@joensuu.fi

Abstract: In this paper orientation and motivation of the Eastern Finland Virtual University Network content production team is studied. Based on a questionnaire, in analysis applying content analysis, the goal was to detect factors affecting understanding and realization of the process of developing web courses. A special attention was paid to the question of understanding the task as production or teaching. The survey shows that the team understands elearning as additional element in teaching, with new insights to the development of teaching. Awareness of pedagogical approaches was low, but respondents were in fact intensively looking for models for more interaction, collaboration, better tutoring and self-directiveness of the student. The production of the web courses was rewarding for the members of the team, especially for those with teacher experience. Small scale production model, where any member of the group was familiar with various tasks in the production process, in supervision of the teaching institution, was a garant for didactic consciousness, and after the first phase of course production team members saw the very importance of careful planning that in the beginning was somewhat neglected.

Introduction

The purpose of this presentation is to study and analyse orientation and motivation of the Eastern Finland Virtual University team in the development of web-based courses. A special accent is going to be given to the matter, how the professional members of the group comprising of fourteen instructional designers, teachers and technical supporting staff, stand to central issues affecting elearning. Those are the background and attitudes of the team, grade of virtual learning in study courses, pedagogical approach, infrastructure and support services, and quality of learning. Special attention is going to be given to the question whether the virtual university personnel considers their task more from the point of producing digital study materials or adding to the traditional way of teaching.

Background

The Eastern Finland Virtual University Network (EFVU) started up at the beginning of 2001 as part of the Finnish Virtual University (FVU), financed by the Ministry of Education. The program is linked to the national ICT-strategy (Education, Training and Research in the Information Society 1999). In the content production team of the EFVU work around 15 persons in the fields of Computer Science, Applied Mathematics, Environmental Technology, Business Administration and Economics. Around 60 credit units /study weeks of web-based courses are being produced in the team.

The Study

In June 2002 a survey was conducted with the purpose to discover experiences and orientation of the virtual university team engaged in the development process of web based learning in the EFVU. Fourteen persons working in different areas of expertise and in technical and pedagogical support answered the questionnaire, most of them in a seminar intended for the team of the EFVU. Those unable to attend the seminar filled in the questionnaire afterwards. The questionnaire was submitted to contents analysis, but also some basic quantitative methods were applied. In the team there are experts from subject departments of the universities and from the Learning / Educational Centres. Nine out of fourteen persons represent subject departments and five these support units. At least some background as teacher do have six persons of the team.

Findings

During the first half of the three-year Eastern Finland Virtual University Network -project, half of the respondents, including both teaching staff and support persons, have produced web-courses carrying the main responsibility. Before the project of Eastern Finland Virtual University Network over one third (n=5) of the respondents had gained experience in web-course production, most of them in more than six courses. Two of this group had produced web-courses having the main responsibility of the production process. A clear majority of the respondents were familiar with various roles in the production of web courses.

The respondents' involvement in the development of e-learning was mainly due to the fact that web-course production was included in respondent's job description and respondent's own enthusiasm for web-course development. The next important motives were person's interest in pedagogy and ICT.

All the respondents consider web-course production very meaningfull or meaningfull. The respondents with a background as teacher (6) considered course development very meaningful (5/6), those in supporting activities somewhat less (3/8). Odd, though, that persons with teacher experience gave as the most important reason to their engagement in e-learning, their job description or order of the head of the department. On the third place was given the will to develop teaching. The reason to this order of importance is not clear, if general obedience or dependence on institutional structures, on the other hand, in the case of a new learning culture, a certain mental dependence could be an asset for the teacher himself/herself; as he/she knows to work on behalf of the Institution. [See Table 1].

In the light of the above it is, though, an interesting point that persons involved in e-learning before the project period of the EFVU, were strongly motivated and directed by their own enthusiasm, whereas persons without early experience placed almost to the top the duty character of their role in the development of e-learning. These persons are mostly the teachers of the team, as described above.

Interest in pedagogy *and* technology were in the group of persons with previous experience (n–5) even, almost at the top of the appreciation, whereas in the group of persons without previous experience (n=9), interest *either* in pedagogy *or* technology was not decisive at all (ranking 45). In this group pedagogy got just three mentions altogether, and just the place five on the list of seven factors. Considered that the group of team members without prior experience was greater than that with experience, the figures show a clear accent.

	Persons with previous experience (n=5)			Persons with no previous experience (n=9)		
	Mentions	Range	Order of importance	Mentions	Range	Order of importance
An order of a superior	1	8	7.	3	1-2	2.
Own enthusiasm for web-course development	5	1-3	1.	6	1-3	3.
Web-teaching is "trendy"	1	5	5.	1	4	6.
Previous experience in audio-visual production	1	6	6.	0	0	-
Web-course production included in job description	2	1-7	4.	6	1	1.
Interest in pedagogy	5	1-3	2.	3	2-5	5.
Interest in technology	5	1-4	3.	7	2-4	4.

Table 1: Reasons leading to engagement in web-course production.

The respondents assessed they have very good or good ICT-skills in creating and editing www-pages, in integrated use of different programmes (eg. text transfer) and in WebCT, which is the standard platform in the institutions of all team members. Skills in transferring video into the net and video editing were most often considered fair or poor.

Text is the most often used and most valued web-course tool. There are no differences between teachers and supporting staff in this place. Text is for them informative and available and readable with technical solutions of low level. Discussion, when related to the subject, enhances the learning process. It provides with social connections, which were considered very important in a web-course. Tests were appreciated as self-evaluation tools. Animation was considered informative and illustrative. Video was still quite little used and appreciated, due to technical limitations and lacking expertise.

As the most important advantage of a web-course was considered the possibility to study over distance and time. This enables eg. personal learning schedules. Diversified material can be included – if there are enough resources for production. Other advantages mentioned were the possibility to use experts from outside and to insert illustrative elements to a course (eg. animation, photos, video etc.)

The respondents rank very high the possibility to personal learning style and offering tutoring to the students, regardless of the respondents' background as teacher or support person. On the other hand diversity and personalized learning path was pretty poor taken into account in the courses already finished.

Half of the respondents, especially persons with longer experience, have constructed web-courses on a certain approach. Majority of teachers and supporting personnel considers web-based learning supportive to the face-to-face teaching. Awareness of the chosen pedagogical approach of a web-course is not very high, as about half of the respondents planned the course according to a specific pedagogical approach. There is practically no difference here between teachers and supporting staff. Opinions as follows were given as descriptive to the issue of pedagogical approach: *"Open, problem oriented, contextual"*, *"Learning by doing. Rapidly in to the practice"*, *"Exploratory learning."*

As to the issue of collaboration in the courses realised by the team members, a clear statement shared by almost all respondents was that just little, at the best some, collaboration was gained. As descriptive for collaboration were given such statements as "discussions in the web" (4 mentions), "shared goals in a group" (3 mentions).

The role of the teacher in web-based learning is a generally known issue. In this study the question was formulated as follows: "Which role at the best would be your choice: teacher, tutor, expert, service provider?" The respondents tended to appreciate the role of a tutor / mentor. After the role of a tutor, secondly that of a teacher and thirdly an expert was given without any great difference in the background of the respondent.

The survey shows that emphasis in course production has moved from technical and practical matters to careful planning, considering the course as an entity, its' structure and interactive elements as well as visualization. The role of technology has become less important, although technical matters are still carefully considered in order to find the best technical solution to each course. The goal is to produce web-courses with readable, illustrative and interactive content, which is technically reliable and easy to access. Thus the most time-consuming phases in course production are producing and editing material into electronic form, suitable for the chosen learning environment. This includes planning and producing course contents, examples and animations.

Over half of the respondents (n=8) have nowadays a little more positive attitude towards web-learning than they had in the past. Considered that the team members do their job out of their one choice, also when appointed by the institution, and find their task meaningful, this is not a surprise. One fourth (n=3) have nowadays a lot more positive attitude towards e-learning than before. Three respondents stated that their attitude has not changed. Experience in web course production seems to have no effect on the change of attitudes. The somewhat reserved attitude towards virtual learning, experienced by many respondents has not discouraged the team members, anyway. The colleagues at the respondent's department have a positive and curious attitude on web-based learning, but also prejudices towards "new and unknown". Also students have a positive stand with some reserve.

One factor that affects the experience in the team is the expectations towards quality of web based learning. Over half of the respondents (n=8) estimated that the quality of web-courses is fairly good compared to traditional learning. Six respondents argued the quality to be good or very good. Careful planning and production reflects to the quality. There are several critical factors related to the quality of web-learning. According to the respondents the material should be readable and illustrative. Technical solutions are not the main issue in course production, but should be considered carefully to find reasonable and functional solutions for each course. Material should be easily accessed over distance and time. Technical and pedagogical support for teachers is of crucial importance. Guidance and support of students has to be organized. ICT-skills of students and teachers reflect to the progress of the course. Although web-courses attach value to teaching being available over distance and time, a timetable and some dates have to be given according to the respondents.

Conclusion and Discussion

The group of respondents seems to take a cautious start in virtual learning. They combine the elements of traditional face-to-face teaching with the modern technical facilities, with the will to keep on personal contact, tutoring and collaboration. In the practice, anyhow, personal contact and collaboration was poorly realised. Altogether in the EFVU project it handles a small scale production of learning materials, where members of the team are familiar with various tasks. The task is generally seen very meaningful. In the present stage of development this seems a rational arrangement, also if there is, of course the question, how much academic staff should be involved in www-page productions etc. (See Ryan et al 2001, 71-72) In this form e-learning is an additional element in teaching. No meaningful differences were detected in different areas of the study in comparison between respondents with teacher background or supporting staff. For the first group developing web courses is more rewarding than to the others, though. The members of the team with longer time experience are strongly directed by personal enthusiasm, whereas newcomers see their job more regulated by the institutional side. This is a signal of a more institutionalized dimension and growing acceptance. The team members show quite little awareness of the pedagogical approach in web course design. A constructivist approach in pedagogy could be acknowledged as a primary orientation in the team (compare with Salmon 2000, 35-36), on the other hand this is not specific at all. It seems, anyhow, that after the first 1,5 years of work this could be changing, and more attention will be paid to careful planning, also with didactic aspects in the production process. On the other hand the closeness of web course production to the teaching and teaching institutions is a garant for didactic consciousness, a matter that not so easily could be detected through the questionnaire.

As noticed above, much attention should be paid to the careful planning. This is also a point Ryan et al (2001, 77-78) recommend, with the help of concept maps and such, for team members to facilitate project management. Documenting the process would also be of great importance.

Some of the findings above could be reflected to the general trends in web-based learning. The will to take diversity into account is somewhat similarly reflected by the team members as for instance the study of Institute for higher education policy (Quality on the Line 2000) shows. Major institutions in e-learning in their specifications do emphasize student centredness but leave personalised learning aside. One has to acknowledge, though, that learner style adaptation is a debated area also when in many ways learners are different, starting from visual, auditory or kinesthetic learning preferences (see McVay Lynch 2002, 16-17).

The role of the teacher is in a lively stage. The group concerned in this study might not be so far that they would name the teacher e-moderator (see Salmon 2000), but they are eager to find new approaches in teaching. The point of view is pedagogical, in any case, not just technological one.

The quality of web-based courses done in the team was not evaluated by any systematic criteria. The comparison between the traditional teaching was more a numerous matter, of credits given. The idea of e-learning quality as a matter of system including elements of student and faculty support, infrastructure etc (see Quality on the line 2000) were not thoroughly considered. The focus of this study, anyhow, was more to find out the orientation of the team members, after 1,5 years of work, and in this function the findings are useful for the further development and becoming conscious of factors important in the process.

References

Education, Training and Research in the Information Society. (1999). A National Strategy for 2000-2004. Ministry of Education, Finland. http://www.minedu.fi/julkaisut/information/englishU/2/1.html

McVay Lynch, M. (2002). *The Online Educatior. A Guide to Creating the Virtual Classroom.* RoutledgeFalmer Studies in distance education. London and New York.

Quality on the Line. Benchmarks for Success in Interner -Based Distance Education. (2000). Prepared by the Institute for Higher Education Policy. April 2000. (www.ihep.com)

Ryan, S., Scott, B., Freeman, H., & Patel, D. (2001). *The Virtual University. The Internet and Resource-Based Learning.* Kogan Page.

Salmon, G. (2000). *E-moderating. The Key to Teaching and Learning Online.* Kogan Page.

A Pervasive Computing Solution to Asset, Problem and Knowledge Management

Suman K. Kalia, Charles C. Tappert, Allen Stix, and Fred Grossman
School of Computer Science and Information Systems
Pace University, USA, ctappert@pace.edu

Abstract: A pervasive computing approach to asset, problem, and knowledge management reduced the average time to complete all major helpdesk tasks, and led to faster data availability, improved data quality, improved help desk effectiveness, improved help desk Return on Investment (ROI), lower overall Total Cost of Ownership (TCO), and increased user satisfaction. We describe the conceptualization, design, and construction of wireless laptop and PDA-based asset, problem and knowledge management systems. The systems work on a Lotus Notes/Domino-based server, supporting both wired desktops and wireless laptops and personal digital assistants (PDAs), to assist in the management of a divisional desktop support team across the U.S.

Introduction

The following quote (IBM Pervasive Computing Website 2002) indicates the importance of pervasive computing in managing information: *"Information is the new currency of the global economy. We increasingly rely on the electronic creation, storage, and transmittal of personal, financial, and other confidential information, and demand the highest security for all these transactions. We require complete access to time-sensitive data, regardless of physical location. We expect devices – personal digital assistants, mobile phones, office PCs and home entertainment systems – to access that information and work together in one seamless, integrated system. Pervasive computing can help us manage information quickly, efficiently, and effortlessly."* Although the term "pervasive computing" is relatively new, its concept has historical precedence. Companies like IBM (IBM Redbook 1995) and United Parcel Service (Brewin 2002) implemented pervasive computing infrastructures as far back as 1982, and the IBM system was developed, as was our system, to improve the effectiveness of Field Technical Support personnel. Pervasive computing is all about access to your information, anytime, anywhere, from any device.

The system described here was developed for a company, hereafter referred to as ABC Company, that spends more than three billion dollars a year to procure technology. A major portion of this expense is for new desktops, servers, and associated peripherals. In spite of such a huge yearly investment, there has been no system to consolidate the technology procurement and to track the assets throughout their life cycle, making it difficult to compute the TCO of the assets. Also, there was no knowledge transfer of the kinds of problems encountered and the procedures followed by different support groups on such hardware/software throughout the organization. This is not only ABC Company's problem, but also one that is much broader and requires the attention of the industry

This paper summarizes a dissertation (Kalia 2002) that studied the effects of pervasive computing on the management of a technology Help Desk environment. The research activities included the conceptualization, design, and construction of wireless laptop and Pocket PC 2000 Operating System PDA based asset, problem and knowledge management systems to assist a divisional desktop support team across the U.S. The systems worked on a Lotus Notes/Domino-based server supporting both wired desktops and wireless laptops and PDAs. First, we created a baseline from our desktop computing Help Desk environment. Then, we established a pervasive computing implementation and measured the change in the quantity and quality of Help Desk calls handled. We hypothesized that the pervasive computing implementation would reduce the time to complete the helpdesk tasks, speed data availability, improve data quality, improve help desk effectiveness, improve help desk ROI, lower overall TCO, and increase user satisfaction.

Pervasive computing has its limitations, and one source (Grimm 2000) lists three scope-limiting areas: user interface and form factor limitations, network constraints, and multiplicity of administrative domains. We have removed, or at least lessened, the effect of these constraints by applying suitable limitations on the scope of our implementation. We addressed the user interface and form factor limitation by limiting the devices used to the Compaq iPaq PDA that uses the Pocket PC 2000 operating system, desktop and laptop computers running current versions of the Microsoft Windows operating system, standardizing the laptop selection on the IBM ThinkPad. We addressed the network constraints issue by limiting the network architecture to our corporate Intranet with its wired Ethernet and wireless 802.11b access, and no access was made available from outside this infrastructure. We addressed the multiplicity of administrative domains limitation by limiting a user logging on to the network from a desktop, laptop, or PDA to a single network identity (User ID and Password) for authentication.

Methodology

The project was divided into two phases: baseline and pervasive computing. For the baseline phase, January through December of 2001, we developed a suite of asset, problem and knowledge management applications in Lotus Notes and implemented them in a pure desktop-centric client/server environment. In the baseline phase, we captured the asset, problem and knowledge management data from the three sites: Tampa, FL, Boston, MA and New York, NY. In the pervasive computing phase, January through April of 2002, we used the handheld computers and collected similar data for comparison purposes. All data were replicated across the WAN at regular short intervals and made available across the country to 5,000 plus users through Lotus Notes.

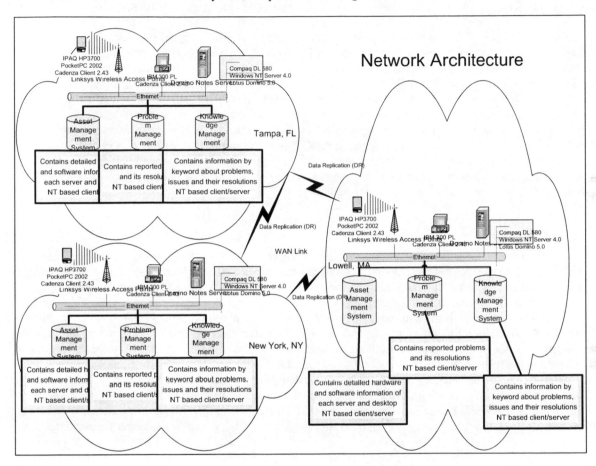

Figure 1: Network Architecture

Figure 1 shows the overall network architecture used for this application in the three supported locations, the configuration of wired Ethernet LANs at each location, and the Wireless Access Points that allow wireless laptop computers and PDAs to be an integral part of this network. It also indicates the positioning of the Lotus Notes servers that house the applications and databases, and the data replication topology used to keep the databases at all locations in synchronization. The PDA clients consisted of two models of the Compaq's iPaq PDA using the Pocket PC 2000 operating system. The desktop and laptop client application development was all done using Lotus Notes development tools. Lotus Notes is a workflow development tool, which integrates, e-mail, text databases, workflow, and forms. The downloading and reformatting of Lotus Notes data to fit on the smaller PDA screen was done using Cadenza, a PDA based Lotus Notes client developed by Common Time, Ltd., that reshapes the data presentation to fit on the smaller presentation area of a PDA screen to integrate with Lotus Notes.

Asset, problem and knowledge management systems were designed, developed, and deployed in a client/server environment to provide a suite of Help Desktop applications supported by a set of corresponding back-end Lotus Notes databases. The Asset Management System was developed to provide an on-going tool to capture desktop hardware and software asset information. We used Lotus Notes because all users had Lotus Notes on their desktops and Lotus Notes servers were already present to support these applications. The Problem Management system is a workflow application developed in Lotus Notes and used to record all incoming desktop problem calls. Each desktop has a Problem Management icon to invoke the application. The application enables a desktop user to enter his own problem calls; or optionally call one of the helpdesk agents and have them record the call on his behalf. Once recorded, a call may be viewed from New York, Boston, or Tampa instantaneously. A recorded problem is also automatically reported to the assigned engineer for immediate action. An engineer has multiple ways to find out about, and address, a reported problem. He may use a hyperlink in the e-mail message to jump directly to the problem record in the Problem Management system, call up the Problem Management application itself and select only his calls, and/or he may even review and accept other people's calls and address them. The Knowledge Management system feeds off of the Problem Management database and is merely a reporting mechanism. It allows a Field Service Engineer to immediately retrieve information on past problems by category (printer problems, LAN problems, etc.), and provides a basis to perform more extensive analyses of problems, solutions, and trends.

The client/server architecture supported the suite of applications. Clustered Compaq servers hosted the various Lotus Notes/Domino servers that supported the Notes based applications. The components consisted of Lotus Notes/Domino Web Server clusters, LAN/WAN/Wired/Wireless Network infrastructure, and Clients. We chose to use the Lotus Notes/Domino servers as our data repositories and Web servers for simple seamless data replication across our locations, for faster development, and for easy future enhancements. The standard Lotus Notes E-mail architecture across the company made it a convenient platform for the research and implementation. The network infrastructure was based on the existing infrastructure at ABC Company, augmented with new wireless capabilities. Data synchronization was necessary to present the same view of the data at all locations, and was a key objective of this project. The three Lotus Notes/Domino server clusters were located on the ABC Company Corporate backbone and thus shared the same wide area network across the country.

Results

During the baseline and pervasive phases, we collected approximately 12000 Lotus Notes records, each corresponding to a help desk call and containing the following information: the engineer responding to the call, the date and time the call was initiated, the date and time the call (task) was completed, and the support category of the call. We downloaded these records into a spreadsheet and removed those of calls not completed within the day received – that is, where the date of the call did not match the date of completion – because they may not accurately represent the time to completion that we were interested in analyzing. We discarded about 2400 records through this data cleansing process, leaving 9662 records suitable for our comparison testing. The records were sorted by date and divided into two groups to represent the baseline phase (Jan-Dec 2001) and the pervasive phase (Jan-Apr 2002).

We then sorted the calls by category and found that more than ninety percent of the total 9662 records belonged to fifteen dominant categories according to total sample size, and that these categories were reasonably represented in both the baseline and pervasive phases. The remaining 731 records not in the fifteen dominant categories were consolidated into a single "catch all" category. Most of the categories (all but 3 and 4) fall under Gartner's technical support category (Berg et al. 1998). The sixteen categories are: LAN connectivity problems, Lotus Notes install, printing problems, hardware – equipment procurement, new software installations, LAN password resets, in-house application support, software – problems, hardware – new installations, Internet support, Lotus Notes ID creation, new user set-ups, LAN account lockouts, relocations, mobile PC support, and the remaining categories combined.

Table 1 lists the sixteen categories by descending sample size – that is, the sum of the number of help desk calls in both the baseline and the pervasive phases – and, for each category, presents the total sample size, the baseline sample size, the baseline average time to completion, the pervasive sample size, the pervasive average time to completion, the decrease in the average time to completion in moving from the baseline phase to the pervasive phase, the percent decrease, the corresponding Chi Square statistical test value, and the corresponding null-hypothesis probability (p) value as a decimal and in scientific notation. The totals and overall statistical test values (for all 16 degrees of freedom) are also shown at the bottom of the table.

All categories benefited from a decrease in the average time to completion of the tasks, with the percentage decrease ranging from 3 to 62 percent. From the p values it is clear that the benefit of moving from the baseline to the pervasive implementation is statistically significant for most of the categories; eleven of the sixteen category decreases were significant with $p < 0.05$, and most of these, as well as the total, were significant with much lower p values. Therefore, the move to the pervasive implementation to handle help desk calls was highly beneficial. The engineers spent less time commuting, worked on more complex problems, and their productivity increased to handling three times as many calls per month.

Task	Total Sample size	Baseline Sample size	Baseline Avg Time (sec)	Pervasive Sample size	Pervasive Avg Time (sec)	Time Decrease (sec)	% Decrease	Chi-Square	p (decimal)	p (scientific)
1	1544	827	2525	717	2363	162	6.4	1.47	0.22532012	2.25E-01
2	1419	555	5075	864	4678	397	7.8	5.29	0.02140613	2.14E-02
3	1068	521	5544	547	5031	513	9.3	5.12	0.02361844	2.36E-02
4	884	386	5982	498	5784	198	3.3	0.64	0.42231671	4.22E-01
5	809	321	4384	488	3014	1370	31.3	41.22	0.00000000	1.36E-10
6	808	541	1588	267	1006	582	36.6	11.24	0.00080256	8.03E-04
7	645	391	4769	254	3675	1094	22.9	12.58	0.00039088	3.91E-04
8	549	256	3990	293	3778	212	5.3	0.65	0.41972157	4.20E-01
9	375	180	7598	195	4440	3158	41.6	50.49	0.00000000	1.20E-12
10	252	95	3170	157	3016	154	4.9	0.23	0.63025296	6.30E-01
11	153	34	5075	119	1928	3147	62.0	45.81	0.00000000	1.30E-11
12	113	38	3837	75	2630	1207	31.5	5.62	0.01777955	1.78E-02
13	112	25	1492	87	813	679	45.5	5.30	0.02128186	2.13E-02
14	109	53	3550	56	2410	1140	32.1	4.04	0.04431985	4.43E-02
15	91	28	5458	63	3471	1987	36.4	8.99	0.00271397	2.71E-03
16	731	342	3368	389	3045	323	9.6	2.38	0.12312043	1.23E-01
Total	9662	4593	59805	5069	51082	16323	27.3	201.08	0.00000000	1.28E-34

Table 1: Average Completion Time of Baseline Versus Pervasive Phases for 16 Task Categories

Conclusions

We can now determine how closely our results match our hypotheses. From the statistical test results, there is no question that that the benefit of moving from the baseline to the pervasive implementation *reduces the time to complete the helpdesk tasks.* Compared to the first four months of the baseline period, the number of calls handled from the four months of the pervasive period tripled to *speed data availability and improve data quality.* A trend analysis showed that we could handle more calls because there is less commuting, a wider Knowledge Base, and remote access to all tools, *improving the effectiveness of the Help Desk.* The more effective Help Desk handled three times the number of calls with the same staff, clearly *improving ROI and TCO.* The increased number of calls is also a good indicator that the implementation of pervasive computing *improves user satisfaction*, which was verified by feedback from the engineers who worked during both the phases.

We provided an integrated suite of asset, problem and knowledge management applications and found that these three solutions, taken together, provided benefits greater than the sum of the benefits that these applications would have provided individually. With the TCO of a desktop computer estimated at $10,000, the non-purchase factors far outweigh the cost of purchase (Berg et al. 1998). The only way to reflect these costs accurately is to keep asset and problem management data together so that we can see how the cost of ownership increases as the hardware and software age.

As a further benefit of centralizing these data, we were able to evaluate the effectiveness of our Field Service Engineers. These data also provided a free source of training for them, since they could see the types of problems that they were likely to encounter in practice and the solutions to those problems, and this free training resulted in significant savings in training expense and enabled the company to utilize engineers with a lower skill set.

References

Berg, T., Kirwin, W., and Redman, B. (1998). *TCO: A Critical Tool for Managing IT*, Gartner Group research report.
Brewin, B. (2002). *UPS takes Wireless Application to Asia*, Computerworld, February.
Grimm, R. et al. (2000). *A System Architecture for Pervasive Computing*, Dept. Computer Science & Eng., Seattle State Univ.
IBM Pervasive Computing Website (2002). *What is pervasive computing?* http://www-3.ibm.com/pvc/pervasive.shtml.
IBM Redbook (1995). *An Introduction to Wireless Technology*, IBM Redbook SG24-4465-01.
Kalia, S.K. (2002). *A Pervasive Computing Solution to Asset, Problem and Knowledge Management*, Doctor of Professional Studies Dissertation, School of CSIS, Pace University.

WebKANEcts

**Building on constructivism
to create
a learning-centred strategy
for e-learning.**

Catherine Kane
Centre for Learning Technology / Information Sysytem Services
Trinity College Dublin
Ireland
Catherine.Kane@tcd.ie

Abstract: This research explores the development of a new strategy for e-learning. A strategy based on aspects of constructivism, that allows the learners to build their own learning environment based on new learning material, prior knowledge and experience. I call this new strategy **WebKANEcts**.

The methodology of WebKANEcts pulls together many existing ideas and strategies into a new focus for education. It is closely linked to the WebQuest strategy (Dodge, 2000). Resources to support the learning are designed as Learning Objects (Bannan-Ritland et al, 2000) and the environment is delivered using an Expert System, **Exesys Corvid** (http://www.exsys.com/1.2NR.html). My strategy takes what is best from other systems and makes the 'WebKANEections' necessary to empower the learner and the teacher.

An artefact has been developed for and tested by second year Botany students at Trinity College Dublin, Ireland. The strategy has also been examined by three experts working in the field of IT in Education.

Introduction

If we are to embrace the challenge Information Computer Technologies (ICT) in education presents us with, then I believe we need to examine new methods of learning and teaching. We need strategies that embrace these new technologies while still taking into consideration established theories on education and learning. I want to develop and test a strategy that enables the learner to compile his/her own learning objectives, where content, context and assistance support the learner and help him/her make sense of the ever more complex world we live in. This strategy should also encourage the learner to draw from his/her own experience and knowledge to create new knowledge. It should go above and beyond the use of educational theories used in traditional text-based learning environments.

Needs survey

In the course of my profession as a Trainer in the Department of Information Systems Services, Trinity College Dublin, and from working with new entrant student annually, it has become apparent that many students enter College with little or no IT skills. Earlier research in this area (Kane 2001) had highlighted this problem. I hoped to build on this research while developing a new strategy for e-learning.

A needs survey of 200 second year Biology students showed the following results. 35.7 % of the students reported having no previous experience with e-mail, 27.1% reported having no Internet experience, and 22.1% reported no experience with Word Processing.

Based on this information I decided to develop an artefact that would support these students in the use of College computers to complete assignments.

Structuring the Learning Environment

I structured the artefact in the same format as a WebQuest.

Figure 1 - Screen shot of system showing all sections.

The Resources section consists of IT resources that may be helpful in completing the task. These resources have been developed as individual learning modules. The student is asked to pick the modules he/she thinks will help them to complete the task. This is where the students build their own learning environment. If the student knows how to perform a task then he/she can choose not to select that module. Subject related resources could also be made available. For our test all resources were IT based.

Figure 2 - Shows a list of Microsoft Word Help choices available to the student

Note: "Filestorage" in Trinity College is a protected central storage area independent of the networked computer from which files are saved. Each user is allocated 30 MB of private "Filestorage" space.

Figure 3 - A student's personal learning environment.

Each learning object deals with one small chunk of information. Text and animations are used to teach the procedure.

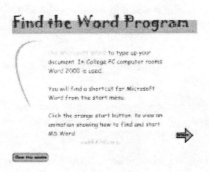

Figure 4 shows a screen shot for the help item **Find the Word Program**.

Findings

Students were asked to fill in a questionnaire to establish how helpful they found the system

Taking a look at the number of times *not helpful*, *helpful* and *very helpful* had been selected across the full survey. There were a total of 161 responses. 90.7% of these responses had found the learning modules either *helpful* or *very helpful*.

Category label	Code	Count	Pct of Responses	Pct of Cases
Not Helpful	1	15	9.3	75.0
Helpful	2	94	58.4	470.0
Very Helpful	1	52	32.3	260.0
Total responses		161	100	805

10 missing cases; 20 valid cases

In a second phase of testing three experts in the field of IT in Education were asked to examine the strategy. I asked them to use the system and at the same time talk about their experiences, feelings and emotions. This type of research is referred to as verbal think aloud analysis (van Someren M.W. et al, 1994).

The three experts were Dr Bryn Holmes, Ms Valerie Carroll and Ms Catherine Bruen. Dr Bryn Holmes is the course director of the M.Sc. in IT in Education at Trinity College Dublin and has a PhD in Information Technology in Education from the University of Cambridge. Ms. Valerie Carroll and Ms. Catherine Bruen are Educational Technologists at the Centre for Learning Technology, Trinity College Dublin.

All three experts had very positive things to report on the strategy. They highlighted the overall look and feel of the project as been very professional.

Holmes and Bruen both referred to the system as being like your friend or buddy.

> *This would be my buddy. Once I'd learn these 9 or 10 things I'd use them again and again for other assignments.*
>
> (Bruen 2002)

Both felt the students might turn to this system rather than asking a friend. Holmes suggested that this system might not be used as I had first envisaged but that students might be inclined to return to it later for short pieces of help when needed.

Holmes felt a system such as this that laid down what the task was, what standards should be followed and what needed to be done was comforting. She felt a strength of the system was how it was suited to both expert and novice users.

> *Although certain courses might be well suited to beginners and others to experts they tend not to be the same course, but this structure offers this advantage.*
>
> (Holmes 2002)

Holmes felt both novice and expert could use the system in the same room at the same time and while working on the same task. She added that while most people come to a subject with some experience a structure such as this allows them to build on that previous experience and motivates the learner to expand their knowledge.

Bruen said she would find comfort in having a system she could visit and revisit as needed. She liked the fact that the resources were limited to what was needed in order to complete the task and reported having difficulties at times with help systems built into programs.

> *...help never works. I can never find what I am looking for. This on the other hand is tailor made to support the task.*
>
> (Bruen 2002)

On a more negative note all experts reported finding the navigation slightly confusing. The students had been given a run through the system before they had to use it. Carroll suggested that the system relied too heavily on the students having attended this orientation session and that not enough help was built into the system. She suggested prompting the students with some questions such as:

> *Do you need to brush up on your computer skills? Then check out IT Resources.*
>
> (Carroll 2002)

As someone who has worked extensively with the WebQuest strategy she felt elements of the WebQuest strategy had not been utilised enough to guide the student, in particular the Process section.

Carroll also suggested that examples or sample reports that showed what was expected would be helpful. She suggested using the Evaluation Section for this purpose. She would also have liked some way to integrate this program into the task so the students could try things for themselves without leaving the environment.

> *I would like to be able to try this for myself. There should be some way to integrate this into the task.*

(Carroll 2002)

Further Research

I believe that as technology becomes more available to our students and our institutions we have no option but to embrace this new tool and look for new ways to integrate it into our teaching and learning. Firstly our students must know how to use the technology and secondly the technology itself must be seen as a tool for teaching and learning in other disciplines. I am interested in embedding the transfer of IT skills through subject related topics. I believe my new strategy is one possible way of advancing this aim. I based this strategy on sound educational theories of constructivism and closely examined current trends, but I believe I have also pushed out the boundaries in search of something new.

The Department of Information Systems Services are supporting a team, lead by myself to develop a set of resources on using College Computing Facilities that will follow my strategy of delivery and design. These resources will support an already established induction course run by the department for new entrant students each year.

Once developed these resources will also be available to the Centre for Learning Technology for inclusion in projects that support the use of ICT in Education. Projects similar to the Botany project (the pilot for this study) will benefit. All resources will be developed as short modules dealing with specific tasks that can be compiled in different combinations for different contexts and to achieve different learning outcomes. Standards in design and implementation will be set to make the reuse of resources possible.

In order to establish whether or not this strategy is successful, I believe it is necessary to build many more learning objects and to test their use and reuse over several tasks and assignments. Records on how students are using the modules, whether they are building on previously used modules to solve new tasks or revisiting old modules, and establishing what connection they are making between old and new resources, will be necessary. This type of ongoing research will take time and cooperation from a target group of students.

I believe there is also a need to build a specific tool to support the construction of these learning environments. This tool might allow the student or the academic to build their own environments, allowing them to add resources that could be shared and used alongside built-in resources. Such a tool would need to be easy to use both for the Academic and the learner and I believe, should not be tied to any one content type or subject.

References

Dodge Bernie, (2001), *Online Retrieved: April 5th 2002, from the World Wide Web*
http://edweb.sdsu.edu/webquest/webquest.html

Dodge Bernie, (2002), , *Online Retrieved: April 5th 2002, from the World Wide Web:*
http://edweb.sdsu.edu/people/bdodge/bdodge.html

Kane C, (2001) *Online Retrieved: April 5th 2002, from the World Wide Web:*
http://www.cs.tcd.ie/Catherine.L.Kane/meta/essay/index.html

March Tom,(1998) '*Why WebQuests?, an introduction*', Online Retrieved: 5th April 2002 from the World Wide Web,
http://www.ozline.com/webquests/intro.html

Van Ryneveld L, http://hagar.up.ac.za/catts/learner/lindavr/lindapg1.htm *Online Retrieved: April 5th 2002, from World Wide Web*

Wiley, D. A. (2000). Connecting learning objects to instructional design theory: A definition, a metaphor, and a taxonomy.
In D. A. Wiley (Ed.), *The Instructional Use of Learning Objects: Online Version. Retrieved December, 18th, 2001, from the*
World Wide Web: http://reusability.org/read/chapters/wiley.doc

An Analysis of the Capabilities of a Self-study Support System for Network Education

Satoshi KASHIHARA, Shinichi FUJITA, ChunChen, LIN, Ming YIN Seinosuke NARITA
Waseda University
3-4-1, Okubo, Shinjuku-ku Tokyo, Japan
601c0319@mn.waseda.ac.jp

Abstract: A great number of pieces of research are being conducted on introducing computers into conventional face-to-face education to make it more effective. The present writers also have successfully developed a system for language lessons conducted at school as well as for reviewing the lessons. This system has the capability of providing learners with videotaped contents of language lessons, so that they can use them for their self-study. This system, however, has recently been confronted with a problem, which was raised by the learners, of being unable to provide them with excerpted information that they need. Although learners are required to spend more time on reviews than lessons or preparations in order to acquire a foreign language, no effective system for reviews has been proposed yet in reality. This thesis describes the present situation in which school education networks are being used, and also makes an analysis of the capabilities of the aforementioned network-based effective system for self-study, taking the state into consideration.

1. Introduction

Education, including e-learnig, may be classified into two types according to whether or not it is carried out under time constraints; education that is carried out under time constraints is categorized as synchronous education, and education that is carried out otherwise is categorized as asynchronous education. Synchronous-type education refers to education that requires every learner to simultaneously take part in lessons. There are two subcategories of education of this type; interactive synchronous systems, which include SCS (Space Collaboration System) (see [4] below), and pseudo-interactive synchronous systems, which include Waseda Learning Square (see [5] below). SCS is well-known as an interactive synchronous system that networks higher education institutions throughout Japan, including national, public, and private colleges, universities, and technical colleges, by the use of a communications satellite. Asynchronous-type education refers to education that allows learners to study whenever they like under no constraints of time, and includes paper-based correspondence education that used to be popular before the Internet gained popularity as well as WBT (Web-based training).

In the area of educational engineering, research is currently being conducted on asynchronous-type lessons, and there are some groups that are making practical use of this type of education. Education of this type, which allows learners to study at their own pace, is considered to be suitable for self-study for reviewing lessons, self-study that aims to acquire and fix knowledge, and drills that learners are required to do repeatedly. The writers have repeatedly mentioned this type of education has the advantage that it can be carried out under no constraints of time. At the same time, however, the writers cannot avoid pointing out the disadvantages of this type of education. In the concrete, there is apprehension that it may not make learners feel they are participating in lessons for the following reasons; teachers cannot easily grasp the situation with regard to each learner's understanding and learning, and learners cannot easily grasp the situation of other learners, either. Accordingly, this type of education may not key learners up to concentrate their attention on lessons. There is also apprehension that this type of education, which may not allow learners to know the situation of others, cannot easily raise motivation. Although there are some defects in the synchronous-type network education, it is still widely used .

Although the aforementioned synchronous-type network education is widely implemented, emphasis is laid, for the time being, only upon giving lessons through networks without any consideration of its functions. Particularly, there are few systems with a well-examined self-study system that can closely relate lessons to preparations and reviews that learners have to do. The following take the case of the self-study support system that was developed and has been practically used by the writers, namely, EDLIN, in order to discuss how to relate school-based lessons to self-study that has to be done by each learner.

2. The Issue of EDLIN's Self-study Support System

The study group that the writers join developed a LAN-based integrated education support system named "EDLIN" (Educational system Developed for Learning on the Internet and an intraNet), and then has used it practically on the scenes of lessons.

According to the aforementioned classification, lessons conducted with EDLIN are categorized as synchronous-type education. EDLIN is intended for a lesson conducted at a computer room where a teacher and student are each provided with a computer on a LAN to communicate with each other, and aims not only to support the lesson being conducted at school but also to comprehensively help the students do their preparations for lessons as well as review lessons. In order to support the lesson being conducted at school, EDLIN includes various capabilities as follows. First, EDLIN includes the capability of serving as an electronic blackboard, which allows a teacher to input what should be written on a blackboard with a keyboard and then to distribute it to the students via an electronic medium, or the aforementioned network. Second, EDLIN includes the capability of transmitting data files, which allows a teacher to transmit data files necessary for his/her lesson. In addition, EDLIN includes the capability of allowing students to use electronic notebooks through keyboard entry, so that they can take notes of a lesson as they like, and that they can refer to them to review the lesson afterwards.

The following describe the aforementioned self-study system in a little detail. The study group the writers join constructed a self-study system, which aims to help learners do their preparations for lessons and review lessons at home, on a typical information providing system of the Internet, namely, the Web. Any student who has access to the Internet at home can use this Web-based system to do his/her preparations for a lesson as well as to review a lesson whenever he/she likes. This system also has the advantage that it enables those who have developed and used it to keep providing students with the latest version of the system by promptly updating a Web server with modifications made to the system. This is the outline of what the system realized by the writers is like and how students can use the system to do their preparations for lessons and review lessons at home. When the aforementioned system was practically used for preparations for lessons, students could study in advance what was going to be dealt with during the lessons at home or somewhere else by the use of its database system for words and grammar and its system for drills and exercises, both of which were made available to them on the Web by the aforementioned study group.

The system uses streaming distribution technology to provide, on the Web, students with not only videos of the lessons that were actually conducted but also data that was input on an electronic blackboard by a teacher, so that the students can review lessons with them. When the system was practically used, students could review lessons by getting access to the streaming data distributed on the Web. EDLIN includes the capability of synchronizing the images of ideotaped lessons and the text data prepared on an electronic blackboard with a teacher's application as well as the capability of automatically uploading the synchronized data to a Web server. These capabilities make it possible to create Web contents available for review almost automatically, and therefore save the teachers who use this system time and labor. This is an original feature of EDLIN.

Figure 1   window for review in EDLIN

Figure 1 shows a screen that displays the contents distributed by EDLIN. It is a real screen that was used for review. An electronic blackboard and an image of a videotaped lesson, both of which are synchronized, are displayed in the left and right sections of the screen, respectively.

EDLIN, which enables students to review the contents of lessons conducted at educational institutions such as schools by getting access to the Internet, was considered to be a very effective self-study support system. However, there occurred an issue concerning this self-study support system when students reviewed lessons with their electronic notebooks. The point at issue was that the students could not excerpt the part that they needed to watch again. In other words, the students had to watch the whole videotaped lessons from beginning to end in order merely to review the part they could not understand. In reality, the students must have wanted to excerpt the part that they regarded as questionable or the part that was regarded as related to the aforementioned part when they actually reviewed lessons with their notebooks. Taking this into consideration, the writers must admit that this system, which compels the students to watch the whole videotaped lessons when they review, is extraordinarily inefficient. The writers are now determined to construct a better self-study system by drawing upon the analysis that has been made up to the previous paragraph. In the concrete, the writers intend to construct an education system that would be available to lessons as well as self-study through a network. This education system enables students to excerpt the images and sound of the part that is related to what they cannot understand when they review lessons while referring to the notes they took with their electronic notebooks during the lessons. This feature would help the students review lessons efficiently.

3. How a Self-study System for School Education should Function

The writers would hereafter discuss how a self-study system for school education should function, taking into consideration the results of the analysis of the capabilities of EDLIN's self-study system. The flow of a study system for school education can be divided into the following three steps; the first step that corresponds to a preview, the second step that corresponds to a lesson conducted at school, and the third step that corresponds to a review. In learning, each step is so important that any of them must not be skipped. Moreover, each step determines how learners relate to their teachers, how the system helps learners and teachers, and what role should be played by learners, teachers, and the system, respectively. When the self-study system being herein discussed is used in a lesson, it shall help one teacher and a number of students have bidirectional communication smoothly, so that a lesson can be conducted more efficiently. When the system is used for students to make preparations for lessons, it shall help them use their notebooks and skim through their textbooks, so that they can grasp the gist of what is going to be dealt with in the following lessons as firmly as possible. When the system is used for students to review lessons, it shall help them deliberate on what they have taught by their teachers and try to understand on their own. If there is anything ununderstandable to the students, they may wish to listen again to what their teachers have explained in order to get a grasp of it. In this case, the students may not wish to listen to the entire lessons but wish to focusing on what they cannot understand.

Up to now, EDLIN has helped students review lessons on their own by distributing the entire part of videotaped lessons on the Web. This method is very helpful to students who missed lessons and those who cannot understand the contents of the lessons at all and therefore wish to take lessons from beginning to end again. However, this method is not so helpful to students who need to review only several parts that they could not understand during the lessons. As stated before, such students do not need to listen to the entire part of what their teachers explained during the lessons but desire to listen to the excerpted part that they need to review. In order to "excerpt the required part", each videotaped lesson shall be given indexes of the following two types:

1. a time index that can be linked to each time point a student took a note with his/her electronic notebook during a lesson
2. a keyword index based upon the topics prepared by a teacher; this type of index can link each part of the contents of a lesson

Each student can use the former type of index simply by making his/her electronic notebook memorize the time he/she takes a note of a matter explained by his/her teacher. The electronic notebook is designed to record the time a note is taken in such a manner that the aforementioned time corresponds to the time period from the beginning of a lesson to the time point a note is taken. Accordingly, the student can pinpoint when the matter he/she took a note of was explained during a lesson. The electronic notebook has the capability of searching the notes that were taken with it. With this capability, the student can search for the matter that he/she needs to review, pinpoint when it was explained by his/her teacher with the index, and then directly access the applicable part of the videotaped lesson for reference.

The latter type of index is based upon the topics that would suggest what is being explained by a teacher. The teacher prepares these topics, and then marks the applicable part of the videotaped lesson with them, so that each topic can be timely linked to the applicable part of the videotaped lesson.

As stated up to now, it is required to construct a system that would enable each student to efficiently review the part that he/she could not understand during the lesson with his/her electronic notebook or by searching videotaped images for the applicable topic prepared by a teacher. See Figure 2 for reference.

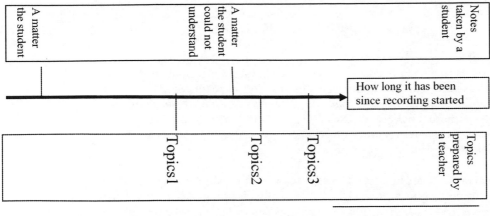

Figure 2 Two Methods of Establishing a Link to Videotaped Images

The following exemplify how the revised version of the present EDLIN is expected to function. The revised EDLIN may provide students with a system that would record each time a note is saved. Every time a student saves a note that he/she took on a matter explained in a lesson with the aforementioned system, the system would record the time, with which the student can establish a link to the applicable part of the lesson contents. The system is also expected not only to establish a link between the text data prepared by a teacher, such as the aforementioned topics, and lesson contents but to have the capability of searching the aforementioned text data. If these expectations are realized, it will become possible for each student to access the lesson contents that he/she really needs through the aforementioned link. As stated before, it is required to construct a system that would enable each student to efficiently review the part that he/she could not understand during the lesson by the use of his/her electronic notebook or by searching videotaped images for the applicable topic prepared by a teacher.

4. Conclusion

In this thesis, the writers have made an analysis of the capabilities of EDLIN, which they developed and have used, in order not only to discuss the importance of self-study as part of school education but also to examine the capabilities of the system that would usefully support self-study. Self-study is a stage of learning that cannot be skipped. It is no exaggeration to say that how efficiently a student can do his/her self-study may determine to what degree the student can understand the contents of a lesson. For the time being, most pieces of research being conducted are focused on how to use networks in order to conduct conventional-type face-to-face lessons at classrooms. Therefore, the writers must admit that there are few systems that relate the contents of lessons to self-study, and also that there are few systems that are constructed on the basis of a learning model of learners. Research on how to introduce computers and networks into conventional face-to-face education may be in the primary stage of the research on e-learning, and research of this kind has already become matured. It is high time for researchers to aim at developing a system that would help learners study with efficiency not only at classrooms but also at home. At the end of this thesis, the writers would conclude the system proposed hereinabove, which may allow learners to make the most of the contents of lessons to study by themselves, not only to keep up with the time but also to be very useful and considerate to learners.

5. References

[1] Makoto Nakayama, Integrated CAI System for Language Education, October 2000
[2] Keihide Kanenishi, Distance Learning in Information course
[3] ChunChen Lin, An examination of the functional capabilities of different user environments in networked classes and the development of a school-based language lesson and self-study system based on this examination, June 2002
[4] SCS, http://www.nime.ac.jp/SCS/index_j.html
[5] Waseda Learning Square, http://www.wls.co.jp/

Although the role of the superintendent is commonly cited as a keystone in school improvement, it is not the traditional role of times past. This presentation puts forth a more encompassing and collaborative perspective on leadership, suggested by Peter Senge (1999), that it is the ability of a group (not an individual) to sustain the purpose it has begun. This session presents the World Wide Web as a conduit through which superintendents can deliver mo re timely, more extensive, and more contextually appropriate resources to their administrative teams and teaching staffs.

The superintendent is not only the organization's chief executive officer for the learning experiences of children and youth, but the motivating agent and facilitator of adult learning for the administrative team, teaching staff, and community. These multi-dimensional tasks demand attention to the informating role that superintendents play for their varied constituencies. Informating, a term coined by Shoshana Zuboff (1988), is a useful concept for professionals who play such connective roles in the learning success of others. In contrast to the automating technologies that make our work more efficient, informating efforts stretch people to think differently about the work they do and then to use technology in improving that work. How then can the educational CEO keep his or her team connected with each other, and with resources that support the district's mission and that reflect "world class" standards?

The presentation uses a conceptual framework based on Rosabeth Moss Kanter's findings about "world class" organizations. Kanter points to three primary factors accounting for this level of successful group effort. They are: 1) improved thinking and problem-solving, 2) improved performance reflected by results, and 3) improved networking of individuals within the organization. She claims that world class organizations whether they are corporate, medical, or educational all support such an amalgamation of thinkers, makers and traders.

This presentation takes these three categories as organizing units from which to explore available electronic resources through which superintendents can connect the administrative and teaching staffs with information to stretch their thinking, improve their performance, and expand their connections to gurus in their field and to each other.

Integrating the web into a superintendents assistive approach to the learning of others exemplifies to a community a "marketing" as opposed to "sales" approach (Schlechty, 1997) to education. The traditional mindset for most organizations is looking at what exists in our warehouses and designing our offerings to reflect an existing product. Like many products, the shelf life of information in education too exceeds its limits. A major dilemma for veteran educators today is that those practices which accounted for their own professional success and the success of their former students grow increasingly obsolete. In both its informative and communicative capacities, the Web enables superintendents to foster a marketing approach linked to best practices and attention to the development of thinkers, makers, and traders, in any organization.

It creates a leadership arena less shaped by policy and bureaucracy and more connected with others on whose success the ability to sustain positive initiatives depends.

The Cost-Effectiveness of an Online Electric Circuits Course

Edward John Kazlauskas
Rossier School of Education
University of Southern California
United States
kazlausk@usc.edu

Hans H. Kuehl
School of Engineering
University of Southern California
United States
kuehl@usc.edu

Lawrence O. Picus
Rossier School of Education
University of Southern California
United States
lpicus@usc.edu

Abstract: This paper describes an e-project in a college-level introductory electric circuits course. Online materials were developed using the Mallard® course management system. The project is acquiring empirical and other data on two critical issues: 1) Whether the course with its substantial online asynchronous components is as effective as a primarily synchronous course; and 2) The comparative costs of the new mode of online instruction, which replaces pen and paper exercises mediated by graders with self-help online instructional exercises and asynchronous online discussion. The project is comparing the modified online version of the course with a traditional version, and the overall design of the project can be considered a pre-test/post-test, control group design with a follow-up qualitative study. The paper then presents initial results of the project.

Introduction

A semester long university-level course on Introductory Electric Circuits establishes a foundation for the understanding that is required in circuit design and includes: an introduction to primitive circuit elements and basic circuit types derived from them; the application of key physical laws (e.g., Ohm's, Kirchhoff's laws) to circuit analysis; and the application of calculus and differential equation skills in analysis of circuit design. There was the recognition that this traditional synchronous course was to some degree "broken." To fix it, the heart of the course needed to be addressed – the paper and pencil homework problems, which are directly or indirectly related to 80% of the course grade and clearly related to student retention and overall success. As a result, an e-component was developed to address this issue.

The Course Management System

The principal software used in the project- is Mallard®, a course management system (CMS). Mallard® and other central CMS software at the university, such as Blackboard®, reside on a robust server serving some 30,000 users. Mallard® is web-based, allowing easy deployment into residential and non-residential environments. As a CMS, Mallard® is similar to others packages, but is especially useful for various types of math problems because it has the mathematical and computational functionality to evaluate and grade most types of problems in this course

The online course materials, the homework, is written in the extended HTML of Mallard®, are intended to replace the cumbersome and unsatisfactory process of solitary exchanges of paper problems with course graders. Online materials have been created that engage students, prepare them for future courses in circuit design, and provide for the potential of improved retention. While the broad content of the online course materials is adapted from a paper text source, the new materials are pedagogically and methodologically unique. For example, the complex equations and other aspects of the problem solutions submitted online by students are evaluated instantly. Further, the online problems are carefully deconstructed versions of the paper originals, which allow students to work to mastery through each element of the problem and at each point are provided detailed and immediate feedback on their mistakes. Students experiment and discover answers themselves and, when needed, have access to email where they can immediately query other students and the instructor for help. Some of the specific features of the online course materials include the following; Capability to program random values into problems so individual students get different numerical values in their problem statements; Immediate evaluation and grading of students' submitted problem solutions and return; Mallard® graded problem scores are automatically recorded; If solution is incorrect, student can rethink the method and submit another solution (10 times without penalty before the due date); Student can then pinpoint more easily where an error lies, and submit a corrected answer; Other student grades, such as exam scores, paper-and-pencil homework scores, laboratory scores, can be uploaded.

Project Description

A project, using the revised e-version of the Introduction to Electric Circuits course, was secured through funding by the Andrew W. Mellon Foundation Cost-Effective Uses of Technology in Teaching (CEUTT) Initiative that focuses on the cost and effectiveness of technology in higher education and whose goal is to identify and disseminate good practices, regarding methods of instruction, and measures of cost-effectiveness. The project is now acquiring empirical and other data on two issues: 1) Whether the course with its substantial online asynchronous components is as effective as a primarily synchronous course with similar material but delivered entirely by a standard lecture, recitation, homework, exam format; and 2) The comparative costs of the new mode of online instruction, which replaces pen and paper exercises mediated by graders with self-help online instructional exercises and asynchronous discussion mediated by the instructor and the students themselves. The plan is to compare the modified online course with a traditional course on the same material, and to measure cost and learning outcomes. The intent is to conduct this comparison working with current and upcoming enrollees in the course (three semesters of data).

The overall design of the project can be considered a pre-test/post-test, control group design with a follow-up qualitative study. In addition, the approach utilizes an entry-level assessment, non-intrusive data gathering throughout the project, post-course assessment, and a follow-retention test. Students in the course are divided into two groups, randomly assigned: (1) Group A and (2) Group B. During the first half of the semester Group A receives training and access to Mallard®, and is known as the 'Mallard group'; Group B is the traditional 'paper' group. In the second half of the semester, Group A no longer has access to Mallard® and switches to be the 'paper' group; Group B then receives training and access to Mallard®, and is the Mallard group. All students receive the same examinations, including the Final. Procedures are established to minimize any leakage across the groups, such as by controlling students' access to Mallard® for only certain parts of the semester. In addition to these two groups, a paper-only group and a Mallard-only group were established to satisfy requests from students who did not wish to partake of the regular 'experiment.' Although the number of students involved in these additional groups is small, the data do provide additional data analysis opportunities.

Data gathering consists of the following. (1) A pre-course instrument intended to measure the students' existing knowledge; a pre-course survey of attitudes; a pre-test instrument intended to measure the students' knowledge of content prior to receiving the course content; a post-test instrument intended to measure the students' knowledge and skill mastery after the course; a post-course attitudinal survey; and a retention test administered at a scheduled time during the semester after the course. (2) Grades on homework and exam; and numbers of time online homework submitted; number of interactions with teaching assistant; amount of time logged-in; etc. (3) But in addition, other approaches may be employed further along in the project, including the use of performance data, such as grades from course prerequisites, unstructured and structured interviews, observations of learners and instructors, examination of student work, and the administration of other instruments. The summative evaluation will consist of the aggregation of data gathered from the three offerings of the course but also emphasizes evaluation in terms of attaining the objectives of the project and of a more detailed analysis of student learning and outcomes.

Initial Effectiveness Results

Results in the Fall 2001 semester from both groups indicate a majority of students were 20-21 years of age (with a range of 19-38); were mostly male; and with English the primary language but with 7 other languages represented. The groups differed in terms of their majors; and a large majority of students were not freshmen or sophomores, although the course is recommended at this level. For the most part, prerequisite coursework was taken or being taken. The majority of students indicated no experience in analyzing or designing electronic circuits. There was variability between groups in terms of the amount of prior experience. A majority had some or a lot of interest in the topics of the course. For the most part students were positive in their self-assessment of the course-related content questions. Data were collected for Spring 2002 and compared to the earlier group. The Fall 2001 groups were slightly younger in age than the Spring 2002 groups, and, although English was the primary language of the majority of students, the Fall 2001 groups exhibited more language variability. Fall 2001 represented electrical engineering and biomedical engineering, and other majors, while Spring-enrollees were mostly electrical engineering majors. Although Fall 2001 students represented a variety of academic levels most Spring 2002 students were second-semester sophomores. A large percentage of Fall 2001 enrollees had not take CSCI 101L, the majority of Spring 2002 students had taken this course. Fall 2001 students exhibited variability in amounts of experience, while the majority of student in Spring 2002 groups had no experience.

Quantitative results for the Fall 2001 semester indicate that Group A and Group B performed differently on the various mid-term exams, but Group B seemed to perform better that Group A irrespective of their use of Mallard® or paper. The combined Mallard® and 'Mallard only' groups performed better overall on Midterms. The Paper Only Group did not perform well on exams when compared to Groups A, B, or 'Mallard Only.' For the most part, the homework grades of the Mallard group were higher. At this point in time, the means are not significantly different between the groups on the homework. For Spring 2002, there were no differences in the test performance of the groups on the same examinations; there was little difference between groups on homework performance.

Various qualitative and other results indicated that interest in the course was intensified. Student felt that it was "them against computer" instead of against the instructor. Some students couldn't sleep until they got the correct answer. The instructor of the course received more e-mail, office visits, and phone calls about homework than ever before. There were much higher homework grades, many were 100%. Students liked the immediate grading and appreciated that they didn't have to wait a week for graded results. If a submitted solution is wrong, students liked being able to resubmit a solution up to 10 times without penalty before the due date. They felt that they learned from their mistakes while reworking problems. The majority of the students think that Mallard® should be continued in the electric circuits course.

Initial Cost Results

This project also has a cost focus. The approach to measuring costs in a project of this nature is to use Levin and McEwan's (2001) ingredients approach. This is accomplished by specifying the "ingredients" of each option considered, and by estimating the costs of each ingredient. Costs measurement is more than simply the expenditures (accounting systems typically report resource flows by object) involved in providing each ingredient, but also includes the concept of economic or opportunity costs (measures of what must be foregone to realize some benefit). For this study, expenditures and costs are being gathered for personnel, and for all other resources. In measuring the cost of personnel, much of the analysis focuses on opportunity costs.

One of the primary costs of development of the Mallard® system was the time of the instructor with an average of 159 hours spent per semester. As anticipated, over time the number of hours spent in development activities has declined. However, it should be noted that much of the development time for the fall 2001 and spring 2002 semesters was due to the study itself. In engineering courses using only the paper and pencil method, students traditionally are given homework solutions after turning in their assignments so they can determine if their methods and resulting solutions are correct or not. On the other hand, in courses using only Mallard® homework, solutions are generally not distributed to students because Mallard® automatically informs them of the correctness of their submitted answers. Assigned Mallard® problems can be used again in subsequent semesters since their solutions are not available from previous semesters. It was decided at the beginning of the study, to furnish homework solutions via the class Web site to both groups, i.e., everyone in the class. –As a result, solutions to all of the Mallard® problems assigned during the semester–are available to everyone in the class and in future classes, requiring the coding of many new problems. The instructor indicated that if all students in the class were using Mallard®, there would be virtually no costs for the development and coding of new problems. An additional development cost is that of teaching assistant time to learn Mallard and to code problems into Mallard. A total of 518 hours of teaching assistant time was spent in development activities.. Individual rates of pay ranged from $7 per hour to $16 per hour. None of the teaching assistants appear to have received tuition remission in addition to their hourly pay for these activities. Note that *no* teaching assistant costs for development were incurred in the actual last two semesters (Fall 2001 and Spring 2002

Regarding instructional costs, allocation of instructor's time during the Fall 2001 and Spring 2002 semesters included preparation of lectures and exams, and coding of problems. As discussed previously four groups existed, thus other costs also includes creating and maintaining three Web sites and a paper-only database as well as shifting students from one format to another during the semester. It was therefore necessary to keep track of and administer four groups instead of two. This cost will be eliminated with the move to a Mallard® only format.

It is in the analysis of teaching assistant time that the most substantial differences in the cost of Mallard® and paper homework become apparent. There was no grading of Mallard® homework but, for example, in the spring 2002 semester, one teaching assistant whose time sheet shows a total of 125 hours in grading for the paper homework grading. If paper homework assignments were eliminated in favor of Mallard®, then most of the grading time would no longer be needed (teaching assistants would still have to grade the tests). Thus, the savings in time – and hence costs.

Data on student time on class activities are also available. Our hope was to compare the time students in the Mallard group spent on class activities to the time other students spent. But, student participation in this data collection activity was limited during one of the semesters, and we are continuing to ascertain the quality of the data by attempting to determine how consistent students were in turning in or not turning in the data collection sheets, and in allocating their time correctly to learning activities.

Maintenance and support costs are also being gathered, such as the Mallard® licensing fees (currently $1,000 per year), installation and maintenance costs, and user support costs (for faculty, teaching assistants, and for students). Unfortunately it may not be possible to get detailed breakdowns of the time spent by computer personnel in supporting Mallard and in providing user support. But it appears that as it relates to the entire university computer operation, the costs are relatively small. In particular, Mallard® is today a stable product that is not upgraded regularly, and is not widely used across campus.

Concluding Comments

The project is gathering data from at least one more iteration of the course (fall 2002); and is securing advice from a project Advisory Board that is reviewing the planning and design efforts, and the results.

References

Levin, H, M., McEwan, P. (2001). *Cost Effectiveness Analysis: Methods and Applications*. Thousand Oaks, Sage.

Acknowledgements

The evaluation efforts of the online electric circuits course was funded by the Andrew W. Mellon Foundation Initiative on the Cost Effective Uses of Technology in Teaching (CEUTT)

Blended Learning at a Leading Executive Education Institute: State of the Practice

Alim Khan
Karen Lindquist
IMD – International Institute for Management Development
Lausanne, Switzerland
alim.khan@imd.ch
karen.lindquist@imd.ch

Abstract: A review over five years has shown the emergence of blended programs – combining face-to-face and ICT at a distance – at one of the world's leading executive education institutes. A review of current practice shows a wide variety of ICT employed in programs. We take a deeper look at how and why ICT is used, through a broad analysis of ICT use in programs, complemented by a case study of a design for a specific program. The analysis reveals that a range of ICT tools have been deployed, and further, that their use differs according to type of program. The case study suggests that rather than the proliferation of ICT tools itself, or the improved technology or bandwidth that accompanies this phenomenon, it is close attention to client business and learning objectives in program design that is driving adoption of ICT in programs.

Making use of ICT in Executive Education Programs

IMD (International Institute for Management Development) is an executive education institute that provides management development programs for middle to senior level managers. For its first few decades of existence, all of its programs were run in classrooms and meeting rooms on its campus in Lausanne, Switzerland, or at client locations. This face-to-face model of high-touch program delivery served the needs of its clients well enough for IMD over the years to be ranked among the leading executive education providers worldwide.[1]

In 1997, IMD began to use Internet and communications technologies (ICT), and especially program websites, to enhance its face-to-face delivery of executive education programs. In their earliest form, these program websites were a convenient repository for depositing program materials. However, it was quickly realized that a flexible solution that offered additional capabilities, especially in peer-to-peer communication, would allow these program websites to develop into a broader platform that would more substantially support learning objectives. Having evaluated leading solution providers' products such as Lotus LearningSpace, WebCT, and Blackboard, IMD chose to develop its own proprietary platform. This custom platform allowed some components that are mostly superfluous in an executive education environment to be eliminated entirely (e.g. grading), and afforded enhancement of others (e.g. tools to allow participants to network and collaborate virtually while not co-located).

The evolution in use of ICT at IMD

Five years on, we knew that use of this platform had increased greatly among programs. We wondered to what extent, and further, sought insight into the variety of ICT tools being used in various program components. Finally, we wondered how program directors, who are responsible for overall program design and execution (including the use of ICT in programs), went about the process of incorporating ICT when designing programs. We followed the creation of a program proposal and present this case study, to address the latter question. Our prior questions lend themselves to a more quantitative approach, and we therefore have gathered and analyzed statistics from log files, program archives, and reports, to provide a view of the use of ICT in programs.

Our overall five-year review showed steady and dramatic growth in the number of programs that have made use of ICT (table 1).

---

[1] e.g. Financial Times rankings of international non-degree executive education have ranked IMD among the top ten providers worldwide since the survey's inception in 1999.

*2002 figures Jan-July only	2002*	2001	2000	1999	1998	1997
Programs supported with ICT	36	42	32	16	2	1

Table 1: Programs Using ICT, 1997-2002

As we have noted above, initially programs used websites consisting of static pages, with content in HTML format and links for downloading content in other formats. To see the richer set of ICT currently in use, we gathered information across all programs during the first half of 2002 which were classified as blended programs, those combining face to face with virtual components (since IMD does not run completely virtual programs, while its face-to-face programs make minimal use of ICT). We examined the program websites, discussion logs, and conducted interviews with the program directors involved. These 36 blended programs represented 40% of all programs conducted by IMD during the period studied.

We classified these programs as either single module or multi-module. In this latter case, there is an opportunity for technology-mediated interaction between the face-to-face modules. We found that there was a variety of ICT tools employed directly (e.g. online chat) or embedded in program activities (e.g. online assignments), and that multi-module programs did indeed make greater use of these tools and activities (table 2).

	TOOLS AND ACTIVITIES	Total	Single	Multi	Total	Single	Multi
	TOTAL PROGRAM POPULATION	36	20	16	100%	56%	44%
TOOLS USED	Content library	28	13	15	78%	65%	94%
	On-line surveys	14	8	6	39%	40%	38%
	Industry Analysis	19	7	12	53%	35%	75%
	Selected research	13	10	3	36%	50%	19%
	Participant-generated content	12	5	7	33%	25%	44%
	Forums	19	5	14	53%	25%	88%
	Chat rooms	4	2	2	11%	10%	13%
	On-line assignments	8	2	6	22%	10%	38%
	Situated project work	14	3	11	39%	15%	69%
	Supplementary CD-Rom	4	0	4	11%	0%	25%
	Community photos	17	5	12	47%	25%	75%
	Electronic follow-up	2	1	1	6%	5%	6%
	Average number of tools used	4	3	6			

Table 2: ICT Tools and Activities Using ICT in Programs, January – July 2002

We indeed found a broad portfolio of ICT in use in programs today: **Content library** consists of the schedule and all readings to be covered throughout the program, as well as logistics information and participant profiles. **On-line surveys** are organizational diagnostic or personal psychometric surveys administered on-line, usually in preparation for a face-to-face module that will include a debriefing of the results of the survey. **Industry analysis** is an online, highly collaborative tool that is part of a process for analyzing an industry and a company's competitive position within it. **Selected research** refers to research reports custom-selected from external commercial research providers. **Participant-generated content** refers to captured, recorded and posted participant-generated learning points and conclusions from learning activities, in electronic text, graphic, or digital image form. **Forums** are asynchronous threaded discussion forums for conversation and constructive debate.[2] **Chat rooms** are a synchronous text chat facility that can be used independently by participants (self-organized) or as part of an organized exercise. **On-line assignments** are problem-solving exercises or assignments that require results and feedback to be posted on the platform as a learning activity in the program. **Situated project work** is a current strategic project, chosen by client companies and carried out by that company's program participants to help these participants meet both learning and business objectives. **Supplementary CD-ROMs** are computer-based training programs that ensure all participants have a basic knowledge of topics such as introductory corporate finance, so that discussions can begin at a higher level than would otherwise be possible. **Community photos** are digital photos taken of participants while they are on campus, working or socializing, and posted on the platform as a reminder while participants are working at a distance. **Electronic follow-up** occurs after the program has ended. Participants share how they have applied new learning in work activities. It typically happens through web conferencing.

[2] We have excluded forums that were made available but not used.

A Spectrum of Blended Learning – From Content to Collaboration

A further exploration of the difference between single and multi-module programs yielded more insights. We found that single-module programs tended to use fewer ICT tools and activities (average 3 per program) and were more focused on content delivery than multi-module programs, which were characterized by project work, an emphasis on collaboration, and used more tools and activities (average 6 per program). Figure 3 below contrasts the emphasis on content and collaboration in both types of programs across selected program components.

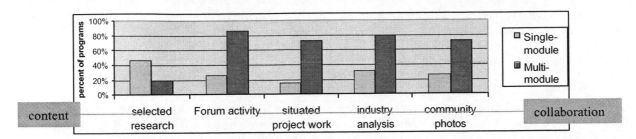

Figure 3: Content and Collaboration in Single and Multi Module Programs

Focusing on forums, we found that the average number of discussion postings in multi-module program forums was higher too, as expected given the greater opportunity to post messages between modules (table 4).

Participants and Discussion forums	Total	Single module	Multi-module
Number of Participants	1691	514	429
Number of Forum messages	2186	169	2016
Postings per participant (average)	1.29	0.33	4.70

Table 4: Average Number of Postings in Discussion Forums

Blended programs at IMD appear to fall across a spectrum. At one end are single module programs in which ICT provides convenient access to content. At the opposite end are multi-module programs in which ICT is also used for collaboration and shared learning. As Figure 5 shows, many programs fall somewhere in between.

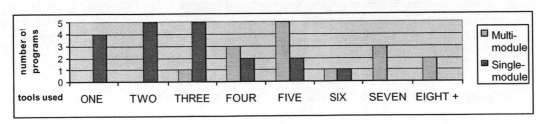

Figure 5: Number of Tools and Activities Used by Program Type

Case study: Program Proposal for a Global Financial Services Organization

With this spectrum in mind, we sought to understand how programs are designed with respect to the use of ICT tools. How does a blended program emerge? To provide some insight, we conducted a case study on a proposed design for a complex multi-modular program.

Background: Client Company's Objectives

The client company is a global financial services company. One of its key objectives is to improve its capability to innovate and implement ideas quickly across organizational boundaries. To achieve this objective, it identified its middle management as needing to develop the following: an awareness of the organization's strategic imperatives; customer-driven thinking as opposed to internally generated thinking; innovative ideas and heir implementation to close the gap between the current practice and strategic imperatives; and improved effectiveness in working in global teams.

To develop its middle managers along these lines, the company decided to partner with a top-tier business school. But the traditional "week at business school" program would not be sufficient to induce deep understanding and the required behavioral change among the target group. Neither could the company spare its managers for long periods of time away from work. Tuition, travel and lodging costs would also be an issue. While the company recognized the value of taking managers out of their daily business routines to be exposed to new ways of thinking, this practice alone was seen as too abstract. Also, the difficulty of transferring, translating, and applying these new ways of thinking to business issues back at the office would remain.

Proposed Approach: "Extending the Learning" Philosophy

To address these objectives given the constraints, much of the learning would be built around participants' business projects. This project component would give meaning to the learning, and participants return to work with immediate "take home value" in the form of progress made on their projects. The use of ICT tools to support collaboration in such an approach would therefore be considered a critical part of the program.

This blended design would also afford strategic awareness, because it would allow for the longer timeframes that strategic considerations often require. Rather than instant but intangible insight, participants could develop an appreciation for strategy as grounded in their own specific business situations. Similar arguments apply to the other objectives, such as customer centred thinking, development and implementation of innovation, and global teamwork objectives. In addition, the cost-effectiveness of continuing to work together at a distance via ICT, without the travel, time, or expense required to meet in person, would allow cost and time concerns to be addressed. Figure 6 illustrates how all of the components would come together.

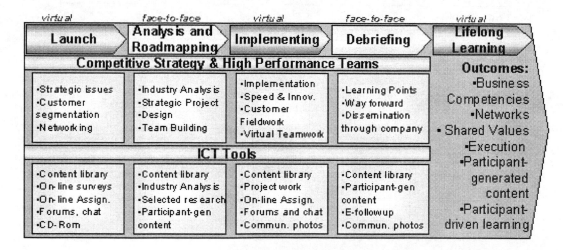

Figure 6: Program Map

Conclusion: Learning and Business Objectives Drive ICT Usage in Programs

From an ICT point of view, the program described above is a good example of selective use of a variety of tools. The program would also have a deep and transformative impact on the organization's management, through extensive collaboration among participants and coaching by IMD through ICT. In this case, the strategic use of ICT in the program design helped achieve challenging client objectives. The proliferation of ICT tools appears to be a response to such demanding client objectives. In this case, it appears that demanding client objectives, rather than a technological focus, are driving adoption of ICT in this program. Anecdotal evidence from other programs and conversations with program directors reveals similar patterns. Thus, we would expect future technological innovations to be adopted not for their ability to replace or enhance face-to-face experiences – but for their strategic fit in meeting client objectives.

Interest Required for Online Courses

Caroline King

School of Computing and Information Technology

UNITEC Institute of Technology,
Auckland, New Zealand
+64 9 415 4321 ex 8659

chking@unitec.ac.nz

Mae McSporran

School of Computing and Information Technology

UNITEC Institute of Technology,
Auckland, New Zealand
+64 9 415 4321 ex 8658

mmcsporran@staffmail.unitec.ac.nz

ABSTRACT

In common with most developed countries, 'New Zealand's learning environment is being transformed by new advances in technology, electronic media and the Internet.' (Beckford and Fitzsimons, 2002) The result is that teachers in this ever-changing environment have to be adaptable. This paper discusses how to keep true to pedagogical strategies whilst managing the technical issues encountered when porting courses to the web.

Our primary aim in education is to facilitate the acquisition of knowledge by our students. Whereas, in the past, lecturers could stand up at the front and deliver a series of notes with an occasional diversion of a discussion, we teachers (tutors, lecturers) today are compared to the "edutainment" industry, where our students are very likely to switch off if not kept entertained. Our colleagues in learning psychology have long ago proved that concentration spans of today's students are reduced and that we must involve our audience. Just as we continually think of new activities in the classroom, we must think of ways to port these to online teaching. As the growth of this area explodes, we must examine the pedagogical strategies that can be used for online teaching.

INTRODUCTION

Use of the new technologies of e-communication, internet access and online courses, is having a profound affect on how society is learning (Bonk et al, 2000) Peer networks, virtual learning space and collaborative learning circles are some of the new techniques being employed. Once the initial mastery of these is achieved, the transformation to teaching online should make us more creative. It is time to look at who adapts best as an online teacher, and the techniques that will enhance the chances of success. The transition for teachers is not simple. Some tend to concentrate on the technology and forget the pedagogy of learning. Some simply hate change, and claim ideals are rarely achieved. Some teachers put a great deal of time and effort into unsuccessful ventures. 'Initial costs in staff time...high and returns are speculative.'(Swindell, 1999).

The role of the instructor is increasingly changing but the aim is the same – to make the delivery methods work for one hundred per cent of the students in one way or another. In a face-to-face class, a good teacher will watch carefully for the facial expressions of affirmation. Online, the affirmation comes through the written communication channel rather than the visual senses.

THE ROLE OF THE INSTRUCTOR

Many instructors are unsure of the online environment. According to De Fazio et al (2000, p 146), 'Academic support is often a complex role requiring a mixture of knowledge of the subject, language and study skills. In addition, there is a people or strong pastoral element that underlies the very nature of the work'. This is difficult enough in a face-to-face situation, but via a computer, 'however, retaining or attaining a sense of human interface between the teacher and the student... can be rather challenging' (De Fazio et al,2000 p 151). Instructors need to be innovative and proactive in the adoption of online strategies and the evaluation of pedagogical strategies. Their role is not just to employ new technologies, but also to maximise the achievable benefits from them. Their role is to prepare the students for the next stage in their learning.

Successful management of background tasks is important if the instructor wishes to enhance the learning. Administration of a web based course brings with it new challenging decisions about resources, tools, partners and markets. Being in love with new technology does not generate new students or class satisfaction. Good old-fashioned passionate teaching enamours students to rave about the usefulness of your course. Boring, non-passionate reading of notes drives them out of the classroom and the same disinterest to online resources results in non-participation, the silent class. If this is a base level course, the flow on effect could jeopardise the offering of higher level courses. Therefore the instructor has an obligation to tailor the use of technology to the course in question. As O'Keefe and McGrath (2000 p 378) state, 'Lecturers need to be aware of the models of teaching and learning which they implicitly or explicitly adopt, and to critically consider the role of technology both in the development of the curricula and the delivery of the material'. Whether online or offline, the interaction between the teacher and learner is a core element of learning. Feedback is required. 'The teacher is an important mediator in the process of constructivist academic learning' (O'Keefe and McGrath , 2000 p 377 citing Laurillard,1993), particularly in e-learning. Discussion boards have been used successfully for many years, but they are not the only tool and tend to be over used. To make this tool viable requires considerable input from the instructor. It is the instructor's role to promote collaboration, a necessary pre-requisite of on-line discussion. If students are not interested in helping others, and cannot see the benefits, the discussions will die. 'This means that a groupware application is not enough for changing the teaching-learning processes.....but simultaneous attempts to change the whole collaboration culture of the classroom are also needed.'(Lehtinen et al ,2000 p 35)

Instructors must take a lead role in the pedagogical strategies attempted in a course, but also need a mentor with whom to discuss new ideas, and preferably one with more experience in online teaching. Continual improvement can only occur if pedagogical and technical strategies that have been successful are repeated or developed further, and those that were less than successful are analysed as to their shortcomings and either discarded or reshaped. For this to happen, course documents providing reflective comments written at the time of delivery or shortly thereafter, must be available. The instructor's role in a course is preparation, delivery and most importantly, reflection, evaluation and improvement, thereby monitoring students' interest and maintaining their own.

STRATEGIES FOR FULFILMENT OF ROLES

Campbell and Hawksworth (1999) point out that the introduction to online learning is important. In our experience a conversational role taken by the instructor allows more participation by the students. Formal or directive statements like an email directing students to discuss their chosen research topic online will result in very few postings other than a declaration of the topic the student is intending to pursue. According to Green and Eves, (2000,p76), 'discussing information that the student is familiar with is essential to the establishment of confidence ... As confidence grows, students become willing to respond to the postings of others ..so the lecturer must bolster confidence during online chats and by the tone of responses to postings' . When online instructors are more interactive and spontaneous and have a genuine concern for the wellbeing of their students, this caring attitude is transferred whether in class or online and results in more interactivity.

Peer assistance should never be underestimated. Instructional conversations can be time consuming but Frequently Asked Questions (FAQs) can be stored and used again and again when appropriate. By actively encouraging the students to participate and by showing a personal interest, the instructor can facilitate the gain of significant advantages for all, by allowing the students not only to post questions, but also to provide answers. However, the postings must be monitored and mediated. The lecturer must not allow incorrect answers to go unquestioned or leave requests for help and challenges to postings to go unanswered. Weekly newsletters can be stored, edited and re-cycled where appropriate. Personalising articles and providing social reporting achieves a familial atmosphere, enhancing learning. (Campbell and Hawksworth, 1999)

One of the easiest ways to avoid overuse of any tool or strategy is to use a graph when formulating lesson plan strategies, drawing attention to usage. Variety is the key as espoused by Bonk et al (2000)

In Class	Online
Ice Breaker 8 noun activity (describe partner)	Ad hoc groups made - same exercise
Peer Feedback Roles Critical Friends	Via email Via discussion "groups"
Reading Reaction Class groups, Case Studies	Discussion Group online
Structured controversy	Whole class discussion (Points)
Brainstorming, Concept Mapping	Use of the Whiteboard (Groups)
Scavenger Hunt (library)	Use the web to get resources
Role Play (paper handouts)	Make script available to certain students. Use "avatar" names
Discussion of sound vision (resources)	Voicemail, video via net (slow) CDs or tapes (digitised)
Guest Experts (in class expensive	Use of new conferencing software

THE PRACTICE OF THE THEORY.

Current tertiary courses use a range of online facilities, with success varying from absolute success to dismal failures. Our study of one successful course with much online content, a second year paper that prepares students for customer support roles in industry, gives an insight into the use of different techniques and strategies. Originally the online resources were used to alleviate the administration load of a Co-operative Education unit, however this course was re-engineered to actively promote online learning within and outside the classroom.

In this course, initial sessions were used to familiarise the students with the tools that are required for online discussions. Blackboard (an online teaching shell) was set up to facilitate class discussions, personal diaries, file management, task completion, course notices and home pages of the student s. Tasks involving collaboration with other students were assigned. These required the use of various technical equipment e.g. scanners, digital cameras and various software, the end focus being on the production of a personal home page and familiarity with the Blackboard utilities. Many different (computer) programs have been used to facilitate collaborative learning making it an important pedagogical tool. (Lehtinen et al, 1999 p16). Very early on, the students were required to conduct online discussions, even though they are physically in the same room. Here the instructor's role was critical. Digital Pictures were used so that participants could have an image of the person they were speaking to. Humour was also used, (cartoons) together with motivational snippets. A heavy focus on sharing resources found on the web was encouraged. To enhance problem solving abilities, small working groups were set up on Blackboard and each group given a similar but different brain-teaser problem. The tools within Blackboard (whiteboard and chat) allowed the participants to draw diagrams and discuss whilst being physically separated. This began in the classroom and continued remotely. The purpose of this non-assessable exercise was to encourage the metamorphosis of the student from face-to-face customer support to remote customer support, the most common implementation nowadays. Weekly tasks were set up in order to evaluate the students' ability to delegate, prioritise and organise. The students were able to view the urgency of a task and monitor/flag their own progress in private, whilst still allowing the lecturer to monitor progress. This was a practice advocated by O'Keefe and McGrath , (2000, p 375 citing Burley and McNaught,1997) 'In online courses it was necessary to retain the high degree of interaction and clarification that face-to-face tutorials provide'

The initial weeks were for the building of a learning community, which then flowed on to become online and supportive whilst they participated in their work-based placement. The use of the online support and social interaction was to raise confidence in their ability to become online commuters, giving them the skills to perform, completely online, other tasks, such as the required organisation of a training day, with no input from the lecturer until the actual training day. Monitoring of the students' communications continued, however, with the lecturer ready to step in if necessary.

All class activities and course documents were put online and visible to the students, except the Lecturer Course Portfolio document. This was a document written after (or updated) each session, providing useful information about the course and the educational context in which it was completed. The instructor's honest reflections were critical, since disasters can be as important as "golden moments". Immediately summarising a lesson overcame academic amnesia. Reading the portfolio before a session avoided pitfalls and boring repetitive teaching. Ideas on the use of appropriate online strategies linked to the student learning needs (after Laurillard), modified through experience by Mae McSporran, are as follows:

Level	Student Learning Needs	Online strategy
1	Motivation & Orientation	Clear and current information
	Information Handling Skills	FAQs, Sharing, Online resources
	Individual choices	Negotiation of topics for study
2	Independent learning Skills	Use of Personal diary, quizzes
	Developing Understanding	Collaborative tasks, problem solving exercises
	Linking theory to practice	Embed Multimedia and simulations, Use Students as mentors
3	Practising Discussion of ideas	Online debates, sharing etc.
	Rehearsing Skills	Interactive activities
	Practising Teamwork	Peer work and actual projects

EVALUATION OF THE COURSE COMPO NENTS

Useful indicators of the effectiveness of the teaching are 'students' satisfaction about how the course was taught and what they believed they learned from it' and 'how a teacher assessed their own teaching' (Yates et al,1999) As promulgated by Yates et al (1999), a high standard of teaching is expected and the process of online teaching is more public and transparent than many anticipate. 'Expectations about what is quality service in providing education are different in a web environment' (Beckford and Fitzsimons, 2002).

The lecturer course portfolio proved to be a valuable resource in providing reflections on both successful and unsuccessful strategies. Comments from this have confirmed the findings of Lehtinen (1999) that the most successful strategies are those involving student collaboration, with timely and constructive feedback and encouragement from the lecturer. From the evaluation of this course and others, it appears that many of the qualities appreciated in face-to-face teaching are also those appreciated in online teaching. The strategy of varying the techniques in the exercises and tasks was instrumental in the success of this course. 'What has contributed to the success of the venture into online teaching has been the adaptations that teachers have made to their prevailing practice.' (Yates et al,1999) The adaptation of in-class exercises to online exercises in the course studied retained the hands-on approach. This required continual monitoring and the workload was not insignificant. However, care and attention to online questions and requests for help and guidance delivered their own rewards, that of effusive thanks from appreciative students. The porting to online of previously face-to-face class intensive lessons in interpersonal skills, and the total online and remotely controlled exercise of the training day have shown that with good monitoring, interaction and genuine interest in the students' progress, unlikely subjects for online teaching can be adapted successfully.

CONCLUSION

In order to improve delivery, documentation of the social, managerial and technological actions that instructors take are just as important as the pedagogical strategies used by online instructors. For this, the lecturer course portfolio or similar is ideal. Online teaching requires as much commitment to the students as face-to face teaching, albeit via a different medium. Appropriate interactivity is the key to success in online teaching. Students need to be allowed to discuss without intervention, unless help is needed. When help is needed, it should be timely and constructive, and this is why the instructors need to monitor the sites closely. Encouraging messages never go amiss. Lecturers always put their own flavour on any lesson, and experienced ones will devise innovative ways of using technology. But most important is the total commitment and interest of the instructor. The successful online instructors have 'built up a reputation for having staff that are enthusiastic about their teaching' (Yates et al,1999). As such, they will have provided variety in the course material and will have taught a useful variety of techniques. Online teaching requires interesting material and interested staff.

REFERENCES

Beckford, N., Fitzsimons,M. (Eds) (2002) *Highways and Pathways: Exploring New Zealand's E-Learning Opportunities*, The Report of the e-Learning Advisory Group, Wellington, New Zealand, March 2002

Bonk, J., Kirkley, J., Hara, N, Dennen., V.,(2000) *Advances in Pedagogy, Finding the Instructor in Post-Secondary Online Learning*, Learning and Teaching Online, New Pedagogies for New Technologies, Expert Seminar, Middlesex University, England, 7 –8th September, 2000 (no page numbers)

Burley,H., McNaught,C. (1997), *Providing Flexibility and Support to students with electronic lectures and tutorials in economics* In McNaught, C. (1997) Conference Proceedings of Teaching with Technology at LaTrobe, pp 31 – 37, Academic Development Unit, LaTrobe University, Bundoora, Australia

Campbell, N. and Hawksworth, L (1999) *The Nuts and Bolts of Learning with the Internet in Indigenous Contexts*, Computers in New Zealand Schools Journal November, 1999, 11,3: 34-37

De Fazio,T., Gilding,A., Zorenon,G.(2000) *Student Learning Support in an Online Learning Environment*, ASCILITE 2000, Proceedings of the 17th Annual Conference of the Australian Society for Computers in Learning in Tertiary Education, Nov 2000

Green,J., Eves,C. (2000) *Structuring Discussions in an Electronic Forum on a Distance Education Course* Short paper, ASCILITE 2000, Proceedings of the 17th Annual Conference of the Australian Society for Computers in Learning in Tertiary Education, Nov 2000

Laurillard (1993) *Rethinking University Education* In Ryan y. (1998). Time and Tide: Teaching and Learning On-Line. The Australian Universities Review, Vol 41: 14-19

Lehtinen, E, Hakkarainen, K, Lipponen, L, Rahikainen, M., Muukkonen, H, (1999) *Computer Supported Collaborative Learning: A Review*, University of Helsinki, online document accessed January 2002. http://www.kas.utu.fi/papers/clnet/clnetreport.html

O'Keefe,S. McGrath,D. (2000) *On-Line Delivery in Higher Education: What Questions Should We Be Asking?* ASCILITE 2000, Proceedings of the 17th Annual Conference of the Australian Society for Computers in Learning in Tertiary Education, Nov 2000

Swindell, J. (1999) *Developing Open Learning Systems: Moving Painlessly from the Classroom to Distance Teaching*, Alt-C99, Proceedings from the 6th International Conference, University of Bristol, September 1999

Yates, R., Campbell, N., McGee, C (1999) *Its not out with the Old and in with the New: The challenge to adapt to Online Teaching*, School of Education, University of Waikato (Private correspondence)

Creating Dialogic Enquiry in an Online Community

Jayne Klenner-Moore, PhD. (ABD)
King's College
Mass Communications & Media Technologies
Wilkes Barre, PA. USA

Abstract: This paper presents ongoing research into creating dialogic enquiry in an online community. There is evidence that the dialogic approach provides for better understanding of key concepts necessary for complex problem-solving in the traditional classroom (Wertsch, 1997). Does this hold true for online communities? Here the research is limited. Wells (personal correspondence, 2002) says that there is a definite potential for this area of research and that he has found that by providing what he calls "activity objects" into the online discourse students have more interesting debates. The problem of enhancing problem-solving skills, becomes increasingly important as we move more and more courses online, or add an online component to a traditional classroom (A blended environment). This paper will provide a model for implementing activity objects into a blended learning environment, and creating an environment that is conducive to dialogic enquiry, knowledge structure, and enhancing problem-solving skills.

Context

The purpose of this paper is to describe findings and observations from ongoing research done in a small liberal-arts college, criminal justice course, working with a blended learning environment. Dialogic enquiry includes a five-step model based on the work done at the inquiry home page site (http://www.inquiry.uiuc.edu/index.php3) (see fig 1.) and includes a combination of the problem-based learning cycle. Activity objects (Wells, 1995) are used to structure the dialogue and provide a goal-oriented activity to engage and promote the dialogue between students and instructor in an online community. This dialogue will mediate the knowledge structuring, which will then enhance problem-solving.

Jean-Paul Bronchart (in Wertsch, Del Rio, and Alvarez, 1995 p. 82) tells us that one of the meanings of mediation can be explained as "discourses formed have the status of open works – works on whose foundations subjects build their understanding of the world". This project was designed to help novice criminal justice students to understand the world of crime scene investigations. What do practitioners do in the field? The online community and dialogue helped students to develop questioning skills that helped build problem-solving skills germane to this field.

Meaningful action is formed by speech, and can be reflected upon by using textual representations such as those allowed for in message boards and chat rooms – features of an online community. "Discourses shape the educative action that is actually carried out within the framework of didactic systems" (Bronchart, 1995 p. 84). The question still remains how to design the activities in an online community that will be most productive in structuring students' knowledge about a subject so that they may become better at solving ill-structured problems. We based our activity objects around real crime scene photographs and allowed students to investigate on their own and with their peers, what those photographs represented. They then reflected on their discussions and were prompted to formulate analyses of these photographs to determine what had possibly transpired, to "solve" the crime.

A goal of this model is to develop optimal conditions for teaching in blended learning community where discourse is a primary ingredient in the blended environment teaching system. In this paper a model for achieving that goal, through the development of activity objects that can be used to spark the online discussion and aid in pushing the students through the enquiry cycle will be presented.

Sign, Symbol, & Language

Language is the medium through which we communicate ideas and come to know about the world around us. It is culturally mediated throughout the lifetime of the individual and meanings change through social interaction. Although, as Engström admits in his discussion of Russian theorist Bakhtin, and Wittgenstein's ideas of language, Activity Theory has only begun to properly integrate the idea of discourse. This model of dialogic enquiry is hoped to integrate Activity Theory and language as the main cultural tool to help students develop better problem-solving skills. In an online community language takes on the form of artifact, as it is now written and may be saved for later retrieval, as well as becoming a tool for reflection. Therefore, in our model for developing activity objects, there is requisite, a place for dialogue, both written text and oral dialogue which may take place in the traditional class as well as online. The forms of which dialogue help for reflection of the culture (Bruner, 1990), as well as reflection of the course content. It is this dialogue which shapes the learning and the construction of knowledge within the community of learners.

Practice

It is with the inclusion of the activity object, which provides for goal-oriented activity, that a community of practice, in this case an online community will stimulate the dialogue and promote knowledge structure. Engström and Miettinen give us the definition of practice as stated by Dewey:

> It means that knowing is literally something which we do; that analysis is ultimately physical and active; that meanings in their logical quality are standpoints, attitudes, and methods of behaving toward facts, ant that active experimentation is essential to verifications. (Deweyin Engström, Miettinen, Punamaki, 1999 p. 6).

Activity theory is concerned with practice as it is the outward exemplification of the outcome of the activity as well as the place where we can study the interaction of culture, division of labor, community, and rules among other things. Practice is one of the biggest areas currently under investigation among Activity Theory researchers.

Developing the Activity Objects

In 1996 King's College began to look more closely at building a "classroom without walls" (Mech conversations, Teagle Grant project). One of the ways that we started this march was through the addition of list serves to the classroom environment. We discovered much to our chagrin that students just didn't talk much online unless the teacher directed them to the discussion. We needed to find a way to "prime the pump, so that students would begin to use the technology to enhance the classroom experience.

What was needed for this course were activity objects that would stimulate the dialogue in the online community and allow for students to follow the inquiry cycle as noted in figure 1, below. The model that we employed brought together the traditional classroom and the online community to facilitate the enquiry cycle.

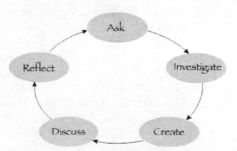

Figure 1 Enquiry Model from: <u>http://www.inquiry.uiuc.edu/index.php3</u>

In the classroom environment, students were introduced to course content and concepts for criminal investigations. They discussed various methods for interpreting what they saw in simulated crime scenes. In this course they became what is often referred to as a "community of practice", (Wenger, McDermott, Snyder 2002) also referred to as communities of learners or COLs (Jonassen, 1999). A community that shares a goal oriented environment. The practice that these students were involved in was the practice of crime scene analysis. The goal for students was to develop problem-solving skills related to this practice.

For the online community we used WebCT where students had the use of chat rooms for discussion, a form of instant messenger, as well as links to course content and the activity objects. Our activity objects were taken from real crime scenes and created on a web page. Students viewed the web page and then went into their assigned chat areas to discuss the photos. You may view the exam page, which includes the crime scene photos and the exam questions at http://www.kings.edu/jkmoore/cj/exam/. [1] Each activity object was developed following the same format as the exam questions. This allowed students to solve novel problems (Jonassen, class notes) using the same mental models that were constructed during the dialogic enquiry phase of the learning experience.

Students then followed the stages of the enquiry model. In this course we utilized a teacher-directed (Barell, 1998) discussion form. Other models will include student-directed, and student-teacher-directed (Barell, 1998) forms of dialogue.

In order to "solve" the problem that is presented by the question, students use the activity object as a tool to ask questions of each other. They begin by *asking* questions about the activity object (photo), then using class notes, other web sites, and the library try to *investigate* information that will help to answer the question. It is during this investigation stage that the students begin to take ownership of the learning process and to synthesize information that will carry them to the next stage (Inquiry Home Page, 2001). In the next stage, *create*; students now begin to formulate a solution using prior knowledge and creativity to come up with the new possibilities for a solution. Now that each student has some idea of what a possible solution may be, there ensues another dialogue where each student presents his ideas to the group, at this point the dialogue take the shape of a debate. And it is here that the social co-construction of knowledge begins within the community. Simultaneously, students are able to *reflect* on their own and others solutions. This then brings our cycle back to the "start" and more questions and dialogues begin.

It is important to note that this process will follow the cyclical routine not once but many times until the problem is solved by the students. In addition, each domain will require that the instructor who wishes to employ this system study the community of practice from which this domain springs.

Future Explorations

At King's College we will be continuing the work with two additional courses in the criminal justice department to test the validity of our instruments and the specific form of dialogic enquiry which will work best online. In addition we have enlisted the aid of several different departments to test this theory and model across domains. We will be developing activity objects for courses in accountancy, philosophy, theology, history and mass communications. It is our hope that a model for development can be made available to all departments on campus who utilize an online community in any form.

References:

Barell, J. (1998). PBL: An Inquiry Approach. Arlington Heights, IL. SkyLight Training and Publishing, Inc.

---

[1] Plese be advised that these are very graphic photos and may cause some distress to the viewer. And please only use my office phone if you wish to contact anyone regarding questions on this site.

Bronckart, J-P. (1995).Theories of action, speech, natural language, and discourse. In J.V.Wertsch, P. Del Rio, A. Alvarez (Eds.), *Sociocultural Studies of Mind* (pp. 75 – 91). Cambridge: Cambridge University Press.

Bruner, J. (1990). *Acts of Meaning*. Cambridge, MA: Harvard University Press.

Engeström, Y., Miettinen (1999). Introduction. In Y. Engström, R. Miettinen, R-L, Punamaki (Eds.), Perspectives on Activity Theory (Learning in Doing: Social, cognitive, and computational perspectives) (pp. 1 – 18). Cambridge: Cambridge University Press.

Inquiry Home Page: was retrieved from http://www.inquiry.uiuc.edu/index.php3 on 20 August 2002.

Jonassen, D.H. (1999). Designing Constructivist Learning Environments. In C. M. Reigeluth (Ed.), *Instructional-Design Theories and Models, A New Paradigm of Instructional Theory Vol II.* Mahwah, NJ. Lawrence Erlbaum Associates, Inc.

Wegner, E., McDermott, R., Snyder, W. (2002). *Cultivating Communities of Practice: A Guide to Managing Knowledge*. Boston, MA. Harvard Business School Press.

Wells, G. (1999). *Dialogic Inquiry: towards a sociocultural practice and theory of education*. Cambridge: Cambridge University Press.

Wells, G. (in press) Dialogic inquiry in education: Building on Vygotsky's legacy. Invited presentation at NCTE, Detroit, November 1997. To appear in C.D. Lee and P. Smagorinsky (Eds.) *Vygotskian Perspectives on Literacy Research*. Cambridge University Press.

BUILDING THE LEARNING COMMUNITY THROUGH TEAMING AND TECHNOLOGY

Cheryl S. Knight, PhD., Director
Dianne B. Barber, Ed.S., Coordinator

Adult Basic Skills Professional Development
Appalachian State University
Boone, North Carolina 28608

ABSTRACT

The Adult Basic Skills Professional Development Project (ABSPD) is a collaborative effort between the North Carolina Community College System and Appalachian State University. ABSPD is committed to enhancing the quality of Basic Skills instruction in North Carolina through providing relevant, timely, accessible, and effective professional development for program faculty and volunteers, create a cadre of Certified Resource Specialists, and develop better instructional skills for the classroom in community colleges and community-based literacy organizations. ABSPD accomplishes this mission by using a team approach to produce multi-media train-the-trainer materials and workshops to build a successful learning community. The presentation will model the teaming approach used to produce training materials. Samples of project media will be featured.

INTRODUCTION

The Adult Basic Skills Professional Development Project (ABSPD) began in 1988 as a one-year project funded by the North Carolina Community College System. ABSPD is housed at Appalachian State University in the Department of Curriculum and Instruction. It is now in the 15th year of providing state-of-the-art professional development to enhance the quality of Basic Skills instruction in North Carolina through building the capacity of community colleges and community-based organizations to provide relevant, timely, accessible, and effective professional development.

ABSPD uses the team approach to produce multi-media train-the-trainer materials and workshops to build a successful learning community. This paper presents the teaming approach used to produce multimedia in a train-the-trainer program to enhance a collaborative teaching effort in the learning communities of community colleges, higher education, and literacy-based organizations.

THE TEAM

The ABSPD team consists of four full-time, one part-time and two graduate students team members housed at Appalachian State University. Each member plays an indispensable role in the planning and production of training media and events. The team meets twice a year with an Advisory Board and consults with the State Office Basic Skills staff on a regular basis. The team meets weekly to discuss progress and future goals.

THE TEAM APPROACH

The planning and production of training media and events is a team effort in which each member plays an indispensable role. From the brainstorming of ideas for content and layout to the final evaluation, each team member makes significant contributions. When the Advisory Board request a training product the team begins reading, generating ideas, and taking notes. The team members convene to share thoughts as they piece together the puzzle that will result in a quality media production. Next one team member takes primary responsibility for writing a script, outlining a plan, or putting structure to the project. Rough drafts are distributed to the team for editing, changing or rewriting. The team meets in a seminar to discuss the draft and add ideas for incorporating graphics, sound, video or other media enhancement to the product. The input is then incorporated into the writing of the next draft while team members, among their other responsibilities, video tape scenes, search for graphics, music, etc. After several meetings to present findings and refine the script, it is time to work on the artsy domain, the designing of storyboards and preparing mockups to provide a visualization of the training concepts. Again the team convenes to give feedback, each member contributing questions and answers from his or her own prospective.

Now is the time to begin the media product, but again the team effort is imperative. From experience, we have learned that waiting to view until the product is thought to be complete is a poor procedure. Too many changes must be made and often they seem to constitute a total makeover. The ABSPD team meets at least weekly to view progress, redesign, discuss changes, and reach consensus on acceptability. Often between meetings emails are circulated requesting feedback on a frame, a video clip, selection of graphics, or any other detail that impacts the quality of the media.

At last edits are complete. Time has come for the grand showing. The team gathers to view the culmination of our collaborative efforts, be it a video or the opening of an institute. As the event begins, we witness ideas come to life as the product unfolds on the screen capturing its audience through sight, sound and touch.

THE TRAINING

Multi-media productions include videos and CD ROMs. The training videos are accompanied by a manual and viewing guide. Annual institutes provide training in techniques of professional development, cutting edge research, integration of skills with a contemporary theme, and an infusion of technology. The ABSPD project plans and presents regional, individual community college and literacy organization workshops in which multimedia programs dominate. In addition, the ABSPD team publishes quarterly newsletters, maintains a current web page, presents at professional conferences, and consults with basic skills professionals throughout the United States.

During 2001-2002, training for professional development and other major activities consisted of the following:

- Developing technology support through video productions and web page accessibility;
- Writing Instructor Training Manuals;
- Producing a CD ROM;
- Providing assistance in planning and presenting professional development with community colleges, community-based organizations and Basic Skills programs;
- Designing the 2002 Summer Institute, "Focus on Cultural Awareness Through Writing."

The ABSPD team produced three videos emphasizing GED 2002: Writing and Reading, Social Studies and Science, and Mathematics and the Scientific Calculator, featuring information necessary to properly teach for successful completion of the GED 2002 Test. Each video begins with a history of the GED and information applicable across testing areas. Videos are designed for use both in individualized professional development and formal group training. They present complete information for preparing an instructor for teaching adults in GED programs. Integration of critical thinking in all skills and academic areas is emphasized. A printed viewing guide accompanies the videos to enable interaction and processing of content in both individual and group settings.

The project team published a three volume series, <u>Adult Basic Skills GED Training Manual</u>, coordinated with the video series. The manuals contain a narrative chapter, lesson plans, glossary and resources, all compiled in 3-ring binders for easy use.
Because instructors must apply generic skills and information across the curriculum, chapters entitled "Critical Thinking" and "Adult Characteristics" are included in all three manuals. For each content area the narrative and lesson section can be pulled out and used individually. The lesson sections contain suggested activities that teach content and skills. They are not intended to be inclusive, but do model integrated multi-level instruction, a model that must be implemented in our adult classrooms if students are to learn to think critically and make application both on the test and in life.

The ABSPD team wrote and produced a CD-ROM that focuses on using the scientific calculator. The first section introduces the calculator as a tool. The second section teaches the use of the calculator to perform basic and intermediate functions. The third section teaches the use of the calculator to perform advanced functions. Practice is provided for each key. The CD-ROM is designed to train instructors in using the calculator with Level I Basic Skills through Adult High School math students. Instructors can also adapt the CD-ROM for student use.

The team collaborates with the North Carolina Community College System office to provide assistance in planning and presenting professional development for community colleges. We consult with national projects, state programs, and community-based organizations. The team incorporates technology to provide training through a Certified Resource Specialist Retreat and numerous GED 2002 workshops. This year we presented formally and informally at conferences using multi-media, shared media products with other programs across the United States, and made ABSPD products available for purchase outside North Carolina.

The team collaborated to design the 2002 Summer Institute, "Focus on Cultural Awareness Through Writing" for 120 directors, instructors and literacy volunteers. Due to the North Carolina budget crisis, it was cancelled May 9, two weeks before the Institute was to begin.

The rapid shift of societal expectations for home, school, and community has placed a heavy focus on technological changes that allow faster and more efficient communication. As all of us become more dependent on technology as a communication tool, educators recognize the impact technology has on instructors and their students. Meeting the challenge of technology requires a respect of each team member's expertise.

The ABSPD web page is available on the Internet. It provides immediate information about the ABSPD project and Adult Basic Skills education across the state and country. New and updated information is continuously added to the site. For convenience and efficiency, it is linked with the North Carolina Community College Literacy Resource Center and other literacy locations.

The Impact

Impact on the community college Basic Skills programs and community-based organizations provided by the ABSPD Project as communicated by directors and participants includes the following:

- Provides participants with the competencies for conducting on-site training
- Provides quality training in areas of need
- Enriches instructors' knowledge of instruction
- Provides individualized training
- Mentors colleagues
- Organizes professional development opportunities
- Teaches trainers how to customize training
- Conducts training in new instructor orientation
- Prepares instructors for leadership roles
- Provides specific instruction on teaching the adult learner
- Motivates increased learning, informed teaching and collaboration
- Builds confidence in trainers and instructors

A survey, conducted annually, request respondent to rate the usability of the materials produced by the ABSPD team. The respondents rate the products as meeting their training needs. Several directors left blank the columns for advanced technology related training products indicating a need for greater support, referring to adequate hardware, software, and training, in using the web and CD-ROMs as training devices.

CONCLUSION:

Collaboration between ABSPD and the North Carolina Community College Adult Basic Skills staff provides multiple ideas and approaches that otherwise would have never been voiced. The synergy generated verifies that ideas added to ideas generate a sum greater than the parts.

Morph Chat: A Multimodal Instant Messaging System[1]

Nupura Kolwalkar
Auburn University
Human Centered Computing Lab
Computer Science & Software Engineering
107 Dunstan Hall
Auburn, AL 36849 USA
nupura@eng.auburn.edu

Juan E. Gilbert
Auburn University
Human Centered Computing Lab
Computer Science & Software Engineering
107 Dunstan Hall
Auburn, AL 36849 USA
gilbert@eng.auburn.edu

Abstract: The acceptance of Instant Messaging Systems (IMS) is increasing within the outreach education community with the growing popularity of distance learning. Instant Messaging Systems such as WebCT chat (2002) have become a part of distance learning in many schools in America. Morph Chat, a multimodal IMS, is the next generation of instant messaging. It is multimodal in the sense that it makes use of audio as well as visual communications to convey information to the users. The research described below, talks of a multimodal IMS, which uses animated agents (Johnson 2001) as the virtual representatives of users.

Introduction

Instant Messaging Systems (IMS) are the ideal means of communication for short and focused queries where an answer is needed quickly. With instant messaging the user knows before asking a question that the recipient is available to answer. IMS lead to instant feedback versus the traditional e-mail where, a question is asked and then answered possibly at a later time. The answer may result in another question. Getting to the final answer may take some time. With instant messaging, the user's question is answered in real time so s/he can quickly respond and get the final answer. This platform has proven to be crucial in distance learning environments such as WebCT chat. These IMS give the enrolled students a virtual presence out of the classroom. It is more interactive than video taped classes since it gives the outreach students a chance to interact not only with the professor but also with their classmates. However current IMS are text based and require constant user attention.

Traditional instant messaging has been deployed as a textual dialogue. Then came the computer-to-computer and computer-to-phone vocal conversations, where users were allowed to make calls from the computer to another user's computer/telephone and talk via computers. This system needed extra hardware, i.e. microphone. A close observation of the existing IMS show that none are multimodal interfaces.

Multimodal Interfaces

Traditional Web browsers visually render Web pages written in HTML, and user interaction is primarily done through the keyboard and a pointing device such as a mouse, roller ball, touch pad or stylus. In contrast, voice user interfaces, present information using a combination of synthetic speech and pre-recorded audio, and allow interaction using spoken commands or phrases. The input options are speech, keypads and pointing devices and electronic ink. The output options are speech and audio, plain text and visual displays. By using two or more of these input and output options a multimodal user interface is created.

Multimodal interfaces can be exploited a few different ways. A couple of them are:

- **Usage of more than one output mode to present complementary information**: In many cell phones, voicemail notification is done using a certain pre-set beep as well as a graphic showing an envelope opening or closing. This presents the same information using two different modes.
- **Choice of selection between different modes depending on the context**: Cell phone users are given two options to send a textual page. One is to type in the message using the keypad or call a call center and speak out the message, which will be typed in by a representative as text to be sent to a specific user(s). So users can switch between modes of input depending upon convenience and necessity.

Morph Chat — A multimodal interface

The two output modes used by Morph Chat to communicate information are visual and auditory. The visual output mode uses text messages and facial expressions. The auditory output mode uses synthetic voices through text -to-speech. Upon entry into the Morph Chat system, users will be prompted to select a random name to use as an identity for sending messages. When the user selects the name and enters the system, s/he is prompted to select a persona from a pop-up window. The user will see the controls of the chat outlet in the parent window are disabled. The user has to select a persona from the pop-up window to be able to send instant messages. As soon as the user clicks on an image representing a persona, this pop-up window is closed and the initially disabled controls in the parent window are made active. At this state the user can send and receive messages to/from the other users who are online.

As users log in, the persona representing them will come up to tell all the other users, that this person has logged in.   At the same time a green box will be added to a set of similar boxes to announce the arrival of the new user, David (see figure 1). These boxes represent the chat names of the users and default to the color red.

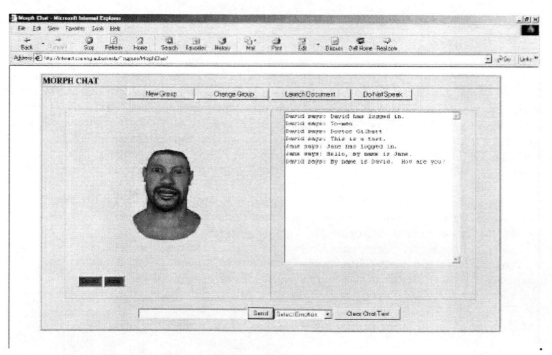

Figure 1: Morph Chat Interface

Users send messages by typing in text and pressing the Send button or the return key. When David sends a message, the persona that represents David appears on every users screen and speaks the typed message on everyone's screen. To use this application, users need not be pre-registered.

Figure 1 and Figure 2 show a conversation between two users David and Jane. David logs in first and then Jane. Jane's login is announced. Figure 2 shows Jane represented by the persona she selected. A green box with Jane's name on it indicates that Jane is talking at the moment.

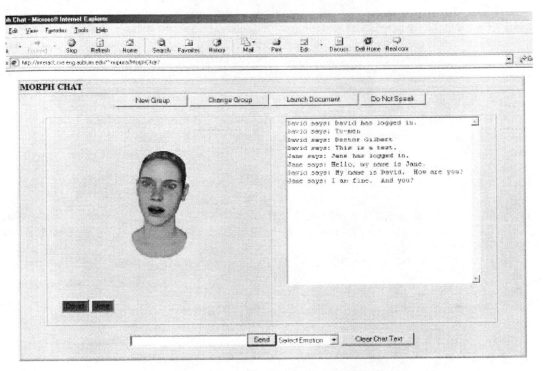

Figure 2: Morph Chat Interface

The Morph Chat system does not require extra hardware for use. The users do need to download Haptek plug-in to be able to send instant messages. Haptek has provided a free version at http://www.haptek.com. If a user does not have this software, Morph Chat offers a download option from within the application window.

Morph Chat – The Architecture

On the server side of the Morph Chat application, a database stores all messages. Though the users are not expected to pre-register and provide personal information, the identity can be proven through the IP address of the workstation used. Hence it is very important that the users know that privacy is restricted. This application is completely time dependent. Each user's action is time stamped. Every message, emotion and/or document sent across from one user to all the other users becomes a row entry in the database. Each entry has a time stamp. The table is sorted in descending order with the latest time to be the last entry. Messages are selected based upon their time stamp every two seconds or when the client side message queue becomes empty.

At the client end, there are two local queues, which get data from the server: the user queue and the message queue. The user queue contains the data of all the user names of the users currently logged in. This queue is locally parsed into each individual name, which is then displayed as a green box on each user's screen. The message queue contains the user name, the persona ID, the message to be sent, emotions and the Web document address of a Web page to be launched on each user's machine. A variety of functions parse this queue in the order of the data received. First the persona representing the sender of the message is displayed, then the green box turns red, the persona speaks the message, expresses the emotion if any and last the message is displayed in the text area of the application. This process is recursive in its functioning until all the messages in the message queue are processed. When all of the messages are processed, the client's machine will go to the server to retrieve more messages. If there are no messages in the database queue, the client will check for messages every two seconds.

Conclusion

As Instant Messaging Systems (IMS) increase their presence in distance learning environments, Morph Chat will prove to be a crucial tool as a multimodal IMS application. Morph Chat will give users an opportunity to choose between the modes of communicating and thereby reduce the stress of constant user attention. Users can listen to the messages sent by an instructor in addition to reading the messages. The Morph Chat interface provides users with an interactive, animated instant messaging environment that proves to be entertaining as well as effective.

The important features and usability of the Morph Chat system will be clearly demonstrated during the presentation. The presentation will include a demonstration of the Morph Chat environment with multiple participants. The architecture and implementation will be discussed during the presentation as well.

References

1. Johnson, W.L., Rickel, J.W., and Lester, J.C. Animated Pedagogical Agents: Face-to-Face Interaction in Interactive Learning Environments. *International Journal of Artificial Intelligence in Education 11* (2001), 47-78.
2. WebCT. (2002) WebCT.com. [Online]. Available: http://www.webct.com .

[1] This research is supported by the National Science Foundation grant #EIA-0085952.

A Unified Content Strategy for Learning Materials

Pamela Kostur
Senior Consultant
The Rockley Group
Toronto, ON Canada
kostur@rockley.com

Abstract: A unified content strategy is a repeatable method of creating consistently structured content for reuse, managing that content in a definitive source, and assembling it to meet diverse needs. A unified content strategy applied to learning materials means that you can serve the needs of different learners and learning objectives, and potentially, deliver dynamic content adapted to learners' unique styles and objectives. You can also unify learning materials with other information products such as brochures, reference manuals, and user guides, so you write content once and use it wherever it is required.

What is a unified content strategy?

A unified content strategy is a repeatable method of creating consistent content for reuse, managing that content in a definitive source, and assembling it to meet diverse needs. A unified content strategy applied to learning materials means that you can serve the needs of different learners and learning objectives, providing learners with content adapted to their unique style and objectives. A unified content strategy also connects authors throughout the organization, allowing content from one area to be used in materials created in another area and reducing authors isolation, creating content that other authors may also be creating content for.

In a unified content strategy, all information requirements are identified up front (e.g., learning content, objectives, evaluation, instructor's guide, supplementary materials). Content is broken into "elements" or reusable learning objects (RLOs) that are stored in a single source or location, such as a database. Elements are identified by metadata describing such things as what objectives they satisfy, who the intended audience is, the information product in which they belong (e.g., student guide or instructor's guide) and the type of learning they support (e.g., receptive, guided discovery). Once elements are defined and described, they can be used wherever they are required. Elements can also be published dynamically to support learners' individual needs (such as experience, language, learning style) and to respond to how well they are doing as they progress through the materials.

A unified content strategy also means that learning materials can be "unified" with other information products such as brochures, reference manuals, and user guides. Elements that are used in the user and learning materials can be pulled from the database and reorganized into marketing materials such as brochures, press releases, and customer demonstrations. In this way, wherever the same content is used, it is consistent. For example, while analyzing one organization's materials in an attempt to unify content across nine different courses, we found four different definitions of the same term, in all nine courses. In another case, we discovered a course description in a brochure that differed significantly from the course description provided in the actual course. These kinds of inconsistencies can result in confusion (caused by students learning incorrect information), they can damage your organization's reputation, and they can also result in accidents and law suits.

Benefits of a Unified Content Strategy

A unified content strategy is a coherent content strategy. Organizations can rely on content being the same wherever it appears, providing both internal and external customers with a consistent message, brand, and accuracy. No longer do organizations have to worry about contradicting themselves with differing information; where duplication occurs, it is the same content. Additional benefits include faster time to market, better use of resources, reduced costs, and improved quality of content.

Faster time to market is achieved through shorter content creation and maintenance cycles. Authors spend less time repeatedly authoring content because they reuse existing content wherever possible, supplementing it where appropriate. For example, the steps that appear in a product user guide can become the same steps in the training materials, supplemented with objectives, examples, and exercises. Reviewers also spend less time reviewing content because they only have to review the content that is new or changed; content that has already been reviewed and signed off doesn't need to be reviewed again. In the case of reusing steps from user guide to training materials, reviewers would only have to review the steps once instead of in two different places—after all, they're the same steps.

In a unified content strategy, you make better use of your resources because the repetitive processes of creation and maintenance are reduced. Because they are required to do less repetitive work, everyone involved in the content creation process can do more value-added work or respond to new requirements. For example, instead of cutting and pasting materials from one document into another one (e.g., from student workbook to instructor's guide), authors create the reusable element once and use it wherever it is required. When they have to update the reusable element, authors don't have to search for all the places it appears. Instead, the element is updated automatically (or, depending on the technology to support your unified content strategy, authors are notified when an element they have reused is updated). Because the often tedious work of cutting, pasting, and tracking content is reduced, authors can spend their time on what they do best—supporting learners with good learning materials.

Because repetitive tasks are eliminated, the costs of creating and managing content are also reduced. Less work is required to get a product to market, not only decreasing internal costs, but potentially increasing revenue. Content is modified or corrected once instead of multiple times, reducing maintenance costs. Translation costs are also reduced because reusable content is translated only once instead of multiple times.

A unified content strategy even helps to improve the quality of content. Content is clearly modeled for consistent structure; increasing its readability and usability. Most importantly, content is accurate and consistent wherever it appears. Issues of inaccurate content, inconsistent content, or missing content are reduced or eliminated.

A unified content strategy also supports SCORM (Sharable Content Object Reference Model), an initiative of the ADL (Advanced Distributed Learning Network) whose primary goal is to provide high quality instruction anytime, anywhere, tailored to individual learners' needs. SCORM accomplishes this by modeling information for different uses and ensuring individual components comply with certain standards for reuse. The SCORM standard is an XML-based industry formalization of the concept of single sourcing. It is similar to the information modeling approach we follow in our unified content methodology.

Applying a unified content strategy to learning materials

To apply a unified content strategy to learning materials, you need to figure what content your learning materials consist of, determine everywhere that content is used and can potentially be reused (within one course, across courses, as well as across other information products), then build a model that supports sound instructional techniques as well as content reuse.

The pedagogical model

Effective instructional design includes three components: prepare (read/view material), do (perform learning activities), and reflect (consider what was learned; apply skills). To develop a pedagogical model that supports these components, you need to:
- Define information types and the learning architectures appropriate for the materials
- Define and incorporate interactivity
- Design learning activities
- Create a course structure that guides learners through the materials, allowing them to work through the materials in a manner best suited to their needs and the type of information they are learning

The unified content component of the pedagogical model requires that you go beyond building a solid course structure. Added to that structure is metadata, indicating in which course or courses each RLO belongs, as well as what type of learning it supports and which learning activities will be used to support it.

Types of information and learning architectures

Information type refers to the content's purpose. Two primary types of information are:
- Near-transfer – methodical, done the same way each time, such as a calculation
- Far-transfer – analytical, done differently depending on situation; similar concepts applied to different situations

Learning architecture refers to the way in which instruction is designed, at a macro level. The learning architecture describes the overall approach to the materials. The four learning architectures are:
- Receptive

- Behavioral
- Guided discovery
- Exploratory

In a unified content model, you tag elements as receptive, behavioral, guided discovery, or exploratory materials and delivering them to support the types of information and learners they are best suited for. In a receptive architecture, learners absorb knowledge and skills from listening to a lecture, watching a video, or reading text. Learners take information in, but there is no externally prompted interaction. Information is presented in text sequences, examples, analogies, visuals, etc. Receptive learning can cause cognitive overload (especially in learners with poor metacognitive skills) if other learning strategies aren't incorporated with it. It's good for building up a good source of information, but—especially for novice learners—it must be balanced with other approaches to ensure the information is absorbed into LTM (long term memory).

The behavioral architecture assumes that learning occurs by a gradual building of skills and information, strengthened by interactions imbedded into the instruction. Learners are provided with small chunks of instruction (basic to complex), followed by an interactive session after each chunk. This approach is widely used in computer-based learning. It manages cognitive load and encourages encoding of information into LTM through frequent interactions. It works very well for teaching procedural (near-transfer) information. However, it's sometimes tiring for learners with more experience. Also, by providing metacognitive regulation, learners don't get an opportunity to build their own metacognitive skills.

Guided discovery emphasizes the building of unique knowledge through case-based learning. Guided discovery is a more "constructivist" approach to learning; the instructional materials provide learners with the resources and experiences required to construct new knowledge. The emphasis is on construction instead of acquisition (which is the basis of the behavioral architecture). Learners are provided with a realistic problem or scenario, and access an array of resources to solve the problem. Guided discovery works well for far-transfer information, but it demands that learners have good metacognitive skills. However, it also helps learners to develop their metacognitive skills and to transfer their knowledge to the "real world".

Exploratory learning accommodates higher learner control. The assumption is that learners (especially in an internet environment) will access the information that best suits their needs. Depending on the amount of information to explore, overload can result, but keeping topics brief and adding frequent, optional practice, can help to manage the cognitive load. Exploratory architecture works well for both near- and far-transfer information, with other strategies employed within the architecture. However, the danger is that learners get lost while exploring. It also assumes that learners have the metacognitive abilities required to make the right learning choices.

There is rarely pure implementation of a single architecture. A combination of architectures is usually required to accommodate varying abilities, balance cognitive load, encourage learners to develop their own metacognitive skills, and teach different types of information (near- and far-transfer). With a unified content strategy, you can outline a number of different learning activities to support various learning architectures, types of information, as well as learner preference.

The unified content model

A unified content model should indicate how architectures will be combined, using metadata to indicate not only which course a learning object belongs in (as well as which other information products it can be used in, either identically or derivatively), but also, what type of learning (and learners) it supports and what learning activities will be used to support it. For example, in a recent project, we were tasked with building a model to accommodate nine different courses that were being moved online. During our initial analysis of the paper-based materials, we discovered much repeated material within courses and across courses. Sometimes, the repeated versions of content were inconsistent from course to course, and even within a course. In fact, learners often complained about the repetition and the inconsistencies. We determined that by reusing elements, we could reuse approximately 35% of the content and potentially, eliminate unnecessary repetition, making the courses more consistent and easier to work through.

The unified content model we developed for this project tells authors how each course should be constructed (hierarchically, based on the pedagogical model and type of information), what an element is (e.g., topic heading, learning content, learning activity, objective, knowledge check question), all the places where that element belongs, and which supplementary information should accompany it. Accordingly, the model includes metadata that describes in which course an element belongs (output) as well as additional descriptors, such as how well learners must "master" an element. (Metadata is simply information about information; in a unified content strategy, it allows authors to provide additional information about how an element is used and to track it.)

The metadata representing "output" tells authors (and the database in which elements are stored) where to publish a particular element. When developing storyboards for learning materials in which content is reused, we include a field for the metadata; authors simply enter the metatags representing the courses in which an element belongs. Metadata to identify output is critical in unifying content beyond learning materials. The same content can appear in a number of different places (e.g., the instructor's guide, the brochure) with more or less detail. Metadata defines everywhere that content will be used.

Additional metadata may not affect output (i.e., where an element is published), but it can be used to provide further information about each element. For example, some elements have to be learned at a particular "mastery" level. While the mastery level does not affect the output, it's essential to identify so that authors can tie evaluation directly to mastery level. There may be three mastery levels, all of which appear in one course. To pass the course, learners may have to acquire general knowledge of one topic (mastery level 1), but must have more applied knowledge of another topic (mastery level 3). Both topics, however, appear in one course. The element that requires mastery level 1 must be taught and evaluated at level 1; the element that requires mastery level 3 must be taught and evaluated at mastery level 3. By identifying mastery level as metadata, authors can easily identify what type of evaluation and learning activities to provide for each element. Further, if mastery levels must change, authors can quickly find all elements tagged with a particular mastery level and update them accordingly. Additional metadata may include such things as:

- Type of information
- Type of learning activity
- Learning architecture it supports
- Date
- Author
- Status
- Version

The unified content process—a summary

Implementing a unified content strategy involves:
- "deconstructing" all content from all courses into elements or RLOs
- assigning elements into outputs, based on learning objectives
- developing standards for and rewriting elements so they follow a consistent structure (consistency is critical in a unified content strategy) and conform to your instructional model that defines which learning architectures best support your content, objectives, and learners' needs
- compiling courses (and other information products) from their required elements, providing supplemental information as required to accommodate different learners, different mastery levels, and even different information products.

A unified content strategy requires much up front analysis; you need to break content down to determine how and where it can be reused and determine how best to write it to support its various uses and users. However, once the analysis is complete, courses can be easily constructed and kept up to date. Also, wherever an element is used it is consistent, eliminating unnecessary repetition.

References

Choi, Ikseon and David H. Jonassen. "Learning Objectives from the Perspective of the Experienced Cognition Framework." *Educational Technology*, November/December 2000.

Clark, Ruth Colvin. "Four Architectures of Instruction." *Performance Improvement*, Volume 39, No. 10. November/December 2000.

Kostur, Pamela and Jane Aronovitch. "From Information to Instruction: Transforming Textbooks into Online Learning Materials." *IPCC Proceedings*, 2001.

Rockley, Ann with Pamela Kostur and Steve Manning. *Managing Enterprise Content: A Unified Content Strategy*. New Riders, 2002. (due out October 2002, ISBN 0735713065)

Watson John B. and Allison Rossett. "Guiding the Independent Learner in Web-Based Training." *Educational Technology*, May/June 1999.

Issues of Transclusions

Harald Krottmaier
Institute for Information Processing and
Computer Supported new Media (IICM)
Graz University of Technology, Austria
hkrott@iicm.edu

Denis Helic
Institute for Information Processing and
Computer Supported new Media (IICM)
Graz University of Technology, Austria
dhelic@iicm.edu

Abstract: Transclusions were first mentioned in the early 1960 by Ted Nelson. Generally speaking transclusions are a method of reusing parts of a document without duplicating these parts. In the proposed implementation authors of documents will be informed (on request) if parts of these documents are reused elsewhere. Authors using transclusions are informed about changes in the reused document. Reused document fragments are marked in both documents to help readers while exploring documents. The concept is old but implementations are still not available to authors and readers. After a short introduction this paper shows some applications of transclusions. Thereafter ideas on how to implement transclusions using a second generation hypermedia information system are presented.

Introduction and Problems

The idea of transclusions was born in 1960, when Ted Nelson invented Xanadu, a revolutionary information- and document management system. "Reuse without duplicating document fragments with the original context available" ([Nelson, 1995]) is the key issue of the transclusion concept. Newly assembled documents are also called *compound documents*, on the other hand, documents reused in one or more compound documents are called *transcluded documents*.

As there is no duplication of document fragments when reusing content many advantages over ordinary cut-and-pasting of data arise (see e.g. [Krottmaier and Maurer, 2001]). In the following we are going to to numerate some of the advantages.

Intellectual Property: Parts of a document are not 'stolen' but simply 'reused in another context'. It must be visible to the reader of a document that parts of the document are no original contributions, but references or inclusions of some other work. Dependent on the electronic format of the compound document this is easily implemented by adding hyperlinks to the original work before and after the inclusion of the reused material. Please note that in HTML documents it is possible to reuse whole images in any context stored on any server system. The reader of the document will not notice this fact without reading the source-code of the HTML document.

Disk Space: Since parts of a document are not copied into a new document there is no need to save the reused part more than once. Surrogates of the reused parts must be stored in a predefined format. There will be no waste of disk space, if the surrogate definition requires less disk space than the referenced part. It is obvious that transcluded documents must be available to the system when assembling the document. Without coping the reused part and without sophisticated caching mechanisms this fact may limit the applications of transclusions to intranet or even intra-server applications.

Update: There is simply no need of manually updating referenced parts because the content is always requested from the *original source*. Since this is an advantage in many applications (e.g. a collection of different course material which is automatically up-to-date) there are drawbacks in some other applications where many people are responsible for the content and access control is not an issue. Some action must be taken if reused parts are changed. At least the author of the compound document must be informed (e.g. via email) by the system if there are any changes in the reused part. While there is no need to update a document it might be a time-intensive task to assemble a compound document. Therefore reusing a document which reuses parts of another document (which itself reuses parts of other documents etc.) must be limited to a certain level. Nevertheless, improvements in network infrastructure and processing speed will reduce this problem.

Two Way Reading: When displaying the transcluded document the system must add additional navigation facilities around the quotes in the compound document. This action is necessary to indicate the reuse of content (see 'Intellectual Property'). Links to the original source of the transclusion are provided. This makes it possible for the reader of a document to take a look at the original context of a quote. The reader of the transcluded document on the other hand has the ability to explore which parts of a document are no original contributions. If a fragment of a document is reused it is very likely that this fragment is important!

These are some of the most important advantages and drawbacks when using transclusions. Authors of compound documents must be aware of the risks when using this technology. The information system where these documents are stored must support authors in many ways (i.e. creation of transclusions, notification of changes, types of changes [Francisco-Revilla et al., 2001], etc.).

Applications of Transclusions

With the knowledge of the concept many existing applications can be improved. This section lists three possible applications. Please note that many other applications will profit from the idea of transclusions.

Electronic Publishing: Scholar papers often quote paragraphs or sentences of other already published papers. When using transclusions readers of the new paper are able to jump directly to the context of the quote (i.e. to the original paper). It is therefore possible for the reader of the compound document to explore the reused quote in the original context. This issue is especially useful for novices in a topic. The author of the compound document may create a special 'view' of a topic. Readers who are interested in the details may read also the original contributions to the topic. Readers of the transcluded document on the other hand are able to see which parts of a document are reused in other documents. This is a very important information! If a part of a document is reused in some other document, it is very likely that this part is very important. This additional 'meta-data' ("This part is also used in some other document(s)...") is a kind of implicit rating of a fragment of a document. In addition to attributes in link-objects (whether the part is used as a positive or negative example) useful information is added to the transcluded document!

Discussion Forum: In electronic written communication (especially in electronic discussion forums like bulletin boards or news groups etc.) many new postings refer to previous postings. These postings are (usually) immutable. In electronic journals or libraries this kind of communication is also very common (e.g. 'letters to the editor' often refer to parts of previous published articles). Referring to parts of an article should be possible by simply mark the fragment to be included in the new document or posting. Readers of the new article can be sure that the referenced part is not modified by the author of the new article. Also readers of the 'old' (i.e. transcluded) document are able to see which parts are discussed later in some other posting. On the other hand it is very likely, if the system is used in the right way and uses are used to it, that questions will be asked not more than once. A much more efficient communication will be the result when using transclusions in this kind of application. Time will also be saved because of additional structure in discussion threads.

Course Material: Very often existing course material is simply a collection of (unidirectional) links to related material stored on different server systems. Unfortunately it is not possible with current web technology to link to parts of existing material and to create links back to the collection. A very simple example will clarify this situation: imagine a single very important paragraph in an article of 100 pages. The author of the course material may add a link exactly to the paragraph, but can't include a link in the (remote stored) material *back to* the collection! Therefore the author of the collection has to cut-and-paste paragraphs of existing material into new documents. The original contexts of these paragraphs are lost.

These three applications showed the need for transclusions. Systems supporting transclusions will have a great impact in may areas. Proper use of transclusions and interoperability between these systems may help authors and readers of content stored on the web.

Requirements and Implementation

In scientific publishing the usage of quotes and references are very common. Readers of those publications have to do a lot of work if they want to explore a reference and want to find the original context of a quote used in another document. Systems like ResearchIndex ([NEC Research Institute, 2002]) are able to answer questions like "Where (i.e. on which page) is this reference used?" but it is not possible to explore the original context of the reused quote! Therefore we are motivated to implement this feature in the Journal of Universal Computer Science ([J.UCS, 2002]). In the publishing system used for serving J.UCS content is offered in several electronic formats to the readers. At the time of writing these formats are HTML, PostScript and also PDF. We consider the implementation of XML formated documents and also eBook-formated content.

In a first implementation we are going to support HTML documents (for both, source and destination document format) with additional hyperlinking information. The source and destination document(s) will be stored in a Hyperwave Information Server (HIS, see e.g. [Hyperwave, 2001] or [Maurer, 1996]), where it is possible to add link objects *without* being the owner of a document. Please note that inserting hyperlinks to HTML documents implies editing of the document itself. Note also that a link in HTML is unidirectional! A successor of the implementation will also consider other document formats (like PDF) and other source systems (like ordinary HTTP-server systems). Let us now sketch ideas related to the involved participants and systems:

Author of the original document: If parts of the document are reused in other documents this participant may want to be notified by the system. If the author wants to change a transcluded part of the document, the related parts should be marked. Note that in the original design of Xanadu (see e.g. [Nelson, 1995]), a "write once – read many" system was considered. Therefore it was prohibited to remove documents. Editing of documents was allowed *only* if the old version was still available and accessible by the system.

Author of a document using transclusions: It must be easy for the author who is using transclusions to determine the fragment of a document to be transcluded. Therefore easy to use tools must be implemented supporting the user in the creation of a new document. In a first implementation a simple JavaScript-based implementation will be used. While there are many drawbacks of this approach the user must not install a separate software and a prototype implementation will be available very soon. The selected part will be represented by links following the XPointer-specification (e.g. [DeRose et al., 2001b], [DeRose et al., 2001a]), therefore the selected fragment may be defined in many ways (e.g. use the 5'th paragraph, or use the first paragraph after the 3rd heading etc.). The links will be stored using objects on the server system.

System, where the transcluded document is stored: The system must be able to serve parts of a document. If documents are mutable, a version control system must be integrated to make old versions of the document accessible. Additionally, the system must provide the reader of the document (depending on personal preferences) with navigation facilities which indicates transcluded parts. If the author of a transcluded document edit some part of the document, the system is responsible for informing other authors using parts of the document about the change. Please note that bidirectional links are an absolutely necessary requirement for the system to perform this task. In the first implementation we consider a HIS as server system because of the many advantages over ordinary web-systems without link management and bidirectional link concept.

System, where compound documents are stored: This system is responsible for assembling the compound document. Navigation facilities must be included by the system to support the reader of the document. If the transcluded part has changed also the reader may be informed about this change. The author of the document has to define whether the user should be informed or not. In our first implementation also this server system will be a HIS.

Reader of assembled documents: It must be easy for the user to notice the reused parts of a document and to jump immediately to the original context of the reused parts.

Since there are many issues to consider, the first implementation will be very limited in terms of supported document formats and server systems. Nevertheless, future extensions are considered in the design of the software.

Conclusion and Future Work

This paper has shown that transclusions have many advantages for the web community and that there is a need for an easy to use system. Readers of a compound document have the possibility to *explore the original context* of the used quote. Authors of compound documents are able to easily *reuse existing material* and do not have to update reused document fragments. Finally, authors of transcluded documents knows *which parts are used* by other authors due to the bidirectional behavior of the used link mechanism. Transclusions have many advantages over conventional cut-and-paste reuse of content.

Future work is addressed to a first implementation in the Journal of Universal Computer Science. Thereafter usability tests and user responses will be evaluated. After successful tests authors of the journal will be able to use transclusions of articles published in J.UCS.

References

[DeRose et al., 2001a] DeRose, S., Maler, E., and Daniel Jr., R. (2001a). XML Pointer Language (XPointer) Version 1.0. available online `http://www.w3.org/TR/2001/CR-xptr-20010911` .

[DeRose et al., 2001b] DeRose, S., Maler, E., and Orchard, D. (2001b). XML Linking Language (xlink) Version 1.0. available online `http://www.w3.org/TR/xlink` .

[Francisco-Revilla et al., 2001] Francisco-Revilla, L., Shipman, F., Furuta, R., Karadkar, U., and Arora, A. (2001). Managing change on the web. In *Proceedings of the first ACM/IEEE-CS joint conference on Digital libraries*, pages 67–76. ACM Press.

[Hyperwave, 2001] Hyperwave (2001). Hyperwave Informatino Server. `http://www.hyperwave.com`.

[J.UCS, 2002] J.UCS (2002). Journal of Universal Computer Science. `http://www.jucs.org` .

[Krottmaier and Maurer, 2001] Krottmaier, H. and Maurer, H. (2001). Transclusions in the 21st Century. *Journal of Universal Computer Science*, 7(12):1125–1136. `http://www.jucs.org/jucs_7_12/transclusions_in_the_21st`.

[Maurer, 1996] Maurer, H. (1996). now Hyperwave — The Next Generation Web Solution.

[NEC Research Institute, 2002] NEC Research Institute (2002). Researchindex. `http://www.researchindex.com` .

[Nelson, 1995] Nelson, T. (1995). The Heart of Connection: Hypermedia Unified Transclusion. *Communications of the ACM*, 38:31–33.

More than Passive Reading: Interactive Features in Digital Libraries

Harald Krottmaier
Institute for Information Processing and
Computer Supported new Media (IICM)
Graz University of Technology, Austria
hkrott@iicm.edu

Denis Helic
Institute for Information Processing and
Computer Supported new Media (IICM)
Graz University of Technology, Austria
dhelic@iicm.edu

Abstract: At the moment it is not very common to actively work with material stored on an Internet server system. Once the right information resource is found, only passive information consumption of documents is provided by a majority of information systems. While this is appropriate for a kind of reading material, this is a limitation for scientific articles. Scientific articles are often read more than once, are usually annotated while they are explored, and are often the root of further investigations. In this paper we explore two features which will be available in the Journal of Universal Computer Science (J.UCS). These features will support the reader in exploring articles and will make it much easier to turn information into knowledge.

Introduction

Digital libraries are often the source of information. Three common steps are necessary to turn information into knowledge:

1. Find the right information.

2. Explore this information.

3. Apply the information.

Several tools are available to support scientists in finding the right information: search engines (such as Google) and directory services (such as Opendirectory) are often used as 'entry to the web'. While search engines are often used by users *who know exactly what they are searching for* and directory services are used by users *who do not know exactly what they are looking for*, there are also some system specific notification mechanisms available, which 'directs' users to sources of information. In the context of digital library systems this kind of service is called 'Alert Service'. These tools are currently well known and heavily used in the Internet community.

A few highly sophisticated features (such as 'find similar information resources') are already integrated in search engines and are inherently available in directory services . Other specialized application specific features are available in the server systems providing the information. In this paper we are going to discuss two features: an annotation feature and a personalization feature. We illustrate implementation details of these features. Annotations are available in J.UCS ([J.UCS, 2002]) since the beginning (1994). The personalization feature is currently under development and will be released in the near future. In J.UCS we use a Hyperwave Information Server (HIS, [Hyperwave, 2001]) to make the implementation of these features as easy as possible. In the following sections we explore some aspects of these features.

Annotations

It is very common to write handwritten annotations on paper or mark some regions of text as important or unimportant for understanding, especially in personally owned material ([Marshall, 1997]). "Dog-eared" books are *highly customized books* and the turned-down corner may be of great value to the "creator" while trying to find an interesting part of the book again! No matter what type of content (text or graphic) on whatever position may be annotated in a traditional library environment. It is obvious that it should be possible to annotate also material stored in a digital library environment.

Unfortunately not all digital library systems support the reader in the creation of electronic annotations although electronic annotations are much more powerful than "analog" annotations in a traditional environment. The following list illustrates features of electronic annotations:

Private Annotations: if the digital library system provides the user with an identification facility, it is very easy to support private annotations. Private annotations must be visible only to the author of the annotation.

Shared Annotations: if annotations are stored in an intermediate- or server system, it is possible that users share annotations. Therefore many users may explore the content by using annotations very quickly. There are many applications of this kind, especially if users are working in groups and/or are exploring online-available literature.

Typed Annotations: types like 'Question', 'Answer', 'Problem', 'Solution', 'Rating' etc. are needful in selecting whether to read or not to read the annotation or even the content. Additional attributes like 'User who wrote the annotation' may be very helpful.

Rated Content: A document may be rated by special annotations. Users may decide to read just articles with top ratings and may not waste their time in reading (obviously) poor written articles. Actual content (i.e. recently published content) must be treated in a special manner.

Nevertheless, some technical problems have to be solved and tools must be created to support users in writing and managing annotations. Let us now discuss some approaches and problems in conjunction with the annotation feature. There are different possibilities of the storage location of the annotations. Annotations may be stored on 1.) client-side systems, 2.) intermediate systems and 3.) server-side systems ([Krottmaier, 2001]).

Annotations in J.UCS are stored on the server-side, therefore they are easily accessible to all users or to a group of users. Annotations in J.UCS are 1.) indexed and therefore search able, 2.) interlinked via special link-types with the content and 3.) physically separated from the content.

We mentioned the term *information source*. This kind of source is a collection of documents which all represents the same content. I.e. if content is available to users in different formats (e.g. in PDF, PostScript and HTML) we talk about *one* information source but different formats of the content.

This fact introduces another problem: Annotations to the HTML-representation of the content should also be presented to users when looking at the PDF-version of the content and vice versa. On the other hand, not every reader of the PDF-version is able to create annotations because the annotation feature is not available in Acrobat Reader. The Adobe Acrobat API-license prohibits development of plug-ins supporting annotations. Therefore another solution without using the PDF-inherent annotation facility must be developed. Currently we explore two approaches to solve this problem: feedback forms for *each page* in the document and hyperlinks from *each section* to an annotation server application.

There are many applications of annotations. One application is the '*active documents*' concept ([Heinrich and Maurer, 2000]). Active documents introduce a system which may automatically answers questions. Users may ask any question at any position in a document stored on the server system. The system either answers the question automatically (by searching for answers to similar questions), or forwards the question to the author or maintainer of the document. If there are many users of the library and if the tools are easy to use, there is an enormous power in using this idea of active documents! But also other applications are possible: e.g. an *intelligent automatic summary* of a document. This summary can be as easy to implement as collecting and displaying all highlighted document fragments which are created by the readers of the document. Again, many users may increase the quality of these summaries.

There are many studies about how annotations are written in an electronic environment (e.g. [Marshall et al., 2001]). Many web based based environments (e.g. [Rosenstock and Gertz, 2001], [Kahan et al., 2001]) are using annotations. Annotations are a necessary feature in every system providing information to a large community.

Rearrange Documents and Document Fragments

Organizing whole content entities or parts of content in a user defined way is essential when improving the usability of digital libraries ([Krottmaier, 2001]). We are currently implementing such a *server-side personal data collection* in the environment of the Journal of Universal Computer Science. This makes it easier for readers *to work with the content* of the library. In the upcoming prototype it will be possible to simply select information sources (in our case articles and article collection) stored on the server and link them to a personal collection. As a result of the integrated link database, the collections will remain up-to-date even if objects are moved to some other location on the server. Therefore the infamous 'HTTP-error 404' ('Page not found') cannot appear when accessing objects stored in the database.

Such a personalized data collection may be static or dynamic. The example above showed a static collection, where each article must be selected and linked to the collection. If there is the request to visualize 'all articles by author XXX' or 'all articles in category YYY', this approach is not very effective. Therefore other possibilities must exist: to answer the first question (articles by author), so called *query objects*, i.e. objects, representing a search query in the database, will be used. When these queries are executed, all matching objects will appear in the listing of the personal collection. The second question (articles by category) can be answered by linking the appropriate category-collection organized by the administrator to the personal collection of the user.

Since we are using an object-oriented database system (Hyperwave Information Server, HIS) which supports inherently users and groups, it is possible to implement *public* and *private* collections of articles simply by assigning the proper 'rights'-attribute. Public collections may be used as a kind of *public bookmarks* already implemented by a lot of services (e.g. [MyBookmarks, 2001]). But there are several other advantages, including accessibility, when saving bookmarks on the server-side rather than on the local file system in some browser-specific format.

Organizing objects stored *on* the server system (*local objects*) is obviously not sufficient in the context of an open digital library system. It must also be possible to organize objects stored on any other system (*remote object*) like HTTP-server systems, other internet based systems, and even files stored on the local file system.

To enable structuring of remote objects a surrogate object must be created in the database. This object (in Hyperwave terminology also known as 'remote object') is then used as handle for further operations. Since the control of the referenced part is completely up to the remote server administrator, tools (such as link checkers and content watchers etc.) must be integrated to support the user while working with remote objects.

Structuring a single document as one unit is easy compared to the task of structuring parts of a document. Resources are usually addressed by URLs (Uniform Resource Locators, [Berners-Lee et al., 1994]). Depending on the document format, more granularity is possible.

We should not limit this discussion of fragments of a text based document (such as HTML, XML and PDF). A user may address the upper left part of an image, or the first 5 seconds of a video, etc. There is much work to do, to implement this feature.

Conclusion and Future Work

In this paper two necessary features were described in the context of the Journal of Universal Computer Science. Problems and issues of the well known annotation feature were presented and ideas on how to personalize documents and document collections were discussed.

In the current implementation it is not possible to add annotations *at any position* in the HTML representation of the information resource. Only whole content objects may be annotated at the time of writing. Although this approach is suitable for small documents, it is inappropriate when working with large documents. Therefore future work is addressed to make it possible to addannotations to parts of documents – simply by selecting a corresponding document fragment. Sharing annotations between different document formats is also an issue in the prototype.

The current working prototype does support rearrangement of locally stored objects, but does not support restructuring of document fragments. The next step is therefore to organize and restructure parts of documents.

References

[Berners-Lee et al., 1994] Berners-Lee, T., Masinter, L., and McCahill, M. (1994). Uniform Resource Locators. available online `http://www.w3.org/Addressing/rfc1738.txt` .

[Heinrich and Maurer, 2000] Heinrich, E. and Maurer, H. (2000). Active Documents: Concept, Implementation and Applications. *Journal of Universal Computer Science*, 6(12):1197–1202. `http://www.jucs.org/jucs_6_12/active_documents_concept_implementation`.

[Hyperwave, 2001] Hyperwave (2001). Hyperwave Informatino Server. `http://www.hyperwave.com`.

[J.UCS, 2002] J.UCS (2002). Journal of Universal Computer Science. `http://www.jucs.org` .

[Kahan et al., 2001] Kahan, J., Koivunen, M.-R., Prud'Hommeaux, E., and Swick, R. R. (2001). Annotea: An open rdf infrastructure for shared web annotations. In *Proc. of the WWW10 International Conference*.

[Krottmaier, 2001] Krottmaier, H. (2001). Improving the Usability of a Digital Library. In Hübler, A., Linde, P., and Smith, J. W., editors, *Electronic Publishing*, pages 178–182, Canterbury, Kent, United Kingdom. International Council for Computer Communication (ICCC) and International Federation for Information Processing (IFIP).

[Marshall, 1997] Marshall, C. C. (1997). Annotation: From paper books to digital library. In *ACM DL*, pages 131–140.

[Marshall et al., 2001] Marshall, C. C., Price, M. N., Golovchinsky, G., and Schilit, B. N. (2001). Designing e-books for legal research. In *Proceedings of the first ACM/IEEE-CS joint conference on Digital libraries*, pages 41 – 48. ACM Press.

[MyBookmarks, 2001] MyBookmarks (2001). `http://www.mybookmarks.com` .

[Rosenstock and Gertz, 2001] Rosenstock, B. and Gertz, M. (2001). Web-based scholarship:annotating the digital library. In *Proceedings of the first ACM/IEEE-CS joint conference on Digital libraries*, pages 104 – 105. ACM Press.

Use of Social Navigation Features in Collaborative E-Learning

Jaakko Kurhila[1], Miikka Miettinen[2], Petri Nokelainen[2] and Henry Tirri[2]

[1]Department of Computer Science
University of Helsinki, Finland
jaakko.kurhila@cs.helsinki.fi

[2]Complex Systems Computation Group
Helsinki Institute for Information Technology, Finland
firstname.lastname@hiit.fi

Abstract: EDUCO is a system for collaborative learning that uses real-time direct social navigation. Social navigation means making the navigation of other users visible to everyone else in the system. The paper discusses the social navigation features of EDUCO and reports empirical results regarding the collaborative behaviour of the students in a university-level Web-course. Contrary to our research hypothesis and the common wisdom in the research area, the data gathered showed that making other users' navigation visible did not have an effect on navigation in this experiment.

Introduction

Social navigation (Munro, Höök and Benyon 1999) provides interesting opportunities in collaborative e-learning. When simplified, social navigation means that the users of an environment are dynamically provided with the information of the actions of other users of the same environment. A trivial example is a counter on a Web page, showing how many other people have visited the page. In their seminal book about social navigation, Munro et al. (1999) use an on-line grocery store as an example when classifying different types of social navigation: if people visiting the store are given recommendations what other people have bought, it is a form of *indirect social navigation*. If a shopper in the grocery store has a sense of other people moving about the store and can engage in seeking e.g. assistance, it is a case of *direct social navigation*.

Experiments with social navigation in educational setting have mostly fallen into the category of indirect social navigation (see e.g. Dieberger 1999). However, EDUCO is a system for collaborative learning to employ real-time direct social navigation. Real-time aspects of EDUCO create the feeling of live companions in the system (Kurhila et al. 2002). Other important facilities include tools for synchronous and asynchronous communication, and support for forming study groups and publishing their work. The purpose of the paper is to demonstrate how the tool was applied to a real-life situation, and describe how the features of social navigation are empirically evaluated from a data gathered from a university-level course of 46 students.

System Description of EDUCO

EDUCO is a system for both the learners and the teachers, to be used with standard web-browsers. From a technological point-of-view, EDUCO consists of a socket server along with cgi-scripts, and a Java applet for every user. From the user point-of-view, the key issues are navigation towards useful information, synchronous and asynchronous communication, group forming and publishing group works.

There is no direct metaphor for the use of EDUCO in traditional classrooms. A learning area in EDUCO consists of the EDUCO tool itself, a view to a document, and comments for the document. The user interface of EDUCO tool consists of different views of which only one is visible at a time. The most important views are map, chat, search and alarm (Fig. 1).

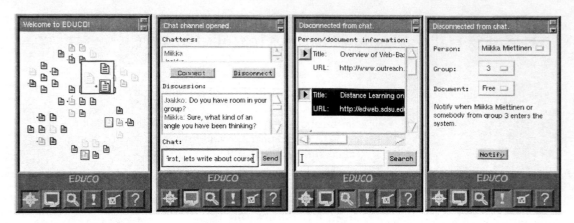

Figure 1: From left to right, four different views of EDUCO: Map, Chat, Search and Alarm.

Map view presents documents currently available in the learning environment and provides a way to navigate to them directly. By double clicking a document a user can open it in the rightmost frame in the browser window. A user is represented as a coloured dot around the document he or she is currently viewing (Fig. 1). Other users are visible to every user in real-time, so that their navigation is visible to everyone present.

The documents change their brightness level and colour on the map depending on how much they have been viewed relative to the other documents, as seen in Fig. 1. The total time all users have spent viewing each document is recorded every hour. The change in the brightness and in the colour of an individual document are determined by the distance of its moving average for the last 24 hours from the same average for all documents.

In other words, map view provides the users of EDUCO two social navigation features. Colouring the documents according to how much they have been viewed is a form of indirect social navigation. Presenting users as moving dots next to the documents they are currently viewing is a form of direct social navigation. Both of these features can help the users to follow the footsteps of the others. The direct social navigation also adds to the sense of not being alone in a web-course (Kurhila et al. 2002).

EDUCO has a built-in *chat* functionality integrated to he map view to enable synchronous communication between peers and other users of the environment. The chatters can be picked up from the map view by clicking the dots representing users. The number of participants in the discussion is unlimited, but one person may use only one chat channel simultaneously. Figure 1 shows an example of the use of chat. In addition to synchronous discussions, EDUCO uses two types of document-specific *asynchronous communications*: areas for general comments and hierarchical newsgroup-type discussions for meaningful knowledge building.

The *search* function of EDUCO can be used in finding persons or documents. The search is targeted to the titles of documents and names of users, both online and offline. The search results are shown in the search view (Fig. 1), but also in map view by highlighting the document with a blue rectangle, as it can be seen in Fig. 1.

The *alarm* offers each user a possibility to set "triggers" into the documents, groups and the overall system. In other words, a user can set EDUCO to alarm when certain conditions occur. This feature is useful in a case where a user searches for a companion showing interest to a certain document or topic, or wants to contact a particular person when he or she enters the system. The alarm function also enables making combinations of triggering events. Figure 1 shows an example of a combination of triggers: the alarm will beep if "Miikka Miettinen" or somebody from group 3 enters the system".

An important feature in EDUCO is the *support for forming groups*. Alarms, chat and navigational patterns can be used when screening for potential partners for group work. Another feature is a list of available (not yet in any group) participants in a Web-course. Every user can form a group by dicking a button "Add a new group". Other people can join an already existing group, or they can start a new group. After producing a joint work, it can be published in EDUCO for comments.

The group-forming feature of EDUCO is designed for Web-courses where the learning process involves writing reports in groups. Document icons in the "map view" of EDUCO can each represent a collection of student reports.

Empirical evaluation
Study setting

A valuable feature in systems like EDUCO is that they make it possible to accumulate large amounts of interesting information through completely unobtrusive observation of the users' activities. Whenever someone moves to another page, starts a chat discussion, joins a group, or uses any other of the available functions, the details of the event are registered in the log. This allows extensive re-construction of the conditions under which the action took place, and facilitates the analysis of the users' behavioural patterns as they occur in real-life e-learning situations.

The data set was collected during the Spring 2002 semester from a course entitled "Computer Uses in Education" with a subtitle of "Web-based learning'". The course was given at the Department of Computer Science, University of Helsinki, Finland. The course was a web-based course without face-to-face meetings and the use of EDUCO was mandatory. Forty-six students were active in the course. Some of the students were adult learners with varying backgrounds and degrees but most of them were Computer Science majors.

The format of the course was unique compared to the other courses at the Department. The students had nine weekly reports to produce from nine different topics. It was not allowed to produce the report alone. At least a working pair was required, and a group of three was also recommended. Moreover, the groups were not allowed to stay the same during the course. A student had to be involved with at least three different groups.

Apart from the documents containing the reports of the student groups, the documents in EDUCO map discussed the issues covered during the first eight weeks. The documents were organized to eight different clusters under a common theme. The themes were close to the weekly topics but not completely the same. The document cluster sizes varied from two to ten, giving a total of ca. 40 documents. The exact amount of documents varied during the course, since new resources were added occasionally.

Results

In this paper, our empirical analysis focuses on social navigation and the formation of groups. We first attempt to examine if the presence of one or more users around a certain document attracts others to navigate to that document as well. This is the real-time aspect of social navigation as implemented in EDUCO. As stated earlier, the document icons also change their brightness/colour based on their popularity. In order to evaluate the role of the colouring mechanism, we compare overall navigation patterns to periods when a new weekly assignment was published so that the colours had not yet changed to influence the users by guiding them to the most relevant documents.

The idea of our analysis of real-time social navigation was to compare the frequencies and lengths of visits to documents that were already being read by at least one person ("occupied documents"), and visits that started without there being others present at the particular document ("unoccupied documents"). Only a rough indication of the tendency of people to move together could be obtained this way, since there were other factors with obvious effects on the results. In particular, the assignments given during the course directed most of the activity to a small number of documents, making social navigation almost unavoidable during the busiest periods. The validity of data gathered from a real course more than compensates for the lack of control, however, when it comes to evaluating the usefulness of a real system.

In order to calculate the relevant statistics, we re-constructed the navigation activity that took place during course from the log file. This involved stepping through the log one row at a time and moving users from one visitor list to another the way they moved when they were actually using the system. The number of visits to occupied and unoccupied documents as well as the lengths of the visits were computed along the way. Our hypothesis was that occupied documents would be somewhat more popular than unoccupied ones. Another intuitive guess was that visits to occupied documents would be shorter, because people would go and take a quick look at things that others seem to find interesting.

Table 1 shows the main results of the re-construction. The 48 students are sorted into 5 groups according to the distribution of their visits to occupied and unoccupied documents (group 5 has 8 students and the other groups 10). The last row of the table contains the overall figures for all students.

	Occupied % of visits	Occupied Average length	Unoccupied % of visits	Unoccupied Average length
Group 1	60%	11	40%	8
Group 2	53%	11	47%	7
Group 3	49%	10	51%	5
Group 4	43%	9	57%	5
Group 5	32%	10	68%	5
All	48%	10	52%	6

Table 1: The number and average length of visits to occupied and unoccupied documents.

The numbers in Table 1 do not indicate a preference to occupied documents over unoccupied ones, since the proportions are practically equal in all groups. The minor differences in the average lengths of the visits do no justify any conclusions either. Therefore, the log data did not provide support for our idea of the usefulness of real-time social navigation.

Another essential mechanism for social navigation is the colouring of the document icons according to their popularity. During the course, there were almost always some documents shining brighter than the others. Since they were generally the most relevant documents for the weekly assignment, the amount of guidance provided by the colouring could not be assessed in isolation under normal conditions. However, after a new assignment was published, there was a period of a few hours, during which the documents that had just become important did not stand out yet. Our analysis is based on comparing the navigation patterns observed during the first six hours following the publication of an assignment to the average patterns of the entire course.

According to our hypothesis, visits should be shorter on average when the colouring does not guide the users directly to the most useful documents. Unfortunately, it turned out that this is not the case. The average length of a visit was 7.5 minutes for periods following the publication of an assignment, and 7.2 minutes in the whole data set. From an intuitive point of view, colouring should help finding relevant documents, but as in the case of real-time social navigation, the log data did not provide support for our intuitive views.

Conclusions

The paper presented a system for collaborative Web-based learning that supports social navigation and described a real-life situation where it was used. Common wisdom has been that allowing a user to see the navigation steps of other users has an effect to the navigation of the user, although valid empirical evaluations are somewhat lacking. However, the effects of synchronous and asynchronous features of social navigation in EDUCO appeared to be non-existent in this study. The result was surprising, especially when a previous study with the same system (with less functionality) showed slightly opposite results (Kurhila et al. 2002). Further studies are necessary to separate the effective factors.

References

Dieberger, A. (1999). Social Navigation in Populated Information Spaces. In A. Munro, K. Höök & D. Benyon (Eds.), *Social Navigation of Information Space*, 35-54. London: Springer.

Kurhila, J., Miettinen, M., Nokelainen, P., & Tirri, H. (2002). EDUCO - A Collaborative Learning Environment using Social Navigation. In P. de Bra et al. (Eds.) *Proc. Adaptive Hypermedia and Adaptive Web-Based Systems (AH 2002)*, 242-252, Berlin Heidelberg: Springer.

Munro, A., Höök, K. & Benyon, D. (1999). Footprints in the Snow. In A. Munro, K. Höök & D. Benyon (Eds.), *Social Navigation of Information Space*, 1-14. London: Springer.

Obtaining Realistic Information on the Context of Use of E-learning System

Masaaki KUROSU[*1] and Hideaki TAKAHASHI[*2]
National Institute of Multimedia Education
Japan
PFD00343@nifty.com [*1] hide@nime.ac.jp [*2]

Abstract: By applying the fieldwork methods such as the interview and the observation, we started our study for obtaining more realistic information about the context of use of e-learning system for the purpose of establishing the full list of system requirements. The information derived from the fieldwork will surely provide us more realistic requirement of the future e-learning system.

Introduction

Besides the university students, there are many people who would like to learn something more than they have learnt at the university or at the high school. Different from the university students, people working in the office, people working at home or people who have retired spend their lives in a variety of situations. In order for the e-learning system to be more usable, effective and satisfactory to these people, it has to be flexible and adaptive for their context. In other words, we have to obtain the contextual information on how they are spending their life in order to clarify the requirements for the e-learning systems in terms of the time course, the contents and the use of media. Although we have many research results on the requirements for the e-learning system quantitatively, most of them are based on the questionnaire. It is frequently pointed out that the questionnaire and the statistical analysis based on the quantitative data such as the questionnaire reveal just a part of the whole requirements. This is the reason why we conceived of applying the fieldwork techniques to specify the context of use information of people who have the need for e-learning.

Importance of Context of Use Information

In ISO standard numbered 13407 (ISO 1999), i.e. "Human-centered design processes for interactive systems", it is clearly stated that the interactive systems should follow the design process as follows (Figure 1).
a) to understand and specify the context of use
b) to specify the user and organization requirements
c) to produce design solutions
d) to evaluate designs against requirements

In the standard, the context of use is defined as "user, tasks, equipment (hardware, software and materials), and the physical and social environments in which a product is used". It is undoubtedly necessary and important "to understand and specify the context of use", because this process is positioned at the top of all processes. Because the system design should put an emphasis on the traceability, the information specified at the first process should be kept and followed by subsequent processes. This is the prerequisite for an interactive system to be usable, i.e. effective, efficient and satisfactory.

Of course, the e-learning system is no exception. If we don't have the adequate information about the context of use of the e-learning system, the system might not fit to the user's needs and situational requirements.

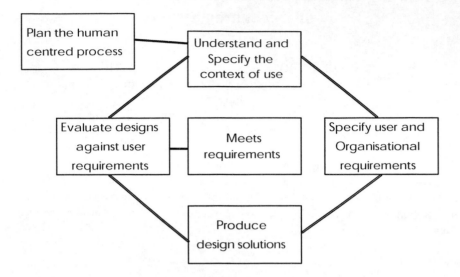

Figure 1: Human centered design processes for interactive systems in ISO 13407

Field Work Methods

Based on ISO13407, a Technical Report ISO TR16982 (ISO 2000) "Ergonomics of human-system interaction — Usability methods supporting human centered design" was issued in order to recommend adequate usability methods for each of the design process. This TR includes such methods as the observation, the performance-related measures, the critical incidents, the questionnaires, the interviews, the thinking aloud method, the collaborative design and evaluation, and the creativity methods for supporting the design processes proposed by ISO13407.

Among them, the interview and the observation are especially recommended for the first process for obtaining the contextual information. Although these methods was developed and have been mainly used by the ethnographers in their fieldwork, their importance and effectiveness are now recognized in the field of HCI (Human Computer Interaction) as two of the main methods for designing interactive systems. Thus it is expected that the use of such methods will fulfill the list of requirements for the e-learning system that is now insufficiently and poorly filled with because of the previous use of the quantitative methods such as a questionnaire.

Focus of Interview and Observation

Before starting to obtain the information on e-learning system by the use of interview and observation, we considered about the focal points as follows.
(a)   Demographic characteristics – age, gender, occupation, academic background, etc. as the basic general information.
(b)   Current situation – activity in terms of the temporal and spatial dimensions, i.e. how the user is spending his/her time of the day, and the days of the week in which location (home / office / public places, etc).
(c)   Expected carrier path – if the user have a clear image of his/her life in the future, e.g. to get a job, to become a social worker, etc.
(d)   Obstacles – what kind of barriers there are
(e)   Other – any additional information

Obtaining Realistic Information

For the purpose of obtaining realistic information, we thought that the interview and the observation should be conducted in the real field of the user as far as possible. This is similar to the concept of the contextual inquiry method proposed by Beyer and Holtzblatt (1998). Natural artifacts around the user will ease the user and will give us more realistic information, thus it was decided that the interview and the observation will basically not be held in the experimental settings but in the real life situation.

Trial Research

We started our study by applying the fieldwork methods to a housewife who has just started attending some e-learning courses. As far as we knew from our earlier study: she has graduated the doctoral course but not yet obtained the Ph.D. She is busy now for taking care of her children of 3 years and 8 months. Hence,

Time	Activity	Time	Activity
7:00	Wakes up in the morning	19:00	Comes back home
7:15	Child care	19:15	Child care
7:30	House work	19:30	Dinner
7:45		19:45	
8:00		20:00	Child care
8:15	Child care	20:15	
8:30		20:30	
8:45	Takes the child to nursery school	20:45	
9:00		21:00	
9:15		21:15	
9:30		21:30	House work
9:45		21:45	
10:00	Comes back home	22:00	
10:15	Child care	22:15	
10:30		22:30	Accesses the mail software
10:45		22:45	
11:00	House work	23:00	
11:15		23:15	
11:30	Puts on the PC	23:30	
11:45	Accesses the mail software	23:45	
12:00		0:00	Accesses UCLA e-Learning site
12:15		0:15	Starts e-learning
12:30	Lunch	0:30	
12:45	Accesses UCLA e-Learning site	0:45	Submits an assignment
13:00	Starts e-learning	1:00	
13:15	Visits the discussion Board	1:15	Visits the discussion board
13:30		1:30	
13:45	Child care	1:45	
14:00		2:00	
14:15		2:15	
14:30		2:30	
14:45		2:45	
15:00	Access UCLA e-Learning site	3:00	Goes to bed
15:15	Starts e-learning	3:15	
15:30		3:30	
15:45	Reads the course documents	3:45	
16:00	Homework	4:00	
16:15		4:15	
16:30		4:30	
16:45		4:45	
17:00		5:00	
17:15		5:15	
17:30		5:30	Child care
17:45	Goes to the nursery school	5:45	
18:00		6:00	
18:15		6:15	Goes to bed
18:30		6:30	
18:45		6:45	

Table 1: Timetable of a housewife who is learning by UCLA web site

her studying time is separated during the day and she sometimes accesses the course during midnight (e.g. 2-3 AM) as can be seen in Table 1 and Figure 2. She frequently studies the course material on the bed or on the dining table as well as in front of the PC. But she has a strong motivation to get a position at the university in the near future and this motivation lets her cope with the difficult situation for learning.

Figure 2: The situation of the housewife using her PC

Future Direction

We are planning to start some other researches for students of broadcasting university courses and the e-learning courses as well as to continue the study with this woman. It is expected that we will be able to summarize the information to propose a sufficient list of requirements for the future e-learning system.

References

Beyer, H. and Holtzblatt, K. (1998) *Contextual Design*. Morgan Kaufmann

ISO13407 (1999) *Human-centred design processes for interactive systems*. International Organization for Standardization

ISO/TR16982 (2000) *Ergonomics of human-system interaction — Usability methods supporting human centred design*. International Organization for Standardization

Managing Time Thresholds in Mixed-Initiative Learning Environments

Dimitris Lamboudis, Anastasios Economides
University of Macedonia
Thessaloniki, Greece
dimlamb@uom.gr, economid@uom.gr

Abstract, The effectiveness of pedagogical agents, in terms of their believability and adaptivity, in mixed-initiative learning environments can be considerably affected by the "timing" of agents' actions. This paper describes an approach to manage time thresholds, which takes into account the response "style" of each individual learner. The proposed approach has provided very positive results in the context of an agent-based, mixed-initiative learning environment, which we are currently developing.

Introduction

Mixed-initiative problem solving lies at the heart of knowledge-based learning environments, aiming to provide an individualised learning experience. Learning environments, which are inhabited by animated pedagogical agents, constitute one of the most prominent paradigms of mixed-initiative systems (Johnson, 2000), (Johnson et al, 2000), (Andre et al, 1999). While learners are actively engaged in problem solving activities, agents monitor their progress and provide to them feedback which is according to their individual profile, aiming to increase learning effectiveness and efficiency. Typical scenarios include an introduction to the subject by the agent, followed by a test, or a task to be accomplished, to evaluate the learner's level of knowledge acquisition (Lester et al, 1999). While the learner tries to perform the task in hand, the agent monitors his/her actions, and continuously evaluates various factors in order to engage and assist. The pedagogical agents' potential to couple feedback functionalities with a strong visual presence, makes them an ideal examp le for studying mixed-initiative interactions (Shaw et al, 1999).

Mixed-initiative systems must consider a set of key decisions in their effort to support joint activity, including: *when* to engage learners with a service, *how* to best contribute to solving a problem, *when* to pass control back to users, and *when* to query users for additional information (Horvitz, 1999). In order to reach to *situated* decisions, agents make "guesses" about learners' needs. These "guesses" usually depend on the evidence obtained through the "keyhole" of the user interface, collaborative statistical data about the learner (Zuckerman and Albreciit, 2001) and explicitly asked information, most commonly in the form of a query the user has to go through in the beginning of a session.

Moreover, in the context of such systems, there are many additional parameters and principles that should be taken into account by the agent in order to reach a turn taking decision (Horvitz, 1999), (Lester et al, 1999), (Bates, 1994). For example, the personality and the emotional state of the agent, the advisory history, the idle time elapsed etc.

This paper focuses on a specific aspect of agent behaviour in this context, namely *timing*, which is directly connected (among others), to *time thresholds*. Time thresholds are defined as the amount of time the learner is allowed to spend in order to successfully complete a task without the agent's help.

Idle time is one of the main variables used by the agents to infer that the learner has difficulties in understanding, solving and, in general, successfully proceeding in the learning procedure. Idle time is usually defined over a predefined time threshold, i.e. agents compare the time elapsed until the learner response, with a predefined time threshold. The actual value of this threshold is most of the times derived from statistical data and corresponds to the "mean time" that learners spend for the completion of the particular task (Lester et al, 1999).

It can be argued, however, that this approach has two main limitations:

- The pattern of the agent's behaviour is soon revealed to the student; this fact may considerably compromise agent's believability, and therefore, agent's effectiveness (Lester et al, 1997a).
- It does not take into account the individual learner's characteristics (it is rather targeted to the "average learner"), which is the main objective in personalized learning environments (Sampson, Karagiannidis, Kinshuk, 2002)

This paper proposes an alternative approach for managing time thresholds in agent-based, mixed initiative learning systems. The proposed algorithm takes into account the response of each individual learner, and has provided very positive results in the context of an agent-based, mixed-initiative learning environment, which we are currently developing.

The Proposed Algorithm

Our approach attempts to overcome the limitations identified in the previous section. The algorithm, instead of spontaneously engaging the agent when idle time exceeds a predefined time threshold, allows the learner to have "a second chance" by extending the threshold. This second chance (the extension of the predefined time threshold) is not provided unconditionally, since this would be equivalent to just set another rigid threshold, although greater than the initial one. Instead, when the threshold is reached, the agent decides to extend it by some probability P_e and not to extend it by some probability $P_a = 1-P_e$. Thus, in the "worst case", the agent will behave conventionally, i.e. like in the existing systems. However, there is a possibility, which is partially defined by the designer, at least as far as the initial value of P_e is concerned, that the agent will give the learner a second chance. Yet, if this possibility is heavily depending on the initial value of P_e, it would be just another ad hoc intervention of the designer, lacking any adaptive characteristics.

Instead, the probability of extending the time threshold (i.e. the definition of P_e), is determined by the agent, through the algorithm which checks if this extension of time has any affects on the learning procedure, that is, if it helps the learner to achieve his/her goals. In case it does, it reinforces the value of P_e. In the long run, this means that independently of the initial values of P_e and P_a the system will favour the option that actually helps the learner.

In more detail, the algorithm is shown in (Fig. 1). The corresponding notation and assumptions are as follows:

- A learning procedure that can be represented by a set of n hierarchically ordered Tasks, $T=\{T_i, i=1...n\}$;
- A set of corresponding time thresholds, $t=\{t_i, i=1...n\}$;
- An initial value of P_e^0 (the corresponding $P_a^0 = 1 - P_e^0$);
  Where $P_e^0 = P$ *(extend time threshold in T_1 / $t > t_1$)*, i.e. the conditional probability of extending the time in the first task, given that the time threshold has been reached;
- A constant $?p$ to represent the reinforcement of P_e^{i-1};
  Where $P_e^{i-1} = P$ *(extend time threshold in T_i / $t > t_i$)*, i.e. the conditional probability of extending the time in the i_{th} task, given that the time threshold has been reached;
- A constant $?t$ to represent the extension amount of the time threshold; (Both $?p$ and $?t$ can be either constant values or percentages);
- A Boolean e, to serve as a flag to declare if there has been a time extension $e=1$ or not $e=0$;

Given these assumptions the algorithm receives t_i and P_e^{i-1} as input and process them as follows:

While (there is no positive response) Do
   if (e=1) then
      act and proceed to Task (t_i-?t, P_e^{i-1})
   else
      If (t > t_i) then
         $t_i = t_i$ + ?t by P_e^{i-1} and e=1;
         act by P_a^{i-1} and proceed to Task (t_i-?t, P_e^{i-1})
  end while
  if (e=1) then
    $P_e^i = P_e^{i-1}$ + ?p
    $P_a^i = 1 - P_e^i$
  Next Task (t_{i+1}, P_e^i)

Note that in case of action-taking by the agent, the algorithm remains to the same task but with a decreased threshold. Since the learner has received help he/she should be able to complete the task in less time. The agent is assumed to provide exhaustive help if needed; thus the algorithm ends with a positive response and avoids stack overflow.

The proposed algorithm can overcome the shortcomings of existing approaches:

1. The use of probabilities, instead of a predefined time threshold, increases the possibility that the agent behaviour will not be revealed to the learner, thus the believability of our agents can be enhanced.

2. Moreover, the time thresholds are dynamically adapted to the individual learner response, thus contributing to a learning experience which is driven by the learner characteristics

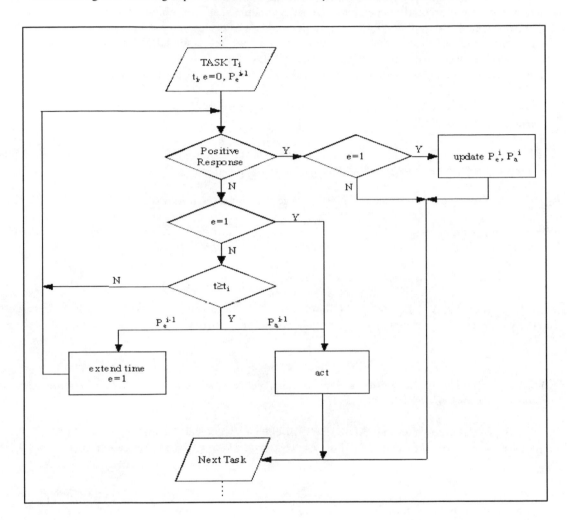

Figure 1: The proposed algorithm for managing time thresholds in agent-based, mixed-initiative learning systems

It is important to note that:

- The algorithm controls *when* an intervention will occur and not if the intervention will take place or not. The agent *will*, after all, engage if needed. Thus the algorithm maintains the pedagogical mainstream of decisions but introduces small variations to adapt to the particular user's style.

- The case of decreasing the value of P_e is not concerned. It seems rational to do so if the agent receives positive feedback before the threshold is reached but this would have the affect of balancing the value of P_e close to the initial value thus cancelling the adaptivity of the algorithm. After all, in the worse case, the agent will wait a bit longer before acting.

- Keeping the sequence of P_e ascending may lead to a value close or even equal to the unit ($P_e = 1$). This should not be avoided in general, since it actually means that the need of the user for extra time is very strong. However, in order to maintain the second characteristic of the algorithm (hiding the behaviour pattern), the designer could incorporate a control for the upper limit of the value of P_e.

Discussion

This paper has proposed an algorithm for managing the "timing" of agents actions in the context of mixed-initiative learning systems. The idea of the algorithm is to modify the timing of agents interventions, based on a probabilistic model, which takes into account the responses of each individual learner.

The proposed algorithm is being implemented in the context of an agent-based, mixed-initiative learning environment that we are currently developing. We have conducted some preliminary experiments with students of our department to evaluate the algorithm. In particular, we interviewed students using the system with pre-defined time thresholds, against students using the system where thresholds follow the proposed approach. This informal evaluation provided very positive feedback: the fact that agent's behaviour cannot be easily determined by the students, makes the agent believable, and enhance their learning effectiveness.

References

Andre E., Rist T., and Moeller J. (1999). Employing AI Methods to Control the Behaviour of Animated Interface Agents. *Applied Artificial Intelligence Journal*, *13* 4-5.

Bates, J. (1994). The Role of Emotion in Believable Agents. *Communications of the ACM*, 37 (7), 122-125.

Horvitz, E. (1999). Principles of Mixed-Initiative User Interfaces. *Proceedings of CHI '99, ACM SIGCHI Conference on Human Factors in Computing Systems, Pittsburgh, PA, May 1999.*

Johnson W. L. (2000), *Pedagogical Agents. MIT Press.*

Johnson W. L., Rickel J. W., Lester J. C. (2000). Animated Pedagogical Agents: Face-to-Face Interaction in Interactive Learning Environments. *International Journal of Artificial Intelligence in Education 2000,* 11, 47-78.

Lester, J. C., Converse, S. A. Kahler, S. E. Barlow, S. T., Stone, B. A. and Bhogal, R. (1997a). The Persona Effect: Affective Impact of Animated Pedagogical Agents. *Proceedings of CHI '97 (Human Factors in Computing Systems,* pp. 359-366.

Lester J.C., Stone B.A., and Stelling G.D. (1999). Lifelike Pedagogical Agents for Mixed-Initiative Problem Solving in Constructivist Learning Environments. *User Modelling and User-Adapted Interaction,* 9, (1-2), pp. 1-44, 1999.

Sampson D., Karagiannidis, C., Kinshuk, (2002). Personalised Learning: Educational, Technological and Standardisation Perspective. *Interactive Educational Multimedia,* number 4 (April 2002), pp. 24-39

Shaw E., Ganeshan R., Johnson W. L., and Millar D. (1999). Building a Case for Agent-Assisted Learning as a Catalyst for Curriculum Reform in Medical Education. *International Conference on Artificial Intelligence in Education.*

Zuckerman I., and Albreciit D. W. (2001). Predictive Statistical Models for User Modeling. *User Modeling and User Adapted Interaction,* 11.

Acknowledgements

Part of the R&D work reported in this paper is carried out in the context of the "EP.E.N.D.Y.SH" project, partially funded by the Greek Ministry of Education.

Hard Choices: Selecting a Course Management System

by Bruce Landon, Ph.D.

Choices are difficult because there are *too many products*

The situation is reminiscent of the early automobile industry when there were over a hundred automakers. Like the early auto industry many other competitors will not survive in the long run. The current front-runners: WebCT and BlackBoard started out as small almost personal projects a few years ago and are now multi-million dollar enterprises that span the global education marketplace. There may well be others out the current products that will evolve into the major brands of tomorrow as the market matures. The point of this analogy is that selecting a learning management system is much more complicated than selecting a new car, in part, because there are so many competing models. There are over 100 products in this marketplace that range from relatively simple limited function applications like WebBoard which just provides threaded discussions and chat to complex enterprise wide learning systems that link to backend databases and administrative data systems used by colleges and universities. Previously in 1997, I had attempted to characterize these products as components or suites by this categorization turned out not to be useful because there were so many variations from product to product he became difficult to classify new products. Also, the products in this marketplace evolve quite rapidly with a new model or version almost every year, like automobiles. So to deal with this rapidly changing market it seems better to characterize products in terms of the features that they provide.

Too little working memory in decision-makers

Nobel laureate, Herbert Simon (1979) characterized the human decision making capacity as having "Bounded Rationality" (also see Gigerenzer & Selten, 2001). When people face decisions they operate within the bounds or capacities of the human mind. They are limited by fallible perceptions, wandering attention, faulty memories, and fluctuating information-processing abilities. People don't optimize, but instead resort to simplifying rules of thumb in order to proceed with their decision-making. These limitations have been investigated for decades with the repeated finding that working memory limitations play a major role in limiting the ability to make rational decisions.

When facing difficult decisions, people encounter overload and then they resort to ways of coping that involve cognitive shortcuts. When overloaded, they are more susceptible to cognitive Illusions (Kahneman and Tversky, 1996). Cognitive illusions are similar to perceptual illusions in that they stem from the fact that in both types of illusions the person can focus only on a small part of the situation at one time. In the case of perceptual illusions this is because the fovea of the eye that sees fine detail encodes only a small segment of the spatial panorama at each fixation. In the case of cognitive illusions this is largely because the conscious working memory can hold only a few "things" and the rest must be inferred or extrapolated in ways that are sometimes biased. In both types of illusions the person is not necessarily aware of any "illusion" at all and may believe that they are "seeing everything correctly."

Too many Cognitive Illusions in Decision-Making

The discrepancies associated with cognitive illusions may be seen a little more clearly in contrast to an idealized rational decision process. In the idealized process, one starts by selecting relevant features/criteria and then assigning an importance weighting to each of those features. Next one evaluates each choice option on each of those important features and assigns a suitability score. Finally one makes the rational decision to choose the option with the highest weighted average suitability score (the average of the weights for a feature multiplied by the feature's suitability score). Choosing the option with the best score is the rational decision (Keeney and Raiffa, 1976 as cited in Roe, Busemeyer and Townsend, 2001). With only a couple of optional choices and a few important features it is likely the limitations of working memory would be overwhelmed even if one were able to do the mental multiplication part. When one is overwhelmed by the size and complexity of the decision situation then one is susceptible to a host of cognitive illusions. A few of the major ones are: Availability Heuristic, Representativeness Heuristic, Hindsight Bias, Gambler's Fallacy, the Framing Effect, Similarity Effect, Decoy Effects, and Overconfidence Effect. When the decision situation is simple and small, on the other hand, most people can and do make good judgments unaffected by these cognitive illusions.

Making the decision situation smaller and simpler can circumvent these obstacles. Dividing up a complex decision into several small and simpler decisions keeps the load on working memory within normal capacity and then decision makers can be quite rational in making good decisions. Donald Norman (1999) has made the case that human-computer interactions can and should be designed to take account of normal human fallible perceptions, wandering attention, faulty memories, and fluctuating information-processing abilities. With good design of decision-making processes that keep the in-the-head part small and simple, a system can be optimized to enable quality decision-making. The normative weighted averaging strategy can be easily divided up into small and simple component parts and then later recombined (outside-of-the-head) into a rational decision process that leads to the "best option." There is a powerful decision-making synergy in combining the focused judgmental prowess of people with the memory and computational prowess of computers.

How people normally Make Decisions: The 5 Basic Strategies

There are five basic decisions strategies (Payne & Bettman, 2001) for choosing among options (products, services etc.) based on features or aspects of the options. All of these five strategies are compromised by the reality that the set of options is limited to those known to the decision-maker and the "best" option may be simply missed in the whole process. While the names of these strategies on may be unfamiliar is quite likely that everyone has used all of the following strategies at one time or another:

> One Reason strategy (aka lexicographic, pick the best)
> Elimination by Aspect strategy (aka pick the last)
> Satisficing strategy (aka Bounded Rationality Model)
> Equal Weight strategy (aka scoring strategy)
> Weighted Averaging strategy (aka weighted adding strategy, grading model)

The One Reason strategy involves two steps: selecting the most important feature and then picking the product from all of the options that is best on that one feature. There is no requirement for the features to be expressed as numbers. If there is a tie then the decision maker simply repeats the process on the second most important feature. This non-compensatory strategy does not allow for some features of an option to make up for other less adequate features. The only involvement of a second feature is in the case of a tie that is broken by considering the next most important feature and selecting the option that is best on that feature.

The Elimination by Aspect strategy is a simple screening strategy involving two steps: setting the requirements for each of the features and then eliminating options one at a time which do not meet any one of the requirements. The decision maker examines the features of each option one by one and the option is eliminated as soon as a feature is found that does not meet the requirements. This popular strategy does not need for the features requirements be expressed as numbers and is easy-to-use. The elimination by aspect is a non-compensatory strategy so that once an option is rejected on any feature that option is eliminated from further consideration. This strategy does not necessarily result in a single best option since more than one option may pass on all of the requirements. Including any features that are irrelevant or biased in favor of one of the options compromises this process.

The Satisficing strategy (Simon, 1955 cited in Gigerenzer and Selten, 2001) is more psychologically developed model of sequential decision-making that includes setting requirement cutoff levels for each feature. An option is examined until it fails to meet one of the cutoff levels then it is rejected and the next option is considered. The first option that passes on all of the features is selected. If none of the options pass all of the cutoff requirements, then the requirements are reduced to new lower cutoff levels and the process is repeated. The satisficing strategy is non-compensatory and effected by the order in which the options are presented as well as the aspiration level of the initial cutoff requirements.

The Equal Weight strategy is comprehensive and considers all of the features on all of the options. The suitability values of one (passed) or zero (failed) are assigned to each to each feature on each option. The total suitability score for each option is the simple sum of the feature suitability values for that option (all features are weighted equally). The option with the highest sum of the values is selected. This strategy is directly analogous to multiple choice test scoring where correct answers are awarded one, wrong answers are awarded zero, and the highest sum score identifies (selects) the best student on the test. This compensatory numeric strategy enables some features assigned one's to compensate for other features that were assigned zero's. This strategy is more useful when there are many features because there is less risk of a tie for best score.

The Weighted Averaging strategy is a more complex version of the simple sum score model where each feature is also assigned an importance weighing. This idea implies that the decision maker is willing to make trade-offs to arrive at the selected option. The process involves five steps: (1) setting the importance weights for each of the features, (2) for each option then determining the numerical suitability value for every feature, (3) multiplying the feature suitability value times the feature weight, (4) then summing these weighted features subscores into an option total score, and (5) finally selecting the option with the highest average score. The averaging of the weighted option total scores simply returns the scores to the scaling metric of the feature suitability value units (which are often on a rating scale such as 1=poor to 9=excellent). This strategy is directly analogous to the grading model where different parts of the grade are weighted differentially (or subsections of an exam are weighted differentially) to arrive at the final mark. The weighted averaging strategy is compensatory in two ways: high scores on one feature compensate for low scores on another feature and a lower importance weight on one feature is compensated for by a higher importance weight on another feature. This strategy is less likely to result in ties between options than is the equal weight strategy when using a relatively small number of features. Furthermore, the weighted averaging strategy is considered the normatively rational decision process because it uses all of the information available in a consistent manner to arrive at a selection. This model is similar to the multiple linear regression model used in statistical analyses and suffers from some of the same shortcomings, most notably it is compromised when irrelevant features are used and when unreliable suitability values are used.

Decision makers often make use of combinations of the above strategies. In combined strategies the decision is made in phases. The initial phase is often to screen out some of the potential options in order to reduce the complexity of the situation to as short list of options. This phase is followed by a more thorough consideration phase to select the best option from a short-list of candidate options. The primary reason that everyone does not use the weighted averaging strategy all the time for all decisions is because it would be too mentally difficult and too time consuming. Other strategies are heuristic attempts to make good decisions with less effort and in less time and sometimes they seem to work well enough.

Thinking in terms of product features

Within each of the three audiences the features of the products can be further grouped into clusters of features and this can reduce the complexity further. On the Online Educational Delivery Applications site (http://www.edutools.info/landonline/) the following conceptual groupings have been used to provide targeted views for the learners, learner support, and technical administrator audiences respectively:

Learner Tools (for learner audience)
>   Communication Tools
>   Real-time Tools
>   Productivity Tools
>   Student Involvement Tools

Support Tools (for learner support audience)
>   Administration
>   Curriculum
>   Instructor

Technical Specifications (for technical administrator audience)
>   Pricing/Licensing
>   Standardization
>   Technical Administration
>   Hardware/Software

Within each of these conceptual categories there would be a small number of specific application tools or features. Altogether there were 52 such specific features that could be a part of an individual application. The complete listing of application features inside of the above conceptual structure attempts to organize the otherwise overwhelming list of features: (adapted from http://www.edutools.info)

No product had all of the possible features and no institutional situation needed all of the features either. The Online Educational Delivery Applications site was intended to help institutions find products with the features that they need and for vendors of products to be discoverable on the basis of the product functionality in the context of a rapidly developing marketplace. The list of product features also turns out to be a moving target over time as new technologies are incorporated into the evolving applications.

Screening phase of decision-making based on requirements of Individual Situations

The elimination by aspect strategy is a screening strategy involving two steps: setting the requirements for each of the features and then eliminating options one at a time which do not meet any of the requirements. To be able to decide which features are important the conventional approach is to conduct some sort of needs analysis of what is required in the institutional setting. This analysis often reveals the uniqueness of the needs of the future users of the online system. At this stage it can be beneficial to involve the stakeholders: students, faculty, student support personnel, and the technical administrators to gain later acceptance of the eventual decision as well as to become aware of needed features that might have been otherwise overlooked. Politically it can be beneficial to even involve representatives from the governing board of the institution when this decision will represent a new pedagogical direction or is expected to involve significant long-term resource commitment.

Making a Short List of Application Options

Using the web tool described above greatly speeds up this elimination by aspect process for those applications that are reviewed on the site. The elimination by aspect is a non-compensatory strategy so that once an option is rejected on any feature that option is eliminated from further consideration. This strategy does not necessarily result in a single best option since more than one option may pass on all of the requirements. The usual outcome of the elimination by aspect strategy is to result in a short list of possibly acceptable options that become the narrowed focus for a more discriminating decision strategy. It may be prudent for comparison purposes to include in the short list any applications that are used by consortia where the local institution is a member or in the case of community colleges the application that is used by local universities where the college has special relationships.

Evaluating product suitability as part of the weighted averaging strategy

Evaluating products (or externally hosted product options) can be a very large task. The greater the number of products and the greater the number of important features multiplies quickly into a potentially overwhelming product research task. This task can be partially shifted to the vendors by structuring a competition among the likely candidates where they are invited to bring the information to the decision makers rather than the decision makers seeking out the vendors and trying to find out the most current product information. The market has matured enough so that most vendors are capable of responding to a request for proposal (RFP) to supply the desired product functionality. Many institutions already have RFP procedures but may never have used them for a situation as complex as selecting an online educational delivery application.

Inviting the shortlist of vendors to competitive presentations/proposals (RFP model)

The RFP model has been described for web software acquisition recently (http://www.technologynews.net/rfp/infotech_rfp.doc) as a necessary part of the decision process. The RFP model offers several advantages over less formal product selection processes including: all vendors get the same information and have a fair opportunity to compete while the decision makers get a proposal document that can be used to assess both the vendor interest and competence. The RFP would be sent to the short list of possible vendors. The vendors will likely have questions as they prepare their proposals so it is useful to have a designated contact person who can supply consistent clarifying information to all of the vendors' requests for information. When the proposals are received there is often another round of elimination by aspect strategy to determine which proposals are in the competitive range. The US Department of Defense (http://web.deskbook.osd.mil/reflib/mfarsups/072ua/009/072ua009doc.htm) further advises that a proposal may be considered outside of the competitive range if (1) it does not address the essential requirements, (2) has a substantial technical drawback the would essentially require a new proposal to fix, or (3) the proposal contains major deficiencies, omissions, or out-of-line costs. They also advise that these proposals are part of a negotiation process and at the end of negotiations, the competitive vendors should be provided with one additional final opportunity to submit a revision known as the "best and final offer."

The RFP method is a time-consuming and involving process both for the institution and for the potential vendors that can be used to produce a fair vendor competition where the best candidate is selected and the social goals of rational decision-making are accomplished. The Online Educational Delivery Application site provides web tool support for the Weighted Averaging Strategy calculation part of the of decision-making. This decision engine tool is little more than an automated score sheet that combines the feature importance and the feature suitability scores into an appropriate total product score. The tool does however enable the decision-makers to use the most rational strategy of decision-making, which would be impossible to do in one's head. The following example illustrates the decision engine web tool using two vendors (WebCT and BlackBoard) with three features (accessibility for persons with disabilities, student help, and instructor help).

References

Gigerenzer, G. & Selten, R. (2001). Rethinking Rationality. In Gigerenzer, G. (Ed.) & Selten, R. (Ed.), (2001) Bounded rationality: The adaptive toolbox. (pp1-12) MIT Press, Cambridge.

Kahneman, D. & Tversky, A. (1996). On the reality of cognitive illusions. Psychological Review, 103(2), 583-591.

Norman, D.A. (1999). The invisible computer: why good products fail, the personal computer is so complex, and information appliances are the solution. MIT Press, Cambridge.

Payne, W.J. & Bettman, J.R. (2001). Preferential Choice and Adaptive Strategy Use. In Gigerenzer, G. (Ed.) & Selten, R. (Ed.), (2001) Bounded rationality: The adaptive toolbox. (pp. 123-146). MIT Press, Cambridge.

Roe, R.M., Busemyer, J.R. & Townsend, J.T. (2001). Multialternative Decision Field Theory: A Dynamic Connectionist Model of Decision Making. Psychological Review, 108(2), 370-392.

Simon, Herbert, (1979). Models of Thought, Yale University Press, New Haven.

Developing, Delivering, and Managing Legal Compliance eLearning Courseware in a Corporate Environment

Teresa Lau
Sun Microsystems Inc.
Menlo Park, CA
USA
teresa.lau@sun.com

Abstract: The paper describes Sun Microsystems' implementation and management of a mandatory online legal course, Business Conduct Overview, for a global, corporate wide audience beginning in July 2002. Sun created an eLearning environment to help employees access customized content, track their progress, report course completion, assess content comprehension, and send e-mail reminders to employees who haven't completed the mandatory training. The various components of the eLearning environment, implementation of the online course, and future plans for delivery and management of online legal compliance training at Sun are discussed.

1. Introduction

Throughout its 20-year history, Sun Microsystems has committed itself to the highest standards of business integrity. Because of increasingly complex legal and regulatory environments in the many countries in which Sun does business, Sun must make every effort to promote its employees' compliance with standards of business conduct. To raise employees' legal and ethical awareness and provide them with resources they need to make the right decisions and take effective actions, Sun's Business Conduct Office has developed an online learning course that is mandatory for all salaried employees to complete. To provide an easily accessible and effective eLearning environment, Sun Microsystems developed a suite of tools to deliver and manage online learning. The eLearning environment includes several unique features, such as the following:

- Automatic e-mail notifications to employees and their managers regarding scheduling and completion of mandatory training; e-mail reminders to those who haven't completed mandatory training
- Automatic launch of personalized content by job type, geographical location, and language preference
- Tracking and reporting
- Online quizzes to test and enhance retention and comprehension

The training is being rolled out in phases. Employees and their managers are notified when to begin the training. At present, nearly one-third of the targeted employee audience has completed the online training.

2. eLearning System Features

2.1. Automatic E-mail Notification

To accommodate the 40,000 Sun employees required to complete the legal training, the Business Conduct Overview course is being rolled out in phases that cut across organizational lines. The integration of the training system and Sun's human resources and e-mail systems allow customized e-mail notifications and reminders to be generated and sent automatically to employees and their managers when various events occur:

- An employee is scheduled to begin the mandatory training.
- An employee has completed the training.
- An employee has not completed the training although the deadline for completion has passed.

The customized e-mail messages serve as a means of communication between the Business Conduct Office and the global Sun community. This helps employees and managers take responsibility for managing their own training.

2.2. Personalized and Localized eLearning Content

To deliver customized content to employees that is tailored to individual responsibilities and needs, the system uses an up-front user profile survey to gather user information (Figure 1). The system can then dynamically generate personalized content based on an employee's job type, geographical location, and language preference.

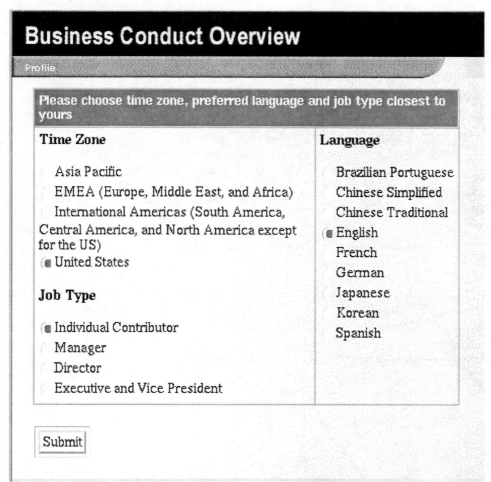

Figure 1: User Profile Survey

2.3. Tracking and Reporting

User progress tracking and management reporting are two important components of the eLearning environment for legal compliance training. To enable tracking, it is necessary to authenticate the user by his or her employee login and password against the human resources database connected through the eLearning system. Once an employee has logged into the system, all activities at the course level are tracked, and completion data is automatically collected and stored. The tracking data is assembled in real time into reports organized at the employee, manager, and organizational level. Real-time user tracking and reporting has proven valuable in managing Sun's mandatory legal training.

2.4. Online Testing and Assessment

To test employees' comprehension and retention of key concepts, short quizzes with feedback are embedded in each section of the course. At the end of the course, employees take a final test. After they have completed the final test, employees receive their test results with incorrect answers highlighted (Figure 2). They are also given additional references that correspond to the questions missed. The final test demonstrates the employee's mastery of content and is required for the employee to receive a completion status. The testing tool also includes comprehensive reporting features: for example, the summary scores can be used to analyze the effectiveness of the online instructional content.

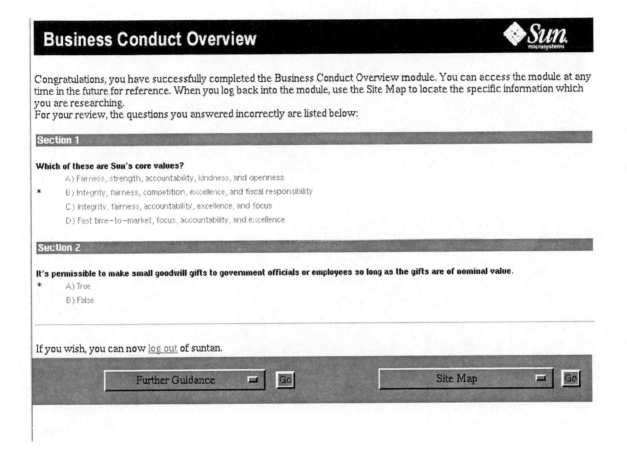

Figure 2: Test Feedback

3. Conclusion

Sun Microsystems has designed, developed, delivered, and managed an online legal compliance course for its worldwide workforce. Since the initial rollout in July 2002, more than one-third of eligible employees have successfully completed the mandatory training. The eLearning environment created for the delivery, administration, and management of the online course has proven an efficient, robust, cost-effective, and reliable way to deliver and manage online legal compliance training for a large enterprise. The success of online training for an internal audience will pave the way for Sun to launch the same legal training for our partners next year.

4. References

General Counsel Roundtable (2000). *Affirmative Defense: Innovative Approaches to Practicing Preventive Law.* Washington: Corporate Executive Board, 2000.

General Counsel Roundtable (2000). *On-Line Compliance Training Systems.* Washington: Corporate Executive Board, 2000.

Streaming, Plug-in Free PowerPoint™ Playback over the Web

Introduction

Microsoft PowerPoint is the most popular authoring tool for creating business presentations and training content. And for good reason – it's easy to learn and to use. It supports narration, animation, transitions, embedded video, as well as the ability to hyperlink or to navigate to specific slides within a single presentation, to other PowerPoint presentations, to Web pages (URLs) and to other content.

The only problem with PowerPoint is that the output files are too large for delivery over the Internet or through e-mail, and too numerous to manage easily.

That's where *impatica* comes in. Simply put, *impatica* **for PowerPoint** extends the reach of PowerPoint by providing an easy to use tool for delivering PowerPoint presentations over the Internet or through e-mail. And unlike PowerPoint's "Save as HTML", "Save as Web Page" or other options for Internet delivery, *impatica* **for PowerPoint** retains the rich media functionality of your presentation

This document describes how *impatica* **for PowerPoint** works, explains how the "*impaticized*" content is efficiently delivered and highlights the resultant benefits.

Conversion for Streaming Delivery

impatica **for PowerPoint** is a desktop software application that reads Microsoft PowerPoint files and transforms the file into an efficient streaming format that can subsequently be read and "played" by a small Java applet on the viewer's Internet device.

impatica **for PowerPoint** dissects the PowerPoint file and identifies each audio, text, shape, and picture. Each media object is compressed or otherwise optimized for Internet delivery.

- Audio is converted to Sun AU format and then compressed using *impatica*'s proprietary compression algorithm. (Sun AU audio is the only audio format currently supported by Java.)

- Pictures and other images are converted to GIF format (if 8-bit or less) or to JPEG format (if greater than 8-bit). JPEGs are compressed according to a Translation Option set by the content developer in the Graphical User Interface for *impatica* **for PowerPoint**.

- Pictures are further optimized by discarding any picture elements that have been removed through cropping. (Even if cropped, PowerPoint retains the entire original picture.)

- Text objects are rendered as images during the translation process. While this transformation is not necessarily optimal in terms of file size, it is a crucial step to ensure that all text will be displayed identically on all viewers' devices, regardless of hardware, OS, or browser platform.

- Wherever possible, autoshapes are retained as dimensioned objects; however, some compound autoshapes are rendered as images at translation time.

impatica **for PowerPoint** files typically achieve 90 to 95% compression of narrated, animated PowerPoint presentations, meaning that the resultant *impatica* file will be only 5 to 10% of the size of the original PowerPoint file. Note, however, that the actual compression achieved on a particular PowerPoint file will be dependent on the relative proportion of audio, text, autoshapes and image objects.

The optimized media objects are then organized into the *impatica* streaming file format, in the order of appearance in which the objects are required. That is, the objects required for the first slide are placed in front of the objects required for the second slide, and so on. Note that, in presentations that include hyperlinks between slides, since it is not possible to anticipate the order in which the viewer will choose to view the slides, the streaming *impatica* file is always organized in the physical slide order.

Wherever possible, *impatica* **for PowerPoint** will reuse objects that appear multiple times throughout the presentation. This pertains to all object types, including audio, text, autoshapes and images.

Playback in a Browser

Once translated, the *impatica* file must be uploaded to a Web server from which it can be played by *impatica*'s Java applet. Specifically, playback is initiated by opening a Web page that contains HTML code pointing to *impatica*'s applet and *impatica* file.

```
<APPLET CODEBASE = "appletlocation.com" CODE = "com.impatica.ImPlayer.class"
ARCHIVE = "ImPlayer.jar" WIDTH =504 HEIGHT =288>

<PARAM NAME = "FILE" VALUE="Intro">

</APPLET>
```

(Note that, if the *impatica* content and applet code are located in the same folder as the HTML page that invokes playback, the "CODEBASE" attribute is not required.)

When the Browser opens the Web page, it launches the applet which, in turn, opens and begins to stream the *impatica* content file. As soon as the first *impatica* objects have been received, the applet begins to display and play the *impatica* presentation while the remaining content objects are being streamed in the background.

Provided that the Internet connection is fast enough to stream the remaining content faster than it is required for playback, the *impatica* presentation will play without pause or hesitation. Normally, continuous playback can be achieved within a 2K stream, i.e., over a 28.8 kbps connection.

Note that when playing presentations that contain hyperlinks to specific slides within the presentation, pauses may occur if the viewer clicks on a hyperlink that jumps ahead several slides. The likelihood and extent of the pause will depend on the speed of the Internet connection, the "richness" of the PowerPoint content, and the number of slides jumped over by the hyperlink. However, these delays can be essentially eliminated through effective content design, using "tips and tricks" explained in the *impatica* for PowerPoint Users Manual.

Unlike other streaming technologies that require special server-side software to "push" the content to the browser, *impatica* content is read by the applet (within the browser) from any standard HTTP server. This approach has the additional advantage that *impatica* content will be automatically cached by proxy servers and caching network strategies thereby reducing the load on the main server. Because there is no server side software, the only playback bottleneck at the server end is the raw throughput of the server cluster and the corresponding connection to the Internet backbone.

Delivery through E-mail

Delivery of *impatica* content through e-mail is essentially the same as viewing *impatica* content from a Web page. The actual e-mail message is a small, simple HTML document that contains the <applet> tag and related information required to launch the applet and stream the *impatica* content from the server over the Internet.

The fundamental advantage of this approach is that the actual e-mail delivered to the recipients' inbox is tiny – generally only 2 to 3K, including all headers and addressing information. There are no bulky attachments that must be downloaded and that would typically clog up the recipients' in-box.

Only when the e-mail is opened, and as long as the user is then connected to the Internet, is the *impatica* content accessed and displayed as it is being streamed in from the server.

Scalability and bandwidth requirements

With reasonable content design, most narrated, animated *impatica* content will play within a 2Kbps stream. That bandwidth requirement is approximately the same as a well designed web page that contains a reasonable mix of text and graphics. One thousand concurrent hits to a web page that contains *impatica* content would require an aggregate throughput capacity of 20 Mbps, disregarding for the moment any savings that result from proxy servers or other caching schemes. That load would be well within the capability of a competent Web server. On the client side, the other important benefit of the high compression ratio is that the quality of the streaming presentation is acceptable at the very least, and high at best, over a standard modem connection (33-56Kbps).

These features represent major bandwidth advantages over other multimedia content delivery streams, such as Macromedia Flash and QuickTime or other video streaming technologies. In a large educational or corporate environment, the reduction in bandwidth can easily translate into thousands of dollars of savings on a monthly basis.

Storage requirements

Another benefit of *impatica*'s aggressive approach to compression is a significant reduction in the amount of disk space required to host PowerPoint content on the server. On average, *impaticized* PowerPoint files require only 10% of the storage capacity for PowerPoint files, whether they are stored as .ppt files or saved as HTML or as Web pages. Because *impaticized* PowerPoint presentations are stored as simple content files on an HTTP server, without any special server-side software, there is no additional overhead beyond the actual small *impatica* file.

The bottom line

impatica's unique and powerful technology combined with its intuitively simple user interface delivers important benefits to anyone wishing to publish their PowerPoint presentation over the Internet:

- **PowerPoint users become empowered as online publishers;**

- **The time, cost and complexity of producing online training and other content is substantially reduced;**

- **Presentations can be delivered to the widest possible audience, without regard for hardware, OS, browser or Internet connection speed;**

- **Plug-in free delivery ensures hassle-free, spontaneous delivery.**

- **Narrated, animated, interactive rich media content provides an engaging message – people remember more when they SEE, HEAR and INTERACT with the content;**

Diabetes and Your Eyes: A Pilot Study on Multimedia Education for Underserved Populations

Kimberly Lawless, Ph.D.[1]; Ben Gerber, M.D.[2]; Louanne Smolin, Ed.D.[1]; Irwin Brodsky, M.D., M.P.H.[2]; Mariela Girotti, R.N.[2]; Lourdes Pelaez, M.D.[2]; Arnold Eiser, M.D.[2]

[1] College of Education, University of Illinois at Chicago, Chicago, IL
[2] Department of Medicine, University of Illinois at Chicago, Chicago, IL

INTRODUCTION

The development and implementation of technology as a vehicle for instructional delivery to health care patients is on the rise (Health on the Net Foundation, 2002). More than ever, individuals are searching for more health knowledge and questioning their medical management through Internet derived mechanisms (Pew Foundation, 2002). Providers sensitive to these changes may suspect that acquired information is more valuable to patients when complimented or endorsed by their own health providers (Clement, 1995). In fact, both parties may potentially benefit, with providers saving time for education.

More recently, touch screen 'kiosks' are being investigated in clinical environments. Kiosks have been described as an easy, convenient, and preferable medium for learning (Glasgow, McKay, Boles et al., 1999). Example applications have included cancer therapy, support for individuals with brain injuries, and chronic disease management such as diabetes (Lewis, 1999). However, there are significant barriers to widespread use among vulnerable populations.

A digital divide persists in the United States, where specific low-income urban as well as rural geographic areas have less access despite overall growth in the US (National Telecommunications and Information Association, 2002). Besides having access to technology, computer skills make current applications more difficult to use (Eng, Maxfield, Patrick, et al., 1998). Few interfaces have been able to accommodate the diverse levels of capability among patients. Also, health literacy remains a barrier. In a study of 25 common health web sites, all of the English and 86% of the Spanish web sites required a high school level or greater reading ability (Berland, Elliott, Morales, et al., 2001). Health information that requires a higher level of literacy will exclude the 40 or more million Americans who are functionally illiterate. In response, recent computer applications have begun to address literacy, and subsequently received favorable responses in pilot testing (Castaldini, Saltmarch, Luck, et al., 1998).

One of the potential benefits of multimedia learning environments on patient education is the ability to target individual needs and preferences. Unfortunately, there are few quality resources available that target African-American, Latino, and other ethnic minority groups. According to Rosenthal and Bandura (1978) "attribute similarity generally increases the power of modeling influences even when the personal characteristics may be spurious indicants of performance capabilities" (p. 656). As such attending to salient characteristics of the population such as age, gender, education level, socioeconomic status, race and ethnicity can increase the impact of the learning materials (Bandura, 1997). Because multimedia environment invite the inclusion of video, users are able to see "themselves" in the educational materials, and can more easily provides appropriate modeling opportunities to minority populations where they might not otherwise be accessible.

This proposal details the development and implementation of a new multimedia application for an underserved patient population with diabetes. A pilot study was conducted to evaluate program use by participants, as well as patient attitudes regarding diabetic eye disease. The main outcome sought from using the program was to increase compliance with annual dilated eye examinations (the standard of medical care).

METHODS
Software Application Development
Prior to developing the application a needs analysis was undertaken. Research examining African-American and Latino diabetic patients was reviewed, especially regarding barriers to obtaining yearly eye examinations (e.g., Walker, Basch, Howard, et al., 1997). In addition, currently available information regarding diabetic eye disease was obtained through the National Eye Institute and National Eye Health Education Program and the Core Curriculum for Diabetes Education.

A lesson plan was created based on the ultimate objective of patients obtaining eye examinations. The lesson plan included 5 segments: (1) An introduction to diabetic eye disease (via patient testimonial), (2) A tutorial on how diabetes affects the eye, (3) A series of patient testimonials relating the barriers to obtaining eye examinations, (4) An interactive portion where the user is tested regarding the needs for an eye exam based on patient testimonials, and (5) A tour of the ophthalmology clinic where eye examinations are performed. The lesson plan was translated into Spanish by two bilingual researchers.

To complete the multimedia, digital images from the National Eye Institute were obtained. In addition, patients were recruited to provide videotaped testimonials. Consented individuals discussed their experiences with diabetic eye disease, or with eye examinations. A total of 16 African-American and 16 Latino diabetic patients were recorded in English and Spanish respectively, answering open ended questions freely without scripting. Example barriers discussed by patients included: fear, denial, religion/faith, pain, and insurance.

Clinical Pilot Testing
Patients arriving for their scheduled medicine or diabetes clinic appointments were recruited. Inclusion criteria include history of type 1 or type 2 diabetes, English or Spanish speaking, and responsibility for diabetes self-care. Consented patients were taken to the computer in the clinic and were instructed regarding the use of the touch screen. They were allowed to view the program at that time, or after their visits with their providers if more convenient. Participants were able to complete the program in approximately 15-20 minutes.

After viewing the multimedia program, a brief 20-question survey was completed regarding attitudes toward computerized patient education as well as diabetic eye disease. In addition, follow-up surveys were conducted 3 months and 6 months later by telephone.

RESULTS
A sample of 56 patients viewed the multimedia application and completed the initial survey (Table 1 includes demographic and descriptive information). Twenty-seven patients, primarily African-American (18/27), completed the English lesson, while 29 Latino patients completed the Spanish version. Overall, a majority of these subjects had no more than some high school education (70% of the English group, 83% of the Spanish group); and many had never had taken any diabetes

education classes before. With respect to standard of care, only 15 (56%) of the English group and 15 (52%) of the Spanish group have undergone dilated eye examinations. Finally, many have reported limited or no computer usage previously (48% of the English group, 14% of the Spanish group).

Of the initial 56 patients, 34 responded to the 3-month survey, and 30 responded to the 6-month survey. A repeated measures ANOVA with language (English/Spanish) as a between-subjects factor was employed. When necessary the Huynh-Feldt correction for degrees of freedom was used.

In the first of these analyses, difficulty of using the computer program (1 = Very Easy; 5 = Very Hard) was used as the dependant measure. Results of the analysis indicated a significant Time X Language interaction ($F_{(2, 52)} = 8.73$; $p < .01$). Examining a v-plot of this interaction, a quadratic effect for difficulty of use over time between languages was identified. Those participants who viewed the English version of the program rated computer usage significantly more difficult at the time of the three month follow-up, while the Spanish version participants maintained a consistent rating over time. Main effects for Time and Language were also significant ($F_{(1,26)} = 7.71$, $p < .01$); $F_{(1,26)} = 12.51$, $p < .01$, respectively), but interpretation was set aside in favor of the interaction.

For most of the attitude questions regarding diabetic eye disease, responses did not show a trend over time. However, significant main effects for time were observed with 'diabetes can result in blindness' ($F_{(2, 52)} = 3.48$; $p = .038$) and 'you can have eye damage with no symptoms' ($F_{(2, 52)} = 3.94$; $p = .025$); both with agreement lessening over time.

There was a small but significant difference between language groups with respect to attitude towards seeing the eye doctor every year ($F_{(1, 26)} = 5.04$; $p = .034$). The group viewing the Spanish program were more likely to strongly agree with this item.

Finally, a significant interaction between Language and Time toward being 'afraid to see the eye doctor', ($F_{(2, 52)} = 4.734$; $p < .05$). Main effects for Time and Language were not found to be significant. Examining a plot of the interaction we saw that the English group had an increase in reported fear to see the eye doctor at three months, but returned to baseline after an additional three months. However, the Spanish group remain consistent immediately following and at the three month follow-up, with a sharp increase in fear at the six month survey.

DISCUSSION

Despite common barriers to accessing health information, there was clear interest and use by the underserved patient groups represented in our sample. Most individuals felt the multimedia was 'easy' or 'very easy' to use; yet there was still a small minority who had difficulty with the English version. Some individuals expected the kiosk to act like a television, running continuously without user input. The reduced level of computer skills may increase the difficulty in actively engaging users. Unfortunately, activities that may better translate a message and provide education require more interaction than simple directions (such as touching the screen). Given the potential benefit of behavioral change, we need further research to improve the user interface.

There was a significant trend toward having greater difficulty using the program reported by subjects at 3 and 6 months. Some individuals may be more likely to report interest and enthusiasm immediately after experiencing a novel intervention. This may be an important concept to consider in additional evaluations where attitudes may change over time.

Attitudes towards diabetic eye disease and eye examinations were positive; though the study did not capture behavioral change from the intervention (the study did not include pre-testing). Differences between English and Spanish groups may represent inequalities in the program, particularly with patient testimonials. For example, some of the Spanish video sequences may stress specific ideas more strongly; or the English video clips may be less clear or influential. In either situation, the cultural differences in the program may contribute to expressing different messages resulting in different outcomes.

The data collected on attitudes post-intervention will be applied towards further development of the lesson. For example, the idea that faith alone may prevent eye disease was common in both English and Spanish groups; despite the majority disagreeing with it. Addressing faith is very important in education on prevention.

The greatest advantages cited by patients include: ease of use of the computer program, the educational nature of the audio narration, and the video testimonials of patients. Some of the users wished to unplug the headphones to so friends or family members can simultaneously view the multimedia. Having more headphones available at a kiosk may be worthwhile.

Implementation in the clinical environment is a significant challenge for interactive kiosks. Since the study has been completed, the computer has continued to collect data regarding patient usage. Further data analysis may offer solutions on how to integrate education into clinical flow. For example, prior to visiting a health provider, there is often an undesirable waiting period possibly serving as an opportune time for self-education. However, after an encounter with a provider, interest in personal health is piqued, and additional reinforcement via the computer may be a powerful component to the office visit (Gerber and Eiser, 2001).

Limitations to the study include small sample size, and large number of individuals unable to complete the telephone call survey. High levels of drop out in follow up surveys may result in overestimating the ease of computer use, if these individuals were less likely to provide positive attitudes about the program in follow up.

Increased resources are necessary to provide tailored information to people of different ethnicity, educational background or gender. Besides the creation of a second version of educational materials in Spanish for the Latino population, further work may still be considered to distinguish between people from Mexico, Puerto Rico, South America, or other Latin American regions. Further research is needed to better understand the cost/benefit ratio between cost of production and implementation and benefit of tailoring material to a target audience.

REFERENCES

Anderson, R. M. , Barr, P. A. , Edwards, G. J. , et al. (1996). Using focus groups to identify psychosocial issues of urban black individuals with diabetes. Diabetes Educ, 22, 28-33.

Bandura, A. (1997). Self-efficacy: The exercise of control. New York, NY: W.H. Freeman and Company.

Berland, G. K., Elliott, M. N., Morales, L. S., et al. (2001). Health information on the Internet: Accessibility, quality, and readability in English and Spanish. JAMA, 285 (20), 2612-2621.

Castaldini, M, Saltmarch, M, Luck, S et al (1998). The development and pilot testing of a multimedia CD-ROM for diabetes education. Diabetes Educ 24(4), 285-296.

Clement, S. (1995). Diabetes self-management education. Diabetes Care, 18, 1204-14.

Eng, T. R., Maxfield, A., Patrick, K. et al. (1998). Access to health information and support: A public highway or a private road? JAMA 280(15), 1371-1375.

Gerber, B. S., Eiser, A. R. (2001). The patient physician relationship in the Internet age: future prospects and the research agenda. J Med Internet Res 3(2), E15.

Glasgow, R. E., McKay, H. G., Boles, S. M. et al. (1999). Interactive computer technology, behavioral science, and family practice. J Fam Pract 48(6), 464-470.

Health On the Net Foundation. HON's Fifth Survey on the Use of the Internet for Medical & Health Purposes. URL: http://www.hon.ch [accessed Feb. 20, 2002].

Lewis, D. (1999). Computer-based approaches to patient education: a review of the literature. J Am Med Inform Assoc 6(4), 272-82.

National Telecommunications and Information Administration. *A Nation Online: How Americans Are Expanding Their Use Of The Internet*. URL: http://www.ntia.doc.gov/ntiahome/dn/index.html. [accessed Mar. 2, 2002].

Rosenthal, T. L., & Bandura, A. (1978). Psychological modeling: Theory and practice. In S. L. Garfield & A. E. Bergin (Eds.), *Handbook of Psychotherapy and Behavior change: An empirical Analysis* (pp. 621-658). New York: Wiley.

The Pew Internet and American Life Project. The Online Health Care Revolution: *How the Web helps Americans take better care of themselves.* URL: http://www.pewinternet.org/ [accessed Feb. 1, 2002].

Walker, E. A., Basch, C. E., Howard, C. J., et al. (1997). Incentives and barriers to retinopathy screening among African-Americans with diabetes. Journal of Diabetes and Its Complications 11, 298-306.

ACKNOWLDGEMENTS

Support from this project came through a grant from the Agency for Healthcare Research and Quality (U18-11092).

A New Baseline for Faculty Knowledge of Educational Technologies

Tracey Leacock, PhD
Simon Fraser University, Canada
leacock@techbc.ca

Abstract: As the pressure to use new technologies in the delivery of education increases, institutions should strive towards agreement on a new baseline level of faculty knowledge of learning technologies and an understanding of the impacts of technology on education. At TechBC, we developed a process that included an up-front investment in bringing current faculty up to the new level as well as the development of a culture that will help incoming faculty achieve the new level quickly. The key aspects of the approach include fostering a culture that encourages innovation in the use of educational technologies -- when and where they are appropriate -- and the formation of faculty into clusters for development and delivery of courseware.

In the past, there have been two extremes that described many potential users of educational technology: the technophobes and the technophiles. As the pressure to use new technologies in the delivery of education becomes ubiquitous, institutions should strive to move adherents at both extremes towards agreement on a new baseline level of knowledge for faculty and an understanding of the impacts of technology on education. At The Technical University of British Columbia (TechBC), we developed a process to do just that.

The TechBC Story

TechBC (now SFU-Surrey) uses a hybrid system (Nesbit 2002), in which face-to-face classes are mixed with online activities, to deliver degree programs in Information Technology and Interactive Arts to undergraduate and graduate learners. All courses have a significant online component delivered through our course management system (CMS), a proprietary system designed for content delivery, conferencing, etc. CMS content typically includes a combination of text, animations, links to external resources, video, interactive activities, etc. (Humphrey 2001). In the face-to-face sessions, faculty lead small group activities that enable learners to interact with and deepen their understanding of the content they are working with.

We are fortunate to have been in the position of having new programs and being able to hire faculty who have self-selected themselves as having an interest in the use of technology to improve the quality of education. However, behind the statement of interest, we have found that our faculty bring a variety of levels of technical expertise. In many cases, there has been more interest than first-hand experience.

Once we realized that not all of our faculty were comfortable with the whys (pedagogical considerations) or hows (technical considerations) of using the new technologies available to educators, we initiated an intensive and multi-faceted approach to increasing the baseline level of knowledge in these areas for all current faculty. We designed the process to become largely self-sustaining, with minimal institutional investment in across-the-board training after the initial start-up phase.

TechBC's unique situation made it easier to bring about such an approach, but the same ideas would be of great value to any institutions dealing with resistance or uncertainty around the increasingly prevalent role of technology in education.

Why Change the Baseline?

At one time, faculty could happily get by with just a pen and paper. In recent years, typing – or more appropriately, keyboarding – and even general computer literacy have become accepted basic skills.

Institutions expect that faulty will know how to send an email and how to find information on the web. The next logical step is to expect faculty to have some basic knowledge of how principles of instructional design can be applied to create solid courseware using new technologies. This knowledge must also be tied in with a good understanding of when the use of the technologies is appropriate and why.

The approach we took was designed to make this expectation explicit. By investing in "educational programs to foster these skills" (Advisory Committee for Online Learning 2001), we have changed what constitutes basic knowledge at our campus. Our goals were to improve the overall quality of courseware, increase the confidence of the faculty in working with new technologies, and establish strong working relationships between faculty and various areas of specialized support (e.g. media developers) who would be available to assist when faculty wanted to try projects that required a high level of technical expertise.

Our Approach

We used a multi-faceted approach to the initial development of the knowledge needed for this new baseline. The four main categories of effort included: faculty orientations; a mandatory course on educational technology and learning; ongoing workshops; and a formalized cluster structure for development and delivery of course materials.

Orientation. All new faculty attend an orientation session that provides an overview of what we do, how we do it, and whom to talk to about specific questions. This sets the stage in a number of ways. It clearly establishes our philosophy of teamwork – we're not sending anyone out on their own into uncharted waters. It also makes clear that we expect everyone to look for new and innovative ways that technology can *improve* learning – we aren't looking for bells and whistles, but we're not looking for the *status quo* for its own sake either. Finally, faculty have an opportunity to meet the people who can provide more advanced support, so they know what help is available. Typically, these orientations are held as group sessions just prior to the start of each term. This provides all new academic staff with a solid grounding, and allows continuing staff an opportunity to drop in to remind themselves of any services that they may not have used recently.

METL. All faculty are required to take a one-semester course called Mastering Educational Technology and Learning (METL). METL covers topics ranging from the design of measurable learning objectives, to the effective use of asynchronous conferencing, to how to integrate learning objects into online content to improve learning. This course uses the same delivery methods that faculty will use in their own classes – a combination of online resources and activities and face-to-face sessions where they can apply their new knowledge. Learners (faculty) work together in small groups, using courseware that they are currently developing or delivering as examples for discussion and activities. (See Stacey 2001 for a review.)

Ongoing workshops. TechBC also offers optional workshops on topics such as designing concept maps for content; matching learning objectives, content, and assessments; and moderating online conferences. The topics are flexible and depend on the needs of participants. These workshops may be offered by members of our Educational Technology & Learning unit or by faculty who have gained experience in particular technologies or delivery methods. The workshops are typically informal and may be as short as a brown-bag lunch or as long as a full day, depending on the needs of the topic.

Clusters. The most innovative aspect of our attempts to raise the baseline on knowledge of new technologies in education has been our use of clusters (Leacock 2001). This is also the aspect that will have the biggest impact on the self-sustainability of the process. We use clusters both for development of courseware and for delivery of courses that have many sections. Both types of clusters are formed on a term-to-term basis.

Development clusters typically consist of 4-10 developers (faculty), an instructional designer, and a project manager. Other specialists are also available as resources to the cluster on an as-needed basis (Fig. 1). The cluster is responsible for the development of a set of courses (up to 6-credits per cluster member), and the group has to follow a general pattern and timeline for development. Within these constraints, there is flexibility for different approaches. The cluster members provide ongoing feedback and insights that are directly related to each other's current development assignments.

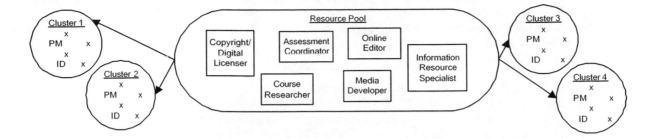

Figure 1: Structure of Development Clusters at TechBC.

Members of a cluster generally meet synchronously on a weekly basis, using a combination of face-to-face meetings and teleconferencing. They also communicate through email and informal meetings regularly. The cluster members share their experiences with using the TechBC delivery models (Course Delivery Models 2001) and available technologies in different teaching contexts. This feedback helps developers to learn from and build on what their peers have already tried, and it fosters a culture of open communication and knowledge-sharing.

Developers have a single four-month cycle in which to complete an assignment. There are three supra-cluster checkpoints: specifications review, quality circles, and the final show & tell. Each cluster may decide to implement additional internal checkpoints. At the specifications review, a university planning committee reviews the detailed plans for the courseware to ensure that they fit with the intentions of the overall programs and institutional needs. (See Module Specification System 2001.) At the quality circles checkpoint, an interdisciplinary team that includes a content expert, an instructional designer, an assessment specialist, and others reviews a sample unit of each course and provides feedback that the developer can use to improve that unit and inform the development of the remaining units (Belfer & Leacock 2002 unpublished raw data). Finally, the clusters present the completed courseware in a show & tell session that is open to all members of the university community.

The results of this cluster development process have been exciting. When we introduced this approach, many developers were new to the online environment and were not familiar with the concepts of instructional design. The feedback from within the clusters tended to be at a low level. However, after completing the METL course and going through the cluster development process once, most developers showed a marked improvement in their choice of technologies, activities, and assessments. This also meant that they were able to provide one another with better feedback as well.

We recently extended the cluster concept to the delivery of our high-enrollment courses by formally grouping all instructors of each course into clusters and encouraging them to communicate regularly on what they were doing in their sections. This helps newer instructors to learn from their more experienced peers, and it increases consistency across sections.

Outcomes

Now that we have a large percentage of experienced faculty who have achieved a new baseline level of knowledge, they automatically use that knowledge when interacting with new faculty, thus, increasing the baseline knowledge of their peers. The result is a self-sustaining culture that understands the benefits and limitations of current technologies in educational delivery and that is prepared to look for and evaluate new and innovative ways to improve education through technology and better instructional design. The tangible results include increased productivity, reduction in the overassessment of learners, strong peer-peer support networks, and more effective use of specialized support services for technically challenging projects.

Productivity. Prior to introducing this approach, course development tended to stretch over multiple terms, and was more likely to trickle over into delivery. Only a few courses would be developed by a few faculty in any given term. In the first semester of using this approach, we increased productivity to approximately 90 credit hours worth of courseware, developed by 19 faculty in six clusters. (Most of these faculty also held teaching responsibilities during this term.)

Assessment. At TechBC, we had identified a problem with overassessment, due to the modular nature of content delivery (courses are delivered in 5-week, 1-credit chunks, each with a transcripted grade). The quality circles and peer feedback have led to more effective ways to assess learner progress that reduce learner and faculty time commitments, while improving the validity of the assessments (Belfer 2001). The material that is developed is also more integrated across the curriculum, has better agreement between objectives, content, and assessments, and has lead to improved ratings by learners during and after delivery.

Peer Support. By changing clusters each term to meet operational needs, faculty get an opportunity to work and develop relationships with many others with similar or related interests. Faculty who studied together during METL or worked together to create courseware also tend to continue to collaborate during later development cycles and to openly discuss issues that arise during delivery.

Specialized Support. Our Educational Technology & Learning unit provides specialized support for development and delivery needs. This unit is now able to allocate its resources to new and innovative projects, as most faculty are able to take care of more basic tasks themselves.

Conclusion

At TechBC, we consciously chose to make an up-front investment in increasing faculty knowledge of the new technologies available to educators. We implemented an approach that had some mandatory components, covering basic information that applied to everyone's teaching, and some optional components that allowed those who were interested to work with certain technologies or activities more closely. The result has been as much a cultural change as a technical change. We have created an environment that encourages innovation in the search for better ways of fostering effective learning. We have created informal peer support structures that promote collaboration, rather than lone ranger or competitive approaches. Finally, we have succeeded in raising the bar on what constitutes basic knowledge of educational technologies.

References

Advisory Committee for Online Learning, The (2001). *The e-learning evolution in colleges and universities*. Ottawa, ON Canada: Industry Canada.

Belfer, K. (2001). *Evaluation Practice Guidelines*. Retrieved July 2, 2002 from http://www.etl.techbc.ca/data/0079EvaluationMethodsDraft/EvaluationModelsMay-02.pdf

Belfer, K. & Leacock, T. (2002) [The effect of quality circles on the courseware development process at TechBC]. Unpublished raw data.

Course Delivery Models at TechBC (2001). Retrieved July 2, 2002 from http://www.etl.techbc.ca/data/0005DeliveryModelsSummary/DMSummaries.pdf

Humphrey, D. (2001) *CMS Orientation*. Retrieved July 2, 2002 from http://www.etl.techbc.ca/data/0001CMSOrientation/index.html

Leacock, T., Farhangi, H. Mansell, A., & Belfer, K. (2001). Infinite possibilities, finite resources: The TechBC course development process. *Computers & Advanced Technology in Education,* 2001, International Association of Science and Technology for Development, Banff, AB. 245-250

Module Specification System (2001). Retrieved July 2, 2002 from http://www.hub.techbc.ca/mss

Nesbit, J. (2000). *Innovation @ TechBC*. Retrieved July 2, 2002 from http://www.etl.techbc.ca/data/0032InnovationAtTechBC/index.html

Stacey, P. (2001, May 25). E-learning – Authoring, instructional design and teaching. *T-net British Columbia*. Retrieved July 2, 2002 from http://www.bctechnology.com/statics/pstacey-may2501.html

Peer and Self Evaluation for Improving Student Collaboration in Online Courses

Lars Leader

Lorraine Schmertzing

Department of Curriculum & Instructional Technology
Valdosta State University
U.S.A.
lfleader@valdosta.edu

Abstract: Although student collaboration for projects offers advantages, especially in the online environment, too often student contributions to a team effort are not equitable or effective. This study addressed that problem by incorporating both peer and self-evaluation into collaborative projects undertaken by graduate students in an online course on evaluation and research methods. In one experimental group, students anonymously evaluated themselves and other team members on their collaborative efforts. Differences between this group and a control group on subsequent project grades and perceived collaboration within project teams suggested that self/peer evaluation could promote group collaboration. Survey responses indicated that after completing self/peer evaluations, students increased the frequency of communication within teams. Implications for promoting online group collaboration and further research are discussed.

Introduction

Project-based learning and the use of project work for students in general have been implemented in recent years in many schools and training organizations. Learner collaboration on the frequently complex tasks in projects is at the heart of this instructional technique. Studies provide considerable evidence that the joint problem solving in these situations is associated with better use of higher-level thinking skills, such as planning, reflection, and metacognition (O'Malley, 1995). Computer-mediated communication in distance learning has also been shown to promote critical thinking by incorporating technologies such as asynchronous discussion boards, which foster revision and reflection in the learning process (Barab, Tomas, & Merril, 2001). With the increase in instructional use of the World Wide Web, learners now often collaborate online for projects. This provides the opportunity to involve students in higher-order learning tasks while taking advantage of the practical benefits of distance education.

However, there is also a downside to student collaboration in project work. Students in collaborative groups frequently complain about some members of the group not "pulling their weight." This decrease in individual effort when performing in a group compared with working alone was termed "social loafing" by Falchikov and Goldfinch (2000). Social psychologists suggest that slacking by members of collaborative groups can be discouraged through individual accountability in the group environment (Myers, 1990). Various ways to identify the contribution of individual group members can be incorporated into assessment of project work. Yet, this is often difficult to administer, especially in an online course where it is often impossible to observe the work of the groups. Trying to identify each group member's contribution may lead to negative attitudes among students if they are asked to judge each other's contribution and make that evaluation available to the group. Or students may collude to provide inflated evaluations of each other to the instructor. The present study considers an alternative approach intended to promote better collaborative effort within project groups. The main research question in this ongoing study is, "When online project team members each anonymously evaluate the collaborative effort made by themselves and other members of their team, what are the effects of these evaluations on project quality and team member attitudes?"

Method

The students in this study took a graduate course in evaluation and research methods at a regional southeastern university. This is a required course within a totally online Instructional Technology program. Participants were graduate education students at the Masters and Educational Specialist levels. The 5 males and 23 females were nearly all of the students in two sections of the course during the years 2001 and 2002.

Among the course requirements were three major projects in which the students worked collaboratively and were assessed by a group grade on each project. The first project involved each team observing an activity, writing descriptive notes on it, and interviewing one of the participants. The team report of this qualitative fieldwork included coded excerpts, data display, and interpretation of the meaning of behaviors in the observed activity. The second project was a team evaluation of an educational or training program. This mixed-method evaluation included testing, observation, and survey. The third project was a proposal for an instructional intervention to address a concern within the evaluated program. The product for this project was a PowerPoint presentation developed by the team. The students self-selected the members of their two- or three-person teams.

For the study design, the teams were randomly assigned to two groups. During each course the primary investigator was not informed as to the assignment of particular students to the groups. Students in the intervention group ($n = 14$) anonymously evaluated themselves and their other team members after the first course project; those in the control group ($n = 14$) did not. The online evaluation form consisted of 12 statements with Likert-style responses. These statements described characteristics of a team member that would facilitate effective collaboration within the project team. One statement asked if "This teammate shared fairly in the production effort." Another statement was "This teammate communicated effectively." Another was "This teammate helped the team to effectively use the strengths of each team member." Each participant completed a separate form on each member of the team. For the self-evaluation, each participant completed a form with the same statements reworded as in this example: "I provided accurate information for the report of this project." Options for responding to each statement were: strongly agree, agree, disagree, and strongly disagree.

The dependent measures were (1) the group grades on the three projects and (2) the individual student responses to a survey completed after the first project and again after the third project. Each project was graded on points for content, format, and clarity by the primary investigator. Students worked on the second and third projects after the intervention group performed the self/peer evaluation. Therefore, the grades on these two projects were combined for analysis. The student survey consisted of 20 Likert-style questions. Some questions asked about skill in using online communication tools. An example is "What is your present level of skill using chat room discussion?" Other questions asked about the frequency of interaction using these tools, for example: "While working with your teammate(s), how often did you communicate by WebCT personal mail?" Another type of question asked about teamwork. For example, one question was "How often did problems concerning the responsibilities that members of your team were to assume affect the quality of your project?" An open-ended question at the end of each survey asked the students to comment on team project work in the course.

Both grade and survey data were analyzed using t-tests. An alpha of .05 established significance. Descriptive statistics were obtained for the survey and self/peer evaluation responses. The open-ended question responses were analyzed qualitatively for trends and themes.

Results

On the first project, the grades for the intervention group ($M = 18.29$) did not differ significantly from the grades of the control group ($M = 18.14$), indicating pre-intervention equivalence of groups. On the second and third projects, which followed the peer/self evaluation of collaboration, the grades for intervention group ($M = 41.64$) were higher than the grades of the control group ($M = 40.00$). However, this difference only approached significance, $t(1,26)$, $SE = .84$, $p = .06$.

On the first student survey no significant difference was found between the groups on their responses to any of the items, again indicating pre-intervention equivalence of groups. Responses to the second student survey, which was administered after completion of the third project, indicated significant differences on three of the 20 items. All three items asked student how often they had communicated with their teammate(s) while working on the second and third projects. Response options (and values) were: never (1), less than once per week (2), 1-2 time per week (3), 3-6 times per week (4), and daily or more frequently (5). On the item that asked about team communication by telephone, the means were 2.92 for the intervention group and 2.15 for the control group, $t(1,24)$, $SE = .36$, $p = .04$. For the item that asked about team use of a chat room, the means were 1.92 and 1.38 respectively, $t(1,26)$, $SE = .23$, $p = .03$. The third item asked about team communication by WebCT personal mail. The means were 3.61 for the intervention group and 2.69 for the control group, $t(1,26)$, $SE = .42$, $p = .04$.

Description of student survey responses for the groups combined was also obtained. When they started the course, almost half of the students were looking forward to being on a team, with the rest about equally divided between a dislike based on bad previous experiences and ambivalence over the prospect of group work. On a Likert-response scale that ranged from 1 = very uncomfortable to 4 = very comfortable, the students were, on the average, comfortable with group work in the course after the first project ($M = 3.44$) as well as after the third project ($M = 3.26$). When asked about grouping for project work, 78% on the first survey wanted to work in a group rather than individually and 72% on the second survey preferred group work. The students responded that for their own learning the team project work was effective ($M = 3.27$ on the first survey and 3.42 on the second one), with a four-point scale from very ineffective to very effective.

A general analysis of the qualitative data from the open-ended survey questions revealed several major themes. One of the prominent ones focused on the benefit of having someone to use as a "sounding board". It is interesting to note that this theme appeared much more regularly in the comments block of the early survey than the later survey. Students identified a variety of ways that having the "sounding board" was beneficial, such as: "I like having someone I can bounce my ideas off of," "Working in my team has been conducive to brainstorming, has provided different viewpoints leading to better ideas, and it has helped us to begin to grasp complex concepts by talking them out," and "Getting another person's input has helped me to see some other dimensions that I would not have picked up on alone."

Another recurring theme was related to individuals and how their own traits either helped or hindered the team experiences. Routine comments regarding team members like, "when all members pull their weight, group work could be effective," "[often] you end up with one or two people doing most of the work (if not all)," and "If all partners contribute to the work load, the learning experience can be invaluable" were present. However, there were also a number of students who chose to emphasize the importance of each person's involvement in a more positive manner: "I work well with a team when I have the freedom to work with whomever I choose [which was the case in this project]," "both of us seem to compliment each other," "the grouping was great," and "grouping should be done carefully." Students chose to make the point somewhat differently, but either in the early survey or the late survey most students either blatantly stated or eluded to the idea that the success of teamwork lies in the natural ability of the team to "fit" together. We chose to include the word, "natural" ability because there was only one comment that indicated a process of working to create a team fit. Other than the admission that, "at times coordination was a bit confusing (due to my work schedule) though successful due to my partner's coordinating and communication skills," no other student indicated a shift from a difficult working relationship to a beneficial team relationship.

Based on a curiosity about how the intervention might change the descriptive language students used in their comments on teamwork, a simple analysis was done to compare the responses from the intervention and control groups. Each comment was examined for words or phrases that may demonstrate strong emotion and/or a more personal tone in the context of the sentence. Some of the key words were friend, feel, personally, excuses, unhappy, stressful, joy, nice, and fear. It did not appear that the intervention changed the descriptive language. Rather it was fairly consistent that students who used emotional language on the early survey were the same students who used it on the later survey and it did not matter whether they were in the control group or the intervention group.

Discussion

The focus of this study was on how peer and self-evaluation for collaborative effort in online project teams might affect project quality and team member attitudes. For project quality, the results indicate that the effect was borderline. Grades for the intervention group on the projects which they undertook and completed after their peer and self-evaluation only approached being significantly higher than the grades of the students in the control group. On the evaluation forms the students responded to statements that were meant to serve as criteria for effective collaboration. Responding to these rating criteria was anticipated to have beneficial effects on team members. The self-evaluation was expected to promote personal development and improve interaction among team members. It was also meant to compel team members to direct their individual efforts in ways they otherwise might have ignored or omitted. Similarly, the peer evaluation was expected to provide direction for improving group collaboration. As explained by Haas and Hass (1998), reflecting on the various criteria that make for an effective collaborative effort and evaluating how other members of the team measure up may suggest to the student evaluator opportunities for improving the group effort.

However, the only measures that did differ significantly between the intervention and control groups were student responses on three of the student survey items. Each of the three items concerned the frequency of interaction between students when using communication tools. Students in the intervention group reported that they communicated with others on their teams significantly more frequently by telephone, chat room, and e-mail than did the students in the control group. This finding appears to indicate that the self/peer evaluation promoted more communication within teams. It may be that students' awareness of the importance of communicating frequently with others on the team was positively influenced by the rating criteria on the evaluation forms. Two of the evaluation items focusing specifically on communication within the team were "This teammate met (in-person or online) when needed" and "This teammate communicated effectively." The thought occurs to us that this increase in frequency is one of the easier changes to realize for improving collaboration. As our analysis of the open-ended comments suggested, students in neither the intervention group nor the control group indicated that the quality of their collaboration improved in such areas as fair distribution of effort, suggesting ideas and accepting others' ideas, and effectively using the strengths of each team member. Inculcation of these characteristics of superior collaboration may require more direct methods, such as training focused on effective collaboration.

This research is an on-going effort. We plan to continue the study with additional participants in the current and future sections of the evaluation and research methods course. With data obtained from more participants, the effectiveness of using peer and self-evaluation to promote online collaboration in student teams should become clearer.

References

Barab, S., Thomas, M. & Merril, H. (2001). Online learning: From information dissemination to fostering collaboration. *Journal of Interactive Learning Research, 12*(1), 105-143.

Falchikov, N., & Goldfinch, J. (2000). Student peer assessment in higher education: A meta-analysis comparing peer and teacher marks. *Review of Educational Research, 70*, 287-322.

Haas, A. L., & Haas, R. W. (1998). The use of self-rating and peer-ratings to evaluate performances of student group members. *Journal of Marketing Education, 20*, 200-210.

Myers, D. G. (1990). *Social psychology* (3rd ed.). New York: McGraw-Hill.

O'Malley, C. (1995). *Computer supported collaborative learning.* Berlin: Springer.

Academic Administration and Organization Model of Digital Distance Universities

In-Sook Lee, Sejong University, 98 Gunja-dong, Gwangjin-gu
Seoul, Korea, inlee@sejong.ac.kr
Seyoung Chun, Chungnam University, Korea, sychun@cnu.ac.kr
Yeonwook Im, Hanyang Cyber University, Korea, yeonwook@empal.com
Heok Heo, Sunchon University, Korea, hoheo@sunchon.sunchon.ac.kr

Abstract: Digital distance education system has become a growing form at the higher education sector. This study suggests a model of academic administration and organization for digital distance universities, which would serve as a corner stone for early successful establishment and enhancement of educational quality. This model shows that distance universities should be equipped with services in both the faculty and staff sides of academic administration, instruction-learning support, student support and welfare, and educational evaluation and these services also need support in the form of organization. The model also emphasizes flexibility and dynamism that connects services and organizations and enables timely provision of services and top-level receptiveness.

Introduction

Digital distance education system has become a growing form at the higher education sector. In Korea, the Ministry of Education and Human Resources permits the establishment of digital distance universities, as part of lifelong education initiatives, and further tries to extend the scope of those universities. The governmental supports have accelerated distance education systems in terms of quantity: Now it is a high time for more attention to be paid to 'quality'. It definitely needs to study a framework of academic and organizational systems that can embrace the diverse needs of learners, the pedagogical considerations of various technologies, and the various instructional services.

The purpose of this study is to suggest a model of academic administration and organization for digital distance universities, which would serve as a corner stone for early successful establishment and enhancement of educational quality. This study was accomplished through the following methods: Content analysis of related documents through which a theoretical framework for the model has been derived. Surveys on three different types of research subjects, which include 15 national and 4 international digital distance universities, 2 national distance education companies, and 18 experts.

Results and Suggestions

Eight Propositions

Based on the reflections on all results of literature review, surveys, and benchmarking, the following eight propositions were suggested that the academic and organizational model of digital distance universities has meant to satisfy:
1) Strategic goals driving digital distance education can vary and organizational structures, governance, programmatic emphases, and financial models should be compatible with the strategic goals. 2) To be successful and competitive, digital distance education will require a governance model with a level of dynamism and flexibility dramatically different from the traditional faculty governance model. 3) Organizational governance should create right mixes about the responsibilities and agreeing on who make what decisions. 4) Governance and organizational structures for attracting and retaining qualified teaching faculty and instructional support personnel are emphasized. 5) Providing appropriate academic and student services to learners is a critical quality issue. 6) With distance education, partnerships are essential. 7) A multitude of policy issues associated with digital distance education exists - ownership of intellectual

property, workload, accessibility, appropriate use, conflict of interest, to name a few. 8) Digital distance education can be an expensive proposition so that only institutions with significant investment capacity should establish distance education.

Suggested Academic Administration and Organization Model

On the basis of above eight propositions, we propose an academic administration and organization model for successful educational service (Figure 1).

Figure 1. Academic administration and organization model

This model shows that distance universities should be equipped with services in both the faculty and staff sides of academic administration, instruction-learning support, student support and welfare, and educational evaluation and these services also need support in the form of organization. The model also emphasizes flexibility and dynamism that connects services and organizations and enables timely provision of services and top-level receptiveness.

Academic administration covers the ideas of academic term system, curriculum operation model, academic organization, tuition and fee, admission and registration, learning quality control, and enrollment size. Instruction-learning support deals with the issues of curriculum quality control, content quality control, instruction-learning process quality control, appropriate technology infrastructure, and faculty support system. Student support and welfare deals with the issues of academic information, learning support service, requests and complaints handling, and technology infrastructure. Educational evaluation introduces various key ideas for quality control in distance education. Teaching and administration support organization suggests that instructional support, system management, marketing and public relations are given more emphasis in distance universities than in traditional offline universities. Organizational structure exhibits more diversity in institutions that provide services in partnerships than in institutions that provide all services by themselves.

A variety of support organizations are needed in distance universities for quality control of various aspects of the institutions including the following (Figure 2): (1) curriculum development and assessment (curriculum development, quality control in curriculum, assessment of education effectiveness); (2) contents development (instructional design, graphic design, web programming, multimedia development); (3) student support (academic information, learning evaluation system, evaluation system for learning process, learning progress checking, etc.); (4) faculty support for instructional development (instructor training, consulting, instructional resource development); (5) marketing and promotion (student recruiting, promotion and sales of educational services, faculty recruiting); and (6) system management (system development and operation, technical support services).

Figure 2. Professional Support

References

AAUP (1997, November). Report on distance learning. Presented by the subcommittee on distance learning. http://www.aaup.org/govrel/distlern/dlrpttxt.htm. Accessed 02/26/2002.

AFT (2000. September). Guidelines for the evaluation of electronically offered degree and certificate programs. Washington, D.C.: AFT.

Berg. G. A. (2001). Distance learning best practices debate. WebNet Journal. 3(2). 5-6, 17.

Council for Higher Education Accreditation (2002). Accreditation and assuring quality in distance learning. CHEA monograph series 2002, number 1. Washington, D. C.: CHEA

Eaton, J. S. (2001. 10). Core academic values, quality, and regional accreditation: The challenge of distance learning. Washington, D. C.: CHEA. http://www.chea.org/Research/core-values.cfm.

Gellman-Danley, B. & Fetzner, M.J. (1998). Asking the Really Tough Questions: Policy Issues for Distance Learning. Journal of Distance Learning Administration. 1(1). [Online] http://www.westga.edu/~distance/danley11.html

James C. Taylor, J.C. & Swannell, P. (2001). An Euniversity for an E-world. International Review of Research in Open and Distance Learning.htttp://www.irrodl.org/content/v2.1/usq.html

Kidwell, J., Mattie, J., & Sousa, M. (2000). Preparing your campus for E-business. In the E is for everything, R. Katz and D. Oblingor (Eds.). San Francisco: Jossey-Bass.

McLendon, E. and Cronk, P. 1999. Rethinking Academic Management Practices: A case of meeting new challenges in online delivery. Online Journal of Distance Learning Administration. 2(1). http://www.westga.edu/~distance/mclendon21.html) (5/25/99)

Moore, M.G. (1994). Administrative Barriers to Adoption of Distance Education. The American Journal of Distance Education. 8(3).

NCES (1999). Distance Education at Postsecondary Education Institutions: 1997-98 [PDF file] http://www.ed.gov/Technology/reports.html. Accessed 07/30/2001.

Oblinger, D. G., Barone, C. A., & Hawkins, B. L. (2001). Distributed education and its challenges: An overview. Washington, D.C.: American Council on Education.

ODLQC. Standards in open and distance learning. http://www.odlqc.org.uk/odlqc/standard.htm. Updated May 2001.

Delphi Study on Competency Model of

Online Instructor

Online instruction has greatly changed the learning environment and learning process in comparison with traditional instruction. It requires a new kind of roles and competencies in instructors (Oh, 1998; Berge, 1996; Kearsley et al., 1995; Kearsley, 200; Reeve & Reeve, 1997). Nonetheless, many studies have been made on technology related to online education and its potential, whereas few studies have been conducted to identify what instructors actually do online (Salmon, 2000). Therefore, there is a need for a systematic and comprehensive study of online instructer's roles and competencies.

This study attempted to provide one indicator for training, selection and placement of future online instructors by identifying online instructor's roles and competencies in a more systematic and comprehensive way. To attain this goal, the following research questions were set:

First, what major roles and competences are required of online instructors?

Second, what role cluster by each role is required of online instructors?

Third, what is the descriptive competency model synthesizing online instructors' roles and competencies?

To fulfill these study questions, the current study conducted the questionnaire research three times with the use of the Delphi technique, especially the Modified Delphi technique which is a research method of finding out the consensus by extracting and synthesizing an expert group's opinions and judgement.

Based on the study results, the following conclusion was drawn:

First, the major role and competency required of online instructors were as follows: 6 major roles required of online instructors include 'interaction facilitator and manager', 'information manager and user', 'classroom evaluator', 'collaborator', 'subject matter expert', and 'planner'. The items rated as the core competency of online instructors totalled 15 items, of which 5 items were found to be 'subject matter expertise', 'interaction facilitation and management', 'instructional design', 'online communication', and 'learning activity evaluation'.

Second, 18 competencies were adopted as the competency cluster of the 'interaction facilitator/manager'. 21 competencies were adopted as the competency cluster of the 'information manager/user'. 14 competencies were adopted as the competency cluster of 'classroom evaluator'. 19 competencies were adopted as the competency cluster of 'collaborator'. 16 competencies were adopted as the competency cluster of 'subject matter expert'. And 16 competencies were adopted as 'planner'.

Third, 5 finally identified core competencies included 'subject matter expert', 'interaction facilitation and management', 'instructional design', 'online communication', and 'learning activity evaluation'. Basic common competency is what becomes commonly fundamental in performing every role adopted in this research. It was found that 7 finally identified basic common competencies. And 'role-related competency' is the competency necessary in carrying out a particular role and refers to the competency partially applied according to 6 roles. It was found that the 'role-related competency' of the online instructor accounted for 14 competencies.

Time and Resource Issues Pertaining to the Design and the Management of Course Materials for a WebCT-Based Project with Engineering Students

Geneviève Légaré
Concordia University, Montréal, Canada
legare@vax2.concordia.ca

Abstract

This paper describes a project using WebCT with engineering students registered in the course "Impacts of Technology on Society" at Concordia University, Montréal. Students carried out five individual assignments that were posted and returned using WebCT. The assignments were used to provide practice in writing as well as to develop critical thinking skills. More specifically, WebCT was used primarily as a mode of delivery to post and to receive student assignments. While a content analysis study was subsequently conducted to analyze the incidence of critical thinking skills in student assignments, the purpose here is to address some of the practical aspects of using WebCT. Thus, the focus of the paper is on the issues of time and resources required to carry out instructional activities using WebCT.

Introduction

Background

The course "Impacts of Technology on Society" is a required course for all fourth year engineering students registered at Concordia University. The course is specifically designed to address social, environmental, ethical, and political issues pertaining to the role of technology in society. Typically, the assignments consist of two short papers (5-7 pages), one major report carried out in teams and a class presentation. Instructional approaches include class discussions, lectures and case presentations. Eighty-five students registered in two sections of the course participated in this project.

One of the challenge with teaching the course is that the students come in with very little experience in writing and expressing ideas. To address this issue, the instructors decided to use WebCT primarily as a mode of communication, which allowed for more writing practices. In the revised version of the course, the short papers were replaced with five written assignments, that is, two essays and three case studies of increasing difficulty. The WebCT assignments were designed and managed by the teaching assistant/researcher, while all other activities were handled by the course instructor.

WebCT Features

From an instructional point of view, WebCT offers a number of interesting features. One can present on-line course materials (documents, lectures notes, course outlines, exercises etc.); provide glossaries for specific terms and concepts; develop quizzes and surveys; communicate by e-mail and create discussion groups; manage student files (for example, to post grades or to track their on-line visits). Course materials can be created as a multimedia package which may include, in addition to the usual text, images such as photographs or graphics, sound and video excerpts, and links to external websites. In addition, design features such as limiting access, determining availibility date and other control features are also available. One of the main advantage of WebCT is that the course content is restricted to the students registered in the course and available at the user's convenience. In short, WebCT presents a series of advantages for the instructor who wishes to go beyond the traditional lecture approach and develop richer and more complex course materials.

Given our needs and our means, we used WebCT primarily as a communication device rather than as a fully developed interactive tool. Consequently, we used the interface mainly to introduce course materials, to communicate to students by e-mail and to post grades. We also used the quizz feature to collect student's feedback about the instructional approaches. For the purpose of this presentation however, only the issues pertaining to the posting of course materials will be addressed.

Characteristics of the Course Materials

The assignments were two essays and three case studies pertaining to the issue of food production technologies. The case studies were specifically designed for the course, using Leenders and Erskine's model of case writing (1989). The documents were quite complex and voluminous, ranging from seven to 20 pages. We designed the case studies in the typical constructivist fashion (see, for example, Cognition and Technology Group at Vanderbilt, 1990; Lave & Wenger, 1991). Multiple perspectives were provided to the students using different visual media. Thus, all information necessary to identify problems and to make recommendations was provided either as articles, links to relevant websites, graphics, images and statistics. Students had to sift through the information, identify the problem (s) and offer possible solution (s). All course materials were created using Claris HomePage and then were saved as a "zip" file.

Time and Resources Issues

While the integration of communication and information technologies such as WebCT in a course offers a great instructional potential, one should not neglect the time involved in creating and managing the materials and additional resources required to use such means in an efficient and effective manner. These issues are discussed below.

Time Issues

While designing materials for instructional technologies may require more time than regular print-based material, using WebCT entails that more "person-time" will be required to deal with logistics issues such as uploading and testing the materials and managing students' files. Thus, four general steps may be considered: 1) Designing the materials; 2) Preparing the material for the WebCT environment; 3) Organizing the logistics involved in using WebCT and 4) Conducting the instructional activities per se.

1) Designing the Materials for a WebCT Environment

The time spent on this step depends more on the type of document to be prepared for the course than the use of a communication technology such as WebCT. Traditional print-based materials such as lecture notes for example, will require less designing time than a case study or a Web page that introduces images, graphics and links. In WebCT, the usual steps involved in the design of interactive materials have to be covered: searching for content, organizing the information in a meaningful way for the learners, validating the content with subject-matter experts and conducting a formative evaluation. In other words, creating an interactive document that includes several media involves more design time than print-based materials. However, the instructor who wants to use WebCT in an interactive fashion will have to learn how to use a web page design software.

2) Preparing for the WebCT Environment

After the material has been created, one has to upload the course materials in WebCT. First, the instructor needs to become familiar with the designer's view options of the shell. In other words, the instructor has to understand the logic behind the design of the WebCT shell. This logic is not totally intuitive. For example, the zipped materials first have to be uploaded in the management tree, then unzipped in the desired folder. All images and links have to be verified to make sure that they have been uploaded and then successfully unzipped. Then one has to verify that all the links work. The next step is to give the students access to the document. This means that while the material may have been uploaded in WebCT, the document is still not accessible by the students. Toggling from the designer's view to the student view is probably the most time-consuming step since one has to go out entirely from the browser and then enter as a student to verify that all the links and the images really appear.

In short, the steps involved in uploading the materials include zipping and unzipping the file, verifying that all the images have been uploaded, organizing the files in the management tree, verifying that the file does appear in the student mode, setting up the access for students and finally, testing the document in student mode. In our project, uploading the course materials and testing the set up required an average of three hours for each assignment. Finally, in the 3.11 version, it was not possible to upload the same material for two sections at once. In other words, when one teaches two sections of the same course, the uploading procedures have to be repeated twice. It is not possible to "duplicate" or to dispatch the materials and the set up to a running course.

3) Organizing the Logistics

Organizing the logistics surrounding the use of WebCT is another issue worth considering before using WebCT. One has to ensure that everybody has access to a computer either from home or from a lab and that all students create their account by a given date. One also has to do some trouble shooting and updating with the students who are experiencing difficulties. Yet, the most time-consuming task in terms of using WebCT in the classoorm is the management of students's assignments. In this project, the teaching assistant/researcher had to : 1) open up the e-mail messages and the attachments; 2) verify the format and the filename; 3) return a reception notice; 4) file the assignment in the proper folder and; 5) assign a participation grade to the student. Although the WebCT part of the course was also designed for research purposes (i.-e. an increased number of assignments) creating and receiving even a lesser number of assignments in WebCT would still require quite some time. To illustrate the point, the task of managing student assignments, despite the application of systematic procedures, required 1.5 days of work per assignment for 85 students.

4) Conducting the Instructional Activities

The use of WebCT does not directly affect the amount of time dedicated to the instructional task per se. In other words, the grading and the provision of feedback is as time-consuming in a WebCT environment as it is in traditional approaches. However, one observation about our experience is that we had the feeling of spending too much time on the logistics and the management of the student files and not enough on the instructional tasks themselves.

Resource Issues

Technical Support for Students

In order to facilitate the students' use of WebCT it is essential to offer proper technical support, especially if it is their first experience with such an environment. In our case, a handout outlining the steps about how to log on to the system was distributed in class. A help line was also made available for the students, as well as a drop-in session for trouble-shooting. In addition, a class presentation of the environment was presented at the beginning of the term.

Clear instructions are essential for submitting electronic files. Such instructions should contain information as to how to give a filename (using the student's last name of the student and their first initials as well as the assignment number); what type of document is accepted (e.g. Word, Word Perfect, PDF, etc.); an explanation about the meaning of the extension (e.g. ".doc", ".pdf"). At first, we perceived this information as being trivial, but we were surprised to find out that quite a few students had little knowledge about the type or the version of word processing software.

Technical Support for Instructors

Learning to navigate in WebCT is not as intuitive as it could be. Some time and energy have to be invested prior to designing the course materials or the course interface. Instructors, teaching assistant and facilitators have to be supported in order to develop the course. In our experience, we were a team of five people. The head instructor with the help of the Information and Instructional Technology Service staff, created the interface for the course and chose the icons and the features to be used; the teaching-assistant/researcher created the materials to be uploaded, debugged and organized the set-up, as well as managed the students' assignments; and finally, two instructors managed the mail and the student grades to be posted. In essence, the instructors, in order to be successful and efficient with WebCT, need some form of technical support from the university, as well as some teaching assistance resources dedicated to the magement of the course in WebCT.

Conclusion

In conclusion, the use of complex and voluminous case studies containing graphics, images, texts, references, and links to relevant websites was facilitated by the WebCT environment. However, as our experience demonstrated, more person-time was dedicated to the design, the logistics, and the management of student assignments than on the instructional activities per se. This implies that whenever planning to use WebCT, one has to expect that more time will be spent on non-instructional task. Consequently, when planning to use an interface such as WebCT, careful planning of physical and human resources has to be considered in order to ensure a successful and relevant integration of WebCT in a course.

References

Cognition and Technology group at Vanderbilt. (1990). Anchored instruction and its relationship to situated cognition. Educational Researcher, August-September, 2-10.

Jones, K. (1985). *Designing your own simulations.* London: Methuen.

Lave, J., & Wenger, E. (1991). *Situated Learning: legitimate peripheral participation.* Cambridge: Cambridge University Press.

Leenders, M. R., & Erskine, J., A. (1989). *Case research: The case writing process* (third ed.). London, Ontario: School of Business Administration, University of Western Ontario.

Thiagarajan, S., & Stolovitch, H. D. (1978). Instructional Simulation Games (Vol. 12). Englewood Cliffs, NJ: Educational Technology Publications.

Teaching about Mythic Kings: How Integrating Multi-Media Presentation Technology with Traditional Essay Writing Has IIelped Students Learn More History

Abstract of Brief Paper Proposal for the Association for the Advancement of Computing in Education, World Conference, October 15-19, 2002, Montreal, Canada

By David Walter Leinweber, Ph.D.
Associate Professor of History
Oxford College of Emory University

OVERVIEW OF THE PROPOSAL

This brief paper highlights experiences and issues related to incorporating multi—media technology into a special topics course I am teaching this Spring Semester at Oxford College of Emory University – *HST 385: Mythic Kings*. A major feature of the course is the preparation of a multi-media presentation prepared by students, based on a significant historical essay they have written. I have found this fusion of traditional essay writing with modern multi-media technological capacities to add an exciting and enriching dimension to students' learning about history.

In a brief presentation to the World Association for the Advancement of Computing in Education, I would like to share some of my experiences using multi-media technology with *HST 385:Mythic Kings*, including some illustrations/examples taken from students' work. I would also like to share some of the practical and philosophical issues I addressed as I configured technology into this course in a very central way.

Having each student convert major written essays into major multi-media presentations has helped them integrate art, music, architecture, and literature into a larger historical framework. The result is a much deeper level of learning that shows students how disparate peoples, places, and periods relate to each other. In addition, technology has helped students directly see how such considerations as music and art are important parts of history, not discrete entities to be considered only by artists, musicians, or art and music historians.

BACKGROUND REGARDING THE COURSE

HST 385: Mythic Kings is a special topics class designed for a rather small group of students who have completed the pre-requisite of *HST 101: Western Civilization Through the Reformation*. There are seven students in this course, all very well-prepared for the discussion, special projects, and research that the course requires. This is important, as it allows us to assume some general familiarity with the various periods discussed, as well as a certain seriousness one brings to the topic.

Also, *HST 385: Mythic Kings* was designed and supported based upon work done by the instructor while a 2001 participant in The Teaching, Learning, and Technology Institute (TLTI), sponsored by Oxford College of Emory University. TLTI expert instruction was directly designed around the proposed course syllabus. The expert support of Oxford's technological staff was a critical element of this course, both as I developed it, and as students proceeded towards completing it.

Other key elements of the *HST 385: Mythic Kings* syllabus are itemized below.

INDIVIDUALIZED SYLLABI

In addition to mundane matters of course administration, the syllabus for HST 385 provided a list of particular "mythic kings." Among these were included Osiris, David, Priam, Theseus, Alexander the Great, Arthur, Charlemagne, and Napoleon. Each student selected his or her own Mythic King from this list, and was provided with an extensive list of references for that particular figure. These references included major primary sources on the historical figure in question, as well as literary, artistic, and musical works that reflected the monarch's enduring legacy in culture and myth. Below you will find a sample of the syllabus references given for one of the student's projects, Theseus as a Mythic King.

A. **Theseus**

Literature: Boccaccio, Giovanni, *Teseida;* Chaucer, Geoffrey, "The Knight's Tale" in *Canterbury Tales;* Dante, *The Inferno*, Canto XII; Euripides, *Hippolytus;* Hawthorne, Nathaniel, "The Minotaur," in *Tanglewood Tales;* Ovid, *Metamorphoses Book VIII;* Plutarch, *Theseus;* Seneca, *Phaedra;* Shakespeare, William, *A Midsummer Night's Dream;* -- *Two Noble Kinsmen*

Music: Richard Strauss, *Ariadne on Naxos* (1912); Milhaud, Darius, *L'Abandon d'Ariane* (1928); --*La Déliverance de Thésée* (1928); Britten, Benjamin, *A Midsummer Night's Dream* (1960); Mendelssohn, Felix, *A Midsummer Night's Dream* (1876); Roussel, Albert, *Bacchus et Ariane* (1930).

Note that an important component of the course was the inclusion of much classical music – operas, oratorios, piano concertos, symphonies, and ballets. Several students chafed some at this. But they are learning to see music (and art) as not just something for people in music departments, but as an important part of the historical record. I viewed the inclusion of music in the syllabus as essential, and have remained firm that students consult the various works related to their particular topics. Music was an important part of the course in the basic sense; but it also presents one of the most exciting potentials for the multi-media component of the course.

TRADITIONAL RESEARCH AND ESSAY WRITING

The central feature of the syllabus was that each student would prepare a major and quite traditional research essay of 15-20 pages in length. Due on the last day of class, the essay focuses on the historical and cultural legacy of a particular mythic king. These are footnoted papers, with bibliographies.

Before completing this major essay, students would write a series of short papers in preparation. Assigned topics for these shorter papers were: The Historical King (e.g. Arthur); Sources of Knowledge about the Historical King; The Image of the King in the Arts; The Kingly Ideal.

Having completed these very serious and meticulous papers, students can generally speak with true authority on their particular king. They are therefore grounded in a serious body of content knowledge that they can then import into their Multi-Media presentations. This grounding in a rather traditional approach to history is very important, and adds enormously to the exciting and creative work they can then incorporate into the technology component of the course.

MULTI-MEDIA PRESENTATION

The essay completed by students is converted into a major multi-media presentation that summarizes its major points, and illustrates them with a wide variety of materials, including maps, music, art, and key passages from literature. This conversion of the written essay into a very carefully structured and thoughtfully conceived multi-media presentation is a critical component of the *HST 385:Mythic Kings* course. The presentations are scheduled for 45 minutes each, so they constitute a major segment of the student's work for the semester.

As a critical sub-component of the Mythic Kings multi-media presentations, students select appropriate and relevant music clips from a variety of musical sources. They integrate the music into the larger framework of important themes and images drawn from the life and times of their particular king. Slides featuring art, architecture, portraits, and other relevant images are organized thematically into sub-presentations that highlight the relationship between history and the Fine Arts

This key musical aspect of the Mythic Kings course has helped students relate such "musical" figures as Palestrina, Purcell, Handel, Berlioz, or Britten, to the larger historical context of their times. It has highlighted for them, and me, how a Handel Oratorio from the eighteenth century can relate to Renaissance Art, which can also relate to famous literary passages from Ovid, or Vergil, or the Bible, or great buildings of the world. The use of PowerPoint technology has illustrated this for them in powerful ways that I could not have imagined even seven or eight years ago.

CONCLUSION

As a rather traditional history teacher, I am very pleased that technology has provided an enormously enriching dimension to my special topics course. Technology has not conflicted with the content of the course. It has not replaced solid learning with bells and whistles. Multi-media technology, coupled with the completion of a serious traditional essay, has enabled my students to gain a much broader sense of how common figures, stories, images, and themes can connect disparate peoples, places, and periods. This has made a very significance difference in my class.

In my presentation to the World Conference for the Association for the Advancement of Computing in Education, I would like to share some of my experiences with using multi-media technology in *HST 385: Mythic Kings* at Oxford College of Emory University.

Reusable Learning Objects: Hazards, Hi-Performance, and a New Convergence

Juan Leon, Ph.D.
Vice-President, Learning and Knowledge Management Strategies
Intelli-media
U.S.A.
juanleon@comcast.net

Abstract: This paper addresses the growing gap between the promise of Reusable Learning Object (RLO) based content development and the sometimes disappointing reality of RLO performance in deployment. After reviewing the principal causes of these disappointments, the discussion outlines strategies for maximizing the benefits of RLO approaches. The first strategy applies most to Instructional Design processes. It demands special attention to curriculum driven training development. The second strategy applies most to Knowledge Management techniques. It demands a sophisticated understanding of metadata schemes and rule-based automation. The discussion concludes by reviewing the social forces and industry trends that are driving the evolution of RLO based systems. Of these, the increasing use of competency-based models of organizational development is seen as the trend most likely to complement RLO based approaches to content creation and management.

The past year was in some ways a good one for realizing return on investment (ROI) with e-Learning. e-Learning delivered new product information to sales forces in the field, reducing their time out of action. For other geographically dispersed employees, classes and discussions normally held at a central site were held over the Web. Collapsing distance in these ways, e-Learning's web-based mode of delivery trimmed training travel budgets across numerous industries.

Not uncommonly, the e-Learning windfall is being reinvested by training departments through the purchase of Learning Management Systems (LMSs) or Learning and Content Management Systems (LCMSs). Will these major investments produce comparably outstanding results by way of the course and content management they offer? The answer may depend in part on how successfully these systems can be stocked with high-quality, standards based course materials. Without the content, the systems will be no more than administrative tools, a great convenience at course registration time, but of no direct consequence to training itself. Without the standardization, these systems will deliver little by way of useful content capture and reuse.

With regard to both these issues, the most promising and problematic feature of the new LMSs and, especially, the LCMSs, is the "Reusable Learning Object" (RLO). "Create once, use many" has been an--admittedly awkward--RLO tagline throughout their evolution. The tagline expresses the idea that instruction can be systematically decomposed into small units and then stored in accordance with internationally agreed upon standards for "packaging". Appropriately labeled, this unit of instruction can function as a piece of "LEGO" in an open and growing world of such LEGO pieces. Each piece is ready to be combined and recombined with others to suit multiple training and information exchange purposes.

Thus, the RLO approach to content creation and management can promise several things, among them:

- Personalized learning
- Collaborative authoring
- Easily modified content libraries
- Efficient management of instructional assets (typically achieved by housing them in a database of RLOs)

Designed to be modular, sharable, and reusable, RLOs are conceived as the basic units of a component based learning (and knowledge management) strategy that can produce remarkably high returns on investment.

Inherent Difficulties

However, RLO based training development systems have often proven difficult to implement. "A great idea, but it doesn't work in reality", has too often become the RLO adopter's refrain. What tends to give rise to this kind of disappointment? The following are frequently unanticipated yet all-too-common difficulties:

- RLO based development brings with it technical challenges that are not only more daunting than those posed by e-Learning or other forms of technology based training but are *different in kind*.
- RLO based development requires more planning up front than training departments are accustomed to or may have the time for.
- Instructional designers don't like RLO based approaches, or remain dubious of their benefits.

There are also larger organizational hurdles. In many organizations content functions and training functions are widely fragmented across business units; and there is not enough understanding of what standards based development involves. These organizational issues must be addressed before real economies of scale can be seen in RLO based content development and content management.

Where to Begin for Training Departments

Responding to these new technical and organizational challenges will require greater levels of cooperation among training departments and IT or IS groups. Training departments will increasingly need to think of the IT or IS group not as a source of "support" alone, but as a partner in enterprise-wide communications, education, and knowledge management efforts. While developing these enhanced intra-organizational relationships, the training department will have to contend with challenges proper to training development itself. The greatest of these is the challenge of achieving coherence in RLO based course construction.

Coherence is that subjective experience that is created by a course composed of well-integrated parts. This sense of coherence is fundamental to understanding and learning. We experience coherence when a course maintains:

- subject matter consistency and natural progression
- logical consistency and natural progression
- thematic consistency and natural progression
- aesthetic wholeness (including consistency of style)

Because RLOs are designed to function as stand-alone units independent of any context, when linked together into courses they tend to produce discontinuities in subject matter, in logic, in theme, and in the "look and feel" of course components. Consequently, course coherence is not likely to be the result of a hastily conceived RLO based development strategy.

An Effective Approach

The answer to this particular challenge is not to create RLOs according to a pre-defined formula—that would defeat their special purpose—but to design them within the framework of a well-planned curriculum, one that incorporates standards compliant classification schemes allowing for consistent labeling of RLOs and efficient retrieval of the RLOs from databases. The curriculum must also be specified in detail sufficient to allow each RLO to target its own clearly focused learning objective.

Wyeth Pharmaceutical's successful implementation of an enterprise learning and content management system last year took a still more radical approach that is instructive. Before building a new curriculum they stepped back and built up a competency model. Their motto: "Design your curriculum in light of your competency model." Doing so helped turn training development into an efficient, enterprise-wide process, moving it away from the purely project driven model of production that had resulted in a "jigsaw puzzle" of training materials created ad hoc. (See Dr. Roshan's paper on e-Learning at Wyeth for more on that organization's integrated approach to training, knowledge management, and organizational development.)

Working toward related goals, Pfizer's training groups have championed efforts to collaborate with Human Resources in developing an enterprise-wide capabilities model. The model supports curricula that are both more comprehensive than in the past and more attuned to the needs of the individual learner. Particularly noteworthy, Pfizer's capabilities model and new curricula support training follow-up and career-long professional development.

Another Effective Approach

The challenge of RLO based course coherence can be further addressed through the use of RLO authoring and management tools that aid in the creation and maintenance of coherence. These tools do so, in part, by enforcing classification schemes, conducting intelligent searches against RLO databases, guiding course designers in the final selection of course components, and helping in the real-time authoring of transitional material unique to a particular course under construction. They help turn instructional design expertise into useful "rules" that can be applied semi-automatically.

Finally, instructional designers may need to learn to think and work in new ways, producing more compact and carefully structured units of instruction while keeping a close eye on curricular objectives.

Consequential Convergences

Producing high-quality RLO based content may be difficult, but the challenge is not likely to be withdrawn anytime soon. Today's explorations of training development based on RLO models comes as a natural consequence of five on-going social and industry trends:

- E-Learning is becoming a commonly used tool, one essential to the smooth operations of critical business processes. Findings from a recent survey of training professionals indicate that over 45% of the organizations polled now use e-Learning as an essential part of their business operations (SRI, 2002).
- "Blended" learning is being increasingly favored. (Driscoll, 2002)
- Both training content and performance support resources are being integrated with organizational IS and Knowledge Management efforts.
- Standards for content packaging and uniform labeling conventions are being widely adopted. It is now difficult to find a serious developer of e-Learning related tools or content that does not comply (to some degree) with AICC, SCORM and / or IMS standards and specifications for interoperability.
- Intranets and the Internet are increasingly taken for granted as communications channels, as are the consistency in technical formats and standards they provide.

When it comes to the growth of RLO based training development, these five trends will continue to provide the push, the pull, or both. Some of the reasons for this include the following:

- Materials digitized for e-Learning are ready to be placed into Learning Objects, and e-Learning now housed in databases --instead of books and binders --is only a small conceptual distance away from RLO course components housed in databases.
- Blended approaches require training materials that can be rapidly used in smaller chunks and quickly customized, while corporate CIOs are more alert than ever to the possibility of capturing and exploiting the knowledge produced by training departments.
- As the corporate world moves toward standards-based content development and exchange, no one will want to be left out or stigmatized as "incompatible".
- The continued evolution of ubiquitous computing will only increase demand for the kind of just-in-time training and information that are the forte of RLO based systems.

Despite the challenges inherent to RLO based content development, then, it is very likely that the training industry will continue to move in the RLO direction. While caution and even skepticism are warranted, we may expect that RLOs, in some form, are soon likely to begin populating efficient learning and content management systems. Experience with RLO implementations may lead to greater successes as we increasingly fulfill the promises of well-made, well-managed and well-used digital content libraries. In particular, the on-going development of competency and capabilities training models will better support the design of the comprehensive curricula essential to practical success with large-scale RLO implementations.

Looking to the horizon, how might the convergence of RLOs and competency model trends further evolve?

Standards and specifications bodies such as the IEEE Learning Technology Standards Committee (LTSC), the IMS Global Learning Consortium (IMS), and others will need to develop the taxonomies through which competencies will be defined and mapped in and across competency management systems. This will be a far more difficult task than that of specifying an RLO package's structure or the metadata to be used in RLO tagging.

Note, for instance, the complexity—and breadth—of any reasonable working definition of "competency", this one crafted by the HR-XML Competency Workgroup last year:

> A specific, identifiable, definable, and measurable knowledge, skill, ability and/or other deployment-related characteristic (e.g. attitude, behavior, physical ability) which a human resource may possess and which is necessary for, or material to, the performance of an activity within a specific business context. (Bork & Kiel, 2001)

Rather than agreeing upon packaging conventions and the kind of classification information that is important to know about a Learning Object, creating complete taxonomies of workplace competencies would involve defining and mapping *all relevant human actions and attitudes as they pertain to carrying out a given task in a given sphere of business activity.* Little wonder, then, that competency specifications and standards groups are having trouble pursuing their goals and that the HR-XML Competency Workgroup makes a point of rejecting taxonomy building altogether.

Instead, it takes on the more manageable burden of creating an XML Schema that provides practical means to exchange information about competencies in a variety of business contexts. The Schema allows competencies to be defined one at a time, a step-by-step approach thay may allow for the piece-by-piece creation of comprehensive, coherent RLO libraries available in the future workplace.

References

Barron, Tom. (May, 2002). SRI Consulting Business Intelligence, "Learning Object Approach is Making Inroads". http://www.sric-bi.com

Bork, D., & Kiel, P. (December, 2001). "HR-XML Consortium: December 7, 2001, Interoperability Summit" [presentation] Contact: dan@ixmatch.com paul@hr-xml.org

Driscoll, M. (March, 2002) "Blended Learning". *e-learning magazine*, p. 54.

Roshan, V. (February, 2002). "How One Corporation Got a Charge out of e-Learning." http://www.cpsnet.com/reprints/2002/02/elearning.pdf

An Empirical Investigation of Student Satisfaction with Web-based Courses

Peter Leong
Department of Educational Technology
University of Hawaii at Manoa
United States
peterleo@hawaii.edu

Curtis P. Ho
Department of Educational Technology
University of Hawaii at Manoa
United States
curtis@hawaii.edu

Barbara Saromines-Ganne
Leeward Community College
United States
bsg@hawaii.edu

Abstract: Electronic communication has become an integral part of higher education. Along with the growth of electronic communication is the rise of Web-based courses. This empirical study surveyed 128 students enrolled in 29 courses offered entirely over the Internet to determine the dimensions which underlie student satisfaction with Web-based courses and examined how these dimensions can be used to predict student satisfaction levels. This study also examined the relationship between demographic variables, such as gender, year in school, students' prior computer, email, and Internet proficiency, as well as, Web-based course experience and their satisfaction levels with Web-based courses. The implication of this study is that instructors of Web-based courses may be able to increase their online students' satisfaction by addressing the appropriate factors underlying student satisfaction.

Introduction

The Internet has impacted the way we learn. More and more courses offered by institutions of higher education are delivered via the Internet. A recent survey by the U.S. Department of Education's National Center for Education Statistics (NCES) found Web-based distance education to be the most widespread mode of delivery (Lewis, et. al, 1999). At least 58 percent of institutions which offered distance education used Web-based courses, compared to 54 percent that used two-way interactive video and 47 percent which used one-way pre-recorded video. Because Web-based distance education is a fast-growing area, it is imperative that we gain a better understanding of this mode of distance education delivery. Most of the current literature about Web-based learning is based upon anecdotal experience or qualitative study (Kearsley, 1998). Many researchers agree that one of the greatest problems with online learning is the lack of empirical research and quantitative studies (McIssac & Gunawardena, 1996; Schlosser & Anderson, 1994; Sherritt & Basom, 1997). Numerous studies in the field of distance education have focused on the comparisons of student performance in distance-education courses versus traditional face-to-face courses (DeLoughry, 1988; Souder, 1993). The general conclusion reached by these investigators is that there is "no significant difference" between the performances of students in distance-education courses compared to traditional face-to-face courses (Russell, 1999; Schlosser &

Anderson, 1994). More recent research efforts have focused on student attitudes rather than the previous emphasis on student performance (Biner, et al. 1994). Biner, Dean and Mellinger (1994) contend that student satisfaction play an important role in determining the success of distance-education courses. The authors argue that sustaining positive student attitudes can result in a number of student benefits such as lower student attrition rates, and higher levels of student motivation.

The Study

This empirical study surveyed 128 students enrolled in 29 courses offered entirely over the Internet to determine the dimensions which underlie student satisfaction with Web-based courses and examined how these dimensions can be used to predict student satisfaction levels. This study also examined the relationship between demographic variables, such as gender, year in school, students' prior computer, e-mail and Internet proficiency, as well as, Web-based course experience and their satisfaction levels with Web-based courses. This research attempted to provide valuable information on the factors that influence the satisfaction of students participating in Web-based courses. The intent of the researcher was to obtain results from a quantitative study that would guide in the design and development of Web-based courses that would fulfill the needs of distance learners, thus ultimately leading to their success in distance-education courses.

The participants consisted of students who were enrolled in 29 Web-based courses in the University of Hawaii system, Hawaii Pacific University, Baker College, Michigan and Nova Southeastern University, Florida for the Fall 2000 semester. The 29 courses spanned a wide range of content areas: two Anthropology courses, one Astronomy course, one Biology course, four Business Management courses, six Computer courses, three English courses, two Educational Technology courses, one History course, one Japanese course, one Journalism course, three Mathematics courses, two Medical courses, and two Political Science courses.

Survey Design

A review of the existing literature on student satisfaction with Web-based instruction, distance education courses and general student course evaluations yielded eight dimensions and 47 question items for the survey questionnaire to ascertain the factors that underlie student satisfaction with Web-based courses. The eight original dimensions were instruction, instructor's aspects, management/coordination, technological characteristics, interaction, experience with system, workload/difficulty and expected/fairness of grading.

The survey questionnaire was divided into two sections. In Section A, students were given a list of 47 statements that addressed the eight dimensions that could potentially affect their satisfaction with Web-based courses. For each statement, students were asked to evaluate the extent of their agreement with each statement. Throughout the survey instrument, a five-point, Likert-type scale ranging from "Strongly disagree" to "Strongly agree" was used. In Section B, students' satisfaction, demographic and individual information was collected. Student satisfaction was measured based on students' responses to two survey questions: overall satisfaction with the Web-based course, and comparison of the course with traditional face-to-face classroom courses (DeBourgh, 1999). Information about students' prior experience with computers, the Internet, e-mail and Web-based courses was gathered. Demographic data collected included gender and year in school.

Procedure

A letter to solicit for survey participants was sent via e-mail to 29 professors who taught Web-based courses, who then forwarded it to their online students. Recruitment of participants was on a voluntary basis, although some instructors provided additional incentive for students to participate in this study by offering extra course credits for completing the survey. The primary method to obtain data was through an online survey questionnaire that was made available to the students from December 11 to 23, 2000. Overall, there were 508 students in the 29 Web-based courses surveyed. A total of 128 usable survey submissions were received, giving a response rate of 25.2 percent.

Data Analysis

All data was analyzed with the use of the SPSS® Version 10.0 for Windows statistical software package. Prior to any data analysis, negatively phrased items were first transformed to ensure comparability of data. Descriptive statistics such as means and standard deviations were calculated for the student satisfaction variables, levels of satisfactions, and the demographic data collected.

Factor analysis was performed on the 47 variables that were expected to underlie student satisfaction with Web-based courses to establish the major dimensions of online student satisfaction. Varimax orthogonal rotation was used. After applying factor analysis, the study examined the relationship between the dimensions of student satisfaction and the overall student satisfaction. Stepwise multiple regression was used to identify dimensions that significantly predict overall student satisfaction with Web-based courses. The dependent variable was a summated scale that consisted of two items: overall satisfaction with the Web-based course, and comparison of the course with traditional face-to-face classroom courses (DeBourgh, 1999). Independent variables were the five dimensions extracted by factor analysis. In addition, t-test and univariate analysis of variance (ANOVA) were used to answer the other research questions in this study.

Results & Implications

Of the initial 47 items in the original survey, only 26 items emerged after factor analysis was performed and they loaded on five factors that were named – interaction, instructor, system-wide technology, workload/difficulty, and function-specific technology, see [Table 1]. The interaction factor was comprised of seven questions measuring respondents' satisfaction with the interaction they experienced throughout the duration of the Web-based course. The instructor dimension was comprised of six questions that measured respondents' satisfaction with the instructor of the online course that they took. The three items that comprised the workload/difficulty dimension measured students' satisfaction with the workload and the level of difficulty of online courses. The system-wide technology dimension included six questions that addressed the general technological aspects of Web-based course systems, such as ease of access and navigation, "user friendliness", online enrollment/registration, and assignment submission. The function-specific technology dimension consisted of four items that dealt with specific technological functions or features that are common to most Web-based course management tools, such as online grade book, assessment, audio/video components, and online lecture presentations.

Dimensions of Online Student Satisfaction

Dimensions	Number of Questions
Interaction	7
Instructor	6
System-wide technology	6
Workload/Difficulty	3
Function-specific technology	4

Table 1: Five dimensions of online student satisfaction involving 26 question items

Regressional analysis performed revealed that the five proposed dimensions of online student satisfaction were related to overall student satisfaction. Overall student satisfaction is apparently influenced primarily by four dimensions: instructor, system-wide technology, workload/difficulty and interaction. None of the demographic factors examined, such as gender and year in school, had any significant impact on overall student satisfaction with Web-based courses. Similarly, students' prior experience with computers, email, Internet, and Web-based courses did not have any significant impact on overall student satisfaction.

The implication from the results of this study is that instructors of Web-based courses may be able to increase their online students' satisfaction by addressing the appropriate factors underlying student satisfaction. For example, it may be possible for online instructors to alter how satisfied their students are with this aspect of their online course by providing more timely feedback, and making themselves more accessible to their students. Additionally, student satisfaction with Web-based courses could be improved by ensuring that general technological aspects of Web-based course systems, such as ease of access and navigation, are improved. Biner, Dean and Mellinger (1994) argue that student satisfaction plays an important role in determining the success of distance-education courses. Therefore, understanding these factors that underlie online students' satisfaction can lead to increased success of online courses.

References

Biner, P. M., Dean, R. S., and Mellinger, A. E. (1994). Factors underlying distance learner satisfaction with televised college-level courses. *The American Journal of Distance Education*, 8(1), 60-71.

DeBourgh, G. A. (1999). Technology is the tool, teaching is the task: Student satisfaction in distance learning. (Report No. IR019596). (ERIC document No. ED 432 226)

DeLoughry, T. J. (1988). Remote instruction using computers found as effective as classroom sessions. *Chronicle of Higher Education*, 34(2), 15-21.

Kearsley, G. (1998). A Guide to Online Education. Retrieved August 13, 2000 from the World Wide Web: http://home.sprynet.com/~gkearsley/online.htm

Lewis, L., Kyle, S., and Farris, E. (1999). Distance Education at Postsecondary Education Institutions: 1997-98. National Center for Education Statistics (NCES), U.S. Department of Education, NCES #2000-013. Washington, DC: U.S. Government Printing Office.

McIssac, M. S. and Gunawardena, C. N. (1996). Distance Education. In D. Johassen (Ed.), *Handbook of research for educational communication*. (pp. 403-437). New York: Macmillan.

Rainie, L. and Packel, D. (2001). More online, doing more. The Internet & American Life Project. Retrieved March 1, 2001 from the World Wide Web: http://www.pewinternet.org

Russell, T. L. (1999). *The no significant difference phenomenon: as reported in 355 research reports, summaries, and papers*. Raleigh: North Carolina State University.

Schlosser, C. A. and Anderson, M. L. (1994). *Distance Education: Review of the Literature*. Washington, DC: A.E.C.T

Sherritt and Basom, (1997). Using the Internet for Higher Education. (ERIC Document Reproduction Service No. ED 407 546)

Souder, W. E. (1993). The effectiveness of traditional vs. satellite delivery in three management of technology master's degree programs. *The American Journal of Distance Education*, 7(1), 37-53.

Implementing Library Instruction for Freshman Composition on WebCT: The Oakland University Experience, 2001/2002

Frank J. Lepkowski
Kresge Library
Oakland University
United States
lepkowsk@oakland.edu

Abstract: In 2001 the library at Oakland University decided to supplement classroom instruction for freshman composition classes with WebCT modules. This web-based instruction included library basics, using the Voyager catalog system and an introduction to the FirstSearch databases. Using this new instructional modality caused striking changes in the relationship between the library faculty and the Rhetoric program, in the librarians' practice of classroom instruction, and in students' perception of the learning outcomes. Librarians were extremely ambivalent about the WebCT instruction and came close to canceling it for the next academic year; Rhetoric faculty consistently evaluated the WebCT module more favorably than the librarians' classroom performance; students frequently approached their library instruction after WebCT with an assumption that they had already learned whatever was needed through online instruction. The most successful outcomes came when a.) librarians and Rhetoric faculty collaborated closely; b.) Rhetoric faculty ensured that their students completed WebCT before arriving in the library; c.) librarians forged ahead with new content in the classroom instead of reviewing what had been covered in WebCT; d.) the students arrived in the library ready to do research with a topic area for investigation already identified.

Introduction

Oakland University is a growing suburban commuter university located in Rochester, Michigan, some 25 miles north of Detroit. Historically the library has been quite pedagogically active, teaming with other teaching faculty to deliver course-related instruction that in recent years has reached more than a quarter of Oakland's 16,000 students annually. In 2001/2002 the library joined in the University's campaign to use WebCT to deliver online instruction. What follows herein is an admitted unscientific yet, it is to be hoped, objective and analytical report on the program's effects on students, writing faculty, and the librarians.

Organizational Context

At Oakland University, all students are required to take a sequence including Rhetoric 160, or Composition II, the crowning focus of which is the consummation of writing a research paper. For many years, the library has provided a full week (roughly 3.5 hours of class time) of instruction in research techniques for this course. In 2000/01, due to the increasing number of sections and a static number of librarians, the library was forced to reduce its contact hours per section from 3.5 to 2. After teaching for one semester with greatly curtailed content, the library attempted to replace some of the lost instructional time with a library instruction course using WebCT.

The University had committed itself to WebCT some time previously, and was sponsoring a big push to have instructors create content for online courses. Over the course of summer 2001, a WebCT module was created covering the basics of library layout and procedures, basic searching in the online catalog Voyager, and introduction to the use of FirstSearch full-text article databases. In order to deliver this to all Rhetoric students, the decision was made to create a WebCT course for each Rhetoric section, into which the library module was then inserted. Previously an online course would only have been created on a individual basis for those sections of Rhetoric where the instructor wanted to develop online material.

Thus the adoption of this module of online library instruction resulted in the web-enhancement of the whole Rhetoric program, including the classes of many instructors who were not otherwise interested in web development.

In particular the Rhetoric faculty had the essential role of ensuring that the students in each section had absorbed all of the online content before arriving at the library for 2 contact hours of classroom instruction by a librarian. Many of the rhetoricians were first-time users of WebCT and were it not for us would not have been placed in the position of having to be familiar with it. The library held training sessions for them and distributed assistive documentation both for the instructors and their students. As can readily be imagined, we found widely varying degrees of commitment to or even understanding of this task among the 30 or so Rhetoric instructors. Similarly the library faculty also needed training in the use of WebCT. Everyone involved was forced to come to terms with this new manner of delivering instruction.

Consequences of Implementation

For the librarians, the creation of this WebCT component altered fundamentally aspects of the pedagogical situation. For the first time, we had to assume prior knowledge on the part of our students, the absence of which had been axiomatic to (and a realistic basis for) our previous manner of instruction. In fact we were forced to make a great leap of faith that in fact the students would actually *learn* from the WebCT module and would bring to the library with them a base level of knowledge upon which we would build. This assumption led us into two principal and somewhat paradoxical areas of difficulty.

The first difficulty was with ensuring the students' completion of the WebCT portion of the class before arriving in our classrooms. Some of our colleagues in Rhetoric were most wondrously effective in extracting compliance from their students, and in sections like that we had 80-100% completion rates. In other sections the instructors showed minimal commitment to this goal, with the result being that some sections would arrive with only 5-20% having done the assignments. Occasionally we found a section where nary a blessed soul had done so, and not infrequently we considered a success a class with a 50-60% completion rates.

The conundrum for the librarians given this wide variance in the amount of preparation by our students was that of choosing a level to pitch the class to in our instruction. We librarians are a service-minded crew and we hate to have any lambs stray from the flock as we guide them through the steep paths and perilous desfiles of the research process; there is also the matter of confronting slack-jawed incomprehension as we try to forge onward. We had been used to trying to sense the level of our audience and calibrating our approach to what we found there; now we had an expectation which we were powerless to enforce upon which the level of instruction was predicated. The more hard-nosed librarians proceeded with planned instruction assuming the students had done the required preparation, and those more sensitive to the gulf of understanding tried to compromise by reviewing content from WebCT to a greater or lesser extent related directly to the incomprehension level in the class. This created not infrequently a profound resentment among those students who had done the work, and the faculty who had made some efforts to ensure their having done so.

The second difficulty was paradoxical in relation to the first. For a certain category of students it seemed that completion of the WebCT module conveyed not the gratifying sense of having learned the bare minimum necessary to begin library research, but rather an illusion of mastery of the topic which made further instruction otiose. Thus it was that some of these students became resistant to further instruction and did not seemingly understand how rudimentary their searching skills still were. A question for further inquiry is whether completion of online instruction leaves the student feeling he or she has learned more than the old, in-person mode of conveying knowledge—a prospect which cannot help but cause an tremor of uncertainty in even an experienced teacher's breast. In our experience it seemed to create resistance to further learning in some cases. It is perhaps not surprising that given the difficulties of implementing the new program and the uncertain position occupied by the librarian with respect to the material that a certain amount of resentment and negativity towards WebCT began to occur.

As the academic year ended, the library faculty considered the future of WebCT instruction and the Rhetoric faculty were asked to contribute to a frank assessment of the effectiveness of the library instruction program. Evaluation of the WebCT library module was consistently positive and its continued use strongly backed, which rather surprised us considering how negative our own view of it was. In fact, the rhetoricians were overall less positive about the classroom performance of librarians. This was especially true when librarians had been seen to cover material in class which had already been done on WebCT. Both the students who had done the work and their instructors who had worked energetically to ensure that they had felt betrayed by librarians' concession to the ignorance of the irresponsible students. Clearly librarians need to make adjustments to their instructional practice to capitalize on the opportunities offered by online instruction, by accepting the accountability of students for their work, and proceeding from the WebCT content as a starting point.

Practices Conducive to Success

Through discussion among the librarians, and also with the Rhetoric faculty at their retreat, elements were identified which seem to be essential to successful library instruction in the current environment. *First,* a close working relationship between the librarian and the rhetorician is extremely important. They need to be communicating well before the class comes to the library, working on the goals for the classroom instruction, sharing information about the topics of student research. *Second,* it is essential that the Rhetoric instructor require the students to work the WebCT module, preferably with a grade attached to it; students seem to take more seriously schoolwork that is in some direct way involved with their GPAs. The librarian should assist in this process by monitoring the progress of students in a section and informing the Rhetoric Instructor when there are laggards as the date for classroom instruction approaches.

Third, students must have a sense of their research topic before receiving the classroom instruction in the library. To see that what they have to learn is meaningful to them, even after having completed the wonderful WebCT module, there needs to exist a clear and ineluctable link between what they need to do for the instructor who will be giving them their grades, and what they have to learn in the library. The most reliable predictor of a successful, productive library session is when students have an impetus and specificity to their research needs. *Fourth,* librarians need to accept students' accountability for their actions and resist the temptation to cover basics that should have been learned through WebCT. The best means of doing this seems to be minimizing the amount of exposition at the outset of the library classroom teaching, and instead involving them in practical searching exercises involving their own research topics.

Thus, in order to be successful, course-related library instruction through WebCT needs to rely upon a close and committed collegial relationship between the librarian and the instructor of record, potent incentives for students to actually do the work, and classroom followup which is directly related to their research projects. In this blended mode of instruction, as rhetoricians are obliged to ensure students undertake the basic level of library instruction, so librarians are obliged to adapt their classroom practice in the light of a presumption of student accountability. Both sides of the instructional team benefit from this, as do, most importantly, our students.

The Global and the Local:
policy and policy processes for education

Brian Lewis, Simon Fraser University
Jennifer Jenson, York University
Richard Smith, Simon Fraser University

"It's like riding the front car on the roller coaster. . . It may look like you're steering the cars, but in fact you're just holding on."

A New Policy Context

This is how the head of the US House Telecommunications and Finance Subcommittee, Rep. Edward Markey, described his role as a key policy maker in 1994. It is an cautionary statement, reflecting graphically the type of shell shock we have witnessed among teachers, principles, boards, and bureaucrats involved in education policy-making across Canada, even today.

An information revolution has shaken the world. The effects of this revolution are visible on micro and macro levels-- from the details of the way people live their lives every day, to the highest decisions of government. The *Economist* (1996) put it this way: "by reducing the cost of communication, IT (information technology) has helped to globalise production and financial markets. In turn, globalisation spurs technology by intensifying competition and by speeding up the diffusion of technology through direct investment. Together, globalisation and IT crush time and space.

Most countries are greeting the emerging communication technologies with new sets of globally harmonised regulatory and economic policies. In the formulation of these policies, they are facing the simultaneous turmoil induced by a series of related fundamental global trends: world-wide policy deregulation in telecommunications, the collapse of traditional national market barriers, economic concentration in truly transnational companies, and breathtaking technological innovation, as communication technologies converge into a digital sea.

This has led to profound questions about the role and nature of policy itself. Are the old values attainable -- or even desirable-- anymore? Policy makers everywhere have begun to find their traditional policy contexts inadequate, indeed irrelevant, to their work.

Policy decisions are crucial here. But never have policy makers seemed so overcome with events, so dazed, in such disarray. The information revolution has challenged the functions and capabilities of policy itself.

Policy is that set of written and unwritten rules and guidelines which institutionalise and put into operational forms the social contracts which define our institutions and organisations. Policy is at work at both macro and micro levels of governance and control: in government at all levels, and in virtually all other public and private institutions, including our universities and our school systems. Policy addresses both institutional procedures and institutional goals. It provides a framework for the structure of decision making within an organisation, and it rationalises the decision-making process in the context of substantive and idealized value sets which represent the goals of the organisation.

Policy can take progressive or conservative forms. In its progressive aspects, policy will be flexible and it will map and steer the development of the organisation in light of evolving social perspectives and goals. In its more conservative aspect, policy tends to entrench established institutional practices and power relationships in favour of stability.

Conservative policy becomes dysfunctional when it works against the recognition of the underlying changing realities of an organisation, and in favour of protecting the status quo. Dysfunctional policy assumes that the agreed-upon procedures and goals are fixed and natural—it denies the reality of the institution or organisation as an historical reality, and denies its own role as the operational form of evolving social and institutional relations. A conservative policy is dysfunctional when it is used to defend bad decisions on procedural grounds, when it is used to bolster an institution and its powers against beneficial change and evolution, when it becomes exclusionary and non-inclusive.

But policy breakdowns can occur at the progressive end of the spectrum as well. A progressive policy becomes dysfunctional if it is too far out front, if it is uninformed, short-sighted, pressure-group driven and non-inclusive.

Policies addressing the information revolution are largely meant to be progressive policies by their implementers—that is, they are intended to map, steer and facilitate institutional change in light of the promise of a technological and economic revolution. They are often "out-front" policies, leading social change.

Education Policy: The Global meets the Local

The "education revolution" must be understood as a critically important part of a more general information revolution—one front in a larger campaign. In this micro realm we find the same transformation of policy and the same transformation of values which we which find in the larger macro-economic and information policy spheres.

Policies addressing the implementation and use of new technologies within education find themselves firmly entangled within overall information and economic strategies. Increasingly, education policies find themselves straddling boundaries between educational and economic objectives, even subordinate to them. The "ivory tower," if it ever existed, exists no longer. (See also *The Tower Under Siege*, Brian Lewis, Richard Smith, Christine Massey, McGill-Queen's University Press, 2002)

In our work we have identified and clarified some of the most pressing issues arising from the implementation of computer-based technologies in schools. These questions include: technological, infrastructure, human resource and learning policy issues; questions of sustainability; questions of gender; and questions of public policy in an increasingly technocentric and commercial education environment.

Each of these issues speaks to the need for strategies designed to address how and why choices are made, who makes them, and to what effect, both intended and unintended. Too often the reverse happens: technology changes rapidly and decisions are made in a more or less ad hoc fashion, as administrators scramble in response to the initial promises of technology. And then these same administrators, as well as teachers, students and parents, must face unforeseen problems and demands triggered by its implementation. The cart drives the horse.

There is a critical need for an approach to the implementation of technology in our schools that pays attention to questions of policy, organizational culture, politics, and decision-making practices. That is the approach we have taken in our work. Technology for whom, why, when, where? What value does technology add to the educational experience? How are the decisions made? By whom?

These can all be understood as "local" questions, grounded in the needs of real people, in real circumstances and real contexts. Yet these local questions-- answers to which we believe are key to the successful implementation of any plan for education, technology or otherwise-- are too often subsumed by the global issues, objectives, and assumptions of plans to develop "knowledge workers for the knowledge economy."

In fact, it is as if a major social fault line has shifted: there has been a shift in our relationship to almost all social activity—which seems increasingly judged and evaluated against a touchstone of macro-economic objectives and priorities. Education has not escaped this shift. If education had once been an objective, a goal, a final cause, for many of its leaders, movers and funders, it has now become much more purely a means to the end of a more efficient and competitive economy and workforce, captured within the notion of the "knowledge economy."

Is policy important?

Our fundamental notions of the purpose and value of education have been drifting, migrating from a primary interest in civic, moral and individual development, from service to families and communities, to the interests of a developing economic and technological infrastructure. Education as a goal in itself, and as a vehicle for the development of the individuals and citizens has been largely devalued in the context of these global changes. Technology policies tend to reflect this shift in basic assumptions: technology policies for schools have been developed, implicitly or explicitly, in alignment with a larger, fundamental shift in values which tends to privilege economic activity and technology as ends, and which tends to favour one-size-fits-all solutions to diverse problems.

But while policy drift reflects social drift, it is not a one-way process, nor is it a simple, one-on-one relation. The global never entirely subsumes the local and the particular. The local is always grounded in the reality of peoples' lives, and it is always potentially a site of resistance and creativity. Policy decisions made at the lower levels—the classroom, the school, the district, the region-- feed back in to the system, and ultimately help determine the direction of change and the velocity of change. And the way in which policy decisions are developed encourages or discourages the buy-in of its participants and stakeholders. Ultimately, local policies assure or discourage the sustainability of change.

Policy-makers and administrators at the school, school district and governmental levels have a decisive impact on the direction of any school reform (Glennan, 1998). Parents are also important: often the key driver for technology in the classrooms, parents need information to judge the educational "value" of different types of learning resources. They would ideally be part of the policy-making process. And in the classroom, teachers must be given the ultimate responsibility for determining the appropriate application of these tools. It is where we find this type of process that we find successful technological implementation and practice.

Technology Policy for Canadian Schools

The overall picture we would paint of a progressive, healthy, policy-making process for education is one in which an enabling, supportive context for experimentation comes from the top, while specific applications and innovations coming from the bottom, fully grounded in an understanding of local learner needs.

Policy makers must first ask WHY? What is the vision, the reason for change? What are our goals? Where do we want to go? These are the fundamental questions which should be driving technology policy for our schools. Defining and co-ordinating this vision is the first task of policy leadership. Provinces should have technology plans, with clear goals. Boards should have plans. Schools should have plans. And good planning should be rewarded with resources, up and down the chain. These plans have to be grounded in local and regional concerns: what do what do we want our children to learn? What works best as a learning strategy, a learning technology — why and for whom?

Policy makers must see technology as a means, not as an end. They must adapt a VALUE-ADDED approach to technology. There is no single solution because there is no single problem. Technology-enhanced learning must not be understood as a alternative to the traditional and legitimate teaching, training, service and community functions of a school, but as a way to add value to each of these functions in specific cases. How can the introduction of technology enhance learning, help build community and citizenship, expand the horizons of our learners, add value to the education experience and help us achieve our traditional educational goals, as well as new objectives?

Policy makers must ask HOW? A transparent and inclusive policy process is essential. At each level, managers needs to think carefully and consciously about the appropriate process for the development of policy. These processes need to be seen to be, and in fact must be, transparent and inclusive. They must locally appropriate—fit the institution and its history and culture. They must embody local/regional knowledge. They must include an implementation strategy. We are no longer entirely pioneers—we have a considerable body of successful and unsuccessful practice in front of us and we can learn from those examples. A first step should always be to attempt to foresee the problems, generate possible best practices, critique these practices in light of the local circumstances, and attempt to generate local solutions.

And finally, policy makers must be prepared to ask WHAT IF? We must reward experimentation, make room to play and grow, make room to fail. We need to increase the critical mass of examples of successful practice, at the local level. Good teachers teaching great courses, made better through new tools. Schools should encourage and legitimize innovation, create an environment which encourages risk-taking, and publicize it. The end result should be a critical mass of good examples, well publicized—as well as mistakes made and lessons learned (equally valuable). Policies have to be formulated which support innovation and make it sustainable, once achieved— incentives for innovation, professional development policies and policies designed to sustain both the technical and human resource infrastructures which are required.

A transparent and responsive policy practice combined with a value-added approach to technology will enable teachers to feel in control of these technologies, and encourage them to become innovators themselves, in their own attempts to fulfil the goals of their professional practice.

References:

Economist, (1996, September 28) "The Hitchhiker's Guide to Cybernomics,", p. 1.

Glennan, T. K. (1998). "New American schools after six years." MR-945-NAS [WWW document]. URL: http://www.rand.org/publications/MR/MR945/MR945.pdf.

Lewis, B., Massey, C. and Smith, R. (2001). *The Tower Under Siege: Technology, Power and Education*. Montreal & Kingston: McGill-Queen's University Press.

Enabling open network access during exams

Michael Chiles, Luby Liao, John Paul, Jeff Wright
University of San Diego
San Diego, CA 92110
`mchiles,liao,jpl,jhwright@sandiego.edu`

Abstract This paper presents our experiences of giving students open network access during exams while guarding against cheating. The practical information presented should be of interest to would-be practitioners and technological conservatives who can test their pedagogies with an aim to give their students the best education while ensuring academic integrity.

1. Introduction

A question frequently asked by instructors in an increasing number of disciplines is how to give an exam that allows students limited and controlled access to the Internet from classroom computers. The following question posted on the ACM SIGCSE Forum mailing list on May 5, 2002 is typical:

'Has anyone tried giving a programming exam for some of your intro-level courses in a lab? I always get complaints from students that it is not fair to write code on a piece of paper without using the tools they normally use (and they are right about that). So, I want to block a lab for 2 hours, and assign a few programming problems to work out, and let them do it. However, I want to somehow avoid them sharing efforts, so that might means having every machine disconnected from the network. What other issues are there? Has anyone tried this? Has it worked? Do students do better than in paper exams? ...'

This paper details one possible solution to this problem in the context of an Engineering Math course. Our approach addresses the poster's problem without disconnecting machines from the Internet.

In the Spring semester of 2002, Jeff Wright taught two sections of Math 110A: Engineering Math using Maple 6, a well-known computer algebra system in a lab equipped with Apple Macintosh computers. To run Maple, each computer must obtain a license from a remote license server which limits the total number of Maple users on the USD network at any given time. While students use Maple in class and during exams, they are encouraged to access the class web site where Jeff maintains copies of relevant Maple worksheets and other items of interest. To summarize, Jeff's problem is to allow students access to the remote license server and the class web site, but disallow other uses such as chat, email, instant messaging, and other unauthorized Net access.

On the flip side, the ideas presented here may be useful to people who for one reason or another believe that giving students any network access during an exam is a bad idea for pedagogical reasons other than the possibility of cheating. Our approach allows these hypotheses to be tested in a more direct way.

2. A conceptually very simple solution

Our solution is outlined in the following steps:

Publicize network access policy to students. Students are told that that they can use Maple and access the class web site during exams. Other intentional outbound traffic such as emailing is considered a violation. We further tell students that during an exam the inbound and outbound traffic of their machines will be captured and later analyzed for evidence of violation.

Exam time reconnaissance. During an exam, we record students' communication in the form of IP packets with other computers. The result is stored in a file that typically amounts to megabytes in size.

Post-exam analysis of the captured network traffic. Using the multi-megabyte file obtained in step two, together with the web access log of the USD web site, we generate various reports to identify possible network access violations.

3. Miscellaneous considerations

The campus network at USD is based on secure switched Ethernet, effectively transforming traditional Ethernet from a broadcast technology to a point-to-point technology. In this case the only packets a machine can normally see are its own and those broadcast packets sent by other computers in the same local area network. Hence, the arbitrary sniffing of all IP traffic on the network described above cannot be implemented until the campus network administrator performs a configuration procedure known as port mirroring [2]. Port mirroring involves copying all packets in and out of all the monitored machines to a specific monitoring machine, known as the 'sniffer'.

A separate issue at USD is a strong privacy policy that prohibits unauthorized sniffing of IP packets. We address this by performing the following steps before giving an exam we wish to monitor:

- request that the network administrator performs port mirroring to enable exam time reconnaissance.
- notify Academic Computing that we will be sniffing packets during exams.
- let the students know that we will be sniffing their packets during exams.

4. Technical details

1. First, we obtain a list of the Media Access Control (MAC) addresses of the classroom computers from the campus network administrator. Every campus computer connects with the campus network using an Ethernet card. Every Ethernet card has a permanent and unique MAC address of the form hh:hh:hh:hh:hh:hh, where h is a hexadecimal digit. Note that 'MAC' should not be confused with the Apple Macintosh computer. The relevance of MAC addresses lies with the fact that our lab computers obtain their IP addresses from a DHCP server when they are powered on. These IP addresses are dynamic as opposed to static because they can potentially change from time to time rather than staying fixed. MAC addresses, on the other hand, remain fixed and serve to identify the computers and the students using them.

2. Immediately before the exam, we run the following command on the designated 'sniffer' computer on the same local area network running Redhat Linux 7.2:

```
tcpdump ether host 00:05:20:C5:67:40  or 00:05:20:96:3F:2E or ...
```

Note the use of MAC addresses to specify the monitored machines in this command, rather than the potentially transient dynamic IPs. Here '...' stands for the remaining long list of other MAC addresses. What follows the tcpdump command is an example of a filter expression. In practice, since the filter expression is very long, we use a more convenient form:

```
tcpdump -F tcpdump_exp
```

where tcpdump_exp is a file that contains the filter expression and -F instructs tcpdump to read the filter expression from the file. This command will capture all inbound and outbound packets from all the machines listed in tcpdump_exp.

Tcpdump is a freeware packet-sniffing program available for Unix and Windows machines. Tcpdump can be installed with the following simple rpm command on computers running Redhat Linux:

```
rpm -Uvh tcpdump-3.6.2-12.i386.rpm
```

A fragment of the output from the tcpdump command follows:

```
07:29:09.967237  xyz203.sandiego.edu.1612  >  www.sandiego.edu.http:  P
607407960:607408445(485) ack 2259258923 win 32768 (DF)

07:29:09.973142  xyz203.sandiego.edu.1611  >  www.sandiego.edu.http:  P
607340903:607341388(485) ack 2259236870 win 32768 (DF)
```

The first line says that at 7:29 AM, the machine xyz203.sandiego.edu sent a packet from its port 1612 to the USD web server machine www.sandiego.edu which listens on the well-known port 80, symbolically named http. '>' visually indicates the direction of the communication. For details of the meaning of the output line components, we refer the readers to the documentation for tcpdump, and [1].

Even though we specify MAC addresses in the `tcpdump` command, the `tcpdump` output identifies machines using their DNS names and not MAC numbers. At USD the DNS names of the monitored machines are programmatically mapped to their dynamic IPs in an intuitive way. For example, `xyz203.sandiego.edu` has IP address `192.215.84.203`. Thus, we need a table that maps the MAC address of each machine to its dynamic IP during the exam. We use another freeware packet sniffing program called `ettercap` to produce this table. The command is

```
ettercap -Nl
```

The output columns, aside from the first, are IP address, MAC address, and fully qualified domain name of each lab computer:

```
14)  192.215.84.172        00:05:02:37:24:9F     xyz172.sandiego.edu
15)  192.215.84.190        00:05:02:F5:2B:04     xyz190.sandiego.edu
16)  192.215.84.205        00:50:E4:05:DA:55     xyz205.sandiego.edu
17)  192.215.84.207        00:05:02:1E:D0:6F     xyz207.sandiego.edu
```

3. The final step is to analyze the `tcpdump` output. Visually scanning it is instructive, but since the readable output file is megabytes in size, it is useful to write scripts to generate reports from the `tcpdump` output file. We used the Python programming language to develop these scripts, but any language with strong text processing support, such as Awk or Perl, could be used. As an illustration, we show fragments of two HTML reports we generated. The next two tables in the first HTML file report on two machines, `xyz157` and `xyz159`. These tables show outbound traffic of each machine. The three columns of the tables are the source port used, the destination machine and the destination port.

Outbound traffic from xyz157.sandiego.edu

src port	destination	dst port
netbios-ssn	lsanca1-ar22-4-33-006-054.lsanca1.dsl-verizon.net	2463
1857	http://www.sandiego.edu/	http
netbios-ssn	adsl-66-125-108-220.dsl.scrm01.pacbell.net	2487
netbios-ssn	66-105-104-140.customer.algx.net	2843
1861	http://www.sandiego.edu/	http
Bootpc	dhcp1.sandiego.edu	bootps
1865	http://www.sandiego.edu/	http

Outbound traffic from xyz159.sandiego.edu

src port	destination	dst port
netbios-ssn	lsanca1-ar22-4-33-006-054.lsanca1.dsl-verizon.net	2459
netbios-ssn	adsl-66-125-108-220.dsl.scrm01.pacbell.net	2483
netbios-ssn	66-105-104-140.customer.algx.net	2839
http	211.219.112.180	3267
Bootpc	dhcp1.sandiego.edu	bootps
netbios-ssn	HSE-Ottawa-ppp240974.sympatico.ca	1798
netbios-ssn	64.128.149.45	1875
http	218.11.130.38	4820

Immediately we notice that the student machines contacted various *targets* that appear suspicious or require further investigation. To wit,

1. on line 1, `xyz159` talked to the server running on port `2459` of `sancal-ar22-4-33-006-054.lsancal.dsl-verizon.net`. Is this a violation?

2. on line 2, `xyz157` talked to the USD web server listening on port `80` (symbolically named `http`) of `www.sandiego.edu`. In this case, further investigation is needed to decide whether xyz157 was accessing Jeff's home page at `http://www.sandiego.edu/~jesper` legally, or someone else's web site such as `http://www.sandiego.edu/~cheater` illegally.

Note that in the first case, `xyz159` talked to its target using a privileged port `139`, symbolically named `netbios-ssn`. This contact was not initiated by the student and therefore does not represent a violation. In the second HTML report we generated, such irrelevant records are filtered out.

To answer the second question, a simple programmed scan of the USD web site access log will suffice. To emphasize the importance of this simple but essential procedure, imagine the following scenario. Student A prepared his cheating group by training the members to use Netscape editor to publish to a common web site http://www.sandiego.edu/~cheater. During an exam, all the group members open Netscape editor to constantly publish their solutions to the site for their members to see. A simple Unix command `grep` applied to the web access log will catch this.

As promised, the next HTML report excludes irrelevant information from the report.

Outbound traffic from xyz157.sandiego.edu

src port	destination	dst port
1857	`http://www.sandiego.edu/`	http
1861	`http://www.sandiego.edu/`	http
1865	`http://www.sandiego.edu/`	http
1865	`http://www.sandiego.edu/`	http
1870	`http://www.sandiego.edu/`	http
1882	`http://www.sandiego.edu/`	http

Outbound traffic from xyz159.sandiego.edu

src port	destination	dst port
49152	`dns.sandiego.edu`	domain
49158	`ftp08.apple.com`	ntp
1367	`http://www.sandiego.edu/`	http
1363	`http://www.sandiego.edu/`	http

Line 1 of xyz159's table is the result of a contact to the Domain Name Server of USD, typically triggered by a web page request. Line 2 is a request from xyz159 to ftp08.apple.com, a time server, to synchronize the computer's system clock. Neither of these packets could be used by students to carry out clandestine communications.

5. Conclusion

After the post-exam analysis, we found no evidence of cheating. We feel that our method is effective for empowering students while preventing them from abusing their power. This practice enriches Jeff's teaching method and benefits his students. Our successes have encouraged us to continue to work to improve and streamline our approach and to experiment with new ones. The Python programs we have written to generate the reports are not refined enough to be published, but they can be useful to some people as examples. Feel free to email `liao@sandiego.edu` to request copies.

6. References

[1] S Northcutt & J Novak, Network intrusion detection, New Riders, 2001

[2] R Seifert, The switch book, Wiley computer publishing, 2000

Development of Web Server Surveillance Software

Introduction:

In early 1970s, David Bell and Leonard La Paula developed a model for secure computer operations. This model was based on the concept of various levels of classified information (Unclassified, confidential, secret and top secret) and various levels of clearance. If a person had a clearance level that dominated the classification level of a file, that person could access the file. If the persons clearance level was lower than the file's classification, access would be denied. This was used in the defense. The Trusted Computing System Evaluation Criteria (TCSEC) also known as Orange Book in 1983 defines Computer System accord in the following scale:

D-the minimal protection or not rated

C1-Discretionary Security Protection

C2-Controlled Access Protection

B1-Labeled Security Protection

B2- Structured Protection

B3- Security Domains

A1- Verified Design.

The other attempts are the German green Book in 1989, the Canadian Criteria in 1990, the information Technology Security Evaluation Criteria (ITSEC) in 1991 and the Federal Criteria in 1992. The concept was that common application environments could develop their own profiles for security functionality and assurance levels. The profile would then be used by some authority to certify the compliance of computer systems.

When Computers are networked together, new security issues arise and old issues arise in different ways. The Orange Book did not address the issue of networked computers. The Trusted Network Interpretation of TCSEC (TNI) took all the requirements of the Orange Book and attempted to address a networked environment of computers. Few systems were evaluated under TNI and it did not achieve commercial success. Hence it appears that none of the solutions by themselves solved all of the security problems. A good security system proposed is a mix of all of these solutions and many more. The intent is to prevent legitimate users from using the server for sending and spreading information harmful for the human society.

Security Essentials:

Computer security (COMPUSEC) is necessary to control access on our computer systems and Network Security (NETSEC) is needed to control the security of LAN. Together all of these concepts provide information Security (INFOSEC). Technology has progressed too fast for most of the proposed process. The anti virus software, Access controls like user ID, smart cards, biometric and Firewall are some preventive methods. A firewall cannot prevent an attacker from using an allowed connection to attack a system. If a webserver is allowed to be accessed it is vulnerable to an attack, since the user is already in the internal network.

Security Threats from legitimate users:

Intrusion Detection Systems (IDS) were once treated as the solution to the entire security problems. Intrusion Detection Systems (IDS) have existed for a long time. No longer it is needed to protect our files and systems, but just identify when someone was doing wrong and stop them. Some IDS have the ability to stop attacks before they were successful. No IDS is foolproof. They cannot detect legitimate users having incorrect access to informations. There are 2 types of IDS.

1.Host based H-IDS

2.Network-based (–IDS)

These have well defined criteria for what constitutes a penetration attempt and what constitutes the security perimeter. This perimeter can be defined by fire walls, telecom demarcation points,

The Defining Goals are :

- Detection of attacks
- Prevention of attacks
- Detection of policy violations
- Enforcement of use policies
- Enforcement of connection Policies
- Collection of Evidence

Proposed Web Server Surveillance:

The proposed Web server Surveillance System is shown in Figure.

Monitoring mechanism ensures that the users are constantly checked for the content of the traffic without violating the privacy policy. Policy Management schemes choose on what to monitor.

IDS schemes are used to detect any malicious intent. Pattern Recognition schemes can be used for comparing with harmful patterns. Natural language Processing is also used.

When suspicious activity occurs, there are five steps that can be taken to determine the nature of the activity. These are:

1. Identify the systems using IP addresses.

2. Log additional traffic between Source to Destination.

3. Log all traffic from the Source S.

4. Log the contents of packets from the Source

5. Calculate the vulnerability and threat level.

Following each of the steps, a determination should be made as to whether sufficient evidence has been found to identify the activity as an attack.Choosing how to respond is critical. Setting Thresholds are necessary to compute Vulnerability and threat The response can be Passive response or Active response If the event occurs once and does not repeat, it is very difficult to confirm. Some anomalies are almost impossible to completely investigate.

GUI tools are used to prepare daily/weekly/monthly reports.

Conclusion:

This Web Server Surveillance Software will prevent users from wrong use of the powerful tool of Communication, the Internet. Also it will prevent Web Server hosts to monitor legitimate users indulging in spread of violence using the server facility.

The Effect of E-mail Project on Enhancing EFL Learners' Academic Writing Skills

Huifen Lin
Department of Adult Education, Instructional Systems, Workforce Education and Development
Penn State University
United States
huifen5612@yahoo.com.tw

Abstract: This paper aims to report the findings of a study conducted to examine if E-mail is an effective tool in enhancing EFL students' academic writing skills. The participants in this study consisted of 8 college students majoring in English as a foreign language in a senior college in Taiwan. Each student was assigned one or two key-pals from eight countries. The findings suggested that although e-mail was proved to be an "authentic communicative writing activity" (Weasenforth &Biesenbach-Lucas 1998), it provided little or no benefits in improving students' overall academic writing skills. However, E-mail exchange provides an authentic audience that promotes two-way communication and its spontaneous nature and "informal conversational texts"(Marcus 1995) responds to most EFL professionals' belief that language acquisition is more likely to take place when there is a purpose to communicate and there exists an anxiety-free circumstance to do so.

Literature review

With the advent of the era of information, new technologies have been explored extensively in the business, commerce and educational field regarding the effectiveness, potential applications and implications they can bring to benefit the life, work and learning of human beings. The impact of technologies on education has, in particular, received increasing research interest when gathering amounts of findings suggested that if appropriately employed, technology can enhance learner involvement (Warschauer,1996;Kelm,1992), promote collaboration among learners and provide learning environments or tasks that traditional classrooms cannot offer. Computer-mediated Communication (CMC), among other technologies, provides tools that vastly transform means and nature of communication which EFL instructors can take advantage of and integrate into a communication-oriented, learner-centered language classroom. The most appealing feature of CMC is its creation of learning environments in which communication can be engaged beyond geographical boundaries and time constraints. Asynchronous type of CMC, for example, e-mail and BB, involves interactions to occur at different times; on the other hand, synchronous mode, including chat, IRC, and MOOs, enables communication to take place at the same time (Sussex & White 1996).According to Murray (2000),CMC, as "a salient mode of communication" has taken on a new role as a facilitator in the English language learning and instruction. Overall, the realities and potential of electronic communication for reducing learner frustration, easing learning process and creating self-paced learning environment have been recognized through the 1990s by proponents for Communicative Language Teaching (CLT), a method that emphasizes the acquisition of communicative competence being the goal of language instruction. Many ESL/EFL professionals have conducted in-depth research on the effect of e-mail on language teaching, hoping to take advantage of the unique features of the electronic text that this medium generates to assist students' learning of the target language. Research findings do suggest the implementation of e-mail projects in L2 classroom improve students' participation (Kamhi-Stein & Browne-del Mar 1997) and furthermore, foster a "student-student interaction"(Ady 1999;Kern 1996).Sakar (2001) on his research on the cross-cultural effects of e-mail on EFL students also suggested that e-mail exchange provided foreign language learners opportunities to be exposed to both reading and writing practice of the target language and also had great influence on learners' perception and attitudes toward the target language culture and people. Task-based or content-based approaches have been a center of discussion among ESL/EFL professionals and instructors, who believe that by dealing with real-life activities or projects, students gain access to "authenticity"-authentic materials and interactions and become highly motivated, as opposed to the artificial or pseudo interactions created from traditional language classrooms (Wolff, Universitat &Wuppertal 1998). Compared to traditional snail mail, e-mail has become more and more popular with its obvious advantages such as the high speed, low cost and ease of editing and revising. Numerous websites nowadays provide service for people or institutions looking for key pals to conduct projects or collaborative works. These e-mail exchange projects or tasks create a process-oriented, learner-centered language learning environments in which students can practice their reading and writing and oral skills indirectly if the task is appropriately designed.

The Study

The setting for this study was a course titled "Project-based Language Learning" in a five-year senior college English department in Taiwan. A successful complement of the course will lead to partial fulfillment for a Bachelor's degree in language and arts. The course objectives include (a) to provide opportunities for meaningful use of the target language on a task or project basis (b) to integrate previously learnt knowledge in different disciplines such as international business, English teaching methodologies, survival English,etc into the project or task design (c) to recognize the value of collaborative work on the process of language learning and (d) to demonstrate to the department faculty that students have achieved a more-than-satisfactory level of English by successfully turning in the final product of the project and orally present and defense it in front of faculty members and their fellow students. After a preliminary research and productive brainstorming process, the class decided the topic of the project," You've got mail-multicultural exchange" and specified the objectives of the project as "to further improve our English ability, especially writing and reading skills. To be exposed to different cultures, accept them and then develop open-mindedness toward cultural diversity; to reduce conflicts resulting from misunderstandings and to try an alternative way to learn a language". (cited from the project preface written by students). This project included three major stages. First, the preparatory stage, the author guided students to log on the net and browsed websites for interested e-pals. Students were advised to look for at leas 3 e-pals from the target culture he/she was interested in and were practicing sending practice e-mail to each other and to the author before starting the e-mail exchange with international e-pals from U.S. Britain, Austria, Korea, Japan, Germany, Argentina and Sweden. The duration for this project was 3 months, covering 8 topics specifically related to culture. Each participant in the project was required to write and reply to each e-mail message at least one time per week. Second, students turned in off-line essays featuring the cultural topics of the e-mail exchange by making reference to the information given by their e-pals, materials collected from school library or searched from the Internet. At the end of the project, the author expected to receive 8 essays from each of the participants, which were then used to compared with the transcripts of the e-mail messages to examine any significant difference in speech registers employed in both types of writings and in particular, to identify the linguistic features employed in academic writings. Finally, questionnaire and interviews were conducted to draw students' feedback on this e-mail exchange project and the aspects of language learning students especially benefited from this activity.

Findings

64 essays and 64 e-mail messages from participants were analyzed according to the linguistic features or speech registers associated with academic writings specified in Table 1. Several insightful findings can be drawn here.
• Paraphrasing, summarizing and giving examples were composing techniques that were used more frequently in both writings.
• Quotation and supporting claims with evidence were two skills that were the least employed in both writings, compared to the other six techniques.
• In e-mail messages, it's easier to appeal to the emotions of the writers/readers as opposed to the paper-and-pencil essay writings.
• There was no significant difference in terms of the frequency of the speech registers associated with academic

writing used in both types of writings.

•The scripts of e-mail messages revealed more carelessly-made errors such as subject-verb agreement, spelling and run-on sentences that mostly would not take place in traditional essay writings.

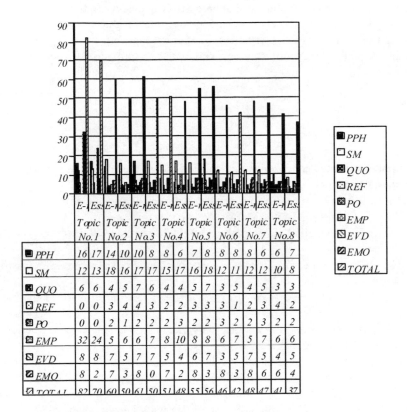

	E-m Topic No.1	Essay Topic No.1	E-m Topic No.2	Essay Topic No.2	E-m Topic No.3	Essay Topic No.3	E-m Topic No.4	Essay Topic No.4	E-m Topic No.5	Essay Topic No.5	E-m Topic No.6	Essay Topic No.6	E-m Topic No.7	Essay Topic No.7	E-m Topic No.8	Essay Topic No.8
PPH	16	17	14	10	10	8	8	6	7	8	8	8	8	6	6	7
SM	12	13	18	16	17	17	15	17	16	18	12	11	12	12	10	8
QUO	6	6	4	5	7	6	4	4	5	7	3	5	4	5	3	3
REF	0	0	3	4	4	3	2	2	3	3	3	1	2	3	4	2
PO	0	0	2	1	2	2	2	3	2	2	3	2	2	3	2	2
EMP	32	24	5	6	6	7	8	10	8	8	6	7	5	7	6	6
EVD	8	8	7	5	7	7	5	4	6	7	3	5	7	5	4	5
EMO	8	2	7	3	8	0	7	2	8	3	8	3	8	6	6	4
TOTAL	82	70	60	50	61	50	51	48	55	56	46	42	48	47	41	37

Table 1: Number of occurrence of academic writing features
Note: PPH-:paraphrase; SM-summarize;QUO-quote;REF-making reference; PO-taking positions; EMP-giving examples; EVD-supporting claims with evidence; EMO-appealing to the emotions

Questionnaires and interviews conducted shortly after the project indicated that participants, in general, believed that e-mail as a writing tool (a) introduced them to a world that they can engage in real, authentic interactions, (b) motivated them to write more and regularly and overcome the language difficulties to get meanings crossed, (c) provided permanent records or resources that they can retrieve or make use of for later work, (d) allowed them to write for real readers/audience instead of writing for the sole reader- the instructor and (e) gave them opportunities to be in contact with more colloquial, informal or dialectal use of the target language, which would be otherwise impossible under the circumstance of traditional language instruction.

Conclusions

This study has shown valuable insights into how EFL students responded to the use of e-mail as a writing tool and the results appeared to suggest that although no significant evidence could be identified to prove that EFL learners improved their skills for writing for academic purposes via involving in the e-mail exchange project, it's still widely recognized that "e-mail provides a context-rich, meaning focused, authentic communicative writing activity" (Weasenforth & Biesenbach-Lucas 1998). Students demonstrated an unexpected level of involvement and enthusiasm towards communicating via e-mail to increase their cultural awareness and language practice opportunities. Cummins (2000) has provided a framework for academic language learning which suggests that focusing on meaning, language and use is essential in language instruction "in order to develop students' access to and mastery of academic registers". Email exchange provides an authentic audience that promote two-way communication and its spontaneous nature and informal conversational texts responded to most EFL professionals' belief that language acquisition is more likely to take place when there is a purpose to communicate and there exists an anxiety-free circumstance to do so. No doubt, e-mail exchange activity could be appropriately integrated into language instruction given the features and advantages derived from this study; nevertheless, further research on its potential in promoting language learning compared to other CMC tools can be conducted to provide instructional suggestions for EFL instructors..

References

Ady, J. (1999).Computer-mediated communication in a high school global education curriculum: A brochure project. Social Studies, 90,159-164.

Cummins, J. (2000). Academic language learnin, transformative pedagogy and information technology: Towards a critical balance. TESOL Quarterly, 34, (3), 537-547.

Hartfiel, V.F., Hughey, J.B., Wormuth, D.R. &Jacobs,H.L.(1985).Learning ESL composition. Rowley,MA: Newbury House.

Horowitz, D.M. (1986d). What professors actually require: Academic tasks for the ESL classroom.TESOL Quarterly, 20,445-462.

Kamhi-Stein, L.D., & Browne-del Mar, C.(1997).EFL teachers and e-mail instruction: Perceived language and professional benefits. CAELL Journal, 7(4).14-19.

Kelm, O. (1992). The use of synchronous computer networks in second language instruction: A preliminary report. Foreign Language Annals, 25,441-454.

Kern, R. (1996). Computer-mediated communication: Using e-mail to explore personal histories in two cultures. in M.Warschauer (Ed.), Telecollaboration in foreign language learning (pp.105-119). Honolulu: University of Hawaii Press.

Macus, S. (1995).E-mailiorating student writing. Electronic learning. January 1995.18-19.

Murray, D.E. (2000).Protean communication: The language of computer-mediated communication. TESOL Quarterly, 34(3), 397-421.

Sakar, A. (2001). The cross-cultural effects of electronic mail exchange on the Turkish University students of English as a foreign language. CALL-EJ Online,3(1),Retrieved from http://www.lerc.ritsumei.c.jp/callej/6-1/sakar.html

Spack, Ruth. (1988).Initiating ESL students into the academic discourse community: How far should we go? In T.Silva & P.Matsuda (Ed.),Landmark Essays on ESL Writing (pp.91-108). NJ: Hermagoras Press.

Sussex. & White. (1996). Electronic networking. Annual Review of Applied Linguistics 16, 200-225.

Warschauer, M. (in press-a). Millennialism and media: Language, literacy, and technology in the 21st century. In Proceedings of the 1999 World Congress of Applied Linguistics. Tokyo:Waseda University.

Warschauer, M. (1996). Comparing face-to-face and electronic discussion in the second language classroom. CALICO Journal, 12,7-26.

Weasenfoth, D., Biesenbach-Lucas, S.(1998)The appropriateness of E-mail in composition instruction- linguistic and rhetorical analysis.Retrieved July 30,2002 from INSA-Lyon scientific and technological university website: http://www.insa-lyon.fr/Departments/CDRL/use.html

Wolff, D., Universitat, B. &Wuppertal, G.(1998)The use of e-mail in foreign language teaching. Retrieved July 30, 2002, from INSA-Lyon scientific and technological university website: http://www.insa-lyon.fr/Departments/CDRL/use.html

A STRUCTURED APPROACH TO PROGRAM EXPANSION FROM ON-CAMPUS TO DISTANCE DELIVERY

Marilyn Lockhart, Richard Howard, Larry Baker
Montana State University
Bozeman, MT   USA

Introduction

The decision at higher education institutions to expand programs and classes from on-campus to distance delivery often has not been made using a systematic, structured approach. Instead, the change at most institutions, particularly those with limited resources, has been driven by political forces, with state legislators, governing boards, and administrators issuing directives to implement the delivery of courses and programs through computer media. These mandates are passed on to deans and department heads, who in turn, look to faculty members to make distance delivery a reality. Arguments of resource savings and enrollment increases seem to be the primary motivation for these mandates. The directives have been presented with minimal consideration or understanding of the impact on faculty. Often, faculty are expected to design and deliver the courses under assumptions and resources similar to those of delivering on-campus classes. A recent review of selected institutions in a state university system revealed that over the past three years, the progress of transitioning from on-campus course delivery to on-line class delivery has been slow, often resulting in faculty and administrator frustration. Gaps between what administrators have promised external constituents and what faculty have delivered have been significant. As external expectations of distance delivery increase, institutional administrators are experiencing increasing pressure with limited ideas about how to enhance the delivery of on-line courses and programs at their institutions.

The purpose of this paper is to present a model of a structured approach to designing and delivering distance education. Adopting a structured approach to identify issues and solutions associated with the development and implementation of distance delivered courses and programs will result in enhancing the campus's ability to meet external expectations, while providing administrators and faculty with a mechanism to identify and recommend needed processes and required resources to deliver quality distance education.

Overview of Structured Decision Making

Structured decision support offers an avenue for the creation of sustainable and positive innovation, in this case, the expansion from only on-campus course delivery to on-line delivery. This structured approach enables college and university administrators to produce a link to faculty and students, increase performance, improve quality, and streamline processes that are easier to manage. Rational or structured decision support typically reflects analytical processes in which models are built that reflect various alternatives that a decision-maker can make and assess potential outcomes. In general, these analyses are quantitative in nature and revolve around the relationships of desired outcomes and needed resources. While these models provide important information, their usefulness in the decision making process should be viewed as a starting point. A process of structured or rational decision-making reflects the creation of information (quantitative and/or qualitative) that is integrated into the knowledge base of the decision makers and other constituencies across the campus. The results of this integration are the creation of intelligence, which is then brought to bear on the decision that needs to be made. In this process, the empirical information is analyzed, interpreted, and integrated into the knowledge base of the decision makers. The resulting intelligence is the integration of both the results of the data analysis and the decision maker's existing knowledge about the context in which the decision is to be made. Once a decision is made, assessment of the impact of the decision provides the campus with increased organizational intelligence. Critical in this process is the ability to access valid and reliable resource and productivity/outcomes data, and through appropriate analyses, create quality information that is communicated effectively to decision makers.

Using The Structured Approach to Distance Delivery Decision Making

Since the motivation for distance delivery often comes from forces external to the institution, mentioned earlier, often there is a resulting disconnect between administrators and faculty. This structured approach provides a method of eliminating this disconnect or gap between administrators and faculty, as well as providing an avenue for creating the knowledge and information needed for making decisions about distance education. The specific model presented below modifies and simplifies a business redesign process developed by the National Association of College and University Business Officers (NACUBO) and has been used by the authors for examining and improving other academic and administrative processes. The approach should function well in expanding higher education offerings from on-campus to on-line delivery.

The structured approach to making decisions about distance education should begin with several underlying mission values formulated and articulated by senior management. These would include the formation of partnerships between administrators and faculty, the delivery of quality programs and classes, and the use of technological and financial resources to their fullest advantage; all in support of the mission of the institution. The approach includes a three-tiered hierarchy, with continual communication among individuals in the different levels of the hierarchy.

The first tier consists of a "Steering Committee", composed of senior level administrators, charged with providing guidance and oversight to the institution-wide endeavor. Their role is to assess institutional readiness/administration, develop a long-range distance delivery plan, and approve policies, procedures, resources, and other support needed to move efforts forward.

The second tier is a "Process Owners Group" which consists of members from areas of the institution that are directly involved in the processes that "own" implementing distance delivery. Administrators and faculty from the colleges/departments and individuals from information technology center, faculty development, student services, and other key areas should be represented in this group. The "Process Owners Group" forms the work teams, writes project charges, and reviews and approves team recommendations.

The teams are composed of a mixture of faculty and administrators who are actually involved in carrying out the distance education initiatives. Some topics that teams might address include faculty services, instructional design/course usability, student readiness and support, and student learning outcomes and retention. The teams could answer questions such as:

- How does the institution prepare the faculty pedagogically and technologically to teach on-line course? What improvements are needed in this area?
- What incentives are and should be provided to faculty?
- How do faculty need to be supported during instruction?
- How do we prepare students to take distance classes?
- How user friendly is the technology to students?
- What services, such as library, registration, and ongoing help is available to students? How effective are these services? What are the additional student support needs?
- How should we measure learning outcomes?
- What are the outcomes of distance classes?
- What are the retention rates of on-line students?

The groups operate as teams, rather than as committees, receiving training in team work and structured decision making. Potential team members are interviewed in advance of appointment to assess available time, commitment to the project, and the ability to be a "team player." Team leaders receive in-depth training on the structured approach to decision making and group dynamics. Characteristics of good teams, such as having clear and identified team roles and responsibilities, conducting open discussions, possessing high levels of trust, displaying cooperation and collaboration, exploring and confronting differences, sharing of decision making, and participating equally, are described and developed among group members by the team leader. Collaboration among teams and between teams and the rest of the campus is encouraged and fostered by scheduling communication/progress reports.

Teams may redesign current activities or create new ones. Practices at other institutions are researched and compared to the context of the home institution. Some teams may distribute surveys to key groups (internal and external) in order to obtain data related to distance delivery. Some may conduct interviews with key stakeholders to gather in-depth, detailed data. Following the structured decision making process, recommendations based upon these data are created. Each team is expected to design a business plan that includes personnel and resource implementation requirements, benefits, potential barriers, and an assessment strategy for each set of recommendations.

Plans are presented to the "Process Owners Group" and "Steering Committee" for final approval.

Conclusion

A structured approach to the development and implementation of distance delivery on a campus can eliminate the gap between external expectations and campus realities. Some institutions may discover they should move more cautiously towards distance delivery than others. A structured approach is more likely to be received favorably by faculty because realistic support requirements have been identified and recognized by administers and faculty. The result will be realistic expectations of a distance education program that is consistent with the campus's resources to support it. In addition, through this structured process, identification of the campus's capacities to deliver distance education provides substantive information for discussions with external constituencies about needed resources.

A Feedback Model and Successful E-Learning

Yiping Lou
Department of Educational Leadership, Research and Counseling
Louisiana State University
United States
ylou@lsu.edu

Helena Dedic & Steven Rosenfield
Vanier College & Concordia University
Montreal, Canada
dedich@vaniercollege.qc.ca & rosenfis@vaniercollege.qc.ca

Abstract: Based on the literature concerning feedback, self-regulated learning and cooperative learning, this paper discusses a model of effective feedback that can be used to support student learning in computer-mediated environments. The model portrays the learner and teacher/peers as actors who both provide and receive feedback in interlocking loops during learning activities. Findings from two illustrative examples in science and social science classes indicate that while e-learning settings offer the opportunity to enhance feedback during the learning process, effective feedback structures are not automatically a part of interactive simulations, computer-mediated communication or other e-learning settings. Effective feedback in e-learning requires careful design and experimentation.

Introduction

This paper discusses a model of effective feedback useful in supporting student learning in computer-mediated environments. The word feedback is often used loosely. In this paper we define feedback as an informational message sent by one element of a system to another element, with the expectation that the receiving element will use this message to modulate its performance. For example, a home heating system consists of thermostats, a control switch and a heat source. The thermostats compare room temperature to a predetermined desired temperature, and then send messages to the switch telling it to either turn the heat source on or off (Doig, 2000). Such a system is only functional if: appropriate messages are sent to the switch; the switch correctly interprets messages; the heat source responds effectively to the situation. Thus, feedback is a message sent with the intent of moving the recipient from a current state to a goal state. We will refer to effective feedback as feedback that meets four conditions: 1) feedback recipients have a clear understanding of the gap between their current state and their goal state; 2) appropriate corrective messages (feedback) are sent and received; 3) feedback is interpretable by its recipients; and, 4) recipients possess prerequisite prior knowledge, motivation, and strategies to respond effectively to the feedback. We will first describe our model of effective feedback that is rooted in research on: feedback, self-regulated learning, and cooperative learning. We will then describe two situations drawn from science and social science classes that will illustrate the differences inherent in computer-mediated learning environments and standard face-to-face settings, when viewed through the lens of our model.

A Model of Effective Feedback

From a constructivist perspective, learners build knowledge by cognitively elaborating new information, by reconciling with previously held views both the data gained through their own observation and experimentation, and through external feedback. Similarly, teachers as course designers function as self-regulating systems when they construct new task and feedback structures in a process involving elaboration and experimentation, as well as reconciliation of previously held views with feedback information provided by actions and performance of learners.

Research on feedback has accumulated a wealth of information concerning the impact of feedback on student learning. Several meta-analyses (*e.g.*, Bagert_Drowns et al., 1991; Azevedo & Bernard, 1995) synthesizing this research found that providing feedback versus not providing feedback has a significant positive effect on student achievement, however, the effects of elaborate feedback with explanation were generally found to be significantly larger than simple feedback without explanation. This research has primarily focused on external feedback, as provided by a teacher either directly or via a computer, after student performance.

Research on self-regulated learning (*e.g.*, Butler & Winne, 1995) suggests that learners generate internal feedback during the cognitive process of monitoring. Self-regulated learners monitor their own academic performance, affect and learning strategies. They rely on internal feedback to guide the selection of appropriate strategies and corrective action if their goals are not being met. They seek external feedback when they cannot resolve problems on their own.

Research on small group cooperative learning indicates significant positive effects of small group learning over whole class or individual learning if appropriately structured (Abrami et al., 1995; Lou et al., 2001) and that those who gave or received peer explanations tended to achieve higher than others (Webb, 1989). This research suggests that peers can be another source of external feedback.

Based on the above three areas of research as well as constructivist theories of learning, we have created a model of effective feedback that incorporates all three sources: self, teacher and peers (see Figure 1). In the model, learning/teaching involves simultaneous feedback loops, one centered on the learner and another (completed by the dashed line) centered on the teacher/peer. Solid arrows indicate feedback, while hollow arrows represent corrective actions in response to feedback. Note that a teacher's/peer's corrective action is simultaneously external feedback for the learner. To portray this duality we use both solid and hollow arrows flowing from the teacher/peer to the learner.

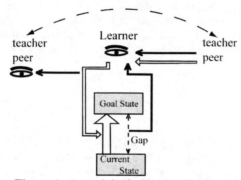

Figure 1. A model of effective feedback

In this model learners are viewed as active self-regulators, who seek feedback and then respond to it. Learners depend on the instructional setting to provide both the tasks from which they can draw data, and the feedback structures that allow them to gauge their performance (Pintrich, Marx & Boyle, 1993). In turn, teachers who create these same task and feedback structures need feedback from learners regarding the effectiveness of the structures. Thus, effective teaching depends on teachers being sent appropriate messages by the students; the ability of teachers to interpret those messages; and, teachers having appropriate skills to respond effectively to messages. That is, teachers, as course designers, form another self-regulating system that initiates changes based on feedback gathered from the actions and performance of learners. Alternatively, peers who offer constructive criticism, form another self-regulating system that interacts with that of learners.

While this model applies both to face-to-face and computer-mediated learning environments, there are vital differences in the type, timing, and sources of feedback used in these different learning settings. For example, in face-to-face classrooms, feedback to individual learners during the learning process tends to be short and simple due to time constraints. More elaborate feedback may be provided to the whole class, but targeting a mythical "average student". Public feedback aimed at an "average student" discourages and bores high-ability students while confusing less apt ones. However, when elaborate feedback is one-on-one, between teacher and an individual student, no student other than the individual involved in the interaction benefits. In the computer-mediated environment individual feedback need no longer be private, nor must public feedback be targeted at the "average student". For example, with discussion boards, public feedback provided by the teacher to an individual student can benefit other students with similar misconceptions. This knowledge motivates teachers to provide more elaborate feedback, which leads to higher performance standards in the class. On the other hand, teachers and learners in face-to-face settings have the advantage of synchronous verbal and non-verbal communication. In face-to-face settings, a good instructor constantly "reads" the class and modifies instruction to maintain student involvement. In computer-mediated settings this type of information is absent and new ways of "reading" involvement must be used.

With two very different e-learning settings, one in science classes using Web-based computer simulations, and one in social science classes using Web-based discussion boards, we will illustrate and draw lessons concerning the interlocked loops of learner and teacher; and then the interlocked loops of learner and peer.

Feedback and Web-Based Simulations

Interactive simulations are frequently used in computer-mediated instruction with the intention of allowing learners to rapidly generate many "instances" of a particular phenomenon. Learners are expected to discover a pattern or rule that explains the phenomenon (hypothesize), and then to verify their hypothesis by interpreting visual (graphical) feedback. For example, in our Calculus course students were asked to observe an animated tangent line moving along a graph of a given function, and then to predict the shape of the graph of the derivative of the given function. Then, a simple modification caused the animation to rerun with the addition of a plot of a graph of the derivative function, thus providing immediate feedback for the student's prediction. After a few tries some students discovered the true nature of the relationship between a function and its derivative, in fact gaining a more general mathematical thought process as well.

In face-to-face classrooms the teacher explains such a relationship, but students rarely discover it in this deeper manner. However, teachers obtain feedback from classroom discussion and non-verbal messages students send, aiding teacher assessment of the depth of conceptual understanding the students have attained. In response to such feedback the teacher can modify instruction immediately. In a computer-mediated environment, where students interact with a computer simulation, the teacher does not get this same feedback.

On the surface it appears that the use of simulations, with visual feedback, enhances student understanding at the expense of feedback for the teacher. However, the situation is more complex. The use of simulations to facilitate learning complex concepts imposes demands on learners not encountered previously in face-to-face settings. First, some students may lack even basic computer skills necessary for learning in a computer-mediated environment. While the number of such students is rapidly decreasing, any such students may actually find that this context hinders rather than facilitates learning. Second, many students may have developed a rigid method of monitoring their own understanding in a subject, and thus may not value feedback that is delivered through the computer interface (Dedic, Rosenfield, Cooper, & Fuchs, 2001). Finally, the ability of students to interpret complex visual messages is often limited. Our work highlighted two ways of helping students to understand such feedback: deliver visual messages in stages, with initial messages being visually simple, and layers of complexity gradually added; and, augment visual feedback with elaborative textual feedback (Alalouf, Klasa, Dedic, & Rosenfield, 2002).

Providing feedback to teachers is a problem in computer-mediated environments for two reasons: the teacher does not obtain such information directly from students, and modifications to the environment require preparation time, therefore resulting in a delay in teachers' responses to any feedback that is obtained. We found that both students' answers to pop-up quizzes, and perusal of student activity log files can generate the requisite teacher feedback. Our research demonstrates that students' answers on pop-up quizzes correlate with achievement after the activity, thus feedback in the form of answers to pop-up quizzes allow us to predict how students are developing conceptual understanding. Further, access to log files allows teachers to trace students' activities during the use of simulations. However, both of these mediums for obtaining feedback must be built into the environment (*e.g.*, Winne, 1989).

Feedback and Web-Based Discussion Boards

CMC tools, such as web-based discussion boards, are increasingly being used in distance education courses or as a supplement to traditional face-to-face classroom teaching and learning, especially in social science courses. One common usage of discussion boards is to enable group/class discussions on topics and issues related to the course. This asynchronous communication provides students with opportunities to reflect and respond to each other thoughtfully. Another effective use of discussion boards is for teachers to provide public and elaborate feedback to either an individual student, or the whole class, so as to benefit more students. For example, in group/class discussions, the instructor can monitor discussions and provide feedback when misconceptions arise. In our social science classes we also used discussion boards to provide detailed feedback on each individual or group project, and to encourage all students to read and comment on the work of others, as well as reading the instructor's feedback. Thus, students not only learned from each other, but also developed a better perception of their learning gap, and consequently helped make feedback effective.

Few studies have been conducted to document how, using CMC, peer feedback between and among students working on different projects can be structured successfully. The primary concern has been that learners are unable to provide each other with quality feedback (Latham, 1997). Our work in a graduate course in instructional design and an undergraduate course in educational technology integration, however, indicates that if appropriate structures and guidance are provided, peer feedback during project-based learning can be beneficial to both the provider and the receiver of the feedback. The strategies used to provide guidance, modeling, and scaffolding in the two courses using class discussion board and group spaces on Blackboard (2000) included: instructor modeling during the early part of the course; the provision of evaluation rubrics; and, the development of common criteria for best projects. In the midterm and end of course evaluations students responded very positively to the structured peer feedback approaches used in the class. Peer feedback placed students in the position of providing feedback, not just receiving it. This promoted student meta-cognitive and critical thinking skills and helped students develop multiple perspectives, thereby increasing achievement motivation and improving self-regulation in learning.

Conclusion

At the core of this paper lies our model of effective feedback involving interlocked feedback loops, portraying learners and teachers/peers as actors who both provide and receive feedback. The model, based on constructivist learning theory and self-regulated learning, emphasizes the importance of gathering learners' process and performance data, and providing feedback during the learning activities so that learners will be effectively guided toward achieving their desired learning goals.

Our findings concerning feedback in science and social science classes indicate that e-learning settings offer the opportunity to enhance feedback during the learning process so that student learning outcomes and affect are improved. However, it is important to note that effective feedback structures are not automatically a part of interactive simulations, CMC or other e-learning settings, and that teachers must actively design them in, and recursively continue to refine them through experimentation.

References

Abrami, P.C., Chambers, B., Poulsen, C., De Simone, C., d'Apollonia, S., & Howden, J. (1995). *Classroom connections: Understanding and using cooperative learning.* Toronto, ONT.: Harcourt -Brace.

Alalouf, E., Klasa, J., Dedic H. & Rosenfield, S (2002). *Conceptual understanding versus algorithmic computation in Calculus: Strawman or real conflict.* Paper presented at the annual meeting of the Association de la Recherche Collegial, Quebec, PQ, Canada.

Azevedo, R. & Bernard, R. M. (1995). A meta-analysis of the effects of feedback in computer-based instruction, *Journal of Educational Computing Research, 13,* (2), 111-27.

Bangert-Drowns, R. L. Kulik, J. A., & Morgan, M. T. (1991). The instructional effect of feedback in test-like events, *Review of Educational Research, 61,* 213-38.

Blackboard, Inc. (2000). *Blackboard, version 5* [Computer software]. Washington, DC: Blackboard.

Butler, D. L, & Winne, P. H. (1995). Feedback and self-regulated learning: A theoretical synthesis, *Review of Educational Research, 65,* 245-81.

Dedic, H., Rosenfield, S., Cooper, M., & Fuchs, M. (2001). "Do I really hafta? WebCAL, A look at the use of livemath software in web-based materials that provide interactive engagement in a collaborative learning environment for differential calculus." *Educational Research and Evaluation, 7*(2-3), 285-312.

Doig, S. M. (2000). *Developing an understanding of the role of feedback in education.* http://www.tedi.uq.edu.au/conferences/A_conf/titles.html, accessed Feb 28, 2002.

Latham, A. S. (1997). Learning through feedback. *Educational Leadership, 54,* p. 86-7.

Lou, Y., Abrami, P. C., & d'Apollonia, S. (2001). Small group and individual learning with technology: A meta-analysis. *Review of Educational Research, 71,* 449-521.

Pintrich, P. R., Marx, R. W., & Boyle, R. A. (1993). Beyond cold conceptual change: The role of motivational beliefs and classroom conceptual factors in the process of conceptual change. *Review of Educational Research, 63,* 167-199.

Webb, N. M. (1989). Peer interaction and learning in small groups. International Journal of Educational Research, 13, 21-39.

Winne, P.H. (1989). Theories of instruction and of intelligence for designing artificially intelligent tutoring systems. *Educational Psychologist, 24,* 229-259.

The Development of a Web-Based Continuing Education Course for Camp Nurses

Jo Lynne Lundy, RN, M.S. Ed.
Doctoral Candidate
Nova Southeastern University
USA
lundyjo@nova.edu

Abstract: Camp nursing is a growing area of specialized nursing practice and there are very few continuing education courses available to the nurse preparing to assume the camp nurse role. Approximately 10,000 camps are currently in operation in the United States and nurses are the most common healthcare providers for those camps. Camp nurses cannot rely on traditional medical equipment and supplies; they must use their own skills, clinical knowledge, critical thinking and problem-solving abilities to make independent decisions and nursing interventions. This research study focused on the collection of data in order to design, implement, and evaluate a Web-based continuing education course for camp nurses. The goals of this study were to determine if camp nurses are receiving specific educational interventions and role orientation prior to assuming camp nursing duties, and to use that information to develop a Web-based course that would enable nurses to bridge the gap between what they know and what they need to know in order to function effectively in the camp nursing role.

Introduction

Nursing is a dynamic process with the opportunity to practice in a variety of clinical settings. The traditional hospital-based practice is the most common, but there are many areas of practice that require specialized education. Camp nursing is one nursing specialty that is experiencing rapid growth. The American Camping Association (ACA) estimates that approximately 10,000 camps are currently in operation in the United States, and an estimated 9 million youth attend camps annually (ACA, 2001). Each accredited camp is required to have a healthcare provider on the property when campers are present, and this provider is most often a registered nurse.

Most nurses are unfamiliar with the outdoor milieu and must learn to adapt clinical skills and patient care to the camp setting. Camp nurses cannot rely on traditional medical equipment and supplies; they must use their own skills, clinical knowledge, critical thinking and problem-solving abilities to make independent decisions and nursing interventions. Due to varying geographical locations, local cultures and customs, and differences in communities, each camp presents unique nursing challenges (Erceg & Pravda, 2001). The nurse working in a camping environment must be prepared to deal with illnesses and injuries in the prehospital setting, and must be adequately trained to handle emergencies of all types.

Two key elements of camp nursing practice are a specialized educational program and a role orientation that will prepare the nurse to practice independently and competently in that specific nursing role. Without a standardized approach to camp nurse education, there can be no consistent standard of outcomes in clinical decision-making, and ultimately in the quality of patient care (Goodman, 1997). The Association of Camp Nurses (ACN) has published *The Scope and Standards of Camp Nursing Practice* (ACN, 2002), but there are presently no national educational standards or standardized courses to prepare nurses to function in this clinical environment.

Nurses enter the camp healthcare environment with a wide variety of backgrounds and experiences. Most nurses practice alone at camp, and without specialized education and role orientation, nurses assuming the role of the primary health care provider in a camp setting do not possess the knowledge base to be successful in that role. An educational course for entry-level camp nurses should include these essential elements: specifying the role and work setting, identifying competencies required to care for specific illnesses and injuries, writing performance criteria, implementing educational programs, and developing evaluation methods to determine when the performance criteria have been met (Alspach,

1990). Two other factors important to the success of a camp nursing course are planning and implementing the program effectively, and selecting an appropriate instructional delivery method (Phelps, 1996).

Goals and Research Questions

Very little has been written in professional nursing literature regarding educational courses for camp nurses. The few references to this topic tend to be standard-setting statements by camping organizations or "how-to" reports from camp nurses themselves. Camp nurses are usually hired for the position without ever having seen the camp and with just a phone interview with a camp administrator. It would seem appropriate for camp administrators to hire only the most experienced nursing candidates, but this may not be a viable option. Employment of experienced nurses in the camp setting may be difficult due to nursing salary expectations that camps are unable to meet, expanded autonomous role challenges that may be beyond the nurse's scope of practice, and the anxiety associated with increased patient acuity in a nontraditional nursing environment (Author).

Nurses seeking to practice in the camp environment should have access to a course designed specifically for the camp nurse, and an orientation to camp nursing practice prior to assuming that role, that is sufficient to enable them to practice safely (Maheady, 1991). This may be difficult because traditional nursing courses and orientation programs are usually not available in the camp clinical setting. Most camp nurses have to accept on-the-job training and orientation to the new role. Nurses in this situation must be accountable for self-assessment of their knowledge and skills deficits and for using self-study mechanisms in order to meet established practice standards. Before any deficit of knowledge, skills, and attitudes can be identified, it is essential to know which of these are necessary in order to deliver a high quality of care (Lindner, 1998).

The goals of this study were to determine if camp nurses are receiving specific educational interventions and role orientation prior to assuming camp nursing duties, and to use that information to develop a Web-based course that will enable nurses to bridge the gap between what they know and what they need to know in order to function effectively in the camp nursing role. This study attempted to answer the following research questions:

1. Are entry-level camp nurses being prepared for the camp nursing role?
2. How are camp nurses preparing for the role of camp nurse?
3. What is the essential course content for a Web-based course for the entry-level camp nurse?
4. How can the effectiveness of a Web-based course for the entry-level camp nurse be evaluated?

Methodology

A descriptive survey design was utilized for this study. The executive committee of the Association of Camp Nurses reviewed and approved this project, and the roster of membership of the ACN was provided as the study sample (n=346). The sample possessed the characteristics and qualifications from which the required data could be obtained, and was representative of the target population. Due to a lack of literature and research on camp nursing, no previously existing instrument was available, and no existing nursing instrument was suitable for adaptation. The survey questionnaire *Camp Nursing: A National Survey* was developed using currently available nursing literature and professional standards for camp nurses published by the ACN. In order to answer the research questions proposed in this study, the survey topics included camp nurse demographics, characteristics of camp health centers, camp nurse job descriptions, the process for and content of camp nurse orientation, and the evaluation of camp nurse orientation outcomes.

Prototype Web-Based Course

The inflexible nature of nursing practice and rapidly changing healthcare reform present challenges to camp nurse education; traditional classroom options do not usually meet the needs of camp nurses. The World Wide Web (the Web) offers many opportunities to deliver quality basic and continuing education; however, barriers to Web-based delivery of an educational course for camp nurses include access to the course from a remote camp setting (not all camps have computers or Internet access available), financial resources of the camp and the camp nurse, obtaining the resources and expertise to build and implement the course, maintaining technical support, and Web hosting issues such as security, sufficient storage space, and knowledgeable system administration (Horton, 2000).

A prototype course was designed using the data collected from the review of literature and the content portion of the survey. The course was delivered via the *Blackboard* course creation Web site (www.blackboard.com). The data obtained from the content section of the survey was used to determine the content that was included in the camp nurse course. A pilot course was developed offering three modules of instruction; the three content topics receiving the highest percentage of response in the survey were included in the prototype course: role of the camp nurse (94.8%), asthma management (93.6%), and management of routine illnesses and injuries (91.8%). Evaluation of the prototype course was performed by six camp nurse evaluators from various disciplines; they were given user names, passwords, and the instructions required to access the course.

Findings

The data analysis revealed that full time camp nurses and seasonal camp nurses did not have statistically significant differences in their responses to the content portion of the survey; both groups of nurses generally agreed that the topics queried were important, although the full-time nurses appear to agree more strongly. Both groups felt camp issues were more important than medical knowledge, although nurses who were not full-time camp nurses appear to feel more strongly about this. The mean number of years of nursing experience of the respondents was 21.3. The mean number of years of camp nursing experience of the respondents was 8.5. Only 22.7% of those responding had taken an online course prior to completing the survey, but 98% of those who had taken an online course indicated that they would take another online course in the future. 56.8% of camp nurses reported that they did receive some type of orientation; however, this orientation was described as including as little as a camp tour, to a one-week comprehensive orientation. Methods utilized by nurses in preparing for the camp nurse role include reading the camp policy and procedure manual (78%,)reviewing nursing and medical textbooks (48%), reading journal articles (49.1%), and taking a tour of the camp (49.0%). 82.8% of camp nurses received only on-the-job training for the camp nurse role.

Conclusions

The findings suggest that camp nurses are utilizing self-directed learning methods in order to prepare themselves for the camp nursing role. The survey results indicated that camp nurses prefer for initial and annual updates to be accomplished via face-to-face workshops/seminars, Association of Camp Nurses conference presentations/standards, and reviewing textbook information. Online courses were identified as being important for annual continuing education updates, but most of the respondents preferred face-to-face continuing education offerings for initial preparation.

Until there are educational courses specifically designed for camp nurses, this population should continue to use self-directed study methods to prepare for the camp nurse role. Each camp has unique medical, geographical, and cultural concerns, and the camp nurse must be prepared to care for that specific camper population. The nursing profession is based on human contact and many of the respondents indicated that the preferred delivery method for continuing education offerings is in the traditional face-to-face setting. However, those respondents who were more comfortable with computer skills indicated a preference for online continuing education.

References

Alspach, J. (1990). Critical care orientation: A discussion of survey results. *Critical Care Nurse,* 10(6), 10-16.

American Camping Association (2001). *American Camping Association.* Retrieved September 15, 2000 from the World Wide Web: http://www.acacamps.org/.

Anderson, D. (2000). *Internet and Web Design for Teachers: A Step-by-Step Guide to Creating a Virtual Classroom.* New York: Longman Publishing Group.

Association of Camp Nurses. (2000). Scope of Practice Statement. *Compass Point,* 10(4), 12-13

Bitter, G., & Pierson, M. (1999). *Using Technology in the Classroom.* Boston: Allyn and Bacon.

Blakeley, J, & Curran-Smith, J. (1998). Teaching community health nursing by distance methods: Development, process, and evaluation. *The Journal of Continuing Education in Nursing, 29*(4), 148-153.

Erceg, L., & Pravda, M. (2001). *The Basics of Camp Nursing.* Martinsville, IN: American Camping Association.

Goodman, D. (1997). Application of the critical pathway and integrated case teaching methods to nursing orientation. *Journal of Continuing Education in Nursing, 28*(5), 205-210.

Horton, W. (2000). *Designing Web-Based Training: How to Teach Anyone Anything, Anywhere, Anytime.* New York: Wiley.

Lindner, R. (1998). A framework to identify learning needs for continuing nurse education using information technology. *Journal of Advanced Nursing, 27*(5), 1017-1020.

Maheady, D. (1991). Camp nursing practice in review. *Pediatric Nursing, 17*(3), 247-250.

Phelps, S. (1996). Off to a successful start! The use of self-study for hospital-wide nursing orientation. *Journal of Continuing Education in Nursing, 12*(1), 7-12.

Vaughn, T. (1998). *Multimedia: Making It Work* (4th ed.). New York: Osborne McGraw-Hill.

Acknowledgements: This project could not have been accomplished without the advice and encouragement of Dr. Gertrude Abramson, my mentor and dissertation advisor at Nova Southeastern University, the Association of Camp Nurses (with special thanks to Linda Erceg), and Darek Nalle, PhD (University of Nevada-Reno) who provided invaluable statistical advice.

E-learning pedagogy: The reveal of value adding learning processes. Definitions and Implications for dynamic learning content delivery

Miltiadis D. Lytras
Athens University of Economics and Business, Greece
Department of Management Science and Technology
Email: mdl@aueb.gr

Abstract

E-learning seems to suffer from the heritage of many "e" things that in the last decade formulate the new business environment. The overestimation of the role of technology causes a misunderstanding concerning the key issues in e-learning (Lytras and Pouloudi 2001). Our approach for e-learning recognizes three dimensions as the critical pillars that have a direct impact in e-learning performance: E-learning pedagogy (Lytras and Doukidis 2001), (Lytras and Doukidis 2000), knowledge management (Lytras and Doukidis 2000), (Lytras, Pouloudi et al. 2002), (Lytras, Pouloudi et al. 2002) and Application Integration. This paper focuses on E-learning pedagogy. Our intention is to provide a thoroughly analysis of parameters that justify a pedagogical strategy for e-leanring exploitation. The ultimate objective is to investigate the role of specific learning process in the exploitation of learning content and in the support of dynamic unique learning experiences.

1. Introduction

The case of human resources management in business environments is of vital importance for the establishment of business strategy (Carter and Scarbrough 2001). Knowledge exploitation and learning capability (Ryan 1995), seem to be two integrated aspects of the same phenomenon: The establishment of continuous improvement flexible mechanisms for the exploitation of the intellectual capital in business and academics environments (Coulson 2000). In this context where the investigation of the performance of the undertaken effort is of critical importance for the justification of investments, the detailed analysis of success factors in e-learning is of critical importance. The Multidimensional Dynamic E-learning Model (MDL model) (Lytras and Doukidis 2000), (Lytras and Odman 2001), summarizes a hypothesis, that in e-learning the overall performance can be overviewed in the mass of a cube which boundaries are determined by three parameters. The e-learning pedagogy dimension, the Knowledge Management sophistication and the application integration dimension.

The Multidimensional Dynamic e-Learning (MDL) Model is based on three complementary dimensions: ▣ The Knowledge Management dimension ▣ The e-Learning dimension ▣ The application integration dimension. Each of these describe in synopsis detailed considerations that confront the e-cooperation platforms such as knowledge management systems with embedded e-learning pedagogy and capacity of dynamic integration with other crucial business applications. To be more specific we will use three explanations for the three dimensions of MDL model. The **Knowledge Management Sophistication** summarizes the ability of the e-learning platform to manage learning content in various formats, to re-use learning modules and to support knowledge management processes such as knowledge creation, knowledge codification, knowledge transformation and knowledge diffusion. The **E-Learning Dimension** stands for the ability of an e-learning system to construct effective learning mechanisms and learning processes that support the achievement of different educational goals. With no doubt this dimension incorporates issues like learning styles, learning needs, learning templates as well as learning specification settings. The **Application Integration Dimension** summarizes for the e-learning platforms the capacity of collaboration with other business applications in order to obtain learning content from real business operations. This dimension seems to be the less detected on the common platforms and this causes a number of gaps for the effective implementation of cooperation systems. The critical issue of insufficient content in many situations is due to the inability of the organizations to establish a knowledge generation mechanism through the operation of information systems that support the most important business processes. Our paper is trying to explain further the e-learning pedagogy dimension. The detailed analysis of each dimension formulates an analytical tool where the delivered value in an e-learning collaboration can be represented in the surface of the cube.

2. Describing methods for Learning Value classification

One of the major obstacles in e-learning is the static approaches to the delivery of learning content. If we assume that in an e-learning system we can obtain sufficient content then the key question is how do you diffuse it to learners and how can we establish effective motivation mechanisms?

For this purpose we decided to analyze the propositions of well-known researchers such as (Bloom and Krathwohl 1984), (Shuell 1992). The key idea of their work seems to has a direct impact in every implementation that refers to learning. But let start our syllogism concerning their relevance of their propositions in learning. The traditional approach in e-learning is mainly focused on the development of session and their delivery through internet usually through a Learning Management System. Unfortunately these platforms do not prove their learning capability. A hypothesis whenever we refer to information systems is that the users of systems require the fulfillment of several needs and potentially this fulfillment is based on a value realization. In other words transforming this general statement in e-learning context we can claim that an e-learner demands the reveal of value components when he/she interacts with the e-learning system. This value realization can be investigated in different level: Technology, content, functionalities, processes, communication etc. But irrelevant of the level, the key understanding is that e-learning is mainly a learning phenomenon. From this perspective the value that the engagement of information and communication technologies promote in e-elearning has primarily to be realized through the learning sophistication of the whole system. The cataloguing of learning objects in a database (which is several packages such as WebCT is not as simple) does not mean that learning is guaranteed.

The main this of the e-learning is the specification of engagement mechanisms with the learning content. If we establish capabilities that will set an environment where learners feel motivated and are engaged in learning content exploration then their perception of value is increased. In this direction three concepts not novel , but quiet interesting are putting in detail analysis: Namely educational objectives, learning processes and learning functions.

2.1 Bloom's & Shuell' s Approaches

The limited space of this paper do not give as the opportunity to discuss in detail two approaches that have for many supported the educational design. The development of a classification framework for writing educational objectives was the main contribution of Bllom in three domains Cognitive, Affective and Psychomotor. Especially in the cognitive domain the hierarchy opf educational goals incorporates: **Knowledge, Comprehension , Application , Analysis , Synthesis.** The taxonomy is hierarchical in the meaning that levels increase in difficulty and sophistication as well as cumulative since each level is based on previous levels or it assumes them as cornerstones in a step b step process that promotes the achievement of well defined objectives.   Additionally the 6 levels can be used as an investigation basis, which promotes the learning performance and the highest possible degree of learning content exploitation. Especially in an e-learning environment a such starting point is very crucial. The dispersed learning objects can be packaged using a value adding proposition through learning processes with specific life cycles overstepping the uncertain learning outcomes in the traditional approach where a hierarchical structure of linked modules sets a static learning scenario. The combination of different learning processes and the justified enrichment with metadat a of the various learning objects in order to support different learning processes seems to be an effective knowledge and learning management mechanism. . More over if we accept this scalable qualitative distinction of learning processes   then we can un derstand why the attachment of metadata admit personalized learning since each learner could exploit learning objects in the basis of the selection of specific learning processes. The cognitive level of learners in this way, becomes the value driver for increased learning performance. Shuell identified a set of psychological processes, such as raising attention, expectations and motivation, activating prior knowledge and perform monitoring, that foster effective learning in the student. The perception of t he learning function as "*an attribute of the learning material in a specific context*" is highlighting the purpose of our research in e-learning. If we can justify several learning processes that are based on the research findings of Bloom and Shuell then t he context for the exploitation of the learning content is secured. In this case for each piece of learning material the author or the knowledge provider has to state the learning processes it serves for the various learners. The list of the 12 learning functions determined by Shuell is: Expectations, Motivation, Prior knowledge activation, Attention, Encoding, Comparison, Hypothesis Generation, Repetition, Feedback, Evaluation, Monitoring, Combination, Integration, Synthesis

2.2 The MDL value proposition for e-learning pedagogy

The contributions of Shuell & Bloom propositions facilitate our research. The integration of their approaches can provide a value -oriented approach concerning the delivery of learning content. The distinction of different educational goals and learning functions that promote a goal-oriented delivery of content promotes a dynamic parameterization in an e-learning environment. The dual concern of Shuell model, the fact that the specified learning functions can be utilized both by learners or educators influences and our approach: In an e-learning environment the content is provided by authors and is exploited by learners. But the packaging mechanism of content has to based in metadata that promote the dynamic nature of learning content exploitation.   If we try to integrate the main ideas that underlie in the two approaches (Bloom, Shuell) , then we have to admit that there is a qualitative distinction of learning performance which is promoted through specific functions or processes that prerequisite different cognitive skills and promote different value to learners. From this perspective the key issue of how to organize and package the learning content and how to engage learners in an e- learning environment can be derive sophistication through the establishment of dynamic learning processes. The combination of learning processes that have specific life cycle set the context for learning scenarios. The advantages of this approach is that if we specify metadata that support more than one learning process then this increases the exploitation capabilities of a learning object and promote a personalized learning environment. In our model can be added more learning processes if we model them. The underlying logic is that the learning object is packaged through its adaptability to the context of specific learning processes. In our research approach we have investigate 9 learning processes (Lytras, Pouloudi et al. 2002) , and we propose them as the basic value carrier in e-learning environments. These learning processes do not demand a magisterial role but set a base for further exploitation. Namely these learning processes are: **Presentation, Analysis, Synthesis, Evaluation, Reasoning, Explanation, Relation, Problem Solving, Cdlaboration.**

3. Detailed presentation of the proposed e-learning Pedagogy scaling

Our basic syllogism is that e-learning performance is directly related to learning processes, which are value carriers for the learners. The first implication is the requirement to model each learning process and consequently to specify metadata for each process in order the linguistic concept of learning process to get empower from descriptive information that can be promoted to learners using ICTs. The ultimate objective is the understanding that reusability of learning resources is not panacea not even a promise for higher learning value except a number of metadata justifies the reusability in terms of diffused value.

An initial statement is that the value in each process is not objective but subjective since each learner pays different importance to processes according to his cognitive level and previous experiences. More over the life cycle of each process has to be analyzed from the perspective of learners and authors. The distinction of several phases does not assume a sequential flow of tasks but rather an indissoluble whole of integrated parts. In the next pages are promotes through tabular synopsis the life cycles and the implications of Shuell and Bloom's work in our research.

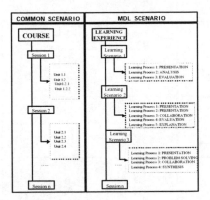

Figure 1. The proposed revision in e -learning content delivery method through value adding learning processes

4. Conclusions

Our approach is setting a context for further exploitation. With no doubt the current situation in e-learning market does not represent the fascinating issue of the incorporation of information and communication technologies in education. Many people use the e-learning term and presuppose the presence of a PowerPoint presentation accompanied with audio as the technological infrastructure for e-learning realization. The MDL framework is being evaluated for more than two year and the findings are very promising. The achievement of higher student satisfaction is only one of the key findings. Finally we have to say that this model is also very demanding. It's realization requires a lot more efforts from both academics and knowledge providers that seem to forget the nature of learning when they prepare learning material. For more information about our research unit you can visit our web site (www.eltrun.aueb.gr) . For comments concerning this paper please send an e-mail to the following address (mdl@aueb.gr).

MDL Learning Processes

Bloom's Taxonomy / T. Shuell Learning Functions	Presentation	Synthesis	Analysis	Evaluation	Reasoning	Problem Solving	Collaboration	Explanation	Relation
Expectations	?	?	?	?	?	?	?	?	?
Motivation	?	?	?	?	?	?	?	?	?
Prior knowledge activation	?	?	?	?	?	?	?	?	?
Attention	?	?	?	?	?	?	?	?	?
Encoding	?	?	?	?	?	?	?	?	?
Comparison		?	?	?	?	?	?	?	?
Hypothesis Generation		?	?	?	?	?	?	?	?
Repetition	?	?	?	?	?	?	?	?	?
Feedback	?	?	?	?	?	?	?	?	?
Evaluation	?	?	?	?	?	?	?	?	?
Monitoring	?	??	??	??	??	??	??	??	??
Combination, Integration, Synthesis		?	?	?	?	?		?	?
Knowledge	?	?	?	?	?	?	?	?	?
Comprehension	?	??	??	??	??	??	?	??	??
Application			?	?	?	?	?	?	?
Analysis			??	??	??	??		??	?
Synthesis		??	??	??	??	??	?	??	?
Evaluation		??	??	??	??	??		??	??

? : Learning Process is influenced by / can support

? : Metadata of General Purpose

? : Metadata Specific in Each Process

 : Learning Scenario

?

Page 1829

References

Bloom and Krathwohl (1984). <u>Taxonomy of Educational Objectives, Handbook I: Cognitive Domain</u>. New York, Addison-Wesley and Co.

Carter, C. and H. Scarbrough (2001). "Towards a second generation of KM? The people management challenge." <u>Education + Training</u> 43(4,5): pp. 215-224.

Coulson, C. (2000). "Developing a corporate learning strategy." <u>Industrial & Commercial Training</u> **Vol. 32**(No. 3): 84-88.

Lytras, M. D. and G. I. Doukidis (2000). <u>Applied Knowledge Management in Education: E-school Architecture.</u> In Dan Remenyi (Eds) proceedings of the 1st European Conference on Knowledge Management (ECKM 2000) , October 26-27, 2000, Bled, Slovenia, pp. 115-122.

Lytras, M. D. and G. I. Doukidis (2000). <u>'E-learning evaluation criticism. The Multidimensional Dynamic e-Learning Model'.</u> The Fourth IASTED International Conference on Internet and Multimedia Systems and Applications (IMSA 2000) [CD Proceedings], ,November , 20-23, 2000, Las Vegas, Nevada, USA, pp. 368-373.

Lytras, M. D. and G. I. Doukidis (2001). <u>'E-Learning Pedagogy: Define the Value'. Technology in Education International Conference & Exposition (TechEd 2001), March 26-29, 2001 Southern California ,USA</u>.

Lytras, M. D. and H. Odman (2001). <u>Fulfilling organizational learning on concurrent enterprises: The Multidimensional Dynamic Learning model for knowledge management exploitation.</u> 7th International Conference on Concurrent Enterprising (ICE 2001), June 26-27, 2001, Bremen, Germany.

Lytras, M. D. and A. Pouloudi (2001). <u>E-learning: Just a Waste of Time</u>. In Strong, D., Straub, D. & DeGross, J.I. (Eds) Proceedings of the Seventh Americas Conference on Informaton Systems (AMCIS), Boston, Massachusetts, pp. 216-222.

Lytras, M. D., N. Pouloudi, et al. (2002). "Implementing knowledge management in learning: an advanced framework for technology and learning convergence in work environments." <u>Journal of International Forum of Educational Technology & Society and IEEE Learning Technology Task Force, (accepted for publication in the special issue of April 2002)</u>.

Lytras, M. D., N, Pouloudi, et al. (2002). "Knowledge Management Convergence: Expanding Learning Frontiers. Journal of Knowledge Management,." <u>Journal of Knowledge Management</u> **Vol. 6**(1): 40-51.

Ryan, M. (1995). "Human resource management and the politics of knowledge:linking the essential knowledge base of the organization to strategic decision making." <u>Leadership and Organizational Development Journal</u> **Vol. 16**(No. 5).

Shuell, T. J. (1992). <u>Designing instructional computing systems for meaningful learning</u>. In M. Jones & P. H. Winne (Eds.), Adaptive learning environments: Foundations and frontiers, New York: Springer-Verlag, pp.19-54.

Community Action/interaction Management System
(A Course/Group Management System that Fosters Community)

By Brian G. Mackie
OMIS Department
Northern Illinois University
USA

Norbert Ziemer
OMIS Department
Northern Illinois University
USA

Abstract: Most course/group management systems are designed from the perspective of the facilitator or the administrator. Since these systems have been developed with an emphasis on administration, student ease of use and student-to-student interaction is frequently an afterthought instead of a design requirement. A student-centric course/group management system (CAMS) has been developed, in order to improve learning outcomes. This system allows participants to interact with one another, and makes the interaction process user-friendly. It is intended to help participants become acquainted with their cohorts quickly, whether the course is on-line or web-enhanced. The core of the system is a fully developed database. The software is open-source, requires minimal configuration and is currently being beta-tested with web-enhanced courses, fully online courses and online community groups.

Background Info/Impetus

Many Northern Illinois University faculty had previously used other commercially available class management systems such as WebCT and Blackboard. Observations by faculty members and student feedback from those learning experiences were used as a basis for the CAMS project. Certain learning challenges were found to be more prominent within an online or web-enhanced learning experience. One problem was the fact that the human elements and visual cues from a face-to-face experience were all but eliminated. Another problem encountered was the ease of navigation and use for both the participants and the facilitators. It was noted that there were times when a user was required to make seven or more mouse clicks to navigate to the desired feature or link. Faculty also experienced system drawbacks, such as the inability to efficiently transfer files from other applications and the limited level of customization allowed.

Deficiencies found with Current Systems

Human elements

The human element deficiencies are crucial to the success of an online learning platform, since the first impression when a participant enters the system can be a lasting one. The online learning environment, by definition, utilizes a different learning environment. This interface can offer advantages over a more traditional face-to-face format, but also has drawbacks including the lack of visual cues (Salmon 2000). The environment may feel less "warm" and welcoming to the participant, since frequently he or she cannot see or hear the facilitator and/or other participants. The inability to associate a name including phonetic pronunciation with a face has been a disadvantage of online Course Management Systems (CMS) compared to face-to-face learning environments. Another deficiency is that participants feel isolated or disconnected within the online learning environment. These deficiencies must be addressed by any viable CMS as they strongly influence student retention and learning outcomes.

Navigation, Learning Curve, Ease of Use

Many of the systems evaluated have lacked easy and consistent navigation and interaction. Systems can become so complex that a participant may be required to navigate through seven or more screens to locate/access a desired feature. Navigation deficiencies can slow down the learning curve and possibly become a deterent to the participant.

Flexibility/Customization

A drawback to many other CMS applications is the restricted movement of data. Either the inability to incorporate data from other sources into the system or export data to other sources are limitations caused by not being able to easily access and reuse information within the system. These limitations are major deficiencies of many CMS applications.

CAMS System Components Addressing These Deficiencies

When participants log onto the system, they are presented with a course/group selection page. Beginning with this page the individual's picture is displayed and they are immediately drawn into the community. Upon course/group selection, the participant is transferred to the main course page. Salmon notes that it is important for participants to contribute. The main course page (see figure 3) contains the following information and links to information that the student can **update**:
- Picture of each student in the class
- Phonetic spelling of student's name
- e-Mail address
- Personal website link
- Bookmarks link
- Book exchange Link

The system includes additional components, accessible from the main course page:
- Faculty picture and Faculty comments
- Most recent Class Announcement and a link to all announcements
- Class Information including Office Hours, Book information and Syllabus
- Class Notes link
- Class Assignments link
- Discussion board link (with pictures displayed on discussion board)
- Chat link (the chat program attaches the participant' picture to his or her message as it is sent) see Figure 1
- Display grades link (complete grading program/grade book) with input/export capability see figure 2

Figure 1

Figure 2

The grading program allows the faculty to enter grade types such as quiz, test and project scores. The system is designed to allow weighted grades, so each area can be given a different weight. The faculty creates an assignment and posts a complete assignment description for student viewing. There is also a provision for the facilitator to enter comments for any student grade. There are two comments for each grade; one is available the student, the other is not. When working with student grades the students' pictures are visible. In addition, from the Class main page the students are able to view their scores to date for the class.

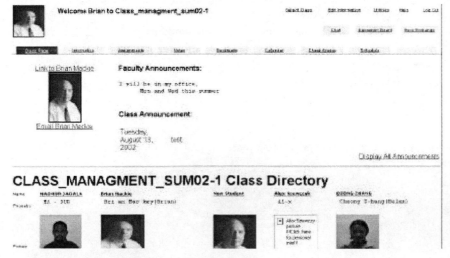

Figure 3

It was decided that the course/group management program would minimize the number of page visits required to reach a desired feature. It was also decided that users should not need a large amount of training to access and use CAMS. Where possible, all selections, modifications and/or additions would use the same techniques. Therefore, all information is updatable whether by participant or facilitator through simple web page forms. The participant or facilitator can update the information using html tags to produce exact formatting; or they may opt to enter the data as text with carriage returns and spaces. If entered in the latter format the system will automatically maintain the format. Participants are allowed to add and update both their personal information and bookmark categories of interest. Additionally, they are allowed to create bookmarks for the class including comments for each bookmark. This is another way of keeping the participant engaged.

Current Status

The CAMS application has been through two levels of beta testing, in both web-enhanced and fully online courses. A community group of approximately 130 OMIS department graduate students is currently being tested. It is anticipated that the CAMS application will be used by many courses in at least two colleges at Northern Illinois University and several other locations.

We are currently monitoring system performance and researching facilitator/participant satisfaction with the system. The system is very robust and ready for expansion to other institutions.

Future Research

It is hoped that other institutions will recognize the potential of the community based and participant-centric system (CAMS) and will contact us to become part of this ongoing research.

Literature References

McVay, Marguerita (2002). *The Online Educator: A Guide to Creating the Virtual Classroom.* New York, NY: RoutledgeFalmer.

Salmon, Gilly (2000). *E-Moderating; The Key to Teaching and Learning Online.* London, UK: Kogan Page Limited.

Stephenson, John. (2001). *Teaching and Learning Online: New Pedagogies for New Technologies.* Sterling, VA: Stylus Publishing, LLC.

A perception of Next Generation E-learning in Australia

Venkatesh Mahadevan
Information and Communication Technology Group
Faculty of Engineering
University of Technology Sydney
Australia
mahadevn@eng.uts.edu.au

Professor Dr Robin Braun
Information and Communication Technology Group
Faculty of Engineering
University of Technology Sydney
Australia
Robin.Braun@uts.edu.au

Anthony Kadi
Information and Communication Technology Group
Faculty of Engineering
University of Technology Sydney
Australia
Anthony.Kadi@uts.edu.au

Abstract: E-Learning has been viewed as technology enhanced and delivered learning in Australia for many years. By extracting the best of the traditional classroom experience and technological infrastructure we could lead to an integrated learning called Blended Learning. Education have became globally accessible; the Blended Learning now needs number of enhanced collaboration features in terms of pedagogical instructions that sets it apart from those existing e-Learning opportunities. This paper explores some of the educational issues underpinning the possible uses of CeNTIE's high broadband network and Telecollaboration software being under development at UTS on an exploratory basis. This paper argues that the e-Learning in the Australian higher education sector is best conceptualized as a collaborative process with educational outcome measurement and the technology (media) does influence the learning provided the participants create their confidence in the use of underlying technology.

Introduction

" E-Learning describes the way new information and communication technologies (ICT) are set to re-invent education and learning in a digital world. In short, it means Internet enabled learning: an exciting range of opportunities for educators and learners alike to use new skills and tools to prosper in an information society" (Arthur Anderson, 2000). Australian universities have undergone profound changes over many years in terms of their commitments to provide quality e-Learning opportunities to their students. In recent years e-Learning has been an integral part of wider use of University's teaching and learning practices and policies. For instance, although most Tele-teaching lectures in the past proceeded smoothly, there were issues like connection problems, time delays in transmission of material and interaction among the participants in the lecture. When it comes to e-Learning, the **REAL** learning is in **LEARNING** *not* in "e" (Russell Thea, 2001). The research at Monash University, Melbourne reveals that apart from the disadvantages such as reduction in learning time, increased potential for disruptive student behavior and reduction in access to lectures, students at remote sites did not feel part of the lecture and have experienced a reduced concentration span. The investigators also found that there appeared to be always weakest interaction between learners compared to content-learner interaction and instructor-learner interaction. They also pinpointed the areas that needed particular attentions are improvement of staff tele-teaching skills and technology (Abdel Halabi, Juhani Tuovinen & Jodie Maxfield, 2000). The advances in digital networks have now leaded us to the creation of new and innovative telecollaboration environments worldwide. Today there are numerous telecollaboration software tools that have helped the educators to broadened their base and allowed them as facilitators, to innovate and customize new education models to implement their new ways of teaching and learning activities. CSIRO's Centre for Networking Technologies for the Information Economy (CeNTIE) and recently received funding from the Australian government and industry collaborators to build a next generation research network linking the key research institutions in Australia is in progress. It recently completed the first metropolitan trial of 10 Gb/s Ethernet network in the Asia pacific region demonstrating shared virtual environments running a surgical training system. The CSIRO is working with the psychologists and educators from three Australian Universities including University of Technology, Sydney (UTS) to identify the appropriate uses in higher education for this high-capacity broadband network system. By embracing a new telecollaboration environment in Australia's higher education sector, UTS is hoping to challenge both the educators and technologists to adapt themselves in a situation to oversee this unpredictable surge of constantly challenging innovation.

Why Collaboration beyond Lecturing?

A common base of all collaboration is Learning. Task oriented collaboration involves the *back grounded learning* and the collaborative (peer) learning involves both the tasks as well as the *fore grounded learning.* Recalling Vygotsky's theory of social constructivism, where students construct knowledge based on interactions with others, it is evident that telecollaboration helps the participants to work together (interact) on a common, shared goal despite of their physical separation. There are five structures for learning that may or may not occur in a traditional classroom scenario. For instance, use of facilities such as information banks, construction kits and the task managers. (Salomon, G., Perkins, D., & Globerson, T, 1991). Collaboration beyond "lecturing" means designing interactive collaborative learning experiences for all the participants involved and facilitating them throughout their learning processes through those experiences (engagement theory). In which case students would be expected to play their role not just as passive observer but an active constructor of knowledge by taking responsibility of their own learning (out-of-box thinking). "Rich environments for active learning" or REALs are constructivist based and designed to encourage student responsibility and motivation (Dunlap & Grabinger, 1996). Now we have reached into a stage of collaborators sharing the application or white boarding apart from involving synchronous and/or asynchronous communication through audio, video, and/or text and reviewing their course material both synchronously as well as asynchronously. Our research on reviewing numerous collaborative models and theoretical frameworks, shows that currently, there is no one system that plugs the user into the remote site where an individual can perform complex group tasks and feel the sense of presence and contribution with the help of set of collaboration tools and utilities that they may choose to use according to their personal preferences and work patterns (student centred learning). Some of the important collaboration service elements been described in our mock up, helped us to visualize our ideas like joining and leaving a session, pointing to shared objects and communication between many-to-many users (reflective conversations).

According to the Workshop on New Visions for Large-Scale Networks: Research and Applications held in Vienna, Virginia, 2001, collaborative environments need to support transparent, intuitive human interactions with services such as automatic configuration, ubiquitous access, security, multimedia capabilities, immersive environments, expert consultation, and side conversations by providing proactive, intelligent, dynamic and "natural" interactions among the participants. It also says the future collaboration environments will need to deal with unpredictable and emergent changes, meet hard real-time constraints, and handle asynchronous events as they occur. This involves a clear understanding of all the participants involved in the collaboration processes to know the need for collaboration (Dale Spender & Fiona Stewart, 2002). Identification of telecollaborative strategies by the facilitator of future telecollaboration session would maximize the learning opportunities of all the participants involved. This is well matched with the vision of our telecollaboration project at UTS.

Does technology (media) influence the learning?

Technology always has been a strategic investment in the higher education sector to validate its missions. Though the technology plays a major role in driving the revolutionary changes, the challenge for the educators to keep pace with those changes still remains the same. To challenge the traditional teaching paradigms, the technology (media) needs to play a major role. These are the two areas of "islands of innovation" due to many different constraints. The development of digital networks now justifies the need for further emergence of development, maintenance and calibration of those options been identified by those areas as pathfinders of our future telecollaboration session. Online education makes it very rich information medium, not simply because of the multimedia capacity, but it is interactive. Online learning is not so much about taking in existing information, but connecting and creating new resources, actively assembling information and engaging in problem solving. This information in turn can be "checked out" by others. Technologies are not to be treated just to read or receive the information, but needs to be used and "repurposed". As all digitally connected individuals can make information, there are multiple voices, rather than one voice, so there is no one right answer but many possibilities (Dale Spender & Fiona Stewart, 2002). For example technology would enable us in rapidly describing or instantiating new shapes, performing simulation and animations of processes and illustrating the transitions. Encouraging the use of multiple modes of representation (different mediums) is one among the "seven pedagogical goals" of constructivist, learner-centered environments (Honebein, 1996). The technology has been always more powerful in terms of providing transmission and sharing of the content and encouraging more out-of-class student reflection. Our main aim is that the proposed technology would help our educators to make further focus shift from content to the contemporary approach (from surface level learning to deep level learning and from independence to interdependence). Some educationalists strongly believe that learning outcomes in the main are not affected by the technology. Some even view technology as a tool for decontextualized drill. But to others like researchers at UTS, technology is an opening door for creative expression and higher-order thinking skills. In all our debate, we rarely take the time to explore whether there are several ways that may effectively contribute to a good education (David D. Thornburg, 2002). It is sad that many educators until today have little understanding of the limitations and constraints of the technology they use. They need to realize the fact that with the proper understanding of use of technology the participants can perform well in a more easier and productive way. One of the critical concepts of Salomon's theory is that the effectiveness of a medium depends upon its match with the learner, the context and the task (Salomon, 1977).

There are just two remaining hurdles that have thus far prevented the widespread adoption of such a practice. The first hurdle is the multimedia interaction requires broadband networking that is economically accessible. Moreover, the resources of the network must be either in abundance or carefully controlled and used in real-time to ensure that the multimedia interaction is of sufficient quality to prevent the technology from becoming a hindrance to the collaboration. According to the e-Learning user survey been conducted in April 2001 at e-Learning conference & expo held at USA, 53% of the respondents said that the lack of bandwidth is the major challenge to the current eLearning techniques (For example, the problem of having unintelligible audio and jerky-motion video etc). Even with the supply of enormous bandwidth that CeNTIE would offer, we as both educators as well as technologists should know the accountability of its uses. One of the most important technical issues here is just by increasing the bandwidth we will not solve the multimedia burstiness problem. In increasing the bandwidth in distributed multimedia computing, the user acceptance of high degree of perceptible quality of multimedia data is always significant factor. The notion of quality of service (QoS) is central and still receives significant attention among the multimedia network researchers. This includes maximal or minimal resolution, the average throughput, allowed error rates and timing requirements etc. For instance research on real-time text editing and the task of distributed synchronization between multi media data could solve some of the problems of QoS requirements in a telecollaboration scenario.

The second major hurdle is the unavailability of set of software tools and utilities to support and enable our future collaborative interactions. The available ones found to be designed for specific contexts and thus, do not adapt well to other situations. Furthermore, many are constrained by capabilities that were available at the time of their design and implementation, but the rapidly changing ICT field has quickly rendered these obsolete. And finally, and probably most importantly, our collective understanding of collaborative processes and the interactions necessary to make them effective is in its infancy – so the design of software tools to enable, support and perhaps even enhance collaborative outcomes is ignorant of the basic requirements for such tools. The platform-independent software under development for the above purposes would allow integration of transmission and sharing of contents along with pedagogical instructions. By being very easy to use, proactive, and engaging it would provide some intelligence. For instance, the development of special tools such as color deficiency tool, sign language modeling etc would be very helpful for the disadvantaged students.

Today's e-Learning infrastructure is still immature in the tools to analyze and measure results to correlate them into your organization metrics (Bersin Josh, 2002). The purposes of intended outcomes in a telecollaboration scenario are never unchanged. The technology would force us to do certain new things or perhaps do things that we would otherwise not be able to do. Outcome based measurement is critical and time consuming. This is because of the reason that the range of possible outcomes that people in different context might want to achieve is very large. This arises the need of a highly adaptable, large spectrum of outcome measurement techniques that could be available to the range of possible outcomes.

Conclusion

Many factors such as difference in motivational factors, skills, pacing and concentration shifts of the participants that affect the e-Learning are areas of further study. The researchers at UTS are expected to deliver a product (technology), which involves numerous collaborative processes that would solve some of the existing educational problems. This project mainly aims at developing a set of high- engagement, high-performance and high- impact remote access tools, utilities and the appropriate technologies that would be capable of providing a flexible framework for active pedagogical teaching and learning approaches. There is a shared understanding among the researchers at UTS of how to build and use telecollaboration software that would encourage the educators to try new forms of teaching and learning and help them to learn how to utilize the latest technical possibilities. This includes identifying the factors to succeed in spite of the barriers created by this new exciting technology.

References

Abdel Halabi, Juhani Tuovinen and Jodie Maxfield (2000). Evaluation of Educational Interactions in Accounting Tele-Teaching. Monash University, Melbourne, Australia.

Arthur Anderson (2000). The e-Learning Funding Guide: a guide to planning and funding e-Learning in schools, Microsoft.

Bersin Josh (2002). How can you justify your investment. E-Learning Magazine.

David D. Thornburg (2002). A Focus for Educational Reform, http://www.pbs.org/teachersource/thornburg/thornburg0301.shtm.

Dr Dale Spender and Dr Fiona Stewart (2002). Embracing e-Learning in Australian Schools. Report sponsored by Common Wealth Bank of Australia.

Dunlap, J. C. and Grabinger, S. (1996). Rich environments for active learning in the higher education classroom. University of Colorado, Denver, CO, USA.

http://www.ngi-supernet.org/conferences.html, (2001). Workshop on New Visions for Large-Scale Networks: Research and Applications. Vienna, Virginia, USA.

Honebein, P. (1996). Seven goals for the design of constructivist learning environments. In B. Wilson (Ed.), Constructivist learning environments: Case studies in instructional design, New Jersey: Educational Technology Publications. USA.

Russell Thea (2001). E-Learning: The opportunity to challenge the paradigm of traditional methods of education by putting the learner in control. 15th Australian International education Conference, Sydney, Australia.

Salomon, G., Perkins, D. and Globerson, T. (1991). Partners in cognition: Extending human intelligence with intelligent technologies. Educational Researcher, 20(4), 2-9.

Talk and Chalk digital

Carmem Maia
Núcleo of Colective Inteligence applied to Education
Departament of Interactive Higher Education
University Anhembi Morumbi
Sao Paulo, Brasil
Carmem@anhembi.br

Abstract: Is e-learning a modern or, better, a digital version of the already traditional "talking...talking... and chalk" which we witness in the model classroom?

Are we not merely reproducing in a digital way the same traditional education models which are known to us, ignoring the means and possibilities of methodological and curricular innovation which interactive technologies allow?

Are we not repeating the same phenomenon which occurred during the early 80s with the emerging of Informatics laboratories - hermetically closed classrooms with a large number of aligned computers -, which in practice did nothing but copy the same model of lessons given in the classroom with traditional desks?

Introduction

Presently, Higher Education Institutions (IES) are being pressed to develop and use new communication and information technologies for Brazil's students as a way to improve or develop traditional higher teaching through quality. The fever of "e-learning", is now a "hype" that is invading the Brazilian higher education market, has compelled many "IES – Instituições de Ensino Superior" (Higher Education Institutions) to try and modernize their technical staff, ignoring their prime human resources (professors) and the main purpose of their business (teaching-training).

With the increasing technological progress of the tools for delivery of courses and disciplines, are we not running the risk of moving towards the mere digitalization and storing of information and contents, without, necessarily, in the majority of cases, preoccupying ourselves with, and taking major care of, those actors which are on both sides of this screen, that is, professors and pupils?

The question is: how must Higher Education Institutions prepare themselves; how must they focus the development of distant higher education interfaced by the interactive web communications, how can they win the challenges of an ever growing production of topics for an ever increasing number of students and yet have their mind focused on ROI in a way to preserve and maintain all efforts focused on the teaching-training process of the student and all the possibilities referring to innovation, curricular integration and cooperative working formation which available technologies and tools can offer.

How can we develop and implement courses and higher education projects at a distance with the proper tools but with distinct adequate characteristics, adapted to the methodologies and cultural features of each region, and allow professors to maintain their pedagogical and methodological identity even if focused on "mass" education, using one proper tool for the implementation of courses and disciplines?

The challenge is to keep e-learning focused on teaching-training, based on the development of truly cooperative and collaborative methods for an ever increasing number of students, including an integrated management of the topics involved, working efficiently and producing satisfactory proven results, from a pedagogical point of view as well as an institutional point of view.

What is going on

Recent decree 2253, institutionalized by the Ministry of Education and Culture, on 18th of October 2001, literally emphasizes the preoccupation of governmental organs with regard to increasing technological progress, of which higher education cannot be kept afar.

On the one hand, we have statistics about the number of outgoing pupils of higher education wanting to enter university and we know that something has to be done to facilitate the access to these universities.

On the other, we know that the traditional educational model of teaching leaves much to be desired from a qualitative point of view, mainly, in "mass" institutions, where very often more than 100 pupils are gathered in one classroom. What type of interactivity or relationship can exist between pupils and teachers in such a space and during the short time of a traditional lesson ? (50 minutes lesson means basically 30 minutes of real lesson, subtracting all delays by the teacher and pupils, starting the lesson, ending it, etc...). Besides, the model of curricular development of a graduation course, for example, also requires reformulation. To merely create a curriculum, disciplines and classes and wait for integration is not sufficient. The model for higher teaching we know of does not attend any more the pupil's formation requirements and professional performance, and should be reformulated, re-invented.

On the other hand, we have an avalanche of technologies and tools being developed and offered by the teaching institutions. Very often the IES are quite satisfied with the technological resources and automation of contents and do not dwell on the needs and necessities of teaching-training. Technologies should be a means of improving the training process, they should be considered as powerful tools for the necessity to re-invent higher education; however, technological resources are not enough, there should be an educational intelligence behind any system, a powerful brain knowing how to use technologies intelligently with a view to meeting training requirements; otherwise, we are just, and once more, repeating the old and antiquated model of the traditional "talk, talk...chalk" in the classroom, and what is worse, running the serious risk of potentializing - once we are on web and the web is a potentializer - a model which we already know is obsolete and does not meet any longer the requirements of pupils, teachers and the institutions themselves.

By means of decree 2253, legislation clearly shows that the path to follow revolves around a mix of what is being called Click and Brick, that is a mix of the factual presence and the virtual; however, to this end, the academic spheres of the IES (higher education institutions) should re-organize and orient themselves towards this new paradigm. This decree stimulates the use and implanting of technologies for improving this process, thus allowing institutions to provide 20% of the course or discipline duration, by way of distant education, through interactive communication technologies, which in practice means re-orienting educational course projects and teaching plans towards a new format satisfying the requisites of this mix.

The tools and technologies being developed strive to show that in the quest for productivity and attendance to an increasing number of beneficiaries, the relation between the cost of this benefit and the ROI must be taken into account when choosing a technological tool and to this intent, the institutions themselves should be aware of what their business and intelligence point at in relation to the development of the disciplines contents, thus leading to the improvement of training and knowledge and not merely to the development of a technology.

University Anhembi Morumbi e-learning Case

University Anhembi Morumbi is a private university located in the Southeast of Brazil, in Sao Paulo city. It has been founded 35 years ago, implementing the first Tourism Bachelor course in Brasil, and during all this decades, the University have been pioneers and innovative in the Higher Education System in Brasil, which is a very traditional academic system, very resistant to changes.

In the beginning of the 80´s, the university begins the implementation of the Department of New Technologies in Education, created to think and implement new strategies and new methodologies, using or not technologies in education. This means the training of all the faculty staff in new technologies and researching during all this years the use of new possibilities to optimize the traditional methodology of the face to face classrooms.

In the 90´s, with the advent of Internet, the University creates the Dept of Interactive Learning, to research the net interactive possibilities to Higher Education. During this last decade, many courses , short courses and pos graduation courses have been created and developed by this department, and the University have been recognized as one of the pioneers in the implementation of a successful "mix" between online learning and face to face classes. During the framing and implanting of on-line and interactive processes at Universidade Anhembi Morumbi, we opted to develop first of all favorable conditions for the improvement of teaching nearly 10 years ago, at a time when there were no virtual training environments or the present educational tools for the development of courses.

For about 5 or 6 years we worked on the research and development of this tool, the result being that we acquired the know-how and expertise in efficient methodologies related to distant training, which in turn led us towards the development of new courses and disciplinary contents not to be given by way of the traditional "talk..talk..chalk".

During the last two years, with the configuration of this new motion opening for the Institutions many other possibilities to improve our classes, we realize the necessity of a system that could manage more than 3000 sincroniusly, and we had to face a serious problem regarding management of the contents and small bugs in the system which cannot occur in large scale teaching.

The challenge now is and will be in the use of a teaching automated authoring tool, like Blackboard, highly efficient and with high quality distant education methodologies so as not to reproduce the traditional educational model requiring the student's presence. Once solved the problem of technological bugs, we shall have to pay attention to the development and training of human resources, integrated contents, know-how and virtual "animators" so that, although at a distance, students and teachers should feel motivated and stimulated to pursue their training and that we do not make poor use of the potentiality of human and technological resources.

Authoring Tools – A knife of two edges?

During this last two years we have been looking and researching for authoring tools which could help us to be more efficient and productive in the delivering and in the content production of the courses. We realized that our logistic system of production the e-learning courses were not efficient and It demands a tool which the teacher could manage the course content the way he wants to, with no technical assistance.

However, our concern was in do not create the same traditional model of the information delivery, now digitally, and one of the purpose for this is work with the teachers in a way that he or she could be a content manager, orienting the students to build their own knowledge and not just replyng the old paradigm of the traditional classroom.

The authoring tool, Blackboard, WebCT, Docent or any other, have two faces: Could be very useful and a helpful hand to be more productive and automatized, because they are very user-friendly and easy to learn, but in other way, this tools could be also a knife of two edges, which must be used very carefully, not only focusing the scalability and the managing of the students, but mainly in the process of learning that the student will be involved during the course.

Unfortunately, what we have been realizing during this research is that it is not easy changing cultures and changing minds, mainly the academic areas. Teachers are used with the face to face methodology and sometimes are not so receptive to chaging paradigms. The use of this authoring tools will create new roles for faculty, we believe that it will be very profitable for all: Institution, Faculty and students.

do not want to improve or There lies the big challenge of the new educational technologies and paradigms.

E-Learning for Distance Learners – Does it work?

John Chi-sang MAK
School of Business & Administration
The Open University of Hong Kong
Hong Kong (SAR), CHINA

email: jmak@ouhk.edu.hk

Abstract: This paper reports the use of Information Technology (IT) for enhancing distance learning in Hong Kong. The challenge of Lifelong Learning and the knowledge-based economy require us constantly upgrading and expanding our skills to meet the future, professional and workplace needs. A survey was conducted to investigate the impact of e-learning from distance learners' perspective, that aims at studying how distance learners might view their (1) course performance, (2) IT fear and anxiety, (3) feedbacks on e-tutoring, and (4) comments on course administration during the e-Learning process. Through a case study in the Open University of Hong Kong, this paper describes in details how an online course is designed, delivered and evaluated. The results indicate that with the opportunity for e-Learning distance learners can enjoy the online teaching and learning process. Although fear and anxiety are initially reported, they could be resolved and manageable during the course. Both tutoring and course administration could be improved through online technology.

Introduction

The Open University of Hong Kong (http://www.ouhk.edu.hk), formerly the Open Learning Institute of Hong Kong (OLI), was established by Government in June 1989, aiming to provide higher education opportunities for adults by open and distance education. OUHK offers more than 100 post-graduate, degree and sub-degree programmes in April 2002. The University recruited about 4500 new students in October 2001 and currently has about 26,800 students (OUHK, 2001a). The majority of them are aged between 22 and 35. On average, they take about nine credits per semester, equivalent to about half of the workload of a full-time student. The University uses a flexible credit system under which students earn credits for each course and accumulate credits towards a degree. Currently, most OUHK courses are print-based. There are also trained tutors who hold tutorial sessions, comment on and mark assignments, and answer students' queries by telephone and correspondence.

There is a vast amount of e-Learning initiatives currently taking place in Hong Kong, including PolyU's CyberU, HKU's SOUL, and CityU's iMBA. Many of the continuing education institutions are also claiming to offer e-learning programmes. However, the aims and objectives of 'e-learning' vary among the institutions. For simplicity, terms such as 'e-Learning' and 'online learning', 'e-course' and 'online course' are used interchangeably throughout this research. E-Learning can be viewed as a virtual classroom, incorporating a set of modern training tools, such as a study guide, notice board, student forum, online mentoring, and an interactive, multimedia courseware, e-library, which are aimed not only at the individual learners, but also at training institution. The virtual classroom provides many of the benefits of the traditional classroom while enjoying the major advantages of training delivered over the Internet that can be accessed at any time from any place. At many institutions, the effectiveness of e-Learning has not been well researched prior to its adoption. Daley et al. (2001) indicate that students' attitudes and perceptions of technology influence their ability to acquire and integrate knowledge, extend and refine knowledge, and use knowledge meaningfully. Understanding the factors affecting students' adoption of e-Learning should be a fertile area for research. Learners' willingness to adopt technology is of vital importance to the design and delivery of e-courses by distance education providers.

Research Questions

This study tries to better understand distance learners' attitude toward online teaching and learning. Also, the effectiveness of e-tutoring and course administration are being evaluated. It aims at studying (1) how distance learners might view their performance, (2) what fear and anxiety they may feel, (3) how they evaluate e-tutoring, and (4) how they evaluate online course administration.

Research Design

An IT-based e-courses with Web-based instruction design beginning in April 2002 was selected for evaluation. During the course, students received printed materials by ordinary mail and supplement online course activity and materials through a Web-based course server. An evaluation is then conducted to measure both the learners' perceptions and the effectiveness of course administration:

Subjects

An electronic version of the questionnaire contains 40 questions asking for quantitative information. The evaluation was conducted in July 2002. Seven hundreds and three adult distance learners enrol B121 course, which is running on-line throughout the semester. A total of 238 replies (33.86%) are collected and all of these responses were considered usable for this study after data validation and checking for excessive missing values. The average daily OLE user logins is 94.57 (11.63%) with average daily hits of 4823.23. The total user logins in June 2002 is 622 users (76.51%). Students connected to the OLE server in different ways: OUHK student dial-up kits (2.17%), OUHK Sub-nets (45.67%), and external Internet Service Providers (52.17%).

Method

A set of questionnaires on a study of how the online technology affects on students and tutors has been designed. The questionnaire is broken down into four brief sections, in which raw items have been developed reflective of (1) course performance, (2) computer fear and anxiety, (3) e-tutoring, and (4) online course coordination. The questionnaire used a 5-point Likert-type scale for each item (1=Strongly agree, 2=Agree, 3=Neutral, 4=Disagree, and 5=Strongly Disagree) to solicit students' feedback. The evaluation was conducted in mid-semesters of the course. Some of questions in the evaluations are based on the work of Zane Berg (1996) and Diehl (1989), whereas others are developed to meet the aims of the research. Details of the questionnaires are available upon request.

Course server

The online courses selected for the research include is B121 Business Computing with Internet Applications. It is a semester, 5-credit, and foundation-level course that comprise the Bachelor of Business Administration (BBA) degree programme. B121 aims to introduce learners to microcomputers and their applications in business; and enable them to develop, through hands-on experience, the knowledge and skills necessary to use common microcomputer software applications in business. Learners are required to make regular access to the Web-based course server via a dial-up modem or an Internet connection during their study. OUHK has developed a Web-based online delivery system, called the Online Learning Environment (OLE), to enhance e-learning experience. Based on WebCT 3.1.3, the OLE provides an interactive learning environment for communication among students, tutors and the Course Coordinator. The OLE is locating at URL: http://www.ouhk.edu.hk/ole, which consists of eight major students' components, including News, Administrative Information, Course Materials, Assignments, Interactive Tools, Personal Folder, Evaluation, and Help.

Major Findings

How students might view their performance in online courses (see Table 1.1)

Table 1.1 Issues	Frequent (%) (1=strongly agree, 5=strongly disagree)					Mean	Mode
	1	2	3	4	5		
Q1. Felt motivated to use IT in the learning process	18.5	55.5	23.1	2.9	0.0	2.11	2
Q2. Enjoy online learning via the OLE	12.7	38.8	40.9	7.2	0.4	2.44	3
Q3. Always read Course News	12.3	29.2	35.2	20.3	3.0	2.72	3
Q4. Like to work with classmates via online interaction	8.0	24.9	43.0	22.4	1.7	2.85	3
Q5. Read messages more than post messages	19.4	54.4	19.4	6.3	0.4	2.14	2
Q6. Perform better with group members online	6.7	26.1	53.4	12.6	1.3	2.76	3
Q7. Can better understand how the course was organised	22.9	46.6	22.5	7.6	0.4	2.16	2
Q8. Invest time to learn how to use IT	14.8	59.1	24.1	1.7	0.4	2.14	2
Q9. Perform well with the aid of IT	11.8	50.8	34.0	2.1	1.3	2.30	2
Q10. Felt much better prepared for the workforce	13.9	57.4	25.3	3.0	0.4	2.19	2

A great majority (74%) of respondents felt motivated to use IT in the learning process. They also agreed that the Internet could assist them in learning more about the subjects that interest them. As a result of learning how to use technology in the course(s), 71% of respondents were much better prepared for the workforce. With the course materials placed on line, 70% of respondents were able to more effectively understand how the course was organised. Reflecting on the experience, students (74%) thought the course(s) challenged them to invest time learning how to use technology benefited their study. It has been time well spent to learn how technology could be applied to their specific learning demands. All respondents were asked if their expectations of performing well with the aid of technology in the course(s) have been met. Here 63% of respondents indicated that it was, while less than 3.4% of respondents replied that it was not. One of the interesting findings is that 74% of respondents spelt more time to read messages from than post messages onto the Discussion Forum. They tend to receive than contribute to the e-Learning process.

What fear and anxiety students may feel in the online courses (see Table 1.2)

Table 1.2 Issues	Frequency % (1=strongly agree, 5=strongly disagree)					Mean	Mode
	1	2	3	4	5		
Q11. The biggest anxiety is not communicating well	3.8	29.4	45.8	18.9	2.1	2.86	3
Q12. The fear is not being effective in using emails	4.6	13.4	32.4	36.1	13.4	3.40	4
Q13. Don't like to be responsible for learning IT	0.0	7.6	49.6	36.1	6.7	3.42	3
Q14. Create more problem than it solves	1.7	12.0	35.0	39.7	11.5	3.47	4
Q15. Had some serious doubts to perform well initially	1.7	17.4	25.5	41.7	13.6	3.48	4
Q16. Not easy use the OLE system	1.3	13.6	30.9	46.6	7.6	3.46	4
Q17. Felt troubled to learn both IT and subject matters	1.7	13.1	42.4	34.7	8.1	3.34	3
Q18. E-communication skills prevent me from sharing	1.7	13.1	42.4	34.7	8.1	3.34	3
Q19. E-learning is suitable for my learning style	11.5	41.3	31.5	13.6	2.1	2.54	2
Q20. Could not overcome the anxiety and fear	0.9	9.8	32.9	46.2	10.3	3.55	4

A question asked if students were anxious about communicating on line in an open discussion forum. Overall, 21% of respondents indicated that they were, 44% of them expressed their disagreement, and 46% were neutral. All respondents were asked to give their view on the statement "My biggest fear in using a computer is not being effective in using emails". Eighteen percent of respondents indicated their agreement, 32% of them were neutral, and 50% of them disagreed. Responding to the statement "Using the OLE for study created more problems for me than it solved", 51% of respondents indicated disagreement and only 14% agreed. Another question asked of all respondents was about the anxiety of using OLE. The statement "when I found out that this course was heavy on technology use I had some serious doubts about my ability to perform well" received a positive response, with 55% of respondents indicating disagreement and 19% saying that they agreed. In response to the statement "I am troubled by the idea of having to learn how to use technology while at the same time learning my subject matter", 43% of respondents disagreed and 15% expressed their agreement. Overall, students felt not too afraid or anxious in online courses. Instead, the statement "The idea of learning on line is suitable to my style of learning" drew agreement from 53% of respondents, while almost all the rest express a neutral opinion (32%) rather than outright disagreement of 16%.

How students evaluate the effectiveness in the tutoring process (see Table 1.3)

Table 1.3 Issues	Frequency % (1=strongly agree, 5=strongly disagree)					Mean	Mode
	1	2	3	4	5		
Q21. Tutors are knowledgeable about e-learning	18.5	55.5	23.1	2.9	0.0	2.11	2
Q22. Tutors give detailed explanations through e-tutorials	12.7	38.8	40.9	7.2	0.4	2.44	3
Q23. The interest in IT for learning has grown	20.1	51.3	23.9	3.4	1.3	2.15	2
Q24. Hands-on tutorials in using IT are appropriate	14.5	54.0	29.8	1.3	0.0	2.17	2
Q25. Tutors email to clarify queries and course requirements	11.1	36.3	44.0	7.3	1.3	2.51	3
Q26. Tutors always reply emails promptly	9.0	27.4	60.3	2.1	1.3	2.59	3
Q27. Tutors are patient with learners	12.0	41.9	44.0	1.3	0.9	2.37	3
Q28. Tutors make use of 'Discussion' for e-tutoring	5.6	28.3	55.8	8.6	1.7	2.73	3
Q29. Tutors are effective at e-tutoring	8.2	39.2	47.8	3.4	1.3	2.50	3
Q30. E-tutoring increases more interactions	8.2	45.9	40.3	3.9	1.7	2.45	2

A great majority of respondents (74%) agreed that their tutors were knowledgeable about OLE. Tutors were found helpful in providing detailed explanations in tutorials. During the course(s), 71% of respondents agreed that their interest in use of computers and the Internet technology is growing. All of the respondents were asked if their tutors replied to email promptly. Thirty-six percent of respondents agreed while 60% of them were neutral. The statement "My tutor was effective at e-tutoring". Forty-seven percent of respondents agreed while 49% of them were neutral. Finally, 54% of respondents agreed that "e-tutoring increases interaction between tutors and students when compared with other print-based courses". Only 6% of them expressed their disagreement.

How students evaluate the effectiveness of course co-ordination (see Table 1.4)

See Table 1.4 Issues	Frequency % (1=strongly agree, 5=strongly disagree)					Mean	Mode
	1	2	3	4	5		
Q31. The OLE server could easily be reached	17.8	53.0	23.5	4.8	0.9	2.18	2
Q32. The response time of OLE is acceptable	11.7	61.3	20.9	5.7	0.4	2.22	2
Q33. The supplementary course materials are helpful	18.3	59.1	20.4	2.2	0.0	2.07	2
Q34. Communication and collaboration can be enhanced	10.4	50.9	33.9	3.9	0.9	2.34	2
Q35. E-learning can help extend students' knowledge	11.3	53.0	31.7	3.9	0.0	2.28	2
Q36. It is effective at administrating the course online	17.0	42.8	37.2	1.7	1.3	2.48	3
Q37. It is better than that of other print-based course	16.1	38.6	40.9	3.5	0.9	2.54	3
Q38. TMA could be submitted, assessed and returned online	20.2	49.1	23.7	5.7	1.3	2.19	2
Q39. Prefer to take an online course again	15.0	46.7	31.3	6.2	0.9	2.31	2
Q40. E-learning meets the professional and workplace needs	20.0	53.0	24.3	2.6	0.0	2.10	2

Most of the time, respondents (71%) could reach the course server to access course materials. When connected to the server, the response time was acceptable to them. The supplementary course materials, such as presentation files, tutorial notes, course information, etc were found to be helpful. Regarding the course coordination, 60% of respondents agreed that the course was being effectively administrated and 37% of them were neutral. Sixteen percent of respondents agreed that the course coordination performed much better than if they were in an ordinary setting while 41% of them were neutral. Respondents (69%) believed that assignments could be submitted, assessed and returned online. When a choice is given, they (62%) would prefer o take an online course again. All respondents were asked to give their view on the statement "Overall, I would ate e-Learning as useful to my future, professional, and workplace needs." The response is strongly positive. Seventy-three percent of respondents agreed, 24% neutral, and 3% disagreed.

Conclusion

The challenge of Lifelong Learning and the knowledge-based economy require us constantly upgrading and expanding our skills to meet the future, professional and workplace needs. Technically, e-Learning is feasible for distance learners. Although anxiety and fear in using IT during the e-Learning process were reported initially, technical support, e-tutoring, and e-course administration could reduce these problems substantially during the course. It is well validated that the e-course could improve not only the quality of teaching and learning but also the cost-effectiveness of course administration.

Contact Details

John MAK is an Assistant Professor at the Open University of Hong Kong, where he teaches Information Systems courses, including Business Computing, Advances in IT, and IS Audits, Security & Control. His primary research interests are the applications of Internet Technology in Business Environment and Distance Learning Technology. He can be reached at +852 2768 6922 or via email at jmak@ouhk.edu.hk. His office is Room A821, 8th Floor, Block A, School of Business and Administration, the Open University of Hong Kong, 30 Good Shepherd Street, Homantin, Kowloon, Hong Kong (SAR), CHINA.

References

Available upon request.

The use of Internet in a PBL course at ITESM.

Ma. Magdalena Maldonado Avalos.
Instituto Tecnológico y de Estudios Superiores de Monterrey
Campus Estado de México
mmaldona@campus.cem.itesm.mx

Abstract: This paper is about how the Internet can improve the process of solving problem in a course design with the didactical technique called PBL (Problem based learning). Firs I presented the differences between the new model and the traditional. Second, what is PBL and the characteristics of good problems. And finally, the 7 steps of the process of solving problems and the use of Internet.

Introduction:

At Instituto Tecnológico y de Estudios Superiores de Monterrey (ITESM), we are working in a new model called "Rediseño" (redesign), this model was designed in order to achieve the Mission 2005. The principal characteristic of this model is a new different role of the student: he or she has the responsibility of his or her learning.

In the next scheme it is possible to see the difference between the Traditional model and the new model:

	Teacher	*Student*
Traditional model	Transmit knowledge He is the only who evaluates He decides what and how is the process	Teacher's dependence Receptive Individualist
New model (Mission 2005)	Planner and designer Facilitator and guider Share with the students the decisions of the process.	Autonomous Participative Collaborative Engaged with the learning process.

So the students need learn to learn, this implies their role is active. That´s the reason why there were select four didactical techniques:
- ✓ PBL (problem based learning)
- ✓ POL (project oriented learning)
- ✓ CASES (cases method)
- ✓ CL (collaborative learning)

I am working in the Marketing Department. The class I teach is Marketing Services, and I decided to use PBL as the main didactical technique.

Characteristics of PBL

PBL is any learning environment in which the problem drives the learning. That is, before students learn some knowledge they are given a problem. The problem is posed so that the students discover that they need to learn some new knowledge before they can solve the problem.

The big deal is to design a problem that motivates the student, so they can understand why they are learning the new knowledge. Learning in the context of the "need to solve a problem" also tend to store the knowledge in memory patterns that facilitate later recall for solving problems. Problem solving is the process used to solve problem, so the students working in a PBL environment should be skilled in problem solving or critical thinking.

Characteristics of good problems

Some factors that are essential for good problems are:

1. An effective problem must first engage students' interest, and motivate them to probe for deeper understanding of the concepts being introduced. It should relate the subject to the real world, so that students have a stake in solving the problem.
2. Good problems require students to make decisions or judgments based on facts, information, logic and/or rationalization. Students should be required to justify all decisions and reasoning based on the principles being learned. Problems should require students to define what assumptions are needed (and why), what information is relevant, and/or what steps or procedures are required in order to solve them.
3. Cooperation from all members of the student group should be necessary in order to effectively work through a good problem. The length and complexity of the problem or case must be controlled so that students realize that a "divide and conquer" effort will not be an effective problem-solving strategy.
4. The content objectives of the course should be incorporated into the problems, connecting previous knowledge to new concepts, and connecting new knowledge to concepts in other courses and/or disciplines.

Relation between Internet and a PBL Course.

The model "rediseño", also known as The New Model, means that at ITESM we are working not only in the academic topics, we are considering also abilities, attitudes and worths. Also, this implies the use of a technological support that can be: Lotus Notes - Learning Space. (LN-LS), or Blackboard (BB).

In order to teach a class in this model required that all the design and the material that will be used during the period of classes be in the (LN-LS). Before to teach a class in this model a teacher must work in the design of the class. Next table show the database that are used in LN-LS and BB.

Database	LN- LS	BLACKBOARD
Schedule - Start Here - Weeks - Calendar	Here we can find the programming of all kind of activities divided per week. (Our courses have 16 weeks)	Course Information Assignments Course Calendar

Media Center	Here we can find all the material that supports the course: Videos, abstracts, presentations, printed advertising, etc.	Course Documents Course materials External links
Course Room - Discussion - Assignments	This is the space designed for make and send the homework (assignments) and the discussions, and also through this database the teacher can graded the tasks.	Discussion Board Virtual classroom Digital Dropbox
Profile - Instructor - Students - Groups	Here we have all the information about the participants of a course (instructors and students). And also here the students can know their grades and the annotations that the teacher made related to their work.	Staff information Use /modify users Groups
Assessment -Questions -Assessments	This space permits to create different types of evaluation like : quiz, exams, survey, self-Asses.	Assesments Pool Manager Online gradebook

Each course is created in a server at each campus. Then each student needs to replicate the course in his or her Laptop through the use of the WEB or the Intranet. So all the activities that a course implies are in the technological support. (LN-LS or BB).

The most important thing in PBL is the relation between the knowledge and the students, Internet is the most easy way of getting knowledge. The student can get information from his laptop, in the moment that he need the information, he can travel through Internet and get it.

In order to solve the problems, the methodology implies 7 steps.

Steps	Description	Use of Internet
1.Clarifyng terms (In groups)	Have the same information. Identify if there are some terms that need to be investigated.	To search the terms that are not clear.
2. Defining the problem (In groups)	Delimitate the topic	
3. Brain storm (In groups)	Give different alternatives to solve the problem, that need to be investigate.	
4. Classification of ideas (In groups)	Classification of ideas and their relations.	
5. Formulating the learning objectives. (In groups)	Based on the explanations, define what knowledge will be investigate.	
6. Self study (individual)	Make the investigation	Each student make this point, Internet is a good way to find the

		information.
7. Oral or written report by group.	Participate in the discussion in order to make the report.	The students share the information they found, and they can use the information that they found in Internet.

Conclusions

As a conclusion, the process of solving problem without Internet, it could be possible, but it takes a long time to get the information. Fortunately, nowadays we have Internet, so the process of solving problems of PBL, is quickest and more interesting to the students, and let them to have contact with the real world and how the knowledge can be used, some of the characteristics of good problems of PBL.

A Distributed E-Learning Tool Based on Learning Objects

Marco Grossi, Mauro Marinilli and Alessandro Micarelli
Università di Roma Tre, via della Vasca Navale 79
Rome, Italy
contact@marinilli.com

Abstract: We present in this paper an intelligent educational system employing a distributed, agent-based software architecture implemented using intelligent agents, P2P and collaborative CBR techniques. The system answers to user information needs by proposing a tailored sequence of learning objects on the given topics found over the Internet. Such learning objects are packed according to a pedagogical approach and the user characteristics. The system can be seen as an intelligent information searching engine at a higher abstraction level, capable of solving extemporary or continuative information needs by means of user-customized presentations (sequences of one or more Learning Objects, tailored to the current user). Instead of presenting documents passively gathered throughout the Web as current search engines do, it tries to explain the requested information need by means of a sequence of learning objects, found in a collaborative way by querying its fellow agents over the Net.

Introduction

Emerging specifications in E-Learning content representation have the power to foster a whole new host of intelligent services, though such potential is still largely unexploited. Our objective was to design from scratch a new intelligent educational system, that took advantage of adaptive technologies while adopting novel E-Learning specifications, as well as employing a distributed, network-centric software architecture. We used these techniques in an attempt to enhance the quality level of the Internet search process (using annotated learning objects instead of simple documents) while enhancing the quantity of the retrieved material (by using a P2P-based, distributed approach).

We are developing a distributed E-Learning system based on collaborative CBR (Case-Based Reasoning [Aamodt1994]) and User Modeling employing standard specifications for Learning Objects (as prescribed in ADL SCORM and IEEE LOM) and other related standards. The system can be seen as an information searching engine at a higher abstraction level, capable of solving extemporary or continuative information needs by means of user-customized presentations (sequences of one or more Learning Objects, tailored to the current user). Hence, instead of presenting documents passively gathered throughout the Web as current search engines do, it tries to explain the requested information need by means of a sequence of learning objects, found in a collaborative way by querying its fellow agents over the Net. The system is also able to create elementary Learning Objects that encapsulates simpler documents, providing a degree of reliability based on user satisfaction. Also solved information needs (known solutions to cases posed by users) are kept in the local agent library for future use so enlarging the overall available knowledge on the given domain. We used a collaborative CBR approach to manage the information needs. We employed CBR for creating new solutions re-aggregating parts of old ones using P2P networks of domain experts agents. We found this approach well-suited for the inductive nature of our information-rich problem-solving situation. The system is currently used as an extemporary information searching facility, on a restricted domain of interest where a human expert has provided a set of annotated Learning Objects. The system integrates such course material with documents extracted from a well-known Web search engine.

The typical scenario could be the following. A student wants to know more about a given topic, "Java Server Pages". After posting the query to the User Agent, this latter one invokes the Pedagogical Agent that creates a particular Infoneed representation (the current problem representation in our CBR system) relying on the user model, the chosen pedagogical approach and the user input. This data is submitted to a Domain Expert Agent, that coordinates a group of interacting experts (such experts are implemented as peers in a peer-to-peer network) that implements a collaborative CBR process. Each expert peer using its local CBR engine provides a set of candidate solutions (a given sequencing of learning objects plus other pedagogical data) that are newly adapted by the leader domain expert agent. The resulting solution is adapted again by the Pedagogical Agent for appearance and to match the current user needs. The final result is proposed to the user. that can give some feedback that is used to tune both the user model, the pedagogical approach chose and the content. We adopted a distributed algorithm based on the classic CBR nearest neighbor case retrieval technique for case indexing and retrieval. From a CBR point of view the system performs a complete, distributed CBR lifecycle (composed of the four steps Retrieve, Adaptation, Revise and subsequent Retain).

Architecture

The architecture can be described adopting the following functional decomposition:

- the **User Agent**. It acts on behalf of the user, provides the GUI to his/her and interacts with the Pedagogical Agent in order to solve the current information need. It uses a User Model in order to better suite the End User needs. Its proactivity is achieved in two ways. One towards the End User, following the user interface agent approach (as in [Maes1994]). The other is towards the Pedagogical Agents, querying autonomously for new information needs on behalf of the End User.

- the **Pedagogical Agent**. It is responsible of refining the information needs posed by the User Agent, to negotiate possible solutions with Expert Agents and to adapt the found solutions to the current User Agent. The Pedagogical Agent is responsible to bridge the information need as perceived by the user into an annotation suitable for automatic indexing by means of a CBR indexing module. For doing this, it uses other information apart from the user model and the information need he / she devised: a pedagogical strategy, and other context data. In future versions we plan to adopt different pedagogical strategies.

- the **Expert Agent**. It is the knowledge warden, organized as a case library. When queried for some information need it is capable of performing a distributed search among its fellow peers over the Net in order to find the most suitable Learning Objects. It adopts a specialized collaboration CBR algorithm. There are several different types of such an agent. The standard one, that acts as a pro-active CBR library for solving known information needs based on the past experience. Another type is interfaced with a standard authoring tool for allowing human experts to input Learning Objects (though this is a temporary solution, future version will use a specialized User Agent for knowledge input). Other dedicated Expert Agents versions are specialized in wrapping existing rudimentary online data sources (such as traditional search engines, news sources, etc.) on-demand. For a better quality the system elects a leader agent.

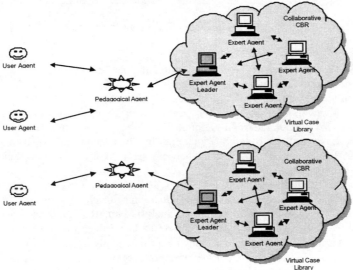

Figure 1. The Architecture

Such an architecture takes advantage of the latest Internet technologies in order to provide a flexible yet robust functional decomposition among the various software modules composing an E-Learning system. Given its top-down, high level approach, this architecture also turns out to be easily understood by non-technical people facilitating their interaction with the system.

Conceptual Model

Our conceptual model is centered around the *Infoneed* concept (an information need posed by the User). This is represented both at an abstract level, and as its concrete implementation (a given sequencing of learning objects provided by the Domain Experts Agents). Figure 2 below describes some of the details of our conceptual model using a UML notation.

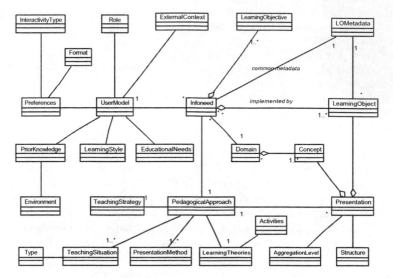

Figure 2. The higher-level conceptual model

In our system an Infoneed is represented as a CBR case comprising the following information:
-   *User Model.* It is made up of some parts: the *role* (teacher, author, learner, manager, etc.), the *preferences* (type of interactive, format of the resource,...) the *prior knowledge* defined by the *environment* (primary education, secondary education,...,university first cycle,...), the *external context* (type of connection, type of computer, geographical zone,...), *educational needs,* the preferred *learning style* (constructivist, predefined) and other data.
-   *Domain information.* It is composed of information regarding the content of the query posed by the user.
-   *Learning Objectives.* This comprises information about the target skills, the competencies and the knowledge to be acquired.
-   *Pedagogical approach.* It describes a theory of learning and education (empirical, rational and constructivism).the approach is composed by three elements: a teaching situation, a teaching strategy and a presentation method. A lesson consist of four *situations*: an introduction, an analysis part (that contains concepts, definitions, rules, the problem solving strategy,...), a reinforcement and a test. The strategy is implemented by a set of activities (observing, describing, analyzing, experiencing, studying, problem-solving, practicing, exploring, predicting, answer questions,...). The presentation method decides the format of the resources (video, mpeg, ht ml document,...)
-   *Learning Object Metadata*, as of the widely accepted IEEE LTSC LOM [IEEE2001].

Conclusions and Future Work

Our system is aimed at filling the gap of intelligent educational presentation, exploiting the best of the two worlds: dedicated, high-quality teaching material (traditionally strongly implementation-dependent) and the wealth of information the Web offers now and it will offer in the near future, when the E-Learning standards will be widely employed. Despite that, given the system capability of encapsulating pre-existing data sources and documents, it can be effectively employed at present time as an ELearning system specialized in some given domain of interest, with the ability to extract (possibly with a lower quality) information from the Web. Furthermore, E-Learning courses and the related material is represented in a standard and reusable way, to allow exchange with other systems.

As regards future works in the agenda we are evaluating the porting of the system to the EDUTELLA framework [Nejdl2002] as a priority issue. Then we will explore the collaboration mechanisms between different Pedagogical Agents in order to promote a better pedagogical adaptation enhancing the overall learning experience.

References

[Aamodt1994] Aamodt, A. & Plaza, E. (1994). "Case-Based Reasoning: Foundational Issues, Methodological Variations, and System Approaches. AI Communications".

[SCORM2001] ADL Team (2001), "SCORM Specification", Version 1.2. http://www.adlnet.org

[IEEE2001] IEEE Learning Object Metadata Specification (2001) Working Draft 6.1. http://ltsc.ieee.org/wg12/index.html

[Lorraine2001] Lorraine McGinty and Barry Smyth (2001), "Collaborative Case-Based Reasoning: Applications in Personalized Route Planning", ICCBR'01 Proceedings.

[Maes1994] Pattie Maes, Yezdi Lashkari and Max Metral (1994), "Collaborative Interface Agents", Proceedings of AAAI '94 Conference, Seattle, Washington.

[Koper2001] Koper, Rob (2001), "Modeling Units of Study from a Pedagogical Perspective: the Pedagogical Meta-Model Behind EML". Technical report of the Open University of the Netherlands.

[Nejdl2002] Nejdl Wolfgang et al.(2002),"EDUTELLA: A P2P Networking Infrastructure based on RDF", WWW2002 Proceedings.

Theoretical framework: Towards a Grid for the Pedagogical Analysis of Online Courses

Martine Chomienne
Cégep@distance
Montréal-Canada
mchomienne@cegepadistance.ca

Abstract: After a review of reports on online learning and the evident lack of conclusive studies comparing online learning, traditional distance learning and classroom learning, a research team funded by the PAREA program of the Ministère de l'Éducation du Québec has developed a tool for comparing various online courses. This is based on the theoretical principals of multimedia communication, online collaborative learning and online instructor/student roles. The tool is applied in the learning impact assessment of a virtual program in the natural sciences.

Introduction

E-Learning has become a buzzword in the field of training and education where it is employed loosely to designate a wide variety of teaching situations. Industry Canada in a report from the Advisory Committee for Online Learning published in February 2001 said: "Online learning can be defined as what occurs when education and training (typically credit but also non-credit) are delivered and supported by networks such as the Internet or Intranets. Learners are able to learn any time and any place. In this report, we use the terms "online learning" and "e-learning" interchangeably. In either case, we mean both distance learning and the provision of technology -enhanced learning within a traditional classroom, lecture hall or lab." Therefore, on the one hand, we talk about online courses in which students have more or less infrequent access to web sites associated with classroom teaching and, on the other hand, courses designed entirely to be delivered via the net and followed from home.

Theoretical Framework

The theoretical framework adopted is based on Depover's (et al.) three dimensional model for interactive multimedia (1998), Henri's (and Lundgren-Cayrol) online student collaborative learning model (2001), and Teles' (2000) and Salmon's (2000) online instructor/student roles.

Student/Teaching Material Interactivity. Depover et al. define educational interactive multimedia as the computer-generated integration, distribution, and management of sound, text, and graphic. An interactive multimedia teaching material gains the attention of the learner through the *perceptive channels* (hearing, sight, etc.) and is composed of interactions between the machine and the user. This later must know what the system expects of him in order to navigate properly into the multimedia. Furthermore, interactive multimedia facilitates the *intellectual activity* of the student by proposing *teaching strategies* and by structuring the learning content into different kinds of knowledge representations. It includes all the information needed to build a model *representing the student* and to propose appropriate activities. Each of these intervention levels (perceptive, transaction-driven, cognitive, pedagogical and evaluative) must satisfy clarity, coherency, pertinence, analogy, redundancy and control criteria.

Student/Other Participant Interactivity. The interactivity between the student and the other participants is influenced by collaborative learning and by the role of the instructor. We have regrouped the student collaboration model by Henri and Lundgren-Cayrol (2001), the instructor role by Teles and the stages of student progress in online learning situations by Salmon (2000) into four components describing activities, tools and participant interventions.

Access and motivation allow students to become technically operational and to prepare themselves psychologically for active participation in their learning experience.

Online involvement and socialization consist in building a real sense of belonging to a virtual community and the development of group working methods.

Communication of ideas or information exchange, knowledge building and learner development constitutes the actual learning components.

Coordination includes all the operations that the instructor and the students do for managing the learning experience.

Each component implies interventions made by students and the instructor to be taken into account in some cases at the design phase of instructional material and for others during the delivery phase.

Steps for the Application of the Tool to Online Courses

To assess an online course with regard to teaching, one must examine the student/educational material interaction by determining first the symbolic systems in play. One must then determine the function of each of the system elements as to the five levels of interactivity (perceptive, transaction-driven, cognitive, pedagogical and evaluative) described by Depover et al. (1998). This is the first step and allows us to put together Table 1.

In the second step one must apply the six quality criteria (clarity, coherence, pertinence, analogy, redundancy and control) as proposed by Giardina and Mottet (1996) to each of the elements and for each level of interactivity.

And finally, in the third step, one must determine the elements making up the student/students and student/instructor-expert interactivity. This allows us to produce a series of tables for each component of this dimension. As an example Table 2 illustrates the dimension of Online involvement and socialization.

Conclusions

The tool has been applied to several courses in the virtual program in the natural sciences and has revealed an interesting progression in the use of the internet teaching potential. Courses designed in 2000 were more interactive than those designed in 1998-1999.

Furthermore, the tool is still at the final validation stage with a number of experts in the field. These people are testing it in an iterative process in other courses of the virtual DEC as well as in courses of Cégep@distance.

References

Depover, C., Giardina, M, and Marton, P, (1998). *Les environnements d'apprentissage multimédia – Analyse et conception.* Paris: L'Harmattan

Ducharme, R. Lizotte, F. and Chomienne, M.(to be published*). Évaluation du DEC virtuel.* Research report presented to the PAREA program of the ministère de l'Éducation du Québec

Giardina, M. and Mottet, M. (1996). Unpublished document

Henri, F. and Lundren-Cayrol, K. (2001). *L'apprentissage collaboratif à distance.* Québec: Presses de l'Université du Québec

Industry Canada (2001). The e-learning evolution in colleges and universities. A Pan Canadian Challenge Report from the Advisory Committee for Online Learning, p.25

Salmon, G. (2000). E-moderating: The key to teaching and learning online. London: Kogan Page

Teles, L. (2000). Investigating the Role of the Instructor in Online Collaborative Environments. Project 5.25 TeleLearning, project report

Acknowledgements

This paper reports on work undertaken as part of a project funded by the PAREA program of the ministère de l'Éducation du Québec (Canada).

Symbolic Systems	Perceptive	Transaction-driven	Cognitive	Pedagogical	Evaluative
Sounds : words, music, reading texts, songs, oral expression, etc.	Hearing (tone, pitch, volume)	Multimedia navigational information (written or oral commands, page-number indications in the section scrolling arrows.)	Explain, detail, specify, (adapted for the target population)	Determine the teaching objectives. Present the content and activities.	Present teaching and summative evaluations. Allow users to know their level of achievement of objectives, etc. Evaluate progress.
Texts (attributes)	Sight			Define and expose	
Attributes of letters (fonts, style)				Define and expose learning strategies, cognitive and meta-cognitive teaching strategies. Bold and capital letters, etc. are often used to attract attention, to accentuate something.	
Hypertexts, Drop-down menus		Click-on prompt	Define		
Pop up		Click-on prompt	Detail Specify		
Shading (colour changes)		Indicates places already visited.			
Flashing		Indicates who should intervene and where			
Colours		Indicate a section, a module, a unit	Hold a cultural meaning.		
Graphic	Sight				
- Icons		Can (but not necessarily) be click-on prompts	convey a command.		
- Hourglass		Indicates that the system is busy			
- Drawings		Can (but not necessarily) be click-on prompts	convey a notion, a concept.		
- Photographs		Idem	convey a notion, a concept.	Can be used to attract attention.	
- Diagrams		Idem			
- Comic strip, Animation		Idem			
- Trees		Idem	Structure content.		
- Tables		Idem			
- Arrows	Hearing and sight	Forward or backward prompts			
- Video		Combine media effects	Combine media effects	Combine media effects.	

Table 1 : Student/Teaching material Interactivity

Components	Sub-components	Tools	Activities	Role of the Host-Instructor		Comments
INVOLVEMENT (HENRI AND LUNDGREN) ONLINE SOCIALIZATION (SALMON)	Group cohesion	Forum Chat Directory (student list) Visitor card Resums Messages	Participate in a forum or in a chat room, fill out the visitor card, Get to know the other participants.	Encourage the students to participate, to share their motivation and their expectations, to give personal information (hobbies, civil status, etc.), to consult the visitor cards of every participant.	Communication space offered to everyone. Room for personal information on everyone.	This activity prepares the setting up of the teams.
	Belonging	Forum with interactivity sociograms	Training at collaborative learning:	Organise and supervise a group negotiation session concerning the collaborative model and the conditions which will apply in order to carry out the training activity (participation rhythm, frequency, intervention size, team constitution, kind of contributions from everyone, parameters or characteristics of group or team productions, work schedule and any other development which applies). Bring back those who tend to remain apart from the group, etc.	Public communication space	The group discovers, understands and evaluates its needs in order to later define the way in which the collaboration will work and which jobs will be done. The instructor studies the interactivity sociogram to intervene with those who do not participate sufficiently.
	Perception of group productivity	Forum Tool for following up projects. Instant questionnaires.	Fill out work-progress questionnaires regularly by the students.	Release the results of the questionnaire to students, informing them of their progress as a group and allowing them to reflect on their team effort.	Public communication space.	

Table 2: Student/Other participant Interactivity

Supporting Elearning in Engineering Education

Constantino Martins, Isabel Azevedo, Carlos Vaz de Carvalho
Instituto Superior de Engenharia do Porto (ISEP) - Portugal
const@dei.isep.ipp.pt

Lígia Ribeiro
Faculdade de Engenharia da Universidade do Porto (FEUP) - Portugal

Abstract: The purpose of this paper is to present the project "Supporting Elearning in Engineering Education". This project addresses research questions related with the identification of the requirements and evaluation of Web-based learning environments used in an on-campus context, to complement the traditional teaching and learning in engineering institutions of higher education. A set of undergraduate and postgraduate courses of the Porto Polytechnic Scholl of Engineering (ISEP) and the Faculty of Engineering of Porto University (FEUP) will be used as test beds.

Background

The accessibility and easy of use of information and communication technologies (ICT) to develop teaching and learning environments, accessible through a Web interface, is being increasingly explored by academic institutions and companies operating in the education "market" ([Flanagan, 2000] [Collis, 1998]).

The use of these environments as a complement to traditional education in undergraduate and postgraduate courses deserves increased attention. As a result diverse models and patterns have been developed and implemented ([Nachmias, 2000] [Seufert, 2000] [Cardoso, 2001]). Especially because studies show that on-line learning is economically sound and convenientOn-line learning is an important financial market for universities and access to education is enhanced and opportunities are expanded from a political point of view through distance learning opportunities.

Like most higher education institutions, ISEP and FEUP have launched a few e-learning initiatives on an experimental basis, whose results are being evaluated. However these initiatives have not been conducted in a systematic way and have not been integrated with existing information systems, taking profit of the management and communication facilities offered by them. Our view is that Information Systems also constitute an important tool to support the evolution of the pedagogical process (David, 2001). Their interconnection with e-learning systems is expected to have a value added contribution to the continuous education effort.

Objectives

The project will be conducted during the 2001/2002 academic year, focusing on a set of one-semester courses of ISEP and FEUP.

The **first phase** goal was to identify the requirements for a Web Based Environment, which advantageously complements the traditional learning process. For this purpose, a set of tools was designed to provide this information, taking into account the nature of the stakeholders (higher education institutions, teachers, and managers).

We synthesized these studies on these tools as well as case studies in other academic institutions. These results will be published elsewhere (Martins Constantino).

The **second phase** of the project (currently ongoing) will look into the adequacy and advantages of integrating the Web Based Learning Environment with existing Information Systems. The evaluation will take into account the defined requirements and analysis of cost/benefit.

The first step of this phase was the selection, acquisition and installation of a Web Based Learning Environment (WBLE) for each Institution, based on the fulfillment of the requirements identify in the first phase. In order to assess the advantages of the integrating the WBLE with the IS, one of the environments selected (ISEP) will not be integrated with an IS, while the other (FEUP) will be integrated with the existing IS of the Institution, SiFEUP (Ribeiro, 1997).

The next step in this phase has been the analysis of the facilities available on SiFEUP and the advantages of integrating the WBLE with it. This phase is currently under development.

Simultaneously some pilot courses were selected (and a corresponding teaching/learning methodology) in each Institution that will be used to test and evaluate the efficiency of each Institution environment. The assessment, through questionnaire, of student's technological profile was conducted before the beginning of the courses.

As it is difficult to demonstrate that a change in practice or in knowledge over time can be attributable to a single isolated resource (the WBLE+IS, in our case), the Integrative approach therefore looks at how the resource is used in conjunction with all the other resources that are available to its users. It will focus on users' opinions and level of use of the resource, and on how it is embedded into the course as a whole. The opinions of the administrative staff and technicians involved in this study will also be taken into account

Expected Results

The expected results are twofold: identification of the requirements and evaluation of the effectiveness of an integrated e-learning/information system environment in engineering education.

The results of this project may be useful for other engineering institutions of higher education that wish to create, manage access and share Infrastructures of "campus-learning", in an integrated and extensible fashion.

Conclusions

The Results of this project, here summarized, may be useful for other engineering institutions of higher education that wish to create, manage, access and share Infrastructures of "campus-learning", in an integrated and extensible fashion. We also think that the experience of this work represents an alternative view about the role of learning Web-based environments/systems in educational processes.

Learning is facing new challenges in the electronic age, and with no doubt on-line educational communities is one of those challenges where we want to focus ours research work. We think, by exploiting online learning communities, for the complement of traditional education, the academics institutions must consider the learning Web-based environment a strategic instrument of development and research.

References

Flanagan M., and Egert, C. (2002). *Courseware quality and the collaborative classroom: implementing IOS courseware to generate seminar-style interactions.* IMEj, 2(1);

Collis B. (1998). *WWW-Based environment for collaborative group work.* Education and Information Technologies, 3, 231-245;

Nachmias, R. et al.(2000). *Web-Supported Emergent-Collaboration in Higher Education Courses.* Educational Technology & Society 3(3);

Seufert Sabine (2000). *The NetAcademy as a Medium for Learning Communities.* Educational Technology & Society 3(3);

Cardoso Eduardo Luís, Altamiro B. Machado (2001). *A Problemática da Adopção de Ambientes de Ensino Distribuído no Ensino Superior.* 2ª Conferência APSI;

David Gabriel, Lígia M. Ribeiro (2001). *Impact of the Information System on the Pedagogical Process*. Proceedings of the 7th International Conference of European University Information Systems, EUNIS 2001 - The Changing Universities, The Role of Technology, pp. 249- 251, Berlin, Germany, 28-30 March;

Karaliotas Y. (1997). *Learning on and over the Internet: Dynamics and Limitations*. August 1997;

Martins Constantino. *Infrastructures of "campus-learning": applicability in the education of Engineering*. MSc. Thesis, in publication;

Ribeiro Lígia M., Gabriel David, Ana Azevedo, J. C. Marques dos Santos (1997). *Developing an Information System at the Engineering Faculty of Porto University*, Proceedings of the European Cooperation in Higher Education Information Systems, EUNIS 97, pp. 282-287, Grenoble, France, 9-11 September;

Teaching Argumentation in Secondary School Through Computer Based and Face-to-face Debate[1]

Miika Marttunen, Leena Laurinen and Timo Salminen
University of Jyväskylä, Department of Education
Finland
miika.marttunen@edu.jyu.fi

Abstract: This article describes a study in which 28 Finnish secondary school students engaged in a 12 week argumentation course. The course consisted of theoretical studies and exercises on argumentation, and argumentative debates in pairs through computer chat and face-to-face. The students' argumentation skills were tested before and after the course. The students also wrote an individual argumentative text before the face-to-face and computer debates and modified their text after the discussion. The test results indicated that the students developed in their argumentation skills during the course. The quality of argumentation in the students' texts improved from the text written before to the text written after the debate. Thus, the debates stimulated students' argumentative thinking and helped them reflect on the topic in question from multiple perspectives.

Introduction

In order to take part in argumentative discussions students are invited not only to construct and transform their own knowledge (Bereiter & Scardamalia, 1989) but rather to co-construct and create new knowledge structures together (Dillenbourg, 1999). For this reason argumentation is a very effective means to learning. Unfortunately, the prerequisites for argumentative co-construction of knowledge are not necessarily met simply by asking students to debate some argumentative topic because, instead of exploring the issue from different perspectives by considering the pros and cons of their arguments, students start very easily to dispute. Although argumentation skills are emphasised as one goal of school education, there is a limited provision in curricula of most countries to teach them. In this paper we present research results based on a teaching experiment aiming at teaching argumentation to secondary school students. The study focuses on the following research questions: 1) Did students' argumentation skills develop during the teaching experiment? 2) Are there any differences between students' individually written argumentative texts before and after the argumentative discussions by either face-to-face or by using chat-tools?

Method

Subjects and Measurement of Students' Argumentation Skills

The data of the study were collected in the teaching experiment (12 weeks, 56 hours) carried out in one secondary school in Middle Finland. Before the experiment the argumentation skills of the students were measured by the pre-test. The students of the experimental group (n = 28) participated in the argumentation course while the control group (n = 27) did not study argumentation. The argumentation skills of both the experimental and the control group were measured again after the experiment by the post-test. The pre-test and post-test focused on the students' skills to a) analyse argumentative text by choosing the main claim and the supporting grounds from numbered sentences of the text, b) present their own grounded view (claim and supporting grounds) on a given topic, c) comment on an argumentative writing, and d) to choose valid grounds and correct conclusions from several choices (see Marttunen & Laurinen, in press).

---

[1] The research reported here was carried out within the SCALE project (Internet-based intelligent tool to Support Collaborative Argumentation-based LEarning in secondary schools, March 2001 - February 2004) funded by the European Community under the 'Information Societies Technology' (IST) Programme. Information on the project can be found at: http://www.euroscale.net/

Argumentation Course

The argumentation course was cross-curricular in nature and practically it was a combination of three sub-courses, one in Ethics and two in Mother Tongue. Two of the courses were obligatory (Power of Language and Good and Evil in Man) and the third course (Argumentation) was optional when it comes to the Finnish secondary school curriculum.

The first six week period of the course was based on the combination of the obligatory courses *Power of Language* and *Good and Evil in Man*. Studies during this period followed partly the text books and exercises included in the worksheets of the books. The first period was divided into introductory, theoretical and practical parts. During the practical part the students practised argumentative communication through two topics (Racism and Sexuality) by engaging in informal discussions, drama-sessions, group discussions and group debates.

The second six week period of the experiment was a specialization course of Mother Tongue (Argumentation) during which the students debated in pairs both face-to-face (20 minutes) and by using a synchronous chat tool DREW[2]) (40 minutes). The themes treated were Capital Punishment, Nuclear Power, and Genetically Modified Organism In this paper the focus is on the argumentative chat and face-to-face discussions about *Nuclear power*. The studies in both chat and face-to-face environments proceeded according to a four phase task sequence during which data were collected on students' performance both before and after the discussions in pairs (see SCALE project, 2002a). The *training phase* included one double-lesson (90 minutes) for practicing the use of the DREW software. In the *preparation phase* the students were given newspaper and web articles (5 in total) on nuclear power. They analysed the argumentative structure of the articles in small groups of 3 – 5 students, and presented the results of the analysis to the whole class. After working with the articles the students wrote their first individual text (total of 24 texts were collected). In the *debate phase* the face-to-face group (n = 10) debated on the topic about 15–20 minutes, and the computer group (n = 16) chatted with DREW about 30 – 40 minutes. After the debate the students reflected on the debate by filling in a graph on the debate collaboratively. Finally, in the *consolidation* phase students modified their original individual text as a function of the debate that had taken place. The articles were not available for the students when they wrote their individual texts.

Data Analyses

Analysis of Students' Individual Texts

The analysis examined how wide the space of debate in the students' texts was. The space of debate is wide when the text provides many relevant arguments with respect to the question, and takes into account the multiple points of view that can be held in the debate The analyses of the students' texts are based on a QED (Qualité de l'espace du débat; Engl. Quality of the Space of Debate) analyses method[3]. QED is a numeric measure which is calculated on the basis of the following analysis criteria of the text (for details see SCALE project, 2002b): 1) *Richness:* the text is rich when several arguments are presented; 2) *Elaboration (classification categories: poor, medium, high):* the text is highly elaborative when arguments are provided with sub-arguments, examples, and explanations; 3) *Balance:* the text is balanced when both pro and against arguments are presented; 4) *Coverage:* the text has a wide coverage when the arguments cover many different topics of the question. Coverage is the ratio of the covered topics in a given text with respect to the number of all different topics found when all the texts written by the students are taken into account; 5) *Coherence:* Coherence is the distance between the general opinion of the student (rather *pro*, rather *against* or *shared*) and the general balance of arguments in her/his text .

Pre-test and Post-test Analyses

---

[2] Drew (Dialogical Reasoning Educational Web too) is a collaborative Java environment designed by Universities of Lyon and St. Etienne during the European SCALE project. For more information on Drew see http://www.euroscale.net/

[3] The QED method was elaborated by M. Quignard (GRIC, Lyon), in collaboration with M. Baker (GRIC, Lyon), J. Andriessen and M. van Amelsvoort (Utrecht University). Details can be found in Deliverable 8 of the SCALE project, at: http://www.euroscale.net/

In the analyses of the students' answers to the task of *analysing an argumentative text* the text included one correct sentence which indicated the main claim of the text, and two partly correct sentences. The correct and the partly correct options were awarded by points. The grounds the students had selected were scored on the basis of relevancy to the selected claim. In the analysis of the task of *composing one's own arguments* the analysis of the claims clarified whether the claim a student had composed was understandable and clear in focus. The analysis criteria for the students' grounds were relevancy and sufficiency (see Bacig, Evans, Larmouth & Risdon, 1990; Walton, 1989). The analysis of the *students' comments on a short biased argumentative text* clarified how analytical their comments were. In the analysis of the *judging tasks of grounds and conclusions*, the different possible choices were scored on the basis of rational reasoning.

Results

The students produced higher quality argumentative texts after the debate compared to the text they wrote before the debate (Table 1). The texts after the debate were more covered with respect of the topics, included more and better elaborated arguments, and were more balanced in terms of arguments in favour and against. Consequently, the general QED scores were also higher in the texts written after the debate compared to the texts before. The improvement was equal in face-to-face and computer chat conditions.

Table 1. Differences (paired samples t-test) of the quality of the space of debate and related variables between face-to-face and computer chat environments

MODE OF STUDY		VARIABLE					
		COV	WSA	WSAP	WSAA	BAL	QED
		% (M)	f (M)	f (M)	f (M)		
Face-to-face (n = 9)	Text before	35.2	6.8	2.3	4.4	30.11	10.6
	Text after	51.2	14	4.1	9.9	39.11	17.9
	p	.081	.000	.043	.002	.025	.030
Computer chat (n = 12)	Text before	38.8	7.5	2.0	5.5	27.7	10.9
	Text after	48.6	12	2.8	9.3	38.5	19.3
	p	.028	.000	.108	.000	.024	.017
Total (n = 21)	Text before	37.2	7.2	2.1	5.0	28.7	10.8
	Text after	50.0	12.9	3.3	9.5	38.8	18.7
	p	.006	.000	.008	.000	.001	.001

COV = Coverage; WSA = Weighted Sum of Arguments; WSAP = Weighted Sum of Arguments Pro; WSAA = Weighted Sum of Arguments Against [The weighting is based on the level of elaboration]; BAL = Balance); QED = Quality of the space of debate.
Note: the range of variables COV, BAL and QED is from 0 – 100.

Table 2 Differences (paired samples t-test) between the students' pretest and posttest results

VARIABLE	EXPERIMENTAL GROUP (N=28)					CONTROL GROUP (N=27)				
	Pre-test	SD	Post-test	SD	p	Pre-test	SD	Post-test	SD	p
Identifying claims	.92	.39	.92	.39	ns.	1.11	.42	1.15	.36	ns.
Identifying grounds	.31	.62	.69	.74	*	.70	.78	.56	.70	ns.
Composing a claim	1.08	.84	1.85	.37	**	1.63	.56	1.70	.54	ns.
Composing grounds	1.21	.74	1.83	.39	**	1.62	.57	1.92	.27	*
Analytical approach	.76	.83	.96	.84	ns.	.55	.70	1.04	.71	**
Judging grounds	1.58	.58	1.50	.51	ns.	1.67	.68	1.37	.63	ns.
Judging conclusions	1.44	.71	1.64	.76	ns.	1.19	.75	1.54	.81	ns.

Note: The range of the variables is from 0 to 2.

Table 2 indicates that the students of the experimental group improved in their skills in *identifying grounds* from an argumentative text (pre-test score .31, post-test score .69), *composing a claim* (1.08 vs. 1.85), and *composing grounds* (1.21 vs. 1.83). All the differences were statistically significant. The control group who did not take part in the combined argumentation course did not differ between the pre-test and post-test results in variables *identifying grounds* and *composing a claim*. However, the post-test scores of the control group in the variable *composing grounds* were higher than their pre-test scores. It is, however, worth noticing that the task relating to composing grounds was different in the pretest and post-test: the theme on which the students were asked to compose the grounds was easier in the post-test. The easier theme in the post-test may have affected the students' better scores in the post-test both in the experimental and control groups. For this reason, in the experimental group the difference between scores of variable *composing grounds* in the pretest and posttest was corrected by the effect of the easier posttest task (i.e. control groups .30 improvement in the task), and the difference was tested once again (one sample t-test). The result indicated that the difference remained statistically significant ($t = 2.27$ $df = 25$, $p = .032$; missing values were replaced with the mean).

The students of the control group achieved higher scores in the posttest also in the case of variable *analytical approach* (1.04 vs. .55 in Table 2). The better scores of the control group are most obviously due to a test-wise effect (Borg & Gall, 1989 p. 644) since the task concerning this variable was the same in the pretest and posttest. The improvement in the scores of the experimental group (although not in terms of statistical significance) also supports this conclusion.

Conclusions

The students' texts after the debates included richer topical and more balanced argumentative structure than the texts they wrote before the debate. Thus, students benefited from both face-to-face and computer based debates on the topic. Argumentative discussions during which new approaches and points of view are aroused seem to stimulate students' argumentative thinking and help them reflect on issues in question from several perspectives.

The pre-test and post-test results showed that the students improved in their argumentation skills during the argumentation course. This result suggests that argumentation skills in general can be taught successfully during 12 week teaching interventions. The results are consistent with previous results that have shown that students learn argumentation skills even during shorter (6 weeks) teaching periods (Wesp & Montgomery, 1998). The results are also in harmony with the results of students' improved QED scores in their texts in this study since they support the assumption that during the argumentative debates the students not only improved in their space of debate, but learned argumentation skills as well.

References

Bacig, T. D., Evans, R. H., Larmouth, D. W. & Risdon, K. C. (1990). Beyond argumentation and comparison/contrast: Extending the Socrates CAI design principles to classroom teaching and the interpretation and production of other forms of discourse. *Computers and the Humanities*, 24, 15 – 41.

Bereiter, C. & Scardamalia, M. (1989). Intentional learning as a goal of instruction. In L. B. Resnick (Ed.) *Knowing, learning, and instruction: Essays in honor of Robert Glaser*. Hillsdale, NJ: Erlbaum, 361-192.

Borg, W. R. & Gall, M. D. (1989). *Educational research: an introduction* (5th ed.) New York: Longman.

Dillenbourg, P. (Ed.) (1999). *Collaborative learning: Cognitive and computational approaches*. Amsterdam: Pergamon.

SCALE-project (2002a). European Commission, project No IST-1999-10664. *First Year Deliverables. Deliverables 1 & 2*, 51 – 55. Available at http://www.euroscale.net/

SCALE-project (2002b). European Commission, project No IST-1999-10664. *First Year Deliverables. Deliverable 8*, 134– 141. Available at http://www.euroscale.net/

Marttunen, M. & Laurinen, L. (In press). Argumentation skills of secondary school students in Finland, Hungary and United Kingdom. *Proceedings of the Fifth Conference of the International Society for the Study of Argumentation*. University of Amsterdam.

Walton, D. N. (1989). *Informal logic. A handbook for critical argumentation*. Cambridge: Cambridge University Press.

Wesp, R. & Montgomery, K. (1998). Developing critical thinking through the study of paranormal phenomena. *Teaching of Psychology*, 25(4), 275-278.

LLC Lecture Capture and Editing Tool for Online Course Delivery

Mark Apperley, Sam Jansen, Amos Jeffries, Masood Masoodian,
Lance Paine, Bill Rogers, Tony Voyle

Department of Computer Science
The University of Waikato
Hamilton, New Zealand
M.Masoodian@cs.waikato.ac.nz

Abstract: This paper describes a system for the capture and editing of live lecture presentations for redelivery locally or over the Internet. The system captures both audio from the presenter and the annotations made to the contents of the presentation material. For lecture capture, the system works in conjunction with standard PowerPoint™ presentation software. The audio editing is done using a stand-alone application, while the redelivery is done directly in PowerPoint™, or over the Internet and using a standard web browser. The captured version of the presentation includes the original lecture slides, graphical annotations made by the lecturer during the lecture, the audio recording of the lecture along with controls and indexing methods which allow easy access to different segments of the presentation. Presentations can be replayed in part or in full as required, preserving all of the content of the live lecture.

Introduction

In recent years the use of software such Microsoft PowerPoint™ has become an integral part of lecture preparation and delivery. Lecturers often prepare their material using some kind of presentation software, and then either deliver their lectures directly using the presentation software, or print their notes on transparencies and use overhead projectors for the actual delivery of the lectures. One of the main reasons for the use of printed transparencies, rather than the presentation software, is because it is easier to annotate the lecture material on transparencies during the course of a lecture. Although most presentation software allow annotation of slides during presentation, it is generally more difficult to use a computer mouse to draw or write on a slide than it is to simply use a pen to annotate a transparency. Also, in most presentation software, such as PowerPoint™, the annotations aren't added to the slides, which means that when one moves from one slide to the next then all the annotations on the previous slides are lost.

A further problem in the use of existing presentation software is the lack of support for redelivery of the lecture material. Conventional presentation software at best allows one to convert the lecture notes to Web pages and put them online for students to use after the lecture. However, this is clearly less than satisfactory because the students then only get the notes without the annotations, and more importantly the audio presentation of the lecturer. There is an additional cost here that is not immediately obvious. If it is not possible to annotate or if it is undesirable to put significant content into annotations because it will be lost in redelivery, the lecturer is forced to put significantly more time into preparation, and given a disincentive to vary content at delivery time in response to the questions and needs of the audience. With a good redelivery system, a lecturer could choose the level of advance preparation freely. In particular they could choose to do no advance preparation, except perhaps personal notes.

Although there is software which allows recording of lectures, both annotations and audio content, the majority of these tools place significant overheads on the lecturer to develop their material in a suitable form or using a special application (Jesshope, 2000; Gehne and Jesshope 2000). These overheads often divert the presenter from the real purpose, the delivery of the content, and focus attention on the form. The effort required is typically far in excess of the preparation of the same material for live delivery.

This paper describes the LLC (Lightweight Lecture Capture) software, developed to support the recording of lecture presentations for subsequent review and redelivery, requiring little or no effort in addition to that for the original live presentation. LLC is based on a standard presentation package, PowerPoint™, and requires only that the original presentation be produced in PowerPoint™ format. Capture is based on large interactive display surface technology, while review and redelivery require only a conventional desktop computer.

During this research we have developed a low-cost Large Interactive Display Surface (LIDS) which we utilize for lecture delivery and capture (Apperley et al., 2001). A typical LIDS system is an office whiteboard-sized

Figure 1: A prototype LIDS system as used for lecture delivery

screen functioning as a computer display, with a Mimio™ (Virtual Ink Corporation, 2002) digitization equipment at the front allowing the users to directly interact with the screen using a pen (providing similar functionality to a mouse). A standard data projector and a rear projection screen are used so as to allow the users to work directly in front of the screen without occluding the image. A prototype LIDS system is shown in Figure 1.

Lecture Capture and Redelivery

The Lightweight Lecture Capture (LLC) software acts as an overlay to PowerPoint™, allowing the presenter to make annotations and additions to the individual slides during live presentations using Mimio™ pens. The presenter's voice is also recorded by the LLC software, and together with the annotations is written back into the original lecture notes at each slide transition in standard PowerPoint™ format. Annotations are inserted with timing information and PowerPoint™ animation settings to roughly approximate the time and manner of their drawing.

Figure 2a shows an original slide from a typical PowerPoint™ presentation, while Figure 2b shows the same slide after it has been annotated by the presenter (a circle and an arrow have been added to the image). Figure 2b also includes a set of controls at the bottom of the slide which have been added by the LLC software. These controls (enlarged in Figure 3) include a timeline of the recorded audio track (usually with a few words recognized and shown in the rectangular boxes), arrows giving an indication of the progression of the audio recording when it is being played back, and a set of indicators showing when the slide was annotated.

A simple gesture recogniser within LLC allows the Mimio™ pen to be used to control the presentation.

a   b

Figure 2: a) the original slide b) annotated slide with LLC controls added

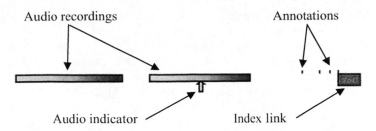

Figure 3: The controls added by LLC

Typical gestures include a right facing arrow to advance a slide, a left facing arrow to retreat through the presentation, and a scribble action to delete an annotation on the current slide. Gestures can also be used to edit aspects of the original PowerPoint™ file during the presentation.

During review or redelivery, which can be carried out on a conventional display screen, the presentation can be indexed at the individual slide level using the standard PowerPoint™ slide sorter view, or the LLC generated slides table of contents. Within an individual slide, animation and audio are synchronized according to elapsed time, although as mentioned earlier, individual graphic components are only crudely animated in themselves. Provision is made to have long silences in the audio minimized to one second, and the annotations resynchronized, again using elapsed time. Further, within a slide, a mouse click will skip forward to the start of the next graphic animation, allowing rapid browsing of both the graphic elements and audio at the annotation level.

The PowerPoint™ presentation, as updated by LLC can be reviewed by students, using either directly using the standard PowerPoint™ system, or as Web pages with imbedded audio and animations, generated by LLC.

Audio Editing

Since the annotations, additions, and audio contents are written back into the PowerPoint™ lecture notes, it is very easy to further review and edit the slides after the presentation. A stand-alone audio editing tool has also been developed to allow editing of the audio recordings of the lecture presentations (Apperley et al, 2002).

The audio editor reads the contents of a given audio file and uses Microsoft Speech Recognizer to make transcriptions of each audio segment contained in the file. The sound segments are listed in the leftmost pane of the editor window (Figure 4). The example presentation shown in Figure 4 has six separate sound samples. Clicking on a sound sample brings its transcript up in the main text window, and shows a graph of the sound wave in the top window. Selection of text, by click and drag, highlights not only the text, but also the corresponding part of the sound graph. In Figure 4 "h(n)umerous butchery and cooking sites have been found by archaeologists" is highlighted. Selection snaps to whole words because the smallest unit on which the editor can operate is a word, as recognized by the recognition software.

A selected portion of sound can be "dragged and dropped" within the text area. The editor then performs the corresponding operation on the sound file. Spaces between words in the text file have no significance. They are

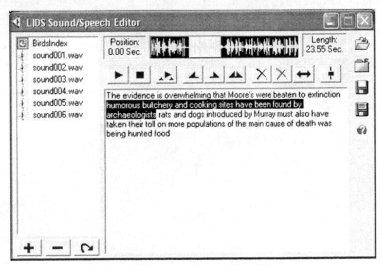

Figure 4: The audio editor

added to improve readability. In the sound file long spaces have no mapping in the text file. Short spaces are taken to be part of the immediately following word.

Command buttons are provided to allow playback of either the entire sample, or the sample from a selected point, or the highlighted section. It is often necessary to select and play sections in order to find out what the spoken word actually was meant to be, because the speech recognition is not perfect. The middle group of command buttons adjust the selected area. Sometimes it is inconvenient to drag over a large selection. These buttons allow separate selection of either end of the selected region. The buttons labeled with a cross symbol are provided to delete either the selected segment, or all but the selected segment. The latter operation is the natural one to apply when selecting a small message from a longer text. In using this, it is often convenient to make a rough cut first, taking more than the required length of sound, and to then trim unwanted words from the beginning and end.

As one may notice from the transcribed text in Figure 4, the speech recognition software far less than perfect. However, since the purpose of transcribed text is only to allow locating and editing the sound itself, it is satisfactory enough for the editing purposes. If the user is unsure of a segment of the transcribed text then he/she can easily play it back by selecting it.

Conclusions

This paper has described a prototype system called LLC which has been developed to provide a lightweight capture mechanism for lectures. LLC allows the capture of both graphical annotations as well as the audio content during the original presentation with little or no additional effort on the part of the presenter. Although LLC is normally used with a large interactive display system during the presentations, the captured content can be reviewed and redelivered using the standard PowerPoint™, or a web browser if the content is converted to a suitable form.

A preliminary study of the LLC software in real lecture settings has demonstrated its effectiveness in capturing the annotations and audio contents of presentations. This study has also shown that the students find LLC generated slides very useful for reviewing the contents of presentations after the lectures.

Acknowledgements

The research described in this paper has been carried out with the support of the Foundation for Research, Science and Technology under the New Economy Research Fund contract number UOWX9910.

References

Apperley, M, Dahlberg, B., Jeffries, A., Paine, L., Phillips, M., & Rogers, W. (2001), Applications of Large Interactive Display Surfaces, Proceedings of SIGCHI NZ Symposium on Computer Human Interaction, Palmerston North, New Zealand, 3-7.

Apperley, M., Edwards, E., Jansen, S., Masoodian, M., McKoy, S., Rogers, W., Voyle, T., Ware, D., (2002), Applications of Imperfect Speech Recognition to Navigation and Editing of Audio Documents, Proceedings of SIGCHI NZ Symposium on Computer Human Interaction, Hamilton, New Zealand, 97-102

Elrod, S., Bruce, R., Gold, R, Goldberg, D., Halasz, F., Janssen, W.; Lee, D., McCall, K., Pedersen, E., Pier, K., Tang, J., and Welch, B., (1992), Liveboard: A Large Interactive Display Supporting Group Meetings, Presentations and Remote Collaboration. Conference Proceedings of ACM SIGCHI 1992, 599-607.

Gehne, R., and Jesshope, C. (2000), Tools for the Production of Small-Footprint, Low-Bandwidth, Streaming Multi-Media for Distance Education, Conference Proceedings of Lifelong Learning 2000, 240-244.

Jesshope, C. (2000), The Use of Multimedia in Internal and Extramural Teaching, Conference Proceedings of Lifelong Learning 2000, 257-262.

Smart Technologies (2002), http://www.smarttech.com/.

Virtual Ink Corporation (2002), http://www.mimio.com/.

Supporting Online Meetings between Research Students and Supervisors

Saturnino Luz
Department of Computer Science
University of Dublin
Trinity College
Dublin, Ireland
luzs@cs.tcd.ie

Masood Masoodian
Department of Computer Science
The University of Waikato
Hamilton, New Zealand
M.Masoodian@cs.waikato.ac.nz

Abstract: Face-to-face meetings between research students and their supervisors are very common. These meetings not only include the verbal interaction between the participants, but also often centre on research documents such as technical papers and reports. Therefore online meeting support systems need to facilitate audio communication as well as shared documents between meeting participants. Although currently there are systems which support audio interaction and sharing of documents, these generally do not provide any linking facilities between the recorded audio and textual contents of the online meetings. This paper discusses the results of a simple pilot study which shows that there is often a close link between the verbal communication and shared document interaction of research meeting participants. A prototype system called COMAP is being developed to allow indexing the recorded audio and textual contents of meetings based on the concepts of *temporal* and *contextual* neighbourhoods.

Introduction

Many university students, particularly at the postgraduate level, often conduct research work in collaboration with supervisors as part of their studies. The students generally meet face-to-face with their supervisors on a regular basis to discuss, plan, and monitor the progress of their research activities. In addition to verbal communication which forms an integral part of face-to-face meetings, research meetings also very often rely on written documents as the basis for discussion. Even when there is no shared document such as a technical report to focus on, the students or their supervisors are likely to take notes for future reference. These shared meeting documents, or personal notes would normally be annotated to include things such as changes, additions, responsibilities, future tasks, and so on which could then be used after the meeting to follow up on things that need to be done.

The audio content of meetings, on the other hand, is usually not recorded, and therefore lost. It is not uncommon for the meeting participants to forget details associated with some part of the meeting which is needed at a later stage. In some cases such details can be retrieved from meetings notes, if there are any, but often it might be necessary to contact the other meeting participants to find out if they remember the details. Clearly in the context of research activities, details or small bits of information can be critical.

An increasing number of students work on research projects with more than one supervisor, who may be located in different institutions or even different countries. In these situations it is not always possible to have face-to-face meetings, and as such, meetings may be conducted over the Internet. However, Internet-based remote meetings suffer from similar problems to those of face-to-face ones. Although there are systems which allow Internet-based audio conferencing, along with access to shared documents across distance, in most cases even if it is possible to record the audio and shared document contents of the meetings, it is not generally possible to link the audio recordings and shared documents.

The objective of this paper is to demonstrate that during research meetings verbal utterances of the participants are closely linked to their interactions with the contents of collaborative documents which form the shared group workspace. It is argued that due to this relationship it is useful to allow meeting participants to randomly access segments of the audio recordings using the indexed links between the audio and the contents of shared document. It is envisaged that such access would be valuable to users searching for information after the meeting. A prototype system is being developed to provide access to audio recording of the meetings using the contents of shared textual meeting documents. The system is based upon the concept of temporal and contextual neighbourhoods (Masoodian & Luz, 2001).

Nature of Research Meetings

The nature of group activities is largely dependent on the type of group task being performed by the participants. The range of research activities undertaken by research students in collaboration with their supervisors is diverse. Any system which aims to support online interaction between students and their supervisors needs to facilitate all these activities, which can be categorized as the following:

- Informal encounters where a shared textual tool acts as a focal point and serves as a medium for exchange of low level details. For instance, when people meet an exchange references, email addresses, etc.
- Formal meetings where a shared textual component acts as a focal point or as a collaboratively built lasting record of the transient speech interaction. For instance, research planning meetings.
- Document evaluation and revision meetings, particularly those supported by shared real-time editors in which text is loaded onto the collaborative tool at the beginning of the meeting, receiving only minor modifications as the meeting progresses. For instance, meetings to discuss a written thesis.
- The variants of collaborative writing described in (Posner & Baecker, 1993) as following a *joint writing strategy* in which people compose the text together, and even small components of the text are decided by group effort. For instance, when a research paper is being written.
- Shared projects, in particular the initial phases of such projects during which people discuss and agree on an interpretation of the problem, define their goals and plan their work, as well as the *integration phase* during which group members integrate their individual inputs. An example of this might be when a students and a supervisor are conducting an experiment.

What is common to all these activities is that they revolve around sharing information in the form of documents. Even when documents are not the focus, in most cases some form of a text artefact is used, such as minutes and action tables. Such documents generally assist people in working on collaborative activities, for instance by reminding them of the responsibilities they may have undertaken during the meeting, or perhaps providing them with information without which carrying out their task may be impossible. It is therefore clear that in many collaborative research scenarios, combinations of speech and text play a central role in the interaction process.

Participant	A	B	C	D	E	F	G	H	Average	Stdev
No. Utterances	225	192	121	125	214	163	126	155	165	39
Duration Speech /2700 Sec (s)	1681	1784	1932	2032	1202	751	499	587	1308	589
Duration Speech %	62	66	72	75	45	28	18	22	48	22
No. Text Activities /2700 Sec	34	74	99	72	37	10	36	63	53	27
Duration Text Activities /2700 Sec (s)	256	605	598	349	426	52	427	533	406	175
Duration Text Activities %	9	22	22	13	16	2	16	110	15	6
Total Duration Speech and Text Activities /2700 Sec (s)	1937	2389	2530	2381	1628	803	926	1120	1714	655
Total No. Speech and Text Activities /2700 Sec	259	266	220	197	251	173	162	218	218	37
No. Simultaneous Speech and Text Activities /2700 Sec	42	96	85	74	48	6	36	27	52	29
Duration Simultaneous Speech and Text Activities /2700 Sec (s)	189	341	562	329	226	17	99	69	229	167
Duration Simultaneous Speech and Text Activities %	7	13	21	12	8	1	4	3	8	6
Duration Inactive /2700 Sec (s)	952	651	732	648	1298	1914	1873	1649	1215	507
Duration Inactive %	35	24	27	24	48	71	69	61	45	19

Table 1: Summary of the analysis of the text and speech interaction between meeting participants

Pilot Study

A small pilot study was conducted to investigate the presence of patterns in the speech and text interaction during research type meetings which might be usefully exploited by an online meeting support system. Pairs of academics took part in four physically remote meetings whose goals were to plan and discuss research and teaching. Meeting were supported by an Internet-based audio conferencing tool, and a shared text editor. The duration of these meetings varied from approximately 20 to 90 minutes. All interaction events were recorded and time stamped. A summary of the analysis of the text and speech interaction between meeting participants is shown in Table 1.

Interleave Factor

The data gathered in the pilot study shows a pattern of co-occurrence of speech and text events which may provide valuable clues for information retrieval. In order to assess the impact that these clues might have it is necessary to quantify the extent to which an action conveyed by the speech medium is accompanied by another in text. A metric based on the degree of "interleaving" of text and speech events during meetings, which is call *Interleave Factor* or IF (Luz, 2002) can be used for this purpose.

The meetings evaluated in the pilot study received varied IF scores. Figure 1 shows sample step function plots of audio and text activity for two participants (*A* and *B*) over a 600-second interval. The meeting segment on the left hand side received an IF score of 0.067 while the one on the right hand side received 0.242. It was observed that, in general, the higher the IF of a segment the greater the likelihood that that segment contained relevant information about a particular item, as opposed to low-IF segments where that particular item also occurred. This observation motivates content mapping technique described below.

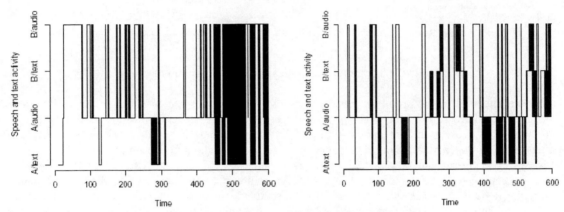

Figure 1: low (left) and high (right) IF segments.

Temporal and Contextual Neighbourhoods

A meeting support tool called COMAP (COntent MAPper) has been designed to allow indexing and retrieval of audio meeting contents using shared document contents. COMAP allows meeting participants to divide the contents of a meeting document into *logical sections*. These sections are then automatically linked by the system to different *segments* of the audio recording using the concept of *neighbourhood*. COMAP defines two types of neighbourhood:

- **temporal neighbourhood:** a segment of audio is in the temporal neighbourhood of a document section if that audio segment was recorded while the section was being *created*, *changed*, or *discussed* by the participants. There can be multiple audio segments in the temporal neighbourhood of a document section, each corresponding to different points in time when that section was *active* (see Figure 1).
- **contextual neighbourhood:** an audio segment is in the contextual neighbourhood of a document section when it shares a number of keywords with that section. There can be multiple audio segments in the temporal neighbourhood of a document section, each corresponding to different points in time when that section was *active* (Figure 2).

COMAP targets two basic scenarios: the system may act as a *listener* while the participants interact through the tools provided by COMAP, or the system may act as an *assistant* for browsing the meeting document along with the audio communication. Currently, COMAP assumes that the shared meeting documents will be textual. Since the text produced as a result of a meeting represents a more structured record of the information exchanged during the meeting, text is the starting point for the content indexing and browsing tools.

COMAP Prototype

A prototype has been built that explores one of the types of information mappings described above, namely, temporal neighbourhoods. The most attractive feature of temporal neighbourhoods from an implementation perspective is the fact that their extraction from a meeting record does not require any speech processing. Time stamps and keyword spotting are all that is needed. Figure 2 illustrates a text and an audio widget linked via temporal mappings. The timeline widget indicates presence of speech by means of horizontal bars stretching along the time axis. The words and phrases highlighted on the text pane are the starting point of the browsing activity. When related clusters of text are selected, the speech event viewer highlights the relevant segments.

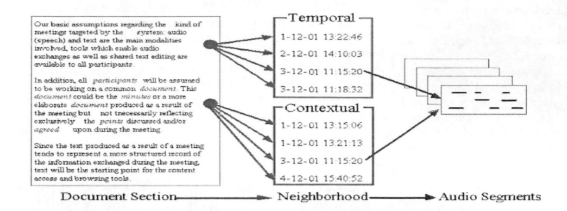

Figure 2: Temporal and contextual neighbourhood mapping

The architecture of the prototype basically consists of a *meeting memory server* and workstations which support a real-time shared editor and multi-party audio conferencing. During a meeting, both text and audio are multicast among the meeting participants using the RTP protocol (Schulzrine et al., 1999), and the COMAP server acts as a passive RTP listener, decoding RTP packets and recording audio and text on disk. After the meeting, these recordings can be accessed via the COMAP client. The shared text editor uses XML technology for tagging text segments and keeping track of document change history. At present, consistency is handled by allowing users to lock a particular node in the XML document tree. In this prototype, users are only allowed to lock paragraph nodes, since we have assumed that paragraphs are the relevant textual unit in temporal neighbourhoods. The audio client uses remote procedure calls to activate playback of audio segments linked to a particular paragraph, and the playback itself is performed via IP multicast. Both the shared text editor and the audio client are written in Java, which guarantees a certain degree of platform independence.

Conclusions

This paper presented an approach to structuring and accessing remote collaborative meeting audio and shared textual documents contents. It builds on notions of contextual and temporal neighbourhoods suggested by the levels of activity interleaving in trial data of student-supervisor meetings.

It is proposed that that our prototype COMAP system will be more useful for meetings which have a high text and audio activity interleave, measured using our notion of Interleave Factor (IF metrics). Future research directions include collecting a larger corpus of speech-and-text meeting data in order to further establish the relationship between IF and effectiveness of information access under varied circumstances, as well as the characteristics of temporal mapping in the presence of richer interaction logs.

References

Luz, S. (2002). Interleave Factor and multimedia visualisation interfaces. Proceedings of 16th British HCI Conference. London, UK. (in print)

Masoodian, M. & Luz, S. (2001). A content mapper for audio-mediated collaborative writing. *Proceedings of HCI International 2001* (pp. 208-212), M. J. Smith et Al. (eds.), New Orleans, LA, USA.

Posner, I. & Baecker, R. (1993). How People Write Together. *Readings in Computer Supported Collaborative Work* (pp. 239-250).

Schulzrine, H., Casner, S., Frederick, R. & Jacobson, V. (1999). RTP: A Transport Protocol for Real-Time Applications. *IETF Internet Draft.*

On-Demand Learning: Infrastructure Design and Management

Enid McCauley
Director, Product Development and Research
Open Learning Agency

Abstract:
On-Demand Learning: Infrastructure Design and Management, a research infrastructure grant from the Canada Foundation for Innovation and the British Columbia Knowledge Development Fund have provided the Product Development and Research Group at the Open Learning Agency the opportunity to explore new models for K-12 and post-secondary content development, storage, production, and sharing. It has also expanded the role of the Agency in the area of standards development nationally, and provided ways for us to address the issues of cultural change within the organization.

In 2000, the Open Learning Agency received infrastructure funding from the Canada Foundation for Innovation and the BC Knowledge Development Fund to further research and development initiatives into digital learning object design, development, and implementation. This five-year research and development project has had significant impact on the Open Learning Agency both in the way it conducts it's course development activities, and in its ability to play a substantial role in the area of standards development internationally.

The research focus of the CFI/BCKDF initiative is the design and implementation of instructional content, both SGML/XML structured content, and digital video content. It also focuses on learning environments and applications that provide on-demand, self-directed learning. This includes establishing and implementing an enterprise-wide repository for the development and management of "learning objects" (text, image, audio, and video), defining ways to effectively re-purpose and re-package these objects to meet the education and training needs of individuals, and designing web-based learning management systems that provide the learner with the ability to create their own "learning path" from the repository of objects.

The infrastructure being acquired to continue our research into effective strategies for the development and use of "learning objects" at an enterprise-wide level, and even more broadly in terms of sharing information, strategies and resources with partner institutions and programs across Canada, includes:

- Installation of Lightspeed's Astoria digital object repository and iEngine management system
- Development of prototype learning management systems (e.g. Learning Lab) and integration with existing learning management systems (e.g. WebCT)
- Hardware and software for development of digital media objects and structured course content.
- Publishing applications to move from structured information to the web or print.
- Web interface tools for distributed authoring directly into the repository.

Our research and development program addresses the critical design and management challenges facing education and training organizations as they begin to exploit new information technologies. These include:

- How to use structured information models in the design, development and delivery of distributed learning programs
- How to design granular learning objects (text, image, audio, video) that facilitate multiple pedagogical models and enable multiple user requirements in an on-demand fashion
- How to develop multiple output formats to meet particular and individualized client needs from unified development processes
- How to use metadata classification systems to facilitate open learning pedagogy and the transfer of assets between academic and business partners

- How to re-purpose and re-package "learning objects" to meet the education and training needs of individuals and organizations
- How to incorporate an enterprise-wide approach into the design, development, and management of "learning objects".
- How to manage the changing culture of post-secondary content development and delivery from the "cottage industry" to the "learning object" models.

The Open Learning Agency research and development initiatives into structured information are becoming core practice as we begin to change the traditional post-secondary development model. This difficult cultural change requires that a proven prototype in which traditional course designers and faculty can become involved be available for "practice", it requires significant staff training, it requires participation and buy-in from a wide variety of staff, and it requires strong leadership.

The Open Learning Agency research and development plan focused on three major projects to develop and test the model. Initially, we began with structured development in our K-12 program, developing 14 senior secondary courses in SGML for output to the web and to print. This major project, OSCAR, provided a wealth of learning for staff, and became the basis for all our further SGML work.

From this basis, we developed a resource-rich teacher education program using open source technology for self-directed learning (The Learning Lab), and a competency-based business program (the New Management Degree). As more and more post-secondary course development is beginning to follow the structured information process, the key issues which confront us are staff development, implementation of production workflow, output from the repository to high-quality web and print formats, and template design.

This presentation will provide an overview of the CFI/BCKDF project to date, and address the cultural change issues we face as we move towards a learning object economy.

Description of Project:

This project addresses the issues of university pre-service and K-12 teachers' perceptions concerning technology and the role of collaboration in utilizing technological applications presented in professional development sessions offered at the university. The dimensions addressed include Higher Education and K-12 in the *Application* domain, Human-Computer Interaction in the *Technology* domain, and Collaborative Learning and Work in the *Strategic Focus* domain. Through funding provided by a PT3 grant (Preparing Tomorrows Teachers to Use Technology Today) at the University of Houston-Clear Lake, university pre-service teachers in their first semester of internship were paired for technology training with their mentor teachers from the public schools. The two groups met at the university for numerous one day workshops which provided training and instruction in areas such as: creating web pages, exploring websites with teacher resources, the use of chat rooms, technology applications in the one computer classroom, numerous technology software packages, and various other computer applications.

After the semester long training, a questionnaire designed by the researcher was administered to 15 pre-service teachers and their public school mentors. The instrument focused on four major areas: 1) technology use 2) attitudes toward technology 3) role of collaboration in learning about and utilizing technology, and 4) perceptions of student engagement potential. Items listed in the questionnaire were determined by examining background literature as well as similar studies. To help validate the instrument, three Instructional Technology professors provided feedback and suggestions on the survey instrument used in the study. After administering the questionnaire, themes and patterns which emerge will be discussed and implications for future research will be noted.

Major Aspects:

The major aspects of the project include a review of the relevant literature and the findings from the questionnaire. The literature review focuses on pre-service and mentor teachers' attitudes toward technology, the ways in which they explore and learn about technology, how teachers incorporate it into their classrooms, and the role of collaboration in becoming literate in the area of technology. The major research questions for this project are:

What types of technology applications do teachers and pre-service teachers utilize?

What types of attitudes do teachers and pre-service teachers have about learning technology-based applications?

What differences, if any, are there among teachers' and pre-service teachers' perceptions about the impact of technology on student learning?

What types of interactions and collaborations (if any) take place as teachers seek to learn about and incorporate technology tools into their classroom communities?

Review of Literature

The review of the literature focuses on three major areas, primarily teachers' perceptions and attitudes dealing with technology, teachers' perceptions of the role of collaboration in learning technology, and teachers' perceptions of the effect of technology on student engagement levels. While there is much written about the evidence that the educational benefits of technology abound (Fletcher, Hawley, and Piele, 1990; Garner & Gillingham, 1996; Kulik & Kulik, 1991), relatively few teachers utilize technology regularly in their teaching (McKinsey, 1996; OTA, 1995). One part of this study seeks to identify the types of applications that teachers and pre-service teachers are familiar with and utilize.

Simply receiving training in technology, though, is no guarantee that it will be infused into the learning environment of the classroom. In a 1998 survey by the U.S. Department of Education, 78 percent of teachers reported that they had participated in professional development about integrating technology into the grade or subject they taught during the last twelve months. In spite of this level of participation, only 20 percent said they felt well prepared to integrate technology into their day to day teaching (National Foundation for the Improvement of Education, 2000).

Perhaps one way to address this issue is to facilitate collaborative efforts within the scope of professional development opportunities. In the process of learning about new technology related applications and making the shift to actual using the information, collaboration can serve as a pivotal force in implementation. Our training at the university sought to do this by allowing the mentors and pre-service teachers to attend the training sessions together. There is much research to show that more sophisticated learning occurs when collaboration takes place. Teaching and learning become interwoven and the learning environment becomes one that is designed for exploration and interaction, and learners are given the opportunity to creatively apply new information (Ferguson & Kopp, 1998). In addition, teachers working together to explore the teaching and learning arena is directly linked to effective schools (Johnson, 1986; Glatthorn and Fox, 1996).

Ideally then, teachers can experience some of the same things we want public school students to experience- engagement with the experience at hand.
Support for this view comes from various sources, starting with the work of Jean Piaget who found that children who are actively engaged assimilate new information more efficiently. The trend in education is moving toward a constructivist view which contends that learning is achieved through relevant, hands-on, socially constructed activities (Ferguson & Kopp, 1998).

The socially constructed nature of learning and the importance of experiential experiences are tapped into to bring about a shift in learners' technological schema. In addition, technology has the added benefit of being a motivational tool. Used appropriately, the use of technology has the potential to affect student engagement. In Means' case studies of 17 classes which incorporated computer usage at nine reform-oriented schools (collected during 1991-1993), it was found that the most common or nearly universal teacher reported effect on students was an increase in motivation (Means and Olson, 1995)

Another promising piece of research shows that exposing teachers to the notion that technology can be an empowering tool to facilitate higher level learning activities can be enough to bring about incremental change. Heath and Burns et al (2000) found that for many teachers knowing how computer technology could be used to enhance learning and being able to plan effective learning activities were more important than having strong personal computer skills. In other words, even teachers who do not feel that they have totally mastered technological applications can begin to think of ways to use technology to advance higher order thinking in their students.

Technology has already had a hand in reshaping business, industry, and the global economy. It has the power to reconfigure the world of education by providing a tool to enhance teaching and learning; but to do this, teachers who currently work in our schools as well as those pre-service teachers who are the future of our schools must be supported and provided with appropriate arenas to explore and implement technology into classroom communities.

References

Ferguson, K.M. & Kopp, O. P. (1998). Technological collaborations: K-12 and Higher Education. Phi Delta Kappa Fastbacks, no. 4387-41.

Fletcher, J.D., Hawley, D.E., & Piele, P.K. (1990). Costs, effects, and utility of microcomputer assisted instruction in the classroom. American Educational Research Journal, 27 (4), 783-806.

Garner, R., & Gillingham, M. (1996). Internet communication in six classrooms: Conversations across time, space, and culture. Mahwah, NJ: Erlbaum.

Glatthorn, A. A. & Fox, L.E. (1996). Quality teaching through professional development. Thousand Oaks, CA: Corwin Press, Inc..

Johnson, S. M. (1986). Incentives for teachers: What motivates, what matters. Educational Administration Quarterly, 22 (3), 54-79.

Kulik, C.L. & Kulik, J.A. (1991). Effectiveness of computer based instruction: an updated analysis. Computers in Human Behavior, 7, 75-94.

McKinsey, I. (1995). A nation of opportunity: Realizing the promise of the information superhighway. A report prepared for the National Information Infrastructure Advisory Council.

National Foundation for the Improvement of Education (2000). "Professional Development and Information Technologies." <u>Connecting the bits: A reference for using technology in teaching and learning in K-12 schools</u>.

The Canadian Design Website:
An Evaluation of Process and Product

Laura April McEwen, Department of Education, Concordia University, Canada, laura@education.concordia.ca

Gretchen Lowerison Department of Education, Concordia University, Canada, gretchen@coreidea.com

Lydia F. Sharman, Department of Design Arts, Concordia Univeristy, Canada, lydia@vax2.concordia.ca

Abstract: The Canada Design Website is a pedagogical resource project located at http://design.concordia.ca/canada_design/. Initially, conceptualized as a pedagogical resource focused on Canadian industrial design, the project has expanded to include the collaborative efforts of undergraduate, graduate and faculty members of the Department of Design Arts at Concordia University. Currently at the end of the second phase of the project, a review of the site to date and an evaluation of the process engaged in by student contributors was initiated. Preliminary findings revealed that learners gained valuable practical experience through this innovative learning initiative but felt that this positive experience might have been enhanced with more clearly defined roles and responsibilities. Several important recommendations from the media/pedagogical expert for improvements to the site included navigation instructions for visitors and enhanced interactivity.

Introduction

A common purpose of course related websites is to serve as an information-delivery medium (Hall, 2002). The World Wide Web has allowed innovative ways to present material. Learners can be presented with text, graphics, animation and multiple ways to navigate through the site. In this multi-media environment, there is an opportunity to engage the learner and enhance the educational experience (Kuh and Vespers, 2001). However, the effectiveness of the media will dependent upon how it is designed in connection with the curriculum (Whitston, 1998).

Hypertext can be used as a cognitive tool. When the learner is presented with material in a hypertext environment, such as the World Wide Web, the locus of control shifts from the designer to the learner. Within this context, learners stand to gain greater control over the learning environment (Hutchings, et al. 1992). Such advantages are dependent upon characteristics of the site design. For example, material might be linked to learning activities that would allow the learner to become proactive, promoting deep-level learning. However, in a more static site, the learner remains passive, knowledge is more declarative and learning is more surface-level.

Background

The site is a scholarly information site presenting Canadian industrial design content. The pilot project was conceptualized in 1996 by Dr. Lydia F. Sharman. As a professor in the Department of Design Arts at Concordia University, she struggled with the lack of pedagogical resources and often drew on personal archive to support her pedagogy. Out of this practical pedagogical need grew the idea for Canada Design Website (CDWebsite). The web offered a particularly appropriate medium as it made it possible to present, in a dynamic form, designers and their products as well as external links to sites of relevance.

During Phase One of the project, content was drawn from Dr. Sharman's archives assembled over a thirty years period. Phase Two of the project involved student researchers developing content from archives and additional primary sources.

An evaluation of the process engaged in by student contributors and the CDWebsite is currently underway. This paper presents the results of the media/ pedagogical expert's review of the site and the preliminary findings from interviews with graduate and undergraduate learners regarding their experiences as content developers. Site development is ongoing and additional data collection and analysis is planned.

The Website Evaluation
Objectives

The purpose of the Website evaluation was to examine the quality of the product to date. The goal of the evaluation was to provide recommendations for improvements to the site.

Methods
Instrument

Evaluation Rubric: The rubric used to evaluate the Canadian design site was developed by the media/pedagogy expert based on the work of Rathswohl, (2002). The following six general areas of focus were identified: (a) General features such as name, URL, author and contributors, (b) Purpose and objectives of the site such as scholarly versus personal, clearly stated purpose and target audience, (c) Navigation and Accuracy such as ease of access, modes of access, internal and external links and accuracy of content, (d) Structure, such as display, quality of graphics and professional design qualities, (e) Pedagogy, such as locus of learner control, interactivity, communication, context, sensory features and information, and (f) Coding features, such as accessibility and browser support of material.

Procedures

Website Evaluation: To meet the objective of ascertaining the pedagogical value of the site, two types of expert reviews were planned: (a) content, and (b) media/ pedagogical. Guided by the evaluation rubric, a media/ pedagogical expert reviewed the presentation and effectiveness aspects of the site. Content reviews with university professors from outside Concordia are planned, as well as several one to one reviews with student volunteers to establish end-users perceptions.

Results

Navigation	<ul><li>Should be more intuitive, currently visitors must rely on trial and error to discover how to gain access to material.</li><li>Links should be uniform throughout the site and easily identifiable as hyperlinks/graphics.</li><li>A navigational option other than the browser back key should be incorporated to facilitate returning to the start page.</li></ul>
Pedagogy	<ul><li>More learner control is recommended. Information is presented fairly linearly, visitors may choose the order of module presentation, but are unable to explore the content of the module prior to selecting it.</li><li>Instructions should be made available to visitors unfamiliar with rollover functionality.</li><li>Adding an element of interactivity would allow the users of the site to be more dynamically involved and perhaps to exchange information and opinions. This would increase the learning potential of the site.</li></ul>
Coding Structure	<ul><li>A document type declaration should be added.</li><li>The use of frames may cause accessibility problems for those without frame capable browsers, and potentially lead to navigational problems for visitors with disabilities.</li><li>ALT tags should be used to describe images on pages for people using non-visual browsers</li><li>A title for every page should be included</li><li>To facilitate maintenance of the site and reduce the size of HTML files, cascading style sheets could be used to specify font, size and color.</li></ul>

Table 1: Findings and Recommendations

The Evaluation of Process
Objectives
The purpose of the evaluation of process was to explore the process engaged in by student contributors. The goal of the evaluation was to (a) define roles and responsibilities, (b) identify the type and sources of support, (c) determine the personal impact of involvement in project and (d) describe personal learning gains.

Methods
Procedures
To meet the objectives listed above, interviews were conducted with three categories of learners. The details of the process evaluation are presented in Table 2. Learners' responses to interview questions were compiled in tabular form in order of their occurrence and then grouped into categories that emerged from the data. Examples of some direct quotes are included in Table. Ongoing informal interviews with Dr. Sharman also provided information regarding learner support. The instructor of the course *History of Canadian Design* also completed a questionnaire, however these results are not included in this paper.

Results

Information gathered	Category of Learner		
	Former Design Arts student	**Graduate student, Design Art**	**Undergraduate (UG) Students in *Canadian Design History***
Type of Contribution	Web Designer	Research Assistant/ Content Developer	Content Developers
Define role and responsibilities	Evolved from site developer to include project management aspects and learner support.	Reported initial confusion regarding role and responsibilities. Had anticipated taking on a site development role.	Strictly content development role, ▪ "write short factual summaries on various aspects of the Montreal Metro's design"(UG1), ▪ "Condense research paper, define segments of intensity"(UG2) Both students hoped the project would allow them the opportunity to engage in web development.
Identified types and sources of support	▪ Provided guidance to graduate student regarding issues of accessibility related to site design. ▪ Developed template for student contributions. ▪ Provided guidance regarding the focus and organization of content.	Team meetings ▪ held every one and a half months. Dr. Sharman ▪ individual content focused meeting. ▪ Editing via email was fast and informative. Web Designer/Project manager ▪ Discussed web design issues (re: image selection, file format)	Canadian Design History Instructor ▪ provided strong support for the development of research skills. Dr Sharman ▪ provided examples of other contributions and links to completed modules on the site. ▪ Ongoing feedback on drafts via email. Web Designer/ Project manager ▪ offered guidance regarding file formatting, image selection ▪ provided supported for the content development stage Team meeting—were invited once and found this to be very advantageous.
Determined personal impact of involvement in project	Launched career in Web Design.	"I learnt that design with Dreamweaver is not what I'd want to do for a living"	UG1: access to designer of Montreal Metro for personal interview. UG2: "The opportunity to work with Dr. Sharman, someone with such extensive knowledge and interest in Canadian Design".
Describe personal learning gains	Gained important project management experience.	Improved English language writing and research skills.	▪ Developed Interview skills (UG1) ▪ Both learners mentioned access to primary source material

Table 2: Preliminary Interview Results

Concluding Remarks
The Canadian Design Website

The Canada Design Project is a very professional looking site. It serves as an information-delivery medium rather than a dynamic site. A search through Google (http://www.google.com) indicates that this is a unique resource for Canadian Design content. In order for the site to become an effective learning tool interactivity needs to be increased.

It is important for the designer to accommodate students' different learning rates and styles as well as diverse background knowledge. In order for the site to be effective, it should attract the attention of the learner but not be so overwhelming that the material is distracting. Hannafin, et al. (1996) points out that students can have trouble navigating in a hypermedia environment when the environment is new. For this reason, it is important to include navigation instructions.

The Evaluation of Process

According to preliminary findings, all categories of student contributors gained substantially from this innovative learning experience. Proponents of constructivist pedagogy support the use of project-based learning initiatives such as these, based on this potential diversity of learning gains (Linn & Burbules, 1993). However, learners' responses indicate a degree of confusion and disappointment regarding respective roles and responsibilities at the outset of the project. Additional data not included in this report would suggest that this confusion was the result of unanticipated challenges related to (a) learner competencies and level of engagement, and (b) limitation in terms of access to technology tools. This inevitably resulted in the subsequent scaling back of student involvement in the web design aspects of the project. Given the obvious enthusiasm for this aspect of the project, it is highly recommended that additional resources be allocated to ensure students more hands on experience with web design in the future.

References

Hall, R. (2002). Aligning learning, teaching and assessment using the web: an evaluation of pedagogic approaches. British Journal of Educational Technology, 33(2), 149-158.

Hutchings, G.A., Hall, W. Hammond, N.V., Kibby, M.R., McKnight,C. & Riley, D. (1992) Authoring and evaluation of hypermedia for education. Computers and Education, 18, 171-7.

Kuh, G.D., & Vespers, N. (2001). Do computers enhance or detract from student learning? Research in Higher Education, 42(1), 87-102.

Linn,C. and Burbules, N.C. (1993). In Tobin, K. (Ed.). The Practice of Constructivism in Science Education. AAAS PRESS: Washington, DC.

Rathswohl, E. J. (2002). A technique for teaching website effectiveness in undergraduate I.S. Classes, InSite, June 2002. Available online at http://ecommerce.lebow.drexel.edu/eli/2002Proceedings/ papers/Raths238techn.pdf

Whitston, K. (1998). Key skills and curriculum reform. Studies in Higher Education, 23(3), 307-319.

Acknowledgements

We would like to acknowledge Concordia University and the McConnell Family Foundation for the on-going funding of this innovative pedagogical resource.

Personality as a theoretical construct for the development of effective school leaders

Lead Presenter
Dr. Michael L. McFrazier
Director of Graduate Programs
Assistant Professor, Ed Leadership and Counseling
Prairie View A and M University
P.O. Box 2355
Prairie View, TX 77446 2355
Michael_McFrazier@pvamu.edu

Co Presenter
Dr. Pamela Barber Freeman
Prairie View A and M University
P.O. Box 4349
Prairie View, TX 77446 4349
Pamela_Freeman@pvamu.edu

According to research, the personal attributes of effective leaders have been examined for decades. In fact, during the turn of the 20th century, theorists believed that leaders were born not made (Davis 1998). This premise is no longer accepted in institutions of higher education because of the large numbers of educational leaders graduating from colleges and universities. This research project examined, via technology, the personality strengths and developmental needs of students enrolled in their first semester of course work at Prairie View A and M University.

After almost two decades of school reform efforts in America, there are still millions of children being left behind. Specifically, the Texas Public Schools Statistic (1999) indicates that African American students comprised 18.7 percent of dropouts while Hispanic Americans made up 51.3 percent. According to research, one reason for this failure is due to the quality of leadership as well as the lack of sensitivity to the cultural dynamics within our nation (Wallace Reader's Digest 2000; Astin and Astin 2000).

There is a critical need for educational leaders to develop a keen understanding of the challenges faced by students. Today's students come from a variety of cultures, religions and economic levels; consequently, arriving to school at different ability levels. In addition, environmental conditions may have circumstances that challenge students' time and attention that could or should be devoted to learning. To cope effectively and creatively with these emerging trends, future leaders will need to possess new knowledge and skills as well as displaying a high level of emotional and spiritual wisdom and maturity (Astin and Astin 2000). As the public sector becomes more sophisticated, as well as impatient, critical questions are being asked and stringent limitations will be placed on institutions of higher education. Institutions of higher education play a major role in developing and shaping the quality of leadership in modern American society (Astin and Astin 2000). Thus, it is imperative that institutions of higher education begin to develop a conceptual framework to train and support leaders who will expand the variety and character of their school district's educational programs. After all, it is character, not money that fosters prosperity.

The face of our society is literally being altered due to the tremendous changes in the economic, educational, and demographic forces. The rapid change in the demographics of the United States has made diversity one of the most significant social facets of our society. Due to differential birthrates and immigration patterns, America is experiencing a major ethnic shift with increased numbers of African Americans, Hispanic Americans, and Asian Americans becoming more evident within our schools. In Texas, African Americans and Hispanic Americans youth constitute 53 percent of the school age population and have the highest dropout rate of any other ethnic group within the state. In postsecondary institutions enrollment of the diverse groups are declining. With the continuous increase of a diverse population, it becomes quite apparent that the dynamics of the culturally heterogeneous world have become both complex and problematic. In fact, one of the most compelling needs of our time is to reach for the "forgotten half" of our population who have the capability of leading but are being left behind by the new economy. Specifically, educational leaders do not begin to reflect public school diversity with only 12 percent of the nation's superintendents being female, and only 5 percent being people of color. In addition, leadership positions are expected to increase by 16percent by the year 2008, making it the largest increase of any other major occupation (U.S. Department of Labor, 2000). Thus, creating a greater need for more inclusion of all ethnic groups who have the theoretical and methodological tools to help frame and answer questions that concern all Americans.

Accepting the premise that higher education is the pipeline for developing productive citizens, academia must take the opportunity to lead the way and demonstrate to the rest of the nation how to accept and nurture a diverse community of leaders. Consequently, the question is whether institutions of higher education are up to the challenge of meeting the needs of this diverse population. Therefore, it seems practical as well as necessary for those institutions (HBCUs) that are graduating the largest numbers of diverse students to become an active and viable component in developing leaders, in reforming curriculum standards and providing training for personnel who will lead and educate America's future citizenry. Because education is a continuum (not just Kthrough12), it is imperative that programs/institutions that educate and train preservice and inservice leader become active with educational reform. Since HBCUs facilitate the largest numbers of diverse leaders on the educational continuum, there are needs for leadership centers on HBCU campuses to provide our nation and the world with leaders equipped with new knowledge and strategies for educational reform.

During the sixteenth century, Martin Luther is noted for stating, "...when a man knows his own heart, he knows the heart of other men." Specifically, if educators have a strong grasp of their attributes, learning styles and personality preference they become more in tuned to their students regardless of ethnicity. Consequently, this research was based on the above premise in order for future educational leaders to reach their educational, professional and personal potential, they must be actively involved in developing and implementing instructional models. The primary outcome sought through this research was to promote what Franke, Carpenter, Fennema, Ansell, and Behrend (1998) call "selfsustaining, generative change." Selfsustaining, generative change is when individuals make changes to improve their methods of leadership and instruction to ensure continued growth and problem solving. To ensure that selfsustaining, generative change is on going, a personality assessment was conducted. One's personality is without question the most important driver influencing career choice, relationships, health and sense of well being (Shaughnessy, 1998). To understand the full potential of one's personality, it is critical to first measure and then gain insight into your strengths and developmental needs through examining the results of personality.

In 2001, The American Association of Colleges for Teacher Education (AACTE) cited Prairie View A and M University as fourth in the nation in the production of school administrators. Prairie View, the 2nd oldest institution of higher education in the state of Texas, is committed to providing state of the art training to individuals who will lead and educate America's future citizenry. Data for this research project were gathered during the month of July during the 2nd summer session at Prairie View. One hundred educational leadership students enrolled in their 1st semester of course work were used as research participants for this study. Each student was asked to complete a personality assessment (Keirsey) via technology. Ninety three usable personality assessments were returned. Research participants were also asked to provided additional data in the following areas: Age: 0 through 24, 25 through 35, 36 through 45, 46+; Gender: Female, Male
Career: Elementary, Middle, Secondary, Other; Race: African American, Caucasian, Hispanic. Currently, the data are being analyzed and prepared for presentation. The preliminary findings suggest that over 50 percent of the students assessed are Guardians, which indicates that they have the temperament for leadership!

Distance learning supports: The intentionality of pre-assessment surveys

Patricia McGee
University of Texas at San Antonio
Department of Interdisciplinary Studies and Curriculum and Instruction
The University of Texas at San Antonio, US
pmcgee@utsa.edu

Abstract. One response to high attrition rates in distance learning has been strategies devised to support the learner during their course and, in some instances, before they begin a course. Pre-assessment surveys are the most common pre-course support. This study investigates the content of surveys used in higher education as they relate to research on successful learner attributes. Findings indicate that most surveys are designed, whether intentionally or not, to discourage or eliminate learners who do not posses successful skills, knowledge, or attributes and which may account for reported low dropout rates.

Attrition rates remain higher than in campus-based courses (Phipps & Merisotis, 1999; Kelman, 1997; Naidu, 1994; Garland, 1993; McKinnon, 1993), and tend to be higher for first-time distance learners (Morgan, 2000). Research suggests that although attrition rates are high in distance learning courses, the reasons for these rates are not clear and research has not conclusively identified causes (Sheets, 1992, Thompson, 1997; Parker, 1999). Often demographics (Thompson, 1997) are attributed to attrition, such as learner maturity and motivation, age, gender or instructor experience and expertise (Carr, 2000). Other factors include conflicts with work schedules (Henke & Russom, 2000), poor time management skills, and ill-defined educational goals (Parker, 1995). In those cases where attrition rates are low, explanations are suspect because there is little evidence that success in a distance learning course is nothing more than a matter of learner characteristics. Even for the experienced distance learner there is no guarantee that the context, interactions, or conceptualization of content will resemble previous course experiences. Most distance learning programs attempt to provide services that support the distance learner once they are enrolled in a course to reduce drop-out rates (Oliver, 1999; Morgan, Dingsdag, & Saenger, 1998; Portier & Wagemans, 1995; Wright, 1991).

One commonly used pre-course service is a self-assessment tool that either allows the student to measure his or her preparedness for taking a distance learning course or serves as an anticipatory set[1] by intimating the nature of a distance learning course. Such self-assessment tools are typically in the form of a 10-15 question survey in which the respondent answers 'yes' or 'no' to a series of learner behaviors attributes, or competencies such as those identified by Rowntree (1995): computer skills, literacy/discussion skills, time management skills, and interactive skills. These types of self-assessment instruments assume that the learner will (a) complete the survey, (b) reflect upon and honestly respond to the queries, and (c) take in consideration the analysis when determining to take a course. However, there is no assurance that potential students use the survey to determine whether or not they should take an online course but may serve to eliminate students that do not fit a successful profile.

This study examines US university-delivered distance learning courses, (rather than programs) which are offered as options to brick and mortar campus course offerings. If pre-course surveys are intended as a support to the learner then they should identify skills, knowledge, and abilities necessary for successful completion of the course. An initial review of such surveys (McGee, 2001) suggests that such instruments are written to identify the traits of the *successful* distance learner and whether intentionally or not, serve as a self-selecting tool to eliminate those learners who do not have the desired attributes. The research question is: What content are pre-course surveys derived from?

Method

After searching online course directories, 50 institutions that offered distance learning courses and had Web sites were identified. Each site was examined for online supports to prepare the distance learner; typically these were in the form of a survey or a Frequently-Asked-Questions page. From the 50 sites identified, 38 offered pre-assessment surveys. All 38 were selected as the study sample. Survey items from the 38 pre-assessment surveys were analyzed and categorized holistically. Since many of the items from different surveys were ver batim, it was not difficult to group like items. Categories were determined based on existing ontologies of disciplinary concepts, i.e. motivation, learning style, self-regulation, etc. A literature review identified characteristics of (a) successful distance learners and (b) learner

---

[1] Relates prior experiences to new learning.

practices for success in a distance learning course. These attributes where then correlated with topics identified through data analysis.

Findings

A topical analysis of survey items identified three major areas of skills, abilities, and knowledge: environmental preferences, learning preferences, and cognitive skills, see Figure 1. Many surveys were identical suggesting that surveys had been borrowed or copied form similar sources. Due to space limitations, only significant findings are reported here.

Figure 1
Pre-assessment Survey Analysis (N=38)

Traits	#	Literature
Environmental Preferences		
Technology Preference	20	Eastmond (1995); Willis (1994)
Flexible time schedule	29	Liviertos & Franks (1996); Willis, (1994); Hyatt (1992); Hezel & Dirr (1991)
Convenience	13	Willis, 1994; Hezel & Dirr, 1991
Self-Regulation[2]	31	Parker (1995); Laube (1992)
Independent learner	15	Suet (1998);Cook, (1997); Hardy & Boaz (1997); Barrell (1995); Biner, Bink, Huffman, & Dean, (1995); Burge (1994) Diaz, (2000);
Internal locus of control[3]		Dille & Mezack (1991); Jonassen & Grabinger (1988); Stone (1992)
Motivation	26	Burge (1994); Schlosser & Anderson (1994); Souder, (1993); Laube (1992);Office of Technology Assessment (1989)
Time Management	31	Hardy & Boaz (1997); Stone (1992)
Technology Proficiency/Comfort	18	Gunawardena (1992)
Learning Preferences		
Interaction	14	Coggins (1998)
Classroom Discussion	16	Powers & Mitchell (1997)
Instructor	16	Burge (1994)
Cognitive Skills and Abilities		Smith & Dunn, (1991)
Reading Literacy	28	
Writing Ability and Comfort	13	Stovalt, Kelly, & Lieberman (1998)

Discussion

Findings indicate that pre-assessment surveys focus on either research-based characteristics of the successful learner or extrapolations from the same. For example, maturity is often cited characteristic of a successful online learner. Maturity is often cited as an indicator of persistence, motivation, and responsibility. However, if maturity is often defined in terms of age rather than other indicators which may more accurately define maturity, such as decision-making or problem-solving abilities. Research that explores more deeply into the reported experiences of the learner and their characteristics suggest that learners' reported data might not be reliable (Rubenson & Woodley, 1987). Morgan and Tam (1999) found that when questioned at length about reported reasons for not completing a course or their poor performance, learners often gave very different reasons from what was specified on a questionnaire or survey[4]. Clearly pre-assessment instruments are self-selecting tools to recruit learners with the most likely traits for success. More importantly, few contingencies or supports exist (in most online learning environments) that can aid a potential distance learner in acquiring skills or knowledge necessary to succeed in an electronic learning environment. Without these supports novice distance learners may be at risk of failure (Dille & Mezack, 1991). Additionally, there is no evidence

---

[2] Self-regulation as it relates to academic settings involves the abilities to plan, organize, and manage learning experiences while accessing appropriate resources, and self-evaluate progress (Bandura, 1997 as cited in King, Harner, Scott, and Brown , 2000). Includes persistence.
[3] Although locus of control is not directly stated in any of the surveys, the attributes of internal locus of control were evident, including: takes responsibility, independent, self-motivated, persistent, and proactive.
[4] Morgan and Tam found that barriers to success and course completion fell into one of four categories: situational, institutional, dispositional or epistemological.

that accommodations for a range of abilities, skill levels, or learning styles are part of distance learning course design. It is a one-size fits all approach assuming that distance learners are a homogenous group. Yet the notion of distance learner as "static" rather than dynamic is increasingly questioned and believed to be invalid (Thompson, 1997; Holmberg, 1995).

The increasing trend toward transforming face-to-face courses into virtual ones with little or no preparation on the part of the course instructor necessitates informed, calculated, and strategic study and implementation of effective adragological approaches to teaching online as well as providing seamless supports and alternatives for all learners.

References

Bandura, A. (1997). *Self-efficacy: the exercise of control.* New York, NY: W. H. Freeman and Company.

Barell, J. (1995). *Critical issue: Working toward student self-direction and personal efficacy as educational goals.* Retrieved on May 27, 2001, from http://www.ncrel.org/sdrs/areas/issues/students/learning/lr200.htm.

Biner, P., Bink, M., Huffman, M., and Dean R. (1995). Personality characteristics differentiating and predicting the achievement of televised-course students and traditional course students. *The American Journal of Distance Education 9* (2), 4 - 18.

Brent, F.L. & Bugbee, A.C. (1993). Study practices and attitudes related to academic success in a distance learning programme. *Distance Education, 14* (1), 97-112.

Brown, B. M. (1998). Digital classrooms: Some myths about developing new educational programs using the Internet. *T.H.E. Journal* [online}. Available : http://www.the journal.com/magazine/98/dec/feat04.html

Burge, E. J. (1994). Learning in computer conferenced contexts: The learners' perspective. *Journal of Distance Education, 9* (1), 19-43.

Carr, S. (2000, February 11). As distance education comes of age, the challenge is keeping the students. *The Chronicle of Higher Education.* pp. A39-41.

Coggins, C. C. (1988)). Preferred learning styles and their impact on completion of external degree programs. *The American Journal of Distance Education, 2* (1), 25-37.

Cook, K. (1997). Locus of control and choice of course delivery mode at an Ontario community college Unpublished research report. Retrieved on April 1, 2000 from http://www.oise.utoronto.ca/~kcook/qrp.htm

Diaz, D. P. (2000). Comparison of student characteristics, and evaluation of student success in an online health education course. Unpublished doctoral dissertation, Nova University, Fort Lauderdale, Florida. Retrieved on March 2002 from http://www.LTSeries.com/LTS/pdf_docs/dissertn.pdf

Diaz, D. P., & Cartnal, R. B. (1999). Students' learning styles in two classes: Online distance learning and equivalent on-campus. *College Teaching, 47* (4), 130-135.

Dille, B., & Mezack, M. (1991). Identifying predictors of high risk among community college telecourse students. *The American Journal of Distance Education, 5* (1), 24-35.

Eastmond, N. F. (1995). *Alone but together: Adult distance study through computer conferencing.* Cresskill, NJ: Hampton Press.

Egan, M.W., Sebastian, J., & Welch, M. (1991, March). *Effective television teaching: Perceptions of those who count most...distance learners.* Proceedings of the Rural Education Symposium, Nashville, TN. (ED 342 579)

Garland, M. R. (1993). Student perceptions of situational, institutional, dispositional, and epistemological barriers to persistence. *Distance Education, 14* (2), 13-24.

Gee, J. P. 1990. *Social linguistics and literacies: Ideology in discourses.* London:Falmer Press.

Gunawardena, C. (1992). Changing faculty roles for audiographics and online teaching. *The American Journal of Distance Education, 6* (32), 58-71.

Hardy, D., & Boaz, M. H. (1997). Learner development: Beyond the technology. *New Directions for Teaching and Learning, 71,* 41-48.

Henke, H, & Russom, J. (2000). Factors Influencing Attrition Rates in a Corporate Distance Education Program. *Education at a Distance Journal, 14* (11). Retrieved on April 4, 2002 from http://www.chartula.com/ATTRITION.pdf

Hezel, R., & Dir, P. (1991). Understanding television based distance education: Identification of barriers to university attendance. *Research in Distance Education,3* (1), 2-5.

Holmberg, B. (1995). *Theory and practice of distance education.* New York: Routledge.

Hyatt, S. Y. (1992). *Developing and managing a multi-model distance learning program in the two-year college.* Paper presented at the Annual Conference of the National Institute for Staff and Organizational Development on Teaching Excellence and Conference of Administrators, Austin, Texas.

Jonassen, D. H., & Grabinger, R. S. (1988). *Independent Study: Personality, cognitive and descriptive predictors.* (ERIC Document Reproduction Service ED 295 641).

Kelman, A. (1997).Distance learning at the LSE with virtual tutorials. *IT Review, 7* (1). Retrieved on June 1999 from http://elj.warwick.ac.uk/jilt/sw/97_1lse/default.htm

King, F. B., Harner, M., Scott, & Brown, W.. (2000). Self-regulatory behavior influences in distance learning. *International journal of Instructional Media, 27* (2), 147-155.

Laube, M. R. (1992). Academic and social integration variables and secondary student persistence in distance education. The American Journal of Distance Education, 15 (2), 279-290.

Livertos, B., & Frank, J. (1990). Alternative learning modes: Spring '92 telecourse and weekend college enrollees. Columbia, MD. (ERIC Document Reproduction Service ED 385 311).

McGee, P. (2001). *Novice Distance Learners: A Web-based Simulation-game Orientation.* Technical Report written for the Joint Advanced Distributed Learning Co-Lab. Orlando, Florida.

McKinnon, N. C. (1993). *An assessment of using technology and learning contracts with adult learners in distance education.* Unpublished doctoral thesis, University of Toronto, Ontario.

Morgan, B. M. (2000). *Is distance learning worth it? Helping to determine the costs of online courses.* Retrieved on June 27, 2001 from http://www.marshall.edu/distance/distancelearning.pdf

Morgan, C. J., Dingsdag, D., & Saenger, H. (1998). Learning strategies for distance learners: Do they help? *Distance Education, 19* (1), 142-156.

Morgan, C. K., & Tam, M. (1999). Unravelling the complexities of distance education student attrition. *Distance Education, 20* (1), 96-108.

Naidu, S. (1994). Applying learning and instructional strategies in open and distance learning. *Distance Education, 15,* 23-40.

Office of Technology Assessment, U.S. Congress. (1989, November). *Linking for learning: A new course for education.* Washington, DC: U.S. Government Printing Office.

Oliver, R. (1999). Exploring strategies for online teaching and learning. *Distance Education, 20* (2) 240-254.

Parker, A. (1999), A study of variables that predict dropout from distance education, *International Journal of Educational Technology, 1* (2).

Parker, A. (1995) Distance Education Attrition . *International Journal of Educational Telecommunications, 1* (4) 389-406. Retrieved on April 4, 2002 from http://www.aace.org/pubs/ijet/v1n4.html

Phipps, R. A., & Merisotis, J. P. (1999). *What's the difference? A review of contemporary research on the effectiveness of distance education in higher education.* Washington, DC; American Federation of Distance Learning in Higher Education Association.

Portier, S. J., & Wagemans, L. J. J. M. (1995). The assessment of prior knowledge profiles: A support for independent learning? *Distance Education, 16* (1), 65-87.

Powers, S., & Mitchell, J. (1997). Student perceptions and performance in a virtual classroom environment. Chicago, IL: American Educational Research Association. (ERIC Reproduction Service No. ED 409 005).

Rowntree, D. 1995. 'Teaching and Learning Online : a Correspondence Education for the 21st Century?'. *British Journal of Educational Technology* 26: 205-215 (3).

Rubenson, K. (1986). Distance education for adults: Old and new barriers for participation. In G. van Enckevort, K. Harry, P. Morin, & H. G. Schutze (eds.), Distance higher Education and the Adult Learner: Innovations in Distance Education, Volumne 1 (pp.39-55). Dutch Open University, The Netherlands.

Schlosser, C. A., & Anderson, M. L. (1994). *Distance education. A review of the literature.* Ames, IA: Iowa Distance Education Alliance, Iowa State University. (ERIC Document Reproduction Service ED 388 159).

Sheets, M. F. (1992), Characteristics of adult education students and factors which determine course completion: A review *New Horizons in Adult Education, 6* (1), pp. 3-19.

Smith, P., & Dunn, S. (1991). Human and quality considerations in high-tech education. *Telecommunications for Learning, 2,* 168-172.

Souder, W. E. (1993). The effectiveness of traditional vs. satellite delivery in three management of technology master's degree programs. *The American Journal of Distance Education, 7* (1), 37-53.

Stone, T. E. (1992). A new look at the role of locus of control in completion rates in distance education. *Research in Distance Education, 4* (2), 6-9.

Stovalt, I., Kelly, M., & Lieberman, J. (1998). *What makes a successful online student?* Retrieved March 2000 from http://www.ion.illinois.edu/IONresources/onlineLearning/StudentProfile.html

Thompson, E. (1997), Distance education drop-out: What can we do? In Pospisil, R. and Willcox, L. (Eds.), *Learning Through Teaching,* Proceedings of the 6th Annual Teaching Forum, Murdoch University, February, 1997, pp.324-332. Available online: http://cleo.murdoch,edu.au/asu/pubs/tlf/tlf97/thom324.html

Thompson, G. and Knox, A.B. (1987). Designing for diversity: Are field-dependent learners less suited to distance education programs of instruction? *Contemporary educational psychology* 12(1). 17-29.

Willis, B. (1994). *Distance education: Strategies and tools.* Englewood Cliffs, NJ: Educational Technology Pubs.

Wood, H. (1996). Designing study materials for distance students. Retrieved on July 2001 from http://www.csu.edu.au/dvision/oli/oli-rd/occpap17/design.htm

Woodley, A. (1987). Understanding adult student drop -out. In D. Thorpe & D. Grugeon (Eds.), Open learning for adults (p. 68). Essex: Longman.

Wright, S. (1991). Critique of recent research on instructional and learner support in distance education with suggestions for needed research. *Second American Symposium on Research in Distance Education.* University Park, PA: Pennsylvania State University.

The Calibrated Course: Considering the Limits of Standards and Standardization

Online courses at post-secondary institutions are proliferating faster than the statisticians can count. With better than 78% of all higher education institutions offering distance education in some form (nearly 60% offering online learning, National Center for Education Statistics, 1999), it is understandable that issues of quality in distance education should arise. Like the Internet itself, online course offerings have generally come about almost randomly as distance learning programs have produced an online course in whatever subject there was an instructor willing to teach online; hence, developers, administrators, faculty–all seek guidelines in this new instructional medium. Early adopters, entrepreneurs, professional organizations, consortial committees, but rarely faculty and institutions themselves, began issuing an almost steady stream of "best practices" or standards, each claiming to be the definitive guidelines for distance education. In their best use standards have been applied intelligently to complement the criteria worthy institutions already have in place for quality assurance. In less effective use the standards have been recast as a template, enabling a distance learning unit to calibrate its production machinery, cobbling courses for mass production that subscribe to the letter, if not the spirit, of distance education. As Howard and Discenza (2000) point out, "Technology does not replace the human factor in education....technology is not as important ...as some other factors that affect the learning process such as student motivation, learner characteristics, and the professor" (p.153).

While regional accrediting agencies have distance education criteria, those standards issuing from educational organizations hold considerable credence because they are viewed less as evaluative measures and more as development measures. Standards from *DETC, WICHE, SREB, NACADA, ACE, for example, detail pedagogical theory, measurable outcomes, course elements, and other distance learning accoutrements, seeming to suggest definitive molds into which course content and instruction can be poured. A comparison of the lists will reveal very similar approaches to distance education standards. For example, on all lists institutional purpose is a touchstone: "Program is consistent with the institution's role and mission (WICHE)." "Institution has a clearly defined and simply stated mission that describes the general purpose and specific objectives of the institution (DETC)." "The program or course is consistent with the institution's role and mission (SREB)."

Why Do the Rules Sometimes Fail?

There is a common thread running through each list–the classroom model. The assumption appears to be that an online course should feel, look, and sound as much like a classroom course as possible–only "virtual." The underlying premise is that students learn best in a classroom setting; therefore, the more the online course emulates the classroom course, the better. At the same time, detractors of distance learning determine by circular argument that the Internet cannot duplicate the classroom setting and, therefore, cannot provide equivalent instruction. By allowing standards to be rooted in the classroom model, even online course advocates are in effect undermining online instruction.

There are other reasons why a rigid set of rules for online instruction fail to assure quality education. Among them is faculty and course individuality. With the exception of basic courses, seldom does an academic department prescribe how a body of material in the discipline is to be taught. It is assumed that the faculty–the content expert–is the best judge of the sequencing, selection, organization, and presentation of material. This assumption is sometimes optimistic, as few faculty have had pedagogical training. However, most faculty do fair-to-excellent jobs of teaching, simply because teaching involves common sense. The faculty who does not offer students multiple ways of learning, means of assessment, explanations, opportunity for questions, and other aspects of effective teaching usually does so not out of ignorance of method, but of a conscious choice to teach in a particular way. The imposition of standards in these cases legitimately falls as the responsibility of the academic department, not with the distance learning unit. Sensitizing faculty to students' learning needs, not a set of rules, makes for improved teaching online or in the classroom. For the rest, the faculty may well craft the online course to be uniquely his/hers.

Gilliver, Randall, and Pok (1999), like Williamson (1996), insist the act of teaching has not fundamentally changed, but is only assisted by the new educational technologies; "technology provides nothing more than a framework and delivery infrastructure to enable educators to be as imaginative, creative, and flexible as they wish" (p. 18). Some view "best practices" as rules circumscribing a uniform model that may ignore not only faculty individuality, but students' personal learning traits, and even subject matter characteristics. For example, WICHE asks "What provisions for instructor-student and student-student interaction are included in the program/course design and the course syllabus?" The ideal distance learning course or program "provides for appropriate interaction between faculty and students and among students," SREB states. Both of these criteria overlook truly independent study courses, which do not operate with a cohort group, or the fact that group discussions may not be appropriate in courses where learning content does not require peer interaction. As Oblinger, Barone, and Hawkins (2001) point out, "The future of distributed learning—and of higher education—will not be a one-size-fits-all approach" (p. 2).

Why Are There Rules Anyway?

Why rules indeed! Has not the Internet grown like Topsy because it was unfettered and in the hands of the masses? Though the growth of the Internet has seemed entirely spontaneous, the provision of academic credit-bearing courses does require some regulation to assure students of quality. The rules after all are about quality, and to suggest that the some rules are unfounded or may be unnecessarily complicated, tedious, and punitive rather than motivational, is not to suggest that rules themselves are unnecessary. Without rules, anything in HTML could be an online course. Even if it is agreed that a new medium calls for a new orientation outside the classroom model, the growing body of knowledge about learning confirms some generally held beliefs about how learning takes place, and learning is the goal of all courses–online or otherwise.

An online course grounds its quality in appropriate instructional objectives. A course is a quality course in direct proportion to the extent it enables students to meet those objectives. A point here about the relationship between technology and learning: While most distance education programs understand technology and learning are not equivalent terms, there is a still a disjunct between technology and the presentation of content. The assumption that media generate courses implies that games, animations, color, and layers of programming make learning happen better than simple screens with minimal text and straightforward organization. The actual difference in degrees of course quality lies between engaging the learning so that learning may take place and dazzling the learner so that the attention, but not the intellect, is stimulated. It is on this point that standards for production make good sense. Building on a general ambience of simplicity-- "less is more," the quality of production should focus on the basics first, such as ease of navigation, intuitive screens, limited distractions, grammatical accuracy. At this point the technology should become transparent, and the content paramount.

So What Are "Best Practices"?

Best practices are rules-of-thumb generally designed to be emulated; therefore, they are often based on what another institution has done with some degree of success. Best practices can involve the macro-level of institutional or even system planning, or on the micro-level the development of a single course.

At whatever level, best practices should have little to do with trappings and everything to do with the facilitation of actual learning. A quality course, for example, may have or may not have a bulletin board, essay questions, a grade archive, or multiple web links; as Ken White and Bob Weight in *The Online Teaching Guide* say, "teaching is about student learning and deals with establishing conditions for facilitating" (p.vii). Best practices must be thought of in terms of the learner–how does it change him or her? At the least a course presents the material, concepts, skills to be learned. No amount of flash, pedagogical theory, or artificially created community can substitute for a course's prime responsibility to the student–show him/her what is to be learned.

Second, it could be suggested also that a quality course involves metacognitive skills, that is, stimulates the student to think about what he/she is learning, because "learning" is more than cerebral digestion; it is learning to learn. Via the course the student might learn to

a. Connect the content of the course to the larger body of knowledge
b. Demonstrate what she/he has learned
c. Find resources for additional skills, remediation, review, further information
d. Understand the application, particularly the transferability of what he/she is learning

Conclusion:

The online environment is *sui generis*. Its possibilities as a learning environment are limitless. As more advanced technologies become standard on newer computers, succeeding generations of students and faculty will be completely at home in this environment. It is time to take off down new avenues of instruction. It can be assumed that an infinite number of ways of presenting material and of learning material will be possible, that faculty will know distance communication as second nature, as they now know classroom communication techniques, and that students will become completely comfortable with independent learning. Standards and standardization will be only the handmaidens of learning, not ends in themselves.

*Distance Education and Training Council, Western Interstate Commission for Higher Education, Southern Regional Education Board, National Academic Advising Association, American Council on Education; see respective websites below

References

1. Gilliver, R.S., B. J. Randall, and Y.M. Pok (1999). The orbicular model–cognitive learning in cyberspace. *Educational Technology Review* (12), 18-22.
2. National Center for Education Statistics. *Distance Education at Postsecondary Education Institutions: 1997-98*. U. S. Department of Education: Office of Educational Research and Improvement, December 1999.
3. Oblinger, Diana, Carole Barone, Brian Hawkins. Distributed Education and Its Challenges: An Overview. ACE, 2001 http://www.acenet.edu/bookstore/pdf/distributed-learning/distributed-learning-01.pdf
4. White, K. and B. Weight. (2000). *The online teaching guide*. Needham Heights, MA: Allyn and Bacon.
5. Williamson, S.R. (1996). When change is the only constant: Liberal education in the age of technology. *Educom Review* 31 (6), 22-25.

Organization Websites

American Council on Education
http://www.acenet.cdu/
Distance Education and Training Council (DETC)
http://www.detc.org/
National Academic Advising Association
http://www.nacada.ksu.edu/
Southern Regional Education Board–Electronic Campus
http://www.electroniccampus.org/
Western Interstate Commission for Higher Education
http://www.wiche.edu

Mobile What? The Educational Potential of Mobile Technologies.

Thomas Fox McManus, Ph.D.
Assistant Professor of Educational Technology
Saginaw Valley State University
7600 Bay Rd.
University Center MI, 48710
(517)790-4060
mcmanus@svsu.edu
http://www.svsu.edu/~mcmanus

Abstract: Each new technology brings with it a certain potential for teaching and learning. This potential is based, in part, on the unique characteristics and capabilities of the technology. What can a learner or instructor do with the technology that they cannot do as well with any other? The advent of mobile technologies has sparked a trend, occasionally called m-Learning, or Mobile Learning, which is being touted as the next thing in learning. In this article we present a picture of what mobile technologies and environments may look like in the next few years. We examine the theoretical implications of mobility and ubiquity, the primary characteristics that separate these mobile technologies from other learning technologies. And we discuss the search for a pedagogical model for the creation of collaborative mobile learning environments.

What is Mobile Learning?

Mobile learning is effectively a sub-category of the larger concept of e-Learning. According to Clark Quinn mobile learning is "the intersection of mobile computing and e-learning: accessible resources wherever you are, strong search capabilities, rich interaction, powerful support for effective learning, and performance-based assessment – e-learning independent of location in time and space" (Quinn, 2000). The difference between e-learning and m-learning is an addition of capabilities and limitations, more evolutionary than revolutionary. Briefly defined, mobile learning is the combination of mobile technologies and appropriate pedagogy to allow learners to interact with learning environments, and other learners, at any time from any location. To expand upon this definition, it is first necessary to describe the sorts of technologies and pedagogies used.

Mobile Technologies

Mobile technologies include any system or device that allows a learner to access information or to communicate without the limitations of power cables or network wires. The term could encompass such technologies as radios, portable cassette players, calculators, dictation devices, or alphanumeric pagers. In most cases though, at the current time, the term mobile technologies usually refers to one or more of wirelessly networked laptops, WAP enabled mobile phones, or handheld computers. Future developments of mobile technologies are likely to include convergence, or the combination of several functions in to a single device, eventually leading to a pervasive or ubiquitous computing environment.

Wireless networking, which allows computers and peripherals to share data without being in physical contact, uses electromagnetic airwaves (radio and infrared) to communicate information from one point to another (WLANA, 2001), is becoming more common in educational settings. Handheld Computers are another new technology that is beginning to be seen in educational settings. Handheld computers, sometimes referred to as Personal Digital Assistants (PDAs), are small devices designed to fit in one's hand or pocket. While many companies produce these devices, there are three widely used operating systems (OS) which act as almost generic names; the Palm OS, the PocketPC (formerly WindowsCE) OS, and the EPOC OS. While most handhelds are capable of interfacing with a desktop computer through a synchronization cradle, many of the newer handhelds are being offered with built-in or add-on wireless connectivity. This allows them to connect to the Internet at anytime, greatly enhancing their utility as an educational tool. Mobile phones, and their attendant technologies such as WAP (Wireless Application Protocol, SMS (Short Messaging Service), and mobile Internet connectivity are the other class of mobile technologies that are being used in learning environments. The next generation of messaging services,

MMS (Multimedia Messaging Service) will extend the capabilities of these devices by adding media to the messages. This system has yet to be proven in wide scale use.

The Future of Mobile Technology

The current trend towards a single device being capable of handling multiple functions and media types is called convergence. This tend is already visible in the recent release of smartphones such as the Nokia Communicator (www.nokia.com) or the Handspring Treo (www.handspring.com), which combine the functionality of mobile phones, WAP, and SMS with the data processing capability of an Internet connected handheld computer. The idea behind convergence is that phone, computer, audio, video, and Internet can all be combined into one easily portable device. The prototype CyPhone, developed at Finland's University of Oulu (http://www.ee.oulu.fi/projects/CyPhone/), is just one example of such a device. Many futurists predict an era of what is called "ubiquitous computing" where computers are everywhere, in everything, constantly interacting in the larger digital world. Computer will cease to be discrete devices, their capabilities being integrated into most technologies. Ubiquitous computing means a fundamentally different way of interacting with the tools and appliances of our daily lives; and of their interacting with each other (Burbules, 2000). In educational terms this has the potential for tremendous impact. As students become more accustomed to this digital world they will expect, and demand, to see it reflected in the schools.

Unique Characteristics of Mobile Technology

In discussing the merits and capabilities of any technology for use in education it is essential to determine its unique characteristics (Kozma, 1991). The unique characteristics of mobile technologies differ with each type of technology you examine. For instance wireless laptops, PDAs, and mobile phones all have significantly different processor, input, and display capabilities. But they also have certain things in common. The most notable of these, and most important for mobile learning, is their mobility.

This begs the question of what characteristics of mobility may have some effect on learning or teaching. The UniWAP Project (UniWAP, 2002) is looking at the added value of mobility in higher education. They have described three aspects of mobility that impact education: convenience, expediency, and immediacy. Convenience, in their work, deals with the fact that mobile technologies allow a person to engage in educational activities from anywhere they happen to be, even while moving. They point out that while this characteristic seems to have little pedagogical relevance, it does effect how the technology is used. Expediency describes the capability of a learner or teacher to be mobile in some particular place or context that is relevant to the content being studied or taught. Immediacy describes the capability of mobile technologies to allow us to access learning environments or to engage in learning activities at any time, from anyplace, not just when we are sitting at a desk bound computer.

There are other characteristics that can be used to describe mobile learning technologies. Elliot Solloway of the HI-CE project (www.hi-ce.org) often touts the affordability of inexpensive handheld computer, as compared to laptops, or desktop systems currently used in K12 schools. He asks what it means for schools when every student has access to computing technology in the learning environment. While this is a good point it is not always true. At the time of writing, it is possible to buy a handheld computer for under $200, well under the cost of any other computer system with the equivalent versatility. But the more capable devices, those with wireless access and multimedia capabilities can cost more than $600. While still cheaper than even the low-end laptops, this price is equivalent to that of a low-end desktop computer. Perhaps the most intriguing characteristic of mobile technologies it the current trend towards ubiquity. The idea of a person having constant access to a computing device has several theoretical implications.

Mobile Pedagogy

When looking at the use of mobile technologies for learning it is important to determine a pedagogical paradigm that suits the characteristics and capabilities of the technology and the content. The use of modern technologies in education has always allowed the learner to place a certain amount of the cognitive load onto the computer (Scardamalia, Bereiter, Brett, Burtis, Calhoun, & Lea, 1992). Spreadsheets, for example, allow students and scholars to concentrate their limited cognitive resources on drawing conclusions from data rather than spending the cognitive energy performing complex statistical calculations. New wireless and handheld technologies have the potential to increase this effect many times. What will it mean when a learner, whether in a classroom or in the field, has access to the near unlimited information of the Internet, voice and data connections to any number of experts or collaborators, and the data storage and processing power of a modern mainframe; all in the palm of her hand? What will the "effects with" such a technology be? How can we, as educators, design learning environments to take full advantage of these synergistic effects? Distributed Cognition, Situated Learning, and Cognitive Apprenticeship are some of the learning models that researchers are looking at as the basis for a mobile and ubiquitous pedagogy.

Distributed Cognition (Salomon, 1993) looks at the interaction of learners with each other and with the technology itself. Distributed Cognition emphasizes how cognitive efforts are distributed across not only artifacts and internal and external representations, but across individuals and groups as well. In doing so, it dissolves the traditional divisions between the inside/outside boundary of the individual, the technology, and the group. If a learner always has a mobile learning device with him or her, the learner and the device begin to interact, in essence becoming more than the sum of their parts as the learner offloads some of the cognitive effort onto the device, enabling the learner to free up more cognitive resources for learning. If the same device enables the learner to keep in touch with a larger community of learners then the cognition can be distributed over the entire community, as well as their devices, allowing for larger scale social construction of knowledge.

Situated Learning theory (Cognition and Technology Group at Vanderbilt, 1993) is based on the idea that learning that takes place in an authentic context is more likely to transfer than learning that happens in an artificial environment. The Cognitive Apprenticeship model (Järvelä, 1996) is also stresses the idea of situating learning in a realistic context. This means creating learning environments that either mimic the authentic environment where the skills and information learned will be used, or creating a learning environment that actual incorporates the authentic environment. Technology allows for either of these goals to meet more easily. Because mobility allows for learners to go to the authentic environments for their learning, it may be possible to design mobile learning environments that follow the tenets of Situated Learning theory and the Cognitive Apprenticeship model to help support the students' learning. This could lead to the development of location or context dependent learning. That is learning that is greatly enhanced when it happens in a particular location or context. Imagine scientific field work or visits to historical landmarks as the context and think of how a mobile device could allow learners to access pertinent information, remediation, evaluation, or suggested further study as the learner comes in proximity to a location.

Research Findings
Most published articles dealing with the use of mobile technologies incorporate training or K12 and Higher Education been anecdotal rather than research oriented. There have been a few more scholarly examinations of mobile learning, but the field is still very new and in-depth scholarly research takes time to perform and disseminate. Earlier studies looking at the use of laptops, though not specifically looking at laptops with wireless connectivity, showed some benefits and trends which may be reflected, or even increased when those laptops are freed from their stationary connections to the Internet. Some studies noted a shift toward more student-centered classroom environments (Stevenson, 1998; Rockman, 1998), increased student motivation (Gardner 1994, Rockman, 1998), and improved school attendance over students not using laptops (Stevenson, 1998). According to Rockman (1998), a majority of teachers in laptop schools reported an increase in both project-based instruction and cooperative learning. Fisher and Stolarchuk (1998), in a study involving the use of laptops in middle school science classrooms, found that emphasis on the process of inquiry positively impacted student learning and attitudes. Roschelle and Pea (2002) examined the way mobile devices change the way people collaborate and the creation of shared knowledge spaces. Perhaps the largest study to date is the Palm Education Pioneers (PEP) Program (Crawford, Vahey, Lewis, & Toyama, 2002). The report is based on data collected from more than 100 schools around the US who received PEP grants. Teachers using the PDAs gave evaluations of the use of PDAs as instructional tools, with responses over 90% positive. Portability and ease of access were cited as benefits, as were the integration of the handhelds into a variety of instructional activities, the increase in student motivation, and the use of collaborative and inquiry based instructional methods. It must be noted that this research was funded by a handheld manufacturer. Nonetheless, the findings are encouraging for the acceptance of the technology into the traditional classroom.

Conclusions

Distance Education has always been about allowing learners access instructional environments that they could not otherwise access. Mobile Learning is another answer to the same need. But it also provides the opportunity for learners to access those environments at any time or from any place. This extra opportunity for ubiquitous access is the value that mobile learning adds to the educational mix. Mobile learning has the necessary characteristics to become a basic element in the structure of learning and education. The increase in access and the flexibility associated with mobile learning will move students from passive to active roles. They will be able to tailor the content and framework of the qualifications they require, and determine the mode, pace and delivery of study that is best suited to their own personal circumstances. While mobile learning research is still in its infancy, it is obvious that the trend towards ubiquitous computing needs to be matched with a sound theoretical model for educators to make the most of the new technologies.

References

Burbules, N. C., (2000), "Why Philosophers of Education Should Care About Technology Issues," Retrieved March 5, 2002, from http://faculty.ed.uiuc.edu/burbules/ncb/papers/philtech.html

Cognition and Technology Group at Vanderbilt (1993). Anchored instruction and situated cognition revisited. *Educational Technology, 33(3),* 52-70.

Crawford, V., Vahey, P., Lewis, A., & Toyama, Y., (2002). Palm Education Pioneers Program: March 2002 Evaluation Report Retrieved April 6, 2002, from http://www.palmgrants.sri.com/ PEP_R2_Report.pdf

Fisher, D., & Stolarchuk, E. (1998). The effect of using laptop computers on achievement, attitude to science and classroom environment in science. "Proceedings Western Australian Institute for Educational Research Forum 1998." Retrieved April 23, 2002 http://cleo.murdoch.edu.au/waier/forums/1998/fisher.html

Gardner, J. (1994). "Personal portable computers and the curriculum." Edinburgh, Scotland: Scottish Council for Research in Education. (ED 369 388)

Järvelä, S. (1996). Qualitative features of teacher-student interaction in a technologically rich learning environment based on a cognitive apprenticeship model. *Machine-Mediated Learning, 5,* 91-107.

Kozma, R. B. (1991). Learning with media. *Review Of Educational Research, 61(2),* 179-211.

Larkin, J. H., & Simon, H. A. (1987) Why a diagram is (sometimes) worth ten thousand words. *Cognitive Science,* 11, (1)

Quinn, C. (2000) "mLearning: Mobile, Wireless, In-Your-Pocket Learning" Retrieved January 12, 2002, from www.linezine.com/2.1/features/cqmmwiyp.htm

Rockman, et. al. (1998). "Powerful tools for schooling: Second year study of the laptop program." Rockman, et. al: San Francisco, CA. Retrieved May 26, 2002 http://rockman.com/projects/laptop/

Roschelle, J., & Pea, R. (2002). A walk on the WILD side: How wireless hand-helds may change CSCL. In G. Stahl (Ed.), *Proceedings of the CSCL (Computer Supported Collaborative Learning) 2002.* Hillsdale, NJ: Erlbaum

Salomon, G. (Ed.) (1993). *Distributed cognitions. Psychological and educational considerations.* NY: Cambridge University Press.

Scardamalia, M., & Bereiter, C. (1991). Higher levels of agency for children in knowledge building: A challenge for the design of new knowledge media. *The Journal of the Learning Sciences, 1(1),* 37-68.

Uniwap, (2002). "The UniWAP Project" Retrieved May 26, 2002, from http://ok.helsinki.fi/sivut/inenglish/ENuniwap_mlearning.html

The Simulation Game: Discussing the Educational Potential of Online Multiplayer Games.

Thomas Fox McManus, Ph.D.
Assistant Professor of Educational Technology
Department of Educational Leadership and Services
Saginaw Valley State University
College of Education 160
7400 Bay Road
University Center, MI 48710
(989) 964-4060
http://www.svsu.edu/~mcmanus/index.html
mcmanus@svsu.edu

Abstract: Computers and games are a natural pairing. And these computer games occasionally have real implications in educational technology. In part this is because new technologies are often utilized in computer games long before they make their way into the class room or training lab. In this article we discuss the rise of a new class of computer games, the Massively Multiplayer Online Role Playing Game, and its possible implications for the development of complex social simulations for education and training.

Introduction

New technologies are often utilized in computer games long before they make their way into the class room or training lab. Distributed interactive virtual environments, have long been a goal of educational technologist. Immersive graphical environments where learners from all over the world could interact with each other and with the environment: this goal has been achieved in the online gaming industry and has far reaching implications for education and training. The rise of the Massively Multiplayer Online Role Playing Game (MMORPG), such as Everquest, Ultima Online, and Acheron's Call, has shown that the technology to build this sort of complex virtual world works. The problem is that it is still far too complex for a teacher or an instructional designer to create or run one of these virtual worlds. Recently new games have been released that include a tool set which allows a user to create a virtual space, stock it with artifacts, people it with characters, and run numerous other users through it in real time. Currently the tool set is being used for user created game content. But the same tools can allow a teacher or instructional designer to create a social simulation and adjust it in real time based on the interaction of the learners as they go through the virtual world. These tool sets may turn these games into real instructional tools.

The Origins of Online Games

Before discussing the characteristics and capabilities of current online role-playing games (RPG) it is important to have some idea how they developed and the traditions from which they arose. There are three components that go into the make up of online role-plying games; the traditional role-playing game, the computer game, and the Internet. Today's RPGs developed from more realistic war games, which have been around, and used instructionally, for some time. Napoleon used war games to help train his officers. War games in this case refer to table top games, simulating troop placement and interaction with counters on a map. Chess is a simplified exa mple of a war game. More complex and realistic war games require some sort of rules to determine the results of actions and interactions. There have been many such rule sets over the years. For example, in 1913 H. G. Wells wrote **Little Wars,** a set of rules for war gaming.

But there is a difference between war games and role-playing games. RPGs incorporate the idea of actions and outcomes defined by rules with the setting and narrative quality of traditional literature. Perhaps the most important influence on modern role-playing games has been the J.R.R. Tolkien's **The Lord of the Rings** trilogy, published in 1954. This very popular series introduced a generation to a rich environment of traditional archetypes and mythical narrative structures. After the resurgence of fantasy literature sparked by the popularity of Tolkien's works, there were several attempts to combine the fantasy characters and settings with complex war gaming rules. In 1974 Gary Gygax published the first edition of the **Dungeons and Dragons** rules. This became the first widely popular fantasy RPG. Though over the years since, many other rule systems and genres have achieved popularity, it could be argued that no other game has been as influential in the field as **Dungeons and Dragons (or D&D)**, indeed many use the name D&D to refer to the entire field of role-playing games.

Computers and games are a natural match that has existed since the early days of the technology. In 1962 students at MIT developed what is thought of as the first computer game called **Space War**. In 1969, **Adventure**, a text based fantasy game was introduced. It combined the fantasy setting from the popular literature with the computer's ability to present interactive environments. Once graphic displays became available, games gained graphical features. **Pong**, which first appeared in 1972, is widely thought of as the first "video game". In 1979 Richard Garriot developed **Akalabeth**, one of the first graphical fantasy games. It attempted to be D&D on the computer.

In the years since there have been a plethora of role-playing games on the computer. These games have had certain advantages when compared to table top, or face to face, RPGs. Games on the computer usually include high quality graphics, often immersive 3d graphics that present a world of beauty and grandeur matching those described in books or presented in movies. The story line of these interactive narratives can also be extremely complex with dozen of non-player characters (NPCs), that is characters that are run by the computer rather than the player, with whom the player can interact. And, unlike face to face games, which require that you gather several people into a room together at the same time to play, computer RPGs allow a person to play any time they wish regardless of the availability of other players. On the other hand these games have limitations which are impossible to overcome, based on the fact that the game and all its structure are created long before the player begins play. If a player wants to interact with an NPC, he or she is limited to those interactions predetermined by the game creators. This can lead to a sense of limited choice, as well as social isolation.

The Internet, the world's largest computer communications network, seems like a natural venue for relieving this sense of social isolation, and it has proven so. Since the early days of the Internet, it has played host to various sorts of online gaming. Play by email, where all interaction is non-synchronous and takes place via email, is a modern equivalent to the venerable tradition of play by mail gaming. MUDs, Multi-User Dungeons, are text based game spaces that allow players and game masters or story tellers to interact with each other over intercontinental distances in real time. Virtual Worlds bring graphics to the idea of the MUD. But most Virtual worlds are simply chat spaces with pictures. They lack the rules and narratives of the RPGs. That is what led to the Massively Multiplayer Online Role-playing Game (or MMORPG).

The Massively Multiplayer Online Role-playing Game

The MMORPG combines many of the aspects of its predecessors into an immersive, persistent, gaming environment where dozens, or hundreds, of people from, all over the world can play and interact in real time. These games are characterized by complex storylines and character development, where a story arc can take months of real time to resolve and characters grow and interact for years, instead of the days or weeks most other computer based games last. This long term character persistence leads to complex social interaction and group dynamics. In an MMORPG there may be thousands of players online at any given moment. While the worlds portrayed by these games are large enough that those players are spread out and usually not interacting with all the other player at one time (a recipe for pandemonium when it occurs), they are still interacting with other characters, played by real people, as opposed to dealing only with computer controlled NPCs. This sort of real interaction leads to the growth of complex social structures, some of which are supported by the design and genre of the game, and some of which are not. For instance in some game worlds player characters (PCs) will join together to form ad hoc teams to defeat powerful enemies or pursue difficult goals, while in other games there are formal structures, often called guilds or alliances, where members can benefit from the growth or success of other members.

There is also the potential for negative social interaction as well. Some players choose to use the relative anonymity and freedom of the game worlds to act out anti-social fantasies. This can range form verbal (or in most cases textual) attacks on other players to character assault, murder, and theft. Most MMORPGs are based on some type of heroic adventure genre. And, as in most adventure literature, violence and conflict play important parts of the story lines. In many games it is possible for a player character to attack another player character, even killing them, in game. As players put a lot of time and effort developing a character in these games, character death is seldom permanent. But it usually has some negative consequences. When a PC kills another PC it can cause various levels of consequences to the murdered character, including loss of in game money or goods, as well as taking the player's time and attention. It is even possible for these in game social misdeeds to have real world consequences. Part of the story line common to most MMORPGs is the hunt for treasure. Certain treasured items are very rare and highly desirable in the game world. This has lead to a booming economy in the real world sales of virtual artifacts. For instance a magical sword may be very useful to a character in a game. If one character accumulates more than one of these swords they may choose to sell the surplus. Often this is done on eBay, or some other real world auction service. A virtual magic sword may sell for $100 real world dollars. It is even possible for a player to sell an entire character or account. If a player has spent several months or even years playing a character until that character is very powerful, many choose to then auction that character, sometimes for several hundred real world dollars. This means that if an anti-social character kills a PC who had this desirable magic sword, they might steal it, then sell it for real money on eBay. Some of the social structures in many of these games have evolved to deal with these sorts of undesirable character actions.

There are currently three popular, successful MMORPGs that have been around for several years. The most popular in the US, with membership nearing half a million players, is **Everquest**. It is occasionally facetiously referred to as EverCrack, as it is said to be almost addictive in its draw for its players. It is a traditional fantasy RPG environment based loosely on the D&D game. The second most popular in the US is **Ultima Online**, based on one of the most popular computer based fantasy RPG series. It differs from most of the others as it uses a 2d interface instead of the more common 3d. It is also the oldest of the popular MMORPGs. The third of the "Big Three" is **Asheron's Call**, distributed by Microsoft. It is also a fantasy game, though the environment is original rather than based on some other property. There are several new games that have reached some popularity in the last two years, many which move away from the fantasy genre, and there are dozens of new games under development, including updated versions of the big three.

The Future of MMORPGs

Two trends in new technologies are most likely to affect the shape of MMORPGs in the next several years; the increase in graphics capabilities and the increase in network bandwidth. Combined with the like advent of head mounted displays and kinesthetic feedback systems, immersive virtual reality will take on a new meaning. As the verisimilitude of these virtual worlds increase, so will the involvement of the players. Even as each game becomes more realistic, the development of social structures and game design combine to create more complex interpersonal interactions. What are sometimes called "next generation" games often include mechanisms to discourage or prevent anti-social behaviors. The popularity of, and revenues from, theses sorts of games often lead people to call MMORPGs the entertainment form for the next century. Whether this is more than mere hype, only time will tell.

It is also possible; likely even, that the basic technology that is the backbone for the MMORPGs, the persistent, shared virtual world based on large scale network systems, will spawn other, non-game related applications. In industry it is easy to imagine virtual meeting spaces where groups from around the world meet and interact with high fidelity avatars. It has also bee suggested that this sort of interface could be combined with tele-control systems to have simulated factories building real products or with tele-presence systems to enable real long distance medical procedures. It has even been proposed that this sort of technology be used for virtual conferences where hundreds of people meet, interact, watch or make presentations, complete with slides and video. Tele-government is another potential use of this technology,. Where legislatures and other government bodies meet and vote in a virtual space, which is in turn open to any voter who wishes to attend.

Creating Educational Simulations

One of the most interesting of the new games, and possibly the most important from an education al point of view, is **Neverwinter Nights** (NWN) from Bioware. This is a multiplayer online role-playing game setting in a traditional fantasy setting. It is based on the Dungeon and Dragons rules (3rd Edition) and allows up to 60 players to interact in the environment in real time. The thing that makes NWN so different, and so interesting, is the inclusion of the **Aurora Toolset**. This toolset allows a user to create their own online 3d immersive environment, people it with NPCs, and most importantly, manage the environment in real time as the players run their characters through it. This means a game master (GM) can design a city, dungeon, or landscape, populate it with people and monsters, giving each a series of preset interactions and responses to the characters and their actions, but if those presets prove ineffective, the GM can, in real time, take over the NPC and cause it to reply or act in the manner most appropriate to the player's actions. This sort of control turns the game into a potential tool for powerful immersive, distributed social simulations.

There are four basic types of simulations: physical simulations, which simulate physical objects, i.e. a frog or a machine; procedural simulations, which simulate a particular activity such as flying an airplane or performing heart surgery; situational simulations, in which the learner is a participant in the larger situation, and can interact with and change the environment; and process simulations, in which the learner sets variables then watches the results of a process. The Aurora Toolset seems best suited for developing situational simulations. If an instructor or designer can shape a virtual environment with complex social interaction, then educators can create social and historical simulations, virtual field trips, even virtual classrooms where the learners can interact with each other as well as with the instructors and preprogrammed characters. One example might be a discrimination awareness simulation where the learners take the role of a discriminated minority with in a society. The reactions of the non-player characters, as well as those controlled by the instructors would should both subtle and overt examples of differential treatment for the learners' characters, all with in the context of a larger society. Or it could be possible to reenact the original Constitutional Convention, with learners each taking the role of a delegate from a particular state, trying to represent the views of that state on the important issues being discussed.

Currently the Aurora toolset is both complex to use and limited in its capabilities. The most noticeable of its limitations is the inability of the content creator to break away form the medieval/fantasy graphics inherent in the game. It is likely that a tool, provide either by Bioware, or by a third party developer, will overcome that limitation in the near future, but for the moment any environment or character created will have a definite fantasy flavor to it. One of the questions being addressed in this research is the importance of verisimilitude in these sorts of simulations. How distracting, or detrimental, is it to learners to have the simulated Abraham Lincoln and Jefferson Davis; look like knights in armor or elves, when seated at a simulated peace conference table. At the time of writing, the author and his colleagues are using the Aurora Toolset to develop educational social simulation environments. Later publications will explore the use of the toolset and the effectiveness of the simulation environments.

The Psychological Dimensions of Communities of Practice and their Relation to Online Learning

Dr Donald W. McMurray
School of Social and Workplace Development
Southern Cross University
dmcmurra@scu.edu.au

Abstract: In 1998, Southern Cross University adopted an action research methodology to design and deliver online units. Each action research cycle involves learning and reflection wherein necessary changes are instituted and the outcomes evaluated to assess the efficacy of online learning compared to conventional distance education learning (Hayden, Saenger & Parry, 1999). Feedback was mixed especially with respect to collaborative learning (McMurray & Dunlop 2000).

In a subsequent iteration of the action research cycle a community of practice concept was promoted where students were encouraged to organise themselves into a community of learners with the goal of supporting each other in their learning (Wilson & Ryder 2001).

In the most recent cycle, a conscious effort was made to simulate the culture and climate of real-world organisations (? ? ? ? ? ? ? ? ? ? ?? ? ?). It was found that the sense of community for online students was in many ways richer than that experienced by face-to-face students.

INTRODUCTION

The notion that the E-classroom adds increased flexibility to the delivery of distance education is well established in higher education institutions today. Distance is vanishing, time is collapsing and relationships are becoming central to success (Olson 2001). There is also some evidence that the opportunity to interact and collaborate leads to richer learning experiences (Lander 2001; McMurray & Dunlop 2000). It is argued that the effectiveness of online learning activities rests on the manner in which they encourage interactivity and collaboration in establishing a community of learners. This paper examines evidence for the existence of a community of practice concept in an online setting as compared with a face-to-face class studying the same unit.

THE INITIAL ACTION LEARNING CYCLES

Staff within the School of Social and Workplace Development adopted an action research methodology to design and deliver online units within the Bachelor of Social Science. Each action research cycle involves learning and reflection wherein necessary changes are instituted and the outcomes evaluated. The process resembles a hermeneutic spiral (Gummesson 1991) where each turn of the spiral builds upon the understanding flowing out of the previous turn.

Since first semester 1999 when five units were offered completely online, there has been an increase in demand by traditional distance education students wishing to utilise this communication technology. Presently 176 units are being delivered online all of which contain discussion forums and group collaborative work areas. In preparing units for online delivery, there has been a deliberate repositioning of the instructor away from the role of knowledge transmitter to that of facilitator, coach and resource guide. Emphasis is given to engaging the collaboration of the students in creating their own knowledge.

At the end of each semester units were evaluated to assess the efficacy of online learning compared to conventional distance education learning (Hayden, Saenger and Parry 1999) using a questionnaire adapted by Dunlop (1999) from Creed (1996). Initial feedback showed that while distance learning students value the interaction with and access to the lecturer, they found collaboration with each other to be problematic, especially where it led to a shared grade.

It was decided to pay more attention to each learner's basic communication needs when operating in a group. Computer supported communication is devoid of important social cues that are important for message validation and, therefore, the building up of trust (Collins & Berge 1996). Moreover, according to Dunlop and Scott (2001), online groups need sufficient time to become acquainted with each other and develop cohesion (King 1999) as well as the necessary social protocols. Only then can successful collaboration take place which, in turn, can lead to the facilitation of shared meaning (Allen & Griffith 1997).

THE PREVIOUS ACTION LEARNING CYCLE

The reflective phase of the initial action learning cycles led to a decision to create a community of practice for online learners since this has been found to be lacking amongst distance education learners (De Vries & Wheeler 1996; Martin

1999). Communities of practice describe informal settings in which people learn by doing. It has its epistemological roots in constructivism which assumes meaning is jointly constructed and arises out of ongoing activities of a community of learners. Here knowledge as well as action is fundamentally social in origin (Henning 1998). Stamps (1997) claims that communities of practice are not actually created but emerge as a function of people becoming united as they work collaboratively towards a common goal.

Accordingly, with the online launch of an undergraduate unit entitled *Organisational Communication*, it was once again decided to focus on a requirement for the students to interact and collaborate. In previous units of study the setting up learner centred groups had been undertaken by the instructor. In this iteration, however, the process of organising themselves into groups was left entirely to the students, including the naming of their virtual organisations. This was an unhurried process that occupied the first two to three weeks of the semester and produced a number of communicative activities, ranging from one-to-one dialogues using email and the telephone to the use of the discussion area inside the course delivery shell by the whole group. Very little instructor-to-learner communication occurred at this stage and this proved to be beneficial for the groups in forging a sense of community amongst themselves.

Once the online groups were established the asynchronous chat room quickly became the vehicle for conducting and archiving discussions. Many exchanges occurred between the two organisations as members explored boundaries and developed a sense of cohesion in and around their new 'organisation'. Initially these discussions were almost exclusively social and yet the creation of this social community served as an important bridge to the formation of the academic community that was to follow.

The evaluation of *Organisational Communication* at the conclusion of semester 2, 2000 confirmed the growing appeal that online learning holds for distance education students. The frequency of visits to the student discussion areas in this unit was almost three times as great as that recorded in two earlier surveys (McMurray & Dunlop 2000). It is contended that this increased interactivity was a product of the community building that took place at the outset of the unit. What began essentially as social interaction transformed into exchanges of a more academic nature. The students could see the merit in interacting with each other in this way. Eighty-six per cent of students rated the real-time chat sessions with other students as having "great value" or "very great value" (Newton & Ledgerwood 2000). In its virtual chat room *CourseInfo* records threads of conversation as online discourse in a way that allows every thought to be captured for future examination, reflection and extension by their peers (Owston 1997). The result is richer, more thoughtful discussions arising out of shared understandings which in turn contribute to a different kind of knowledge building from that which students are able to accomplish on their own.

Reflecting on this action learning cycle it was realised that if meaningful and useful collaboration is to become an integral part of computer assisted education, it is essential that the students are motivated to participate (Prendergast 1996). Further, it appears that for collaboration to be truly successful, the learning environment should be structured by the participants themselves. This includes reaching agreement about shared goals as well as the purpose of the collaborative enterprise.

THE CURRENT ACTION LEARNING CYCLE

The reflections flowing out of the second action learning cycle led to a number of important determinations. First, interactivity which occurs online is qualitatively different from that which takes place in a face-to-face environment. For example, a sense of immediacy is missing, along with an absence of non-verbal cues. For this reason it was decided to encourage the current cohort to make greater use of the virtual chat room. It was hoped that this real-time contact would promote a shared understanding of concepts and allow them to experience diverse and multiple kinds of feedback ahead of that received from the unit instructor. It was also hoped that this kind of interactivity would serve the dual purpose of fulfilling both academic and social needs of a geographically disparate group of adult learners.

The group of students presently studying *Organisational Communication* are all female and include two from the USA. They refer to their organisation as *CyberF.com*. From the outset the instructor once again maintained a relatively low profile while the group set about the business of developing their community of practice. While the instructions were clearly stated in the unit outline, control of the decision making process concerning how unit objectives were to be achieved was placed in the hands of students. Interestingly this type of instructor style was interpreted by one of the students as being somewhat laissez faire.

Towards the end of the unit members of *CyberF.com* were surveyed to ascertain what happens when students congregate to provide mutual support for their learning. The instrument used was designed to reflect perceptions of organisational climate. Moran and Volkwein (1992) see

??????????????????????? [as]? ???????????????????????????????????????
???????????????????????
??????????????????????? Views? ???
????????????????????? -
??
?????????????????????????????????????
???

???
????????????????????
??p.??

At the same time students studying via conventional distance education techniques were also surveyed as to their perceptions about the climate as determined by their learning mode. Differences were found between the two groups with respect to 'cohesion', 'support' and 'trust'. For example, only 21% of distance education students reported feelings of cohesion with the school or their fellow students as compared with 90% of *CyberF.com* students. Similarly, almost twice as many online students felt supported in the studies as compared to external studies students.

Overall, the results provide evidence for the existence of a healthy climate amongst the online group that was not found in the conventional distance education mode. It is suggested that these factors are important requisites to the formation of a community of learners and are themselves the products of sustained interaction and collaboration.

BUILDING LEARNING COMMUNITIES ON THE WEB

There are a number of techniques that can be identified for those wanting to develop effective online courses. First, online learning needs to be viewed as a process not a sequence of structured activities. Action learning offers an appropriate lens through which to view these processes as they unfold.

Second, there should be a deliberate attempt to provide an environment that is intimate, inviting and authentic if quality learning is to occur. Ideally, this can occur within a community of practice. Hill (2001) outlines a number of strategies for establishing online communities of practice. These include:

- appealing to their sense of adventure from the outset by providing a vision that causes an air of excitement;
- providing communicative mechanisms that facilitate interaction;
- ensuring a safe and protected environment free of outside criticism and interference;
- assuring them of a constant connection with the instructor as needs dictate;
- enabling them to interact and communicate in a number of different ways; and
- working hard to avoid or remedy technological problems that may potentially thwart their community building.

Third, encourage a diversity of participants since geography does not matter in an online community. Nevertheless, adequate attention needs to be paid to cultural demographics. Finally, as instructor, it is important to provide the human touch by visiting the chat rooms, staging teleconferences, recording audio messages and sending e-mails. The prime objective here is to encourage students to reflect on their own learning and to analyses these metacognitive activities for future reference.

CONCLUSION

This paper has traced the emergence of a sustained positive shift in attitude towards collaborative online learning for distance education students over a number of action learning cycles. It is concluded that the establishment of a virtual community of practice involving common goals and a desire to learn from each other are key drivers behind the shift. Technology, in and of itself, does not foster collaboration. As Adams and Freeman (2000) found, the establishment of a community of practice serves the purpose of supplying the necessary human infrastructure for the creation of knowledge with the Web providing the technological tool. Student feedback suggests that collaborative online learning yields richer learning than simply requiring individuals to interact with materials that have been web-mounted (Hiltz & Benbunan-Fich 1997).

REFERENCES

Adams, E. C. & Freeman, C. (2000). Communities of practice: Bridging technology and knowledge assessment, *Journal of Knowledge Management*, 4, (1), 38-44.
Allen, D. & Griffith, R. (1997). Vertical and lateral information processing: The effects of gender, employee classification level and media richness on communication and work outcomes, *Human Relations*, 50, (10), 23-31.
Collins, M. & Berge, Z. (1996). Facilitating interaction in computer mediated online courses. Paper presented at the Florida State University Distance Education Conference, Tallahassee, FL, June. http://star.ucc.nau.edu/~mauri/moderate/flcc.html.
Creed, D. T. (1996). Project ADEPT (Assessment of Distance Education Pedagogy and Technology). http://www.users.csbsju.edu/~tcreed/adept/desrv1.html

DeVries, Y. E., & Wheeler, C. (1996). The interactivity component of distance learning implemented in an art studio course, *Education*, 117, (2), 180-184.

Dunlop, M. (1999). *The Impact of Computer Delivered Distance Education on the Participation.* Unpublished BSocSc(Honours) Thesis, Southern Cross University Press: Lismore.

Dunlop, M. & Scott, D. (2001). An Examination of the impact of aspects of online education delivery on students. In Treloar, A. and A. Ellis. (Eds.). AusWeb01, Proceedings of The Seventh Australian World Wide Web Conference Southern Cross University Press: Lismore, 269-283.

Gummesson, E. (1991). *Qualitative methods in management research.* Newbury Park: Sage.

Hayden, M., Saenger, H. & Parry, S. (1999). *An evaluation of online units delivered in first semester 1999 at Southern Cross University.* Report compiled by *The Teaching and Learning Centre.* Southern Cross University: Lismore, NSW.

Henning, P. H. (1998). Ways of learning: An ethnographic study of the work and situated learning of a group of refrigerator service technicians. *Journal of Contemporary Ethnography, 27,* (1), 85-136.

Hill, J. R. (2001). Building community In Web-based learning environments: Strategies and techniquies. Paper presented at Ausweb 01- Seventh Austyralian World Wide Web Conference, held at Southern Cross University, Coffs Harbour, NSW April, http://ausweb.scu.edu.au/aw01/papers/refereed/hill/paper.html

Hiltz, R. & Benbunan-Fich, R. (1997). Supporting collaborative learning environments in asynchronous learning networks. Invited Keynote Address for the UNESCO/Open University Symposium on Virtual Learning Environments and the Role of the Teacher. Milton Keynes, England April 28 1997. http://eies.njit.edu/-hiltz/CRProject/unesco.htm.

King, K. (1999). Group dynamics for the online professor. Paper presented at AusWeb99, Fifth Australian World Wide Web Conference, Southern Cross University, Ballina, April, http://ausweb.scu.edu.au/aw99_archive/aw99/papers/king/paper.html.
??????? ? ??????? ?? ? ? ?(??? ?). I?????????????????????????????????????? ? ?????? , ? ? ? ? ? ? ? ? ? ? o? s, 44, (3), ? ? ? ? ? ? ? ?

Lander, D. (1999). Online learning: Ways to make tasks interactive. *UltiBASE,* 24 May 1999. http://ultibase.rmit.edu.au/Articles/may99/lander2.htm.

Martin, W. A. (1999). Being there is what matters. *Academe,* 85, (5), 32-36.

McKey, P. (2000). The total student experience. Keynote presentation at ASCILITE 99, Queensland University of Technology, Australia, December 6-8.

McMurray, D. W. & Dunlop, M. E. (2000). The collaborative aspects of on-line learning: A pilot study. *UltiBase,* July. http://ultibase.rmit.edu.au/Journal/journal.html.
? ? ? ? ? ? ? ? ? ? ? ? ? ? ? ? ? (? ? ? ?) . T ? m? ? ? ,? ? ? ? ? ? ? ? ? ? ? ? ? ? ? ? 24 5, (1), ?? ? ? ?

Olson, R. (2001). Looking to 2010 and beyond. *Association Management.* 53 (8), 78-84.

Owston, R. D. (1997). The world wide web: A technology to enhance teaching and learning? *Educational Researcher,* 27, (2), 27-33.

Newton, D. & Ledgerwood, T. (2000). School of social & workplace development online student feedback survey, October 2000. Unpublished Report, Southern Cross University, Lismore.

Prendergast, G. (1996). *Using Computer Supported Cooperative Learning to Deliver Effective Work Place Training.* University of Melbourne Press: Melbourne.

Stamps, D. (1997). Communities of practice, *Training,* 34, (2), 34-43.

Wilson, B. & Ryder, M. (2001). Dynamic learning communities: An alternative to designed instructional systems, unpublished paper at http://carbon.cudenver.edu/~mryder/dlc.html (accessed 1 May 2002).

WEBQUESTS: INSTRUCTIONAL and DESIGN TECHNIQUES

Donna J. McNierney
Beeghly College of Education
Youngstown State University
United States
mcnier@zoominternet.net

Abstract: Using multimedia and computer generated web-based instructional activities; such as the WebQuests is a non-traditional instructional approach for teaching subject area content. This instructional method is designed to meet the learning needs of the student related to visual literacy, problem solving, discovery, and critical reflectivity. Transforming traditional instructional methods using critical pedagogy, promotes the teacher to examine current practice and ways to integrate technology with classroom instruction.

Introduction

This paper has two primary purposes. The first purpose is to review current research related to visual learning and learning theory and to discuss the resulting critical pedagogical implications within teacher education methodology and technology courses. The second is to describe the design of WebQuests as a learning activity so that teacher education students will learn the importance of integrating technology with instructional use in their classrooms as a web-based instructional tool. The learning experience for the students of designing WebQuests helps to challenge the teacher to engage in critical reflectivity of lesson planning and to promote the learner's ability in visual learning, problem solving, and discovery. Inherent in a review of the research is an understanding of the importance of the critical reflectivity process itself. Critical pedagogy theorists argue that teacher education programs must include methods in the curriculum which engage education students in a critical reflective process - a process which results in their discovery and examination of traditional teaching and current practices. Engaging students in this process, using theoretical frameworks from researchers such as Dewey, Jung and Wink, ultimately assists in setting the parameters for designing successful instructional and methodologies which include the integration of technology. As a teacher educator at the university level, my education students in the technology courses need to learn that "critical pedagogy forces educators to look again at the fundamental issue of power and its relationship to the greater societal forces that affect schools" (Wink, 1997). Students need to know how current teaching practice that is enhanced with appropriate and challenging web-based activities, such as WebQuests, changes the teachers role but also gives power back to the students by challenging them using a constructivist approach by using problem solving and inquiry based learning.

Dondis stated that the traditional educational system places too much emphasis on the "verbal mode to the exclusion of the rest of the human senses and with little sensitivity to the visual character of the child's learning experience" (Dondis, 1973). Teaching and learning with visual images is usually of secondary importance in a curriculum. Many educators believe that when students are engaged in a visual learning activity, the learning is often passive, not personal or interactive. The dominant teaching style in traditional classrooms then remains teaching by telling.

How do we provide both the ideological and physical conditions important and necessary to educate all future citizens? How do we challenge all students in the dynamics of critical literacy, constituting a basis for a well-informed citizenry in a democratic society? (Giroux, 1988).

For example, if lecturing remains a popular method in our traditional classrooms, how do we know if it is the most egalitarian? How do we know if most of our students learn by listening through the auditory senses? How do we know that they can apply the principles and concepts of their subject matter merely by hearing? The answer, apparent to most informed educators, is that we do know and the answer is that most students do not and cannot learn merely by listening. How much of the students' learning is through the visual?

Jung's research, however, on psychological type helps to illustrate the importance of visual learning by identifying how students prefer to perceive and interact with their world. Jung's definition of the psychology and structure of consciousness yields "four basic functions which are constitutionally present in every individual: thinking, intuition, feeling and sensation" (Jung, 1992). These functions are also referred to as the functions of consciousness or typology.

John Dewey, another prominent educational theorist, contributed interest and effort to the learning process. Dewey (1985) stated that the learning experience of the student is enhanced when interest is "secured in a given set of factors or ideas; we can be perfectly sure that the student will direct his/her energies toward mastering them" (p.159). According to Dewey, the level of interest in a given topic and the amount of effort it takes to complete that task, "necessitates that genuine interest is the accompaniment of the identification through action, of the self with some object or idea, because of the necessity of that object or idea for the maintenance of a self-initiated activity" (Dewey, 1985, p.159).

Interest is first active; second, objective; and third, personal. To be interested in performing a task, students must have a direct concern in it and recognize that because of this required personal commitment the outcome is important to them. Students must identify the task/idea as their own and thereby achieve both a sense of pride as well as a positive self-concept when their goals are met. Due to the personal interest attached to the attainment of the goal, students are willing to put forth the effort. The cliché, time flies when you are having fun, is appropriate in describing the students' interest level.

Nowhere are Dewey's ideas more pertinent in today's educational process than in how they relate to visual learning. How many times have students failed to correctly answer a geometry question but won a friendly game of pool? To play the game first hand requires both visual and critical thinking of the laws of physics and geometry and an interest. Students who cannot successfully memorize the mathematical formula for a passing grade can successfully envision a bank shot into the corner pocket. They understand the concept of angles and speed and apply them first hand -- because they are interested and because they are visual. In essence, they are successful in decoding the images.

For a lifetime of learning and literacy that extends far beyond the walled boundaries of a school, the learned ability to accurately recognize, identify and interpret visual messages, actions, objects, and symbols encountered in the world is an important critical element in encouraging the processes of reflectivity and critical literacy. Visual images are a language, visual literacy is the ability to understand and produce visual messages (Heinich, 1996). Recent research and study in the field has focused on the importance of the development of teaching and learning strategies to increase students' abilities to evaluate, create and think critically about the images presented. Findings from the visual literacy field of research are increasingly important because due to the ever-widening role of the mass media in our society, students need to be informed and knowledgeable so that they can decode both wanted and unwanted communicated message

All prospective teacher educators in this multi-dimensional information age need to develop and transform instructional methods by integrating technology and web-based activities. As a teacher educator, it is important that I model instructional methods and develop activities in the classroom which centers on students to rethink how their subject/content area can be taught in the future.

The Design

According to Dodge, developer of the WebQuest strategy, the World Wide Web has become a popular wide ranging method for students to browse for factual information, online graphics, cyber communication, and global awareness. Using the Web "can revolutionize student learning." (Dodge, 2002) "WebQuests were designed to address the dilemma of using progressive learning theories, such as, constructivism, authentic assessment, cooperative learning, and scaffolding by integrating them together for effective teaching practices into one integrated student activity." (Dodge, 2002)

WebQuests engage students curiosity and often increase their motivation to learn to make conceptual connections that are related for example to a particular topic, theme, or problematic situation. Depending on how the WebQuest is designed by the teacher, students may need to respond to real world problems, confront issues, or work cooperatively with peers. (Dodge, 2002) The primary goal of using WebQuests as an instructional and learning tool is to engage students in higher order thinking skills. A good website to use as a framework for the development of the WebQuest is located at http://webquest.sdsu.edu. Included in that website are the six elements necessary for designing and formatting the structure of the WebQuest. They are the following:

1. Introduction
2. Task

3. Information sources
4. Process
5. Guidance
6. Conclusion

The website is particularly good because it defines the six elements needed to create the WebQuest in addition the site provides great examples of short and long term WebQuests for diverse susbject areas and grade levels.

http://www-bioc.rice.edu/precollege/k12resources/webquest/links.html (Marty Daniel, Oct. 10, 2001)

Once familiar with the construction of the WebQuest and the situation or scenario for the basic framework for the students to investigate is planned, a web editor or software needs to be chosen. One of the more sophisticated and highly recommended web editors available is Macromedia's Dreamweaver. The ability to design in layout view is a powerful feature for creating a web page because it is visually stimulating for the designer and because writing code or being a programmer is not the major factor in the overall creation. Dreamweaver does have a valuable function that allows for both views to be observed, code and design.

Another aspect to Macromedia's web editing software is the easy integration with Fireworks and Flash. The graphics, images, or video the designer may want to include is made possible with Macromedia's software packages that integrate seamlessly with one another.

Conclusions

The traditional definition of literacy has referred only to the reading and writing of verbal information. However, in today's world the concept of literacy assumes a much broader meaning in interpretation. "The term visual literacy refers to the learned ability to interpret visual messages accurately and to create such messages" (Henrich, 1996).

This paper had two primary purposes. The first purpose was to review current research related to visual learning and learning theory and to discuss the resulting critical pedagogical implications within teacher education methodology and technology courses. The second was to describe the design of WebQuests as a learning activity so that teacher education students will learn the importance of integrating technology with instructional use in their classrooms as a web-based instructional tool.

The created learning experiences which are first-hand, which are of interest, and which incorporate the students' prior experience and knowledge are engaging visual literacy skills that are strengthened by using a multimedia approach to learning. WebQuests add to the instructional and learning environment for the student because of the non-traditional approach to teaching as well as encouraging students to use higher order thinking skills to achieve the task.

Teacher educators, in their technology and methodology courses, should take a leadership role in the use of computer technology and media. Such multimedia approaches, as the WebQuest, can contribute to visually-oriented thought-provoking lessons. The design of instructional technological lessons identifies teacher educators as significantly transforming their own teaching in the classroom, through reflection, action, and the recognition that, indeed, a picture is sometimes worth a thousand words.

References

Dewey, John. (1985). *Essays on Philosophy and Psychology 1912-1914*. Carbondale and Edwardsville: Southern Illnois University Press, 159.

Daniel, M. WebQuest Links Oct. 10, 2001

Daniel, M. Teaching With WebQuests Oct, 12 2001

Dondis, Donis A. (1973). *A Primer of Visual Literacy*. Cambridge, Massachusetts, and London, England: The MIT Press, 9.

Dodge, B. The WebQuest Page at San Diego State University Oct. 21, 2001)

Ellsworth, Elizabeth and Marianne H. Whatley. (1990). *The Ideology of Images in Educational Media, Hidden Curriculums in the Classroom.* New York: Teachers College Press.

Gardner, Howard. (1983). *Frames of Mind.* New York: Basic Books, 336.

George, Paul, Gordon Lawrence and Donna Bushnell. (1998). *Handbook for Middle School Teaching.* New York: Longman, 86.

Giroux, Henry A. (1988). *Teachers As Intellectuals.* New York: Bergin & Garvey, xxxiii.

Heinich, Robert, et. al. (1996). *Instructional Media and Technologies for Learning.* Englewood Cliffs, New Jersey: Merrill, 67.

March, T., ozline.com - Why WebQuests? Aug.1,2002

Pascal, Eugene. (1992). *Jung To Live By.* New York: Warner Books, Inc., 16.

Vygotsky, L.S. (1978). *Mind in Society.* Cambridge, Massachusetts: Harvard University Press,.

Wink, Joan. (1997). *Critical Pedagogy.* New York: Longman, 36.

Sustaining Instructional Design Strategies to Enhance E-learning Among Learners at Open University Malaysia

Mustafa Md. Hanafiah
Associate Professor Dr. Abtar Kaur
Center for Instructional Design and Technology
Open University Malaysia
Malaysia
mustafa1@hotmail.com
abtar@pc.jaring.my

Abstract: The OU Malaysia views the use of advance technologies, especially e-learning as important as the University espouses a life-long learning culture with the intention to produce knowledge workers. This paper will showcase how the implementation of e-learning efforts in OU Malaysia through three methodologies: providing basic information, providing multimedia content and conducting online interactions. These efforts are in use to cater the different needs and expectations of the learners. This paper also explores on the various attributes in WebCT that are exploited to create a culture of e-learning. The e-learning design process, the adoption of the constructivist and objectivist approaches and the attributes of motivation are further described in this paper to sustain the instructional design strategies to enhance e-learning among learners at OU Malaysia.

Introduction

OU Malaysia was officially established on 10 August 2000 and our first program was offered in August of 2001. Our mission is to provide flexible, easily accessible and affordable life long learning opportunities to open and distant learners. Currently OU Malaysia has 12 undergraduate and diploma programs offered through five schools, that is School of Business & Management, Information Technology & Multimedia Communications, Education & Humanities, Science & Foundation Studies and Engineering. To support our learners we have thus far produced an estimate of 60 print-based modules and four sets of multimedia courseware (on CD ROM) and another four sets of multimedia clips for the web. To cater for all this needs, the Centre for Instructional Design and Technology was set up on January 1 2002. Its main responsibility is to assist the schools develop open and distance learning materials that are used in their programs. The center has been given the task to create more e-learning materials. Thus to start the discussion on our paper, we will look at a definition of e-learning that will help keep us focused on our e-learning efforts.

According to Rosenberg (2001), e-learning refers to the use of Internet technologies to deliver a broad array of solutions that enhance knowledge and performance. It combines both the online and knowledge management attributes. Some of the success factors for e-learning includes creation of a learning culture, receiving support of leaders, creating a nurturing environment, sustaining change throughout the organization, having formal instruction but goes beyond it, is happening all the time, has intellectual capital build-up and the individual and organizational performance is increased. In creating and exhorting the e-learning culture, the instructional design (ID) process employed must be sustained throughout the learning continuum. Instructional Design according to Reigeluth (1985) is 'the process of deciding which methods of instruction is best for bringing about desired changes in student knowledge and skills for a specific student population'.

E-Learning Efforts at OU Malaysia

E-Learning efforts at OU Malaysia are implemented through 3 methodologies: a) providing basic information about the course that is being offered, b) providing multimedia content and c) conducting online interactions. The purpose of this variety is to cater for as much individuality as possible in terms of learning styles, aptitudes and time constraints. WebCT is the learning system that has been adopted by OU Malaysia and most of the e content is uploaded into the WebCT.

Providing Basic Information

Basic information consists of putting up course information such as syllabus, course objectives, readings, relevant websites and announcements. In OU Malaysia, e-executives carry out this function for those courses where faculty is not permanently with us. For those faculty which are permanently with OU Malaysia, they upload the information on their own.

Providing Multimedia Content

Multimedia content consists of two types: courseware and stand-alone multimedia clips. Courseware is created for those subjects that are difficult to understand and need a lot more e-support. The courseware is normally loaded onto CDROM. With courseware, the learner is allowed to practice a lot more and feedback is given to help the learner attain learning objectives. Courseware also consists of problem-solving strategies whereby the learner is able to immediately check his/her understanding. Stand-alone clips are normally loaded into the WebCT and the purpose of the stand-alone multimedia clips is to allow the learner to view/listen to it and then discuss the issue related to the clip using the online discussion board in WebCT. A team of experts consisting of multimedia programmers, graphics artist, animators and audio and video specialist creates the multimedia content. The content is first visualized and designed by a team of instructional designers and subject-matter experts. In the process of developing courseware, Gagne's Nine Events of Instruction are adopted by OU Malaysia. Gagne (1992) suggests that learning tasks for intellectual skills can be organized in a hierarchy according to complexity: stimulus recognition, response generation, procedure following, use of terminology, discriminations, concept formation, rule application, and problem solving. The primary significance of the hierarchy is to identify prerequisites that should be completed to facilitate learning at each level. Prerequisites are identified by doing a task analysis of a learning task. Learning hierarchies provide a basis for the sequencing of instruction.

Conducting Online Interactions

Online interactions are crucial in e-Learning efforts especially for open and distance learners as these interactions allow them to discuss shared experiences, which may otherwise be lacking. Online interactions are conducted via the WebCT learning system. Two of the most popular interactions are the email system and the online discussion board. The online moderator is the face-to-face tutor who meets the students once a fortnight at OU Malaysia's selected learning centers. Each online moderator has between 20-25 students. The online moderator has two important roles to play. One, is to answer student queries related to content. For this the students are advised to use the email. The other role is to moderate online discussions related to the content under study. As each subject is divided into 5 study units, the discussion is designed in such a way that, every two weeks, there is a discussion on one of the units. In this way, issues related to the subject is covered quite adequately.

According to the official WebCT website, WebCT has five attributes which can be applied to the innovation of technology in our university. The attributes are relative advantage, compatibility, complexity, trialability, and observability. The table below describes the five attributes. These attributes also contribute to sustaining of instructional strategies to enhance e-learning among learners in OU Malaysia and are elaborated in the section below.

Attribute	WebCT as innovation
Relative Advantage	• Automated marking of tests (multiple choice, short answer, matching and calculated questions) • Easy course administration • Communication (synchoronous and asynchoronous) between lecturer-students and students-students
Compatibility	WebCT is used for both residential (via the Intranet) and distance (via the Web education)
Complexity	WebCT is very user friendly and lecturers/tutors find it easy to use
Trialability	Lecturers/tutors can choose which WebCT functions they want to use, e.g. • Provide access for students to the current teaching material, study guides in the form of text • Communication via the Bulletin Board, E-mail, Chat rooms, • Testing which is graded by the computer and the grades are statistically processed • Course management, e.g. the student class list, student tracking
Observability	• Any function which the lecturer/tutor wants to use, is immediately available to view

Table 1: WebCT attributes that sustain instructional design strategies.

E-learning Design Process

According to Shank (2002), the key step in the e-learning design process is the creation of the plan for "interaction design". A series of criterion are considered before embarking on the plan: a) To determine what kind of courseware to create in the first place b) The size of the content to be developed c) The kinds of activities it should cover d) The kinds of coaching and support should it include.

The steps taken to determine concretely what needs to be taught with the solution being expressed in a specific work product are specification of teaching points, design theme, project timeline, prototype, production plan, implementation review, and functional specification.

The first activity is to gather data on what the specific need is. To get teaching points, experts and practitioners are interviewed. Teaching points are a refinement of information gathered during weeks of research and interviews. The goals of the course are to be described, and written documentation must be examined. In order to make an impact on performance when teaching, one needs to identify impact behaviors that will have the greatest effect on learners' performance and success on the job.

In determining a design theme the development team essentially chooses certain design architectures and past project experience as a style of interaction to use. A general approach 'hypothesis-driven investigation' is then adapted to assist in the designing of theme. This also involves in the planning out and dividing the design into tasks or activities and the time spent for each activities or tasks.

Before a task is designed it is structured by choosing a sample problem which is taken from a book. A learner's input is taken into the design process by having some learners work the problem using the books with the involvement of the tutors. A graphical representation of a design is done at this stage. A simple checklist is created in the forms of bulleted lists as a specific sense of how the core task is to be structured in the content.

At the production stage it describes what to be taught and how we plan to teach it. There are several decisions yet to be made as the design is structured - How will the details of the interaction be staged? What specific materials will be required to implement the interaction? How will the specific decisions the user makes be structured? How will the user be led to generalize from the specific scenario to the overall task?

After decisions have been made a walkthrough using a simple template is created. This creation is actively done by the design team members, to subject matter experts and in some cases, a representative of the user group. The design team and subject matter experts at the implementation review stage pose several review questions such as: a) Will this be an effective design? and b) How much effort will it take to create?

The final step of the e-learning instructional design process is to convert the walkthroughs into an overall learning system to the users. This also involves getting feedback from the learners and deciding on the solutions to the feedback. Adjustments are then made to improve and also to make the development of e content a cost-benefit content.

Sustaining the Instructional Design

Instructional design of e-learning is sustained by adopting a constructivist as well as an objectivist approach to learning. This is crucial as open and distance learners at OU Malaysia come from various backgrounds, experiences, and learning abilities. Constructivist learning strategies will suit the more advance learners, those who are in-charge of their learning and are ready to move forward. On the other hand, students who need to be lead, coached and monitored closely, may use the multimedia courseware to help them attain their learning needs according to their styles. These students may also use more of the emailing system to take advantage of the one-to-one coaching. However, this does not mean that they stay completely away from the online discussions. In fact online moderators are trained to identify learners who are not very active and coerce them to join the discussions. Instructional design of e-learning is also sustained when students are encouraged to contribute discussion topics for online discussion. In this manner, the student curricula is also met.

In a more physical sense, instructional design of e-Learning is sustained by providing students with computer facilities at OU Malaysia's learning centers. This is especially crucial in remote areas especially on the Borneo Island where students do not have ready access to Internet and computers.

According to Moshinskie (cf Rossett, 2002), organizations implementing e-learning projects are facing high attrition rates. During the online course, several strategies can be adapted to create and maintain motivation. These include a) maintain a conducive environment – is related to how learner is influenced by environment factors, people support, learning design strategy, and technology accessibility, b) proper chunk of information – this includes review of pre-requisites, an overview of objectives, interactive presentation of materials, job-related exercise, and a summary, c) build on the familiar- interest is build on by incorporate learners' beliefs and examples, d) vary the stimulus – vary information presentation by using audio, video, and animations, e) provide human touch – chat rooms, email, electronic office hours, video streaming and online mentoring can supply the human touch not only from tutors, also from fellow learners.

Future Plans

With the increased number of students using the WebCT, OU Malaysia has set an incredible pressure on the infrastructure, and more specifically on the availability of computers for our remote students. With the growing number of our Learner Support Centers in Malaysia it is hoped that the involvement of learners with technology will immensely improve their knowledge acquiring capabilities. This will ensure the implementation of WebCT or alternative learning system as part of a broader strategy to guarantee the creation of an e-learning environment. What we are therefore seeing as emerging is an integrated approach to sustaining instructional design strategies to enhance rich e-learning experiences in the flexible and affordable environment.

References

Gagne, R.M. Briggs, L.J. & Wager, W. (1992). *Principles of Instructional Design, (5th Edition)*. New York:Holt. Rinehart and Winston.

Reigeluth, C.M. (1983). Instructional Design: What it is and Why is it? In C.M. Reigeluth (Ed.), *Instructional Design Theories and Models: An Overview of Their Current Status*. Hillsdale, NJ:Lawrence,Eralbaum

Rosenberg, M.J. (2001). *E-Learning – Strategies for Delivering Knowledge in the Digital Age*. New York: McGraw Hill.

Rossett, A. (2002) *The ASTD E-Learning Handbook - Best Practices, Strategies, and Case Studies for An Emerging Field*. New York: McGraw Hill.

Schank, R.C. (2002). *Designing World-Class E-Learning - How IBM, GE, Harvard Business School, and Colombia University Are Succeeding at E-Learning*. New York:McGraw Hill.

WebCT Resources, Available: http://www.webct.com/wyw (20 August 2002).

Acknowledgements
We would like to thank Halimatolhanin Mohd Khalid, Hamitha Abd Kader, and Sharifah Sariah Syed Hassan for making initial contributions towards this paper.

A New Paradigm For OnLine Science Laboratory Learning Environments

Gerald W. Meisner, Physics Dept., UNC Greensboro, US, jm@curie.uncg.edu

Harol Hoffman, Physics Dept., UNC Greensboro, US, hh@curie.uncg.edu

Mike Turner, Physics Dept., UNC Greensboro and Guilford County Schools, US, mturner@curie.uncg.edu

Abstract Robust online courses in the sciences must be based on: (1) sound, research–based pedagogy, (2) rich laboratory environments with skills and operational knowledge transferable to the wet lab, (3) a paradigm that is economically scalable. LAAPhysics courseware meets these challenges in the distance-learning field, using server/client technologies to develop and build a complete online physics laboratory learning environment comprised of equipment and instrument objects and interactive curriculum modules. Client/server data includes dialog (guide agent/tutor and student), white board discussions with virtual peers, assessment and capstone investigations. Complete portfolios of student performance are generated, permitting individual and aggregate analyses not only of conceptual understanding but also of peer to peer interactions and student understanding of various representations of experimental data.

LAAPhysics courseware is being authored to provide rich laboratory-based learning environments in the sciences for those unable to obtain such experiences in traditional college and secondary school settings. One problem the science education research community faces is the lack of data on the effectiveness of good online science laboratories. The reason for that lack of data is that no one has solved the problem of how to successfully port the science laboratory to a meaningful online environment. Without good online laboratories, we lack the necessary tools to conduct basic research on student learning in these settings. This is a recipe for a closed loop. To date, there has been no sustained and successful effort to bring together experts in content, technology, design and discipline-based education research to address these two interrelated problems. LAAPhysics uses internet-based technologies and physics education research results to create pedagogically sound teaching and learning laboratory online courseware environments. This approach will increase opportunities for individuals who currently lack them and transform the current limitations imposed by traditional classroom settings. It will also make available to pre-service and in-service teachers a research based 'online textbook' which can both increase their content knowledge and influence the way in which the discipline can and should be taught.

The LAAPhysics *system* consists of a number of innovative subsystems, which are now in various degrees of completion. All are in at least alpha stage, with beta testing of selected introductory physics 'tutorials' incorporating many of these subsystems to start during the fall of 2002. We are:

- developing open-ended 3D laboratories for the physical sciences that permit exploratory student investigations in which students are interactively engaged with their environments of space, equipment, instruments and data analysis tools. These laboratories will use research-based guided inquiry pedagogies from the science disciplines (such as *Workshop Physics*, the *Modeling Method*, and *Physics By Inquiry)* along with the most appropriate current computer technologies. A virtual tutor will guide students, as would an expert modeler, in, say, Hestenes' Modeling Workshop. We are initially authoring in Mac OS X, with Windows XP to follow.
- using a research model pedagogy to script interactive and guided laboratory-based tutorials in physics, chemistry and astronomy for students of diverse populations in diverse settings. LAAPhysics permits students to experience the scientific investigation paradigm in the context of a guided learning

experience, with branching logic enabling faculty to accommodate students of various backgrounds and levels of understanding.

• assessing student content understanding within the tutorial settings under varying conditions. Students are exposed to both higher-level concepts/tasks in which they deploy their developed models in novel situations, and lower level tasks in which they learn how to use instruments and equipment, or how to identify dependent and independent variables in an experimental investigation. Assessment and evaluation (A&E) questions are currently being authored which go beyond the common algorithmic questions at the 'end of the chapter'. Online environments permit a richness of A&E not possible with hard copy texts, provided appropriate courseware tools are authored for faculty and student to use. We have authored a variety of tools which permit faculty access to instantaneous qualitative A&E grading tools hitherto lacking: LAAPgraph, LAAPAnalysis, LAAPVector and LAAPMotionMap. These are being beta tested in the coming months. As with all online developments, midcourse corrections can be easily and quickly executed. The extensibility of the LAAPhysics approach, along with authoring tools we are developing, will permit a community of developers to quickly emerge, both here and in other countries.

LAAPhysics will not be an encyclopedia of all possible subject matter, which could be discussed, in an introductory, algebra-based course. We will author those which are most appropriate for constraints imposed by pedagogy, medium, funding and 'less is more' philosophy.

LAAPhysics uses selected IT tools, current advances in cognitive science, pedagogy research, and user interface design considerations from both the scientific and the entertainment sectors. From this array, LAAPhysics is developing an integrated software package composed of the following modularized interconnected components:

• a Physical Reality Engine (PRE)©™ that re-creates real-world phenomena in a simulated 3D environment. The open-ended laboratory workspace will contain virtual laboratory equipment and apparatus objects, the parameters of which can be varied by the user in an experimental setting. The open-ended nature of the lab space will provide enhanced environments suitable for visualizing abstract concepts, and will allow users (students and faculty) to employ the environment in unlimited creative ways;

• an Interactive Engagement System (IES)©™ that serves as the central management system of the application. The IES provides interactive content to the learner within a collaborative learning environment where students work together asynchronously with 'virtual peers' guided by a virtual tutor/guide agent. The IES monitors student progress and dynamically responds to student input with contextual modifications that individualize instruction. Through the script branching features, the IES thus guides the learner through appropriate sections and activities within each learning module, providing remedial experiences where needed;

• a System Tools Package (STP) that contains Learner Tools (LT) and Authoring Tools (AT). Each tool is a stand-alone component that can interface with various other components of the application. LT are student research tools that include graphing and data analysis tools. AT include an XML-based editor and development tools that will enable faculty to modify and extend either the engine environment or the content environment with minimal programming skill or knowledge;

• an Information Storage System (ISS) that sorts and stores student and course data on a remote server and furnishes that information to the IES for display to the user (student and/or faculty).

We are in the early stages of:

• developing research methodology on the effectiveness of LAAPhysics learning approach compared to traditional methods of teaching. We will assess both content knowledge (using accepted instruments) and laboratory skills of students who learn in the online environment, comparing this to those students from various conventional learning situations. .

• developing research methodology on the interface between student and machine in this interactive environment. Student interaction, such as use of graphs, tool selection, mouse actions, time on task and data analysis strategies, will be stored in databases that can serve as a research base for understanding important user interface and design issues.

• investigating techniques to enable those students with visual impairments to use and benefit from LAAPhysics.

The beneficiaries of the LAAPhysics approach to online laboratory based courses are:

• Students: Underrepresented populations: inner city minorities, native Americans, and others missing from the MSET mix; whose labs are inadequate or missing: from poor regions of the country, economically strapped community colleges, under-funded high schools, and colleges with inadequate space; those with scheduling difficulties due to work, family or geographic location; those who are ill, injured or who have disabilities.
• Faculty: who are interested in conducting research on student learning in online environments; who are interested in conducting research on student conceptual learning by means of a detailed LAAPhysics portfolio which is automatically created for each student; who want the option of "customizing" course material, and those who want to adopt the role of mentor rather than dispenser of information.
• Institutions: where economic realities make it unfeasible to pay for the high cost of laboratory space; where there is a conflict between lab space and other space demands; where the number of well trained lab instructors is limited; where home schools or struggling charter schools are used.
• Distance Learning Community: where the current absence of scientific laboratory work places severe constraints on distance learning.

LAAPhysics is a generalized simulated 3D laboratory learning environment that models an open-ended laboratory and thus facilitates the transfer of skills and experience from the virtual program space to real world classrooms and laboratories. The system allows students the freedom to make errors, which will be corrected through a further dialog between mentor (written script) and student. The modifiable software package is modularized and designed to provide an extensible interactive online learning environment for authoring introductory laboratory courses in physics (now), astronomy, and chemistry (in the future) and for conducting research on student learning in web-based environments. Our claim is not that the LAAPhysics is better than *in situ* guided inquiry laboratory based courses. Rather, LAAPhysics addresses those instructional situations where *in situ* introductory courses are less than ideal: those that are based on lectures alone, or where students have limited access to laboratories outside of scheduled class time, and/or where students may lack the apparatus and instruments that have been central to scientific investigations of the 20th century.

The Use of Course Mentoring Websites for Collaborative Curriculum Design and to Support Adjunct Faculty Teaching For Lesley University

By Dr. Linda Mensing Triplett Ed.D.
And
James A.J. Triplett M.S.

April 8, 2002

Abstract

Course mentoring websites (CMW's) have proven to be powerful vehicles for providing support and professional development to adjunct faculty teaching required courses for the Technology In Education Department at Lesley University. Adjunct faculty teach courses in many different locations across the United States, using a variety of course delivery models (delivery models include face-to-face courses that meet once a week, weekend courses, online courses, and hybrid combinations of online and face to face instruction). CMW's provide adjunct faculty with access to experienced professors who serve as online course mentors. CMW's are accessible to all the faculty members and furnish a medium for defining and publishing course standards, for giving faculty access to high quality instructional resources, and for maintaining consistency in the delivery of required courses. In addition, CMW's foster a sense of intellectual community among the faculty teaching each course. The goal is for each faculty member to consider themselves an active participant in an ongoing, online curriculum development process. CMW's provide the online context for communication and collaborative course development, and they can be constantly adapted to changing needs, to advancing technologies, and to the realities of diverse teaching environments.

Experienced faculty serving as course mentors establish and are responsible for the continued development of each CMW. The faculty mentor communicates and collaborates with all other faculty members teaching the same course, to gather resources in an ongoing way, and for the purpose of continually improving the CMW.

CMW's are organized to provide faculty with easy access to a variety of resources. Lists of pre-requisite skills that students taking the course will need in order to participate in a meaningful way are made available, as is a set of resources that can be provided to students who feel they need to work on these prerequisite skills. The framework being used for online curriculum development requires that each course have a list of overarching goals related to NCATE/ISTE standards, and that each of these overarching goals be accompanied by an essential question and connected unit goals. Each unit goal has a set of suggested activities which can support the achievement of that goal. These sample activities can be used by faculty for creating course syllabi. Unit goals also have a set of outcomes and/or culminating performances that will help both the instructor and the students determine if goals have been achieved. Performance assessments accompany each activity (i.e. a set of scoring rubrics). The website lists software and technologies that are to be used in the course and a set of technical skills that will be learned. The website also includes an updated set of sample syllabi from adjunct faculty, as well as the

URL's of course websites that have been developed by faculty and are used for teaching the course.

CMW's are built upon technologies that provide access to information and resources, and support both communication and collaboration. Each CMW includes technical tools for collaboration between faculty. These tools are designed so that it is easy to create and continually modify curriculum. Tools include message boards and discussion forums, chat rooms, and visual cues as to when and who last updated a particular part of the course. Publication space is provided for all faculty. Curriculum materials and resources, such as worksheets and handouts can be attached, and these can be made available for various computing platforms (i.e. Mac and PC). Links to web pages are provided, as are NCATE/ISTE standards pages and appropriate help for integrating these standards into the course. Each CMW has built-in support for using technologies to enhance teaching of the course, including models and examples of technology integration in the curriculum. Models of effective pedagogical methods and principles are also provided. Examples of exemplary student work on major projects are included in each CMW, with accompanying performance assessments.

Faculty responsible for developing CMW's recognized the need to develop online course content in a production mode similar to computer software programming. Thus is was determined that CMW's would be designed in "course content modules". The Sharable Course Object Reference Model (SCORM) under development by Advanced Distributed Learning Network (ADL) provided an example and standards for construction of course content modules. Reusable course content modules are appealing because - although Lesley University is a traditional academic institution where individual faculty offer learning experiences that are unique and result from their own expertise and creativity - the productivity, richness, and high degree of maintainability of "course content modules" and the ease of sharing these among faculty members via web technologies has begun to change traditional academic thinking. Economic and competitive pressures, as well as rapid expansion of programs within the Technology In Education Department have also driven online development of course content modules.

Initial CMW design efforts were built on the Blackboard Course Management System because it facilitated web delivery while providing as set of integrated tools for communication, access to publishing spaces for faculty, and resources for measuring course outcomes. However, Blackboard uses a proprietary approach for constructing course modules, as well as for importing and exporting course content. Its template oriented framework did not provide the necessary flexibility or allow for development of course content modules that could be easily utilized by faculty working in a variety of other web formats.

For these reasons, it has been necessary to move away from the use of a Course Management System like Blackboard for this project and to establish technical standards that would permit interoperability and free exchange of content developed in various software packages. The recent development and deployment of tools for building websites and web-based information systems that are usable at all levels of expertise gives Lesley University the opportunity to builds it's systems on Internet-standard technologies using commonly available free or inexpensive tools.

Starting with a standard shared-server Unix-based website, one can layer open-source software systems to provide the desired functionality. Basic requirements for a CMW include easy upload and download using FTP or tools such as MS FrontPage or Macromedia Dreamweaver; a dynamic webpage creation environment using a scripting language such as PHP; and an SQL database such as MySQL accessible from that scripting environment. Because this platform is commonly used throughout the Internet, it is easy to build a user environment with sophisticated features like user-personalization, discussion forums, and individual upload capabilities, using freely-available software packages. For their course development work, faculty are able to use inexpensive commercial packages like FrontPage or Dreamweaver, or free tools such as Arachnophilia or CuteHTML.

Learning Cubes: A Model for Online Education

William P. Messier
Coordinator, Multimedia Management and Production
McLennan Community College, Waco, TX, United States
wpm@mcc.cc.tx.us

Abstract: This paper describes how a faculty development project was designed for the World Wide Web. The paper also describes interactions that took place between faculty to illustrate how collaborative learning and problem solving can be facilitated and implemented by the web. The project assignment content focused on instructors (students) being immersed in an authentic learning environment. The students actually experienced a form of technology based learning while undertaking specific tasks. The paper concludes with some pedagogical discussion about the use of cooperative learning as a teaching strategy for online education.

Introduction

Online learning is a relatively youthful field, which is still being classified as a discipline. As Administration and faculty members struggle with decisions about how to structure online courses for collaborative, cooperative learning, faculty perspectives of successful strategies can provide valuable insights for decision-making. Few studies have been conducted that examine the impact of the collaborative teaching/learning strategies in the distance-education setting (Hardwick, 2000). This paper presents general research findings pertaining to collaboration in online learning along with personal insights into what makes a project-based online assignment successful as a collaborative learning experience.

While online learning offers administrators, faculty, and students many advantages over traditional campus-based learning, problems do exist. Attrition is one such problem for online learners. Attrition is brought about in large part by a sense of isolation (Adelskold, Aleklett, Axelsson, & Blomgren, 1999). One teaching/learning strategy, which can improve this sense of isolation, is cooperative or collaborative learning. Collaborative learning involves students in social communication, as groups work together to discover knowledge, think critically, communicate effectively, reflect, and solve problems. Social interaction among learners plays an important part in the learning process, in fact, it can have a significant impact on learning outcomes. (Jonassen, et. al. 1995, Eastmond and Ziegahn 1995, Berge 1995). Students in online education programs, though separated spatially, can gain a sense of community as they distribute and simplify ideas, actively contribute to a team, and cooperatively solve problems (Cecez-Kecmanovic & Webb, 2000).

With progress in telecommunications and computer technologies, it is now possible to offer collaborative learning experiences in a cost-effective way. In the past, collaborative approaches to distance learning were limited by the cost and sophistication of the technology. Recent advances in technology coincide with a general shift in educational theory to a collaborative origin of learning, which recognizes the learner's need to share control and assume responsibility for problem solving in the context of a peer group (Anderson & Garrison, 1998). Collaborative learning is an outcome of cooperative learning, in that students must develop cooperative learning skills in order to use them in self-directed, high-performing teams. These collaborative groups conduct free investigation and members jointly discover and solve problems. Success in cooperative learning is grounded in the skills students develop within the context of the academic organization provided by the facilitator/instructor. More importantly, in distance learning, students must possess or develop the technical skills necessary for online communication, as well as acquire and practice social skills necessary for collaboration (Kemery, 2000). Cooperative learning involves requiring individuals be accountable so that each participant does a fair share. It involves effective cooperative social skills, effective and appropriate communication skills to bring the task to completion. Research shows that such cooperative learning practices lead to more efficient and effective processing, increased achievement, positive relationships among students, and efficient exchange of information (Johnson, Johnson & Smith, 1997).

Overview of the Model

Since collaborative learning is an outcome of cooperative learning, learning cubes is a product of both teaching strategies. Learning cubes is another name for peer learning and teaching, peer tutoring or team learning. The major difference between these learning strategies and leaning cubes is who is delivering and the amount of information delivered to the student at one time. With learning cubes one student will take responsibility for a certain prescribed amount of information and teach it to a small assigned group of students. This prescribed amount of Information disseminated by the group will be small, challenging, and productive. Prescribed information can be layered assignment to assignment allowing connections of previous taught material to be made while threading new ideas or skills to be learned from the group. Group size for the learning cube is usually small between two or three students. This size increases effective interaction between students while extending the learning process. Some positive interdependence is built in to the experience so that members need one another to accomplish common goals of constructing knowledge. Learning cube, team learning, and peer tutoring works best for some students and it may not work well for all but in most cases students increase learning while not hindering the learning of others (McKeachie, 2002, Larson, 1984). Students become active partners in the learning process and may learn effectively from interacting with their peers. Instructors may need to spend more of their time in the role of facilitator, organizing students, managing students, and helping students work together effectively.

Within a faculty development classroom, nine newly hired McLennan Community College (MCC) educators participated in an online collaborative project-based assignment. This faculty development was mandatory for all newly hired instructors. The educators taught in various fields of study. All educators were given two preliminary workshops using Blackboard, the e-learning course management system software.

As students, the instructors were given two weeks to complete the assignment. As learners via the web, the instructors could interact with one another from different geographical locations either in synchronous (real time) or asynchronous (delayed) mode via text-based communication for the purpose of dialogue. All members of the group had to complete the activities assigned. For assessment purposes, students were required to demonstrate newly learned skills in two pieces of work: 1. after learning how to create a web page from a Word document, each student must create a HTML document reflecting the pros and cons of cooperative learning, and 2. another HTML document reflecting upon items given on their pre-survey.

Model Structure

Within Blackboard the interface structure was designed for ease of use. There were eight categories of interactive buttons designed on the left side of each web page. The categories were in the following order: 1. *Announcements* – this category welcomed students online, reinforced what the emphasis of the activity is about, gave minor reminders about the use of Blackboard and the assignment, allowed students to take a pre-survey, and gave day and times the assignment help desk could be accessed for technical support. 2. *Course Information* – this category gave clear and precise responsibilities for the groups teachers and students. 3. *Course Documents* – this category gave clear and precise instructions for downloading a digital streamed video movie. 4. *Assignments* – this category allowed students to take a pre-survey, study a streamed movie, apply new knowledge learned to a simple activity, and teach this new knowledge to the group. 5. *Books* – this category gave references as books and websites about cooperative, collaborative, and team learning. 6. *Communication* – the communication category gave students access to e-mail or a real time virtual chat room. 7. *Virtual Chat* – this category allowed students to browse the archives for a previous virtual chat room sessions as well as access to the virtual chat room. 8. *External Links* – finally, this category allowed students to access educational data bases like ERIC.

As group members mastered making a web page using Word, each member of the group had to demonstrate new knowledge by completing their own HTML documents. Completed assignments were then forwarded to an email address on the assignments web page.

Pre-Activity Assessment

For feedback purposes, each member of the group was asked to participate anonymously in a pre-activity assessment. The survey was designed to stimulate thoughts concerning the topics of cooperative learning. All survey questions were designed using Blackboards management system. At the end of the required assignment, this survey will be used as a reflective evaluation. The following questions are from this pre-activity assessment: 1. Do you feel that high quality learning can take place without going to a traditional educational facility? Why or why not? 2. Do you like the idea of sharing your work, life and educational experiences as part of the learning process? If your answer is yes or no explain why? 3. Do you think it is possible for increased learning to take place when work/knowledge/life experiences are shared with peers? Why or why not? 4. Do you accept the value of facilitated learning as an advantage over the more traditional lecture based learning process? Why? 5. Have you incorporated cooperative learning into instructional methods? If so, how?

Faculty Interaction: Pre-Activity Assessment

To **question one**, do you feel that high quality learning can take place without going to a traditional educational facility? Most faculty members felt that high quality learning outside the traditional educational facility happens all the time such as people learning at the work place, reading/learning at home, or people learning about a new sport. Many instructors still feel that there is distinct value in face-to-face communication with students and teachers. **Question two**, do you like the idea of sharing your work, life and educational experiences as part of the learning process, most instructors commented positively? All instructors felt that their rich learning experiences should be shared with their students. **Question three** asked, do you think it is possible for increased learning to take place when work/knowledge/life experiences are shared with peers? All respondents had positive statements about this question. **Question four** inquired, do you accept the value of facilitated learning as an advantage over the more traditional lecture based learning process? The comments for this question were mixed positively and negatively. For the most part, many instructors felt that it would depend on the circumstances. **Question 5** asked, have you incorporated cooperative learning into instructional methods? This question also got mixed responses. Five instructors answered positively saying that they have used this teaching strategy before. Some faculty used cooperative learning a little, while others did not use it all for instruction.

Faculty Interaction: Post Survey

At the end of the two weeks, all instructors involved in the project-based assignment were given a simple post survey. The post survey primary contained open-ended questions about the direct impact this assignment had on the users as teachers. The questions were: 1. How were you actively engaged? 2. What aspect of the project-based assignment will you immediate incorporate into your teaching? 3. What was missing that would make this project-based assignment more valuable to you?

Most instructors completed the online collaborative project-based assignment within two weeks. Instructors who had experience using computers or the software program Blackboard had finished the assignment early. Faculty who had limited computer experience took the full two weeks to complete. Although the participants did not choose their own group members their post survey answers indicated that they were actively engaged in the project-based assignment. This was primarily because of the pre-activity assessment, the watching of the streamed tutorial movie, and the engagement of making a HTML document from within a Word document.

Instructors also commented on what aspect of the project-based assignment would they immediately incorporate into their teaching. Most commented positively.

Instructors also commented on what was missing that would make this project-based assignment more valuable to them. One instructor commented, "perhaps a little more detail on the value of cooperative and its integration to be used in web pages." Two instructors said, "I would have liked to learn this from a traditional classroom setting." While most instructors commented that nothing really stood out, a few still had problems following directions or working with the methodology. These instructors commented, "a little hard following instructions," "this was very time consuming," finally, "it was too hard to get into this."

Pedagogical Issues

Cooperative or active learning methods may not be appropriate for every institutional setting (e.g., part time students working full time). For new teachers beginning to implement cooperative strategies, the idea of using students' as instructors teaching small amounts of information may be somewhat intimidating. If you are teaching specific content or cognitive processing, each session must facilitate an environment conducive to collaboration. For learning cubes, team learning, peer tutoring to work, the groups and the content delivered must be small and effective. Further, the team project or assignment must be challenging enough to insist teamwork. Besides, challenging assignments replicate real world situations and help prepare students to be productive life-long learners.

To have effective group members, instructors should provide guidance for students on how to work successfully in collaborative teams. The social characteristic of successful teams should be clearly taught and not assumed. Successful teams will have certain member qualities. Among those sought-after qualities are an interest in other team members beyond the task at hand, the capacity to clarify and commit to goals, an open and honest evaluation of team performance, an understanding of others' perspectives, a wish to confront conflict positively, a commitment to make decisions inclusively, the valuing of individual differences, a willingness to freely contribute ideas and encourage that in other team members (Robbins & Finley, 1995). Group members play an important part in the success of the assignment. From the group's perspective, clear and distinct roles for each member can aid in the groups communications. Among group members, a clear understanding of assignments and work responsibilities can make task management easier for each student. Tasks and authority in the given areas of responsibility must be well defined. Individual team members may be given more decision-making authority in their various areas of expertise.

In planning your courseware design for online education the instructor must provided the following: 1. provide effective technology workshops for students if new hardware and software will be used in the session 2. provide a technology help desk with appropriate days and times users can receive help 3. provide students purposeful asynchronous and synchronous help sessions 4. provide useful creative chat sessions for office hours with appropriate days and times. Additionally, flexibility in meeting assignment requirements facilitates students to develop ownership of the assignment, aids in the development of critical thinking and problem solving skills, imparts room for originality, and encourages a sense of group individuality and unity. Providing a plan for group formation is imperative for team success and cannot be underestimated. Helping students choose team members intelligently will aid in the formation of group member roles, allow members of the group to fill needed areas of expertise, and provide a solid foundation for shared esteem among group members.

In a collaborative group effort, certain individuals may be chosen as project manager for the purpose of setting task deadlines or resolving conflicts of opinion. Once set, group members should hold each other responsible for meeting deadlines with weekly meetings and encouragement. In every group effort there will be differences of opinions. Decisions must be based on ideas and not on personalities.

Conclusion

This brief paper has provided insights into the nature of cooperative learning as a teaching strategy for online education. Online collaborative project-based assignments can be a rewarding experience if certain factors are incorporated into the teaching strategy. A skillful facilitator, capable of balancing guidance with flexibility is one crucial factor. Another is a group with the skills, both technical and social, to truly collaborate the learning process. When those crucial factors as well as other pedagogical issues come together in a learning setting, collaborative online assignments can result in a product exceeding the expectations of the teacher. It is hoped that a useful model will be developed to enable instructors to use online software management systems like Blackboard. It is also hoped that the pedagogical issues of teaching online discussed throughout this paper will be used by educators. As higher education institutions seek to make decisions about how to structure online courses for collaborative, cooperative learning, it is hoped that administrators and faculty alike can gain valuable perspectives and insights for the decision process.

References

Adelskold, G., Aleklett, K., Axelsson, R., & Blomgren, J. (1999). Problem-based
distance learning of energy issues via computer network. Distance Education, 20(1), 129-143.

Anderson, T. D. & Garrison, D. R. (1998). Learning in a networked world: New roles and responsibilities. In Gibson, C.C. (Ed.), Distance Learners in Higher Education: Institutional Responses for Quality Outcomes (pp. 1-8). Madison, WI: Atwood Publishing.

Berge, Z. L. (1995). Facilitating Computer Conferencing: Recommendations From the Field, Educational Technology, January-February, 35(1), 22-30.

Cecez-Kecmanovic, D. & Webb, C. (2000). A critical inquiry into Web-mediated collaborative learning. In Aggarwal, A. (Ed.), Web-based Learning and Teaching Technologies: Opportunities and Challenges (pp. 307-326). Hershey, PA: Idea Group Publishing.

Eastmond, D., and Ziegahn, J., (1995). Instructional Design for the Online Classroom. In Computer Mediated Communication and the Online Classroom, Volume Three: Distance Learning (Eds. Berge, Z. L. and Collins, M. P), 1995, Hampton Press Inc., New Jersey, p29-36.

Hardwick, S. W. (2000). Humanising the technology landscape through a collaborative pedagogy. Journal of Geography in Higher Education, 24(1), 123-129.

Johnson, D. W., R. T., Johnson & K. A., Smith M., (1997). Academic Controversy: Enriching College Instruction Through Intellectural Conflict. Washington, DC.: ASHE/ERIC.

Jonassen, D., Davidson, M., Collins, C., Campbell, J., and Haag, B.B., (1995). Constructivism and Computer-Mediated Communication in Distance Education. The American Journal of Distance Education, 9(2), 7-26.

Kemery, E. R. (2000). Developing on-line collaboration. In Aggarwal, A. (Ed.), Web-based Learning and Teaching Technologies: Opportunities and Challenges (pp. 227-245). Hershey, PA: Idea Group Publishing.

Lai, K. W. (1999). Net-Working: Teaching, Learning & Professional Development with the Internet. Dunedin, New Zealand: University of Otago Press.

Larson, C. O., et al. (1984). Verbal Ability and Cooperative Learning: Transfer of Effects. Journal of Reading Behavior, 16, 289 295.S

McKeachie, W. J., et al. (2002). Teaching Tips: Strategies, Research, and Theory for College and University Teachers. Boston, MA: Houghton Mifflin Company.

Robbins, H. A., & Finley, M. (1995). Why Teams Do Not Work: What Went Wrong and How to Make It Right. Princeton, N.J.: Peterson's/Pacesetter Books.

Public Relations Writing Moves from the Classroom Online:
An Experience Report

by Alton Miller
Fellow, Center for Teaching Excellence
Acting Director, Public Relations Studies
Columbia College Chicago
United States
amiller@colum.edu

and Margaret Sullivan
Chair, Marketing Communication Department
Columbia College Chicago
United States
msullivan@colum.edu

Abstract: Distance learning techniques developed according to previously existing Internet models do not always produce educational tools that serve students well. Rather than adhere to the "supermarket" templates typically used by commercial Web sites seeking to attract and dazzle consumers, which require users to master the rules of navigating among a range of global options, I have found that a *linear* model based on email communication conventions better addresses students' needs. The complex challenges associated with learning public relations writing via the Internet are made simpler through the use of relatively low-tech online presentations. The emphasis is on creating relationships with and providing prompt feedback to students, and sharing information among students, to better replicate many successful pedagogical techniques of the classroom. I hope that my experience teaching writing courses in the classroom and online simultaneously will provide valuable comparisons of useful techniques for teachers in other disciplines.

Introduction

I teach public relations writing. In today's marketplace of ideas, the craft of public relations writing is an important tool for effective advocacy. Public relations writing is often more than a necessary skill in the global arena of contesting ideas – in many cases it *is* the arena itself.

Public relations writing is a complex process involving three sets of skills: research and organization ("pre-writing"); the writing itself, necessarily the product of an individual talent; and rewriting, often a consensus effort requiring a process of compromise among several interested players.

To develop these skills, students employ several styles of learning. As they are introduced to techniques of research and organization, they are acquiring and assembling information and putting it into practice, much as a physics student might. As they discover the disciplines of editing and rewriting, they are internalizing an essentially social process involving both interior and interpersonal negotiation, much as an actor or dancer might. And as they develop skills in the "actual writing," they are working individually, under the eye of a master, to perfect technique, much as a medieval crafts-guild apprentice might.

Writing as a Process

Public relations writing is made more complex by the fact that public relations writers actually serve not one but three masters – the story, the editor and the client. To tell any story, students must acquire basic writing skills; sadly, this is not a given in today's undergraduate population. By basic writing skills I mean not only the ability to develop a theme, paragraph by paragraph, but even the awareness of what constitutes a good paragraph. Second, students must learn to express themselves within the disciplines of journalistic style, a style for which most English composition classes have not prepared them. A generation ago, a general familiarity with news style was naturally acquired, through habits of newspaper reading; this is no longer the case. Third, students must learn to persuasively focus a client's message in terms that please the client, as well as in a style acceptable to news editors.

Thus the process of public relations writing implicates three sets of skills, and three different objectives for the writer. The order in which these activities unfold is ultimately not important – the professional writer will develop personal work styles out of individual preferences. But I have found that my students avoid confusion and do their best work when they acquire these skills in a certain order, advancing to the next stage only after demonstrating an understanding (though not yet mastery) of the preceding one. The details of the order are less important for my present point, than the fact that there exists an optimum order for the presentation of the elements of an education in this discipline.

Substitute Techniques

In the classroom experience, that optimum linear order is maintained in real time, by the content of each class discussion and exercise, and by attentive monitoring of students' progress. (Also important is the fact that Columbia limits each writing class to fifteen students.) Online I have had to develop substitute techniques.

Objective assessment indicates that my in-class students progress from mediocre to very good over the course of each fifteen-week term, and their level of accomplishment serves as the basis by which I make evaluations of my online students. This comparison is made easier by the fact that I teach both sections simultaneously using the same syllabus; I am able to monitor, week-by-week, the progress on both sides.

When I undertook to create an online course at Columbia College Chicago, I established as a key principle that the online experience would be asynchronous and strictly online. That is, students would be able to sign on and do their coursework at any hour, independently of whether I, or other students, were online at the same time; and there would be no requirement for a personal meeting (with the possible exception of a final exam), nor would students be required to chat with me or with each other in real time. A student should be able to complete my course from a computer on the moon. My purpose was to develop a genuine distance learning system – I had already long been providing online enhancements for my in-class students, and did not intend merely to shift from a preponderance of classroom instruction to a preponderance of online instruction.

The other guiding principle was that my online students should be afforded all the advantages that my classroom students enjoyed, though it was clear that this would call for some ingenuity in devising recipe substitutes. While my online colleagues will recognize this as an inherently impossible objective, they will also appreciate that with a little redefinition, nothing is impossible.

The three most difficult amenities to substitute were the teacher's personality in conveying information, the benefits of continual evaluation and feedback, and the students' ability to learn from other students. My success online, as well as in the classroom, I am convinced, depends upon the quality of the teacher-student relationship I am able to foster; continual feedback; and the dynamics by which students learn from other students ("If he can do that, so can I.")

Email Relationships

I began by rejecting the "supermarket" template typically used by commercial Web sites seeking to attract and dazzle consumers, which requires the user to master the rules of navigating among a range of global options. Like any teaching activity, an online course must work to engage students; but it need not "sell" them. Put bluntly, the online student is a captive audience and the combined effect of design and language can be put to the service of educating rather than capturing attention and convincing the user to keep turning the page.

I decided, instead, to build on the observation that young Internet users develop real relationships with others via email and real-time chatting; and the related fact that the easiest and most intuitive Internet activity is the use of email. My first communications with each student are personal email messages, in the week or so before classes begin. I provide general orientation, and also pose questions that require a response from students. In some cases (depending on how quickly they respond to each message) I have exchanged as many as six rounds of email before the first lesson.

Some of these email messages – and, later in the course, some email messages that complement the lesson material – are group messages, not personally composed. But from the standpoint of the student, they appear to be individually directed. I achieve this illusion without undue deception, simply by addressing the email message to my own address, with "blind" copies to the student list. I maintain my email relationships strictly in the second-person singular.

Once the student is provided with a username and password, the focus shifts to the lessons posted online. In Week One, only Lesson One is available – and not via the syllabus/lessons links (which will be activated later), but as a "Next Page" link from the introductory page of the course site. Even though the student has now been launched into the course trajectory, I continue to maintain an email correspondence – usually simple, short messages – especially when I think the student will benefit from a little prodding.

Personalization + Interactivity = Feedback

To make my system more personal, I chose to use a "stand-alone" course site, physically located on the server at Columbia College Chicago. Rather than begin at a course management Web address, students reach their lessons by clicking on a link in their email (taking them to http://prwriting.columbiacollege.net, a URL I personally own, aliased to redirect to the Columbia site). Students arrive immediately at the first page of the course. The design is crisp and clean and easily legible, uncomplicated by any row of icons leading to an array of options; above all, the Web pages are low-tech, without extraneous graphics, devoid of animated features. Each page loads quickly.

The first page is illustrated with a casual photo of the instructor, and a personal message, signed with my handwritten signature. The message is, in style, theme and content, a continuation of the email correspondence we – the student and I – have already enjoyed. Each week's lesson begins with a similar page and, of course, a fresh message introducing the work at hand.

From the outset the pages are laid out in a one-way sequence: they may be read only in one clear narrative path. In the navigation bars there are links to a variety of resources, but initially each of those links evokes only a firm but gentle admonition that these resources are not yet available. In the first week, the student advances from page to page in a strict sequence.

Lessons average about seven Web pages, of varying lengths. Every two or three pages there is provision for some interactivity – a questionnaire to complete, an interactive exercise demonstrating a principle, or a page calling for a short essay response to an online article. Every lesson also includes a quiz, which doubles as a review device. Though they are disguised as various forms of online communication, these interactive interruptions are all simple HTML forms which, when submitted, automatically generate an email response to me. By tracking these responses I am able, not only to evaluate each student's understanding of the lesson material, but also to follow his or her progress through the lesson. I know when students have signed on, and how quickly they are advancing, and I am able to email a student who is not leaving a trail, and inspire him or her to get with the program – or consider dropping the course.

Online educators are familiar with the problem of otherwise able students losing their way in an online course. My experience is that students need to be told repeatedly, while they are still able to drop the course without penalty, that an online course will make serious demands on them. I have developed a short litany of admonitions, delivered within the initial sequence of emails as well as in the introductory lesson material, to the effect that there is no shame in dropping a course you can't handle, but no excuse for falling behind once you've confirmed your commitment to the course. Online courses are flexible (study when you want), but there are deadlines (turn in assignments when I want), and late assignments are just as late for online courses as for in-class courses (or clients' expectations.) I have found that when I stress these points early, those students who remain in the course perform to higher expectations.

Another important lesson for me has been the students' need for immediate feedback. There is a tendency among online instructors to manage the workload by batching certain types of work and responding, by category, on the instructor's timetable. My system encourages me to treat my students as I would any other email correspondents. I acknowledge receipt of their assignments as soon as I notice their arrival; I address, point for point, every email message, almost always on the same day; and I edit and annotate students' assignments (see below) as soon as possible, almost always by the following day's end.

Students Learn from Students

Links on the navigation bar become effective in the second or third week, and students may then browse through a wide range of examples and other resources. After all the students' first assignments have been completed, they may take a look at how other students have solved the same problems. When I begin assigning letter grades (usually not until the fifth week of the fifteen-week course) they may study examples of real student work that earned an "A," a "C" and an "F." Though I have the capability of putting classmates' papers online, I use examples from previous semesters, rendered anonymous. In these and similar ways, I share students' work with students, without requiring them to interact with one another.

I have experimented with real-time chats among students, and a "Conference Room" where students could post asynchronous messages to one another. I have also experimented with a system whereby students could post responses to a question posed, and read one another's replies. These capabilities were derived from course management systems I had investigated. They seemed to be desirable features – until I questioned the premises of that desirability. I have not found that students were in any way assisted by these hoops through which I asked them to jump, and I have discontinued all efforts to create the illusion that students are together in a "class." In fact, I find such efforts counterproductive to the more important objective of creating a teacher-student, editor-writer relationship.

Often, during the first or second week, a student will email me asking for a further explanation of lesson material. This is a natural extension of the email relationship we have cultivated, and the request is not unreasonable. In the classroom, one way a student learns from another student is to hear a question asked and answered; both the question and the answer are educational. I should add, the question can also educate the teacher, and sometimes the emailed question will cause me to reconsider how I have presented the lesson. However, if the online student's question has already been addressed in the lesson, it is usually the case that the student is asking for private tutoring beyond the scope of the class. In such cases – and they are the norm – the students will find that their questions are answered with questions – "Look again at Lesson 2, page 2, and tell me what *you* think." – and my questions are not rhetorical: I follow up and insist on answers to questions raised by their questions. I have found that this additional demand on the student's study time gently but firmly nudges him or her toward the full use of the online material and away from an expectation of private tutoring, or other abuse of the one-on-one email relationship.

By the final weeks of each semester, students are producing drafts of press releases and other public relations writing, and I am editing and returning them as quickly as I receive them. This calls for a system of folders to keep them sorted, and a system of renaming files before sending them back. I require students to use a strict system of nomenclature – a standard prefix ("PRW"), a hyphen, their last name, another hyphen, and the assignment identifier – in both the attached filename and the "Subject" field of their email message. For example, "PRW-Smith-HeartPR" identifies a press release on "From the Heart" by Smith. After editing I simply append a hyphen and a letter grade (or, early on, an "x") to each filename, before attaching and returning it.

When I edit a student's work, I use an open file of "Notes" adjacent to the student work on my computer monitor. "Notes.doc" is a Microsoft Word document containing twenty or so "Text Box" comments representing the most frequently called-for observations and edits. I drag appropriate comments from the "Notes" file to the student's work, and always personalize at least one of them, and sometimes otherwise tweak them. I also make free use of the "Rounded Rectangular Callout," "Strikethrough," "Arrow" and "Highlight" features for my comments. I then email the marked-up assignment to them as an Microsoft Word attachment.

Conclusion

There is a consensus among online teachers I have interviewed, that unless the course is carefully managed, an online course can require significantly greater work output per student, than an in-class course. This is not surprising: there's a reason why we collect students together in one room for group work. If online education is to be a viable alternative to in-class education, the workload issues must be addressed. However, high-quality standards of online education are unsupportable if the course is simply an interactive textbook. The techniques I have developed are work-saving devices that support genuine one-on-one relationships without going overboard in the direction of private tutoring. I continue to experiment with ways to promote those relationships, without which genuine education cannot take place – and to complement the course material with the means for expeditious feedback, and ways for students to learn from other students.

"Virtualizing": A Brazilian Initiative for Upgrading Media Knowledge of K-12 Public School Teachers

Nilson Modro, MEng.
Distance Education Laboratory,
Graduate Department of Production Engineering,
Federal University of Santa Catarina, Brazil
modro@led.br

Leslie Paas, MEng.
Distance Education Laboratory,
Graduate Department of Production Engineering,
Federal University of Santa Catarina, Brazil
leslie@led.br

Alejandro Martins Rodrigues, Dr.
Distance Education Laboratory,
Graduate Department of Production Engineering,
Federal University of Santa Catarina, Brazil
martins@led.br

Ricardo Miranda Barcia, PhD.
Distance Education Laboratory,
Graduate Department of Production Engineering,
Federal University of Santa Catarina, Brazil
rbarcia@led.br

Abstract: This paper describes a project-in-progress for upgrading Brazilian public school teachers' media literacy skills. The project, called "Virtualizing", is currently being applied at a municipal level, in the city of Florianópolis, Santa Catarina (Brazil), to 180 K-12 teachers with generally little or no knowledge of computers and the internet. An constructivist educational design strategy was developed in partnership with the Distance Education Laboratory (LED) of the State's Federal University (UFSC), aiming at maximizing the teachers' exposure to informatics and internet technologies via the use of an online learning environment (VIAS-K). After describing the program circumstances, objectives and strategies, the authors focus one of the program's courses (AVA II), designed specifically to further demystify new media and give teachers a renewed sense of control and participation in the information society.

Virtualizing: Project Circumstances & Objectives

Reality of the Brazilian Public School System and Recent Legislation

In Brazil, there is a 2-tiered education system: private and public. While private schools in Brazil are comparable in quality to those of the North America, Public Schools at the K-12 level tend to have fewer resources, with lower teacher education levels and technology available. However, efforts have been made to improve these differences. For example, in 1997 the Brazilian Ministry of Education decreed that computers and access to the internet be issued to all public schools, under the condition that the schools present an appropriate pedagogical strategy [MEC 2001]. This has made the public schools' concerns the same those concerning all educators around the globe: how to appropriately use computers and networks in the classroom? Another law recently implemented decrees that all school teachers must have at least an undergraduate uiversity degree. At least 50% of the Brazilian school teachers will have to upgrade their skills.

This paper describes a constructivist strategy for upgrading 180 Brazilian K-12 public school teachers' skills, via demystifying computer and internet technology. The authors participated in the instructional design and system design process, aiming toward objectives and results that could be examplary for both public and private school teachers, throughout Brazil and around the globe.

Virtualizing Project Objectives

The Virtualizing project is a partnership between the Ministry of Education of the Municipality of Florianópolis and the Distance Education Laboratory (LED) of the Federal University of Santa Catarina (UFSC). The program consists of courses for 180 teachers from 19 elementary and junior high schools with computer labs. The teachers were selected from various subject areas: Language Arts, , Geography, Mathematics, Biology, etc. The principal objective of the program is to encourage, via immersion in an e-learning environment, a culture of technology use and appropriate pedagogical strategies for the municipality's public education system.

VIAS Knowledge

VIAS Knowledge (VIAS-K) is an educational platform that offers a broad set of interactive models, including learning environments for users, multimedia content, tools for collaboration, support and system management. The platform unites state-of-the-art information technologies with appropriate pedagogical methodologies. It aims to attend to the growing demand for education in Brazil and is modeled toward continually improving efficiency during the learning process. [Freitas et al 2001]. VIAS-K was conceived in October of 1999. In March of 2001 it was ready to support its first users - a 1 year distance education program for 600 students (teachers from the areas of maths, chemistry, biology and physics who had not yet finished undergraduate studies).

Since many of the learners are new to computers and networks, an important aspect of the VIAS-K learning environment is its user support system. In addition to online support tools and information, every course offered via VIAS-K relies on the added support of live course tutors. The tutors help students and professors to use the technology and act as facilitators in the communication and learning process.

Another aspect of the VIAS-K platform worth highlighting is its model for accessing the system. The first screen the student accesses is a Portal of information related to the course, managed and automatically updated by administrative members (in this case, member of the Ministry of Education) through online forms allowing for the upload of text and graphics. The Portal model serves to keep the group informed as a whole, with timely and relevant information, as well as providing news to the public in general. The Portal also contains the point of login for students, professors and tutors. Upon entering a valid user ID and password, users have direct and unlimited access to course content and support tools. Fig 1. illustrates this access dynamic.

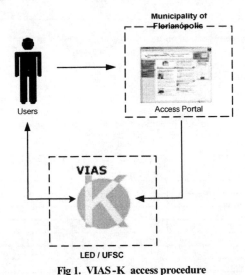

Fig 1. VIAS-K access procedure

Fig. 2 presents the VIAS-K main page and its elements: 1. navigation content tree (a graphic organization of educational content); 2. content area (once a topic is selected in the navigation content tree, it is shown in this area); 3. user identification; 4. tools (divided into 5 categories: personal tools, administrative tools, collaboration tools, support tools and on line-help); and 5.logout area.

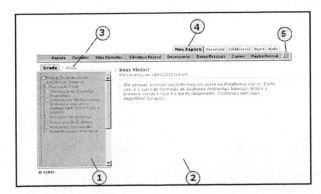

Fig 2. VIAS-K main page and its elements

Fig. 3 to follow shows some screen shots of the Virtualizing program.

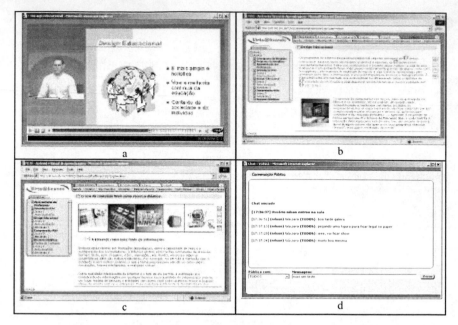

Fig. 3 Virtualing Program screen shots: a) online video being viewed; b&c) content in hypermedia documents; d) chat tool in action.

Strategies

The 180 teachers were divided into 6 groups. Each group selected a course according to their interests / needs. The courses mixed face-to-face and on-line learning, as shown in table 1 below, during a period of 3 months (April 25 – August 30, 2002).

Group #	Courses	Total Number of Participants	Total Hours	Hours F-t-F	On-line
All	Virtual Learning Environment I	180	20	14	6
1	Media and Knowledge	30	40	17	23
2	Accessibility and Technologies	30	30	9	21
3	Digital Workshop: constructing texts	30	20	6	14
4	Digital Libraries and Knowledge Management	39	40	17	23
5	Virtual Learning Environments II	30	30	9	21
6	Multimedia production technologies	30	20	6	14
Total number of Hours		200			
Total hours Face -to-Face		34 meetings / 64 hours			
Total hours on -line		136			

Table 1: Virtualizing course structure

The Virtualizing program began with the all participants taking the course "Virtual Learning Environments" - I (AVA - I), divided into their respective groups, ten hours per week for a period of 2 weeks (April 25th to May 10th, 2002). The objective of this course was to facilitate the digital immersion of all the participants into the program. The mainconcepts covered included basics of on-line learning, and how to operate and collaborate in the program's virtual environment (VIAS K). This was an important first step, since nearly all of the teachers in the program were novice computer users.

The authors, involved in the instructional design and systems design process of VIAS-K for the Laboratory of Distance Education, were responsible for designing a subsequent course AVA II for the Virtualizing program, highlighted in grey in table 1 (above), and discussed in detail to follow.

Course AVA II

The course Virtual Learning Environments II -AVA II, was specifically designed to extend the teachers' knowledge of virtual learning environments and digital resources in general, aiming to empower them with the knowledge and attitude necessary for managing classrooms in today's information society. The course was divided into 6 modules: Introduction; Components of Virtual Learning Environments; Educational Design for the Information Society; Strategies for Technology Use in the Classroom; Using the Web for Didactic Resources; Methodology for Constructing Virtual Learning Environments. The information in each module was offered in 3 distinct ways: 1. A descriptive hypermedia document, containing images exemplifying ideas and links to various related sites/documents; 2. A fictitious narrative about a grade school student's experiences interacting in a futuristic learning environment; 3. Tests for auto-evaluation, and instructions for relevant individual or group activities. Activities included contributing reflections on provided literature in an online discussion forum and chats, evaluating online educational material and creating an annotated bibliography of internet sites relevant to each participant's subject area, creating a basic home page for the subject area (via online forms), and devising a strategy for a classroom activity which would use the internet.

The content was made available on the VIAS-K platform in a non-linear manner - each user could access any part of the modules in any order he/she wished. However, a suggested course chronogram was provided to guide users towards course completion. The course chronogram was designed so that topics covered in synchronous meetings (chats, videochats and face-to-face) coincided with AVA II course content and activities in a progressive way. Evaluation was informal (critical feedback without giving a grade), geared toward encouraging and helping participants to successfully complete the course activities. A motivational strategy was designed based on project exposure - each participant was expected to publish his/her site on the Virtualizing Program Portal, thereby making their findings available to local colleagues and teachers around the world.

Long-term Objective: Sustainability and Growth

The authors designed AVA II with long-term objectives in view. Each time the course AVA II is completed by a group, the number of teachers' sites published on the Portal will increase, annotated lists of internet resources will be updated and participants experiences documented, thereby creating a rich data base of useful and relevant information. These long-term objectives are designed to give a sense of continuity to the program, and are expected to be a motivational factor as the knowledge constructed by participants in the program is exposed and shared.

Final Considerations

The basic premise of the Virtualizing program is that the best way for teachers to upgrade their computer skills is through immersion in digital environments. For many participants of the program, logging on to the system and accessing course materials were major first steps. In the course AVA II, many of these novice internet users took seemingly giant leaps forward by conducting searches and evaluations of educational internet sites, and creating their own home pages and classroom strategies for internet use, something most of them couldn't conceptually imagine being able to do in the weeks preceding the course. The hands-on approach helped to demistify the media as well as give a sense of empowerment to the teachers. However, an indispensable element of the instructional design is the mixture of face-to-face and online activities and the support of tutors, to clarify difficulties and avoid feelings of isolation that can arise in pure distance education settings.

References

CISCO Systems, Inc (2000). *Reusable Learning Object Strategy: Definition, Creation Process, and Guidelines for Building*. in http://www.cisco.com

MEC Ministério da Educação (2002). Programa Nacional de Informática na Educação. http://www.mec.gov.br/seed/proinfo.shtm (accessed July 2002)

Freitas, J. O. J., Martins, A., Barcia, R. M., Pacheco, R. C. S., Martins, J. G., Tissiani, G. (2001).VIAS Teaching Environment. *7TH. International Conference on Virtual Systems and Multimedia*,. Berkeley, CA, USA.

Tschang, F.T. & Della Santa, T. (2001). *Access to Knowledge: New Information Technologies and the Emergence of the Virtual University UNU/IAS*. Elsevier Science Ltd. Oxford, UK.

Valente, José Armando. (1993). *Diferentes Usos do Computador na Educação*. http://www.proinfo.gov.br/prf_txtie2.htm.

Visser, Jan. (1999) *Changing Learning Environments: The Real and Not so Real of Reality and Virtuality* http://www.unesco.org/education/index.html

Technological Applications in a Graduate Special Education Program
Le Petite Technology

Maribeth Montgomery Kasik, Ph.D.
Governors State University
University Park, Illinois 60466, USA

Technology usage in higher education classrooms for service delivery has increased tremendously over the past 30 years. As an illustration of this point, this writer offers the following timeline as an example. As an undergraduate student in the late 60s and early 70s the only technology required of students was perhaps a calculator and typewriter. Professors lectured in large lecture halls with the use of chalkboards, overhead projectors, slide and movie projectors. This technology requirement for the "beginning teacher" was to be prepared via the "AV" da jour. Classroom teachers were equipped much the same way as the university professor. The public schools this writer experienced between 1970 and 1981 did not offer to their teachers or students computers for service delivery. There were initial computer hook ups at some schools in the city of Chicago that were linked to mainframe computers at the University of Illinois. However, these large computers were reserved for an elite few and not available to the general student and faculty populations.

As a student, the very first course in computer technology experienced was in 1969. The room was filled with keypunch machines and monitor-less keyboards "hooked up" to a main frame 200 miles away. There equipped with our plastic flow chart stencils, and computer paper, we learned the basics of "computer-speak" such as FORTRAN, COBOL, Pascal and of course BASIC. The fun everyone waited for was the opportunity to insert their cards into the key punch machine. The terror came waiting to see if those punched cards would actually run the program that we created.

At this very same time that the computer was emerging into the general population, the technological advances for the computer were being used in government agencies and some industries. As a college student in education, computers were not something essential if one was to be a teacher, let alone a teacher of students with special needs. Faculty really did not give computers any thought about being part of their daily existence. The next encounter and first university requirement to use computers in higher education for this writer came in 1977 as a graduate student where statistical research had to be entered into the computer mainframe using keyboards (this time connected to monochrome monitors) while sitting on a stool bolted to the floor in a large modern computer lab. After one's data was entered, one would wait at the job bin for their "job" to be processed.

Not until 1981 while a doctoral student at Southern Illinois University at Carbondale did PCs enter into this writer's daily reality. Statistical data was still entered into the university mainframe at this time; faculty did not have computers on their desks (nor did the staff). The IBM Selectric typewriter was the main technology for word processing. One day an Apple IIe computer showed up in the department office. It sat in a box for months because no one wanted to set it up or learn how to use it. With permission from the head of the department, this writer, on her way to becoming a certified "geek" set this computer up and running with little effort. Yet, it was not until 1984 that money was available to purchase her first Apple IIe computer for personal use.

Concurrently, this professor began teaching at Governors State University in Illinois where she re-designed a graduate program in Multicategorical Special Education. This program was to be a state of the art program for Master teachers to provide them with the skills that would make them and their students the most successful. As part of that curriculum, she developed a course: Educational Applications of Microcomputers in Special Education. The initial intent of this course was to help teachers see the need for computers; the uses for computers; learn of assistive technology and overcome any fears of computers.

Very rapidly through the 80's and 90's one could barely keep up with the almost daily advances with computers and technology. Computers began appearing in the public schools and university classrooms. There were personal decisions to be made about commodore, apple series and IBMs. As much as this user of technology loved the Apple series, in 1992, the IBM series leaped ahead. Presently used as a favorite is a Present Dell Laptop with 1 Gig Processor and 40 Gig Hard Drive 256 Meg RAM.

The early years of this course found the professor spending a great deal of time working on the elimination of basis techno-phobias among graduate students. Early lectures and class applications included learning Apple Basis, Logo, DOS, How to turn the computer on and off, Simple Assistive Devices, Computer Assisted Learning, How to Initialize a disk, etc. Students appeared excited in the university classroom about using the computer in their jobs, but found resistance came on the part of administrators and parents who felt that the computer was a toy such as Atari and just games like PacMan. Students could not learn if they were allowed to play games. Many graduates would report back that they were not able to use the school computer lab or that there wasn't time to use the computer sitting in the back of their classroom. For many years, this was the only exposure to technology that students in the graduate program would find.

During the 1990s the emergence of computer labs began to flourish and develop further. The computer was just beginning to be seen as something that could be used daily rather than once in a while by students and faculty. There were those that resisted even using telephones with voice mail systems at our institution. Many have memories of a professor stomping his telephone into pieces while proclaiming how he hated technology and would never use it. Even this professor had a change of heart when the day came that he could bring up his New York Times on the screen in his office.

Today we have technology standards, initiatives and guidelines. Students at several universities are required to have Personal Digital Assistants (PDA)s to bring to class with them. Some school districts are sending teachers to technology workshops to learn to use PDAs and other emerging technologies. Universities are finding it necessary to have "SMART" classrooms with projectors and internet connections and PCs for each student. Teachers and Professors have to be intelligent consumers of technology and the internet.

As of today, the use of technology has spread rapidly throughout the entire graduate program in special education. What began as just one course with technology has now grown to using the same applications in the majority of the classes. In 1984, 10% of the program was devoted to or delivered via technology. Today over 80% of the activities for the program require technology.

Hardware and software exist to deliver educational and vocational benefits to those with disabilities just as they exist for other people. Microcomputers as tools to which the effectiveness of depends upon the training and understanding of the use. with the changing educational environment as a result of the microcomputer, the special education uses of microcomputers have become endless as the technology, special educators need to be competent users of the resources available to them.

What follows are some of the slides that will be part of the PowerPoint presentation to accompany the text for this paper. The slides are illustrations from the current WebCt version of Educational Applications of Microcomputers in Special Education. WebCt is used by the professor as a supplement to the course. Included in the presentation are sample of student PowerPoint presentations and other technological applications.

(Please e-mail author for copy of slides)

Slide 1 My WebCt Support

Slide 2 Home Page

Slide 3 Sample Assignment Page

Slide 4 Sample Assignment Page 2

Slide 5 Calendar Page

Slide 6 Course Map

Slide 7 Graded Student View

Sample Student Projects

[A powerpoint is available for each of the listed topics]

- 1 Assistive Technology
- 2 Memory
- 3 Managing the Learning Environment
- 4Learning Strategies
- 5 Managing Classroom Environment
- 6 Coping with Tragedy September 11, 2001
- 7 Visual Strategies and Autism
- 8 Web Design Techniques

For further information or a copy of the PowerPoint presentation please e-mail
Dr. Maribeth Montgomery Kasik at m-kasik@govst.edu

CardioResearch: Supporting Knowledge Management in an Academic Cardiology Environment.

Mariella A. Montoni[1], Catarina Rocha[1], Marcus V . de Souza[1], Kathia Oliveira[3], Ana Regina Rocha[1], Álvaro Rabelo Jr.[2] , Lísia Rabelo[2], Beatriz Salvador[2]

[1]COPPE Sistemas - Federal University of Rio de Janeiro
Caixa Postal 68511 – Cep 21945-970 - Rio de Janeiro – RJ

[2]Fundação Bahiana de Cardiologia/ Unit of Cardiology and Cardiovascular Surgery
Federal University of Bahia - Rua Augusto Viana S/N – Cep 40140 -060 - Salvador-B a

[3]Catholic University of Brasília
SGAN 916 Asa Norte– Cep 70790-160 – Brasilia - DF

email: {mariella,darocha}@cos.ufrj.br, {kathia}@ucb.br

Abstract: Knowledge management offers support in decisions making through the capture of the acquired knowledge in the organizational processes and on new technologies, the access to the domain of the business model, collaborative work and knowledge reviews among the employees. CardioResearch is a web-based tool that supports scientific research activities in an academic cardiology environment. Cardio Research can help physicians and cardiologists in decisions making during the execution of their tasks, and it can also help students gaining new insights while the organization preserves its intellectual capital. CardioResearch is part of a knowledge management environment, CardioKnowledge, configured and adapted according to *Fundação Bahiana de Cardiologia/Unit of Cardiology and Cardiovascular Surgery*'s goals and particularities.

1. Introduction

The ability to systematically capture and manage the intellectual capital of an organization regarding its employee's experience, understanding, know-how and skills is emerging as the central theme in business [1], [3]. In an academic environment, there are new scientific findings every day, which means that knowledge is being generated faster than ever before. Medical knowledge is estimated to increase fourfold during a professional lifetime, that means physicians cannot practice medicine without constantly updating their knowledge [3],[4].

According to [1] and [2], the *Fundação Bahiana de Cardiologia/Unit of Cardiology and Cardiovascular Surgery* can be considered, in cardiology domain, as an academic Research and Development (R&D) organization. Its focus is scientific research in cardiology and development of medical informatics software.

R&D, in *Fundação Bahiana de Cardiologia/ Unit of Cardiology and Cardiovascular Surgery* takes place in four different aspects: (i) participation in Clinical Trials; (ii) research in master and Phd thesis; (iii) research while providing medical assistance to patients in the ambulatories; and, (iv) research in medical software developing.

These four aspects require from the physicians skills in various areas, including application domain, computer science technologies and research methodologies [1].

Motivated by these aspects, CardioResearch has been implemented to support scientific research activities in an academic cardiology environment, helping physicians and cardiologists in decision making, helping students in generating new knowledge and the organization in the creation of innovative and creative solutions.

2. CardioResearch

Taking knowledge management as quality differential in the process of organizations with different business types, such as consultancy, medical assistance and research and software development, a knowledge management environment named CardioKnowledge has being configured and adapted according to *Fundação Bahiana de Cardiologia/ Unit of Cardiology and Cardiovascular Surgery*'s goals and particularities.

CardioKnowledge aims to support knowledge management's main functionalities[7]: (i) *knowledge identification*, identifies organization's goals in a way to be configured and adapted for it; (ii) *knowledge acquisition*, captures, in a structure way, organization's internal and external knowledge; (iii) *knowledge use*, uses the knowledge acquired in a way to support business organizational process; (iv) *knowledge creation*, creates new knowledge through use and reuse of existing knowledge; (v) *knowledge dissemination*, defines manners to deliver relevant knowledge in the right moment to the right person; (vi) *knowledge valuation*, utilizes metrics to evaluate knowledge; and (vii) *knowledge maintenance*, eliminates irrelevant and obsolete knowledge.

In this context, a web-based tool of the environment CardioKnowledge, named CardioResearch, has being developed to support knowledge creation functionality, as illustrated in Figure 1. This supports is given through knowledge use and reuse in a basic environment in terms of innovation and creativity.

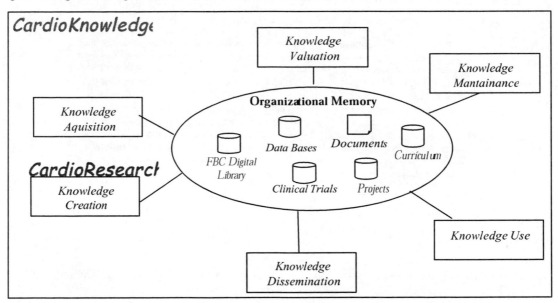

Figure 1: CardioResearch, a web-based tool to support knowledge creation functionality.

The *Fundação Bahiana de Cardiologia/ Unit of Cardiology and Cardiovascular Surgery* (*FBC/UCCV*) does four types of research: (i) participation in Clinical Trials; (ii) research in master and Phd thesis; (iii) research while providing medical assistance to patients at the ambulatories; and (iv) research in medical software developing.

CardioResearch can support the activities, at clinical trials participation and research in the ambulatories.

"Clinical Trials are a type of research study that tests how well new medical treatments or other interventions work in people. Such studies test new methods of screening, prevention, diagnosis, or treatment of a disease. The study may be carried out in a clinic or other medical facility." [8].

The ambulatories of *FBC/UCCV* have the following objectives: (i) provide cardiologic attendance to the patients; (ii) promote cardiology teaching to students of the Federal University of Medicine of Bahia and the residents of cardiology at *FBC/UCCV*; and (iii) to accomplish scientific researches.

The *FBC/UCCV* participates in several clinical trials studies and accomplishes a great amount of researches in the ambulatories, thus the research in a cardiology domain is knowledge intense process. Such knowledge, at *FBC/UCCV*, is easily lost, because it is not documented in its organizational memory; besides that, this knowledge is distributed in the employees and doctors' mind, hindering the accomplishment of the researches.

With the purpose to support cardiology researches in decision making while executing their tasks, the CardioResearch tool was proposed. It is integrated into the knowledge management environment CardioKnowledge, which seeks the explicit representation of the *FBC/UCCV*'s organizational memory, see Figure 1. CardioResearch can support the research activities in the following ways:

First, in order to form a qualified team to participate in clinical trials is necessary to combine physician's experiences to clinical trial's particularities. CardioResearch indicates qualified physicians combining key-words in their curriculum with clinical trial's characteristics filled out, previously, in forms. CardioResearch storages and retrievals documents in a document repository located in the organizational memory, in that way, clinical trial's results can be documented and shared allowing exploitation of experiences acquired from past trials and consequently avoiding repetition of mistakes. CardioRes earch also provides tutorials to train the clinical trial time. This tutorial contains the workflow process of the clinical trial and varies according to its purpose.

Second, to start a research project through patient's assistance in ambulatories, research's requirements are identified, a team of physicians and medicine students are defined, and an infrastructure is prepared to support research in the project. In this context, CardioResearch offers a module to help physicians organize research's information (e.g. research's main goals, project team, results, etc) through hypermedia forms. All this information is stored in and can be retrieved from a project repository in the organizational memory. To help selecting qualified students to set a team, CardioResearch promotes calls for participation with forms that are filled by students and evaluated by the coordinating team. To train selected students CardioResearch provides manuals describing procedures that must be following facilitating knowledge reuse.

Third, CardioResearch also promotes a learning environment where the student can be involved in patient cardiologic care receiving specific training. At this moment education, takes place in two ways: in the ambulatory, physicians and students discuss and analyze patient's records in order to reach a conclusion of patient's therapeutic plan; and in clinical meetings, where students and cardiologists discuss critical analysis, statistical results of clinical cases and current cardiology issues, correlating them with ambulatory cases. CardioResearch also uses a personalized digital library [5], adapted to *FBC/UCCV*, named, CardioLibraryFBC, with the purpose to capitalize knowledge gained by the students after finishing their degrees. This tool stores students' thesis and scientific papers facilitating organization's library collection management and literature's research and study. This helps students in gaining new insights performing and achieving the state of the art in their academic works.

Four, to prepare an infrastructure for research in patient's assistance ambulatory, medical software development is required. In order to provide that, a software engineering team develop medical databases used by CardioResearch to provide chart analysis to demonstrate research solutions and results in classes, conferences and meetings.

3. Ongoing Work

CardioResearch is still a work in process; the approach that is being used integrates knowledge management concepts and organizational processes.

The approach includes the following phases: (i) knowledge identification, in this phase requirements were identified building relevant knowledge; (ii) organizational process's identification and knowledge acquisition; (iii) process modeling through workflow; and, (iv) development of CardioResearch. The first and the second phase were completely finished and we are on the third phase validating the processes of *Fundação Bahiana de Cardiologia/Unit of Cardiology and Cardiovascular Surgery*, in meanwhile we are specifying CardioResearch's development.

4. References

[1] von Wangenheim C., G., Lichtnow D., von Wangenheim A., (2001), "A Hybrid Approach for Corporate Memory Management Systems in Software R&D Organizations", In Proceedings: Software Engineering Knowledge & Engineering 2001, pp. 326 – 330.

[2] von Wangenheim C., G., Lichtnow D., von Wangenheim A., Comunello E., (2001), "Supporting Knowledge Management in University Software R&D groups", K.-D Althoff, R.L. Feldmann, and W. Müller (Eds): Learning Software Organizations, Lecture Notes in Computer Science 2176, pp. 52-66.

[3] Fuka K., Syrjänen E., Hanka, R., (2000), "Knowledge Management in Helthcare", In: Proceedings of IRIS 23, Laboratorium for Interaction Technology, University of Trollhättan Uddevalla,2000.

[4] Dove R., (1998), "RealSearch: A Framework for Knowledge Management and Continuing Education", Presented at IEEE March 1998 Aerospace Conference, pp. 1-19.

[5] Rocha C., Xexeo G., (2002), "MyLibrary: a Web Personalized Digital Library", To be publish in Proceedings: Ed-Media 2002, July 24 th – 29th, Denver Colorado.

[6] Abecker A., Bemardi A., Hinkelmann K., Kühn O., Sintek, (1998), "Towards a Technology for Organizational Memories", May/June 1998, IEEE Intelligent Systems, pp.40-48.

[7] Probst G., Raub Steffen, Romhardt K., 2000, "Managing Knowledge – Building Blocks for Success", John Wiley & Sons, Ltda, New York, 2000.

[8] http://www.phoenix5.org/glossary/clinical_trials.html

Developing a WICeD® Team

Peter Moodie
WICeD®
The University of Waikato
New Zealand
p.moodie@waikato.ac.nz

Abstract: The University of Waikato has a very successful e-learning story to tell. This paper looks at how the Waikato Innovation Centre for e-Education (WICeD – pronounced 'wicked') team develops elearning software and explains why it has been so successful since its formation. A research project highlighted some particular tools and techniques used daily in WICeD to focus development efforts on the teaching and learning rather than on the technology. This paper reflects on the use of those tools and makes suggestions for the formation and development of any e-learning development team as a result.

Introduction

This paper is not about elearning tools, systems or even specifically about the pedagogy of elearning. It examines the establishment of a successful and innovative e-learning development team in a university environment. By taking a close look at the development of one component of our e-learning environment we have discovered some important points about the way in which an e-learning development team can be constructed and can work together to produce very successful results. In this paper I will outline the processes which led to the creation of our e-learning programme and development team and will propose some key points to keep in mind for the development of any e-learning development team.

The University of Waikato has been formally involved in online teaching and learning since 1996 when we ran our first pilot online course. Before this the University had not been involved in teaching at a distance either online or via correspondence. I was involved in the establishment of the pilot and took on the role of the technical specialist. Following the success of the pilot, my involvement in the technical development of online learning grew until I became Learning Systems Manager at the beginning of 2000. I have taken and adapted this role to focus specifically on developing our online capabilities through the development of online communities. My role is now that of the E-Learning Systems Development Manager in the Waikato Innovation Centre for Electronic Education (WICeD).

Developing our roots in e-learning

Since the inception of elearning at Waikato growth has been enormous. We have moved from providing one course fully online with 30 students to providing 130 courses fully online with over 800 students. In addition to this, we now also have over 700 campus based courses utilising e-learning technologies – catering to over 5000 students. The original focus of our e-learning activities was in the field of teacher education and has continued through to other disciplines that tend to be taught in a collaborative mode. It is this growth, along with both solicited and unsolicited feedback from learners and teachers, which has led us to believe that our elearning programme has been a success.

The information and communication technology used by the University has matured over the period we have been learning to teach online. When we began online teaching we, like so many others, started by trying to teach using a software package designed for the "transmission" model (TopClass). It taught us a lot about teaching and learning in the elearning mode. The key lessons were that learning always comes before technology, that the transmission model of teaching was no more effective in the online environment than face-to-face and that the strengths of our institution were in the field of collaborative and community based e-learning.

In retrospect these conclusions seem fairly self evident. They will not come as a surprise to any experienced e-learning institution. However, the process by which we learned these facts was important for the formative years of WICeD and the development of its in-house e-learning tool ClassForum™.

By 1999, TopClass was proving to be inappropriate for supporting the collaborative style of online teaching and learning developed at Waikato. The search was on once again for a tool which would allow us to concentrate on teaching and learning activities – picking up particularly on the collaborative and community based approach to learning – without being forced into a rigid courseware framework. Several tools seemed to meet many of our needs, however, none of them was designed specifically as a Learning Management System (LMS). The final selection criteria, therefore, was the ability to programmatically adapt the tool and build in links to student administration, authentication and assessment systems.

ClassForum, conceived early in 1999 at Waikato, was born in late 1999 and is based on *Web Crossing 4.1* which is a powerful and fully customisable online community package. ClassForum, along with the underlying Web Crossing technology, has undergone a great deal of evolution and enhancement since we began. Development started with simple enhancements to assist in classroom management such as class lists and user interface changes. Then came the development of more sophisticated teaching and learning tools such as peer assessment modules and personalised workbooks. Development is now underway on the ClassForum Learning Object Library (LOL) which is a means of collecting and sharing innovations and teaching methods and tools within the ClassForum teaching community.

Also, during 1999 the University re-visited its strategic goals and as a result of the review listed "Leadership in E-Learning" as one of the "five key strategic objectives by which the University will achieve its vision and strategic intent"(Gould 2000). One of the main outcomes of this focus in strategic direction was the formation at the beginning of 2001 of the Waikato Innovation Centre for Electronic Education, which is referred to as WICeD. In the year leading up to the formation of WICeD the development and growth of the ClassForum system continued in the Campus Media unit of the ITS Division.

Reporting directly to the University Vice-Chancellor, WICeD is a team of 17 staff who are dedicated to furthering research and development in the field of e-learning. Many of the WICeD staff were recruited from the ITS division – including the Director, who gave up his long term role as Director of ITS to take on this new venture. The staff of WICeD include: four Learning Designers, three software developers, an e-learning systems manager, a video producer, audio developer, usability specialist, 3D modeller, two graphic artists and two administrative staff.

Designing a new e-learning support tool

In 2001 I completed a Postgraduate Certificate in Tertiary Teaching. This was to further my understanding of teaching and learning in Higher Education and because I recognised the need for ever improving approaches to development within my workplace environment. As a result, an assignment component of this qualification was a research project in which I examined techniques for developing e-learning tools within a Higher Education organization. The title of which is *Focussing on Teaching and Learning in the Development of an E-learning Tool*. It examines the process of developing a new set of tools within ClassForum by the development and learning design team in WICeD. What follows comes from this research.

Initially, I assumed that I would be involved with, and reporting on, a fairly typical user centred software development process. The aim of the development was to design, program and implement a wizard based tool to enable teaching staff to create complex teacher-to-student and student-to-student group discussion systems within their online teaching space. The prototype system had been developed by myself in 2000 in conjunction with one teaching staff member who had requested a tool to create private teacher-to-student 'Portfolios' which allowed for a space in the asynchronous discussion tool shared only between the individual student and their teachers.

Now that WICeD was established and there was a very skilled team of professionals available to work on the enhanced project I expected a larger, more robust and flexible Portfolio type system to be developed. This new system was to be known as the Electronic Workbooks System (EWS). In the process of developing the EWS I made a number of interesting discoveries.

The first key educational issue was determining the extent to which teachers should be involved in the development plan. Would using a team of teachers on this development project lead to an outcome suited to the needs of the majority of eventual users? My initial thoughts on this were that it had to be an improvement over having the opinion of just one user participant in the design process, as had happened with the prototype tool. However, the difficulties of such an approach seemed equally obvious based on our experience in several previous design and development projects. The process of forming a user (teacher) consulting group would immediately present two problems which could compound the initial problem. The group would be self-selecting. Teachers who volunteered would very likely do so for one, or both, of the following reasons. There is a high likelihood that they would be keen users of the software and early adopters of new technology into their teaching practice. Secondly, those who took the time to be involved would be more likely to have their own specific needs in mind and, therefore, may approach the task with a narrow focus while WICeD enjoys the luxury of having an overview for the whole University.

In the case of those who were typically early adopters of new teaching technology, the feedback may not clearly reflect the needs and approaches to using software that a 'typical' teacher might have. Their prior experience, and often even enjoyment of using new tools, where they had to explore and learn from mistakes, could cloud their judgement in favour of a system more complicated than is ideal. For those with their own specific needs in mind, many aspects of a tool's use might be ignored in favour of the specific need they identified. The final problem was, of course, the fact that time considerations during the development 'window' meant that there was a high likelihood of not being able to get enough time from any teaching staff. This debate regarding representation is central to questions about finding the balance between technology and educational needs.

It was this difficulty, and the approaches we took to alleviate it, which led to the discoveries we made and to clarifying why our approach to the development of e-learning tools has been so successful.

Using WICeD expertise in the design process

Early in the design phase of the EWS project the decision was made by the development team to include a wide group of teachers later in the development process than we would normally feel comfortable doing. This was as a result of the difficulties in finding that elusive character, the perfectly representative teacher. The plan was to design and develop a working version of the tool using our own ideas and knowledge of the problem teachers were trying to solve – then test our understanding against a group of teachers in a formal usability study.

Given the risk of failure this posed, we had to use some techniques to attempt to maintain our user and pedagogical focus throughout the design and development process. Two techniques, role playing and conversation, were used to try and do this.

The first technique was to use role play during the design and development phases of the project. This was part of the action research approach I had adopted. My official role in the development team was 'architect and project manager'. Another member of the team was one of our learning designers and his role in the development process was to maintain focus on the pedagogical aspects of the development. Aside from our formal roles in the project, we both agreed at the outset to deliberately role-play as teachers who would use the software throughout the development process. During the project development cycle we did not mention this decision to the other members of the team.

Secondly the meetings throughout the project were conversations held between colleagues with a common goal in mind rather than formal agenda based meetings. Clark (2001) says of a good conversation; "Good conversations demand good content ... good conversation resists the bounds of definition ... is voluntary ... happens on common ground ... requires safety, trust and care ... good conversation develops" and "good conversation has a future". The meetings held during the development of the new Portfolios tool displayed all these general characteristics of good conversation.

Using conversation in the development process was not a new phenomenon for WICeD, but evaluation of transcripts of these conversations did demonstrate that the conversation style of meeting allowed for more 'thinking aloud' which led to many holes in the product being plugged before implementation. The combination of role-playing and using conversations led to a very good representation of the characteristics of the general user community.

User feedback after four months in operation has been consistently positive. Requests for enhancements and additions to the EWS system are now the norm rather than requests for assistance in creating workbook equivalents. Faculty have gone on to use the EWS in ways that even the original design and development team had not imagined. This has demonstrated to us that the flexibility and robustness of the tool which was enabled through the thinking aloud and role playing techniques has been effective.

Conclusions

Evaluation of the development process for the EWS led to a very important discovery about how the way WICeD was formed, and the way it works is applicable to other e-learning development teams. The WICeD team was established as a result of the organization recognising the need at a strategic level for central funding to establish the development of an e-learning innovation centre. Of the 17 staff who currently work in WICeD, eleven have had some, or in many cases, considerable teaching experience in the Higher Education sector. Those members of the development team consistently approach their work with teaching and learning foremost in their minds. For a technology development unit this is exceptional – for an e-learning technology development unit perhaps it should be the norm.

Without keeping teaching and learning at the forefront of e-learning developments, the results will continually drift towards technologically 'tidy', but pedagogically lax results. The supportive and proactive climate at the University of Waikato, which led to the formation of the WICeD team from a group of pedagogy aware technologists and technically aware teachers, has proven to be a successful model for the formation of an e-learning development team. Innovative approaches to teaching and learning are set to continue at a pace in WICeD.

References

Clarke, C. (2001). *Talking Shop* – authentic conversation and teacher learning. Teachers College Press: New York

Gould, B. (2000). University of Waikato Strategy Statement. Web Publication:
        http://quality.waikato.ac.nz/strategystatement.shtml (accessed 9 April 2002)

Increasing Teacher Certification through a Multi-Campus (Blackboard) Praxis Network

William E. Moore, Willa M. Moore, Ann W. Henderson and Mous Diack
Colleges of Education and Sciences
Southern University
Baton Rouge, Louisiana 70813 USA
billsubr@aol.com

Abstract: In this paper we describe the development and implementation of a test preparation network for students enrolled at four universities in the state of Louisiana. The network uses the course management software *Blackboard* as a medium for test preparation, posting resources, and conducting collaborative projects among universities. The network has a strong accountability component and provides for good statistical tracking of student activities. One noteworthy and unique feature of this project is that the network enables students from four universities to benefit from the general strengths and faculty expertise from four institutions. We will illustrate several of the local instruction models we have developed and indicate how the methods may be implemented on a larger scale.

Introduction

The popularity of e-learning is evidenced by the unusual proliferation of online courses and degree programs. Despite this unprecedented growth, controversy prevails regarding the effectiveness of this mode of instruction (Chamberlin 2001). Two years before this date, we had begun to capitalize on a middle-ground approach that combined face-to-face instruction and online learning. We then extended this methodology to include a network of four universities (The J. K. Haynes Consortium) addressing the common problem of preparing students to pass threshold examinations for teacher certification. Initially activities were confined to individual campuses and we reported our findings in annual faculty development and planning conferences. The participating institutions included Grambling State University and Southern University Campuses at Baton Rouge, New Orleans and Shreveport.

In the summer of 2001 we discovered that our consortium of schools possessed an ideal infrastructure for establishing a web-based network. For example, it could provide learning resources for students, serve as a medium for faculty development and program planning, and provide opportunities for collaborative learning among campuses. Equally as important, the network would allow the consortium to fill gaps in knowledge so that we could witness higher passage rates on the Praxis examination. To this end, we elected to use the course management software system, Blackboard, as the central tool for implementing the network. The uniqueness of this collaborative network is that students from four campuses benefit from the faculty expertise from these universities and that it provides a medium for the rich exchange of ideas among students and between students and faculty. The archives also provide valuable documentation and elements of accountability. In this paper we describe model activities that were carried out on the Baton Rouge campus of Southern University.

The Study

In our local model, we chose to employ the middle-ground approach involving students from four different classes. This arrangement included two sequential six-week Saturday workshops with an average of 47 students per six-week session. This program was part of the J. K. Haynes outreach initiative and the sessions involved regular university students and some commuters who traveled as much as 130 miles to receive face-to-face instruction. The second component involved two eight-week reading classes that were offered concurrently in the summer of 2002. One class was devoted to teaching reading for elementary school and the other reading class focused on teaching reading at the secondary level. A third component of the local network involved a *Blackboard* faculty development thrust designed to create a Praxis-based e-learning culture. For clarity, these initiatives will be discussed separately.

The Saturday Outreach Workshops

The class associated with this activity met four hours each Saturday (9:00 a. m. to 1:00 p. m.) for six successive weeks. During this time period, four faculty members offered instruction around the various components of the Praxis II examination. The first week was devoted to administering a diagnostic test and familiarizing the students with features of Blackboard. The former enabled faculty to determine student deficiencies requiring intensive work or individual attention. The latter was designed to enable students to begin using Blackboard immediately. For this purpose, we created a test bank of approximately 860 discrete multiple choice test items. By the end of the first week, students could access the available test items at their convenience. The faculty could monitor student progress and use the information to determine appropriate types of intervention. When we analyzed the Blackboard statistics, we began to see a strong correlation between usage and performance on the actual Praxis Examination. A student who had average scores on 12 of 15 Blackboard exams showed a greater likelihood to pass Praxis than one who had high scores, but only took three of fifteen exams during the same time period. In short, the intensive Praxis based instruction the students received on Saturdays proved to be an appropriate complement to Blackboard usage during weekdays.

The Summer Reading Classes

In the summer of 2002, .approximately 29 students were enrolled in each of the two reading classes for education majors to learn methodologies for teaching reading at the elementary and secondary levels. For the purpose of Blackboard activities, the classes were placed in the same Blackboard classroom. However, they were not physically combined and students never met one another except through a non-class coincidence. In this way, the students were able to take advantage of available test items and which gave the faculty the opportunity to experiment with collaborative learning across the physical boundaries of brick and mortar classes.

In the collaborative learning project, students were divided into groups of six each, with three students coming from each of the reading classes. Each group was given a name (Piaget, Bloom, Montessori, Locke, etc) and placed in the Discussion component of Blackboard. Access was restricted to members of a given group.

The entire *Blackboard* class was given 15 analytical reasoning problems and instructed to solve them collaboratively. They were informed that each student was required to provide leadership in discussing three problems and was required to participate in the discussion of all problems. They were given a deadline of midnight July 23, 2002, to complete the problems and submit a consensus report .In this section student interaction was high but some did not complete the consensus reports. More than 70% of the students indicated that they benefited from the asynchronous cross-fertilization. In an earlier study we had conducted in a similar class, the consensus reports were much higher -- largely because we had grade bonus points attached to acceptable completion of the reports.

Students in the reading classes were also required to develop home pages and place Praxis relevant material at these respective sites. These included case histories and other activities involving reading and writing skills. We found that some students had significant gaps in knowledge regarding human development, assessment and education in the courts. To this end, we created Power Point review activities and placed them in the course document section of Blackboard..

An important aspect of the reading activities was that seven faculty members were placed in this combined class as observers who could also engage in exchanges with students and offer them advice or cues to their respective problem. This part of the model is a scaled down representation of what would happen at four universities across the state of Louisiana. In this case we envision a group of students from four universities working on an assignment and having faculty members from these universities provide clues, mentoring support and insight through the Blackboard discussion forum. The preliminary results we have received suggest that there is vast potential in this application (Horton 2000).

Discussion

The results we have obtained from the four classes we have studied locally suggest that Blackboard can serve an important role for creating a culture that will accommodate e-learning and teacher certification. The creation and use of the 800-plus item test bank provides evidence of its utility. We have also demonstrated that asynchronous, peer-based collaborative learning is an important tool for filling gaps in knowledge. We further show that there is a strong positive correlation between frequency of Blackboard usage and performance on the actual Praxis examination. We are equally convinced that web-based faculty development is workable and that it provides a powerful means of exchanging ideas and teacher certification resources.

The next step in the Praxis preparation process is to implement the multi-campus network. This will include faculty development, local face-to-face instruction and a robust combined Praxis virtual classroom for students of the four campuses. We will track course statistics and provide rigorous evidence of the effectiveness of the various components of this classroom.

References

Chamberlin, W. Sean. (2001). Face –to – Face versus Cyberspace. *Syllabus* 15:5

Frayer, Dorothy A. (1999). Creating a campus culture to support a teaching and learning revolution. Cause/Effect 22:2.

Horton, Sarah (2000). Web Teaching Guide: A Practical Approach to Creating Course Web Sites. Yale University Press.

McCormack, Colin, & Jones David (1998) Building a web-based education system.. New York:Wiley Computer.

Acknowledgements

This work is supported by a planning contract from the Louisiana Board of Regents Distance Education Initiative (LA-DL-DEI-07-01/02). This project also received generous support from the Southern University Office of Technology and Network Services.

The authors gratefully acknowledge the technical assistance of Ryan Knight and Evan Thomas for creating and maintaining the examination data base.

Developing and Integrating Resources in a Virtual Learning Environment

Raul Morales and Yoneo Yano
Information Science and Intelligent Systems Department
Tokushima University
2 – 1 Minami Josanjima-Cho, Tokushima 770, Japan
{raulms, yano}@is.tokushima -u.ac.jp

Abstract: This paper presents an approach to develop and to integrate highly diverse resources in learning spaces via personalizable interfaces and virtual collaboration areas. Digital libraries comprise vast digital repositories and wide range of services, users' environments and interfaces, all intended to support learning and collaborative research activities. We are developing a distributed learning environments for which services and interfaces include, for example, web-based learning systems using annotation environment, adaptive WBL, agents-based asynchronous virtual classrooms, computer assisted language learning using video and annotation, teacher support environment in web-based training system, videoconference-based CSCL environments, user agents for video information retrieval and access to digital documents that support specific courses and projects. In order to assist users in dealing with this complexity, we are designing environments, termed collaborative personal and group spaces, which provide users with means to access and control all available resources in a uniform fashion from a single vantage point.

1. Introduction

This paper analyzes some of the majors problems faced by users when using collections and services provided by network learning environments or digital libraries and presents an approach for the integration of learning environments resources which is based on the concepts of personal and collaborative learning spaces. We posit that users should have at their disposal means to create virtual areas within the learning environment in which they can place information objects that are relevant to their interest and ongoing tasks. We refer to this sort of virtual space as a collaborative personal space (CPS). Additionally, digital libraries and learning environments should also provide users that usually work remotely with virtual spaces where they can meet to discuss objects and topics of interest and to work collaboratively on group projects while maintaining the capability to access materials in digital collections. We refer to this second category of virtual place as a collaborative group space (CGS).

Our group has been conducting research in the areas of computer supported collaborative learning (CSCL) and digital libraries (DL) and has produced advances both in the construction of digital contents and in the provision of e-learning for users in the context of distributed system architecture. In this context, we are designing and implementing one version of collaborative personal spaces and other of collaborative group spaces. We report our design and development experiences in this particular area of our learning environment.

2. Environment Context

One part of our group has been working in a system architecture for a learning environment in a Digital Library that addresses the needs for information management, communication and collaboration among a highly distributed community of users. We have aimed to build both a practical, functional learning environments and a testbed for research of open issues in the field, including aspects of personalized and groups interfaces, collaborative work and information visualization.

The realization of our learning environment has called for research and developed efforts in three major areas: building content, designing components that provide general infrastructure such as information retrieval services, multimedia management and agent essentials, and user interfaces and environments. Our advances in the area of general infrastructure include a distributed framework that integrates services and interfaces, with implementations using KQML, servlets and RMI as well as components implementing various popular information retrieval mechanisms. Finally, in the area of user interfaces and collaboration environments, our work has resulted in various access and visualization mechanisms.

One distinctive element of our work in leaning environments is our view of information and collaboration spaces as comprising both the digital and physical realms. We believe the needs posed by learning activities can be satisfied if traditional resources as well as the novel digital facilities are accessible to users at any given time in a seamless fashion. In this regard, we have been integrating traditional on-line learning material and user services in to our new developments. As can be expected, software components such as CoCoA, AVC, Sharlok and LeComm consider that both digital and physical resources should be accessible to users.

Even though each software component may facilitate seamless access to some learning resources, the diversity of such components as well as the size and dynamic nature of digital collections and user communities have the potential to make the digital library a complex and unwieldy environments for end users. Means are needed to ensure that individual users have access to exactly the resources they are entitled to according to their roles, needs and preferences. Providing more that a user needs unnecessarily increases the system's complexity and the user's cognitive overload. On the other hand, limiting access excessively would result in system under-utilization and user frustration. The needed compromise should be the result of electing and addressing every user's needs and preferences. Learning environments users typically need to work collaboratively as in a school or in a physical library. More often than not, a given user belongs to more than one regular group of users. It is also possible that learning or library resources are disjoint for every group a user belongs to, or that some materials need to be used in several work groups. Thus, for example, a user may participate in a class discussion for which he is the instructor or facilitator and also in a technical committee that is reviewing a paper submitted to a conference. For him class, he may suggest a reading (available at the digital library) which happens to be, say, a missing reference in the paper being reviewed by the other group in which he participates.

The work described in this paper aims to advance along these lines: facilitating the creation and maintenance of personalized areas (which we call collaborative virtual spaces) that integrate resources relevant for a given user , and making possible for users to easily move from personal to group areas sharing digital content in an adaptive video-CSCL environment.

3. Collaborative Virtual Spaces

In the context of a learning environment, we define collaborative personal space as a virtual area that is generated, owned and maintained by a user to persistently keep resources like objects, agents, etc. or references to resources which are relevant to a task or set of tasks the user needs to perform in the learning environment. Collaborative personal spaces may thus contain digital documents in multiple media, personal schedules, visualization tools, and user agents. Resources within collaborative personal spaces can be pre-assigned according to the user's role. For example, a research student would have access to research-specific topic materials, visualization tools and interfaces to communicate (video, audio or text based chat) with his colleagues. Agents may be available for recommending research or library materials that are relevant to the research topic and the collaborative personal space could be enriched by the agent's suggestions.

Similarly, we define a collaborative group space as a virtual area in which learning environment users can meet to conduct collaborative activities synchronously or asynchronously. Explicit collaborative group spaces are created dynamically by a group leader or facilitator who becomes the owner of the space and defines who the participants will be. Implicit collaborative group spaces can be generated automatically when a number of users have been detected to have similar user profiles or interests around a given topic or task. In addition to direct user-to-users video-communication, users should be able to access research and learning materials and make annotations on them for every other group participants to see.

4. Implementation

We are developing prototypical implementations of collaborative personal and group spaces concepts in order to provide a homogenous interface to the various user services and environments described in last section. We based our designs on the well-known room metaphor [Greenberg and Roseman 1998; Henderson et al. 1986]. Collaborative personal spaces are thus conceived as rooms that every user may configure and adapt by defining some characteristics as color, furniture, layouts and by adding learning resources that are used frequently or support user tasks. We also have emphasized the role of every user in our prototypical interface design [Shineiderman and Plaisant 1994]. When users register to access the learning environment, they specify the role(s) the will be playing in the system. Typically, a user selects or is assigned a combination of the various existing roles; research, graduate or undergraduate student, full time or part-time professor, research staff, or system administrator. The initial collaborative room configuration is determined by the user's role.

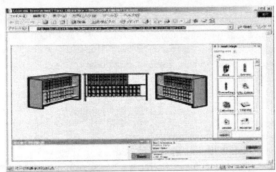

Figure 1. The interface of Hyzone – 1 for CPS.

Our first CPS prototypical implementation, which we termed Hyzone-1, is being developed to users in Java applets that could be downloaded and run at the client level. Figure 1 illustrates the interface of Hyzone - 1. The idea is straightforward: Users may configure their collaborative personal space by changing a room's physical characteristics and placing sheets icons (representing learning resources) into bookshelves that can be added and moved around at will. Drag-and-drop functionality can be applied practically to any element in the prototypical interface. The figure also shows icons for search tools and recommender agents. Menus include options for adding and removing elements from a room, associating learning resources with icons, sending instant messages to active users (same interest) and new elements can be shared by clicking pull-down menu.

Our current version of Hyzone – 1 implements explicit collaborative group spaces (as per our definition in the previous section): any user of the learning environment may create a CGS and send invitations to users who are members of a team or who are potentially interested in a particular discussion subject.

Figure 2 illustrates a session of five users who have started a discussion in Hyzone -1. Upon entering the "room" representing the CGS, every user sees a picture or video of himself, images or videos of the other users currently logged in, as well as icons that represent learning environment, which have been brought to the room to support the discussion. Users participate in the discussion by posting their comments via text interface and pointing to learning resources. Users can make annotations on shared materials (images and videos) and see other users' annotations. The entire discussion can be saved so latecomers may join a meeting and get up to speed quickly, or the discussion may be suspended and retaken by the group at different time.

In Hyzone -1, users can drag their own image or video and drop them near another user, group of users or learning resources. This is intended to reflect natural positions in a discussion in a visual fashion that can be perceived by all group participants. Alternative, new rooms or sessions may be created to include different sets of users for addressing sub-topics or new discussion topics.

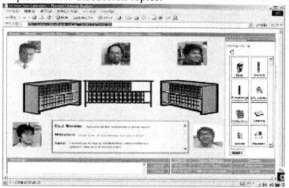

Figure 2. The interface of Hyzone – 1 for CGS.

Our ongoing-work implementations of collaborative personal and group spaces have undergone various usability and performance test with encouraging results. We have focused initial tests to our main target communities: college students, professors and research staff. For our tests we have used small collection of digital videos, articles, technical information and online information.

In addition to usability inspections test, we have been observing users experiment with the prototypes. With only minimal initial guidance, users of Hyzone – 1 have been able to personalize their information space by creating rooms, changing their appearance, and more importantly, by gathering learning materials and references (online entries) and placing them in bookshelves. From their collaborative personal space, users also have been able to open digital documents and launching applications such instant messaging and videoconference tools. However, some of the services and applications described in this paper have become available more recently.

From our results thus far, we believe collaborative personal and groups spaces are a promising approach to the integration of highly distributed, heterogeneous information spaces. Our design and prototypical implementations shows that our approach may effectively help users in coping with the size, complexity and dynamism of digital learning content.

REFERENCES

Ellis, C.A., Gibbs, S.J., & Rein, G.L. 1991. Groupware: Some issues and experiences. *Communications of the ACM* 34, 1, 38-58.

Henderson, D. Austin, and Card, Stuart. 1986. Rooms: the use of multiple virtual workspaces to reduce space contention in a window-based graphical interface. *ACM Transactions on Graphics* 5, 3, 211-243.

Lakos A., Gray C. 2000. Personalized library portals as an organizational culture change agents: Reflections on possibilities and changes. *Information Technology and Libraries 19*, 4 (December), 169-174.

Morales, R., and Yano, Y. 2002. Effective collaboration in a videoconference-based CSCL environment. *World Conference on Educational Multimedia, Hypermedia & Telecommunications.* (in progress).

Sanchez, J. A., Leggett, J. L. 1997. Agents services for users of digital libraries. *Journal of Networks and Computer Applications 21*, 1, 45-58.

Shneiderman B., Plaisant, C. 1994. The future of graphic user interfaces: personal role managers UMD CS-TR-3285, CAR-TR-713, ISR-TR-94-48 People and Computers IX, British Computer Society's HCU 94 (Glaswow, Scotland, Aug.) CU Press (Cambridge, U.K.) 3-8

The Use of Virtual Learning Environments in UK Higher Education - Are VLEs Supporting Student-Centred Learning?

Sue Morón-García

Institute of Educational Technology, The Open University, United Kingdom

s.d.moron-garcia@open.ac.uk

Abstract: This paper reports on doctoral work in progress investigating whether Virtual Learning Environments (VLEs) are being used to support student-centred learning in UK Higher Education (HE). VLE is the term used to describe the package of integrated software tools that make use of Web or Internet-based technologies and are used to put courses online. The focus of the research is the lecturer (HE teacher), because it is they who set up the learning environment for the student. The findings of a pilot study into the use of Web and Internet-based technology to support learning in HE were used to develop a main study which concentrates on the use of VLEs by humanities and social science lecturers in face-to-face education.

Introduction

This research investigates whether lecturers are moving towards a more student-centred model of teaching, facilitated by the use of Virtual Learning Environments (VLEs). The aim is to identify factors relating to the VLE, the context in which it is used and a lecturer's pedagogic model that may support or prevent this happening. The research questions are:

- Can Virtual Learning Environments support student-centred learning and how does the functionality of the system affect lecturers?
- What are motivating factors for lecturer use of Virtual Learning Environments and what prevents them being used?
- How are lecturers using them, what methods are they using, and how does this fit into their overall pedagogy?

The focus of this research is the lecturer (HE teacher), because it is they who set up the learning environment for the student. The findings of a pilot study into the use of Web and Internet-based technology to support learning in Higher Education (HE) were used to develop interview questions for a main study concentrating on the use of VLEs by humanities and social science lecturers to support face-to-face education. The main study also used the Approaches to Teaching Inventory (ATI – Prosser and Trigwell, 1999) to help identify a lecturer's pedagogic model.

Virtual Learning Environments

The most recent manifestation of Web and Internet-based technology packaged for educational use and promoted as a way for universities to get their lecturers online is the Virtual Learning Environment (VLE). The two most commonly used VLEs in the UK currently are WebCT and Blackboard. Some VLEs are based on specific pedagogic models, for example COSE (Stiles 2000), emphasising the use of communication and collaboration tools. The aim is to encourage a different model of teaching and a move away from the uploading of large amounts of content (the first stage of use for many lecturers) and the replication of what can already be achieved through print. According to a recent report the institutional motivation for the adoption of VLEs ranges from increased efficiency to the enhancement of teaching and learning, greater flexibility and a move towards distance education (Jenkins *et al*, 2001).

The Benefits of Using Web and Internet-Based Technology

Much of the writing and research relating to the use of Web and Internet-based technology deals with the perceived benefits for the learner. Those highlighted include the enhancement of study skills and the ability to participate in subject activities (Martin and Fayter, 1997) as well as the creation of transferable skills (Harrison, 1994). It is claimed that the new collaborative tools and new media actually afford a better learning experience for students (Gibbs, 1999), aiding understanding (Pimentel, 1999) and facilitating the sharing of knowledge (Harasim, 1989). It is claimed that the use of Web or Internet-based technology can facilitate the creation of a student-centred learning environment (Collis, 1996) and the adoption of a student-centred method of teaching (Westera, 1999). Student-centred approaches are advocated as a way of equipping students with the skills they need to survive in today's complex world.

Factors Affecting a Student-Centred Approach to Teaching

It is widely argued that student-centred teaching approaches encourage students to adopt higher quality approaches to learning - what Biggs and Moore (1993) among others call a deep approach to learning - and aid the development of critical abilities. It is argued that student-centred learning and learning environments designed with reference to constructivist theories of learning will produce in students the critical and cognitive skills that Higher Education aims to develop (CNAA, 1990, Jonassen *et al*, 1993, Thorpe, 2000). However, there may be pressures on lecturers to use particular approaches in their teaching. Trigwell and Prosser (1997) found that lecturers who felt that they had more control over their teaching (what is taught and how) were more likely to adopt student-focused approaches. These approaches were affected detrimentally if the class size was thought to be too large, student diversity too great and workload too heavy.

Elements in the institutional environment may affect lecturer usage of the Web and Internet-based technology such as access to equipment, training and support. Barnard writes about an obstacle course of barriers that have to be overcome if teachers are to move "from being non-users of technology to being fluent users who could integrate technology into their teaching" (1999, pg. 352). These include anxiety, unfamiliarity with the technology, resourcing, perceived usefulness, personal philosophy, the influence of colleagues and classroom dynamics.

Lecturers' beliefs about teaching and learning and how to create the most effective learning environments are fundamental to improving student learning. Previous research has shown that lecturers' conceptions of teaching correlate with teaching approaches that in turn correlate with student learning approaches and learning outcomes (Kember, 1997 for an overview). Trigwell *et. al.* (1999) built on previous research to show that lecturers' teaching methods correlate with the approaches to learning of their students and that student-centred methods are linked to deep learning approaches in students that in turn are linked to better learning outcomes.

The Pilot Study

The pilot study was conducted in order to find out what was actually happening in Higher Education (as distinct from what the literature indicates may be happening):
- Were lecturers using Web and Internet-based technology?
- What sort of technology and how?
- Was pedagogy influencing the use of the technology?
- Were lecturers aware of their pedagogy?

The objective was to develop a series of interview questions that would facilitate the collection of data to answer the research questions.

Twelve lecturers from four universities were interviewed about their teaching and their use of Web and Internet-based technology, including VLE use. Consideration was given to the possibility that some lecturers may be more comfortable with the use of Web and Internet-based technology and that some lecturers may be more able to explain and justify their pedagogy. For this reason education lecturers and those teaching computer science were interviewed. A third category of lecturer, social science or humanities, with no obvious reason to feel comfortable with the technology or a reason to be familiar with pedagogic terms was also interviewed.

Findings

- The use of VLEs is not widespread, even within those universities that support use. The newer universities were more likely to have an institutionally supported VLE and have an institutional policy that encourages use.
- Use is restricted by access issues, student and lecturer IT literacy, student expectations and colleague use, time available to create resources and to become familiar with technology.
- The 'electronic filing cabinet' was thought to be valuable – it was convenient for both students and lecturers.
- The use of e-mail as a means of communication was becoming the norm, discussion forums were used with varying degrees of success, but there was some resistance from students and lecturers were unsure how to make best use of it; 'chat' was only used by one lecturer.
- Technology was used to support group work, reflection, contact with the lecturer, sharing of work, engagement with materials and content outside class time.
- Teaching methods adopted by lecturers were dependent on class size and influenced by the way in which they were taught, observing others and any training they had received, but the same method (for example, a lecture) meant different things to different lecturers.

Developing questions for the main study

There were discipline differences in the way Web and Internet-based technology was used that made comparison difficult, therefore it was decided to focus on the social science and humanities discipline areas where it was hoped there might be more of a pedagogic pull than a technology push.

It had proved difficult to identify a lecturers' teaching model, the same method, for example a lecture, could mean different things to different people and talk about VLE use had often been mixed up with talk about general teaching. Research relating to teachers' and lecturers' conceptions of teaching indicates that there is a disjunction between lecturers' conceptions of teaching and their claimed educational practice; so even if lecturers say that they are using student-centred methods they may not be in practice. Prosser and Trigwell (1999) developed the Approaches to Teaching Inventory (ATI) to overcome this disjunction and aid in identifying the intended and actual strategies used by lecturers. It was decided to use the ATI as one of the instruments for the main study. Lecturers were asked to focus on a specific example of VLE use when completing the ATI and to talk about the way in which the VLE supported and facilitated the teaching methods used in that context.

Questions in relation to a lecturer's level of IT literacy had not worked well, personally defined levels of expertise are highly subjective and mean little in comparison to other's self-claimed levels. It was decided to ask lecturers to define (and give examples of) their own comfort level with software applications and tools relevant to VLE use, for example a word processing package, a presentation package, Web authoring software and computer mediated communication tools. The data had also indicated that there were a number of other factors that influenced the use of a VLE such as the types of students being asked to use the VLE and the ethos of the department and institution in which the lecturer works.

Thirty-two lecturers across ten universities were individually interviewed about their use of their university's VLE (three of these were trial interviews, as part of the process of developing the interview instrument). The interview data is currently being analysed.

References

Barnard, J. (1999) *Factors Affecting the Use of Computer Assisted Learning by Further Education Biology Teachers.* Unpublished PhD thesis, The Institute of Educational Technology, Open University, Milton Keynes, UK.

Biggs, J.B. and Moore, P.J. (1993) *The Process of Learning*. 3rd ed., Sydney, Australia: Prentice Hall.

Collis, B. (1996) *Tele-learning in a Digital World*. London: Thomson Computer Press.

Council for National Academic Awards (1990) First degree courses in computing in polytechnics and colleges, June 1990 *quoted in* Council for National Academic Awards (1992) *Case studies in student-centred learning*. London: The Council for National Academic Awards.

Gibs, G.R. (1999) Learning how to learn using a virtual learning environment for philosophy. *Journal of Computer Assisted Learning*, 15(3), pp. 221-231.

Harasim, L. (1989) On-line Education: A New Domain *in* MASON, R. and KAYE, A. Eds. (1989) *Mindweave: Communication, Computers and Distance Education*. [Online] Available: http://icdl2.open.ac.uk/mindweave/chp4.html [30th July, 2002].

Harrison, C. (1994) The role of learning technology in planning change in curriculum delivery and design. *Association for Learning Technology Journal*, 2(1), pp. 30-37.

Jenkins, M., Browne, T. and Armitage, S. (2001*) Management and implementation of Virtual Learning Environments: A UCISA funded survey* [Online] Available: http://www.ucisa.ac.uk/TLIG/vle/welcome.htm [30th July, 2002].

Jonassen, D., Mates, T. and McAleese, R. (1993) A Manifesto for a Constructivist Approach to Uses of Technology in Higher Education In T.M. Duffy, J. Lowyck and D.H. Jonassen (Eds.), *Designing Environments for Constructivist Learning* (pp.231-247). Berlin: Springer-Verlag.

Kember, D. (1997) A Reconceptualisation of the Research into University Academics' Conceptions of Teaching. *Learning and Instruction*, 7(3), pp. 255-275.

Martin, A. and Fayter, D. (1997) Cross-curricular tools for university students: developing an effective tool. *Association for Learning Technology Journal*, 5(1), pp. 70-76.

Pimentel, J.R. (1999) Design of Net-Learning Systems Based on Experiential Learning. *Journal of Asynchronous Learning Networks*, 3(2) [Online] Available:http://www.aln.org/alnweb/journal/Vol3_issue2/pimentel.htm [30th July, 2002].

Prosser, M. and Trigwell, K. (1999) *Understanding Learning and Teaching: The Experience in Higher Education*. Buckingham: SRHE and Open University Press, 1999.

Stiles, M.J. (2000) *Effective Learning and the Virtual Learning Environment* [Online] Available:http://www.staffs.ac.uk/COSE/cose10/posnan.html [30th July, 2002].

Thorpe, M. (2000) Pedagogical implications of flexible learning. In Jakupec, V. and Garrick, , J. (Eds.) *Flexible Learning, Human Resource and Organisational Development: Putting theory to work* (pp. 175-192). London: Routledge.

Trigwell, K. and Prosser, M. (1997) Towards an understanding of individual acts of teaching and learning. *Higher Education Research and Development*, 16, pp. 241-252.

Trigwell, K., Prosser, M. and Waterhouse, F. (1999) Relations between teachers' approaches to teaching and students' approaches to learning. *Higher Education*, 37(), pp. 57-70.

Westera, W. (1999) Paradoxes in Open, Networked Learning Environments: Toward a Paradigm Shift. *Educational Technology*, 39(1), pp. 17-23.

E-Learning & the Global Interface

This short paper begins with effective communications principles in contemporary multicultural and multinational classrooms and differing national and personal styles of discourse, and proposes their broader application to e-learning environments.

It examines several instances of their embodiment in sound screen and website interface design principles.

The paper closes on some design issues for new technologies (beyond the desktop Web browser) that will impact learning, stimulated by the author's Summer 2002 semester as an exchange professor in Japan.

Michael R. (Mike) Mosher has been an interface, Web and instructional animation designer for Apple Computer, IBM Almaden Research Center and Cisco Systems. He is now Assistant Professor of Art/Communication Multimedia at Saginaw Valley State University. Mike is the author (with R. Shepherd) of Creating Web Graphics, Audio and Video, Prentice-Hall Publishers, 2002.

Collaboration as a Response To Individualism

Robert Muffoletto, Ph.D.
College of Education
Department of Curriculum and Instruction
Appalachian State University
Boone, North Carolina

Abstract: This paper addresses issues related to the conception of collaborative learning as a design form for the Internet environment. Collaborative learning is positioned in opposition to the liberal/modern notion of the individual. In other words, how we construct the individual within a collaborative learning environment counters how western industrial society's attempt to construct the notion of the individual as a free agent responsible for their own success or failure. This paradigm counters how we think of students within a traditional learning environment—one based upon merit and the business model.

Introduction

The Internet and related technological developments have allowed educators and students alike the opportunity to consider alternative forms of educational environments ranging from traditional instruction centered environments to community-learner centered learning environments. This paper will begin to outline a context for issues related to ideas concerning the individual in light of these movements. In doing so I am not taking a technological determinist perspective, but position technology as a systematic relationship to various processes and devices, woven together through ideologically based theories of application and practice, working within and through society.

There is no denying that developments in computer related technologies have effected how we think about education, leading to a paradigmatic shift framing teachers, students, and knowledge in a different manner. The Internet as a multi-mediated learning environment is providing "design forms" to educators through which to engage their students in the active pursuit of knowledge and application. The traditional classroom, the role of students and teachers, have been questioned and challenged as the result of the teaching and learning paradigm shift. It is now possible to create learning environments, over instructional environments that re-define the definition of teaching, learning, and the classroom. As we consider educational possibilities that include collaboration and cooperative models of interaction and learning, we need to re-think how the resulting learning environment constructs and re-constructs the idea of the individual within a perceived community of learners, over the autonomous individual within a crowd.

To consider the development and definition of collaborative learning environments we need to move beyond the "common sense" notion of technological and educational neutrality. We need, in a reflective manner, to contextualize the "idea" of collaborative learning communities within a historical and geographic construct. Not to do this will further lead to the mystification of process and the glamorization of technology as progress.

Why Talk About Collaboration

Talk concerning collaborative learning environments attempt to localize collaboration as a response to a history in the United States of "rational individualism" in education and educational technology. In other words, to consider learning environments based upon a notion of collaboration is in itself a direct response to the environment found in classrooms that is competitive, centering the curriculum within an instructional framework.

In thinking about a collaborative learning community, it is important that we see it in opposition to and different from, a non-collaborative environment centered on liberal individualism, progress, and technology. In education, liberal individualism is present in neo-behaviorist learning theory, which is centered on merit and individual measurable achievement. From this perspective, progress or learning in education is based upon presumed objective, measurable criteria, resulting from individual effort, and natural intelligence.

From this perspective, our educational system in the United States has been built upon an ideology of progress, science, and control. Education in the United States has been constructed on late 19th century and more developed 20th century models of management and control over labor and knowledge. In the modern world of the twentieth century we have witnessed how the individual was engineered by capitalism and a business ideology as an object to be controlled for the perceived good of a few over the needs of the many. In the post-modern world, where questions of identify and social justice drive much of the thinking, the individual is recognized as a member of a larger community bound together through history, language, culture, and geography. Post-modernism in education moves the discussion away from the individual as an object to be formed, to the individual as an emerging subject.

The construction of the individual from an object on the assembly line to the individual, as defined in an individualized, self-paced integrated learning system is a small step, but a major element in hegemony of the "ideology of the self" within a capitalistic, competitive merit based society. It is an ideology where the individual is held responsible for her or his development and progress. A progress defined by the system itself. This notion of progress is found in the current movement towards a standardized curriculum and high stake testing.

Contrasting the notion of the individual found in the community formed within the modern urban industrial society, to the concept of the individual as found in rural America, southern and eastern Europe, we see the individual woven into the fabric of the rural community. The individual in the rural agrarian community, gained her identity within the life of the community, and in return had responsibilities to that community. Whereas, the individual in the urban industrial community was defined by the system as an objectified object, a free agent, an independent contractor, who is responsible for his or her own condition and future. In one instance, the community engaged the individual within its own survival and definition, where in the other case, the individual existed in solitude in control of its own destiny.

If we reflect on the "idea" of the individual as an autonomous being, responsible for its own condition, it is radically different from understanding the individual as a member and defined by a community. In this case, the community shares responsibility for the individual, and the individual is responsible to the community. These forms of communities are held together through religion, family history, economic ties, and various practices. Communities of practice define their members, not as individuals, but as members. We can find examples of communities of practice in different locals. Individuals who share common labor practices, shared physical space, shared ideological perspectives, history of oppression, histories of wealth, team members, and class mates, all have borders (discourses) of different thickness and depth which unify them into communities.

In an educational system and its focus on the merits of the individual student, the individual teacher, and the individual school, the student, as well as the teacher, is constructed not as a member of a community of practice, but as an individual, who is judged by their behaviors in light of pre-determined outcomes and economic needs.

To speak of collaborative learning environments is to speak in opposition to the current dominant paradigm, which hosts individualism, competition, and an objectified measurable knowledge base. To speak of collaborative and cooperative learning environments is to embrace notions of democracy, community, shared responsibilities, and diversity. To speak of collaborative learning environments in traditional face to face classrooms, or in geographically dispersed ones, moves education away from an historically grounded, "instruction centered" paradigm, to a "learner centered" one. In a collaborative learning environment the shift is away from the search for "a" truth, to the recognition of truth and meaning as socially constructed, resulting from an understanding of history, the boundaries of geography, membership, and reflective analysis.

Any discussion or analysis of learning communities, collaborative learning environments, or democratic classrooms found on the Internet or not, is not a simple matter. Any discussion of collaborative learning is an analysis and critique of the established discourse and collective consciousness which benefits certain "ways of knowing" and the construction of individuals as objects. To reflect on what appears to be a "common sense" reality of educational practice is as complex as attempting to understand reality from any perspective.

Educational Technology as a Method of Control

In the first part of this paper I attempted to create a framework for considering the notion of the "individual" in education. I would like to now shift our attention to a brief discussion to contextualize the field of educational technology as a discourse of control and benefit. First of all, technology is about systems not objects or devices. Educational technology emerges out of a systematic approach to the identification of educational needs or problems, and their solutions. Educational technology systems frames a relationship between hardware or devices, software-the curriculum, and theories of instruction and learning which also draws from the fields of communication, learning, evaluation, and information design.

Before 1940, various devices served the classroom teacher as an aid to their instruction and as an enhancement to the learning process. Audio Visual aids, or AV, served the classroom teacher in her attempt to bring the world to the classroom, as seen with film and still images (with accompanying sound). Most of devices from this time period were seen as "aids" to the teaching process, not as a delivery system of instruction and the curriculum.

After the 1940s and into the 1950s there was a shift away from audio visual aids to a technology of instruction. Educational technology was a merging of engineering principles and devices – with roots in the social engineering movement of the late nineteenth century; psychology- with its roots in behaviorism, and education given the responsibility of preparing our youth to be productive and participate in the modern world (which usually meant the world of labor), educational technology could provide a scientific rationale and process for making education more efficient, effective, and accountable to the dominant culture and their perception of a good society.

Out of the merger of engineering, psychology, and education, emerged the current field of educational technology. As far back as the first decade of the 20th century we have witnessed the merging of system concepts with educational needs. Taylorism applied to education is a good example of that effort to separate the "conception and development of curriculum" from its delivery in the classroom, as well as the management of the educational factory. In the 1920s and beyond, we find in the work of Franklin Bobbit, WW Charters and others, the efforts to bring a scientific process to the development of curriculum. But it was not till after World War II that we witnessed the emergence of a technology of instruction to address what was seen as the weakest link in the educational endeavor—the classroom teacher.

I feel it is important that we contextualize our thinking about "collaborative learning environments" within this history because it is this history that student centered, collaborative education is in opposition to.

Collaborative Learning Environments

From what I have argued above, collaboration, people working and learning together, is in opposition to a system which constructs individuals as autonomous isolated objects.

How we (the collective we) construct educational environments through the Internet will be dependent upon the paradigm brought to our endeavors. The environment we create will be dependent upon the paradigm we employ, the constructs of knowledge we elicit, and the educational philosophy we practice.

Educational environments created on the Internet will define the individual as either an autonomous agent or as a member of a community of learners. In either case, the nature of knowledge, the vision of futures, and the identity of the self, will be formed respectively. Classrooms located on the Internet or within the walls of the institution will look differently. Each will define through its own framework the notion of legitimate knowledge and what it means to learn.

Issues related to building and practicing collaborative learning environments (communities) begin with opposition to the concept itself. Teachers, administrators, and learners have internalized the dominant definitions of what it means to teach, learn, and hold class. Questions concerning teacher work and student evaluations will arise. Issues related to a fixed or constructivist view of knowledge will need to be discussed and reflected upon. In short, collaborative learning engages the whole notion of what it means to teach and learn. It brings everything into question. There is no safe ground when the status quo is questioned and challenged. A guiding question within the debate will be: "Who benefits from the way education is now and who will benefit if it changes?"

The Internet offers to us who have access to it, a world of possibilities to increase democratic practices and to redefine what it means to teach and learn. A collaborative learning community challenges dominate forms of knowing, allowing those who have been marginalized an equal voice in constructing social reality.

E-Learning: "Self Service" Does Not Equal "Self-Directed"

By Felicity Mulgan
Content Alive
felicity.mulgan@contentalive.com

Abstract: This paper examines the distinction between self-service learning and self-directed learning in relation to e-learning strategies. Based on the findings of a series of case studies of Canadian corporations with e-learning strategies, it argues that e-learning alone is not the solution for businesses that want to nurture and grow their knowledge capital. Rather, e-learning in conjunction with a deliberate strategy to increase employee self-directedness is a more effective solution. It further argues that although traditional e-learning strategies may bring about small, incremental improvements towards greater employee self-directedness, these will only occur on a wider scale if an organization sets out to develop more of what Rosenberg terms a "learning culture" (2001).

Introduction

As more organizations adopt e-learning strategies, training delivery is moving towards a self-service model, where learners are expected to take more responsibility for taking and completing required training.

The self-service model offers many benefits to organizations, particularly in terms of cost and efficiency. Gone are the expensive classroom courses and the costly trainers. Gone are the days when the course schedule determined when training took place, or when enforcing training consistency across the organization was a challenge. Organizations can now administer standardized training from a learning management system, establish job-related curricular, track employee progress and enjoy the efficiencies of disintermediation that e-learning affords.

While benefits like cost savings and efficiency may appear to be worthwhile goals in the short-term, it is pertinent to ask whether the typical self-service e-learning model that business organizations are adopting is really providing them with the learning system they need to meet the demands of doing business in the 21st century. Our series of case studies of Canadian corporations with e-learning strategies suggests that despite implementing e-learning, many organizations still take a traditional approach to training. Our findings also suggest that a key barrier to change lies with organizational attitudes towards learning, and that e-learning in conjunction with a deliberate strategy to increase employee self-directedness is a more effective way to ensure knowledge and skills are developed and shared within organizations.

E-learning Strategies and Self-Directed Learning

Current theories of e-learning identify two opposing paradigms: the traditional approach reflecting a "training culture", where knowledge and skills are transmitted to learners, and the value drivers for the organization are cost, efficiency, access and consistency; the progressive approach reflecting a "learning culture", where learning takes a "transformation" approach, and where the value drivers for the organization are "synergistic", and include the ability to create more self-directedness, build communities, share knowledge capital and integrate employees more fully in the business (Berge 2000, Pearson 2002, Rosenberg 2001).

The progressive approach, it is argued, is a better response to the ongoing social, economic and technological changes that organizations now face. A workforce of flexible, self-managing and self-directed employees is a critical part of this approach. This belief is supported by studies that have found a positive correlation between self-directed employees and improved workplace performance (e.g. Guglielmino & Guglielmino 1988, Long and Morris 1995).

E-learning provides organizations with the means to support and develop self-directedness amongst employees in a way that was never available before, but not all e-learning is created equal in this regard. Within the range of e-learning practices and strategies, it is possible to find both traditional and progressive approaches to training/learning, and to find strategies that are more about enhancing self-service than self-directedness. This is an important distinction to make, since self-service and self-directedness meet different organizational needs. The former is a method of administering learning that cuts out the "middle man", and provides some flexibility to learners within an ultimately controlling environment. Indeed LMS's can be a boon to organizations that want to tighten control over who learns what and when, and keep track of employee development. The latter, self directedness, means employees play a greater role in shaping their own personal development, setting their learning goals, and managing their own development. It means developing in employees what Senge has called "personal mastery" (1990), and embracing the concept of continuous learning.

To illustrate, many e-learning practices, such as online courses, continue to reproduce the standards of more traditional delivery mechanisms (linear structure, fixed content, completion through a test, etc.), while the typical learning management system perpetuates the concept of training as a series of pre-determined one-time events rather than as an ongoing process that is responsive to individual needs (Harrison 2000). By contrast, e-learning practices that can encourage greater self-directedness have less in common with traditional delivery mechanisms, and include self-assessment tools, performance support tools, collaborative learning spaces, online mentors, online resources, decision support tools, content development tools and knowledge management systems. Used as part of a strategy that encourages self-directedness, they can be powerful tools for both employee and organizational development (Rosenberg 2001).

To understand why many organizations have not adopted the more progressive practices of e-learning, it is necessary to examine the role of self-directed learning in the workplace. Knowles defined self-directed learning as "a process in which individuals take the initiative, with or without the help of others, in diagnosing their learning needs, formulating learning goals, identifying human and material resources for learning, choosing and implementing appropriate learning strategies, and evaluating learning outcomes" (1975). Two concepts here, learner control and learner initiative, have rarely been a feature of workplace learning. However, much of the literature on self-directed learning finds that for self-directed learning to take place, learner control and initiative are among the critical success factors (e.g. Tough 1979, Candy 1988, Guglielmino et al 1988, Morris Baskett 1993, Bouchard 1994). The challenge for business organizations, therefore, is to foster these traits in employees in a way that is meaningful to the success of the organization. This usually means aligning the employees' desire to learn with the goals of the organization.

A useful framework for measuring the degree to which training or learning is self-directed in the workplace is Piskurich's Self-Directed Learning (SDL) Continuum (1994). His assertion that at a certain point along the continuum, the locus of control shifts from the organization to the employee/learner, ties in with the traditional/progressive paradigms discussed earlier. If we analyse the e-learning practices of an organization in relation to the continuum, we can easily identify how far the organization is organized upon the principles of employee self-directedness. The locus of control concept also helps to identify practices that are more about self-service than self-directedness.

Findings of Study

Our series of case studies of e-learning strategies at Canadian corporations looked at how far their e-learning strategies were promoting employee self-directedness. It found that in the majority of cases, the strategies were focused around basic online course delivery, usually via a learning management system. Though these strategies were promoting the self-service model, they were not promoting the concept of employee self-directedness. No practices were identified that belonged far enough along Piskurich's SDL Continuum for the locus of control to have shifted to the employees. A summary of findings include:

- Standard, linear tutorial type courses were most common
- Tutorials were typically presented in 30 minute or longer chunks of information at the subject or competency levels, rather than at task levels
- Courses were expected to have a shelf life of over a year, so were not always tailored to immediate needs
- Courses had associated tests; passing a test was deemed to indicate that the skill or knowledge had been acquired
- No specific training or tools were offered to help employees become more effective learners
- Training interventions were limited to job-related skills and knowledge

- Opportunities to take training outside a job-related curriculum were almost non-existent
- Employees were rarely able to identify own learning needs
- Knowledge management or knowledge sharing was either not practiced or was in its infancy, and took on a "push" characteristic, not a shared characteristic

An investigation into the culture and attitudes towards learning at these organizations further underlined the finding that these organizations were promoting self-service, rather than self-directedness. In all cases, although learning was considered a strategic necessity, it was also considered distinct from productive work, and was therefore thought of as an organized type of activity that employees participated in, rather than as an integral part of work that could happen at any time, with any one. These organizations were only prepared to sponsor or underwrite learning interventions that could be clearly linked to specific job skills, and all personal development was tied strictly to an employee's current position or to the development of skills in preparation for a particular career move. Employees were offered virtually no e-learning opportunities to explore other avenues of knowledge, particularly those that had less direct relation to the organization, and there were no examples of the use of e-learning practices such as collaboration, two-way knowledge sharing, and other methods associated with the progressive paradigm. Although the implementation of LMS's had successfully reduced the gate-keeping role that managers used to play in relation to employee training, managers continued to set work priorities and remained strongly focused on traditional notions of productivity, which were seen as distinct from learning.

On a more positive note, our study also found signs that employees appreciated the independence that self-service learning gave them. Other small, incremental changes in relation to self-directedness were also discernible, which may lead to greater expectations of learner autonomy in the future. At the more senior levels, employee expectations around personal development were also found to be high, and organizations were thus under pressure to provide more access to training and learning opportunities. This reflects a more general trend identified in relation to employee training and retention (e.g. Moss Kanter 2001), and one that is likely to trickle down through all levels of the organization as the population in general grows used to being able to find the information it needs online.

Conclusion

A workforce of self-directed learners is an asset to an organization that wants the flexibility to respond to the pressures of today's economy. However, self-directed learning is partly about control: who controls what, when, how and why an individual learns, and who determines whether they have reached an appropriate standard. Currently, e-learning strategies appear to mirror the culture of the organizations in which they are implemented, particularly in terms of who controls learning goals and resources. The results of this study of a sample of Canadian organizations suggest that the implementation of e-learning does not, in itself, transform an organization from having a training culture to a learning culture. Despite e-learning's potential to change the way employees learn, e-learning is viewed by some organizations as a cost efficient alternative delivery mechanism rather than a vehicle to overhaul approaches to learning, and control over learning goals and resources remains firmly in the hands of the organization.

Organizations such as those featured in this study may be missing opportunities to develop a more flexible, self-managing, self-directed workforce that can respond effectively to ongoing change. All those involved in developing e-learning strategies, from training managers, to e-learning vendors and consultants, can play a role in helping organizations see that e-learning is not a homogeneous solution to training a workforce, and that sometimes more fundamental organizational changes need to take place in order to develop the best and most effective employees.

References

Berge, Z. (Ed.) (2001). *Sustaining distance training:Integrating learning technologies into the fabric of the enterprise.* San Francisco: Jossey-Bass

Bouchard, P. (1994). Self-directed professionals and autodidactic choice. In H.B. Long, & Associates (Eds.) *New ideas about self-directed learning.* Norman, Oklahoma Center for Continuing Professional and Higher Education, University of Oklahoma.

Candy, P. (1991) *Self-direction for lifelong learning.* San Francisco: Jossey-Bass

Guglielmino, L.M., and Guglielmino, P.J. (1988). Self-directed learning in business and industry: An information age imperative. In H.B. Long & Associates, *Self-directed learning: Application and theory.* Athens, Georgia: Adult Education Department, University of Georgia.

Harrison, R. (2000, July-Aug). Learner managed learning: Managing to learn or learning to manage? *International Journal of Lifelong Education, 19,* (4), 312-321.

Knowles, M.S. (1975). *Self-directed learning.* Englewood Cliffs, NJ: Prentice Hall.

Long, H. B., and Morris, S. (1995). Self-directed learning in business and industry: A review of the literature 1983-93. In H.B. Long & Associates (Eds.), *New dimensions in self-directed learning.* Norman: Public Managers Centre, College of Education, University of Oklahoma

Morris Baskett, H.K. (1993) *Workplace Factors which enhance self-directed learning.* Paper presented to 7th International Symposium on Self-Directed Learning, West Palm Beach.

Pearson, R. (2002, February). *E-learning. Is all the hype warranted?* Paper presented at the Human Resources Professional Association of Ontario Annual Conference, Toronto, Canada.

Piskurich, G.M. (1994). The current state of SDL in business and industry. In H.B. Long & Associates, *New ideas about self-directed learning.* Norman, Oklahoma: Oklahoma Research Center for Continuing Professional and Higher Education.

Rosenberg, M. J. (2001). *E-Learning: Strategies for delivering knowledge in the digital age.* New York: McGraw-Hill.Senge, P. (1990) *The fifth discipline.* New York: Doubleday.

Tough, A.M. (1979) *The adult's learning projects.* (2nd ed.) Toronto, Canada: Ontario Institute for Studies in Education.

Analysis of Students' Eye Movement in Relation to Contents of Multimedia Lecture

MURAKAMI Masayuki
Faculty of Foreign Studies, Kyoto University of Foreign Studies, JAPAN
Email: masayuki@murakami-lab.org

KAKUSHO Koh MINOH Michihiko
Academic Center for Computing and Media Studies, Kyoto University, JAPAN

Abstract: In this article, we report our analysis about relation between the content of lecture and the students' eye movement in order to clarify the criterion to capture image information for distance learning. We classified content of lecture into nine instructional process categories: introduction, presentation, explanation, illustration, assertion, query, reply, question, and response. As the result of analysis, we get the characteristic of students' eye movement in each instructional process category in practical lecture. And our research suggests the practical guide for selecting of image information for distance learning

1. Introduction

The rapid advancement of the Information Technology (IT) such as the Internet has been changing education, particularly distance learning. In the case of distance learning, lecture with multimedia material is shot by some cameras, and the image information is recorded and transmitted. It is necessary to convey the content of lecture effectively, so we need the criterion to decide what we should capture by camera.

In the previous work, they proposed some automatic shooting systems and archive systems for lecture (Kameda et al.,2000, Onishi et al., 2000). These works were interesting in the visual point of view. But, we propose that it is important to consider contents of lecture for selecting of image information. Since students depend on contents of lecture in order to decide what they look at, we pay attention to students' eye movement.

Our purpose is to clarify the criterion to select image information for distance learning and WBT. Then, we report our analysis of how the students' eye movement is affected by the content of lecture.

2. Instructional process category

Lecture with multimedia material consists of lecturer, material and students. Multimedia material continues to be shown during the lecture. Students choose an object (material, lecturer and the other students) at which they look to get information. We define the style of this lecture as "multimedia lecture". In this multimedia lecture, the roles of lecturer and material change according to the situation. In this research, we examine the roles of lecture and material which affect students' eye movement.

A criterion is necessary to partition the multimedia lecture into parts based on contents. Then, we define "Instructional Process Category" referring to the past research of instructional analysis (Flanders, 1970, Hough et al., 1970, Mizokami et al., 1998) and teaching method. We classified contents of lecture into nine categories: introduction, presentation, explanation, illustration, assertion, query, reply, question, and response.

Introduction: Lecturer tells students about the preliminary knowledge and the outline of lecture so that he/she expects students to be motivated the lecture. In this process, lecturer gives students advanced organizer. We define this part as "introduction".

Presentation and explanation: We propose that the process of learning multimedia material classifies into two parts, referring to process of learning text (Kintsch, 1994). First, they learn of multimedia material. They try to recognize and understand the multimedia material in order to construct text-based model to replay and summarize the contents. We define this part as "presentation". Next, they learn from multimedia material. They try to integrate information and knowledge in order to construct situation model to apply the integrated knowledge. We define this part as "explanation".

Illustration: Lecturer shows a concrete example to help students understand. We define this part as "illustration".

Assertion: Lecturer asserts his/her argument and tells his/her experience. We define this part as "assertion".

Questions and Answer (query, reply, question and response): Lecturer often interacts with students by verbal communication in the lecture. We call this part "questions and answers". We classify this part into four parts in detail. When speaker is the lecturer, we define as "query" and "reply". On the other hands, when speaker is a student, we define as "question" and "response".

3. Experiment

We have practiced TIDE (Trans-Pacific Interactive Distance Education) project between University of California Los Angeles (UCLA) and Kyoto University (Yagi et al., 2000, Murakami et al., 2001).

"Japanese Economics" were offered from April to June 2001. Several professors of Kyoto University give this course. For Kyoto University students, this lecture is regarded as usual multimedia lecture. In this research, we select this distance lecture as experimental lecture.

Figure 2 shows the figure of classroom of Kyoto University. Left screen shows Web material, and right screen shows students of UCLA. Lecturer makes the lecture on the center of the classroom. In this situation, students' eye movement changes depending on what they look at, among lecturer, students of UCLA on the screen, and material. Two cameras in the front of classroom recorded students so as to catch the direction of their eye movement. Whereas the camera behind the classroom recorded lecturer and two screens in order to check the contents of lecture. And, the first author attended all lectures and recorded the state of classroom in field notes. After that, we classified the recorded lecture into instructional process category.

We select two lectures as experimental lectures among course. Two lectures were practiced by different lecturer. Table.1 shows time of each category.

We extracted 9 students from each lecture as target of analysis. We checked what students look at per 10 second. Additionally in order to analysis in detail, we select some parts of lecture, which cover all categories, so we checked per second about the select data.

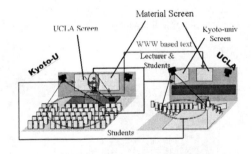
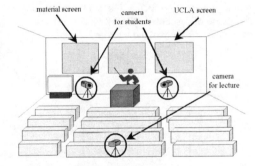

Figure 1 Distance Lecture System   Figure 2 Classroom of Kyoto University

Table 1 Time of Each Instructional Process Category

We consider ratio of observation and pattern of eye movement as indicator. The ratio of observation is calculated by (the number of students looking at the object)/(the number of all students). The pattern of eye movement is based on cycle of eye movement and what student looks at first. We define cycle of eye movement as (when he/she looks at lecturer) + (when he/she looks at material next), or in the case of reverse order. We think that the continuous is important factor, so that we analyze the data by the following methods. If student looks at different object in only a second (for example, lecturer in 3 seconds, material in 1 second and lecturer in 4 seconds), we regard that student looks at same object continuously (above example, lecture in 8seconds).

4. Analysis

4.1 Result

	introduction	presentation	explanation	illustration	Assertion	query	reply	Question	response
lecture1	4:30	11:10	18:30	4:30	8:30	0:30	7:10	7:20	1:40
lecture2	4:00	20:00	12:30	9:40	5:20	2:00	5:30	4:00	3:00
Average	4:15	15:35	15:30	7:05	6:55	1:15	6:20	5:40	2:20

Firstly, in order to clarify the character of ratio of observation on each category, we calculated average of the ratio of observation per 10 second on each category. The result shows Table 2.

Table 2 Ratio of Observation on each Instructional Process Category

	introduction	presentation	explanation	illustration	assertion	query	reply	question	response
material	41.3%	81.3%	50.1%	93.5%	24.3%	22.2%	8.6%	6.6%	4.5%
lecturer	47.9%	17.4%	48.0%	6.5%	71.2%	57.8%	59.3%	20.3%	37.7%
students	10.8%	1.3%	1.8%	0.0%	4.5%	20.0%	32.1%	73.0%	57.8%

Secondly, we analyze eye movement of each student on each category. Results of analysis about introduction, presentation and explanation show figure 3-5. In these figures, 2 of y-axis shows looking at lecturer, 1 shows material and 0 shows no object.

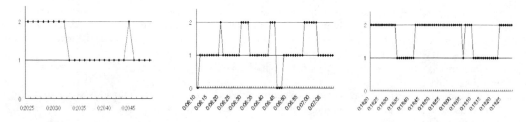

Figure 3 Introduction   Figure 4 Presentation   Figure 5 Explanation

Thirdly, we sampled cycles in these data, and add up them on each category. Histogram of cycles about presentation and explanation show figure 6,7. The x-axis shows time of cycle and the y-axis shows the number of times. The average of cycle of presentation is 11.60 second and standard deviation is 3.38, whereas the average of cycle of explanation is 20.21 second and standard deviation is 6.85.

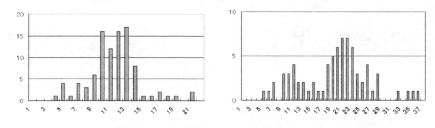

Figure 6 Cycle about Presentation   Figure 7 Cycle about Explanation

4.2 Relation between Category and Eye Movement

We discuss the relationship between instructional process category and eye movement from the results of analysis described in 4.1.

Introduction: The ratio of looking at material is much the same the ratio of looking at lecturer from Table 2. As concerns the pattern of the eye movement, students gazed at lecturer at first, and next looked at material from Figure 3. It is thought that they tried to acquire advance organizer from the lecturer.

Presentation: The ratio of looking at material is very high, 81.5%, from Table 2. From Figure 4 and Figure 6, students mainly stared at material for about 15 seconds and sometimes peered at lecturer for about 3 seconds. They learned of multimedia material during presentation, so that they mainly stared at material. And they looked at lecturer in order to complement understanding.

Explanation: From Table 2, the ratio of looking at material is close to the ratio of looking at lecturer. From Figure 5 and Figure 7, the cycle of eye movement is about from 19 seconds to 29. The cycle is the longest than other course process categories. They learned from multimedia material during explanation, so that students stared at the object which they regard as important to understand the lecture.

Illustration: The ratio of looking at material is the highest, 93.5%, from Table 2. As the reason of high ratio, it is thought that material offered main information source.

Assertion: The ratio of looking at lecturer is very high, 71.2%, from Table 2. They gaze at lecturer because of interaction between lecturer and students.

Question and answer: Generally, students looked at speaker. But in the case of "query" about material, they change their focuses on material and lecturer by turns frequently. It is thought that students tried to grasp information of lecturer and material in order to answer to the question.

4.3 Guideline

Based on the result of analysis, we discuss the practical guide for select of image information. In introduction, we should select image of lecturer for several seconds first in order to give advanced organizer. In presentation, we basically select image of material, but we occasionally insert image of lecturer. In explanation, we should present image of material and lecturer by turns for about 20 seconds. In illustration, we should select image of material. We should select image of lecturer in assertion. In questions and answers, we basically select image of lecturer, except the case of the query about material. In query about material, we should alternate image of lecturer and material frequently.

5. Conclusion

In this article, we report our analysis about relation between the contents of lecture and the students' eye movement in order to clarify the criterion to select image information for distance learning and WBT. As the result of analysis, we get the characteristic of students' eye movement in each instructional process category in practical lecture. And based on these results of analysis, we propose to apply these results to selecting image for distance learning.

Reference

Flanders, N. A. (1970) Analyzing Teaching Behavior, Addison-Wesley

Hough, J.B., Duncan, J.K. (1970) Teaching: Description and Analysis, Addison-Wesley

Kameda, Y., Ishizuka, K., Minoh, M. (2000) A Study for Distance Learning Service - TIDE Project -, IEEE International Conference on Multimedia and Expo, Vol.3, pp.1237-1240.

Kintsch, W. (1994) Text Comprehension, Memory, and Learning, American Psychologist, Vol.49, No.4, pp.294-303

Mizokami, S., Ozaki, H., Hirakawa, J. (1998) Aimed at Analyzing Teaching Process with Students are Satisfied, Kyoto University Researches in Higher Education, Vol.4, pp22-64 (in Japanese)

Murakami,M.,Yagi,K.,Kakusho,K.,Minoh,M.(2001) Evaluation of Distance Learning Course shared by UCLA and Kyoto University., ITHET2001

Onishi, M., Izumi, M., Fukunaga, K. (2000) Blackboard Segmentation Using Video Image of Lecture and Its Applications, The Transactions of the Institute of Electronics, Information and Communication Engineers D-I, Vol.83-D-I, No.11, pp.1187-1195 (in Japanese)

Yagi,K., Kameda, Y., Nakamura, M., Minoh, M., M, A, Abdalla.(2000) A Nobel Distance Learning System for the TIDE Project, ICCE2000, Vol.2, pp1166-1169

ON-LINE STUDENT SUPPORT SERVICES (OSSS)
A Pre-Testing Opinion Survey of Distance Learners on OSSS

Dr. K. Murali Manohar
Professor of Distance Education and
Programme Director, DEQSTI, SDLCE
Kakatiya University, Warangal (AP) India

Distance Education (DE) is known for its 'learner-centeredness' and precisely due to this reason it evolves and provides all possible support services through every possible means to facilitate the learners complete their 'learning objectives'. Most of the DE institutions provide a wide variety of support services to reach each and every student based on their needs and requirements. The institution may use print or telephone or other mode to interact with the students for various purposes ranging from providing information and other services from pre-entry level to post-entry to after-course completion levels. The students under distance mode of learning will naturally seek endless information raising a number of questions, doubts and various other queries time and again till they get satisfied. In the recent times most Universities are found to have been using Internet and web technologies to maintain on-line communication with the students.

In a traditional system of ODL, there will be a Reception / PR Centre or Academic Services Division which would deal with the academic questions and problems of students and resolve them instantaneously on its own or by referring to the administrative units concerned. In a modern ODL system instead of doing these activities manually or through correspondence, it will provide the services concerned through electronic means via website. Under this system each University will have an interactive website while facilitating the students to have exclusive access to the On-line Student Support Services (OSSS) system. It would provide access to students via Internet about any information (being updated every time) regarding the courses and programmes available, with full particulars and details of eligibility conditions, academic schedules, fee and its procedure for payment including on-line payment of fee via credit card, submission of receipts, confirmation of admissions or cancellations, academic counseling, information relating to Regional/Study Centers and their activities on-line chat rooms with faculty members involved instructional materials (with down loading facility), assignments, feedback forms, news letters, student forums, all types of academic time tables, results, grades, marks, certificates and messages relating to deadlines, general information and other academic details in which the students may be interested to know or the institution may be interested to make others know.

The system can provide all possible information, clear options, needed access with 'dos and don'ts' or 'proceed or do not proceeds' and other instructions and instantaneous resolution of problems and 'on-line acceptance or rejections' with full opportunity to students to continuously interact, make alterations needed and get other related things done. It will provide access to services while increasing one to one interaction and enabling self-based learning. Further it gives complete security of information and protection from hackers on on-line transactions with student access No. and password facility to activate the system any time, from any where and for any purpose and facilitating the students to seek needed support and guidance at all levels of their study. There will be automatic mail-back system, messaging, remainders to students e-mail account, auto-reply system on all simple and programmed queries, answers to any general or specific or frequently asked questions etc. At appropriate levels and stages, audio and video facility also will be made available for appropriate institution - student interaction. As things move and as facilities improve more and more information could be added thereby and the OSSS system is continuously upgraded and strengthened. The institution under this system may provide free Internet access points in all Regional and Study Centers or at appropriate places where study centers are not available for student free access and use and this will relieve the student's burden. Since the Internet facility is available everywhere and in every town and city and not being very expensive in the open market, more and more student's 'will come forward' to use it. Provision for a little more skill or training can make the student more perfect in 'accessing and approaching' the institution by activating the OSSS. This system is new to Indian ODL institutions and except to some extent at IGNOU, a few IITs and other technical institutions which provide distance mode of education, no full-fledged OSSS system is now available any where in India's University education system. Thus the introduction of OSSS in any University system in India would still be an 'experiment' and in this connection Indian ODL Institutions are to learn many lessons from the experience of advanced institutions.

Present Study: 'The What and Why' Issues

The present study deals with the concept and a model of on-line student support services system (OSSS) and makes an attempt to elicit student's opinion on a programme specially proposed (at the pre-introduction-level) of an on-line student support services system at a 10 year old Duel Mode University operating in Southern part of India with 62 programmes (from Certificate level to Ph.D. level) and 36,000 students to its credit. It has already setup a website and permitted students to seek answers from the institution through e-mails. It is found that an estimated 30 per cent of post-graduate students had e-mail account and interestingly eighty per cent of them had the account with yahoo.com, around 12 per cent in their offices, 2 per cent in their homes and the remain with other companies. It is estimated that to create and setup a dynamic website with necessary staff at the Head Quarters and Internet facility along with necessary equipment in around 50 study centers it will cost a one-time capital expenditure of around Rs. 20.00 lakhs and an annual recurring expenditure of Rs. 8.00 lakhs which is in any case not a burdensome proposition to the institution which had Rs. 600 lakhs annual revenue income to its credit. The institution under reference recently took a decision to introduce the system and hence the survey to know its feasibility.

The University under reference thus based on its proposals to introduce a system called OSSS, a 'pre-induction' survey has been conducted both by using electronic mail and printed questionnaires while contacting 300 students via e-mails and 300 students by pre-paid postal media for collecting their opinions and responses on various connected issues of 'creation, induction and implementation of OSSS scheme'. For the purpose of the survey, all the respondents chosen were drawn from urban and semi-urban areas pursuing post-graduation courses through distance mode. The response rate is relatively high through electronic media (about 212 out of 300) which is a healthy sign as far as the 'introduction of the proposed system' is concerned. About 180 (out of 300) responses were received by postal means which is also not much discouraging. The responses indicate that students seem to have felt very much happy for approaching them and showing concern like this and extended full cooperation to respond to a wide variety of questions with a feeling of involvement and a sense of responsibility. To be straight and brief, the main results of the survey are summed up below while highlighting various aspects covered.

Availability of Internet Facility

An overwhelming majority of students as around 82 percent (95 percent of Internet users and 62 percent of correspondence respondents) had said that Internet facility is available in their places and they are for introduction of OSSS response system in the University. Most of them however pleaded that 'free Internet access' with a little training for handling it may be provided to them and all study centers/regional centers/ other centers may extend such services to all the bonafide students. Further 18 percent of the students had already had the Internet facility in their homes/offices which they can make use of and around 30 percent of the students had the experience of using Internet earlier for different purposes.

OSSS and its Need

An overwhelmingly 88 percent of students supported the idea of OSSS, provided it does not effect the prospects of other support services and replace the old one. Almost all the respondents believe that Internet is increasingly a fast penetrating medium replacing the phones, fax and mail as a preferred method of communication and offers quick, easy, powerful and timely response to the users. It is significant to observe that most of the students had already had some idea about the on-line services available 'outside' and in different western universities. A majority of them have had the access to different computer and Internet magazines and through which they had learnt the benefits of the system. Most of them had even developed a liking for the system.

Coverage of OSSS

Majority of respondents had felt that OSSS scheme should offer a package of services that should be comprehensive enough to cover the entire gamut of support they needed. Coupled with the facilities already available at study centers, they think that it should serve as a 'full-fledged information support system' to be guided constantly by the 'net'. They said that 'individualized redressal of grievances' and 'a continuous and active flow of information' is possible through OSSS. Thus, apart from serving the purpose of an 'information provider', OSSS system may also offer the facility of processing and confirming admissions, accepting credit card or on-line payments, making needed altercations of programmes / centers / combination of courses, supply of additional instructional materials other than the course materials supplied available as well as on-line, in print form, handling assignments, declaration of results, providing score cards, marks sheets etc., the respondents added. It should otherwise provide a virtual campus facility keeping in view of the changing needs of the students on the one had and encouraging creativity, independent thinking and problem solving on the other.

Cost Component

Majority of the students however seem to have 'vigilant and cautious' as far as the matters relating to the 'cost component' is concerned. A vast majority of the respondents said that it should not involve any additional cost on their part and impose any additional financial burden to meet the expenditure towards this purpose. More respondents who had no Internet accessibility at home and office, pleaded that necessary equipment must be provided at the study centers with full and free accessibility of the net service. They should also be provided a minimum knowledge of technology - both hardware and software in a specially conducted induction programme.

Some Apprehensions

In the overall analysis, though a couple of apprehensions were also raised especially about the need for increased access to technology, increased speed in connectivity, greater-band width, its relevance and applicability to all courses, availability of required hardware and software at the study centers, data up gradation and improvements, promptness of service and quality of maintenance of OSSS system, there is widespread agreement on the need for such a support service.

Implications and Conclusions

On-line delivery of support services making use of new information and communication technologies has a lot of potential for providing quality and prompt on-line support service to the students. The response from the students towards the need for a system called OSSS is overwhelming and they were willing to accept the use of Internet and web technologies for strengthening the institutional student support system. Since Internet facility is available everywhere in the open market with costs decreasing, it appears that provision for OSSS in any University and especially the University under reference is feasible and manageable. the willingness and commitment on the part of the institution to strengthen the student support services and its level of efficiency in managing it would give greater results for the benefit of both the institution as well as the students. But the issues relating to the cost component and preparedness of the ODL institutions to provide the service, provision for necessary budgetary allocations, creation of additional inputs such as expertise to man the service and provision for machines at the HQs and study centers etc., still, remain matters of serious concern for the institution to offer. The whole programme seem to be still dependent upon various other factors such as the design, facilities and maintenance of the website of the institution, the bandwidth, greater penetration of information and communication technologies, greater access and increased speed in connectivity, openness to cultural variables affecting the machine-human interactivity etc., still remain as crucial issues. In spite of all these, the positive results of the feedback from the students provide a valuable data on how these programme could be introduced and implemented with facilities available outside and in the open market, costs decreased and access increased, coupled with appropriate and need-based changes in the whole programme, introduction of OSSS will be of great use to the students and provide a strong base for a complete on-line education in the near future.

References:

Cahoon, B., (1997) 'Exploring the World-wide web', [http://www.gactr.uga.edu/exploring/]

Carr - Chellman, Alison and Duchastel, Philip (2000) 'The On-line Course', British Journal of Educational Technology. 31(3) : 229-241.

Carswell, Linda et.al (2000) "Distance Education via the Internet: The Student Experience', British Journal of Educational Technology, 31(1): 29-46

Harasim, LM, Calvert, T. & Groeneboer, C (Eds), 1997, 'Virtual-U: a Web-based System to Support Collaborative Learning', (Vol.I), Englewood Cliffs, NJ: Education Technology.

Hiltz, S.R. (1994). The Virtual Classroom: Learning without Limits via computer Networks, Norwood: NJ Ablex Publishing Corporation, Human-Computer Interaction Series.

Joshi (2000), 'Information Technology-Advantage India', http://www.isda.india.org/an-aproll.html

McAlpine, Iain (2000) 'Collaborative Learning On-line', Distance Education, 21(1): 66-80

McCartan, Audrey (2000) 'Use of IT in a Postgraduate Distance Learning Course: Part-I: Students' Experiences', Innovations in Education and Training International, 37(3), August 2000: 181-191

Morgan, Christopher (1998). Tutoring via Electronic Mail, Open Praxis 1:26-28.

Oliver, Ron (1999) 'Exploring Strategies for On-line Teaching and Learning', Distance Education, 20(2): 240-253.

Owston, Ronald D (1997). The WWW: A Technology to Enhance Teaching and Learning. Educational Researcher, 26(2), 27-33.

Prasad, Janardhan (1999), 'Modern Media and Education Practice. New Delhi, Kanishka.

Srinivasa Kumar, P & Subhash Maji (2002): 'Meet of Internet and Worldwide Web (WWW) in Distance Education', paper presented at IX Annual Conference of Indian Distance Education Association, 13-15 March, 2002, Jammu University, and Jammu.

Subramanyam, VV: M. Learning - A Mobile Learning Era, paper presented at IX Annual Conference of Indian Distance Education Association, 13-15 March, 2002, Jammu University, Jammu.

Venkateshwarlu & Subhash Maji, 'E-Learning in Distance Education', paper presented at IX Annual Conference of Indian Distance Education Association, 13-15 March, 2002, Jammu University, Jammu.

Internet-based Distance Learning in Slovakia

Klara Nahrstedt*, Julius Bajcsy

(*University of Illinois, USA - klara@cs.uiuc.edu, **Slovak Technical University Bratislava Slovak Republik-julius@pluto.elf.stuba.sk)

Abstract

Many universities in USA, Canada and West Europe have extensive experiences in offering distance education courses to remote students and utilize the advanced Internet and multimedia technology for appropriate interaction. In Eastern Europian countries, the Internet-based distance learning programs are being setup only recently, however for different reasons and under different conditions when compared to programs in Western Europe, Canada and USA. Having learned from past experiences of Internet-based distance learning programs at top ranked universities around the world, we present a design of an Internet-based distance learning program for technical universities in Slovakia. We discuss the overall design process through the case study program, initated at the Slovak Technical University in Bratislava.

1. Introduction

There has been an explosive growth of multimedia computing, communication and educational applications during the past years, extensively utilized in Internet-based distance education at various universities (e.g., University of Illinois, Stanford, McGill). Internet-based distance education represents an educational form where students are located outside of the classroom and reach educational material as well as the instructor via remote multimedia electronic tools such as video conferencing such as NetMeeting from Microsoft, Web service, email, ftp service, and others. Current computing and communication environments, consisting of high-end PCs, cable modems, Ethernet LANs, or DSL communication lines, at many universities and homes allow for interactive communication and on-demand multimedia information access. Instructors of distance learning programs are able to (1) distribute their teaching material, auxielary papers, detailed instructions to the remote students via web, email, ftp services, (2) receive comments, and questions via email and newsgroups, and (3) conduct discussions via newsgroups and other chat programs. Remote students of distance learning programs are able to (1) access all teaching material remotely through web services, and other Internet services, (2) communicate easily with instructors and their local student fellows, and (3) conduct remote experimentation, using expensive equipments on the campus, during their laboratory work.

Many universities in USA, Canada and West Europe such as Open Universities (e.g., in England), Stanford, UIUC, McgGill, and others, have extensive experiences in offering distance learning courses to remote students in other countries and utilize the advanced Internet and mu ltimedia technology for appropriate interaction [1,2,7]. However, many top ranked universities have also reserved attitude about offering distance learning programs such as master programs to remote students in foreign countries [3]. In Eastern Europian countries, the Internet-based distance learning programs are being setup only recently, although for different reasons and under different conditions when compared to USA, Canada, and West Europe. Having learned from past experiences of Internet-based distance learning programs at top ranked universities around the world, we present a design of an

Internet-based distance learning program for technical universities in Slovakia. We discuss the overall design process through the case study program, initiated at the Slovak Technical University (STU) in Bratislava.

The paper outlines in Section 2 the history of distance learning at STU in Bratislava. In Section 3 we present the goals, justification and implementation of the Internet-based distance education program at STU, and in Section 4 we discuss organization and business issues of the distance learning program. Section 5 concludes with leassons learned from other distance learning programs that will be seriously considered during the execution of the STU experiment.

2. History of Distance Learning at STU

Distance Learning at STU in Bratislava has a long tradition and history [4,5]. The first form of distance learning program started during the school year 1952/53 through the Resolution of the Slovak government about extraordinary forms of study, November 11, 1952. The department of Electrical Engineering at STU established the Consultative Center for Remote and Evening Study, which was directed by the Institute of Remote Study at STU. In 1956, the organization and control of the distance learning programs was moved from the Institute of Remote Study to the departments (to the associate dean for educational technologies).

The distance learning program took on three different forms:

- **Six years distance learning undergraduate study** (during 1983/84 this program was renamed to Distance Learning on the Job). The student was able to finish the first two years of study any time in consultative centers, established outside of the university.

- **Six years evening dstance learning undergraduate study.** This study was organized and possible for resident students on the campus of the university who worked during the day and took classes during the evening hours.

- **Three years specialized suplement distance learning study for teachers of secondary teachnical trade schools.** This program started in 1976/77.

All three forms of the distance learning program required that the students met twice a month with the instructor (Friday and Saturday), as well as at the end of the semester, they would go through laboratory exercises of courses that required experimental skills. The students of these distance learning forms used the same lecture material, such as books, papers, provided by the instructor, as the regular registered students on the campus. The last set of students who graduates via these distance learning program forms graduated in 1994/95.

3. Internet-based Distance Learning at STU

The goal of the Internet-based distance learning program at STU in Bratislava is to provide undergraduate bachelor degree to remote students outside of STU and Bratislava. There are several reasons for the demand of Internet-based distance learning: (1) For many students outside of Bratislava, the **cost of living** in Bratislava is too high; (2) There is an **acute shortage of professors and teachers** in technical disciplines at technical universities outside of STU; (3) The **cost of traveling** for teachers and students is very high; and (4) The **equipment budget**, universities receive from the Minis tery of Education, is very low, therefore sharing and remote experimenting with expensive laboratory equipment is neccessary. Hence, due to the reasons above, and due to the modern Internet-based technology development, which allows not only paper material distribution, but also interactive electronic communication (e.g., email, web service, multimedia conferencing) with remote students and remote experimentation with laboratory equipment, the distance learning program at a new level is neccessary in Slovakia. In 2001/ 2002, the Department of electrical engineering and information technology at STU[1] in Bratislava started to offer an undergraduate degree via Internet-based distance learning program in the area of electrical power engineering. The department plans to expand the areas and to offer an undergraduate degree in the area of automation in 2002/ 2003.

To implement successfully the distance learning degree programs in power engineering and automation, the STU set up three local centers for distance learning throughout Slovakia in Bratislava, Zvolen and Kosice six years ago. These centers were prepared and participated in the development of the technical infrastructure, needed for Internet-based distance learning. The material and technical infrastructure setup were strongly supported by international projects TEMPUS, PHARE and LEONARDO [6]. The centers gained alot of experiences by organizing various preparation courses for entrance exams in the area of mathematics, physics and chemistry, as well as provision of courses in industrial management.

4. Organization and Financial Support of Internet-based Distance Learning at STU

For a student to complete the undergraduate degree via the new Internet-based distance learning program, it is planed to take six years. The first two years of the educational plan are already clearly outlined, and plans for the next four years are in preparation. Long-time experienced teachers are contracted and are working on creating the electronic and traditional educational ma terial for the Internet-based program. The requirement is to deliver the requested educational material to the centers one year before teaching of the course is offered[2].

The remote students receive advising and other help for their course work through Internet-based communication with the course instructors directly or through Internet-based communication with the teaching assistants assigned to the course. All teaching personel in the Internet-based distance learning program is contracted and the conditions for usage of Internet services when communicating with remote students are clearly defined, including financial agreements for performed activities.

The financial support for the Internet-based distance learning program comes from three sources: (1) **fixed cost** for creation of the teaching material, honorarium for authors/instructors, and financial support for a center comes from the internal departmental budget, which is given to the department by the Ministery of Education according to the number of students (Undergraduate degree for every student is paid by the Slovak government), from sponsorship donations, and from international projects; (2) **variable cost** for written material, mail, telephone cost and others come from the students who purchase educational material; and (3) **other direct cost** for equipment, used in laboratories, comes from the departmental budget.

5. Conclusion

The Internet-based distance learning in Slovakia is in progress and it is now matter of time to show its successful path as well as lessons learned. The program was established on sound base of many experienced international programs[1,2,4,6,7], hence there is an optimism that this distance learning effort will (1) **save the living and**

---

[1] In Slovakia, the official name for the Department of Electrical Engineering and Information Technology is the *Faculty of Electrical Engineering and Information Technology.*
[2] The material, delivered one year ahead, is only conceptual material, not the final electronic delivery format.

transport cost of many new students, (2) **address the current shortage** of instructors and teachers at technical universities in Slovakia, and (3) **allow students to share** expensive and advanced laboratory equipment via Internet-based technologies.

6. References

[1] Quantum Master Degree Distance Learning Program, http://www.cs.uiuc.edu

[2] Distance Learning Program at Stanford University, http://www.stanford.edu

[3] Faculty Minutes about Quantum Program, January 2002, University of Illinois at Urbana-Champaign

[4] From bulb till Internet. Publis her: Slovak Technical University, Bratislava 2001

[5] Faculty of Electrical Engineering and Information Technology - Annual Report 2001. Edited by S. Milovska, Bratislava 2002.

[6] Local Center of Distance Learning, http://www.kar.elf.stuba.sk/lsdv

[7] Distance Learning Program at McGill University, http://www.mcgill.ca/distance

Putting the E to Work in E-teaching

John C. Nash
School of Management
University of Ottawa
Canada
jcnash@uottawa.ca

Abstract: We consider university teaching from a viewpoint of the activities in which students and professors engage while taking or giving courses. We seek to apply software and procedural tools to make these processes more efficient, following in general terms Deming-style process improvement. Our ultimate goal is to have technology that is so familiar and obvious that students and professors use it naturally without training. Tools we have developed or improved to date include homework submission (with identification and automatic routing by section), random "volunteer" selection (PICKSEAT), image grab and send, a simple web forum for consolidating student and professor contributions, and image consolidation and captioning. None of the above tools is new in concept, but we believe there are important benefits from the level of simplicity achieved.

Motivations

In teaching statistics to business students, we have found it highly effective to "teach from the back of the room", even in classes as large as 80 students. This tutorial style allows the professor and other students to witness mistakes or gaps in student background and provides an opportunity to correct the deficiencies. At the same time we show that problem-solving requires a willingness to learn from mis-steps. We would like to adapt this teaching style on the Web, especially if the sessions could be saved for replay as web-pages. To limit resource demands, we seek a low-bandwidth solution. We also want system components to be useful in themselves so that we can use developed software as soon as possible, in particular to deal with the province of Ontario "double cohort" (www.oecta.on.ca/pdfs/ontdblcohort.pdf). The components described below may succeed even if the totality, named *E-tutor*, does not.

Consider the activities in which students and professors engage while taking or giving courses. From this viewpoint, we seek to apply software and procedural tools to make these *processes* more efficient, following in general terms Deming-style process improvement. "Efficient" in our context is measured by comparing the relative or marginal time, effort and resources needed to accomplish a given task in different ways. That is, we accept existing infrastructure as given and apply relative costings. Our ultimate goal is to have technology that is so familiar and obvious that students and professors use it without training and without taking particular note of it. Some of the tools we have developed or improved to date include:

- File uploading by students for homework submission and subsequent downloading or retrieval by the professor or teaching assistant. The software must modify file names to identify the student and also permit block download by the professor or assistant.
- Choosing a "volunteer" to solve a problem in class (PICKSEAT) in a way that is random so that there is no favouritism or victimization.
- A web forum to allow students to pose questions and/or answer queries by others (CO4).
- Image grab and send (ET-GRASED), needed to allow a student to communicate written or drawn material to the professor and the class, since at low-bandwidth we do not wish to use video.
- Simple web forum for consolidating student and professor contributions.
- Image consolidation and captioning.

None of the above tools is new in concept, but we believe the level of simplicity we have achieved – by efforts that belie that ultimate simplicity – has been worthwhile. Moreover, the tools are usable alongside or within other e-teaching systems and will be made available under an open-source licence. We intend that they be consolidated into the full E-tutor system, which is the long-term objective. The design for E-tutor was proposed by the author in 2000 and reviewed and assessed in early 2001 (K. Leblanc, 2001). An exchange of ideas with other practitioners, particularly those whose starting point is pedagogy, is welcomed. In the spirit of continuous improvement, we consider all our efforts to be in a state of development.

Experience to date

The School of Management has operated a simple file archive (called DocDepot) since 1999 which has proved extremely useful for supplying information to students on a full-time, 24/7, basis. It has been very popular among students. For example, it eliminates much of the concern about lost or misplaced course outlines or assignment documents, and saves students travel time and parking costs to obtain such materials. Indeed, the success of DocDepot has raised student expectations so that professors are essentially forced to put materials there. However, we still need better mechanisms for upload, control, and deletion of files by professors and others in a sensible manner.

DocDepot has allowed the posting of student work. Students may read and learn from others, and are encouraged to cite any ideas they use. Marks are *not* included, but students quickly judge which work is good. While not provable, we believe posting all work provides a brake on plagiarism. Work that we would term a "disaster" due to misunderstood assignments has largely disappeared. We have observed the incentive to excellence a couple of good papers provide.

Delivery of assignments is therefore an important task. In large, multiple section courses, delivering the student work to the right marker, with proper identification, is an annoying clerical task that creates many difficulties. Homework uploading, with proper sorting and identification, has proved very helpful, and much simpler than either email or diskettes. We have now used a simple file uploader in roughly twenty tasks across a variety of courses plus the first round of the 2001 National Advanced Technology Management Competition, where the competitors were geographically distant.

Students submit material in Adobe Acrobat format (PDF files). We provide documentation and links so such files may be prepared without the need to purchase the Adobe Distiller or PDF Writer. The major advantage of such files is that they are not dependent on the printer definition used in document creation. The marker reads the document (either on-screen or printed out) in the layout and style that the student prepared. Two particular features of our homework submission tool(s) are worth mentioning. One is that the student log-in provides the student number, and this is pre-pended to the filename of the submitted file so that "noname" assignments are not possible. The other is that the marker can choose to download all the submitted work for a given task as a zip file. This saves time during downloads.

Overall, both students and professor have been very happy with the submission tools. Students can work from home, saving time as well as travel and parking costs. The professor similarly does not have to travel to retrieve submitted homework. We found that the typical cycle time from submission of homework to reporting of marks to students dropped by a factor of three. Students had positive comments about this. To date, we have had very few technical problems. Indeed the major "glitch" concerned omission of student names from class lists provided by the administration, so a couple of students could not log in.

Students generally are reluctant to step forward to attempt the solution of a problem. To choose a volunteer" in a way that is random, PICKSEAT was developed. It requires the seat arrangement for each classroom to be set up as a simple character graph in an ordinary text file. If a chosen seat is empty, we proceed to the (professor's) right and then forward row by row until an occupant is found. The program is executed on the classroom display computer. Students seem to regard it as a sort of game, and acceptance has been smoother than anticipated.

Automated consolidation and captioning of images is useful in building some teaching and related materials. We first developed FOTOHTML for use in organizing family photographs in a large genealogical collection. We found it particularly important that the tool assist in verifying that both the image collection and caption list match properly. It is also helpful that the resulting HTML files each display a small number of images (default 10) so the files do not take too long to load in a Web browser.

Other tools are still undergoing tests, but we hope some results will be available by October 2002.

Methods and approaches

We have been developing two variants of the homework submission tools: ETPRL, a tool to handle just one assignment or task, implemented as simple scripts in the Perl programming language, and ETPHP, which is programmed in the PHP programming language and makes calls to the MySQL database system. So far, all experience has been with versions of ETPRL. A design requirement is that the system be very simple and obvious to use, that is, that the affordances of the user interface be intuitive (Norman, 1990 and 1992). For students such clarity has been achieved. The major deficiency discovered was that each task required a separate set of directories and files for both the programs and uploaded files, making setup awkard as well as inefficient of disk space. This is being rectified by the author and a new, streamlined version is undergoing tests.

The CO4 collaborative web forum was programmed in Perl for a Windows web-server by a student, Lawrence Taylor, as a course assignment. Using a general set of requirements provided by the author, he did an outstanding implementation. CO4 allows a set of users to collaboratively build a web page by inserting, adding to or editing sections. There are facilities to insert images or more general file links. The file display is set up to display only a few sections at a time to reduce the time to load the page. CO4 proved quite easy to port to Linux, but so far is lacking in access control. We intend to re-implement in PHP for easier maintenance.

All these tools are implemented using server-side scripts and a single cookie. They are largely unaffected by the firewall protections that were increased after September 11, 2001, while systems relying on client-side scripts have been blocked. Such systems include the WebCT e-teaching system, as well as Hotmail and similar email hosts.

Image grab and send (ET-GRASED) is a tool needed to allow a student to communicate written or drawn material to the professor and the rest of the class. This tool has been developed to the stage of proving capability. The client program is for Microsoft Windows only and written in Visual BASIC, while the server software is a script in PHP for Linux-based servers.

PICKSEAT is already available as a project within the sourceforge system (sourceforge.org) , while FOTOHTML can be obtained via a link from www.nashinfo.com. Both are written in Pascal; while Turbo Pascal was used for development, we believe Gnu Pascal will compile and run these codes.

Future developments

We plan to use ETPRL and/or ETPHP in courses led by professors other than the author, so that reaction and ease-of-use for professors and teaching assistants can be verified and, if necessary, improved. We also hope to launch some trial applications of CO4. PICKSEAT and FOTOHTML are already available to others, but we have had very little reaction communicated to us yet.

We decided very early in the design to release the "products" of the work reported under either the Gnu Public License (www.gnu.org) or similar arrangement. This means that others may use and improve the software, with resulting improvements themselves being available to others. To alert others to this work, and also to learn what choices are being made elsewhere, the author has actively sought to meet workers with similar interests. These exchanges, carried out during personal or professional travel, as well as by telephone and e-mail, have proved very helpful in refining ideas and in gauging the value of design choices. Very recently (April 2002), it has been possible to let such colleagues actually test prototypes of some of the tools. For the most part, the reaction has been exceedingly positive, but it has also revealed some potential improvements and possible "glitches" related to as -yet-unresolved issues with particular Web browsers on particular operating systems.

Conclusions

The tools described above have largely met their design goals. For example, the assignment uploaders have proven very simple for students to use, to the extent that they are almost "invisible". They shorten the waiting time for the professor or marker to receive student work, offering opportunities for quicker correction and assessment that students appreciate. There is also a reduction in the clerical effort of the marker to organize and file papers, especially if students have omitted identification. All the tools are small and relatively simple in design and implementation. Improvements are clearly possible and desirable, but at present we perceive none that require major reworking of the programs.

Acknowledgements

A Teaching and Learning Grant from the Centre for University Teaching of the University of Ottawa paid for programming by Patrick Suwalski and Markus Svilans. Lawrence Taylor and the author also contributed code. Woody Suwalski supplied the Rebel Netwinder server used in initial experiments of ETPRL, while the School of Management has provided innovation funds for the courses.gestion.uottawa.ca server that will be hosting ongoing tests.

References

Leblanc, Karen (2001) *e-TUTOR*, University of Ottawa, Faculty of Administration, macnash.admin.uottawa.ca/~etutor/k_leblanc.pdf

Norman, Donald (1992) *Turn Signals are the Facial Expressions of Automobiles*, Reading MA: Addison-Wesley

Norman, Donald (1990) *The Design of Everyday Things*, New York: Doubleday

Faculty Institute: A Model For Online Success

Susan Moak Nealy
Carl Perkins Programs
Northwestern State University of Louisiana
United States of America
nealys@nsula.edu

Darlene Williams
Coordinator of Electronic Learning
Northwestern State University of Louisiana
United States of America
darlene@nsula.edu

Kathy Autrey
Assistant Professor of Mathematics
Northwestern State University of Louisiana
United States of America
autrey@nsula.edu

Abstract: This project was developed to provide a roadmap for setting up online courses. A series of workshops was designed to help instructors improve upon and expand their use of technology as an instructional tool. Topics included pre-course development, interactivity, converting a traditional course to an online format, assessment, and using web-based materials to supplement a traditional course. Through the use of a web resource, material from these workshops is accessible to anyone interested in developing an online course or supplementing a traditional course with online materials. As a result of this project, 43 of the 47 participants surveyed were more likely to supplement their traditional courses with Blackboard and 42 were more likely to participate in the development of an online course.

Introduction

As the leader of Electronic Learning in the state, Northwestern State University of Louisiana encourages its instructors to make course offerings available online and to integrate technology into traditional classroom courses. The goal of this project was to provide face-to-face and online support for instructors whether they were already working with an online or hybrid course (traditional classroom with online supplements), or just starting to explore these instructional media. While technical aspects of the program were based on a Blackboard platform because it is the platform currently utilized by our university, much of the information can be used with any electronic learning platform.

The Program

A cohesive program of five broad topics was identified as essential to electronic instruction. Six experienced faculty members were identified to present workshops as part of a professional development series on integrating technology and education. These peer mentors were all seasoned veterans in the area of electronic learning, including online and hybrid courses. Faculty members developed a workshop on their assigned topic. Presentations were not limited to a presenter's specific discipline but were developed to be relevant to all participants. Workshops included presentation, group discussion, and small group discussions. Participants were allowed to register for one to six workshops, dependent upon their interest and schedule. Each workshop therefore had to be an independent session but still fit into the overall program. All workshops were presented in the university's compressed video classroom and broadcast via compressed video to two of the university's satellite campuses to allow for broader participation. Two workshops were held each month for three months and a practice course was set up in Blackboard during that time for participants to review examples and practice what they were learning.

Upon attendance at their first workshop, participants began to build their Online Faculty Resource Manual. The manual consisted of a program binder with in-house printed materials for each session, as well as additional relevant materials (tips, guidelines, etc.) to be placed in the appendix. The manual contained a section for participants to add their own materials as well, to customize the resource so that it was useful for them.

Because participants represented a variety of backgrounds and experience levels, we knew their reference needs might vary. In addition to the resource manual, participants were allowed to select materials through an online bookstore that would meet their own individual needs relating to the integration of technology and instruction. The amount of resources available to each participant was based on participation in the series, at a maximum of $250 per participant.

Through the University's web site, a web presence for the seminars was created. Web Developers were contracted to build the template that was used as an interface for this project, making this important information available to educators worldwide. At Perkins Presentations, visitors can review the handouts for a particular session, the computerized presentation (if applicable), or the actual presentation itself. Each session was also preserved on compact disc and video cassette tape with a copy placed at each campus's library, so that anyone on campus could review the material without accessing the web site.

Session I encompassed Pre-Course Development. Participants were provided with checklists for starting a new course and continuing to present that course in subsequent semesters. Sample letters and other relevant items were also provided. Session II was entitled Converting A Traditional Course To Online Part I. This session reviewed the theory or "thinking" part of converting a traditional face-to-face course to an online version. Participants brought in a syllabus for one of their own courses and completed some of the exercises necessary to complete this process. Session III, Converting A Traditional Course To Online Part II, dealt with the "buttonology" of converting a course. This session worked extensively with Blackboard, the university's platform for online learning. Its goal was to take participants through the process, step by step, of loading lectures, tests, announcements, etc. The subject for Session IV was Building Assessments. Participants discussed matters related to online testing and evaluation, including minimizing academic misconduct and importing test pools into the university platform. Course Facilitation was the topic for Session V. Various electronic methods for increasing student communication and interaction were discussed. Session VI, Using Blackboard as a Supplement, was chosen as the final workshop. Participants were able to draw on the technical information presented in the first five workshops and see how to use it in a more limited, supplemental fashion.

The Results

Participants evaluated each session individually as well as the program as a whole. Of the 48 respondents who completed the evaluation process, 76% had 5 or more years of traditional teaching experience; 17% had taught for 1 to 2 years and 7% had 3 to 5 years experience. Twenty-three of the participants (59%) had no prior online teaching experience and 36% had no experience using technology as a supplemental tool in a traditional classroom setting. The majority of the participants were from the main campus (60.4%) and 45.8% attended all six sessions.

Although 7% of the participants surveyed were undecided, the remaining participants indicated a willingness to supplement their traditional courses with technology (specifically Blackboard) and 92% expressed an increased likelihood of developing an online course in the future. The resource manuals as well as the web site were found to be extremely useful tools as well as the opportunity to interact with other professionals who had already designed online courses and supplemental materials. Forty percent of the participants indicated a preference for more "hands-on" type sessions with specific examples of ways to incorporate the technology into the classroom. According to one participant, " . . . I would actually like to sit down in a lab and design an online class or shell with assistance from the gurus. . ."

The ratings from the individual sessions mirrored the overall program ratings. Those sessions that incorporated more technological skill were more highly rated than those dealing with other areas. This finding is in keeping with the high percentage of participants who rated their skill at the level of novice. More experienced participants rated the sessions highly as well; however, their concerns were more related to issues of evaluation and assessment of current courses and conversion of traditional courses.

Conclusions

Given these findings, future plans include the development of workshops for both novice and experienced individuals. These will include more opportunities for "hands-on" experience as well as opportunities to discuss issues related to specific disciplines. The overall concept is one of an online institute in which individuals would be able to choose from a variety of offerings based upon their specific needs.

Acknowledgements

The Project, *Northwestern State University: A Model For Online Success* was funded through a Perkins III Postsecondary Leadership Grant awarded by the Louisiana Community and Technical College System. Additional assistance and support was provided through The President's Office, The Graduate School, and Barnes and Noble Bookstore at NSU.

THE ISSUES FACED BY TRADITIONAL CLASSROOM TEACHING STAFF WHEN CONVERTING COURSES FROM FACE TO FACE TO ONLINE.

Jenny Newby-Fraser, Manager, Centre for Learning Technologies, Waikato Institute of Technology, Hamilton, New Zealand   jenny.newbyfraser@wintec.ac.nz

Introduction

Wintec, a traditional face to face teaching institution, identified a need to move into online teaching (OT) and learning. Wintec teaching staff have a lot on their plate and converting some of their courses to contain an online component causes anxiety for many. The Centre for Learning Technologies (CLT) was established to support the institute's OT initiative. Its role is to work with teaching staff, (the content experts and content developers), and support them with project management, instructional design, curriculum development, WebCT technical and design issues.

As Rogers (1983) predicts, Wintec has staff at the five stages of motivation: Innovators, Early Adopters, Early Majority, Late Majority and Laggards. Approximately 70% of Wintec staff are in the Early and Late Majority categories and these cohorts are more conservative and averse to risk. Most staff are in the Early Majority category however and all need support, reassurance, motivation and guidance (Newby-Fraser, 2000). There are many issues associated with the introduction of OT. A previous evaluation by the author found human concerns, rather than technical concerns, came through strongly. Boettcher and Conrad (1999) state that, *"Change is difficult. It takes time, energy, resources and altered attitudes"* (p.12). This paper concerns itself with how such changes affect teaching staff.

Methods

The study was both qualitative and quantitative and involved 17 staff completing questionnaires incorporating the following 12 statements:

S1: I was given sufficient CLT support in the development of my online course.
S2: I was given sufficient time release to develop my online course.
S3: I did sufficient professional development to make me feel comfortable prior to starting OT course development.
S4: Converting my course to online has made me review my course content.
S5: Converting my course to online has made me review the content of my assessments.
S6: Establishing a sense of community within my online course is essential.
S7: Compared to face to face teaching my online teaching has been as effective.
S8: Taken overall I am satisfied with the online component of my course.
S9: I get a buzz from teaching online.
S10: Converting my course to online has affected my face to face teaching practice.
S11: After converting my course to online but before I actually taught it I felt comfortable about online teaching.
S12: After teaching my course online I felt comfortable about online teaching.

Each statement had a Likert scale (Strongly agree = 1 to Strongly disagree = 5) and provision for open comment and suggestions. Verification of the results of the questionnaire was obtained by asking a volunteer focus group outside the questionnaire group. Likert scales were analysed for their mean, median and mode. Those statements scoring above a mean of 2.0 were examined for future action.

Results

Of the 12 Statements regarding staff concerns during conversion of their courses to OT, the means of five statements (S2, S3, S7, S10, and S11) were above the 2.0 "Action Line" (Fig. 1).

Figure 1. Mean Likert Values of Evaluation Statements

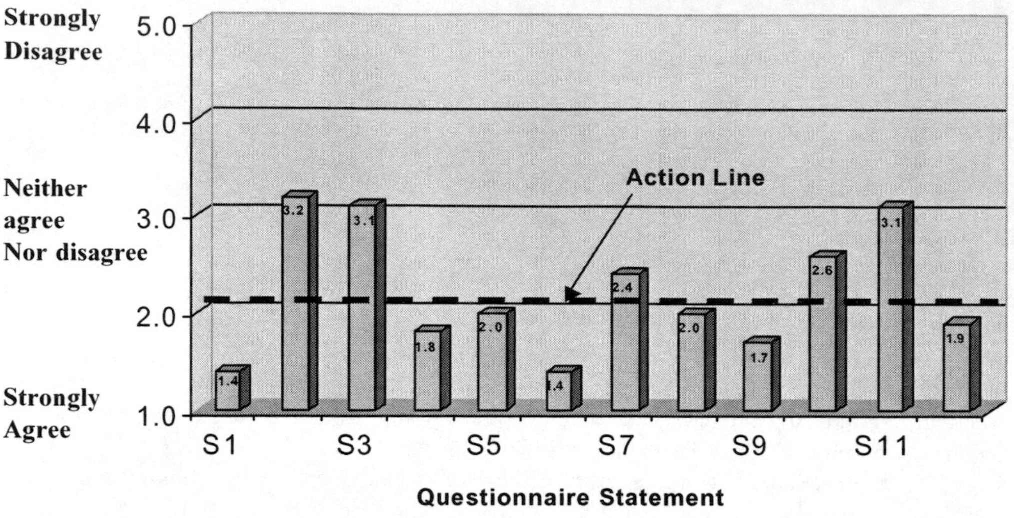

In Statements 2 (release time) and 3 (professional development), a good proportion of staff did not agree. In Statement 7 (online teaching is as effective as FTF), although the mean was 2.4, the mode and median were both 2 and this indicates that scores were skewed below the mean. The mean may therefore be a slight overestimate of the average results. In Statement 10 (online has affected FTF), although the mean was 2.6, the mode and median were both 2 and indicates that scores were skewed below the mean. There appears to be a strong dichotomy of opinion among the staff on this statement as there is a gap between the majority of staff answers and the four staff who strongly disagreed. In Statement 11 (comfort prior to teaching online), both mean and median were 3.0 and the mode 2. This indicates that scores were fairly evenly distributed around the mean and the mean is a fair estimate of the average result.

Confirmatory Interviews

The three interviewees agreed in general with the questionnaire scores and comments. The only factor stressed more heavily by interviewees was the importance of course ownership.

Discussion

For change in delivery to be successful, the majority of staff must see some benefit from participating in a mixed mode delivery initiative, e.g. Release-time, technical and pedagogical support, professional development, promotion opportunities. (Newby-Fraser 2000).

Greater release time (a precious commodity) is a clear staff need. I agree with Oblinger (1999) that, a mixed mode initiative cannot be successful unless a substantial portion of mainstream staff buy into it. Without release time, they won't buy. Ideally, staff should have release time from some of their regular teaching commitments to work on their course redevelopment, or development, on negotiated allocated days in the CLT.

Then there is the issue regarding the time allocated for OT, although perhaps this is only an issue the first time it is taught, and perhaps it is highlighted if the course design is inappropriate.

"I did not realize the amount of time I would need, never having done this before. I did not allow time to learn about "how to manage" the course."

Staff do need to learn new skills to facilitate online teaching (Vardi & Bunker 2001).

Both the scores and comments in Statement 4 confirmed that much of the release time staff have been given for OT development is spent changing their content and updating their material. Although much of this work needs to be done for their FTF teaching, for a number of reasons it often does not get done. Staff comment on how much easier it is to "fly by the seat of your pants" in a FTF class than it is online. In the online world materials need to be prepared well beforehand. It is important for staff, and management, who are planning on course delivery redevelopment to know that staff need time to do this. It will be interesting to see if these figures change over time as staff become more familiar with OT. One of the interviewees highlighted the formative assessment tools (eg. quizzes, matching exercises, cloze procedure) that are used increasingly by staff who teach the lower level courses. She commented, *"Self-marking more immediate."*

The results also clearly indicate that staff need more professional development in the online world. Successful online teaching and learning depends on teachers acquiring new competencies. Staff need to learn how to facilitate online, to learn new competencies in designing effective online learning environments and facilitating online (Palloff & Pratt, 2001) however many of the respondents would agree that many of these competencies are the same no matter what the mode of teaching.

The strategies and techniques staff use in their FTF teaching remain very relevant. *"Good teaching, is good teaching."* (Ragan, 1998,) Staff were asked to list the qualities of an effective online teacher and they provided a very long and comprehensive list. They believe that the requirements of an effective online teacher are actually a subset of effective and competent FTF teachers (Newby-Fraser, 2000). As one staff member commented, they were,

"Willing to try a variety of delivery methods based on recognized teaching theories and practices."

Staff need to learn how to communicate and facilitate online. Students too need to learn how to communicate online, however they can be guided, facilitated, supported into this through thoughtful course design and teaching. We are mindful that student satisfaction depends more on the quality and effectiveness of the instructor and the instruction than on the technology (Johnson, Aargon, Shaik, & Palma-Rivas, 2000). One staff member who hadn't done any professional development commented, *"I did not know what I did not know!"* I think staff need to experience being an online student themselves. For a reflective practitioner this is a very valuable experience to have.

The results show staff are aware of the importance of a sense of belonging among the students in their course. *"Fruitful learning experiences don't happen by chance"* (Kimball, 1995) cited in Murphy & Cifuentes (2001, p.297). To build an online community, groups must share who they are *"as people...to build that container of trust"* (Pallof & Pratt 1999, p.7). On a sense of community some staff commented, *"Essential for student interaction and discussion. This is time consuming but very important".*

The staffs' perception of the effectiveness of their OT in comparison to their FTF teaching (Statement 7) scored a mean of 2.4. Wolfe (2001), a Wintec midwifery online teacher, commented on the *change of roles* for her with OT. In the FTF classroom she is often the most "active participant" and enjoyed the various roles "teacher, director, organiser, actress". Online she found her students often interacted with each other, expanded on ideas, shared online resources and sometimes almost excluded her! Becoming an online teacher for many has been quite a learning curve. This is well documented in the literature.

"The role of the instructor is still key but changed." (Harasim et al, 1999, p.9).

Overall, staff were happy with their OT efforts and some wanted to take their OT to greater heights:

"It has been challenging but has reinforced the basics, especially of planning, of good teaching practice. The feedback from students confirms this."

Most staff got a buzz from OT. Harasim *et al.* (1997) agrees and says teaching staff should be motivated sufficiently to start online conversions and satisfied when they are finished. I was very interested in knowing if teachers who enjoyed being in the FTF classroom with their students still felt that same excitement when working online with them. Generally from these results there seems to be an energy, excitement, and motivation related to teaching online, even when staff are unhappy about release time (not enough of this) and professional development opportunities (not enough of these). It appears therefore that staff who enjoy traditional FTF classroom teaching also enjoy working in the online classroom. It is the challenge and also the opportunity to extend themselves into doing something different.

In FTF teaching we get our "buzz" from being in the classroom among students. As two staff members put it,

"I just love it!"

"Definitely gives a sense of satisfaction. Ability to quickly change online notes."

Although the scores of Statement 10 indicated a dichotomy among staff opinion on whether OT affected their FTF teaching, based on qualitative comments alone, I perceived staff strongly agreed that it did.

"I have found that having to change material for online has made me look ahead in my face to face teaching - look at the effect of what I do."

"Positive spin-offs for your teaching generally."

Many staff definitely felt anxious before delivering their OT course. This was expected because the majority of staff participating were "first-timers" in converting courses to OT. Perhaps more professional development would help alleviate some of this anxiety although anxiety levels related to teaching online dropped markedly after staff had actually taught online. This is in line with what many experienced OT teachers say about OT, and indeed I would say about FTF classroom teaching. After we have taught a course once we are much more comfortable. One staff-member encapsulated it nicely:

"It is always stressful trying something new."

The study confirmed that: human aspects are the main concerns of Wintec staff; release time and staff professional development need further attention; and with knowledge of the specific causes, apprehension in teaching staff can be minimised. Technology issues take a back seat. I agree with Epper and Bates, (2001,) *"Probably the most important finding from the study is that best practice institutions keep their focus on teaching and learning issues and not on the technology itself "* (p.144).

References.

Boettcher, J.W., & Conrad, R. M. (1999). *Faculty Guide for Moving Teaching and Learning to the Web*. C.A: League for Innovation Community College.

Brandon, P.R. (1998). Stakeholder participation for the purpose of helping ensure evaluation Validity: Bridging the gap between collaborative and Non-collaborative Evaluations. *American Journal of Evaluation, 19*(3), 13.

Epper, R.M., & Bates, A. W. (2001) *Teaching Faculty How to Use Technology. Best Practices from Leading Institutions*. Westport CT: Oryx Press.

Harasim, L. Hiltz, S.T. Teles, L., & Turoff, M. (1997) **Learning Networks. A Field Guide toTeaching and Learning Online.** Cambridge Massachusetts. The MIT Press.

Harasim, L. (1999). What are we learning about teaching and learning online: An analysis of the virtual u field trials. Conference Proceedings. International Distance Education and Open Learning Conference.

Murphy K., & Cifuentes L. (2001). Using Web Tools, Collaborating, and Learning Online. Distance Education 2001, Vol. 22, No 2, pp. 285-305. ODLAA Inc

Newby, M., & Fisher, D. (1997). An instrument for assessing the learning environment of a computer laboratory. *Journal of educational Computing Research,* 16,179-190.

Newby-Fraser, J.B. (2000). A New Zealand Polytechnic's Implementation of New Learning Technologies: A Human Perspective. Paper presented at Learning Technologies 2000 Conference. Noosa, Queensland, Australia, 25-28 October 2000. http://www.videolinq.qld.edu.au/

Palloff, R., & Pratt, K. (2001). *Online learning in the New Millenium. Lessons from the cyberspace classroom: Realities of online teaching*. Jossey-Bass. San Francisco.

Ragan, L.C. (1998) Good Teaching is Good Teaching: An Emerging Set of Guiding Principles and Practices for the Design and Development of Distance Education. DEOSNEWS Vol. 8. No 12. http://www.ed.psu.edu/ACSDE/

Rogers, E.M. (1983) *Diffusion of Innovations*. New York: The Free Press.

Vardi, I. and Bunker, A. (2001). The Relationship Between the Perceived Value of Supplementary Online Components, and Student Roles and Responsibilities. Conference Proceedings, ASCILITE 2001, Melbourne.

Wolfe, E. (2001). The Oldest Profession in the World – Online. Learning Technologies Conference. "Surviving the Odyssey". Noosa, October 2001.

Single–click Interactive Java Programming Tutorials on the Web

Jan Newmarch, School of Network Computing
Monash University, Australia, jan.newmarch@infotech.monash.edu.au

Abstract: Teaching programming is often best done by running and demonstrating programs, both by instructor and student. Programming environments are often very complex, and may hinder understanding of a lesson that does not involve the environment. This paper describes how the environment can be hidden, so that program compilation/execution is reduced to a single–click from a Web page. Programs can be modified within a Web page and re–executed again with a single–click, improving prospects for experimentation and student–centred learning.

Introduction

One of the major features of the Web is the ability to follow links to a wide variety of content using a single–click. This feature has proved so desirable that ecommerce models built on "single–click purchases" have even been patented.

The Web has been used for conveying teaching materials, and there is a huge literature on the courseware available on the Web (previous WebNet or any other Web conferences such as Asia–Pacific Web have conference sections devoted to the use of the Web for education). A large amount of this literature is concerned with techniques and application of learning models for structuring the courseware so that single–click navigation is profitable. Some literature uses plugins of various kinds (such as ShockWave) to deliver certain effects judged to be of educational value.

Computer programs are represented statically, but can only be understood by dynamic execution. Teaching programming is often regarded as a laboratory subject due to the need to run and to experiment with programs. Courseware on the Web (as with other media) is unable to aid directly in this, and there is often a means of accessing complete working programs, either by cut–and–paste or by FTP downloads.

An experienced programmer will not have difficulties in copying and pasting example programmers into their favourite programming environment, and will put up with various arcanities such as the Java main() method in order to play with new concepts.

The novice on the other hand faces a large number of difficulties just in dealing with any programming environment
*   how does the editor work?
*   how are individual programs or projects of many programs dealt with?
*   how are programs compiled and linked?
*   how are programs run?

It is common for the first few weeks of any introductory course to concentrate of getting students familiar with their local environment (such as an IDE or Unix command line tools). Educational systems such as BlueJ for Java (Barnes, 2002) are often used to try to remove as many enviromental issues as possible to allow concentration on pedagogical issues only.

This paper reports on a project to aid in learning Java by offering single–click compilation and execution of programs displayed in Web pages. The programs are given in TextArea's within browsers so that they can be displayed and edited (for experimentation). A single–click then delivers these to a server where they are compiled and the class files returned to the browser to be run as WebStart applications (webstart, 2001). The editing environment is familiar to users from previous experience with forms, while the compile and execution environments are hidden.

Previous work

In (Newmarch, 1996) we reported on a scheme to allow C programs to be displayed in a browser, edited and then compiled and run back on the browser side. There are many security and trust issues involved in this:

- If the browser can edit and send a file to a server, then the server will not want to perform any potentially dangerous operations such as executing code from an external source. Certain operations such as compilation may be safe, but execution may not be
- If the browser receives code from a server, then it must trust the server before it should execute it
- Any messages between internet nodes can be tampered with, so should be signed if there are possibilities that hostile code may be introduced by a third party

In addition, there are many environmental issues. Simply, C code is usually compiled to code native to a particular processor, and is not portable between either processors or operating systems. This generally means that compilation and execution must be done on the same machine. This machine would either be the server (too risky) or client.

The scheme used in Newmarch did solve the problem, using proxy servers running on each browser machine. It used a security exploit on the servers that made them execute code locally rather than transmitting it. This was extremely complex to set up, required administrator access to student machines, and was fragile in use. The scheme was used successfully for a few years, and then broke due to an unknown cause and could never be made to work again.

During the period in which it was working, both I in my lectures and students in labs used the mechanisms extensively. One click live demonstrations of programs proved very effective, especially when they could be edited in place to show variations, re-executed with just another click.

Requirements of single-click execution

A program needs to be displayed in a browser or plugin called from the browser and executed locally. Intermediate steps may involve compilation to executable or intermediate code, and may or may not involve round trips to a server.

Local execution means that the program must be run on the same machine as the browser, preferably in the same execution environment as the browser. It should be possible to interact with a program using keyboard and mouse. These rule out a number of possible technical solutions such as remote execution or using a proxy running as a different user.

Local compilation and execution may be preferable for client-side security. However, the variety of possible compile and execution environments makes this infeasible for all but the most common interpreted environments. Programs in a language such as C, with a multiplicity of compilers, need a high degree of local customisation. Languages with platform independent intermediate forms such as Java and Emacs Lisp can be compiled on servers and delivered to local platforms for execution (once the location of the local interpreter is known).

Execution of all but the most trivial programs will require access to local resources, and this may be problematic for security reasons. For example, a Java applet cannot be used to demonstrate file I/O using the standard applet sandbox security model since file I/O is disallowed under this model. There are weaker forms of the sandbox model that can be used in recent versions of Java. This requires trust in the executing code, and this trust must be present for all other possible solutions.

WebStart

The Java Network Launching Protocol (JNLP) is designed as a way to download and run Java applications by clicking on a particular kind of URL. URL's with extension .jnlp are associated in a browser to a helper application webstart. A JNLP file contains information about jar files and any other files (such as appropriate version of the Java runtime) required to run the application. The helper checks local system resources and downloads any required classes or resources before starting the application.

JNLP allows a one–click method of downloading software and running it locally. It takes care of ensuring that dependencies are met and a suitable runtime is present. It will download just the minimum to ensure this.

It has a security model that restricts code to a sandbox model unless the code is signed, in which case it may be allowed to run with no restrictions. This is a very coarse–grained security model, with far less options than are allowed with the Java 2 security model. The options are not appropriate for Jini code, for example, which should often run in a "sandbox with networking". Nevertheless, the all–permissions model does allow trusted code to run and do interesting things locally.

Interactive Web programs

By combining the ideas from our earlier work with WebStart, we can get a one–click interactive environment for demonstrating Java programs. The "compile once, run anywhere" property of Java means that most of the complications of languages that compile to native code can be avoided. The one–click environment is built from the following components

- A TextArea is used to display a Java program within an HTML Form. This can be edited to demonstrate variations, or submitted as is
- Form submission calls a CGI script/servlet/etc on the server which attempts to compile the program
- Errors are reported back in text/plain format
- A correct compile results in generation of a signed jar file containing the compiled classes
- A JNLP file is returned to the browser, which needs to be configured to hand this to a WebStart helper
- The WebStart helper uses the JNLP to download any needed files from the server
- The program which originated from the browser is then run in the browser's environment, allowing full user interaction

Engineering aspects
Lifetime
The Java source files are extracted from the Form data, compiled and used to create a jar file. Essentially, this is an atomic action, and after creation of the jar file the source and class files are no longer needed.

A response can then be sent as a JNLP file back to the browser, which references the jar file. The browser will call WebStart which will fetch the jar file after checks on the local system. After this, the jar file is no longer required on the server.

Managing this bumps into the standard web problem of stateful access in a stateless system. The response of a JNLP document ends a request session from the browser, and the interaction between WebStart and the server is a separate session. The current implementation handles these issues in the following manner

The "atomic" operation of creating the Java source files, compiling them, building the jar file and deleting the source and class files is protected by a file lock

The jar file is given a unique name for each session, and this jar file is stored persistently in the file system

After some "reasonable" time it can be assumed that WebStart has fetched what it needs of the jar file, and it can be deleted. This is similar to a cookie "timing out" and releasing a resource on the server

Visibility

To illustrate a programming concept it may not be necessary to show a full program. A couple of classes, or perhaps just some methods of a class might be enough. The current implementation uses the class as minimum unit. That is, one or more classes can be shown in TextArea's for editing. This may not be enough to actually run a program, and additional classes may be needed.

These may be included in two ways
- as hidden fields within the Form
- as references to jar files held on the server

Non-GUI programs

WebStart makes the assumption that downloaded programs use a GUI interface. This is not in the specification, and is just ignored as an issue. The Sun implementation of WebStart just discards I/O involving System.{in,out,err}. Other possibilities might have been a flag within the specification to include this environmental possibility, or to have an equivalent of the Netscape "Java Console" to handle this form of I/O.

There are many situations where one might want to avoid this assumption
- A lesson on a basic topic such as Vector would not want the complication of GUI code
- Some versions of Java – the J2ME restricted environments – do not even have the AWT or Swing classes
- Lessons on the JDK1.4 new I/O classes may not want GUI code complicating things

Objects such as System.in are declared final and so cannot be reassigned directly. However, there are methods such as System.setIn(...) that can be used to reassign these objects. Using these methods, it is not too hard to build a "GUI wrapper" that consists of a Text or JText with I/O linked to System.{in,out,err} by pipelines. The wrapper can be used as the main controller from a hidden field so that it need not be visible to the student.

Results

I currently teach a subject "Distributed Programming using Java". The Web lecture notes for this subject are being modified to allow one-click execution of programs (after WebStart has been installed). A sample lecture is at http://jan.netcomp.monash.edu.au/distjava/socket/lecture.html

Using this, it is straightforward to demonstrate even multithreaded and network programs using clients and servers, and modify the code in place. The subject will next be taught in August, and usage of this will be monitored throughout the teaching period.

Conclusions and future work

A system is running and is being used to modify existing teaching material of the author. Some parts of the online Java Tutorial are also being modified (in private copies) to demonstrate that this system is not tied to a particular teaching style.

There has been substantial work done on a teaching environment called BlueJ. This is a standalone system at present. Investigations are being made into integrating BlueJ and WebStart technologies to allow Java courseware on the Web to be imported into the BlueJ teaching environment.

References

Newmarch, J.D (1996) Client–Side Execution of Programs Proc AusWeb96, Southern Cross University
Barnes, D.J (2002) *Objects First with Java*, Prentice–Hall, 2002
WebStart (2001) Java WebStart, http://java.sun.com/products/javawebstart/

Building a Hybrid Learning Community

Submitted by Thanh Nguyen

As email, synchronous and asynchronous threaded discussion boards have increasingly become important communication tools for students and teachers, building a hybrid learning environment plays a critical role in enhancing student learning. "Hybrid" is the term commonly used nationwide to describe courses that combine face-to-face classroom with computer-based instruction. Activities in a hybrid course could be a mixture of Web-based and face-to-face discussions, or virtual classes where students could upload and share their works online before presenting theirs to others in the face-to-face learning environment. Also after their presentations, others could review their works for feedback. Because a hybrid learning environment allows students to have more time in giving their opinions, students could express their thinking and learning without being limited by their shyness or learning disabilities. For example, a near-blind student could take the time needed to read others' responses, or an English as a Second Language student could take time to understand other's writings.

Teaching with a hybrid format allow instructors not only having activities for usual face-to-face meetings, but also up loading a course syllabus, files, assignments, PowerPoint presentations with voice and sound recorded, streaming videos, posting grades and tracking student works. The instructors could make announcements or send messages to each or all students through the message board. Once class information was uploaded onto the class website, instructors would know for sure that students could get access to the information without worrying about student's losing their works or instructions. Using this hybrid format, students can take more responsibility in their own learning. For example, they can upload their assignments onto the course site, share their work with the class or with members of a work groups at their choice, or can search the web and email each other directly using clickable email aliases embedded in the course pages.

The threaded discussion forum allow instructors to check on students' knowledge through conversations exchanged on the forum or from topics covered through reading assignments. Best of all, the discussion forum allow students to share ideas with other students in class, extending the work during in-class discussions. Here is what students say:

- I enjoyed using the threaded discussion board for various reasons. It helped to create a thoughtful dialogue as each person carefully thinks over their answers. I enjoyed hearing from each of my classmates. My classmates writing often give me something to respond to in my writing. Sometimes I feel like it was kind of impersonal since I couldn't always connect the writing with the actual person in the room. Overall, however, I think it is a successful tool.

- I have really enjoyed having access to this online site where the class can find information, share ideas, contact our classmates etc. It is something new and I enjoy exploring its different features.
- I really like typing my responses and reading the comments of my classmates. First, I like that I don't have to do some extra journal before class. I like coming and applying what I read. It helps me see if I understood it after awhile and also serves as a refresher for the class discussion. I like reading everyone else's comments as well. They are written highly intelligently and sophisticated. I find I get more out of my classmates written and synthesized thoughts than if we just had an oral discussion. In an oral discussion, not many people talk and those that do always talk. It's nice to hear shy people's thoughts as well as boisterous ones, because they are all very important and have contributed significant insights to me.
- I think the threaded discussion board has worked fairly well -- it gives everyone in class the opportunity to express his/her opinion thoughtfully and everyone has a chance to be heard. Too often, one or two voices dominate class discussion but the online discussion eliminates that problem.
- I like this web-based environment as a tool for this class. It is convenient to get assignments online and respond to discussions online. As far as learning, I can't say that I've learned a completely new concept but it adds a new dimension to the course.

Technology Leadership Academy

The Technology Leadership Academy is a project funded by the U. S. Department of Education's *Preparing Tomorrow's Teachers to Use Technology* (PT3) Initiative. The mission of the Academy is to develop a collegial network for the infusion of technology into teacher preparation within the four-state area of Kansas, New Mexico, Oklahoma, and Texas. Academy partners include the higher education community, state agencies involved in teacher education, and the corporate sector. This presentation will showcase how the Academy has developed an online learning community for technology infusion and how faculty members can create this collaborative environment at their universities and in their regional areas to elevate faculty teaching and improve adult learning. Additionally, the Academy's online tutorials for faculty development will be highlighted.

The mission of the Technology Leadership Academy, a component of the Technology Leadership Institute, is to develop a learning community among teacher preparation programs. During the past three years it has grown from an abstract concept to an organization with around 450 members within the four-state area of Kansas, New Mexico, Oklahoma, and Texas. The Academy's membership throughout the world spans to 2,000 members. From the beginning, the goal was to build a collegial and collaborative organization to provide mutual support and sharing of resources in the challenging task of infusing technology into teacher preparation. The first organizational meeting, hosted by The University of Texas in January 2000, was attended by key officials from 85 universities and state educational agencies from the four states. Activities included: finalizing the Academy's organizational structure; establishing priorities; dividing into task groups (each concentrating on one aspect of the Academy's mission); nominating chairs of each Task Group (to serve on the Steering Committee and oversee the Task Group's functioning); and identifying a set of directives and recommendations for the Task Groups.

The Steering Committee, comprised of deans, faculty and technology directors, provides direction and oversight of the Academy's activities and meets several times a year to review progress and discuss future plans. There has been a shared responsibility in the development of the Academy, even though the distance across these institutions makes this task even more challenging (and yet so rewarding).

Each Task Group is chaired by a Steering Committee member and consists of volunteer faculty or staff from the member institutions and state educational agencies. Each Task Group is responsible for determining and coordinating its specific part of the Academy's functioning. Eight Task Groups emerged from the organizational meeting of the Academy. These included: Assessment and Planning, Academy Web Community, Consultants Database, Fall Institute, Policy and Leadership, Professional Development, Regional Conferences, and Technology Integration. Last year, the Academy formed a ninth committee, the Digital Equity Task Group, to ensure that the other eight Task Groups were addressing digital equity issues in their efforts.

The Academy facilitates an online tutorial process to provide on-going professional development opportunities. The Academy Web Community Task Group has developed a Faculty Mentor and Faculty Subject Area Mentor. These projects are unique resources that use a question and answer format to allow faculty members access to relevant online faculty technology professional development resources, models, and research. The Subject Area Mentor has four content area components: English-as-a-Second Language, Mathematics, Science, and Social Studies.

Academy members are represented on the Educational Technology Coordinating Council which developed the State of Texas Master Plan for Educational Technology 2000-2003. The mission of the ETCC is to ensure the cooperation and coordination of the state's efforts to implement education technology initiatives. The State of Texas Master Plan for Educational Technology is aimed at pre-service and in-service training in technology integration for teachers and librarians. The Master Plan includes eight goals and objectives which identify the organizational infrastructure and data requirements necessary to measure successful implementation. Included in the goal descriptions are definitions, levels of impact, lead agencies, participating agencies, objectives, limitations, and due dates. One of the most significant sections in the Master Plan recognizes 12 Recommendations which serve as an implementation plan for achieving statewide collaboration for educational technology.

Although competition within universities can be used in a positive manner, the focus of the Academy is to instill close, working relationships among and across institutions. The Fall Institute, the Academy's annual conference, is an activity used to accomplish this goal. Teams of 3-5 individuals from member institutions participate in a 3-day conference focused on infusing technology into teacher preparation programs. Academy members also participate in organizing Regional Conferences on member campuses to strengthen the face-to-face component of the continued attempted by the Academy to provide a structure that fosters community and resource sharing.

The Academy has devised a project to recognize outstanding faculty members who are effectively infusing technology into the curriculum. The purpose of the Consultants' Database is to develop a comprehensive listing of faculty with expertise in various areas who have agreed to be featured on the Academy website in a biweekly segment and to be part of a database of resources.

This session will be an interactive experience, whereby mutual benefit will exist between participants, between the participant and the presenter, and vice versa. The following objectives guide this session:

For participants to

1. Become familiar with the mission, goals and objectives, and components of the Technology Leadership Academy;
2. Participate in a discussion regarding issues involved in building an online learning community;
3. Learn about the process that the Academy took to develop this community (discuss benefits and challenges of certain strategies taken);
4. Contribute ideas on how the Academy can reach more faculty members.

Our overarching goal is for the participants to share ideas with the presenter on how to encourage more faculty members to become involved in the Academy and how to continue to meet our members' needs.

Please visit the Academy website at http://www.edb.utexas.edu/academy

Online Learning 'Assumes' Online Delivery Skills

John O'DONOGHUE – Senior Research Fellow

National ICT Research Centre for Education, Training and Employment
University of Wolverhampton.
Shropshire Campus
Telford TF2 9NT
UK

j.odonoghue@wlv.ac.uk
Voice: 01902 323854
Fax: 01902 322836

Abstract

Research suggests that education needs to embrace IT, use it to provide quality, flexible teaching and learning. In order to be competitive the organisational structures need to reflect the environment, this means a change from the rigid, inflexible internal/stable structure. Findings suggest that, technological developments will change the role of the lecturer.

The expectations and learning styles of students and staff are increasingly diverse. Learning is regarded as a lifelong activity. Distance learning is becoming commonplace. Increasingly there is an emphasis on lifelong skills.

The solution is simple! Introduce technology, video conferencing, labs of PC's with powerful software. Significant investment has been made in technology within Education to enable students to use a very powerful computer to word process assignments and 'surf' the Net! Staff are little better, intrigued or disillusioned with video conferencing, seeing it as 'glossy' or at best futile in the context of learning delivery. This paper considers some of the issues raised and addressed by the development and implementation of our own in-house Virtual Learning Environment.

It is often said that we are entering or even part of the Information Age. This coming period could equally be called the Age of Learning: The sheer quantity of learning taking place in the world is already many times greater than in the past. For example, not very long ago, and in many parts of the world, young people would learn skills they could use in their work throughout life. Today, in industrial countries, most people are doing jobs that did not exist when they were born. The most important skill determining a person's life pattern has already become the ability to learn new skills, to take in new concepts, to assess new situations, to deal with the unexpected. The competitive ability is the ability to learn. Information technology, from television to computers, affords an opportunity to enhance the learning experience.

Children have seized this opportunity, they have entered a passionate and enduring love affair with the computer. What they do with computers is as varied as their activities. The greatest amount of time is devoted to playing games, with the result that names like Nintendo™ have become household words. They use computers to write, draw, to communicate, to obtain information. Some use computers as a means to establish social ties with other cultures, while others use them to isolate themselves.

However with all the technology and the ability to access it where or what has changed, in terms of a teaching and learning environment. If a party of time travellers from an earlier century descended on us what would they see. If they consisted of surgeons and teachers. The surgeons, irrespective of their competence, might recognise that some operation was taken place, but there would have no idea of the environment, or the technology or of the strange devices and tools which the present day surgeon would be employing. The rituals of antisepsis and anaesthesia, and even the bright lights, would be utterly unfamiliar to them. The teachers would respond very differently. They might be puzzled by a few strange objects, and there will be some debate about standard techniques which had changed, but would be reasonably comfortable with what was being attempted and may even be able to take over the class. This is particularly true of some of the more traditional subjects.

Why, through a period when so much human activity has been revolutionised, have we not seen comparable change in the way we help people learn?

To date, classroom enhancements have replaced traditional apparatus rather than the process or didactic model of teaching:

⇒ The chalkboard replaced the slate;
⇒ the whiteboard replaced the chalkboard;
⇒ the OHP replaced the whiteboard;
⇒ software (Microsoft PowerPoint™ et al) replaced the OHP

Teachers/ lecturers felt comfortable with these changes as they were replacing the quill with the keyboard, the delivery mechanism, process and interface was essentially the same. So how to progress, there is a need to enable staff to consider the pedagogic implication of the on-line learning environment rather than the content.

The Internet potentially provides an opportunity to change all this.

According to Graziadei et al (1998), in order to implement and sustain remote, distance based computer mediated courses with a high probability of success, the following should be considered as the critical areas:

• enhancing/extending autonomous learning and productivity in the face-to-face traditional classroom setting
• creating a Web-presence with easy access to 'basic' information about online courses and interactive learning materials
• discovering/developing tools and standards to support new learning environments
• advancing our understanding of the virtual and distance university
• increasing community/off-campus access to the teaching-learning community
• providing evidence of the viability of these concepts

Staff are currently being asked to develop material for on-line delivery. This is an anathema to them. Not because of any motive other than competence in the pedagogy, technology environment etc. They generally teach the way in which they have been taught. As tutors they feel in control of this environment of physically teaching students, they are 'happy' with the quality and control and standard of the 'interface'. To introduce another medium is quite threatening and may well affect the quality of the experience.

If I could elaborate. I personally feel that something such as video conferencing (VC) is not as successful as perhaps it ought to be due to the 'tablet looking for something to cure..' syndrome. Have we developed a real use for VC? I would suggest not, so we create environments where VC can be used. This is surely not the thing to do. From my own experience setting up e/mail in schools for pen pal use failed miserably. This was because I introduced e/mail and then something to do on it…However I rapidly learnt a lesson. In a number of other schools I introduced the staff to e/mail and provided an opportunity for them to exchange pictures/ letters/ curriculum ideas and projects. These were via e/mail and more traditional means of communication. These teachers then developed local, regional, national and international databases and information exchange systems, the important fact being that *they* exchanged, *they* decided, *they* owned, developed and delivered. I provided and enabled a platform for them. The issues are about how teaching and learning are perceived within the organisation.

However we must maintain quality within our content and delivery. According to the literature, quality is concerned with meeting a defined specification(s). Clearly then, for learning to be considered as quality learning, it must also meet prescribed and accepted criteria. Nightingale and O'Neil (1994: p. 54), suggest that the indicators of high quality learning having taken place are:-

• being able to discover knowledge for oneself
• long term retention of knowledge (implying that there is understanding)
• being able to perceive relations between old and new knowledge

- being able to create new knowledge
- being able to apply knowledge to solving problems
- being able to communicate one's knowledge to others
- wanting to know more

But, they add the caveat that it is only possible to achieve this specification where certain pre-requisites for quality in learning are in existence:-

- the learner is ready to meet the demands of the learning task(s)
- there is a reason for learning (acceptable reason, to the student)
- the learner is active during learning
- adequate support is provided by the environment in which that learning occurs

The adoption and implementation of such a model by staff in developing for an on-line delivery platform or for an on-line supported delivery platform will require a greater understanding of both the learning process itself, and also the most appropriate means to facilitate that process (O'Donoghue et al, 2001). This understanding is a pre-requisite for effective course design. But, I would suggest that at present, part of the problem is the differing conceptions held by academic staff as to exactly what; a) learning is, and b) what on-line facilitated learning is. But perhaps more importantly, future developments in course design, structure and delivery will continue to be at best misguided, and at worst potentially damaging to the quality of the learning experiences that are offered.

The challenge is to develop a curriculum which can emphasise interconnections between learning pathways, the practical application of knowledge in a variety of contexts and flexible relationships between core and specialist knowledge. It must be based on sound pedagogy. The focus on tutors is not on the training but on the facilitation of central processes of learning which too often is interpreted as something which is transmitted to people rather than an activity for which they themselves have responsibility. The teachers of tomorrow must have some involvement, experience and opinion of 'student-centred learning', 'flexible learning', 'open learning', 'active learning', 'on-line learning' etc.

Effective learning within this environment is:-

1) a function of the interaction between, *and* the interdependence of, 3 groups of factors
2) and a cause of that interaction

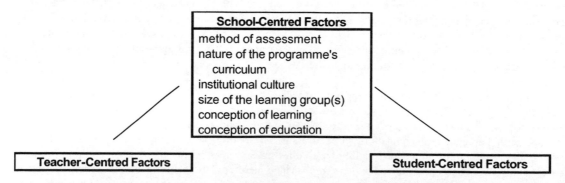

```
┌─────────────────────────────┐                    ┌──────────────────────────────┐
│ teaching style              │                    │ student motivation           │
│ teacher motivation          │                    │ learning style               │
│ degree of learner autonomy  │                    │ level of anxiety             │
│ nature of new knowledge in  │                    │ learning skills              │
│    relation to previous     │                    │ learner self-confidence      │
│    knowledge                │   STUDENT LEARNING  │ approach to learning adopted │
│ method of teaching used     │                    │    by the learner            │
│ nature of the learning      │                    │ previous knowledge           │
│    environment              │                    │ conception of learning       │
│ degree of learner           │                    │ conception of education      │
│    involvement in the       │                    │                              │
│    learning process         │                    │                              │
│ conception of learning      │                    │                              │
│ conception of education     │                    │                              │
└─────────────────────────────┘                    └──────────────────────────────┘
```

Robotham, 1996

The approach of the tutors in allowing cross fertilisation and conceptual development of the student and tutor and technology must be fostered. It must allow various "partnerships" into which students will enter. Successful learning depends on success in establishing and developing such partnerships - with tutors and with collaborators.

However, such an attitude is not free of complication. It may be argued that one important goal of formal education is to cultivate a capacity to learn independently; in a sense to find some release from learning - as - partnership. Now, claims of this sort introduce an element of tension: we wish to develop partnerships for purposes of socially mediated learning, but we also wish to cultivate in the learner a certain autonomy. Tension of aims need not imply conflict of aims. Indeed, far from being in conflict there may be necessary developmental relationships between socially organised cognitive functioning and that which is 'private' or autonomous to the individual (Vygotsky, 1978). Nevertheless, at a practical level of formulating strategies for teaching, there does remain a tension to be handled. Thus, in practice, one thing teachers must surely consider is how they should manage the learning process in terms of a balance of emphasis between pupil autonomy and interpersonal exchange.

References

Graziadei, W., Gallagher, S., Brown, R., & Sasiadek, J. Building Asynchronous and Synchronous Teaching-Learning Environments: Exploring a Course/Classroom Management System Solution. http://horizon.unc.edu/projects/monograph/CD/Technological_Tools/Graziadei.asp. Accessed July 2002.

Nightingale, P., & O'Neil, M. (1994). Achieving quality learning in higher education. London: Kogan Page.

O'Donoghue, J., Singh, G., Caswell, S. & Molyneux, S. (2001). Pedagogy vs. Technocentrism in Virtual Universities. Journal of Computing in Higher Education. Volume 13, Number 1. October, 200.

Robotham, D.(1996). Effectiveness of self directed learning (Thesis).

Vygotsky, L. S. (1978). Mind in society : The development of higher psychological processes. Cambridge. Massachusetts. Harvard University Press.

A Model for an Open, Flexible Website to Aid Classes at University: the Student Interface.*

Lia Raquel Oliveira & Elías Blanco
Curriculum and Educational Technology Dept.
University of Minho
Portugal
lia@iep.uminho.pt & eblanco@iep.uminho.pt

Abstract: In the context of a research-development study in progress, a website prototype was created (dynamic, interactive and multimedia data base) with the purpose of providing support to any subject-matter in teaching and learning at university. The aim is to make classes more flexible in the terms of space and time, providing a classroom virtual environment, based on "good pedagogical practices" of sharing and cooperative construction of knowledge. The model is briefly presented and the interface to be used by students is discussed.

Introduction

The new technologies of information and communication, and more specifically the Internet, have radically transformed the ways in which information is accessed and produced, as well as the scale of its diffusion. At the same time, forms of communication have changed, too. Universities, as generators of knowledge and agents of human resources development, are not dissociated from these phenomena and play a determining role within them. Both society and available knowledge are experiencing change and, consequently, workplaces demand flexible professionals with autonomous learning skills, ability to adapt and a cooperative enterprising capacity. In this context, the university needs to reflect upon the kind of education and the forms of learning it provides. Thus, we believe it has to undertake some changes in its pedagogical practices. One of these changes includes the effective use of the web as a didactic device for teaching activities. This implies not only transposing study material into the web, but also, and above all, creating and developing environments which aid methodologies and strategies so as to improve meaningful learning. We are not dealing with the issue of long-distance teaching but rather with the reconceptualisation of formal education through the use of technology at hand and its potential for communication and distribution. In fact, it is precisely due to this technology that we have witnessed a steadily increasing convergence between the two forms of teaching, which tend to complement each other both in education and training.

Intention and Objectives

The context of this project is a research-development study in progress, whose primary objective is to discuss and understand the process of conceiving and implementing a device for education/training. This objective distinguishes the project from other similar undertakings, which may concurrently occur over time. The purpose it to provide a working tool which will allow an essentially pedagogical and didactic reflection on the use of this technology in this context, in addition to a reflection on the technical, administrative and logistic aspects of the prototype.

A website was designed, aimed at providing support for any subject-matter related to learning at university. This prototype is to be used outside the classroom and/or in the classroom and provides support, both as a model and an example, for the subject of Educational Technology (3rd year of training for prospective secondary school teachers), which is taught in a laboratory regime, with special emphasis placed on project methodology and portfolio assessment.

The purpose of the website is to make attended classes more flexible, in terms of time and space management, by creating a virtual environment based on "good pedagogical practices" which can be translated into the notion of community (group, the feeling of belonging), sharing and the cooperative construction of knowledge. Flexibility will allow students to possess greater autonomy in their learning process because, during their training period, they have access to an interactive reference online regarding the subject and may use it in accordance with their personal characteristics (learning styles and pace).

More concrete objectives include the way in which access to relevant information is facilitated, making thematic communication more dynamic (students-students and students-teachers), promoting the development of information literacy skills, and simplifying some of the teacher's administrative and organizational tasks, thus contributing to improved quality in learning.

The Process of Creating the Device

The process of creating the device was undertaken in three phases: conception, development and implementation (analysis and assessment are currently under way).

The conception phase started with a literature review on the subject and a search on the web for related undertakings. From the analysis of available platforms (paid or gratuitous) for "virtual lessons", we concluded that they were either too complex for what was required (although some were extremely interesting) or excessively directed towards distance-learning. However, we found various specific undertakings which closely matched our intentions. We proceeded with some preliminary research on the existence of sites possessing these features, at Portuguese state universities, for the teaching of the subject under study (Educational Technology or other related subjects) (Oliveira & Blanco, 2001).

We then made decisions about specific objectives, the contents to be made available and the formats to use, the approach to communication/aesthetics, and the types of communication and interaction. The idea of "good pedagogical practices" previously mentioned was turned into a metaphor inspired by the categories of narratives (since Man is a consumer/producer of stories): elaboration of a story (i.e. construction of knowledge) in a specific dimension of time and space, by someone who makes something, using the resources required to meet common objectives and depending on some conditioning factors (Laurel, 1991, Depover et al, 1998). The communication/aesthetic options were as minimalist as possible, respecting the criteria of simplicity, easy use, clarity, consistency and induced credibility. The architecture of the final information was managed by resorting to the "post-it" technique (Boling & Frick, 1997) and the result is presented in the following flowchart (Fig.1).

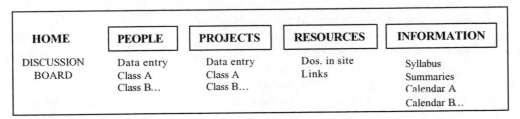

Figure 1 - Flowchart of the student interface.

The development phase - the technical execution of the site itself - counted on the collaboration of professionals from the areas of Systems Engineering and Communication Design (programming and surface structure). After elementary testing and site installment, we undertook usability tests not referred to at length here, which were fundamentally based on the analysis of "think aloud" individual protocols registered on video (Schriver, 1997), involving five participants representative of the intended users (Nielsen & Landauer, 1993, Reeves & Carter, 2001). Some changes were made as a result of these tests.

The website was implemented for a semester (2002) and was used by approximately seventy students from teaching degrees (languages and science). At present, we are analysing opinions gathered from these users (through questionnaires and interviews) and we expect to make the results available soon, especially those relating to the pedagogical interest of using the model in the given situation.

As for the system, the site has two interfaces: the student interface, that is, the shared environment (students and teacher) and the administrator interface (teacher) for updating and managing the information on the site. To make this possible, the online content is dynamic and is fed by an information system created by Microsoft Access (using Dreamweaver, Ultradev, HTML, ASP and Java Script). We are, therefore, dealing with a data base whose interfaces allow data uploading without authorized access to the server. We consider this aspect to be important for real interactivity at the level of both interfaces, so that the platform is not reduced to unidirectional communication (teacher-students) and directive discourse. Access to any of the interfaces requires login and a password.

The student interface is made up of five sections: Home, People, Projects, Resources and Information. These sections aim to reflect the adopted metaphor.

The Home section (Fig.2), presented as the site map (deeper information is accessed after a maximum of three clicks, due to the use of pop-down menus) proposes a type of simplified forum - a discussion board. A statement is under discussion (weekly suggested by the teacher) and the comments introduced are automatically inserted using a click (bypassing identification). These comments may be used to start a discussion at the beginning of a class. The principles underlying this option are reflectivity and voluntary participation. Thus, the Home is supposed to generate interactivity and participation.

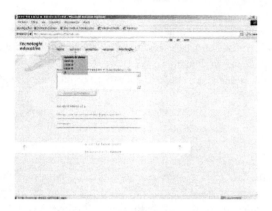

Figure 2 - Home and navigation menu.

The People section allows four entries: data entry and three classes.

In the data entry, students will find a form where they fill in personal data (photography included) which become available on a personal page made accessible via the course page. The teacher is part of the page since she/he integrates the group/community, although she/he obviously has different objectives from those of the students.

The Project section also allows four entries: data entry and three courses.

The data entry is also a form where students are asked to fill in synopses of the work projects in which they are involved. Their names (nicknames identifying them in the group) are connected with their personal page.

The Resources section allows two entries: resources on the site and external resources. The latter are traditional *links* of interest, which are progressively updated by students' contributions (the *links* are inserted by the teacher). At present, these are grouped as national and international.

The resources on the site are grouped according to the type of document: written texts (.doc), powerpoint presentations (.ppt), video extracts (.mpeg), still pictures (.jpg and .gif) and exercises (various formats). At present, these are presented on run-on pages (with *links* for the top of the screen and for the category) since it is difficult to predict the number of documents which can be inserted.

Various reference texts were made available, also powerpoint versions of some of them, assessment grids for projects to be undertaken as well as for various types of performance (student participation, teacher's activity), autonomous presentations in powerpoint, video extracts of documents seen in class, a set of images and a few exercises on computing tools. This possibility of insertion and the availability of multimedia documents constitutes an inevitable requirement due to the obvious advantages, for the process of learning, of using diverse symbolic systems to represent information (Depover et al, 1998).

All the documents are posted on a new window on the *browser* so that they can be seen immediately and may be recorded at the source of application.

The links to other sites use the same process of posting a new window on the *browser*, avoiding, on the one hand, an involuntary exit from this site (due to URL change) and, on the other, preserving their authorship (one of the many reasons why frames are not used).

The Information section summarizes institutional and administrative aspects: the formal course syllabus, summaries and calendar (for each course).

The syllabus page occupies one screen (containing a summary of it) and one can *download* from the respective file (.doc) as well as from a specific file concerning assessment norms, criteria and methods.

The Summary page is similar and allows one to download from the respective file.

The Calendar, as the name indicates, schedules the activities over the time-period estimated for attendance of the course. It is divided into months and days (on a run-on page) and presents a guiding summary for the activities to be developed.

As for possible forms of communication, apart from the initial discussion board which can be used in an asynchronous or synchronous manner, priority is given to the use of electronic mail. All the members of the class-community introduce their electronic mail address on their personal pages, which then becomes available for communication from this interface.

Electronic mail, as we know, allows private communication from one person to another but also from one to various people (e.g. mailing lists). It also allows one to send attached files in various formats. On the other hand, e-mail applications allow one to establish rules for message reception and dispatch (e.g. various filters) as well as to file, register and confirm reception. Thus, we believe that this mode of communication is the most suitable in this kind of situation, ensuring the privacy, speed and general efficiency required in the exchange of messages. Furthermore, it is via electronic mail that the transmission of assessment results takes place (formative and summative) both by the teacher and the students, through the use of selective mailing lists (individual, small group or course groups). This option is based on the fact that we consider evaluation, in any of its forms, to be a context-sensitive process which concerns the people involved and that, therefore, a certain degree of discretion and privacy must be ensured. This, in fact, occurs in the traditional academic context of publicizing results (posting marksheets). It is our belief that using electronic mail for this purpose over the learning period contributes to higher degrees of personalization, transparency and fairness in the assessment process.

Final remarks

No technology can be educational on its own. To understand this, you need only to use it (Jacquinot-Delaunay, 2001). The conception, development, implementation and evaluation of educational and training devices for the web necessarily demands deep reflection and discussion, not only regarding the computer software and communication aspects of operating those devices, but also and above all, concerning the pedagogical, didactic and curricular purposes and intentions which support them. With this text, we hope to contribute to this discussion and promote the transdisciplinary approach that this medium of communication requires.

References

Boling, E. & Frick, T. W. (1997) "Holistic Rapid Prototyping for Web Design: Early Usability Testing Is Essential". In, Khan, B. H. (Ed.), *Web-Based Instruction* (pp. 319-328). Englewood Cliffs, NJ: Educational Technology Publications.

Depover, C., Giardina, M & Marton, P. (1998), *Les Environnements d'Apprentissage Multimédia. Analyse et Conception*. Paris: L'Harmattan.

Jacquinot-Delaunay, G. (2001) "Avec Internet, finies les télévisions éducatives?" (pp. 72-73). In *MédiaMorphoses*, 1, Janvier. Bry-Sur-Marne. INA.

Laurel, B. (1991) *Computers as theaters*. Reading: Addison-Wesley.

Nielsen, J. & Landauer, T. K. (1993) "A mathematical model of the finding of usability problems" (pp. 206-213). In Proceedings of ACM INTERCHI'93, Amsterdam, The Netherlands, 24-29 April.

Oliveira, L.R. & Blanco, E. (2001) "Apresentação de informação educativa na *Web*, no contexto universitário português: análise de disciplinas *online* de suporte à lecionação" (pp. 421-429). In Silva, B. D. & Almeida, L. (Eds.) *Actas do VI Congresso Galaico-Português de Psicopedagogia*. Braga, Portugal: CEEP.

Reeves, T. C. & Carter, B. J. (2001) "Usability Testing and Return-on-Investment Studies: Key Evaluation Strategies for Web-Based Training"(pp. 547-557). In Khan, B. H. (Ed.) *Web-Based Training*. Englewood Cliffs, NJ: Educational Technology Publications.

Schriver, K. A. (1997) *Dynamics in Document Design*. USA: John Wiley & Sons, Inc.

*This work is financed by the portuguese Foundation for Science and Technology (FCT) with the reference SFRH/BD/1297/2000.

WHAT ARE FACULTY'S THOUGHTS ON ASYNCRONOUS TEACHING? A CASE STUDY OF ONE COMMUNITY COLLEGE IN UPSTATE, NEW YORK.

Carol Oliver, MA
The Graduate School, The City University of New York
Environmental Psychology, Sub-Program in Psychology
New York, New York, USA
oliverc126@aol.com

Abstract - This research paper critically looks at professors' everyday work experiences teaching courses online, their work responsibilities as faculty within the larger university system and the issues that affect these faculty members. The paper illustrates how their experiences with asynchronous teaching have an affect on their professional and personal work experiences. The methods used for this study primarily involved qualitative research design and some quantitative analyses. Surveys and one-on-one interviewing were used for the collection of data. This paper is only a preliminary introduction to some of the data analyzed from interviews conducted with faculty.[1]

Introduction

The academic profession operates as a mentoring-training ground for professions, which include, doctors, lawyers, architects, engineers, and representatives of other advanced crafts or non-professional training (Clark, 1987). The academic profession involves varying dimensions of academic work, such as teaching, research, mentoring, evaluation of students' work, supervision and evaluation of dissertation work, administration and public policy work (Cahn, 1994; Clark, 1987; Markie, 1994; McKeachie, 1994). The question *what do academics do* is difficult to answer because it varies by discipline, institution, professional seniority, teaching styles and by personality traits, like temperament. The work of the professor involves teaching, mentoring, administration, and research, but these tasks vary greatly by person, institution, and seniority. Research and publishing serve as the primary basis for prestige in many disciplines and in the profession as a whole, and it is bound to play a substantial role in major universities (Clark, 1987, p.70). In addition, professors spread themselves beyond these two major tasks; some formally counsel students, some work in administration, some are heads of departments and others are active members in committees where they can vote on university policies and procedures (Cahn, 1994; Clark, 1987; McKeachie, 1994). Despite this range of activities, the workload of academics is usually defined by "teaching load" (Clark, 1987). In some cases, the workload may include supervision of students (both in the professor's research and in activities such as mentoring, studio work, dissertation work etc.) but teaching remains the institutional obligation for which hours can be specified. In graduate schools dissertation supervision is also considered part of the faculty workload and "research load" (for which one can get "released time" from teaching) is often assessed as a formal duty that is required for retention and promotion.

A review of the literature on the academic profession looks at "workload" in terms of "productivity,"(Green & Gilbert, 1995; Massy & Wilger, 1995; Robinson, 1997; Wulf, 1995). With the evolving use of information technology in academia, the work of professors is being measured by how much is produced within a specified time. Since information technology is allowing professors to do their work, including teaching, at a distance, the question of productivity has taken on new dimensions and in some learning institutions has become a concern. With email, distance learning, Internet technologies and fax, the method of delivering "*teaching*" or "*what professors will be doing,*" will change as information technologies change the environment of professors' "work" and their access to students. While the

---

[1] *The data for this paper is part of a larger data set that is currently being analyzed by the author for the completion of the dissertation.*

research on distance learning continues to grow many programs and universities are continuing to develop this medium to 'deliver' educational courses (Blumenstyk, 1997; Curtis , 2001; Frenette, L. 1997; Jaffe, 1998; Jellinek, 1988; Luke, 1997; Maurizio, 1997; Margolis, 1998; Noble, 1997; Novek, 1998;).

Technological advances in education are still met with skepticism by both educators and higher education administrators and teacher unions, (as reviewed in PSCcuny Clarion, 2000 Vol 29(6):5 -article entitled *"CUNY is not ready for distance learning"*). However, some academics and higher education administrators feel that distance education is a wonderful new teaching tool for learning because it offers flexibility of time and space and students can have access to professors by email and other online methods. In addition, distance learning education, can be attractive to the non-traditional learner (Ben-Jacob, et al., 2000). According to the article, *The Learning Environment of the 21st Century (Ben-Jacob. et al, 2000),* "the typical 21st century student will be an adult learner who is mature, more likely to be financially secure and more serious academically than today's student. A great number of these students will be employed full time and will pursue further education as a requirement of employment or for career advancement" (Ben-Jacob et al., 2000, p 8.). Distance learning will capture the interests of these different types of students because it provides flexible arrangements responsive to their time constraints (Ben-Jacob.et al, 2000, Berg, 2000). Conversely, some faculty members feel that distance learning is not *"a real education"* because students need to have face-to-face contact with educators. They view the online courses as inferior to the traditional classroom lecture, because they assume that distance courses cannot be rigorous enough to be academic (Ben-Jacob, et al., 2000). Faculty are concerned with *workplace* issues, such as the time that they spend designing their traditional courses online and how they will be compensated for the time they spend preparing a course. They are concerned with issues regarding evaluation for tenure and being retrenched by these new methods of teaching along with issues like publishing online, proprietary work and mentoring. Other ethical issues, such as universities becoming diploma mills, have become major concerns in the academic community ("An on-line experience," 1995; Curtis, 2001; Guernsey, 1997; Novek, 1996; Robinson, 1997; Young, 1997).

Currently, distance learning technologies are being used by professors as another teaching tool and not as a replacement to their practice of teaching. Questions of how professors use distance learning technologies in their work, if in fact, these technologies alter their teaching practices, and how teaching online may differ from teaching in the classroom, are important in looking at the profession in the context of professors' work lives when they use information technology. While some empirical studies on these questions have been done, studies have not looked at the teaching strategies that professors use when teaching online, nor has further consideration been given to issues of the professors' work environment. This research will examine these issues and will critically evaluate all aspects of the work lives of faculty that teach in online learning environments.

The Study

This paper is a result of one-on-one interviews that were done with faculty from a community college in Upstate New York. The faculty members at this community college were interviewed on issues relating to their online teaching *work* and *personal space issues* when teaching at a distance. This research was based on a larger data set, where 299 surveys where sent to faculty's homes asking about their experiences with computers and questions about online teaching. From the 299 surveys sent, 112 responded and 20 faculty members returned a postage-paid postcard that was attached to the survey, indicating that they would participate in the one-on-one personal interviews. The faculty members were contacted by email and given two weeks to respond to a date and time for the interview. Seventeen out of 20 professors responded and were interviewed. The interviews were taped and transcribed. The preliminary results that follow come from the interview data.

Preliminary Findings

The following is a grouping of preliminary findings that are currently being further analyzed.

What faculty favored about asynchronous teaching:

- Faculty members (n=17), in general were happy with the work they were doing using distance learning technology to teach. They enjoyed teaching online and felt that they had close-knit relationships with their students.
- Faculty expressed that they knew their students far better than they knew their face-to-face students. They had a stronger one-on-one relationship with their students because of the increased interaction they had with them online.
- Faculty stated that this was due to the more time they were spending evaluating individual student's work. They had to answer enormous amounts of email and discussion questions with each individual student.
- Despite the fact that the literature, and many non-distance learning teachers say that they do not teach online because they need the face-to-face interaction, these teachers felt that they knew their students far better than their traditional classroom students. They felt a special bond with the students and there was a *special* "virtual" communication that happened online between the student and the instructor.
- Faculty stated that students who took online courses were more reflective with their answers and homework assignments. Their writing was far better and they took more time to give well, researched answers.

What faculty concerns are regarding asynchronous teaching:

- All 17-faculty members stated that the number of students enrolled in their classes was *too* many. Student enrollment for an online class was the same as in a face-to-face class in this community college. For example, if a psychology class has a 30-student enrollment, then the department expected that the online class should have the same number of enrollments as well. All faculty (n=17) expressed that if enrollment was capped at an average of 15-20 students, it would be more manageable and less time consuming. Currently the community college has about 30-35 students enrolled in online classes at the time of registration, by the first weeks of class students enrollment drop to approximately 20 –25 students. *Faculty stated that the number of students made a <u>major difference</u> in the amount of hours they spent online!*
- One faculty member compared the amount of time and work in an online class with the classroom in a ratio of 4:1. The instructor said, *"For every hour I spend in the classroom, I spend four hours online."*
- Three faculty members reported ergonomic issues e.g. carpal tunnel syndrome; back pain; neck pain.
- Faculty stated that students who were not successful online were students who needed discipline, maturity and students who needed to be organized and structured in order to make their online experience rewarding and successful.
- Faulty reported that students, who dropped out during the first three weeks of class, needed more hands-on training as to the mechanical aspects of online course. They stated that they hope that the administration and the technology people could work together to give students more tutorial experiences.
- Two faculty members admitted that they were not happy with their dl experience because they were not utilizing the technical support adequately (by choice). These two faculty members reported that they were meeting with students online once or twice a week and giving them test --- they had no discussions with students online nor did they develop and online dialogue.
- Faculty stated that getting release time for teaching online or getting extra compensation for designing, preparing, or upgrading a course was <u>optimal</u>.
- Faculty stated that it was important to get more compensation because of the endless amounts of time they spent online evaluating student's work, participating in threaded discussions and answering large amounts of email messages.
- Two faculty members suggested that the university should be able to provide for the paid-Internet service at home, since they did all of their online teaching at home.

References

An "online" experience. Discussion group debates why faculty use or resist technology. (1995). In, *Change* Vol. (27)2 March/April

Ben-Jacob, M.G., Levin, D. S., and Ben-Jacob, T. K. (2000). The learning environment of the 21st century. *Educational Technology Review*. Spring/ Summer 2000, No.13, P.p. 8 –12.

Berg, G. A. (2000). Distance learning in the middle of trends in higher education. *WebNet Journal. Internet Technologies, Applications & Issues*. April-June 2000, Vol. 2(2), P.p. 5-6.

Blumenstyk, G. (1997). Some elite universities get serious about distance learning. In, *The Chronicle of Higher Education*. June 20, 1997. Pp. A23.

Cahn, S. M. (1994) *Saints and scamps. Ethics in academia.* The Graduate Center. The City University of New York. Maryland: Rowman & Littlefield Publishers, Inc.

Clark, B. R. (1987). *The academic life. Small worlds, different words.* The Carnegie Foundation for the Advancement of Teaching. Princeton, NJ: Princeton University Press.

CUNY is not ready for distance learning. (2000). PSCcuny Clarion. Vol 29 (6), p5.

Curtis, M.P. (2001) *Incentives and obstacles for nursing faculty in choosing to teach via distance.* Dissertation. The Graduate School of Saint Louis University.

Frenette, L. (1998). Distance learning takes off at SUNY. In, *The Voice*, Vol. (25) 5. Pp. 11-12.

Green, K. C., and Gilbert, S. W. (1995) Great expectations. Content, communication, productivity and the role of information technology in higher education. In, *Change* Vol. (27) 2 March/ April, p8.

Jaffe, D. (1998). The opportunities of anytime/anywhere learning. In, *Aft On Campus*, February 1998, Pp. 9.

Jellinek, D. (1998). Distance Learning/Digital Degrees, *The Guardian Weekly,* Vol (Pp.21).

Luke, T. W. (1997). The culture of cyber schooling: Information technology, digital discourse, and the political economy of university restructuring. *Presented at the Annual Meeting of Anthropological Association, November 19-23, 1997.*

Margolis, M. (1998) Brave new universities. (The future of the academy?). *First Monday*, Vol 3 (May 4, 1998) Issue 5. Also, [On-line] http:/www.firstmonday.dk/issues/issue3_5/index.html.

Markie, P.J. (1994). *Professor's duties. Ethical issues in college teaching.* Maryland: Rowman & Littlfield Publishers, Inc.

Massy, W. F. and Wigler, A. K. (1995). Improving productivity. What faculty think about it-And it's effect on quality, in *Change,* Vol (27)4 July/August p 10-20.

McKeachie, W.J. (1994). *Teaching tips. Strategies, research and theory for college and university teachers.* (Ninth Ed). Massachusetts: D.C. Health and Company.

Noble, D. F. (1997). Digital diploma mills: The automation of higher education. (http:/www.hronline.com/forums/labour/9711/0271.html).

Novek, E, M. (1996) Do professors dream of electronic sheep? Academic anxiety about the information age. Paper presented at the *79th Annual Meeting of the Association for Education in Journalism and Mass Communication, Anaheim, CA. August 10-13, 1996.*

Robinson, P. (1997) Awash in technology. Will the rising tide lift all boats? in *Aft on Campus*, Vol (17) 3. November 1997. P.6-8.

Thompson, H., (1999). The impact of technology and distance education: A classical earning theory viewpoint. Wulf, W. A. (1995). Warning: information technology will transform the university.[On-line journal] *Technology*, Vol (2) 53, p15-52. SIRS Researcher

Young, J. R. (1997). Rethinking the role of the professor in the age of high-tech tools, In, *The Chronicle of Higher Education*, October 3, 1997, Pp. A26-A28.

Doctorate at a Distance (D@D): In Search of Serendipity

Nadine Ozkan, Jacqueline Bourdeau and France Henri
Télé-Université, LICEF
4750 Henri-Julien, #100
Montreal, QC.
Canada H2T 3E4
Ph. : (1 514) 843-2015
Fax: (1 514) 843-2151
nozkan@licef.teluq.uquebec.ca , bourdeau@licef.teluq.uquebec.ca , fhenri@licef.teluq.uquebec.ca

Abstract: Distance higher education is a rapidly growing and evolving phenomena, which is actively promoted in many countries. Despite this, there is a relatively small proportion of this effort devoted to the distance PhD: distance PhDs programs are relatively new and experiences are scarce, specific, and hard to generalize. How, then, can we approach the design of a distance PhD program? This is the focus of the paper. Issues addressed include the following:

What are the pedagogical motivators of distance PhD programs? Here, we attempt to understand the benefits of such programs in terms of learning outcomes and of target population.

What are the specific challenges linked to distance PhD programs (as compared to other distance university degrees), and how can we attempt to address them?

What methods should be explored in order to ensure quality of learning but still favor autonomy and creativity?

Introduction

We are concerned with the design of distance PhD programs. Within PhD programs, we can distinguish those aimed at training highly skilled specialists, and those aimed at training researchers. Our focus is with the latter: the PhD process as research training.

The doctorate at a distance (or D@D) is a topical area, which currently fuels much interest from governments and universities (Averous and Touzot, 2002) (FU.NT Expert Work group, 2002) (National Science Board, 2002). Benefits sought include:

- An increased accessibility for potential students, which is a motivator for distance education in general, but which is specially relevant at the PhD level, in the context of "knowledge economies";
- The merging of PhD programs which, individually, may have a small number of students, but which attain critical mass when merged;
- The promotion of distributed research, which is actively encouraged and rewarded by research funding organizations. Distance PhD programs can help introduce a new generation of researchers to the practice, tools and methods of distributed research.

Despite this interest, there is currently little work in this area, either theoretical or in terms of best practices from the field. Indeed, work in distance university training focuses on *professional* training rather than on *research* training, and work in such areas as virtual research communities focuses on the *practice* of research rather than on the *training* of researchers. As to actual experiences, there are some existing distance PhD programs, but no synthesis – guidelines or principles – that might help guide the design of such programs. A reflection on distance research training remains to be done, and we hope that this paper constitutes an initial contribution.

Initial Reflections On the Nature of Research Training

In this section, we attempt to understand the nature of training for research, in order to assess whether a systematic approach to instruction design for the D@D is possible.

At a high level of abstraction, we consider the objective of research training to be the development of the capacity to contribute to the advancement of knowledge in a given area (which may be multidisciplinary), according to the norms defined by the research community. These norms, which are defined in a collective and consensual way, must thus be known and applied to the advancement of knowledge.

We consider the advancement of knowledge to be manifested in two ways: by conducting research projects that respect these norms, and also by the critical application of these norms to research projects conducted by others. In the first case, the contribution of the researcher is direct and active, and must be submitted to peer assessment. We qualify this as the *active* role of the researcher. In the second case, the researcher must apply meta-knowledge: the quality norms of research must be sufficiently understood and mastered to allow the constructive appreciation assessment of research projects. We qualify this as the *assessor* role of the researcher.

In the active role, in order to carry out a research project, the researcher must first conceive a research problem, which means identifying and stating a problem which is new, for which there is no obvious solution, which can be investigated using a scientific method, whose relevance can be convincingly argued and which builds upon existing scientific knowledge. The next step is to plan and execute the research project: design ways to approach the problem, choose one or several appropriate methodology/ies, execute the plan in a correct and ethical fashion, interpret results and draw conclusions. The last step consists in communicating research results in the appropriate channels, using the format of scientific communications.

In the assessor role, the researcher must be able to apply the norms of the scientific community to the activities that pertain to the carrying out of research projects (as described above), and to communicate the assessment (in order to advance the community).

In addition to these basic research skills, the doctorate student must also be trained in skills that are required from the context in which research will be undertaken in their professional life. Here, we can distinguish academic careers from organizational - industrial or public (governmental) - careers. Future academics should be trained in pedagogical skills and in raising grant funding. Future industrial researchers should be trained in issues pertaining to the commercialization of research results, including the protection of intellectual property, and in the management of research teams.

Finally, researchers should also have a deep knowledge of their domain area, of its concepts, theories and state of the art, and of that of the sub-domains that constitute it.

We have found that these reflections on the role, nature and activities of research lend themselves very well to their encapsulation in a hierarchical competency profile. We are currently developing such a profile, developing and building upon the initial reflections we have exposed here[1]. To our knowledge, there is currently no competency profile for researchers. Our undertaking, presented partially in this section, is the result of a synthesis of the following sources:

- general objectives for doctoral training (Prégent, 2002),
- requirements for admission into post-doctoral training, and criteria for the granting of post-graduate grants and scholarships (Economic and Social Research Council, 2001), and
- the definition of training objectives for some PhD programs (e.g., Missouri University, 2002).

Further Challenges

In addition to training of the specific competencies that researchers must demonstrate, as sketched in the previous section, PhD training displays specific features that distinguish it from other types of training, and that should have consequences for the design of distance PhD programs. We review them here.

- PhD programs aim at training self-directed, autonomous workers, who can demonstrate leadership. Indeed, PhD graduates are often required to supervise or guide undergraduate or

---

[1] Lack of space prevent us from showing an extract of our competency profile, but this will be shown in the presentation at the conference.

master students. PhD training should include components specifically linked to the development of autonomy and leadership.

- The interaction between PhD students and their research environment (peers, researchers, seminars, facilities, etc.) is an essential aspect of the training. In a distance mode, tools and facilities that support the emergence and maintenance of communities of practice and of communities of learners should be investigated.

- Another essential aspect is their interaction with their research supervisor and with their mentor (who may not be the same person. In fact, studies suggest that these interactions are more effective when mentor and supervisor are indeed not the same person (McCall and al., 2000). Studies show that the reactivity, relevance and regularity of these interactions are factors that can influence the success or failure of PhD studies (Muirhead, 1999), (Council of Graduate Schools, 1998) (Walker, 1998). Studies also show the importance of establishing trust early in the process ("swift trust" – (see Hiltz and al., 2002).

- The writing of the thesis is a critical stage in PhD studies. Indeed, it is at this stage that most of the "drop-outs" occur (National Science Board, 2002). The writing stage should be a time for monitoring and encouragement, notwithstanding the next point.

- PhD training requires "mental space" for the elaboration and maturing of ideas. A training environment where student progression is monitored too closely is not conducive to research training objectives, and can be a de-motivation factor for adult and autonomous students.

- The undertaking of a PhD program is a process that is deeply personal and meaningful, and that requires a high level of commitment (Prégent, 2002). The aims, activities and resulting career paths of PhD programs should be strongly coherent with the personal project of the PhD student.

These specificities all point to the fact that vital to successful PhD studies are a sustained contact with a stimulating research community, peer interaction, mentoring and the guidance provided by the supervisor. Learning outcomes should emerge naturally from these contacts, interactions and supportive relationships within the PhD environment, in a process that we qualify as *serendipitous*. The challenge in the design of distance PhD programs will be in the delicate balance between *engineering* learning outcomes, which is a proven way to ensure quality, and making room for *serendipity*, required at the PhD level.

Conclusion

This paper points to the need to assess the scope of applicability of an instructional design approach to the design of distance PhD programs. We have argued that an instructional design approach can be possible and beneficial, provided that it makes room for serendipitous creativity, which is the essence of research apprenticeship.

References

Averous, M. and Touzot, G. (sous la direction de). (2002). *Campus Numériques. Enjeux et perspectives pour la formation ouverte et à distance.* Rapport de Mission sous la direction de, à l`attention du Ministère de l`Éducation Nationale, du Ministère de la Recherche et de la Délégation à l`Aménagement du Territoire et de l`Action Régionale. Avril 2002. France. www.education.gouv.fr/rapport/foadenjeux.pdf

Council of Graduate Schools, Task Force on Distance Graduate Education. (1998). *Distance Graduate Education : Opportunities and Challenges for the 21st Century.* Washington. Sept. www.cgsnet.org

Economic and Social Research Council. (2001). *Postgraduate Training Guidelines.* Third Edition.. Jan. http://www.esrc.ac.uk/esrccontent/downloaddocs/sectionae.pdf

FU.NT Expert Work group (Formation Universitaire et Nouvelles Technologies). (2002).*Création d'un campus virtuel suisse.* Suisse. http://www.edutech.ch/edutech/publications/rapport_final_f_f.asp

Hiltz, S.R., et Turoff, M. (2002). What Makes Learning Networks Effective? *Communications of the ACM*, april, vol. 45, no. 4, pp. 56-59.

Institute for Higher Education Policy, National Education Association. (2000). *Quality On the Line: Benchmarks for Success in Internet-Based Distance Education.* US, April. www.ihep.com/Pubs/PDF/Quality_.pdf

McCall, L., Schattner, P. et Piterman, L. (2000). *Supervision of research by distance methods. Department of Community Medicine and General Practice*, Monash University, Australia. http://www.com.unisa.edu.au/cccc/papers/non_refereed/mccall.htm#Abstract

Missouri University. (2002). *Doctorate in Information Science and Learning Technologies (PhD) Competencies and Products*.. www.coe.missouri.edu/~sislt/programs/phd_comp_chart.html http://www.coe.missouri.edu/~sislt/phd/research.html

Muirhead, B. (1999). *Attitudes Toward Interactivity in a Graduate Distance Education Program: A Qualitative Analysis*. PhD dissertation, Capella University, April 13th, Dissertation.Com Publishers. http://www.dissertation.com/library/1120710a.htm

National Science Board. (2002). *Science and Engineering Indicators 2002*. http://www.nsf.gov/sbe/srs/seind02/pdfstart.htm

Prégent, Richard. (2001). *L`encadrement des travaux de mémoire et de thèse*. Presses Internationales Polytechnique, Montréal, Canada.

Walker, R. (1998). Experiments in Virtual Supervision. *ED-MEDIA/ED-TELECOM 98* World Conference on Educational Multimedia and Hypermedia & World Conference on Educational Telecommunications Proceedings, Freiburg, Germany, June 20-25.

A Model LAN to Mimic the Networking Environment in Hong Kong Primary and Secondary Schools for Teaching and Learning

Ka-man Pang and Simon So

Department of Information and Applied Technology

Hong Kong Institute of Education

10 Lo Ping Road, Tai Po, N.T.

Hong Kong SAR, China

E-mail: {kmpang | swwso}@ied.edu.hk

Abstract: With the surging demands for the use of network-based learning environment in primary and secondary schools, the knowledge and practical skills on school LAN management is increasingly critical for our pre-service and in-service IT teachers. Many of our IT graduates will assume the role of IT coordinators in their employed schools on top of their regular teaching duties. Training on network concepts and hands-on communication skills are essential to them. As the prime business of our Institute is teacher training, it is impractical to provide the students with the comprehensive network training similar to network engineers. We should focus on the training to the prescribed network infrastructure in our government-funded schools. In this paper, we describe our model LAN project for teaching and learning. The model LAN stimulates a school's networking environment so that our student teachers can acquire the relevant knowledge and practical skills very close to the real school networking environment.

Introduction

Under the Hong Kong Government's five-year strategy for IT in education to promote the use of IT for the enhancement of learning and teaching (Education and Manpower Bureau HKSAR, 1998), the majority of primary and secondary schools in Hong Kong have well-established and fairly standardized network infrastructures. The networked areas include 1) Staff Room (limited to two only), 2) Computer Room, 3) Library, and 4) Multimedia Learning Centre (MMLC) if available. Some schools may have multiple access points installed in their classrooms. The computing facilities are predominately PC-based. Microsoft Windows NT Servers or 2000 Advanced Servers are used to support the client-server environment. The configuration and the cabling system for a school (Education Department HKSAR, 2002) is specified by the Education Department as illustrated in Figure 1.

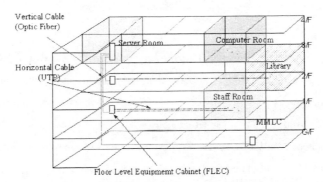

Figure 1. The Configuration and Cable Infrastructure for a school in Hong Kong
(Education Department, HKSAR)

Given the unique characteristics for the school network requirement, the Hong Kong Institute of Education (HKIEd) offers a number of modules for our IT students in the areas of School LAN Management and Network-supported Learning Environment. Students are exposed to network theories, network configuration, operating system setup, web-based learning sites and a range of intra- and inter-networking concept and knowledge relevant to the school environment.

In the 2001-2002 academic year, we taught these modules and students' feedback are highlighted in Table 1. Students (over 80%) indicate that they want to practice their knowledge in a real school network which is not feasible at present. This reveals a pressing need from us to provide an authentic learning environment and, hence, the idea of a model LAN to mimic the real school environment is formulated. We proposed to the Institute for a model LAN establishment and the project has been accepted and funded.

Questionnaire(Further Comments)	Responses
The most useful aspects of this module were:	Recognize the essential network knowledge and principle
Why are they useful?	Help me understand the school network, how to setup a network-based learning environment, more confidence in teaching computing related subjects such as IT and very helpful on future self-development.
What can be changed to help students learn better:	More lectures and workshops. Doing more practice in a real network environment. Organize visit to HK school to get more exposure on a real school network. Provide a better workshop environment.
Why are these changes would help?	Practice can enhance the learnt knowledge and skill. Can understand better if learning in a real school network environment rather than from books and Internet.

Table 1. Highlight from 50 Students' Feedback

In this paper, we provide the overall design, the configuration and the salient features of our model LAN. The chief objective for this project is to foster an authentic teaching and learning environment for our students. The design is also flexible enough to allow us to explore, reconfigure and extend beyond the current school networking environment.

Overview of the School Networking Environment Model (Model LAN)

In order to design an environment suitable for teaching and learning and, at the same time, provide an experience for our students close to a real school, we started with the recommendation found in the Procurement Guidelines from Education Department HKSAR (1999) as well as our experience on students' teaching practices in schools. We come up with the design topology of the school model LAN as illustrated in Figure 2. The model LAN stimulates the typical architectural design of a school in a laboratory. Four computers are grouped together in a subnet of a star topology to imitate an individual floor of a school. Each subnet is connected to the backbone switch using optical cables to mimic the vertical cabling of a school. This forms a star-to-star topology for the entire school.

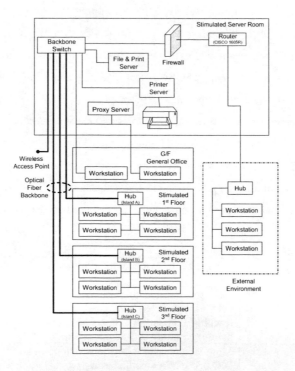

Figure 2. The Topology of Model School LAN Project

Since this is a teaching and learning LAN model, consideration must be given to the students on what the daily operations can likely be occurred in schools. Therefore, the salient features of our design include the following:

1. External access: We need to stimulate the external environment on accessing the network. Therefore, a stimulated external subnet through a router is protected by a firewall. All the traffic

from the simulated external subnet will be monitored by the firewall. Students will learn the important concept of security and the firewall setup activities.

2. Flexible configuration: We need to demonstrate to the students that it is possible to detach the three individual star networks / floors from the backbone switch. This is a very likely scenario in a large network when some segments are failed. Students can learn how to keep the network alive. Furthermore, by separating these star networks, we can support three small group workshops on the client-server networking model simultaneously.

3. Expandable features: We need to accommodate the latest development in schools. Campus-wide wireless communication is getting popular in schools. Therefore, the provision of wireless access point connected to the backbone switch allows the students to learn the configuration and setup of accessing the servers through wireless notebook within an accessible range. Traffic from this access point is monitored and coordinated by the proxy server. The concept of setting up a web-based portal in relation to the proxy server can also be learned in this configuration.

Conclusion and Future Work

This paper describes the model LAN project is currently undertaking in HKIEd. We are confident that this project can enhance the learning of our students on school LAN management. The model LAN will be used in the 2002-2003 academic year. By then, we can assess the learning outcome of this project.

The School Administration and Management System (SAMS) developed by the Government forms an integral part of the daily operations for teachers in schools. In the future, we need to enhance our model LAN by attaching another Virtual LAN to our model LAN to facilitate this type of networking facilities.

Acknowledgement

The authors would like to thank Stephen Ho for his technical support to this project and the IT Strategy Committee, Dr. Kar Tin Lee (ITADC), for the approval of this project.

References

CISCO (2001). Writing the Classroom Rules: An End-to-End Network for Delivering Broadband in Primary and Secondary Environments. Retrieved on 5th July 2002, from http://www.cisco.com/warp/public/cc/pd/si/casi/ca3550/prodlit/sndsy_dg.htm

Education Manpower Bureau HKSAR (1998). *Information Technology for Learning in a new Era Five-year Strategy 1998/99 to 2002/03*. Hong Kong: HKSAR.

Education Manpower Bureau HKSAR (1999). *Technical Guidelines for School LAN Implementation under the Information Technology in Education Project.*. Hong Kong: HKSAR.

Education Department HKSAR (2002). Retrieved on 4th July 2002, from http://www.ited.ed.gov.hk/English/ITinschool/Site_preparation/work_sitepreparation2_english.htm

Adaptation Architecture for Adaptive Educational Hypermedia Systems

José M Parente de Oliveira
Clovis Torres Fernandes
Computer Science Division, Technological Institute of Aeronautics
Brazil
{parente, clovis}@comp.ita.br

Abstract: Several Adaptive Educational Hypermedia Systems (AEHSs) have been described in the literature. In general, the adaptation mechanisms are presented but the architecture of these systems do not clearly separates the several components involved. As a consequence, these architectures neither facilitate the understanding and reproduction aiming at implementing new models of AEHSs nor offer a frame of reference for comparison and analysis. This paper presents a proposal for a generic architecture for AEHSs. On the basis of the analysis of AEHSs using the proposed architecture, it is expected that the architecture be a safety reference for the analysis and implementation of new AEHSs.

1 Introduction

Nowadays there are several Adaptive Educational Hypermedia Systems (AEHSs) available. The literature present them with their respective adaptation mechanisms [Brusilovsky et al., 1996; Fernández, 2000; Henze, 2000; De Bra and Calvi, 1998; Barbeiro, 2001; Weber et al., 2001]. In general, the architecture of these systems do not clearly separates the several components involved. As a consequence these architectures neither facilitate the understanding and reproduction aiming at implementing new models of AEHSs nor offer a referential for comparison and analysis. The main focus of this paper is to present a proposal of a high level architecture for AEHSs.

The paper is organized in the following way. Section 2 presents the proposed architecture. Section 3 presents some preliminary findings from the analysis of some AEHS using the architecture. Finally, Section 4 presents some concluding remarks.

2. Proposed Architecture for AEHS

To incorporate several adaptation aspects, the architecture of the AEHSs have to clearly separate the roles of the involved components. Adaptation includes aspects of adaptivity and adaptability [Opperman 1994; Opperman et al. 1997]. Adaptive systems have the capacity of automatically modifying their own characteristics with base on their perception of the user's necessities and personal characteristics. Adaptable systems offer tools that allow the user to explicitly set certain system characteristics in order to adapt the system to user's behavior.

Figure 1 shows the proposed high level architecture for AEHSs. Such an architecture is the result of the analysis of the architecture of AEHSs and adaptive systems described in the literature [Brusilovsky et al., 1996; Fernández, 2000; Henze, 2000; De Bra and Calvi, 1998; Barbeiro, 2001; Weber et al., 2001; Opperman, 1994; Opperman et al., 1997; Karagiannidis et al., 2001]. The explanation of the Interface Component is out of scope of this paper. The architecture's components are described next.

Interaction Analyzer

The Interaction Analyzer has two main functions [Karagiannidis et al. 2001]:

- To monitor learner-system interaction in order to get information on links that have been followed, selected tools, etc.

- To infer relevant conclusions on the learner's behavior, as for example if the learner wants to relate a giving concept with another one, wants more details, etc. Depending on the learner's actions the Interaction Analyzer draws conclusions that can be of adaptativity or adaptability types.

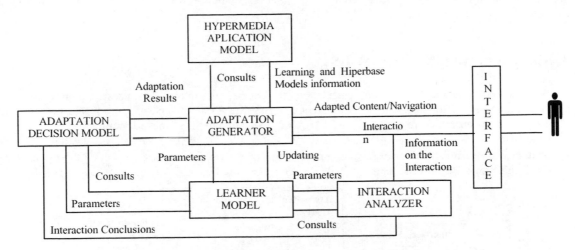

Figure 1: Proposed Architecture for AEHS.

Adaptation Decision Model

The Adaptation Decision Model is responsible for deciding *what* the system should do and *how to do* it. These decisions are based on the conclusions draw by the Interaction Analyzer. Examples of what to do are to present more details, related concepts, etc. The *how to do* part includes the selection and the activation of the corresponding adaptation mechanisms. Among these mechanisms are the two main adaptation types identified in Brusilovsky [1996, 1998]: adaptive presentation and adaptive navigation. The function of the adaptive presentation is to adapt the content of an information node of the application domain to the current knowledge level, goals and other characteristics of the learner. The function of the adaptive navigation is to help the learners to find their navigation routes throughout the information hyperbase. The system provides this last adaptation type by presenting the links for the goals, knowledge level and other characteristics of the learner.

As to adaptability, the Adaptation Decision Model simply carry out the action requested by the learner. Adaptability includes the several tools the systems offers to the learner with respect to interface, content and navigation adaptation, as well as to inspection of the learner model.

Learner Model

The Learner Model is the structure that contains the information on the learner's characteristics during the interaction with the AEHS, that allows the system to adapt to these characteristics. Among the main learners' characteristics to be considered for adaptation are knowledge level, goals, previous knowledge, experience and preferences [Brusilovsky, 1996]. Another aspect that can be added to this list are the personal characteristics that define a learner as an individual, as for example personality factors, cognitive factors and learning styles [Brusilovsky, 2001].

Hypermedia Application Model

The Hypermedia Application Model comprises two submodels: Hyperbase and Learning Submodels. The Hyperbase Submodel includes aspects related to domain modeling, metainformation on the domain and the way information is internally represented. The stored information include the concepts to be learnt, examples, exercises and distinct ways of learning evaluation. The Learning Submodel includes pedagogical aspects, guided and unguided presentation, etc. This submodel represents the type and the way the learning activities should be realized, which actually determine the learners's behavior during the activities.

Adaptation Generator

The Adaptation Generator is responsible for generating what will be presented to the learner as a result of processing the information received from the Interaction Analyzer, Adaptation Decision Model, Learner Model, and Application Model.

3 Analysis of Adaptation in AEHSs

Besides being useful for the implementation of AEHSs, the architecture presented in Figure 1 also provides subsidies for the analysis of the adaptation in AEHSs. As an example, Figure 2 presents the result of an analysis of the architecture of the AEHS ELM-ART, according to the proposed architecture.

ELM-ART, an acronym for *Episodic Learner Model – Adaptive Remote Tutor* [Brusilovsky et al., 1996], is an adaptive system for supporting learning programming in Lisp. Even though ELM-ART be considered an AEHS in this work, Brusilovsky et al. [1996] refer to it as an Intelligent Tutoring System for the WWW.

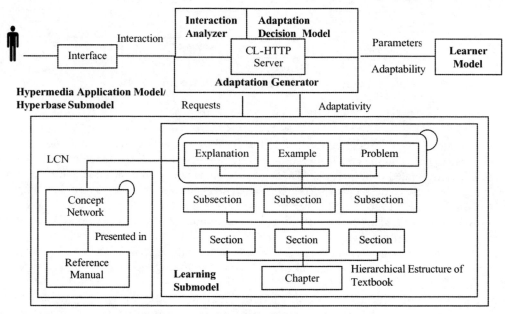

Figure 2: A possible structuring of ELM-ART's architecture according to the proposed architecture.

In Figure 2, the Hypermedia Application Model comprises the Hyperbase Submodel and the Learning Submodel, but in fact the Hyperbase Submodel corresponds to the whole Hypermedia Application Model. The Hyperbase Submodel consists of two main components: The Lisp Concept Network (LCN) and the Learning Submodel called also the Hierarchical Structure of Textbook. The LCN represents all the concepts used in the course, as well as the relations among them. Every concept in LCN corresponds to a page in the reference manual. In the textbook, each terminal unit, defined as Explanation, Example and Problem, treats the concepts of the textbook sections. In addition, each textbook section is indexed by the concepts of the LCN.

Since the Learning Submodel is entirely integrated to the Hyperbase Submodel, any change in the Learning Submodel in fact entails changes to the Hyperbase Submodel.

The CL-HTTP Server performs all the functions proposed in the Interaction Analyzer, Adaptation Decision Model and Adaptation Generator. Such a integration may cause some problems for carrying out system maintenance and improvements.

Besides ELM-ART, the following systems have been analyzed [Oliveira, 2002]: HEZINET [Fernández, 2000], KBS Hyperbook [Henze, 2000], AHA [De Bra and Calvi, 1998], CHA [Barbeiro, 2001] and NetCoach [Weber, 2001]. The analysis presented in Oliveira [2002] includes possible structuring of these systems using the proposed architecture, similar to the one showed in Figure 2. The following recurrent problems were noticed:

- There are no clear separation between the hyperbase submodel and the learning submodel. To some extent these two submodels are put together in a single one.
- Personal characteristics that define a learner as an individual, as previously mentioned, are not explored in these systems.
- Adaptability aspects are poorly explored. Basically they are limited to allowing the learner to define personal preferences in terms of information media and to change some aspects of the learner model related to the learner's perception of the concept mastery level.

4 Conclusion

Besides being a useful model for the implementation of new AEHS, the proposed architecture can be considered as a high level framework for the analysis of the adaptation in AEHSs. The proposed architecture fulfills the lack of a common frame of reference to such an analysis. Though the proposed architecture can drive the analysis work, it is still difficult to analyze AEHSs because of the poor system descriptions available in the literature.

The adaptation concept for AEHSs maybe could be more explored on the basis of the Hyperbase Submodel, Learning Submodel, Adaptation Decision Model, Adaptation Generator, Learner Model and Interaction Analyzer, at least to improve the systems descriptions. Maybe this can open up space to explore different levels of adaptation between the concepts of adaptativity and adaptability.

References

Barbeiro, Raul S. G. (2001). Characterizing and Modeling of Adaptive Hypermedia Courses. National Spatial Researching Institute (INPE), Master Degree Dissertation. (Available in Portuguese).

Brusilovsky, Peter (1996). Methods and Techniques of Adaptive Hypermedia. *User Modeling and User Adapted Interaction*, v.6, n 2-3, p 87-129.

Brusilovsky, Peter (1998). Adaptive Educational Systems on the World-Wide-Web: A Review of Available Technologies. *Proceedings of Workshop "WWW-Based Tutoring" at the 4th International Conference on Intelligent Tutoring Systems* (ITS'98), San Antonio, TX, August 16-19, 1998.

Brusilovsky, Peter (2001). Adaptive Hypermedia. *User Modeling and User Adapted Interaction*. Kluwer Academic Publishers, v.11, pp. 87-110.

Brusilovsky, Peter; Schwarz, Elmar; Weber, Gerhard (1996). ELM-ART: An intelligent tutoring system on World Wide Web. In C. Frasson, G. Gauthier, & A. Lesgold (Eds.), *Third International Conference on Intelligent Tutoring Systems, ITS-96* (LNCS, Vol. 1086). Berlin: Springer-Verlag, p 261-269.

De Bra, Paul; Calvi, Licia (1998). *AHA! An Open Adaptive Hypermedia Architecture*. The New Review of Hypermedia and Multimedia. Taylor Graham Publishers, v. 4, p 115-139.

Fernández, Tomás A. Pérez (2000). *Un Hiperentorno Adaptativo para el Aprendizaje Instructivo/Constructivo*. Universidad del País Vasco, Departamento de Lenguajes y Sistemas Informático, Memoria para el Grado de Doctor en Informática.

Henze, Nicola (2000). *Adaptive Hyperbooks: Adaptation for Project-Based Learning Resources*. University of Hanover, Department of Mathematics and Informatic, Doctoral Dissertation.

Karagiannidis, C; Sampson, Demetrios; Brusilovsky, P. (2001). Layered Evaluation of Adaptive and Personalized Educational Applications and Services. *AI-ED 2001*, Workshop on Assessment Methods in Web-Based Learning Environments & Adaptive Hypermedia, May 19, 2001, p 21-29.

Oliveira, José M. P. (2002). Adaptation Model for Adaptive Educational Hypermedia Systems. Technological Institute of Aeronautics (ITA), Computer Science Division. Doctoral Thesis Proposal.

Opperman, Reinhard (1994). Adaptively Supported Adaptability. *International Journal of Human-Computer Studies*, 40, 544-472.

Opperman, Reinhard; Rashev, Rossen; Kinshunk (1997). Adaptability and Adaptivity in Learning Systems. *Knowledge Transfer*, vII, p173-179.

Weber, Gerhard; Kuhl, Hans-Christian; Weibelzahl, Stephan (2001). Developing Adaptive Internet Based Courses with the Authoring System NetCoach. *Twelfth ACM Conference on Hypertext and Hypermedia – Hypertext' 01*. Arhus, Denmark, August 14-18.

Every Word a Click: The Hypertext Being Smart

Young Park (yp85@columbia.edu),
Instructional Technology & Media, Teachers College, Columbia University

Abstract: Hypertext, one of representatives of Internet is well known for its unique features for knowledge generating activities. Now, the new types' smart hypertext is appearing to overcome current hypertext's limitations. They seem to be promising since they start developing recognizing the current Internet users' needs. The study's purpose is to investigate the new hypertext's meaningfulness on knowledge activities and to propose hypertext's future direction. And it calls researchers' attentions by asking its interrelationship with cognitive development.

The Problems

The hypertext is well known as a tool to represent rich semantic relationships. A learner builds up her memory structure by adding a new object to existing memory structure. So some factors such as proper visual association, meaningful relationships or appropriate category are very significant to enhance learning. For this reason, hypertext is very suitable to support knowledge activities.

The current hypertext is built up only by links created by a web author. It is incomplete in terms of user-centered information environment with the following reasons. Very often a web page's information can be interpreted as very different anchors from information author's original intention. It could mean that it does not provide the right response or feedback according to users' inquiry. Immediate response is one of very important factors in knowledge activities because otherwise, a user might lose her curiosity or even forget soon what she would look for. Thus, with some kinds of aids, if a user is able to construct her own hypertext-links for herself, presumably, she is able to follow her own curiosity and to facilitate knowledge activities. It could also encourage a user's flexible and creative thinking process. On the basis of such a point, I propose that the current hypertext should be more developed to be more user-centered, context-oriented and learning-focused. On the basis of this perspective, I searched the Internet and found out three new types' hypertext applications, Atomica (www.atomica.com), Flyswat (www.flyswat.com) and Microcosm (www.microcosm.com) reflecting my perspective.

The Example

Among them, Atomica, a free shareware is an exemplary one to demonstrate the above perspective. Its key point is the simple human computer interaction, which is that one just clicks on the word you want defined or explained. When a user clicks a word on where it is available, whether you're using, for example, an e-mail client, a word processor or a spreadsheet as well as Web, Atomica automatically searches its relevant information as well as definition and then opens a small window to show the list.

There is an example for understanding its features. Suppose that a user was reading an article on the Web, or an e-mail and she came across this sentence: "The abstemious people from Woonsocket invested aggressively in companies like Tecumseh Products, hoping to become as rich as their idol, John Kluge." And suppose she had no idea what "abstemious" meant, where Woonsocket was, what Tecumseh Products did, or who Mr. Kluge was. To find them out quickly using the Internet, she needs to look up each term individually, which requires her to leave the document that she was reading and laboriously type in each term for multiple searches, probably at multiple sites. Instead, she could use Atomica that fetches such answers from the Internet, without leaving the text she was reading. Also, Atomica combines the ability to search multiple information sources simultaneously with a natural intelligence that helps to ensure targeted results. Users don't have to memorize Boolean logic or even construct an English language query. For the kinds of information Atomica is designed to parse-word definitions, language translations and company profiles-it works well.

Finally, one of the most distinguishable elements of Atomica is trying and guessing the entire phrase or context of a word that a user clicks on although it is still very limited. If, for example, a user clicks on either word in the phrase "Supreme Court," the program pops up with an answer about the highest court in the U.S., not a definition of either word on its own. And it pays attention to capitalization. It knows that the word "polish" is something a user does to furniture, but Polish is a language and culture (Wall Street Journal, 2000).

However, the service is still a work in progress. First, it doesn't work with text inside an image. Second, it is not able to search multimedia-based information such as mp3 files or quicktime movie files. Third, while it draws on a host of reference works and Web databases, it doesn't use premiere sources, such as the Encyclopedia Britannica and major newspapers. It tends to rely on almanacs, single-volume encyclopedias and little-known reference sites, though it does use major dictionaries (Wall Street Journal, 2000).

The Suggestions and Discussion

I conducted the small pilot study with five graduate students in Teachers College, Columbia University in order to explore for the new hypertext's future direction. Based on Atomica's functions and the results of the pilot study, I propose the following directions.

First, hypertext is merging with a search engine. With it, hypertext is becoming more effective and is able to reduce users' information seeking efforts considerably.

Second, the future hypertext's success empowered by a search engine depends on, I believe, how much it understands users' intention. Namely, they should be smart enough to understand not only what a user is looking for but also the whole context where a user is. The findings of a pilot study support it. Its subjects merely used very simple search formulations. What they wanted to obtain was simply the quick and effective search results and not-so-complicated human-computer interaction. Hence, the concept of 'agent software' is inevitable one so that it can play a role like a secretary or a task manager reducing human users' cognitive overload to a certain degree that they feel comfortable. At the same time, such agents will restrain information overload by filtering and analyzing information on web pages.

Third, when the smart agent, hypertext provides advice or a hint to users by being modeling and doing scaffolding exactly like a teacher in a classroom, I assume that it could reduce users' unnecessary search behaviors and assist developing their' meta-cognitive process. Atomica's 'did you mean?' description or its additional key words' list can be exemplary.

Finally, while more successful information seekers seem to be able to initiate their search behaviors on their own, less successful ones need a structure to help them search and do knowledge activities. Hence, it will be worth to consider if hypertext can provide different levels' gateway or interface design according to information seeker's search capability consisted of novice, intermediate and expert.

Such a new hypertext seems to be worthy for further consideration to influence users' information search behavior. Although I have explored mostly the positive impacts of it but there should be negative impacts such as users' dependence on its smart functions. Thus, it should be pondered critically to what degree and in what ways it would support human beings' Internet search. That is, we should investigate its multi-dimensional aspects carefully. I hope that this study could draw educational researchers' attention to explore its roles and potential to build up the enhanced learning environments.

References

Choo, C. W., Detlor, B. & Turnbull, D. (1999). Information Seeking on the Web – An Integrated Model of Browsing and Searching, 1999 ASIS Annual Meeting contributed Paper.

Mossberg, W. (10/05/2000). No Need to Leave the Page As Atomica Fetches Answers, *Wall Street Journal.*

Unz, D. C. & Hesse, F. W. (1999). The Use of Hypertext For Learning *Journal of Educational Computing Research*, v20, n3, 279-295.

Generic simulator model

for training and learning in virtual laboratory environments

Pierric PERMEZEL [1], Olivier MARCOUX [1],
Hamadou SALIAH-HASSANE [2], Maarouf SAAD [3], Chahe NERGUIZIAN [4]

[1] ENSEITH, pierric.permezel@free.fr
[2] Télé-université & LICEF/CIRTA Research Center, saliah@teluq.uquebec.ca
[3] École de Technologie Supérieure, msaad@ele.etsmtl.ca
[4] École Polytechnique de Montréal, Chahe.Nerguizian@mail.polymtl.ca

Abstract : Designing and developing simulators as a learning tool is an essential aspect of computerized learning systems. Yet such computerization must be well thought out and simulators designed for this purpose must be a useful and effective alternative to using the real systems they simulate. We therefore propose a simulator design method based on a simple, modular and above all generic and reusable architecture. This design method can therefore be applied to a broad range of fields and offers an efficient solution to various problems such as 1) economic factors, since a simulator is often less expensive than the system it simulates; 2) geographic constraints, since it can be utilized almost anywhere; 2) grasping certain concepts, since it can focus on interesting aspects and results by getting rid of numerous technical problems; 3) lastly, it lightens the educator's workload by assisting the student using the system. As well, the widespread use of *Java* allows for a quick, simple and efficient implementation of such simulators, especially due to its multi-platform properties, the modular nature of its *JavaBeans*, the ease with which the encapsulation of variables is executed and the inherent self-analysis possibilities of this language. Yet it should be pointed out that *Java* still exhibits problems, especially in regard to sluggish execution speed and insufficient security management.

Introduction

Over the last few years, there has been an explosion and widespread use of communication technologies, and of the Internet in particular. Thus there is an easier access to these new technologies, from an intellectual and an economic point of view. Educational and teaching institutions have welcomed this electronic revolution, since some educators have long dreamed of the benefits of computerizing learning systems (Paquette et al, 1996). In fact, they have in many cases already explored this approach, and have encountered numerous problems: an inadequate and heterogeneous infrastructure of materials and software, insufficient processing capabilities and above all, insufficient design and development tools. As a result, numerous specific learning objects have been created independently: on-line courses, student evaluation tools, interactive tutorials or virtual laboratories systems often based on simulations or remote access to real apparatus (Saliah et al, 1999). Let's recall that a virtual laboratory is a space where several people can run experiments based on real or simulated data and materials, while being totally free of geographic constraints This paper will deal with the latter type of computerized learning system. Developing reusable pedagogical and modular software simulators of real systems offers several advantages: 1) It helps students grasp the fundamental concepts of a system by getting rid of material problems such as bad contacts in electronic circuitry, handling hazardous products, lengthy and laborious handling of material; 2) It offers automatic assistance during the learning process by providing students with advice and relevant information at the appropriate moment; 3) Lastly, it resolves economic or physical problems involved in accessing to costly materials, by simulating and integrating real materials within the context of *virtual laboratories*.

Software solutions have been available for some time and propose remote access to various devices (National Instruments, 1998) and (Sigmon and Davis, 2001), yet they incur numerous problems: utilization limited to a specific field, complicated utilization, difficult integration with a computer-assisted learning system (CAL) (Saad et al, 2001). As a solution to these problems and requirements, in this paper, we are proposing a generic simulator model for training and learning within virtual laboratory environments based on reusable Java components (Matena et al, 2001). In the following sections we will describe the architecture of the proposed modular and generic simulator model.

A Simple Case Study: An Helicopter Altitude Control System Simulator

Requirements
In order to clearly describe the basic components and advantages of our model, we propose designing an helicopter control system simulator. We wish to develop a Distributed Computer Aided Learning application that copes with the specification described in table 1. These specifications let us henceforth predict the functions that should exist in our simulation application.

Table 1: Specifications and Functions Sought

Specifications	Functions Sought
To simulate an helicopter altitude control system	• simulation functions of the system based on mathematical algorithms and equations modeling the proposed filters. • set of variables representing the simulated system state
Lets the user interact with the system parameters during the simulation	• user interface reacting at any time during the simulation • immediate feedback of any modification • control of transition states from setting to setting, as required
lets the simulation be conducted automatically according to a pre-established scenario	• scenario manager
can run this simulation in real time by means of a real data acquisition system; Data can be acquired from a remotely located site through computer networks can export simulation results to an external software.	• input/output control • capability of importing signals, doing calculations and exporting results in real time; and configurable data acquisition system

Generic Model Proposed
The generic interface has three windows (Figure 1). The first allows the input of the physical model's parameters. All the controller parameters are defined in this window and they can be changed during the simulation. The second window is designed to animate the physical representation of the system. For example, figures 2, 3 and 4 shows respectively simulators of a tank, a submarin and an helicopter control system within the same interface framework. Finally, the third window gives a brief explanation of the theory related to the system, the diagram bloc and the time domain results. The diagram bloc illustrates the control loop. In the case of the helicopter altitude control simulator (Figure 4), R(z) is the set point signal, E(z) represents the error between the set point and the measured output Y(z). The error is then applied to the controller to compute the control to be applied to the system. In the case illustrated above, the controller structure is a PD type controller with the following transfer function $G_c(z)$ in the z-domain:

$$G_c(z) = K_P + \frac{K_D}{T} \frac{z-1}{z}$$

where K_p and K_D are the proportional and derivative controller gains and T the sampling period. The output Y(z) is related to the control U(z) by the following relation

$$\frac{Y(z)}{U(z)} = K \left[\frac{T}{z-1} - \tau \frac{(1 - e^{-\frac{T}{\tau}})}{z - e^{-\frac{T}{\tau}}} \right]$$

This architecture is comprised of the following five main modules:

The System State Module
The *State variables* contain the information representing the simulated system state. These values are memory-resident and can be consulted and modified via the *Simulator, Input-Output, GUI* and *Scenario*

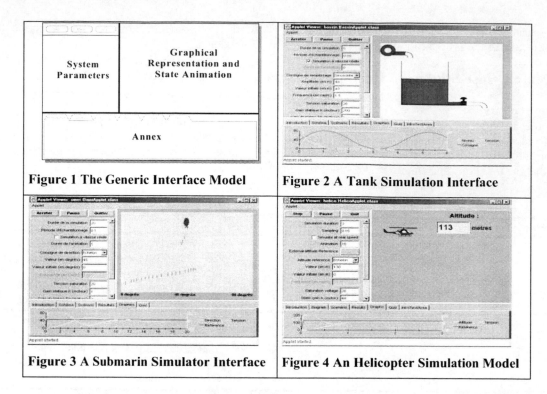

Figure 1 The Generic Interface Model	Figure 2 A Tank Simulation Interface
Figure 3 A Submarin Simulator Interface	Figure 4 An Helicopter Simulation Model

Manager modules. In the highly unlikely event that a state variable might be simultaneously modified by two modules, protecting concurrent access to the variable by means of mutual automatic exclusion would be advisable. The *write controller* sends events to other modules when the value of a variable being utilized has been modified

The Simulator Module

How this module works can be clarified in figure 7. The *simulation model*, specific to each application, contains the code needed for the simulation itself. This simulation will generally be based on a set of mathematical formulas and other constants. The *GUI pilot*, also specific to each application, gives a graphical rendering of the simulated system state by driving the *GUI*.

The Graphical User Interface

The *GUI construction module* represented in figure 8 utilizes set data to define all components to be loaded on starting the application. It creates the startup screen and all windows or components that could be utilized during the simulation. The *standard and intelligent component library* provides various types of visual or non-visual components. Each component will possess some input data (title, style, etc…) and output data (values). Interacting with these components (click, value modification or entry) will automatically generate a *system state* modification, according to the new state of this component.

The Input/Output Module

The *exported data management* module exports data generated by the simulator. It controls the entire process such as the connection with external applications, the accessibility, data transfer (sending) and traffic flow security. The *imported data management* module, on the other side imports data generated from external sources and useful to the simulator. It also controls the entire process but deals with the received data instead.

The Scenario Manager Module

The scenario manager's role is to drive the simulator according to a pre-established scenario or according to a user-generated scenario. Here, the Graphical User Interface (GUI) Pilot is a set of functions allowing the user to edit scenarios and control their execution.

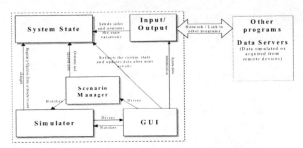

Figure 5 The Simulator System Architecture

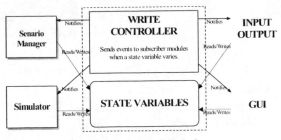

Figure 6 The System State Module

Conclusion

Computer Aided Learning applications are fast becoming an essential learning tool. Simple, modular and generic simulators represent a solution for various problems: economic factors, geographic constraints, grasp of certain concepts (understanding the fundamental notions involved), avoidance of having to deal with real equipment, efficient follow-up of student progress. We have used JAVA, a computer language, to demonstrate our concept of generic control system simulator. The model can be used for applications other than learning. This design method is not limited to the teaching area and can very well be utilized in developing all types of simulators, be they stand-alone or part and parcel of a virtual laboratory.

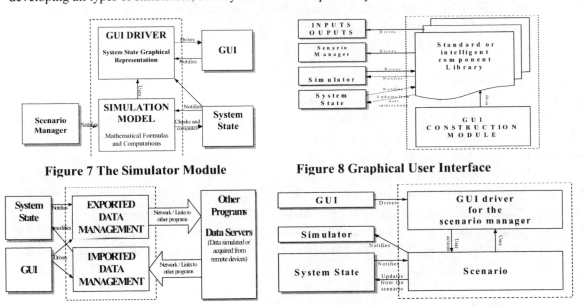

Figure 7 The Simulator Module

Figure 8 Graphical User Interface

Figure 9 The Input/Output Module

Figure 10 The Scenario Manager Module

References

Paquette, G., Ricciardi-Rigault, C., Paquin, P., Liégeois, S., Bleicher, E., (1996), *Developing the Virtual Campus Environment, Proceedings of Ed-Media 96 World Conference on Educational Telecommunication,* (pp. 244-249), Boston, USA.

Saliah, H. H., Abecassis, A., Nurse, E., (1999), *Design of a Generic, Interactive, Virtual and Remote Electrical Engineering Laboratory, Frontier in Education Conference 99: Designing the Future of Science and Engineering Education,* San Juan Puerto Rico.

National Instrument, (1998), *LabVIEW Basics 1 Hands-on Course,* National Instruments, Austin.

Sigmon K, and Davis K., (2001), *Matlab Primer - 6th Edition,* Chapman and Hall/CRC Press

Saad, M., Saliah, H. H., Hassan, H., El-Guetioui, Z., Cheriet, M., (2001) *Synchromous remote accessing control laboratory, 2001 International Conference on Engineering Education; Interfacing the World,* Oslo/Burgen, Norway.

Matena, V., Stearns, B., (2001) *Applying Enterprise JavaBeans: Component-Based Development for the J2EE Platform, The Java Series,* Sun Microsystems, Inc.

Title: A District in Transition: Information and Decision-Making in a California
Community College
Authors: Dr. Lisa Petrides and Sara McClelland, Teachers College, Columbia University
Email: lap52@columbia.edu

BACKGROUND

Information systems play a critical role in assessment and accountability. In order for educational institutions to develop effective methods to evaluate strategies that improve student outcomes, a reliable and accurate system must be in place for collecting and disseminating data. These data, in turn, must be readily accessible and put into formats that are easily understood and used. Finally, staff must be willing and able to use data and have the ability to inform and modify policy and practice accordingly. Unfortunately, most community college districts have no reliable methodology to evaluate the effectiveness of resource allocation in improving student learning. However, state and national trends are clearly moving in that direction—improvement of assessment and accountability research.

This study examines the ways in which faculty and staff within a community college district interacted with student information in making day-to-day decisions and engaging in long-term planning. The goal of the research was to better understand the intersection of cultural, political and technological forces within the district as they faced an increased demand to use data, information, and knowledge to account for monies spent and decisions made. Current organizational change research shows that effective use of data and information can raise performance, productivity, and outcomes at all levels – for students, faculty, administration, and governance. Therefore, an institution that collects and uses data on student performance can proactively make decisions about investments in programs and services, target remedial assistance, eliminate duplication in programs, and ensure higher rates of student success.

METHODOLOGY

Due to the increase in state-mandated accountability measures and the desire for internal research, this study examined the use of data to inform decision-making in one California community college district. We were interested in identifying the issues that arose out of the desire to use information about students to inform decision-making; specifically, the types of student information that were required, how information was produced or accessed, the quality or usability of the information, and how the information was used once it was received.

The research team conducted 49 in-depth interviews with administrators, faculty, and staff at one community college district. We used the critical incident technique that allowed us to elicit examples and outcomes by gathering information about actual behavior that relied upon specific recall, thereby bypassing opinions and hypothetical situations. By asking people to recall specific incidents, gathering information about the context of those incidents and asking whether the incident had a successful or unsuccessful outcome, we were able to take a snapshot of what types of information had been requested over the past year and to identify the processes undertaken by information seekers to get information on students. We selected our interveiw samples based on a cross section of administrators, faculty, and staff members who were chosen because of their involvement in decision making processes. The critical incident methodology allowed us to examine: 1) the beginning and ending of a critical incident; 2) a task or goal of a user just before critical incident occurred; 3) expectations of user just before critical incident occurred; 4) a detailed description of critical incident (what exactly happened, what caused it); and 5) the severity and frequency of the critical incident

We employed a non-random selection process that included:

1. Administrators: The high level officials who oversee the management of the campuses
2. Faculty: The teachers who are also involved in decision making bodies on the campus such as deans and program coordinators
3. Staff: The assistants and aides who support the faculty and administrators and therefore are often the ones who do the legwork to find out student information

FINDINGS

The first theme that we found was the presence of a very strong research culture within the district. Individuals have a strong desire to find out how they can help students and a highly developed ability to craft insightful and focused inquiries. However, historically necessary data and resources have not been readily available. As a result, this desire to improve outcomes has often been hindered as faculty, staff and administrators struggle to find data that can be used to make informed decisions concerning students. Said one participant:

> I can't even tell you how many students survive a class here. I have no idea. Does this make me feel good as a manager? Absolutely not. I feel like I'm trying to manage in one of those black hoods where you're just kind of feeling - is this an elephant? Is this a giraffe? What do I have a hold of? And I'm trying to do my best guess.

Instructors and administrators alike have a strong desire to acquire meaningful data to become more effective in their jobs, yet this desire has not been appropriately supported or aided by the existing student information systems. More often than not, data are fragmented, scattered, and incomplete. One participant commented:

> [T]here's more than one system tracking student data and they don't -- they're not the same. They don't yield the same data. So is it valid? Is it reliable? Can you count on it? Can you do projections? Can you do reports accurately? Probably not.

Additionally, access to and flow of information remains inconsistent across departments. Technology infrastructure and capabilities are insufficient to support the increasingly complex needs for meaningful information. As a result, existing data fails to inform its users in ways that enable them to decide where to invest resources and which programs need to be improved. Most are forced to rely on hunches about student performance rather than rely on multi-variable student data that are continuously collected and analyzed. This translates to lost opportunities on each campus—lost time and energy having to create smaller but more accurate systems, lack of long-term planning data, difficulty with enrollment management, problems in assessing student outcomes and establishing benchmarks for comparison, and an inconsistent ability to substantiate needs for further funding. This ultimately impedes progress in the development of appropriate learning environments or interventions for students.

This culture of inquiry has been historically hindered by the lack of available data resources. In the face of this deficiency, many individuals have developed ways of working around this problem and have created their own data, in the form of separate databases, internal student data, and sometimes resorting to methods such as hand counting students in classrooms because they believe an accurate and timely count could not be retrieved using the existing technology.

> *Well, we all use Excel. We all use our own spreadsheets. We do all that. I mean, that's what we do.*

Although this means there is a strong desire to acquire meaningful data in order to be effective educators and administrators, this desire has not been appropriately supported or aided by the existing student information systems. This translates to lost opportunities on each campus—lost time and energy having to create smaller but more accurate systems, lack of long-term planning data, difficulty with enrollment management, and an inconsistent ability to substantiate needs for further funding. This ultimately impedes the district's progress in the development of appropriate learning environments or interventions for their students. They are forced to rely on hunches about student performance rather than rely on multi-variable student data that is continuously collected and analyzed.

> *Interviewer: How are you able to, I mean, what are examples of situations in which you find yourself needing to make a decision, needing data, and what mechanisms do you devise in order to do that?*
> *Participant: Shoe leather, conversation, and just my best guess. That's all I've got.*

All of these factors impact this community in a number of important ways. First, students are not served to the fullest. Second, this district is not spending its limited resources effectively. If staff are forced to hand count students, this is time and energy that is taken away from many other important tasks. Third, they cannot plan for the future when they are not sure what has worked in the past. They cannot develop new strategies for growth and change with the times when they do not know what programs are shown to positively impact student success. They simply do not have enough information to know what works and what does not.

> *Interviewer: And are you able to notice any distinguishing characteristics among those students who are failing? Is that kind of information--*
> *Participant: That's the information that we're not getting. We're not breaking it out. We're not breaking it out by ethnicity, or by course, or by gender, or any of those kinds of things. That would be helpful information to know how to target what to look at, are there special populations that are encountering these kinds of issues. And if so, then you identify the population and look at that population and say, 'Well, what are the barriers? What can we do to create interventions?' But we're not getting to that depth utilizing the research information to get to that depth to problem solve.*

CONCLUSION

We believe that the ability of administrators, staff, and faculty to obtain the information they need to make informed decisions about their academic programs and services is criticial to student success. As researchers, we started with a basic assumption that the accumulation of data is influenced by the core values of the organization, and that these data, through human interaction, take on significance as information. Our findings indicate the importance of research in the field of education that can help us understand how and if data are transformed into information and then knowledge, and finally, how this process informs decisions that contributed to positive student learning outcomes.

Research concerning how groups manage data and information in order to make decisions has long been popular in other contexts, outside of higher education. There has been a great deal of recognition in the business world, for example, that information and knowledge management can be vital tools in organizations. However, it is only recently that institutions of higher education have begun to look at how they might more effectively use information systems for better management practices, as well as in teaching and learning environments. Because much of the literature on knowledge management in business is focused on economic utility and consumerism, studies that focus on the field of education are important in order to ensure that issues of student success in terms of democracy (such as information sharing) and social justice (such as access and equity) are kept in the forefront.

CORE SOLUTIONS: A TRIFECTA FOR EDUCATION

Jennifer Platt
University of Central Florida/Orlando
College of Education
4000 Central Florida Blvd.
Orlando, Florida 32816 USA
platt@mail.ucf.edu

Mem Stahley
University of Central Florida
Brevard Campus
1519 Clearlake Road
Cocoa, Florida 32922 USA
mstahley@mail.ucf.edu

Abstract: In the central Florida area, the School District of Osceola County, the Valencia Community College and the University of Central Florida have designed a partnership program to give employees of the school district the opportunity to complete a baccalaureate degree. This paper addresses the current shortage of qualified teachers, the need to recruit and retain teacher education candidates through a mutual effort by universities, community colleges, and school districts, and the need to attract a more demographically representative minority population to teaching. The paper also presents the existing connectivity and technological tools that support and enrich the academic experience. The program, named CORE (Creating Opportunities and Resources for Educators) is described. The presentation will include a live demonstration of the technological infrastructure affording access to library and Internet resources for all CORE students and faculty.

The CORE Program

Osceola County has a reported population of 172,493 residents. The School District of Osceola County has a population of 37,774 students in K-12 with a growth rate of 12% annually. Of these students, 35% are Hispanic and about 22% have language problems. The school district identified as one of its highest priorities the recruitment of a diverse pool of teachers to meet the needs of a diverse group of students. To accomplish this, the Superintendent of the School District of Osceola County and the President and Provost of Valencia Community College contacted the Dean and Associate Dean of Education at the University of Central Florida to form a partnership that would give employees of the school district (non-instructional personnel) the opportunity to complete a baccalaureate degree in Education.

The CORE Program (Creating Opportunities and Resources for Educators) is a collaborative partnership formed by a metropolitan, research university, a community college (a Hispanic serving institution), and a school district with a Hispanic population of 35% that is experiencing a critical shortage of teachers. The purpose of the CORE Program is to address the critical shortage of qualified teachers by assisting non-instructional personnel in the district to pursue a degree in teaching. It is based on the premise that the accountability for solid educator preparation relies on the mutual efforts of university, community college, and school district faculty and administrators; business leaders; legislators; members of the media; private foundations; counselors; advisors; and financial aid officers. The purpose and outcomes of CORE underscore the need for collaborative efforts among diverse partners to address the national shortage of qualified teachers. The CORE Program has promoted the success of all its students by assisting them to overcome the obstacles of distance and time, learning in isolation, problems accessing technology, and difficulty with paying tuition.

CORE participants who live and work in the county have excellent access to lower division college classes at the local community college. The community college campus is located in the heart of the county's most populous area. The CORE Program offers a class schedule that accommodates the needs of the participants who are faced with the difficulties of working full-time, meeting their family commitments, and taking classes. CORE participants also have access to specially designed online classes that facilitate flexible time scheduling. For many potential teachers, the prospect of completing their studies at a senior institution is complicated by the fact that the local university is over 40 miles away. For CORE participants, the university offers the baccalaureate degree right on the community college campus with selected courses provided through distance education. In addition, CORE participants complete required field experiences and internships in their own school district.

One of the greatest challenges non-traditional students face is the fact that they have to fight the uphill battle of getting an education without an extensive support network. The CORE Program has created a community of learners by giving every participant a mentor, a teacher or administrator who works in the same school. CORE participants stay connected with others through their own dedicated web page (http://faculty.valencia.cc.fl.us/CORE), which contains a discussion board for their exclusive use. In addition, a community college member stays in contact with each of the students each semester to make sure that everything is going smoothly and the university sends professional advisors to the community college campus to provide advisement. CORE participants complete the program as members of a cohort making it possible for the participants to form study and support groups.

Students cannot take advantage of web pages, online classes, or the riches of the Internet if they do not have computers. Every CORE student who needs one is able to have a computer at home. The community college provides the computer and the school district equips the computers with modems, thus helping to close the digital divide between the technology haves and have-nots.

Since time is critical for CORE students, it is essential to provide them with a fully articulated curriculum. The CORE program provides participants with the opportunity to earn an Associate of Arts degree, thus guaranteeing them junior status at the university. Furthermore, this curriculum meets every transfer requirement for the university's Bachelor of Science degree in Elementary and Exceptional Education. The CORE Program guarantees a seamless transition between the two academic institutions.

Closing the Digital Divide

Convenient efficient program models, realistic course loads, mentoring, and schedules tailored to meet the needs of working adults are essential to student success. Academic information, i.e., electronic access to student services and to academic and library resources, is also crucial. Particularly in the CORE program, many of our students reside outside the metropolitan area in communities where they maintain employment and families. A large part of our commitment to high quality education rests on developing technological tools and staff training to provide convenient remote access to multiple information services. In an earlier work the authors discussed access to admission, class schedules and registration (Stahley and Platt, 2001), the following portion of this presentation will examine live, online information access strategies in place at the community college and the university to afford access to proprietary educational resources, library catalogs, and help services.

As CORE students begin their coursework in pursuit of the associate's degree in education, their best option for electronic research access is Valencia Online (VO), http://west.valencia.cc.fl.us/distance/lrc.html, a site brimming with useful information including bookmarks for style guides, and full-text and citations databases accessible to any user equipped with an Internet Service Provider (ISP). Valencia Online was designed for distance learners. The site, however, and supporting links present not only LRC catalogs and proprietary database gateways, there are also countless tutorials and guidance services tailored to meet any research need. As such, VO is an invaluable asset for meeting the needs of all VCC students and faculty.

For example, the VO page includes a hierarchical menu of resources beginning with the Library Card link. Here is found is information about the 14-digit number required for access to licensed databases, as well as a listing of the other services and resources that require a library card. Next is a search guidance hyperlink to the community college catalog. The Online resources link leads to research bookmarks and electronic databases chart. Research Bookmarks presents a tabular list of indispensable reference works for the student researcher ranging from APA and MLA style guides, to full-text encyclopedias, to a multimedia archive of photos, audio clips, and graphs dating back to the 1920s. The electronic databases link is the gateway to a matrix listing of databases, complete with subject coverage, information type, update frequency, format, and a hot link to the database. One of the most valuable links at the Distance Learning site is to be found at the Internet Resources page. After a succinct caveat related to evaluating Internet information, the list begins with an 4part information literacy tutorial on selecting a topic, searching for information, and evaluating and documenting resources. Several other useful and relevant links are on the list, including a step-by-step research guide, a search engine strategies chart, and a guide for citing electronic resources. Last, the Distance Leaning page describes "bread and butter" services, such as document delivery services, and descriptions of each Valencia Campus Learning Resources Center Collection, with areas of subject emphasis to give students and faculty an idea of "what is available and where."

Once students make the seamless transition to their upper division CORE studies, the knowledge, skills and experience acquired from Valencia Online provides the foundation for utilizing the University of Central Florida library and information services. The countless resources of UCF libraries are accessible via the Internet. The size and complexity of the available databases makes them slightly less intuitive and user-friendly than Valencia Online. Still search guides and user assistance are generously sprinkled throughout the system. In addition, like the VCC system, UCF licensed information is protected and accessible only by students, faculty, and staff. Several levels of system entry are available, ranging from baseline ISP access, for book catalogs and non-proprietary databases, such as ERIC, to proxy access to most information and services, to full-blown, comprehensive access to every database and service via the University's network, Pegasus server.

For CORE students, the University Libraries homepage, http://library.ucf.edu/, is the starting point for education resources access. Corresponding to VCC's resources pages, the UCF library's page lists a hierarchical index of resources beginning with book catalogs and WebLUIS services. Following is a link to journal articles and other resources. Clicking the articles and other resources link takes the researcher to a tabbed listing of 18 subject-specific resources links beginning with popular databases and ending with social sciences databases. Clicking on the education subject tab takes the researcher to a hot-linked listing of full-text and citation databases designed to fill the research needs of students and educators. In the Education page header is a link to a dozen user guides for education classes. Some of the most useful educational resources links are the six areas mentioned in the table below below. All of the guides are worth examining.

UCF Online Education Resources			
Link Title	**Access To**	**Comments**	**Hyperlink to Resource**
Education and Elementary Education Resources	Book catalog by classification range and subject databases and indexes for education topics.	Includes description and access needs.	http://library.ucf.edu/Instruct/Education/UserGuides.htm
Education Webliography	Comprehensive access listing of 28 education-oriented sites, including curriculum and instruction, elementary education and middle school, technology in K-12, mathematics and science, and multicultural education.	Most sites include annotation.	http://library.ucf.edu/Instruct/Education/eduwebsites/education_webliography.htm
Internet Tools	Hot linked listing to research resources for searching and evaluation of Internet sites, and an annotated list of popular and meta, image, and education search engines. Also includes children's search engines and a site for search engine comparison and evaluation.	An irresistible gateway to everything you always wanted to know about Internet searching but did not know how to ask.	http://library.ucf.edu/Instruct/Education/EDF6481/internet_tools.htm
Music Webliography	Comprehensive access listing of 25 music education-related sites, including church music, American music, composers, ethnomusicology and world music.	Many sites are annotated. Also include sites for lyrics and public domain music. Note: ".com" usually designates a pay-for-access commercial site. Look for ".edu," ".gov," or ".org" sites.	http://library.ucf.edu/Instruct/Education/music webliography.htm
Psychology Subject Guide	Comprehensive listing of 13 psychology guides, including access to online journals, texts, APA resources, directories and associations.	Many sites are annotated and include resources at other universities.	http://library.ucf.edu/Instruct/Education/psychology_subject_guide.htm

Table I: Illustrates online education resources available from the UCF Library Homepage.

Conclusion

CORE is a program that exemplifies the role of shared accountability in education implemented by university, community college, and school district partners in central Florida as they identify potential teacher candidates and shepherd them to successful completion of a collaborative teacher preparation program. The CORE Program is dedicated to the mission of finding potential teacher candidates and helping them become successful, while at the same time relieving the shortage of qualified teachers that exists in the community. To ensure that CORE students have optimal access to resources, and ultimate success in their educational pursuits, VCC and UCF have designed and engaged a system of electronic and Internet access and resources tailored to suit education-specific lower and upper division coursework.

Handouts will include the presentation slides and a list of partnership, and education resources web sites.

References

Anderson, B. T., & Goertz, M.E. (1995). Creating a path between two and four year colleges. *In Teaching for diversity: Models for expanding the supply of minority teachers* (pp. 48-71). Princeton, NJ: Educational Testing Service.

Brennan, S., & Bliss, T. (1998). Increasing minority representation in the teaching profession through alternative certification: A case study. *The Teacher Educator.* 34(1), 1-11.

Chambless, J.R, Sweeney, M.V., & Thompson, W.D. (1999). *The Mississippi teacher fellowship program: A state-based initiative for the recruitment and retention of teachers in critical shortage districts.* (ERIC Document Reproduction Service No. ED 437348)

Darling-Hammond, L. (1998). *How can we ensure a caring, competent, qualified teacher for every child? Strategies for solving the dilemmas of teacher supply, demand, and standards.* Presentation to Shaping the Profession that Shapes the Future: An AFT/NEA Conference on Teacher Quality, Washington, DC.

Dilworth, M.E. (1990). *Reading between the lines: Teachers and their racial/ethnic cultures.* Teacher education monograph: No.11, Washington DC: ERIC Clearinghouse on Teacher Education and American Association of Colleges for Teacher Education.

Gonzalez, H. (1999, October). *The teacher shortage in Texas: How are school districts coping?* Paper presented at the annual conference on School University Partnerships, San Antonio, TX. (ERIC Document Reproduction Service No. ED 434 113)

Haselkorn, D., & Fideler, E. (1996). *Breaking the class ceiling!: Paraeducator pathways to teaching.* Belmont, MA: Recruiting New Teachers, Inc.

Stahley, M. and Platt, J., "Knowledge Management and Access in a Multi-Campus System: Collaboration, Communication, and Innovation," a professional paper for presentation at the Webnet 2001 World Conference, Orlando, FL, October 23-27, 2001.

Stewart, D. (1999). 10 Ways to recruit teachers. *Techniques: Making Education and Career Connections.* 74, 20-22.

Villegas, A.M., & Clewell B.C. (1998). Increasing teacher diversity by tapping the paraprofessional pool. *Theory into Practice.* 37(2) 121-130.

Yeager, M. (1999). Better pay, benefits would help fix shortage. Globe News [On-line]. Available: *http://www.amarillonet.com/stories/090198/new_134-2038.002.shtml*

Online Learning Forum:
An RPInteractive Professional Development Model

Linda Polhemus
Center for Initiatives in Pre-College Education (CIPCE)
Rensselaer Polytechnic Institute

Karen Swan
University at Albany

Michael Danchak
Computer Science
Rensselaer Polytechnic Institute

Lester Rubenfeld
Center for Initiatives in Pre-College Education (CIPCE)
Rensselaer Polytechnic Institute

Abstract: This paper will describe the Online Learning Forum (OLF), a k-12 professional development program. This RPInteractive professional development model provides teachers with the opportunity to learn new technologies, work collaboratively, communicate with their peers, and develop projects for their classrooms. With the advent of distance learning, online teaching and learning allows educators to participate in such experiences at their own pace, in their own environments, on their own time. This model has been developed to facilitate a community of learners, where the transfer of existing technologies and the development of new technologies are integrated into an RPInteractive experience unlike any other.

Background

This model of online professional development is a work in progress, where new technologies and new approaches to online teaching and learning inspire new pedagogies. The Capital Area Technology and Inquiry in Education (CATIE) mentoring program, also developed by CIPCE, provides a basis for the online learning forum. The CATIE model situates educational technology experts in schools and classrooms to work directly with teachers (Swan et. al., 2002). The situated professional development model is based on a constructivist approach to technology integration, in which educational technology mentors work jointly with teachers to design computer-supported lessons that incorporate technology into existing classroom curricula.

We are adapting this model into the online environment. However, the Internet's current limitations as a medium of instruction, including its reliance on text and still graphics or low-quality audio and video would seem to restrict instructors' abilities to form motivational relationships with their students (LaRose and Whitten, 2000). Research on classroom teaching in higher education found that *teacher immediacy* behaviors that increase the perception of closeness between instructors and students can increase affective learning, which in turn increases cognitive learning (Rodriguez, Plax & Kearney, 1996). Mediated instruction can also evoke teacher immediacy, but only live interactive video (Hackman & Walker, 1990) and videotape recordings have been (Guerrero & Miller, 1998) proven effective. Research on computer mediated communication (Walther, 1996; Lombard & Ditton, 1997) calls our attention to the socio-emotional deficits imposed by mediated instruction.

Although there are deficits imposed by mediated instruction, the development of new technologies and approaches to online instruction challenge us to create better web courses. To improve the 'behavior' of the computer, RPInteractive presents a new approach to online course development.

RPInteractive is an approach to e-learning being developed at Rensselaer that seeks to enhance learner-content, learner-instructor, and learner-learner interactivity for distance students (see Danchak paper submission to ELearn). As a natural extension of the Studio model (Wilson, 1994) of instruction in the face-to-face science and engineering classrooms integrates mini-lectures, collaborative learning, inquiry and direct experience, reflection, and conceptualization, in a sequence not unlike the Kolb Learning Cycle, RPInteractive transfers these techniques, as well as existing and new technologies into the online environment. The role of the instructor/coach in this model is to gauge students' understanding, listening and questioning them to develop desired knowledge (Cupp, et al, 2001). In the online learning forum, a course Mentor guides students through an experience and models an interactive, student-centered approach to instruction.

Our Unique & Innovative Style

Integrating tools with content is the pedagogical foundation of everything that the Online Learning Forum attempts to achieve. The components described in Table 1 are integrated into the context of a topic(s) and/or a software application to meet course objectives, where communication, collaboration, and activity-based learning are facilitated.

Component	Description	RPInteractive Element
QuikQuiz©	This tool, unique to the Online Learning Forum, addresses the issue of immediacy behaviors, where the Mentor poses a question regarding a given topic, and students are to respond, after which they are immediately able to view the responses of their fellow participants. The course mentor can then view which participants are on task, and make necessary adjustments.	Communication Collaboration
Interactive animation	Another unique component of the Online Learning Forum that permits participants to follow along as the animation proceeds to sequentially access commands in the computer application being taught online.	Activity-Based Learning
Video	Camtasia is also integrated into the online learning forum experience. This allows participants to watch a demonstration of a specific objective in short clips.	Activity-Based Learning
Problem solving	These scenarios are integrated into the context of a learning activity. Project development is supported by the integration of problem-solving situations where the participants are required to analyze and critique situations.	Activity-Based Learning
Threaded discussion	This communication tool permits participants to interact with the course Mentor and course participants to share, discuss and reflect on teaching and learning with technology. Participants have the ability to access these discussions and a tree-like structure will permit them to respond to any of the comments.	Communication Collaboration
Technical orientation	This prerequisite may be completed online or in-person with a course mentor. This orients participants to the online environment and provides them with all plug-ins and downloads necessary for a successful OLF experience. Teacher attitudes and beliefs, which may affect their confidence in dealing with advances in technology and their perception of change, are also addressed.	Activity-Based Learning
Capstone project	Participants complete a project that can be integrated and implemented into their classroom and/or school environments.	Situated Learning

Table 1: Online Learning Forum Interactive Components and Descriptions.

Findings

The online, asynchronous six week experience aims to provide a forum for interaction between educators where they are able to reflect individually and as a group on technology integration, to build a network of fellow educators to develop and disseminate technology-rich resources, to share new learning and to provide hands-on experience with software applications. During the Spring 2002 semester, 27 area educators enrolled in two different online courses. An end of session online survey was distributed to course participants to determine their perceptions of the course's structure, format, content, and design.

Participants in the Online Learning Forum courses were satisfied with the course objectives, structure and course mentor. All of the participants indicated that the components provided them with the opportunity to interact with the course content at a level comparable or higher than a traditional workshop setting.

Feelings about learning online when you enrolled in the course were first captured. All participants reported reluctance, as well as excitement. Comments included:

".... anticipated it would be a great way to learn at my own pace at home!"

" I was excited about learning how to do this work."

" I was excited by its flexibility and wanted to try it!"

" I was nervous at first. I thought that it would be confusing."

" I was very curious as to how the lessons would be taught and how much I would be able to do."

As a result of the online courses, students also reported the ways their feelings changed, or remained the same, as a result of taking this course. Comments included:

"I still think it has the advantage of being able to work at your won convenience but there is also a matter of self-discipline creating the time."

"I am more confident in taking another course online. Even though I did miss people direct contact."

"I am pleased with what I have learned and the experience of it via distance learning."

"I am amazed at how informative the course was! The examples were very clearly portrayed. I was able to apply them right away!"

In addition, participants revealed that having an initial face-to-face orientation to the online environment course would have enhanced their experience. For these participants who have not taken online courses before, this would alleviate any initial hesitation and frustration. Participants stressed the importance of problem solving scenarios and examples. In future and existing courses, revisions will be made to include more interactive, problem solving scenarios as well as an integration of more examples of how to apply give software programs.

Conclusion

Most of the participants in the online learning forum have never taken an online course prior to this experience. Although the online learning forum allows educators to engage in technology-rich activities to enhance their face-to-face instruction, some teachers are skeptical as to whether an online experience is for them. Learning new technologies in an online environment requires that participants not only learn given content, but also become familiar and comfortable with the course design. Future efforts will be given to finding solutions to issues such as these, in addition to a continued pursuit to integrate new technologies that will improve online professional development.

References

Cupp, E., Danchak, M., Foster, K., and Sarlin, D. (2001). "The RSVP Unibrowser: Bringing Interactivity to e-Learning", Intenational Conference on Advanced Learning Technologies, Madison, WI, Aug., 2001.

Guerrero, L.K & Miller, T.A. (1998). Associations between nonverbal behaviors and initial impressions of instructor competence and course content in videotaped distance education courses. Communication Education. 47(1), 30-42.

Hackman, M.Z. & Walker, K.B. (1990). Instructional communication in the televised classroom: the effects of system design and teacher immediacy on student learning and satisfaction. Communication Education 39 (July), 196-206.

LaRose, R. and Whitten, P. (2000). "Rethinking Instructional Immediacy for Web Courses: A Social Cognitive Exploration" , Communication Education, 49 (4), pp. 320-338.

Lombard, M. Ditton, T. (1997) At the heart of it all: The concept of presence. Journal of Computer Mediated Communication. 3(2).

Rodriguez, J.I, Plax, T.G. & Kearney, P. (1996). Clarifying the relationship between teacher nonverbal immediacy and student cognitive learning: Affective learning as the central causal mediator. Communication Education 45(4), 293-305.

Swan, K.,Holmes, A., Vargas, J., Jennings, S., Meier, E., & Rubenfeld, L. (2002). Situated Professional Development and Technology Integration: The Capital Area Technology and Inquiry in Education (CATIE) Mentoring Program. Journal of Technology and Teacher Education. 10 (2), 169-190.

Walther, J.B. (1996). Computer-Mediated Communication. Communication Research. 23(1), 3-43.

Wilson J.M (1994) The CUPLE Physics Studio. The Physics Teacher, 32, 518-523

Student Roles in Online Learning Communities:
Navigating Threaded Discussions

Linda Polhemus & Karen Swan
University at Albany

Abstract: This paper discusses navigation strategies affecting the interactivity of a graduate level course's asynchronous online discussion with a focus on the development of a learning community and knowledge building. This qualitative analysis reports on an exploratory investigation of student interviews and observations while interacting with the online discussion board. Observations of graduate level students in education courses from the State University of New York Learning Network (SLN) in the 2001-02 academic year revealed that students were interacting with the content vicariously and that the integration of multiple perspectives facilitated the construction of knowledge both individually and communally. Routines for reading and responding to discussion board messages also suggest that first students negotiate through the threads created, then based on personal criteria interact directly or vicariously with the content of messages.

Purpose

Quantitative research provides valuable information for online teaching and learning, however, the emphasis on grade/test score improvement does not really explore what is really going on in an online learning environment. How can we identify factors that increase participation and the quality of an online discussion? How can we evaluate the navigation patterns and their influence on the dynamics of the online community only assumed in an online discussion? This study presents the development and implementation of a research and evaluation protocol that analyzes online course participation for community building indicators and perceptions of learning. Specifically, it examines the way in which a user navigates the online discussion board interface, uses 'dialogue' to compose messages and construct and develops a perception of community online.

Literature

Many believe that the defining characteristic of the computing medium, if one can think of the computer as a single medium at all, is its interactivity (Bolter, 1991; Landow, 1992; Murray, 1997; Turkle, 1997). Recent research has focused on the general topic of student interaction within four defined categories: (a) learner-content, (b) learner-instructor, (c) learner-learner, (d) learner-interface (Hillman, Willis, and Gunawardena, 1994; Moore, 1989). When at least one of these forms of interaction is incorporated into teaching, student achievement and satisfaction are enhanced (DeVries, 1996; Fulford & Zhang, 1993). a fifth interaction, that of (e) 'vicarious' interaction (Sutton, 2001) whereby students do not interact directly at all, but observe and process both sides of direct interaction between two other students or between another student and the instructor has also been suggested.

Research focusing on community describes 'legitimate peripheral participation' as a means for knowledge building (Wenger, 1998). Although peripheral participation is assumed as a result of online communication, evidence for this assumption have not been determined. In addition, working together in an online discussion is also facilitated. Students are required to respond to each other to reach course goals. This produces the externalization of the thought processes, the comparison of alternative perspectives, social facilitation, better learning, high self-esteem and more positive attitudes toward the learning experience (Salomon & Globerson, 1989).

Method

The students who volunteered to participate in this exploratory study were enrolled in graduate level courses. Over the course of two semesters, different students from different courses discussed and participated in their online courses as they 'normally' would. Our protocol involved first students responding to questions regarding discussion board participation and online community. Second, students were asked to 'think aloud' while reading and responding to required discussion for that particular module or week. Third, students were asked follow-up questions regarding their interactions with the discussion messages, why they made such decisions and what they think about the community.

Instructor expectations for threaded discussion integration into asynchronous courses are as follows:
- To make thought visible
- Negotiate meanings around content
- Exposure to multiple perspectives
- Articulate positions
- Elicit reactions
- Critically analyze content, experiences and beliefs

To determine a student's level of participation in terms of 'learning,' we analyze not only the content of their messages, but also their reaction and interpretation of the messages of others. Examples of knowledge building in online threaded discussion is dependent upon the triangulation of community development (social presence), multiple perspectives, and routines for navigation.

Community Development	Multiple perspectives	Routines for Navigation
"I feel a part of the online community of all people who've taken online courses and also a part of the smaller community that is my online course I'm taking now."	"I am excited that the information in this module correlates with an ETAP course I took last summer! I have the opportunity to draw on prior knowledge."	"First I check to see if anyone has responded to any postings I have made. Then I check out new postings. I respond to several postings, sometimes I do this randomly as to not respond to the same person all the time."

Table 1: Examples of Knowledge Building in Online Threaded Discussion

In the observations, student interactions with the structure of the discussion board, the content, their peers and the instructor were found to reflect the learning community's dynamics. In a traditional classroom setting, students are integrated with all discussions (by listening), however, their engagement with those discussions are unknown and perhaps limited. On the other hand an online discussion provides students with the opportunity to experience the interactions of others based on their own personal interests and goals. In a traditional classroom, time may not permit all students to actively participate in these experiences, nor may students be attending to what others have to say even when they are present in the classroom environment. In the online interactions we observed, when a student clicked on (and read) another's message, he or she was then either motivated to respond or not. Observations and interviews indicated that students were more motivated to read and respond to a message with which they identified culturally, professionally, or personally; to meet course requirements; to make others feel a part of the course; to anyone who responded to them; to those messages that integrated multiple perspectives.

Similar to Salomon & Globerson (1989) students reported that learning took place in the comparison of alternative perspectives. Also, as indicated by Gunawardena & Zittle (1997) and others, students were aware of other student's social presence based on immediacy behaviors. During observations, students made mention of other's negotiation patterns (such as how, where, when and to whom they posted), experiences and cultural backgrounds. In addition, students used the discussion board to 'prime' their thought processes when composing messages to others.

Video-taped sessions of students 'thinking aloud' provide evidence for the following:

1. Setting for diverse thought

2. Navigation: reading other reactions, then forming own

3. Social presence evident in posting patterns

4. Priming: reading other messages, composing, then thinking of a new response to a previous message

5. Affect: laughing out loud at the message

Follow-up interviews revealed that students feel a part of their course's learning community, as well as, part of the community of all online learners.

Discussion

When students were navigating through the discussion, they were making decisions. First, they were making decisions about which messages to read. When students entered the discussion, they first interacted with the interface of the threaded discussion. Most students re-read the instructor's question, and then scrolled through the discussion. Students interacted with those messages from students with whom they could identify. Over time students who integrated themselves at a high level were able to make predictions of the nature of another's message. These students described the posting habits of other students, as well as made assumptions about the contents of their messages. As a result, during the semester, an online learning community was built. An integrated role in the online community is supported by student navigation patterns when students are able to acknowledge another's tone in dialogue (e.g. social presence), and identify with another student culturally. When students navigated the discussion board, the above characteristics are what influenced their feeling of a learning community in that they could connect with another student.

Disagreements also influenced student interactivity and student roles. When controversy took place online, disagreement between learners created an opportunity for others to mediate or oppose another's view. As a result, students were more likely to read and respond, thereby increasing interactivity. However, in the online discussion board, unlike a traditional classroom, not all students witness an argument or disagreement. One student we interviewed, who was segregated in the online discussion, was not aware of the argument. She did not read and respond to many messages, only to a limited few.

The roles that are taken in an online discussion vary. In an online course students are given the opportunity to participate in many threads of the discussion for a broad perspective (integrate themselves), or participate in only a small amount for deeper engagement (segregate). The two experiences are not necessarily mutually exclusive, however, student roles and expectations may facilitate one experience over another.

Students did not respond to all messages that they read. Also known as, 'lurking,' this vicarious interactivity (Sutton, 2001) also supported knowledge building. Those students who identified other student's as 'higher-level' participants, often read those messages to interact with the content. Although students did not always respond in written form, they sometimes printed these messages for future reference.

Finally, all students perceived they learned about diversity and multiple perspectives from the online discussion. Students reported that diversity and multiple perspectives provided the most evidence for learning, which was delivered in the form of feedback in the online discussion.

Conclusion

Bangert-Drowns & Pyke (2001) define learning engagement as the strategic mobilization of cognitive, volition and affective processes to foster personal meaning-making. We will continue to conduct more interviews and observations to investigate the possibilities of cognitive processes (and knowledge building) in terms of message content, volition (decision-making, the student's rationale for reading and responding or not), and affect (the integration of social presence). Some limitations to this particular study include the 'think aloud' process and the protocol for interviewing and observing student participation. Time, as well as other variables, limits the validity of the observation and interview process. However, the observations and interviews also provide insight into online communication for further research with a broader range of disciplines and a revised protocol.

References

Bangert-Drowns, R. L., & Pyke, C. (2001) *A taxonomy of student engagement with educational software: An exploration of literate thinking with electronic text.* Journal of Educational Computing Research, 24 (3), pp. 213-234.

Bolter, J. D. (1991) *The Writing Space: The Computer, Hypertext and the History of Writing.* Chapel Hill, NC: University of North Carolina Press.

Fulford, C. P., & Zhang, S. (1993). *Perceptions of interaction: The critical predictor in distance education.* The American Journal of Distance Education, 7(3), pp. 8-21.

Gunawardena, C. & Zittle, F. (1997) *Social presence as a predictor of satisfaction within a computer mediated conferencing environment.* American Journal of Distance Education, 11 (3), 8-26.

Hillman, D. C., D. J. Willis., and C. N. Gunawardena. (1994). *Learner interface interaction in distance education. An extension of contemporary models and strategies for practitioners*. The American Journal of Distance Education 8 (2): 30-42.

Landow, G. P. (1992) *Hypertext: The Convergence of Contemporary Critical Theory and Technology*. Baltimore, MD: Johns Hopkins University Press.

LaRose, R. & Whitten, P. (2000) *Re-thinking instructional immediacy for web courses: a social cognitive exploration*. Communication Education, 49, 320-338.

Moore, M.G. (1989). *Three types of interaction*. American Journal of Distance Education, 3 (2), 1-6.

Murray, J. H. (1997) *Hamlet on the Holodeck: The Future of Narrative in Cyberspace*. New York: The Free Press.

Richardson, J. & Swan, K. (2001) *An examination of social presence in online learning: students' perceived learning and satisfaction*. Seattle, WA: Paper presented at the annual meeting of the American Educational Research Association.

Rourke, L., Anderson, T., Garrison, D. R. & Archer, W. (2001) *Assessing social presence in asynchronous text-based computer conferencing*. Journal of Distance Education, 14 (2).

Salomon, G., Globerson, T. & Guterman, E. (1989). *The computer as a zone of proximal development: Internalizing reading-related metacognitions from a reading partner*. Journal of Education Psychology, 89,620-627.

Sutton, L., (2001) *The Principle of Vicarious Interaction in Computer-Mediated Communications*. International Journal of Educational Telecommunications, 7(3), 223 – 242.

Turkle, S. (1997) *Life on the Screen: Identity in the Age of the Internet*. New York: Simon & Schuster.

Community and Constructivism: Implicit Pedagogical Models in Virtual Learning

Richard Pountney, School of Education, Sheffield Hallam University, UK
r.p.pountney@shu.ac.uk

Liz Aspden, Learning & Teaching Institute, Sheffield Hallam University, UK
e.j.aspden@shu.ac.uk

Abstract: Communal constructivism attempts to move beyond social constructivism and capture specific elements of the additional value that ICT applications bring to the learning and teaching environment. Case studies of elearning implementations at Sheffield Hallam University are used to examine whether the advent of new educational technologies such as virtual learning environments warrants a new kind of educational theory, or whether they perhaps lure teachers into affordance (Tolmie and Boyle 2000). Properties of one VLE, *Blackboard*, which allow certain actions to be performed and which encourage specific types of behaviour, are examined and the attributes of effective models of online communities of learners are considered.

Introduction

Recent approaches towards teaching practices have seen a shift towards an acceptance of constructivist principles (Dalgarno, 2001). Although constructivism does not represent a single outlook, and is better understood as a continuum (Doolittle, 1999), the various different viewpoints unite around central core beliefs, and stand in stark contrast to behaviourist thinking. Whereas behavioural psychology is associated with an objectivist epistemology, where reliable knowledge about the world exists and can be transmitted from teacher to (passive) learner, constructivists acknowledge the active role of the learner in creating knowledge. So, for example, although cognitive constructivism does believe in the existence of an external reality, it is concerned with the construction of mental structures about this reality, rather than merely a passive assimilation of facts.

Of the different types of constructivism, social constructivism is often perceived as the more holistic viewpoint and, as the name suggests, its epistemological underpinnings emphasise the importance of social context, interaction, and dialogue in knowledge construction. It is these beliefs that Holmes et al have suggested need updating in order to account for the "synergy between more recent advances in information technology...and advances in virtual learning environments" (2001). What they propose is communal constructivism, where students create knowledge not only for themselves, but also for others who are not involved in the initial knowledge construction process. It is suggested that it is the particular attributes of ICTs and VLEs (such as the increased potential for communication, and storage of a variety of data types) that allow this to occur. Rather than passing through the educational system and leaving no trace, students' learning processes and products are available to learners in subsequent years, and potentially to the wider learning community (ie: those not involved in the initial knowledge construction).

Communal constructivism doesn't represent a radical departure from social constructivism in that many of the teaching practices advocated are precisely those that would be used in social constructivist environments. However, where the two do seem to differ is in the scope of influence that students are allowed, and it is suggested that the main interest is in the ways in which "ICTs can be creatively used to bring new life into...diverse ideas" (Holmes et al, 2001). By examining some of the activities taking place across Sheffield Hallam University (SHU), this paper aims to assess the strength of communal constructivism as a theory, as well as asking whether some of the developments could, potentially, be understood in terms of technical affordance.

Technical affordance

The term affordance was coined by J J Gibson (1979/1986), and is a central concept in the approach to perception and action within ecological psychology (Stoffregen, 2000). Behaviour is afforded by the environment, and affordance can be defined as the "properties of the environment of an animal that have consequence for the animal's behaviour" (Stoffregen, 2000). Affordances can be positive or negative and are effected by their context (Barnes, 2000); they are not necessarily deterministic - rather, they are opportunities (Barab et al, 1999, cited in Barnes, 2000) which guide behaviour. In her discussion of affordance of electronic conferencing in relation to distance education, Barnes uses the analogy of a path in the woods to illustrate this - the existence of a path "does not imply that this is the only place we can walk. However, it does provide an easy place to walk as well as providing a direction to walk in" (2000).

This clearly illustrates both the negative and positive aspects of affordance: the path allows the walker to travel more easily through the wood (positive), but may not lead the walker in the direction he wishes to go (negative). It is in this context that we talk about teachers being 'lured' into affordance by the particular attributes of a system: VLEs and ICTs have their own attributes that act in the same way as paths in woods. Email, for example, affords asynchronous communication (one-to-one; one-to-many); the use of electronic conferencing affords closed group discussions to take place online, either asynchronously or synchronously.

In their examination of two contrasting case studies, where CMC has been used to supplement campus based study, Light et al state that the introduction of computer mediated communication "can encourage both tutors and students to examine their existing roles and practices" (2000). In their conclusion, they agree that "As Harasim et al (1995) put it, CMC offers a *customisable* networked learning environment, *tailorable* to a wide range of purposes...even in this medium (and even when they are trying not to) tutors still have a critical role in shaping student learning experiences" (Light et al, 2000). What this paper aims to assess is how much influence the structure of the VLE could have over the individual decisions made by the tutors.

Case study background

As part of ongoing research at Sheffield Hallam University, members of staff who have been using the VLE *Blackboard* have been asked to contribute case studies outlining their use of the available technology, and their motivation behind this. Course tutors were asked to 'self-identify' how the VLE had been used to supplement teaching and learning activities by indicating which of a series of modes of usage could be applied to their course. At one end of the scale are purely content driven sites (or 'support' modes), where the site is used to display copies of essential documents, important dates, contact details for unit leaders, etc. More interactive sites introduce elements of communication (synchronous or asynchronous; one-, two-, or multi-way), assessment (formative or summative; single or multiple attempt), and resource provision, combining these with face-to-face teaching to a lesser or greater degree. The findings from the first phase of case study collection (total of 20 cases collected) have been used to support the conclusions of this paper in relation to the relevance of affordance and communal constructivism, and also to begin identifying attributes of effective online communities.

General findings

Both communal constructivism and technical affordance acknowledge that the availability of ICTs have a profound impact on teaching and learning. For Holmes et al, the emergence of new technologies "force the teacher to undertake a radical reassessment of the way in which they teach" due to the "enormous flexibility" offered (Holmes et al, 2000). This places the emphasis on the decisions made by individuals. The affordance theory, on the other hand, would assume that the availability and adoption of a VLE would guide tutors towards a particular style of teaching. So, the available features would "push behaviour in certain directions" (Tolmie & Boyle, 2000). At a general level, there is little to suggest from the collected case studies that the affordances of the VLE are guiding tutors to adopt practices that they would not necessarily wish to use. In fact, there was a strong sense of variety, with tutors choosing to adopt styles of site organisation that fitted in to their personal view of teaching and learning: there was no wholesale, widespread adoption of a particular feature, or set of features. Additionally, there are instances of tutors actively reassessing the practices they have adopted, rather than continuing in any particular way. These findings seem to assert the strength of the individual in the decision making process, and the following section outlines some general observations that support this, as well as providing a more in depth look at three undergraduate units.

Discussion

Barnes suggests that "The main issue concerning affordances of ICT and education is how and when ICT is an appropriate medium that enhances the learning process or learning outcomes" (2000). Comments from tutors at SHU such as "ICT is used alongside teaching, rather than being the driving force" were common, showing that they were interested in using particular functions to support their own aims. Appropriate use of the features of the VLE, and awareness of the need for this, has been highlighted throughout the case studies with tutors actively selecting - and amending their use of - particular features. So, for example, we can examine one affordance of the VLE - the potential for multi-way communication to occur - and compare three different units, all of which have tried to introduce some element of this. In the first case, the synchronous discussions proved extremely successful, leading to the conclusion that online communal learning has the potential to work well at undergraduate level. In the second case, the synchronous communication was not used ("if the students are on campus at the same time anyway, it makes more sense for them to be together in a 'physical' environment"; quote taken from case study), but the asynchronous discussion area has been used extremely effectively. This has been done to the extent that it has fostered a sense of community, with students happy to share thoughts and ideas in this environment. In the third case however, where the students were all professionals in full time work, the use of secure Discussion Boards for asynchronous communication is being discontinued. It is felt that "the commitments of a full time job and study leave little time for engaging in what is perceived as non-essential dialogue" (quote taken from case study). This pattern suggests that, even if tutors are being led down a particular path by the availability of certain functions, they are tailoring their use of the VLE to their own ideas, and the needs of the students: it supports the assertion of Light et al (2000) that "there is not *one* way, or even perhaps a *best* way of using CMC to support student learning".

We will now turn to a more descriptive look at three undergraduate case studies. The first of these - *ICT in an Educational Context* - is a specialist, level 3 unit taught over 7 weeks. In a previous paper (Pountney et al 2002), the manifestation of the nine critical elements of situated learning contexts as identified by Herrington & Oliver (see Herrington & Oliver, 2000) was examined, with the conclusion that it provided a highly effective environment for social constructivist learning activities: It provided authentic contexts and activities, alongside access to expert thinking and different perspectives; the environment allowed students to collaborate in knowledge construction, to reflect on their work, and to articulate their beliefs; it allowed for the integration of authentic assessment, and for the teacher to provide scaffolding at critical times. In looking at whether it could be re-described in terms of communal constructivism, the authors remained sceptical, and whilst acknowledging that communal constructivism does provide a useful framework for ensuring that networked learning is appropriately employed, they felt that it did not depart radically enough from social constructivism to warrant being a new educational theory (Pountney et al, 2002).

One of the fundamental tenets of communal constructivism is students developing a body of knowledge that will potentially benefit other learners, and teachers, thereby allowing the students to leave their mark on the course. By examining a second case study, where undergraduate students are involved in collecting fieldwork relating to tourism in the City of Sheffield, we can find support for the Holmes et al's belief that "the synergy between the more recent advances in information technology...and advances in virtual learning environments" (Holmes et al, 2001) does allow new educational opportunities. The information collected by the students in one year is stored in a hierarchical database, which has been packaged within *Blackboard*. This allows students in subsequent years to access and use this data alongside their own to map longitudinal changes in tourism provision. So alongside the authentic contexts already provided by the unit (eg: use of fieldwork, and collection of data reflecting how information is used in real life), it could be argued that the particular use of ICTs in this unit enable an additional layer of authenticity to be added to the learning process, as students can see how knowledge created at one point in time can be used in the long term, by others, as it would be in industry, for example.

Communal constructivism also argues that students can be "actively involved in creating knowledge that will benefit other students" (Holmes et al, 2001), an idea that is echoed in the development of a body of knowledge to be used over time. In our final case study we look at an instance that supports the idea of students collaborating, and creating knowledge for themselves and others, in a way supported specifically by the use of the VLE. Second year undergraduate students have been demonstrating high levels of engagement with the networked learning opportunities afforded by the *Blackboard*. This has been particularly well demonstrated in the use of the Discussion Board, where they have regularly been posting thoughtful messages, including suggestions for useful resources that they have found outside of the scope of those suggested. One point is particularly relevant here in relation to communal constructivism: although students could just as easily communicate, collaborate and pass on information on a one-to-one basis, or within controlled groups, the exchanges and processes could potentially remain invisible to the tutor. However, within the secure environment offered by the VLE, the students feel comfortable sharing their ideas within the whole group, and the elements of the collaboration are made visible to the tutor as well as to other students who may potentially have been excluded from individual exchanges. Thus, it could be argued that the particular features of the VLE allow these exchanges to be made available to a wider community.

The above three case studies illustrate units where the pedagogic strategies employed have created effective online communities of learners. A possible interpretation of this is that the particular features of the VLE have encouraged particular types of behaviour. The availability of multi-way communication, and the ability to store data, might have prompted tutors to use these facilities to supplement their learning and teaching strategies simply because they were there: they might have provided a particular path through the woods. Where the affordances have proved successful, they have been developed and integrated to supplement the teaching in effective ways. However, as in the instance mentioned briefly above, where they have been felt to be negative or unnecessary, they have been reassessed and their use discontinued.

Conclusion

It is apparent that the opportunities offered by ICTs do provide the opportunity for tutors to actively reassess their teaching practices, and it could equally be suggested that the availability of certain features do suggest particular strategies. However, to argue that it is the facilities themselves that push behaviour in certain directions is to ignore the role of the tutor - and the students - in the process of developing the course. In the cases collected at SHU the positive (or not) engagement of students and tutors with the technology has as strong an influence over the development of the course as does the availability of certain features. Tutors are actively involved in the decisions made about the course, rather than being just passively guided by the opportunities offered by the technology.

References

Barnes, S. (2000) What does electronic conferencing afford distance education? In *Distance Education*. Vol. 21, No. 2.

Barab, S. A., Chekes-Julkowski, M., Swenson, R., Garrett, S., Shaw, R.E. & Young, M. (1999). Principles of self-organization: Learning as participation in autocatakinetic systems. In *The Journal of the Learning Sciences*, Vol. 8., Nos. 3-4.

Dalgarno, B. (2001) Interpretations of constructivism and consequences for Computer Assisted Learning. In *British Journal of Educational Technology*, Vol. 32, No. 2.

Doolittle, P (1999). Constructivism and Online Education. 1999 Online Conference on Teaching Online in Higher Education. Available at http://edpsychserver.ed.vt.edu/workshops/tohe1999/text/doo2.pdf

Gibson, J. J. (1986) The ecological approach to visual perception. Hillsdale, NJ: Lawrence Erlbaum Associates, Inc. (original work published 1979)

Harasim, L., Hiltz, S. R., Teles, L. & Turoff, M. (1995) *Learning Networks: a field guide to teaching and learning online*. Cambridge, MA: MIT Press.

Herrington, J. and Oliver, R. (2000). An Instructional Design Framework for Authentic Learning Environments. In *Educational Technology, Research and Development*, Vol. 48, No. 3, pp23-47.

Holmes, B., Tangney, B., FitzGibbon, A., Savage, T., and Mehan, S. (2001). Communal Constructivism: Students constructing learning *for* as well as *with* others. Proceedings of SITE 2001, Florida.

Light, P., Nesbitt, E., Light, V., and White, S. (2000). Variety is the spice of life: student use of CMC in the context of campus based study. In *Computers & Education*. Vol. 34, Nos. 3-4.

Pountney, R., Parr, S. and Whittaker, V. (2002) Communal Constructivism and Networked Learning: Reflections on a case study. In Banks, S., Goodyear, P., Hodgson, V. and McConnell, D. (eds) Proceedings of the Third International Conference Networked Learning 2002, pp497-506. Sheffield University, England.

Stoffregen, T. A. (2000) Affordances and Events. In *Ecological Psychology*. Vol.12, No. 1.

Tolmie, A. and Boyle, J. (2000) Factors influencing the success of computer mediated communication (CMC) environments in university teaching: a review and case study. In *Computers & Education*. Vol. 34, No. 2.

Williams, C. (2002) Learning On-line: a review of recent literature in a rapidly expanding field. In *Journal of Further and Higher Education*. Vol. 26, No. 3.

An Efficiency Improvement Scheme for Content-Based Image Retrieval Systems

Wichian Premchaiswadi*, Nucharee Premchaiswadi**, Sutasinee Chimlek*,
Wichai Premchaiswadi***, Seinosuke Narita****
*Faculty of Information Technology, King Mongkut's Institute of Technology Ladkrabang,
Bangkok, 10520, Thailand
**Faculty of Information Technology, Dhurakijpundit University, Bangkok, 10210, Thailand
***Faculty of Engineering, Khon Kaen University, Khon Kaen, Thailand
***School of Science and Engineering, Waseda University, Tokyo, Japan

Abstract: This paper presents a scheme for improving an efficiency of image retrieval systems. The image indexing and retrieval technique based on the combination of the autocorrelogram method and color difference correlograms method is proposed. Color filtering technique is used for quantization of the RGB colorspace into 64 colors to reduce the complexity and calculation time. Then, both color and spatial information are employed to build the index of each image by using autocorrelgram and color difference correlogram. The distance measure technique is used to retrieve target images from the database. Experimental results suggest that this method can index and retrieve images which different views of the same scene, large changes in appearance. The performance of the image retrieval system is also improved significantly when compared with both color histogram and color correlogram method.

Introduction

Content-based image retrieval system is one of the popular techniques for retrieving image from image databases. There are two steps that are common used in most image database information retrieval systems as followings: indexing and searching (Huang et al., 1997). In indexing process, each image in a database, a feature vector capturing certain essential properties of the image is computed and stored in a feature-base. Then, in searching process, given a query image, its feature vector is computed, compared to the feature vectors in the feature-base, and images most similar to the query image are returned to the user. In a content-based image retrieval system, color (John et al. 1995, Swain 1991), the most recognizable element among image contents, is usually used for various image database applications. Color histogram, however, does not provide enough spatial information such that different images may have similar color histogram. To handle the weakness of color histograms several new features that strive to integrate both color and spatial information have been proposed (Huang et al., Pass et al., Markus et al., Hsu et al.)

This paper proposes a scheme that makes use of both color and spatial information for the image indexing and retrieval system. The effectiveness of the proposed scheme is confirmed by the experimental results and compared with both color histogram and color correlogram method.

Image Indexing Scheme

The process consists of three steps namely: color filtering, autocorrelogram (AC) and Color different correlogram (CDC).

1. Color Filtering

The process is used for quantization of the RGB colorspace of each image into 64 colors to reduce the complexity and calculation time in the following processes.

2. Autocorrelogram

A color correlogram expresses how the spatial correlation of color changes with distance [1] and is defined by the formula shown in Eq. 1 and Eq. 2.

Let I be an $n \times n$ image. The colors in I are quantized into m colors $c_1, ..., c_m$. $H_c(I)$ is number of pixels of color c_i in I. For a pixel $p = (x,y) \in I$, let $C(p)$ denote its color. Lets $I_c = \{p| \ C(p) = c\}$. The distance between 2 pixels, i.e., for pixels $p_1 = (x_1, y_1)$, $p_2 = (x_2, y_2)$, defined $|p_1 - p_2| = max\{|x_1 - x_2|, |y_1 - y_2|\}$, let $[n]$ denote the set $\{1, 2, ..., n\}$. Let a distance $d \in [n]$ be fixed a priori. $i,j \in [m]$, and $k \in [d]$.

$$\gamma_{c_i, c_j}^{(k)}(I) \cong \Pr_{p_1 \in I_{c_i}, p_2 \in I}[p_2 \in I_{c_j} \ \| \ p_1 - p_2 \ |= k] \tag{1}$$

$$\gamma_{c_i, c_j}^{(k)}(I) \cong \frac{\Gamma_{c_i, c_j}^{(k)}(I)}{H_{c_i} \times 8k} \tag{2}$$

The autocorrelogram captures spatial correlation between identical colors only and defined by Eq. 3.

$$\alpha_{c_i}^{(k)}(I) \cong \gamma_{c_i c_i}^{(k)}(I) \tag{3}$$

3. Color Difference Correlogram

Color difference correlogram (CDC) is the scheme that is modified from the texture description technique (Robert et al., Manjunath et al., Randy, Nepal et al.). Color difference correlogram of an image is graph or table that indexed by color difference value, where the k-th entry for $Diff_i$ specifies the probability of finding color difference value $Diff_i$ of pixels at distance k from any pixels in image. The color difference value between two pixels having distance equal to k is defined by Eq. 4.

$$Diff_i = | \ C(p1) - C(p2) \ | \qquad \text{where } |p_1 - p_2| = k \tag{4}$$

The color difference correlogram is calculated by the formula in Eq. 5.

$$\tag{5}$$

$$Cdf_{diff_i}^k(I) \cong \Pr_{p_1, p_2 \in I}[| \ C(p_1) - C(p_2) |= diff_i, \ \| \ p_1 - p_2 \ |= k \ ]$$

$$Cdf_{diff_i}^k(I) = \frac{\beta_{diff_i}^k(I)}{n_1 \times n_2 \times 8k}$$

Image Retrieval Scheme

The process is used to retrieve images from the image database. The technique of distance measure (Huang et al., 1997) is employed in the process. This paper use d_1 distance measure for comparing histogram, autocorrelogram, color difference correlogram, and AC/CDC because it is "relative" measure of distance.

d_1 distance measure for histogram, autocorrelogram, color difference correlogram and AC/CDC is defined by Eq. 6 to 9.

$$d_1(h) = | \ I - I' \ |_{h,d_1}$$

$$\cong \sum_{i \in [m]} \frac{| \ h_{c_i}(I) - h_{c_i}(I') \ |}{1 + h_{c_i}(I) + h_{c_i}(I')} \tag{6}$$

$$d_1(\gamma) = | \ I - I' \ |_{\gamma, d_1}$$

$$\cong \sum_{i,j \in [m], k \in [d]} \frac{| \ h_{c_i}(I) - h_{c_i}(I') \ |}{1 + h_{c_i}(I) + h_{c_i}(I')} \tag{7}$$

$$d_1(CDC) = | \ I - I' \ |_{CDC, d_1}$$

$$\cong \sum_{diff_i \in [diff], k \in [d]} \frac{| \ CDC_{diff_i}^k(I) - CDC_{diff_i}^k(I') \ |}{1 + CDC_{diff_i}^k(I) + CDC_{diff_i}^k(I')} \tag{8}$$

$$d_1(\gamma, CDC) = d_1(\gamma) + d_1(CDC) \tag{9}$$

Performance Measures

The performance of the scheme is measured by using the parameters the same as described in (Huang et al.,

1997) as follows.

$$r - measure = \sum_{i=1}^{q} rank\,(Q_i^{'})$$

(10)

$$Avg\ \mathrm{r\,\text{-}\,measure} = \frac{\mathrm{r\,\text{-}\,measure}}{q}$$

(11)

$$p_1 - measure = \frac{1}{\sum_{i=1}^{q} rank\,(Q_i^{'})}$$

(12)

$$Avg\ \mathrm{p_1\,\text{-}\,measure} = \frac{\mathrm{p_1\,\text{-}\,measure}}{q}$$

(13)

Experiment Results and Conclusion

The proposed scheme is implemented by using Visual Basic version 6.0 and Microsoft Access Database. The experimental image database is a heterogeneous image database. It consists of 10,204 images in varieties formats such as JPEG, BMP and GIF and varieties sizes. The number of color in each image is quantized into 64 colors. Thus, color difference of 64 values are computed, set {0, 1, ..., 63}. The distance measure is performed by d={1}, d={1,3}, d=(1,3,5}, ..., d = {1, 3, 5, 7, 9, 11, 13, 15, 17, 19}.

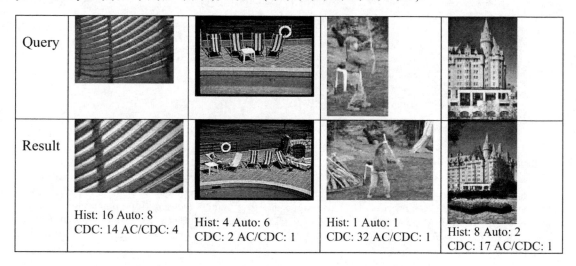

Figure 1. Sample queries and answers.

For the performance evaluation, one hundred queries, each with a unique correct answer, are used in the experiment. Figure 1 shows sample of some queries, query results and ranking of the result in various method namely: color histogram (Hist), autocorrelogram (Auto), color difference correlogram (CDC) and autocorrelogram and color difference correlogram (AC/CDC) methods. It can be seen that the AC/CDC scheme performs better performance than the other compared schemes. The scheme can also retrieve images with different views of the same scene, large changes in appearance.

The performance of the proposed scheme is also compared with other methods, color histogram, autocorrelogram and color difference correlogram. The comparison of average r-measure values and average p1-measure for each method are shown in Figure 2 and 3, respectively. From the experimental results, it could be concluded that the use of autocorrelogram and color difference correlogram for indexing and image retrieval that could improve the performance of the image retrieval system.

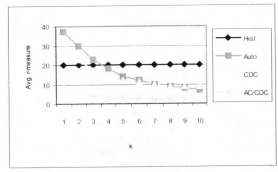

Fig. 2. Average r-measure.

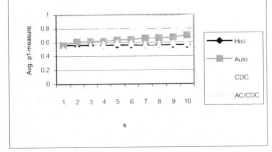

Fig. 3. Average p1-measure.

References

Huang J., S. Kumar, M. Mitra, W.J.Zhu, and R. Zabih (1997). Image indexing using color correlogram. Proc. of IEEE Conf. on Computer Vision and Pattern Recognition, pp.762-768.

John R. Smith and Shih-Fu Chang (1995). Single color extraction and image query. Proc. IEEE Int. Conf. on Image Proc., pp.528-531.

Michael Swain and Dana Ballard (1991). Color indexing. International Journal of Computer Vision, 7(1), pp.11-32.

Robert M. Haralick, K. Shanmugam, and Its'hak Dinstein (1973). Texture feature for image classification. IEEE Trans. on Sys, Man, and Cyb, SMC-3(6), pp. 610-621.

Manjunath B. and W. Ma (1996). Texture feature for browsing and retrieval of image data. IEEE Transaction on Pattern Analysis and Machine Intelligence, 18(8).

Randy Crane (1997). A simplified approach to Image Processing. New Jersey, Prentice-Hall.

Pitas I. (2000). Digital Image Processing Algorithms and Applications. New York: WILEY INTERSCIENCE.

Nepal S., M V. Ramakrishna, J A. Thom (1997). Image Retrieval Using Pixel Descriptor and its Applications to Region Extraction. Technical report, Royal Melbourne Institute of Technology.

Stephan Bres and Jean-Michel Jolion (1999). Detection of interest points for image indexing. 3rd Int. Conf. on Visual Information Systems, Visual 99, Springer, Lecture Notes in Computer Science, 1614, pp.427-434.

Greg Pass, Ramin Zabih, and Justin Miller (1996). Comparing images using color coherence vectors. In Proceedings of ACM Multimedia 96, Boston MA USA, pp. 65-73.

Greg Pass and Ramin Zabih (1996). Histogram Refinement for Content-Based Image Retrieval. Workshop on Applications of Computer Vision.

Markus Stricker and Alexander Dimai (1996). "Color Indexing with Weak Spatial Constraints. SPIE Conference, San Jose, CA.

W.Hsu, T.S.Chua and H.K.Pung (1995). An Integrated Color-spatial Approach to Content-based Image Retrieval. The ACM Multimedia Conference, pp. 305-313.

Selecting a Course Authoring System

Dr. Robert V. Price, College of Education, Texas Tech University
Bob.Price@ttu.edu

Abstract

Selecting a Course Authoring Tool (such as WebCT or Blackboard) that best meets the needs of the course author or instructor is an important consideration in creating quality online instruction. This paper reviews the features and considerations which course authors and instructors should consider when selecting a course authoring tool. An evaluation rubric is presented which those evaluating course authoring tools may use to guide them in their selection of the most appropriate system for the intended use. The rubric includes features common to course authoring tools, a rating scale of their ease of use, and a rating scale for the relative importance of each feature to the course author.

Providing course materials and information through the Web is a new frontier for many educators. *Course authoring tools* (CATs) are vital for the development and maintenance of course Web sites. A CAT is a computer program that is used by a course developer to design, develop, and maintain learner based web sites. Course authoring tools such as *WebCT* and *Blackboard* provide designers the means to distribute course materials, content, and tests to learners through the Internet. These tools use program components that allow course designers to design and deliver courses online, provide course material updates, and effectively deliver instructional modules to learners through standard web browsers.

The use of course authoring software for developing and maintaining courses has become a necessity. Course issues are important because they determine which course authoring tool is best suited for the job at hand. Selection of an authoring tool will have a direct affect on course development and the achievement of program goals.

Features of Course Authoring Tools

The selection of a course authoring software program is simplified if the user is aware of the features needed for course development. The software features considered here include course development, course collaboration, and course management (Gray, 1998). These software feature categories stem from typical activities that occur in the instructional environment and are shown in Figure1.

Course Development	Course Collaboration	Course Management
Content: lectures, materials and homework are developed for delivery through the web. Delivery: course development is conducted to include content. Forms of delivery include text, HTML, video, animation, and audio.	Access: course materials are accessed through learners' Internet service providers. Interaction: learners interact using own Web browsers. Support for e-mail, document sharing, learner homepages, discussions, etc.	Assessment/Feedback/Administrative: grade books, quizzes, exams, course related reports, course security, and software support.

Figure 1: Class activities that fall under software tool features (Aggarwal, 2000)

Tools for Course Development

Some features to consider for course design include:
- Site search tools,
- Course participant homepages, and
- Course development (templates).

Search tools help learners find useful information they need. Search tools can be invaluable for prospective learners who may be interested in online course offerings. *Learner homepages* are one way to help learners get to know each other. Learner home pages help because they allow the participants a chance to share personal information and interests. They provide learners with opportunities to help reduce the psychological effects produced by the distance between them.

A *course-authoring template* allows the developer to construct an online course using a pre-designed format. Templates are easy to apply to specific course development applications and adapt to changing situations. Templates help a designer get a new course up and running in the shortest amount of time possible. When a designer has a custom course template, it can be shared among divisions or departments to provide standard course interfaces and visual consistencies. The ability to develop and distribute a custom template design will help an organization accomplish this task.

Tools for Course Collaboration

Some of the main tools provided for course collaboration are:
- Chat rooms,
- Message boards,
- E-mail for course participants,
* Whiteboards support, and
* Special workgroup features.

Course discussions may be conducted either asynchronously or synchronously. Asynchronous discussions are usually threaded and allow learners to respond when it is convenient. This type of discussion typically takes place over several days, or longer, for each topic. Synchronous, or real-time discussions, allow learners to participate in a virtual classroom session and communicate to others who are logged on at the same time. Instructors can designate a specific time for discussions or workgroup activities.

Electronic bulletin boards allow course instructors to post announcements related to the course that learners can visit periodically to check for new information. E-mail provided through course management programs gives learners private e-mail accounts that are specific only to the courses for which they are enrolled. E-mail is very useful for receiving course assignments and corresponding with learners on an individual basis. Some instructors prefer web based private mail to regular email because it eliminates the need to maintain a class email list, and the problems that may be associated with learners working from a variety of ISPs.

Whiteboards allow the instructor to provide course participants with visual information (i.e., computer graphics) from the computer or a physical whiteboard (i.e., drawings). Instructors can use whiteboards to enhance synchronous discussions.

Finally, web-based *workgroup features* can help provide collaborative elements to learners. This is done through a special workgroup option that provides group members with web-based resources that might include a workgroup homepage, a private discussion area, or file transfer options for the workgroup.

Tools for Course Management

Some features to consider for managing a course include:
- Course grade books,
- Assessment tools (such as quizzes and exams),
- Course access control,
* Software support, and
* Course related reports.

Web-based course *grade books* provide a means for grading and tracking learner progress. Some course authoring tools provide tests, grade books, and other data handling options. Assessment tools provide a variety of options to the course instructor, such as, the ability to generate standard or random tests and quizzes for online assessment. Grading and other forms of feedback can be provided immediately to learners, if desired.

Course access control provides a means to secure course sites and learner access. Course authoring software should provide for course sites that are easy to access by authorized users, yet guard against unauthorized use. The most common methods of access control are user names and passwords.

Learner tracking features provide the ability to generate various reports concerning learner activities in a course and the use of online course resources. Such reports help instructors and designers evaluate the effectiveness of course delivery and design, and help instructors evaluate learner participation.

Evaluating Course Authoring Programs

There is no one best program which is best for all situations. The various software features discussed previously will vary in importance to individual course authors. While many tool features are common to most software programs, the quality of these varies from one program to another. The rubric below is provided as a framework for evaluating course authoring software. Course authors and designers could use this tool to help select the authoring tool that will work best for their needs.

Authoring Software Tool Evaluation Rubric

Program Title:		Version:	
Publisher:		Price:	
Reviewer:		Date:	

Tools for Course Development:	Importance Rating 0-4	Quality Rating 0-4	Score 0-16
Site Search Tools			
Participant Homepages			
Course Development Features			
Ready-Made Templates			
Custom Templates			
Quick Start Features			
Tools for Collaboration:			
Synchronous Chat Capability			
Message Board			
Private E-Mail Capabilities			
Whiteboard Capabilities			
Workgroup Capabilities			
Tools for Course Management			
Course Grade Book			
Assessment Tools			
Course Site Security			
Course Reports			
Student Progress			
Site Resource Use			
Course Evaluation			
Software Support			
Total Score			

Figure 2: Authoring Software Evaluation Rubric

The rubric lists the primary features of authoring programs. To use the rubric, the reviewer should first decide how important the features listed are to them. Using the following scale, enter a number from 0 to 4 for each listed tool. If there are other important tools which are not listed, they can be added to this form.

0 = Not Important
1= Minor Importance   3=Very Important
2= Some Importance   4=Extremely Important

After rating the importance of the tools, review the actual authoring software program or a demonstration version of it and enter your assessment of the quality of each tool using the scale below from 0-4. Consider ease of use, power, and flexibility in your assessment.

0= poor quality or not available   3=Good
1= Weak   4=Excellent
2= Fair

After evaluating the features of a software program, multiply your **Importance Rating** by the **Quality Rating** and enter the result in the **Score** for each tool. Tools which are rated 0 in importance will receive a 0 regardless of the quality rating so the reviewer can pay little attention to these tools. Either lower importance ratings or lower quality ratings will cause the score for a tool to be low. The highest overall ratings will result from those tool features which have ratings of both high importance and high quality. After evaluating all of the features of an authoring tool program, total scores for each item can be totaled by adding up the scores of all the tools and entering the result in the **Total Score** cell. After reviewing all of the authoring software programs available or reviewing those selected for further indebt consideration, the total scores and individual scores can be compared and a final selection made.

Use of this evaluation rubric forces reviewers to decide which features are important to them as well as providing a framework for evaluating the features of the programs being considered. This tool could be used by a selection committee or by individual designers or instructors to help them select the authoring tool which is most likely to meet their needs.

Conclusion

Use of this evaluation rubric by course designers will help them evaluate the course authoring tool options available to them and to select a tool which will work best for their unique needs.

Building Worldwide Mentoring Tools: Content Analysis of Visited Web Page and Matching

W. Curtiss Priest, Ph.D., Director, Center for Information, Technology & Society
Jared Luxenberg, Center Fellow
August 21, 2002

Abstract

Peer-to-Peer (P2P) Communications has become increasingly more recognized as a powerful tool for learning. In a project supported by Cisco Academies we have designed, built and are testing a new tool for P2P. We wished to have online mentors matched to online learners, but, the problems of successful matching, taking into account the current interests of the learner is challenging. Our design is to: 1. Give K-12 learners web-based learning resources 2. The student has a hover button that tracks their journey and says "Find me a Mentor" 3. They press that buttons: a. The contents of the currently visited web page is read b. We interpret the key concepts or topics of the visited page c. We employ a sophisticated matching tool (like the "find similar" for web pages at Google) to get a ranked list of relevant mentors d. Using an intermediate server, we find which of these mentors are online e. We make the match within seconds and place the learner in touch with the mentor via IM

Background

Mentor-Matcher is a knowledge sharing tool. To grasp how it performs knowledge sharing, it is useful to put this tool in perspective of other knowledge sharing tools. Once it is defined in those contexts, the technique for constructing the tool is addressed, followed by how it is currently being piloted.

The history of computer-based knowledge sharing tools goes back to the creation of online databases, such as by Lockheed Dialog, which terminals could connect to via packet networks in the early 70's.

Also created in the early '70's was a knowledge sharing tool called EIES by Murray Turoff at the Stevens Institute of Technology. Called computer teleconferencing, this tool and others like it permitted an asynchronous dialog among a group of participants where, again, using a dial-up terminal, users could dial to a central computer and post notes to a set of discussion topics.

Quite separately, on the UNIX side of computing, a hodgepodge of "news feeds" were created called Usenet. Either using telephone connectivity, directly, or by obtaining a "feed" from a computer networked to other computers, the user would receive a stream of messages sent to the "group" on the local machine. The user could either reply to a message (called threading) or open a new subject of discussion by announcing it in the subject line of the message.

Yet another mode of knowledge sharing was the Bulletin Board System (BBS). Here permanent messages could be posted in "Forums" and some of the first online chat sessions and chat rooms were created using software such as PCBoard. Other knowledge sharing occurred through the exchange of freeware and shareware files, also placed under topic headings (or directories).

In the '80s, with the prevalence of the PC, it was now possible to distribute knowledge sharing systems -- a form of communications which in the '90s was called Peer-to-Peer communications (P2P).

This author developed (and patented) the first P2P knowledge sharing system that combined e-mail communications, a knowledge database, and a topic structure. A topic structure (or controlled vocabulary) need be thought of as no more than a set of directories containing messages sent in the "context" of the topic.

A later implementation of such a P2P knowledge sharing system was Microsoft's Outlook which permitted the user to exchange information within "categories." Like the Priest implementation, both the category and the information were bundled into a header, a header different from a typical e-mail header.

With the advent of the Internet (net), a wholly different form of knowledge sharing grew, which actually resembled the original online database format more than later P2P implementations.

The net permitted thousands of different sites to flourish, and each contained knowledge of one kind or another. Early pioneers such as Yahoo and Lycos saw the need to comb these sites for information and provide a portal to an index of this information via web-based search engines. The technique behind the scene was the "webcrawler" which gathered words from site after site, stuffing them into a single searchable index. So these tools resembled the early text database tools of the '70s except that the "databases" were much more widely distributed.

On the net, the BBS chat rooms gave way, first to IRC (Internet Relay Chat) and then to P2P chat such as AOL Instant Messenger.

Mentor-Matcher Design

In a prior project we had designed a desktop agent (Tracker) that followed K-12 students using the web for learning resources. In that 81% of a student's time is spent outside of school (P. Kenneth Komoski, "The 81 Percent Solution," *Education Week*, January 26, 1994, p. 52), the goal was to provide a way to encourage learners to use the net to learn more. And, hopefully, the more passive activity of watching around six hours of television a day might be reduced and replaced with something more constructive.

A learning resource portal site was constructed (http://www.eLearningSpace.org aka eLs) with support from the U.S. Department of Education. Students receive a "learning credit" for each hour spent learning at some 4000 identified resource sites and can exchange those credits for donated goods (such as brand name shoes, etc.) via an online auction site (much like eBay).

Cisco Academies showed interest in this work and have been constructing the backbone of a knowledge sharing system for the 8000 or so academy sites around the world. We suggested that the time was right to combine knowledge sharing tools in a way that merged the abilities of web-based search engines and instant messaging.

The design problem was "how to elicit mentoring strengths of online mentors and match those abilities with the current learning needs of the learners "

The national standards efforts had produced a set of topics and sub-topics in the area of math, science, and reading. So, using Javascript we built a topic/sub-topic list where sub-topics and sub-sub-topics can be display by clicking on a plus sign next to the higher topic – a technique used in Acrobat and other indexed lists.

This approach works well because mentors have a well defined set of strengths that do not change much over time. However, a student's learning interest changes by the hour.

Somehow we needed to make a match between a topically defined person – the mentor, and a learner who is selecting and viewing web resources.

This problem is similar to the web search engine problem of finding web pages similar to the currently viewed web page. Ah, but the mentor topics were stored in a database; how to make these behave like web pages?

To solve this problem we create a set of local web pages with a key for each page back to each mentor. But how to populate the pages with lots of words?

Since several encyclopedias are online, we could build a tool that "expanded" a knowledge topic – say "planets" – into a web page of up to 30,000 words discussing planets. To do this we built an intermediate tool called "WordScooper."

After the mentor signs on to the project and provides a set of topics and/or sub-topics, the server immediately has WordScooper query Microsoft's Encarta for words on that subject. We created rules where WordScooper behaves a bit like a webcrawler, taking words from various levels of encyclopedia pages by following the links on the top page. We ignore pages that are not subordinate to the top web page.

So, now we have reduced the design problem to trying to match the learner's currently viewed web page (an indicator of their knowledge needs) with our locally stored set of web pages (which are keyed back to the mentors).

Knowing that there are several dozen web search engines and that many of these are available in several ways to search one's own web pages, we went to http://kresch.com/search/search.htm which lists all known search engines and their features. While the feature of "find similar" was **not** in their summary of features, they **did** have active links to sample sites employing the particular engine. Using this we reduced the list to four possibilities. Of these, the engine by Thunderstone (Webinator) appeared to be widely used by colleges and universities and, best of all, one could obtain the search engine software and run it under the local server's OS (in our case NT5). This is free, provided the server can access the Thunderstone site to receive authorization to run. [Alternatively, the entire text-based, SQL featured search engine (called Texis) can be purchased for $11,000 (U.S.).]

The matching and messaging process operates as this: 1.) Webinator is instructed to bring down the web page currently viewed by the learner and convert the page to plain text; 2.) Webinator is instructed to use its "metamorph" facility to create an internal set of thirty frequent and unique words which define the content of the web page; 3.) a search engine query is submitted with that list, searching all of our local web pages of mentor-related word-expanded topics; 4.) a rank order list of relevant mentors is returned; 5.) an intermediate server of ours determines which mentors are currently online, and displays a list to the learner of online mentors and the word that caused the match – each item in the list is a "link" to each online mentor; 6.) the learner clicks on one of the links; our online AOL-IM-like server sends a message to the mentor including the student's name and a display of the URL the student is currently viewing; the mentor may accept or refuse the "assignment;" if he "yes"," our intermediate server sends a message of acceptance to the learner and a two-way chat occurs; 7.) we log the entire chat session and its duration so that the learner can receive learning credits (as above) by verifying that the sites are on the list of educational web pages approved by eLs and logging the minutes in the student's eLs portfolio. The data gained by tracking the student's web browsing had to be detailed (keystrokes, etc.) and be in a form that was easily accessible from ASP scripts.

In first researching tools, we wished to use client side Javascript to track web browsing. This approach presented some control issues. Netscape would not allow tracking outside of the domain the Javascript page was hosted on, and some of the features of the script did not work properly in Internet Explorer (IE). Since Javascript implementations vary from browser to browser, and some users have Javascript turned off, this solution was not feasible. We looked for other ways to track web surfing. We looked at server-side solutions, such as a backwards proxy, but the overhead associated with these out weighed their benefits. We eventually found a way to automate IE on the client side, eliminating the need to run Internet traffic through a central server.

Microsoft provides an ActiveX interface to launch an instance of IE. Events are fired when the user visits URLs, closes the window, reloads the page, etc. This allows total control over the browser, and it provided the degree of control we needed.[*]

The field test stage has begun, and the tool has met and exceeded all expectations for performance.

In summary, the project illustrates a useful way to combine two different ways of accessing knowledge: 1.) use of keywords or a controlled vocabulary, and 2.) full-text searches. The choice of one and/or the other relates to the ability or inability to use a controlled vocabulary as pieces of this design problem have demonstrated.

―――――

[*] The authors express their concern that "all roads" seem to lead to IE and await the U.S. Justice Department suit results against Microsoft in this regard.

Using Animated Pedagogical Agents to Teach Entomology

Haiyu Qi[1]
University of Maryland
CALCE Electronic Products & Systems Center
College Park, MD 20740 USA
qihaiyu@calce.umd.edu

Juan E. Gilbert
Auburn University
Human Centered Computing Lab
Computer Science & Software Engineering
107 Dunstan Hall
Auburn, AL 36849 USA
gilbert@eng.auburn.edu

J. Wayne Brewer
Auburn University
Entomology & Plant Pathology
242A Animal Dairy Science
Auburn, AL 36849 USA
brewejw@auburn.edu

Abstract: Animation technologies are widely used in the areas of entertainment, such as video games. Animation technologies have also been implemented in education in the form of animated pedagogical agents (Johnson, 2001). In this paper, animated pedagogical agents are used as teachers in an introductory level CD-ROM based Entomology course at Auburn University. The designed course is self sufficient, as the animated teachers go through the lectures, provide quizzes and communicate verbally with the students. This new CD-ROM based course has several advantages, such as inspiring, attractive, flexible, cost saving and students evaluated this course to be very effective as teaching tool.

Introduction

The CD-ROM Entomology course, figure 1 is based on Entomology 2044 – An Introduction to the Study of Insects. This course is an independent study course created by Dr. J. Wayne Brewer, Professor in the Department of Entomology at Auburn University. This course consists of sixteen lessons contained in a course book and a series of videos. Each lesson includes a reading assignment in the required textbook, a set of lesson objectives, a written lecture on the assigned subject, written exercises to be submitted for grading and a set of practice test questions. The completed lessons, quizzes and exams are submitted to the instructor through the Auburn University Distance Learning Center for grading. From September 2001, the authors worked together to redesign the original Entomology course to one CD-ROM course. In this new course, there is an animated pedagogical agent (Johnson, 2001) who represents the traditional instructor. The agent addresses the lecture, provides quizzes and corrects practical test questions instead of a human teacher. All course contents are on one CD-ROM, which will be delivered to the students by the Auburn University Distance Learning Center. The CD-ROM course has the following advantages:

1. More inspiring - Instructor can add any inspiring contents, like questions, quizzes easily as compared with video tapes traditionally used for distance learning courses.
2. Attractive – Teaching by agents (animated teachers) can be fun for students if designed appropriately.
3. Flexible - Students can design their own learning process based on the necessary requirements.
4. Feedback - Educator can communicate with students easily and in time. All feedback can be processed quickly and precisely.

5. Cost saving – Educator and students can save money on tedious video recording, shipping or mailing.

However, there are also some limitations on this new CD-ROM course design:
1. Text-speaking technique – Though the text-speaking technique has improved, it can not compare with the real human voice.
2. Third party developer - Educators or students need a third party for the agent development, such as multimedia specialists.
3. The basic requirement for students –The student should have a computer with necessary support system together with the working knowledge of simple computer operations.

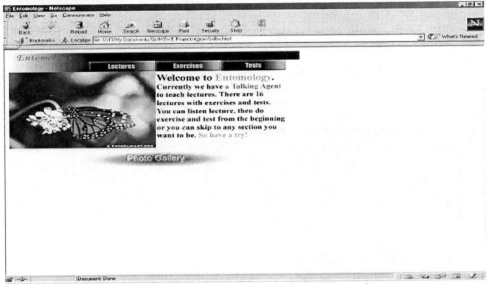

Figure 1: Entomology CD-ROM Interface

In the following section, the imp lementation, architecture and importance of the proposed CD-ROM course will be discussed.

Implementation

The Entomology course is implemented using JavaScript, HTML and a third party plugin. All contents are on one CD-ROM. When the student inserts the CD into a Windows computer, the application runs automatically .

Haptek Plugin

This project was built using the Haptek VirtualFriend 4.1 plugin, which is available as a free download from the Haptek website (Tech News – Haptek.com, 2002). JavaScript is used to control the VirtualFriend plugin. The core channel of communication with the plugin is a function called *SendText()*. *SendText()* simply sends a string of text to the plugin. If the string is simple text then the VirtualFriend will speak the text via speech synthesis. However, the VirtualFriend has a set of special commands that can be embedded in any sentence used to control the plugin, these commands are called Haptek Hypertext. The Haptek Hypertext commands can direct the plugin to download a new texture, perform an animation sequence, morph, or even load an entire new scene. For convenience, most of the Haptek Hypertext commands have been encapsulated in a set of easy to use JavaScript functions.

Architecture

The physical architecture of the CD-ROM entomology course begins with a root directory. The root directory contains images, software needed such as Microsoft Speech API, Microsoft TTS Engine

(Tech News – Microsoft.com, 2001), Haptek Plugin, Cygwin and three subdirectories – Agent, NoAgent and Animation directories. Considering some computers may not have the minimum system requirements, there is a version of course without the Agent in the NoAgent directory.

In the Agent version, an animated teacher goes through the lectures, provides quizzes and communicates with the students verbally. The No-Agent version presents the same content and explanations as the Agent version but the Agent is not present. The Entomology course interface is organized into four sections: Lectures, Exercises, Tests and a Photo Gallery, which is shown on Figure 1.

There are sixteen lessons in total. Students can access each lesson by clicking the corresponding link. Each lesson's interface consists of two frames: Navigation frame (left) and Content frame (right). In the navigation frame, there is one animated instructor and several function icons. Students can control the agent's speaking, choose different lessons, and skip to exercise or test sections by clicking the function icons. To help students master the content easily and fast, the content is divided into small concepts. Each concept is further subdivided into many small scenes so that agent can speak sentence by sentence. Between each concept there is a short question related to the previous concept. Students are required to correctly answer the short question. If the student can not answers the question correctly, he/she will not be permitted to proceed to the next concept in the lecture. Students can go back to the previous concepts to find answers. Figure 2 shows the lesson interface with the short question.

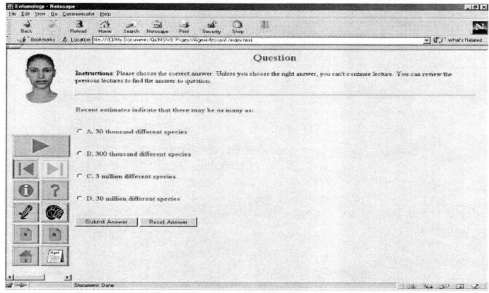

Figure 2: Short Question Interface

There are also sixteen written exercises in total. Each exercise is related to each lecture and includes three parts: definition responses, discussion responses and short question responses. Students can check their answers for correctness by clicking on the "compare answer" icon. In the navigation frame there are six icons: *Introduction*: is linked with an HTML page to explain the exercise section. *Definition responses*: is linked with an HTML page to show some terms needed to be defined. *Discussion responses*: is linked with an HTML page to show some discussion questions to be answered. *Short question responses*: is linked with an HTML page to show ten short questions and after students fill all the blanks they can click the compare answer button leading to a pop up dialogue box showing the percentage of correct answers. *Menu*: by clicking this icon the current exercise interface switches to an exercise list interface so that the student can choose different exercises from the links. *Back*: by clicking this, the current exercise interface switches to the lesson interface.

There are also sixteen self tests in total, each test is related to each lecture or written exercise and includes two parts: *multiple choice* and *true-false*. Students can compare their answers with standard answers after they finish any of two parts. In the navigation frame there are five function icons: *Introduction*: it is linked with an HTML page to explain the test section. *true-false*: it is linked with an HTML page to show ten true-false questions to let students choose true or false. *Multiple choice*: it is linked with an HTML page to show ten multiple -choice questions to let students choose one right answer.

Menu: by clicking this button the current self-test interface switches to self-test list interface so that students can choose different self-tests from the links. *Back*: by clicking this button the current self-test interface switches lesson interface. The self-tests interface is shown on Figure 3.

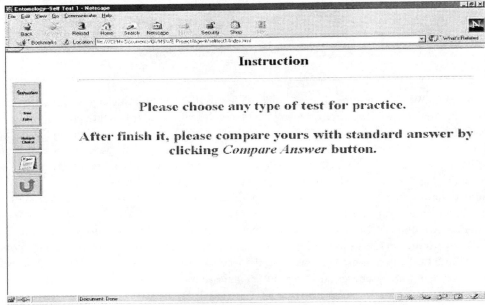

Figure 3: Self Test Interface

The Photo Gallery section, links an HTML page with nine insect images to provide some direct impression of insects to students. There is a separate Animation Directory. It includes two graphics animation applications written in OpenGL. One is a butterfly and the other is a dragonfly, the students can control these by using the keyboard.

Conclusions

The CD-ROM Entomology course has animated pedagogical agents to represent the course instructor role. Course contents are organized into four sections: Lectures, Exercises, Tests and a Photo Gallery. With text-to-speech technology, Haptek VirtualFriend 4.1 plugin and software development, students can be instructed as verbal and visional ways simultaneously. There are several significant features in this course, such as inspiring course contents, attractive teaching style, flexible study arrangement, and cost-savings for both students and educators. All those features satisfy the high education trend in the new centaury. This CD-ROM Entomology course proves to be a good teaching tool as evaluated by one of the students of this course. According to this success, this new education style may be considered to apply on various courses in CALCE Electronic Products and Systems Center, University of Maryland in the near future.

References

1. Johnson, W.L. (2001). Pedagogical Agents. [Online]. Available:
   http://www.isi.edu/isd/carte/ped_agents/pedagogical_agents.html
2. Tech News – Microsoft.com (2001), Text To Speech [Online]. Available:
   http://research.microsoft.com/srg/docs/intro2tts.html
3. Tech News – Haptek.com, (2002), VirtualFriend 4, [Online]. Available: http://www.haptek.com

[1] Mr. Haiyu Qi is a Ph.D. student at CALCE Electronic Products & Systems Center, University of Maryland directed by George E. Dieter Professor Michael Pecht and Dr. Michael Osterman.

Open Goal-Based Scenarios: An Architecture for Hybrid Learning Environments

Lin Qiu and Christopher K. Riesbeck
Department of Computer Science
Northwestern University
Evanston, Illinois 60201 USA
{qiu, riesbeck}@cs.northwestern.edu

Abstract: We describe a software toolkit called Indie, for building hybrid Investigate and Decide (Indie) learning environments. In Indie learning environments, students can run simulated experiments, construct reports arguing for different claims, and submit these reports for critiquing. The Indie learning environment is one example of the Goal-based Scenario (GBS) learn-by-doing environments. Previous examples of GBS systems have been self-contained software-based learning environments. The content of the learning environments is always pre-defined, which leaves little space for open-ended activities. We overcome this problem by creating an architecture for hybrid GBS's that provide the option for having human coaching in the learning environments. This brings the possibility of having open-ended activities in GBS's as well as the opportunity for incrementally augmenting the content at instruction time. Indie has been used to construct Corrosion Investigator, a learning environment for engineering undergraduates in the domain of biofilms.

Introduction

The Goal-based Scenario (GBS) (Schank, 1994; Schank, Fano, Bell, Jona, 1993) framework for computer-based learn-by-doing (Dewey, 1916) environments is designed to engage learners in active purposeful learning (Bransford, Brown, Cocking, 1999). A GBS begins by giving learners some large realistic problem that needs to be solved. With support from the learning environment, students learn target skills and underlying concepts in pursuit of goals within a context rich environment. The content of a GBS system is authored in advance based on real-life cases, common pitfalls, war stories, and so on. GBS's provide not only a simulated world for interaction, but also modules for expert coaching and critiquing, so that the learners are not limited by the availability of domain experts.

In order to support such computer-based coaching and critiquing modules, GBS's have to be closed world systems. The vocabulary of operations and situations has to be specified in advance so that rules can be written to provide accurate and timely feedback. Once deployed, learners can only do what the GBS has been prepared to support, so designers have to anticipate every action a student might want to do, and the most appropriate feedback for such actions in all situations. GBS's require significant upfront design, implementation, and piloting by content developers working with domain experts and test subjects, in order to provide learners with a rich challenging environment. There is no easy way to add new operations, coaching, or critiquing later in order to incorporate new developments in the domain or locally relevant content. Furthermore, it is difficult for GBS systems to accommodate the interests of open-ended teaching and learning paradigms (Collins, Brown, Newman, 1989; Gardner, 1991; Papert, 1993).

To overcome the above difficulties, we have been creating an architecture for hybrid GBS's and applying it to a subclass called Indie (Dobson, 1998). In Indie learning environments, students learn how to solve problems by running experiments and using the results to support or refute possible diagnoses. A hybrid Indie learning environment does not only have traditional support in a GBS from the computer, but also allows human experts in the feedback loop to handle totally open-ended inputs from the students that previously are not allowed and understood by the system. Open-ended activities are therefore made possible with the help from the human expert. Meanwhile, new material can be introduced in the interactions by students and faculty during the running of the GBS. There no longer exists a point where the system content is frozen. Introducing a human expert into the learning environment makes both the learning environment and the development of the learning environment open.

Indie Architecture

Indie is a content-independent Java-based software toolkit that includes a content authoring tool and a runtime learning environment (Fig. 1). The content authoring tool provides a user-friendly knowledge input interface for experts to enter content knowledge into a knowledge base, e.g. scenario challenge, experiment options, result generation methods, and domain background information. The Indie Learning environment reads in content files and become instantiated to a web-based learning environment. The Indie learning environment has a common interface, including support for a splash screen, a welcoming "challenge" document, a "background" screen where students can browse materials describing the scenario and domain content, a "lab" interface where students can order tests and collect results, and a "report" interface where students can construct arguments for and against possible diagnoses, using the evidence gathered from the tests. Indie learning environments automatically generate lab test results based on requests from students and provide scaffolding for students to construct arguments. Working as middleware between the students and instructor, it tracks student working progress for the instructor and lets the instructor role-play characters in the scenario.

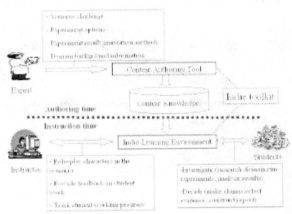

Figure 1: Architecture of the Indie toolkit

Though authoring time and instruction time in Figure 1 respectively refers to the time when the expert inputs knowledge into the system and the time when the instructor works with the students through the learning environment, they are not necessary separate periods. In other words, the instructor can work as the expert to augment the system while engaging in working with the students. Having the instructor working in the learning environment keeps the system from totally depending on pre-defined content, which is crucial when the content knowledge in the system is still under development.

An Example: Corrosion Investigator

We used Indie to build the Corrosion Investigator application, a learning environment for engineering undergraduates in the domain of biofilms. In the learning environment, students take the role of consultants to help a company determine the cause of pipe corrosion. Students need to make conscious decisions about which tests to run and which test results support the claims they make in order to solve the problem in a timely and economical manner. This requires students fully understand the purposes of the tests and the implication of the test results.

To run tests, students go to the Experiment page (Fig. 2). Here, students can look for tests by entering test names into a textbox. Tests matching the name will be shown. Students can view the description of the tests and possible variable values for the tests. Currently, there are five tests in Corrosion Investigator. A few more will be added. If no test matches the name that students enter, students will be asked to try another name, or email the Scientific Consultant, a character played by the instructor in the scenario, for help. Using an open-ended interface for test names forces students to research and brainstorm about what tests might be relevant. It also allows tests to be used that the scenario authors hadn't predicted. Hence, the problem solving activity is more open-ended and closer to real life situations. Such activities help students develop adaptive expertise (Bransford et al., 1999). New tests and results can then be incorporated into the system for reuse by future students. This approach does require an expert in the loop, though, to interpret reasonable but unexpected test names, and to generate plausible test results on the fly.

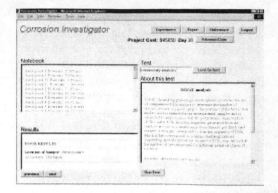

Figure 2: The Experiment screen in Corrosion Investigator.

When the test results become available, they appear in both the Notebook and Test Results area (Fig. 2). Test Results area displays the test results in a readable manner. The Notebook records all the test results that the user has received in a list that can be used for constructing a report. Most of the numbers in the test results are generated randomly based on constraints specified in the domain files.

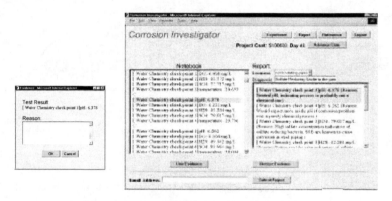

Figure 3: The Report screen in Corrosion Investigator.

When students feel they have gathered enough information, they can go to the Report screen (Fig. 3), make claims, and apply evidence in the Notebook towards that claim. Students need to specify the reason for using a test result as evidence. They also need to use many pieces of evidences to support their claim, because the strength of the argument, and its freedom from irrelevant evidence, is a key area for critiquing. After finishing constructing the argument, students click the Submit button to submit their reports. The system emails the report and the data in the Notebook to the instructor. The instructor reviews the report and emails feedback to the students. Students then continue working based on the feedback.

Related Work

A previous version of Indie was developed in Lisp on the Macintosh by the Institute of Learning Sciences (ILS) at Northwestern University. Over a dozen of Investigate and Decide learning environments were built with the old Indie (see Dobson, 1998). Our new version is Java-based for portability and web-delivery, and uses XML files to represent the domain content. Most imporantly, the new Indie supports human coaching and critiquing as well as much more complex tests, and random test result generation.

See Dobson (1998) for more related work.

Future Work

Six first-year graduate students in the Civil Engineering Department in Northwestern University used Corrosion

Investigator in a class in May 2002. After using Corrosion Investigator for 3 weeks, students completed a survey regarding their experience. Their average score to the statement that "overall, this is an excellent system for doing the project" was 2.16 on a scale of 1 to 5 (1 stands for Strongly Agree, 5 stands for Strongly Disagree). The question "How difficult is it for you to find out the right test to run?" got the most negative score, 3.83 on a scale of 1 to 5 (1 stands for Very Easy, 5 stands for Extremely Hard). This shows that the most difficult aspect of the interface to use was the mechanism for finding tests to run. Improving the interface for finding tests to run thus becomes one of our future research issues. Other parts of the system were considered not difficult. As for the professor of the class, the software significantly reduced his work during the project phase, especially on test result generation.

The content knowledge for Corrosion Investigator was written in XML format directly without using the Indie authoring tool because the tool is still under development. We are using a class-based dialog box approach that proved quite successful in the previous Indie for building the tool.

Acknowledgements

This work was supported primarily by the Engineering Research Centers Program of the National Science Foundation under Award Number EEC-9876363. Matthew Parsek, an assistant professor in Civil Engineering, developed the original biofilm course that Corrosion Investigator was based on. He later expanded and refined the content in his course for Corrosion Investigator. Ann McKenna, a post-doctoral fellow in the School of Education and Social Policy, guided the development and evaluation of the original course.

References

Bransford, J. D., Brown, A. L., & Cocking, R.R. (Eds) (1999). *How people learn: Brain, Mind, Experience, and School.* Washington, DC. National Academy Press.

Collins, A., Brown, J.S., & Newman., S. (1989) *Cognitive Apprenticeship: Teaching the Craft of Reading, Writing, and Mathematics,* In L.B. Resnick (Ed.) *Knowing, Learning, and Instruction: Essays in Honor of Robert Glaser,* Lawrence Erlbaum Associates, Hillsdale, NJ

Dewey, J. (1916) *Democracy and Education,* The Free Press, New York.

Dobson, W.D. (1998). Authoring Tools for Investigate and Decide Learning Environments. *Ph.D. thesis.*

Gardner, H. (1991) *The Unschooled Mind, How Children Think & How Schools Should Teach,* BasicBooks, New York.

Papert, S. (1993) *Children's Machines: Rethinking Education in the Age of the Computer,* BasicBooks, New York

Schank, R. (1994). Goal-based scenarios: *A radical look at education.* Journal of the Learning Sciences 3, 4, 429-453.

Schank, R., Fano, A., Bell, B., & Jona, M. (1993). The Design of Goal-Based Scenarios. *Journal for the Learning Sciences* 3:4. 305-345.

Making Your Online Learning Environment a Success
Clemson University's Approach

Carla Rathbone
Director of Collaborative Learning Environment
Clemson University
United States
bone@clemson.edu

Abstract: A popular topic of discussion in higher education is online learning environments. Everyone wants to collaborate, learn anytime and anywhere and do this with little or no experience required. Competition between commercial versions of online class environments, locally developed versions and a hybrid of the two has inundated our educational institutions. Regardless of the choice, how do you make it succeed? More importantly, what makes faculty and students buy in to this new way of teaching and learning? This article looks at how Clemson University is addressing these issues of what makes an online learning environment useful and how to encourage the innovative use of this environment. We will conclude with a look at how we have been able to expand our services to a portal concept that addresses the computing needs of all users at Clemson and extends these personalized tools and services for use in the classroom and the workplace.

Introduction

Clemson University is a public, land-grant research university with a total enrollment of 17,465 students and approximately 1200 faculty. Clemson's Collaborative Learning Environment, better known as MyCLE, was created in 1997 to lead the university in incorporating technology into the teaching and learning process, providing a wide range of technological services for use in the classroom. This online learning environment was developed internally to provide collaborative work space and web tools for all 6000 class sections each semester with no administration required by the professor. This system integrates information from our legacy Student Information system, Novell Directory Services and numerous customized applications. Access to the online learning environment is through a single computer user ID and password. Membership in the class workspace is automatically maintained through a dynamic link to the Student Information System. Each class has a consistent suite of course tools and file folders with common folders for turning in and reviewing homework, storage of class materials (such as course syllabus and assignments), public web folders, team folders, student surveys, grading, discussion boards and library reserves. In support of both synchronous and asynchronous learning, Clemson University's online learning environment is globally accessible from both our network and the web.

Background

The Collaborative Learning Environment department is department of the Division of Computing and Information Technology (DCIT) and was established with support from the Provost office with a $150,000 annual funding. We have continued to receive this funding every year to support training positions, provide faculty incentives and purchase new hardware and software for training and faculty development labs. Additionally, DCIT restructured its academic support to focus on supporting this new learning environment. Currently the CLE department consists of 12 full-time employees, six to eight students and two faculty fellows to promote and support the use of MyCLE.

Clemson University's Approach – Support and Services

Communication and support have been the cornerstone of the implementation process of our online learning environment for both faculty and students. The approach used by the CLE has itself been a collaborative effort and included many departments and groups across campus. Partnerships have been formed, new training programs established and student and faculty labs upgraded as outlined below, all as part of creating and supporting a successful collaborative learning environment at Clemson University.

Partnerships

- Office of Teaching Effectiveness and Innovation (OTEI) and CLE share office space and work together to assess the technological needs of faculty in teaching and learning. Joint workshops and seminars are provided on a regular basis.
- Student Government and CLE worked together to produce a syllabus repository for students. This repository of course syllabi allows students to research class descriptions prior to registration. It also allows faculty to automatically upload their class syllabi to MyCLE.
- The University Library and CLE developed a process to allow the library to post class reserves electronically through the university's online learning environment.
- CLE works with the Office of Off-campus, Distance and Continuing education to determine standards and tools for distance learning and co-sponsor seminars for faculty to learn how to use these tools.
- CLE Advisory Board (consisting of 2 faculty representatives from every college and student representation) evaluates the needs of faculty and students in the use of the online learning environment.
- CLE faculty fellows (faculty members who are given additional funding to serve) act as mentors to their colleagues in the use of technology. The faculty members sponsor workshops, address discipline-specific needs, write articles for the faculty newsletter and assist in beta testing new tools and features of the online learning environment.

Training and Support Programs

- A computer literacy program was designed and implemented for 100 level courses, specifically English 101 to introduce students to Clemson's computing environment.
- In-class training for course-specific instruction may be requested by faculty and is held during the regularly scheduled class period.
- Short courses are offered each semester to all faculty and students
- One-on-one consulting is available to assist faculty and students in the use of MyCLE.
- A newsletter, Faculty Directions, is published quarterly that showcases the work of faculty using technology in the classroom.
- Faculty training classes are scheduled each semester covering the use of MyCLE and supported web and multimedia application.
- Faculty Laptop development program is implemented this Fall to address faculty use of laptops (required this year in College of Business and Behavioral Science, College of Engineering and Science undergraduates and also for the first year MBA students).

Labs

- A faculty development/multimedia lab was created for scanning of text files, images/slides, video capturing and editing; color printing, digital media and web page creation.

- A "virtual laptop" environment was developed allowing students to have access to files, programs, email, bookmarks, etc. from any lab computer on campus or dorm room
- Over eighty classrooms have been converted to "smart classrooms" and equipped with a podium containing a network-connected computer, VCR, cable TV connection, and with a ceiling mounted high quality projector.
- Laptop requirements have been implemented this semester to include freshman in College of Business and Behavioral Science, College of Engineering and Science and also for the first year MBA students.

Conclusion

This level of services and support throughout the CLE, combined with the ease of use and availability of our online learning environment, has proven to be successful with faculty and students. Currently 85% of all students and teaching faculty representative of all five colleges use some components of the online learning environment in their classes. As more faculty and students become comfortable using the tools and features, the gradual transition to online learning becomes a reality allowing more flexibility and alternative methodologies in the teaching and learning process.

The CLE continues to develop and expand the services offered in order to meet the needs of the Clemson University campus users. Over the past year we have been able to implement the portal concept to extend and personalize these services to administrative units across campus because of the successful use in the classroom. Work groups are automatically created in addition to scheduled classes to provide access to these tools and services in the classroom and workplace. This includes various web tools, shared file space, personalized applications and access to university systems. Some of the current uses for work areas include our SACS Self Study groups, student organizations, administrative business units and student advisory committees.

For more information go to http://cle.clemson.edu. For a look at the online learning environment, contact cle-l@clemson for a guest account and enter at http://mycle.clemson.edu.

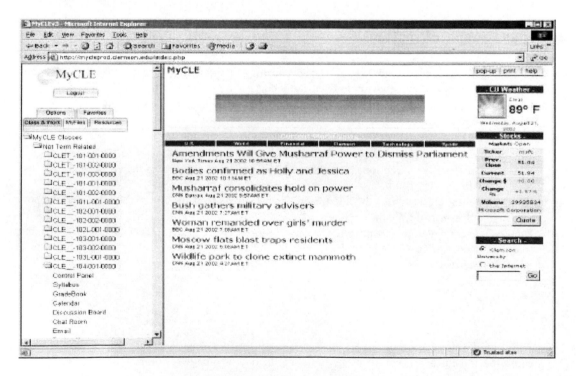

Figure: 1: Clemson University's Online Learning Environment (MyCLE)

Without any doubt, there are special challenges to providing adult education as such in a developing country.

The first and foremost challenge is to spread a relatively scarce resource - knowledgeable content providers (i.e., lecturers) - over a huge geographic area. Another challenge is to find the necessary financial resources to fund the delivery of adult education in the face of pressing basic necessities such as providing primary health, welfare, and safety care. On top of this, in South Africa there is the added imperative of an urgency to empower millions and millions of illiterate adult black South Africans due to the educational backlog because of the previous government policy of apartheid.

Against this background, a new company with the apt name of *eDegree* was formed in South Africa with a capital investment by PricewaterhouseCoopers three and a half years ago, with the specific objective of harnessing the advantages of e-learning as one of the most viable solutions to meeting the above-mentioned challenges.

In many ways, in retrospect, it was a case of "fools rush in where angels fear to tread". I believe we were one of the very first companies/institutions in the world to deliver a fully-fledged Bachelor of Commerce, as well as an MBA degree, completely online. At the other end of the spectrum, our Adult Basic Education and Training programme (i.e., a fast track for illiterate adults from grade 1 to grade 9) delivered on CD was surely a world first.

I would like to share my company's experience in providing e-learning to the African continent (and, more specifically, in South Africa) with you. During this time, we have learnt to move at lightning speed, to redirect and re-engineer every two to three months, to navigate through uncharted waters, building new models as we progressed and, yes, also from time to time looking back in amazement at our ignorance 30 days before.

By utilising e-learning, the expertise of the relatively small pool of high-level content providers who are able to contextualise knowledge within local circumstances is being distributed on a national level.

Furthermore, course delivery via a virtual classroom (text and/or audio), synchronous and/or asynchronous, lends itself admirably to bringing learners into contact with peers and lecturers all over the country and continent, drawing on one another's unique yet comparable third-world circumstances. (Bandwidth restraints in Africa limit the use of streaming video to a very large extent at this stage.)

On top of this, e-learning now provides African learners with direct access to the best international resources available through the WWW or by means of e-mail for the first time.

It is important that one should recognise that there are different categories of adults who would benefit from online learning. Young undergraduates have learning requirements that are quite different from those of highly motivated mature learners in the professional workplace. And how on earth does one go about teaching a completely illiterate adult to use a computer? Does it make any sense at all to use such a highly sophisticated piece of technology to educate somebody who has never even used a pen or pencil?

An understanding of the relevance of learning requirements and styles must precede the design and implementation of learning programmes. The learning environment and the facilities available to support the learner, both online and off-line, should reflect the elements of sound pedagogy relevant to the groups concerned.

Developing a training course for the South African market requires developers and providers to create courses that are not simply didactic, but that also reflect the principles of learner-centredness, lifelong learning, flexibility in learning provision, the removal of barriers of access to learning, recognition of prior learning, provision of learner support, relevance, differentiation, redress, nation-building and non-discrimination, critical and creative thinking, flexibility, and progression.

It is neither desirable nor appropriate for large numbers of academic staff (even should they be available) to become experts in the use of authoring software. In any case, the design of effective courseware materials involves much more than the use of an authoring tool. In our opinion, it is more appropriate in the development of materials that subject matter experts should be creative and work with and advise experts in instructional design, in graphical design, in the production of audio and video materials, and in a range of other services to ensure courseware of high quality than for them to try to do everything themselves.

Therefore, the core business of *eDegree* is to assist public and private higher education institutions and companies to redesign and package their course content to optimise the e-learning capabilities to the full. This we do by training faculty in e-learning instructional design principles and, thereafter, digitalising their courseware on a five-tiered scalable index according to different parameters such as cost, target population, and technical considerations.

At *eDegree*, we also take responsibility for the administration and management of the delivery of the e-learning courseware if the client so prefers, with the academic institution at all times the custodian of all matters pertaining to academic standards.

e-Learning courseware design

Partly to help economise on development costs, increasing interest is being shown in the concept of reusable "learning objects" defined as the grain size of the smallest unit of production within learning material. We use the term "learning object" to refer to the smallest study unit that a learner might wish to take: full courses should be structured by combining such small units. Structuring course content in the form of independent learning objects implies that multiple learning outcomes and, therefore, multiple curricula needs can be met by re-using the same learning objects. This has the advantage that different qualifying authorities (universities, colleges, and companies) can select relevant outcomes or objectives for learners from the same pool or repository of carefully constructed learning objects. The learning objects are relatively self-contained from a learner's perspective and are structured to enable the learners them to be assessed.

To provide this level of flexibility, the ideal is that *eDegree* will need to make available stand-alone learning objects for learners throughout the African continent, which could form part of a fuller course leading to an award, or they could simply be independent units prepared for a specific market. This will enable potential consumers to select learning objects, either separately or in combination, to suit their needs – albeit with guidance about their coherence and about the possibilities for an award.

Developing material in the way we propose requires subject expertise to be combined with a range of skills associated with instructional design. The development process is time-consuming and expensive, which is one reason why these scarce resources are centralised in one specialised service provider such as *eDegree*.

Constructing courseware by means of learning objects implies that no duplication – and, therefore, unnecessary use of an expensive limited resources – takes place. On the contrary, extensive reuse of knowledge is made, packaged in such a way that immediate updates at relatively low cost can be done quickly.

This way of organising knowledge does, of course, have enormous implications for courseware design. But even more importantly, it demands a whole new way of thinking about curriculum development and structuring of qualifications.

One of the outcomes of this approach is that the World Bank has awarded us a grant for developing a world-first Online Authoring course, i.e., an individualised online programme to train subject matter experts in the unique instructional design methodology necessary for designing an online learning experience, enabling them to transform their existing content knowledge to optimise the benefits of the online learning environment. This has been a formidable challenge and a tremendous opportunity.

We have succeeded in developing a curriculum design through a flexible modular architecture built on the learner's personal (lecturing) profile, his/her target audience, different learning styles, etc. In practical terms, this means that instead of a linear approach, SMEs are prompted to follow a non-linear route through the learning material in a way that best serves their needs and those of their target audience. By first assessing which learning outcome a learner lacks, he or she is then branched to the specific learning object underlying success in mastering the outcome.

Within the course content, different instructional design principles and how they impact on learners from varying cultural and educational backgrounds are addressed. Not only does this add to the applicability of the programme within the different educational contexts worldwide, but it is also believed that from our experience gathered in the multicultural South African educational environment, we are uniquely positioned to develop a novel product of this nature.

In order to add functionality to the front-end tools, the use of artificial intelligence to automatically evaluate the didactic applicability of selected multimedia features has been developed – also a unique attribute of this programme.

An unique e-learning challenge

It is imperative that, given the African education scenario, special attention is given to training of adults on lower levels also. It is with this in mind that *eDegree* has put a very special effort and millions of rnads into developing an Adult Basic Education and Training (ABET) programme, essentially training illiterate adults to read and write.

The term "ABET" connects literacy with basic, general adult education and with training to enable income generation. ABET learners exist in a wide range of learning constituencies, including organised labour in the formal economy, self-employed and underemployed people, the unemployed youth and adults in urban areas and settlements, the rural unemployed, and women heads of households in both urban and rural areas.

The ABET audience is diverse. It is also located in the dynamic world of globalisation and technological advance. It is vital then that material provided to meet ABET learning needs is flexible, so that it works within a wide range of contexts. Our programme lends itself to two modes of delivery: the traditional classroom-based method and the computer-aided method guided by the facilitator. The computer-aided approach to ABET aims to bring together classroom-based and distance learning, taking the best from both approaches and forming a new method focused on meeting individual learner needs.

While ABET learners can never be expected to complete courses independently, the lessons learnt in forming sound distance learning principles relate to the independent nature of self-paced learning. Incorporating multimedia into the learning equation enables learners to learn at their own pace, while still enjoying the support and guidance of a facilitator and the camaraderie of fellow learners.

The benefits of e-learning in an ABET context are many and varied: over and above the benefits of monitoring capabilities, and providing independent, self-paced learning, instruction given is standardised, and e-learning allows for easy adaptation of material. The endless capabilities of multimedia with sound, animation, and graphics make explaining concepts to learners at lower levels far easier. A learner who is able to watch the animation of different shapes moving together to form letters, letters moving together to form sounds, and sounds moving together to form words is able to "experience" a new concept, rather than accept static representations of the concept, filling in the blanks where necessary. Reference tools come alive in front of learners' eyes – an alphabet library, combining the name of each letter, the sound it makes, how to write it, and an associated picture, makes learning to read and write more than memorising lists of sounds and shapes; it becomes an integrated learning *experience*.

The process of developing an effective e-learning programme becomes significantly more complex when South African developers are faced with the challenge of providing programmes in 11 official languages.

The challenge is compounded when the programme being provided is essentially one enmeshed in language, such as an ABET course. Teaching someone to read and write in English is vastly different from teaching someone to read and write in another language. Think of a literacy course in French. The French language is bound by grammar rules such as the masculine and feminine gender of nouns. Simply translating a French literacy course into English will not produce a meaningful programme. It is not only grammar rules that cannot simply be translated – think of idioms, poetry, and humour specific to the English language. Before the process of developing content for courses in 11 languages can begin, generic components must be isolated, language-specific components for each language identified, and a way forward mapped out. Translators and language experts become vital new members of the team.

But the challenge does not end here. Instructional designers, graphic designers, and programmers require an understanding of the content in order to mould it into a meaningful learning experience. The answer cannot be to simply form a team for each language, where each member speaks the language concerned. How would one control quality and consistency? The likelihood of finding a person who speaks all 11 official languages AND with enough knowledge and experience to manage 11 multimedia production teams is slim. Furthermore, quality control and monitoring of programmes in 11 languages once these programmes have been implemented is no easy task.

Conclusion

With Africa and, more particularly, South Africa having been relatively isolated from the rest of the world for very long for various reasons, we take special care to keep at least up to date in terms of fast-moving international best-of-breed e-learning practices.

Globalisation demands high productivity, an advanced skills base, and a competitive edge. We should maximise our potential in focus areas, while taking advantage of international skills in other areas. Globalisation offers us the opportunity to compete in world markets for the first time. This enables us to make use of state-of-the-art technology, while sharing knowledge and ideas with specialists who have a common passion and purpose.

Life on the Bleeding Edge: How Emerging Technologies Can Help New Teachers

Pamela Redmond
Teacher Education Department
University of San Francisco
Redmond@usfca.edu

David Georgi,
Teacher Education Department
California State University, Bakersfield,
dgeorgi@csub.edu

Abstract: The Teaching Learning Interchange (TLI), a federal Preparing Tomorrow's Teachers to Use Technologies project, will be in its second year of applying several emerging technologies to help new teachers in several ways. This presentation will report actual second year results compared with the first year expectations listed below.

The Teaching Learning Interchange (TLI), a federal Preparing Tomorrow's Teachers to Use Technologies project, will be in its second year of applying several emerging technologies to help new teachers in several ways. This presentation will report actual second year results compared with the first year expectations listed below.

The target population consists of "preintern teachers," a designation in California for teachers who are not credentialed and have not passed subject matter competency. The intent of the preintern program is to provide a way for those wishing to enter the teaching profession to attain subject matter competency and a credential while they are working in the classroom. The program originated because of a severe teacher shortage in California.

TLI has partnered with 15 county offices to have access to preinterns and corporate partners who are developing new technologies.

ClearPhone provides software for conducting video conferences among small groups anytime/anywhere via Internet access. TLI identified a number of subject matter science specialists (the area of greatest need) from the Exploratorium. They are being connected with preinterns who need to attain subject matter competence. Each participant will be given a net cam, whiteboard and software. Online meetings will be conducted in which several preinterns can meet with a specialist and discuss topics covered on the Praxis science test. The whiteboard allows participants to share lesson plans and student work samples.

Expectations are that both the specialists and preinterns will give ClearPhone high marks in the ability to meet from distant locations. Those in rural areas with long distances are expected to have similar benefits to those in congested urban areas, notably the efficiency of meeting without the disadvantages of travel to a common location. The preinterns in the project are expected to score higher on Praxis than preinterns in general.

Lesson Lab provides online video of classroom practice that is particularly useful in helping preinterns understand and plan for the complexities of classroom management and lesson delivery. LessonLab has a unique software package that allows instructors and preinterns to time index a video of classroom practice while online. For example, an instructor can create an assignment to demonstrate a particular teaching practice, like responding to the efforts of learners. The assignment can provide a link to where an example, say at 12 minutes 32 seconds of a 60 minute video. The assignment can then require preinterns to view all or some of the entire video and mark where they see examples of effective or ineffective practice and write narrative descriptions of their perceptions. When the assignment is completed by all the preinterns, a chart showing all the examples marked by preinterns can be displayed, forming the basis of a dialog on examples marked by many and those marked by only one or two. The advantage of this approach is that teaching is shown within a realistic context including both effective and ineffective teaching practice. Preinterns can explore practice via synchronous and asynchronous online discussions to obtain deep levels of understanding of the complexities of teaching. Both instructors and preinterns are expected to report that this technology is helpful in improving their classroom management, lesson planning and delivery.

Apple Computer recently redesigned its Apple Learning Interchange (ALI) to include video cases along with Units of Practice for particular lessons and links to related resources. A search engine is included on this portal that links Units of Practice to state and/or subject standards. Preinterns will be given structured access to the ALI. They are expected to report that the ALI is useful in obtaining and adapting lesson plans, viewing examples of successful practice and accessing resources and standards.

In conclusion, the experiments of the TLI in providing such state-of-the-art technology to new teachers is expected to produce a wealth of useful applications that have great potential in future teacher preparation programs, as well as identifying a number of potential problems that go along with such innovations.

Diversify, Diversify, Diversify! Why Gender Mainstreaming in Educational Media Does Not Mean one Size Fits All.

Bernd Remmele

Bernhard Nett

Frank Roehr

Britta Schinzel

Benjamin Stingl

Tanja Walloschke

Institute for Computer Science and Social Studies
Dept. 1: Modelling and Social Impacts – RION Rechtsinformatik Online
University of Freiburg, Germany
remmele@modell.iig.uni-freiburg.de

Abstract: Distant Education and Internet-supported classroom education pose specific problems to the establishment of gender equality in Higher Education. Instead of discussing these problems from the perspective of insufficient competencies among women, it is stressed that the specific media have to allow different (also female) user strategies. Especially the integration of presentational and communicative functions into educational software promises to show general (ungendered) success. These assumptions will be rested on experiences of the Internet based teaching network RION.

Introduction

'RION – Rechtsinformatik Online' is an Internet based teaching network of nine German universities and three different disciplines, i.e. law, informatics, and economics (Rechtsinformatik is the German expression for computer and law - C&L). It is designed to create an Internet platform including a learning space for the field of computer and law. [1] This field is gaining more and more importance with the new media and it is constantly changing with them, however it does not fit into the traditional structure of German law teaching. So there are some gaps, which RION tries to fill with its interdisciplinary, and ICT based approach.

The authors, who are an interdisciplinary group (computer science, law and sociology) themselves, are responsible for the didactical consulting, the gender mainstreaming and the evaluation of the whole project. One main objective of our evaluation is therefore the problem of gender and new media. Though we raise data about computer literacy according to the present computer practice and get the expectable result (i.e., the male practise is 'more advanced' than female), we do not think that this is mainly question of deficient female competencies. The statement that there are such differences between the sexes in the usage of ICT in Higher Education does not mean women have to become like men; rather we have to reconsider the interaction structure of the media and the practises they allow in order to promote the implementation of software that can be used successfully by different users. Why should different user groups (there are more differences then that between men and women) adapt to the media instead of adapting the media to the different interest and the relating competencies.

From this perspective computer literacy has to be seen in the framework of a definition of media competence, which is conceptualised in a more complex way than just by superficial present practise. A timely definition of media competence has to add contextual knowledge about the media to the limited determinations of mere ICT handling; this involves some critical faculty especially regarding the social dimension of the media and their usage (Cf. Baacke 1999). We want to point out that this comprehensive conception also involves another perspective on the C (commu-

---

[1] http://www.ri-on.de
RION is financed by the Federal Ministry of Research and Education in the framework of the sponsorship programme „New Media in Education". RION is a cooperation of the Universities of Freiburg, Oldenburg, Münster, Karlsruhe, Berlin, Hannover, Göttingen, Darmstadt and Lüneburg.

nication) and its connection with the I (information), because the ways communication is organized in educational software – if at all – do not reflect the whole spectrum of services and features, demanded by different user interests. Of course this does not sounds really new, as most of it complies with constructivist pedagogics. Constructivism also focuses on contextuality. Information has to be framed in a given context to be meaningful, and this means also that it is socially situated. So when contextualization was discovered as a chance for education in the nineties, constructivism became popular in pedagogics. Therefore regarding ICT in (higher) education the interactive potential of the computer should be moved into the center of interest. Students should no longer be considered as mere consumers. Instead, their involvement ought to be promoted by making it decisive in regard of what happens (Cf. Siebert 1999; Specht 1998).

As gender mainstreaming is an enterprise that goes to the roots of organizational and technological structuring, it is clear that gender mainstreaming is directly concerned with possible user strategies in the realm of educational software. One of our basic assumptions is that the disciplinary (learning) culture of informatics is decisive for the learning models implemented in educational software (regardless of the design of the user interface and similar apparent qualities, which are mostly expressions of an analogous production process). This model is determined by the singling out of the learners (i.e. no grouping in the strict sense of the word takes place), assumed standardized basic knowledge, and clear-cut separation from other scientific disciplines and practical usage. In the respective software we thus have mainly space for lecture-scripts, and - if at all - communication-tools, which are somehow stuck on to the central presentational core, without building a functional unit.[2] This obviously is not constructivist.

Evaluation Results

A basic survey carried out at the beginning of RION showed in regard to the (Western) Internet-standard-applications more or less equal results for men and women. However there were significant differences in advanced computer use or - to say it in another way – in male domains, like hardware, programming, games and discussion boards to the disadvantage of female participants. These results are supported by the fact, that in discussions of male students the computer is an issue more often than among female ones: so technical expertise is exchanged more frequently within male dominated networks.

Certain internet tools tend to support gender-specific communication styles, and especially discussion boards do so in a way, that has often lead to frustration of female participants (Cf. Herring 2000). With the data of our survey we can establish the thesis that gender-specific user profiles, in consequence of specific media biographies, correlate with diversified self-conceptions: In regard to the self-estimation of their computer competence, female students rate themselves significantly lower.

"I know, that I can handle my computer well."				
	exactly	rather correct	rather not correct	no
female (20)	10.0%	50.0%	40.0%	0.0%
male (49)	40.8%	49.0%	10.2%	0.0%

We asked students of law and economics from different universities, who are studying C&L,[3] with a questionnaire to rate the assertion "I know, that I can handle my computer well." As the table shows no one answered 'no' and half of the women as well as half of the men choose 'rather correct'. However 40% of the female said 'rather not correct' whereas the same percentage of the male answered 'exactly'. This clear difference regarding the 'computer self efficacy'[4] and the respective gendered satisfaction pattern leads of course to lesser practice in this field, so that we get a vicious circle of less experience and lacking contentment.

Experiences with the MOO used by RION (called JurMOO) may point at a way out of these circumstances.[5] To understand this claim we first have to know what makes a MOO so special. A MOO is a Mud (multi-user-domain) object oriented. This means that the whole setting including the "characters" is programmed in an object-oriented manner - and the users themselves may change all these elements. If you look at the user interface of a MOO[6] -

---

[2] Kirkup & Prümmer (1997) also connect gender problems with the design of communication features. "For distance education to take this seriously, systems must have designed into them connection networks among students with the chance to communicate and meet."

[3] Though in general the proportion of sexes in law and economics is balanced, where there is the choice more men are taking courses in C&L.

[4] Cf. http://www.chssc.salford.ac.uk/healthSci/selfeff/selfeff.htm

[5] http://lem.iig.uni-freiburg.de:7000/

[6] Basically a MOO can be used via Telnet; the JurMOO of RION can also be accessed via a browsable Java emulation (http://lingua.utdallas.edu/encore/).

which admittedly needs some familiarization - there are three 'frames'; on the right side there is something like a web page, the 'rooms' of the MOO; and on the left side there are the two frames – a big one on top, a small one at the bottom -, which are something like a mixture of a chat client and a command line. With the different commands you can change the structure and the content of the 'rooms' and objects. Everybody is represented by an individual character. MUDs and MOOs are normally used for text adventures, with battle lines and quests created by the players themselves in the framework of some fantasy plot; but they also find some usage in Higher Education contexts.[7] So MOOs are bad means for simply distributing traditional top-down teaching (Bruckman & Resnick 1995), but instead are able to support active groups of learners.

Depending on the structure of the MOO there is a diversity of possible things to do: usually 'move' from one 'room'/web page to another, give a message to all in the same room ('say'), give a message to one specific character, write mails, and describe, change or build rooms or objects; but there also special things to do like marry (one or more persons), smoke a cigarette, cuddle etc. … 'Move' and 'say' are of course the mostly practised actions. And because these actions are tightly interweaved on the user interface, it can be said that the distinctive feature of a MOO is that it directly combines communicative and presentational functions. This complex condition allows diversified user strategies. Thus the potential of the MOO is its combination of information and communication, and the easy shifts between them (Hoadley 1999).

Among other purposes RION used its JurMOO for the preparation of a two-day-workshop on broadcast law for law students.[8] For several weeks before the workshop the participants discussed the subjects of their presentations with each other and with tutors, and they built a 'room' where they put their table of contents etc. for annotation.[9] The development of the whole course was evaluated by questionnaires (e.g. regarding computer literacy and self efficacy), interviews and analyses of the server log of the MOO.

	'move' - first 150	'move' - total	'say' - first 150	'say' – total	actions all together
female (16)	53 %	56 %	37 %	36 %	100 % (8762 actions)
male (18)	73 %	67 %	21 %	26 %	100 % (8827 actions)

The most striking result of our evaluation is the existence of different however converging user strategies for females and males.[10] The table shows the percentage of 'move' and 'say' in relation to all used commands specified by the sexes, in respect to the first 150 actions of each person and to their total amount. Obviously women 'say' more and 'move' less than men at the beginning; women still 'say' more on the long run (Also female messages in average are longer, so that a female did 'say' almost twice as much as a male during the whole course.[11]) While organizing the common task the gendered preferences converge however to a certain degree. There is a development especially with the male participants. Whereas women only 'move' a little bit more with time, men clearly 'move' less and 'say' more.[12] This convergence of user strategies throughout the virtual seminar was however only made possible by the special characteristic of MOO, the integration of communicative and presentational functions. And it were the men who 'adapted' primarily.

Thus concerning the satisfaction pattern, there is another interesting result. Female students were more content with the use of this tool than the male ones. Comparing the ratings of male and female students, both evaluated JurMOO´s influence on the quality of the individual presentations for a final face-to-face situation and the overall help provided by the tool pretty equally. In contrast, a relatively strong positive deviation of the ratings of the female students existed for JurMOO´s contribution to the understanding of co-students and their presentations (in the mean 5.4 for women to 4.3 for men out of a 0-10-scale), while positive deviations of the male ratings are related to the

---

[7] E.g. http://clark.colgate.edu/dhoffmann/text/ACTFL2000/moovass1.htm, telnet://moolano.berkeley.edu:8888/; cf. Holmevik, & Haynes 2000.

[8] http://www.uni-muenster.de/jura.tkr/alte_version/lehre/materials/Verlaufsplan Seminar WS0102.pdf

[9] Due to the constraints of German mass faculties like law, to discuss a presentation in advance is more than unusual. Normally nobody has an idea of the connections of his subject with that of a fellow student, therefore he has also quite little interest in the presentations of others.

[10] Regarding gender-different but converging learning styles cf. Campbell 2000, p. 137.

[11] The average length of messages was for females: 35,39, and for males: 31,78.
In average a female did 'say' 7081 signs, whereas a male did 'say' 4191 signs.

[12] This table shows the development in smaller steps.

	0-49	50-99	100-149	150-199	over 200
female 'move'	50 %	54 %	54 %	56 %	57 %
male 'move'	69 %	79 %	71 %	50 %	66 %
female 'say'	39 %	37 %	35 %	35 %	36 %
male 'say'	23 %	17 %	24 %	43 %	27 %

coordination impact of JurMOO for the seminar (5.2 to 5.7). One possible interpretation could be, that female students welcomed the more communicative style, whereas male students saw the seminar preparation by JurMOO more as a measure to improve the overall teaching quality of the seminar. The promotion of the mutual understanding regarding what each is doing and learning contributes of course also to the development of an actual learning group, which is one of the big problems of distant education.

Conclusion

Our results regarding the possible convergence of user strategies and the higher female contentment with the mutual understanding support the assertion that the use of a MOO-like tool can be a promising instrument for gender mainstreaming in distant education. The gender gap (regarding in possession/access of, assumed knowledge about, and usage of new media technology) can be smoothed by a systematic integration of communicative and presentational functions, because the changed status of the communicative function directly affects the participation structure and with it the satisfaction of women.

To allow the convergence of these different strategies and the establishment of a learning group sharing its knowledge this technical side has however to fit in an overall didactical setting, where e.g. the incentives have to be tuned in a much more deliberate way than in classroom education. The conditions for (equal) participation in scientific discourse furnished by educational multimedia can be substantial for didactic success, because in this way the contextualization of each owns contribution is provided. So this approach first set by the interest in gender equality fits into the general realm of constructivist learning theory. The fact that men 'adapt' to a more participatory style, if the didactical and technical setting stimulates it, shows the general potential of this approach.

References

Baake, D. (1996): *Medienkompetenz als zentrales Operationsfeld von Projekten, in:* Baacke, D. e.a. (Ed.): *Handbuch Medien: Medienkompetenz,* Bonn Bundeszentrale für politische Bildung.

Berszinski, S., Messmer, R., Nikoleyczik, K., Remmele, B., RuizBen, E., Schinzel, B., Schmitz, S., & Stingl, B. (2002): *Geschlecht (SexGender). Geschlechterforschung in der Informatik und an ihren Schnittstellen,* in: FifF-Kommunikation 3/02.

Bruckman, A., & Resnick, W. (1995). *The MediaMOO Project. Constructivism and Professional Community,* Convergence

Campbell, K. (2000): *Gender and Educational Technologies: Relational Frameworks for Learning Design,* in: Journal of Educational Multimedia and Hypermedia 9(2), pp. 131-149.

Haynes, C., & Holmevik, J.R. (1998): *Highwired. On the Design, Use, and Theory of Educational MOOs,* UMP, Ann Arbor

Herring, Susan, 2000: *Gender Differences in CMC: Findings and Implications,* in: CPSR Newsletter 18 (1), http://www.cpsr.org/publications/newsletters/issues/2000/Winter2000/herring.html.

Hoadley, C.M. (1998): *Between Information and Communication, Middle Spaces in Computer Media for Learning,* in: Hoadley, C., & Roschelle, J. (eds.:) *Proceedings of Computer Support for Collaborative Learning, CSCL 1999,* Stanford Univ., Palo Alto, California

Holmevik, J.R., & Haynes, C. (2000): *MOOniversity. A student's guide to online learning environments.* Allyn and Bacon, Boston, London, Torronto, Sydney, Tokyo, Singapore

Huber, B., & Remmele, B. (2001): *Ein Fall fürs Internet. Didaktische Überlegungen zu einem kooperativen Lernkonzept für eine instruktionistische Fachkultur,* in: Wagner, E., & Kindt, M. (Ed.): *Virtueller Campus. Szenarien – Strategien – Studium,* Münster Waxmann.

Kerres, M. (1998). *Multimediale und telemediale Lernumgebungen: Konzeption und Entwicklung.* München Oldenburg.

Kirkup, G., & Prümmer, Chr. v. (1997): *Distance Education for European Women,* in: The European Journal of Women's Studies 4, pp. 39-62.

Nett, B., Huber, B., Knirsch, S., Meyer, L., Remmele, B., Röhr, F., Schinzel, B., & Stingl, B. (2002): *Tailoring Educational Elements for Academic Teaching - The JurMOO,* in: Proceedings of the Information Science and IT Education Conference IS 2002, Cork, http://ecommerce.lebow.drexel.edu/eli/2002Proceedings/papers/Nett078Tailo.pdf

Schinzel, B. (2001): *e-learning für alle: Gendersensitive Mediendidaktik,* in: Ernst, U. (Ed.): *Gender und Neue Medien,* Innsbruck, http://fem.uibk.ac.at/nmtagung.html

Schulmeister, R. (1997). *Grundlagen hypermedialer Lernsysteme: Theorie, Didaktik, Design,* München Oldenburg.

Siebert, H. (1999). *Pädogogischer Konstruktivismus. Eine Bilanz der Konstruktivismusdiskussion für die Bildungspraxis,* Neuwied Luchterhand.

Specht, M. (1998). *Adaptive Methoden in computerbasierten Lehr-/ Lernsystemen,* GMD Research Series, 1998, No. 24, GMD, St. Augustin

Stingl, B., & Remmele, B. (2002): *Das JurMOO - Kommunikation und Kooperation in der virtuellen Seminarunterstützung,* in: *Virtueller Campus 2002,* Münster Waxmann.

Faculty Rewards and Incentives for E-Learning

Judi Repman
Randy Carlson
Department of Leadership, Technology, and Human Development
College of Education
Georgia Southern University
Statesboro, GA USA
jrepman@gasou.edu
rcarlson@gasou.edu

Abstract: This brief paper provides an overview of successful strategies and policies related to faculty rewards and incentives that promote participation in distance learning. Best practices and suggested strategies related to faculty motivation for e-learning will be presented.

Introduction

In his classic work on the diffusion of innovations, Everett Rogers offers this definition: "*Innovativeness* is the degree to which an individual…is relatively earlier in adopting new ideas than the other members of a system" (1995, p. 22). Rogers goes on to classify adopters into several categories: innovators, who are ahead of the curve; early adopters, who follow innovators and are often seen as opinion leaders within the organization; the early majority, who typically make up about one-third of the members of the system; the late majority, who tend to be skeptical about innovations; and, the laggards, who make decisions based on "the way we've always done it" (1995, p. 261-265).

Many E-learning attendees fall into the categories of innovators and early adopters. You embrace e-learning enthusiastically and lead your organization in creatively applying cutting edge technology in the teaching/learning process. Can you keep going it alone or in small numbers? The answer is probably not. Unless members of the early and late majorities (about two-thirds of the organization) begin to participate in e-learning, your efforts may be marginalized. E-learning will not be seen as part of your organization's mission or vision, nor will its value be recognized or rewarded. Since the participation of the early and late majorities is critical to the success of any innovation, we're going to examine characteristics of these groups. We'll also examine some possible rewards and motivators for higher education using Rogers' diffusion of innovations categories as the framework for the discussion. Those of you in corporate e-learning environments where tenure and its security are traded for other rewards can translate the following arguments to those that are meaningful to your organization.

Motivation

Incentives and rewards are closely related to motivation. Motivation theory supports the notion that incentives don't come in a "one size fits all" model. Intrinsic motivation, when an individual's desire to learn something or do something becomes rewarding in and of itself, is certainly a critical component of adoption of an innovation like e-learning. It plays an important role in the risk-taking behavior exemplified by innovators and early adopters. These groups embrace e-learning because it offers new and different ways to address teaching and learning issues and it promises to improve the efficiency and/or the effectiveness of instruction. Extrinsic motivation has its source external to the individual. Money in its various forms (cash, promotion, time off) is probably the most powerful and common extrinsic motivator.

However, some people are motivated by praise or recognition from their peers or supervisors. In a school setting, grades are the most common extrinsic motivators for students. While members of the early and late majorities may come to feel the same intrinsic motivation to participate in e-learning as time goes on, some kind(s) of extrinsic or external rewards or incentives might need to be used to get the process started (Bower, 2001).

Early and Late Majority Adopters

A large body of research in areas ranging from prescribing new drugs through the spread of educational technologies supports our earlier statement that most members (60-70%) of any group can be classified as early or late majority adopters (Rogers, 1995). The early majority adopters don't want to be the first to try something, nor do they want to be left behind. This group relies on the judgment of people that they consider to be opinion leaders. After observing the behavior of the opinion leaders, the early majority will usually go ahead and give the innovation a try. A little extra support and/or encouragement may be needed for the early majority to move beyond trial to adoption of an innovation. Late majority adopters are more skeptical. They may wait until there is little other choice but to adopt an innovation. Peer pressure may have to be considerable to initiate action (Rogers, 1995). One interesting consideration is that resistance to change is an important part of the natural cycle of the diffusion process. "Even those who approve of an innovation are likely to find some aspect of their cultural or social identity challenged, and some professional or psychological comfort zone intruded upon" (Ellsworth, 2000, p. 166). To be receptive to the value of e-learning, early and late majority adopters must first resist it. Whether or not they get past this resistance phase may depend on the rewards and incentives available. The first area that must be addressed is very basic: Do faculty think that e-learning is relevant to the mission of their organization?

Centrality to Mission

The rapid growth of e-learning has taken many institutions by surprise. Higher education has its fair share of laggards in leadership positions, so it isn't surprising that few institutions specifically mention e-learning, distance learning or distributed learning in their mission statements. Yet it is crucial for members of the early and late majorities to see the link between e-learning and the institution's mission. In a survey of Management faculty, Rahman found that the most important reason given against online teaching was that faculty believed that it was not part of the university's mission (2001). The same study found that e-learning adopters *did* believe that e-learning was part of the university's mission! Centrality to mission is important in building intrinsic motivation for e-learning. If the mission statement doesn't clearly discuss e-learning, Rahman suggests that less direct phrases like "student centered university" and "access" be highlighted as supportive aspects of the mission. Georgetown University's Research, Curriculum, and Development Group page (http://www.georgetown.edu/uis/rcd/index.html) provides an example of a direct link between a university's teaching/learning mission and faculty technology use. No matter how the link is made between the mission and faculty practice, the connect/disconnect becomes overt when faculty try to figure out how the primary reward system (promotion and tenure) accommodates e-learning and faculty development.

The Higher Education Reward System: Promotion and Tenure

While many educational institutions actively seek to hire junior faculty with both the skills and the desire to engage in e-learning, these new roles and responsibilities are not reflected in promotion and tenure policies or guidelines (Wilson, 2001; Young, 2002). One important consideration is the weight given to course development and delivery in promotion and tenure criteria (Prestera & Moller, 2001). Some call this movement "the scholarship of teaching" and suggest that examination of relationships between teaching activities and student performance should be part of the higher education reward system (Bass, 1999; Cambridge, 1999). We don't want to stifle the creativity and energy of faculty who are excited about high-tech possibilities for learning, nor do we want to set them up to fail under the existing system.

Many faculty who are enthusiastic users of instructional technologies still value traditional definitions of research and service. At the same time, the diffusion of e-learning offers many possibilities for faculty and administrators to take part in a dialog about promotion and tenure. Early and late majority adopters may need to have these issues out on the table before they are even willing to try e-learning. If these groups are already hesitant about new technologies, their reluctance will only be reinforced if they feel that the reward system might actually punish them (i.e. denial of promotion and/or tenure).

Many e-learning innovators see themselves as educational entrepreneurs. As noted in the ACE/Educause report *Distributed Education and Its Challenges: An Overview*, "Some faculty may be willing to trade security (i.e. tenure) for greater economic opportunities and payoffs." (2001, p. 13) The entrepreneurial faculty member may not even want to work for an institution where the primary reward system (i.e. promotion and tenure) is based on the face-to-face classroom model of teaching and traditional definitions of research and service. This problem is compounded when many potential early and late majority adopters are untenured and thus at the greatest risk for personal failure in terms of this reward system.

Extrinsic/External Motivators

Promotion and tenure is the most visible extrinsic reward system in higher education. Faculty members who don't earn promotion from assistant to associate professor and tenure in the required 5- or 6-year cycle find themselves looking for their next job. But promotion and tenure aren't the only external motivators around. Three categories of external motivators have been widely used to promote change in higher education: monetary incentives, workload incentives, and training and support.

When 1500 faculty members in Kentucky were surveyed about incentives for distance learning, financial incentives were ranked lowest (Wilson, 2001). Rahman's (2001) study demonstrated the same surprising finding, although in his study junior and adjunct faculty members ranked financial considerations higher than senior faculty. What does this mean to administrators trying to promote e-learning? It means that, unlike the movies, faculty aren't sitting in their offices screaming "Show me the money!" into the telephone. We're sure that most faculty wouldn't turn down money if it is offered, but it does seem that faculty actually consider other factors to be at least as important as money.

Workload considerations do seem to be more important to faculty members, primarily because of the amount of time required to design and deliver instruction using new tools and instructional strategies. Conference presenters demonstrating distance learning modules or courses almost always mention how long the development process took -- and if they don't mention it someone in the audience will ask. Casual hallway conversations about on-line courses focus on the amount of time it takes to respond to the flood of student e-mails and threaded group discussions. Common workload incentives include summer grants and release time for course development (Rahman, 2001). Release time may be as little as one course for one semester, which supposedly is adequate to get a course ready for web-based delivery. This release time vanishes once the course is on the web. Given the emphasis placed on publication in refereed journals that is the cornerstone of many promotion and tenure systems, it isn't surprising the early and late majority adopters are reluctant to invest large amounts of time mastering new technologies and reconfiguring courses and student learning activities.

The same faculty surveys report that training and support for e-learning are critical (Rahman, 2001; Wilson, 2001). Bower notes that "fear of appearing incompetent may cause faculty to resist involvement in any activity for which they have not had the proper training" (2001, p. 2). There are many models for faculty support. Some institutions employ teams of instructional designers who will consult with faculty and basically do all of the technical work associated with changing to an on-line format. Other institutions offer group training sessions and individual consultations for faculty members, but the faculty member has the primary responsibility for doing the work. Using students to provide this support is an increasingly popular option.

The University of Central Florida (http://reach.ucf.edu/~coursdev/) offers all of these services through the UCF Course Development and Web Resources Virtual Development Team. This kind of centralized model might not fit the style of all institutions but it does save faculty members from trying to figure out who to call to answer a certain kind of question. Many institutions have adopted approaches recommended by the Teaching, Learning and Technology Group (http://www.tltgroup.org/) to support faculty use of educational technology. Making these kinds of resources available and appealing to early and late majority adopters is critical. Innovators and early adopters need to share their expertise and insight through institutional support systems—even if attendance at workshops, chats, etc is not always high.

Conclusion

As the ACE/Educause report notes, "In an era when many students have never known life without the Internet, when time is constrained for adult learners seeking additional education, and when worldwide demand for education is at an at all-time high, the classroom no longer bounds the learning environment" (2001, p. 2). Many faculty have heard this directive and have acted on it. Now it's time to get other faculty on board, focusing on the early and late majority adopters. Innovators need to fight the tendency to say "nobody paid *me* any extra money or gave me any help when *I* taught my first on-line class" and recognize that external motivators may be needed to move the process along.

References

American Council on Education (ACE) & Educause. (2001). *Distributed education: Challenges, choices and a new environment.* Washington, DC: ACE. Retrieved April 15, 2002, from http://www.acenet.edu/bookstore.

Bass, R. (1999). The scholarship of teaching: What's the problem. *Inventio, 1*(1). Retrieved April 15, 2002, from http://www.doiiit.gmu.edu/Archives/feb98/randybass.htm.

Bower, B.L. (2001). Distance education: Facing the faculty challenge. *Online Journal of Distance Learning Administration, IV* (II). Retrieved April 15, 2002, from http://www.westga.edu/~distance/ojdla/summer42/bower42.html.

Cambridge, B. (1999, December). The scholarship of teaching and learning: Questions and answers from the field. *AAHE Bulletin.* Retrieved April 15, 2002, from http://www.aahe.org/Bulletin/dec99f2.htm.

Ellsworth, J.B. (2000). *Surviving change: A survey of educational change models.* Syracuse, NY: ERIC Clearinghouse on Information and Technology.

Prestera, G.E., & Moller, L.A. (2001). Organizational alignment supporting distance education in post-secondary institutions. *Online Journal of Distance Learning Administration, IV* (IV). Retrieved April 15, 2002, from http://www.westga.edu/~distance/ojdla/winter44/prestera44.html.

Rahman, M. (2001). Faculty recruitment strategies for online programs. *Online Journal of Distance Learning Administration, IV* (IV). Retrieved April 15, 2002, from http://www.westga.edu/~distance/ojdla/winter44/rahman44.html.

Rogers, E.M. (1995). *Diffusion of innovations.* (4th ed). New York: The Free Press.

Wilson, C. (2001). Faculty attitudes about distance learning. *Educause Quarterly, 2*, 70-71.

Young, J.R. (2002). Ever so slowly, colleges start to count work with technology in tenure decisions [Electronic Version]. *Chronicle of Higher Education, 48* (24). Retrieved April 15, 2002, from http://chronicle.com/free/v48/i24/24a02501.htm

Empowerment Through Equitable Access:
Middle School Students Developing Strategic Skills
In E-Learning Environment

Reynolds, Thomas
National University
USA
treynold@nu.edu

Serdyukov, Peter
National University
USA
pserdyuk@nu.edu

Abstract: Infusing technology in school is successful when it is a convergent process: a technology-based environment is created to provide computer and Internet applications in all classes, and, at the same time, computer or information literacy programs integrate strategic skills with technical skill development. Such a synergetic approach combines practical computer-based assignments in the computer literacy class together with complex intellectual activities. This paper describes such a symbiotic e-Learning project for middle school students.

Information and Computer Technology (ICT) plays a dual role in education: it is the object of learning and, at the same time, a tool for learning. As part of school curriculum, it is intended to help students to master the use of computers and the World Wide Web. This goal is pursued through computer or information literacy programs in schools that assist students in learning how to use contemporary technology. Remarkably, computer literacy in schools is often regarded as a goal in itself and as a particular subject area. However, ICT is also used as a teaching and learning tool in practically all classes and in students' independent work. Computers help to enhance students' learning activities and empower them to solve higher order cognitive tasks. This is why infusing technology in school is successful when it is a mutually beneficial process: on the one hand, a technology-based environment is created to provide computer and Internet applications in all classes, and, at the same time, computer literacy programs integrate strategic skills with technical skill development. Such a synergetic approach combines practical computer-based assignments in the computer literacy class and complex intellectual activities. The students then are engaged in solving cognitive tasks in accordance with K-12 Content Standards (1) while developing basic computer and Internet skills.

The task of teaching computer and information skills together with developing higher order skills is aggravated by limited access to information technologies and Web-based educational resources in schools located in low-income multicultural areas (2). Consequently, it is crucial to provide equitable opportunities for disadvantaged students from these areas to use contemporary educational resources and technologies in order to fully benefit from the mainstream school instruction.

This paper describes an e-Learning project being jointly developed by Marston Middle School, San Diego Unified School District, and National University, La Jolla. In this program that was initiated in 2001, the University professors together with student teachers teach an ethnically and culturally diverse class of 15 students of 12-14 years of age. The class takes place on Saturday mornings and lasts 2.5 hours. The goal of this project is to create a specific e-Learning environment to help diverse school students become computer and Internet literate and, at the same time, develop their cognitive and social skills that will contribute to their mainstream learning. Specific objectives of this project are:

- Build a model of instruction for a symbiotic information literacy and developmental program.
- Implement K-12 Content Standards in a Flexible School Program.
- Help students develop computer and Internet skills.
- Create conditions where students will apply their knowledge and skills acquired in the regular class to real-life problems solved by using ICT.
- Teach students to solve cognitive tasks while learning to use e-Learning tools.
- Bring about positive side effects in reading and writing.
- Develop a collaborative community of learners.
- Train schoolteachers and student teachers to effectively run the program.

The model of learning we are investigating now consists of five steps:

1. Task Setting. A problem is described and the task for students is defined.
2. Model presenting. Students are explained and shown ways to solve the problem using a computer and the Internet. This is where various computer uses are demonstrated and skills taught.
3. Individual work. Individual information search and processing
4. Small group work. Students share the information they collected and created, and collaboratively develop a project.
5. Whole class work. Project presentation and discussion.

In the process of this program implementation, several tasks are being solved: students learn to pose questions, to define intellectual tasks, to find and process online information, to solve problems and develop projects, to work collaboratively in a group, and present their findings to the class.

ICT is explored and applied in its many roles: as a tool for learning, for solving problems, for information search and processing, for electronic computer-mediated communication and as a game machine for developmental purposes.

The students' learning outcomes will be assessed in the end of the year. In the meanwhile, we observe students' evident success in mastering e-Learning tools together with growing interest and motivations for learning. They are able to solve more complicated cognitive tasks today than in the beginning of the year. The next step will be to improve the model and to expand the current effort to include new schools, with concomitant recruitment of both students and teachers.

The importance of this program goes beyond the framework of the current project: our intent is not only to expand it to other schools across the school district, but also to use it in preparing teachers at National University as a practical example of equitable access to education provided for diverse student population through an e-Learning program.

References:

1. California Department of Education. Educational Technology Office. California Technology Assistance Project Summary of Year 2000. Statewide School Survey Findings. June 2000. California Statewide Report. http://www.cde.ca.gov/edtech/ctapsurvey.htm

2. A Commitment to Standards-Based Education for California's Middle Grades Students http://www.cde.ca.gov/middle/tcs.html

A Multi-Disciplinary Framework for the Design and Evaluation of Computer Supported Learning-Environments

Christoph Richter, Heidrun Allert
Learning Lab Lower Saxony, University of Hanover, Germany
{richter, allert}@learninglab.de

Abstract: This paper outlines a framework for the design and evaluation of information and communication technology in learning environments. This framework is intended to support multidisciplinary cooperation during the entire project lifecycle. In contrast to other approaches it does not merge the distinct approaches but links them via a common communication platform. An extended scenario-based approach is outlined to meet the special requirements for this purpose. The domain specific approaches are interpreted as special views on the common artefact. The framework integrates the design of the social learning environment with the development of adequate technology based support. Additionally, an elaboration of this framework in form of a conceptual toolbox is drafted.

Motivation

We specify a framework for the design and evaluation of information and communication technology in learning situations. This framework has its origin in our experiences in consulting different projects within the Learning Lab Lower Saxony [L3S]. The Learning Lab Lower Saxony is a multidisciplinary research lab that focuses on the development of innovative learning technologies and is a member of the Wallenberg Global Learning Network. Within the L3S the main task of the eTeam (evaluation team) is consulting and coordinating design and evaluation of distributed projects in collaboration with the project members. The concept of theory-based evaluation is guiding this work (Nash, 2001).

Conceptualizing design and evaluation of information and communication technology in learning situations is a multidisciplinary enterprise and is accompanied with specific challenges. While it is often stated that multidisciplinary approaches are crucial in this field, there is a lack of concrete methods to facilitate this cooperation.

The diverse disciplines, which contribute to the development of technology supported learning environments, apply specific methods of modelling, implementing and evaluating domain specific artefacts. These distinct approaches and methods are widely used within each discipline. An approach, which connects these methods is still missing. The framework we present facilitates the combination of the different approaches without losing the specific advantages of each method. To respect each domain specific method facilitates multidisciplinary cooperation.

Problem Description

The following disciplines are mainly involved in the development of technology supported learning environments: computer science, media design, learning science, program evaluation. Within multidisciplinary projects any of these disciplines make unique contributions that cannot be compensated by any other discipline. Beside their distinct focuses every discipline has developed specific methods to model, implement and evaluate the artefacts they produce.

- In computer science various concepts taken from the field of software engineering are widely used. While the Unified Modelling Language (UML) is a common approach to model different aspects of software artefacts, methods such as usability testing are used to assess the artefacts.
- In educational science specific teaching and learning models to design learning environments are in use. Instructional principles such as PBL, Case-Based learning, Competency-Based learning e.g. work as

frameworks for design. Beside this methods of pedagogical evaluation that focus on motivational and instructional aspects e.g. are applied.

- We understand program evaluation as a separate discipline because it provides unique methods for describing projects, ways to guide the development and also provides concepts for assessment and evaluation. For example in theory-based evaluation methods have been developed to describe an evaluand including the views of all stakeholders (Strömdahl & Langerth Zetterman, in process). Program evaluation has been applied in fields as diverse as education, economy, health care, ecopolitics and many more (e.g. Wottawa & Thierau, 1998).

Any of the mentioned disciplines have developed concepts that can be used during the whole project process from planning to a completing summative evaluation of the artefact. But every single approach focuses on domain specific aspects and neglects other. While approaches in the field of software engineering are specialized to support the development of technical systems, they are often unsuitable to describe sociotechnial systems (see e.g. Goguen 1994). On the other hand methods to model educational settings focus on social processes and tend to view technology only from a user perspective. While methods of program evaluation are applicable to support any kind of project they strongly require clear and unambiguous description, which can only be provided by the projects themself.

Towards a Solution: a Scenario-based Communication Platform

While there are attempts to develop approaches specifically addressing the design of technology supported learning environments it has been argued that it is not useful to build a unified framework that subsumes several approaches from distinct disciplines (e.g. Bannon, 1994). In contrast our framework provides a method to explicitly link the already existing domain specific approaches without subsuming them under one theory. We consider any of these domain specific approaches as specific view on the common artefact (the intended educational setting). The crucial point in linking the different views is to establish a communication platform that can be used by any stakeholder. Also it has to be ensured that all stakeholders can translate the joint description of the artefact into their domain specific models.

The scenario-based approach provides this communication platform (see Fig. 1). Scenarios have been used in many different domains. For example in different areas within the Computer Science (e.g. Rolland et al., 1998) as well as for purposes of strategic planning in fields as business, economics, politics (e.g. Kahane, 2000).

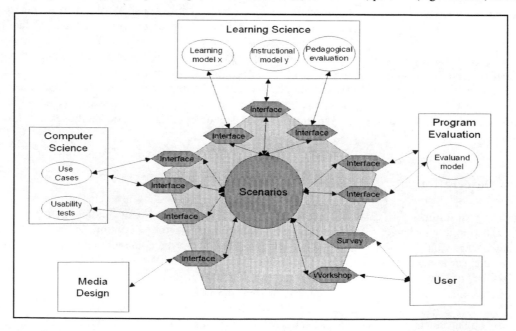

Figure 1: The core elements and interrelations of the *scenario-based communication platform*

We refer to the definition of scenarios proposed by Carroll (2000): A scenario is a concrete story about use. Scenarios include protagonists with individual goals or objectives and reflect exemplary sequences of actions and events. This definition is much broader than other definitions of scenarios and more comprehensive than the concept of use cases proposed by Jacobson et al. (2001).

The use of natural language as the basis for the communication platform helps to introduce domain specific knowledge into the discussion on the joint artefact. On the other hand narrative stories can be told on any level of abstraction as well as any level of granularity. Scenarios can also be written and discussed by the end users of the artefact.

In order to use scenarios to link several domain specific design approaches it is necessary to extend existing scenario-based approaches. On the one hand scenarios have mostly been used in projects dealing with work and not with learning. On the other hand scenario-based approaches do not systematically address socio-technical and social aspects of the artefact. Some scenario-based approaches (e.g. Benner et al. 1993; Kyng, 1995) actually broaden the scope, but do stress the importance the context in general and lack a definition of context. Those, which provide a well elaborated framework focus on work.

The core elements and interrelations of the *scenario-based communication platform* are illustrated in Fig 1. The elements in the domain-specific boxes represent some examples. The domain-specific concepts are related to the shared scenarios via interfaces. In this context an interface is a specific method that allows to transform domain-specific concepts into scenarios and vice versa. Some of these interfaces have already been outlined. Carroll (2000) describes how to link scenarios and use cases. Bødker et al. (1995) have developed a work-oriented checklist that helps to identify and reflect about core aspects of a concrete work situation described in a scenario. While this checklist links the sociological CSCW literature to scenarios similar checklists to link instructional models to scenarios are conceivable. We also recognize a lack of interfaces between scenarios and program evaluation. The interfaces to the user are formed by surveys, workshops or other methods that help to reveal the users point.

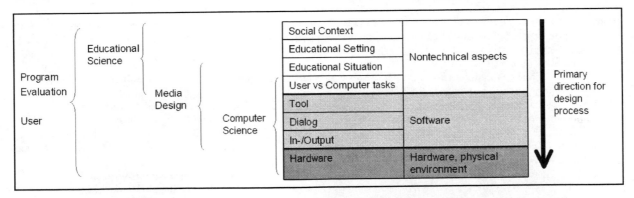

Figure 2: levels of granularity (based on a diagram by Koch et al. 1991, p. 30)

Scenarios, which are concrete stories of human activities, can be told on different levels of granularity. Fig. 2 lists 8 levels that are relevant to the design of technology supported learning environments. According to Koch et al (1991) we presume that the design of computer supported systems has to start on the social and organizational levels. Later within the progress of the project, scenarios also address the technology that supports learning and teaching. This does not eliminate the necessity to reflect on the social effects evoked by the technology. This proceeding does ensure that technology supports the learning situation and not vice versa. Fig. 2 also shows that the different groups of stakeholders with their different views on the learning situation contribute at different layers. As a consequence of this not all stakeholders are involved during the whole process to the same degree. A typical problem we are confronted with: At the beginning of a project the computer scientist does not realize what the learning scientist focusses on. Later the learning scientist cannot estimate whether the implementation the computer scientists works on does exactly meet the requirements of the proposed learning environment.

Conclusion and Further Work

The proposed framework provides several advantages compared to approaches that try to merge different domain specific methods. The use of a common communication platform and interfaces enables all stakeholders to use their domain specific methods without modification. This helps to conserve the unique advantages of the different methods and enables multidisciplinary cooperation at the same time. The framework is useful to develop sophisticated evaluation strategies, which can combine a broader range of variables, survey methods and data. Therefore this approach facilitates the concept of triangulation, called for in the field of evaluation and empirical research methodology (see e.g. Worthen et al. 1997; Mayring 2002). Understanding the design and evaluation of educational settings as a multidisciplinary challenge reflects the complexity of this task.

At the moment we already use scenarios in consulting several projects at different stages of the project lifecycle. Our next step will design, apply and evaluate a conceptual toolbox for the design and evaluation of educational settings supported by technology. The tools are intended to support projects but also provide a framework for those who consult projects. Basic tools will describe and facilitate the writing and management of scenarios at the centre of the communication platform. Further tools will form the interfaces: we will draw into account already existing methods, like workshops, checklists etc. but also design completely new methods. For example: The interfaces of learning science will provide prototypical scenarios, which explicitly represent specific instructional models, learning theories and paradigms. These scenarios will correspond to several sets of educational metadata. These sets of metadata will explicitly model learning paradigms, principles and theories and therefore allow to share and re-use conceptual structures. On the other hand this interface will support consulting: often projects state a specific learning theory or learning paradigm (constructivism e.g.), but do not actually address it in their design. Scenarios help to discuss the relevant aspects.

Furthermore we will create interfaces that link the scenarios with program evaluation. These interfaces will support the design of appropriate evaluation plans. The results of evaluation provide feedback to all stakeholders and help to refine the existing scenarios.

References

Bannon, L.J. (1994). Problems of Interdisciplinarity. *Interdisciplinary Foundations of System Design and Evaluation.* Position Papers for Dagstuhl Seminar 9348. pp. 8-9. http://iug.uni-paderborn.de/iug/veroeffentlichungen/1995/rks_dagstuhl.

Benner, K. M.; Feather, M.W.; Johnson, W. L.; Zorman, L.A. (1993). Utilizing Scenarios in the Software Development Process. *Information System Development Process*, Elsevier Science Publisher B.V. (North-Holland), 117-134. http://citeseer.nj.nec.com/benner93utilizing.html.

Bødker, S.; Christiansen, E.; Thüring, M. (1995). A conceptual toolbox for designing CSCW applications, COOP '95, *International Workshop on the Design of Cooperative Systems*, pp. 266-284, Juan-les-Pins, January 1995.

Carroll, J.M. (2000). *Making use: scenario-based design of human -computer interactions.* Cambridge: MIT press.

Goguen, J.A. (1994). Requirements Engineering as the Reconciliation of Technical and Social Issues. In: Jirotka, M.; Goguen J.A. (eds). *Requirements Engineering: Social and Technical Issues.* London: Academic Press. pp. 165-199.

Jacobson, I.; Booch, G.; Rumbaugh, J. (2001). *The Unified Software Development Process.* Boston: Addison-Wesley.

Kahane, A. (2000). *How To Change the World: Lessons for Entrepreneurs from Activists.* Global Business Network Publications. http://www.gbn.org/public/gbnstory/articles/ex_kahane.htm.

Koch, M.; Reiterer, H.; Tjoa, A.M. (1991). *Software-Ergonomie: Gestaltung von EDV-Systemen; Kriterien, Methoden und Werkzeuge.* Wien: Springer.

Kyng, M. (1995). Creating Contexts for Design, In: John M. Carroll (Ed.) *Scenario-Based Design: Envisioning Work and Technology in System Development*, pp. 85-107. John Wiley and Sons.

Mayring, P. (2002). *Einfuehrung in die qualitative Sozialforschung - Eine Anleitung zu qualitativem Denken.* 5. Aufl. - Weinheim: Beltz.

Nash, J.B., Plugge, L.; Eurlings, A. (2001). Defining and Evaluating CSCL Evaluations. In A. Eurlings & P. Dillenbourg (Eds.), *Proceedings of the European Conference on Computer-Supported Collaborative Learning* (pp. 120-128). Maastricht: Universiteit Maastricht.

Rolland, C., Ben Achour, C., Cauvet, C., Ralyté, C., Sutcliffe, A.,Maiden, N.A.M., Jarke, M., Haumer, P., Pohl, K., Dubois, E., Heymans, P. (1998). A Proposal for a Scenario Framework. In: *Requirements Engineering Journal.* Vol. 3, No. 1, Springer Verlag pp.23-47.

Strömdahl, H.; Langerth Zetterman, M. (in process). *On theory-anchored evaluation research of educational settings within ICT environments.* http://www.skeptron.ilu.uu.se/MonicaLZ/arkiv/tea-slutmanus.pdf.

Worthen, B.R.; Sanders, J.R.; Fitzpatrick, J.L. (1997). *Program Evaluation : Alternative Approaches and Practical Guidelines.* 2nd ed. New York: Addison Wesley.

Wottawa, H.; Thierau, H. (1998). *Lehrbuch Evaluation.* 2. vollst. ueberarb. Aufl.- Bern: Huber.

Inclusive Workforce Development in an *E*-learning World

Creating a Fully Inclusive Twenty First Century Workforce System

(For workforce development programs and their business customers), e-learning holds the potential of contributing to significant gains in worker skills, productivity and performance. E-learning also can deliver significant cost savings when compared to traditional types of (workforce) training. Equally important, e-learning can provide access to high-quality training content from countless sources throughout the world. This, in turn, can lead to improvements in individual and organizational performance. (For workforce communities) e-learning's promise rests in its potential as a driver of value-added economic growth. By opening the door to dramatic boosts in business performance, productivity and the number of skilled workers, e-learning can play an essential role in economic development initiatives at all levels. (For individual citizens), e-learning can broaden opportunities for skill development and employment in high-quality jobs for all segments of the population, contributing to income growth, improved lives for Americans, and a more informed and contributing citizenry. A Vision of E-Learning for America's Workforce, Commission on Technology and Adult Learning (2001)

Lessons Learned

We have recently completed a century and a millennium. Our Old World in the twenty-century has come to an end and a new world is upon us. We now relate differently, play differently, learn differently and work differently than our parents. While this is true for most of us, many are still stuck in the twentieth century depending on an old world workforce system. "The world is fast polarizing into two potentially irreconcilable forces: on one side, an information elite that controls and manages the high-tech global economy; and on the other, the growing numbers of permanently displaced workers, who have few prospects and little hope for meaningful employment in an increasingly automated world" [i]

"Just as e-learning presents a number of opportunities for individuals, organizations and society, it also poses some serious questions for the future, including: How do we ensure consumer protection and high-quality learning in an open e-learning environment? In a learner-centered system, what is the best way to assess what individuals are actually learning? How can we best certify learning results? And how do we promote equitable access to the technologies and the high-quality.[ii]" The digital divide is one of the most important civil rights issues facing our modern information economy. As telecommunications increasingly entwines itself with educational, social, financial, and employment opportunities, those workforce communities lacking access will find themselves falling further behind the rest of society. The Internet has the potential to empower its users with new skills, new perspectives, new freedoms, even new voices; those groups and communities who remain sequestered from the technology will be further segregated into the periphery of public life.[iii]

Within this group of permanently displaced workers are most individuals with disabilities, as employment continues to be the area with the widest gulf between those who are disabled and those who are not, with nearly 2/3 of those that want to work unable to gain access to employment. (Harris, 1986, 1994, 1998 and

2000.) Accessibility problems have increased dramatically with new developments in hardware, software and Web page design. With limited access to the information superhighway, those who could benefit the most are being overlooked.

Workplace diversity is increasingly recognized as an organizational asset. Many companies operate in global markets, and a diverse work-force is more capable of serving a diverse customer base. Moreover, in industries and workplaces that thrive on creativity and innovation, a diverse work force produces different perspectives, different approaches to solving problems, and a richer pool of ideas. As we enter the 21st century, according to the Department of Commerce Office of the Technology Policy, two-thirds of new work force entrants will be women and minorities. Yet, today, women and some minorities including people with disabilities are underrepresented in the technical work force. This outcome partly originates in the current workforce development pipeline.[iv]

During the past decade, university and private entrepreneurs have invested tens of million of dollars and ten of thousands of hours to plan, promote and deliver Web-based and related forms of distance education. Yet, often these initiatives move forward as if it was something new, a kind of unintended consequence of the Internet. While technology, specifically e-learning has raised the aspirations for more automated online workforce development opportunities, the current economic downturn appears to be producing significant on-line enrollment downturns at many educational institutions and a number of dot-com education providers have simply vanished, thus providing early important e-learning development lessons.[v]

First among these lessons is that anytime anywhere e-learning really can expand learning opportunities by mixing convenient access with enhanced, effective customized multimedia content. However, contrary to popular consensus, the next learned lesson is that content is not king, and in absences of a supportive facilitator and an appropriate enabling infrastructure, content has little value. Learning is still change, and people only change when they have to change, when the pain of learning becomes less than the pain of maintaining the status quo. Up to 75% of e-learners drop out of non-instructor facilitated courses before completing them, reports Gerard Prendergast.[vi] "It's the tutoring processes that will determine whether people complete their learning experience successfully," he concludes. Trained tutors also provide a crucial intangible – encouragement, especially for those lacking even basic computer literacy skills that are more likely to served by a one stop center.. He also claims that with trained tutors, the dropout rate in his study of corporate e-learners was reduced from 75 to 8 percent. Mix these trained tutors with high quality, engaging, customized, and validated e-learning content that is easy to view and read, along with high speed Internet connections and computers; and a model for a next generation workforce lifelong learning system begins to emerge.

A Next Generation Workforce Development System Vision

> *I have learned about two ways to think about technology: one is called automating, the other is called informating. One will give you incremental improvement; the other will give you big improvement. Unfortunately training programs and technology tend to focus on automating. The means that you bolt technology on top of what you are already doing... You get very different results when you informate. The real revolution is information and communication, not technology. Let go of the word technology. If you focus on it, then you'll just do what you're already doing. The trick in planning as we move forward is to think about (workforce) information systems, whole systems of the flow of information and communication --- Alan November -from Creating a New Culture of Teaching and Learning.*

Most one stop workforce centers are now taking that first step in getting wired, but they must also consider the needs of the learners, the teachers, and the communities that support them. Access, content, literacy, pedagogy and community—may not be enough to complete the entire digital divide puzzle, but they go a long way in providing a picture of what is at stake. What is needed is a dynamic e-learning culture that embraces the inherent contribution of all people as life-long learners to meet the needs of both the individual and society. Not only do dynamic e-Learning cultures need to address personal, community, and organizational aspects of learning – they also have to attend holistically to what best influences learning for individual learners given the particular knowledge and skill areas being developed. For the optimal development of positive e-learning contexts and cultures, attention is needed to research validated principles that can meet the learning needs of all learners. New roles for workforce center administrators, teachers or learning facilitators, and students must be considered. Envision that traditional concepts will be abandoned as all become learners and interchange roles from learner to expert learner.

Leaders will need adaptive expertise and political leadership to evolve new forms of assessment and accountability in dynamic e-learning cultures. Effective assessment and evaluation practices need to hold workforce training programs accountable for customizing e-learning using activities based on individualized e-learning plans implemented in a workforce community context. Private sector developers are spending millions of dollars to optimize e-learning systems. The workforce system needs to develop private sector partnerships to ensure that universal design principles are incorporated in all next generation learning systems as well as to validate these system with a diverse array of adult learners. Accountability policies for training and job placement, assessment and evaluation practices aligned with core standards and indicators, funding criteria, and articulated outcomes that are balanced for individual and societal needs are required.

> *Issues of learner achievement cannot be separated from issues of teacher expertise, professional development, prevention and intervention strategies, curricular alignment, assessment strategies, leadership, and funding. To be successful, efforts must include changes in all of these areas. It is one thing to embrace the idea that all can learn; it is another thing to make sure they do learn. –from Blueprint for Student Success*

An NSF sponsored study at Western Michigan University evaluating the use of SmartForce e learning with students with disabilities attending community colleges is being conducted. The current e-learning market leader is SmartForce with over 1.5 million online learners world wide including much of the U.S. military provides 24/7 online live mentoring support to supplement an extensive learning management system (LMS). Early results seem to support Prendergast's claim on the importance of trained tutors in the e-learning process. Customers of second chance programs within Workforce system can especially be expected to benefit from the personal encouragement that a 24x7 trained tutor can provide while using a comprehensive, customizable e-learning management system like that being developed by SmartForce.

Recommendations

1. Promote, quality e-learning experiences including the provision of appropriate infrastructure, accessible learning environments, support systems and trained tutors to use with corporate quality e-learning management systems that are both customizable and comprehensive.

2. Create an e-learning workforce culture that supports student motivation, learning, and achievement while also supporting the teacher's (tutor) need to also be a learner.

3. Pursue healthy e-learning networked communities that works for everyone, and encourages rather than eliminates diverse perspectives.

4. Provide the tools and capacity for networked workforce learning communities that can expand and transform notions of e-learning in ways that produce healthy and productive lifelong learners within a larger integrated networked community of learners.

5. Provide new approaches for measuring, certifying and reporting on authentic e-learning outcomes.

6. Ensure equitable access to e-learning opportunities that are available and known to all.

7. Pursue public - private sector partnerships to conduct research and development on how adults learn and how to measure adult learning in meaningful ways.

8. Advocate to all that even the most advanced technology-supported networked learning communities need to be supplemental to the human elements of insight, understanding and encouragement provided by trained tutors (instructors) engaged with the learner in a guided partner relationship. Such a relationship must allow the learner to take ownership of their own career development plans by making informed choices and the taking responsibility for reaching and resetting their careers goals in this brave new e-learning world. [vii]

[i] Rifkin, J. E., (1995), The End of Work: The Decline of the Global Workforce and the Dawn of the Post Market Era, J P Tarcher; London.

[ii] Merrill, S.E. & Wiigenhorm A.W., Introduction, (2001) A Vision of E-Learning for America's Worker, A Report of the Commission on Technology and Adult Learning, ASTD and NGA Center for Best Practices.

[iii] Carvin, A. (2000) Mind the Gap: The Digital Divide as the Civil Rights Issue of the New Millennium, Multimedia Schools, Jan.-Feb., 2000, p.2-4.

[iv] Mearns, C.A. & Sargent, J. F. Jr. (1999) The Digital Workforce: Building Infotech Skills at the Speed of Innovation, U.S. Department of Commerce, Office of Technology Policy

[v] Green, K.C., (2001) Distance Learning: Lessons From the Early Years, Converge: Innovations in High Education 4(10) (60-62).

[vi] Prendergast, G. Online Learning Europe 2001 Conference & Expo in London, England. (2/13/01).

McCombs, B. L. (2000, July). Learner-centered psychological principles: A framework for technology evaluation. Invited paper presented at the U.S. Department of Education's Regional Conferences on "Evaluating Technology in Education," Atlanta. [vii]

Author Index